CASSELL'S

BATTLEFIELDS OF BRITAIN AND IRELAND

CASSELL'S

BATTLEFIELDS OF BRITAIN AND IRELAND

Richard Brooks

WEIDENFELD & NICOLSON

First published in Great Britain in 2005
by Weidenfeld & Nicolson

10 9 8 7 6 5 4 3 2 1

A CIP catalogue record for this book is available from the British Library.

ISBN 0 304 36333 2

Maps by David Hoxley

Design by Gywn Lewis

Printed and bound in Finland by WS Bookwell Ltd

Weidenfeld & Nicolson

The Orion Publishing Group Ltd
Orion House, 5 Upper Saint Martin's Lane, London, WC2H 9EA

www.orionbooks.co.uk

Contents

Acknowledgments

I would like to thank the following people for their valued assistance with the preparation of this book: Ken Brooks, Dave Carson, Nigel Drury, Val Fontana, Ann Greenway, Jeff James, Brendan Kenny, Matthew Little, Wendy Smith, Alison Wareham and Ralph Weaver.

I am particularly indebted to Bill Johnson of the Portland Learning Resource Centre, Portsmouth University, for his invaluable cartographic support; to the staff of Portsmouth Central Library, especially the inter-library loans section; to David Hoxley for drawing the maps with clarity and accuracy; and also to Catherine Cleare at Weidenfeld & Nicolson for her patience.

Introduction

Launching yet another battlefields book onto the market seems to require some excuse, beyond the usual assertions of superior accuracy and scope. Why should anyone in postmodern Britain revisit these unhappy scenes, two centuries since the area's last conventional land battle at Ballinamuck in the modern Republic of Ireland? What do we profit from rediscovering some forgotten battlefield? What do we mean by a battlefield anyway?

A battle is an encounter in the open, between two or more armed forces organized for war. The term excludes riots, massacres, mutinies, sieges and accidental encounters between members of the same army or navy. Large numbers of participants or casualties are not essential. An important medieval battle might be a skirmish by modern standards. Location, on the other hand, is crucial to the concept of battle. Military forces exist within physical space; they occupy positions, and choose their ground. Armies camp in one place, advance to another to deploy, and fight a little further on. Battles are dynamic events, rarely limited to a single kilometre map square. The Anglo-Saxon 'place of slaughter' accurately describes the static infantry fights of the 9th century. Not all battlefields are so circumscribed. Running fights such as Yellow Ford (1598) spread over several miles of countryside. British cavalry taking part in the Castlebar Races (1798) are said to have fled 30 miles (48 km) without stopping.

A few battlefields are known by some noteworthy circumstance, or their date, for example Palm Sunday Field, better known as Towton (1461). This may reflect topographical uncertainty, as with the Alleluia Victory (*c.*429), or the St James's

Day Fight (1666), a naval action spanning the North Sea. However, most battles derive their names from a geographical feature. This might be a watercourse or a hill, as in the case of the Idle River (616) or Hadden Rigg (1542). More commonly the nearest settlement lends its name, profiting hostelries and postcard shops. This process can take some time. Until the 1530s Bosworth Field (1485) was called Redemore, from a wetland 3 miles (5 km) southwest of Market Bosworth.

Fighting occasionally took place inside a town, notably at Lincoln (1217) and St Albans (1455). More often armies met on open ground. Medieval and early modern armies needed clear terrain to manoeuvre without losing formation. The unenclosed grazing land between groups of villages, connected by drover's paths, provided the perfect rendezvous, as at Ringmere (1010), Bramham Moor (1408) or Blore Heath (1459). Sometimes armies fought in the broad fields that surrounded pre-agricultural revolution settlements, producing such battlefield names as Ripple Field (1643). Medieval writers also used 'field' in a tactical sense, as when the Duke of Somerset 'left the felde' at Tewkesbury in 1471, breaking his formation and losing the battle. Lose-Coat Field (1470) reflects this alternative usage. Even battles that take their names unmodified from settlements, such as Northampton (1460), were usually fought in the fields outside. These are now prime development sites, hastening the disappearance of many battlefields under concrete.

But should we care if they do? The contribution of armed conflict to shaping the British and Irish political landscapes is easily missed. Economic growth and development of human rights have driven kings and battles from the historical agenda. Academia despises the drum-and-trumpet approach of traditional battlefield history. Many historians question the very concept of a 'decisive battle' before the 19th century. A historical profession of liberal views averts its gaze from the grim realities of combat, focusing instead on the social or economic aspects of warfare. It is easy to forget the ultimate purpose of armed forces in England, 260 years after the last clash of opposing armies on English soil at Clifton (1745).

The Easter Rebellion of 1916, which altered the whole basis of Anglo-Irish relations, and the Battle of Britain are more recent reminders that battles still act as historical punctuation marks. Some, like Hastings (1066), send the course of history off in new directions, in the old 'decisive battle' tradition. Others proclaim a new but previously unrecognized balance of social and political forces. Charles I lost control of his three kingdoms long before Marston Moor (1644) and Naseby (1645) destroyed his military power. Defensive battles matter for their negative consequences. The Armada's defeat in 1588 did not eliminate the Spanish threat at a stroke, but it did prevent the Counter-Reformation taking root in England. Many battles remain significant for their mythic resonance. Commemorations of the Relief of Londonderry (1689) still provide an annual flashpoint in Northern Ireland.

Apart from their individual meaning, groups of battles possess a more general significance. Historians like to pretend events are unique, none repeating another. This is only half true. Battles form a specific class of events sharing a common set of attributes. Each one fits a similar pattern of approach, encounter, attrition and decision. The Prussian military philosopher Karl von Clausewitz (1780–1831) saw military engagements as very much alike, differentiated solely by their specific purpose. Like other collective events, such as elections and weddings, battles are sufficiently numerous and well documented to permit collection of consistent data about them. This can then be used as a basis for meaningful comparison. The locations of 7th-century battlefields, for example, show Dark Age armies covering remarkable distances. King Cadwallon of Gwynedd in North Wales was killed at Denisesburna (634), within sight of Hadrian's Wall. Oswald of Northumbria probably died near Oswestry at the Maserfelth (641). Penda of Mercia's death on the Winwaed in 654 followed a raid to the Firth of Forth, 250 miles (400 km) from his capital at Tamworth.

Nevertheless, the secondary literature on British and Irish battlefields reveals a surprising lack of consensus. Improbable errors abound, such as the idea that Edward, Earl of March, the most successful commander of the Wars of the Roses, could have been so stupid as to fight Mortimer's Cross (1461) with his back to the River Lugg. Monuments are routinely in the wrong place. The obelisk at Evesham stands a quarter of a mile (400 m) west of the shallow depression said to mark Simon de Montfort's last stand. The Covenanters' memorial at Bothwell Bridge (1679) is the wrong side of the River Clyde.

Received views of many British and Irish battles are inconsistent both with the documentary evidence, and with such scholarly analysis as they have received. Popular history follows its well-trampled path regardless. Reconstructions popularized by Sir Charles Oman in the 1920s or A.H. Burne in the 1950s still persist despite competition from more credible interpretations. Recent paperback editions have given both a fresh lease of life. Burne's practice of using what he christened 'inherent military probability' to fill evidential gaps has proved particularly disastrous in less skilful hands. The challenge for today's battlefield historian is more often to disentangle rival interpretations than set out a handful of recorded facts. The only way to resolve the contradictions of modern accounts is to fall back on contemporary sources. The numerous quotations I have used are intended to limit speculation, allowing readers to focus on what people near the original events wrote about them, and make up their own mind.

Battlefield research questions the basis of our knowledge of the past as sharply as any area of historical investigation. Medieval sources are few and laconic. The more discursive lay accounts that became common during the 16th century are often biased and self-seeking. Pre-gunpowder armies left few traces, beyond a few naked bodies tipped anonymously into a common grave. Broken weapons and equipment were salvaged and recycled. Scotland's most important medieval battlefield, at Bannockburn (1314), has only recently yielded its first 14th-century weapon. The poverty of ancient sources and the carelessness of historians have obscured the location of many battlefields. More than a quarter of Anglo-Saxon battlefields are lost, the great battle of Brunanburh (937) among them. Recent work on Bosworth, a central event in English history, suggests every account of the battle since the 18th century has placed it incorrectly, with writers jumping backwards through hoops to make the contemporary evidence fit the wrong patch of ground.

The location of ancient conflicts is of more than antiquarian interest. Accuracy matters, if history is to maintain its credibility in a scientific age. The contradictions and inaccuracies of much popular battlefield history tarnish history's image as a discipline. Even academics make serious errors. The only modern account of Kilrush, fought in 1642 between Irish Royalists and Catholic Confederate rebels, places it at the wrong end of Co. Kildare. Rival authorities disagree about which way armies were facing, for example at Stoke Field (1487) or Killiecrankie (1689). Such topographical errors are fundamental. The shape of land battles is decided by minor accidents of ground, the direction of the opposing lines of approach, the number of combatants, and the available space. Accurate information about such matters of detail is an essential prerequisite for successful generalization about broader issues. J.E. Morris rendered worthless his analysis of Edward I's Welsh campaign of 1294–5 by confusing Maes Madog near Conwy, in North Wales, with Maes Moydog near Welshpool, in the Welsh Marches. Identification of the *Anglo-Saxon Chronicle*'s nine national fights of 871 with sites in Hampshire and Wiltshire paints a more serious picture of the Viking threat to Wessex than if those battles took place in some peripheral area, remote from the heart of the kingdom. Politically interested parties exploit symbolic events to further their sometimes malign agendas. Culloden (1746) is often misrepresented as an Anglo-Scottish confrontation, when it was really the last act in a British civil war between the Stuart and Hanoverian dynasties. To describe it otherwise slights the memory of numerous Scots who fought for King George, and fuels the wrong sort of national feeling.

The Theatre of War

The ambition of *Cassell's Battlefields of Britain and Ireland* is to include every action fought on British and Irish soil, or at least a higher proportion of them than anyone else. The inclusion of Irish and Scottish battles reflects the strategic unity of an area whose islands are as often joined as separated by the intervening waters. Dublin Vikings fought at Brunanburh (937); Anglo-Normans at Dublin (1171) and Dysart O'Dea (1318); Scottish troops at Faughart (1318) and Benburb (1646). The Irish returned the compliment at Stoke Field (1487), Tippermuir (1644) and Killiecrankie (1689). English fears of foreign influence in Ireland or Irish intervention in England have inspired too many expeditions beyond the Irish Sea to mention.

There is no convenient or generally acceptable name for the two islands that the Romans called Britannia and Hibernia. The former expression means little between the Roman departure and the accession to the English throne – as James I – of the Scottish king James VI in 1603. Readers beyond the Irish Sea may well resent inclusion under the umbrella of the 'British Isles', however innocently intended. The delightful expression 'these islands' is too vague. 'The Four Nations' is altogether too sporting, and neglects the Cornish. The geographical term 'North Atlantic Archipelago' looks cumbersome, but it does combine precision with neutrality.

Modern territorial labels mean little for much of the area's history. Scotland emerged first, with Kenneth mac Alpin's accession to the joint Scottish-Pictish throne in 843. A united England followed with the death of Eric Bloodaxe, the last Viking king of York, killed on Stainmoor in 954. Wales came together just in time to be conquered by Edward I in the 1280s. Ireland remains divided. Expressions like English or Welsh or Irish are used for convenience rather than precision.

The archipelago's geography is a major determinant of its military history. A landscape's physical structure shapes the society that lives there and the armed forces that defend it. Hills, waterways and predominant vegetation constrain the direction, weight and speed of troop movements, and determine the tactics employed when armies meet.

The inclusion of naval actions illustrates the crucial point that Britain and Ireland are islands. The first and last conventional battles in the archipelago were both at sea: Dover (55 BC) was a Roman assault landing; Lough Swilly (1798) a Nelsonic ship-to-ship action. In the latter case, bad weather had already forced the French to turn back, but prevailing westerly winds foiled many earlier invaders. Only three state-sponsored invasions of Britain have succeeded: the Romans in AD 43, the Normans in 1066 and William of Orange's coup in 1688. Insularity does not provide automatic immunity to invasion, however. Contrary winds mattered less to piecemeal immigrants like Saxons and Vikings, who could await a fair wind and tide.

Britain and Ireland have long been a destination for raiders and economic refugees from Scandinavia and the Low Countries. Angles landed in Northumbria and Scotland, Belgae in Essex, Jutes in Kent and Hampshire, Flemings in Munster, and Vikings everywhere. The open beaches and broad estuaries of

Britain's southeast coast favoured such arrivals. Prehistoric migrations left few traces of conflict, beyond hillforts, but the coming of the Saxons was reflected in battles around the Solent and Thames estuary, and at Lindisfarne (*c.*590). In their turn the Saxons resisted Viking landings, most poetically at Maldon (991), and in the earliest recorded English sea fights of the previous century. Not until the 17th century did the islanders become strong enough to hold interlopers at arm's-length, the Royal Navy engaging Dutch and French fleets within sight of the coastline at Dungeness (1652), Sole Bay (1672) and Beachy Head (1690). Over the next century, the development of a fleet able to maintain a continuous blockade of hostile ports would help bring the archipelago's domestic military history to a full stop.

Invaders followed various routes into the interior. Ancient downland trackways lead to battlefields at Barbury Castle (556), Ashdown (871) and Ellendun (825). Roman roads quartered the country, so well built they might have been geological features. Over a thousand years after their construction, armies still marched down them to St Albans and Mortimer's Cross (both 1461), as they had to Reading (871), Abergwyli (1022), the Holme (903), Hastings (1066), Northallerton (1138) and Lincoln (1141, 1217). Good communications encouraged clusters of decisive battles in the Midlands. Boudicca's Revolt (AD 60) may have been crushed in sight of Bosworth Field (1485), and within a forced march of Naseby (1645). Battles on London's doorstep reflect the capital's longstanding political and commercial importance: Barnet (1471), Brentford (1016, 1642), Blackheath (1497), Benfleet (893), Crayford (*c.*456) and Fleet Street (1554), ending with the Battle of Britain in 1940. More battlefields surround England's northern capital at York, including two of England's largest at Towton (1461) and Marston Moor (1644). The Scottish Border, Britain's only international frontier after 1282, has attracted the heaviest concentration: 30 battles out of the British total of 289.

Unvisited by the Romans, Ireland presents a different pattern. The island's centre is flat, wet and fringed by mountains. Bogs and forests hinder inland movement. Most Irish battles were fought near the coast, many in east Ulster and Leinster, opposite Ireland's larger neighbour. The chief town, Dublin, lies in a 50-mile (80-km) gap between the Mourne and Wicklow Mountains. The strategic gateway to Ireland, it was the site of crucial battles: Clontarf (1014), Castle Knock (1171), Rathmines (1649) and the Easter Rising of 1916. Across the Irish Sea lies the Cheshire Gap, the natural route for troop movements between England and Ireland. Relations between Charles I and the Long Parliament had finally broken down over troops for Ireland, but Roundhead victories at Nantwich (1644) and Chester (1645) ensured little help ever reached the king from that quarter.

The rough terrain and poor weather of Britain's western parts have produced one of the enduring distinctions in British social and military history. Lowland and highland zones have been distinct since prehistoric times. The Romans used the Fosse Way from Exeter to Lincoln to separate the more settled and economically advanced southeast from the sparsely populated, pastoral northwest. Later the Pennines and the Dee/Severn line separated Saxon from Celt, and to a lesser extent Parliamentarian from Royalist. Unsettled conditions along the Welsh Marches encouraged more than one military adventurer, as witness battles at Shrewsbury (1403), Mortimer's Cross (1461) and Worcester (1651). The Welsh people, however, relied upon their mountains and climate for defence. Less than a dozen battles arose from Welsh resistance to an invader, between Caradoc's Last Stand (AD 51) and the death of Llewelyn the Last at Irfon Bridge (1282). The Highlands of Scotland on the other hand provided a last refuge for a heroic style of warfare, which embarrassed governments in Edinburgh and London with defeats at Killiecrankie (1689) and Prestonpans (1745). Usually the lowlanders' superior numbers and weaponry overpowered the simpler armies of the Celtic fringes. Bowman and knight crushed unsupported spearmen at Maes Moydog (1295) and Halidon Hill (1333); field artillery and bayonets worsted Highland swordsmen at Culloden (1746).

The physical configuration of Britain and Ireland influenced military operations in other ways. Armies did not blunder aimlessly about the countryside. Strategic bottlenecks channelled armies along well-known routes, simplifying the business of finding the enemy without aerial reconnaissance. They met naturally at topographical chokepoints, such as river crossings: on the Medway (AD 43), the Idle River (617) and perhaps the Meden at Haethfelth (632); on the Avon at Evesham (1265), the Severn at Tewkesbury (1471) and Worcester (1651), and the Ribble at Preston (1648, 1715). Significantly over 20 battlefields include the element 'ford' in their name.

Before the invention of long-ranging field artillery, armies could not force river lines as William III did at the Boyne (1690). Medieval armies let their enemies cross unopposed, as at Maldon (991) and Stamford Bridge (1066). Presumably they hoped to drive them back into the water, as the Scots did to the English at Stirling Bridge (1297) and Myton-on-Swale (1391). Thomas of Lancaster's attempt to storm across the River Ure at Boroughbridge (1322) was unusual, and doomed to failure. Armies sometimes used water obstacles to secure their rear, as the Vikings did at Reading (871). This could lead to disaster, as the Picts found after the Alleluia Victory (*c*.429), the Mercians at the Winwaed (654) and the Lancastrians at Northampton (1460). More commonly, battlefields run along the dry ground of a watershed. Streams flowing outwards, away from the action, protected the flanks of opposing armies at Hastings (1066), Northallerton (1138) and Naseby (1645), and kept the fighting within predictable bounds.

Elizabethan state papers for Ireland refer constantly to bogs, woods and passes. The Moyry Pass (1600) between Newry and Dundalk was typical of many, 'beset on both sides with bogs where the Irish might skip but the English could not go'. Seven-toed Cuchulainn had defended it in the heroic age, and it remains debateable territory. The strategic gateway to the Highlands has always been the Forth/Clyde isthmus. Defended in the Roman period by the Antonine Wall, it saw major battles at Stirling Bridge (1297), Falkirk (1298, 1746), Bannockburn (1314), Kilsyth (1645) and Sheriffmuir (1715). High ground penned armies against the coast, especially in Scotland: Pinkie (1547), Dunbar (1296, 1650) and Prestonpans (1745) all took place on the eastern approaches of Edinburgh, between the Firth of Forth and the Lammermuir Hills. The first and last great battles of Scottish history were fought in the strategic defile between the Grampians and the Moray Firth, at Mon Graupius (AD 83) and Culloden (1746).

Historical Perspective

The geographical proximity of the British and Irish military heritage contrasts with its historical remoteness. The people who fought most of the area's battles inhabited a different world. Life was hard, lacking the most elementary comforts even for the rich. Violence was endemic, making the transition to war less striking than it might be today. Battle was not the sole preserve of princes, as shown by the fight at Nibley Green (1470). The intellectual equipment of combatants who believed in portents and banshees appears laughable, but they were rational beings in their way, as capable of strategic calculation as ourselves, and equally adept at exploiting the military technology of their day.

Few of those who fought on the battlefields of Britain or Ireland were professional soldiers in the modern sense, or belonged to national armies. Warfare remained an upper class game, played with small regard for national identity, long after England and Scotland achieved political unity. For centuries society conformed to Alfred the Great's threefold division between those who worked, those who prayed, and those who fought. Young men of good family and small fortune served their lord for honour, in the hope of material reward: the gold rings offered by Dark Age chiefs, or the knight's fees granted by William the Conqueror. In the absence of modern health care sudden death in battle was far preferable to dying slowly in bed.

Making sense of these ancient battles requires an effort of the historical imagination. Written sources are patchy and difficult to interpret, the passage of time has obliterated physical evidence on the ground, and technological change has obscured the material conditions under which battles were fought. Battles were transient affairs, lasting one or two days, too short a time to be noticed by archaeologists. Archaeology can confirm and enrich the historical record, but its findings are insufficiently specific to form the basis of a narrative. Battlefield history requires written sources.

Documentary evidence presents its own problems, however. Over half the battles in these islands predate William Caxton's introduction of the printing press to England in 1476. For the previous millennium and a half our knowledge depends on manuscript sources. Transcribed many times, these became garbled and incomplete. Their ancient and medieval authors wrote from hearsay, in strange tongues, to an alien agenda. Their purpose was moral not historical. History was a rhetorical exercise aimed more at improving the present than understanding the past. Little reliance can be placed on the unconfirmed words of chroniclers remote in time, place and sympathy from the events they described. Few medieval soldiers kept diaries or wrote letters, so professional eyewitness accounts of battles before the reign of Henry VIII are scarce. The Civil Wars of the 17th century on the other hand take up between a quarter and a fifth of this book, depending whether one counts words or battles. This may reflect the struggle's intensity, or the unprecedented literacy rates of the 1640s.

The topographical framework that constrained commanders has also shifted. Today's landscape is manmade. River valleys have been drained and wastelands cleared. Man's recent destruction of the environment has only accelerated natural processes that had already obscured the setting of ancient battles. Coastlines are notoriously unstable. Shifting channels in the Thames estuary are crucial to our understanding of the campaigns of Julius Caesar and Claudius in 54 BC and AD 43 respectively. Wooded areas can also move, if less dramatically than Birnam Wood's stage advance to Dunsinane, where the real-life Malcolm defeated Macbeth in 1054 without arboreal assistance.

The medieval countryside was less enclosed than today, with fewer forests than historians once thought. The heavy Anglo-Saxon plough had enlarged fields, allowing armies to manoeuvre freely, despite their lack of tactical subdivisions. This was particularly so in the corn-growing Midlands, where cavalry still dominated Civil War battlefields at Edgehill (1642), Cropredy Bridge (1644) and Naseby (1645). Cautious commanders like Sir Ralph Hopton or the Duke of Monmouth refused to expose unsupported infantry on Salisbury Plain in face of superior cavalry. In western England and around built-up areas, Civil War armies fought hedge-to-hedge, not just in the well established bocage of Cornwall at Stratton (1643) and Lostwithiel (1644), but outside Newbury (1643) and Preston (1648). The unimproved agriculture of the Highlands, on the other hand, left open spaces suitable for sudden devastating charges.

The British Isles remained virtually empty throughout the area's life as a theatre of war. Population figures before the 1801 census are conjectural, but the Roman province may have had a million inhabitants, with as many more outside the frontier. These figures may have doubled by the Norman Conquest a thousand years later. The medieval English population peaked at 4–6 million before the Black Death, not recovering until the 16th century. Some 5 million English people lived through the Civil Wars, while about a million Scots witnessed the Jacobite Risings of 1715 and 1745. Only the population of pre-Famine Ireland exceeded today's, more than doubling to 5.5 million in the century between the battles of the Boyne (1690) and Vinegar Hill (1798).

Estimates of numbers engaged or losses inflicted must be set against this background. Armies were small by modern standards. Anglo-Saxon laws defined 7 men as thieves, up to 35 as a gang, and any more as an army. The 29,000 men that Edward I fielded at Falkirk (1298) was an unparalleled effort. The largest Civil War battles were Marston Moor (1644) and Worcester (1651). With 45,000–50,000 combatants they are the largest battles ever fought on British soil. The largest battle ever fought anywhere in the North Atlantic Archipelago was at the Boyne (1690) with 60,000. By contrast, the Duke of Cumberland crushed the Jacobites at Culloden (1746) with less than 8000 men.

Numbers matter, because they determine the space armies occupy, how long they need to deploy, and how long they can resist. Where other considerations are equal, such as weapons and training, superior numbers are usually decisive. A manoeuvre that is easy for 1000 men, however, will be difficult for 10,000, and impossible for 100,000. Professional 19th-century armies with trained staff officers could not move or supply more than 30,000 men along a single road, a figure consistent with the maxima quoted above. Inflated army strengths given by innumerate chroniclers, and repeated by uncritical historians, must be rejected on military as well as demographic grounds.

Small armies were one factor differentiating historical battles from modern ones. Technology was another. Commanders lacked modern communications equipment, making command and control something of a lottery. Lack of ships that could stay out at sea made it difficult to intercept invasions. There were few beach-defence battles after Dover (55 BC), though the defenders' poor showing at Maldon (991) might suggest that fighting an invader at his strongest was not the optimum strategy. Short-range weapons of low lethality determined the shape of battlefields from Julius Caesar's time until the Age of Enlightenment. Armies adopted dense formations and fought at close range, at most a few hundred yards. Only the Romans possessed permanently embodied combat units capable of complex manoeuvres under fire, or of reacting effectively to tactical emergencies. Later armies were slow to acquire the same flexibility, until the rediscovery of drill in the military revolution of the 16th century. Even then they remained clumsy by Napoleonic standards. The Duke of Cumberland formed line of battle twice during his approach march to Culloden (1746), fearing a recurrence of the recent shambles at Falkirk, where Highlanders charged through a hailstorm to sweep away a half-formed British army.

Technology changed slowly. Shifts that we discern in medieval military capability often owed as much to new forms of military organization as to advances in the underlying technology. The Bayeux Tapestry shows little difference between Norman and English equipment at Hastings (1066), except that the invaders rode horses. Anglo-Saxon bows, like those found in the Nydam ship from 4th-century Schleswig, differed little from the ones that shredded Scottish schiltrons at Halidon Hill (1333). The weapon emerged as an instrument of victory because of changing social attitudes to its use, rather than alterations in the basic design.

Short ranges and tactical inflexibility made it difficult to force action upon an unwilling enemy. Battles occurred by surprise, as at Evesham (1265) or Hexham (1464); by pinning the enemy against an obstacle, as at the Winwaed (655); or by consent as at Hastings (1066). Commanders had every reason to refuse action. Armies that fought hand-to-hand had little chance of breaking off a fight without being cut to pieces. Defeat usually precipitated a massacre of the beaten army. The tactical clinch loosened when gunpowder opened up combat ranges, but the fate of Newcastle's white-coats at Marston Moor (1644) was not very different from Harold's housecarls at Hastings (1066). Medieval commanders knew that if they lost they would share the end of Simon de Montfort after Evesham (1265), Harry Hotspur after Shrewsbury (1403) or Richard III after Bosworth (1485) – their mutilated corpses put on display to impress the populace. A willingness to risk everything on a single throw of the dice is not the least quality that separates them from us.

Structure of the Book

Cassell's Battlefields of Britain and Ireland starts with Julius Caesar's expedition of 55 BC, and ends with the Battle of Britain in 1940. It covers 377 battles, from Aberdeen to Yellow Ford, by way of Beachy Head. Their distribution is as follows:

England	204
Ireland	69
Scotland	66
Wales	18
Naval	20
Total	*377*

Individual battles exist within a more general context. Their conduct can only be understood in the light of contemporary military practice, the strategic background that determined where they were fought, the forces engaged on the day and their weapons, organization and training. *Cassell's Battlefields of Britain and Ireland* provides this information through its organization into parts, campaign narratives and battle narratives. This allows the reader to approach the book as a linear narrative, or go directly to whichever lower-level section they require, when in reference mode. The following indexes provide alternative paths into the work:

(1) Battles in date order, showing, year, day, month.

(2) Battles listed by nation and county/unitary Authority, showing name and year.

(3) Battles in alphabetical order, name, year and main page reference.

(4) A general index including commanders, battles, place-names, people, events and weapons.

The eight major parts of the work reflect a broad categorization of the military capabilities of the period covered. Their titles allude to predominant weapon systems, such as Knight and Castle, rather than dynastic labels, such as Tudor or Stuart. Drawn from English political history, the latter are unhelpful when applied to Scotland and Ireland. Each part has an introduction defining its characteristic strategic and tactical conditions. Most parts are illustrated by an overview map showing the location within the North Atlantic Archipelago of every battlefield described in that part. Part 2 (106 battles) has two such maps; Part 8 (2 battles) has none.

Battle narratives are organized within each part into logically related groups. These may represent a specific campaign, such as Montrose's operations of 1644–5, or a less coherent series of battles, like Elizabeth I's Irish wars. Each group of battle narratives is prefaced by an overview providing immediate political and strategic context. Campaign and battle narratives appear in chronological order, except where it makes better sense to separate simultaneous but unrelated actions. Hopton's campaign in the west of 1642–3, for example, is treated independently of concurrent operations in the Midlands.

Battle narratives vary in length, depending on the evidence available, the complexity of the fighting, and the level of disagreement it has inspired. Some battles are consolidated within a single narrative, where their significance or available information does not warrant separate treatment. At the other end of the scale, some particularly significant battles have been treated at greater length: Hastings (1066), Bannockburn (1314), the Spanish Armada (1588), Edgehill (1642), Marston Moor (1644), Naseby (1645), Culloden (1745) and the Battle of Britain (1940).

No short account of an event as complex as a battle can be entirely satisfactory. At best it provides an opening into the subject, indicating key circumstances and points of debate. Sir Richard Bulstrode, a Royalist cavalry officer, commented after Edgehill (1642):

> There is always great Difference in Relation of Battles, which do usually according to the Interest of the Relators; when it is certain, that, in a Battle, the next Man can hardly make a true Relation of the Actions of him that is next him; for in such a Hurry and Smoke as in a set Field, a man takes Notice of nothing but what relates to his own Safety: So that no Man gives a clear Account of particular Passages.

Battle narratives follow a standard pattern describing:

(1) the immediate context, and the approach to battle;

(2) the numbers of troops engaged and their probable location;

(3) the fighting itself;

(4) the result, including comparative losses.

River banks are specified right or left, as seen looking downstream; the right and left wings of armies from the point of view of side under discussion, facing the enemy. Distances are given in yards and miles of 1760 yards for consistency with British speedometers and original sources. Metric equivalents appear in parentheses. Direct quotations often give distances in old British great miles of 2428 yards (2.225 km). Tactical maps accompany 102 battle narratives; the crucial two-day battle at Bannockburn (1314) has two. More detailed information about individual battles and sources quoted can be found in the Further Reading section at the back of the book.

Most battle narratives include the following additional elements, presented in bold or italic type to catch the eye without detracting from the text:

(1) IDENTIFICATION

Battle name (alternative name), day month year
Nation, County, Map sheet and reference

For example:
Newburn Ford, 28 August 1640
England, Newcastle-upon-Tyne, LR88 NZ1565–1665

NOTES

BATTLE NAME: the usual, most commonly recognized version.

ALTERNATIVE NAME: shown where applicable; appears in the alphabetical battles index (referring you to the main battle name).

DAY: omitted when unknown; days of the week or holy days given where they appear in the sources.

MONTH: omitted when unknown.

YEAR: usually AD unless shown BC; modified by *c.* (*circa*) when uncertain; follows battle name in text to distinguish multiple battles, e.g. Falkirk (1298) and (1746).

NATION: England, Scotland and Wales as current political boundaries, or Naval if at sea. Ireland is defined geographically.

COUNTY: generally as current boundaries; English traditional shires sometimes replace modern unitary authorities. It is more helpful to know Blackheath is part of London than within the Borough of Lewisham.

MAP SHEET AND REFERENCE: a unique reference pointing to the appropriate map sheet(s) and one or more 1-km map squares. 'LR' means the British Ordnance Survey's 1:50,000 Landranger series, and 'DS' the Ordnance Survey Ireland Discovery Series (Discoverer in Northern Ireland). British map references use the standard six-character format used in the Ordnance Survey's *Gazetteer of Great Britain*:

(a) Two letters identifying which of the 100-km squares forming the basis of the Ordnance Survey grid contains the battlefield;
(b) Four numbers giving the easting (position 1–2) and northing (position 3–4) of a 1-km square within the 100-km square (specified above) that contains the battlefield. Modern OS maps show these numbers along their top, bottom and sides as appropriate, with the alphabetic codes in the corners in large blue letters.

Irish map references use a five-character format:

(a) A single letter identifying one of the 100-km squares forming the basis of the Irish grid;
(b) Four numbers giving easting and northing.

An oblique stroke '/' between references indicates alternative sites; a dash '–' indicates a single site extending across several map squares; 'and' shows where fighting flared up in separate places. Compare the entries for Cynwit (878) and Rowton Heath (1645) with Newburn above. A question mark shows the site is uncertain, for example Abergwyli (1012). Our map references may diverge from the Ordnance Survey's crossed-swords symbols, which change their position over time, and are limited to a single square.

(2) COMPARATIVE DATA: A STANDARD 'SCOREBOARD' AS FOLLOWS

	Winner	*Loser*
Opponents	Covenanter	Royalist
Commanders	Sir Alexander Leslie	Edward, Viscount Conway
		Lord Henry Wilmot (p)
Numbers	17,000	4500
Losses	*c.*300	*c.*300

NOTES

WINNING/LOSING SIDE: national or tribal origin; faction in civil conflicts.

COMMANDERS' NAMES AND TITLES: indexed by surname, e.g. Leslie, Wilmot.

The Gaelic 'mac' appears:

- separately in lower case for 'son', e.g. Bruide mac Bili.
- as part of an established patronymic, e.g. MacDonald, MacDonnell.

COMMANDERS' FATE: d = died of wounds, k = killed, p = prisoner, w = wounded, x = executed.

NUMBERS/LOSSES: commanders rarely knew their own numbers, let alone the enemy's, particularly in the remote periods when most British battles took place. Differing degrees of uncertainty are indicated by '*c.*' (*circa*) for reasonable approximations, and question marks for guesswork or propaganda claims. Losses means total estimated casualties, including various combinations of killed, wounded or captured. Numbers of wounded are rarely available before the 18th century as the walking wounded might hobble away and serious cases would be knocked on the head. Where possible, figures are qualified in the text. The headings are omitted where data is consistently unknown, as in Part 2.

(3) DIRECTIONS

A brief indication of how to find the site. These are not evidence of public rights of way, and are followed at the user's own risk. Beware dogs at Killiecrankie, MOD helicopters at Edgehill and killer motorists on the A361 at Cropredy. As far as possible the text uses place-names found on 1:50,000 Ordnance Survey maps. These are an invaluable adjunct to the maps provided, and essential for battlefields not so illustrated. Internet users can also access maps for battlefields within the United Kingdom via the Ordnance Survey's *Get-a-Map* facility (http://www.ordnancesurvey.co.uk/oswebsite/getamap/). Enter a six-character map reference to display the appropriate 1-km square from the 1:25,000 Explorer series, from which a zoom facility gives access to the 1:50,000 Landranger and 1:250,000 Travel Map series.

PART ONE

SWORD AND JAVELIN

The Romans in Britain 55 BC–AD 83

The first historical battles in the British Isles resulted from the Roman invasions of 55 BC and AD 43. Archaeological evidence abounds of the warlike propensities of the existing population, in the shape of weapon finds and hillforts, but lack of written sources makes it impossible to guess where, when and how these objects were employed. The *Commentaries* of Julius Caesar, who led the exploratory raid of 55 BC, cut through the darkness like a searchlight, leaving the darkness as impenetrable as before when suddenly extinguished. The Roman historians Tacitus and Dio Cassius provide fitful illumination. Gaps in the sources lend exaggerated significance to those battles or commanders fortunate enough to be recorded. The reputation of Agricola, the victor of Mons Graupius (AD 83) owes much to his son-in-law Tacitus. There are no indigenous accounts of the Celtic resistance, reinforcing pro-Roman bias among classically educated commentators. The narrator of Joseph Conrad's *Heart of Darkness* naturally identified his experiences of the Belgian Congo in the 1890s with those of Britain's Roman invaders: death skulking in every bush, 'a military camp here and there, lost in the wilderness like a needle in a bundle of hay'.

Britain was the helpless object of Roman imperial politics. It was a remote province, taken when the Empire was strong, to be released when weak. The Roman occupation of Britain was the result of a gradual process, provoked by the Celtic sack of Rome in 390 BC. The horrified Romans initiated a policy of expansion, to forestall any further barbarian incursions. By the middle of the 1st century

Land over 200m
Edinburgh
Clyde
Tyne
York
Dublin
Shannon
Trent
Severn
London
Thames
1
2
3
4
5
6
0
25
50 miles
0
50
100 km

BC the Roman Empire stretched from Spain to Syria. Its northern frontier approached the Rhine. Nowhere lay beyond the potential boundaries of an empire that recognized no moral or diplomatic equal.

Roman troops reached the Pas de Calais in 56 BC, and conducted a reconnaissance in force across the English Channel the following year. Political instability in Rome delayed permanent occupation for almost a century, but once established in Britain the invaders stayed for over 400 years, a fifth of the island's recorded history. They founded many of England's pre-industrial cities, built the road network between them, and also built the wall that shadows the border between the modern nations of England and Scotland. Romanization of the economically advanced southeast reinforced the contrast between that area and less developed highland regions. Roman cultural influence was short-lived, however. Unlike Gaul, Britannia lost its adopted language and laws after the withdrawal of the legions. Towns and villas were abandoned. Scotland north of the Forth and the separate island of Ireland remained unconquered, and largely unvisited.

Many aspects of Roman civilization are strikingly modern, not least its baths and central heating. Imperial officials moved regularly between civil and military posts, dispensing justice and raising taxes. Unlike its immediate European successors, the Empire maintained a standing army of permanently embodied professional troops. After the civil war that Julius Caesar provoked, his nephew and successor, Augustus, stabilized the Roman army at 30 legions. These were formations the size of brigade groups, about 5000 strong, with regimental traditions and semi-permanent stations. While the legions recruited in Italy, provincial regiments comprising recently conquered barbarians and Roman officers provided the army's cavalry and light infantry. The troops were paid in regularly minted coins. There were state-sponsored factories, mines and waterworks,

---

KEY

1 Mons Graupius AD 83

2 Menai Straits AD 60

3 Caradoc's Last Stand AD 51

4 Medway AD 43

5 Bigbury Camp 54 BC

6 Dover 55 BC

and a complex interchange of goods across the Empire. Nevertheless, the role of slavery in this commerce is a reminder of the distance between Roman civilization and modern British society.

The political and cultural fragmentation of Britain before the invasion contrasts with Roman centralization and unity of purpose. Celtic-speakers with iron tools and weapons had spread unevenly across Britain and Ireland during the 1st millennium BC, but Bronze Age and late Neolithic customs and artefacts persisted alongside the new Iron Age settlements. Land hunger and political dissension encouraged the spread of hillforts across southern England. Their earth ramparts and maze-like gateways defied chariots and cattle thieves, but were no defence against Roman legionaries advancing behind a barrage of ballista bolts. Hillforts provide physical evidence of the political disunity that preceded the Roman invasion, while it is known that Julius Caesar and the Emperor Claudius both entertained British collaborators, driven from their tribal kingdoms by rival chiefs. The Roman conquest of Gaul and cross-Channel trade further divided British society, heightening tensions between pro- and anti-Roman tribes, as Western power destabilizes the Third World today.

Celtic society was organized for fighting, but hardly for war. Raids in pursuit of women or cattle were commonplace, but these small-scale engagements emphasized individual prowess rather than concerted action. Craftsmen manufactured fine arms and armour for heroes, rather than serviceable weapons for the masses. In the moments before battle champions would step out from the line to challenge their opponents to single combat, proclaiming their ancestors' deeds of valour, while belittling their enemy to undermine his courage. Victors carried off the losers' weapons and ornaments, and took their heads for display, like so many hunting trophies. The Celts had two great passions, 'to be brave in war, and to speak well'. In victory they were arrogant, in defeat desperate to the point of suicide.

British weapons derived from a similar technological base to that of the Romans, but different social structures produced contrasting tactical systems. Celtic individualism demanded skirmishing weapons: javelins and long slashing swords that needed plenty of space. The British fought naked, in the sense that they shunned armour. Their only protection was a hexagonal shield, and magical symbols painted on with woad. Elaborately decorated bronze shields and helmets appear to have been made for display or as religious offerings, not for fighting.

The ultimate platform for individual displays of athleticism was the chariot. Drawn by two ponies, chariots were lightly constructed from wickerwork, their spoked wheels innocent of scythes. At the start of a battle charioteers dashed about hurling javelins, hoping to throw the enemy into confusion. Then the warriors would leap down to fight on foot, while the drivers kept out of harm's way, ready to rescue their master if hard pressed. Such was the skill of the crews that they could operate at the gallop on a steep incline, the warriors running out along the draft pole, and back into the vehicle, as quick as lightning. Chariots were ideal for a sudden descent upon foragers, or for cruising up and down before a battle, but they were too few and too quickly exhausted to sustain a lengthy combat. Once horses and drivers were worn out, the ill-equipped masses of British footmen, without leaders or tactical organization, were helpless.

The Romans were more businesslike. Their central military institution was the legion of ten cohorts of 480 men each, organized in six centuries similar in size and number to the companies of a modern battalion. Cohorts formed up for battle in six ranks, each file occupying a yard (approximately 1 m) of frontage. Depending on tactical requirements, a legion might deploy its cohorts in two or three lines, the *duplex* or *triplex acies*, occupying a front of 650 to 800 yards (600 to 730 m). As in modern tactics, successive echelons kept reserves fresh, outside the zone of demoralization, ready to relieve a front line in difficulties, or respond to unexpected developments.

Unlike their noisy opponents Roman soldiers kept silence in the ranks, and attacked together in response to their commander's signal. They were well equipped for offensive action at short range. Helmets and armour protected heads and bodies, but legs were left bare for mobility. Semi-cylindrical shields of plywood edged with iron provided further protection, from chin to knee. In the testudo or tortoise, soldiers linked shields overhead for cover while attacking fortifications. A bronze boss over the handgrip made the shield an offensive weapon, allowing legionaries to fell their opponents with a punch, before stabbing down or sideways with their short double-edged swords. Legionaries also carried two heavy javelins, or *pila*, thrown before charging. The missile's long iron head was designed to bend after piercing an enemy shield, leaving the latter's owner encumbered even if not injured. Roman weapons and tactics made the legion a deadly killing machine. A concerted charge would closely follow volleys of *pila* at 30 yards (27 m) range, legionaries knocking down their shieldless opponents, trampling them with iron shod sandals, crowding them too close together to use their own long swords, and slaughtering them wholesale.

Auxiliary units protected the flanks or prepared the attack with slings, bows and javelins. Archers from the eastern provinces used composite bows ranging up to 150 yards (140 m). Beyond that, every century had its ballista (catapult) able to transfix an enemy warrior with a 12-inch (30-cm) bolt at 300 yards (280 m). The mounted arm was not capable of shock action against undefeated infantry, but was essential for reconnaissance and pursuit, cutting down fugitives with their lances and long swords. Hardened by continuous training and frontier wars, the Roman army's only weakness was its lack of mobility. Foot soldiers carried a heavy load of armour and equipment, although less than Royal Marines carried in the Falklands Campaign of 1982. More seriously, the shortage of reliable cavalry forced the Romans to entrench every night to avoid surprise, diverting energy from marching to digging, and slowing the pace of campaigns.

Given their tactical superiority, it is not surprising that Roman commanders sought to destroy the enemy's will to resist by inflicting heavy casualties in a decisive battle. If necessary, Roman forces would devastate an area to force the inhabitants to fight, as Julius Caesar and Agricola appear to have done in Essex and Scotland respectively. The superior logistics of an organized army ensured more Romans reached the battlefield than barbarians, whose forces melted away from hunger or boredom. A victorious Roman army would expect to occupy the enemy's chief centres of power, and consolidate their own position by building forts, linked by roads and signal towers. The presence of numerous craftsmen in the ranks paid off in peacetime, as the army became a motor of economic progress, native settlements springing up to service military outposts.

The Britons' strategic response to invasion was not dissimilar to that faced by British soldiers of Queen Victoria's reign. First the natives attacked the intruders' camps and foraging parties. Defeated in the open field, they resorted to passive defence of naturally strong positions, such as rivers or hillforts. Beaten out of these strongholds, they embarked upon guerrilla resistance, harassing Roman 'friendlies', or ambushing dispersed parties building forts or roads. This phase of the struggle would be painful for the invaders, as it set the defenders' strengths, their agility and local knowledge, against the weakness of regular troops facing a popular uprising in a foreign country: lack of mobility and lack of local intelligence. Distance and poverty were a sure defence for the Celts of the Scottish Highlands, and still more so for those beyond the Irish Sea. No battles are recorded for the later centuries of Roman rule in Britain, but there was plainly much fighting. The walls built to mark the northern frontier were destroyed and rebuilt more than once, not least during the *conspiratio barbarica* of AD 367–9. The vagaries of the sources mean that we can only follow the drama of conquest, not the long-drawn anticlimax of retreat.

Julius Caesar's Invasion 55–54 BC

Julius Caesar was one of several aggressive dynasts scrambling for power as the Roman Senate lost its grip during the 1st century BC. Governor of the existing Roman provinces of Cisalpine and Transalpine Gaul from 59 BC, Caesar revealed unsuspected military talents, conquering northern Gaul by 55 BC. The Gauls had received help from Belgic tribes recently emigrated to Britain, so military necessity justified intervention beyond the encircling ocean. Britain was considered a source of freshwater pearls, silver and slaves, the soldier's appetite for plunder providing further economic motivation. As cross-Channel traders provided little intelligence regarding harbours or the opposition that might be encountered, the next logical step appeared to be a reconnaissance in force, perhaps followed by a longer campaign.

The Roman army was not yet the perfect instrument created by Augustus. Lacking regulation mail corselets, Caesar's men had to improvise personal protection from leather or felt during the civil war. The auxiliary troops were bands of ill-disciplined irregulars, often recruited from recently hostile barbarians, still under their own officers. Caesar brought two legions with him in 55 BC and an unspecified number of auxiliaries. The follow-up operation in 54 BC consisted of five legions and 2000 cavalry. The latter expedition was unprecedented in scale, with 600 transports specially constructed for amphibious operations, 28 warships and 200 auxiliary vessels.

The course of the two campaigns reflected the scale of the forces employed. In 55 BC Caesar made a successful opposed landing, but lack of mobile forces prevented the legions breaking out of their bridgehead. Contrary winds held up the cavalry, and there was only the narrowest of strategic windows before the autumnal equinox forced Caesar to return suddenly to Gaul. Next year the Romans landed unopposed, and defeated a combined British army under Cassivellaunus, whose operational skill marks him out as the first great British commander. Caesar crossed the Thames, and took Cassivellaunus' chief stronghold, after a period of guerrilla warfare. However, the approach of autumn led once more to hasty negotiations and departure. The presence in Caesar's entourage of Mandubracius, an exiled prince of the Trinovantes from Essex, hints at a wider agenda. His restoration by force of Roman arms could have formed a useful pretext for future intervention.

The results of Julius Caesar's invasions are debatable. Contemporaries grumbled he had not found one pennyweight of silver. British slaves were worthless, being neither musicians nor secretaries. The later Roman historian Suetonius saw the affair as one of only three occasions when Caesar failed. However, the Senate awarded an unprecedented 20 days public thanksgiving for the first expedition, and it should not be assumed that the agreed tribute was never paid. Reconnaissance in force is the most futile of operations, ending inevitably in retreat, but even as reconnaissance missions, the expeditions were unsatisfactory. Neither found a harbour, and both invasion fleets suffered extensive storm damage off open beaches. The main enemy, as in many later invasion attempts, was not the local defence forces, but the sea and weather.

Dover (Porta Dubris), 26 August 55 BC

England, Kent, LR179 TR3849–52

Julius Caesar's assault landing at Deal in 55 BC was the first recorded battle on English soil, and its inhabitants' first experience of organized amphibious warfare. We have only Caesar's account of the landing, but it convincingly resembles later combined operations. A campaign against the Veneti, a maritime people in Brittany, the previous year had given Caesar the nucleus of a Channel fleet and experience of naval operations in northern waters. However, a German invasion of Gaul, followed by Caesar's crossing of the Rhine, had eroded the 55 BC campaigning season. Caesar had only time for a brief visit to see Britain and its inhabitants for himself.

The expedition of 55 BC was a leap in the dark. A Roman naval officer scouted the south coast, but failed to spot the harbour at Richborough. Meanwhile contrary winds prevented Caesar concentrating his ships at one invasion port. He embarked 10,000 infantry of VII and X Legion in 80 transports at Boulogne, and sailed for Britain at midnight on 25/26 August. The cavalry went further up the coast to Ambleteuse, missed the tide, and put back.

When the first Roman ships appeared off Dover at 9 a.m. next morning, the defenders were waiting on the cliffs, within javelin range of the narrow beach. Their numbers and the unpromising lie of the land dissuaded Caesar from an immediate landing. He spent the morning waiting for his whole force to come up, while lecturing his officers on the peculiar risks of naval operations. Caesar then showed his own grasp of the flexibility of seaborne forces. At 3 p.m. he ran north with the tide to run his ships ashore on the evenly sloping shingle beach at Deal, where Henry VIII would build his castle – 1600 years too late (LR179 TR3752).

The Romans' difficulties were not ended, as British cavalry and chariots had shadowed the fleet along the coast. The transport vessels were not designed as landing craft, and grounded too far off the beach, in deep water. Weighed down with armour, and encumbered with weapons, legionaries were neither trained nor equipped for wet landings. The lightly armed Britons had the advantage, as they dashed through the surf throwing javelins. The legionaries failed to show their customary enthusiasm, and refused to disembark. Caesar's response was to beach his galleys on the enemy's unshielded right flank, where the crews could use slings, bows and artillery to maximum effect.

The British fell back, creating the opportunity for a heroic gesture to break the deadlock. Jumping into the sea the eagle-bearer of X Legion led the way ashore, precipitating a confused struggle along the water's edge. Unable to get a firm foothold or form up in their accustomed ranks, the Romans lost their tactical advantage. Superior numbers of Britons surrounded isolated groups of legionaries, hurling javelins into their exposed right flank. Again Caesar showed his grasp of combined operations, using ship's boats to move a floating reserve of uncommitted soldiers to critical points in the battle line. Once enough legionaries were ashore to form a solid front, they charged, dispersing the enemy with customary efficiency. Lack of cavalry precluded decisive success, as there were no mounted troops to convert the British rout into a massacre.

The victory was enough to persuade local chiefs to seek terms. Caesar was evidently awaiting his 500 cavalry, without whom he could not accomplish his reconnaissance mission. Another storm drove the cavalry transports back to Gaul, and also damaged the ships anchored offshore in the Downs, while high spring tides swamped the beached warships. These natural disasters encouraged the British to resume hostilities. They successfully attacked VII Legion while it was out foraging, but were themselves beaten in a more formal battle outside the Roman beachhead

Dover

	Winner	*Loser*
Opponents	Roman	British
Commanders	Julius Caesar	unknown
Numbers	10,000	unknown

defences. While entertaining fresh peace offers, Caesar took advantage of a break in the weather to sail home. His operations made little permanent impression on the Britons, only two tribes delivering the promised hostages. At home, the Senate's enthusiastic endorsement of the illegal excursion outside Caesar's own province encouraged a further expedition next year.

Directions

Caesar's landing beach extended several miles south from the pier opposite Deal Castle, between the Strand and the sea.

Bigbury Camp, 8 July 54 BC

England, Kent, LR179 TR1157

Cassivellaunus' Fight, 21 July 54 BC

England, Kent, unlocated

Caesar's first expedition to Britain demonstrated the feasibility of transporting an army across the ocean, feeding it from local resources and defeating the natives. The campaign of 54 BC was less equivocal in its outcome. In just under a month Roman troops decisively defeated the Britons, forced a major river and stormed two fortified strongholds or *oppida*.

Caesar sailed from Boulogne at dusk on 6 or 7 July, with five legions and 2000 cavalry, in some 800 ships. He found the previous year's landing beaches undefended, the mass of ships having frightened the Britons away. Caesar's first concern was to bring them to battle. As soon as he had secured a bridgehead, he marched under cover of darkness to attack the enemy's reported position, 12 miles (19 km) away on the River Stour, where he arrived early next morning. The Belgic centre of Bigbury lay on Harbledown, beyond where the city of Canterbury now stands. It was (and still is) surrounded by woods, its earth ramparts crowned with palisades, the gate blocked with felled trees. Brushing aside the defending skirmishers, VII Legion formed a testudo, filled the ditch, and drove the Britons out. Caesar's description of the fighting is brief, but it must have taken most of the day to chase away the chariots disputing the ford over the Stour and to fight up the slopes of Harbledown. Only a few hours of daylight remained, and the need to pitch camp before dark limited pursuit.

Overnight (8/9 July) a storm wrecked 40 of the ships in the Small Downs off Sandwich, and disabled many others. Caesar is often criticized for attacking Bigbury before beaching his ships, but the task could not have been completed before the storm struck. His real error lay in not finding a sheltered anchorage. The ten days now required to bring the fleet ashore gave the Britons time to renew the war on the Stour. They entrusted overall command to Cassivellaunus, a renowned warrior, and probably king of the Catuvellauni from Hertfordshire and Buckinghamshire. British numbers are unknown, but they had at least 4000 chariots, a plausible number considering the problems they caused the Roman cavalry. Cassivellaunus' mobile troops harassed Caesar's return march to Bigbury, fighting in relays so that fresh forces were always ready to replace weary charioteers. When the Romans halted to encamp, the Britons left the woods and attacked the outposts. Even the elite first cohorts sent to retrieve the situation were unnerved, and a military tribune killed, suggesting significant casualties. Legionaries were too heavily armed

Bigbury Camp

	Winner	Loser
Opponents	Roman	British
Commanders	Julius Caesar	unknown
Numbers	*c.*21,000	unknown

Cassivellaunus' Fight

	Winner	Loser
Opponents	Roman	British
Commanders	Julius Caesar Gaius Trebonius	Cassivellaunus
Numbers	*c.*13,000	unknown

for such irregular combat, while unassisted cavalry could not overcome the dismounted charioteers.

Despite these difficulties, the next day gave Caesar his decisive battle. The exact location is unknown, except that the Britons occupied high ground west of the Stour, perhaps covering the route of the future Watling Street. Caesar sent out three legions and most of his cavalry as a foraging party. Two cohorts per legion and 300 horse had probably stayed behind in the bridgehead, suggesting 24 cohorts and 1700 cavalry saw action on 21 July. Caesar may not have been present, as he credits Gaius Trebonius with the command. This time the Britons overcommitted themselves. They swooped down on all sides, pressing their attack right up to the legionary standards, close enough for the Roman infantry to launch an effective and sustained counterattack. Encouraged by the legionaries' success, the Roman cavalry charged, preventing the Britons from reforming to make a stand. British losses are unknown, but they were prevented from taking the field again in such strength.

Cassivellaunus retired across the Thames, probably across a tidal ford between Higham in Kent and East Tilbury on the northern bank. Penned within artificial banks, the modern Thames is much deeper than it was in 54 BC. The ford is now impassable, but a ferry plied there until the Middle Ages. Caesar's traditional crossing place at Brentford seems too far west, while ancient stakes found in the riverbed there are more probably fish weirs than military obstacles. Wherever Cassivellaunus disputed Caesar's passage, the Romans charged through neck-deep water to scatter the Britons, ending conventional resistance. Cassivellaunus kept only his 4000 charioteers in the field. Other Britons submitted, betraying the location of Cassivellaunus' *oppidum*. This lay among woods and swamps, perhaps at Wheathampstead, a 100-acre (40-ha) fortification near St Albans, or at Wallbury, south of Bishop's Stortford. Attacked on two sides, the defenders soon gave way, leaving behind numerous cattle, the movable wealth of the Catuvellauni.

Both sides were now inclined to negotiate. Cassivellaunus had shot his bolt with an unsuccessful diversionary attack on Caesar's bridgehead, while Caesar could not secure unconditional surrender before autumn. Westerly winds that prevented Roman ships returning from the Continent showed the risks Caesar was running. Facing unrest in Gaul, he abandoned plans to winter in Britain. Caesar had won the war, but the Gallic Revolt and Roman civil wars would delay British subjugation for almost a century.

Directions

Bigbury *The A2(T) and A2050 now cut between Harbledown and Canterbury. Turn off the A28 west of Canterbury, and cross the Stour for Chartham Hatch. Walk up through the woods to the hillfort and nature reserve. Alternatively, walk from the centre of Canterbury along Summer Hill and Faulkner Lane.*

Cassivellaunus' Fight *Site unknown. See Medway (AD 43) for Higham.*

The Roman Conquest AD 43–100

The cautious pragmatists who restored peace to the Empire after the Roman civil wars distrusted military adventures. Augustus and Tiberius Caesar left Britain to the traders, encouraging a balance of power in southeast Britain, dimly revealed today in the pattern of coin finds. The Catuvellauni remained hostile, but their long-reigning king Cunobelinus, Shakespeare's Cymbeline, avoided provocative gestures. Relations with Rome only deteriorated after his death about AD 40. His sons, Caradoc (also known as Caradog or Caratacus) and Togidumnus were young and tactless. When pro-Roman chieftains claimed imperial protection, the new Catuvellaunian leaders rudely demanded their extradition. The Emperor

Claudius had to make a choice between unthinkable loss of prestige or military intervention. The hostile biographer Suetonius suggests Claudius' only interest in Britain was a cheap triumph, but the emperor had better motives. There were too many unemployed legions on the Rhine frontier, while slaves and plunder, *pretium victoriae* ('the prize of victory'), would finance a successful campaign.

The Roman army had improved since Julius Caesar's time. Legionaries wore redesigned helmets, strengthened with iron. Flexible iron body armour or *lorica segmentata*, as shown on Trajan's Column, had replaced leather corselets. Roman officers had reorganized the auxiliaries into reliable cavalry and light-infantry units. These would play a key role during the conquest of Britain, spearheading attacks or controlling areas between legionary fortresses. The Britons continued in their traditional state of disorder. Numbers available to fight the Romans would be limited by defections, and the difficulty of feeding large concentrations of warriors. Weapons were unchanged from those found wanting in 54 BC. Cunobelinus had fortified his new capital at Camulodunum (present-day Colchester) with extensive ditches proof against chariot attack, but he was preparing for the last war, not the next.

Claudius' invasion army was approximately twice as large as Julius Caesar's: four full-strength legions, 20,000–24,000 men, and as many auxiliaries. The emperor left initial operations to a solid professional, Aulus Plautius, who conducted them in a thoroughly businesslike manner. The invasion force sailed in three echelons: an assault wave to secure the landing area; an exploitation force to expand the bridgehead; and reserves and stores. They landed at Richborough, just north of Julius Caesar's landing place. It is hard to understand how he had missed the harbour there, unless the Wantsum Channel had been inundated since 54 BC, creating a new anchorage between the Kentish mainland and the Isle of Thanet.

Aulus Plautius crushed a combined British army on the Medway, forced the Thames and took Camulodunum. He quickly established an initial frontier running southwest to northeast, from the Bristol Channel to the Humber, enclosing the economically more desirable parts of Britain. However, the Claudian invasion did not have the clear-cut result for which Roman strategists must have hoped. The politically necessary delay while Claudius travelled to the front allowed Caradoc to escape and become the focus of resistance to Roman rule. The Romans had not known of the fierce tribes and rough terrain in the west and north. The easy success of AD 43 committed the invaders to a wider struggle that was not ended by the defeats of Caradoc and Boudicca, or even Agricola's exaggerated victory at Mons Graupius (AD 83). Britain would be the first Roman province bounded by an artificial rather than a natural frontier.

Medway, AD 43

England, Kent, LR178 TQ6973

The Battle of the Medway in the summer of AD 43 was one of the most significant ever fought on English soil. An unusually protracted operation, it lasted two days and decided the future of lowland Britain for over 300 years.

Nobody opposed the landing at Richborough. Reports of troops refusing to go aboard the invasion fleet had persuaded the Britons that the Romans would not come. Unlike Julius Caesar, Aulus Plautius only moved inland after thorough reconnaissance. The first hostile contacts probably occurred along the River Stour, where the Romans met Caradoc' and Togidumnus' outposts. The Briton's main army probably gathered behind the River Medway, the strongest defensive position before the Thames. Had the Britons fought further to the west, they would have exposed now impassable fords across the lower Thames, leading directly to the Catuvellaunian heartland.

The Romans could approach the Medway by two main routes. The most direct follows Watling Street between the coast and the Downs, and would preserve communications with Richborough. However, the unimproved route would have been heavy going compared with the ancient trade route over open chalk hills further south. A coin find at Bredgar on the north edge of the Downs, a day's march short of the Medway, may suggest Aulus Plautius followed the high ground, leading to Chatham Great Lines, an ideal position to survey the battlefield.

The Britons' position would depend on the location of crossings. Today the Medway below Rochester is 200–500 yards (180–460 m) wide and over 20 feet (6m) deep. More practicable fords upstream at Halling, Snodland and Aylesford led early commentators to place the battle above Rochester, but the Britons probably fought lower down. The Medway, like the Thames, was shallower then, and the British line of retreat lay across the tidal ford at Higham. They needed to defend the lowest possible crossing to avoid being cut off, perhaps occupying Broom Hill above Strood. The general outline of the battle would be similar, in either scenario. The Romans occupied internal lines within the great bend of the river, forcing the Britons to manoeuvre to counter outflanking movements.

Aulus Plautius committed three legions, presumably keeping the fourth in reserve. Had he left two cohorts of each on the lines of communication, as Julius Caesar did, 16,000 legionaries would have been present, with a similar number of auxiliaries. British numbers are unknown, but commonly suggested strengths in excess of 100,000 would have absorbed half the male population of Roman-occupied Britain. Distance and political differences must have limited the call-up to southeast England, and it is hard to believe Britons outnumbered Romans. An overall total of 60,000 combatants still exceeds the numbers at Marston Moor in 1644.

Medway

	Winner	*Loser*
Opponents	Roman	British
Commanders	Aulus Plautius	Caradoc Togidumnus
Numbers	32,000	unknown

Like many primitive peoples, the Britons overvalued physical obstacles. They could not imagine an opposed river crossing, and bivouacked carelessly on the far bank. While they watched the main Roman army, eight cohorts of Batavian infantry from the Netherlands launched a surprise attack, as recommended by the Roman military expert Frontinus. Accustomed to swimming the most turbulent rivers in full equipment, they crossed the Medway below the Britons' left flank, perhaps at Chatham Reach, concealed by the bend in the river. Dio Cassius says they targeted the chariot horses, implying they caught them standing by while their owners swaggered about, or else picked them off piecemeal as they galloped up to deal with the unexpected onslaught.

Once the Batavians had drawn off the chariots, Plautius sent II Augusta and another legion straight across the river, under Vespasian, the future emperor. They may have found a ford, but Dio's words suggest they used some improvised means, such as assault boats made from leather tents stuffed with straw. The Romans surprised the Britons again, but failed to drive them from the field. A third legion reinforced Vespasian's foothold overnight, and the battle resumed the next morning. Fighting must have been heavy, as the senior legate was nearly captured. The Britons finally retreated, exploiting their local knowledge to escape across the Thames marshes. Dio's account of a large pool formed at high tide suggests Hope Reach below Tilbury. References to swamps, a bridge and more than one ford indicate a wide marshy area, intersected by several relatively shallow channels. Oral traditions of Plautius crossing the Thames at Higham survived until the 18th century.

Aulus Plautius had to await the emperor's arrival, before entering Camulodunum in triumph. Suetonius commented that Claudius fought no battles and suffered no casualties in Britain, but subdued a large part of the island, a comment on the decisive effect of Plautius' victory. The 16-day imperial visit was notable for the first recorded appearance of elephants in Britain, and the surrender of 11 kings, but not Caradoc. He had escaped to continue the fight.

Directions

The battlefield is thoroughly obscured by urban development. View the river from the south bank, above the bridge from Centenary Walk, and Limehouse Reach from Ship Road off Rochester High Street. Hope Reach can be seen from the Saxon Shore Way along the Thames's south bank through Higham Marshes to Cliff Fort. Cassivellaunus may have retired this way in 54 BC.

Caradoc's Last Stand (Cefn Carnedd), AD 51

Wales, Powys, LR136 SH0190?

The Catuvellaunian leader's last battle was just one episode in his nine-year struggle against the Romans. We know about it because Tacitus chose this one dramatic episode to illustrate the general course of the war. The continued insurgency suggests this emphasis lends the action, and Caradoc's subsequent capture, a spurious significance.

The Romans quickly overran southern England after the Medway battle. XX Valeria occupied Camulodunum, while the other legions fanned out: IX Hispana up Ermine Street to Lincoln, XIV Gemina along Watling Street into the Midlands. Vespasian's II Augusta cleared the south coast, fighting 20 battles, subduing two warlike tribes, and capturing the Isle of Wight and more than twenty *oppida*. Aulus Plautius returned home to a well-deserved ovation, having consolidated the Empire's new frontier along the Fosse Way.

The boundary (extending from present-day Exeter to Lincoln) was logistically and tactically sound, excluding the wild and unprofitable highlands. It was compromised almost at once by the Silures of south Wales, reinforced and inflamed by dissident refugees from the southeast. Among these was Caradoc, whose guerrilla exploits made him pre-eminent among British leaders. The clumsy response of Plautius' successor, Publius Ostorius Scapula, to a frontier in flames undermined the conquest's political basis. A punitive expedition into the Cheshire Gap offended the friendly Brigantes of the Pennine region. Pre-emptive disarmament of the provincial population provoked a minor revolt, perhaps at Wandlebury in Cambridgeshire. New legionary fortresses at Wroxeter and Gloucester pushed the frontier forward to the Severn, and denied the Silures strategic space, but stripped the interior of the province of troops.

As the net closed around south Wales, Caradoc transferred operations north, into the territory of the Ordovices, nicknamed 'hammer fighters'. Tacitus admits Caradoc was outnumbered, but gambled everything on a final confrontation, having enlisted all those who feared a Roman peace. Perhaps guerrilla operations became unprofitable in the face of overwhelming Roman strength; perhaps Caradoc hoped a defensive victory deep in hostile territory might precipitate a Roman disaster like that in the Teutoberger Wald in AD 9. Scapula may have thought one smashing victory would solve all his difficulties, or he may just have seen another hillside beyond another stream.

The site of Caradoc's last stand is unknown. The plethora of hillforts named Caer Caradog undermines A.H. Burne's compelling location of the battle on the River Clun, between Clunbury and the Black Hill in Shropshire. Various hillforts on the upper Severn have been suggested, but lack conviction. Tacitus mentions improvised stone walls, not continuous earthworks, while isolated hilltops with no emergency exit are inconsistent with Caradoc's reputation as a guerrilla leader. The current favourite is in Powys, 6 miles (10 km) northeast of Llanidloes, at Cefn Carnedd, above Caersws. However, it is too steep for Tacitus' description: a gentle ascent flanked by hills, protected by a minor river across the front

Caradoc's Last Stand

	Winner	*Loser*
Opponents	Roman	British
Commanders	Scapula Publius Ostorius	Caradoc (a.k.a. Caradog or Caratacus)
Numbers	20,000	unknown

that left space on its banks for diehard Celtic warriors to disport themselves. Today's countryside would be quite unrecognizable to Tacitus' informant, however. Marshes and sandbanks choked undrained valley bottoms, forcing armies onto higher ground. Perhaps the most likely area for the battle lies above Newtown (Y Drenewydd) 5 miles (8 km) further east, where ancient trackways approach the Severn.

Scapula had two legions, possibly reinforced by detachments from the other two, say 10,000–12,000 legionaries with as many auxiliaries. The Britons are generally assumed to have outnumbered the Romans several times, but the narrow valleys would have left little room for so many. Their rapid escape and apparently low casualties imply the Britons were less numerous. Tacitus precedes Caradoc's battle with the usual imaginary speeches to dense throngs of suitably defiant savages. His account of Scapula's delay before attacking is more credible, even if it exaggerates the beetling hills and generally grim topography. Scapula would naturally have surveyed the ground before launching a frontal attack. He may have been waiting for the river to subside after a Welsh summer downpour.

The river made a disappointing obstacle, and was crossed without difficulty. As long as the struggle was a long-range exchange of missiles, most of the casualties were Romans. Once their testudo penetrated the stonewalls, however, the Britons did not last long. They fell back up the ridge, pursued by light and heavy infantry, the former skirmishing with their javelins, the latter pushing on in close order, the unarmoured Britons in complete disorder. Tacitus' account then degenerates into stock phrases. No British casualties are claimed, an indirect tribute to Caradoc's choice of ground. Perhaps he only put up token resistance, which Tacitus wrote up as a notable victory. The only substantial Roman gain was the capture of Caradoc's wife and family. Caradoc fell into their hands later, through treachery.

Neither battle nor capture ended the war. The Silures fell upon a legion dispersed building forts, and killed the camp prefect, or third in command, and eight centurions. They cut up foraging parties, and escaped with trivial losses, despite rescue parties of legionaries. Two auxiliary cohorts were wiped out and XX Valeria was defeated in the open field. Guerrilla engagements flared in woods and marshes, decided not by Roman skill or training, but by luck or individual courage. While Caradoc lived in honourable exile in Rome, Scapula died on service, broken down by ill health and anxiety. His notable Welsh victory was a hollow one.

Directions

For Cefn Carnedd take a minor road southwest off the B4569 Caersws–Trefeglwys road. Cross Afon Trannon and turn left at Trewythen, up the hill. At the top follow a track on the left through woods to the fort.

Menai Straits, AD 60

Wales, Anglesey, LR114 SH5571?

Boudicca's Revolt (Mancetter/Paulerspury), AD 60

England, unlocated

The Boudiccan Revolt was a disaster for Roman and Briton alike, the more shameful for the former, having been brought upon them by a woman. Destruction of Roman centres at Colchester, Chelmsford and

Menai Straits

	Winner	*Loser*
Opponents	Roman	British
Commanders	Suetonius Paulinus	unknown

Boudicca's Revolt

	Winner	*Loser*
Opponents	Roman	British
Commanders	Suetonius Paulinus	Boudicca
Numbers	*c.*12,000	unknown

London is well attested by archaeology, but the final battle's location remains unclear.

The Claudian policy of limited occupation had failed by the mid-50s, prompting Suetonius Paulinus, a new governor with a background in mountain warfare, to initiate a more forward policy. In AD 60 he stormed Anglesey after forcing the Menai Straits, most probably at the shallowest part of the waterway near Thomas Telford's 1826 bridge. Anglesey was the granary of Wales, and the last refuge of those who were opposed to Roman rule. Hags in black flitted about the defending throng brandishing torches, while druids showered curses on the invaders, curses that should have turned their bowels to water. The Romans paused as they left their landing craft, refused to be intimidated by a crowd of women and fanatics, and slaughtered the lot.

Paulinus' campaigns on the Welsh extremities weakened Rome's hold on Britain's settled heartland, and while his men cut down sacred druidic groves, the Iceni of East Anglia revolted. XX Valeria's transfer from Colchester to Gloucester had reduced the military presence in the southeast. Their replacement by a colony of uncouth veterans outraged the Britons whose land they took. The last straw was the violent termination of the Iceni client-kingdom on the death of its king, Prasutagus. His property was plundered, his protesting widow Boudicca flogged, and her daughters raped.

The Roman situation was desperate. Forced marching to save Colchester, IX Hispana lost three cohorts in an ambush, perhaps at Wormingford just north of the colony. Paulinus dashed to London with his cavalry, but in the absence of defences or garrison, took the grim decision to sacrifice the city and save the province. He retreated back up Watling Street to meet his legionaries marching down from Anglesey. The model municipality of Verulamium was abandoned to the rebels. Tacitus claimed 80,000 Roman sympathizers died, but archaeological evidence for such casualties is scarce.

Paulinus avoided action, hoping the Britons might disperse, or reinforcements arrive. He summoned II Augusta from Exeter, but hostile tribesmen surrounded the town and the camp prefect refused to march. Eventually Boudicca's approach compelled the Roman commander to fight with the troops in hand. The battlefield lies somewhere in the Midlands, along the line of Watling Street, as far west as would still allow reinforcement from Exeter. Tacitus is hopelessly imprecise, despite eyewitness testimony from his father-in-law, Agricola. Paulinus chose a position approached through a defile that prevented the Britons deploying their superior numbers. A wood, well scoured for infiltrating Britons, secured the Roman rear, while a bare plain in front prevented another ambush.

Several sites for the battlefield have been proposed. Paulerspury southeast of Towcester in Northamptonshire seems too near London. Wroxeter, headquarters of XIV Gemina, lacks good communications south. Mancetter in Warwickshire, not far from Bosworth Field, is a plausible rendezvous, intermediate between London and Chester, lying on a geological fault that might create the conditions Tacitus describes. Unfortunately the fault runs parallel to Watling Street, requiring Paulinus to occupy a flanking position, presenting his right flank to the enemy, and exposing his communications with the Severn valley. A position at right angles to Watling Street would be more credible, somewhere just east of Wall in Staffordshire, a couple of days march further west, still covering the Gloucester road to Exeter.

Paulinus had all XIV Gemina, part of XX Valeria and the auxiliaries from nearby stations – at least 10,000 men, perhaps 7000–8000 legionaries and 4000–5000 auxiliaries. Dio's claim of 200,000–300,000 Britons needs to shed a nought at least. Roman deployment was standard: legionaries in the centre, covered by light troops in front and cavalry on the flanks. They had too few men to match the Britons' front, so drew up in three divisions, to engage the enemy at several different points. The Britons wandered onto the killing ground piecemeal, installing their wives on carts to watch the Romans' final destruction.

Reports of Boudicca's pre-battle speeches are the usual tosh, but Dio's personal description of Boudicca rings true: tall, fierce of eye, harsh of voice, with waist-length tawny hair and tartan tunic. Paulinus' soldierly exhortation to his men is more credible. It was quality not numbers that counted. Only let the soldiers keep closed up and steadily pile up the dead with sword and shield boss, forgetting the thought of plunder: 'once the victory was gained, all would be their own'. The troops can have needed little encouragement to sell their lives dearly, as they were cut off from help and aware of their old comrades' fate at Colchester.

The Romans awaited the Britons in silence until they were within effective range, when they hurled their javelins and dashed forward, breaking into the enemy's ranks. Tacitus suggests the first shock won the day, but Dio describes a daylong encounter. Surrounded by superior numbers, the three Roman divisions faced in every direction. Chariots careered through the melee, scattering close-formed infantry, until Roman archers shot the unarmoured crewmen. Dio describes a mass of writhing bodies and limbs, like a lurid relief on some sarcophagus. As usual Celtic enthusiasm was no match for Roman discipline. The legionaries drove the ill-armed Britons back against the parked wagons, giving no quarter, even to the women or baggage animals.

Roman casualty reports are reasonable: 400 dead implies 10 per cent losses overall, at two wounded to every dead man. British casualties of 80,000 are overstated by a factor of ten. A loss ratio of one to six in favour of the winner is not unreasonable, including many fugitives.

Boudicca poisoned herself soon after the battle, but Paulinus kept his troops in the field, to punish guilty and neutral alike. As famine swept the province, Nero appointed a more conciliatory governor. The military had done their work. Lowland Britain would now experience 300 years of peace.

Description

Menai Straits *Reach the rocks on the Anglesey side via a footpath on the left, immediately after Telford's suspension bridge. View the strait from a viewpoint on the A4080, between Telford Bridge and Pont Britannia.*

Boudicca's Revolt *Site unknown*

Mons Graupius, AD 83

Scotland, Aberdeenshire, LR 38 NJ6825?

Agricola's victory at Mons Graupius appears to complement earlier Roman victories in England and Wales, fulfilling the work of Aulus Plautius and Paulinus. Thanks to Tacitus, we seem to be remarkably well informed about the conquest of Scotland, and the final battle of AD 83. However, Tacitus' *Agricola* was a eulogy, written in memory of a respected father-in-law, not a balanced view of objective truth. The date, location and true nature of the battle are all open to question.

Agricola fought Mons Graupius in the seventh year of his governorship, which probably began in AD 77, but could have been a year later. Archaeology shows him completing the work of his predecessors, consolidating the Roman position in Wales and northern England. He did not extend the province's boundaries until AD 80, when he reached the Forth–Clyde isthmus. Only during operations in Galloway the following year does Tacitus claim contact with nations hitherto unknown. Agricola renewed the advance in eastern Scotland in AD 82.

The identity of the enemy is unclear, Tacitus lumping them all together as Caledonians. Initially they would have been the Celtic inhabitants of Angus and Aberdeenshire: the Vacomagi and Taexali, who reacted violently to Agricola's drive up Strathmore, between the southern edge of the Highlands and the Sidlaw Hills. When Roman forces divided, the locals attacked IX Hispana by night, stabbing the sentries and breaking into the camp. Agricola's arrival with

Mons Graupius

	Winner	*Loser*
Opponents	Roman	Caledonian
Commanders	Agricola Gnaeus Julius	Calgacus/Calgaich
Numbers	25,000	30,000
Losses	c.1100	10,000?

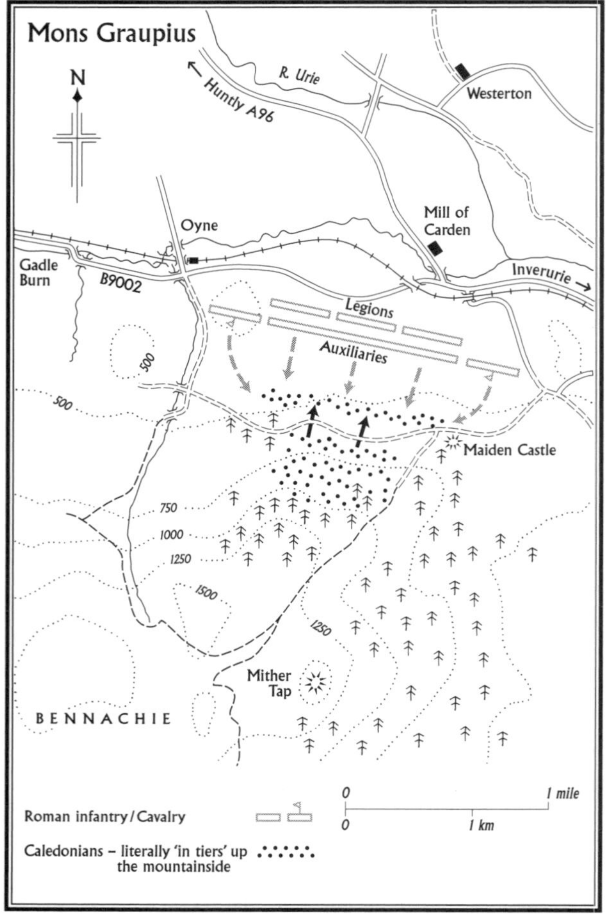

Directions

Bennachie lies 5 miles (8 km) northwest of Inverurie. Take the A96 to Pitcaple and fork left along the B9002, where the Forestry Commission car park at Pittlodrie may lie on the Caledonian front line. A minor road north past Mill of Carden leads to Durno Camp, which is only discernible from the air.

mobile forces saved the day, but he failed to score a decisive success, as woods and swamps covered the enemy's retreat.

The final battle came the following season, after much countermarching over bogs, hills and rivers, the weary troops wondering if they would ever come to grips with the enemy. Caledonian motives for accepting battle are unclear. Warrior aristocrats, lacking foreknowledge of the outcome, they may have been stung into action by the devastation that accompanied every Roman army. Perhaps Agricola's advance threatened their agricultural interests in Nairn and Moray, where subterranean granaries suggest an arable economy. Death in battle was preferable to starvation.

The location of the ensuing encounter is one of the most vexed questions about the Roman occupation of Scotland. The battle's name is unhelpful: Mons does not necessarily mean a mountain, while the Grampians take their name from a later misreading of Tacitus. Attempts to convert Tacitus' rhetoric into topographical detail are foredoomed to disappointment, but everything indicates a far northern location: the lateness of the season, and Tacitus' belief, voiced by his fictive Caledonian leader Calgacus (from *Calgaich*, 'the swordsman'), that there were no more nations beyond them, only waves and rocks.

There are four credible sites:

(1) Duncrub Hill in Perthshire is etymologically equivalent to Mons Graupius, but too far south: 8 miles (13 km) southwest of Perth and 1 mile (1.6 km) west of the Roman camp in map square NO0014.

(2) Meikle Carewe Hill (983 feet/286 m, NO8292) near Stonehaven in Aberdeenshire. However, the nearby Roman camp at Raedykes (NO8390) was probably built much later.

(3) Knock Hill, overlooking the Pass of Grange, where the Grampians' proximity to the sea might have compelled Agricola to attack the enemy's chosen position. It is 10 miles (6 km) southwest of Banff, in map square NJ5355.

(4) Durno Camp north of the massif of Bennachie near Westerton farm, some 20 miles (30 km) northwest of Aberdeen, is the strongest contender. Sepa-

rated from the high ground by the River Urie, which Tacitus fails to mention, it may be too large for the forces at Agricola's disposal. However, it does provide a fine view of the mountain, on whose steep northern slopes the Caledonian ranks would appear as described by Tacitus, below the serrated crest, *summa collium* 'the top of several hills'. The Romans' fighting position would lie south of Gadie Burn, between Oyne and Mill of Carden. A vitrified fort at Mither Tap, which might serve as a backdrop to Calgacus' speechmaking, is not contemporary with the battle. Only fresh and compelling archaeological evidence such as mass burials will resolve the debate.

The burden of the day fell upon the Roman auxiliaries: 8000 infantry in the front line, flanked by 3000 cavalry, and with another 2000 cavalry in support. The legionaries remained in reserve, presumably close behind the auxiliaries, not a mile away, in camp. Three under-strength legions of 4000 would bring Agricola's total numbers up to 25,000. Tacitus claimed the Caledonians fielded over 30,000, drawn from many tribes, united by the Roman threat. They deployed on a gentle slope, foremost ranks on the plain, subsequent ranks in tiers above them, while chariots clattered about between the armies. Agricola opened out his ranks to match the Caledonian front, but refused to commit the legions.

A preliminary missile exchange allowed the Caledonians to display their dexterity in catching javelins on their broad swords, and then six auxiliary cohorts charged, driving the enemy infantry back uphill, with shield boss and sword. Other cohorts joined in, their rapid advance leaving a trail of dead and winded Caledonians. Roman cavalry chased off the chariots and joined the infantry melee, but lost momentum attacking uphill. As the attack stalled, those Caledonians who preferred to see the winner before committing themselves began to come down from the mountain tops. Choosing his moment, Agricola scattered them with his reserve cavalry, who pressed on to take the main Caledonian battle line in the rear. Pinned in front by the infantry, the Celts could not turn to face this new threat, and fled.

The 360 Roman dead suggests over 1000 casualties altogether, 7 per cent of the troops committed. A lower proportion than in Boudicca's defeat is reasonable, as the fighting was less severe. Tacitus probably exaggerated enemy losses for effect, although one in three is not implausible for the losers in a battle fought at sword-length. The German military historian Hans Delbrück (1848–1929) doubted whether the action ever happened at all, viewing the auxiliaries' difficulties and the Caledonian numbers and losses as rhetorical embellishment. In his view the natives were so weak they gave way before the first Roman attack, and the situation never became a real battle, as the failure to commit the legionaries suggests.

Agricola's victory had little permanent consequence. The Roman army abandoned its forts, withdrawing to the River Tweed, 85 miles (140 km) to the south. The emperors Domitian and Trajan had more pressing concerns than conquering a particularly unprofitable corner of a remote island province. North Britain remained unsubdued, beyond complex defensive systems named after the emperors who built them – Hadrian's Wall and the Antonine Wall. An unintended consequence of Agricola's advance was the Caledonian and later the Pictish confederation. They inflicted terrible defeats upon the Romans, including the destruction of IX Hispana, in unrecorded guerrilla actions. Mons Graupius may not have been the climactic victory described by Tacitus, but it was the Romans' last documented battle in Britain.

PART TWO

SHIELDWALL

The Barbarian Invasions *c.*429–1066

The Roman army's departure from Britannia at the turn of the 5th century had far-reaching consequences for the region's military history, even beyond the old provincial frontiers in Scotland and Ireland. Battles became more common with the passing of the *pax romana*, though their details remain mysterious. Sources rarely permit precise location or detailed reconstruction. Nevertheless, they do reveal strategic patterns that lie behind the cultural divisions of the British Isles – the North Atlantic Archipelago – today.

For six centuries the North Atlantic Archipelago was a target for Germanic or Scandinavian invasions. The Romans had regarded such people, living outside the Empire, as barbarians. Their material and political culture appears in many respects inferior to that which they replaced. They lacked writing, leaving the military historian dependent on archaeology, or on poetry handed down orally and not written down until much later. These are sometimes revealing but often dangerous sources. Pots are unreliable evidence for political events, while the importance of a battle may bear little relation to its bardic fame. The earliest written records for what used to be called the Dark Ages are not much better. Military events have to be reconstructed from passing references in genealogies, Easter annals and ecclesiastical histories, many of them written years later by ignorant or partisan scribes. The inadequacy of the historical record is particularly frustrating in the earliest part of the period. The post-Roman economy in Britain collapsed in the middle of the 5th century, towns fell out of use, and coins ceased to circulate. The origins of the English settlement are buried in the wreckage, leaving historians unable to decide between competing interpretations of the settlement as a genocidal catastrophe, or business as usual under new management.

When the dust settled in the late 6th century, a number of Anglo-Saxon kingdoms had emerged in the south and east of England, engaged in slow but persistent expansion at the expense of each other, and of British successor states in Cornwall, Wales, Cumbria and lowland Scotland. Beyond them lay the Picts of the Highlands and, over the Irish Sea, the *Scoti* or Scots, as the Irish were then called. Their depredations faced the Britons with an unwinnable war on two fronts, especially once the Antrim Scots crossed into Argyll to form the kingdom of Dalriada. The chronic divisions of the British do much to explain Anglo-Saxon and Scottish expansion. The most famous battle recorded in the Welsh Annals was Arfderydd (*c.*573). This was an internecine struggle between rival British leaders, not against the Angles of Northumbria or the recently arrived Scots of Dalriada.

Military interaction between Britain and Ireland at this period was generally eastwards. The 5th century was the classical period of Irish piracy, with raids up and down the western seaboard of Britain. Their most famous victim was St Patrick. The first Irish high king, Niall of the Nine Hostages, fell victim to Romano-British coastal forces somewhere off the Isle of the Wight in 405. Some centuries later, the Vikings possessed similar strategic mobility. The grandsons of Ivar the Boneless ruled alternately over kingdoms in York and Dublin in the early 10th century. The first Irish battles recorded in sufficient detail to discuss here were fought against foreign invaders, although the result of Clontarf (1014) was radically different from that of Dover (54 BC) or the Medway (AD 43). The Pictish successors of the Caledonian League that resisted Agricola dominated the Scottish Highlands until the 9th century. Little survives of their material culture, except for their astonishing engraved stones.

The Anglo-Saxon settlers of England and southeast Scotland are generally supposed to have come from various German tribes, whom Bede calls Angles, Saxons and Jutes. By the 9th century these tenuous differences had been subsumed in a common 'English' identity. The Anglo-Saxon kingdoms of that period are most accurately classified as a tetrarchy of four states: Northumbria, Mercia, Wessex and East Anglia. Smaller kingdoms in Essex, Kent and Sussex were

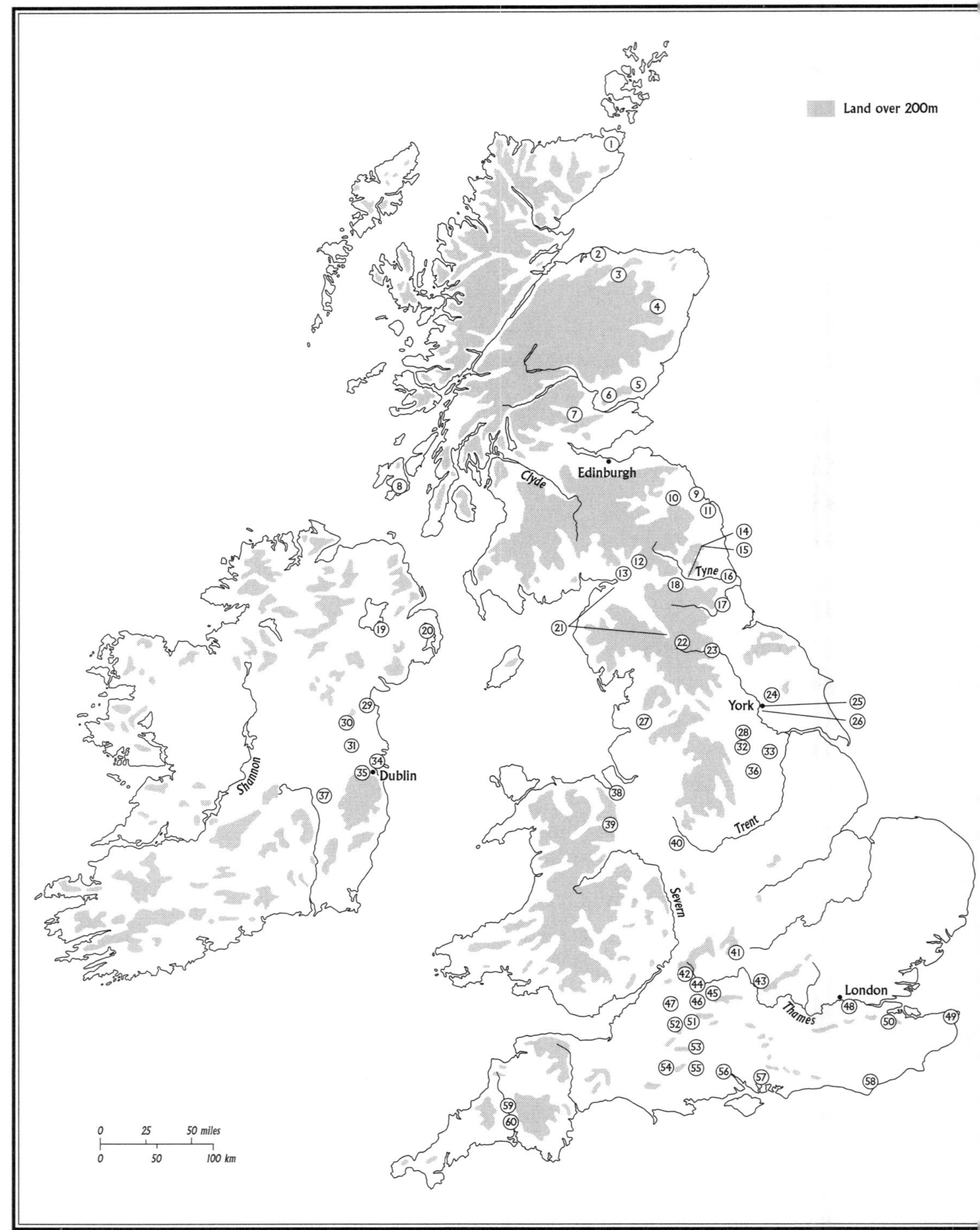
Land over 200m
Edinburgh
Clyde
Tyne
York
Dublin
Shannon
Trent
Severn
London
Thames
1
2
3
4
5
6
7
8
9
10
11
12
13
14
15
16
17
18
19
20
21
22
23
24
25
26
27
28
29
30
31
32
33
34
35
36
37
38
39
40
41
42
43
44
45
46
47
48
49
50
51
52
53
54
55
56
57
58
59
60
0 25 50 miles
0 50 100 km

KEY *Map Left*

1 Skidamyre *c.*995
2 Torfnes 1040
3 Mortlach *c.*1005
4 Lumphanan 1057
5 Nechtanesmere 685
6 Dunsinane Hill 1054
7 Monzievaird 1005
8 Calathros 639
9 Lindisfarne *c.*590
10 Carham 1018
11 Alnwick I 1093
12 Degsastan 603
13 Arfderydd *c.*573
14 Corbridge 914
15 Corbridge 918
16 Don's Mouth 796
17 Durham (Siege) 1039
18 Denisesburna *c.*633
19 Mag Rath 637
20 Strangford Lough 877
21 Burgus *c.*1006
22 Stainmoor 954
23 Catraeth *c.*598
24 Stamford Bridge 1066
25 York 867
26 Gate Fulford 1066
27 Whalley 798
28 Castleford 948
29 Anagassan 926
30 Kells 718
31 Tara 980
32 Winwaed 654
33 Idle River *c.*617
34 Clontarf 1014
35 Dublin 919
36 Haethfelth 632
37 Allen 722
38 Chester *c.*616
39 Maserfelth 641
40 Tettenhall 910
41 Fethanleag 584
42 Cirencester 628
43 Bensington 779
44 Ellendun 825
45 Mons Badonicus *c.*495
46 Beranburh 556
47 Dyrham 577
48 Crecganford *c.*456
49 Wippedsfleot *c.*465
50 Aegelesthrep *c.*455
51 Wodnesbeorh 592
52 Bradford-on-Avon 652
53 Searoburg 552
54 Peonnum 658
55 Cerdicesford *c.*519
56 Natanleag *c.*508
57 Portesmutha *c.*501
58 Anderitum *c.*491
59 Gafolford 825
60 Hengestesdune 838

Unlocated

Alleluia Victory *c.*429
Biedcanford 571
Caer Greu *c.*580
Circinn 597
Glen Mama 999
Strathcarron 642
Trent *c.*678
Wibbandun 568

Battles in Southern England and Wales after the Viking Invasion

Map above

1 Buttington 893
2 Holme, The 903
3 Thetford 1004
4 Ringmere 1010
5 Brunanburh 937
6 Tempsford 918
7 Assandune 1016
8 Maldon 991
9 Sherston 1016
10 Benfleet 893
11 Reading 871
12 Englefield 870
13 Ashdown 871
14 Brentford 1016
15 Aclea 850
16 Rochester 884
17 Thanet 853
18 Sandwich 850
19 Cynwit 878
20 Carhampton 836
21 Carhampton 843
22 Watchet 988
23 Parrett River 848
24 Ethandun 878
25 Meretun 871
26 Kennet 1006
27 Basing 871
28 Farnham 893
29 Pinhoe 1001
30 Wicganbeorg 850
31 Penselwood 1016
32 Wilton 871
33 Winchester *c.*860
34 Portland 837
35 Southampton 837
36 Sea Battle 896
37 Aethelingadene 1001
38 Hastings 1066

pawns in the game, passing under West Saxon control after the Mercian defeat at Ellendun (825). These seven historical kingdoms, the traditional Anglo-Saxon Heptarchy, arose from a process of forcible amalgamation dating at least from the Battle of Wibbandun (568). Viking invasions hastened amalgamation by exterminating all the Anglo-Saxon royal houses except that of Wessex. The 300-year struggle against the Vikings transformed English military structures, leading to the reintroduction of fortified towns, the royal burghs. The unprecedented levels of military mobilization included the most advanced taxation system in Western Europe, used to support a navy and professional infantry force, the housecarls.

The Emperor Honorius had urged British municipal authorities to take responsibility for their own defence in AD 410. Their failure to do so resulted in a fragmented and militarized society dominated by Anglo-Saxon invaders in the southeast and Celtic warlords in the imperfectly Romanized north and west. On both sides of the cultural divide warfare became the main concern of societies dominated by a small warrior elite of petty kings and their hearth-troops. Seven centuries later the Welsh still considered it a disgrace to die in bed, and an honour to be killed in battle. The original of Old Siward in Shakespeare's *Macbeth* was disgusted at dying a 'cow's death' in his bed of straw at York in 1055. Few early medieval kings died peacefully: out of eight male descendants of King Aelle of Deira (in what is now Yorkshire), three died in action, two were murdered, one was poisoned, and two died as children in exile. Thirty sub-kings perished at the Battle of the Winwaed (654) alongside King Penda of Mercia. A king's companions, his *comitatus*, were not expected to survive his fall, and many did not. When the atheling (prince) Cyneheard killed Cynewulf of Wessex during an attempted coup, and then perished himself, both men's companions fought to the death, refusing offers of money and life. One severely wounded man escaped from each party, echoing the solitary survivor of a Celtic force destroyed at Catraeth (c.590). It is unlikely that in the 10th century Earl Byrhtnoth lived and feasted with his followers in the old style, but the poem celebrating their loyalty unto death at Maldon (991) suggests that heroic aspirations persisted even in Aethelred's England.

After the collapse of a money economy during the early 5th century, Celts and Anglo-Saxons alike depended on mixed farming, domestic industry and trade by barter. Similar economic circumstances produced comparable military institutions. Warriors attached themselves voluntarily to leaders of renown in return for arms, food and drink, a share in their plunder, and, if they lived long enough, a grant of land. Close tribal ties between leaders and led were neither essential nor usual. Mynyddog of Din Eidyn's war band, which rode to Catraeth (*c*.590), included both Pictish and northern Welsh fighting men. The lament for Owain ap Urien, one of many heroes whose exploits were filched by Arthur, recalled Owain's style and generosity: 'A fine warrior in his many-coloured harness, / Who gave horses to suppliants'. Earl Byrhtnoth was another giver of horses. Egill Skallagrimsson hopefully described Eric Bloodaxe, a Viking king of York, as 'the giver of gold armlets', dealing out gold to gladden the heart of seamen. To maintain prestige and a constant supply of plunder, leaders led annual 'hostings' (armies) to defend their borders, or to steal a neighbour's cattle. Raids were a necessary evil in a broken-backed economy, devoid of trade or currency, the only way to accrue additional resources or satisfy the heroic aspirations of the *comitatus*. Intended partly as bravado and partly as economic ventures, raids led to continual loss of life and chronic vendettas.

Settled societies remained vulnerable to raiding strategies throughout the first millennium. Marauders who appeared unexpectedly and roved over enormous areas were almost impossible to counter, as they infiltrated through forests in gangs or mounted groups, wherever there were no defenders. They could reduce a countryside to chaos and inflict permanent damage. A life of St Oswald, killed at Maserfelth in 641, described the frontier between Bernicia and Deira, Northumbria's chief components, as waste: 'nothing but a hiding place and home for wild and woodland beasts'. Battles fought by dispersed raiding parties bore little resemblance to later struggles for territorial possession. Raiders lost their advantage when victory brought permanent occupation, as the Anglo-Saxons found when they became the targets of Viking raids.

The barbarian art of war was inferior to Roman practice in technique as well as consequence. Literary and archaeological evidence support the assumption, on economic grounds, that armies were extremely small. The atheling Cyneheard nearly seized power in Sussex with 85 men, lending credibility to the *Anglo-Saxon Chronicle*'s claims that the founders of the early English kingdoms arrived in a mere handful of ships. The 4th-century German ship found at Nydam might have carried 40 people, suggesting Aelle of Sussex, who landed at Selsey Bill with three ships, brought a *comitatus* of around 100 men, while only 300 troopers are said to have ridden to Catraeth. These numbers match the level of utilization of hillforts, which were reactivated on a reduced scale during the 5th century: at Garn Boduan in Gwynedd, for example, a half-acre (0.2-ha) post-Roman site occupies a corner of the 28-acre (11-ha) Iron Age fortress. The Latin term *urbs* lost its association with the Roman or modern idea of a town, and came to mean the fortified dwelling of a leader and his retainers. The unit of defence had shrunk from the tribe to the war band.

Contemporary sources give little reliable indication of the numbers engaged in Dark Age battles. The *Anglo-Saxon Chronicle*'s claims of thousands of casualties inflicted upon the British are simply unbelievable. In the 4th century the total Roman garrison of a unified and prosperous Britannia possibly numbered 6000. German tribes mobilized a higher proportion of their military manpower than the Romans, perhaps a fifth of their population, but the largest Continental Germanic armies numbered only 10,000–15,000. The Anglo-Saxons were fragmented by overseas migration, and decimated by diseases like the plague that reached Britain in the 540s. It is inconceivable that one of the numerous Anglo-Saxon successor kingdoms, or their equally divided Celtic opponents, could have mobilized as many as a thousand warriors. The very early laws of Ine considered up to 7 men thieves, between 7 and 35 a gang, while more than that was an army or *here*. Political consolidation and the reappearance of a money-based economy in the 8th century could have supported larger forces. Viking armies must frequently have exceeded a thousand, in order to man the 200 ships in which the 'Great Army' crossed the Channel in 892, or to defend the 2000-yard (1830-m) perimeter of their winter base at Wareham in 876–877. Fleets of 100 or 200 ships were by no means rare in the 11th century, implying landing forces in the low thousands, not far off the numbers probably fielded at Hastings in 1066.

Early medieval armies were not only much smaller than Roman forces. They were worse equipped, in weapon mix and quality. The Romans had fielded all-arms forces, employing a balanced range of missile and shock weapons. Anglo-Saxon armies consisted exclusively of unprotected infantry, armed with general-purpose throwing/thrusting spears and shields. Few could afford a 3-foot (0.9-m) pattern-welded sword capable of hacking through a shield or skull. Iron was scarce among the Germans, who relied on captured or traded Roman equipment. Helmets and mail were the exclusive possession of kings, while shields were flimsy circles of alder or willow planks, up to 40 inches (100 cm) across, but only a quarter to half an inch (6–12 mm) thick. Unlike the Roman *scutum*, German shields were bound with leather, their only iron component a 6-inch (15-cm) boss in the centre, used as a knuckle-duster. Weapons found with the Nydam ship (*c.*350) suggest the Anglo-Saxons had longbows, but they do not seem to have used them for fighting. The Vikings introduced axes and bows into English warfare, or at least into the poetry: 'Darts splintered and points bit; bowstrings sped arrows from the bow … / The yew bow twanged when swords were drawn.' Bows were busy at Maldon (991), but the spear remained the main English missile weapon: Old English had eight words for spear, while in the Bayeux Tapestry housecarls are depicted carrying up to four spears apiece. Armour and a conical helmet became standard equipment for a professional warrior during the 10th century, although some still fought in everyday clothing, protected now by a kite-shaped shield. The English never adopted the Continental habit of fighting on horseback: they used horses for chasing Vikings cross-country, and for forced marches like those before Stamford Bridge and Hastings (September and October 1066), but still dismounted to fight. Byrhtnoth sent his horses away before Maldon, lest anyone misunderstand his intention to fight it out on the spot.

Like the Anglo-Saxons, the Celtic successor kingdoms had a weak industrial base. Furnaces excavated at British sites are a quarter the size of Roman ones. This metallurgical decline alone discredits the armoured cavalry of Arthurian legend. *Y Gododdin*, the poem that commemorates the Catraeth disaster, describes a warrior showering spears in flight from his bounding courser rather than charging home. It speaks more often of spear thrusts than sword strokes, implying a similar weapon mix to the Anglo-Saxon enemy. British weapon finds have been few, but Irish examples are undeveloped compared with those of the Anglo-Saxons: swords 14 to 24 inches (35–60 cm) long, and 4-inch (10-cm) shield bosses mounted on small target-sized shields, as shown in the Book of Kells. How far the Celts fought on horseback is unclear. Gerald of Wales classified most of his 12th-century countrymen as infantry. Only leaders fought on horseback, perhaps indulging in the flashy skirmishing that characterized Caesar's mounted opponents.

Armies were highly mobile, despite their lack of cavalry. Small forces with simple equipment had limited logistical requirements compared with the millions of bushels of wheat and wagonloads of missiles that Roman armies required. The Anglo-Saxons and their enemies moved rapidly around a network of Roman roads not yet plundered for building material. Four routes were sufficiently important to be labelled 'royal roads': the Fosse Way, Watling Street, Ermine Street, and the Icknield Way, the latter used by the Vikings to reach Reading in 871. Armies covered remarkable distances. King Cadwallon of Gwynedd was killed within sight of Hadrian's Wall, 225 miles (360 km) from his base at Aberffraw in Anglesey. In 654 Penda pursued Oswy of Northumbria to the Forth, 250 miles (400 km) from the Mercian capital at Tamworth. The Viking army of 894 'went at one stretch' from Benfleet in Essex to the Wirral in Cheshire.

Clusters of battles at river crossings or at strategic points of the Roman road system suggest the unfairness of traditional judgements that the military geography of early medieval Britain was too obscure to reveal much strategic ability. More than one Northumbrian leader died fighting for control of the Roman road between Lincoln and Doncaster that bypassed the Humber ferry crossing: Aethelfrith at the Idle (*c.*617), Edwin at Hatfield Chase (*c.*633), Aelfwine at the Trent (*c.*678). Kings understood the value of strategic surprise. Raedwald of East Anglia launched a successful pre-emptive strike against Aethelfrith. Harold Godwinson's rapid advance in 1066 caught a Norwegian army divided and disarmed at Stamford Bridge. Many battles lay deep within hostile kingdoms, suggesting that outnumbered rulers saw the wisdom of delaying a decision until reinforcements arrived, or the enemy had been worn down by his own success. Examples include Maserfelth (641) and, most famously, Nechtanesmere (685).

The scarcity of sieges strengthens the impression that early medieval warfare was mobile and fluid. Anglo-Saxon captures of Roman fortresses at Anderitum and Portchester are rare, and possibly mythical, examples of successful attacks on fortifications. There is no evidence that the identification of prehistoric ringworks with battles, for example at Old Sarum (552) or Badbury Castle (556), was more than a geographical convenience. Chester's Roman walls may have drawn Aethelfrith there in 616, but he certainly did not occupy what the Anglo-Saxons called Legaceaster. The 'City of the Legions' was still in ruins 300 years later. It is more likely that, seeking a confrontation with the Welsh border kingdom of Powys, Aethelfrith simply followed the Roman roads from York, via Manchester and Northwich. The Vikings made good defensive use of fortifications, but neither they nor their English opponents developed effective siege techniques.

The limited range of weapon types available to commanders restricted their tactical options, and restored symmetry to the battlefield. Like the Anglo-Saxons and Vikings with their *bordweall* or *scyldburh,* the Gododdin fought in ranks, behind their fence of shields. Celtic armies once outclassed by the Romans won significant engagements against Anglo-Saxon hosts at Mons Badonicus (*c.*490), Hatfield Chase (633), and Nechtanesmere (685). Battles were brutal hand-to-hand encounters on foot, in which one army fought the other to a standstill in a giant rugby scrum. Morale, cohesion and stamina were more important than clever tactics. A fictitious battle between two sons of Thorkill Skullsplitter illustrates the managerial style required. One had a Scots army hired from Macbeth:

> The Scots were most hot at the beginning of the fight. Earl Ljot bade his men to keep under their shields, but still to stand as fast as they could [to conserve their strength]. But when the Scots could do nothing, Ljot egged on his men, and was himself the hottest ... then the array of those Scots was broken, and after that they fled.
>
> *Orkneyinga Saga* (*c.*1200)

Illiterate thanes left no tactical manuals. Careless translation of the Latin *cuneus* as 'wedge' has suggested Germanic barbarians, including Vikings, fought in a triangular formation. This assumption is tactically insupportable, as the isolated leaders would be cut down on contact, unless the flanking files immediately dashed forward to support them. Either way, the point of the wedge would soon have flattened out. The term 'wedge' must refer to the disruptive effect of the formation on the enemy, rather than its shape. Tacitus and the Byzantine Emperor

Maurice clearly describe Germans attacking in a closely compressed body of equal strength on front, rear and sides, capable of bursting through a shallower opposing line. A *comitatus* of 100 men would have formed a solid square of ten files and ten ranks, capable of rapid movement in any direction regardless of terrain. A larger war band would be deeper and wider, while an army of many war bands would form a line of 'wedges', able to charge in echelon, automatically protecting each other's flanks.

An army on the defensive, like the English at Hastings, could form a continuous line, six or seven ranks deep, the better equipped men in front. When the shield-wall broke, casualties amongst the losers, exhausted and a spear's length from their opponents, would be heavy. Many leaders paid the ultimate price of defeat: Aethelfrith, Edwin, Oswald and Ecgfrith of Northumberland; Penda and Beornwulf of Mercia; Cadwallon of Gwynedd; the Viking Bagsecg; Earl Byrhtnoth; Harald Hardrada; Harold Godwinson and his brothers.

A few leaders refused to leave the outcome to chance or superior numbers. Surprise is particularly effective against small armies lacking adequate reserves against the unexpected. Aethelfrith may have ambushed the Dalriadan host in the narrow defiles of Liddesdale in 603, and Bruide mac Bili certainly ambushed Ecgfrith at Nechtanesmere (685). St Oswald launched a dawn attack at Denisesburna (634), after a night approach march. In such minor operations of war, comparable in scale to modern company attacks, the personal ties and shared experience that bound barbarian armies together would have made an effective substitute for the formal training that they lacked.

The Making of England

The Anglo-Saxon settlement of lowland Britain between the 4th and 9th centuries transformed the area's political and linguistic structure, and perhaps the ethnic composition of its inhabitants. The process took five centuries, compared with the four decades of the Roman conquest, revealing the numerical and political weakness of the Anglo-Saxons. The process was plainly not peaceful, whatever happened to the original Celtic population. Thin documentary evidence permits only summary coverage of the early centuries, although much ingenuity has been devoted to detailed campaign narratives that subsequent archaeological discoveries have blown sky high. The early Anglo-Saxon battles described here range from the foundation myths of the new order through the proto-history of early Wessex to the well-documented warfare of 7th-century Northumbria. In Mercia and East Anglia not even bogus genealogies have survived. Those areas feature only as they interact with Wessex or Northumbria, the homes of surviving narratives.

Adventus Saxonum 410–520

Written sources for the first arrival of the Anglo-Saxons provide remarkably precise indications of its date and location, setting it in Kent between AD 446 and 455, followed by Sussex and Hampshire between 490 and 530. They also suggest a high level of violence. The archaeological record confirms neither the dates nor the trauma. No evidence of general urban destruction has been found, beyond one burnt out house in Caistor-by-Norwich. Germanic people had been peacefully settling coastal areas from the Wash to Portsmouth Harbour since the middle of the 4th century. Many came as mercenary soldiers, *foederati* hired by the Romans to defend the Saxon Shore against their cousins, the Saxon pirates who infested the North Sea. Others followed, as rising sea levels flooded their farms on the mud-banks of Friesland.

The symbiosis between *foederati* and unarmed citizens probably lasted until an economic crisis during the 450s cut off the troops' customary supplies. The resultant mutiny followed rather than preceded the initial migrations. If they operated in a similar way to continental Germans, Anglo-Saxon chiefs preferred looting to fighting. Contemporary literary evidence bears this out. Although barbarians penetrated to the western shores of Britain, they then retired to their eastern bridgeheads. Indecisive skirmishing culminated in Anglo-Saxon defeat at Mons Badonicus (*c.*490), followed by half a century of peace.

The Alleluia Victory, *c.*429

England, unlocated

The Alleluia Victory shows the defencelessness of post-Roman British polities in the face of barbarian incursions. St Germanus of Auxerre was a Gallic bishop, who happened to be in Britain suppressing the Pelagian heresy when a raiding party of Picts and Saxons menaced his hosts. Bede contrasts the Britons' lack of leadership or confidence in their weapons with the enemy's boldness, 'as if they were attacking an unarmed foe'. The disparity between defenceless citizens and well-armed raiders suggests a breakdown in the usual defensive arrangements, perhaps a mutiny by Saxon troops stationed at York. Such *foederati* had cooperated with Pictish raiders before, during the *conspiratio barbarica* of 367, when they overran England as far as Kent, and killed the Count of the Saxon Shore.

The battle is usually associated with St Albans and hence the northern escarpment of the Chilterns, which extend as far as Dunstable 12 miles (19 km) up Watling Street, making them a useful defensive position. It has also been located at Maes Garmon (Germanus' field) in Flintshire. The action clearly took place in a backward frontier area as the saint had to improvise a place of worship from wattles for the baptism of his army. Neither of these points is consistent with Bede's description of an urban setting with piped water and theologically inclined notables. However, the frontier may not have been far away, as roads and drainage systems collapsed and encroaching forests provided cover for banditti.

Germanus had been a Roman army officer, and volunteered to organize the defence. He posted scouts to observe the enemy and reconnoitred the vicinity, while at the same time boosting morale with religious instruction and mass baptisms. Recognizing the weakness of his untried force, Germanus occupied a concealed position among some moderately sized hills, overlooking a valley. Here the British, 'still soaked in the waters of baptism', lay in ambush, watching the enemy draw near. Germanus gave the signal for action, like a Roman general, and the whole army cried out 'Alleluia' – to the consternation of the raiders, who threw down their weapons and fled in panic. Bede ascribed the victory to faith not swords, but Germanus evidently knew his business, for many of the enemy drowned in a river they had just crossed. Had it not been for his chance presence and previous military experience, the raiding party would have met no resistance. Such incidents, reproduced across southern England with less happy results for the citizens, would soon disrupt the civilized existence of town and villa.

The Alleluia Victory

	Winner	Loser
Opponents	British	Picts
Commanders	St Germanus	unknown

Directions

Tactical locations unknown.

Aegelesthrep (Aylesford), *c.***455**

England, Kent, LR178 TQ7258?

Crecganford (Crayford), *c.***456**

England, Kent, LR177 TQ5174?

Wippedsfleot (Ebbsfleet), *c.***465**

England, Kent, LR179 TR3363?

The traditional chronological peg for the coming of the Saxons is the landing of Hengist (or Hengest) and Horsa at Ebbsfleet on the Isle of Thanet in the late 440s, followed by a series of battles that established the basis of the subsequent Kingdom of Kent. This account is deeply flawed, not least because it takes no

Aegelesthrep

	Winner	Loser
Opponents	Saxons	British
Commanders	Hengist Horsa (k)	Vortigern

Crecganford

	Winner	Loser
Opponents	Saxons	British
Commanders:	Hengist	Vortigern

Wippedsfleot

	Winner	Loser
Opponents	British	Saxons
Commanders	Vortigern	Hengist

account of the archaeological evidence for previous Anglo-Saxon settlement. Hengist and Horsa, a suspiciously equine double act, are mythical figures. Their names, meaning stallion and horse, are intended to relate subsequent kings back to god-like heroes of pre-invasion times. The West Saxon compilers of the *Anglo-Saxon Chronicle* garbled Kentish place-names, making their identification uncertain. The Welsh version of the story re-orders the battles, and awards ultimate victory to their own side. Some military information can be salvaged from the foundation myths, however. Contradictory stories may reflect oral traditions recorded at different points of their development, which the annalists strained to give a historical form, without the anthropological skills to do so.

The invasion's political background was the employment of Jutish chieftains as mercenary soldiers by a British ruler named Vortigern. This translates as 'proud tyrant', originally *superbus tyrannus*, which simply meant a leader exercising power outside Roman structures of authority. Hengist and Horsa, or their real-life equivalents, were therefore *foederati* who rose against their employers, when in the *Anglo-Saxon Chronicle*'s words, they realized 'the worthlessness of the Britons and the excellence of the land'.

The first two battles lie along Watling Street, the direct route from Thanet to London. Welsh Annals reverse the sequence of Aegelesthrep and Crecganford, but Aylesford is logically earlier, being nearer the Saxon bridgehead. The ford there would allow an invader to bypass the fortified bridge over the Medway at Rochester. Crayford is the last significant river crossing before London, where Watling Street crosses the marshy confluence of the Rivers Cray and Darent, before climbing high ground to the northwest. The invaders killed 'four troops of Britons' there, which persuaded the British to abandon Kent. Their flight to London is the last report of the city until settled Anglo-Saxon kingdoms emerge in the early 7th century.

The last battle appears out of sequence, if correctly located. The Ordnance Survey marks Ebbsfleet as 'Traditional site of the Landing of the Saxons 449'. In the 5th century Ebbsfleet stood on a narrow peninsula with water on three sides. Now it lies inland, 2 miles (3 km) north of the River Stour, the last remnant of the Wantsum Channel, the tidal waterway that avoided the perils of the North Foreland. The action could, however, represent a British counterattack on the Saxon bridgehead at Thanet. Welsh Annals assure us the barbarians fled to their ships, beside the Gallic Sea, despite Saxon counterclaims of a dozen British chieftains killed. The setback can only have been temporary. The *Chronicle* records a final success for Hengist and his successor Aesc in 573 at an unnamed location where they seized much booty, and the Britons, now described as Welsh, fled from them as if from fire.

Directions

Tactical locations unknown.

Anderitum (Pevensey), *c.* **491**

England, East Sussex, LR199 TQ6404

Portesmutha (Portchester Castle), *c.* **501**

England, Hampshire, LR196 SU6204

Natanleag (Cerdicesleag), *c.* **508**

England, Hampshire, LR196, unlocated

Cerdicesford (Charford), *c.* **519**

England, Hampshire, LR184 SU1718?

The *Anglo-Saxon Chronicle*'s account of Germanic penetration of the south coast shares many of the features that render its description of the Kentish invasion suspect. The military adventurers who took Sussex and Hampshire exist within a mass of chronological contradictions. They have little archaeological support and only tenuous links with historical kings of Sussex and Wessex.

They all arrive with a handful of ships, fight a

battle, kill a local leader to establish their legitimacy and fall into obscurity. Names are suspiciously aetiological: Port at Portchester, the dead British leader Natanleod at Natanleag, or the sons of Aelle who provided names for Cissbury and Lancing in West Sussex. The landings recorded by the *Anglo-Saxon Chronicle* are unhelpful. Identification of Aelle's landfall at Cymen's Shore in 477 with Selsey depends on a forged medieval charter and fails to explain his subsequent advance on Anderitum rather than the much closer and equally Roman Chichester. The West Saxons managed to arrive twice at the unidentified Cerdic's Shore (495 and 514), under different leaders.

The fall of the two fortresses may represent a symbolic moment in the invasion process, when the Britons lost the last sections of the Saxon Shore still in their hands. The storming of Anderitum is the most clearly recorded attempt to defend a Roman coastal stronghold. Archaeological evidence of Anglo-Saxon settlement between the Rivers Ouse and Cuckmere in East Sussex ties up with an unlocated fight at Mearcred's Burn in 485 to provide motivation for Aelle's attack on Anderitum. If Mearcred's Burn represents the Cuckmere, Aelle would have had good reason to storm the fortress and massacre its occupants. He could not tolerate a garrison on his eastern flank, able to raid his settlements at will and then shelter behind the Roman defences. Anderitum was the last and most irregularly shaped of the Saxon Shore Forts. Pevensey Haven now separates its massive walls from the sea, but they still occupy a good defensive position, surrounded by marshy levels. Aelle only got in by treachery, or by smashing down the gate.

Portesmutha most readily equates with Portchester Castle at the northern end of Portsmouth Harbour. The unfortified settlement at the harbour mouth is much later, dating from the 12th century, while archaeological remains suggest Romano-British peasant militia occupied Portchester during the 4th century. Portchester Castle, the Roman Portus Adurni, occupies a similar site to Anderitum, protected by tidal mud flats to seaward. Its capture would provide essential security for the Jutish settlements that left their characteristic 'ingas' place-name endings from Hayling Island to Lymington.

The mass of archaeological evidence for Jutes in south Hampshire leaves little room for Cerdic's traditional landfall at Ower on Southampton Water. The *Anglo-Saxon Chronicle*'s duplication of the earliest West Saxon entries suggests either a failure to reconcile competing oral traditions, or a ham-fisted attempt to legitimize the West Saxon encroachments of the 7th century. Their ancestral leader Cerdic was thus a minor figure, operating on the fringes of Jutish territory. Even the battles at Natanleag and Charford, the only places positively associated with Cerdic, are doubtful. The former appears to duplicate a later battle at Cerdicesleag or Cerdic's Wood of 527, in which case it would follow rather than precede Cerdicesford, supporting Cerdic's later arrival date.

Charford is near the lowest ford across the Hampshire Avon, a navigable route inland for shallow-draft Saxon ships, while avoiding the Jutes. Lack of casualty claims suggests the battle was unsatisfac-

Anderitum

	Winner	*Loser*
Opponents:	Saxons	British
Commanders	Aelle	unknown (k)

Portesmutha

	Winner	*Loser*
Opponents	Saxons	British
Commanders	Port	unknown (k)

Natanleag

	Winner	*Loser*
Opponents	Saxons	British
Commanders	Cerdic	Natanleod (k)
	Cynric	

Cerdicesford

	Winner	*Loser*
Opponents	Saxons	British
Commanders	Cerdic	unknown
	Cynric	

tory, dense woods and numerous hillforts frustrating further Saxon advances. The subsequent action of Natanleag/Cerdicesleag is usually placed at Netley Marsh near Totton. It may have arisen from an attempt to infiltrate between Britons and Jutes, skirting the northern edge of the New Forest. The *Anglo-Saxon Chronicle*'s incredible claim that 5000 Britons were killed may indicate a favourable result.

Directions

Anderitum *Massive remains of the old fortress, just south of the A27 through Pevensey.*

Portesmutha *turn south off the A27 at Portchester shopping centre, down Castle Street. The complete perimeter of the fortress stands on the left, past the old village centre.*

Cerdicesford *Turn right off the A338 Fordingbridge–Salisbury road at Breamore, and cross the Avon near 'The Shallows'. Turn left in Woodgreen, and find a footpath on the left back across the river to South Charford Farm.*

Mons Badonicus (Mount Badon), *c.***495**

England, Wiltshire, LR174 SU2079?

The only contemporary authority for the celebrated Battle of Mons Badonicus is the British monk Gildas (d.570?), whose work passed via Bede into the Anglo-Saxon tradition. Generally held to have delayed the Saxon advance by half a century, Mons Badonicus has probably generated more hot air than any other battle of the period.

As usual with 5th-century events, the sources fail to cohere. Neither date nor location of the battle can be established beyond doubt. Dates range from 490 to 516, the balance of probability inclining to the 490s. The closest equivalent place name is Badbury, but there are five Badburys, distributed from Lincolnshire to Dorset. The Wiltshire occurrence is favourite, alias Liddington Castle near Swindon, where a hillfort guards the intersection of a group of Roman roads and the M4 motorway. Lying on the northern edge of the Downs, it satisfies Field Marshal Slim's dictum that all British battles are fought uphill and at the junction of at least two maps.

Mons Badonicus' chief claim to notoriety is its appearance on a list of 12 stolen or imaginary battles that the 9th-century *History of the Britons* attributed to Arthur. Gildas, the source nearest the event, never mentions Arthur. Arthur's death at the Battle of Camlann in 534 makes him unlikely to have seen action during the 490s, in a period when few warriors reached their forties. Welsh monks remembered Arthur not for his leadership qualities as *dux bellorum* ('leader of wars') but as an avaricious tyrant, whose marital infidelities inspired satirical verses. None of this has curbed Arthur's evidence-defying career, since Geoffrey of Monmouth and Sir Thomas Malory recognized his money-spinning potential in the Middle Ages. As J.N.L. Myres commented: 'No figure on the borderline of history and mythology has wasted so much of the historian's time.'

Arthur's spurious connection with Mons Badonicus should not detract from the battle's historical credibility. Gildas wrote within living memory of the event, and presumably wanted his readers to take him seriously. His description of the battle's geographical setting implies a populated area on the western border of the Saxon settlement, possessing towns whose fortifications required 'engines' or at least tree trunks to break down their gates. Hills and forests sheltered refugees, and at least one port allowed emigration to Brittany. This area was also the home of Ambrosius Aurelianus, the one person that Gildas named in connection with Mons Badonicus. Aurelianus was presumably a Romano-British tyrant, similar to Vortigern, who organized British resistance after the collapse of relations between citizens and *foederati*. J.N.L. Myres domiciled Aurelianus in Wiltshire, where surviving villas might have provided recruits.

Mons Badonicus

	Winner	*Loser*
Opponents	British	Saxons
Commanders	unknown	unknown

He specifically favoured Amesbury (Old English *Ambresbyrig*), a rare example in England of a place-name that commemorates a Roman landowner.

Liddington Castle lies 22 miles (35 km) north of Amesbury, commanding the junction of the Ridgeway, Ermine Street and another Roman road running through Mildenhall to Amesbury. Three miles (5 km) southeast lies the village of Baydon (SU2878), the highest point (764 feet/233 m) on the Roman road to Silchester, allowing an alternative interpretation of 'Mons Badonicus' as 'the Baydon hill country'. Either location would permit an enterprising leader charged with the defence of Wiltshire to intercept invaders from the Thames valley by using the network of Roman roads and ancient trackways. Only the Thames-valley Saxons were strong enough for their defeat to have been remembered as a matter of such consequence.

It is impossible to know exactly what took place at Mons Badonicus. Gildas describes the conflict as a siege, *obsessio montis badonici*, implying a protracted fight. Welsh Annals support this, for what it's worth, with their report of Arthur wearing the Cross of our Lord on his shield, like a regular Roman soldier, for three days and nights. The reported slaughter of 960 Saxons bears no credible relationship to the small forces engaged, perhaps 1000 men a side. Complex reconstructions of manoeuvres and cavalry charges owe more to Geoffrey of Monmouth's 12th-century fairytales than 5th-century reality. British mounted troops would have been lightly armed mosstroopers, not the armoured cataphracts of the Eastern Roman Empire, a form of cavalry that Aurelianus lacked the blacksmiths, riding masters and horseflesh to emulate. The Britons clearly won, but the invaders' loose political structures would have limited the battle's wider consequences. Other Anglo-Saxon groups would have continued to consolidate their position elsewhere, regardless of events on the upper Thames.

Directions

Leave the B4192 a mile (1.6 km) south of Liddington, and walk three quarters of a mile (1.2 km) along the Ridgeway to find the castle across the summit of Liddington Hill on the right.

Building Wessex 550–825

The resumption of the *Anglo-Saxon Chronicle*'s military record in 552 supports the notion of interrupted conquest. The dubious chronology of early Wessex develops fresh coherence with the battles of Ceawlin, the first definite king of the Gewissae, an Anglo-Saxon confederacy operating in the upper Thames valley. Regular West Saxon defeats by the Mercians contrast with their successful expansion into the Celtic West Country, and southwards into Jutish Hampshire and the Isle of Wight. Achieved by dynastic murder rather than warfare, the latter breakthrough established commercial and political links with Charlemagne's empire. Frankish arms shipments and expertise may have contributed to the West Saxons' surprise victory over Mercia at Ellendun (825).

Searoburg (Old Sarum), **552**

England, Wiltshire, LR184 SU1332?

Beranburh (Barbury Castle), **556**

England, Wiltshire, LR173 SU1476?

The truce that followed Mons Badonicus was crumbling by AD 550. West Saxon victories in central Wiltshire form a link between Cerdic's mythical struggles on the margins of the New Forest and the near historical campaigns of Ceawlin that established Wessex as the dominant power in southern England.

Searoburg is the only solo exploit of Cynric, a

Searoburg

	Winner	Loser
Opponents	West Saxon	British
Commanders	Cynric	unknown

Beranburh

	Winner	Loser
Opponents	West Saxon	British
Commanders	Cynric Ceawlin	unknown

shadowy figure who may have been invented to fill the genealogical gap between Cerdic and Ceawlin. The magnificent Roman hillfort of Sorbiodunum, now Old Sarum, controlled the strategic junction of roads running to Amesbury, Blandford Forum and Andover. It dominates the Avon flood plain to the south, where modern Salisbury lies. The action can be interpreted as a major offensive success that established West Saxon dominion over the chalk region of central Wiltshire. Later this area became one of the main foci of the kingdom of Wessex, with its *villa regalis* ('royal hall') at Wilton, and three of the largest Saxon cemeteries in Wiltshire. An alternative interpretation is the successful defence of an existing settlement. The *Anglo-Saxon Chronicle* gives away little, except that Cynric 'put the Britons to flight'.

Beranburh marks Ceawlin's first appearance, his association with Cynric and hence Cerdic legitimizing his taking of the kingdom in 560. Barbury Castle is a prehistoric hillfort controlling the Ridgeway south of Swindon. It lies on Marlborough Down almost 900 feet (275 m) above sea-level, with splendid views north towards Cirencester. The assumed capture of Barbury in 556 is traditionally taken as marking the breakthrough of the Hampshire Anglo-Saxons to the Thames. Hasty male burials intruding into round barrows in the Vale of Pewsey, south of Barbury, may have been battle casualties. The north-facing alignment of the Wansdyke, a mysterious 5th- or 6th-century entrenchment 6 miles (10 km) south of Barbury Castle, implies, on the other hand, that the Saxon combatants at Beranburh came from the north. The geographical distribution of Ceawlin's later battles implies that his power-base lay in the Thames valley. The *Anglo-Saxon Chronicle* says even less than usual. Beranburh may have been an unimpressive victory.

Directions

Searoburg *Old Sarum's remains are 1 mile (1.6 km) north of Salisbury, left of the A345.*

Beranburh *Several minor roads lead south from Wroughton towards Barbury Country Park. Barbury Hill is half a mile (0.8 km) west of the viewpoint (879 feet/268 m).*

Wibbandun (Wibba's Mount), **568**

England, Surrey, unlocated

Biedcanford (Bedford), **571**

England, Bedfordshire, unlocated

Dyrham (Deorham), **577**

England, Gloucestershire, LR172 ST7476?

Fethanleag (Stoke Lyne), **584**

England, Oxfordshire, LR164 SP5628?

Wodnesbeorh (Woden's Barrow), **592**

England, Wiltshire, LR173 SU1163

Ceawlin's career is remarkable for its length and geographical scope. The *Anglo-Saxon Chronicle*'s unusually full entries adopt a poetic tone, suggesting an epic source consonant with Ceawlin's victories and his status as first credible king of Wessex, the second of Bede's *Bretwaldas* or overlords of the southern English. By turns he struck out eastwards down

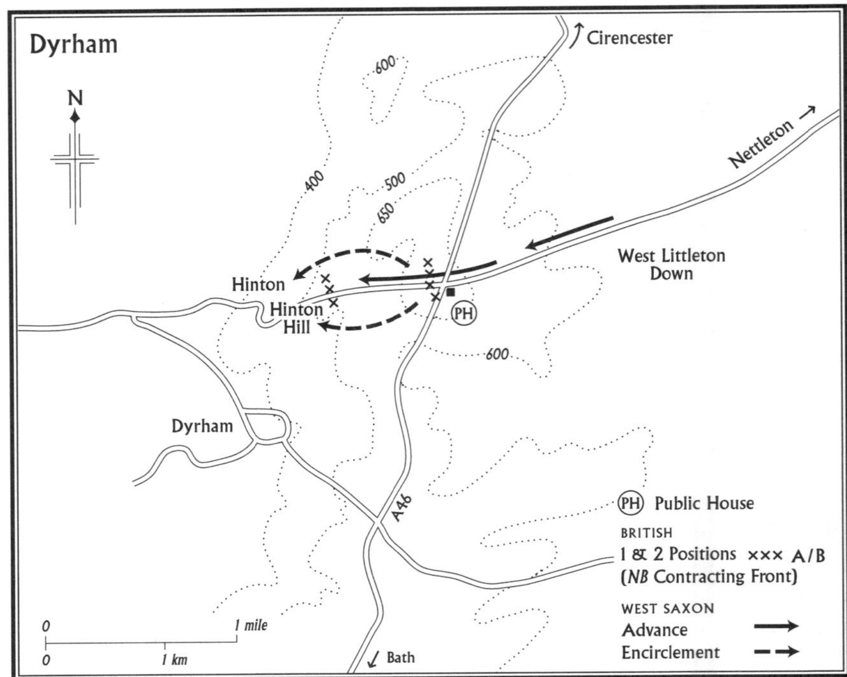

the Thames, westwards into Gloucestershire, north into the Midlands, and then south to meet disaster.

Wibbandun is geographically obscure but politically significant. In a single battle Ceawlin cleared his eastern flank and drove Aethelberht of Kent out of Surrey, reducing Kent to a second-class power. It was the first recorded clash between rival groups of invaders, although probably not the first to have actually taken place.

Biedcanford appears not to fit into this sequence of battles, unless Cuthwulf is related to the Cuthwine and Cutha of the others. The *Anglo-Saxon Chronicle* describes Cuthwulf exploiting his victory by advancing down Icknield Way from Limbury, near Luton, through Aylesbury to Benson and Eynsham on the Thames. Such movements were a feature of an earlier period than the 6th century. J.N.L. Myres wondered whether confused annalists had postdated the whole story by a century. In that case Cuthwulf may have founded the original Anglo-Saxon bridgehead on the Thames in the 470s, approaching overland from the Wash rather than upriver, past London. If Biedcanford does belong in the 570s, it probably represents a mopping-up operation directed against Britons lurking in the Chiltern woods.

Ceawlin's great achievement was his victory at Dyrham in 577, which R.H. Hodgkin saw as the decisive battle of the second stage of the Anglo-Saxon conquest. After nearly a century of gradual progress, the Saxons split the British into two, pressing back the future inhabitants of Wales and Cornwall either side of the Avon Gorge, and opening up the Severn valley to the invaders. The *Anglo-Saxon Chronicle* implies Ceawlin's victims may have been kings of Cirencester, Gloucester and Bath, perhaps successors to Roman municipal authorities, although the archaeological evidence is unhelpful. They were more likely sub-Roman tyrants occupying reconditioned hillforts, copying Roman military equipment and importing Mediterranean luxuries. Large quantities of sub-Roman metalwork found in the area suggests Ceawlin faced a major threat.

Directions

Dyrham Turn right off the A46 three quarters of a mile (1.2 km) south of M4 Junction 18. Follow the minor road to Hinton Hill.

No tactical details survive, but the location is suggestive. Dyrham village lies below the Cotswolds' western extremity, halfway between Roman roads from Gloucester and Cirencester to Bath, which the British could have used to concentrate their forces. Dyrham is as far west as the British could retreat without giving up the high ground and allowing the Saxons access to the Bristol Channel. The prehistoric camp on Hinton Hill, on the edge of the escarpment above Dyrham, is a better place to fight, however. Two low ridges running north–south 900 and 300 yards (800 and 275 m) east of the hillfort form successive lines of defence in front of the camp, where the combatants could leave their impedimenta. The higher, easternmost ridge bars the old track across West Littleton Down from Nettleton where it crosses the modern Bath road, half a mile (0.8 km) south of the M4. Ceawlin's natural approach from the Thames valley would follow that track, avoiding Cirencester and Bath. Despite their ersatz Roman equipment the Britons were defeated, perhaps falling back down the spur to the lower ridge to make a last stand on Hinton Hill, where they became trapped. The contracting British front would release men from the Anglo-Saxon flanks, allowing them to encircle the fort and cut off the retreating Britons, including all three of their leaders.

Wibbandun

	Winner	*Loser*
Opponents	West Saxon	Kentish
Commanders	Ceawlin	Aethelberht
	Cutha	

Biedcanford

	Winner	*Loser*
Opponents	West Saxon	British
Commanders	Cuthwulf	unknown

Dyrham

	Winner	*Loser*
Opponents	West Saxon	British
Commanders	Ceawlin	Condidan (k)
	Cuthwine	Conmail (k)
		Fairmail (k)

Fethanleag

	Winner	*Loser*
Opponents	West Saxon	British
Commanders	Ceawlin	unknown
	Cutha (k)	

Wodnesbeorh

	Winner	*Loser*
Opponents	West Saxon	West Saxon
Commanders	unknown	Ceawlin

Ceawlin's expedition to Fethanleag was less satisfactory. His fellow commander Cutha was killed, and despite the alleged capture of many towns and countless booty, Ceawlin returned home in anger. The *Anglo-Saxon Chronicle* seems to be glossing over a disastrous raid northwards, probing the headwaters of the Great Ouse. Fethanleag or Battle Wood probably lies near Stoke Lyne, west of the Roman road north from Bicester. Near Stoke Lyne the modern road passes between two woods on a ridge (394 feet/120 m) south of an east–west stream that would make a reasonable defensive position. Cutha may have died of wounds on the way home, at Cutteslowe north of Oxford, where King John demolished a burial mound said to be the haunt of robbers.

This first setback may have undermined Ceawlin's power. He suffered another defeat near Wodnesbeorh, a long barrow also known as Adam's Grave near Alton Priors in Wiltshire, near a gap in Wansdyke. The Ridgeway passes close under the western side of the isolated summit where Woden's Barrow stands (659 feet/201 m), making it a strategic spot. Perhaps Ceawlin hoped to recover his position by breaking through the Wansdyke, opening up Dorset and Somerset to his Gewissae. Perhaps Wodnesbeorh was a day of reckoning for Ceawlin's many aggressions. There was much carnage and Ceawlin was driven out. He died next year with two more thanes, presumably the victim of a murderous attack. It was a wretched end to an astonishing career, no doubt typical of many who never entered the historical record.

Directions

Fethanleag *Follow the B4100 3 miles (5 km) northwest from Bicester, towards Banbury, as described in the text above.*

Wodnesbeorh *Adam's Grave is right of the Marlborough–Alton Prior's road, overlooking the Vale of Pewsey.*

Cirencester, 628

England, Gloucestershire, LR163, unlocated

Bradford-on-Avon, 652

England, Wiltshire, LR173 ST8261?

Peonnum (Penselwood), 658

England, Somerset, LR183 ST7531?

Bensington (Benson), 779

England, Oxfordshire, LR175 SU6191?

The two centuries after Ceawlin's death saw numerous conflicts between Wessex and its neighbours. Tactical details are lacking, but the locations and contrasting results of the above sample are strategically illuminating. The key feature is the emergence and subsequent dominance of Mercia. Cirencester, at the junction of the Fosse Way (from Mercia) and Ermine Street (from Wessex), was the first recorded victory of King Penda, who united a patchwork of Midland sub-kingdoms and permanently excluded Wessex from the Severn valley. A century and a half later the great Offa dictated terms to a West Saxon king at the heart of his kingdom: Benson was a West Saxon *villa regalis* ('royal hall') on the Thames, just 3 miles (5 km) from Dorchester, the original diocesan centre of Wessex, and thereafter Offa's appointees replaced Cynewulf's in Kent and Sussex.

Crushing defeats by Mercia compelled Wessex to turn against the less formidable Celts of the southwest. Cenwalh's victory at Bradford in 652, at the eastern end of the Avon Gorge, is said to have forced the Britons back into the Mendip Hills. Cenwalh fought them again at Peonnum in 658, driving them in flight across the River Parret, probably southwards down the Fosse Way to Ilchester, dodging inundations further downstream. The Parret was an important north–south boundary across the Somerset wetlands, but Peonnum may have taken the West Saxons as far as the hills between Devon and Somerset. Locations suggested for Peonnum include Pen Hill in the Mendips, Poyntington north of Sherborne, and the strategically eccentric Pinhoe near Exeter. A more likely location is Penselwood, 'head of Selwood', lying northeast of Wincanton,which is nearer Cenwalh's likely line of advance. It lies on high ground, is well provided with earthworks and covers a plausible line of approach from the centres of West Saxon power, where the prehistoric trackway from Old Sarum to Ilchester crosses the River Stour.

Cirencester

	Winner	*Loser*
Opponents	Mercian	West Saxon
Commanders	Penda	Cynegils
		Cwichelm

Bradford-on-Avon

	Winner	*Loser*
Opponents	West Saxon	British
Commanders	Cenwalh	unknown

Peonnum

	Winner	*Loser*
Opponents	West Saxon	British
Commanders	Cenwalh	unknown

Bensington

	Winner	*Loser*
Opponents	Mercian	West Saxon
Commanders	Offa	Cynewulf

The victory re-established Ceawlin's kingdom, restored Anglo-Saxon control of Wiltshire, and drove a wedge between the British of Dorset and Somerset.

Directions
Tactical locations unknown.

Gafolford (Galford), **825**

England, Devon, LR201 SX4786?

Ellendun, 825

England, Wiltshire, LR173 SU1083–4

Hengestesdune (Hingston Down), **838**

England, Cornwall, LR201 SX3871

West Saxon history came together under King Egbert in 825, when he first defeated the Cornish Britons, then ended Mercian supremacy at one blow.

Gafolford, 'the Tax Ford', has been interpreted as Camelford in Cornwall, which seems rather far west for anything larger than a raid. Galford by the River Lew, northwest of Dartmoor, is a more likely site for an action that the chronicler Henry of Huntingdon (?1084–1155) remembered as 'a great battle between the Britons and the men of Devon ... where many thousands were slain on both sides'. The results of Ellendun were more notable. Beornwulf of Mercia was a man of action, conquering Powys in 823, a vivid demonstration of Mercian power beyond Offa's Dyke. He descended on Egbert's northern frontier to demand homage before the West Saxons could replace their losses in Cornwall, but Egbert's thanes chose iron before dishonour, and the conflict was resolved at Ellendun or 'Elder Bush Down', just inside Wessex. Sir Charles Oman among others placed the battle near Wroughton, a parish that once extended further northwest than now, over low ground crossed by the M4 motorway. A.H. Burne preferred a site near Lydiard Tregoze, on Swindon's western outskirts, drawing on footpath research and the Annals of Winchester. A pre-Saxon track could have brought Egbert that way, passing Barbury Castle, through Uffcot and Salthrop to the roundabout on the Swindon–Wootton Bassett road at point 107. Today the old road is interrupted by housing and the M4, but it once continued north through Lydiard Tregoze to Cricklade, the general direction of Beornwulf's approach. Hay Lane reappears east of Tregoze Country Park, running north from Lower Salthrop, amongst the suburban drives and closes.

The Winchester scribe describes the opponents lining up some hundreds of yards apart. Armies approaching head-on naturally seek ridges across their line of march, in this case the West Saxons around point 107, the Mercians on a convenient elevation some 1200 yards (1100 m) further north, obliquely crossing Hay Lane. It is now occupied by a school. Between the two ridges the ground falls slightly to the junction of Hook Street and Whitehill Way, named after a vanished farm. If both sides advanced they would have met in boggy ground just north of the Freshbrook roundabout (338 feet/103 m). The 350-foot contour on old maps shows the configuration of the two ridges now obscured by buildings. Small streams running behind Beornwulf's position along the eastern edge of Tregoze Country Park became a killing ground for defeated Mercians. For what it is worth, Burne turned up a tradition of ancient fighting on Windmill Hill, on the western flank of his battlefield. Today it is a business park.

The Winchester scribe claimed the sides were unequal in number and skill: 'against a hundred feeble soldiers pale with fright, Beornwulf had a thousand well set-up men browned by the sun'. Nevertheless the Mercians were thrashed, falling 'as thick as rain or hail'. It was hot, and 'many of the fugitives suffocated from sweat rather than blood'. Beornwulf himself took flight, 'and would not have lost his spurs for three pence', which must have been a lot of money then. The mention of spurs and a battlefield littered with dead men and horses reflects later tactical conditions, but coincidentally recalls the losers' mad scramble to horse that followed an Anglo-Saxon battle.

Gafolford

	Winner	*Loser*
Opponents	West Saxon	British
Commanders	Egbert	unknown

Ellendun

	Winner	*Loser*
Opponents	West Saxon	Mercian
Commanders	Egbert	Beornwulf

Hengestesdune

	Winner	*Loser*
Opponents	West Saxon	British/Viking
Commanders	Egbert	unknown

Henry of Huntingdon's evocation of slaughter was equally gory: 'Ellendun's stream was reddened with blood, blocked with the fallen, and filled with the stench. Egbert came away the deadly victor having made the greatest slaughter of folk on both sides'. Neither source explains how Egbert managed to turn the tables on Mercia so decisively. His exile at the court of Charlemagne has prompted suggestions that Egbert imported Carolingian tactics, but the Anglo-Saxons never imitated Frankish cavalry. Dynastic rivalries within Mercia may have weakened Beornwulf, his thanes not wishing to risk their necks for a factional leader.

Ellendun revolutionized Anglo-Saxon power politics. Egbert immediately despatched his son Aethelwulf with some high-powered advisers to take control of Sussex and Kent. Within a year the East Anglians had killed Beornwulf and sought Egbert's protection. In 829 he marched across Mercia to receive Northumbria's submission near Sheffield, and a year later harried the Britons of North Wales. He defeated the Cornish again on the Devon–Cornwall border at Hengestesdune or Stallion's Hill. Hingston Down is a circular hill dominating the lowest crossing of the Tamar, where the Tavistock –Liskeard road crosses the river. Egbert put the Cornish to flight, but they enjoyed the assistance of a 'great raiding ship army' of Danes – a sinister portent.

Directions

Ellendun *Swindon's expansion westwards has overrun Burne's site, north of the A3012, off Junction 16 of the M4. See text above for the relationship between the battlefield and today's man-made topography. The fatal streams still run through Lydiard Park, on Beornwulf's right rear, accessible along a footpath off Hook Street, opposite Park Farm.*

Galford *and* ***Hingston Down*** *tactical locations unknown.*

Building Northumbria 570–685

The best-documented series of Anglo-Saxon battles before the Viking era was in the north. The Venerable Bede, a monk at Jarrow and father of English history, was nearly contemporary with Northumbria's 7th-century struggle with its Celtic and Anglo-Saxon neighbours. Futile British attempts to resist Anglian encroachments in Yorkshire, Northumberland and Lothian made way for civil strife between Northumbria's twin foci in Bernicia and Deira, around Bamburgh and York respectively. The heathen King Penda of Mercia bestrode the military stage like a colossus, winning battles through his 'diabolical art', and killing Northumbria's saintly King Oswald and King Anna of East Anglia 'by guile'. Oswy of Bernicia re-united Northumbria when he terminated Penda's career beside the River Winwaed (*c.*654). Defeats suffered by Oswy's son Ecgfrith on the Trent (678) and at Nechtanesmere (685), however, set permanent limits to Northumbrian power. Lacking an expanding frontier like that of Wessex in Devon and Cornwall, Northumbria fell into decline. The kingdom would be in no state to survive the 9th century Viking onslaught.

Arfderydd (Arthuret), *c.*573

England, Cumbria, LR85 NY4072?

Caer Greu, *c.*580

England, unlocated

Lindisfarne (Medcaut), *c.*590

England, Northumberland, LR75 NU0743

The earliest known battles in the area that became Northumbria were recorded not by the invaders but by Celtic people already living there. British resistance in the north was more protracted and severe than in the southeast, reflecting the difference between the highland and lowland zones. Bards left eloquent images of Anglo-Saxon losses, but tell a story of heroic defeat, hastened by darkest treachery.

Arfderydd is famous for the participation of the bard Merddyn, the historical original of Merlin. Merddyn lost both his patron Gwendolleu there and his wits, becoming a wild man in the forest of Celyddon. The battle was fought near Longtown, perhaps at Carwinley (Caer Gwendolleu) in a bend of Liddel Water, east of its confluence with the Esk. A motte and bailey on the gentle slope down to the river and a group of 'moat' place-names testify to the opinions of later generations regarding the area's strategic value. Arfderydd, however, was part of a civil war between rival British princes, who might have done better to focus on Anglian settlements along the Yorkshire and Northumbrian coast. The victors of Arfderydd soon fell victim to these folk at Caer Greu, an obscure Yorkshire battle attributed to 580.

Northumbria consisted of two competing political units until the early 7th century: Bernicia and Deira. Corresponding roughly to modern Northumberland and Yorkshire respectively, their characters were quite different. The former lay outside the old Roman civil zone, and was the product of military conquest, while the latter arose from agricultural settlement within the civil zone. Adda, victor of Caer Greu, was a successor of Ida, who traditionally founded Bernicia in 547, fortifying Bamburgh with a stockade. This unusual mention of fortifications has inspired a belief that the local British hemmed the Bernicians in against the coast, an idea reinforced by reports of a confrontation at Lindisfarne between 589 and 593.

Urien of Rheged shut up Theodoric of Bernicia on the Isle of Medcaut, or Lindisfarne, for three days and nights, which may just imply a protracted period similar to the three-day 'siege' of Mons Badonicus. Rheged, like other post-Roman political entities, remains obscure. Historians have located its capital variously at Carlisle or Catterick, crediting Urien as the only northern British chief able to organize effective resistance to the Bernicians. His confederates included Rhydderch Hen 'the Old' of Strathclyde, Gwallog or Gualloc, and Morgan, who may all be 9th-century personifications of tribal groupings, invented when *History of the Britons* was written down. British unity was short-lived. Morgan betrayed Urien '*per invidia*' ('from envy'), and had him murdered, 'because he was the greatest war leader of them all'. The foul deed was done beside Aber Lleu,

Arfderydd

	Winner	*Loser*
Opponents	British	British
Commanders	Gwrgi Pryderi	Gwendolleu (k)

Caer Greu

	Winner	*Loser*
Opponents	Bernician?	British
Commanders	Adda	Gwrgi (k) Pryderi (k)

Lindisfarne

	Winner	*Loser*
Opponents	Bernician	British
Commanders	Theodoric	Urien of Rheged (m)

perhaps the River Low's southern outlet, where the allies could have camped on a gentle rise at the landward end of the causeway to Holy Island. The poet Taliesin lamented the dead man's son, Owain ap Urien:

> His sharp spear like the rays of dawn,
> For the equal will not be found.

Like Rheged, Owain did not long survive his father's death.

Directions
Tactical locations unknown.

Catraeth (Catterick), *c.*598

England, North Yorkshire, LR99 SE2298?

Poetry is a poor substitute for historical narrative, but in the case of Catraeth it is all there is. The rambling elegy *Y Gododdin* commemorates a British disaster unknown to history, of uncertain date and location, relating to heroes of uncertain identity. The poem was probably composed in the 9th century, 300 years after the events it purports to describe. Catraeth may even be the same battle that Bede recorded at Degsastan in 603. Accepting a date in the 590s suggests the Catraeth expedition was an attempt to stem the Deiran advance up the Vale of York before Aethelfrith, king from 592, consolidated his position in Bernicia. *Y Gododdin* describes the enemy loosely as Saxons or a mixture of Deirans and Bernicians, but the Celtic protagonists are more definite: a picked multi-tribal war band assembled and led by the Gododdin of Din Eidyn (later Edinburgh), the people the Romans knew as Votadini. After a year feasting by the glow of rushlights and drinking from glass cups, the warriors rode south to pay for their mead. The corrupt and disconnected verses cast flickering sidelights on a blend of heroism and fecklessness:

> Men went to Catraeth; merry was the host
> The grey mead was their drink and their poison too.

Evocative and possibly anachronistic images of war abound: 'Blue their armour and their shields,/ Lances uplifted and sharp,/Mail and sword glinting.' Repeated references to 300 warriors reflect Celtic delight in triads, but the small numbers are consistent with a society deficient in trade, coinage or policy, but dominated by a heroic elite.

The Gododdin approach march of just over 100 miles (160 km) would not be impossible for a small mounted force, moving for the most part through friendly country. Roman roads ran from Edinburgh via Crawford and Carlisle, over the Pennines by Brough in the Eden Valley, to Scotch Corner and Catterick. Brough lay within British territory only 32 miles (51 km) from Catterick, a day's march for mounted troops. There they were intercepted, deep in Anglo-Saxon territory, and annihilated. The poem claims the heathen host numbered thousands, which is not likely, but may reflect an overwhelming combination of Bernician and Deiran forces against the foe in their midst.

The action is usually assumed to have happened in or around the 7-foot (2-m) thick walls of the Roman station at Cataractonium just south of the River Swale. One of the doomed companions 'glutted black ravens on the rampart of the city, though he was no Arthur'. However, the Swale could have been known as the Cataract River from a waterfall three miles upstream at Richmond, near the southern end of Scots Dyke. This east-facing Dark Age earthwork straddles the moorland road from Brough, and may mark the Anglo–British frontier. The last stand of the Gododdin could therefore have occurred on the heights of Richmond, as they turned the southern flank of Scots Dyke, near the medieval castle. Protected with mail coats and whitewashed shields, sporting gold collars and amber, they fought in ranks with swords, spears and throwing javelins, but without arrows. Their panegyrist claimed five fifties

Catraeth

	Winner	*Loser*
Opponents	Saxon	British
Commanders	Aethelfrith?	unknown

fell before their blades, but none returned to their lands. After the shout of battle there was silence. Catraeth ended all hope of a Celtic revival. A two-word entry in an Irish annal to '*obsessio Etin*', 'the siege of Din Eidyn', during the 630s recorded the fatal consequences of defeat: the fall of the Gododdin citadel to the Bernicians.

Directions

Tactical locations unknown. The A6136 to Catterick Camp passes traces of the Roman fort.

Degsastan (Dawston Rigg), **603**

Scotland, Scottish Borders, LR80 NY5697?

Aethelfrith of Bernicia's first historical victory was at Degsastan or Degsa's Stone. It was also the first of a series of battles that, for the first time, brings together the peoples of northern Britain in a coherent narrative with a secure chronological background.

Despite his holy orders, Bede recalled Aethelfrith in heroic terms, a very brave king most eager for glory, who 'ravaged the Britons more extensively than any other English ruler'. No ruler had subjugated or settled more land, after exterminating or subduing the natives – a description that does little for the continuity interpretation of Anglo-Saxon settlement. Aethelfrith's successes inspired opposition from a new quarter: Aedan mac Gabhran, friend of St Columba and first king of the Irish (i.e. Scots) colony of Dalriada based at Dunadd Rock in Argyll. Aedan's Scots had already come into conflict with Anglo-Saxon raiders, who killed his son in the Forth lands in 598. Blood feud sharpened strategic rivalry.

Bede described Degsastan as '*in loco celeberrimo*' ('in a most famous place'), but the site is less well-known today. It is usually equated with Dawston Rigg (i.e. 'ridge') at the head of Liddesdale, although the names are not etymologically related. Dawston Burn flows into Liddel Water from the north at Saughtree, the converging streams separated by the steep spur of Hudshouse Rigg (833 feet/254 m). A minor road follows Dawston Burn and then winds over the Cheviots towards Denholm, the southernmost fort of several that prolong the line of the Roman road from Clydeside, where the water-borne Dalriadans could have left their boats. Dawston lies an hour's march west of Deadwater, the watershed of the Liddel and North Tyne, the course of the latter leading into the heart of Northumbria. Bede wrote of Aedan's immensely strong army, begging the question how such a force could maintain itself in so desolate a spot, among the bare hills of the Border. A strong army of the 7th century, however, would be smaller and travel lighter than a modern infantry battalion. The entire population of a rock citadel like Dunadd numbered only a few hundred, a reminder of the diminutive scale of these early kingdoms.

The narrow valley of Dawston Burn provided a splendid killing ground, between the stream and the spur rising from Beattie's Knowe up to Hudshouse Rigg. The strategically astute Aethelfrith, whom the British knew as Aedlfred Flesaur, 'the Twister', could have lain behind the crest, once the Scots had committed themselves to that particular route through the hills. Beyond the stream Saughtree Fell rises steeply to over 1400 feet, preventing any escape that way. Aedan's army was cut to pieces, the septuagenarian king escaping with a few survivors. Among the casualties was a Bernician atheling, Hering son of Hussa, perhaps Aedan's candidate to replace Aethelfrith. Battles of this period were rarely walk-overs, however. The Scots killed Aethelfrith's brother Theobald before they broke, with all his hearth-troop. Whether Aethelfrith won through surprise or by fielding Deiran auxiliaries, the victory was shattering in its effects. No Dalriadan king dared make war against the English again. Radiating the prestige of

Degsastan

	Winner	*Loser*
Opponents	Bernician	Scots
Commanders	Aethelfrith Theobald (k)	Aedan mac Gabhran

victory over Scots and Britons, Aethelfrith proceeded to subordinate prosperous Deira to the Bernician warzone, creating a new Northumbrian overkingship.

Directions

Saughtree is 8 miles northeast of Newcastleton on the B6357. The road north to Hobkirk runs alongside Dawston Burn, with Hudshouse Rigg up on the right.

Chester (Caer Legionis), *c.***616**

England, Cheshire, unlocated

The results of Aethelfrith's other celebrated victory, fought at Chester somewhere between 613 and 616, were more equivocal. Bede's account focuses more upon St Augustine's religious vendetta against the Celtic Church than on military events.

The main incident for Bede was Aethelfrith's preliminary massacre of 1200 Celtic monks on the commonsense grounds that they were fighting against him with prayers for his defeat. Other details remain obscure. Bede simply records that Aethelfrith collected a great army against Caer Legionis, 'the city of the legions', where he made a grand slaughter 'of that nation of heretics', that is the Welsh. Aethelfrith's acquisition of Deira would have brought him into contact with the Welsh kingdoms of Powys and Gwynedd across the Ribble and Mersey valleys, where Aethelfrith may have been raiding to protect Anglo-Saxon settlements. Deira would have provided additional troops, together with an advanced base at York, whence a Roman road ran through Manchester and Northwich to Chester. The march was not particularly arduous: 100 miles along an established route was well within the military capabilities of the day.

Chester

	Winner	Loser
Opponents	Northumbrian	British
Commanders	Aethelfrith	Selyf ap Cynan (k)
		Cadwal Crisban (k)

Aethelfrith's chief opponent was Selyf or Solomon ap Cynan, 'the Serpent of Battles', a heroic figure often associated with Owain ap Urien. As king of Powys Selyf was the traditional defender of the Dee valley, where lay the monastery of Bangor-is-y-Coed whose monks found martyrdom at Chester. The name of Selyf's personal bard is known, but none of his verses survive to enliven the historical narrative. The only detail Bede gives of the fighting is that Brocmail, in command of the monks' escort, turned his back at the first onslaught, leaving the holy men unarmed and undefended. The Northumbrians then destroyed the rest of the British army, 'though not without heavy losses'. Aethelfrith did not long outlive Selyf, whom the Welsh Triads (a verse form not a criminal organization) consequently reckoned one of three heroes avenged beyond the grave.

Aethelfrith's victory at Chester is often supposed to have separated the Britons of Wales and Cumbria, but the quickest and safest route between the two was always by sea. Brocmail's defection suggests more insidious divisions than geographical separation. Bede's lack of comment implies he saw the battle not as an isolated turning point, but as one incident in a protracted struggle. Aethelfrith may have been the first Anglo-Saxon king to reach the Irish Sea, but to imagine he reoccupied Chester's legionary fortress is to misunderstand the fluid raiding character of 7th-century warfare. The Mercian speech of Cheshire's later Anglo-Saxon settlers shows Aethelfrith's Anglians took their plunder home.

Directions

Tactical locations unknown.

Idle River, *c.***617**

England, Doncaster, LR111 SK6494–SK6593?

As Aethelfrith had lived by the sword, so he died, victim of his own brutal policies. He had secured Deira by marrying the last king's daughter and driving the Deiran heir Edwin into exile. Like other dispossessed athelings Edwin hung about foreign courts, first in Gwynedd then East Anglia, dodging assassins and drumming up support for a coup. He might have stayed in East Anglia indefinitely if Aethelfrith had not approached King Raedwald with a sinister mixture of threats and bribes to have Edwin murdered. Knowing his man, Raedwald of East Anglia raised a large army as soon as the Northumbrian envoys had gone, and marched north before Aethelfrith could assemble his own forces. The quarrel was more than an extradition dispute, however. Raedwald and Aethelfrith were competing for prestige and influence among the Anglo-Saxon communities either side of the Humber estuary that lay between their main power centres.

Raedwald and Aethelfrith resolved their differences in the sensitive border area known as Hatfield Chase. Much of the district between the Trent and Don was marsh before it was drained during the 17th century; a less notorious obstacle than the Fens but just as impenetrable. The key route from east to west was Tillbridge Lane, a Roman road from Lincoln to Doncaster, which crossed the Idle at Bawtry. Bede tells us Raedwald, with a much stronger army, met Aethelfrith and killed him on the Mercian border, on the east bank of the Idle. The battle was not all one-sided, for Raedwald's son Regenhere was also killed.

Bawtry lies on the county boundary of Nottinghamshire and South Yorkshire, the old frontier of Mercia and Northumbria. North of Bawtry the Roman road crosses a low 100-foot (30-m) rise, a sensible position for the outnumbered Aethelfrith to await Raedwald's advance from the southeast. Skeletons were reportedly found nearby at Austerfield during the 18th century. Henry of Huntingdon, a 12th-century chronicler with access to lost northern sources, preserved a local snatch of song: 'Foul ran the Idle with the blood of Anglians'. Ten miles (16 km) north of Bawtry the 'Slay Pits' northeast of Hatfield town may be the battle's culminating point (though see below). Until 1626 the Idle ran north to the Don, not east to the Trent as it does now. A broken army at Austerfield might have fled along the river's swampy eastern bank, coming to grief on Hatfield Moor.

Idle River

	Winner	*Loser*
Opponents	Anglian	Northumbrian
Commanders	Raedwald	Aethelfrith (k)
	Edwin	

Directions

Aethelfrith's proposed position lies left of the A638 Bawtry–Doncaster road. Austerfield is on the right.

Haethfelth (Hatfield Chase), *c.* **12 October 632**

England, Nottinghamshire, LR120 SK5669–70

Edwin's fatal defeat at the Haethfelth in 632 is commonly associated with Hatfield near Doncaster, but there are powerful reasons for placing his death further south, outside Northumbria's borders.

Edwin had imperial pretensions. He built a Roman style assembly hall at Yeavering in Northumberland, and had an imperial standard or *thufa* carried before him. He completed the breach between Cumbrian and Welsh Britons that the Battle of Chester had foreshadowed by eliminating the British kingdom of Elmet near Leeds and by means of naval operations in the Irish Sea. Despite his conversion to Christianity Edwin made numerous enemies. He ravaged Wessex, killing five sub-kings, after a botched West Saxon assassination attempt in 626. Forgetting Welsh kindness during his exile, Edwin became one of the three chief oppressors of Môn (Anglesey), although 'nurtured within the island'. He invaded Anglesey and drove his foster brother Cadwallon of Gwynedd into exile in Ireland, first blockading him on the rocky islet of Ynys Lannog (Priestholm, or Puffin Island).

Cadwallon returned in 632, supported by the pagan Penda, whom Bede described as 'a most

Haethfelth

	Winner	Loser
Opponents	Mercian	Northumbrian
Commanders	Penda Cadwallon of Gwynedd	Edwin (k)

energetic member of the house of Mercia'. The allies defeated Edwin in a fierce battle 'fought on the plain called Haethfelth', where 'the whole of his army was either slain or scattered'. Edwin was killed and his head sent back to Cadwallon's stronghold at Aberffraw on Anglesey. Northumbria broke up into its constituent parts and reverted to paganism. The Welsh remembered Cadwallon as 'ruler of the armies of Britain', who for a brief space raised hopes of snatching Britain back from the Anglo-Saxon invaders.

The popular location for Edwin's disaster since William Camden's 16th-century survey in his *Britannia* has been the 'Slay Pits' near Hatfield, northeast of Doncaster (see above), although the meretricious 9th-century *Historia Brittonnum* refers to '*Bellum Meicen*', perhaps signifying Meigen in Powys. Heathfield is, however, a common place-name found across a wide area in Yorkshire and Nottinghamshire, from the Humber to Sherwood Forest. A more suggestive place-name than Hatfield is Edwinstowe in Nottinghamshire (SK6266), which takes its name from a church dedicated to King Edwin, and associated with a contemporary cult of the martyred king. Further down the Mansfield road, a cross marks the site of a chantry dedicated to St Edwin. A few miles northwest, near the village of Cuckney, farms named Hatfield Grange and High Hatfield provide an etymological link with Bede's narrative. Leeming Lane, the old Mansfield–Doncaster road, crosses Cuckney Hill, 150 feet (45 m) above Meden Vale to the south, forming a defensible position.

The logical rendezvous for Cadwallon and Penda's forces would be Derby, accessible by Roman roads but a safe distance from Northumbrian territory. The allies could then have chosen to march north via Mansfield, meeting Edwin at Cuckney as he moved south to meet them. Drawing troops from much of northwest Britain, Cadwallon and Penda would have outnumbered the Northumbrians, who were marching blind into hostile territory.

The National Coal Board, whose spoil heaps cover Cuckney Hill, provided dramatic support for these speculations in 1950–1 when workmen shoring up the Norman church found a 7-foot (2-m) deep layer of adult skeletons extending under the footings. The burial predates the Norman Conquest, as Domesday Book lists a church already standing on the site. The vicar counted some 200 skulls exposed by trenches in the nave, without allowing for any others still buried inside, or undiscovered beyond the church walls. Some catastrophic event occurred in Cuckney before 1086, other than an epidemic, which would have killed children too. Edwin's devotional and etymological associations with the area make the Battle of Haethfelth a prime candidate. While the fleeing Northumbrians were cut down and buried *en masse* at Cuckney, the king's body was recovered and taken to Edwinstowe, resting briefly on the site of the long-vanished chapel.

Directions

Cuckney is 7 miles (11 km) north of Mansfield on the A60. Edwinstowe is on the A6075 Mansfield–Ollerton road.

Denisesburna (Hefenfelth), *c.*633

England, Northumberland, LR87 NY9056?

The Northumbrian disaster at Haethfelth released 200 years of pent-up Welsh fury. Cadwallon raged through the shattered northern kingdom, as if 'to wipe out the whole English race'. Unable to stomach either Northumbrian dynasty, Cadwallon killed Osric of Deira during a sortie from a fortified town, probably York, and murdered Eanfrith of Bernicia, who had foolishly opened peace talks in person. However, another of Aethelfrith's sons, Oswald, survived in exile. His victory at Denisesburna after a year of Welsh terror reversed the result of Haeth-

Denisesburna

	Winner	*Loser*
Opponents	Northumbrian	British
Commanders	St Oswald	Cadwallon (k)

felth, making certain the eventual outcome of the long Anglo-British struggle.

Denisesburna has a multiplicity of names, most of them misleading. 'The brook of the Denise', now called Rowley Burn, is a 7-mile (11-km) long stream flowing north from Hexhamshire Common into Devil's Water, thence into the North Tyne between Hexham and Corbridge. The Welsh name of the battle was *Catscaul*, a mistranslation of Hexham's Anglo-Saxon meaning, 'village of the young warriors'. The proximity of Hadrian's Wall has encouraged the further misnomer *cath-is-gwaul*, 'the battle within the wall'. Hefenfelth, literally Heavenfield, lies 9 miles (14.5 km) north of the actual battlefield, hard by the wall, which forms its northern boundary. Some authorities place the battle at Hefenfelth, but Bede makes a clear distinction between Denisesburna, where Oswald defeated Cadwallon, and Hefenfelth, where something far more important happened: the definitive Northumbrian conversion to Christianity.

Oswald had been in baptized while in exile at the monastery of Iona, in the Inner Hebrides. He therefore approached the area of operations in 633 from the north. He had to cross Hadrian's Wall before fighting Cadwallon, who stood between Bernicia and Deira, in the heart of Northumbria. Bede tells us Oswald had only a small army 'strengthened by their faith'. This suits Bede's patriotic and evangelical purpose, but may truthfully represent the small hearth-troop that would have shared Oswald's exile, and now acted as the focus of Northumbrian resistance. To encourage his men he set up a wooden cross near Hadrian's Wall, and reminded them they were fighting for a just cause and the preservation of their people. St Oswald's Chapel marks the site near Mile Castle 26, between Chesters and Dere Street, the main road from the north. This was Hefenfelth, the place Bede singled out as still venerated in his own day, distracting attention from the site of Oswald's earthly victory.

St Oswald's Chapel was a day's march from Cadwallon's position beyond Hexham, in the wild hills sloping northwards to the Tyne. Adomnan's *Life of St Columba* of Iona (dating from the 7th century) tells us that two nights before the battle, the saint appeared to Oswald in a vision. Besides moral encouragement, St Columba (once a soldier) offered tactical advice, suggesting a dawn attack. Buoyed up by religious fervour, Oswald's army promised they too would accept baptism when they returned victorious. Adomnan continues:

> The ensuing night ... King Oswald advanced from the camp to battle against many thousands with a much smaller army, and as had been promised him, he was granted by the Lord a happy and easy victory.

Adomnan makes it clear the final approach to battle took place the night after Oswald's dream, so the fighting must have taken place beyond Hefenfelth. Bede confirms the devastating result of the dawn assault, Oswald's men destroying the 'abominable leader of the Britons together with the immense force which he boasted was irresistible'. Cadwallon's army would have dwindled after a year's marauding. It was a long way from home, and vulnerable to a counterstroke. The Welsh, for whom Cadwallon's death was an irretrievable disaster, remembered Oswald as *Lamnguin*, 'of the bright blade'. Bede, on the other hand, made St Oswald the hero of his *Ecclesiastical History*.

Directions

The battlefield is somewhere along Rowley Burn, 4 miles (6 km) south of Hexham. St Oswald's Chapel is on the B6318, where it crosses Hadrian's Wall, 1 mile (1.6 km) east of Chesters.

Maserfelth (Maes Cogwy), **5 August 641**

England, Shropshire, LR126 SJ3025?

Accounts of Maserfelth show how different the contemporary agenda was from that of today. Observers focused on the divine and heroic, neglecting material reality. Bede provides numerous anecdotes of St Oswald's death and subsequent miracles, but fails either to locate the scene of the action, or to suggest its tactical course.

Penda of Mercia had not been involved in Cadwallon's defeat at Denisesburna, and remained Oswald's inveterate enemy. Bede recorded that in 641 the Northumbrian king was killed 'in a great battle by the same heathen people and the same heathen king as his predecessor Edwin in a place called ... Maserfelth'. Traditionally Oswald died praying for the souls of his army. Then his enemies hacked off his head and hands and fixed them on a stake. Oswald's successor and brother Oswy recovered the remains a year later for Christian burial, the head at Bamburgh and the rest at Bardney Abbey in Lincolnshire. In the 12th century Henry of Huntingdon wrote that the battlefield shone with the bones of saints, the loser's casualties left unburied.

Unfortunately Bede gives no further clues to the location of Maserfelth. Since the 12th century Oswestry has been construed as 'Oswald's tree', the stake to which Penda fixed his gruesome trophies. The identification has been encouraged by the assonance between Maserfelth and Meresberie, now Maesbury, the site of a service station on the A5 south of Oswestry. Similar place-names elsewhere have also attracted Oswaldian connections, for example 'Oswald's Tump' at Marshfield near Bath.

The name Oswestry more probably derives from a less sinister tree, used to mark a boundary. Welsh poetic tradition lamented a battle at Maes Cogwy (or Cockboy) that is usually equated with Maserfelth: 'I saw armies on the ground of Cogwy and the battle full of affliction.' There is no evidence for Welsh participation at Maserfelth, however, and no definite correspondence between local Shropshire place-names and those in the literary sources. Oswestry seems rather far west for a battle between kings whose power centres lay east of the Pennines and in the Midlands, unless Oswald had chased Penda as far as the Welsh foothills before bringing him to bay. It is impossible to show the battle was not fought at Oswestry, but neither is there any proof that it was.

Other candidates for the battlefield have attracted little support, for example Winwick north of Warrington, or Epworth in the disputed Lincolnshire corridor between Deira and Mercia, which would be more convenient for translating Oswald's bones to Bardney. The political results of the battle are clear enough, however. The Northumbrian confederation broke up, leaving Penda's Mercia the predominant Anglo-Saxon power.

Maserfelth

	Winner	*Loser*
Opponents	Mercian	Northumbrian
Commanders	Penda	St Oswald (k)

Directions

Tactical locations unknown.

Winwaed (Winwidfeld), *c.* **15 November 654**

England, West Yorkshire, LR111 SE4317?

The Battle of the Winwaed is the high point of Bede's account of the long rivalry between Northumbria and Mercia. It was the subject of his longest battle description, and one of the most decisive actions of Anglo-Saxon history, ending the life of Penda of Mercia as he had done for so many others, and leading directly to Mercia's conversion to Christianity.

Oswy, who succeeded Oswald in Bernicia, continued to suffer Penda's 'savage and insupportable attacks'. Thirteen years after St Oswald's death at Maserfelth, Penda invaded Northumbria with a coalition of Middle

Winwaed		
	Winner	*Loser*
Opponents	Northumbrian	Mercian
Commanders	Oswy	Penda (k)
		Cadafael
		Aethelhere (k)

and East Anglian, Welsh, and even Deiran forces. Oswy retreated to Bernicia's northern limits to a stronghold at *urbs Giudi*. This has been variously located, most plausibly at Stirling, a Dark Age fortress at the head of navigation on the Forth, commanding the Roman road north into Pictland. Oswy tried to buy peace with the treasures of the Bernician royal hoard, the plunder of victories dating from Catraeth. Bede and the 9th-century *Historia Brittonum* disagree over the outcome of this 'Restoration of Iedeu'. Bede says that Penda declined to be bought off, being determined to exterminate the whole Bernician people. According to the *Historia*, Penda distributed the treasure among his followers, and set off home in triumph.

Oswy overtook Penda's army just south of Castleford on the Great North Road. As usual the location is disputed, but Bede specifically places it near Leeds, '*in regione Loidis*', beside the River Winwaed, which was swollen by heavy rain. The little River Went, east of Wakefield, is variously transcribed as the Winned, Wenet or Wynt. It has high banks, floods after autumn rain and auspiciously rises in St Oswald's Pool in Nostell Park. The battle's catastrophic outcome suggests Penda was trapped in the river bend at Hessle, north of Ackworth Moor Top, the Northumbrians blocking his escape, perhaps on higher ground to the west, around Wragby church.

Bede assigns the larger army to Penda, which may be correct as Oswy had felt compelled to negotiate. Penda also had a qualitative edge: 'thirty legions ... experienced in war and commanded by famous leaders'. This agrees with subsequent casualty claims, as long as a legion is reckoned as a tribal warband. Oswy had only his own resources, as his nephew Aethelwald, the Deiran sub-king, was on the other side, guiding the enemies of his homeland. Penda's troops were, however, encumbered with loot and disinclined to fight. Aethelwald withdrew 'in the hour of battle', to await the outcome in a place of safety. Cadafael of Gwynedd crept away in the night, winning the ironical nickname Catbagail Catguommed, 'Battle-seeker, Battle-avoider'.

Oswy's desperate band, with everything to regain, smashed the heathen army, killing most of Penda's 30 '*duces regii*', its commanders of royal rank. Their number agrees not only with Bede's legions, but also with the 30 or so peoples that the Tribal Hidage, a contemporary survey, placed between the Thames and Humber. Penda, the author of the war, was himself cut down, having lost his own troops and his allies. More drowned in the swollen river than perished by the sword. The Welsh named the battle 'Strages Gai Campi', or the slaughter of Gaius' Field. Their poets remembered 'a pool knee-deep in blood, /Twenty hundred perished in one hour'. Henry of Huntingdon breaks into an atavistic victory chant:

> In the river Winwaed is avenged the slaughter of
> Anna,
> The slaughter of the kings Sigberht and Ecgric,
> The slaughter of the kings Oswald and Edwine.
>
> (Sigberht and Ecgric were kings of East Anglia killed by Penda.)

Oswy gratefully dedicated his baby daughter and 12 estates to the service of God. The latter included a hermitage of St James on the hill his troops had occupied before the battle, which after the Norman Conquest developed into Nostell Priory. A charter of Henry I in 1122 confirmed the monks' possession of the surrounding wood of St Oswald, showing the site's association with the Bernician royal house, and affording a strong indication of the battle's location.

Directions

Take the A638 Wakefield–Doncaster road past Nostell Priory on the left, now a Palladian country house. See Wragby church and the ruins of the Augustinian Priory in the park. Turn left at the roundabout into Cross Hands Lane, and right along Hessle Lane, around the bend in Went Beck, where Penda may have met his end. A footpath to Ackworth Old House runs through the low ground and across the Beck.

Trent, *c.*678

England, unlocated

Nechtanesmere (Dunnichen Moss), 20 May 685

Scotland, Angus, LR 54 NO5149

The battles fought by Oswy's son Ecgfrith set the borders of Northumbria for the remainder of its existence. Despite the importance of these two battles, the location of the Trent battlefield is lost, while that of Nechtanesmere has only recently been rediscovered.

The strategic corridor between Lincoln and York remained a focus of conflict. Aelfwine was Ecgfrith's brother and under-king of Deira. His death beside the Trent provided 'good reason for fiercer fighting and prolonged hostilities', according to Bede, but the Northumbrians accepted compensation, and recognized the constraints that Aethelred of Mercia imposed on them. Ecgfrith showed less moderation in the north.

Oswy and Ecgfrith had extended Northumbrian power in Scotland, provoking a Pictish 'revolt' in the early 670s. Eddi (*fl.c.*700), the biographer of St Wilfrid, described the ensuing massacre of the 'rebels', which sheds light on the disaster at Nechtanesmere. Ecgfrith 'got together a troop of horsemen, for he was no lover of belated operations ... [and] attacked with his little band ... an enemy host which was vast and moreover concealed'. So many Picts died that their corpses blocked two streams, allowing their killers to pass over dry-shod. Ecgfrith was evidently a bold and successful commander, accustomed to conducting mobile operations against an intangible enemy. Northumbrian aggression, however, encouraged cooperation between their erstwhile allies in Dalriada and the Picts, shifting the northern balance of power. The victorious Pictish commander at Nechtanesmere symbolized the alliance, being an Irish prince from Dalriada.

In 685 Ecgfrith ignored his ecclesiastical policy advisors, and, according to Bede, 'rashly took an army to ravage the kingdom of the Picts', beyond the Firth of Tay: 'The enemy feigned flight and lured the king into some narrow passes in the midst of inaccessible mountains; there he was killed with the greater part of the forces he had taken with him', his bodyguard cut down with him. An 11th-century claim that St Wilfred sighted two devils carrying the royal soul off to hell remains unconfirmed.

Nechtanesmere's timing is known with rare accuracy. The battle was fought on a Saturday, at about the ninth hour – four o'clock on a Scottish summer afternoon. Where the Anglo-Saxons remembered its site as a swamp, '*stagnum Nachtani*', the Irish called it *Cath Duin Nechtain*, 'the battle of Nechtan's fortress', whence the modern name of Dunnichen. Welsh Annals preserved the original Pictish name: *Gueith lin garan*, 'the battle of the heron's lake'. The site 3 miles (5 km) southeast of Forfar is now well known, although neither swamp nor fortress is prominent. One was drained in the 19th century, the other pulled down for building materials. Unusual winter floods recreated the vanished loch in 1946–7, allowing archaeologists to reconstruct its shoreline along the previously inexplicable curves of a disused road skirting its southern edge. Traces of a medieval chapel provide a clue to its northwestern extremity. Mutilated traces of a walled Pictish settlement on the southern slope of Dunnichen Hill reveal the site of Nechtan's *cashel* or fort, on a small plateau once known as Castle Hill.

Ecgfrith could have reached the area by two routes: one between the Tay and the Sidlaw Hills, turning left

Trent

	Winner	*Loser*
Opponents	Mercian	Northumbrian
Commanders	Aethelred	Ecgfrith Aelfwine (k)

Nechtanesmere

	Winner	*Loser*
Opponents	Picts	Northumbrian
Commanders	Bruide mac Beli	Ecgfrith (k)

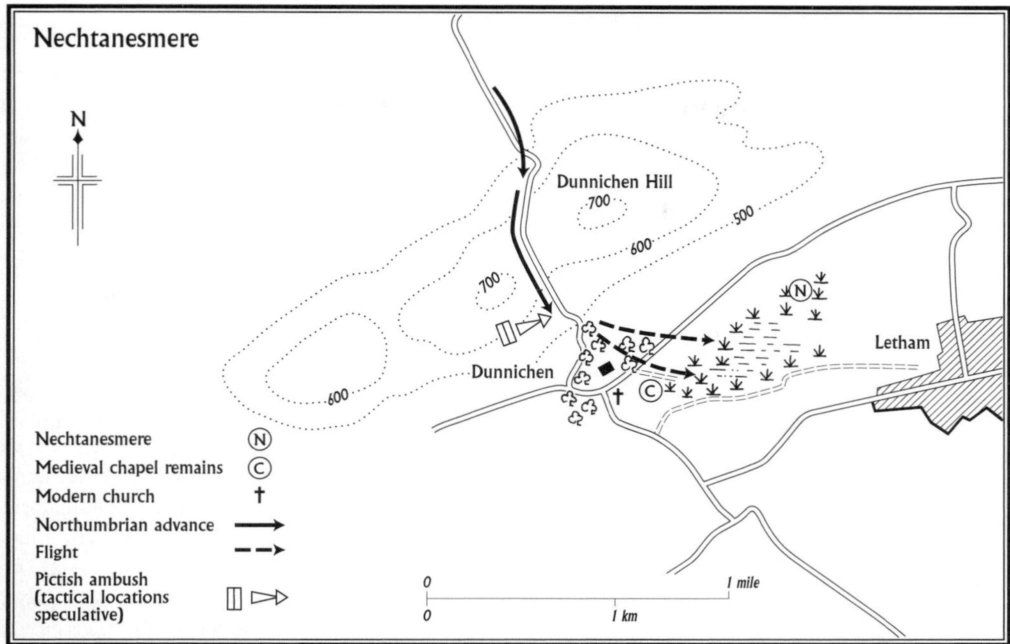

near Dundee to approach the battlefield from the south, the other along a better road up Strathmore, between the Grampians and Sidlaws. The latter suits Bede's description, concealing the tactical hazard of Nechtan's stronghold until the last minute. Turning south at Forfar, perhaps in pursuit of some coat-trailing Pictish light horse, the Northumbrians would suddenly burst out between the twin peaks of Dunnichen Hill, only to find enemy reinforcements hard on their flank. In the absence of better evidence, the direction of the Northumbrian flight would place the ambush on their unshielded right flank. Strung out and breathless the Northumbrians would have had no time to dismount and form a shieldwall, before the 'enemy host which was vast and moreover concealed' drove them downhill into the swamp on their left. The fight would leave few archaeological traces, the victors spoiling the dead and throwing the naked bodies into the 10-foot (3-m) deep mire.

Four miles (6 km) north of Dunnichen, by the porch of Aberlemno church, an inscribed stone may record the story from the Pictish point of view, in rows of figures like a strip cartoon. At the top a larger horseman (Ecgfrith?) chases a smaller (Bruide?); in the middle a group of infantry holds off the large horseman; and at the bottom the smaller mounted man again confronts the larger, who is last seen unhorsed and disarmed, with a raven at his throat.

The Northumbrians never again exacted tribute from the Picts, but nationalist celebration of Nechtanesmere as a decisive point in the development of Scottish independence is misplaced. Bede describes the slaughter and enslavement of Bernician settlers, but Ecgfrith's successor would restore the kingdom. Northumbria held Lothian into the 9th century, ensuring that Anglian speech would persist throughout the area.

Directions

Nechtanesmere *Dunnichen is 3 miles (5 km) south-east of Forfar. Take the B9128, and bear left at Hillend along a minor road, leaving Dunnichen Hill (764 ft/233 m) on the left. Minor roads lead around the vanished loch, in the depression between Mains of Dunnichen and Letham. See the modern monument and replica of a Pictish stone near the church. Also see the Pictish slabs at Aberlemno 4 miles (6 km) north on the B9134.*

Directions

Trent *location unknown.*

The Fury of the Northmen

Viking attacks on the British Isles during the 9th century were a continuation of the Germanic migrations that created Anglo-Saxon England. Contemporary Anglo-Saxon writers now saw the Vikings as barbarians, intruding upon a more settled Christian society. They resented the spoliation of their treasures, the destruction of their libraries, and the slaughter of their leading men. For a few years the very future of English Christianity appeared to be at stake.

'Viking' is an umbrella term for invaders whom the *Anglo-Saxon Chronicle* describes variously as Northmen, heathens or Danes. In Ireland and the Hebrides Norwegians took the lead, and for almost a century sustained a remarkable bifocal kingdom at Dublin and York. Scandinavian emigration may have been driven by overpopulation, climate change or the consolidation of royal power at home. Vikings may even have been the innocent victims of Frankish power politics. In any case, the revived money economies of western Europe, with thousands of silver pennies in circulation, posed an irresistible temptation.

The Vikings revolutionized England's political and cultural structure. In little more than a decade they replaced a patchwork of competing Anglo-Saxon kingdoms with a bipolar division of the country. In the southwest an Anglo-Saxon coalition of Wessex and a rump Mercia survived as the nucleus of the future kingdom of England. In the northeast, beyond Watling Street, the Scandinavian kings and jarls of the Danelaw squatted amidst the ruins of Northumbria and East Anglia. Raids increased in scale as fleets switched between England and Francia, depending on the resistance they met either side of the English Channel. During the 860s Viking objectives expanded from plunder to conquest. Sporadic attacks on coastal targets developed into a deliberate assault that obliterated Northumbria and East Anglia, partitioned Mercia, and nearly overran Wessex. In 871 Alfred bought off the Great Army after a dreadful campaign of nine battles, most of them defeats.

Saxon defeats were not rooted in inferior technology or expertise. Viking weapons were not very different from those of their enemies. Anglo-Saxon armies were not an ill-armed peasant levy, but professional fighting men similar to Vikings in training and equipment, organized by shire, and commanded by royal governors or ealdormen. This was not a job for the faint-hearted. Nine ealdormen from Wessex are known to have died in action during the 9th century, and six from Mercia. The system was slow to mobilize, but provided defence in depth. Historians disagree about the size of Viking armies and the extent of the damage they did. Contemporary sources show two scales of Viking activity: raids by small squadrons of precisely stated numbers of vessels, and major invasions by a Great Army or *micel here*, transported by fleets estimated at hundreds of ships. Continental and Irish sources record a similar pattern. Ships recovered from archaeological sites carried 30–50 fighting men, suggesting that while raiding parties might only number hundreds, Viking armies fielded thousands of men, even if many vessels were auxiliaries, stuffed with loot and wives. These estimates of Viking strengths bear comparison with the numbers of men specified by the Burghal Hidage, a list of garrisons assigned to key points in Wessex. These varied in proportion to the area to be defended, on the scale of four men per pole, or 5½ yards (5 m), of perimeter. Totals ranged from 2400 at Winchester to 150 at Southampton, and are consistent with surviving perimeters, for example at Wareham. The Vikings could hardly have overrun England so comprehensively unless they had fielded at least equal numbers to the defenders, given the similar levels of weaponry and tactics on both sides.

The Vikings' secret weapon was strategic mobility.

Shallow draught longships struck from the sea without warning, and pushed deep inland along rivers. Rivers became strategic fault lines, invasion routes instead of defensive obstacles. When their ships ran aground, Vikings stole horses to keep ahead of defending forces. Scandinavian leaders combined the strategic offensive and tactical defensive with a flair bordering on genius. Repeatedly they wrong-footed the opposition, suddenly seizing key points that would force the enemy to attack at a disadvantage, or suffer disastrous losses of prestige by allowing the Vikings uncontested possession of national capitals and royal estates.

King Alfred's fights with the Vikings are the first English battles recorded by contemporary witnesses. The main source for the period is the *Anglo-Saxon Chronicle* compiled in Wessex by survivors of the war, which they made the main focus of their dramatic narrative. The *Life of King Alfred* attributed to Alfred's friend Bishop Asser purports to be a unique contemporary biography of an Anglo-Saxon king. Its unfortunate mixture of long-winded paraphrase of the *Chronicle* and folkloric hagiography has persuaded some scholars that the *Life* is a forgery, and involved others in convoluted attempts to reconcile the text with common sense. Both sources exaggerate Alfred's reputation at the expense of his elder brothers, who carried the burden of kingship until 871.

Don's Mouth, 796

England, South Tyne, LR88, unlocated

Whalley, 2 April 798

England, Lancashire, LR103, unlocated

Despite the *Anglo-Saxon Chronicle*'s regional bias towards Wessex, its first recorded encounters with Vikings occurred in Northumbria, within easy reach of the sea. *Donemuthan* ('Don's mouth') was the monastery at Jarrow, where the Don flows into the Tyne estuary (NZ3365). A Viking leader was killed, and bad weather wrecked some of their ships, local people polishing off any crew who escaped drowning. Whalley with its medieval abbey lies in the Ribble valley, suggesting the raiders were Norwegians operating in the Irish Sea. The Roman road from Preston to York runs between Ribchester and Whalley, a possible route for local forces to cut off Vikings returning to their ships.

Directions

Tactical locations unknown.

Don's Mouth

	Winner	*Loser*
Opponents	Northumbrian	Viking
Commanders	unknown	unknown (k)

Whalley

	Winner	*Loser*
Opponents	Viking	Northumbrian
Commanders	unknown	Alric (k)

Carhampton, 836

England, Somerset, LR181 ST0042

Portland, 837

England, Dorset, LR194, unlocated

Southampton, 837

England, Hampshire, LR196 SU4211?

Carhampton, 843

England, Somerset, LR181 ST0042

Parret River, 848

England , Dorset / Somerset, LR182, unlocated

Wicganbeorg (Wigborough?), 850

England, Somerset, LR193 ST4415?

Carhampton		
	Winner	*Loser*
Opponents	Viking	West Saxon
Commanders	unknown	Egbert

Portland		
	Winner	*Loser*
Opponents	Viking	West Saxon
Commander	unknown	Aethelhelm (k)

Southampton		
	Winner	*Loser*
Opponents	West Saxon	Viking
Commanders	Wulfheard	unknown

Carhampton		
	Winner	*Loser*
Opponents	Viking	West Saxon
Commanders	unknown	Aethelwulf

Parret River		
	Winner	*Loser*
Opponents	West Saxon	Viking
Commanders	Osric	unknown
	Bishop Ealhstan	

Wicganbeorg		
	Winner	*Loser*
Opponents	West Saxon	Viking
Commanders	Ceorl	unknown

The even results of these clashes suggest Wessex successfully contained the Viking threat during the early 9th century. Numbers of raiding ships remained small: 35 or 25 at Carhampton, 33 at Southampton, implying attacking forces of a thousand at most. Defensive arrangements worked well: men from Dorset and Somerset fought together on the Parret; Devon men made great slaughter of the heathen at Wicganbeorg, probably Wigborough in Somerset. On three occasions out of six the Danes won the field ('held the place of slaughter', in the words of the *Anglo-Saxon Chronicle*), the Saxons claiming victory in the other three. The defensive effort was not cheap: two bishops and two ealdormen fell at Carhampton (836). Ealdorman Aethelhelm's companions died with him at Portland, an unsung echo of the heroic past.

The raiders concentrated on coastal targets until the 850s. Twice they beached their ships in Blue Anchor Bay, to attack the royal estate at Carhampton. Another royal hall at Cannington may have attracted the raiding army that Osric and Ealhstan defeated beside the River Parret. Wigborough lies in a loop of the same river, 22 miles (35 km) from its estuary on the Bristol Channel, but only 7 miles (11 km) from the Parret's head of navigation at Langport. Saxon Southampton or Ham-Wih lay east of the medieval town, spreading 1000 yards (915 m) inland from the River Itchen, with a market around St Mary's Church. The town was the most important trading and manufacturing centre in Wessex, but declined after the attack. Southampton was more fortunate than Quentovic, the great Frankish entrepôt, which disappeared entirely. In both cases Viking assaults brought serious and unwelcome consequences for the local population and regional economy.

Directions

Tactical locations unknown.

Aclea (Oak Glade/Oak Leigh), 850

England, Kent, LR178 TQ7274?

Sandwich, 850

Naval, English Channel, LR179

Thanet, 853

England, Kent, LR179 unlocated

Pressure increased during the 850s. Viking fleets overwintered on the Isles of Thanet and Sheppey in 850 and 855. Three and a half hundred vessels came into the Thames estuary in 850. They stormed Canterbury and beat off Beorhtwulf of Mercia, London's overlord, before suffering a salutary defeat at a place called Aclea at the hands of King Aethelwulf, Alfred the Great's father, and his eldest son. The 9th-century compilers of the *Anglo-Saxon Chronicle* remembered the action as 'the greatest slaughter of a heathen raiding army that we have heard tell of up to this present day'. The site of this memorable victory is sadly unknown. Suggestions range from Oakley (Hampshire), through Ockley (Surrey), to Oakleigh (Kent). The Hampshire location, west of Basingstoke, would suggest Aethelwulf saw off a blow directed at the heart of his kingdom, down the Roman roads from Silchester past Basingstoke to Winchester and Salisbury (LR185 SU5650). Ockley, near Dorking, also has strategic attractions (LR187 TQ1440). It lies near the junction of Stane Street, the Roman road southwest of London, and the Pilgrim's Way, a natural route for an army from Wessex marching to assist Athelstan, another of Aethelwulf's sons and sub-king of Kent. Oakleigh near Higham in Kent is nearest the recorded scene of action, within sight of the tidal ford across the Thames at Tilbury, suggesting a successful counteroffensive driving the Vikings back to their ships.

The first explicitly recorded English naval action came just before or after Aclea, alternative versions of the *Anglo-Saxon Chronicle* giving a different sequence of events. The energetic Athelstan caught a raiding army at Sandwich, probably in the roadstead, where the Ordnance Survey shows 'Bloody Point'. He captured nine ships, but such losses were nothing to fleets numbered in hundreds. Where the combined forces of Dorset and Somerset had won the day at the Parret (848), Kent and Surrey failed to evict a raiding army from Thanet in 853. Many Saxons, including both leaders, were killed and drowned, presumably in the marshes of the Stour.

Directions

Tactical locations unknown.

Aclea

	Winner	*Loser*
Opponents	West Saxon	Viking
Commanders	Aethelwulf Aethelbald	unknown

Sandwich

	Winner	*Loser*
Opponents	Kentish	Viking
Commanders	Athelstan Ealhhere	unknown

Thanet

	Winner	*Loser*
Opponents	Viking	Kentish
Commanders	unknown	Ealhhere (k) Huda (k)

York, 21/23 March 867

England, York, LR105 SE6051?

Energetic countermeasures by the Frankish king Charles the Bald during the 860s persuaded many Vikings in Francia to seek easier pickings across the English Channel. In 865 a great raiding army settled in East Anglia for the winter, where they acquired horses. For the first time the *Anglo-Saxon Chronicle* recorded their leader's name: Iguuar or Ivar, known elsewhere as 'Ivar the Boneless', one of several sons attributed to the legendary Ragnar Lothbrok or 'Hairybreeks'. The Danish historian Saxo Grammaticus claims the Northumbrians had thrown Ragnar into a pit of vipers, suggesting the ensuing battle was a grudge match.

Sensitive to their enemies' political weakness, the Vikings rode for York in the autumn of 866. The Northumbrians were enjoying a succession dispute, and could not raise an army until the following year. Their kings failed to see the risks of tackling an undamaged Viking army behind fortifications, where it had been allowed to dig in unmolested. On Palm Sunday 867 the Northumbrians stormed York's Roman defences, which still stood 10 feet (3 m) high in places. The last kings of Northumbria went down street-fighting, with all the savage fury but none of the guile of Aethelfrith the Twister: 'an immense slaughter was made of the Northumbrians there, some inside, some outside, and both of the kings were killed'. Eight ealdormen died with them, attesting to the totality of the defeat.

Directions

Tactical locations unknown.

York

	Winner	*Loser*
Opponents	Viking	Northumbrian
Commanders	Ivar	Aelle (k)
		Osberht (k)

Winchester, *c.*860

England, Hampshire, LR185, unlocated

Englefield, 31 December 870

England, Berkshire, LR175 SU6272?

Reading 4 January 871

England, Berkshire, LR175 SU7173?

The Great Army invaded Wessex in the winter of 870–1. The previous year the Vikings had wintered in East Anglia, where they martyred King Edmund and left the great abbey at Peterborough 'as it were nothing'. In December 870 another of Ragnar Lothbrok's sons, Halfdan, led a mounted force down the Icknield Way to Reading, intending to add Wessex to the list of obsolete Anglo-Saxon kingdoms. A raiding army at Reading was well situated to receive waterborne reinforcements from the lower Thames, and had a choice of continuing south to Winchester or west along the Thames to Wallingford. Both were important West Saxon centres, allocated large garrisons in the Burghal Hidage. Mercia had recently ceded Berkshire to Wessex, and its king, Burghred, sent no help to his brother-in-law Aethelred of Wessex, the third of Aethelwulf's sons to succeed to the kingdom.

While Halfdan's men dug in at Reading, two of his jarls marauded along the Kennet valley. Beyond the high ground immediately west of Reading water meadows extend from Pangbourne on the Thames to Theale on the Kennet, forming a natural wet ditch. Here the jarls met Aethelwulf, Ealdorman of Berkshire, a veteran Viking-fighter. When 200 shiploads of raiders from the Somme had devastated Winchester in 860, he had led his men into Hampshire to catch them as they returned to their ships. Now he was on the defensive, his hall at Reading in enemy hands. Eight of Berkshire's 20 hundreds were cut off beyond Reading, so Aethelwulf may have fought at half-strength, though he had the better position: the moderately steep hill west of the village of Englefield is covered by boggy ground to its front, heavy going for mounted infantry. Whether the jarls attacked the hill, or Aethelwulf caught their men looting the village, the Vikings were beaten, and one of their leaders possibly killed.

Four days later Aethelred showed he had not appreciated the lessons of the disaster at York, and launched a frontal assault on the defences at Reading with 'a great army'. Halfdan may have calculated that a king of the period could hardly do otherwise, if he were to retain the loyalty of Aethelwulf and his Berkshire thanes. Just a week had elapsed since Halfdan had taken Reading, suggesting only Hampshire and Wiltshire could have joined Aethelwulf in the interval.

Bishop Asser, in his *Life of King Alfred*, claimed the Vikings made a rampart between the Kennet and Thames, a precaution consistent with Viking tactics in Francia. The defences have been identified with the Plummery Ditch, a water-filled dyke that cut off Forbury and King's Meadow east of the town, until the Great Western Railway filled it in to build Reading Station during the 19th century. A kink in the Thames restricts the defensive front there to about 800 yards (730 m). The Burghal Hidage allowed four men per pole of wall, about 4 feet (1.2 m) per man, setting a minimum number of Vikings at 580, besides reserves and lookouts along the river bank. Whether the Anglo-Saxons dashed themselves in vain against the rampart, or, as Asser says, the Vikings burst out of the gates like wolves, the result was a disaster for Wessex. Aethelwulf was killed, a leader King Aethelred could ill afford to lose. According to some accounts the attacking forces retreated eastwards, over the River Loddon at Twyford. This seems unlikely. Converging rivers had forced Aethelred to attack from the west, and he must have withdrawn the same way, probably through Englefield. When the Vikings left Reading four days later, he was ready for them on the Berkshire Downs.

Directions

Englefield *the village is just west of the A340 Pangbourne–Theale road.*

Reading *Halfdan's rampart presumably lies under central Reading, beneath the railway station and public library.*

Winchester

	Winner	*Loser*
Opponents	West Saxon	Viking
Commanders	Aethelwulf	Weland?
	Osric	

Englefield

	Winner	*Loser*
Opponents	West Saxon	Viking
Commanders	Aethelwulf	unknown

Reading

	Winner	*Loser*
Opponents	Viking	West Saxon
Commanders	Halfdan I	Aethelred I
	Bagsecg	Alfred
		Aethelwulf (k)

Ashdown, 8 January 871

England, Berkshire, LR174 SU5381–82

The Battle of Ashdown holds an important place in English national mythology. It was the only significant West Saxon success of the campaign of 871, and the first victory associated with Alfred the Great.

The *Anglo-Saxon Chronicle*'s customary vagueness combined with Ashdown's perceived significance has inspired extensive disputes about its location. The Anglo-Saxon name *Aescesdun* meant a district associated with a man called Aesc, rather than a particular tree-ridden place. Despite numerous attempts to identify the site from place-names, it is impossible to do more than connect it with the northern edge of the Berkshire Downs, an area still referred to as

Ashdown by local shepherds in the 18th century. Asser's explanation of Ashdown as Ash Tree Hill is no help, as it was inspired by a mistranslation.

The traditional site of the battle is at White Horse Hill, at Uffington near Swindon. This is too far from Reading for the defeated Vikings to have returned there the day after the battle, while the chalk carving associated with the battle dates from the Iron Age. A more credible area for the battle lies nearer Reading, between the Icknield Way and the Ridgeway on the line of Moulsford Down and Lowbury Hill, the highest point on the east Berkshire Downs. Lowbury Hill is an excellent landmark for West Saxon reinforcements summoned to replace losses suffered at Reading. Aethelred's main army could await them at the intersection of six trackways near Roden Down, allowing easy movement to counter Viking moves along the Thames valley and the Ridgeway, or further south around his right flank.

Two sites for the battlefield stand out on military grounds: a re-entrant or valley between the spurs of Kingstanding Hill and Moulsford Down, and the stretch of the Ridgeway across Louse Hill further west between Lowbury Hill and Compton. The opposing spurs at Moulsford Down are impossibly steep for 9th-century close-order tactics, while the approach along the waterlogged Thames valley would be impassable in winter. The gentler slopes of Louse Hill would suit contemporary tactical requirements better. It seems more likely that the Vikings would march up the southern dip slope of the Downs via Aldworth, rather than assault the northern escarpment. They knew the southern route through Englefield, and could reach the battle area dry-shod, once across the boggy Pangbourne. Charter evidence and Domesday Book also support Compton. Both sites are a day's march from Reading, implying the combatants spent the night shivering on top of the Downs to make the most of the few hours of daylight available for fighting in January.

Ashdown

	Winner	*Loser*
Opponents	West Saxon	Viking
Commander	Aethelred I	Bagsecg (k)
	Alfred	Halfdan I

A.H. Burne believed local place-names showed the course of the battle. The Vikings occupied Louse Hill, dubiously equated with the Romani for 'Hill of Destruction', before advancing into 'Awful Bottom' to fight. Then they retreated east through 'Dead Man's Hollow', beyond Starveall, where they suffered their heaviest casualties. Burne criticized Aethelred for giving up the higher ground at Louse Hill, but that would have only mattered, given the short-range weapons in use, if the West Saxons wanted to attack. In the event the Viking advance precipitated the battle. They formed up in two divisions, one led by their two kings, the other under the jarls, reflecting the separate identities of the war bands. The West Saxons conformed to this twofold arrangement, Aethelred commanding one wing and Alfred the other. Asser adds unnecessary confusion by giving Halfdan and Bagsecg the centre of their army, '*mediam partem exercitus*', implying a right and left wing to make three divisions in total.

Asser's purpose was not tactical, but hagiographical. His *Life of King Alfred* systematically devalues Aethelred's contribution to the victory, to Alfred's advantage. Almost every modern account has repeated Asser's claim that when the Vikings moved forward Aethelred was deep in prayer, and left Alfred's division to absorb the shock unsupported. The *Anglo-Saxon Chronicle*, written during Alfred's reign, probably at his court, shows this tale is completely untrue. The West Saxon divisions engaged simultaneously, although Aethelred the king takes proper precedence over his younger brother:

> And then King Aethelred fought against the king's force, and there the King Bagsecg was killed; and Alfred his brother against the jarls' force …

After his recent defeat Aethelred might have preferred to await reinforcements. The Vikings, for the same reason, would have forced a decision, while the West Saxons were still shaken. Once the Vikings advanced the West Saxons had to countercharge as a whole. If only one division went forward it would have been

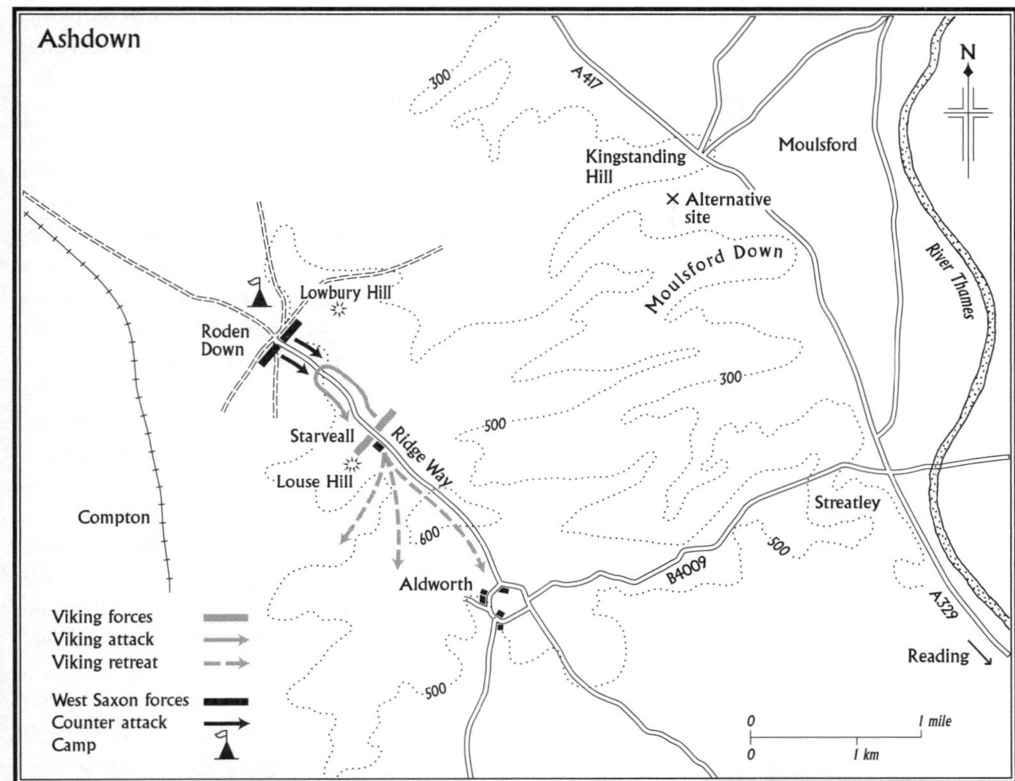

beaten in detail, as Edmund Ironside was at Assandune (1016). The water that collects in 'Awful Bottom' may have slowed the Vikings' charge, leaving them floundering and vulnerable to a counterattack. Pushed back up the long western slope of Louse Hill, they would have been driven over the crest into the deeper mire around Starveall, where they were cut down trying to reach their horses.

Asser provides various details, which are less helpful than they seem. He compares Alfred's attack with that of a wild boar, perhaps an advance in wedge formation, but a common Welsh metaphor of the period. Alfred closed up his shieldwall in proper order before advancing, but it would have been odd if he had not. Asser gives the Vikings the higher ground, which supports the Louse Hill battlefield, but fits Asser's hagiographical scheme too neatly to be accepted without confirmation. Asser's most irritating detail concerns a solitary thorn tree around which the armies clashed, and which he claimed to have seen with his own eyes. A single tree has no tactical significance, while the overwhelming profusion of bent and naked thorns along the Ridgeway renders it valueless as evidence of the place of slaughter.

The *Anglo-Saxon Chronicle* named five jarls who accompanied Bagsecg to Valhalla, an indication of the seriousness of the day's work:

Directions

Take the B4009 from Streatley onto the Downs, and turn right in Aldworth along the Ridgeway. Push on past Starveall, and over the hill to Aethelred's rendezvous at Roden Down. The alternative site at Kingstanding Hill is accessible by a footpath opposite a dangerous junction on the A417, 1 mile (1.6 km) west of Moulsford.

both raiding armies were put to flight, and there were many thousands of killed; and fighting went on until night.

Aethelweard's Latin transcription of the *Chronicle* recalled:

all the nobler youth of the barbarians fell there, so that neither before nor after has such a slaughter been heard of since the race of Saxons won Britain in war.

Aethelred won a significant victory in spite of Asser. He did not end the war, but Ashdown was a gleam of hope through worse days to come, justifying its place in the national consciousness.

Basing, 22 January 871

England, Hampshire, LR185/6 SU6549

Meretun (Merantune), March 871

England, Wiltshire, LR174 SU2860

Wilton, May 871

England, Wiltshire, LR184 unlocated

Vikings hammered at the gateways to Wessex throughout the spring of 871, demonstrating their military superiority in at least three more battles. Taken as a group Basing, Meretun and Wilton form a recognizable campaign with definite objectives on both sides. In Halfdan's case this was the final destruction of Anglo-Saxon England, through a sustained offensive. The operational tempo appears to fall off after Basing, but the *Anglo-Saxon Chronicle*'s summary of the war mentions nine national fights, of which it names only six. If the three unidentified battles occurred between Basing and Meretun, the average interval between confrontations in spring 871 would approach the two quiet weeks after Ashdown. This rapid succession of blows suggests a flow of Viking replacements, and ruthless dominating intelligence on the part of their leaders. The Great Army was a serious menace, not just a bunch of strategically illiterate thugs bent on plunder.

The obvious strategic context for a fight at Basing in north Hampshire is a Viking strike at Winchester, sidling around Aethelred's right flank as he blockaded Reading from the west. Aethelred met the Viking advance in the field, avoiding a repetition of the Northumbrian dilemma at York in 867. The traditional site for the battle is east of Basingstoke, in the northeast corner of Hackwood Park, a long day's march from Reading. One version of the *Chronicle* comments, 'because of their [i.e. the West Saxons'] sins the Danes captured the field'. Aethelweard suggested more prosaically that the Vikings lured the West Saxons into a frontal assault across the water meadows of the River Loddon. A wild guess would put them at Daneshill, a built-up area east of Basingstoke's ringroad. Aethelred did at least prevent their further advance, for the Vikings retired 'without the spoils of victory'.

The site of Meretun is uncertain. Locations range from Merton in Surrey to Marden on the western edge of Salisbury Plain. Neither of these makes strategic sense, as they would have exposed the heart of Wessex to an enemy located at Reading. Martin in Hampshire has been advocated as Aethelred was buried nearby at Wimborne Minster soon after the action. However, important casualties were often removed considerable distances before burial. Marten in Wiltshire is etymologically and strategically sounder. It makes a good rallying point for a West Saxon army defeated near Basingstoke, intermediate between that place and Wilton, the last battle of the campaign. The Inkpen Ridgeway provides good lateral communications south of the Kennet, allowing Aethelred to parry further Viking advances.

If the Vikings could clear Marten, at the western end of the Kennet line, they had a choice of Roman roads to Salisbury or Winchester. Nowhere south of Marten could the West Saxons oppose an advance on their two capitals without dividing their forces. According to this scheme, Halfdan moved west along the north bank of the Kennet, after several abortive

Basing

	Winner	Loser
Opponents	Viking	West Saxon
Commanders	Halfdan I	Aethelred I
		Alfred

Meretun

	Winner	Loser
Opponents	Viking	West Saxon
Commanders	Halfdan I	Aethelred I (w)
		Alfred

Wilton

	Winner	Loser
Opponents	Viking	West Saxon
Commanders	Halfdan I	Alfred

manoeuvres represented by the nameless trio of battles. Southwest of Hungerford the road crosses a narrow pass between Savernake Forest and a steep combe occupied by Shalbourne village. On or behind the ridge stood the West Saxons. The Vikings attacked in two bands, and were finally successful. Casualties included Bishop Heahmund of Sherborne, 'and many good men'. Perhaps the Vikings attacked in successive waves and wore their opponents down. Perhaps the defenders followed up an initial success and were caught in disorder by concealed reserves. Raegnald of York won a battle at Corbridge (918) by a similar ploy. Aethelred died a month later, possibly of wounds.

Now king of Wessex, Alfred soon saw fresh action at Wilton just west of Salisbury. The West Saxons had clearly failed to hold the northern edge of Salisbury Plain after Meretun, retreating into the very heart of the kingdom. Wilton, like Carhampton, Reading and Meretun, was a royal estate. Persistent Viking attacks on such targets suggest a deliberate effort to undermine the kings of Wessex by driving them away from their centres of royal power. The *Chronicle* attributes only a small troop to the new king, suggesting Alfred was taken by surprise, forced to defend himself at short notice. According to Asser, Wilton was on a hill south of the River Guilou, Welsh for the Wylye. Perhaps he meant the fighting took place on the high ground between the Wylye and Nadder, along the continuation of the Roman road westwards from Old Sarum through Grovely Wood.

The *Chronicle* put on a brave face, claiming that Alfred put the enemy to flight, but this is no more likely than Asser's claim that the Vikings ran away, only to rally when they realized the small number of their pursuers. Vikings were just very tough opponents, with a healthy numerical advantage following the arrival of a summer raiding army. The attempt by Asser and the *Chronicle* to gloss over another defeat cannot be credited any more than Asser's blatantly false claim that Alfred was 'victorious in virtually all battles'. Alfred's greatness lay in his steadfast reaction to adversity, not the consistency of his military success.

Later the same year the West Saxons made peace with Halfdan's raiding army, and it withdrew to London. Similar agreements in Francia always involved payment of Danegeld, which West Saxon sources do not mention. Halfdan may have been grateful to achieve a payoff, after a risky advance into deepest Wessex, where he faced total disaster if beaten. For Alfred the agreement was a lucky break that bought precious time to rebuild the defences of Wessex.

Directions

Basing *and* ***Wilton*** *tactical locations unknown.*

Meretun *Marten is six miles southwest of Hungerford, where a minor road (once Roman) crosses the A338 Andover road.*

Alfred's Wars

Alfred the Great faced two Viking invasions after he became king of Wessex. The Great Armies of Guthrum and Haesten, in the late 870s and 890s respectively, were as powerful and as deadly in purpose as Halfdan's in 871. Where Halfdan had probed cautiously at the West Saxon defences, Guthrum and Haesten struck out boldly in search of fresh areas to plunder. Their campaigns traversed the length and breadth of Alfred's kingdom, from Kent to Devon, by way of Dorset and Wiltshire, even penetrating the Welsh border country. Guthrum staged ambitious combined operations against Wareham, Exeter and Somerset with mounted armies and hundreds of ships. Haesten menaced Kent in a great pincer movement that fastened upon Appledore and Milton Regis, near Sittingbourne. Both leaders enlisted veterans of Halfdan's army who had settled in East Anglia, but who were not yet reconciled to agricultural careers. The wars of the 870s and 890s differed from one another, however. While Guthrum brought Alfred to the brink of personal ruin, Haesten's dramatic cross-country dashes resemble the struggles of some marine monster entangled in a net. The Viking threat was no longer beyond control.

Alfred conducted his later wars in a way very different from that of Aethelred in 871. Never again would West Saxon armies seek battle with such naïve enthusiasm. The mature Alfred preferred to shadow Viking forces and to prevent them dispersing to plunder the countryside. When Vikings occupied fortified positions like Wareham (875), Exeter (876) or Chester (893), the West Saxons starved them out. Battles only occurred when raiding parties were caught at a disadvantage encumbered with loot (Farnham 893), when besieged forces faced starvation (Cynwit, 878, Buttington, 893), or in the direst emergency (Ethandun, 878).

This Fabian strategy depended on unglamorous reforms that Alfred may have picked up from the Frankish scholars he invited to his court. The fyrd, the defensive forces of the shires, was divided into two shifts to support extended campaigns without wrecking the economy. Ancient obligations to build and maintain bridges and fortifications were exploited to build a network of fortified towns or *burhs* that protected the population from Viking raids, and deprived raiders of food, plunder and replacement horses. New types of warship were developed, and Frisian naval experts hired to operate them.

The reforms were not always effective. A force besieging Thorney Island in Buckinghamshire in 893 went home before the relieving shift arrived. The leading wave of Haesten's invasion found only a few peasants in a half-finished fort at Lympne. Alfred's new ships revealed serious design faults in action (896). Taken as a whole, however, his strategy wore the Vikings down, while limiting the harm they could do. Eventually they would accept modest payoffs, abandon the Viking way of life, and settle down as farmers in the Scandinavian enclaves in East Anglia and Yorkshire.

Cynwit (Cannington/Countisbury), 878

England, Somerset/Devon, LR182 ST2440 / LR180 SS7449

The Battle of Cynwit is less well known than Ethandun, but it was the prelude to Alfred's supreme victory. The two actions brought a three-year campaign to a successful conclusion, justifying Alfred's unheroic but realistic policy of avoiding battle with superior Viking forces.

The survivors of Halfdan's 871 army separated, after dividing Mercia between themselves and a puppet regime in the West Midlands: Halfdan went to Northumbria, and Guthrum to East Anglia. By 875 the Great Army was ready to finish off Wessex, the last remaining Anglo-Saxon kingdom. Guthrum launched a series of combined operations to seize a naval base in Alfred's rear, first at Wareham (occupied 875–6) and then Exeter (876–7). The loss of 120 ships off Swanage wrecked Guthrum's plans, however. In the autumn of 877 he made the customary exchange of false oaths and doomed hostages, and withdrew to Gloucester in compliant Mercia.

Alfred shadowed Guthrum into north Wiltshire. While the Christians celebrated Christmas at Chippenham, Guthrum lashed out at the thinly defended royal estate, and Alfred ran for his life. The most famous stories of Alfred's reign come from this difficult period of flitting through woodlands and swamps with a few companions, spying on the enemy disguised as a minstrel, or accidentally burning the cakes of a swineherd's wife. Such fabulous tales, with their themes of role reversal, provide a popular but extreme perception of Alfred's darkest hour. The majority of his people cannot have fled overseas, although Ealdorman Wulfhere of Hampshire did. The men of Devon were plainly still under command, for at Cynwit their ealdorman dealt Guthrum's amphibious strategy a final blow.

Ubba, another son of Ragnar Lothbrok, was active in the Bristol Channel with 23 ships. In the winter of 877–8 he was killed in 'Wessex Devonshire' with 800 of his men and another 40 of his personal retinue. The precision of the casualty figures urges their accuracy. Odda's victory is usually placed on the coast, although nothing in the original accounts proves it was by the sea. Two sites are credible: Countisbury near Lynmouth, or Cannington beside the Parret. The first has been dismissed as a phonetic impossibility, but it is tactically consistent with Asser's account. Countisbury stands on a stupendous hill above the shingle beach at Lynmouth, a great ditch and bank cutting through the peninsula from East Lyn cliffs to the sea. Many of Alfred's thanes had shut themselves up there, 'since by the lie of the land that place is very secure from every direction except the east'. True to form the Vikings avoided a frontal attack, and sat down to starve out the defenders. Lacking water, the West Saxons launched a dawn attack and overran the besiegers, who must have experienced severe problems regaining their ships, as the beach is in the opposite direction to the natural line of flight along the combe.

Cannington Park is a strategically more attractive milieu, Cynwit having been equated with nearby Combwich. While Alfred remained in the Somerset wetlands he was safe from Guthrum's mounted infantry at Chippenham, but he was vulnerable to seaborne attack. Ubba was heavily implicated with Ivar the Boneless in the murder of King Edmund of East Anglia, and his longships would have had no difficulty sailing up the Parret to the West Saxon stronghold at Athelney, 'Isle of Princes'. It is hard to resist the implication that Odda was stationed at the mouth of the river to prevent the kind of direct assault on the king's person for which the sons of Ragnar Lothbrok were notorious. Countisbury, despite its spectacular location, is too remote from the campaign's strategic focus.

Cynwit

	Winner	*Loser*
Opponents	West Saxon	Viking
Commanders	Odda	Ubba (k)
Numbers	unknown	1200
Losses	unknown	840

Asser's claim of 1200 Viking dead agrees uncannily with the total crews of 23 ships at 50 men each, but even 840 represented crushing losses. The capture of Ubba's personal banner, known as the Raven, confirms the gravity of the Viking defeat. Stitched by Ubba's three sisters, the Raven, symbol of Odin, the Viking god of war, is the only item of spoil that the *Anglo-Saxon Chronicle* ever considered worthy of specific mention.

Directions

Cannington *On the A39 northwest of Bridgewater. Take a minor road north of the village past the Agricultural College, turn left and right on a footpath to the hillfort (262 feet/80 m) which dominates the low-lying surroundings.*

Countisbury *Asser's site is 1 mile (1.6 km) east and uphill from Lynmouth along either the Southwest Coastal Path or the A39. Both cross the earthworks between Sillery Sands and Wind Hill.*

Ethandun (Edington), May 878

England, Wiltshire, LR184 ST9252?

Ethandun is one of the most important battles fought on English soil, although its exact date (some time between 6 and 12 May) is uncertain. It is rightly the climax of the *Anglo-Saxon Chronicle*'s first section. One of the most dramatic moments in English history, Ethandun had fundamental consequences. Like El Alamein, it broke an endless cycle of defeat, paving the way for eventual victory.

Alfred had been a fugitive in the Somerset Levels since he had fled Chippenham at Christmas 877. St Edmund's horrible death leaves little doubt of Alfred's likely fate if captured, but unlike Burghred, ex-king of Mercia, who sought exile in Rome, he stayed to fight it out. The recovery of Alfred's fortunes began at Easter (23 March) with the construction of a fort at Athelney, perhaps the 'Mump' at Borough Bridge on the Parret. Cynwit had secured Alfred's rear, and he could now carry a guerrilla war to the enemy. Guthrum's strategic position may have been less secure than it looked. The Viking army had lost the initiative, after the failure to trap Alfred and the destruction of Ubba's squadron at Cynwit. Guthrum's offensive had reached a culminating point, with no obvious target at which to strike. A defeat in north Wiltshire, miles from the sea or a navigable river, would expose him to total ruin.

Alfred resumed conventional operations seven weeks after Easter (4–10 May). The *Anglo-Saxon Chronicle* gives a full account of his movements, affording a rare glimpse of how an Anglo-Saxon army might concentrate for battle. Alfred's objective is generally agreed to have been the high ground on the northwest edge of Salisbury Plain. It has been suggested that Ethandun was fought at Edington in the Polden Hills only 7 miles (11 km) from Athelney, but it is hard to see how Alfred could have taken three days to move so short a distance, or how he could then have starved out a Viking army with its back to the Somerset coast.

Most accounts agree that Alfred marched east from Athelney towards Stourhead, along an ancient drover's road, the Hardway or *Herepath*, literally 'the army road'. The rendezvous was at Egbert's Stone, whose location somewhere near Penselwood has never been securely established, though not for want of trying. The site of an 18th-century monument on Kingsettle Hill at Stourton possesses academic credibility and a water supply. Kingston Deverill, a royal estate, has water, a concealed campsite behind Brimsdown Hill, and two stones near the church, associated with Alfred's grandfather King Egbert. All the fighting men of Somerset and Wiltshire met Alfred there, plus a contingent from Hampshire, 'this side of the sea', presumably west of Southampton Water, and 'they were glad of him'. If half the Burghal

Ethandun

	Winner	*Loser*
Opponents	West Saxon	Viking
Commanders	Alfred	Guthrum
Numbers	c.4500	unknown

Hidage establishments were present, the two full-strength counties would have fielded 4000 men, plus several hundred from Hampshire. Guthrum's strength is incalculable. His original mounted army must have been at least 1600 men to occupy Wareham at the Burghal Hidage rate of one man to every 4 feet (1.2 m) of wall. Since then they had been reinforced by sea, suffered several thousand casualties by shipwreck off Swanage, and possibly gained fresh recruits in Mercia.

At Kingsettle Hill the Hardway intersects another trackway, which runs north from Poole Harbour through Kingston Deverill to Warminster, fed by other tracks and Roman roads from east and west. Streams of West Saxon troops could flow together, like tributaries of a river, a safe distance from the Viking army, before marching directly upon the enemy, to come upon him suddenly in prime fighting condition. The main West Saxon army had evidently concentrated before Alfred's arrival, for they were ready to move off next day. They had a short march to their forming-up point at *Iglea* or Iley Oak, a meeting place reliably identified with Eastleigh Wood near Sutton Veny on the south bank of the River Wylie.

North of Iley Oak rises the western extremity of Salisbury Plain, beyond which Edington village lies down in the valley of the Bristol Avon. Had the Vikings failed to picket the heights, Alfred's men could have simply swept down upon their camp at dawn: 'there fought against the whole raiding army, and put it to flight, and rode after it as far as the fortification', presumably Chippenham. Edington was another royal estate, and perhaps the Vikings had drunk too much of Alfred's beer.

Military critics have refused to believe the tactically astute Vikings could have been surprised so easily. A.H. Burne suggested Guthrum occupied the southern edge of Warminster Down (LR184 ST8948), where an ancient embankment bars various tracks leading up from the Wylie, past Battlebury and Scratchbury camps. The British Army's Imber training ground is not far to the east, and the Ordnance Survey appropriately marks Battlebury as a Danger Area. Here the armies fought with customary ferocity and compact shieldwalls, until the Vikings retreated to Bratton Camp on the north edge of the escarpment. However, Bratton Camp was waterless and long demilitarized. It could never have withstood a fortnight's siege, despite a spectacular site enhanced by a white horse that Alfred's victorious troops supposedly carved in the chalk. A more likely scenario has the defeated Vikings fleeing on horseback to Chippenham, 12 miles (19 km) from the battlefield, perhaps after a last stand in the defile between Tinhead Hill and Edington Hill.

Asser wrote of West Saxons hacking down Vikings as they fled, but the *Anglo-Saxon Chronicle* makes no casualty claims comparable with the thousands that littered Ashdown. Ethandun may have been a moral victory, the Vikings running away before they suffered many losses. A low body count would explain Alfred's preferring to negotiate, rather than risk a bloodbath like Reading (871), assaulting a shaken but physically intact Viking host. No epic poems about Ethandun survive, but it was Alfred's finest hour. He had overthrown the Great Army in open battle, ensuring that England would never become a Scandinavian country. Wessex had survived to become the engine of England's unification.

Directions

Edington is 3½ miles (5.5 km) east of Westbury on the B3098. Several footpaths lead up from the village onto Edington Hill (666 feet/203 m), although nobody knows whether the battle was fought there, or on the flat ground below.

Rochester, 884

England, Kent, LR178 TQ7468

Farnham, 893

England, Surrey, LR186, unlocated

Benfleet, 893

England, Essex, LR178 TQ7785–86

Buttington, 893

Wales, Powys, LR126 SJ2408

Alfred's last war against the Vikings in the 890s reveals the strategic revolution he had engineered. The only pitched battle was at Farnham, when Alfred's son Edward the Elder overtook a Viking raiding army on the march. Benfleet and Buttington arose from sieges. Alfred's defensive preparations paid off. None of his *burhs* fell to the enemy. Rochester had set the trend in 884 by holding out against some Danelaw Vikings, the first English town to withstand such an attack. The new Viking leader Haesten never enjoyed the success of Halfdan or Guthrum in the 870s. He was pinned down on the landing beaches and reduced to raiding along the unsettled border between the Danelaw and Anglo-Saxon territory, eventually returning through friendly Northumbria to avoid the increasingly dynamic fyrd.

The Viking challenge of autumn 892 looked as daunting as ever. Two and a half hundred shiploads of men seized Appledore on the south coast of Kent. Eighty more under Haesten, a Viking of legendary renown, occupied Milton on the Thames estuary. Such pincer movements were a common Viking strategy. They threatened wide swathes of territory, in this case most of Kent, and revealed a confidence born of tactical and numerical superiority. Besides his own men Haesten could call on Danelaw Vikings, freed from their treaty obligations to Alfred by Guthrum's death in 890.

Alfred occupied a central position, and watched both Viking armies, ready to attack whichever was first to leave their sheltering woods and creeks. In readiness for a long campaign, Alfred divided his army into two echelons: one in the field and one awaiting their turn at home. This delaying strategy reduced the Vikings to creeping through the forests in small mounted parties. Haesten transferred operations north of the Thames, while the Appledore Vikings rode north with their plunder. Edward the Elder caught them at Farnham, and put them to flight. Why Vikings should ride through hostile territory rather than sail round to Essex is not clear, but Aethelweard's Latin *Chronicle* reports the devastation of Hampshire and Berkshire at Easter 893, suggesting the battle followed a major raid. Edward recovered the plunder, pursued the Vikings north into Mercia, and boxed them in at Thorney (Buckinghamshire), beside Heathrow Airport.

This hot pursuit reveals an important shift in the Anglo-Viking balance of power. The Mercians had sent no help to the West Saxons in the 870s, but a rapprochement between Alfred and Aethelred, the senior surviving Mercian ealdorman, now prevented the Vikings exploiting Anglo-Saxon political divisions. From this time it is possible to speak of English armies, rather than Mercians or West Saxons. When a seaborne raid on Exeter diverted Alfred's field army, it was the Mercian garrison of London that took Haesten's base at South Benfleet. The area is now built up, but in the 1890s the attentive observer might still find suggestive elevations on the low spit of land where the village stood beside the stream across Hope Green and the church. The Viking fleet would have lain in Benfleet Creek, between the mainland and Canvey Island, covered on the landward side by a ditch and palisaded bank. The contemporary Viking fort at Shoeburyness had a ditch 40 feet (12 m) wide and 8–9 feet (2.5–2.75 m) deep outside a 12-foot (3.65-m) bank. While Haesten was out raiding, the Londoners stormed Benfleet, capturing Haesten's family and the accumulated plunder from north Kent. So many ships were taken that the English destroyed them where they lay. A thousand years later, navvies building the London, Tilbury and Southend Railway beside the creek found the charred remains of ships deep in the mud, surrounded by human skeletons.

Haesten pursued the war with fresh vigour. The remains of both raiding armies rode across England, first up the Thames and then 80 miles (130 km) up the Severn, until they were cornered at Buttington near Welshpool. Some accounts place this episode at Buttington Hill (Gloucestershire) on the peninsula between the Wye and Severn, near Chepstow, but this must be incorrect. The *Chronicle* clearly states the English surrounded the Vikings on both sides of the river, although the Severn is over a mile (1.6 km) wide opposite Chepstow, and no contemporary source mentions a fleet.

Aethelred of Mercia took command, as at Benfleet. Thanes from burghal garrisons joined the men of Wiltshire and Somerset, led by Aethelnoth, a veteran of Alfred's darkest hour at Athelney. A fyrd that could travel so far from home and so quickly was clearly not a ragtag assembly of footsore peasants, but a professional flying column. Welsh and Mercian troops from beyond the Severn patrolled the west bank, while Aethelred's main army beset Haesten on the English side. Perishing with hunger the Vikings broke out eastwards. They suffered heavily, but killed many king's thanes on the way. The survivors' escape, having eaten their horses, shows the poverty of Anglo-Saxon siege technique. Had they surrounded Buttington with a continuous line of circumvallation in the Roman style, none of the Vikings could have got away.

Remains of the Viking camp survived round the churchyard and vicarage grounds into the 1920s. Offa's Dyke formed the east side, since levelled for the Leighton road, while the Shrewsbury–Welshpool road has replaced the north side. The western bank sloped towards the boggy riverbank, leaving only the south bank and its partly filled ditch still standing. In 1838 some 300 skulls and other skeletal remains were found in the southwest corner of the churchyard in a series of circular pits, usually regarded as war graves of the period.

Buttington was the decisive action of the campaign. Aethelweard reported that 'these events … were vaunted by ancient men'. Usually terse Irish chroniclers spared a line for the 'English victory over the Danes in which countless numbers were slain'. Like so many Viking defeats the results were ambiguous. Seemingly endless reinforcements sustained Haesten's raiding army until 896, when it dispersed, still a coherent fighting force. Alfred fought no more pitched battles. His detachment from the hurly-burly of hand-to-hand combat indicates his maturity as a war leader. He had learned from disasters at York and Reading (867, 871), to imitate Viking defensive tactics. He built a stable coalition with Mercia and secured support for strategies at odds with the heroic ethos of the day. The battlefield commander of the 870s, who once attacked like a wild boar, had grown into the organizer of victory.

Rochester

	Winner	*Loser*
Opponents	West Saxon	Viking
Commanders	Alfred	unknown

Farnham

	Winner	*Loser*
Opponents	West Saxon	Viking
Commanders	Edward the Elder	Haesten?

Benfleet

	Winner	*Loser*
Opponents	English	Viking
Commanders	Aethelred	unknown

Buttington

	Winner	*Loser*
Opponents	English	Viking
Commanders	Aethelred Aethelhelm Aethelnoth	Haesten

Directions
Rochester *and* ***Farnham*** *tactical locations unknown*
Benfleet *Haesten's camp presumably lay around the High Street (B1014), between the railway station and church. Ferry Road south of the station leads to a footpath between the railway and Benfleet Creek, once choked with burning longships.*
Buttington *1½ miles (2.5 km) east of Welshpool, at the junction of the A458 and the B4388 Leighton road.*

Sea Battle, 896

Naval, Solent?, LR196–7?

Ninth-century Wessex was not a naval power, and never confronted Viking invasion fleets at sea. The few reported naval actions of 870–900 usually involved snapping up stragglers. The most serious confrontation was off Harwich in 884, when the West Saxons took 16 ships in retaliation for a raid on Rochester by Danelaw Vikings, killing all the crews. The first English naval battle of which any extensive account survives was fought in 896, providing a unique glimpse of contemporary naval tactics.

Viking warships of this period usually had between 20 and 30 'rooms', where a pair of oarsmen sat on a thwart mounted above one of the transverse frames that formed the ship. They would carry at least 50 men, although later Norwegian ships had 3 to 8 men per oar, implying much larger crews. As naval actions were resolved hand-to-hand, crew size mattered. Olaf Tryggvason's 34-room ship, built a century later, was 145 feet (44 m) long and carried over 500 men, two watches of 4 men per oar. The *Anglo-Saxon Chronicle* credits Alfred himself with designing 60-oared ships that combined features of Danish and Frisian vessels, formidable capital ships in the open sea. How effective such unhandy ships might be in the shallow coastal waters where most 9th-century naval actions took place is another matter.

Haesten's army had broken up by the summer of 896, but Viking raiders remained active, six ships raiding between the Isle of Wight and Devon. Nine of Alfred's new ships intercepted the Vikings in an unidentified river mouth or harbour along the south coast. Exmouth, Poole Harbour, Hamble River in Southampton Water and the meeting of the Solent and Spithead have all been suggested. The battle site consisted of three areas: an outer bay, a river mouth or harbour entrance, and an upper harbour, which might fit any of the above. The Vikings had beached three ships, presumably while the crews went ashore for plunder or fresh water, covered by three more waiting offshore. The English engaged the latter just outside the harbour entrance and captured two, killing all hands. The third escaped.

Three English vessels grounded during the fight, on the same side of the harbour as the beached Viking ships. The remainder took ground on the other side of the harbour, and played no further part in the action. The ebbing tide exposed dry land between the two hostile groups of three, and Viking landing parties attacked the English ships along the beach. Fighting continued until the flood tide refloated the Viking ships. These were evidently shallower draught than the English units, which remained hard aground while the Vikings escaped. Viking casualties were twice those of the English, suggesting the advantage of larger crews or higher freeboard, but the *Anglo-Saxon Chronicle* names five of Alfred's thanes killed in the fighting, including three Frisians. These men were presumably acting as technical consultants to the unhandy West Saxons, and represented a serious loss.

Only one Viking ship made it home to East Anglia. Exhausted by wounds and casualties, two of their ship's companies were unable to 'row past the land of Sussex'. They were all captured and hanged at Winchester, a salutary reminder of the

Sea Battle

	Winner	*Loser*
Opponents	West Saxon	Viking
Commanders	unknown	unknown
Numbers	9 ships	6 ships
Losses	0 ships	5 ships
	62 men	120 men

limits to Alfred's Christian forbearance. The Ower Banks off Selsey were the most likely place for the two Viking ships to come to grief, with strong currents particularly dangerous for vessels propelled by oars. A shipwreck in Sussex supports a south Hampshire location for the battle, in Portsmouth or Chichester Harbour. The tide flow described by the *Anglo-Saxon Chronicle* strongly resembles that at the mouth of Fareham Creek, off Porchester, the main settlement in the area, and a possible Viking target. Had the fight occurred further west, the oarsmen who failed to weather Selsey Bill might have been expected to be wrecked in the Portland Race or off the Isle of Wight, long before reaching Selsey Bill.

No more is heard of Alfred's big ships. Their mixed showing against a smaller force hardly justified so costly an investment, when Frisian ships and seamen were available for hire. Nevertheless, the king's personal interest suggests an understanding of the importance of naval operations to an island kingdom, vindicating Alfred's reputation as founder of the English navy.

Directions

See Portesmutha (c.501) above for directions to Portchester Castle, and a view of the Harbour.

England and the Danelaw

The period following Alfred's death in 899 saw a gradual reconquest of Viking-occupied England, leading to unification under the house of Wessex. The process was not inevitable. The Danelaw remained a source of instability throughout the first half of the 10th century, and a focus for opposition to Alfred's successors. Edward the Elder had to fight for the throne of Wessex. However, the coalition with Mercia survived, as Edward's sister Aethelflaed, the Lady of the Mercians, succeeded her husband Aethelward in 911. Joint campaigns against Viking settlements in the Midlands and East Anglia reinforged ties between the two rival Anglo-Saxon kingdoms, and Edward's son Athelstan succeeded to both thrones in 924.

Military engagements of the period followed the pattern of Alfred's last war, with few pitched battles. The strategic balance had shifted decisively in favour of the English. Mercia and Wessex were economically and demographically stronger than the northern and eastern parts of England, where real Vikings must have been in a minority. Once settled in the Danelaw, the Scandinavians lost the initiative, becoming as vulnerable to raids as the Anglo-Saxons. Edward and Aethelflaed adapted Alfred's *burhs* for offensive purposes, fortifying strategic points that compelled the enemy either to withdraw, or launch costly and dangerous frontal assaults. The policy was so successful that by 918 Edward and Aethelflaed had eliminated the East Anglian Vikings as an independent political force and recaptured most of the east Midlands.

The Viking kingdom of York was more problematic. The northern Danelaw was remote from the population centres of Mercia and Wessex, and an international flashpoint. Its Scandinavian inhabitants posed an unrelenting threat to the emerging kingdom of the English. The activities of the atheling Aethelwold that culminated at the Holme (902) set the pattern: a warlord would land in the Humber, seize York, and march south with whatever allies he could drum up among English malcontents, or from Scotland. Olaf Guthfrithson's attempts to establish himself at York in 937 provoked the greatest pitched battle of the century at Brunanburh (937), between Athelstan's Mercians and West Saxons, and an alliance of Scots and Dublin Norse. The *Anglo-Saxon Chronicle* celebrated Athelstan's victory in elegiac verse, but another 17 years elapsed before Eadred's final ejection of Eric Bloodaxe from York.

The Holme, 8 December 903

England, Cambridgeshire, LR142 TL1987

The deadly results of the Battle of the Holme show the wisdom of Alfred's combat-avoidance policy. Both sides lost all their chief men, converting Aethelwold's tactical success into a personal disaster.

Succession to the West Saxon throne in the 9th century depended more on political expediency than strict primogeniture. Aethelwold had been a child when his father Aethelred died at the height of the Viking invasion of 871, so his uncle Alfred became king. After Alfred's death in 899, Aethelwold must have thought his claim to the kingdom as good as that of his cousin, Edward the Elder. He barricaded himself in the royal villa at Wimborne with a politically useful heiress abducted from a convent, but lost his nerve and fled to York when Edward camped nearby at Badbury Rings.

Aethelwold's reappearance in eastern England with an army of pagan Northumbrian Vikings shows how social ties between Dark Age warrior chieftains outweighed nationality or religion. Joined by the Vikings of East Anglia, they raided as far as Cricklade on the Thames, taking 'all they could grab'. Edward chased them back up the Icknield Way, ravaging northwards to the Fens, between the Fleam and Devil's Dykes, and the River 'Wusan'. The English then found that it was not so easy to get away. The Kentish contingent lagged behind, despite the king sending them seven messengers with the order to retreat. Aethelwold's army surrounded the stragglers and inflicted a bloody defeat, killing the two ealdormen in command, an abbot, three other named thanes and small fry too numerous to mention. Unluckily for Aethelwold he was also killed, as was his ally Eohric, king of the East Anglian Vikings. Another significant rebel fatality was Beorhtsige, whose name implies a relationship with the last kings of Mercia. He presumably had a claim to part of the old Mercian kingdom, now ruled by Edward's brother-in-law Aethelred. Beorhtsige's presence alongside Vikings from the whole of the Danelaw shows the seriousness of Aethelwold's rebellion, and the importance of the Kentish fyrd's last stand.

The Holme is dated variously between 902 and 904, but spring 903 is the most likely time for Aethelwold's raid into Mercia. The name comes from Old Norse *holmr*, a small island or piece of dry ground amidst marshland. The only Holme surviving along the fenland margin is 2 miles (3 km) east of Ermine Street, southwest of Whittlesey Mere. The modern settlement lies at the east end of an ancient track known as Glatton Way, just within the sea-level contour that marks the old limit of the peat fen. The name 'Wusan' applied to both the Ouse and the Nene, the latter river crossing Ermine Street just north of Holme.

Aethelwold's whole force may have fallen upon the Kentish fyrd as they turned back in accordance with Edward's orders. Pursued down Ermine Street, they could have blundered down Glatton Way by mistake, or seeking concealment. They soon found themselves in a cul-de-sac, the fens hemming them in on three sides. Such an error would account both for the Kentish fyrd's disobedience and for their heavy losses, as the detachment could neither receive messages nor escape. Their sacrifice was not in vain, for Aethelwold's death decisively resolved the succession dispute. Casualties among other commanders began a process of attrition that left the eastern Danelaw leaderless, incapable of organizing its own defence.

Directions

Turn right off Ermine Street, the A1(T), 7 miles (11 km) north of Alconbury, along the B660 to Holme village.

The Holme

	Winner	*Loser*
Opponents	Rebel	English
Commanders	Aethelwold (k)	Sigehelm (k)
	Eohric (k)	Sigewulf (k)

Tettenhall (Wednesfield), **5/6 August 909/910**

England, Staffordshire, LR139 SJ8800?

Tempsford, 918

England, Bedfordshire, LR153 TL1652

Mercian and West Saxon solidarity brought victory over the politically fragmented Vikings of the Danelaw. Viking settlements were as vulnerable to raids as English *burhs*, while on the battlefield Scandinavian forces were consistently outnumbered and outgeneralled.

Tettenhall wiped out the Danelaw's northern leadership, as the Holme (903) had done for the south. A foray by joint English forces against the northern raiding army in 909 provoked reprisals the following year. The York Vikings knew Edward the Elder was busy with his fleet in Kent, so imagined 'they might go unfought wherever they wanted'. They harried through Mercia and across the Severn, returning via Bridgnorth, but they reckoned without Aethelred, Lord of the Mercians, and the English capacity for cooperation and coordination of their forces. Edward reinforced Aethelred with West Saxons, and 'they got in front of the raiding army from behind when it was in flight, and killed many of it'. Another version of the *Anglo-Saxon Chronicle* claimed thousands killed. Aethelweard's Latin *Chronicle* describes the Vikings as recrossing the Severn 'rejoicing in rich spoil', when squadrons of Mercians and West Saxons attacked them, gaining a great victory at Woden's Field or Wednesfield, now a suburb of Wolverhampton. Tettenhall is 10 miles (16 km) from Bridgnorth, and Wednesfield 5 miles (8 km) further down the Vikings' road home, suggesting the battle was a running fight, an idea supported by the *Anglo-Saxon Chronicle*'s reference to the English overtaking the raiding army. The prevalence of such chases encourages speculation that the English fought on horseback before the Norman Conquest. If this is true, it must have been as light skirmishing cavalry, as archaeological remains of Anglo-Saxon horses show they were no bigger than ponies.

The date of Tettenhall is reported as variously as its location: 5 or 6 August in either 909 or 910, the latter being more generally accepted. The battle was the summit of Aethelred's military career, as Edward was not involved. Altogether the *Anglo-Saxon Chronicle* records an unprecedented 12 Viking leaders who 'with other jarls and noblemen hastened to the hall of the infernal one'. Among these were included two or three kings and one Osferth Hlytte or 'Soothsayer', whose skill as a clairvoyant had evidently deserted him. After the earlier disaster at the Battle of the Holme, Tettenhall left the Danelaw leaderless, incapable of effective action to stem the rising tide of reconquest.

The storming of Tempsford in the summer of 917 was the decisive moment in the reconquest of the southern Danelaw. It was also the high point of a campaign that began before Easter (13 April) with Edward the Elder's construction of a new *burh* at Towcester on the Anglo-Danish frontier, and ended with submission of the Cambridge and East Anglia Vikings in November.

Edward's earlier *burh* on the south bank of the River Ouse at Bedford already threatened to cut the Danelaw in two, by preventing Viking movements round the western edge of the Fens. Between Rogation and Lammas 917 (24 June–1 August) the

Tettenhall

	Winner	*Loser*
Opponents	English	Viking
Commanders	Aethelred	Eowils (k)
		Halfdan II (k)

Tempsford

	Winner	*Loser*
Opponents	English	Viking
Commanders	Edward the Elder	Guthrum (k)
		Toglos (k)

Viking armies of Huntingdon and East Anglia fortified Tempsford, 7 miles (11 km) northeast of Bedford at the confluence of the Ivel and Ouse. While their confederates from Northampton and Leicester attacked Towcester, the Tempsford Vikings assaulted Bedford, but both incursions were beaten off.

Edward's reaction was devastating. He collected troops from the nearest *burhs,* presumably Buckingham, Hertford and London, broke down Tempsford's defences, and killed anyone inside who offered resistance. A small square work known as Gannock's Castle still stands southwest of the village of Tempsford, which the *Victoria County History* attributed to this period. Two hundred yards (180 m) from the old riverbank, its ramparts enclose an area 120 by 84 feet (37 by 26 m), and stand at least 12 feet (3.5 m) above the ditch. Fields south and east showed traces of larger earthworks too faint to decipher, the little fort apparently forming an external keep or bastion. Viking casualties reveal the importance of the place: Guthrum, last Viking king of East Anglia, Jarl Toglos of Huntingdon and his son and brother were all killed.

Edward followed up Tempsford by storming Colchester with a 'great tribe' from Kent, Surrey and Essex, killing everyone who could not escape over the Roman walls. To underline Edward's success, his sister Aethelflaed, Lady of the Mercians, simultaneously stormed the Viking stronghold of Derby. All the Viking towns left south of the Humber submitted by the following year. 'From this time forth', proclaimed the *Ramsey Chronicle*, 'the power of the Danes gradually decreased, while that of the English was augmented.'

Directions

Tettenhall *A built-up area around the junction of the A41(T) Wolverhampton–Newport road and the B4161 extension of the A454 from Bridgenorth, the Viking line of approach. Tactical locations are unknown.*

Tempsford *Turn left off the A1(T) 2 miles (3 km) north of Sandy at the south end of Tempsford, past the church, where the Ordnance Survey marks a 'Moat' on the left, towards the river.*

Corbridge, 914 and 918

England, Northumberland, LR 87, unlocated

The fact that there were two battles at Corbridge within five years of each other provides a corrective to Anglocentric accounts of the inevitable reconquest of the Danelaw. The location of these battles near the Roman fort at Corstopitum, where Dere Street crosses the River Tyne en route for Scotland, places Viking activity in a wider context, and helps explain the apparently random comings and goings of the Norsemen. The fighting at Corbridge also provides a clue to the unresolved location of Brunanburh.

Raegnald came from a new generation of Viking leaders, the grandsons of Ivar the Boneless, the executioner of Northumbrian and East Anglian kings in the 860s. Ivar's kinsmen had since harried Ireland, until their expulsion from Dublin in 902. Ten years later Raegnald exploited the power vacuum left by the death toll at Tettenhall to make York a springboard for the recovery of Dublin. He landed on the north shore of the Humber, broke in upon York and killed or drove out its more influential inhabitants. Corbridge's twin battles were probably not Raegnald's only fights in northern England. They are recorded because of their effect upon St Cuthbert's patrimony, the monastic estates in County Durham.

The battles of 914 and 918 are significant for marking Raegnald's departure for Ireland and his subsequent return. Their location and Raegnald's chief opponent suggest the route he took. Tynemouth is halfway between the Humber and the Forth, the latter providing the shortest land transit between the North and Irish Seas, via the Antonine Wall and the Clyde. One of Raegnald's cousins was killed in 904 plundering Dunkeld, and a similar attack on Dunblane preceded Raegnald's return to England in 918. Ivar's grandsons evidently preyed upon the local monasteries as they travelled between their two kingdoms, passing through Scotland rather than making the laborious crossing of the Pennines.

Raegnald ventured into northern England with a multitude of ships in order to occupy the lands of

Ealdred, Reeve of Bamburgh and successor to the defunct kings of Northumbria. Ealdred sought Scottish help, making the First Battle of Corbridge an attempt to evict Raegnald from the area. The action was probably north of the River Tyne, the Viking fleet possibly beached near the remains of the Roman defences. Like most direct assaults on Viking armies, it failed, although the *History of St Cuthbert* attributed the defeat of the Christians to their sins rather than poor dispositions. Despite the claims of Scots chroniclers that their side had the victory, Raegnald put Constantine to flight, and killed all the English nobles, except Ealdred and his brother.

In 918 Constantine was in hot pursuit down Dere Street when Raegnald once more turned to meet him on the banks of the Tyne. The *Annals of Ulster* describe the second battle in unusual detail. As at Ashdown, the Vikings formed up in distinct bodies, one each under Raegnald, his brother Guthfrith, two jarls, and a fourth under some young nobles. Even fighting as allies in a large battle Viking war bands preserved their separate identities. Raegnald's battalion kept out of sight while the Scots and their English allies demolished the other three, killing the two jarls. The Viking reserve then launched into the victors' rear, and slaughtered them until nightfall. No Scottish leaders fell, but Ealdred was less lucky.

The *History of St Cuthbert* ignores Raegnald's subsequent return to York. He died in 920, shortly after 'submitting' to Edward the Elder at Bakewell. The dynastic struggle was not over. Olaf Guthfrithsson used the same route as his uncle in the 930s, precipitating the greatest battle of the age, at Brunanburh.

Directions

Tactical locations unknown.

Corbridge

	Winner	*Loser*
Opponents	Viking	Scots
Commanders	Raegnald I	Constantine II
		Ealdred (k)

Brunanburh (Bruneswald/Wendune), 937

England, unlocated

Brunanburh was the greatest battle of the Anglo-Saxon age, excepting Hastings. Had Olaf Guthfrithsson won, he might have anticipated Cnut's imposition of a Scandinavian dynasty upon England by 80 years. Despite the scale of the battle, Brunanburh's location remains infuriatingly uncertain. Some grasp of its location is essential, however, for proper appreciation of one of the finest Old English battle poems, a triumph-song that eulogized Athelstan's 'undying glory won by the sword's edge'. The *Annals of Ulster* confirm the English view with an unusually long-winded notice of a 'great, lamentable and horrible battle stubbornly fought between Saxons and Northmen, in which many thousands of Northmen beyond counting were slain'.

Brunanburh was the high point of the struggle between the descendants of Alfred the Great and Ivar the Boneless. Athelstan of Wessex had driven Guthfrith, brother of the double victor of Corbridge, out of York in 927. Guthfrith's son Olaf had since made himself master of Ireland by defeating the Limerick Vikings. From his base at Dublin, he now reasserted the family claim to York, where Athelstan's intrusion had alienated Danish settlers. Scots and Strathclyde Britons were ready to join the Dublin Vikings after Athelstan's invasion of Scotland in 934, when he spoiled as far as Edinburgh.

Viking fleets were amphibious forces, readily transferable across land transits from one area of maritime operations to another. Like his uncle, Olaf would have transported his ships overland between the Clyde and Forth estuaries, presumably along the route of the Forth and Clyde Canal, which is relatively level, and would allow them to use the Carron and Kelvin rivers some of the way. The ships could then coast down to the Humber, as the 12th-century chronicler Florence of Worcester says they did. Olaf could then occupy York and await reinforcements. William of Malmesbury (*c.*1095–1143) and the Icelandic skaldic poet Egil Skallagrimsson (*c.*910–990), unlikely associates, confirm the coalition-building that preceded the campaign: the Scots' quiet assent, followed by Northumbrian submission.

An approach from the northeast eliminates all the western sites proposed for Brunanburh, from Galloway to the Wirral, where Bromborough is a frequently canvassed option. The etymological identification of Brunanburh with Bromborough does not enjoy universal support, while there is no lake at Thingwall, the area of the Wirral associated with *Dingesmere*, a water feature across which the defeated Norsemen fled. It seems more likely that Athelstan faced a standard northern invasion down the east coast, the usual focus of Viking resistance, in greater numbers than usual.

Olaf had pulled off one of the most remarkable military concentrations of Dark Age Britain. The result was no frontier skirmish: Brunanburh lay well inside English territory, and Olaf only regained his ships after a daylong mounted pursuit. The king of Scots 'came north to his kin by flight'. All this points to Anglo-Saxon Mercia. William of Malmesbury described destruction Olaf would not have allowed against his Danelaw kinsmen. The West Saxon battle poem emphasizes Mercian heroism at Brunanburh, suggesting the Midlands bore the brunt.

This Midland context excludes two otherwise promising sites east of the Pennines. A.H. Burne favoured Rotherham on the Ryknield Way, which runs from York via Doncaster to the Mercian stronghold at Tamworth, avoiding the swamps of the Trent valley. Three-quarters of a mile (1.2 km) south of the Roman station at Templeborough the road crosses a low hill, where the Rother forms a bottleneck on Olaf's supposed route south. This might once have formed a good defensive position between Brinsworth and Catcliffe, now surrounded by Sheffield airport and a steelworks. C.R. Hart's analysis of place-names led him to Bourne in Lincolnshire, between Car Dyke and the East Glen River (LR130 TF0919). An army marching south from Lincoln down King Street, another Roman road, could be halted there, before they reached English territory at the River Welland. Both sites seem too far forward, however. Had Athelstan occupied Templeborough or Bourne, Olaf could have outflanked him down the Fosse Way.

Brunanburh

	Winner	*Loser*
Opponents	English	Allied
Commanders	Athelstan	Olaf Guthfrithsson
		Constantine II

Further to the south, two transverse roads, Watling Street and the Via Devana, allowed Athelstan to meet Olaf whichever way he came. A.P. Smyth's proposed location for Brunanburh lies between these highways, among the hills of the Northamptonshire–Huntingdonshire border. Some early sources refer to Bruneswald, rather than Brunanburh. This can be identified with a forest of that name, between the Rivers Nene and Ouse, which featured such suggestive localities as Newton Bromswold. This approximate location of the battle is as close as the evidence allows, and a lot nearer than some would accept.

The eulogy in the *Anglo-Saxon Chronicle* brilliantly evokes a battlefield darkened with soldiers' blood, but it is tactically uninformative. Fighting lasted all day, and ended with a protracted pursuit, West Saxon household troops hacking at fugitives with mill-sharp blades. The Icelander Egil Skallagrimsson describes a Battle of Vinheidr, which is cognate with Wendune. *Egil's Saga* places the battlefield between a river and wood, on the English left and right respectively. The ground was level, carefully chosen to accommodate a great host. It sloped down to the river, from east to west, and towards Olaf's start line. Egil's brother, fighting for Athelstan, tried to turn the enemy flank under cover of the wood. Sadly the Saga is neither contemporary (it was only written down in the 13th century) nor reliable. Vinheidr may be a garbled recollection of fighting in Russia, a stock setting beside the River Dvina grafted onto the more famous action at Brunanburh.

All sources agree on the unprecedented numbers present and losses suffered. Olaf is said to have deployed 615 ships, suggesting an implausible 30,000 Vikings fought at Brunanburh. A tenth of the ships would have doubled Ubba's force at Cynwit (878). High-status casualties were impressive enough: five kings and seven jarls on the losing side, including a Christian king from the Hebrides and probably

Owain of Strathclyde, who was put to flight and never heard of again. According to the Old English triumph-song Constantine escaped, 'the hoary man of war ... shorn of his kinsmen ... left his son on the place of slaughter, mangled by wounds'. English losses were also heavy, including two of Alfred's grandsons and the Bishop of Sherborne:

> Never yet in this island
> was there a greater slaughter
> of peoples felled by the sword's edges,
> before this ...
> ... since Angles and Saxons
> came here from the east.

The battle was a personal triumph for Athelstan, but did not outlast his reign. Olaf retook all the Danelaw by political means, after Athelstan's death. Without strong leaders Anglo-Saxon England remained vulnerable to Viking adventurers, who unlike the kings of Wessex could draw on an apparently inexhaustible supply of professional freebooters.

Directions
Location unknown.

Castleford, 948

England, West Yorkshire, LR105 SE4225–26?

Stainmoor, (Stainmore) 954

England, Durham, LR92 NY9012?

The last Viking king of York was Eric Bloodaxe, favourite son of Harald Fairhair of Norway. Twice he held the city under the helmet of his terror, at the invitation of Archbishop Wulfstan of York, leader of Northumbrian opposition to English unification. Without the Scottish support enjoyed by Olaf Guthfrithsson, Eric lacked the military resources to maintain his throne. He was first expelled in 948 when Athelstan's successor Eadred threatened to waste the country after its inhabitants attacked an English rearguard at Castleford. Restored in 952, Eric

Castleford

	Winner	*Loser*
Opponents	Norwegian	English
Commanders	Eric Bloodaxe	Eadred

Stainmoor

	Winner	*Loser*
Opponents	Northumbrian	Norwegian
Commanders	Maccus	Eric Bloodaxe (k)

finally came to grief when Eadred imprisoned Wulfstan, undermining the Norwegian adventurer's political support. Eric fled along the Roman road towards Carlisle, and his awaiting longships. Somewhere on the moors of North Yorkshire he was betrayed by Earl Oswulf of Bernicia, ambushed and killed at a 'certain lonely place called Stainmoor'. The area was still desolate in the 16th century, when William Camden wrote of:

> that mountainous waste tract always exposed to wind and rain ... called Stanemore, all the country around being a desert, except an inn ... in the middle of this stony waste, and near it a fragment of a crosse which we call Rerecrosse.

Snorri Sturluson's collection of sagas, *Heimskringla* (*c.*1220), celebrated a heroic last stand against overwhelming numbers: 'Many of the English folk fell, but ever whereas one fell came three in his place.' At last Eric was cut down by an obscure cutthroat named Earl Maccus. Victorian antiquaries speculated that the Rere or Rey Cross marked where Eric fell. Five kings died with him, and two sons of the Jarl of Orkney. Earl Oswulf did well from his treachery, becoming Eadred's man at York in a unified England. The North remained a source of instability, but the roadside massacre of Eric and his companions had completed the modern map of England.

Directions
Castleford *tactical locations unknown*
Stainmoor *Rey Cross (1467 feet/447 m) is 10 miles (16 km) west of Barnard Castle along the A66, where remains of a Roman camp straddle the road.*

The Northmen Return

Anglo-Saxon England enjoyed less than 30 years of peace after Eric Bloodaxe's appropriately sanguinary end at Stainmoor (954). Viking raids of unprecedented ferocity recommenced in the 980s, but there was no king of stature to withstand them. Aethelred II, still reviled as the 'Unready' or 'Ill-advised', took the throne after the murder of his brother Edward the Martyr in 978. He was quite unable to inspire united or effective resistance to such heroic figures as Olaf Tryggvason of Norway or Swein Forkbeard of Denmark.

When English royal armies took the field they broke up in disarray; the situation was aggravated by Aethelred's inability to choose loyal or competent ministers, and his connivance in political murders. Isolated attempts to resist the raiders in the shires usually resulted in disaster, with a heavy death toll among English leaders, who became understandably chary about closing with the enemy. When Ealdorman Aelfric led an army into Devon in 1003, 'he pretended to be ill, and began to retch so as to vomit, and said that he was ill, and thus deceived the people that he should have led' (*Anglo-Saxon Chronicle*). Unable to respond militarily to the Vikings Aethelred paid Danegeld in hopes they would go away. Even Alfred had bought off Viking raiders, but in the absence of military sanctions Aethelred's largesse was an unqualified reminder to individual Vikings of England's ill-defended wealth. Vast sums were paid out, a staggering £236,000 over 25 years.

The English turned on their persecutors on St Brice's Day in 1002, and massacred large numbers of Danes, including King Swein's sister. Economic motives made way for revenge. In 1013 Swein sailed up the Humber resolved on conquest rather than profit. After years of unremitting defeat the English caved in and recognized Swein as king. Aethelred fled to Normandy, but Swein's sudden death in February 1014 postponed the Danish takeover. A restored Aethelred continued to demonstrate his unfitness to rule until his own death in April 1016. While the leading men in Danish-controlled areas elected Swein's son Cnut as king, London and Wessex chose Aethelred's son Edmund. With his back to the wall Edmund Ironside fought an astonishing campaign in the summer of 1016 that demonstrated the resilience of an Anglo-Saxon state that, after nearly 30 years of defeat and betrayal, could still raise armies capable of fighting Cnut to a standstill. Only Edmund's premature death in November 1016 allowed the Dane to take the whole kingdom.

English defeat arose from political not military weakness. Viking hosts would naturally include a higher proportion of experienced fighting men than the English fyrd, but this had not prevented strong Anglo-Saxon leaders defeating Viking armies at Buttington (893) or Brunanburh (937). The *Anglo-Saxon Chronicle* repeatedly attributed English defeats to treachery, not faulty tactics or equipment. The failure to maintain the *burh* system stemmed from lack of political direction. Walls crumbled and ditches silted up. Garrisons that had reinforced field armies at Buttington (893) and Tempsford (917) had dispersed. London's successful resistance in 994, 1009 and 1016 was exceptional.

The Vikings may have possessed better equipment, despite the *Chronicle*'s reticence. The commemorative poem about the Battle of Maldon (991) describes the gruesome song of English weapons upon Viking armour, but never mentions an English byrnie (coat of mail) turning a Viking blade. Byrhtnoth's men fought without helmets or mail, which may account not only for their defeat, but also for the collapse of morale amongst unprotected English fyrds repeatedly cut to pieces by armoured hosts. In 1008 the king ordered that every eight hides of land, enough to support eight families, should furnish a helmet and byrnie. Such weapons soon began to appear on coins and in the wills of the well-to-do.

Great magnates and their retinues or *hiredmen* continued to provide the elite nucleus of armies, supplemented by wealthier smallholders or thanes. The so-called 'great fyrd' of ill-trained peasants has left little trace in contemporary sources. Armies were select bodies of mounted infantrymen, raised at the rate of one fighting man from every five hides. Men fought alongside neighbours from their shire, hundred or soke, held together by bonds of lordship, strengthened by the oaths of fealty sworn by all fyrd-worthy men. Although the sword was the aristocratic weapon, literary and archaeological evidence agree that the spear remained the most common weapon, equally suitable for missile or shock action. The longbow was the weapon of the unfree. The only one used at Maldon belonged to a Northumbrian hostage. Under the pressure of defeat Aethelred hired mercenaries, such as Thurkil the Tall, who in 1012 undertook to defend his recent victims with 45 ships. Cnut retained similar forces after his accession, paid for by the *heregeld* or army tax.

Maldon, 10/11 August 991

England, Essex, LR168 TL8605

Maldon was one of the most decisive battles of Aethelred II's reign, not because it brought matters to a conclusion, but because it set a pattern of futile resistance and hapless payment, after the damage was done. Maldon is remembered because a nameless poet turned the English defeat into legend with a few hundred lines of accidentally preserved verse, the only extended description of an Anglo-Saxon army in action.

The *Anglo-Saxon Chronicle* confirms that Ealdorman Byrhtnoth fell in action at Maldon in 991, fighting against a Viking fleet of 93 or 94 ships. Their commander was probably Olaf Tryggvason, future king of Norway. The Vikings' motives in Essex were profit: 'Better for you all,' said their messengers, 'that you should buy off this onslaught of spears with tribute money, than that we should join battle so grievously.' The English commander was the premier active ealdormen of the kingdom, perhaps entrusted with the defence of the whole east coast. Despite his white hair, *Liber Eliensis* ('the book of Ely', a later chronicle) depicted Byrhtnoth in heroic terms: 'strong in his power, of the greatest physical size, indefatigable in warfare ...'. Like many of his thanes Byrhtnoth was a local landowner, fighting within sight of his own hearth smoke.

Byrhtnoth may not have realized the odds against him. The Vikings were equipped with helmets and mail, hardened to violence, and commanded by leaders of international renown. At 50 men per ship they could have landed 3500 men, allowing for boat keepers. Hidage figures suggest Essex could have fielded at most 700. Even if Byrhtnoth's personal retinue brought his army up to a thousand, he was outnumbered three-to-one, unless he had picked up reinforcements during the approach march through Cambridgeshire. Monastic tradition recorded visits to both Ramsey and Ely, whose monks carried Byrhtnoth's headless corpse back to their abbey after the battle. *Liber Eliensis* specifically attributes the defeat to lack of numbers.

The poem does not mention Maldon, but it does name the River Pante, now the Blackwater. Maldon stands at the head of the river's tidal estuary, south of its confluence with the Chelmer. The town had

Maldon

	Winner	*Loser*
Opponents	Viking	English
Commanders	Olaf Tryggvason	Byrhtnoth (k)
Numbers	*c.*3500	*c.*1000

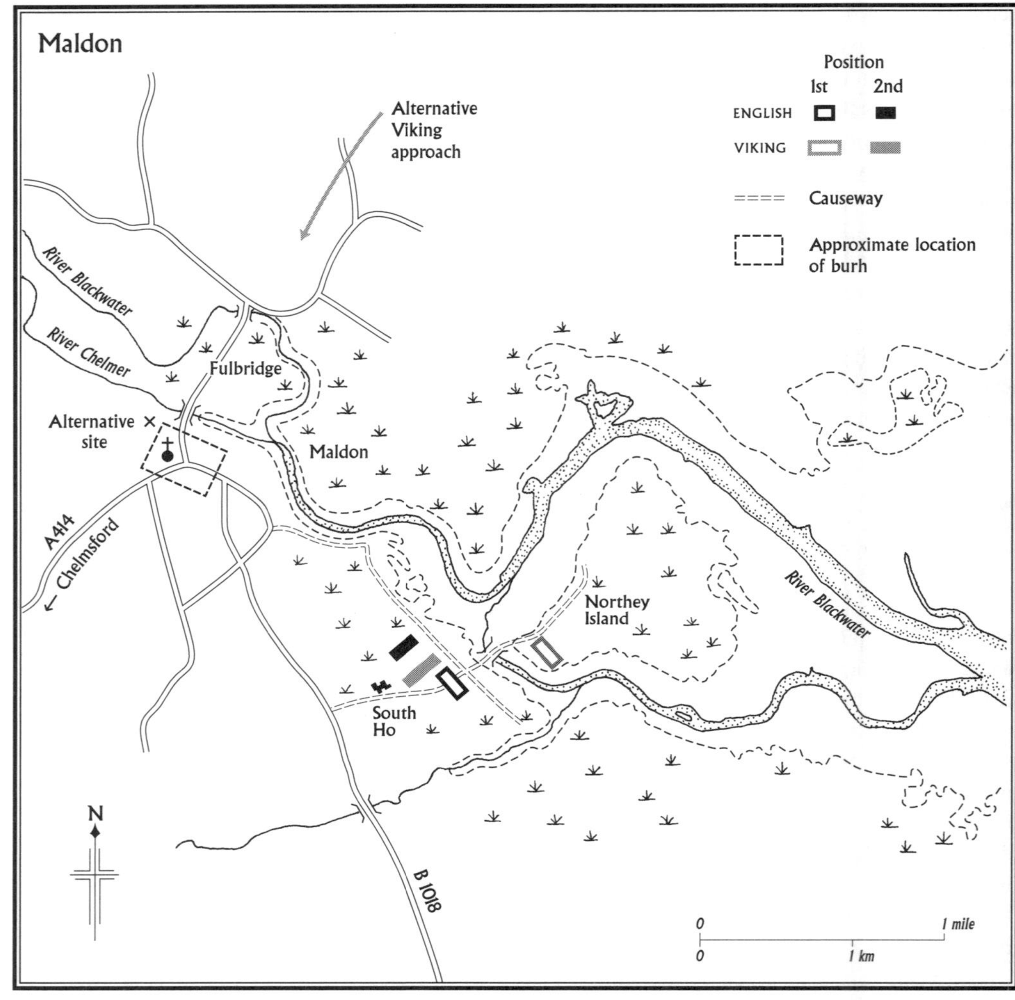

been one of Edward the Elder's *burhs*, and had a mint, a desirable target for a Viking fleet. The battle's generally accepted site is a mile and a quarter (2 km) southeast of the *burh*, at the western end of the tidal causeway to Northey Island, where the Vikings are supposed to have beached their ships. The channel between the island and west bank was narrower than now, permitting verbal exchanges between the two armies across the water. At high tide it was 120 yards (110 m) wide, the causeway under 6 feet (1.8 m) of water, flanked at low tide by soft mud 10 feet (3 m) deep. The turbulent interaction of tidal streams around the island may have inspired the poet's graphic image of these streams interlocking. Northey Island was near enough to Maldon for the raiders to present a clearly visible threat, without approaching the *burh*'s rundown defences too closely. Other cause-

Directions

10 miles (16 km) east of Chelmsford along the A414. Take the footpath from Maldon along the south bank of the Blackwater. The causeway is on the left, and the Ordnance Survey's site on the right at South House Farm.

ways in the area are either not tidal, or do not allow the Vikings to cross '*west ofer Pante*', or place the fighting under the *burh* walls, with insufficient room to swing an axe.

Not all authorities accept this location. Northey Island lacks drinking water, while sticky mud would immobilize ships beached on its east side. Salt marshes along the Blackwater's southern shoreline extended further inland than today, hampering military operations. C.R. Hart has argued that the Vikings landed further east at Mersea Island, as they did in 894, and approached Maldon overland from the north. In this case, the causeway would have been the 'foul, muddy causeway' or '*ful brycg*' that crossed the interlocking Blackwater and Chelmer streams, and became the modern Fulbridge Road. Byrhtnoth, in this case, met his death in Maldon itself, between the Chelmer and St Mary's Church.

The poem's details come from the poet's imaginative recreation of events, enriched by the heroic tradition, and perhaps by Sallust's account of the death of Catiline in 63 BC. Speeches and individual duels probably reflect how a contemporary audience felt a battle should be reported, rather than the actuality of warfare. Its broad outlines are not implausible. The English ride to battle, but send their horses away. Byrhtnoth remains mounted while deploying his shieldwall, then dismounts to join his bodyguard in the centre of the line. A shieldwall is a traditional motif, but may be literally true: the large round shields still in use would naturally form a continuous, overlapping front. The ebbing tide revealed that the English had bottled up the Vikings, who could not force the causeway, defended by champions worthy of memory: Wulfstan, Aelfhere, and Maccus.

Byrhtnoth broke the stalemate by allowing the Vikings across, presumably in the hope of beating them before they sailed off to terrorize somewhere less well defended. If Byrhtnoth knew his business, he would fall back towards Maldon covering his line of retreat, unless he withdrew west onto dryer ground beyond South House. Either way the Vikings risked disaster, fighting with the causeway at their backs. Byrhtnoth's annihilation strategy proved beyond his capability, however. After an exchange of spears thrown or thrust, Byrhtnoth was struck down, and his head hacked off. Panic spread as one of his retainers fled on Byrhtnoth's own horse, encouraging general flight. Some fought to the death, encouraging each other to avenge their dead lord:

> More constant shall be our will,
> More warlike our hearts,
> More powerful our courage,
> As our strength weakens.

The battle was a disaster for the English, soon followed by the first payment of £10,000 Danegeld. Byrhtnoth's death was particularly shocking. If such a thing could happen to him, it could happen to anyone. Contemporary interest was reflected not only in the poem, whose non-defeatist tone implies an early date, but also in a tapestry that Byrhtnoth's widow presented to Ely Abbey. Poem and tapestry created a typical English myth of defeat redeemed by magnificent courage. Legend was founded in reality. Renovation of the choir at Ely in 1769 uncovered a skeleton beneath Byrhtnoth's timeworn effigy. The head was missing, but other bones indicated a man well over 6 feet (1.8 m) tall. Most strikingly, the collarbone had been cut nearly through in a classic axe stroke.

Watchet, 988

England, Somerset, LR181 ST0743

Aethelingadene, 1001

England, W Sussex, LR197, unlocated

Pinhoe, 1001

England, Devon, LR192, unlocated

Kennet, 1006

England, Berkshire, unlocated

Thetford, 1004

England, Norfolk, LR144, unlocated

Ringmere (Rymer), 5 May 1010

England, Norfolk, LR144 TL9087

Viking attacks on England recommenced in the 980s, provoking confrontations with English shire forces, whose wide distribution shows how the raiders once more held the initiative. Their rapid and unpredictable movements regularly took defenders by surprise, before they could gather their forces. Twenty years of turmoil and defeat undermined the Anglo-Saxon state, softening it up for outright conquest.

The *Life of St Oswald* balanced its account of Maldon with reference to a 'savage battle in the west in which our men ... achieved the triumph of victory'. Watchet was a typical Viking target: a royal estate on the coast with its own mint and vineyard. It had been raided in 914, when Edward the Elder's coastal defence arrangements had ensured that 'few came away, except only those who could swim out to their ships'. The defenders were less successful in 988, when Vikings killed the Devon thane Goda, and 'a great slaughter with him'. Unusually 'more of them were killed, and the English had the place of slaughter'.

Swein Forkbeard's operations were unequivocally disastrous for the English. In 1001 he returned from winter quarters in Normandy to raid and burn 'almost everywhere' along the south coast. First he struck at the Hampshire–Sussex border, defeating the Hampshire fyrd at Aethelingadene ('Atheling's valley'). The site of this battle lies in the South Downs in the valley between West and East Dean, a little to the east of the Roman road from Chichester. In 894 a sortie by the *burh* garrison had killed hundreds of Viking raiders, but this time two of Aethelred's high reeves were killed, and 81 other Englishmen. The *Anglo-Saxon Chronicle*'s claim that 'there were many more of the Danish killed' seems unlikely, as they held the place of slaughter.

Swein then sailed westwards to the River Exe. He burnt Kingsteignton on the way, but Exeter's inhabitants held out behind their Roman walls. High reeves Kola and Eadsige 'came against them at Pinhoe with such an army as they could gather', and were put to flight with heavy loss. Another version of the *Chronicle* talks of an 'immense army', but 'as soon as they joined battle the English army gave way'. Pinhoe is 2½ miles (4 km) northeast of Exeter, on the lower slopes of Beacon Hill, where the Roman road from Honiton would cross the swampy valley of the Clyst. Perhaps Swein enticed a relieving army into attacking uphill, with a river at their backs. The *Anglo-Saxon Chronicle* describes Swein's approach as 'a single journey', suggesting his rapidity prevented Kola and Eadsige concentrating all their forces before Pinhoe; in the 12th century Simeon of Durham wrote that 'the Angles owing to the fewness of their soldiers, took to flight, overpowered by the numbers of the Danes'.

Swein's outrages continued unchecked. In 1006 he raided the Thames valley from a base in the Isle of Wight, and burnt Alfred's *burh* at Wallingford. Trailing his coat along Ashdown, he defied old prophecies that no Vikings who reached Cwichelm's Barrow would ever get back to the sea, by brushing aside an English army somewhere along the Kennet.

The East Anglian descendants of earlier Scandinavian settlers were no longer pleased to see their kinsmen. The main focus of resistance, after the destruction of Norwich in 1004, was Thetford, perhaps the scene of St Edmund's fatal encounter with the sons of Ragnar 'Hairybreeks'. In 1004 Ulfcytel Snilling, *Dux* of East Anglia, was prepared to buy peace, as the enemy's sudden appearance had given him insufficient time to gather his whole force. When the Danes broke the truce to attack Thetford,

Watchet

	Winner	*Loser*
Opponents	English	Viking
Commanders	Goda (k)	unknown

Aethelingadene

	Winner	*Loser*
Opponents	Danish	English
Commanders	Swein Forkbeard	Aethelweard (k) Leofwine (k)

Pinhoe

	Winner	*Loser*
Opponents	Danish	English
Commanders	Swein Forkbeard	Kola Eadsige

Kennet

	Winner	*Loser*
Opponents	Danish	English
Commanders	Swein Forkbeard	unknown

Thetford

	Winner	*Loser*
Opponents	Danish	English
Commanders	Swein Forkbeard	Ulfcytel

Ringmere

	Winner	*Loser*
Opponents	Danish	English
Commanders	Thurkil the Tall	Ulfcytel

Ulfcytel gathered an army in secret, ordering 'they should chop up the ships, but those he thought of failed' (*Anglo-Saxon Chronicle*). Thetford's defences were plainly decayed as the attackers easily got inside, raiding and burning the town. When they wanted to return to their ships next day, Ulfcytel was across their line of retreat, compelling them to give battle. Presumably the fighting took place northeast of Thetford, on the way back to Norwich. The English had still not concentrated: 'the chief men of the East Anglian people were killed, but if they had been up to full strength they [the Danes] would never have got back to their ships'. The *Chronicle* had to console itself with the Danes' admission 'that they had never met harder hand play in England than Ulfcytel gave them'.

Ulfcytel's second battle at Ringmere (1010) shows the alteration in English warfare. Uncharacteristically the Danes sought battle inland. Turning up at Ipswich after Easter, they 'went straight away to where they had heard that Ulfcytel was with his army'(*Anglo-Saxon Chronicle*). *Burh* defences had not been repaired despite 20 years of tension, neither Ipswich nor Thetford imposing any delay upon Danish movements. Perhaps for that reason Ulfcytel chose to defend Thetford indirectly by fighting in the open. He assembled his host at Ringmere, a meeting place at the centre of a wide expanse of open heath. A network of drove roads joined together the common lands that lay between population centres, making heaths a natural rendezvous.

Sources disagree about the date of the battle, giving 5 and 18 May, of which the first is more likely. Ulfcytel had assembled troops from most of the southern Danelaw, but the men of East Anglia ran away almost immediately, led by a turncoat Norseman, Thurcytel 'Mare's Head'. Cambridgeshire stood fast and took heavy losses, including five named leaders, 'and many other thanes and countless people'(*Anglo-Saxon Chronicle*), which suggests a general call-up of anyone able to carry a spear. Among the casualties were thanes from Huntingdon and Bedfordshire. Ottar the Black sang how Thurkil's host, 'far from the ships, piled up a heavy heap of slain. Ringmere Heath was reddened with blood. The people of the land ere all was done … fled terrified away'.

Ringmere had more than regional significance. The victorious Danes rode south to the Thames ravaging Oxfordshire and Buckinghamshire, and into Wessex before regaining their ships at midwinter. Nobody was prepared to resist them, despite heavy fines for deserters:

> When they [the enemy] were in the east, then the army was kept in the west; and when they were in the south, then our army was in the north … In the end there was no head man who wanted to gather an army, but each fled as best he could; nor even in the end would one shire help another.

Facing almost certain death in battle, Anglo-Saxon leaders had lost the will to fight.

Directions

Ringmere *is 5 miles (8 km) northeast of Thetford on the A1075, near Langmere nature reserve. Other tactical locations unknown.*

Penselwood, 1016

England, Somerset, LR183 ST7531?

Sherston, June 1016

England, Wiltshire, LR173 ST8487?

Brentford, July 1016

England, London, LR176 unlocated

Assandune (Ashdon/Ashingdon), 18 October 1016

England, Essex, LR154 TL5741–42 / LR178 TQ8693–8793

The Danish conquest of England in 1013–16 was one of the most spectacular achievements of the Viking age. Their final takeover followed an epic struggle between Cnut and Edmund Ironside that raged across the south of England. The odds were stacked against Edmund. Cnut began the campaign with 160 ships. Among his supporters were Thurkil the Tall and the treacherous Ealdorman Eadric Streona of Mercia.

Cnut and Edmund had been ravaging the Midlands and Northumbria, before Aethelred's death at Cosham in Hampshire on St George's Day cleared the field for their personal showdown. At Rogation (7–9 May 1016) the Danes were besieging London, whence Edmund had slipped away to rally support. Cnut moved with typical Viking speed, denying Edmund time to gather his forces. They clashed on the eastern edge of Selwood Forest, a traditional meeting place for the men of Dorset, Somerset and Wiltshire. Kings of Wessex had passed that way before: Cenwalh in 658 and Alfred in 878. The *Anglo-Saxon Chronicle*'s silence on the outcome of the encounter at Penselwood suggests stalemate, but Florence of Worcester (12th century) claimed that with God's help and 'the army which he had been able to collect in so short a time … [Edmund] conquered and put them to flight'.

Another battle followed after midsummer, probably at Sherston in Wiltshire, although Florence placed the fight in Gloucestershire in the country of a people known as the Hwicce. If the Wiltshire location is correct, the battle took place 2 miles (3 km) east of Sherston on the Fosse Way, near the important West Saxon centre of Malmesbury. Florence had access to sources now lost, and gives a fuller account than the *Chronicle*. Edmund's pre-battle speech is probably invention, but significantly the king placed the best men or *optimates* in the front rank. The experienced thanes who served king and magnates led the advance, and took the brunt of the fighting. Their armour would protect the remainder of the fyrd during the initial exchange of missiles, and the first shock of contact with the enemy. Cnut had the assistance of Eadric and other quislings, but withdrew after two days of fighting, too exhausted to continue. Only a ruse had saved him on the second day, Eadric holding aloft a severed head that he proclaimed to be Edmund's, to the temporary astonishment of the English.

Penselwood

	Winner	Loser
Opponents	English	Danish
Commanders	Edmund Ironside	Cnut

Sherston

	Winner	Loser
Opponents	English	Danish
Commanders	Edmund Ironside	Cnut

Brentford

	Winner	Loser
Opponents	English	Danish
Commanders	Edmund Ironside	Cnut

Assandune

	Winner	Loser
Opponents	Danish	English
Commanders	Cnut	Edmund Ironside
	Thurkil the Tall	Eadric Streona
		Ulfcytel (k)

Twice more Edmund raised armies to relieve London or intercept raids into Mercia. Many English were carelessly drowned at Brentford, the lowest permanent ford on the Thames, before Edmund drove the Danes back to their ships at Sheppey, killing as many as he could overtake. At Aylesford he made peace with the weathercock Eadric, the *Chronicle* commenting with embittered hindsight: 'There was no more unwise decision than this was.'

The decisive action of the war took place not in Kent, but at Assandune in Essex. Cnut used his ships to transfer operations north across the Thames estuary, and menace the Midlands. Edmund brought him to battle with a fifth army raised from the entire English nation, but was defeated. It was a turning point, leading to the replacement of Alfred's heirs by an Anglo-Scandinavian dynasty. The battle's importance has fuelled heated debate about its location, extending to the alleged fabrication of archaeological evidence.

Two sites have been canvassed: Ashdon and Ashingdon in the north and south of Essex respectively (TL5741–42 and TQ8693). The latter sounds more like the name given in the *Anglo-Saxon Chronicle*, and has gained general acceptance. However, the etymology is suspect, as are topographical interpretations based upon Florence's account, which he based upon classical battle narratives. A silver penny of Cnut's reign 'found' in Ashingdon churchyard at the height of the debate in 1928 is militarily irrelevant, and possibly put there deliberately. Earthworks at Canewdon, translated incorrectly as 'Canute's Camp', are undated and too small for an army. No authentic Norse names exist in the area. Nevertheless Ashingdon is frequently and uncritically treated as the only possible location.

Ashingdon is at the wrong end of Essex for a raid into Mercia, with few good lines of communication running in the appropriate direction. The seaward approach to Ashingdon, up the River Crouch, is cramped and muddy. It is far less attractive than the Stour, which leads towards Ashdon from the excellent harbour at Harwich, which means 'army base' in Old English. A great earthwork once cut across the narrow peninsula there to create a classic Viking bridgehead. The Stour valley was a well-established route inland with which the Danes were familiar. English notables killed at Assandune came from Cambridgeshire rather than Essex, favouring the northern site. *Liber Eliensis* (12th century) recorded 'many friends of Ely who perished'. Past and present abbots were cut down offering prayers for Edmund's victory: 'The brothers of Ely, who had gone up to the battlefield carrying relics, as is the custom of the church, were slain, and the relics … lost.'

If the battle's location is controversial, its tactics are unknowable. Florence claimed that Edmund drew up on a hill whence he attacked Cnut's army on lower ground. A.H. Burne applied this assertion with customary panache to the spur of high ground which extends from Ashingdon church (*c.*100 feet/30 m) to Canewdon (128 feet/39m), falling to 33–66 feet (10–20 m) in between. Ashdon also lies down a slope, so Florence's inventions favour neither place. According to the *Knutsdrapa* (written *c.*1050),

Assandune was fought north of 'Danoskogar' ('Dane's wood'). This has not been located, but a large tract of woodland did stand on high ground southwest of Ashdon parish, its remnants known as Hales Wood.

Cnut gained the day through treachery: 'Eadric, as he often did, first started the flight with the Magonsaete,' his own people from the Midland–Welsh borders. The 12th century *Ramsey Chronicle* is more explicit:

> Eadric, traitor to country and people, seeing Edmund penetrating the enemy line with lightning fury, the cunning contriver of trickery led his troop in flight, proclaiming Edmund was dead. Whereupon the remainder following in bewilderment and panic, the courage of the Danes increased, Edmund abandoned the place of slaughter ...

Another local source, Henry of Huntingdon (12th century), recorded Eadric's exact words: 'Flet Engle, Flet Engle, ded is Edmund.'

Exposed to Cnut's concentrated efforts, Edmund's casualties were disastrous, including the flower of the English race. Among them was Ulfcytel Snilling, slain by Thurkil the Tall, who married Ulfcytel's widow and succeeded him as Earl of East Anglia. Just over a month later Edmund Ironside was also dead, possibly of wounds, allowing Cnut to ascend the throne. The new king paid off his men with a final Danegeld of £82,500, divided England among his supporters, and purged the old nobility. One victim was Eadric Streona, his corpse thrown over London wall and left unburied – 'very justly', according to Version F of the *Chronicle*.

In 1020 Cnut dedicated a minster at Assandune to the memory of those fallen in the battle. The site is unknown, but Domesday Book shows significant churches at both Ashdon and its neighbour Hadstock before 1066. Ashingdon with one plough and 40 sheep is unlikely to have been able to support a minster served by Cnut's own chaplain. Analysis of field names suggests Old Church Field at Ashdon as the site of Cnut's minster. If Cnut built his church upon the very place of slaughter, as William the Conqueror did with Battle Abbey, it is there one should look for the last stand of Alfred's legitimate heirs.

Directions

Penselwood *and* ***Sherston*** *tactical locations unknown.*

Brentford *See the 1909 monument in the High Street at the junction of Alexandra Road.*

Assandune *sites:*

(1) Ashdon *4 miles (6 km) northeast of Saffron Walden past Hales Woods on the right. Possible site in Church End, northwest of the village, left of a right-hand bend in road.*

(2) Ashingdon *4½ miles (7 km) north of Southend-on-Sea off the B1013 to the right along minor roads. The area is built up, except between Ashingdon church and Canewdon. Turn down the Canewdon road after the church, along the northern flank of the 'battlefield'.*

High Kings and Gentiles

Kells, 718

Ireland, Co. Meath, DS42 unlocated

Allen (Almu), 722

Ireland, Co. Kildare, DS49 N7620

Strangford Lough, 877

Ireland , Co. Down, DS21 unlocated

Ireland lay outside the great upheavals of the first millennium after Christ. Unlike England, Wales and Scotland, it never suffered occupation by the Romans or invasion by Germanic barbarians. Irish culture continued largely unaltered until the 10th century, an archaic survival of a heroic way of life not unlike that of pre-Roman Gaul. The simple spear and shield remained characteristic of the Irish warrior, as they had been for Cuchulainn, hero of the great Indo-European epic *Tain Bo Cuailgne* (*The Cattle Raid of Cooley*).

Irish battles remained prehistoric, like those of Iron Age Britain. There was much violence, but little organized warfare. Legal and social constraints limited intertribal conflict. The absence of weapons from many archaeological sites suggests ordinary people lived in peace. The earliest laws, written down in the late 7th century, contain no reference to warriors. A plethora of minor kings and chieftains shared a fragmented authority. Warfare was an aristocratic affair: an extension of hunting rather than a political activity, with feuds, cattle rustling and ritualistic hostings in search of battle or hostages. Political instability limited the value of success in battle. The victor of the Battle of Kells (fought between two Leinster dynasties) was himself killed by the over-king Fergal mac Maele Duin only two months afterwards.

Fergal died a few years later on Ireland's first traceable battlefield, the Hill of Allen, 5 miles (8 km) northeast of Kildare, although lack of evidence prevents detailed reconstruction. Monastic annalists provided cryptic notes of events, devoid of sustained narrative, barely recording participants and outcome. Professional storytellers, the poets or *na filid*, had little interest in historical accuracy. Their account of Allen emphasized mythological elements such as the singing head of Donn Bo, the Ulster musician, whose words moved the carousing Leinstermen to tears.

The Vikings ended Ireland's isolation in the 9th century. The Irish called them Foreigners, Gentiles or Heathen to emphasize their pagan savagery. Strong but light ships gave the Vikings mastery of the country's waterways, enabling them to bypass the bogs, forests, and drumlins that entangled future Norman and English invaders. Nevertheless, as Irish kings copied or hired Norse war bands, the Vikings

Kells

	Winner	*Loser*
Opponents	Leinster	Leinster
Commanders	Conall Grant	unknown

Allen

	Winner	*Loser*
Opponents	Leinster	Ulster
Commanders	Dunchad	Fergal mac Maele Duin (k)

Strangford Lough

	Winner	*Loser*
Opponents	Irish Norse	Viking
Commanders	Bardr Eysteinsson	Halfdan I (k)

became just one more factor in an already confused situation. Eleventh-century insertions into the *Tain* suggest improved protection for Irish warriors: leather jerkins, waxed linen shirts, and even helmets, reflecting Viking practice. Irish disunity made the country easy to invade, but difficult to subdue. Alliance with one faction guaranteed another's enmity. Unlike the Danelaw Vikings, Irish Norsemen never occupied large areas outside their urban strongholds at Dublin, Limerick and Waterford. The Scandinavian position crumbled as they fought each other. Halfdan I of York, who survived five battles in Wessex, met his death in Strangford Lough, having failed to snatch Dublin from its Norwegian occupants. The Irish never attained the unity imposed by the kings of Wessex in England, but they had contained the threat of Viking hegemony long before Clontarf (1014), the traditional end of the Viking era in Ireland.

Directions

Tactical locations unknown.

Dublin, 15 September 919

Ireland, Co. Dublin, DS50 O1234

Anagassan, 5 January 926

Ireland, Co. Louth, DS36 unlocated

Tara, 980

Ireland, Co. Meath, DS43 N9159?

Glen Mama, 999

Ireland, Co. Dublin, DS50 unlocated

Irish kings were initially helpless before Viking fleets. The high king, Niall Glundub ('Black Knee'), confronted Ragnall Caech ('Squinty') for twenty days on the plains of Cashel in 918, but could not bring him to battle. Viking leaders were as cautious in Ireland as they were in England, and simply waited for opposing armies to disintegrate. The resources of defending kings were limited. The *Airgialla* of north Meath who made up the high king's army in the 9th century acknowledged a maximum of six weeks military service, once every three years.

Niall Glundub was killed at Dublin, emulating Aethelred's attack on Reading in 871. The Viking ship-fortress lay on the swampy south bank of the Liffey, in the angle made with its tributary the Poddle, where Viking trading vessels could anchor in the Dubh Linn or 'Black Pool'. Warships drew up on the beach, west of the present junction of Essex Quay with Parliament Street. The 10th-century town included the high ground now occupied by Christchurch Cathedral and the Castle, suggesting a defensive perimeter between the Liffey and Poddle, perhaps along St Michael's Hill. Niall died outside the defences, fording the Liffey at Islandbridge. The 17th-century compilation entitled *The Annals of the Four Masters* specifies the site as 'Kilmohavoc' near Ath Cliath, the area west of Viking Dublin at the end of High Street. Despite fielding troops from half of Ireland, Niall suffered the most crushing Irish defeat since the Vikings' first appearance off Lambay Island in 795. Twelve sub-kings fell in a disaster that marked the zenith of Viking power in Ireland: 'It shall be called until Judgement Day the destructive morning at Dublin.'

Irish disunity made it impossible for Ragnall to inflict a knockout blow like York (867). Less than a decade after Niall Glundub's death, a new high king, Muirchetach, beheaded 200 Vikings at Carlingford Lough in September 925. He followed up by killing the son of the Norse king of Dublin at Anagassan, and pursuing Halfdan's defeated followers up the Newry River. The Viking position in Ireland crumbled. Of 25 battles fought by Dublin Vikings between 917 and 1014, they won 10. Maelsechnaill II ended the Viking threat at Tara in 980 by defeating Olaf Cuaran Sigtryggsson, king of York and Dublin, who recognized altered times by retiring to Iona. In 988 Maelsechnaill made a joint hosting with Brian Boru, representative of a new power in southwest Ireland, the Dal Cais dynasty of Munster. Together they 'took pledges of the Gaill for their submission to the Irish'.

Brian defeated Olaf Cuaran's son, Sigtryggr Silkenbeard, and his Leinster allies at Glen Mama, near Saggart on the northern fringes of the Wicklow Mountains, at the very end of the first millennium. Both sides suffered heavy losses, the Irish claiming 4000 Viking casualties. Maelmorda hid up a yew tree, and the Vikings were chased back into Dublin, which Brian occupied while his forces mopped up surrounding forts and passes. Sigtryggr Silkenbeard was reinstated as Brian's client, after giving hostages. In 1002 Brian displaced Maelsechnaill II as high king, a move recognized by a marginal note subsequently added to the 9th-century *Book of Armagh* written 'in the presence of Brian *imperator Scottorum* [emperor of the Irish]'.

Dublin

	Winner	*Loser*
Opponents	Viking	Irish
Commanders	Ragnall Caech	Niall Glundub (k)

Anagassan

	Winner	*Loser*
Opponents	Ulster	Viking
Commanders	Muirchetach of the Leather Cloaks	Halfdan Gothfrithsson (k)

Tara

	Winner	*Loser*
Opponents	Irish	Viking
Commanders	Maelsechnaill II	Olaf Cuaran Sigtryggsson

Glen Mama

	Winner	*Loser*
Opponents	Munster	Leinster
Commanders	Brian Boru	Maelmorda Sigtryggr Silkenbeard

Directions

See text for Dublin (919). Other tactical locations unknown.

Clontarf, 23 April 1014

Ireland, Co. Dublin, DS50 O2035–36?

The first Irish battle of which it is possible to write at any length is Clontarf. Celebrated as an Irish victory over the Norse, Clontarf did not remove the threat of a Scandinavian hegemony in Ireland comparable to Cnut's in England. It was more a demonstration of the fragility of Munster's recent preeminence, which ended with Brian Boru's death. Leinster and the Dublin Vikings had already rejected his overlordship, thus provoking the battle.

The most detailed source for the action is the 12th-century *Cogadh Gaedel re Gallaibh* ('War of the Irish against the Foreigners'). It explains the clash between Brian and Maelmorda of Leinster in romanticized terms, Maelmorda being provoked into action by his sister Gormflaith, 'the fairest of women'. Gormflaith had previously been married to two participants in the campaign, Brian and Maelsechnaill II, and was the mother of Sigtryggr Silkenbeard by Olaf Cuaran. Searching for allies, Maelmorda further promised her hand to both Sigurd of Orkney and Brodar, the Manx Viking leader, though neither lived to enjoy the lady's favours.

Every Irish family of note has posthumously swollen the ranks of Brian's army, falsifying the record with the names of ancestors dead years before the battle. Brian probably had fewer men than he had hoped. On the eve of battle Maelsechnaill withdrew his forces after an unexplained quarrel. This left Brian with his own troops from Munster reinforced by the men of Galway, and some Viking allies led by Wolf the Quarrelsome. Precise numbers engaged are unknown. On the other side Brodar brought 20 ships, a landing force of perhaps 800 men. G.A. Hayes-McCoy, the doyen of Irish military historians, guessed at a total of 5000 combatants, less than at

Hastings, but the most powerful force yet seen in Ireland. This would have given Brodar about a third of the allied strength, justifying his command of one of their army's three wings.

Maelmorda's allies concentrated at Dublin on Palm Sunday 1014, and marched out to confront Brian on Good Friday. Hayes-McCoy placed the battle within sight of 11th-century Dublin, somewhere beyond the reclaimed area outside the docks, where the Belfast trains run northeast from Amiens Street station above the suburb still known as Clontarf, north of the River Tolka. Details of the deployment are obscure. The *Saga of Burnt Njal* (*c.*13th century) describes a conventional division of forces on both sides into a centre and two wings. Unfortunately the saga loses credibility by ignoring the Leinstermen, who may have outnumbered their Scandinavian allies two-to-one. The allied army's sub-division resembles that of Viking armies at Ashdown and Corbridge (871, 918) where war bands retained their separate identities in action. Perhaps Sigurd and Brodar formed the allied flanks, while the more numerous Leinstermen took the centre, the saga-maker overlooking their non-Viking leader. Sigtryggr stayed in Dublin to cover the allied rear, the only allied leader to survive the battle. Brian Boru was too old to fight in person. He remained behind his army, leaving overall command to his son Murchad.

The *Cogadh* describes formations 'so dense together in the lines on either side ... that a four-horsed chariot could be driven on their heads from one flank to the other'. The analogy with the packed ranks of the English shieldwall at Hastings is striking. The two sides' offensive weapons are the usual mixture of swords, spears and axes. The Irish also had their characteristic throwing spears, darts with variegated silken strings, thick set with nails, to be violently cast and retrieved using the string. The Vikings were better protected, with mail from head to foot, while the Irish had 'only elegant tunics with smooth fringes, shields, and finely wrought collars to protect bodies and necks'.

Clontarf

	Winner	*Loser*
Opponents	Munster	Leinster
Commanders	Brian Boru (k)	Maelmorda (k)
	Murchad (k)	Sigtryggr Silkenbeard
		Sigurd the Stout (k)

The scribe's heroic conception of battle reduces the engagement to a series of duels described in poetic detail. Murchad slays 15 mail-clad warriors on his left and another 15 on his right, melting the gold inlay on his sword hilt with the heat of his blows, before his last victim stabs him to death. Sigurd's raven flag, borne before him at Skidamyre (995, see below), brings death to all who bear it, until Hrafn the Red cries out, 'Bear thine own devil thyself', and Sigurd is run through wearing his banner beneath his cloak. Portents before and during the battle emphasize the importance of the occasion: a fairy from Craig Liath Sidhe foretells Brian's death; a Caithness man sees a dozen women spinning, with men's heads for loom weights, human entrails for the warp and weft, and a sword for a shuttle.

Returning to reality, fighting lasted from morning till evening, from one full tide to another. As the allies weakened, the larger Munster army overlapped the allied flanks, preventing escape. The allies retreated seawards, 'like a herd of cows attacked by flies ... in the heat of the summer sun'. Many drowned as the rising tide prevented escape along the beach. Casualties during the pursuit included Brian's grandson Toirdelbach, found afterwards in Clontarf weir. Armoured Manxmen broke through the Irish lines, and came upon the old king praying for victory. Brodar split Brian's head with his axe, but was himself trapped in a nearby wood, and killed. A Norseman who stopped to tie a loose shoelace was more fortunate. Asked by an Irishman why he delayed, his honesty saved his life: 'Because I can't get home tonight; I live in Iceland.'

Both sides suffered grievously. Besides the high king, his son and grandson, the victors lost six kings dead, and the losers four, plus Sigurd and Brodar. No foreigner of rank escaped alive. Contemporary sources claimed some 6000 fatalities, more than

Hayes-McCoy's estimate for the entire force engaged. Although the Leinstermen lost the battle, they had scotched the power of Munster, and discovered the value of overseas alliances. When new high kings arose in the 12th century, a future king of Leinster would not hesitate to seek assistance from other Northmen who had conquered the neighbouring island, with fateful consequences for both.

Directions

Turn right off the R105 at Marino along Clontarf Promenade. Suggested locations include Castle Avenue, running north to the Howth Road past the sports ground and Danesfort, or Conquer Hill on the left, after the sailing club slipway, leading to Brian Boru Terrace, as good a place as any for the final stages of the battle.

Scotland Unites

Dark Age Scotland was home to several distinct groups of people. The most powerful were the Picts of the north and east, descendants of the Caledonians who fought Agricola. Remnants of the northern Britons held out in Strathclyde and Cumbria to the southwest, their chief stronghold at Dumbarton Rock. Scottish migrants from Northern Ireland carved out the kingdom of Dalriada in Argyll, its centre at Dunadd in the Great Moss of Crinan. These three peoples were all Celts. Meanwhile Germanic settlers spread northwards into southern Scotland, although they would lose Galloway in the 9th century to Northmen, the *Gall Gaedill* who left the area their name. More Norwegians settled the islands and peninsulas of the north and west: the Orkneys, Hebrides and Caithness. All these people intermarried and fought with one another, but their conflicts have left few traces, except a few scraps of poetry, and the names of unlocated battles.

The Picts gave up chariots in the 3rd century, replacing them with horses for pre-battle posturing, though not for combat, which was predominantly on foot. Sculpted stones show spears, short swords, and a mixture of square and round shields. Bows appear only in hunting scenes. The Aberlemno Stone that commemorates Bruide mac Beli's great victory at Nechtanesmere (685) shows a group of Pictish infantry, perhaps in three ranks. One confronts a mounted Northumbrian with sword and shield; a second levels a spear two-handedly against the horse's chest; a third, perhaps the rear rank, awaits his turn, holding a spear upright. The Northumbrian horseman wears a helmet with nasal (nosepiece) similar to that found at Coppergate in York, but the Picts are bare-headed. Light equipment would suit difficult Highland terrain, and the hit-and-run tactics of domestic Scottish warfare. The 7th-century *Senchus Fer nAlban* ('History of the Men of Alba') shows how the Dalriada raised their armed forces. Three or four kindreds divided the kingdom between them, further subdividing the land into multiples of 5, 20 or 30 households. Every 20 had to provide and crew a pair of seven-benched ships, the total contingent amounting to 140 ships and some 2000 men. As in England it can be surmised that noble kindreds and a few free commoners fought, while the unfree mass fed the hostings.

Viking raids isolated Scotland, cut the Scots off from their Irish roots and drove them eastwards upon the Picts. The slaughter of Pictish aristocracy at an unnamed battle in 839 prepared the way for Kenneth mac Alpin's accession to the joint throne in 843. Few details of this crucial transaction survive: scarcely more than three lines of type. Dumbarton's capture by the grandsons of Ivar the Boneless after a four-month siege in 902 destroyed the North Britons' independent power, with countless prisoners carried off to the Dublin slave markets. Strathclyde kept its cultural identity, as a Scottish satellite. Cut off from their Anglo-Saxon compatriots by the Viking kingdom of York, the Bamburgh Angles drifted under

Scottish influence, as shown by King Constantine's leadership at Corbridge (914 and 919).

The history of Scotland emerges from the shadows in the 11th century with the reigns of Malcolm II (1005–34), Macbeth or mac Beatha (1040–57), and Malcolm III, *Ceann Mor* (i.e. 'Great Chief', 'Bighead' (1058–93). Shakespeare's dramatic genius has blackened Macbeth's reputation for ever, but relations between rival branches of the Scots royal house were more complex than the playwright knew. Macbeth was the last Gaelic king of Scotland. His overthrow by Malcolm III would extinguish Scotland's Celtic character through the introduction of feudalism and the English language.

Circinn (Howe of the Mearns), **597**

Scotland, Aberdeenshire, LR45 unlocated

Mag Rath (Moira), **637**

Ireland, Co. Down, unlocated

Calathros (Dun Nosebridge), **639**

Scotland, Argyll and Bute, LR60 NR3760

Strathcarron, 642

Scotland, Falkirk, LR65, unlocated

Circinn

	Winner	*Loser*
Opponents	Picts	Scots
Commanders	unknown	Aedan mac Gabhran

Mag Rath

	Winner	*Loser*
Opponents	Scots	Scots
Commanders	Domnall mac Aed	Domnall Brec (p)

Calathros

	Winner	*Loser*
Opponents	Scots	Scots
Commanders	unknown	Domnall Brec

Strathcarron

	Winner	*Loser*
Opponents	British	Scots
Commanders	Owen ap Beli	Domnall Brec (k)

The Scots gave their name to all Scotland, but this was not inevitable. Their king Aedan mac Gabhran was beaten by Picts at Howe of the Mearns (597), and by Aethelfrith of Bernicia at Degsastan (603). Domnall Brec of Dalriada, 'the Pockmarked', lost all but one of his eight battles. After the celebrated Battle of Mag Rath ('the Red Pools'), he was captured near Moira on the main road from Belfast to Lurgan, and the Dalriadic Scots lost control of their Ulster homeland. In the Battle of Calathros an unknown Scots competitor drove him from his stronghold at Dun Nosebridge on Islay, in the Inner Hebrides. Domnall Brec's catastrophic reign ended near the River Carron in the strategic Forth/Clyde isthmus. A laconic interpolation in *Y Gododdin*, the poem that commemorated the Battle of Catraeth (598), recalled an array from Kintyre:

> ... who came with the battle shout
> And ravens gnawed the head of Dyfnwal Vrach.

Directions

Tactical location unknown, apart from:

Calathros *3 miles (5 km) southeast of Bridgend in Islay, along a minor road off the A846. Just before Cluanach, take a footpath on the left through woods on the north bank of the River Laggan towards Dun Nosebridge on the southern slopes of Coill a'Ghuail.*

Skidamyre (Skithmore), *c.*995

Scotland, Highland, LR12 ND3257

Monzievaird, 1005

Scotland, Perth and Kinross, LR52 NN8725

Mortlach, *c.*1005

Scotland, Moray, LR28 NJ3239

Malcolm II was a warrior in the heroic tradition: a red-faced 'destroyer of the gaill [foreigner]', 'a king who will redden spear points'. The first king titled *Rex Scotiae,* he was credited with ten battles gained, though only four are remembered.

Kenneth mac Alpin's successors shared sovereignty between alternate branches of the royal house. The crown passed not from father to son, but to a brother or nephew. This Irish system, known as tanistry, moderated succession disputes, but sometimes broke down. Seven out of nine Scottish kings between 934 and 1040 died in feuds, and Vikings killed one of the other two. The crowded battle scenes and neatly stacked corpses of Sueno's Stone at Forres are a reminder of the realities of power, perhaps inspired by King Dubh's death in action there in 966, when his body was concealed nearby, under Kinloss Bridge.

Malcolm II's accession was typical. He emerged from obscurity in 1005 to kill his predecessor, which he did at Monzievaird, the 'Moor of Bards' above Crieff in Strathearn. The chief external threat to Malcolm's position came from Sigurd the Stout, Jarl of Orkney, whose power extended around the west coast to the Clyde. Sigurd had already clashed with Findlaech, *mormaer* or high steward of Moray, at Skidamyre in Caithness. This was apparently by appointment, as Findlaech 'staked in a battle-field for Sigurd on Skidmoor [sic] by a day named'. *Orkneyinga Saga* (*c.*1200) claimed Findlaech had overwhelming numbers, but Sigurd's mother embroidered a magical raven banner 'with mickle needlecraft and famous skill ...' guaranteed to bring victory to the one before whom it was borne, but death to whoever bore it. Three standard bearers were slain before Sigurd, directing operations from the second row of the scrum, was victorious. The battlefield has been identified with a slight rise in moorland (121 feet/37 m) at the defunct Coastal Command airfield of Skitten. The position covers Wick's northwest approaches, its flanks protected by Loch of Wester to the right and Loch of Kilmister to the left.

Norwegian saga-makers ignored Malcolm's dealings with Sigurd, leaving historians dependent on medieval inventions. Hector Boece (*c.*1465–*c.*1536), whose fictitious history of Scotland provided the raw material for *Macbeth*, also embroidered Malcolm's victory at Mortlach. Scots and Vikings allegedly clashed at Dufftown, where Mortlach monastery stood on the western edge of the wooded glen of Dullan Water. Mortlach was a sufficiently important ecclesiastical centre to attract Viking attentions, and to call on the king for defence, although the narrow glen leaves little room for fighting.

The opposing forces approached from east and west: the Scots from Auchindoun in Glenfiddich;

Skidamyre

	Winner	*Loser*
Opponents	Viking	Scots
Commanders	Sigurd the Stout	Findlaech

Monzievaird

	Winner	*Loser*
Opponents	Scots	Scots
Commanders	Malcolm II	Kenneth mac Dubh (k)

Mortlach

	Winner	*Loser*
Opponents	Scots	Viking
Commanders	Malcolm II	Sigurd the Stout

the Norsemen from Strathspey, camping en route at an old hillfort on Little Conval (1811 feet/552 m). An initial Scots charge ran into 'deep trenches full of water and mudde', and only Malcolm's invocation of the local St Moluag saved the day. The more reliable John of Fordun (14th century) says only that the Vikings were 'ramscuttered'. Three of their skulls decorated the church until the 18th century, when schoolboys stole them for footballs. The kirkyard Boece regarded as the battlefield houses the usual anachronistic Battle Stone, 7 feet (2 m) tall and decorated with early Christian and pagan symbols.

Directions

Skidamyre *Skitten Farm does not appear on current OS maps. 4 miles (6 km) northwest of Wick, turn right off the B876 at Biggins (95 feet/29 m), and travel ½ mile (0.8 km) along a farm track. Farmers use the airfield buildings, and a monument commemorates those killed flying from Skitten.*

Monzievaird *2 miles(3 km) north of Crieff fork left off the A822 Amulree road to Monzie, at the foot of the Braes of Monzie.*

Mortlach *The old kirk (14th century) is ½ mile (0.8 km) south of Dufftown centre, on the left.*

Burgus, *c.* 1006

England, Cumbria, LR85/91 unlocated

Carham, 1018

England, Northumberland, LR74 NT8338

Malcolm II invaded Northumbria at least twice, provoking widespread confusion about the dates, locations, participants and results of the ensuing battles.

The *Annals of Ulster* (15th century) recorded a battle between Scots and Saxons in 1005/6: 'And the rout was upon the men of Alba [Scotland], and they left behind them a slaughter of their best men.'

Burgus

	Winner	*Loser*
Opponents	Northumbrian	Scots
Commanders	Uhtred	Malcolm II

Carham

	Winner	*Loser*
Opponents	Scots	Northumbrian
Commanders	Malcolm II Owen the Bald (k)	Uhtred

The conflict has been identified with a siege of Durham, raised by Earl Uhtred of Northumbria, 'a young man of great energy most well suited to war', who mobilized Yorkshire and Northumbria to cut the entire Scots army to pieces. Unfortunately this interpretation depends on a single contentious manuscript. Promisingly entitled *De Obsessione Dunelmensis* ('Of the Siege of Durham', 12th century) it sets its narrative impossibly early, and duplicates details of a better documented siege of Durham in 1039.

The *Obsessione* probably reflects traditions of some other confrontation between Uhtred and Malcolm II, perhaps a conflict arising from a show of strength soon after the latter's accession to the throne. To attract the Ulster annalist's attention it probably occurred west of the Pennines. John of Fordun records an undated and hard won victory over Uhtred in Cumbria, '*juxta Burgum*'. Cumbria lay south of the Solway, suggesting 'Burgus' might be Burgh-by-Sands between Carlisle and Hadrian's Wall (LR85 NY3259), or Brough in Westmorland (LR91 NY7914), where traces of 11th-century fortifications survive above the Roman fort. The area was a Dark Age flashpoint, seeing the death of Eric Bloodaxe in 954, and frequent Scottish raids as far as the Rey Cross on Stainmore.

Malcolm II's victory at Carham in 1018 was different. Numerous sources refer to a great battle '*apud Carrum*', 'at the rocks', the later site of Wark Castle on the River Tweed. East of Wark an otherwise unexplained deviation in the border may indicate a stretch of the southern bank where the battle could have taken place. Much confusion has arisen from attribution of command of the Northumbrians to Earl Uhtred in 1018, as the *Anglo-Saxon Chronicle* dates his death to 1016. Uhtred's murder by Thorbrand the Hold was a major event in the North. It provoked the most celebrated vendetta of the age, culminating in the massacre of all Thurbrand's male descendants bar two, by Earl Waltheof, Uhtred's great-grandson, in 1073. However, the appearance of a comet 30 days before the battle and the subsequent death of Ealdhun, Bishop of Durham, independently support a date for the battle during September 1018. The geographically remote *Anglo-Saxon Chronicle* may have misdated Uhtred's murder, which logically belongs with the purges that followed Cnut's coronation in 1017.

Historians generally assign Carham the significance appropriate to a battle heralded by a comet and a bishop's death. The *History of the Church of Durham* (12th century) described how: 'the whole population from the Tees to the Tweed [excluding Yorkshire] was almost completely cut down while fighting an infinite multitude of Scots'. Cnut had detached York from Uhtred's earldom, leaving him fewer men than in 1006 to face a Scottish army reinforced from Strathclyde.

More recently the action has been represented as a landmark, confirming Lothian's cession to Scotland, and fixing the Border between England and Scotland along the Tweed. The Northumbrians' heavy losses may, however, have been something of a literary effect, like Bishop Ealdhun's death from grief – allegedly 'after a few days', but which in fact occured the following year. English kings had long abandoned southern Scotland, sacrificing Lothian to stabilize Northumbria. Scottish kings raided south of the Tweed throughout the 11th century, showing little respect for the hypothetical frontier. Arguably the Battle of Carham was a typical Dark Age bloodletting with no permanent significance.

Directions

Tactical locations unknown.

Durham (Siege), 1039

England, Durham, LR88 NZ2742

Torfnes (Burghead/Torness), 14 August 1040

Scotland, Moray, LR28 NJ1069–1169

The battles preceding Macbeth's seizure of power in 1040 do not bear out Shakespeare's picture of a bloodstained usurper. It was Malcolm II who killed off his relatives to ensure the succession of his incompetent grandson Duncan. Both Macbeth, son of Findlaech, *mormaer* of Moray, and Thorfinn Sigurdsson, Jarl of the Orkneys, had as good a claim to the throne as Duncan, whose record of military failure demonstrated his unfitness to rule.

Duncan's siege of Durham, after a Northumbrian raid with a 'countless multitude of troops', was a dismal failure:

> a great part of his cavalry was slain by the besieged [presumably in a sortie] and he was put to disorderly flight, in which he lost all his foot soldiers and narrowly escaped with his own life.
>
> *History of the Church of Durham* (12th century)

Four women received a cow apiece for cleaning up the better-looking heads, 'ornamented with braided locks as was the fashion of the time', for display on posts around the marketplace.

Renewed squabbles over Caithness sealed Duncan's fate. *Orkneyinga Saga* records Scottish disasters at Thurso and at sea off Deerness, inflicted by Thorfinn upon Karl 'Son of a Dog', probably a derisive nickname for Duncan. Thorfinn then occupied a post on the Scottish coast as an advanced base for plundering the wretched inhabitants, as other Vikings had done at Benfleet and Dublin:

> Reddened were the wolf's bit edges,
> At a place – men call it Torfnes.

Duncan seems to have made the mistake of attacking a Viking force in a defensive position of its own choosing. Like Aethelred at Reading (871), or Niall Glundub at Dublin (919), he came off worst. Duncan had reinforcements from Ireland, but the Vikings had axes, mail and helmets. They drove off the lightly armed Irish, then repulsed a Scots charge against their centre: 'Karl took flight though some men say that he was slain.'

Torfnes is now Tarbat Ness, the cape between the Dornoch and Moray Firths. Duncan's demise soon afterwards in a smithy at Pitgavenny suggests the battle took place further south, perhaps Burghead on the north Moray coast. This was a major Pictish fort, burnt by Vikings in the 9th century and possibly restored by Thorfinn Sigurdsson. It made an immensely strong position behind the salt flats of Loch Spynie, with its own fresh-water supply. The western ramparts have fallen into the sea, while the modern town has swallowed up the landward defences. The original walls stood 18 feet (5.5 m) high, solidly built from stone, revetted with baulks of timber.

Duncan's cousins ganged up on him, for there is little doubt that Macbeth finished him off. Contemporaries must have been glad to be rid of a king of whom John of Fordun wrote: 'during the short period of Duncan's rule nothing was done of which mention should be made'. The early *Verse Chronicle of the Kings* remembered Macbeth's reign as long and prosperous: 'seventeen years and in his reign there were fruitful summers'. Macbeth's position was so secure that he travelled to Rome in 1050, scattering silver among the poor like seed corn. His downfall resulted from foreign intervention, not domestic upheaval.

Durham

	Winner	*Loser*
Opponents	Northumbrians	Scots
Commanders	unknown	Duncan

Torfnes

	Winner	*Loser*
Opponents	Viking	Scots
Commanders	Thorfinn	Duncan (k)

Directions

Durham *tactical locations unknown.*

Torfnes *Burghead is 8 miles (13 km) northwest of Elgin. Turn right off the A96(T) Elgin–Forres road, and follow the B9013 as far as possible to the remains of the fort, although the battlefield is unlocated. Also see Sueno's Stone at Forres.*

Dunsinane Hill, (Day of the Seven Sleepers) 27 July 1054

Scotland, Perth and Kinross, LR53 NO2131

Lumphanan, 15 August 1057

Scotland, Aberdeenshire, LR37 NJ5703

Alnwick (I), 13 November 1093

England, Northumberland, LR 81 NU1914

Dunsinane is the climactic point of Shakespeare's *Macbeth*, but the dramatist's account of the battle is as inaccurate as the rest of his play. Macduff was no more historical than the Weird Sisters, and Macbeth lived to fight on for another three years. Almost the only elements of the truth in the tale are the names of the Anglo-Danish leaders who restored the exiled Malcolm Ceann Mor on English spear points.

The *Anglo-Saxon Chronicle* records that Siward, Earl of Northumberland, invaded Scotland on the orders of Edward the Confessor, to whose court Malcolm had fled on the death of his father, Duncan. Siward led a combined operation, a fleet following a mounted column advancing up the east coast through Stirling to Perth. *Vita Edwardi Regis* (later 11th century) grumbled at the Scots' refusal to fight properly: 'an uncertain race and fickle ... which trusts rather in woods than in the plain, also more in flight than manly courage in battle'. Dark Age strategists were quite capable of leaving fatigue and disease to do their work for them. Macbeth avoided action until

Siward's proximity to the Scottish royal centre at Scone forced him to fight.

William of Malmesbury (12th century) located the battle at Dundee, where 9th-century earthworks survive outside the city. More contemporary accounts put it nearer the Tay. Six miles (10 km) northeast of Scone, Dunsinane Hill blocks Siward's progress up Strathmore into Macbeth's Moray heartland, as Dundee does not. A triple ramparted hillfort occupies the top of Dunsinane Hill, but Macbeth fought in the open, suffering twice the invaders' losses. Among them were some Norman adventurers, suggesting Macbeth disposed of a few heavy cavalry.

Siward's victory was indecisive, despite English claims of 'such a great war booty as no man had ever got before'. Not only did Macbeth escape, the casualties included Siward's son and nephew, besides royal housecarls. Malcolm was installed in Cumbria, and left to finish the job. By 1057 he was strong enough to mount a coup-de-main, nearly catching Macbeth at Scone. As Macbeth fled north over the Grampians, Malcolm headed him off, driving the doomed king towards the remote settlement of Lumphanan, north of Deeside on the ancient road from Cairn o' Mount to the Don. Contradictory traditions place Macbeth's last stand either at Peel of Lumphanan, a motte and bailey not built until the 13th century, or the prehistoric Macbeth Stone 200 yards (180 m) further south. Macbeth's head was cut off and presented to Malcolm on a spear. But his body was buried at Iona, the proper resting place for a rightful king of Scotland.

It was Malcolm Ceann Mor who was denied burial at Iona, after his death on the banks of the River Aln in 1093. Raiding Northumbria once too often, he was treacherously killed by Normans north of Alnwick on St Brice's Day, in unspecified circumstances so shocking that even other Normans were embarrassed. The presence of these Francophone Vikings on the Border signalled the doom of the diverse societies that had evolved in Britain since the Roman withdrawal. Along with Malcolm died his son Edward and most of their soldiers. Those that escaped drowned in rivers swollen by winter rains.

Dunsinane Hill

	Winner	*Loser*
Opponents	Northumbrians	Scots
Commanders	Siward	Macbeth
	Malcolm III Ceann Mor	
Losses	1500	3000

Lumphanan

	Winner	*Loser*
Opponents	Scots	Scots
Commanders	Malcolm III	Macbeth (k)

Alnwick

	Winner	*Loser*
Opponents	Norman	Scots
Commanders	Richard Mowbray Earl of Northumberland	Malcolm III (k)

Two local people carted the royal corpse away to Tynemouth, there being no Scots being left to do the job.

A Gothic cross half a mile west of the A1 junction at Denwick commemorates Malcolm's death. Dated 1774, the monument may recall earlier traditions of the site. Medieval fragments of an earlier cross survive, and an Anglo-Norman lord of Alnwick founded the nearby Hospital of St Leonard, to sing masses for Malcolm's soul.

Directions

Dunsinane Hill *Take the A94 from Perth to Balbeggie, and fork right onto the B953 through Bandirran. Turn left along a minor road southwest of Dunsinane Hill (899 ft/274 m), and back up a track to the hill fort.*

Lumphanan *From Banchory take the A980 to Lumphanan village, turning left for the Peel. Macbeth's Stone is in the field opposite.*

Alnwick *Follow the B6341 north from Alnwick Castle, past the hospital on the left. Malcolm's Cross and the Ordnance Survey battle site are on the right, before the roundabout.*

The Fall of Anglo-Saxon England

The autumn of 1066 saw a series of battles that changed the course of British history. The Anglo-Saxon kingdom went down in a welter of blood that was decisive in the widest possible sense. The battles of Stamford Bridge and Hastings not only decided which of three claimants should seize the throne of England, but also the linguistic, legal and social forms under which they should rule. The documentation for these momentous events is appropriately abundant, even if most of the authors were called William, like the Conqueror. A range of nearly contemporary sources includes an unusually well-informed account by William of Poitiers, who had been a knight before becoming Duke William's chaplain. Most precious of all is the Bayeux Tapestry, commissioned by the Conqueror's brother Bishop Odo, but worked by English nuns.

The contrast between the obscurity of the battles that carved out Anglo-Saxon England and the blaze of publicity surrounding its destruction suggests the extent of change in the 600 years that separated Hastings from Aegelesthrep (*c*.455). A wealthy and united kingdom had arisen from the impoverished fragments of an abandoned Roman province. Coinage, a vernacular literature and centralized government all placed the Anglo-Saxon state ahead of its continental neighbours. Political instability and military conservatism, however, left England vulnerable to foreign adventurers, as shown by Cnut's success in 1016. The restoration and long reign of Edward the Confessor, son of Aethelred the Unready, concealed English weakness beneath an aura of stability and legitimacy. Edward drew England closer to Normandy, where he had spent most of his early life. He introduced knights and castles to bolster his rule, but failed to limit the excessive power of a few magnates, especially Earl Godwin of Wessex. The situation was made worse by Edward's failure to produce an heir, and by his ambivalence over the succession before his death on 6 January 1066.

Edward had almost certainly promised the crown to his first cousin once removed, William, Duke of Normandy, whom the *Anglo-Saxon Chronicle* unkindly labelled 'the Bastard'. William had the most tenuous hereditary claim. He was related to Edward through the latter's mother, Emma of Normandy, who had no personal right to the English throne at all, although she had married two kings of England. In his dying moments, Edward may have nominated Harold Godwinson as his heir. Already the leading figure in the kingdom, Harold could allege a spurious kinship with Edward, as his sister Edith had married the dead king. Harold's accession immediately after Edward's death was as revolutionary as Swein Forkbeard's coup in 1014, but at least Harold was English. It hardly seems fair that only foreign grandees could bid for the throne of England. Unfortunately Harold had compromised his position during a diplomatic mission to Normandy in 1064, when Norman sources aver he swore fealty to William, and promised to expedite the duke's succession to the English throne. English sources were silent on the issue, though *Vita Edwardi* admitted Harold's regrettable generosity with oaths. As the *Chronicle* remarked, 'he experienced little quietness in it while he ruled the kingdom'.

The contest did not remain two-sided. England's descent into confusion invited intervention from the last great Viking adventurer, Harald Hardrada ('Hard Ruler'). Hardrada had served the Byzantine emperor as a Varangian Guard before seizing the Norwegian throne in 1047. He had even less of a claim to England than the other claimants, but everyone knew from Cnut's example that the country was rich, and could be won by the sword. Hardrada had an unlikely ally. In 1065 the men of York had expelled Harold Godwinson's brother Tostig, placed over them as earl, and replaced him with Morcar, brother of Edwin, Earl of Mercia, the Godwinsons' chief competitor within England. Tostig fled to Flanders, where in the spring of 1066 he raised a fleet and harried the coast from Hampshire to Lindsey, before taking refuge in Scotland. Tostig's attack followed the appearance of Halley's Comet, 'which some men call the haired star'. For once it was a true portent of disaster.

The military build-up either side of the English Channel reveals the gulf separating 11th-century rulers from bandit chiefs like Hengest or Cerdic. William collected or built hundreds of ships, and collected some 7000 troops and 3000 horses from Normandy, Brittany and Flanders. He then maintained them at Dives-sur-Mer throughout the summer from his own resources. Indiscriminate foraging was forbidden. The peasant's flocks grazed peacefully in the fields, while the harvest awaited the husbandman's sickle, untrampled by horsemen. The details of this logistical feat are unknown, as are the steps taken to dispose of the 700,000 gallons of horse urine that flowed each month from so many chargers. Harold Godwinson made a comparable military and naval effort, 'although in the end it was to no avail'. All summer and autumn he lay off the Isle of Wight with the largest fleet the *Anglo-Saxon Chronicle* could recall, 'and a land army was kept everywhere by the sea'. Contrary winds kept William in port, while Harold's logistics fell apart. The five-hide system rationed troops for 60 days, but by 8 September 'the men's provisions were gone and no one could hold them there any longer'. No sooner had Harold's ships dispersed than Hardrada and Tostig 'came by surprise north into the Tyne with a very great raiding ship army – and no little one'. The final agony of the Anglo-Saxon monarchy had begun.

Gate Fulford, 20 September 1066

England, York, LR105 SE6149

Stamford Bridge, 25 September 1066

England, East Yorkshire, LR105 SE7155–SE7255

The battles outside York in September 1066 have been overshadowed by the violent overthrow of Anglo-Saxon England at Hastings three weeks later. Gate Fulford and Stamford Bridge were significant events in their own right. They were the last of the old-style Anglo-Scandinavian slogging matches where heavy infantry fought it out with axe and spear, uninterrupted by archers or cavalry. Politically, the two northern battles marked the last attempt of a Scandinavian adventurer to use the North as a stepping stone to the English throne. Stamford Bridge was also the last victory of a kingdom that still possessed the vitality to conduct two national fights within five days.

Harald Hardrada's rendezvous with Tostig at the Tyne in the late summer of 1066, and their subsequent advance to the Humber, followed a pattern of intervention dating back to the 10th-century Norse kingdom of York, and the battles of Corbridge (914 and 918) and Brunanburh (937). Hardrada could hope to exploit separatist feeling expressed during the 1065 revolt against Tostig, when northerners ravaged as far south as Northamptonshire, killing men, burning crops and houses, and carrying off cattle and slaves. Before reinstalling Tostig, however, Hardrada had to deal with the men who had replaced him, the Earls of Mercia and Northumbria.

The Norwegians reportedly deployed 200, 300, or 500 ships, plus whatever vessels Tostig had left from his earlier raids. Snorri Sturluson's *King Harald's Saga* (13th century) claimed that Hardrada took half the fighting force of his kingdom. The odds deterred Morcar from meeting the invasion at sea. He withdrew his ships up the River Wharfe to Tadcaster, Hardrada following to Riccall. A mile (1.6 km) from the confluence of the Wharfe and Ouse, this was a useful position not only within striking distance of York but also bottling up Morcar's squadron. Two roads lead to York from Riccall through Escrick or Naburn respectively, until an elbow in the Ouse brings them together again

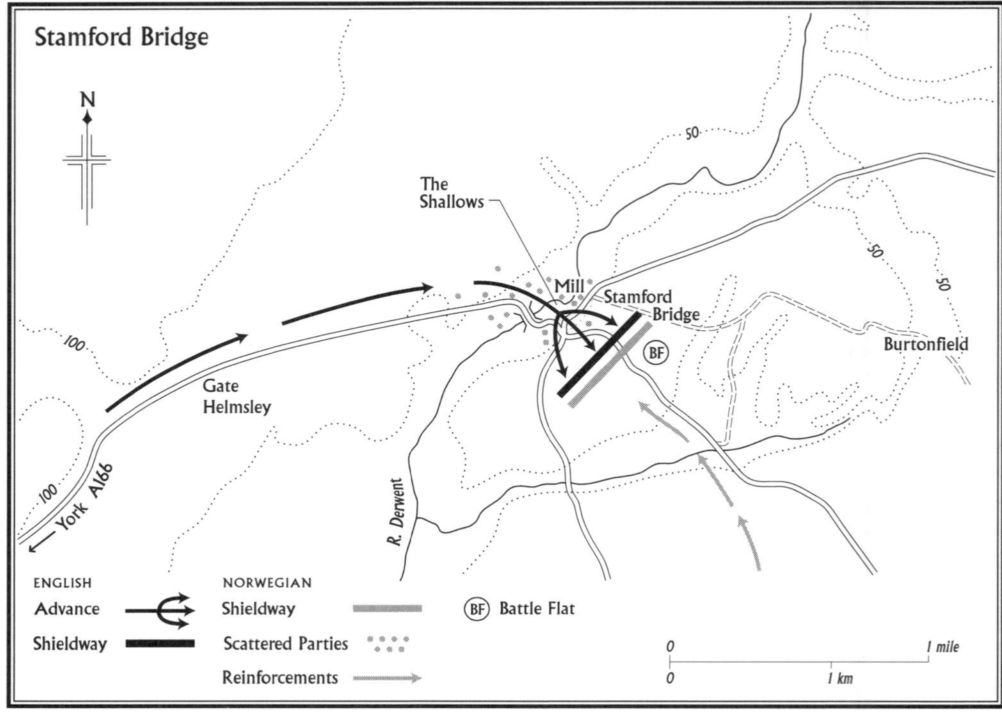

a mile (1.6 km) north of the A64 ring road, just short of Gate Fulford.

Snorri Sturluson's confused account of the action in *Heimskringla* suggests the English drew up across the road, which ran parallel to the river, and some 100 yards (90 m) to the east of it. A ditch and fen beyond the road suggests that the ground further east was also boggy. The whole area is low-lying. A small stream runs at right angles to the main A19 road past the cemetery, across the front of an army drawn up above the 33-foot (10-m) contour, where the suburb of Fulford now stands. The English right rested on the Ouse, their left on the ditch. Edwin and Morcar 'had gathered as great a force as they could get', but their numbers were still too few. Their decision to fight in the open instead of behind York's defences may indicate the poor condition of the walls, doubts about the population's willingness to stand a siege, or an outdated personal preference. Alternatively, the embankment carrying the road between river and fen may have formed a defensible defile, the narrowness of which might offset Hardrada's superior numbers. Estimates of Hardrada's strength vary from 5000 to 18,000. At 40 warriors per ship he could have fielded 8000 to 12,000 men, some of whom must have stayed behind as boat-keepers. While the English pushed back the Norwegian right, Hardrada broke through on the other flank, and rolled up the English line from west to east. Many of the defenders were driven into the fen to drown, while the others fled.

Stamford Bridge *On the A166 east of York. See above for the bridge fighting. Battle Flat is uphill, beyond the village.*

Harald Hardrada was no berserk freebooter. Instead of sacking York he took hostages and 'spoke of complete peace provided they would all go south with them and win this land'. His restraint shows the seriousness of his political intentions, which explain the puzzling location of the next battle. Stamford Bridge lies 8 miles (13 km) east of York, leaving the city open to the southwest, the dangerous side. Four

Roman roads converge on Stamford Bridge, making it an ideal meeting place to exchange hostages with the men of Yorkshire's main population centres: the Wolds, the Vale of York and the Vale of Pickering. The Norwegians went to Stamford Bridge to talk not fight: about a third of Hardrada's men remained at Riccall with the fleet. The day was hot, and many left their armour behind.

The Norwegian cannot have expected so prompt a reaction from Harold Godwinson, held in the south by the Norman threat. The *Anglo-Saxon Chronicle* writes breathlessly how 'in the middle of all this came Harold with all his army on Sunday to Tadcaster … and then on Monday went right through York'. Harold Godwinson's march has attracted general admiration for its speed and decision, but less for the strategic surprise it achieved. At York Harold was between the Norwegian army and fleet, and nearer to either than Hardrada was to his ships. The Viking leader's first indication of the English approach was their appearance over the gentle rise at Gate Helmsley, a mile (1.6 km) or so west of Stamford Bridge. The invaders had to fight with the main enemy army between them and their base. Godwinson may have had longer for his march than is usually allowed. He received the news of Hardrada's landing 'when he came off ship', after returning to London with the disbanded fleet. Harold probably headed north before Gate Fulford, taking a week to cover 200 miles (320 km) from London to York. At nearly 30 miles (48 km) a day this is double the speed of the British Expeditionary Force's retreat from Mons in 1914. An Anglo-Saxon royal army was clearly a mounted force to have maintained such a ferocious pace.

Gate Fulford

	Winner	Loser
Opponents	Norwegian	English
Commanders	Harald Hardrada	Edwin
	Tostig	Morcar

Stamford Bridge

	Winner	Loser
Opponents	English	Norwegian
Commanders	Harold Godwinson	Harald Hardrada (k)
		Tostig(k)

The River Derwent is about 20 yards (18 m) wide at Stamford Bridge, with steep banks and a muddy bottom. Its speed and depth of 8 feet (2.5 m) makes an opposed crossing impossible except at the bridge. The present structure, dating from the 1720s, replaced an earlier that stood 100 yards (90 m) upstream at a point known as the Shallows, just below the present weir. A.H. Burne argued the Saxon bridge was still further upstream at a point more consistent with the original road layout, but the exact location of the bridge makes little difference to our understanding of the fight. A memorial stone pillar and inscribed stone that commemorate the battle stand near the mill, between the alternative sites.

The English caught the invaders scattered either side of the river. Those on the west bank fought for their lives, gaining time for Hardrada to draw up the main body on the other bank. Half a mile (0.8 km) beyond the river the ground rises gently towards an area still known as Battle Flat, between the dismantled railway and a footpath to Burton Fields. A tradition of weapon finds in the area supports the place-name evidence, as does its tactical location, covering the eastern end of the old bridge. Hardrada may have only deployed 6000–7000 men out of his original landing force, allowing for 20 per cent casualties at Fulford, and the boat guard left at Riccall. The English are usually assumed to have been fewer, but they engaged the invaders successively, and beat them in detail.

For a long time a single Norwegian, who had not forgotten his armour, held the bridge. He survived an attempt to shoot him, but succumbed to an Englishman who paddled a swill-tub under the bridge, and stabbed him from below:

> Then Harold, king of the English, came over
> the bridge, and his army along with him, and
> there made a great slaughter of both Norwegians
> and Flemings.
>
> *Anglo-Saxon Chronicle*

The uncontested passage of the bridge after its heroic defence reads oddly today, but resembles other medieval battles at Maldon (991) and Boroughbridge (1322). Passive defence of a river line is unlikely to have appealed to a renowned warrior such as Hardrada, who may have hoped to push the English back into the stream with a well-ordered charge from higher ground.

The circumstantial account by Snorri Sturluson is incorrect in every detail that can be tested. Confusing Stamford Bridge with Hastings, he gives the English cavalry and archers, one of whom shoots Hardrada through the throat in a distorted echo of Harold Godwinson's own fate. Tostig took up Hardrada's 'Landwaster' banner, but when he fell the invading army disintegrated. Fighting continued long enough for Norwegian reinforcements to arrive from Riccall, only to join the casualties. They presumably took a roundabout route to reach the rear of their own army via Wilberfoss, as there is no hint of a flank attack on the victorious English.

The Norwegians' situation was desperate, as their line of retreat lay away from their fleet: 'some of them came to ship, some drowned, and some also burnt'. For once the *Chronicle*'s claims of few survivors can be believed. Seventy years later a great pile of whitening bones still marked the field. Three kings fell there: Harald Hardrada, who won the seven feet of English soil that Harold Godwinson promised him before the battle; his son-in-law Eysteinn Orri who led the reinforcements; and an unnamed Irish adventurer. Only 24 ships sailed back down the Humber. If the year's campaigning had ended at Stamford Bridge, Harold Godwinson would be remembered as one of England's greatest captains. Instead his northern blitzkrieg was a fatal distraction. While the king was away, William of Normandy had landed in Sussex.

Directions

Fulford *1½ miles (2.5 km) south of York on the A19. Follow Minster Way footpath along the Ouse to the south end of the village. Cross the road to see remaining open ground to the east, perhaps the place of slaughter.*

Hastings (Senlac), **Saturday 14 October 1066**

England, East Sussex, LR199 TQ7415

The Battle of Hastings stands at the centre of recorded British history, midway between the Roman invasions and today. Historians have expended thousands of words upon its reconstruction, ensuring that 1066 remains one of the very few memorable dates of English history. The event was exceptional in many ways: in scale and decisiveness, above all in the quality of the evidence for its conduct and location. Nevertheless, Hastings remains controversial. The general course of the fighting is clear enough, but numerous misconceptions persist about its detailed aspects, leaving the casual reader at the mercy of prejudice and speculation.

The Battle of Hastings was the culmination of one of the most remarkable amphibious operations of all time. Estimates of the fleet that carried Duke William across the Channel vary from 400 ships to an incredible 3000. The most plausible contemporary figure was that provided by the Norman poet Robert Wace (*c.*1100–74): 696 vessels of all types, including skiffs carrying arms and armour. William's naval effort may have surpassed that of Harald Hardrada, as the Normans shipped thousands of horses, each requiring four times the tonnage of an infantryman. Norman military intelligence seems to have been good. William took advantage of the English fleet's demobilization in September to move his invasion fleet from Dives-sur-Mer to St Valery-sur-Somme, closer to its objective. He sailed on the evening of 27 September, as soon as favourable winds allowed, landing unopposed at Pevensey next morning. Pevensey Haven then formed a tidal lagoon, a safe anchorage for the fleet, further protected by a Norman garrison left in the Roman fortress. William acted with caution, moving sideways along the coast to Hastings. Unlike Julius Caesar, who pushed inland immediately, William remained near his base. Hastings then lay at the seaward end of a defensible peninsula between the Brede Levels and Bulverhythe lagoon.

William erected a prefabricated fort on the cliffs above the port, securing communications with Normandy. Foraging expeditions ravaged the country, to collect supplies and to provoke whoever emerged victorious from the struggle in the north.

Harold Godwinson heard of the Norman invasion while celebrating his victory at Stamford Bridge. The news cannot have reached York before 1 October, but Harold was back in London on the 7th or 8th, baffling critics who believe the English army consisted of leg-infantry. Housecarls and thanes of the 11th century were gentlemen, and they rode to battle, easily covering 30 miles (50 km) a day. Harold sought an immediate decision, pushing on for the Sussex coast on 11 or 12 October. Commentators suggest he was intoxicated by recent success, or stung by the devastation of Godwin estates in Sussex.

The *Anglo-Saxon Chronicle*'s comment that the battle was fought before all Harold's army had arrived has encouraged suggestions that his rapid movements had exhausted the troops, and left many by the roadside. Modern critics write of them straggling into the rendezvous the night before the battle, although the 60-mile (100-km) ride from London to Hastings in two or three days does not seem excessive for hardened warriors. The lack of Northerners among identifiable casualties at Hastings can be attributed as easily to losses at Gate Fulford as to hard riding.

The Englishman may have misjudged his opponent. During his unlucky visit to Normandy, Harold had witnessed the usual medieval war game of siege, skirmish and devastation. William's reluctance to leave his Sussex bridgehead may have reinforced a false impression of timidity. Unlike the Breton border warfare Harold had seen in 1064, William's position in England demanded that he fight a major action. William's reconnaissance was better than Hardrada's, depriving Harold of tactical surprise. Norman scouts reported Harold's approach late on 13 October, giving William time to recall his foragers and seek out the English at first light the next day. Harold had concentrated too far forward, leaving himself open to a sudden attack, 'before his people were marshalled'.

The differences between the opposing forces at Hastings emphasize the pivotal nature of the battle. They mark the shift away from the simple tactics of the barbarian invasions towards the more flexible mixture of infantry and cavalry that dominated battlefields until the end of Britain's conventional domestic military history in the 18th century. Harold's army consisted exclusively of heavy infantry, expected to fight at close range with axe and spear. A single English bowman appears on the Bayeux Tapestry, in much the same way as the Maldon eulogy (see above) mentions a token archer. The idea that Harold's archers fell behind on the Great North Road because they lacked horses lacks any evidential foundation. The same applies to notions about Anglo-Saxon cavalry. Once an English army reached the scene of action it dismounted, and packed densely together on foot, '*quasi castellum*' ('like a castle'), as Henry of Huntingdon put it. The nearly contemporary *Carmen de Hastingae Proelio* observed: 'The English scorn the solace of horses and trusting in their strength they stand fast on foot.' Robert Wace clearly thought English ignorance of jousting had counted against them.

The Bayeux Tapestry shows two types of English infantry: heavily armed in conical helmet and mail shirt, and lightly armed in everyday dress, protected only by a round or kite-shaped shield. Historians have invented dubious distinctions between 'select' and 'great' fyrd, to explain these differences. Sir Charles Oman dismissed the whole lot as untrained peasants equipped with agricultural implements and 'rude weapons more appropriate to the Neolithic age than to the eleventh century, [such as] great stones bound to wooden handles'. Such a rabble would have lasted no time in the face of Norman archers and horsemen. The duration and quality of the English resistance suggests the lightly armed men were attendants of the prime fighting men, imbued with the same warrior spirit. Only one stone axe appears in the Tapestry, a throwing weapon. The universal weapon is the spear. Heavily armed soldiers also carried swords and double-handed axes. Some of these men would have been thanes, landed gentlemen whose social status depended on military service. The others were housecarls, disciplined soldiers, descended from

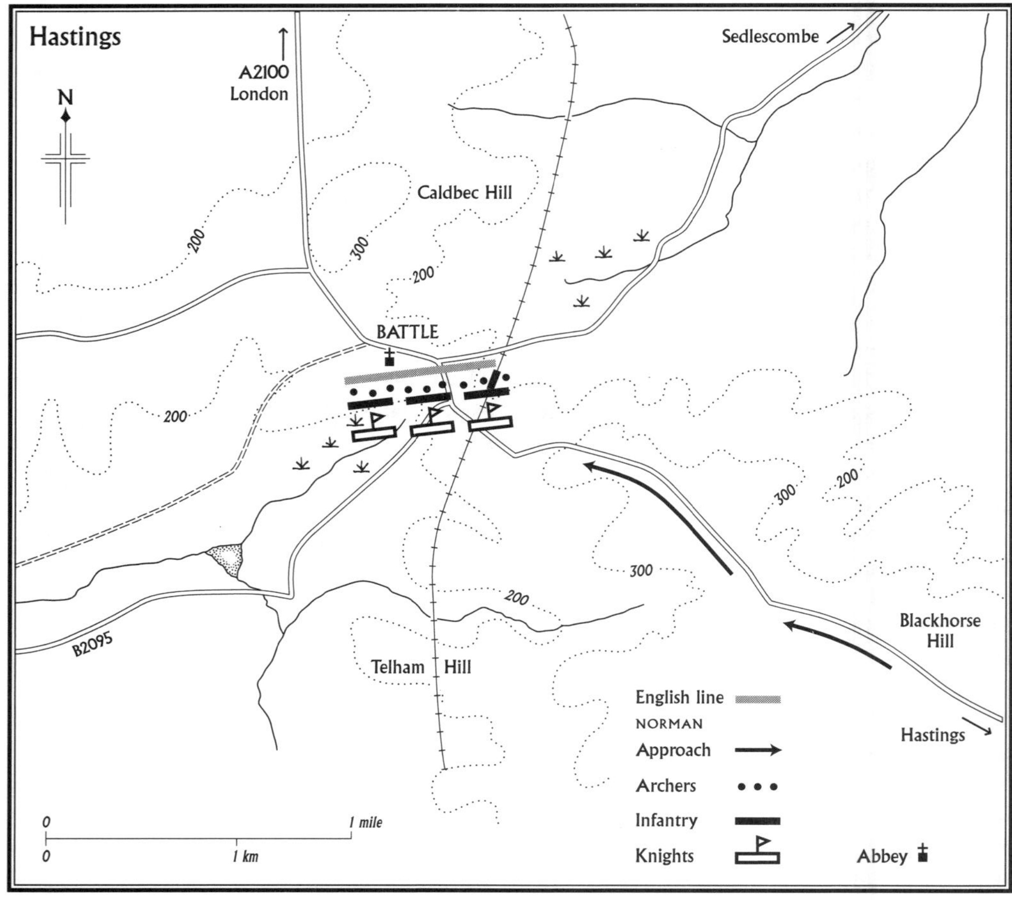

Danish bodyguards introduced into England by Cnut, and related to military brotherhoods like the Varangian guards of the Byzantine army. Cnut and Edward the Confessor had maintained 2500 and 1000 housecarls respectively. At Hastings Harold could have deployed several thousand housecarls, the best infantry of the day. His brothers' retinues and draughts of Danish mercenaries would have balanced any losses at Stamford Bridge. Housecarls and thanes would form the front ranks of the shieldwall, seconded by their retainers to the rear.

The Norman army, by contrast, was an all-arms force of heavy cavalry, archers and heavy infantry. The most significant element, socially and tactically, was the cavalry. The Bayeux Tapestry shows that the

Directions

Left of the A2100 from Hastings, on the slope leading up to Battle Abbey. Reach the battlefield and visitor centre from the village side, to the north.

Norman cavalry had not yet completed their evolution into the fully armoured knights of the later Middle Ages. Similar in appearance to English housecarls, many Normans used their lance overarm, an ancient technique familiar to Roman cavalrymen. Others couched their lances under their arms, using stirrups and high saddles to concentrate the whole momentum of horse and rider into the lance point. The resulting shock was such that the Byzantine princess Anna Comnena considered it would carry a Frankish knight through the walls of Babylon. Only one or two Norman cavalry are shown throwing their lances javelin fashion into the English ranks. The archers' part in the battle is well known. They probably used a mixture of conventional bows and crossbows, although the Bayeux Tapestry shows only the former. The inferior social status of the heavy infantry has obscured their role in the battle, which seems to have been a mixture of missile and close action. William of Poitiers, chaplain to the Conqueror, describes them exchanging javelin shots as well as blows with the English.

Numbers are uncertain, as with all battles of the period. Disregarding the chroniclers' more risible efforts, modern estimates range from 4000 to 15,000 English and 4400 to 10,000 Normans. Most attribute superior numbers to the former, although the impartial William of Malmesbury wrote that 'Harold reached Hastings accompanied by very few knights', adding 'they were few in number, but brave in the extreme'. The *Chronicle* hints at treachery: Harold gave battle only 'with those men who wanted to support him'.

Robert Wace (a Norman) admitted William had more knights and archers. If Harold occupied somewhat less than the whole frontage available to him, with 6 ranks instead of the 10 or 12 estimated by Oman, he would have fielded 6000 men, slightly fewer than the most likely guess of 7000 Normans, including 2000–3000 horsemen. Morale could have been high on both sides. The Normans, salt water at their backs, spent the night confessing their sins. The English, buoyed up by their recent victory, are said to have spent the night carousing in the old heroic style, singing 'Bublie ... Weissel ... and Drincheheil', and it is hard to conceive any 11th century abbot disobeying such an order.

The site of the Battle of Hastings ought to be one of the most precisely located of all medieval battles. By the Conqueror's command the High Altar of Battle Abbey was built at the spot where Harold fell beside the Wyvern banner of Wessex. Today, English Heritage provides a visitor centre and information panels to interpret the battlefield, and the ruined abbey is open to the public. The many advantages of the English position dispose of clichéd characterizations of their commander as an impetuous bruiser. Far from attempting to rush the Norman camp, he deliberately occupied a strong position astride the main A2100 road. The hill where Battle village now stands is about 1100 yards (1000 m) wide and 150 yards (137 m) deep. A narrow isthmus with steep slopes either side joined it to the Wealden hills to the north. To the south it slopes down into the marshy bottom of Sandlake brook. The road originally crossed the hill's highest point, running straight through Battle Abbey. Gardens now obscure the original contours, and there are more trees than in 1066.

Strategically Harold had bottled William up in his bridgehead, while a revived English fleet threatened his cross-Channel communications. Tactically Harold's choice of ground handicapped William's key weapon systems. The gentle southern slope slowed cavalry charges and reduced the effect of arrows, which would tend to go over the defenders' heads or into their shields. Boggy ground on the flanks and woods to the rear inhibited turning manoeuvres. Various interpretations of Harold's tactical deployment are on offer. Differences focus on the frontage occupied and the extent to which the flanks were refused. The most modern studies recommend a straight line more or less along the 250-foot (76-m) contour, extending 400 yards (360 m) west and 200–400 yards (180–360 m) east of Harold's position, perhaps as far as the Chequers inn, or the school down the Sedlescombe road. The only criticism of the position is that it was cramped, preventing casualty evacuation or manoeuvre. However, the ideal medieval formation was one so close that an apple could not fall between the ranks. The tighter the files the more hand-strokes could be delivered from every unit of frontage, the contemporary equivalent of a higher rate of fire.

Duke William's response to Harold's appearance challenges the traditional view of medieval battles as mere scrambles over a convenient hillside. William's complex deployment and subsequent handling of the battle are generally regarded as flawless. His achievement is especially remarkable as Hastings was

William's first experience of independent command in a large set-piece battle. The Norman army marched northwest from Hastings along Blackhorse Hill at dawn, just before 7 a.m., cavalry at the rear of the column, which prevented them outpacing their supporting arms. Visual contact with the enemy would be established about 8 a.m., probably from Telham Hill. While leaders conferred, the knights put on their armour. William had an awkward choice, whether to deploy close to the English position, between Sandlake and the foot of the slope, or further back. The nearer start line (200 yards/360 m from the enemy) avoids the boggy valley bottom, but might expose the Normans to a spoiling attack before they had deployed. The more distant forming up point (600 yards/550 m from the enemy) is safer, but forces the attackers to advance through the marsh. A.H. Burne, with professional caution, preferred the latter. More recent reconstructions place the Normans at the foot of the hill, just outside bowshot.

William's battle plan is celebrated for making best possible use of the forces at his disposal. Three successive waves of archers, heavy infantry and cavalry would soften up, break into and ride down the (by now) disorganized English. Normans formed the centre, with wings of Breton and French allies to left and right. These divisions are conventionally shown as equal in size, although no one knows their actual strengths. The plan did not work as intended. Archers emptied their quivers into the English ranks, whose failure to respond in kind compelled the Normans to cease shooting as they ran out of arrows. Heavy infantry went in, to be crushed by a hail of spears and savage axe blows. Supporting waves of cavalry took their place in the front line, with no better success:

> The English were helped by the advantage of their higher position, which, massed tightly together, they held without attempting to advance. They also had a great numerical advantage and they kept their ranks very close. What is more the weapons with which they fought easily cut through shields and other protective armour.
>
> William of Poitiers, *Gesta Guillelmi ducis Normannorum et regis Anglorum* (late 11th century)

The English drove the Normans back, even wounding those who threw javelins from a distance. William of Poitiers admits the infantry and Breton cavalry 'turned in flight, terrified by this sudden onslaught'. Most likely the Norman knights did too. In the hurly-burly the duke was thought killed, until he rode after his fleeing knights, 'bellowing at them and threatening them with his lance'. He did more than stabilize the position, leading his rallied troops back into the melee to encircle and cut down 'thousands' of pursuing English. The dramatic result of the English advance suggests Harold may have attempted to launch a decisive counterattack, too early in the day. His brothers Gyrth and Leofwine may have been killed at this time, effectively decapitating the English army.

One of the most vexed debates over Hastings has concerned the Norman use of 'feigned retreats' to disorganize the English ranks. According to William of Poitiers, these were a deliberate ploy inspired by the Conqueror's riposte against those English who had left the safety of their shieldwall. Military critics have decried the idea as impossible to organize in the heat of battle. Academic commentators have pointed to other examples of feigned retreats, and to the undoubted expertise of Norman knights in small-unit tactics. In reality, unless a cavalry charge drives all before it, the horsemen must fall back when they lose momentum, before trying again. Cavalry were a novelty on English battlefields; English infantrymen would have been unused to the mobility of horsemen. They might easily have followed retreating cavalry to finish off stragglers or recover missile weapons, only to be outpaced, and cut off from their own lines.

Whatever tactical euphemisms are employed, the second phase of the struggle was a battle of attrition,

Hastings

	Winner	*Loser*
Opponents	Norman	English
Commanders	William, Duke of Normandy	Harold Godwinson (k)

as successive Norman cavalry charges wore down their opponents. William lost three horses killed under him, and fought on foot with a broken lance stump, 'more often heard shouting to them to follow him than ordering them to go ahead' (William of Poitiers). Despite losses, the English continued closely massed on their hill, shouting abuse at their attackers, or the enigmatic battle cry, 'Out! Out!':

> The fighting ... was most unusual, for one side continued the attack in a series of charges and individual assaults, while the other stood firm as if rooted to the ground ... The dead as they tumbled to the ground, showed more sign of motion than the living.
>
> William of Poitiers, ibid.

After six hours fighting, despite the technical superiority of the Norman archers and cavalry, the battle hung in the balance. The Tapestry suggests it was ended by a return to combined tactics. While the knights continue their attacks in the central panel of the Tapestry, an almost uninterrupted procession of 23 archers shoot them in from the lower frieze, with enormous quivers stacked before them. Modern authorities squabble over the relative efficacy of high- or low-angle shooting. The German scholar Delbrück thought the archers plied their bows between cavalry charges, an alternation of missile and shock action suggested by the chronicler's phrase '*sagittant et perfodiant*' ('they shot arrows and thrust spears').

Finally the Normans breached the shieldwall, and slaughtered Harold's bodyguard. One of the Tapestry's most horrible scenes shows a mailed knight grabbing a disarmed Englishman by the hair, before chopping off his head. Two separate figures under the comment '*Haroldus Interfectus Est*' ('Harold is killed') show him shot in the eye and cut down, like successive images in a strip cartoon. Residual stitch marks for an arrow in the second figure's eye suggest they both represent the same person. William of Malmesbury confirms that the leader's death was decisive, as always in medieval battles: 'When Harold fell with his brain pierced by a blow from an arrow, the English fled headlong.' Surviving housecarls were in no state to fight on: 'those who remained were exhausted and at the end of their tether', while 'the Normans seemed as strong as ever' (William of Poitiers). The Tapestry ends with a disarmed rout fleeing on foot or flogging their horses, the urgency underlined by a frieze of naked and dismembered bodies. Many words have been wasted on a final clash at the so-called Malfosse, into which pursuing Normans are supposed to have ridden in the gathering darkness. The incident derives from confused additions to earlier sources, and was too late to affect the outcome.

Casualty figures at Hastings are no more certain than the numbers engaged. Two indicators suggest heavy losses on both sides. William followed up with caution, only entering London after the arrival of reinforcements via Portsmouth and Chichester. The English offered no resistance to the Norman *chevauchée* through the Home Counties that ended with the Duke's consecration as king at Westminster at Midwinter 1066. William I faced revolts and guerrilla warfare, but no further challenges in the open field. After an unsuccessful attempt to rule an integrated kingdom, he eliminated English bishops and magnates from the ruling élite, and their language from the courts.

Historians still debate the results of the Norman Conquest. Carlyle rejoiced at William's overthrow of the 'gluttonous race of Jutes and Angles ... lumbering about in pot-bellied equanimity'. Richardson and Sayles denounced the Normans as barbarians just 'becoming conscious of their insufficiency'. The immediate consequences of William's victory are clearer. A small military caste dominated the country from small, easily defended castles. Norman kings held their throne by force, a point emphasized by the introduction of trial by combat. William's successors counted their precedence from 1066, disregarding Old English monarchs of the same name. William of Malmesbury, a child of both peoples, saw Hastings as 'a fateful day for England, a sad destruction of our beloved fatherland, for it now passed into the hands of new masters'.

PART THREE

KNIGHT AND CASTLE

Feudal Warfare 1022–1328

The period after the Norman Conquest was one of consolidation across the North Atlantic Archipelago, which now developed a distinctive regional identity. With typical energy the Normans hammered into shape the four nations that still define the main political and cultural boundaries of the area. This might have been expected to be productive of armed conflict, and sometimes was. Few battles, however, occurred in England during the two centuries after Hastings, compared with the previous two hundred years. Armed conflict moved to England's borders, or beyond them into her neighbours' territory.

The Norman Conquest strengthened and enriched English central government. The great Anglo-Saxon earldoms of Wessex, Mercia and Northumbria were suppressed, making the county the unit of local administration, too small and numerous to become a focus for dissent. William the Conqueror's atrocious Harrying of the North did at least stamp out the separatism that had tempted so many adventurers, from Olaf Guthfrithsson to Harald Hardrada. A united England became part of a cross-Channel empire, facing south into France instead of north towards Scandinavia. Norman kings and their Angevin and Plantagenet successors conducted their wars overseas, financed by English taxes. Invasions became rarities. A last Danish ship-army refused action in 1075, intimidated by Lincolnshire fyrdsmen who cut their hair short and dressed like Normans. The only maritime invasion of the period was at the invitation of dissident barons in 1216. It collapsed after an infant royal navy intercepted reinforcements off Sandwich (1217). Every one of the pitched battles fought in England during the

12th and 13th centuries occurred during a civil war, when anxiety not to damage their own economic base impelled antagonists to seek prompt resolution of their differences. The contemporary William of Malmesbury wrote of Robert of Gloucester's decision to seek battle at Lincoln (1141) that he 'preferred risking extremities, to prolonging the suffering of the country'.

Battles were a rare and dangerous option for medieval commanders, compelled by tactical necessity and social custom to lead from the front. Victory was considered an expression of God's will rather than the result of tactical skill. To fight a battle demanded unusual confidence in one's relationship with the Almighty. William the Marshal, 'the best knight in the world', only fought two battles in his life, including Lincoln (1217). Edward I, for all his crusades and conquests, fought only three: Lewes (1264), Evesham (1265) and Falkirk (1298). Warfare was less concerned with seeking victory through battle than with exerting economic pressure upon the enemy by laying waste his land, or gaining control of it by capturing his castles. The presence of some 1250 castles across England inhibited mobile warfare, and reduced the significance of victory in the field. Sieges were numerous, and some resulted in battles: Lincoln and Stockbridge (1141), Alnwick (1174), Lincoln (1217) and Bannockburn (1314). The usual experience of war was burnt-out houses, ransacked barns, trampled corn and a terrified population. Nevertheless the importance of battles in medieval warfare should not be underestimated. Often they were the culmination of prolonged hostilities: Lincoln (1217), for example, ended a two-year civil war. The earlier battle there nearly ended King Stephen's career for good. Castles could delay but not prevent full-scale invasions, such as the Scottish incursions that were defeated at Northallerton (1138) and Alnwick (1174).

Replacement of an Anglo-Saxon king by dukes of Normandy had serious consequences for England's neighbours. Later Anglo-Saxon kings did little to extend their rule into Scotland or Wales, broadly accepting the status quo. The Normans were more dynamic, exploiting the military potential of a nation whose territory was half as big again as either of its larger neighbours. Demography was even more biased in England's favour. Medieval population data is speculative, but reasonable estimates suggest there were 2.25 million English in 1066 compared with 1 million Scots and 300,000 Welsh. Ireland came somewhere between, with 500,000 or more.

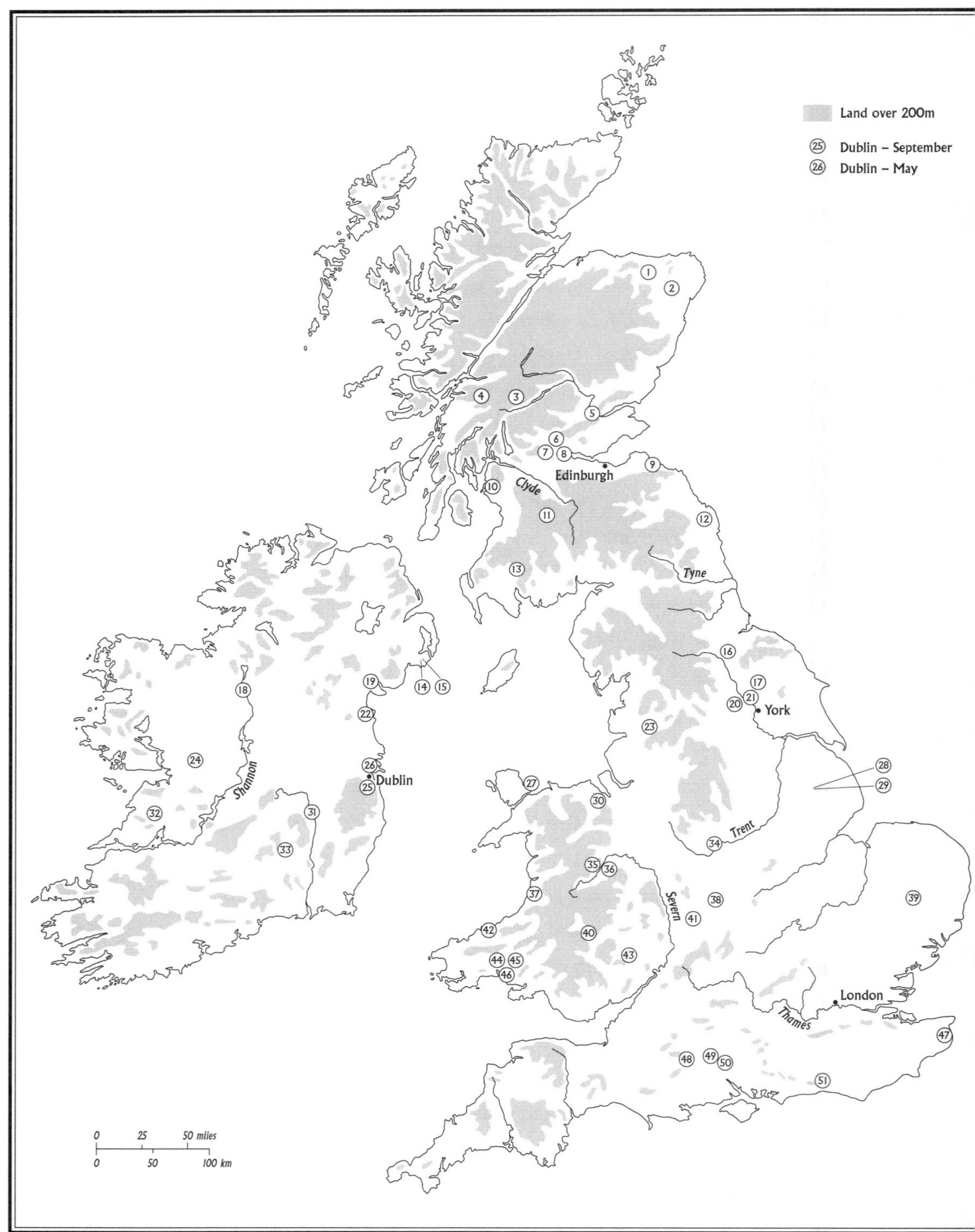
Land over 200m
25 Dublin – September
26 Dublin – May
Edinburgh
Clyde
Tyne
York
Dublin
Shannon
Trent
Severn
London
Thames
0 25 50 miles
0 50 100 km

Responses to Norman aggression varied in style and effectiveness. Kings of Scotland discreetly adopted castles and knight service, becoming Anglo-Norman in culture and manners. Intermarriage between descendants of Malcolm Ceann Mor and William the Conqueror moderated Anglo-Scots conflict; David I was Earl of Huntingdon before he became King of Scots. English superiority usually deterred Scottish adventures south of the Border. William the Conqueror could call on some 5000 knights, while William the Lion of Scotland may have summoned 100 for the invasion that led to his capture at Alnwick (1174). A contemporary reckoned Scotland's chief military assets were difficult terrain and a tough population, 'neither overcome by excess of cold, or enfeebled by severe hunger, putting their trust in swiftness of foot and light equipment' (*Gesta Stephani*). When an English feudal host marched north, prudent Scots commanders avoided action, as David I did in 1136. In 1322 the Scots laid their own country waste before Edward II's invading army, considering a scorched-earth policy less risky than offering battle. Early Anglo-Scots battles arose from Scottish attempts to exploit English preoccupation elsewhere, for example at Northallerton (1138) during the Anarchy of Stephen's reign, or Alnwick (1174) during the Young King's Revolt against Henry II.

Despite Scotland's relative weakness, the blending of feudalism with traditional Scottish society created a stable monarchy and a sound basis for Anglo-Scots relations. In 1237 the Treaty of York renounced Scottish claims upon England's northern counties, confirming the Border as it now stands. For 60 years England and Scotland enjoyed one of the most peaceful periods in their history, until Edward I's insatiable ambition and the accidental extinction of the Scots royal house spawned the horrors of the Scottish Wars of Independence.

KEY

1 Slioch 1307
2 Barra 1308
3 Dail Righ 1306
4 Pass of Brander 1309
5 Methven 1306
6 Stirling Bridge 1297
7 Bannockburn 1314
8 Falkirk I 1298
9 Dunbar 1296
10 Largs 1263
11 Loudon Hill 1307
12 Alnwick II 1174
13 Glen Trool 1307
14 Down I 1177
15 Down II 1260
16 Northallerton 1138
17 Byland 1322
18 Athankip 1270
19 Faughart 1318
20 Boroughbridge 1322
21 Myton-on-Swale 1319
22 Balibragan 1329
23 Clitheroe 1138
24 Athenry 1316
25 Dublin 1171 (May)
26 Dublin 1171 (Sept)
27 Priestholm 1098
28 Lincoln 1141
29 Lincoln 1217
30 Coleshill 1157
31 Athy 1359
32 Dysart O'Dea 1318
33 Clais an Chro 1169
34 Burton-upon-Trent 1322
35 Maes Moydog 1295
36 Rhyd-y-Groes 1039
37 Aberystwyth 1116
38 Kenilworth 1265
39 Fornham 1173
40 Irfon Bridge 1282
41 Evesham 1265
42 Crug Mawr 1136
43 Hereford 1055
44 Abergwyli 1022
45 Cymerau 1257
46 Maes Gwenllian 1136
47 Sandwich 1217
48 Wilton 1143
49 Stockbridge 1141
50 Winchester 1141
51 Lewes 1264

Wales and Ireland were different. Politically divided and militarily weak, they almost demanded intervention. The physical obstacles that hindered invaders also divided Wales and Ireland into a patchwork of mutually antagonistic princedoms. Family relationships – like the Irish *derbfhine*, which permitted four generations of a king's descendants to compete for the succession – encouraged internecine strife in both countries. Between 1100 and 1125 six members of Powys's ruling dynasty were killed, blinded or castrated by relatives. English writers contrasted England's settled society with the barbaric world beyond the Marches: 'a country of woodland and pasture ... [which] breeds men of an animal type, naturally swift footed, accustomed to war, volatile always in breaking their word as in changing their abode' (*Gesta Stephani*). William I's marcher earldoms at Chester, Shrewsbury and Hereford formed the base for a huge pincer movement along the narrow Welsh coastal strips, north and south. Sixty nautical miles (111 km) from the Liffey, Wales provided a stepping stone to Ireland. Henry I's grant of Ceredigion to Gilbert de Clare in 1110, 'if he could win it from the Welsh', was the kind of speculation at local people's expense that became common in Ireland.

The diversion of Norman energy from Wales to Ireland in 1169 left the conquest of both unfinished. Initial advances in both countries were swift, but the locals picked up the invaders' military techniques, or learned to exploit the defensive potential of their impenetrable mountains and bogs. English kings before Edward I lacked the resources or energy to overthrow local Welsh rulers. They preferred to play them off against unruly marcher lords, or left them to fight one another. Independent princes of Gwynedd held out in North Wales until the 1280s, assisted by impossible terrain and horrible weather. In Ireland there were too few invaders to provide more than a feudal veneer, and the Irish Normans went happily native. When Anglo-Norman settlers killed the 'English' Justiciar at Balibragan in 1329, his Irish harper was among the casualties. Outside the far northwest, Irish kings had largely succumbed by the reign of King John, but Gaelic culture survived until that of Elizabeth.

The military superiority that asserted English overlordship across Britain and Ireland depended on two interrelated weapon systems: the armoured cavalryman, known as a knight or *miles*, and the castle. Knights and castles are the classic symbols of medieval warfare. They were a capital-intensive application of resources to war, money and labour pouring into limited numbers of each to achieve a decisive superiority of fighting power. Such was their advantage over traditional modes of fighting that ridiculously small numbers of knights could subdue whole countries: England in the 1060s; Ireland in the 1170s.

The knight rode a specialized horse known as a destrier, bred and trained for war. A long mail coat (hauberk) with a hood protected the rider, supplemented by an iron cap with a nose guard. Armour was impenetrable by arrows fired from over 50 yards (45 m), and provided an immense moral and physical advantage to its owner. Unprotected combatants were described as *inermis* or naked. Mail was little encumbrance to its user. Evenly distributed over the body, it weighed 25–30 lbs (11–14 kg), a fifth of the load British infantry carried during the Falklands War. Accustomed from boyhood to bear arms, a fully armed knight could vault into the saddle or climb a scaling ladder. Offensive weapons were the 10-foot (3-m) lance, increasingly held rigidly under the arm, and the sword, a single-handed slashing weapon with a double-edged 34-inch (85-cm) blade. There was no major change in a knight's equipment between the Norman Conquest and the Scottish Wars of Independence, except for the adoption of horse armour. Mail became more costly and extensive, as the blacksmith's skill extended to mittens and leggings. The kite-shaped shields used at Hastings became curved and shorter, perhaps to facilitate fighting on foot. Heraldic devices appeared during the late 12th century to distinguish combatants encased in a mass of iron. Some knights enhanced their anonymity by sporting the great helm, an enclosed headpiece, which also reduced visibility.

Knights were expensive to equip and run. An early Frankish warhorse cost as much as 23 oxen – nearly three plough teams. A hauberk of King John's reign cost £2, equivalent to 15 oxen. The daily feed for a 14th-century warhorse cost 2d., an infantryman's wages, and every horseman required several mounts. Knights provided military service in return for a parcel of land known as a fee or *feodum*, held of the king or some other magnate. This was the economic basis of what historians have called the feudal system, although arrangements were so unsystematic as to make the term meaningless. Younger sons without a fee might serve for pay, in companies of mercenaries or as household knights. These resembled the ancient German *comitatus*, and provided the permanent core of royal armies. King John had 375 household knights in 1215, Edward I had 800 at Falkirk in 1298, and all great men, even bishops, were accompanied by retinues in proportion to their rank. Stephen's household provided command expertise for the scratch English army at Northallerton in 1138. The expense of knighthood escalated during the 12th and 13th centuries, encouraging the appearance of similar but cheaper cavalry, known as sergeants, *scutifers* or squires. They swelled the numbers of men-at-arms without undermining their social cohesion or battlefield superiority.

Castles provided a force multiplier that allowed 5000 knights to dominate over 2 million English in the early years of the Conquest. Castles were small and highly defensible. Anglo-Saxon burghs of 25 acres (10 ha) were large enough to accommodate a threatened community. Norman castles occupied 2 or 3 acres (0.8–1.2 ha), sufficient to house a leader and his retinue, and to protect them from the local community. The classic motte and bailey consisted of earth embankments topped with wooden palisades, like those illustrated in the Bayeux Tapestry. They could be built quickly using local material and labourers, who thus contributed to their own subjection. Massive square stone structures known as keeps still stand at key points, such as London, Dover or Rochester. Stone generally replaced wood during the 12th century, and a curtain wall with multiple towers replaced the single keep, but some 200 Conquest-period castles were still in use during the civil wars of John's reign. Castles were equally effective along the English frontier. Hundreds of mottes were thrown up along the Marches. Often within sight of one another, they presented an impenetrable barrier to Welsh incursions like that which had led to the English rout at Hereford in 1154. Beyond the Marches, castles set the seal on Norman occupation. Cardigan Castle was the only place to hold out when the battle of Crug Mawr restored Ceredigion to Welsh rule in 1136. Robert Fitzstephen held Carrick-on-Slaney against the men of Kinsale in 1171 with five knights and a few archers, 'whereas they had but a ditch or hedge upon a little stone wall' (*Book of Howth*). He only surrendered when two Irish bishops falsely swore that Strongbow had been massacred at Dublin with all his companions.

Although knights were socially and militarily dominant, most combatants fought on foot. Neglected by sources written under knightly influence, foot soldiers outnumbered their superiors five or ten to one. In the early 13th century the borough of Dunstable provided nine short infantry mail shirts and one long cavalryman's hauberk for royal hosts. The first Norman expedition to Ireland consisted of 30 knights, 60 other horsemen and 300 archers, carried in three ships. Longbows were cheap and potentially decisive weapons. Magnus Barefoot of Norway turned back the Norman advance into North Wales at Priestholm (1098) by shooting Hugh the Fat in the eye. Bows were particularly prominent on the Welsh Marches. The Normans learned from the archers of South Wales, celebrated by Gerald of Wales in the 13th century as being able to pin a knight's leg to his horse through two layers of mail. Edward I's armies included thousands of archers, although many infantry still turned up with swords and daggers. Crossbows were always an oddity on British battlefields, although high rates of pay reflected their elite status. Their accuracy made them especially deadly at Lincoln (1217), where the siege conditions made their low rate of fire a matter of little importance.

Inhabiting rugged terrain and with scant industry, the Celts used little armour. Gerald described the Welsh using 'light weapons which do not impede their quick movements, small leather corselets, handfuls of arrows, long spears and round shields'. A minority possessed iron helmets or greaves. In view of the marshy and uneven terrain, they fought mostly as infantry. The few Welsh horsemen would often dismount, ready to flee or attack. The southern Welsh used the bow, but in the north the spear was supreme.

The Irish were as poorly equipped. As late as 1260 Brian O'Neill was killed with eight chiefs of Connacht in an unequal battle at Downpatrick. As an old poem puts it:

> Fine linen shirts on the race of Conn,
> The Foreigners one mass of iron.

Irish nobles rode barefoot as late as the 1390s. Gerald described the characteristic Irish weapon as the axe, carried like a staff, so that: 'if they have a feeling for any evil, they can the more quickly give it effect'. From the mid-13th century these weapons were used by mercenaries known as *galloglaigh* or gallowglasses imported from the Scottish islands. Their arrival was a turning point in Anglo-Irish warfare. Dressed in knee-length mail shirts and conical iron helmets that came down over the neck, the gallowglass was arrow-proof, and could withstand a Norman charge.

Celtic success on the battlefield usually depended on avoiding confrontation. They did better to wear the enemy out with tiresome marches, or lure them into ambushes, as at Stirling Bridge (1297), Athankip (1270) and Cymerau (1257). When unarmoured Galloway tribesmen charged an English phalanx at Northallerton they were shot to bits, as the English leader predicted in his pre-battle speech. During the Wars of Independence the Scots fought successfully in dense masses of spearmen known as schiltrons, but it was Robert the Bruce's raiding strategy that reduced English statesmen to despair. The stunning Scots victory at Bannockburn was an aberration. William Wallace's defeat at Falkirk (1298) was the more usual result of challenging a mixed army of knights and archers with an outnumbered force of spearmen with few cavalry or missile troops.

Much nonsense has been written about the incompetence of medieval armies and their commanders. An unprejudiced review of such battles as Alnwick (1174), Lincoln (1217) or Evesham (1265) shows that leaders of the period employed sound and occasionally brilliant tactics, appropriate to the forces at their disposal. Medieval armies were rarely larger than a modern brigade group (about 5000), and more often of regimental strength (about 1000). William the Marshal fielded 406 knights and 317 crossbows at Lincoln in 1217, besides foot sergeants. Treaties and payroll data shows that chroniclers grossly exaggerated the size of armies. Henry I hired 1000 knights from the Count of Flanders in 1101, while Henry III's two Welsh expeditions in the 1220s employed 387 and 585 knights respectively. The largest army deployed by a medieval English government was the 28,000 men fielded at Falkirk (1298), at the height of the Scots Wars of Independence. The English population had risen to nearly 6 million since 1066, making earlier armies unlikely to have exceeded those of the 1290s. Celtic armies, with no settled agrarian base, will have been smaller. Claims that Gwynedd fielded 8000 men at Crug Mawr (1136) are laughable. Edward I overran North Wales in the 1280s with forces whose payrolls numbered less than half that.

Lack of numbers inhibited complex manoeuvres and set a premium on rapid decision-making, subsequently criticized as rashness. Medieval commanders needed the qualities of regimental cavalry officers or foxhunters, a quick eye for ground and the sort of dash that pulled off the surprise capture of William the Lion at Alnwick. The skill of such leaders as Robert of Gloucester, William the Marshal, Simon de Montfort or Edward I is the more remarkable as their experience of battle was limited, preventing the accumulation of expertise. Not until the Scots Wars of Independence did leaders fight sufficient battles to develop the tactical understanding that lay behind the changes that ended the knight's predominant role on the battlefield in the early 14th century.

Medieval armies possessed sound tactics, supported by appropriate organization. Their characteristic division into three or four wings or *batailles* is not dissimilar to the structure of modern formations. It allows for refusing a flank in response to outflanking moves, attacking on a broad or narrow front, and withholding a reserve. *Batailles* consisted in turn of squadrons and troops: *échielles* and *conrois* in the contemporary vernacular. Where 20 knights and sergeants might follow a banneret, infantry were led by vintenars and centenars in 20s and 100s. The inappropriate use by monastic chroniclers of outmoded Latin terms has obscured this rational hierarchy. There is no more reason to suppose that their legions and cohorts represent classically formed bodies of infantry than that their *cunei* were triangular wedges. *Gesta Stephani* describes groups of knights fighting as *armatorum cunei* inside Wherwell Priory, where any formation would be impossible. William Rishanger (*fl.* later 13th century) refers to Scottish schiltrons as *cuneos*, although other sources plainly describe them as circular. The major divisions of a medieval army were named according to their position on the line of march: vanguard or vaward, main, and rearward or reregarde. The van typically took the right flank in action, the rearward the left, but neither spelling nor deployment was consistent.

Medieval units lacked the group training of their modern equivalents, but possessed individual bonds of discipline just as powerful. Aristocrats spent their lives preparing for war, in hunting, tourneys or private feuds. The pastoral Welsh were preoccupied with military training, always dreaming of war, climbing mountain peaks, and practising with spears and arrows. Leaders were careful to marshal their forces before battle, as Simon de Montfort did before Lewes (1264), to ensure everyone knew his place. At Wilton (1143) Robert of Gloucester 'in soldierly fashion, carefully divided those he had brought with him in three bodies of men closely packed together, and heavily charging his opponents with the greatest resolution compelled the king to give ground'. *Brut y Twysogion* ('Chronicle of the Princes') criticized the disorderly advance of the Welsh at Aberystwyth in 1116 as 'a villain host'. Close order maximized the fighting power of short-range weapons, concentrating the maximum number of blows on the shortest frontage. Continental sources described 'such close formations that the wind could not blow between their lances'. Knights fought in groups, not as individuals, despite modern claims to the contrary. Royalist knights tried jousting at Lincoln (1141), but were soundly beaten by close-order opponents charging with drawn swords.

Once committed to a melee, a force quickly lost cohesion. Sheer noise prevented communication, and defied thought. An Anglo-Irish *chanson de geste* contained in the 16th-century *Book of Howth* compared the noise of weapons upon helmets to 'hundreds of forges with their smiths and others with hammers and sledges beating upon anvils of steel'. Intelligent commanders provided reserves to compensate for loss of control. Simon de Montfort may have owed his victory over superior numbers at Lewes (1264) to timely deployment of a fourth *bataille* held in reserve. David I's four *batailles* at Northallerton were tactically superior to the solid English phalanx, although he failed to realize their potential. Bodies of infantry might provide a rallying point for disorganized cavalry, although they notably did not at Lincoln (1141) or Lewes (1264). Norman knights were remarkable for their readiness to dismount to support their infantry. During the 13th century, English knights became less willing to do so. At Lewes and Evesham the cavalry preceded the footmen, involving them in their rout when defeated. There is no evidence that Edward I, or any of his magnates, dismounted at Falkirk. The disastrous showing of English chivalry at Bannockburn discredited the mounted charge. Edward II's later years saw the first attempt, at Boroughbridge (1322), to deploy archers supported by dismounted men-at-arms, a technique that proved unbeatable during the following reign.

The Anarchy

The reign of King Stephen (1135–54) is one of the most notorious episodes of English medieval history, when God and his angels memorably slept. Dynastic struggles were common enough in Anglo-Norman England, but Stephen's reign was distinguished by the duration and inconclusiveness of the succession dispute, which lasted almost until his death. The concentration of battles around 1140 was also unusual, underscoring the bitterness of the struggle. Northallerton (1138), Lincoln (1141) and Wilton (1142) were the only formal actions fought in England during the 12th century, supplemented by the remarkable campaign and double siege of Winchester that culminated in the Rout of Stockbridge (1141).

England had been relatively peaceful during the reigns of the Conqueror's immediate successors William Rufus and Henry I. Military operations were restricted to the plundering and minor sieges that accompanied baronial revolts. Henry I fought a few pitched battles in Normandy, notably at Tinchebrai (1106) and Brémule (1119). When the Conqueror's direct legitimate male line died out in 1135, his grandson Stephen of Blois seized the throne at the expense of his cousin Matilda, Henry's daughter and the wife of Geoffrey, Count of Anjou. The usurper faced a series of military challenges from dissident magnates, the most significant of whom was David I, King of Scots and Matilda's uncle. Stephen had confirmed David's son Henry as Earl of Huntingdon, and ceded him Carlisle, but this statesmanlike generosity failed to prevent a devastating series of Scottish attacks. The invaders had advanced within 30 miles (50 km) north of York when local forces defeated them at Northallerton.

The following year Matilda made her bid for the throne, supported by her illegitimate half-brother Robert, Earl of Gloucester, a respected figure and a competent soldier. The Angevins held the Severn valley against the king, but were never strong enough to land a knockout blow. Stephen fell into their hands after the Battle of Lincoln, but Matilda alienated potential supporters, while Robert was soon captured at Stockbridge. An exchange of key prisoners returned both sides to square one. Fortifications built to subdue the English now prevented a swift end to the war. William of Malmesbury wrote of castles throughout England, 'each defending, or more properly speaking laying waste, its neighbourhood'. Indecisive fighting continued for over a decade, while Geoffrey of Anjou overran Normandy. Only the death of Stephen's son Eustace in 1153 broke the stalemate, persuading Stephen to accept the succession of Matilda's son as Henry II.

Weapons and tactics had changed little since Hastings. Helmets covered more of the face, and additional pieces of mail on legs, arms and chest supplemented the basic hauberk. Enhanced protection altered the nature of casualties. Well-armed knights were difficult to kill, opening the prospect of taking prisoners for ransom. Stephen was only captured at Lincoln after being stunned by a rock and wrestled to the ground. Infantry played a significant supporting role in all the major engagements of Stephen's reign, continuing a trend set by Henry I at Tinchebrai, where dismounted knights provided a rallying point for the cavalry.

The most significant shift in military practice was increased employment of mercenaries. Norman kings had always hired individual *milites stipendiarii*, but the civil war's duration encouraged the emergence of permanent mercenary bands, bound together by the terrible things they had done. Where refugees had found peace in Henry I's England, under Stephen freebooters flocked in from the Low Countries 'in expectation of rich pillage'. The most important was William of Ypres, who restored Stephen's fortunes after Lincoln and became Earl of Kent. Robert Fitz-Hubert, on the other hand, was hanged by Robert of Gloucester after burning two dozen monks in a church, and exposing captives smeared with honey to wasps. Henry II's taxation records reveal the economic havoc wrought by such men. The *Peterborough Chronicle* lamented a general catastrophe: 'Then corn was dear, and flesh and butter and cheese, because there was none in the land. Wretched men starved with hunger ... Never before was there more wretchedness in the land.'

Clitheroe, 10 June 1138

England, Lancashire, LR103 SD7441?

Northallerton (the Battle of the Standard), 22 August 1138

England, North Yorkshire, LR99 SE3698

The Battle of the Standard was an oddity. In an age dominated by armoured cavalry, both sides fought on foot, while the outstanding feature of the action was the destruction of unprotected 'Picts' by Yorkshire bowmen. The battle's title came from a ship's mast fixed on a cart and hung with the banners of local saints and the body of Christ, a unique English example of the *carroccio* of Italian city militias. Two local contemporaries, Richard of Hexham and Ailred of Rievaulx, left accounts whose clarity has not prevented widespread misrepresentation of the battle's course. One 19th-century author even reversed the combatants' locations, leaving the Scots facing north.

David I invaded northern England three times in 1138, his nephew William winning an obscure victory at Clitheroe. In July the Scots moved down the east coast, reaching the Tees in mid-August. Archbishop Thurstan of York, assisted by Walter Espec, Sheriff of Yorkshire, and some of King Stephen's household knights under William of Aumale, persuaded local magnates to make a stand. They concentrated at Thirsk, a mixed bag of baronial retinues, civic militias and country people led by their priests. The banners of St Peter of York, St John of Beverley, St Wilfrid of Ripon and St Cuthbert of Durham flew in the centre of the host, reinforcing a crusading atmosphere inspired by the invaders' atrocities. On 21 August, as the Scots crossed the Tees, the English closed up to Northallerton overnight, and deployed about 2 miles (3 km) beyond the village.

The battlefield lies between the A167 Northallerton–Darlington road and the lane from Brompton to Oaktree Hill. The battlefield was then flat and open, '*in campo latissimo*'. A gentle downwards slope falling away towards watercourses on either flank encouraged the Scots to come straight on. Most reconstructions place the English on a hillock beside the roadside monument, facing the Scots on another low hill (217 feet/66 m) half a mile (0.8 km) to the north. A.H. Burne helpfully found both hills were known as Standard Hill. In addition, bone and metal fragments have turned up in Scotpit Lane (variously spelled), behind the supposed English position, suggesting they may have formed up further south, near Firtree Farm, rather than on either Standard Hill.

The English massed in column around their *carroccio*:

> The greater part of the knights, then dismounting, became foot soldiers, a chosen body of whom, interspersed with archers, were arranged in the front rank. The others, with the exception of those who were to dispose and rally the forces, mustered with the barons in the centre, near and around the Standard, and were enclosed by the rest of the host, who closed in on all sides.
>
> Richard of Hexham

As was customary, the English shook hands and swore to conquer or die, sending away their horses to make sure.

Numbers engaged are uncertain. Richard of Hexham's 26,000 Scots is plainly fantastic. Only 5000 appeared at Bannockburn (1314), the largest Scottish effort of the age. More reliable indicators are the 200 knights assigned to Prince Henry of Scots, or the 375

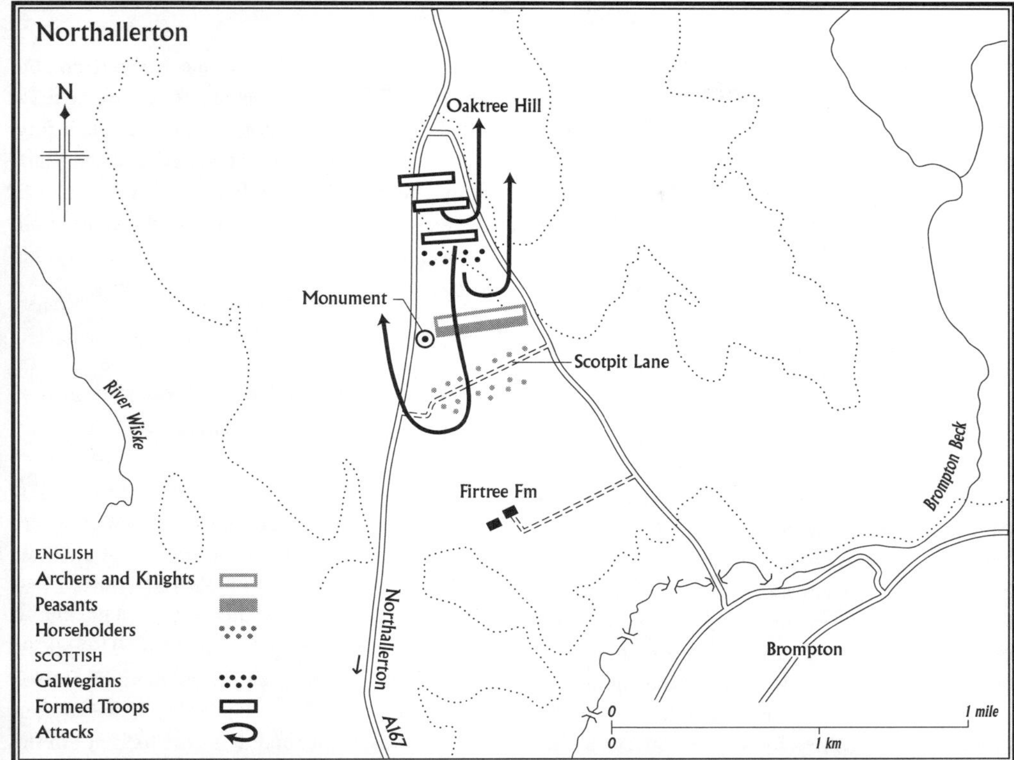

knights' fees owed by those English barons taking part for whom information is available. To them must be added knights sent by the king and archbishop. If both sides fielded several hundred knights, then comparison with later armies suggests their infantry numbered a few thousand each. The English may even have outnumbered the enemy. Contrary to some accounts, the archbishop was not present, being old and physically feeble.

King David intended his knights and archers to lead, but the Galloway men insisted upon their ancient right to attack first, unarmoured as they were: 'What use to the French were mail shirts at Clitheroe?' (Ailred). David gave in, rather than see his coalition of Anglo-Norman Lowlanders, Celtic Highlanders and Galwegians disintegrate. Prince Henry followed the Galwegians with his knights and archers, together with the men of Cumbria. The men of Lothian and the Hebrides came third, while the king held the Highlanders and Moray-men in reserve, with a personal bodyguard of knights.

Directions

Take the A167 Darlington road 2–3 miles (3–5 km) out of Northallerton to find the monument in a lay-by on the right-hand verge. Continue to Oaktree Hill and turn back down the minor road towards Brompton to see the other flank. Several tracks crossing the battlefield from east to west are private, including Scotpit Lane.

Modern accounts usually place the first three divisions in line, Prince Henry on the right, and the king behind the centre, but the sources do not support this. Ailred of Rievaulx describes Prince Henry's force as '*alteram aciem*', the other or second battle line. His narrative suggests the Scottish divisions attacked in succession, one after another, straight down the ridge. Richard of Hexham was less elaborate: 'In front of the battle were the Picts; in the centre, the king with his knights and English; the rest of the barbarian host roaring around them.'

Shrieking their awful war cry or *ululatum* the Galwegians charged with such force they drove the foremost English spearmen back, until rallied by the knights. Galwegian javelins broke against the defenders' shields, while archers shot the attackers to pieces: 'stuck with arrows all over, like a hedgehog's spines, the Galwegians ... waved their swords, now running forward in blind rage ... now beating the air with empty blows' (Ailred). Prince Henry charged through an unspecified English flank like a cobweb, and thinking his friends behind him, pressed on to the English horse lines. The experienced English knights, however, stolidly closed up their ranks. Displaying a conveniently severed head, some wily individual loudly proclaimed King David's death.

Caught between showers of arrows and knightly swords, the Galwegians fled, carrying away the Lowlanders. David dismounted to lead on his reserve, but 'the cowardly Scots' joined the other fugitives, 'so that in a short time few remained around the king'. Prince Henry's glorious survivors rode discreetly back, masquerading as English men-at-arms. Only 19 out of 200 returned uninjured, their equipment intact.

English chroniclers guessed wildly at 10,000–12,000 Scots casualties, more than both sides' combatants added altogether. The battle was over too quickly for such slaughter, being fought between the first and third hours, approximately 6–9.30 a.m. Richard of Hexham thought more perished after the fight than in the battle, as peasants took their revenge: 'wherever [Scotsmen] were discovered they were put to death like sheep'. Only one English notable perished, although Prince Henry must have done for many smaller fry. The victors got little advantage from their success. David resumed the siege of Wark, which surrendered in November. In the longer term Northallerton set a pattern for Anglo-Scots encounters from Dupplin Muir to Culloden, speed and ferocity going down before superior weaponry and tactics.

Clitheroe

	Winners	*Losers*
Opponents	Scots	English
Commanders	William, Prince of Scots	unknown

Northallerton

	Winners	*Losers*
Opponents	English	Scots
Commanders	Walter Espec William of Aumale	David I, King of Scots Henry, Prince of Scots

Lincoln, 2 February 1141

England, Lincolnshire, LR121 SK9671–72

Warfare in the 11th century revolved around castles. Stephen's only major battle in 17 years of civil war arose from a siege. Ranulf, Earl of Chester had treacherously seized Lincoln Castle, and the townspeople's complaints demanded a royal response. Stephen appeared before Lincoln about Christmas 1140, catching 17 of Ranulf's knights in the city, but the earl himself escaped. His wife held out in the castle with a small garrison. Ranulf was 'staunch to neither party' in the succession dispute between Stephen and his cousin Matilda, but he turned to his father-in-law, the Angevin leader Robert of Gloucester, for assistance. Stephen had isolated Matilda's supporters in western England, but his problems at Lincoln opened up a new front, offering Robert a chance of breaking the stalemate.

The two earls probably met at Claybrook in Leicestershire, at the junction of Watling Street and the Fosse Way (coming from Chester and Gloucester respectively), and followed the latter route over Newark's new bridge to Lincoln. Sources for the battle are not as good as those for Northallerton (1138), causing some debate over its site. Various factors point to the west side of the city. The castle lies there, making it the natural line of approach for a relieving army. The rebels crossed the swollen Fossdyke, a channel between the Rivers Trent and Witham that still runs south of Lincoln, and fought with the river at their backs, facing north or north-east. After the battle Stephen's defeated cavalry escaped into open country, i.e. northwards, while his infantry fled into the city. All this suggests the battle took place on the flat ground below the hill, between the city and the Fossdyke. Stephen had the slope in his favour, and may have hoped to destroy all his enemies at once. The Angevins had always refused action; now he seemed to have them at his mercy.

The Earl of Gloucester's willingness to force a battle under such difficulties suggests that the two rebel factions outnumbered the king. Stephen had probably brought few cavalry to a siege, apart from William of Ypres' mercenaries. Numerous earls were in attendance, but they had come without their knights, 'as if to a conference, and not a battle'. Against them were 'the disinherited', whose lands Stephen had confiscated for rebellion. Orderic Vitalis, a contemporary, thought 'the best knights and men-at-arms were in the king's army, but the enemy outnumbered them in infantry and Welsh allies'.

Both sides adopted Henry I's tactics. Knights strengthened infantry centres, with cavalry wings in front or on the flanks. Henry of Huntingdon's contemporary description of Stephen's formation is generally accepted:

> He himself took up position amidst a host of mailed knights, dismounted in close formation. The earls with their knights he stationed on horseback in two battle lines, but these squadrons appeared somewhat thin.

The rebels' deployment is less certain. Henry of Huntingdon enumerated them as if in order of march: first Ranulf of Chester, then the 'disinherited', third Robert of Gloucester. His narrative suggests Ranulf's men deployed on the right, the 'disinherited' forward on the left, and Robert's forces in the centre, the logical

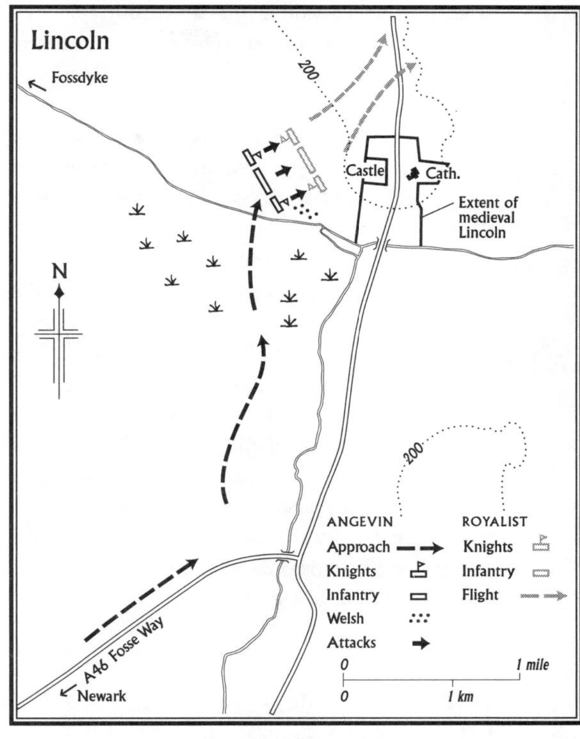

Directions

Follow Carholme Road, the A57 Worksop road, westwards past Brayford Pool. Turn right along Alderman's Walk between West Common and the houses that probably cover the battlefield.

place for the senior commander. Welsh spearmen from Gwynedd skirmished forward on the right flank, 'with more courage than skill at arms'.

The disinherited charged with such force they routed Stephen's earls 'in the twinkling of an eye'. William of Malmesbury said the Royalists had underestimated their opponents, treating the affair like a joust, 'but when they saw that the [rebel] party ... did not attack from a distance with lances, but at close-quarters with swords ... the earls to a man ... consulted their safety by flight'. William of Ypres rode down the Welsh on the other flank, but, encountering Earl Ranulf's battle, 'was scattered in a moment'. William, an experienced soldier

Lincoln

	Winners	*Losers*
Opponents	Angevin	Royalist
Commanders	Robert, Earl of Gloucester	Stephen (p)
	Ranulf, Earl of Chester	William of Ypres

of acknowledged valour joined the rout: 'perceiving that it was impossible to bring succour to the king, he deferred his aid to better times' (Henry of Huntingdon).

Stephen was left with his infantry in the midst of the enemy, who 'encircled the royal army and attacked it from all sides, as if they were assaulting a castle' (Henry of Huntingdon). For a while he defended himself with the two-handed axe of the Danelaw, 'grinding his teeth and foaming at the mouth like a boar'. When the axe broke, Stephen fought until his sword shattered, and a stone hit him on the head. William of Cahaines grabbed the royal helmet and shouted, 'Here, everyone, here! I have the king.' Once Stephen and his household knights were overcome, the remaining infantry surrendered or fled. Only 100 were killed in action, but 500 may have died during the sack of Lincoln. Stephen was carried off a prisoner to Bristol. The Angevins appeared to have won the war at a stroke.

Winchester (siege), **1 August–14 September 1141**

England, Hampshire, LR185 SU4829

Stockbridge, 14 September 1141

England, Hampshire, LR185 SU3535

Wilton, 1 July 1143

England, Wiltshire, LR184 unlocated

The Rout of Stockbridge is one of the most remarkable episodes of the 12th century. It followed a unique 'siege within a siege', staged in the heart of a city second only to London in importance. Scholars have neglected these events, despite their unusual interest and full documentation. This is a pity, as surviving roads and buildings reveal the scenes of action with unusual clarity.

The Angevin victory at Lincoln in February 1141 handed the kingdom to Matilda, Countess of Anjou. King Stephen was imprisoned at Bristol, 'to be kept there until the last breath of life', and his supporters crushed. Matilda's domineering behaviour soon fulfilled contemporaries' worst expectations of a woman ruler, alienating key supporters in London and the Church, especially Stephen's brother Henry of Blois, Bishop of Winchester. Expelled from London, Matilda launched a pre-emptive strike against Winchester, 'to catch the bishop if she could'. As she rode in one gate on 31 July, Henry rode out of another. He left garrisons in his fortified palace at Wolvesey and another at a castle in central Winchester. Wolvesey's remains still stand between the cathedral and the River Itchen. The other building may have been William the Conqueror's palace northwest of the cathedral, suggesting Henry's men occupied the cathedral close in the southeast corner of the city. The Angevins had the royal castle at the top of the High Street, now buried beneath the Law Courts. Firebrands were the 12th-century equivalent of phosphorous bombs, and much of the city was burnt, including St Mary's and Hyde Abbeys, and 40 of its 57 churches.

The siege became a trial of strength. The pro-Angevin William of Malmesbury claimed few barons attended the countess, but *Gesta Stephani* described 'a swarm of warriors', including David I of Scots, and the indispensable Robert of Gloucester, who installed his headquarters near St Swithun's Church. Stephen's faction was anxious to redeem the disgrace of Lincoln. Henry of Blois hired knights with melted silver from the ashes of Hyde Abbey. Stephen's queen, another Matilda, brought 'a splendid body of troops' from the Royalist redoubt of Kent: William of Ypres's Flemish mercenaries, and the remains of Stephen's household knights. A thousand Londoners marched down, 'magnificently equipped with helmets and coats of mail'.

Faced with such numbers the Angevins could neither storm the bishop's castles, nor invest them. The Royalists blockaded the city, reversing the combatants' roles, as the Angevins now found themselves besieged. While the Royalists picketed byroads on

Winchester

	Winners	Losers
Opponents	Royalist	Angevin
Commanders	William of Ypres Henry of Blois	Robert, Earl of Gloucester

Stockbridge

	Winners	Losers
Opponents	Royalist	Angevin
Commanders	William of Ypres Henry of Blois	Robert, Earl of Gloucester (p)

Wilton

	Winners	Losers
Opponents	Angevin	Royalist
Commanders	Robert, Earl of Gloucester	Stephen

the west to stop provisions reaching the city's 5000–6000 inhabitants, their own supplies crowded in from the east. In an attempt to breach the embargo, 200 or 300 Angevin knights fortified the priory at Wherwell on the Test, 10 miles (16 km) to the north-west, hard by the Roman road to Andover and Matilda's sources of supply in the Thames valley. The Royalists reacted with overwhelming force, clearing the church with burning torches. The *Gesta* describes in vivid eyewitness terms the horror of armed men ranging about the house of prayer engaged in mutual slaughter, while nuns ran shrieking through the flames, showered with boiling lead from the roof.

The Wherwell disaster persuaded the Angevins to abandon the stricken city. Collecting their baggage, they marched out of Westgate on 14 September, turning half right to gain the Stockbridge Road, leading westwards to safety. Matilda went ahead with an escort, while her brother covered the rear with 200 knights: 'a chosen few who had spirit enough not to be alarmed at a multitude' (William of Malmesbury). The Angevins started 'in close column, all retreating in one body' (*Gesta*), but superior numbers of Royalist cavalry attacked them from all sides, scattering the host. Earl Robert, 'the chief object of universal attack' (Malmesbury) kept his rearguard together across 8 1/2 miles (13.5 km) of hilly country until the steep slopes and flat marshy bottom of the Test valley crossed his path. Florence of Worcester, who obtained his information from Miles, Earl of Hereford, an Angevin survivor of the battle, wrote that Robert was then captured by Flemings at 'a place called Stolibricge', i.e. Stockbridge.

Persistent local tradition places Robert's last stand at a place then known as 'Le Strete'. This is now a roundabout, where the main Winchester road crosses the Andover–Romsey road, near Old St Peter's Church. A secondary branch of the River Test known as Marsh Stream ran here until it was filled in for the railway, which has also disappeared. Stockbridge itself stands on an artificial causeway described in Domesday Book. It was the only practicable crossing between Romsey and Andover, and gave Robert a chance to delay his pursuers, while Matilda disappeared among the folds of Danebury Down, beyond the Test. Alternatively, broken-down wagons could have jammed the causeway, giving Robert little choice about defending the ford at Le Strete.

Pinned against the Marsh Stream, his left flank open to attack from Andover, Robert was soon forced to surrender. He could afford to do so, being far too important to kill out of hand. Once resistance had ceased, the Royalists fanned out, seeking plunder or prisoners for ransom. Some of the fugitives escaped by throwing away their knightly arms and giving false names. Others found 'sordid hiding places', or were beaten up by peasants. King David was captured three times, bribing his captors to let him go. Matilda, 'superior to feminine softness', rode astride like a man, reaching Gloucester half dead with fatigue and fright.

The *dispersio Wintoniensis* ('rout of Winchester') was the astonishing climax of a seven weeks campaign, so unusual that 'the oldest of men could hardly remember one like it'. Gloucester was eventually exchanged for Stephen, despite his sporting insistence that his co-prisoners were exchanged with him, as a king was more valuable than an earl.

The Anarchy only saw one more significant action in the open, possibly at Wilton House near Salisbury.

Robert of Gloucester surprised Stephen improving Wilton Castle, deep in Angevin territory. The king advanced to meet the enemy, forming mounted squadrons on either flank, reminiscent of Lincoln, but Robert's dispositions or numbers were superior. Carefully dividing his forces in three closely packed bodies he forced Stephen to give ground. As Royalist troops scattered in every direction, the king did not wait to be recaptured, but fled. His steward, William Martel, covered the royal escape, until taken prisoner. Then the Angevins swept through the town of Wilton, 'raging most terribly with pillage and the sword'. Making no distinction between civilians and fleeing soldiers, the victors violated the Abbey of Black Nuns, smashing down the doors to drag out those who had sought sanctuary. William Martel was exchanged for Sherborne Castle, which *Gesta Stephani* considered 'the master-key of the whole kingdom'. It was not. Civil war continued for another ten years, until the deaths of Stephen and his son Eustace.

Directions

Winchester *and* ***Stockbridge*** *In Winchester see the Cathedral Close and Wolvesey Castle. Leave the Westgate, which still stands, by the Romsey Road, and bear right across St Paul's Hill to gain the B3049 Stockbridge Road. Follow the main road into Stockbridge down Winchester Hill, where the A3057 crosses the B3049 at a roundabout, which marks the general area of Robert of Gloucester's surrender. St Peter's Old Church is on the left, south of the roundabout.*
Wilton *Wilton House is 4 miles (6 km) west of Salisbury, on the A3094.*

The Young King's Revolt

Henry II spent most of his life at war, defending the huge Angevin Empire that sprawled from the Tweed to the Pyrenees. He never fought a pitched battle in person, however. The only two English actions of the reign occurred in his absence, and were little more than skirmishes. The brilliant successes of Henry's lieutenants at Fornham and Alnwick reveal the tactical power of armoured cavalry in open warfare. At Fornham Royalist knights scattered superior numbers of infantry before they could form up. At Alnwick the men-at-arms rode boldly through a cloud of marauding Scots to snatch their king from under their noses.

Medieval kings commonly had problems with unruly heirs seeking to anticipate their inheritance. Henry II's pre-emptive coronation of his eldest son, another Henry, as co-regent failed to stifle the Young King's ambition. The latter spent Christmas 1172 in Paris plotting with Louis VII of France to dispossess old Henry, assisted by William the Lion, King of Scots. Revolts broke out after Easter 1173 in Normandy and England. Louis and the Young King confronted Henry II on the continent, while the Scots overran northern England with the usual atrocities. In September Robert, Earl of Leicester landed in Suffolk with a troop of Flemish mercenaries to assist Hugh Bigod, the disloyal Earl of Norwich. Richard de Lucy, the royal justiciar responsible for England during Henry's absence abroad, bought off William the Lion with a truce while he dealt with Robert at Fornham. William resumed operations the following Easter, but was captured outside Alnwick castle, ending the crisis.

Besides the usual ecclesiastical chronicles, Jordan Fantosme celebrated the campaign in a poem. Not only is the source a rare vernacular account (in French), but Jordan actually witnessed the capture of William, and must have spoken with veterans of Fornham. These minor actions mark a dynamic shift away from the interminable sieges of the previous reign. Jordan's verse graphically illustrates the fluidity and excitement of chivalric warfare, and the skills required of its practitioners.

Fornham, 17 October 1173

England, Suffolk, LR155 TL8368

The Young King's supporters held out in two main areas, Cheshire and East Anglia, a belt of royal castles between them. The Battle of Fornham arose from an attempt by the Earl of Leicester to break out of the eastern enclave, to reach his own territory in the Midlands. In mid-October Robert left the Earl of Norfolk's stronghold at Framlingham, heading for the Icknield Way near Bury St Edmunds to pick up the Via Devana westwards through Cambridge. He knew Royalist forces were watching his movements, but his wife urged him on:

The English are great boasters, they do not know
how to fight;
Better they know how with large cups to drink
and act the glutton.

Robert had a few heavy cavalry and a large number of Flemish mercenary infantry; William of Newburgh, a contemporary, reckoned 'eighty picked horsemen and four or five thousand valiant infantry'. Jordan Fantosme described their vulgar motivation and status:

We have not come to this country to pass the
time of day,
But to destroy King Henry, the old warrior,
And to have his wool ...
... the most were weavers,
They did not know how to bear arms like
knights,
But for this had they come, to have gain and war

As they marched they sang one of the oldest recorded snatches of Flemish song:

Hoppe, hoppe, Wilekin, hoppe, Wilekin
Engelond is min and tin.

Flemish greed exceeded their caution. Straggling towards the ford over the River Lark, the rebels unexpectedly met the Royalist army near the now defunct church of Fornham St Genevieve, 4 miles (6 km) north of Bury St Edmunds.

The chief justiciar and Henry's constable, Humphrey de Bohun, had gathered their forces in Bury, and probably moved down the east bank of the Lark to take the rebel column in flank, as it marched east–west. They had 300 stipendiary cavalry plus the retinues of the Earls of Cornwall, Gloucester and Arundel, outnumbering the rebel knights four-to-one. They had few infantry, but their cavalry was in battle order, and gave the rebels no time to disentangle themselves from the boggy water meadows, now occupied by a sewage farm. William of Newburgh wrote how Robert's men 'unable to wheel either to right or left made a virtue of necessity and boldly pushed on with all speed using their cavalry as a screen. And so began a desperate battle, the king's troops fighting for glory and the rebels for safety.'

Earl Robert was overthrown and taken. Dressed in a hauberk his wife fell into a ditch, a Royalist knight saving her from drowning. On the other side Walter fitz Robert attacked the Flemings:

And they resist him, who fear him not.
They were more than he by thousands and hundreds.
So they force him back with his people;
But he did not delay to seek vengeance.

Resistance cannot have lasted long. The *Memorials of St Edmund's Abbey* claimed a thousand soldiers fell outside the town's gates in an hour:

The wool of England they gathered very late
Upon their bodies descend crows and buzzards

Once the knights had scattered the Flemish foot, the country people finished them off with fork and flail, 'By fifteens, by forties, by hundreds, and by thousands'. The *Memorials* bear Jordan out, recording frequent finds of men's bones in the meadows, with marks of violence upon them. Robert of Leicester and his intrepid lady got off lightly, with a spell in Henry II's castle in the old Roman fortress at Portchester.

Fornham

	Winners	*Losers*
Opponents	Royalist	Rebel
Commanders	Richard de Lucy Humphrey de Bohun	Robert, Earl of Leicester (p)
Numbers	unknown	*c.*3000

Directions

Fornham St Genevieve is on private farmland at Fornham Park, between the B1106 and the Lark. The nearest public footpath to the battlefield is St Edmund's Way, beyond the river, accessible from the bridge at Fornham All Saints. St Genevieve's church tower can be seen through trees along the eastern bank.

Alnwick (II), Saturday 13 July 1174

England, Northumberland, LR81 NU1813

The affair at Alnwick was hardly a battle at all, rather a case of a few hundred knights halting a major invasion in its tracks. It is significant for the professionalism it reveals among Anglo-Norman knights, and was the first English battle described by an eyewitness: the poet Jordan Fantosme wrote 'as one who was there'.

Supporters of the Young King's rebellion against his father Henry II resumed operations after Easter 1174. The English rebels were too few for offensive operations, and depended on the king of Scotland, William the Lion. Scottish forces cruelly ravaged Northumberland and Cumberland, capturing seven castles and agreeing terms that might soon give them Carlisle and Wark. The Scots then besieged Prudhoe on the Tyne, which inspired a response like that before the Battle of Standard in 1138. The northern magnates rallied behind the royal sheriffs Robert d'Estouteville of Yorkshire and William de Vesci of Northumberland. They marched to Newcastle, moving with such rapidity that their infantry failed to keep up. The approach of 400 heavy cavalry persuaded William to retreat to Alnwick, his troops vindictively barking Prudhoe's apple trees before they left.

The English were outnumbered, perhaps four-to-one, but their decision to press on was not just knightly bravado. Intelligence reports indicated William's army had dispersed to burn the country, while the king lay at Alnwick 'with a small suite'. Rather than seeking out the main Scottish army, the English struck at its leadership. Prudently they sent a spy ahead, 'to reckon their forces'. The exact time of the resulting encounter is uncertain. Jordan, who took part in the march, spoke of going 'by night closely', while William of Newburgh marched the English off in the morning, 'hastening onwards at such a speed that they appeared to be propelled by some force of nature'. They covered 24 miles (38.5 km) in five hours, 'which seemed scarcely possible for men burdened with the weight of arms', but agrees with 19th-century cavalry manuals. William claimed such dense fog enveloped the column 'that they hardly knew where they were going', but Jordan's eyewitness account omits this graphic detail. Near Alnwick the English hid in a wood to meet their spy, 'who told them all'.

The Scots king and 60 knights were watching Alnwick Castle, 'in complete security and fearing nothing less than an incursion of our men'. William must have been south of the river to do this, allowing the English to observe his movements from high ground further south. Jordan implies they arrived at dawn, but has the Scots king taking his helmet off, 'Because of the heat, which is great', so clearly the day was more advanced. When the English broke cover William mistook them for his own men, returning from pillage. Recognizing the banners too late, he gallantly charged into the middle of them:

> Everything would have gone on well, to my knowledge,
> Were it not for a serjeant who rushes up to him;
> With the lance he holds he pierces his horse.

Pinned beneath his dead charger, William was

Alnwick (II)

	Winners	*Losers*
Opponents	English	Scots
Commanders	Robert d'Estouteville Ranulf de Glanville	William the Lion (p)
Numbers	*c.*400	*c.*100
Losses	unknown	unknown

captured, along with many knights who disdained flight when their king was taken. Jordan's messy details spoil the image of a polite joust:

> Great was the battle and stubborn on both sides;
> You might see darts enough thrown and arrows shot,
> The bold fighting and the cowards flying.
> Of the unfortunate Flemings great carnage was made,
> You might see their bowels dragged from their bodies through the fields;
> Never in their country will they cry, Arras!

Jordan claimed a thousand dead or wounded, clearly a figure of speech, although more Scots were cut off and massacred at Warkworth, where they had cruelly mistreated the monks of St Lawrence. Having achieved their aim of snatching the Scots king, the English hastily retired to Newcastle, taking William with them, his feet tied under a fresh horse. Deprived of their king, the Scots host broke up in disorder, its diverse nationalities fighting each other, as they had after Northallerton. Deprived of external support the English rebels made peace and repatriated their mercenaries. Church bells rang across England in joyful celebration. William the Lion handed over five major Scottish castles, and did homage to Henry II for Scotland, the first Scottish king to do so.

Directions

The battlefield has been transformed beyond recognition by later development of town and castle, now the seat of the dukes of Northumberland. See a remaining fragment of the steep sloping southern bank of the River Aln from the B6341 bridge, north of the town.

The Norman Invasion of Ireland

The first Normans to land in Ireland came ashore on 1 May 1169 in Bannow Bay, Co. Wexford, where the grassy headland at Bagginbun still shows traces of earthworks. Hitherto Ireland had been a threat to her eastern neighbours, a base for native or Scandinavian pirates, who carried off their prey to Dublin's slave markets. Now Ireland became the target for exploitation and conquest.

Hibernia in the 12th century was a geographical not a political expression. Ireland was divided. A few Norse townships occupied desirable commercial sites around the periphery, at Dublin, Wexford, Waterford and Limerick. A patchwork of Gaelic kingdoms competed for the hinterland: Connacht, Munster, Leinster, Ossory, and more. Since the death of Brian Boru their marches and wars, in the chronicler's expressive phrase, had made all Ireland 'a trembling sod'. It was a rough game. Dermot MacMurrough, king of Leinster, killed or blinded 17 of his own chiefs in 1141. When the Hiberno-Norse Ostmen of Dublin had killed Dermot's father, they buried a dead dog with the body, a huge joke. Fifteen years later, facing a similar fate, Dermot fled abroad for help, and ended Irish isolation for ever.

Nationalist historiography casts Dermot as the arch-quisling responsible for all of Ireland's subsequent ills, but Celtic warlords had employed foreign mercenaries before. Norsemen fought for Maelmorda at Clontarf (1014) and a handful of Normans for Macbeth at Dunsinane (1054). The earliest Normans to join Dermot were one more element in the power struggle: 'ninety heroes dressed in mail, and the Gaels set no store by them'. Not until Richard FitzGilbert, nicknamed Strongbow, arrived at Waterford on 23 August 1170 to marry Dermot's daughter, did the agenda shift from hired help to conquest. By the end of the century, Normans were entrenched throughout southeast Ireland, although there were never enough of them to overrun the whole island. Like the Vikings they would remain *Gallaibh*, 'the Foreigners'.

Traditional explanations of Norman success in Ireland stress the superior military capabilities displayed in battles in Ossory (1169–70) and around Dublin (1171). Mailed knights smashed ill-equipped Irish hosts to seize the most profitable parts of the country. The native Irish were not, however, without armour or horses. Kings had often presented followers with *Luirecha* or mail shirts. Laws distinguished between warhorses and mounts used for hunting or personal mobility. Irish armies were sub-divided into horse and foot in the same way that contemporary European armies distinguished between *equites* responsible to a marshal, and *pedites* responsible to a constable. Gerald of Wales describes the Norse as 'born warriors in Danish fashion completely clad in mail ... men with iron hearts as well as iron arms'. The Ostmen, however, lacked cavalry and missile weapons.

The Normans' key advantage was their combination of these two arms. The *Book of Howth* even describes archers riding behind mounted men in order to keep up. At Downpatrick (1177) their arrows broke the impetus of the Irish cavalry, preparing the way for the Norman knights' countercharge. Gaelic throwing darts had no comparable long-range effect, and Irish cavalry fought separately from their infantry. Once the Irish horse were driven off, their unsupported foot were at a loss, for 'always they looked for ... the aid of their horsemen, amongst whom were all their gentlemen, in whom the footmen had all their trust' (*Book of Howth*, 16th century).

Ireland was easily overrun, but it was not an easy country to keep. Towns and the cultivable southeast fell to the invaders, but Gaelic society survived in the less accessible northwest. Irish resistance exploited the difficult terrain, cutting trenches across bog land paths and 'plashing' the edges of woods with entangled undergrowth. Heavily armed knights had less advantage in the plundering expeditions that made up the small change of frontier warfare. Irish annals mention numerous minor actions less favourable to the invaders, actions that the Norman sources pass over in silence. The invaders usually won the pitched battles, but these were only part of the strategic equation.

Clais an Chro (Clashacrow/the Dinin), **1169**

Ireland, Co. Kilkenny, DS60 S4263?

Contemporary and modern historians have exaggerated the importance of the Normans' first actions in Ireland: Gerald of Wales to magnify his Fitzgerald relatives, who took part in the invasion, and Sir Charles Oman to illustrate his battle-oriented view of medieval warfare. The Ossory raids of 1169–70 expose the irregular nature of 12th-century Anglo-Irish warfare.

Robert Fitzstephen's men were present as Dermot's allies; Gerald reckoned only 600 (100 cavalry, 500 infantry) out of the whole column of several thousand were *Gallaibh*. The rest were Irish. Dermot had captured Wexford with Norman help, and recovered his rock-cut stronghold at Ferns, with its library of illuminated manuscripts. After three weeks feasting, Dermot and his friends rode into Ossory, an ancient enemy whose king had blinded one of MacMurrough's sons. Interpretations of the expedition vary. Gerald's heroes fight their battle 'as if on the edge of the country'. Oman set the action beside the River Dinin, after a successful raid through Kilkenny, heading for Leighlinbridge on the River Barrow. Recent consideration of place-names locates the fighting further west, near Freshford in the pass of Achadh Ur, after a drawn-out running fight along the River Nuenna, a tributary of the Nore. The main Ossorian force would have stood west of the River Arigna, at a spot still known as Clashacrow, 'Hollow of the Slaughter', or, more mundanely, Trench of the Shed.

Oman interpreted the battle as a Norman feigned retreat. Dermot's column stalled in a defile between woods and river, before a ditch and palisade, so Maurice de Prendergast withdrew to higher ground, drawing the 1700–2000 defenders from their prepared position. The cavalry then cut them to pieces. Gerald does not support Oman. His description resembles a running fight, the natural resource of a tactically weaker forest-dwelling opponent. The Ossorians pursued the column through trackless swamps and woods, eventually following them out into the open. Fitzstephen's horsemen then turned on them, scattering them across the country. Anyone the cavalry disabled was left to the large-headed axes of the accompanying Irish infantry. Such a riposte would be the natural outcome of a fighting retreat by a heavy column harassed by lighter opponents, and encumbered with loot. It follows the usual pattern of Irish warfare, mounted nobles covering the rear while common folk drove off plundered cattle. There is no need to imagine a cunningly feigned retreat, which would have taken Dermot's force deeper into enemy territory.

Wherever the fight or fights took place, their key feature was the move to dry ground. Even today the river valleys are waterlogged after bad weather, and the whole district must have been a swamp before it was drained. The nearest hard ground to Achadh Ur is Ard an Chro, 'Hill of Slaughter', while nearby Gort na nDeor, 'Field of Lamentation', may commemorate the Norman cavalry charge. Two or three hundred heads were collected for Dermot to admire. One particular enemy he held up by the ears, biting off the nose and lips. The Normans had made little difference to the strategic balance so far. Despite their presence, Rory O'Connor, the high king, forced Dermot to surrender his remaining legitimate son as a hostage against the Foreigners' departure. That was more than MacMurrough could deliver, with dire consequences for his offspring.

Clais an Chro

	Winners	*Losers*
Opponents	Norman and Irish	Irish
Commanders	Dermot MacMurrough Robert Fitzstephen Maurice de Prendergast	Donal MacGillapatrick of Ossory
Numbers	*c.*3000	*c.*2000

Directions

Take the R693 from Kilkenny to Freshford. Turn left onto a minor road for Clashacrow 1½ miles (2.5 km) before Freshford. The fighting took place west of the River Arigna, extending up onto the hill (594 feet/ 181 m) south of Freshford. For the area of Oman's battle, follow the N78 along the Dinin valley.

Dublin, 16 May 1171

Ireland, Dublin, DS50 O1634?

Dublin (Surprise of Castle Knock), 1 September 1171

Ireland, Dublin, DS50 O0836?

The strategic and symbolic importance of Dublin made it an inevitable scene of confrontation between the *Gallaibh* and Ireland's established inhabitants. Every high king required Dublin's submission. Its possession by the Normans gave them access to central Ireland, and secured communication with England. Two battles beneath its walls, separated by a two-month siege, destroyed the authority of Rory O'Connor, the existing Ard Ri (high king), and consolidated the Norman foothold.

The arrival of Richard FitzGilbert ('Strongbow') in September 1170 altered the Norman presence in Ireland from that of allies to conquerors. By treachery and forced marches, Strongbow and his new father-in-law Dermot MacMurrough snatched Dublin from under the noses of the high king and its *mormaer* (high steward) Haskulf Thorgilsson. A joint Irish-Norse counteroffensive in May 1171 was disastrously ill-coordinated. The chronology is uncertain, but Haskulf probably appeared first, and was beaten in isolation.

Dublin

	Winners	Losers
Opponents	Norman	Irish Norse
Commanders	Miles de Cogan	Haskulf Thorgilsson (k)
Numbers	*c.*1150	*c.*2500

Dublin

	Winners	Losers
Opponents	Norman	Irish
Commanders	Earl Strongbow	High King Rory O'Connor
Numbers	600–1000	unknown
Losses	unknown	1500

Rory then blockaded Dublin until the starving Normans sallied forth to disperse the besiegers.

Dublin was a small, fortified settlement between the south bank of the Liffey and the high ground later crowned by the castle. The town extended west to Bridge Street and east to the River Poddle, which now flows under Parliament Street into the Liffey. Haskulf landed below the town at an open space then called the Steyne, now Trinity College. Gerald of Wales reports Haskulf had 60 shiploads of Norwegians and islanders from Man and the Scottish isles, implying a landing force of 2400 men. Casualty figures in the Old French *Song of Dermot and the Earl* add up to 4500, suggesting over 100 ships. The Norsemen had red ironbound shields, and long mail shirts. Among their leaders was John '*agnomine the Wode*' ('that is called Mad or Furious'), a berserker.

The Norsemen clearly outnumbered Dublin's garrison. Maximum Norman strength in Ireland was 250 knights, 500 mounted sergeants or squires, and 1750 infantry. Strongbow was elsewhere, leaving Miles de Cogan in command of perhaps half that number. Despite inferior numbers, he engaged the enemy outside Dublin's eastern gate at St Mary del Dam (named after the mill dam by the mouth of the Poddle), near St Andrew's Church in Dame Street. Driven back to the walls, Miles secretly detached his brother Richard with just 30 knights. Leaving the western gate at the far end of the High Street, Richard rode around the southern edge of central Dublin, to come down noisily on Haskulf's rear. Disconcerted, the Norsemen tried to face in two directions at once. Wavering under a hail of arrows from the walls each side of St Mary's Gate they fled back to their ships.

John the Wode was overwhelmed by numbers and killed, despite hacking one knight's leg off, armour and all, and killing nine or ten other opponents. The *Song of Dermot and the Earl* claimed 2000 Norsemen killed and 500 drowned, leaving only 2000 to escape. Haskulf was captured slipping away on board ship. Held for ransom, he failed to hold his tongue: 'With little power we came now, and this was but an assay of our might; but if I live ere it be so long, there shall come twice as many as these' (*Book of Howth*). Haskulf's exasperated captors cut off his head, but his strategic analysis was accurate enough.

Both sides marshalled their forces. The high king besieged Dublin with four armies, encamped at Castleknock, Clontarf, Dalkey and Kilmainham. Thirty longships maintained the blockade to seaward. The besieging forces cannot possibly have approached Gerald's figure of 30,000 men, who would have soon starved to death. If the Irish population was two-thirds of medieval Scotland's, whose peak effort was 4000–5000 at Bannockburn, Rory might have mobilized 3000. Gerald's kinsmen demanded action, as food ran short: 'Though few men we be, yet well weaponed we are ... Though many they be ... they shall never have power ... to withstand us.' Even if Maurice FitzGerald's words are an invention, they express Norman self-confidence well enough.

The Normans moved out of Dublin's western gate at 1 p.m. and turned right down today's Bridge Street across the Liffey. They deployed in the usual three divisions, moving in column, one behind another, but easily wheeled into line: Raymond le Gros led with 20 knights, Miles de Cogan followed with 30, and Strongbow came last with 40. If mounted sergeants and archers were in the usual proportions, the Normans hardly fielded 1000 men, including a few townsmen. The *Song of Dermot* described even more attenuated forces: 40 knights, 60 mounted archers and 100 foot sergeants to each division.

The Normans advanced rapidly north towards Finglas. At Glasnevin they wheeled left between the Tolka River and the future Phoenix Park, and fell suddenly upon Rory O'Connor's encampment at Castleknock. The Connacht men were too far from their supports at Clontarf to expect any help, and were probably outnumbered at the decisive point. Besides they were taken hopelessly by surprise. Rory was in the bath, and narrowly escaped with his life. Raymond le Gros justified his stout reputation by running his lance through two men simultaneously. Other Normans hunted their victims across 'the green of Ath Cliath', until sunset.

The *Annals of Loch Cé* (16th century) named it the 'victory of the ashes', 1500 Irish falling in exchange for a single English sergeant. The other Irish armies melted away without a fight. Strongbow had consolidated his position just in time. Henry II arrived a month later to impose the first Anglo-Irish constitutional arrangements, possibly at the request of native Irish kings who despaired of restraining the invaders by military action. Not for the last time in Irish politics, an externally imposed settlement would satisfy neither party.

Directions

See text, although tactical locations are unknown.

Down (I) (Downpatrick), **February 1177**

Ireland, Co. Down, DS21 unlocated

Down (II) (Drumderg), **14 May 1260**

Ireland, Co. Down, DS21 unlocated

Henry II's intervention in 1171–2 failed to stabilize the Anglo-Irish frontier. Ireland was empty compared with the rest of 12th-century Europe. Absentee kings of England could no more restrain land-hungry colonists and acquisitive barons than 19th-century administrations in Washington could restrain westward migration across the prairies. One of the most remarkable of Anglo-Irish pioneers was Sir John de Courcy, a Somerset knight, who founded a border kingdom in eastern Ulster or Ulaid. As chief of Ulster, *princeps Ulidiae*, he minted coins, built castles and married the king of Man's daughter – with no regard for any outside authority. De Courcy owed his position to his defeat of the native king of Ulaid in the first Battle of Down. The *Book of Howth*'s chivalric, and possibly fictitious, account conveys the flavour of medieval Irish combat better than more staid authorities.

Bored with garrison life in Dublin, de Courcy organized his own freelance expedition: 20 knights, 50 sergeants and 300 archers, besides an unspecified number of friendly Irish. In the depths of winter he marched 90 miles (145 km) to Downpatrick in three days, 'without let of any of his foemen, unknown to any man but his own'. The tired and hungry Normans arrived early on 1 February 1171, whereupon Rory MacDonleavy 'sped him out of the town'. He was back within a week, allegedly with a host of 10,000, more probably a tenth of that.

Like their Viking ancestors, the Normans had an eye for defensive positions. Downpatrick lies on a peninsula between Strangford Lough and Dundrum Bay, and is only accessible from the west, between the Annacloy (Quoile) and Blackstaff rivers. Presumably de Courcy drew up his 700 men on that side of the town, their right flank on the Quoile, 'where as then a marsh ground was'. His brother Amory took the opposite flank, away from the soft ground, with all 140 cavalry, including 70 archers riding behind the men-at-arms. Sir Roger Power held the marsh on the right with infantry, and de Courcy the centre.

The Irish king rushed ahead with his horsemen, thinking to destroy Amory's handful before the main body of foot came into action. The ground was obstructed, however, by an impassable ditch and hedge, where Amory had placed his archers. As the Irish charged, 'the shot of arrows came on so fast their horses were so galled that [they] began to shrink

Down (I)

	Winners	*Losers*
Opponents	Norman	Irish
Commanders	John de Courcy	Rory MacDonleavy
Numbers	700	unknown

Down (II)

	Winners	*Losers*
Opponents	Norman	Irish
Commanders	Roger d'Auters Roger le Taylleur	Brian O'Neill, of the Battle of the Down (k)

back'. Amory countercharged and chased Rory away, beyond a defile. The Norman archers secured this in the native manner, entrenching the pass and obstructing it with brushwood. The battlefield was very cut up in general, the Irish foot awaiting the outcome of the cavalry action in a 'great truncke' or trench. Sir John now set upon them, 'like a wolf amongst a herd of lambs'. Sir Roger Power dealt severely with attempts to turn de Courcy's right flank through the morass, for 'between him and the main battle there was no way but upon dead corpses, or harness, legs and heads, that lay upon the ground'.

Unable to gain the 'moor' on their left, the leaderless Irish infantry retreated across the open ground to their right. They supposed themselves 'lighter and lustier … in travail and footmanship' than the exhausted Norman cavalry, but were deluded. Roger O'Hanlon kept 200 of them together, until Amory broke them with the last 40 cavalry in a fit state to charge:

> Great work was there at this time with these few horsemen, for Sir Amore was put twice on foot, and was helpen up to horse again, till the third time, being beyond a ford … was unhorsed, and his horse slain. But as God would, three of his men lighted a-foot by him, which took 4 spears which they took of dead men … and kept that ford upon the footmen till Sir John Coursey came…

All this while, the English troops holding the pass against the Irish cavalry were under severe pressure, losing 3 knights. There was more to de Courcy's success than simple technological superiority, for if Amory had not separated the Irish cavalry from their infantry, 'it had not be like the fortune of battle to turn on Sir John de Coursey's side'. The Normans had combined shock and missile action, and taken every advantage of the terrain: 'Policy helpeth good fortune.'

De Courcy's policy ensured English and French speech replaced Gaelic from Coleraine to Cork. He never penetrated beyond the Bann into western Ulster, however, and there were never enough English or Flemish settlers to secure the colony. Conditions remained unstable throughout Ireland. By the 1250s the unrestrained greed of expansionist magnates had inspired widespread opposition. Brian O'Neill, king of Tyrone, claimed the high kingship with support from Connacht and Thomond, and marched on Downpatrick with a great host. He suffered a terrible defeat at Drumderg, not at the hands of any great chivalric figure, but of colonists with such mundane surnames as 'le Taylleur'. Brian fell with 23 other named leaders, and '15 of the principal men of Muinter-Cathain'. Never again would a native ruler claim the title 'King of all the kings of Ireland'. Brian's death marked the end of the invasion period, and a low point in the fortunes of medieval Gaeldom.

Directions

Tactical locations unknown: see the motte and bailey between the town of Downpatrick and the River Quoile.

The Marshal and the Dauphin, 1215–17

The reign of King John was thick with strategic and political revolution. The long-running Angevin feud with the kings of France ended with Philippe Auguste's occupation of Rouen on 24 June 1204. Anjou had already gone the way of Normandy, so John's descendants would be known by their family name of Plantagenet, instead of their old regional name Angevin.

John's unsuccessful and costly attempts to recover his cross-Channel inheritance brought high taxes and disputes over military service. In 1215 dissident barons and ecclesiastical critics of John's methods forced him to sign Magna Carta. They were the first rebels with a cause beyond feathering their own nest, for besides dismantling the Angevin machinery of repression, the magnates proclaimed the rule of law, and the need for consent to precede taxation. John was never likely to accept this, and civil war broke out late in 1215. The baronial party offered the throne to the heir to the king of France, Louis the Dauphin, who was in London by May 1216. Anglo-French rivalry was for a few months fought out on English rather than French soil. In the middle of the crisis John died of dysentery. This was his best possible move, as his departure removed the barons' main grievance.

The new king was a boy, the nine-year old Henry III, but the regent was William the Marshal, Earl of Pembroke and the best knight in the world. He had cleaned up on the tournament circuit as a young knight, but at 70 was about to put on the finest performance of his career. William's political skills equalled his chivalry. In November 1216 he undermined the rebels by re-issuing Magna Carta, less its most objectionable clauses. Nevertheless, the war continued with a haphazard exchange of castles, until in May 1217 Louis split his forces. While he went to besiege Dover, many of his troops headed north, to relieve Mountsorrel Castle in Leicestershire and to besiege the royal castle at Lincoln. William urged his followers to seize their chance: 'It is God's will that we should defend ourselves. Their host is divided ... No more threats but attack them' (*L'Histoire de Guillaume le Maréchal*).

Royalist forces mustered at Newark on Whit Monday, 15 May, moving on to Torksey after three days of discussion and religious devotions. They took a roundabout route to avoid the water obstacles south of Lincoln, approaching instead from the north, probably down the ancient strategic route along Tillbridge Lane and Ermine Street. The combined French and rebel forces were behind city walls and outnumbered the relieving army, but the Royalists won one of the most complete victories of the century. The Dauphin could only continue the war with powerful reinforcements from France, which were intercepted off Sandwich on 24 August. Their flagship was taken, along with its trebuchets and costly warhorses, and the whole fleet captured or chased back to Calais. Within three weeks, on 12 September, the Peace of Kingston brought the war to an end.

Lincoln (Nundinae or the Fair of Lincoln), **20 May 1217**

England, Lincolnshire, LR121 SK9771

The battle of Lincoln was a curious affair. A mounted force stormed a walled city, and cleared it by jousting along lanes too steep for 21st-century vehicles. So few combatants were killed that contemporaries referred to it as the Fair or Tournament of Lincoln. The *Histoire de Guillaume le Maréchal* was written from personal memoirs, but explains neither where the Royalists broke through, nor why their attack was so successful. Roger of Wendover (d.1236) fills the gaps, confirming many of the *Histoire*'s details.

Medieval Lincoln followed the outline of the Roman city, an elongated parallelogram running 3000 yards (2745 m) from the North Gate at Newport Arch. The northern half stood on a steep rocky hill, whence the southern half sloped down to the River Witham. The castle was inside the west wall, separated from the town by a ditch. The Normans had buried the Roman gate under their castle mound, piercing a new entrance just north of the castle, the present Westgate. The castle itself had gates east and west, leading to the town or open country respectively. Nicola de la Hay, widow of King John's castellan and 'an ingenious and vigorous old lady', held the castle in the royal interest.

The rebels besieged the castle from the city, but the town's perimeter was too extensive to defend effectively. This makes their decision not to fight outside difficult to understand. The *Histoire* gives them 611 knights and 1000 foot against William the Marshal's 406 knights, 317 crossbows and at least 200 sergeants. Roger of Wendover gives similar numbers; moderate and probable figures compared with the usual medieval exaggerations. The French commander, the Comte de Perche, ignored suggestions that he meet the enemy on the slope north of Lincoln, and 'catch them like larks in a cage'. He went to see for himself, 'in the Gallic fashion'. Spare banners hung on the Royalist baggage train fooled him into overestimating their fighting strength, and he barricaded himself inside the city. William must have expected more aggression. He had formed his cavalry in four squadrons, one behind another, the crossbows extended across the front to pick off French horses as they charged. The sergeants were detailed to kill their own horses if necessary, as an obstacle. The Marshal was delighted, however, to see men 'ever foremost in the Tourney, hide themselves at our appearance', and sent his nephew John Marshal ahead to make contact with Dame Nicola.

At this point, the *Histoire*'s author admits his inability to reconcile his sources, and entangles his listeners in a confused account of how Peter des Roches, Bishop of Winchester, found a concealed way into the city. This is quite possible. Peter was 'learned in the art of war', and seems to have served as William's chief of staff. However, the poet never visited Lincoln, and makes nonsense of the location of the crucial entry. Topography and Roger of Wendover clarify matters. The Royalists approached from the northwest, probably from Burton, and communicated easily with the castle's defenders, who suggested their postern gate as a way into the city. William's colleagues would not commit their whole force to so constricted a passage, going off to batter the North Gate. They left King John's old mercenary leader Fawkes de Breauté and his crossbowmen to enter the castle, and somehow open a way for the army. For lack of a more suitable opening, this would appear to be the blocked up Westgate. Kate Norgate ingeniously suggests stones had been piled outside the doors, which the rebels, on the inside, did not see being removed until too late.

Suddenly Fawkes de Breauté's crossbowmen appeared on top of the houses and ramparts, directing their deadly bolts against the barons' horses,

Lincoln

	Winners	*Losers*
Opponents	Royalist	Rebel
Commanders	William the Marshal	Comte de Perche (k)
Numbers	900	1600
Losses	2 dead	3 dead

laying their riders helpless on the ground beneath them. Fawkes himself burst out of the castle into the midst of his enemies, momentarily falling into their hands until his men pulled him clear. Meanwhile the king's knights smashed in the city gates, and charged down Westgate and Newport. So complete was the surprise, a French engineer was beheaded reloading his trebuchet. Swords struck sparks from helmets, while crossbows mowed down warhorses like 'stuck pigs'. Turning right into Bailgate the Marshal swept along to the brow of the hill with his own and the Earl of Salisbury's squadron. Here the Comte de Perche made a stand between the castle and cathedral in Minster Yard. Backed up against the cathedral's west front, he was offered quarter, but swore he would never surrender to Englishmen who had betrayed their own king. Infuriated, someone shoved a spear through his helmet eyehole, which did not prevent him giving the Marshal three tremendous sword blows over the head, before falling dead off his horse.

De Perche's friends fled to their left down Steep Hill, regrouping in the lower town. When they counterattacked, the Marshal held them in front while the Earl of Chester's squadron, from Northgate, menaced their right. Other knights fell upon them from the rear, having worked their way around side streets. The surviving rebels fled once more down High Street, to make one last stand beyond Stonebow at Wigford Bridge. In the rush the Marshal's standard-bearer went off the bridge and into the river. Numerous prisoners were taken there and at the Bargate at the south end of High Street. One source says the barrier only allowed one rider through at a time, another that a cow jammed herself in the passage. About 200 panic-stricken knights escaped, seeing Marshals in every bush. Most of the barons who had supported Louis were captured, besides 300 knights. Only five men died in the battle, although peasants polished off the defeated infantry as usual. Lincoln's citizens had been neutral, but were spoiled 'to the uttermost farthing', while numerous refugees drowned in the Witham.

Unable to agree what to do next, the Royalists dispersed to secure their prisoners, but the battle was decisive. Louis broke off the siege of Dover, and moved to protect London. He had lost the initiative, and would soon lose the war.

Directions

See text for locations of fighting. Visit the cathedral and castle, where the Lucy Tower stands on the original Norman motte. Newport Arch up Bailgate is the only Roman gate still used for traffic.

Sandwich, 24 August 1217

Naval, English Channel, LR179

The battle of Sandwich was the first great English naval victory. Strategically it showed that even an established invader, controlling half of England, had to control the sea routes home. Tactically Sandwich was prophetic, demonstrating the capital importance of deploying better ships rather than superior numbers, and holding the weather gauge, i.e. remaining to windward of the enemy. For contemporaries the victory was a miraculous deliverance from the notorious master pirate Eustace the Monk whose unique blend of wickedness and success they could only attribute to necromancy.

Following his setback at Lincoln (see above), Louis the Dauphin sent an urgent plea for reinforcements to his father Philippe Auguste. Without them he could neither continue the struggle in England, nor return home. The Cinque Ports that controlled the Straits of Dover had originally assisted the French invaders. Now they returned to their loyalty and blockaded the Channel, while Henry III's forces tightened their grip on London, Louis's last significant foothold. A major expedition was needed to rescue the heir to the French throne. A fleet of 60 or 80 vessels made ready at Calais, spearheaded by 10 great ships given over to men-at-arms. Eustace was commissioned as fleet navigating officer, responsible for bringing the armament up the Thames. Overall command was given to Robert de Courtenay, the French queen's uncle. Both men sailed in 'the great ship of

Bayonne', so heavily laden with treasure, warhorses and a trebuchet that her decks were nearly awash. The English fleet was smaller but stronger. It consisted of under 40 vessels, but included at least 16 large ships, outnumbering major French units three-to-two. There was also a number of iron-beaked oar-propelled galleys, which the Angevins maintained in a stone-lined dock at Portsmouth, the nucleus of the future Royal Navy. William the Marshal's followers would not let him risk his neck at sea, so command devolved upon Hubert de Burgh, King John's justiciar and the defender of Dover Castle.

The Battle of Sandwich was unusual in being fought at sea and under way, probably in the sheltered waters of the Downs or off Ramsgate as the French headed for the North Foreland. Most naval actions of the day were fought at a standstill, often in a harbour or estuary. The English grasp of naval tactics under sail was therefore remarkable. As the French sailed north up the Channel on St Bartholomew's Day with a fresh following wind, the English fleet tacked out of Sandwich to meet them. Hubert de Burgh led them close-hauled in line astern, luffing between the French ships and English coast: '*obliquando ... id est* loof', as the contemporary chronicler Matthew Paris put it. Thinking the English had refused action, the French sailors sang rude songs, and their admiral ordered Eustace to change course to intercept these 'fishing boats'.

Modern accounts describe the French flagship wallowing behind their fleet, which was massed 'in a close line, as for a set battle'. The *Histoire de Guillaume le Maréchal*, however, specifically places Eustace ahead, and it is hard to see how else he could have fulfilled his role as pilot. As the 'great ship of Bayonne' closed with the English line, the rest of the French passed on up the Channel, getting well to leeward before they realized their admiral's difficulties. Eustace missed the first English ship, running foul of the second. Another three English ships joined the attack, including a great cog. Lightly laden and riding high in the water, she rained down stones, arrows and crossbow bolts on the enemy decks. The closely packed French ships, with the wind blowing them away from the scene of action, were unable to beat back to windward in time to intervene. In any case, more ships under Hubert de Burgh had weathered the French fleet, and were already attacking its rearmost ships.

Unable to force their way on board the French flagship, the English hurled pots of powdered quicklime onto her decks, clouds of burning dust blinding her crew. A sergeant from Guernsey leaped down from the cog, scattering the French ship's leading defenders. More English men-at-arms followed, killing all they found, in accordance with the grim old custom of the sea. Only Robert de Courtenay survived, with 32 knights worth ransoming. Caught hiding in the bilges, Eustace unavailingly offered 10,000 marks ransom. Stephen Crabbe of Winchelsea gave him a choice between having his head cut off on the trebuchet or the ship's side, after which the grisly trophy was stuck on a lance for exhibition ashore.

The English now pursued the French fleet up the Channel, shooting them full of arrows, grappling and cutting down their rigging to prevent escape. The king's galleys joined in, their iron rams sinking target ships in an instant. How any of the French escaped is a mystery, as the English lay upwind, between them and Calais. Many French sailors drowned themselves rather than fall into enemy hands. Allegedly 4000 perished, although the *Histoire* took no responsibility for the estimate. Only 15 French ships reached home, including 9 of the great vessels, too dangerous to tackle when more vulnerable prey abounded. The battle was one of the most decisive contemporary encounters in northern waters, ending the most hopeful but least known French attempt to conquer England.

Sandwich

	Winners	*Losers*
Opponents	Royalist	French
Commanders	Hubert de Burgh	Eustace the Monk (k)
		Robert de Courtenay (p)

Directions

Sandwich is now several miles inland. See the bay from Ramsgate sea front.

The Barons' War, 1264–5

The Barons' War arose from attempts to impose constitutional limits on Henry III, widely perceived as a weak and corrupt king. In 1258 the Provisions of Oxford established a council of barons, headed by Simon de Montfort, Earl of Leicester, but disagreements among the barons allowed Henry to regain power in 1261. Relations broke down irretrievably between the Royalist faction and de Montfort's supporters. The former was led by Prince Edward (later Edward I), and Henry's brother Richard, Earl of Cornwall. The baronial party included the City of London and Gilbert de Clare, Earl of Gloucester. The campaigns that followed provide rare medieval examples of the interplay between what were later known as interior and exterior strategic lines, as Royalist commanders sought to maintain a central position between divided Baronial forces, and crush them in detail. When they failed to do so, at Lewes, they were beaten; when they succeeded, at Kenilworth and Evesham, Edward achieved a double victory.

Civil war broke out in April 1264 as Henry III advanced into de Montfort's power base in the Midlands, capturing Northampton, Leicester and Nottingham. The king's army divided the baronial forces, preventing them making an effectual response until Henry moved south to relieve Rochester Castle. Once in Kent the Royalists could no longer prevent de Montfort concentrating his forces in London and following Henry south. At Lewes de Montfort defeated a stronger Royalist army and captured its leaders. De Montfort maintained a façade of royal authority, but remained insecure, despite summoning the first English parliament in January 1265. In May Prince Edward escaped and made terms with the Earl of Gloucester, who had fallen out with de Montfort after Lewes. Between them they isolated de Montfort west of the Severn, preventing him from joining his son, Simon the Younger. While Edward beat up young Simon's quarters at Kenilworth, the old earl crossed the Severn, but was trapped and killed at Evesham. Constitutional reform died with him. In future unsatisfactory kings would be replaced in a more summary fashion.

Lewes, Wednesday 14 May 1264

England, East Sussex, LR198 TQ3911?

Lewes was a rare example of a medieval battle won by a smaller army on the offensive. Traditional accounts place the action on top of the South Downs, but evidential fragments ignored until the 1980s suggest a location on the lower slopes, much nearer Lewes.

Henry III reached Lewes on 10 or 11 May after an uncomfortable march from Rochester through the Weald. Lewes's castle and walled priory made it a secure base to await the Baronial army coming from London. The River Ouse protected the north and east, while tidal mud flats came up to the walls on the south. The only practical military approach was from the west, where the Downs slope down to the river in three spurs. De Montfort approached cautiously, reconnoitring the Downs west of Lewes, and probing the Offham gap where the Ouse flows through the hills. On the night of 13–14 May he moved west under cover of darkness, to gain the crest of the Downs by a still extant track past Blackcap (676 feet/206 m), avoiding royal scouts posted on the direct route from Offham. Once on high ground, the Baronial army could move southeast towards the

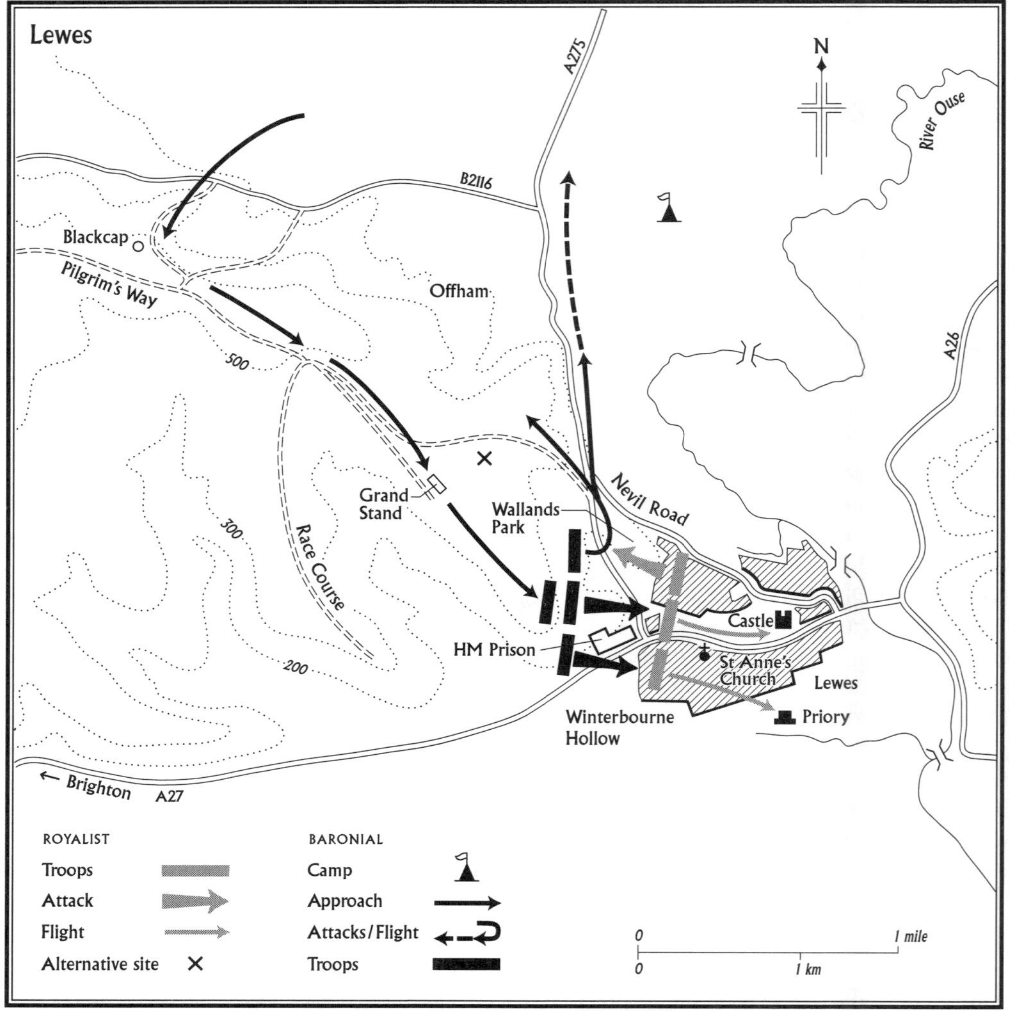

old racecourse, able to observe the Royalist army without being seen.

De Montfort had spent the previous day assigning everyone their place in the line of battle. This was the usual three battles in line, plus a fourth in reserve under himself, presumably behind the centre. A London contingent formed the left wing, described by the contemporary annalist Thomas Wykes as 'an immense mass, ignorant of battle'. Their fate suggests the knights rode ahead of the foot, which may have been true of the other battles. No source mentions archery, suggesting the infantry carried hand-to-hand weapons, despite the 1252 Assize of Arms specifying the longbow as the yeoman's standard weapon. The Royalists formed up in front of their respective billets: Prince Edward from the castle

Directions

Turn off the A275 north of Offham to follow de Montfort's approach march along the B2116. 1¼ miles (2 km) further on fork left up the footpath to Blackcap, turning sharp left again at the top of the scarp. Follow the Pilgrim's Way along the top of the Downs towards Lewes Prison to look down on the battlefield, much of which is now built up. See a monument in the priory, shaped like a knight's helmet.

on the right, Richard of Cornwall and the king from the priory in the centre and left. They had no reserve, which had been left behind to garrison Tonbridge. Edward's wing is said to have included 'the flower of the army'.

Estimated numbers vary wildly, though the king is agreed to have been stronger. The Dunstable Annalist (another contemporary) reckoned he outnumbered de Montfort four-to-one, in line with claims that 500 Baronial knights faced 1500 Royalists with armoured horses. A total of 2000 heavy cavalry resembles the numbers deployed in Edward I's Welsh wars, while 500 cavalry returned with the prince at the end of the battle. A modern reader, lacking the Annalist's faith in miracles, may wonder how the Baronial party won at such a disadvantage. Henry III was certainly surprised by the barons' sudden appearance, and may not have been ready to meet their onslaught. His station with the least honourable left wing and his failure to form a reserve suggest haste and disorder lay behind the Royalist defeat, rather than divine intervention. Nobody was very interested in the infantry, but three pits containing 500 skeletons each were found during the construction of Lewes jail in 1810. If half the loser's infantry were killed and numbers were initially even, there would have been 6000 infantry altogether.

Most reconstructions describe the Royalists climbing the hill to attack de Montfort between Offham pits and the racecourse, where the Ordnance Survey locates the battle. Several considerations, however, place the fighting lower down on the central spur, near the prison and its telltale grave pits. Three chroniclers specifically describe de Montfort's army 'coming down the slope'. Richard of Cornwall took refuge in a windmill known as Snelling's or King Henry's Mill that stood between the jail and St Anne's Church. The mills that battle maps usually show further uphill were built later. The Royalist line of battle probably stood just east of the school opposite the prison, facing the barons as they advanced from the northwest.

The first clash occurred in the Wallands, between de Montfort's left and Edward's cavalry. The prince overthrew the leading 'cohort', and drove them back over the supporting infantry. Some fled over the Downs, smaller grave pits marking their flight. Others fled up Nevil Road, 60 knights drowning in the Ouse. The victorious Royalists chased after them, off the battlefield. Meanwhile the Baronial centre and right caught their opposite numbers on the difficult slope around the prison and near Winterbourne Hollow. Fighting was desperate for a while. De Montfort's standard-bearer was killed, and the king's justiciar suffered 20 wounds before he surrendered. Richard's centre gave way first, perhaps allowing de Montfort to commit his reserve against the exposed right flank of the king's battle. Wykes wrote of an encircling multitude. Henry III was much beaten with swords and maces, and had two horses killed under him before his knights got him safely into the priory.

The *Lewes Chronicle* reckoned the 'greater part' of the Royalist army was destroyed between prime (4.15 a.m.) and noon. Edward reappeared, breathless from mistakenly slaughtering some Royalist hostages held in de Montfort's personal carriage, and joined the king in the priory. Only 4 people of note died, although 2000–2700 smaller folk were recorded as slain. The *Melsa Chronicle* reckoned 3300 dead on both sides. Scores of Henry's supporters stuck in the mud south of Lewes, to be found at low water, drowned in their saddles. The victors were unwilling to risk a bloodbath by storming the well-defended priory. Friars brokered a deal restoring the Provisions of Oxford, subject to arbitration, while Prince Edward, the Royalists' trump card, was taken hostage. De Montfort had won the day, but his unfulfilled promise to negotiate undermined his regime's legitimacy, paving the way for counter-revolution the following year.

Lewes

	Winners	*Losers*
Opponents	Baronial	Royalist
Commanders	Simon de Montfort Gilbert de Clare, Earl of Gloucester	Henry III Prince Edward Richard, Earl of Cornwall (p)
Numbers	*c.*3500	*c.*4500

Kenilworth, 2 August 1265

England, Warwickshire, LR140 SP2772

Evesham, Tuesday 4 August 1265

England, Worcestershire, LR150 SP0345

Civil war between crown and barons resumed in May 1265. Prince Edward and the Earl of Gloucester, the active Royalist leaders, controlled the Severn valley. Simon de Montfort held the king at Hereford, but was cut off from his son, Simon the Younger, who had gathered an army around the Montfortian fortress at Kenilworth. The two Simons might trap Edward in a pincer movement at Worcester, except for the difficulties of coordinating two armies 60 miles (100 km) apart, without modern electronic communications. Edward moved first, catching the younger de Montfort's army 'buried in sleep' outside the castle. Edward had ordered no unnecessary killing, and most of the Montfortian barons were captured, complete with knights, sergeants, horses and harness. Young Simon escaped by swimming the moat.

Edward countermarched the same day to find old Simon had crossed the Severn 4 miles (6 km) south of Worcester, at Kempsey. The two sides rested for a day, before de Montfort sidestepped towards his son's scattered forces. Records of Henry III's oblations show the king reached Evesham with the Baronial army early on 4 August, probably along the A44 via Pershore. Fatally the barons stopped to hear mass at the abbey, and to rest troops and horses who had neither slept nor eaten for three days. Meanwhile, a transvestite spy named Margot tipped Edward off, giving him time to cut the route north from Evesham to Kenilworth, and trap the Baronial army.

A recently discovered eyewitness account has discredited all previous interpretations of Edward's strategy. Most involve a converging approach by two or three separate columns either side of the river, disregarding the complexities of such a manoeuvre at night, without maps, radios or wristwatches. Details differ wildly, except for Mortimore's presence beyond the Avon, blocking the Bengeworth bridge, then the only crossing place.

The new account almost certainly comes from a monk present at Evesham throughout the battle, who wrote for pilgrims visiting the site of de Montfort's martyrdom. He provides the first specific evidence of Edward's and Gloucester's route. Before their final approach, they knighted several of their followers at Mosham, a riverside meadow next to the A4538, between Craycombe and Evesham. Both Royalist commanders then came 'up the hill with their army in three divisions', as one might expect in a conventional medieval battle. Several points in the new source suggest Mortimore was still with them, probably commanding the third division:

(1) The bridge was not blocked when Edward and Gloucester first appear: the Bishop of Worcester retires across it to seek refuge in Blockley church; de Montfort suggests his younger followers, men with wives and children, might also escape that way, a viable option for a few mounted knights, though not a whole army.

(2) Mortimore is specifically named as de Montfort's killer, placing him in the thick of the fight, not the other side of the river. Leading Edward's third

Kenilworth

	Winners	*Losers*
Opponents	Royalist	Baronial
Commanders	Prince Edward	Simon de Montfort the Younger

Evesham

	Winners	*Losers*
Opponents	Royalist	Baronial
Commanders	Prince Edward Roger Mortimore Gilbert de Clare, Earl of Gloucester	Simon de Montfort (k)
Numbers	*c.*4500	*c.*3000
Losses	unknown	*c.*2400

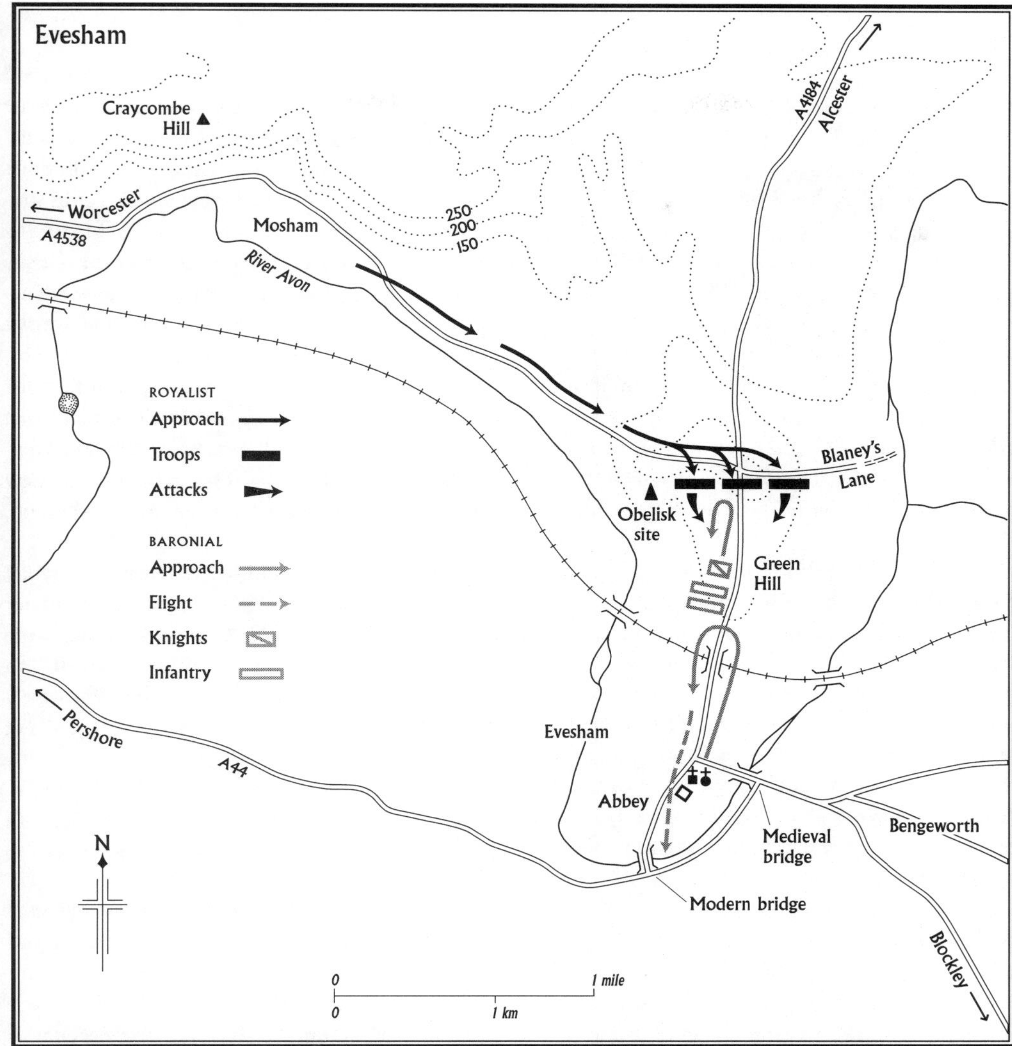

division, Mortimore would have been near the traditional location of de Montfort's death, conveniently located to take the earl's head and other trophies. Mortimore's appearance at the tail of the column satisfies the much quoted statement from Walter of Guisborough that Mortimore's standard was seen '*ab occidente et a tergo*', 'to the west and in the rear', that is on the other flank to Gloucester.

Evesham seems to have been much simpler than historians have imagined. The Royalists followed de Montfort by the shortest route, in the standard formation of three battles, one behind another. Walter of

Directions

From the Abbey take the A4184 Alcester road out of Evesham, across the railway, and up Green Hill. The area is now built up, but some open ground remains on the left, near the Battlewell and obelisk. The fighting was just south of the A4184/A4538 junction.

Guisborough refers several times to them approaching from the north. Once they had occupied the high ground on that side of Evesham, they formed lines facing right, to block de Montfort's escape. He had to come out and fight, or face politically terminal humiliation. Opposing strengths are uncertain, but Edward did not need the three-to-one superiority the *Melrose Chronicle* gives him to carry out the simple plan described by the new source. Baronial casualties, which approached 100 per cent, may have equalled the *Lanercost Chronicle*'s 2400 dead English, although his 5000 Welsh looks like exaggeration. Edward's army could therefore have been nearer the 4500 of Lewes than the 9000 traditionally assigned to him.

Evesham town lies within a deep loop in the Avon, a bad position to defend against the north, with no escape except one narrow bridge east of the abbey. The traditional battle site is Green Hill, across the base of the loop in the river. Side roads join the main Alcester road here, from Fladbury and Offenham, the latter known as Upton or Blayney's Lane. Innumerable bones were found here in the 18th century, and an antiquarian recorded traditions of fighting 'in the road and in Upton lane'. Two features mark the battlefield: an obelisk erected in 1845 stands on a spur a quarter of a mile (0.4 km) west of the crossroads, while 145 yards (133 m) southwest of the junction is a shallow depression known as the Battlewell, said to mark de Montfort's last stand; once the scene of miraculous cures, it is usually dry, and is easily missed.

The Evesham monk confirms the traditional view that de Montfort was in the abbey when Edward appeared, and adds some new details. The thunderstorm that underscores the drama of many accounts had cleared before de Montfort left the abbey. As he rode out, his standard-bearer broke the lance bearing de Montfort's banner on the gatehouse, the earl remarking, 'God help us now.' As the troops formed up on the edge of town the Welsh gave a great shout, in Celtic fashion. De Montfort is always shown leading with the cavalry, followed by the infantry. This may not have been intentional, as he rebuked the infantry commander for lagging behind: 'That's no way to conduct a battle, putting the foot soldiers in the rear. I know well how this will turn out.' When de Montfort saw Gloucester's banner over towards the river, on Edward's left as would be appropriate, he commented, 'How skilfully they are advancing. Our bodies are theirs, our soul's are God's.'

A gap in the Evesham manuscript throws us back on old sources for details of the fighting. The *Westminster Chronicle* says only a stone's throw separated the two sides when de Montfort's troops gained the top of the slope, implying that Edward occupied Green Hill's military crest, south of the crossroads. The Baronial cavalry had formed a deep column, perhaps 8 ranks deep and 50 files wide, to punch through the Royalist line. Edward's division recoiled before the charge, to be rallied by taunts about their performance at Lewes. Graves near the crossroads may represent the culminating point of de Montfort's offensive. Then the overlapping flanks of the Royalist army closed around the barons, forcing them into a 'thick mass in the form of a circle' (Thomas Wykes).

Edward had selected 12 men-at-arms to break through the Baronial ranks and kill de Montfort. One struck de Montfort through the neck with his lance, the Evesham monk resuming his account to say it was Mortimore, 'for he could be recognized by his armour and shield'. De Montfort's head was sent as a trophy to Mortimore's wife at Wigmore, the nose allegedly decorated with his private parts. Many of de Montfort's followers were cut down or were drowned swimming the river. An unprecedented number of knights died, perhaps as many as 200, almost all on the losing side. Even Henry III was wounded as he rode about in a borrowed suit of armour, crying, 'I am Henry of Winchester, your king, do not kill me.' The infantry were slaughtered like sheep, their blood polluting the abbey as it ran down into the crypt from the high altar. Robert of Gloucester sang of 'The mordre of Evesham, for battle it was none'.

The Conquest of Wales

The three centuries spanning the Norman Conquest of England and Edward I's conquest of Wales in the 1270s and 1280s decisively altered the relationship between the two peoples. Independent Welsh princes that Anglo-Saxon kings had regarded as legitimate if inferior rulers were subordinated, then obliterated. Like most medieval conflicts, the struggle was decided not by a few sparkling victories, but by unremitting strategic pressure. Plundering raids, devastation and assassination were more significant than pitched battles. This was especially the case in Wales, where the opponents were unusually ill matched. Welsh survival depended on avoiding formal confrontations, while wearing down more powerful English forces by guerrilla action. Those battles that did occur illustrate the asymmetrical nature of Anglo-Welsh warfare, and the shifting balance between defenders and invaders. Many reflect the fluidity of Welsh tactics, of which their sole idea, as Gerald of Wales wrote, was 'either to pursue their opponents, or else to run away from them'.

Welsh topography presented problems for both sides. Its predominant feature is the central massif, dividing the fertile fringes of North and South Wales. Over a quarter of Wales is above 1000 feet (300 m). One observer of Henry II's campaigns remarked on 'the Welsh amidst their Alps'. Physical barriers reinforced the centrifugal tendencies of Celtic politics. In addition to the major principalities of Gwynedd, Powys and Dyfed in northern, central and south-western Wales, there were other more transient entities. Wales remained an association of culturally allied people rather than a nation, until English pressure formed a new national consciousness in the 13th century.

Divisive terrain hampered invasions. There were few roads, except crumbling Roman routes west from Chester, Shrewsbury, Hereford and Caerleon. Dense oak woods choked the valleys, and favoured ambushes. A short growing season prevented accumulation of food surpluses that might support invading armies, unable to forward supplies along nonexistent roads. Henry II's invasion of 1165 collapsed under its own weight, as it inched across the Berwyn mountain range during the wettest August in living memory. William Rufus had already found heavy cavalry ill suited to mountain warfare: 'For the French could not penetrate the rocks and woods, but hovered about the plains. At length they returned home empty, without having gained anything …' (*Brut y Twysogion*).

Gerald of Wales, writing in the late 12th century, criticized the English failure to adopt methods better suited to Welsh conditions. He recommended employment of lightly armed troops, not weighed down with elaborate armour that was unnecessary against an enemy retreating at top speed through mountain defiles. Fresh troops should follow the leading echelons, to replace them as they grew weary, and keep the enemy moving. Before starting military operations, the English should stockpile supplies in castles, foment Welsh political divisions, and ban strategic imports of corn, salt, cloth and armour. Naval forces should enforce the embargo and safeguard English supply lines.

Until the Normans came, Welsh warfare continued in the old heroic manner. Small war bands roved long distances to overthrow rivals, as Llywelyn ap Seissyl's Gwynedd men did at Abergwyli in 1022. Gruffudd ap Llywelyn opened his reign with a show of force at Rhyd-y-Groes (1039), as Malcolm II of Scotland had at 'Burgus' (1006). The English defeat at the Battle of Hastings substituted 'a crowd of busy pioneers' for what Sir John Lloyd described as 'the sluggish home keeping race' of Anglo-Saxons that Gruffudd defeated at Hereford (1054). A far-sighted cleric at St David's Cathedral lamented the Normans' coming: 'Our limbs are cut off …

liberty and self-will [i.e. independence] perish.'

The conquest of Wales fell into three main stages. Rapid Norman expansion along the coastal strips was followed by a century of military stalemate, combined with cultural and ecclesiastical assimilation. This was followed by a period of rising tension, culminating in Edward I's final solution to the Welsh question. The initial Norman surge receded after an enigmatic Norwegian intervention at Priestholm (1098), but the pattern had been set. Normans dominated Glamorgan and Dyfed in the south. The Welsh held Anglesey and Snowdonia in the north, and would soon reassert themselves in the centre in Ceredigion and Powys, after Crug Mawr (1136). Norman castles, however, made the invaders difficult to shift, even when Welsh forces controlled the countryside, as Gruffudd ap Rhys found at Aberystwyth (1116).

The Welsh benefited from English political instability. Stephen failed to respond effectively to Gruffudd ap Cynan's victory at Crug Mawr, and during the Anarchy Gruffudd's son Owain Fawr advanced the borders of Gwynedd within sight of Chester's red towers, losing ground to Henry II after Coed Eulo (1157). Norman and Angevin kings generally preferred influence to conquest. After the failed invasion of 1165 Henry II developed personal ties with such magnates as Yr Arglwydd Rhys, the Lord Rhys of Deheubarth in southern central Wales. Henry III neglected such linkages, inspiring Llywelyn ap Gruffudd to seek an independence beyond his strength. Llywelyn exploited English disunity to make himself Prince of Wales in 1258, not long after an English column suffered disaster at Cymerau (1257). However, he backed the wrong side at Evesham (1265), and had to do homage and pay compensation to Henry III.

Llywelyn never resolved his feudal relationship with Henry's successor Edward I. If Llywelyn was too sensitive, Edward was too masterful, the first English king with the energy and strategic insight to implement Gerald of Wales's advice. In 1277 he imposed economic sanctions and invaded Wales with relays of infantry and workmen who cut paths through the forests. Overwhelmed by numbers and facing starvation, Llywelyn gave in without a fight. Faced with losing their cherished freedom the Welsh found a new sense of nationhood, presenting Edward in 1282 with a broadly based popular revolt. Edward repeated the measures that brought success in 1277, but Llywelyn was killed at Irfon Bridge before they took effect. The Statute of Wales and Edward's castle-building programme underlined his victory. A last despairing revolt in 1294–5 was suppressed by massively superior force, of which the Battle of Maes Moydog was an incidental side effect. The 900-year struggle against the Saxon had ended with the extinction of the Britons' legal and dynastic independence, though not their cultural identity.

Abergwyli, 1022

Wales, Carmarthenshire, LR159 SN4321?

Preoccupied with theology, early Welsh scholars reduced many secular events to a few unhelpful lines in an annal. The Battle of Abergwyli is an exception thanks to *Brut y Twysogion*'s unusually extended, almost literary treatment of the affair, *sub anno* 1020.

Reyn was a pretender to the principality of Deheubarth, the southern or right-hand Britons, seen from a western viewpoint. 'Yscot' carries its original meaning of Irish, making Reyn one of many Welsh princes to have taken refuge across the Irish Sea. The *Brut* agrees with modern scholars in rejecting his claim to be son of Maredudd ap Owain, 'the most famous king of the Welsh', but the assertion was impressive enough for the men of the South to receive him as lord. It also alarmed Llywelyn ap Seissyl, who had married Maredudd's daughter, provoking him to march the length of Wales to deal with the usurper.

Abergwyli lies east of the Roman station of

Carmarthen, in the confluence of the rivers Gwyli and Tywi. Two Roman roads converge there, joining beyond the Gwyli: Via Julia from Llandeilo to the east, and Sarn Helen from Llandovery and other points north. Llywelyn could have followed either route, before Reyn interposed between him and whatever facilities existed at Carmarthen. No numbers are available for Reyn's battle, but in 1047 the men of the Towey valley, whose fathers could have fought at Abergwyli, killed 140 of Gruffudd ap Llywelyn's *teulu* or household guard in an ambush. The two sides at Abergwyli probably totalled a few hundreds altogether.

Reyn 'boldly led on his host, and after the manner of the Scots [i.e. Irish], proudly and ostentatiously exhorted his men to fight, confidently promising them that he should conquer'. The sentence describes a recognizably oratorical Gaelic approach to battle, reminiscent of saga heroes egging on their men. If the *Brut*'s account is true, the Gwyneddians stood on the defensive, usually the better option in medieval battles. They were victorious after general slaughter on both sides, as would be expected between armies of similar size and armament.

Reyn 'retreated shamefully in a fox-like manner', pursued by the Gwyneddians: 'slaying his men, and devastating the country, pillaging every place, and destroying it as far as Mercia'. He disappeared from the *Brut* as mysteriously as he came, but *Annales Cambriae* baldly record his death in action: '*occisus est Reyn*'.

Directions

Take the A40 Llandeilo road east from Carmarthen to Abergwyli, its later Bishop's Palace lying between the main road and the River Tywi. To follow Sarn Helen take the A485 from Carmarthen to Lampeter.

Abergwyli

	Winners	*Losers*
Opponents	Welsh(Gwynedd)	Welsh (Deheubarth)
Commanders	Llywelyn ap Seissyl	Reyn Yscot (k)

Rhyd-y-Groes, 1039

Wales, Powys, LR126 SJ2400?

Hereford, 24 October 1055

England, Herefordshire, DS149 unlocated

Gruffudd ap Llywelyn maintained a balance of terror along the Anglo-Welsh border throughout the 1040s and 50s. The *Brut* gleefully records how 'from beginning to end, [he] pursued the Saxons and other nations ... and overcame them in a multitude of battles'. Domesday Book leaves no doubt about the consequent depopulation: agricultural land around Oswestry had reverted to forest; Archenfield was of no value; the Wye's southern bank lay empty. Two of Gruffudd's victories were recorded in some detail. Exact locations are uncertain, but both occurred near the junctions of Roman roads.

The modern village of Rhyd-y-Groes, the Ford at the Cross, lies southeast of Welshpool near Forden. Gaer Forden was a Roman auxiliary fort stopping up the Severn valley as it ran west to Cefn Carnedd, where Caradoc may have fought in AD 51. Sir John Lloyd denied that the battle of Rhyd-y-Groes could be more precisely indicated than an unknown ford on the Severn, finding no good authority (except the literal words of the *Brut* and *Annales Cambriae*) for locating the fight '*in vado Crucis*' ('at the ford of the cross'). However, the Roman road from Shrewsbury runs through Rhyd-y-Groes, and seems the logical approach for a Mercian host seeking to block an incursion '*super Sabrinus*' ('beyond the Severn') by the new king of Gwynedd ap Llywelyn. Gruffudd took the Mercians by surprise, '*per insidias*', to inflict a crushing defeat. Perhaps he forestalled them east of the Severn, lying in ambush to cut them to pieces as they emerged from the defile between Long Mountain and Camlad stream. Eadwine, brother of the Earl of Mercia, was killed, 'and very many other good men'.

Hereford lies east of the fortified Roman settlement of Magnis, near Kenchester. In the early 1050s

Rhyd-y-Groes

	Winners	*Losers*
Opponents	Welsh(Gwynedd)	English (Mercian)
Commanders	Gruffudd ap Llywelyn	Eadwine (k)

Hereford

	Winners	*Losers*
Opponents	Welsh (Gwynedd)	English
Commanders	Gruffudd ap Llywelyn Aelfgar	Ralph the Timid, Earl of Hereford
Numbers	*c.*1000	*c.*1000
Losses	none	400–500

it became one of the earliest Norman settlements in England, when Edward the Confessor made his French nephew Ralph, Count of the Vexin, Earl of Herefordshire. Gruffudd may have wished to take the measure of these novel opponents, or he may have been fishing in troubled waters. Earl Aelfgar of East Anglia was outlawed early in 1055, as part of the infighting that disfigured late Anglo-Saxon politics, and driven overseas. He returned with 18 shiploads of Irish Norsemen, and joined Gruffudd in harrying the border.

Earl Ralph intercepted the allies near Hereford, 2 miles (3 km) outside the city. Two Roman roads pass near Hereford: one from the west along the Wye valley, another from the north, where Gruffudd defeated another Anglo-Norman force at Leominster in 1052. The 1055 fighting could therefore have occurred west of Hereford, near Swainshill, or towards Moreton-on-Lugg to the north. Both sides claimed that the other had mobilized 'a very great host'. Aelfgar's ships might have carried 700 fighting men altogether, giving a total allied strength of over 1000. If English casualties were accurately recorded, they must have fielded as many, for their losses could not have been annihilating.

According to the *Anglo-Saxon Chronicle* Earl Ralph ordered his entire force to fight mounted, 'contrary to their custom'. The Norman may have hoped to achieve some sort of tactical homogeneity by this, but the result was catastrophic. The *Brut* says Gruffudd 'attacked them immediately with well-ordered troops', the Anglo-Saxons taking flight after 'a severely hard battle ... unable to bear the assault of the Britons'. The first statement is likely enough, but the *Anglo-Saxon Chronicle* records a sudden rout: 'Before there was any spear thrown, the English people already fled, because they were on horse.' Another version states that 'with a little struggle they were brought to flight'. Florence of Worcester says the Normans ran away first, 'seeing which the English with their commander also fled', earning Ralph his unfortunate nickname of 'the Timid'. Losses were unbalanced even for a medieval battle: 400–500 English plus wounded, against none in return. Such large casualties in a supposedly mounted force suggest the Anglo-Saxons could not even run away on horseback.

The victors pursued with such vigour that they surprised Hereford's garrison eating lunch, and proceeded to burn town, minster and relics, killing or enslaving the entire population. Gruffudd got away with this outrage in the short term. Harold Godwinson had to be content with refortifying Hereford with 'a wide and high bank ... gates and bars', while Aelfgar was reinstated, as part of a short-lived peace agreement. At Christmas 1062, however, Harold led a mounted column in pursuit of Gruffudd, devastating North Wales with such energy that, as Gerald of Wales approvingly quoted: 'he left not one that pisseth against a wall'. Gruffudd's power was shaken, and the *Brut* bewailed the fatal consequence: 'The head and shield and defender of the Britons, fell through the treachery of his own men. The man who had been invincible, was now left in the glens of desolation.'

Directions

For Rhyd-y-Groes take the A490 from Welshpool through Kingswood to the crossroads 1 mile (1.6 km) further on. The battlefield at Hereford is lost beyond speculation.

Priestholm (Anglesey Sound), **July 1098**

Wales, Anglesey, LR114 SH6279

The Normans' first impetus carried them as far as Anglesey, but they could not maintain so forward a position, lacking the stone castles and sea power that Edward I would deploy. Mere accident sufficed to roll them back to the Dee. The curious encounter at Priestholm was also the last significant Viking appearance in Welsh or English military history.

North Welsh resurgence during the 1090s brought together the marcher Earls of Chester and Shrewsbury in an attempt to recover Môn (Anglesey) and mainland Gwynedd. Both christened Hugh, they were distinguished by nicknames, being Fat and Proud respectively. The Welsh avoided action as usual, retreating to Anglesey, which they hoped to defend with the help of an Irish Norse fleet. Unfortunately the wily Norsemen accepted French bribes and ferried the Normans across to torture and maim the inhabitants. The Welsh leaders fled to Ireland, 'for fear of the treachery of their own men' (*Brut y Twysogion*), leaving the Normans to ravage the island. Among other atrocities Hugh the Proud kennelled his hounds in Llandyfrydog church. Retribution was swift.

A Viking fleet led by the king of Norway appeared off Ynys Seiriol, the rocky island of Priestholm or Puffin Island, and for no particular reason attacked the force in possession. Priestholm is an unlikely place for an assault landing. The beach is too steeply pitched to run ships ashore, and consists of large round stones, an insecure foothold for men, let alone horses. *Orkneyinga Saga* describes 'a great battle in Anglesey-sound', suggesting somewhere inside the northern approaches to the Menai Straits. This is consistent with the *Brut*'s reference to the Normans camping at Aber Lleiniog, a wooded valley between Beaumaris and Penmon, whose priory may have been the Viking target. Aber Lleiniog runs down to a gently shelving bay sheltered from the Irish Sea, an altogether more practicable landing place.

Hugh the Proud rode down to meet the invaders and 'dashed wildly into the sea to attack them' (Gerald of Wales). The *Saga*, pursuing its heroic agenda, described an uncertain conflict, while Magnus Barefoot plied his bow from the prow of his ship:

Blood on helmets there was sprinkled
Bowstrings hail on mail came flying
Men fell fast and Harda's king
Seeking land with onslaught hard
Dealt his deathblow to the earl.

The *Brut* describes a more plausible standoff, for 'as they were mutually shooting, the one party from the sea, and the other party from the land, Earl Hugh was wounded in the face, by the hand of the king. And then the king with sudden determination, left the borders of the country.' Magnus had seen the armoured figure at the water's edge, byrnied to the eyes, and shot at him with another marksman: 'One arrow struck him on the nose guard, but the other went in at the eye, and flew afterwards through the head.' Hugh the Proud's men withdrew, unable to recover his mail-clad body until low tide.

The *Saga* claimed a great victory, but like all raiders Magnus did not stay long before he 'turned back by the south course to Scotland'. This nonchalant demonstration of sea power must have rattled the surviving Earl Hugh, for he abandoned Gwynedd's exposed northwest coast, and restored its fugitive princes: 'From that moment onwards,' Gerald commented, 'the English lost their control of Anglesey.'

Priestholm

	Winners	*Losers*
Opponents	Norwegian	Norman
Commanders	Magnus Barefoot	Hugh d'Avranches, Earl of Chester Hugh Montgomery, Earl of Shrewsbury (k)

Directions

Follow the B5109 northwards from Beaumaris, turning right at Llangoed, down a minor road for Aber Lleiniog and Penmon. Continue 2/3 mile (1 km) northeastward from Penmon to view Puffin Island 1/2 mile (0.8 km) offshore.

Aberystwyth, 1116

Wales, Ceredigion, LR135 SN5878–9

The Normans who occupied Ceredigion, anglicized as Cardiganshire, made it a land of castles. These were not just passive refuges, but a base for defensive-offensive operations. Garrisons often combined against larger Welsh forces, which might dominate the countryside but were generally incapable of taking castles. Razo's defence of Aberystwyth neatly illustrates the double function of such fortifications, described with unusual candour in the *Brut y Twysogion* by a local chronicler from Llanbadarn Fawr.

Gruffudd ap Rhys, a footloose prince of Deheubarth, provided a focus for Welsh discontent during the mid-1110s. Numerous hotheads flocked to him, 'instigated by the devil' according to the *Brut*, out of sympathy with 'lunatics' who 'committed indecencies' in the author's own church. Early in 1116 Gruffudd ran amok, terrorizing 'Saxon' settlers brought in 'to fill the country, which previously from paucity of inhabitants, was proudly empty'. He attacked Swansea and Llandovery, destroyed Narberth Castle and burnt Carmarthen town, then moved into Ceredigion, to slaughter the garrison of Razo's fort at Penweddig. Afterwards his army marched on Aberystwyth, camping at Glasgrug, 3 miles (5 km) northeast of the castle, and a mile (1.6 km) from Llanbadarn, whose monastic livestock they ate.

The local chronicler placed Aberystwyth's first castle 'over against Llanbadarn near the mouth of the river called the Ystwyth ... situated upon the top of a hill that shelved down to the river Ystwyth, and over the river was a bridge'. Built by Gilbert FitzRichard *c.*1110, it crowned a slight hill between sea and river, where the Ordnance Survey shows a 'Ring & Bailey'. The later Edwardian castle, within the modern town to the north, was a quite distinct structure.

Aberystwyth		
	Winners	*Losers*
Opponents	Norman	Welsh
Commanders	Razo, Castellan	Gruffudd ap Rhys

The resolution of Gilbert's castellan Razo contrasts with the negligence and indiscipline of his attackers. Although 'moved with sorrow for his men, and for his loss' at Penweddig, Razo sent immediately for reinforcements from Ystrad Meurig castle 10 miles (16 km) to the southeast, who came in overnight. Gruffudd's men do not seem to have expected the castle at Aberystwyth to be defended, for next morning they 'sallied from their tents, without putting their troops in array; and without setting up ensigns, a villain host, like a company of people without counsel, and without a commander'. While they stood around devising some means of breaching the walls, 'the day glided away until it was afternoon'.

At this point the garrison, 'as is the manner of the French to do everything by stratagem', sent some archers down to the bridge in hopes of luring the Welsh across, to be cut off by heavy cavalry. The Britons were clearly North Welsh without bows, for they 'indiscreetly ran to meet them', rather than shooting back. The ploy nearly ended badly for one Norman. A knight fell off his horse rushing onto the bridge too violently, 'and then everybody with spears endeavoured to kill him, but his coat of mail protected him, until some of his party came and dragged him away'. Some of the Welsh chased the discomfited Normans back 'almost to the declivity of the mountain', a few hundred yards. Others awaited events by the bridge. One version of the *Brut* has them acting as a support for their friends, 'in case pursuit and distress should come upon them'. Watching from the hilltop, Razo seized his chance. Suddenly he counterattacked the loosely knit ranks of the Welsh advance party, killing as many as could be caught, and scattering the rest about the countryside.

The insurgency melted away, as participants sought to escape with their looted cattle, or at least their lives. Gruffudd himself found shelter in the impenetrable woods of Ystrad Tywi. Somehow he escaped Henry I's bounty hunters, to take part in the great Welsh victory of Crug Mawr (see below).

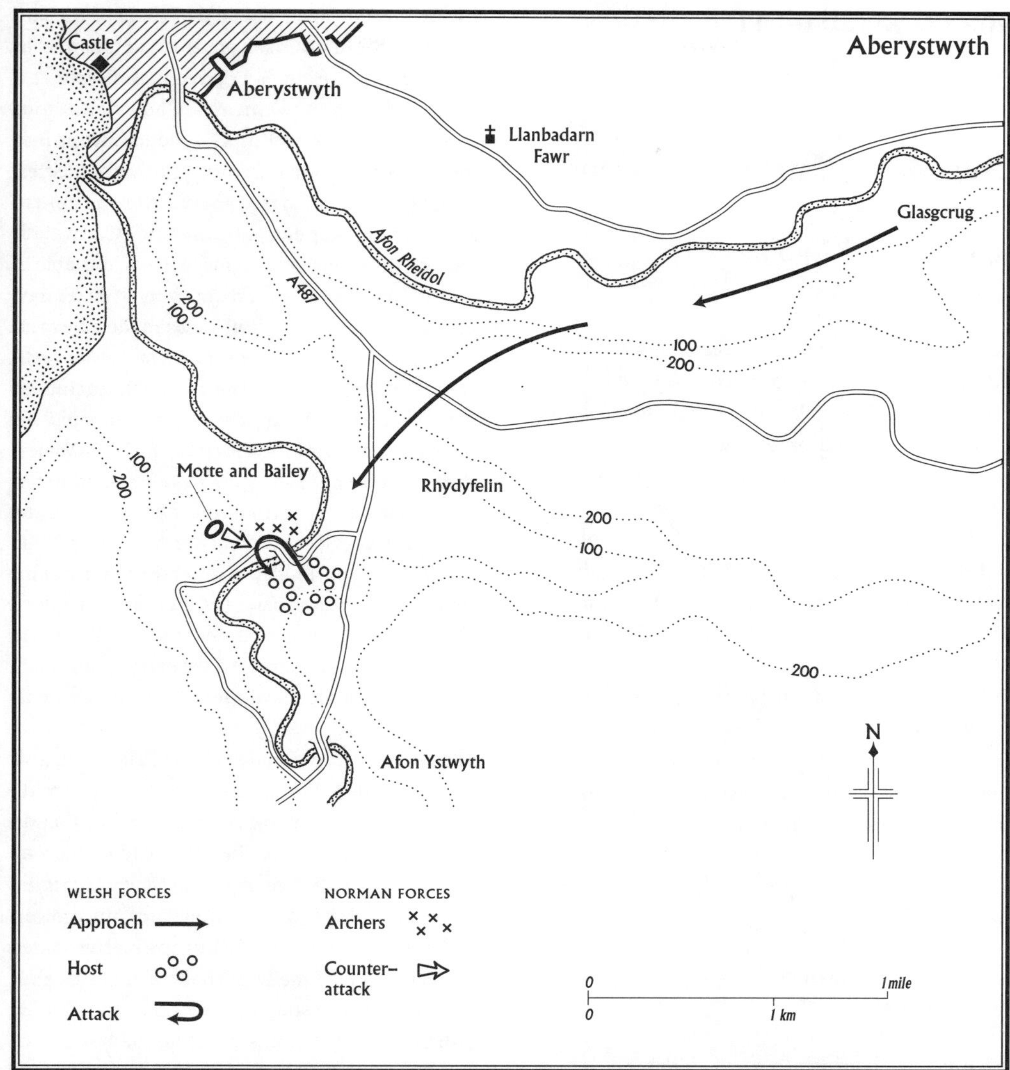

Directions

Follow the A487 south of Aberystwyth. Turn right in Rhydyfelin, down to the river. Buildings now stand between the bridge and the castle's remains on the high ground beyond.

Maes Gwenllian, 1136

Wales, Carmarthenshire, LR159 SN4208

Crug Mawr (Cardigan/Crugmore), October 1136

Wales, Ceredigion, LR145 SN2047

Henry I dominated Wales by personal force, a man 'against whom none can contend save God himself'. His death in December 1135 released tensions throughout the region, as infuriated Welshmen turned upon the Normans and their Anglo-Flemish running dogs. On 1 January 1136, 500 settlers were overwhelmed in battle somewhere between Loughor and Swansea. The men of Deheubarth in South Wales marched on the motte-and-bailey castle at Kidwelly led by Gwenllian, wife of Gruffudd ap Rhys, who had gone to seek help in Gwynedd. Maurice of London cut them to pieces north of Kidwelly, between Mynydd y Garreg and the River Gwendraeth. Ever since, the spot where 'the flower and ornament of all Wales' was beheaded has been known as Maes Gwenllian, the meadow of Gwenllian. In Ceredigion, however, the Welsh won a major success that undid conquests a quarter of a century old.

Maes Gwenllian

	Winners	*Losers*
Opponents	Norman	Welsh
Commanders	Maurice of London	Gwenllian (k)
Numbers	unknown	unknown

Crug Mawr

	Winners	*Losers*
Opponents	Welsh (Gwynedd)	Norman
Commanders	Owain 'Fawr' Gruffudd ap Rhys	Stephen, Constable of Cardigan
Numbers	*c.*4000	*c.*3000

The campaign opened with the killing of Richard FitzGilbert, Lord of Cardigan, at Coed Grwyne, as he rode unarmed from Abergavenny to Brecon, his minstrel playing. Owain and Cadwaladr, sons of Gruffudd ap Cynan of Gwynedd, swept into Ceredigion to capture five of Richard's castles, including Aberystwyth (see above). After a pause to remove their plunder, Owain and Cadwaladr resumed operations in September. The Constable of Cardigan came out to meet them, with all the French from Neath to the Dyfi. Both sides made an exceptional effort. The contemporary *Gesta Stephani* estimated the Anglo-Normans at 3000, including infantry. Gruffudd ap Rhys had collected an immense army with all the great men of Wales, although the *Brut y Twysogion*'s '6000 fine infantry, and 2100 cavalry in armour' must be questionable. The knight service of England was only 5000 horsemen, supported by a much broader demographic and economic base. If Gruffudd had indeed mobilized all the choice combatants of Wales, the Welsh must have outnumbered the enemy sufficiently to pull off a double envelopment, a most difficult operation of war.

The battle's traditional site is at Crugmore, also known as Banc y Warren, 2 miles (3 km) outside Cardigan beside the main Aberaeron road. Gerald of Wales passed south of the battlefield on his way to Lampeter in 1188: 'leaving Crug Mawr, that is the big hill, on our left soon after riding out of Cardigan ... [where] Gruffudd son of Rhys ap Tewdwr gained a great victory over the English in pitched battle'. It was an appropriate spot for a Welsh victory. To the Welsh antiquary Nennius (fl.*c.*800) the tumulus of 'Cruc Maur in Cereticiaun' had been a wonder of Britain. According to *Gesta Stephani* the Welsh 'divided themselves into three terrible bands, well ordered and soldierly, and surrounding Richard's knights on three sides routed them'. The locally compiled *Brut* is disappointingly brief: 'After joining battle, with cruel fighting on every side, the Flemings and the Normans took to flight, according to their custom.'

All sources agree on the disaster that followed, as the Welsh pursued the defeated army back into

Cardigan 'with shouts and arrows'. Some they killed outright, and some the cavalry trampled underfoot: 'the greater part, like fools, drowned in the river' (*Brut*). Many were led off into captivity. The *Gesta* turns the affair into a war crime: 'Others they massacred by driving them violently into a river [the Teifi], a good number they put in houses and churches to which they set fire, and burnt them.' The principal contemporary accounts omit the lurid details featured in modern accounts of the Teifi bridge collapsing under the weight of fugitives, their bodies blocking the stream. Only one notable fatality was acknowledged on the Welsh side, while the *Brut* cheerfully claimed 3000 Norman casualties. The proportion might be compatible with an encirclement battle, except that Gerald's uncle Maurice, who fought on the losing side, lived another 40 years.

Only Cardigan Castle held out, as the rest of Ceredigion fell into Welsh hands. Distrust between Stephen and his marcher lords prevented an immediate counteroffensive, providing an unparalleled opportunity for the Welsh to push back the frontier. As usual they fell out over the spoils, and the southern Normans hung on.

Directions

Maes Gwenllian *See the remains of Kidwelly Castle and Gwenllian's modern memorial, then cross Gwendraeth Fach by the B4308, forking left to Mynyddygarreg. Maes Gwenllian is north of the village, down several footpaths on the left. Old 2½-inch maps show it in the top right corner of the map square specified.*

Crug Mawr *Take the A487 Aberaeron road as far as Banc y Warren 2 miles (3 km) from the centre of Cardigan. A track on the right leads to Crug Mawr farm. Gerald presumably took the B4570 Lampeter road through Llangoedmor.*

Coleshill (Coed Eulo), **1157**

Wales, Flintshire, LR117 SJ2966?

The accession of Henry II in 1154 restored stability to the Welsh Marches. Three years later he attempted to reassert English prestige with a massive expedition aimed at Owain ap Gruffudd of Gwynedd, the chief beneficiary of the divisions and chaos of Stephen's reign. The campaign was a rare occasion when the Welsh felt strong enough to offer battle to an English royal army. The location and course of the fighting have provoked much debate, but the eventual outcome justified the usual Welsh reluctance to risk battle.

Both sides made extensive preparations. Henry called up archers from Shropshire and Welsh auxiliaries from Powys, and concentrated a fleet at Pembroke to rendezvous with him in North Wales. To keep sufficient heavy cavalry in the field, he reduced the number of knights mobilized in exchange for a longer period of service than the usual 40 days. Owain 'called to him his sons and his strength and his army and his power, [and] encamped at Basingwerk, having with him an immense host' (*Brut y Twysogion*). Basing is the northern end of Wat's Dyke, an old frontier defence, blocking the traditional invasion route between the Dee estuary and the Clwydian mountains. Owain had adopted a dangerous strategy, offering battle so far forward against an opponent at full strength, not yet worn down by slogging through rainswept hills: 'And there he fixed an appointment for battle ... causing dykes to be raised, with the design of fighting a pitched battle' (*Brut*).

Henry II could not refuse such a direct challenge, but had more imagination than to run his head against a fortified position. He split his forces, which were large enough to do so without risking defeat in detail. One column advanced directly, 'along the strand towards the place where Owain was'. Henry himself moved around Owain's open western flank, 'with armed troops, the most prepared for fighting ... through the wood ... that lay between them

Coleshill

	Winners	*Losers*
Opponents	English	Welsh (Gwynedd)
Commanders	Henry II	Owain 'Fawr'

and the place where Owain was'. This arrangement has attracted two misguided comments: first that Henry led a flying column of light troops; secondly that he plunged into the woods in a fit of 'youthful ardour and rash enthusiasm' prompted by ignorance of local conditions. The outflanking column was a conventional 12th-century force including at least four barons, while Henry was no military ingénue, after four years restoring order among England's baronage.

Owain's position was traditionally located at Dinas Basing, the ruined priory of Basingwerk near Greenfield, where Gerald of Wales stayed in 1188. However, in 1157 the monastic community occupied a site 3 miles (5 km) further south at Hen Blas (SJ2273) between Cefn Coleshill and Coleshill village, a mile inland from Flint Castle. Several contemporary sources, including Gerald of Wales, name Coleshill as the location of the fighting that broke out as Henry felt his way around Owain's flank. The *Brut*, however, says that David and Cynan, sons of Owain, intercepted the English in the trackless wood of Cennadlog, before their outflanking movement was complete. If Owain was at Coleshill, the ambuscade must have taken place still further to the south. Recent scholarship has shown that Cennadlog is a misreading of Pennardd Alaog, the Wood of Hawarden, or Penarlâg in modern Welsh. When Gerald visited the area, Coleshill had become a name for the whole district between that village and Hawarden. He was therefore giving a more general indication of the location of the battlefield, than the better-informed Welsh chronicler of the *Brut*. Ewloe, from which the battle derives its alternative name, is a mile (1.6 km) northwest of Hawarden at the junction of the A55 and the A494 Queensferry road. The Ordnance Survey's indication saying 'Supposed Site of the Battle of Coleshill' in the immediate vicinity of Flint is thus misleading.

It would appear that while Owain's main forces held their prepared position at Hen Blas, his sons were thrown forward in the extensive woods that Domesday Book recorded at Hawarden. The Welsh army thus formed a huge L-shaped ambush. Henry did well not to walk into the trap, from which the only exit lay across the deadly quicksands of the Dee estuary. As it was, the English outflanking column suffered heavy casualties from Owain's forward echelon, *in primo conflictu*, 'the Welsh lurking in pathless mountain defiles and swamps, as their custom is' (*Osney Chronicle*). Several barons were killed, and the king narrowly escaped death. Henry's personal standard-bearer threw his banner away and fled, for which he was compelled to retire into Reading monastery.

Patriotic Welsh historians have taken their chroniclers' enthusiasm at face value to concoct a great Welsh victory, while ignoring the final outcome. Henry broke through to open ground, encircling the awaiting defenders: 'and when Owain understood that the king was coming upon him from behind, and saw the earls [i.e. the coastal detachment] from the other side approaching ... he left the place and retreated' (*Brut*). *Annales Cambriae* leave no doubt that Owain fell back 'to a safer place' in face of overwhelming forces approaching from behind, '*a tergo imminere*'. Enraged at his losses, Henry pressed on, probably by the route followed by today's A55, to besiege Rhuddlan.

Casualties at Coleshill and a naval disaster at Moelfre in Anglesey persuaded Henry to make peace with Owain, who was lurking at Cil Owen, a mile (1.6 km) southeast of St Asaph. Owain for his part did homage and gave hostages. He had mauled the invaders, and managed to retreat, but had nearly come badly unstuck. When Henry returned in greater force in 1165, Owain refused to fight, leaving hunger and weather to destroy his enemies.

Directions

Tactical dispositions unknown. See text for general locations.

Cymerau (Coed Llathen), **Saturday 2 June 1257**

Wales, Carmarthenshire, LR159 SN5020

The annihilation of an English column at 'Cymerau' was a more typical Welsh fight than Crug Mawr or Coleshill (see above). It was not a pitched battle between armies drawn up at a given place and time, but a running fight over many miles and several days. The irrepressible Welsh of Ystrad Tywi harassed a powerful English force on the line of march, and finally cut it to pieces. For once the victors would not have needed numerical superiority, shooting from cover into a dense column, strung out along the road in the open.

Henry III was frequently at odds with his barons, and Llywelyn ap Gruffudd, last native prince of all Wales, was quick to exploit the English king's distractions. One of Llywelyn's victims was Rhys Fechan, a Welsh collaborator ejected from Dinefwr Castle in 1256 as part of a general uprising against Henry's extortionate taxes. Stephen Bauzan was an experienced royal official, ex-seneschal of Gascony and '*regi carissimus*' ('very dear to the king'). He gathered a force at Carmarthen in May 1257 to restore Rhys, and incidentally to plunder the Tywi valley.

The expedition left Carmarthen on Thursday 31 May, probably by the Roman road along the north bank of the Tywi that has become the A40: 'all renowned men-at-arms with numerous armoured horses, and other instruments of war' (*Annales Cambriae*). Not without difficulty, they made their way to Llandeilo Fawr, bypassing Dinefwr Castle on its hill west of the town, and encamped for the night. *Annales Cambriae* says they did this 'without fear', but they had bitten off more than they knew. The Welsh of Ceredigion had joined the men of Ystrad Tywi, and 'with great shouts gathered around the English on all sides in the woods, forest clearings, and surrounding valleys'.

Next day (Friday) the English remained at Llandeilo, harassed by Welsh javelins and arrows. On the Saturday, Rhys Fechan, seeing the English in a tight corner, slipped quietly away. Still trusting in superior weaponry, the English took the road home, though the annals suggest they would have done better to place more trust in God. The Welsh tormented them from the shelter of the woods all morning, some eight hours at that time of year. At an unknown wood called Coed Llathen, the English lost their baggage train, with the spare arms and horses. Around noon the Welsh burst through the English ranks, boldly tipping them off their armoured horses. English sources confirm the column was let down by its Welsh guides, surrounded on all sides and overwhelmed by superior numbers after the Welsh had killed the horses.

The *Annales Cambriae* say all this happened on the Kerdegaun road, which makes no sense, as Cardigan lies beyond Carmarthen when starting from Llandeilo. Sir John Lloyd placed the disaster at the confluence or *cymerau* of Aber Cothi and the Tywi, 8 miles (13 km) from Llandeilo, more than halfway back to Carmarthen along the Roman road. As the battered column approached the steep crossing at Pont-ar-Gothi, the Welsh were elated by their capture of the supply train. They made a last charge, driving the English off the road and down the spur between the two streams, to be trampled 'in the swamps and ditches' of the valley bottom. The *Osney Chronicle* describes the English caught between swamps and woods, a figure of speech applicable to most Welsh scenery, but appropriate to Bauzan's situation, between wooded hill slopes and marshy river valley.

Few English can have got out. *Brut y Twysogion* claimed the victors 'took the barons and noble knights, and slew upwards of 2000 of the army, that

Cymerau

	Winners	*Losers*
Opponents	Welsh	English
Commanders	Maredudd ab Owain Mareduddap Rhys	Stephen Bauzan (k)
Numbers	unknown	unknown
Losses	unknown	2000–3000

was when the men were slain in mutual engagement'. *Annales Cambriae* claimed an extra thousand, perhaps picked off as they fled. Several thousand does not seem an unlikely strength for a major expedition under an experienced leader, gathered from diverse parts of England, and the losers' casualties could have approached 100 per cent in such a battle. English sources admitted a great slaughter of unknown extent: 'nobles, knights, men-at-arms and infantry, to the number of 1000 and more' (Matthew Paris). Only two named knights survived, one as a prisoner. No such catastrophe had happened for generations, and it was not forgotten. One of Edward I's earliest actions after his conquest of Wales was to place tombstones on the graves of English commanders killed at Cymerau.

Directions

See Dinefwr Castle, then follow the A40 west from Llandeilo to Pont-ar-Gothi, where Bauzan's men came to grief in the Tywi valley on the left.

Irfon Bridge (Orewin Bridge), **Friday 11 December 1282**

Wales, Powys, LR147 SN9950

The death of Llywelyn ap Gruffudd extinguished Welsh independence, and with it the ancient British nation. The sources are sadly unequal to the occasion. In his official despatch Robert L'Estrange starkly informed King Edward that 'Llywelyn ap Gruffudd is dead, his army broken, and all the flower of his men killed.' He left the messenger to fill in the details by word of mouth.

Edward I's nearly bloodless conquest of Wales in 1277 had subordinated Gwynedd to the English crown, leaving Llywelyn as Edward's greatest feudatory lord. Contrary to the Treaty of Aberconwy, aggressive royal officials disregarded Welsh laws, provoking violent popular reaction. Llywelyn joined the general uprising, but misjudged his chances of repeating the successes of the 1250s. Edward I was not

Irfon Bridge

	Winners	*Losers*
Opponents	English	Welsh
Commanders	Edmund Mortimer Robert L'Estrange John Giffard	Llywelyn ap Gruffudd (Llywelyn the Last) (k)
Numbers	*c.*2500	*c.*2000

Henry III. He was determined 'to put an end finally to this matter ... of putting down the malice of the Welsh'.

Edward deployed vastly superior forces in a well-coordinated campaign, which the scattered Welsh were quite unable to resist. By autumn Edward's northern army was poised for an unprecedented winter campaign in Snowdonia, dressed in specially provided warm clothing. Llywelyn struck south into the central marches, hoping to exploit local unrest. Roger Mortimer had died in October 1282, leaving the inhabitants without a lord, 'very fickle and haughty, as if they were on the point of leaving the king's peace'.

Llywelyn had miscalculated again, for he was killed near Llanfair ym Muallt, i.e. Builth Wells. Sadly the last native Prince of Wales did not die gloriously at the head of his army, but unattended, in some disregarded corner of the field. It is not even certain how he came to be alone. Chroniclers hint that Mortimer's heirs treacherously lured Llywelyn to his death. Treasonable letters disguised by false names were allegedly found on his body. The traditional account is that Llywelyn was hurrying back from some parley, when he was intercepted and killed almost by accident.

Most reconstructions follow Walter of Guisborough, also known as Hemingburgh, a circumstantial, but remote and unreliable source writing about 1300. According to him Llywelyn left his army on a hill above the Wye, observing an English force south of the river, beyond Orewin Bridge. The hill has been identified with high ground at Cilmeri, on the north bank of the Irfon. Llywelyn went off with one man-at-arms to test the loyalty of the valley's inhabitants.

The usual traitor revealed a ford, allowing the English to get across during Llywelyn's absence and demolish the Welsh spearmen with a neat combination of shock tactics and missiles:

> The Welsh stood in squadrons on the crest of the hill ... And our men climbing up, shot arrows and many missiles. Having engaged in some close combat many fell to our archers (who were supported between the cavalry) ... At length our cavalry charged up the hill above them, and having cut some down, drove off the rest at speed.
>
> Walter of Guisborough, *Chronicle* (*c.*1300)

Hurrying back from his conference, Llywelyn was slain by Stephen de Frankton, a centenar or company commander from Ellesmere, who only later realized what he had done. From this obscure action Sir Charles Oman traced the development of the English longbow to 'all the glorious continental successes of Edward III and Henry V', making Irfon Bridge part of English as well as Welsh national mythology.

Walter of Guisborough's dramatic narrative is uncorroborated and untrustworthy. No other source mentions a battle at a bridge over the Irfon, or anywhere else. His other place names, 'Helyswath' and 'Thaulveyr', no longer exist. As Walter did not write until at least 1297, he may have concocted his account of Irfon from confused reports of Stirling Bridge and Falkirk that he picked up from soldiers returning from Edward's Scottish wars, hence the opposed river crossing and the mixture of cavalry and archers. By coincidence, a Scots renegade from Irvine did reveal a nearby ford before Stirling Bridge. The assonance with Irfon, where the 'f' is pronounced 'v', is too suggestive to require emphasis.

Almost every other source describes a long and fierce battle with heavy losses on both sides: the 15th-century historian John Capgrave wrote that 'Much harm was done on both sides.' Many suggest an ambush at a pre-arranged spot, '*in loco prenominata*'. Llywelyn was killed very late, 'almost at the hour of vespers'. The contemporary Dunstable chronicler thought Llywelyn died where he was buried, at Abbey Cwmhir, 14 miles (22 km) north of Builth (LR147 SO0571), but otherwise followed the consensus:

> There suddenly fell upon him, after sunset, those who were for the king from the garrisons of Montgomery and Oswestry. Also killed with the prince were three of his magnates and up to 2000 foot; very few horse.

The Peterborough chronicler (another contemporary) gave the names of the three, one of whom was bailiff of Builth, stating a credible Welsh cavalry strength of 160. Incomplete payroll records suggest the English fielded 2000 infantry and 20 paid cavalry under Robert L'Estrange, Edward's commander at Montgomery. The Mortimers were also present with their own, not inconsiderable, retinue. Capgrave describes Edmund Mortimer ransacking the dead, 'and amongst divers hedis that were there he found Levlyn's hed, which he brout to the kyng'.

Whatever the place and circumstance of Llywelyn's death, the result was catastrophic for the Welsh cause: 'All Wales was cast to the ground'. Poets lamented the end of their world, and a head 'which when severed was not avenged by Kymry'. Edward I resumed his inexorable advance, capturing Llywelyn's fugitive brother Dafydd in June 1283. Dafydd died a traitor's death, leaving no direct heirs to continue the struggle, except a little girl shut up in an English convent. In two short campaigns Edward had transformed the political map of Wales, and laid the foundations of how the country would be governed for over 200 years.

Directions

Take the A483 west from Builth Wells. A roadside monument records the spot where Llywelyn is said to have fallen, just past the Prince Llywelyn inn. A footpath runs down under the railway to the demolished bridge at Hendre, though the Welsh must have stood further up the hill north of the main road. The remains of Abbey Cwmhir are on private land 3 miles (5 km) down a minor road left of the A483, north of Llandrindod Wells. See the modern slab at the east end of the nave commemorating Llywelyn's burial.

Maes Moydog (Maes Madog/ Meismedoc), Saturday 5 March 1295

Wales, Powys, LR125 SJ1607

The Welsh revolt of 1294–5 was the last concerted attempt to reverse Edward I's conquest of Wales. The Earl of Warwick broke the back of the revolt at 'Meismedoc' in March 1295. Unfortunately the disjointed evidence has so puzzled students of the campaign that some have placed the encounter near Colwyn Bay in January, 50 miles (80 km) and two months away from its true place and time.

Conscription for overseas military service provoked rebellion throughout Wales in October 1294, Madog ap Llywelyn, a junior member of Gwynedd's old dynasty, playing a pre-eminent part. Edward moved to suppress the revolt with customary despatch. He summoned over 30,000 infantry and marched into North Wales, celebrating Christmas at Conwy. Edward's only setback was in January, when he lost his baggage train and was beleaguered in Conwy Castle. Even the king had to drink water, an embarrassment from which he was rescued by the Earl of Warwick. J.E. Morris, the usually meticulous historian of Edward's Welsh wars, ran all these incidents together. From indirect evidence he deduced the battle was in North Wales, dating it 'a day or two before 24 January'.

Contemporary evidence disproves this. The *Worcester Chronicle*, which first named the action, specifically assigned it to 5 March, when Warwick by his own report was miles away from Conwy as '*chevetayne de la host en les parties de Montgomery*' ('chief of the host in the regions of Montgomery'). Expenses were paid for escorting prisoners to Conwy, after Madog's defeat '*in terra Kerenion*', i.e. Caereinion in Powys. The enterprising Madog had left Edward immobilized by lack of supplies, and like Llywelyn the Last, struck southeast. Warwick was at Oswestry when spies brought intelligence that Madog was nearby. The earl countermarched to Montgomery, doubling back overnight towards Welshpool to defeat Madog next day.

Tradition associates Madog with fighting around Cefn Digoll or Long Mountain, east of Welshpool. Four miles (6 km) west of Welshpool, however, the parish of Castle Caereinion includes the locality of Moydog. This is the chronicler's 'Meismedoc', which historians have wrongly equated with Maes Madoc, the Field of Madog, rather than Moydog. Three farms and a wood share the name, all lying in a small valley atop the high ground between the rivers Vyrnwy and Severn. Trevet's *Annales* confirm how the battle came about:

> The Earl of Warwick hearing that the Welsh were massed in great numbers in a certain plain between two forests, took with him a picked body of men-at-arms, together with crossbowmen and archers, and surprising them by night, surrounded them on all sides.

Moydog is 8 miles (13 km) from Montgomery, a reasonable distance for a night march. Higher ground rises steeply north and south of the valley floor, defining a cockpit 600 yards (550 m) wide by a mile (1.6 km) long, ample room for the small forces deployed. Warwick's payroll ran to 119 heavy cavalry and 2715 Shropshire infantry, besides 13 specialist crossbowmen, paid the premium rate of 3d. a day. Many of the infantry must have carried bows, as missile weapons played an important role in the fighting. Not all fought at Maes Moydog. Warwick only took some chosen knights, '*electa militia*', with him, and had detached a cut-off party.

A contemporary newsletter reveals that for once the enemy took the offensive: 'For the Welsh stood so well and went against our men face to face, and were the boldest and most handsome Welshmen anyone ever saw.' Sir Charles Oman saw the battle's

Maes Moydog

	Winners	*Losers*
Opponents	English	Welsh
Commanders	William Beauchamp, Earl of Warwick	Madog ap Llywelyn
Numbers	maximum 2847	unknown
Losses	7	*c.*700

combination of missile and shock action as another step towards the glories of Falkirk and Crecy:

> Seeing themselves surrounded, they [the Welsh] fixed the butts of their spears in the earth, with the heads pointing outwards, to keep off the rush of the horsemen. But the Earl placed a crossbowman between each two knights, and when by their shooting a great part of the spearmen had been slain, he burst in among them with his horse, and made such carnage as no Welsh army ... had ever suffered before.
>
> Nicholas Trevet, *Annales*

Trevet's 'crossbows' must have included a number of longbows at 2d. a day. There is no evidence, however, that the men-at-arms dismounted, as they would during the Hundred Years' War. Indeed they lost ten horses, suggesting mounted action. The newsletter admitted losses of one squire and six infantry, which the payroll confirms, showing six men paid for wounds suffered in the fight with Madog.

Welsh losses were allegedly enormous: 600 killed or drowned, fleeing north across the Vyrnwy, swollen by months of heavy rain. Madog himself escaped with difficulty. A detached English force intercepted his baggage, killing another 100 men, and capturing 120 pack animals. Warwick had gone to some trouble to cut off Madog's retreat westwards across the Banwy valley, infiltrating troops along the scrappy Roman road north from Caersws on the Severn. Madog's defeat was a turning point. Soon afterwards two Welsh princes surrendered on terms, one of whom was probably Madog. Warwick's brilliant victory had not so much rescued Edward at the end of the winter campaign, as removed the best Welsh army and its leader before the spring campaign had begun.

Directions

Follow the A458 west from Welshpool, turning right along a minor road just short of Cyfronydd for Moydog Fawr farm about 1 mile (1.6 km) north of the main road. Continue along the A458 to Llysyn farm and Llystynwynnan, where the English may have captured Madog's baggage train.

The Scots Wars of Independence

The accidental death of Alexander III of Scotland without an heir in 1286 was a double misfortune: by disastrous coincidence a leaderless Scotland was left facing the most energetic and ambitious English ruler of the Middle Ages. Scotland's succession crisis was for Edward I an opportunity to continue the unification of Britain that he had begun in Wales. The consequences of his intervention in Scotland were disastrous. Scotland and the Border region were devastated, while England was reduced to bankruptcy and civil war. Contrary to Edward's intentions, Scotland reaffirmed its independence in a series of iconic battles, still exploited by politicians and filmmakers.

The war that began in 1296 was not inevitable. Six 'guardians' representing the community of Scotland had resolved the succession issue, at the price of swearing fealty to Edward for adjudicating between rival claimants to the throne. John Balliol was enthroned King of Scots in November 1292, but Edward broke his promises to withdraw from Scottish politics. John was summoned before the King's Bench in London, on trivial and vexatious charges, and treated like a common debtor. War between England and France in 1294 exposed both the reality and weakness of English domination. Edward's demands for military service overseas presented Scots magnates with an unmissable chance to reject his overlordship. Fresh guardians took power from the discredited John, and allied themselves with France.

Unable to ignore the threat to his rear, Edward invaded Scotland, overthrew the guardians, and from Scone Abbey carried off the Stone of Destiny, on which the kings of Scotland had traditionally been crowned. To legitimize his rule Edward behaved as if a kingdom of Scotland had never existed. Resistance was treated as rebellion, subject to the penalties of treason. Edward extracted numerous individual oaths of fealty, but the general community of the realm never accepted his authority, a popular rejection symbolized by William Wallace's homespun leadership in 1297–8. Edward's reign of terror after Robert the Bruce's bid for the throne in 1306 gave Scots little choice but war; according to the contemporary chronicler Walter of Guisborough, 'since … the Scots were to be burned, drawn at horse tails and hanged … with one accord they joined Bruce preferring to die rather than be tried by English law'. Edward's death in July 1307 left his son Edward II with an unwinnable war, a disaffected aristocracy and an empty treasury.

Edward I was slow to realize the strategic problems that Scotland presented, beyond its superficial resemblance to Wales. Both were mountainous and underpopulated, but Scotland was more remote and much larger. Wales lay near medieval England's most densely populated shires, while Scotland was many days' march beyond the impoverished northern counties. Wales was small and easily accessible to ships, but English fleets rarely penetrated beyond the Clyde and Forth, while the Western Isles provided Robert the Bruce with an inaccessible refuge. Wales remained disunited to the last, whereas Scotland's tradition of unity dated from before the Norman Conquest.

Scottish armies were better balanced than the regionally distinct bands of Welsh spearmen or archers, who rarely combined missile and shock action. The Scots could field mixed forces of all arms. Heavy cavalry and archers supplemented spearmen raised from the 'horseless classes'. Contemporary illustrations show Scots infantry with bows and arrows, spears and axes, even swords. Defensive equipment was limited to leather caps rather than bascinets, no one appearing in hauberks or even quilted aketons. Lack of protection made Scots infantry formations vulnerable to English archery. After Falkirk, the Scots refused to compete directly with larger hosts raised south of the Border. They fought a guerrilla war, and developed their infantry. The immobile schiltrons of Falkirk learned to manoeuvre against cavalry in the open, their successful attacks at Bannockburn preceding the comparable Swiss victory at Morgarten by a year. Mounted on nags for mobility and with few logistical needs, such troops ran rings around heavier English forces.

Edward I relied on mass to terrify the Scots into submission. He summoned armies larger than any previously raised in England, forces not surpassed until the Civil Wars of the 1640s. Edward's infantry increasingly carried the longbow, but not through any government initiative. Writs requested foot soldiers skilled in arms, but left their weapons to the responsible local authorities. The government did not even supply ammunition. At Falkirk the English ran out of arrows, and threw round stones which lay conveniently to hand. Towards the end of his reign Edward lost faith in masses of ill-trained infantry, and fielded smaller numbers. Not until Edward III's reign would English men-at-arms fight on foot, or archers take horse to keep up with Scottish raiders.

The only significant fight during Alexander III's reign had been a skirmish with Norse raiders at Largs in 1263. This was scant preparation for the struggle against Edward's veterans, which fell into four phases:

(1) Unavailing Scottish attempts to resist Edward I by conventional means. Their feudal host was dispersed at Dunbar (1296), and a popular array cut to pieces at Falkirk (1298), after a surprise victory at Stirling Bridge (1297).

(2) A 16-year lull between Falkirk and Bannockburn without major actions. Edward forced the national party to surrender in 1304, but Robert the Bruce's murder of John Comyn, its unsuccessful leader, reignited the struggle. Bruce fled westwards after defeats at Methven and Dalry (1306). When he returned his only notable actions were against Scottish opponents: Slioch, Barra, and the Pass of Brander (1307–9). The chief exception was Loudoun

Hill (1307), where Scots tactics may have presaged those used at Bannockburn. Otherwise, the English were evicted from Scotland without a pitched battle, a process hastened by Edward II's domestic weakness, which prevented him campaigning in Scotland except once in 1310–11.

(3) The military vindication of Bruce's kingship at Bannockburn (1314).

(4) A final period of Scottish raids across the Border. Edward II's refusal to accept Bannockburn's verdict led to widespread misery in northern England, with incidental battles at Myton-on-Swale (1319) and Old Byland (October 1322). England descended into civil war, starting at Boroughbridge (March 1322).

Far from uniting Britain, Edward I's aggressive policies brought discord to his own kingdom, and created an inveterate enemy in the north, fiercely aware of its separate identity.

Largs, Tuesday 2 October 1263

Scotland, North Ayrshire, LR63 NS2059?

Alexander III's strategic preoccupations lay to the northwest, not the south. The Hebrides, Orkney and Shetland under Norwegian overlordship remained an ever-present temptation and threat. Scots pressure upon Norse settlements in Skye stirred Håkon IV, 'last of the great sea-kings of Norway', to mount a final expedition. It petered out in Largs Bay, as much a victim of the weather as Scottish skill at arms.

Norway remained northern Europe's dominant naval power. Håkon's 260-foot (79-m) flagship with 37 oars a side and a crew of several hundred was the finest vessel of her day. Icelandic annals claimed that the fleet that left Bergen in July 1263 carried 'the largest army which ever sailed from Norway'. Reinforced from the Isle of Man, Håkon disposed of 'more than 120 ships ... most of them great, and all in good trim both as to men and weapons'. At the end of September, having subdued the Hebrides, the Norse armament lay in Lamlash Bay off the island of Arran in the Firth of Clyde, poised to strike at mainland Scotland.

Alexander III tried to resolve the crisis by diplomacy. Barefoot Friars went to and fro, achieving little. *Håkon's Saga* accused the Scots of bad faith, spinning matters out while summer passed and the weather deteriorated. They talked much of peace, while gathering their forces. When Håkon's men ran out of food, he made 'an end to all truces'. Sixty ships were portaged from Loch Long to Loch Lomond to ravage Lennox, while Håkon closed up the rest into the lee of Great Cumbrae island, within sight of Largs.

The 1890s translator of *Håkon's Saga* followed tradition in placing the fight that followed at Largs, despite 'the actual battlefield being unknown'. In 1912 a commemorative stone tower was erected on the rocky foreshore below Bowen Craig, by public subscription. Meteorological probability may justify popular sentiment, the battle following Norwegian attempts to recover ships stranded by an equinoctial gale. This presumably blew from the southwest, carrying insecurely moored vessels between Cumbrae and the mainland towards Largs beach. During the storm of 30 September–1 October a merchant ship or 'bark' fouled Håkon's flagship, before taking ground on the island. The morning tide floated off the bark, which drove up the Scottish coast before running ashore with three other vessels. Seeing the ships drift in, the Scots gathered on the beach and shot at the crews, leading to a desultory exchange of missiles: 'Sometimes the Scots came on, and sometimes they fell off. There few fell, but many were wounded'

Largs

	Winners	*Losers*
Opponents	Scots	Norwegian
Commanders	Alexander III	Håkon IV, King of Norway
Numbers	500+	800–900
Losses	unknown	unknown

(*Håkon's Saga*). The Scots withdrew before Norse reinforcements, returning after dark to loot the merchantman.

Håkon landed next day to direct salvage operations. When the bark was all but cleared, the Scots reappeared. Some reckoned there were 500 knights on mail-clad horses, others something less. The infantry were poorly equipped, with a mixture of bows and Irish bills or axes. Håkon had 800–900 men, 200 of whom under Ogmund Crow-Dance were forward on the hillside, providing security for the salvage parties. The Norwegian position was unenviable, trapped on a narrow strip of land commanded from higher ground, which runs down almost to the shore. Håkon's men showed their opinion of the risks by sending him back to the fleet for reinforcements, keeping 60 of his bodyguard to stiffen the beachhead.

Ogmund's outlying detachment retreated to the beach, pelted with stones, but in good order, covering themselves with their shields. Panic set in as they reached the brow of the hill, when 'each tried to be faster than the others'. The men on the beach mistook their comrades' hurry for flight, and ran for the boats, some of which upset, drowning their occupants. Others got into the bark, while Ogmund's party crossed the wooded hollow between hill and beach, and ran south along the shingle. With no choice except to defend themselves they rallied around another stranded ship, to begin an unequal struggle against superior numbers, probably not the saga-writer's ten-to-one.

The storm still blew, but a few reinforcements reached the beach party, who pushed the Scots back up the hillside, 'and then there was a lingering fight between them for a while with shot and stones'. Towards evening the Norwegians gathered enough strength to clear their front:

> Brown brand bit the rebels sharply,
> At the mail-moot on the hill;
> Up the 'How' the red shields mounted,
> Till the bearers reached the top.
>
> *Håkon's Saga*

The Scots fled eastwards into the hills of Cunningham, the weary Norsemen rowing back to their ships. The next day (Wednesday) they returned for their dead, and on Friday they burnt the wrecked ships after the weather had improved. Scottish casualties are unknown, as they carried them off.

The Battle of Largs was hardly a famous victory, but it was a fatal blow to Håkon's expedition. Short of provisions and exposed to further storms, the fleet broke up. Håkon's ships suffered more losses rounding Cape Wrath. Worn out by hardship, disappointment or old age, the Norwegian king died at Kirkwall, never reaching home. His successor acknowledged Håkon's failure, for in 1266 Norway ceded the Hebrides and Isle of Man to Scotland. The inconclusive skirmish at Largs has acquired some of the resonance of Bannockburn, as a happy deliverance from invaders. More certainly its removal of Norwegian sea power from the Irish Sea effected an unnoticed strategic revolution, easing Scottish intervention in northern Ireland, and English naval operations against Wales.

Directions

Access either Castle Bay or Largs Bay by footpaths from Largs Pier. These are squeezed against the coast by the A78 to the north (Largs Bay), and the railway to the south (Castle Bay). The 'Pencil' monument is south of Castle Bay, overlooking the marina.

Dunbar (I), 27 April 1296

Scotland, East Lothian, LR67 NT6776

The first action of the Scots Wars of Independence had immediate and apparently decisive results. An advanced detachment of Edward's invading army routed the Scottish feudal host at Dunbar and captured their leaders, appearing to justify Edward's confidence in his ability to unify the two kingdoms by force.

Anglo-Scots hostilities began in March 1296, soon followed by Edward's capture of Scots-held town of Berwick. John Warenne, Earl of Surrey, pushed on

Dunbar (I)

	Winners	*Losers*
Opponents	English	Scots
Commanders	John Warenne, Earl of Surrey	John de Balliol, King of Scots
Numbers	*c.*2300	unknown
Losses	none	3000?

to take Dunbar Castle and clear the coast road to Edinburgh. Under cover of a truce, the Scots brought up a relief force, hoping to catch the English at lunch, *post prandium*, with the help of a sortie from Dunbar. Numbers are uncertain. The *Worcester Annals* claimed 1000 Scottish cavalry, half of them on horses covered with mail, and 40,000 foot, an implausibly high proportion of Scotland's total population. Payroll records show Edward I fielded 11,000 men in 1296, including 1000 heavy cavalry. Contemporaries imagined all of these fought at Dunbar, but a fifth is more likely, reinforced by 100 of the Bishop of Durham's knights, perhaps 300 cavalry and 2000 infantry altogether. Dunbar's decisive result suggests that the Earl of Surrey outnumbered as well as outclassed the Scottish knights, who still rode light rounceys in the 1320s, never the powerful destriers bred for war. Their infantry may have outnumbered the English, some of whom had to maintain the siege. Lightly armed with bows, spears and axes sharpened to a point, Scots infantrymen had not yet mastered the art of manoeuvring in masses without falling into disorder. Peter of Langtoft, an unfriendly contemporary commentator, described them unkindly as 'al route de raskayle' ('a rabble of rascals').

Scots banners appeared on the brow of the Lammermuir Hills south of Dunbar shortly after noon. Had they stayed behind Spott Burn on the steep hillsides, rising to 600 and 700 feet (180 and 210 m), the Scots might have embarrassed English siege operations. However, as Surrey deployed towards the hills, the Scots unaccountably imagined the English were retreating. They rushed across the U-shaped glen that ran along their front, onto the lower ground, shouting 'They flee! they flee!', and losing formation on the almost vertical hillside. Dunbar's garrison offered no help, beyond shouting threats to cut off the Englishmen's tails. Confronted with superior numbers of English cavalry in good order, the Scottish knights broke at the first onset, like quails or straw in the wind said Langtoft, leaving their infantry to be cut to pieces.

Over a hundred knights and squires were captured, and carted off to England in chains. Bipartisan observers counted an unlikely 10,052 dead. The Worcester chronicler claimed that there were 3000 Scots dead, which might be possible, but at the same time acknowledged only two English knights were wounded. Langtoft could not remember a battle where so many had turned their backs, or been slain so suddenly:

For Scottes	For the Scots
Tell I for sottes	I reckon for fools
And wrecches unwar	And wretches unaware
Unsele	Want of luck
Dintes to dele	In dealing blows
Tham drohu to Dunbar.	Drew them to Dunbar.

Dunbar surrendered next day, opening the way for Edward's unopposed progress through Scotland, receiving homage as far north as Elgin and Aberdeen. In July John de Balliol resigned the kingdom to Edward. His ungrateful subjects remembered him as 'Toom Tabard', a cruel reference to his plain surcoat, mercilessly stripped of its royal arms. Edward packed Balliol off to the south with the Scottish royal regalia and records, installed English justices and sheriffs, and no doubt congratulated himself on a speedy resolution of the Scots problem.

Directions

See the remains of Dunbar Castle, slighted and rebuilt since the 1290s, by the harbour. To find the battlefield follow a minor road out of Dunbar through Newtonlees, under the railway. Continue south across the A1, stopping just before the Spott Burn bridge. The slopes down which the Scots advanced are 1/2 mile (0.8 km) further south, beyond the village of Spott.

Stirling Bridge (Cambuskenneth), **Wednesday 11 September 1297**

Scotland, Stirling, LR57 NS8095

Scotland's strategic centre of gravity lies in the Clyde–Forth isthmus. All three major battles of the Wars of Independence were fought there, two within sight of Stirling Castle, watchtower over the ancient road between Lowlands and Highlands.

Edward I's conquest of Scotland in 1296 was too easy to be decisive. Popular discontent broke out in the murder and kidnapping of English officials. The name commonly associated with this widespread resistance is William Wallace. Younger son of a middling landowner from Renfrewshire, he was hardly the blue-faced, kilted ruffian of Hollywood mythology. His name means 'Welshman', linking him with British Strathclyde, rather than the Highlands. Wallace was not the uprising's only leader. English occupation forces were under pressure in the Highlands too, from Andrew Moray. The patriots joined forces near Stirling in late August, isolating English garrisons beyond the Forth.

The English government was ill placed to respond. The king was away, fighting in Flanders. Civil war was brewing between the regency and its senior military functionaries, the hereditary marshal and constable. The Flemish expedition had absorbed taxes raised in Scotland, and few troops were available. Edward I's lieutenants were the Earl of Surrey and his treasurer, Hugh Cressingham. Modern accounts usually give them 300 cavalry and perhaps 10,000 infantry, although the *Melsa Chronicle* says 6000 following earlier defeats. Peter of Langtoft commented that Cressingham's economies drove many of the infantry to desert.

Many Scots knights were captive, while others had recently resubmitted to English rule at Irvine. Wallace and Moray depended not on a feudal host, but on smallholders who owed service for their land. They followed their provincial banners, in companies led by their lords. English sources describe great multitudes of Scots, but they were probably outnumbered as usual. The patriots chose a strong defensive position, commanding the northern end of the causeway that led from the old wooden bridge over the Forth. They concealed their troops in the woods covering the lower slopes of Abbey Craig, the volcanic plug that towers above the flat water meadows by the Forth.

The causeway followed today's main road, although the early medieval bridge was above the 'Old Bridge', itself upstream of the modern road bridge. A loop in the deep-running Forth encloses the causeway on three sides. The ground off-road was not impassable. It was dry enough to grow oats, but heavy going for cavalry. Any column forcing the river had to advance on a narrow front, two or three riders across, as far as the village of Causewayhead. Scots knights serving with the Earl of Surrey pointed out the risks of the enemy cutting off the few men able to cross at a time. They proposed detaching a force upstream to the Fords of Drip, where they could cross 60 abreast.

Hugh Cressingham refused to divide the army. He expected another capitulation, especially as the Earl of Lennox had come in, promising imminent submission. English infantry crossed the river twice during the morning of 11 September, only to withdraw, as Surrey still slept. Two friars, the international mediators of the day, urged Wallace to submit, but he meant to fight: 'Let them come on, and we shall prove this on their beards' (Walter of Guisborough).

An obscure passage attributed to the contemporary William Rishanger describes the English troops finally advancing in a dense mass to attack the Scots, through the narrow defile, and oblivious of the enemy's strategic wiles. As they passed, not expecting anything of the sort, the Scots burst out taking them by surprise, struck home and broke through their ranks. Bartholomew Cotton, another contemporary, adds that the English were not drawn up ready for battle when the Scots came against them, ready in well-ordered ranks. Peter of Langtoft blamed Surrey:

> And that was his folie so long in his bed gan ligge
> Untille the Waleis partie had umbilaid the brigge

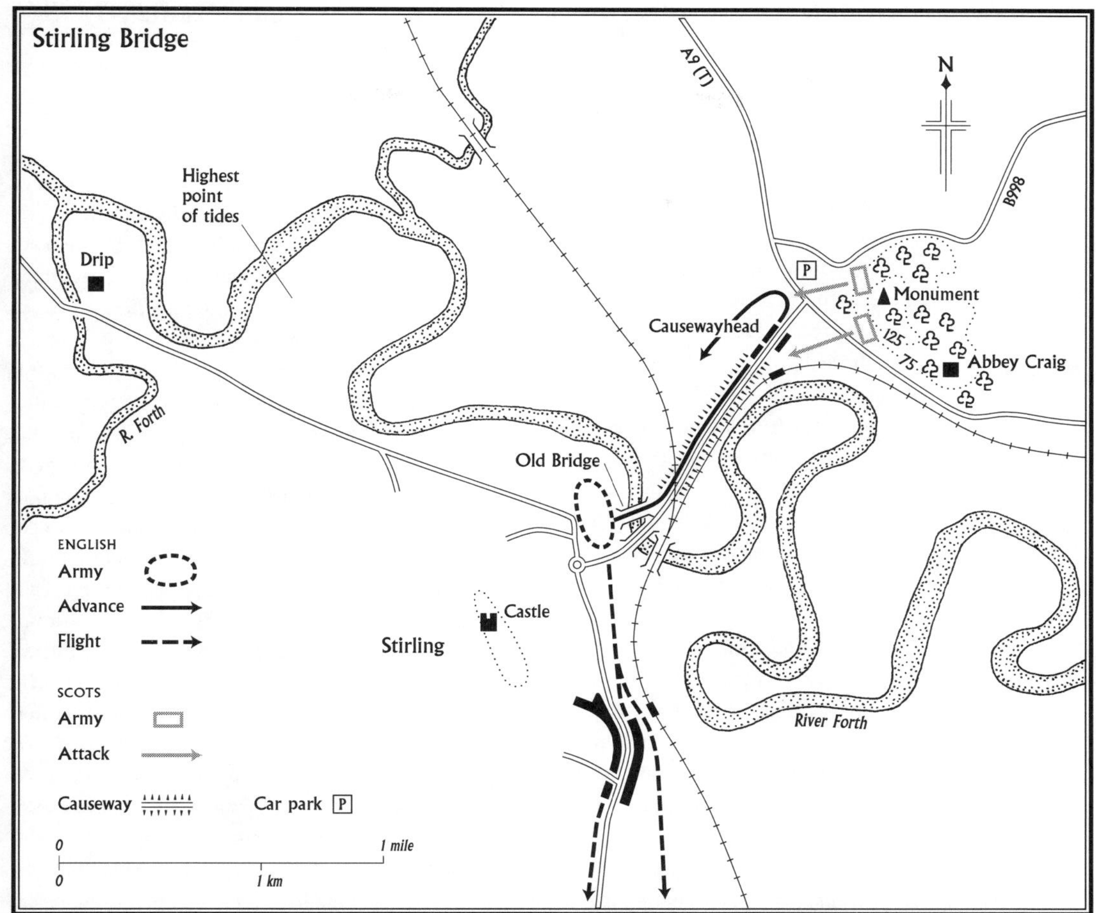

With gavelokkes [axes] and dartes suilk ere was
none sene
Might no man tham departe, ne ride ne go bituene.
(tr. *Robert of Brunne*)

Modern sources ascribe the ensuing slaughter to Scots pikemen blocking the bridge itself, but this is neither likely nor necessary. Everyone agrees the Scots lay at the foot of Abbey Craig, '*sub montibus*', with the English vanguard jamming the mile-long (1.6-km) road between them and the bridge. The chronicles stress the sudden unexpected nature of the onslaught, '*ex improviso*', testimony inconsistent with a 20-minute jog down to the river, in full view of the troops packing the causeway. Starting

Directions

Cross the stone 'Old Bridge', built since the battle, and follow the A9 into Causewayhead. The area between the A9/A907 roundabout and the Forth is now built up, obscuring the ambush site. Visit the Wallace Monument upon Abbey Craig to see the lie of the land.

from the Abbey Craig's southern slopes, the Scots most immediately struck west into the English flank, as they formed up in the open ground around Causewayhead, the literal meaning of Langtoft's words, '*le chef du pount*' ('the head of the bridge'). The lightly armed Scottish left could then cut in behind the

English, to occupy the causeway, and so preventing their retreat. The initial slaughter was probably, therefore, nearer Causewayhead than the river. When Surrey saw the battle lost, he had the bridge cut down, apparently without interference from the Scots, and rode off to Berwick, abandoning a sizeable proportion of his army south of the river.

The bridge was clearly not impassable before then, as Sir Marmeduke Tweng, who accompanied the vanguard, fought his way out that way. Those that could reach the bridge before it was cut down escaped; those that could not did not. Perhaps 100 knights and several thousand English and Welsh infantry were taken or killed, '*aut capti ... aut jugulati*' (*Melsa Chronicle*). More losses were incurred as the English army's leaderless tail straggled down the Roman road to Falkirk, ambushed by the now firmly patriotic Earl of Lennox. Hugh Cressingham was among the dead; cut to pieces by the *ribaudaille d'Escoz* ('the rabble of Scotland'), as Langtoft put it. English propagandists made much of Cressingham's flaying alive, and the circulation of strips of his skin around Scotland as tokens of liberation. However, Scottish losses were not insignificant. Andrew Moray was sorely wounded, his death leaving William Wallace the uncontested leader of the patriots.

Stirling Bridge remains a deeply symbolic Scots victory, because it showed that the country could not be conquered in a single campaign. Unfortunately it did not end the war, only provoking Edward I to redouble his efforts.

Stirling Bridge

	Winners	*Losers*
Opponents	Scots	English
Commanders	William Wallace	John Warenne, Earl of Surrey
	Andrew Moray (d)	Hugh Cressingham (k)
Numbers	unknown	6000–10000
Losses	unknown	c.2000

Falkirk (I), Tuesday 22 July 1298

Scotland, Falkirk, LR65 NS9179?

Falkirk was the dourest and most bloody battle of the Scots Wars. The disaster at Stirling Bridge shocked the English. They deployed one of the largest armies seen in the British Isles before the 17th century, and took their revenge. Falkirk demonstrated English superiority so convincingly that the Scots avoided large battles for 16 years.

William Wallace became sole guardian after Stirling Bridge. When Edward I invaded Scotland in June 1298, Wallace avoided action. Headwinds delayed English supply ships, reducing their army to starvation. As his offensive stalled near Edinburgh, Edward received intelligence that Wallace was six leagues (some 18 miles or 30 km) away at Falkirk, intending to harass the English retreat. 'He shall not come to me,' said the king, 'for I will go to him' (Walter of Guisborough). Marching via Kirkliston and Linlithgow Edward came up with the Scots next morning at the third hour, just after 8 a.m. at that time of year.

The location of Wallace's army is a puzzle. At least 17 sites have been canvassed. Sir Charles Oman placed the battle 3 miles (5 km) southwest of Falkirk at Darnrigg Moss (NS8675), without explaining why anyone should fight in so remote a spot. More recent reconstructions locate Wallace south of Callendar Wood, protected by the Glen and Westquarter Burns, but facing away from Edward's line of approach. None ask why Edward should detour south into the trackless bogs of Muiravonside to attack Wallace's front, rather than continuing along the coast, the route of the Roman road and A9, to arrive conveniently behind Wallace's left flank.

Contemporary sources place the Scots 'on hard ground on one side of a hill beside Faukyrke', and 'this side of Falkirk', i.e. on the east from the English viewpoint. The English saw the Scottish spears directly they left Linlithgow, massed on the hilltop opposite them, statements fitting a position east of Callendar Wood, rather than south. Between the

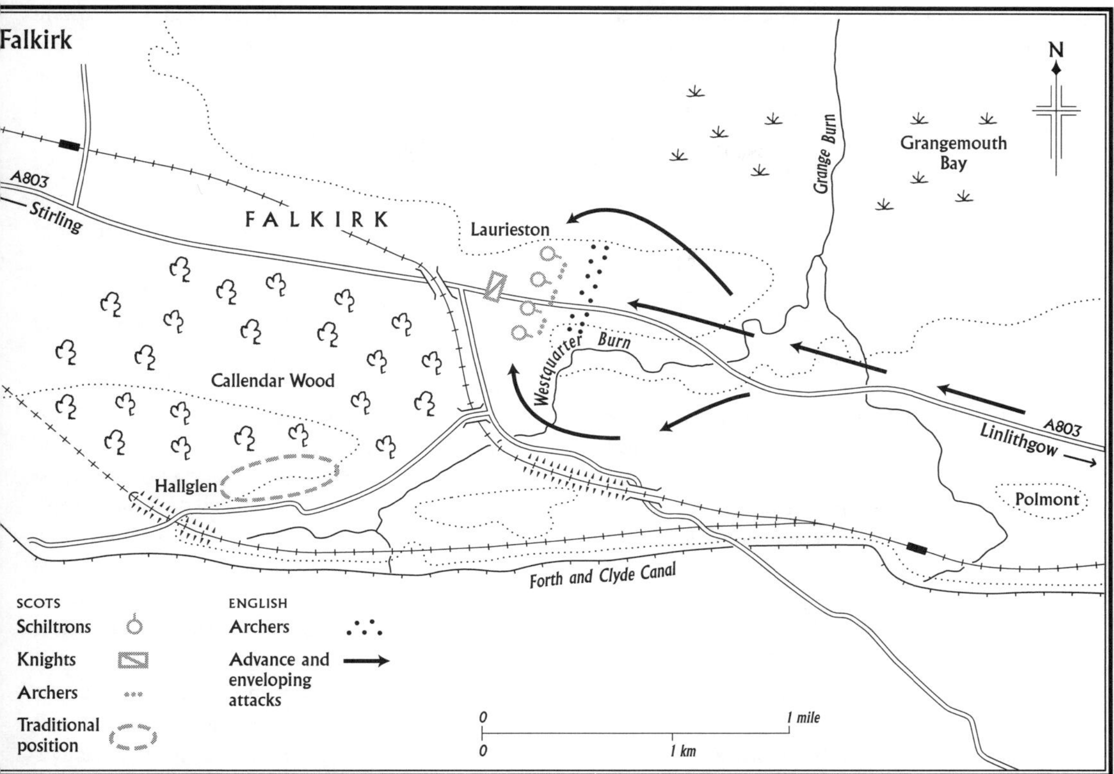

armies lay a swamp, '*lacum intermediam bituminosum*', forcing the English to turn the western and eastern ends of the Scots position, which presumably lay obliquely across the direct route from Linlithgow, the combined Glen and Westquarter Burns flowing across its front into Grangemouth Bay.

An army deployed along the 100-foot (30-m) contour west of the Glen Burn near Laurieston could well be described as 'on one side of a hill', and would command the gap between the hilly uplands south of the main road and the marshy bay. After the battle, surviving Scots retreated through the woods, except those on the left, who drowned '*in pelago*' ('in the sea'), an unlikely fate had they started south of Callendar Wood, which covers the full length of the traditional Scots position.

Wherever it was, Wallace's position was naturally strong. He strengthened it artificially, 'fixing long stakes in the ground,' according to William Rishangar, a contemporary, 'and tying ropes and cords between them in order to obstruct the English attack'. For the first time his infantry formed the dense hedgehogs known as schiltrons (or scheltrouns), designed to resist cavalry:

> In their vanguard back was placed against back,
> And point of lance on point, in squadrons so serried,
> Like castle in plain surrounded with wall.
>
> Peter of Langtoft

Directions

Take the A803 from Linlithgow to Falkirk, or leave the M9 at Junction 4. Stop in Westquarter, just before crossing the Glen Burn, where a footpath runs besides the stream, perhaps the swamp that halted Edward's leading knights. The area is very built up. Turn left in Laurieston before the railway bridge, then right to Hallglen to see the southern aspect of Callendar Wood, and the traditional battle site on the right (NS8978).

Walter of Guisborough describes the Scots 'standing in circles with their spears at an angle and thick like a forest'. There is no evidence the Scots tied their spears together, as some suggest. Wallace had four schiltrons at Falkirk. Their strength is unknown, but about a thousand men each would approach the limit of effective command. Rishanger speaks of their imperfect training: '*disciplinae militaris ignavus*'. Wallace also doubted his soldier's capabilities, 'I have browghte yowe to the ring,' he said, 'hoppe [i.e. dance] yef ye kunne.' Between the pike circles, Wallace stationed his few archers, and in the rear a few hundred horsemen.

Edward's cavalry totally outclassed the Scottish chivalry. It was organized in four divisions led by 110 knight bannerets, about two dozen each in the right, left and rear divisions, the remainder in the centre with the king, who marched third. Reliable estimates suggest Edward fielded 2500 men-at-arms, though not all were necessarily present. On 20 July he had 14,800 English and Irish infantry in pay, and 10,500 Welsh, a total of just over 25,000 foot. The Welsh refused to fight, awaiting the result on a nearby hillside. Even so, English claims that the Scots outnumbered them three-to-one are nonsense.

The fullest account of the fighting comes from Walter of Guisborough. If not an eyewitness, he had spoken to one. He paints a fine picture of the leading English knights riding ahead of the main body, unexpectedly checked by swampy ground in front of the Scots position, and turning the flanks to attack the outer schiltrons. The Scots men-at-arms fled before overwhelming numbers, without a blow struck. The English knights cut down the Scottish archers, but were repulsed by the hedgehogs of pikes. Rather than renew the cavalry attacks, Edward had his infantry soften up the target. Modern historians decry this much-vaunted combination of archers and knights, questioning the tactical capabilities of untrained infantry. However, they had little to do except advance straight against the enemy and discharge their arrows, resorting to stones as they shot away their ammunition, until succeeding divisions of knights were ready to resume the flank attacks. Walter specifically refers to those Scots standing on the edges of the schiltrons being stunned by the barrage, before the cavalry broke their ranks.

Falkirk (I)

	Winners	*Losers*
Opponents	English	Scots
Commanders	Edward I	William Wallace
Numbers	*c.*28,000	*c.*5000
Losses	*c.*2200	unknown

William Rishanger provides irritatingly brief notices of the English breaking through the entanglements to attack both flanks of the Scots army, or even their rear, '*post tergo venientes*'. Horse inventories and payrolls show that Edward's household knights and the English infantry were in the thick of the fight. The former lost over 100 horses, while the latter were reduced to 12,600 a week after the battle, an unusually precise indication of medieval casualty levels. Only two English men-at-arms were slain: the Master of the Temple and his *socius* ('companion') pressed their attack too far, were trapped in a slough, and killed beyond reach of help. Scottish losses must have been heavy among the commoners, although nothing near the chroniclers' 40,000–100,000. Rishanger compared the dead to the blossom from a fruit tree, and Langtoft less kindly to flies. The Welsh joined the pursuit, covering the ground with stripped bodies like snow in winter.

Despite the slaughter the Scots still controlled the countryside beyond the Tay, where Edward burnt Perth and St Andrews to no lasting purpose. His withdrawal in October left only southeast Scotland in English hands. Not until spring 1304 would Edward compel the collective leadership that replaced Wallace to surrender. But no more would the Scots confront an English royal army in open battle. Falkirk marked a turning point, when the Scots abandoned conventional resistance in face of overwhelming English might.

Methven, 19 June 1306

Scotland, Perth and Kinross, LR52 NO0226

Dail Righ (Dalrigh), 11 August (or July) 1306

Scotland, Stirling, LR50 NN3429

Edward I appeared to have extinguished Scotland's independence by spring 1306. King John Balliol was in exile, his cause discredited by the surrender of his leading supporter John Comyn of Badenoch, the Red Comyn. Robert the Bruce, Earl of Carrick, a rival claimant to the throne, was at peace with Edward, after helping to hunt down William Wallace for a show trial and execution at Westminster. In February 1306 Bruce turned Scottish politics on its head by murdering the Red Comyn in Greyfriars Kirk in Dumfries. The Balliol party, previously champions of Scots independence, now sided with the English against Robert the Bruce, who became standard-bearer for the patriotic cause. Bruce was politically isolated, despite his enthronement at Scone in March 1306, regarded as a traitor and a manslayer. Bruce's early battles reveal his weakness. Two were disasters, bringing death or imprisonment to family and friends. His 'victories' lack independent confirmation, suggesting embroidery by John Barbour, author of the eulogistic contemporary verse epic, *The Bruce*.

King Robert – Robyn or Hobbe to his enemies – began operations with a recruiting drive in northern Scotland. Lists of forfeited estates show support from Perth, Angus, Aberdeen, Banff and Moray. When Bruce approached Perth on 18 June he may have outnumbered English forces within the town. They would not emerge, despite the Scots dissembling their numbers and identity by wearing surplices over their coat armour. Facing the ruin of his life's work, Edward had sent Aymer de Valence ('a worthy knight' said the hostile Barbour) with a flying column and orders to 'byrn, and slay, and rais dragoun'. His payroll bore 50 knights, 21 squires, 140 crossbowmen and 1960 archers, reinforced by Scots lords owing fealty to Edward I.

Unwilling to attack Perth's fortifications, Bruce withdrew 6 miles (10 km) to Methven, bivouacking in a wood on the hill (358 feet/109 m) just north of the village. Aymer outclassed Bruce in generalship as well as troop quality. While Bruce's men dispersed, 'to loge thaim her and thar', Aymer took 'the straucht way towart Meffen', and fell on the Scots camp with 300 men-at-arms and some infantry. The action was more rout than battle. The Scots had a lower proportion of heavily armed fighting men to scratch infantry, who soon faltered, despite Bruce's attempts to rally them:

> On thaim, on thaim, they feble fast
> This bargane never may langer last.

Bruce killed Aymer's horse, but soon turned his back and fled, to translate the words of the hostile Peter of Langtoft: '*Robyn le dos luy tourne, s'en fuist aliours.*' Twice he was nearly captured, rescued once by force, and once released by a Scots knight in English employ. Some of Bruce's chivalry got away, leaving the small folk to attract rare sympathy from Edward I as 'the poor commons of Scotland who by force rose against the king', and now had to find their ransoms.

Bruce's mounted party fled west, through the Breadalbane mountains, and north up Strathfillan. Short of Tyndrum the barons of Argyll blocked their escape at Dalrigh, on the River Cononish. Barbour names the hostile commander as John of Lorn, a

Methven

	Winners	*Losers*
Opponents	English	Scots
Commanders	Aymer de Valence, Earl of Pembroke	Robert the Bruce
Numbers	2171	*c.*2500

Dail Righ

	Winners	*Losers*
Opponents	Scots	Scots
Commanders	John MacDougall of Lorn	Robert the Bruce
Numbers	1000	unknown

kinsman of the murdered Comyn, for whom family revenge came before patriotic duty. The Argyll men fought on foot with axes, like gallowglasses. They crippled the royal party's horses, forcing Bruce to retreat to avoid outright destruction. Dail Righ ('king's meadow') and nearby Lochan nan Arm ('tarn of weapons') may derive their names from the action. Casualties were few, but the demoralized fugitives ceased to be an organized force. Bruce disappeared to contemplate arachnids in Arran or Rathlin Island, while his family sought refuge in the far northeast. Here they fell into English hands. The men were executed, and the women imprisoned. Bruce would not see his wife and daughter again until after Bannockburn.

Directions

Methven *From the church in the centre make a circuit of the battlefield anticlockwise. Heading northeast, turn left at the crossroads to Lawmuir, turning left and left again along farm roads to return to Methven from the northwest. The old ¼-inch OS map marked the battle north of hill 109, within the route described.*

Dail Righ *Follow the A82 from Crianlarich for Tyndrum. Turn left into Dalrigh after crossing to the north bank of the Cononish, and follow a track back across the river, bearing right past Lochan nan Arm. East of Strathfillan was a small priory Bruce established later as thanks for his deliverance. Do not confuse Dail Righ with Dalry in Ayrshire.*

Loudoun Hill, *c.* 10 May 1307

Scotland, East Ayrshire, LR71 NS6137

Glen Trool, 12/23 June 1307

Scotland, Dumfries and Galloway, LR77 NX4279

Loudoun Hill

	Winners	*Losers*
Opponents	Scots	English
Commanders	Robert the Bruce	Aymer de Valence, Earl of Pembroke
Numbers	600	1500

Glen Trool

	Winners	*Losers*
Opponents	Scots	English
Commanders	Robert the Bruce	Aymer de Valence, Earl of Pembroke
Numbers	*c.*350	300

King Robert returned to Scotland late in 1306 with hardly enough men to pursue a guerrilla strategy. Pursued like wild game with hounds and horn, he was lucky to avoid serious encounters until Edward I's death in July 1307 undermined English commitment to the war. Barbour's *Bruce* makes much of Scots successes near Loch Trool and Loudoun Hill, though neither left much trace in English records. It is typical of the confusion of this period of Bruce's struggle that even the sequence of these two actions is uncertain.

Bruce hid in the remote and steep-sided Glen Trool, where small English forces sought him out at least twice. A stone tablet in the glen ascribes Barbour's fight to March 1307, but English records favour June. Aymer de Valence approached by night, hoping to take the king – 'That wyst rycht nocht of ther cummyng' – by surprise. Scouts reported Bruce's camp in 'sa strayt a place, / That horsemen mycht nocht him assayle'. Such a description fits the Ordnance Survey's chosen spot, between the northeast end of Glen Trool and the crags of Mulldonoch (1827 feet/557 m). Aymer dismounted under cover of the woods and advanced on foot, sending a female spy on ahead, an indication of the small numbers at his disposal. Inadvertently she alerted Bruce, who had time to form up ready for Aymer: 'his baner gert display, / And set his men in gud array'. Discouraged by their hot reception, Aymer's men fell back quickly with few losses. In English sources the action appears as a few horses lost '*in chacea super Robert Bruce inter Glentruyl et Glenhour*', suggesting Bruce subsequently fled across the hills to Glen Urr.

The location of Bruce's other early success is more certain. Loudoun Hill (1037 feet/316 m) is a round-topped hill north of the main road from Kilmarnock to Strathaven, although the Ordnance Survey places the battle more correctly in the field below, near the farm at Allanton Plains. Oman interpreted Loudoun as a tactical forerunner of Bannockburn, a contest between men-at-arms unsupported by archers, and pikemen using natural obstacles to secure their flanks. Bruce skilfully chose a position where the road ran between two morasses, as it still does at Allanton Plains. He further restricted his front by digging three lines of ditches inwards from the edge of the mosses. The resulting 100-yard (90-m) gap in the centre he stopped with dismounted pikemen, their flanks protected by the ditches and embanked spoil. The night before the action Bruce lay further west, at Loudoun Castle near Galston, where he could observe the English approach from Ayr and prevent premature discovery of his preparations.

Bruce's opponent is supposed to have run his head against these defences with bone-headed feudal élan, although elsewhere Aymer is credited as one of Edward I's more able commanders. Following Barbour, Oman claimed two charges, 'in twa eschelis [squadrons] ordanyt', which left over 100 men-at-arms dead. Walter of Guisborough mentions a few casualties in an unnamed battle, '*infra Lowdyan*', and there are no financial records of horses killed in action, despite Barbour's graphic detail:

... with speris that sharply schar
Thai stekit men and stedis baith
Till rede blud ran off woundis raith.

A contemporary letter mentions royal displeasure at Aymer's retreat before King Hobbe without any exploit, confirming his failure to press the attack. Other documents show Aymer escorted the treasurer of England between Ayr and Bothwell soon after the supposed battle. Bruce may have waylaid Aymer and his financially interesting companion, but was unable to cut the road permanently. Two months after his supposed triumph at Loudoun Hill, Bruce was once more on the run, 'scarcely able to let down his breeches for fear of the traitors seeking a reward for his death'.

Directions

Loudoun Hill *Take the A71 east from Kilmarnock through Darvel. Loudoun Hill is on the left 5 miles (8 km) east of Galston, up a minor road. The pass between the mosses is 1 mile (1.6 km) further along the A71 at Allanton Plains.*

Glen Trool *Pick up the Southern Uplands Way at Glentrool village off the A714 north of Newton Stewart, and follow it through the plantations to Loch Trool, where a forest track leads along the south side of the loch.*

Slioch, *c.*25 December 1307

Scotland, Aberdeenshire, LR29 NJ5439–5539

Barra (Inverurie/Meldrum), 23 May 1308

Scotland, Aberdeenshire, LR38 NJ7926

Bruce's struggle for the crown, like many wars of national liberation, was directed as much against internal enemies as foreigners. In autumn 1307 he turned his attention to the Comyn-dominated country north of the Tay. Castles here were ill defended motte-and-bailey affairs, with feeble garrisons. Edward II paid a mere 30 men-at-arms to defend Scotland from the Orkneys to the Mounth in the southeastern Grampians. Fighting over so vast an area against such trivial forces King Robert could achieve the numerical superiority he needed to crush his domestic opponents at Barra near Old Meldrum, after a brush with death at Slioch.

The locations of these battles are plain enough, but John Barbour, the most detailed source, disagrees with his fellow Aberdonian John of Fordun (d.*c.*1384) about the chronology. Barbour dates Slioch 'after Martinmas [11 November] when snow had covered all the land', assigning Barra to Christmas Day the same year. Fordun places Slioch just before Christmas, and Barra 'in the year 1308', which for him began on 25 March. Most modern historians accept Fordun's dates, which agree with English documents and a verse chronicle specifying Ascension Day, which in 1308 was 23 May.

Slioch is chiefly significant for what did not happen. The fighting fizzled out in a skirmish, and the Bruce did not die of pneumonia. Hearing the king was deep in their territory, the Comyn faction offered battle at 'Slevach', anglicized as Slioch. Their leader, the Earl of Buchan, was the uncle of Bruce's victim at Dumfries. Now just a farm east of Huntly town, in the 14th century Slioch featured a chapel and Torra Duncan, a motte 42 feet by 36 (13 m by 11 m). Barbour calls this a 'strinth', implying palisades and perhaps a stone tower. The Ordnance Survey places its battle symbol between motte and farm, a fair compromise as the site is unknown. The locality comprises a marshy flat-bottomed valley surrounded by such place-names as Boghead, and probably derives its own name from the Gaelic *sliabhach* denoting a marsh. Why King Robert should occupy so unhealthy and indefensible a location is unclear, unless Buchan cut him off making for Strathbogie Castle north of Huntly, perhaps at Battle Hill, the low ridge between Slioch and the town.

Barbour claimed that Buchan outnumbered Bruce's party two-to-one, although the feeble Comyn performance makes such odds implausible. The garrisons on which Buchan could draw were hardly numerous. Forfar Castle for example, 'all stuffit with Inglis men', contained less than 30 soldiers all told. Bruce on the other hand was hot from intimidating the Earl of Ross, who reported to Edward II that Robert had deployed 3000 men against him. The estimate may have been a self-serving exaggeration, but would explain Buchan's loss of confidence at Slioch: 'When they saw the king with his men against them ready for the fray they halted' (Fordun). To ambush a flying column was one thing. A deliberate assault on a powerful line of battle, 'stood in array right closely', was another. The confrontation petered out into three days of bickering with archers, in which Buchan 'the worse had ay'. Fordun thought the two sides observed a truce over Christmas week.

Both chroniclers record that King Robert was very ill, unable to eat or drink, 'borne on a pallet whithersoever he had to go'. While Buchan's forces waxed stronger, Bruce's men starved in the woods around Torra Duncan. At some uncertain moment they formed a dense mass around their sick king, and marched off to warmer quarters in Strathbogie Castle, in full view of the enemy, who watched them go. Buchan's failure to overrun his leaderless and enfeebled opponents is inexplicable, unless he was outnumbered. Perhaps Buchan was unwilling to leave the dry ground on Battle Hill to take his chance in the marshy plain. His inertia would cost him the campaign.

The decisive action in Bruce's recovery of the north was fought at Barra next summer. His supporters had spent their time since Slioch overrunning Comyn fortresses in the Highlands. On the eve of battle, King Robert lay at the Bass of Inverurie, a motte and bailey beside the River Urie. Buchan was 5 miles (8 km) northeast at the 'farmtoun' of Old Meldrum, probably not in the waterless prehistoric fort on Barra Hill labelled Comyn's Camp: 'a full gret cumpany / Off men arayit jolyly [handsomely] ... / A thousand trow I weile, thai war' (Barbour).

A dawn reconnaissance by Buchan's supporters beat up Bruce's outposts, with unintended consequences. The moribund king rose from his pallet calling for his armour, and led his men in hot pursuit, propped up in the saddle by riders on either side. The battle that followed was quickly over. Bruce drove in

Slioch

	Winners	*Losers*
Opponents	Scots	Scots
Commanders	Robert the Bruce	John Comyn, Earl of Buchan
Numbers	700	*c.*1400

Barra

	Winners	*Losers*
Opponents	Scots	Scots
Commanders	Robert the Bruce	John Comyn, Earl of Buchan
Numbers	*c.*700	*c.*1000

Buchan's scouts, scarcely giving him time to arm or array his troops, men-at-arms in front of the rabble. Nevertheless, Buchan 'maid gud sembland [appearance] for to fycht', presumably across the road from Inverurie at North Mains of Barra in the level pasture of King's Field, Barra Hill's steep slopes protecting his left flank.

Buchan's men watched the Bruce 'cum stoutly on', and then flinched, 'a litill on bridill thai them withdrew'. Bruce 'Pressyt on thaim with his baner, and they withdrew mar and mar' into the boggy hollow beside Lochter Burn known as Bruce's Field. At this point the infantry, described in scatological Franco-Scots as 'merdale', lost their nerve and fled, carrying their social superiors away with them. Fordun confirms the rout:

> But when the opposing party saw him [the king] and his men ready for battle, at the mere sight of him they were all sore afraid and put to flight, and they were pursued as far as Fyvie ...

The outcome of the battle is only comprehensible if King Robert once more outnumbered his enemies, having brought up most of the 3000 men that had cowed the Earl of Ross. Scarcely drawn up in time, Buchan's men refused to countercharge Bruce's 'mekill mycht' ('great might'), and were swept away, the inevitable fate of cavalry standing to receive a charge. The subsequent harrying or 'Herschip' of Buchan's lands in northeast Scotland clinched the victory. Fordun had no doubts of Barra's significance: 'From that day the king gained ground and became ever more hale himself, while the adverse party was daily growing less.'

Directions

Slioch *Follow the A96 east from Huntly railway station past Battle Hill on the left. Take the second left down a minor road to Slioch farm, again on the left. Torra Duncan, almost ploughed away, is 1 mile (1.6 km) northwest of the modern farm beyond Knightland Burn.*

Barra *See Bass of Inverurie in the cemetery at the southern end of the town of Inverurie, on the B993. Follow Bruce's probable route along the B9170 from Inverurie to North Mains of Barra, 1/2 mile (0.8 km) outside Old Meldrum. Tracks either side of the main road suggest the general alignment of Buchan's army before they fell back towards Lochter Burn.*

Pass of Brander (Ben Cruachan), **15/23 August 1308**

Scotland, Argyll and Bute, LR50 NN0627

The last domestic obstacle to the Bruce's drive to power was the inveterate hatred of the MacDougalls of Argyll. Once they had fought for Scottish independence, but as cousins of the Red Comyn they became irreconcilable enemies of his murderer. After Barra had secured the Bruce position in the northeast, King Robert moved to protect his western flank. At Pass of Brander he took revenge against John of Lorn for Dail Righ (1306).

There is some doubt whether the fight occurred in 1308 or 1309. John of Fordun's manuscript for 1308 states the king 'defeated the Argyllmen in the heart of Argyll within the octave of the Assumption of the Blessed Virgin', i.e. 15–23 August. Walter of Guisborough reported Bruce's return from the Isles, immediately after the crisis in England over Piers Gaveston's influence over Edward II, also in 1308. Accepting Fordun's specific dating, Bruce would have set out no later than July 1308, a propitious month for a Highland campaign, with good weather and fordable rivers.

John of Lorn, known as Bacach ('the Lame'), reported to Edward II that the Bruce had menaced him with 10,000–15,000 men, while he had only 800 to defend his borders and three castles around Loch Linnhe. John exaggerated his numerical disadvantage, but many Highlanders and Moray-men had joined Bruce's core force, with whom he had subdued the north. Reasonable estimates of the army that invaded Argyll range from 2500 to 5000.

Barbour's only topographical clue is that 'Crechinben hecht [was called] that montane'. The traditional site of the battle lies in the Pass of Brander.

Today this extends several miles along the southern slope of Ben Cruachan, which rises to 3694 feet (1126 m) from Loch Awe in just over a mile. The royal army presumably approached along the route of the Oban railway through Dalmally, rounding the northern end of the loch. John of Lorn sent 2000 men to ambush the track, while he watched from his galley on the loch. Barbour described the way as 'an evil place', so narrow that in places two men might not ride abreast. With rare understatement, Barbour wrote, 'it was hard to pass that way'. Below the pass, according to Barbour, a black crag, high and hideous, fell precipitously into the sea.

Professor A.A.M. Duncan has argued the unsuitability as a battlefield of a mountainside that slopes too steeply for lines of men to stand upright, let alone engage in combat. He suggests Barbour's specific reference to 'the sea', shows that John of Lorn's galleys floated not in Loch Awe's fresh water, but on the salt water of Loch Etive, in touch with their base at Dunstaffnage Castle. In this case the battle took place on the northern slopes of Ben Cruachan, below Barran Dubh, the Bruce army approaching from the north via the Great Glen and Glencoe. However, the absence of any road at all through the tangled mountains north of Taynuilt begs the question whether the alternative site is any better than the traditional one.

Whichever route he took, King Robert knew about mountain warfare. He sent Sir James Douglas – nicknamed 'the Black Douglas' by the English – ahead with all the archers to climb above potential ambush sites, which had to be within bowshot of the road i.e. 100–200 yards (90–180 m). He also had Highlanders in his force, 'men that lycht and delyver [swift] war, / And lycht armouris had on …'. When Lorn's men rose from concealment, 'and schot and tumblit on him stanys / Rycht gret and hevy', Bruce's reaction force rushed up the hill to counter their attack. Simultaneously Douglas's archers appeared above the ambushers, pouring in arrows then closing with cold steel. 'Assaylit upon twa partys,' and with the mountaineer's fear of an enemy further uphill, the MacDougalls fled. They made for Bridge of Awe, the only crossing place, but were followed too closely to break it down before they were overrun. Bruce chased them deep into their own country, capturing their castle at Dunstaffnage.

Pass of Brander		
	Winners	*Losers*
Opponents	Scots	Scots
Commanders	Robert the Bruce	John MacDougall of Lorn
Numbers	2500–5000	2000

Mindful of the awful example of the Herschip of Buchan (see Barra, 1308, above), the MacDougalls soon came to terms, John of Lorn escaping to England by sea. Bruce the rebel and freedom fighter transformed himself into Good King Robert, issuing his earliest surviving acts of government, and in March 1309 calling his first parliament.

Directions

Follow the A85 west from Dalmally north of Loch Awe. The Pass of Brander begins 1/2 mile beyond Falls of Cruachan, and extends about 3 miles (5 km). Bridge of Awe is another mile (1.6 km) further on. The alternative site north of Ben Cruachan is inaccessible by public road, though a track runs north from Taynuilt between the mountain and Loch Etive. See Dunstaffnage Castle on Loch Linnhe, 3 miles (5 km) north of Oban.

Bannockburn, Sunday 23 June–Monday 24 June 1314

Scotland, Stirling, LR57 NS7990–8191

Bannockburn is rightly remembered as a crucial moment in British history. Vindicating Robert the Bruce's claim to the Scottish throne, it set the seal of incompetence upon the reign of Edward II of England. What should have been a walkover for superior English numbers and skill at arms became a rare victory for the smaller army. King Robert extracted every possible advantage from the ground, skilfully combining the elements of his army in a complex two-day action to inflict one of the most lamentable defeats ever suffered by an English army.

The encounter was untypical of Anglo-Scots warfare, and of the Bruce's strategy. Since Methven (1307) he had pursued a guerrilla war. Small forces operating in a friendly countryside launched lightning raids on ill-defended castles, which then were slighted to deprive English counterattacks of an obvious objective. When Edward II launched a major offensive in 1310–11 the Scots hid in caves and wooded places, leaving their opponents to perish through winter cold and lack of forage. Usually English magnates preferred baiting their insouciant and possibly bisexual monarch to winkling King Hobbe out of his mountain retreats.

Circumstances in the autumn of 1313 precipitated a showdown. King Robert gave his Scottish opponents 12 months' notice to come into his peace, or face perpetual disinheritance. Edward II's loyal province of Lothian petitioned him for assistance, without which it must submit, unravelling the whole English position in Scotland. For once Edward II could help, as the faction fighting that had culminated in the murder of his favourite Piers Gaveston had abated, making decisive action possible. In November 1313 Edward II promised to lead an army into Scotland by the following midsummer, to reverse the unfavourable trend of the war and relieve his northern subjects.

The deadline of 24 June 1314 was dictated by availability of forage for English warhorses, and not, as is so often said, the need to relieve Stirling Castle. That complication arose later, after King Robert preempted Edward II's projected expedition by capturing Edinburgh and Roxburgh in February 1314, and besieging Stirling Castle, the last great English stronghold left in Scotland. Sometime in April 1314 Sir Philip de Mowbray, the governor of Stirling Castle, agreed with Edward Bruce (the king's brother) to surrender by 24 June if not previously relieved. This injected new urgency into Edward II's preparations. He first refers to Stirling as an objective on 27 May 1314, in a letter urging prompt despatch of troops to the front.

The surrender terms also exercised King Robert, whose decision to oppose Edward II before Stirling was perhaps the greatest risk of his career. Apart from the uncertainty inherent in any battle, the Bruce's resources were greatly inferior to those of his opponents. Scotland's subsistence economy could maintain only a small percentage of her adult male population in the field, 8000 men at most. Manpower was further reduced by the adherence of many leading Scots to Edward II. The hereditary constable, the Earl of Atholl, sacked Edward Bruce's supply depot at Cambuskenneth the night before the battle. Besides men, the Scots lacked warhorses, persuading King Robert …

> To gang on fute to this fechting
> Armyt bot in litill arming …
> Sen our fayis [foes] ar mar off mycht
> And better horsyt than ar we.
>
> John Barbour, *The Bruce*

Most of his army were lightly equipped pikemen. They had quilted linen armour, which, according to the contemporary *Vita Edwardi II*, 'a sword would not readily penetrate'; the *Vita* goes on to describe how they held 'axes at their sides and carried spears in their hands'. Besides the spearmen, there were 500 light horse under Robert Keith, the earl marischal, and an unknown number of archers. These supporting arms would play a subordinate but essential role.

Contemporary estimates of Scottish numbers at Bannockburn range from *Vita Edwardi II*'s 'great multitudes' to John of Fordun's 'few men'. Professor Barrow proposes 5000–6000: four schiltrons of 1000 each, 500 cavalry and miscellaneous hangers-on. Other estimates fall as low as 3500. According to Barbour, the Scots deployed in four *bataillis*, commanded by Edward Bruce, Thomas Randolph, Earl of Moray, and Sir James Douglas, with the king's division as reserve. Contemporary English sources based on eyewitness accounts unanimously describe only three divisions emerging from the wood in a reverse arrowhead: 'Two columns went abreast in advance of their third, so that neither was in front of the other, and the third, in which was Robert, followed' (*Lanercost Chronicle*). Sir Thomas Gray, whose father was a prisoner in the Scots camp, specifically states that 'at sunrise the Scots marched out of

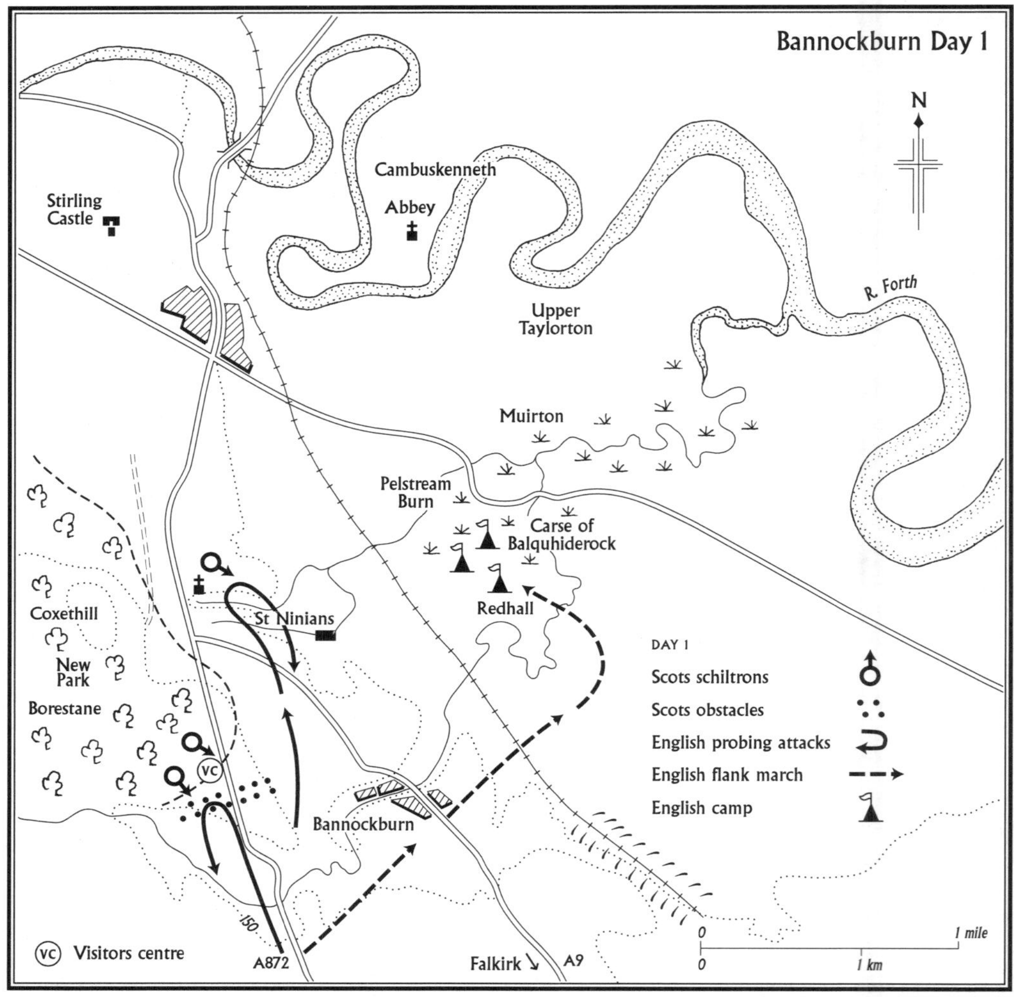

the wood on foot in three divisions'. Barbour may have had a personal interest in overstating the Black Douglas's role at Bannockburn, to the extent of giving him an independent command. Sir James's participation in mounted reconnaissance before the battle and in the subsequent pursuit makes it more likely that he commanded a cavalry force.

Barbour's claim that 30,000 Scots defeated 100,000 English is of course a joke. Edward II summoned over 21,000 infantry from the North, Midlands, Wales and Ireland, but not all of them turned up. Even Edward I could only compel half those summoned to appear. The show rate for Edward II's siege of Berwick in 1319 was 25 per cent. An intermediate allowance of a third for 1314 implies 7000 infantrymen actually served. Edward II was no exponent of archery, however. He wanted mounted action, issuing 890 letters of protection to men-at-arms in baronial retinues. Comparison with other Edwardian armies suggests twice as many heavy cavalry served in all, a total of 1800, consistent with *Vita Edwardi II*'s figure of 2000. Even Barbour's 3000 horse covered in plate and mail only brings Edward's maximum strength to 10,000, half the numbers

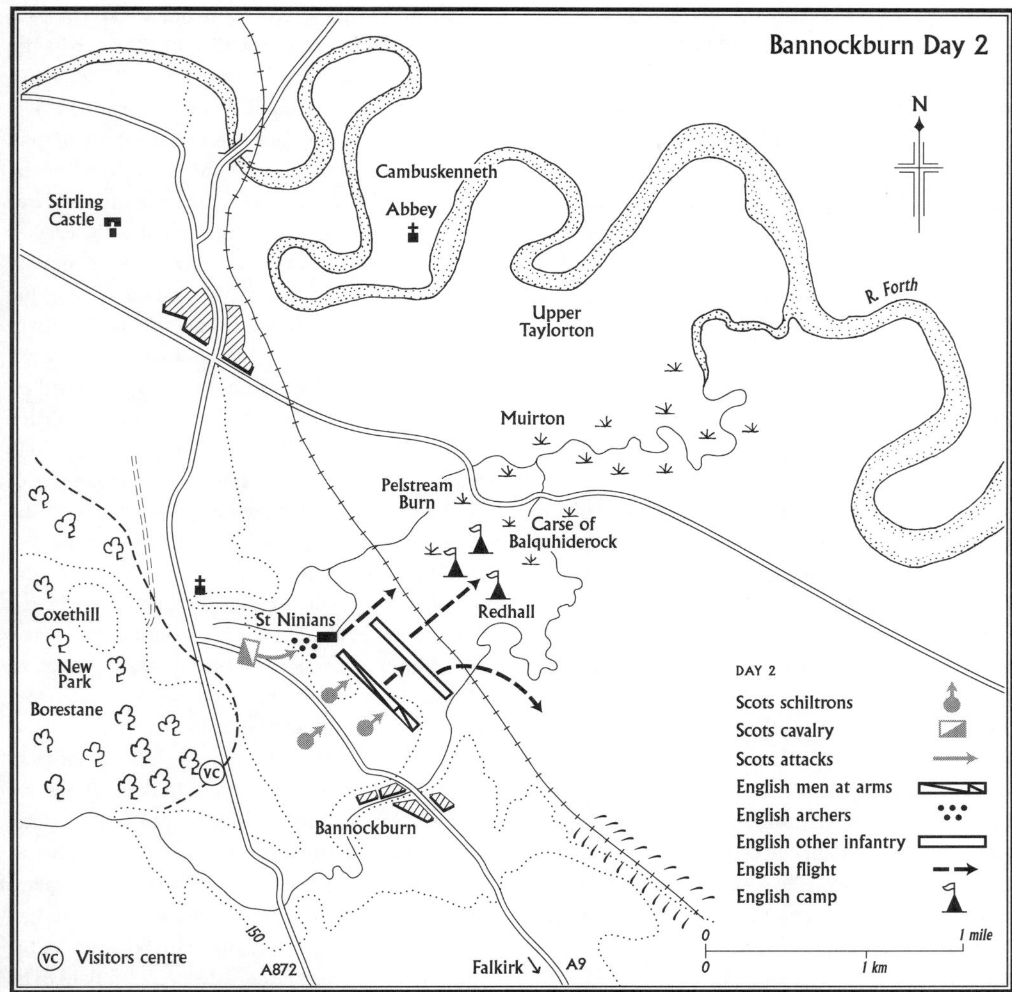

usually assigned to him. Numerous foreign knights signed up, including Giles d'Argentan, reputedly one of the three best knights in Christendom. Edward II had him rescued from prison in Salonika to hold his reins in action. The host's organization is obscure. Barbour writes of ten divisions, but whether of cavalry or infantry or both is not clear, while Gilbert de Clare, Earl of Gloucester, commanded a separate vanguard formed from 500 of his own men.

Contemporaries were most impressed by Edward II's logistics arrangements: 186 units each consisting of a 4-horse caretta and an 8-ox carra, with a total

Directions

From M9/M80 Junction 9 take the A872 to the National Trust for Scotland Heritage Centre at Borestone Brae. Much of the area is built up, but follow the main road to St Ninian's, and turn sharp right onto the A9 to see the Broomridge site described by Professors Barrow and Duncan, and accepted here, on the left. Several roads and paths cross the Carse, including the A905 from Stirling to Grangemouth.

lift of 650 tons, allegedly occupying 20 leagues of road. They were too unwieldy for the steep coastal route through Dunbar, so Edward took the Roman road from Wark through Lauderdale, reaching Edinburgh about 19 June. With nearly 20 hours of daylight in every 24, there was little time for sleep or meals. On Saturday 22nd the English closed up to Falkirk, some 14 miles (22 km) from Stirling.

King Robert summoned his troops to meet at Torwood, an ancient woodland north of the River Carron, where William Wallace had gathered his army. Aware of Edward's approach, Bruce fell back on the Saturday to New Park, a palisaded hunting preserve of uncertain extent on the southern edge of the wooded plateau before Stirling. The Bannock Burn protected his front. This stream was the only serious obstacle between the Rivers Carron and Forth, running down from the road, between 50-foot (15-m) high braes to the low-lying marshes near the Forth, known as the Carse. Wooded broken ground to the west precluded outflanking movements in that direction, and provided a covered line of retreat if English numbers forced a way through to Stirling. Two main roads cross the area today, the A872 (ex-A80) and the A9. In 1314 there was just the Roman road from Falkirk. It passed through New Park by a narrow and uninviting 'Entrye', further strengthened with knee-deep *pottis* dug honeycomb fashion either side of the road. Their exact location has fascinated historians, but hardly matters as they had no discernible influence over the course of the fighting.

King Robert's position between St Ninian's and New Park allowed him to block both the direct route to Stirling and the indirect approach around his eastern flank. Concealed among New Park's trees King Robert's infantry would be at an advantage against the English horse, as they would also be against a turning movement through the Carse: 'Giff that thai will beneath us ga / And our the marrais [marsh] pas.' English military intelligence was nervous of this area. Edward II wrote in May 1314 of the Scots 'striving to assemble great numbers of foot in strong and marshy places, extremely hard for cavalry to penetrate, between us and our castle of Stirling'.

Historians once regarded Bannockburn as a straightforward head-on confrontation across the stream that bears that name: a purely defensive victory for Bruce's dogged Lowland spearmen. The mythical planting of King Robert's royal standard in the Borestone belongs with this static view of the battle. In 1913 W.M. Mackenzie revolutionized our understanding of the battle. The failure of the English advanced guard to penetrate New Park on Sunday persuaded Edward II to turn the position through the Carse: 'a plain near the water of Forth, beyond Bannockburn – an evil, deep, streamy marsh, where the said English army unharnessed, and remained all night' (Sir Thomas Gray). On the Monday Bruce changed front to face east, and drove the English back into the killing ground formed by the meanders of the River Forth. A 15th-century illustration of the battle supports Mackenzie's dispositions, showing the Scots with Stirling Castle on their left, the Bannock Burn to their right. The English are before them, '*outre Bannokburn*'. Far from being a static affair, Bannockburn was a brilliant example of an army going over from the defensive to the offensive, one of the most difficult operations of war.

Advanced elements of the English host approached the Scots position during the afternoon of Sunday 22 June. Once dismissed as unfortunate skirmishes, the resulting clashes were essential preludes to Monday's disaster. The Earl of Gloucester's vanguard probed the southern entry to New Park, while the first echelon or '*prima acies*' of the main body under Sir Robert Clifford swept around the Scots left flank. The two actions were simultaneous but uncoordinated. Welsh troops led by Henry de Bohun screened Gloucester's left-hand prong, presumably light infantrymen for scouring the undergrowth. Thinking Scots troops along the tree line were running away, de Bohun pressed on into the covert, where Bruce himself appeared, drawing up his *bataill*. Seeing the king poorly mounted 'apon a litill palfrey', de Bohun rode against him, only to be slain with a back-hander from the king's axe that dashed out his brains. 'This,' says *Vita Edwardi II*, 'was the beginning of the trouble.'

Clifford penetrated further into the Scottish position. Avoiding New Park he made for Stirling

Bannockburn		
	Winners	*Losers*
Opponents	Scots	English
Commanders	Robert the Bruce	Edward II Gilbert Clare, Earl of Gloucester (k)
Numbers	6000	10,000
Losses	unknown	unknown

Castle, riding around the wood in hopes of cutting off the enemy as they withdrew. He had 300 men, commanded by three bannerets, perhaps one of Barbour's ten divisions. Near St Ninian's at the back of New Park, Clifford met 500 men of Moray's division, placed 'Besyd the kirk to kepe the way'. Spurred on by Bruce's often quoted remark that 'a rose of his chaplete was fallyn', Moray took the initiative, and advanced boldly against the heavy cavalry, something not seen in Britain since the Norman Conquest. Despite the English leaders urging their men to 'let them come on, give them some ground', the knights had no room to work up a charge. When they closed around the Scots, the leading spearmen brought down the horses, while rear ranks threw 'speris dartis and knyffis'. Others 'schout out of their rout', breaking ranks to stab horses and bring down their riders. Lacking archers Clifford could not break the Scots formation. After vainly casting their maces at their opponents the knights rode off, leaving a score of casualties.

The consequences of this double repulse were profound. Gloucester's experience confirmed the advice of Sir Philip de Mowbray, now at Edward II's headquarters, that New Park was too strong to be forced. He advised against seeking battle, as Edward's presence was enough in itself to satisfy the surrender agreement. The king's aim, however, was not to relieve a castle, but to make an end, as his father thought he had done. Clifford's unfortunate reconnaissance appeared to offer an alternative way around New Park, to good fighting ground between the woods and the Carse, where Edward might resolve the broader issue.

The night of 23/24 June the English harboured 'doune in the Kerse', pulling down cottages 'to mak briggis' over the Bannock Burn, and throwing the thatch under their wagon wheels. Commentators dwell on the discomfort of the dejected knights, sat all night in their armour in a swamp, while the infantry got drunk. More fateful was their strategic predicament, from which only decisive victory could extricate them. The English front was parallel to their line of advance, their only retreat lying to a flank across the burn, for the Forth sealed off other escape routes. Edward I must have been turning in his grave, as his feckless son voluntarily placed himself in the same situation that Simon de Montfort had occupied at Evesham.

There are four possible locations for the second day's fighting at Bannockburn. Mackenzie eliminated the traditional Borestone site with its statue and visitor centre. His own site looks impossibly deep in the Carse, in the buckle of the Forth between Upper Taylorton and Muirton. Scottish chroniclers associated the battle with the ancient place-name 'Bannok', placing the fighting further south. Mackenzie was further misled by contemporary references to 'polles'. He mistook these for pools, which he naturally placed near the river. In fact the whole area was known as *les Polles*, meaning the sluggish high-banked streams that cut through the waterlogged peat of the Carse. The Ordnance Survey and National Trust place the battlefield in the confluence of the Pelstream and Bannockburn, conveniently near Redhall, where Oman reckoned the English crossed into the Carse. This area below the 50-foot (15-m) contour is very wet, and lies out of sight of New Park. Contemporary sources make it plain the English frontline could see the Scots when they broke cover before the battle. This suggests that after camping in the marshy area marked by the Ordnance Survey, the English moved up to the 100-foot (30-m) contour before daybreak, forming up where the hard ground slopes down to the Carse. This is confirmed by numerous references to the plain hard field, '*arrida terra*', i.e. the Dryfield of Balquhiderock near Broomridge, three quarters of a mile (1.2 km) east of the traditional pre-Mackenzie battlefield.

Overnight the Scots considered withdrawal, until heartened by a deserter who urged, 'This is the time if ever you mean to undertake to recover Scotland.' At dawn the Scots moved out of New Park in order of battle, Edward Bruce on the right, Moray on the left, and the king in reserve. Their task was to keep Edward II in his tactical cul-de-sac, and if possible press him back into it. Sir Thomas Gray describes the Scots advance '*de tot aleyn de schiltrome*', i.e. aligned on a single unbroken frontage. Unlike their predecessors at Falkirk, the Scots in 1314 occupied the whole front available to them, depriving the English cavalry of any chance of a flank attack.

All accounts agree on the fatally constricted nature of the battlefield. Jammed between Pelstream and Bannock Burn the English could not exploit their numerical superiority, or even move. Gray refers to '*les batailles des Englez qui entassez estoint*': battalions piled up unable to advance, until their horses were impaled on advancing Scots spears. The usual interpretation of the English formation is that Gloucester's van took the left facing Edward Bruce, the remaining nine squadrons opposing Moray. The infantry were behind, unable to deploy, or to shoot without hitting their betters in the back. Two English sources, however, start the battle with an archery exchange. At least some infantry were deployed forward, or on a flank.

The Scots gave the English archers no time to loose their arrows: 'They advanced boldly against the English, records the *Lanercost Chronicle*; their leading division fiercely attacked Gloucester's division (*Vita Edwardi II*); Moray's men vanished among their opponents 'As thai war plungyt in the se'. Combatants fought in grim silence except for grunts and blows that struck fire as if from flints, staining the grass red with blood. Gloucester's death, fighting Edward Bruce, must stand for many:

> Suddenly the Scots make a rush, the earl's horse is killed and the earl falls to the ground ... burdened by the excessive weight of his body [armour] he could not easily get up.
>
> *Vita Edwardi II*

The English archers 'schot rycht hard and grevous', but before they took effect King Robert brought up 500 light horse to deal with them. No contemporary source specifies which flank the Marischal's cavalry had occupied. Modern historians locate them as best suits their own view of events. A refused position on the Scots left towards St Ninian's would keep them out of harm's way, until needed. Outside the archers' arc of fire the Scottish cavalry 'ourtuk them at a sid', and scattered them. Encouraged by lack of opposition, the previously outnumbered Scottish archers 'with all thar mycht schot egrely / Amang the horsemen ... and slew of thaim a full grete dele'.

The battle hung in the balance. The English cavalry were fought to a standstill, unable to deploy their reserves: 'for thar awne folk had na space / Yhet to cum to the assembling [i.e. fighting]'. At this decisive moment Barbour has Bruce commit his own division. Such a deliberate, though unconfirmed, intervention is more likely to have swung the battle than the celebrated appearance of Scottish camp followers over Coxet Hill. The hard-pressed English army began to break up: 'sum of thaim fled all planly' while others 'At gret myschieff mantenyt the fycht'. The rear ranks fell back into the burn, falling over one another in their confusion. Edward II had to use his mace to knock down Scottish outriders snatching at his reins.

Finally the king's minders led him away, much against his will, 'taking the ruin and flight of his men with a bitter spirit,' as the contemporary *Chronicle of Trokelowe* put it. The royal escape route via Stirling Castle was Mackenzie's decisive argument for locating the second day's fighting on the Scottish flank. Without this crucial realignment, Edward would have needed to cut his way through the whole victorious Scottish army to get there. Rightly refused entry to the castle, Edward rode westwards, circling King's Knot, the golf course and New Park to regain Dunbar via Linlithgow. Sir James Douglas chivvied the fugitives along, not giving them leisure 'As any water for to ma [make]'. His party was too few (60 against 500) to capture the king, and end the war at a stroke.

Once the king's banner left the field, the English army collapsed, 'sum slayne sum drownyt war'. Enough perished in the Bannock Burn 'betwixt the braes' to block the stream, allowing their luckier comrades to escape dry-shod. The absolute number lost will never be known. Barbour's claim of 30,000 English casualties is credible as a percentage of the 100,000 he thought present. A third is not an unlikely casualty rate after so catastrophic a defeat, and roughly agrees with the same author's estimate of 200 knights and 700 squires killed out of 3000 men-at-arms. Many were killed or captured wandering about the countryside, sometimes by women. Such heavy losses among the chivalry were untypical and deeply shocking. Over 500 English notables were ransomed, including the Earl of Hereford, who was exchanged for King Robert's wife, daughter and sister, with the veteran patriot Robert Wishart, Bishop of Glasgow, thrown in.

Bannockburn should have ended the war. The Bruce's generalship had amply justified his claim to the crown. Stirling and Lothian fell into Scottish hands, exposing northern England to devastating raids. Unfortunately no vital English interests were at stake in that remote and economically backward region. Scottish attacks would destabilize Edward II's regime, before he acknowledged Scottish independence.

Myton-on-Swale (the Chapter of Myton), *c.***20 September 1319**

England, North Yorkshire, LR99 SE4366

Bannockburn opened a new phase in the Scots War. While Edward II squabbled with his magnates, Scottish raiding parties pressed deep into northern England. These were not indiscriminate border raids, but deliberate blows aimed at key members of the English establishment, with the intention of ending the war. The Battle of Myton underlines the reversal in fortunes. A picked Scots army cut to pieces a scratch force of Yorkshire townsmen and peasants, as Edward I's veterans had once dispersed ill-trained Scottish levies.

The border outpost of Berwick – the first and last of Edward I's conquests – fell to the Scots by treachery in April 1318. Next year Edward II tried to recover it with an army of 8000, including his unreliable cousin Thomas, Earl of Lancaster. They made little progress before the Scots launched a dramatic diversion. Edward had installed Queen Isabella and the Treasury at York, with 21 wagonloads of documents, including Domesday Book. Moray rode deep into Yorkshire, before a captured spy revealed his plan to kidnap Isabella, whose seizure must have brought even Edward II to the conference table. Accordingly, the Archbishop of York and Chancellor John of Hotham led out a force of townsmen, clergy and anyone capable of bearing arms, to rescue the queen and send her away by water to safety at Nottingham.

Unfortunately for the citizens, they did not stop there. Incensed by Scots depredations in the North Riding, the clerical army went out again, meeting the enemy near Myton-on-Swale, 13 miles (21 km) north-west of York, soon after lunch. Local tradition places the fighting in flat meadows west of the River Swale, where the Ordnance Survey marks the battle site. A reasonable position for the Scots lies between Clot House Farm and Ellerthorpe Lodge. No medieval source states explicitly that the English crossed the river, limiting themselves to such expressions as '*prope*' or '*juxta Mitonam*', near or beside the village. However, the northern *Melsa Chronicle* does refer to '*haec discumfitura … inter Mytonam et Thorntonam*'. Thornton Manor (SE4371) is 3 miles (5 km) further up the Swale, on the west bank, where the Scots had been reported after burning Boroughbridge. Many of the English drowned in the Swale. Had they stayed on the east bank, they would presumably have ended up in the River Ure instead.

Historians disagree about the date of the action. Local sources give 12 September; the professional chroniclers at St Albans the 20th. Estimates of numbers vary as wildly: 10,000–15,000 Scots; 10,000–20,000 English. Since Moray avoided Edward II's besieging army, he presumably had less than 8000 men. The sources speak of one or two schiltrons, 3000 Scotsmen at most. The entire population of York may have numbered only 10,000, so the archbishop is unlikely to have fielded more than half that

Myton-on-Swale		
	Winners	*Losers*
Opponents	Scots	English
Commanders	Thomas, Earl of Moray Lord James Douglas	William Melton, Archbishop of York
Numbers	*c.*3000	*c.*5000
Losses	none	1000–4000

figure, including recruits from neighbouring villages.

All accounts agree on the qualitative differences between the two sides. The Scots were picked fighting men, ready for anything, led by experienced and successful commanders. The English were untrained in the art of war, *'inexercitatos et inexpertos'*, as ready to run as to fight, without leaders or anyone of military experience. When the Scots saw them approach in no kind of array, they scoffed: 'These are hunters, not warriors, they won't do much' (*Vita Edwardi II*). Unlike Thurstan's levies at the Standard (1138), Archbishop Melton's men lacked a professional core of knights, who were all with the king outside Berwick.

The Scots were about to decamp when their opponents' disorderly approach encouraged them to stand, forming their usual defensive mass of dismounted spearmen. Smoke filled the air from haystacks fired by the Scots, concealing from the English what awaited them. At three-spears' length, the Scots gave a great yell and charged down on them, in very good order. The astonished English took to their heels, pursued by the Scots, who broke up their schiltron to regain their horses.

Between 1000 and 4000 English were killed or drowned, including the Mayor of York. Many were carried off for ransom: a senior Treasury official fetching 2000 marks. So many clergy were slain the Scots called the affair the Chapter of Myton, or the White Battle, from the surplices of 300 dead priests. One trophy evaded the Scots, as the archbishop's crucifer (cross-bearer) swam his horse across the stream and pulled himself into a willow tree, before hiding his silver cross. A peasant found it and kept it wrapped in baling twine, until a nagging conscience moved him to return the sacred emblem.

The Scots continued south to Pontefract, devastating Ayrdale, Wharfedale and Craven. The siege of Berwick, bedevilled by secret machinations, broke up, achieving Moray's immediate objective. The political results of the Chapter of Myton were out of all proportion to the forces engaged. Chroniclers denounced Edward II's notorious infamy, his torpor, cowardice and indifference to his great inheritance. Rumours spread that he was not Edward I's true heir at all, preparing the way for Thomas of Lancaster's outright challenge to royal authority.

Directions

Turn left off the A19 9 miles (30 km) north of York, and take country roads through Tollerton to Myton, where the modern bridge is west of the village. On the far side follow a footpath north and then west to Clot House Farm, to view the battlefield.

Burton-upon-Trent, 10 March 1322

England, Staffordshire, LR128, unlocated

Boroughbridge, Tuesday 16 March 1322

England, North Yorkshire, LR99 SE3967

Edward II's humiliations at the hands of the Scots contributed to a short but savage civil war, ending in the defeat of the rebel Earls of Lancaster and Hereford. Troops loyal to the king intercepted them on the River Ure in a battle sometimes seen as a step in the tactical developments that culminated in victory for English longbowmen at Crecy.

Thomas of Lancaster was Edward II's cousin and the richest landowner in England. He was the natural leader of opposition to the king's favourites Piers Gaveston and later Hugh Despenser the Younger, 'who was, as it were, the king of England's right eye' (*Lanercost Chronicle*). Lancaster had Piers murdered in 1312, and drove Hugh into exile, with support from Hereford and other Welsh marcher lords. When Edward reinstated the Despensers, Lancaster attacked the royal castle at Tickhill, and Edward moved north with an army reportedly 60,000 strong. The rebels held him up at Burton Bridge for three days, until Lancaster and Hereford took fright at the numbers of Royalists, and withdrew in confusion. The leaders and nine score men-at-arms retreated through Pontefract, intending to join Scots forces lurking on the Border.

Andrew Harcla, Sheriff of Carlisle, was well informed of rebel movements. He assembled 4000 men from Cumberland and Westmorland and marched to Ripon, 6 miles (10 km) from the earl's route up the Great North Road. Receiving intelligence that Lancaster would be at Boroughbridge next day, he advanced overnight to forestall him. Sending his horses to the rear, Harcla stationed archers and dismounted spearmen at the northern end of the wooden bridge and ford across the River Ure. The latter were formed, 'in scheltrum after the Scottish fashion, to resist the knights and horses upon which the enemy relied' (*Lanercost*). Professor Tout believed Harcla had invented the combined-arms tactics used in the Hundred Years' War, but his arrangements are no more than the commonsense approach one might expect from a competent soldier, *miles providus,* wishing to defend a river passage. The Ure is a serious obstacle at Boroughbridge, 60 yards (55 m) wide. Harcla's archers on the higher northern bank commanded both crossings.

The *Lanercost Chronicle* says Lancaster turned up next day, but *Vita Edwardi II* suggests the earls were already installed in billets south of the river, which makes Harcla's manoeuvre all the more dramatic. Realizing Harcla had enough Borderers to wipe them out, the rebels formed two columns to cut a way through: Hereford on the left against the bridge; Lancaster on the right against the ford, a few hundred yards downstream.

Hereford attacked first on foot, the narrow wooden bridge proving unsuitable for a mounted assault. The leading men-at-arms met a hedge of pikes, thrust from all sides. A Welshman beneath the bridge poked a spear through a crack into Hereford's groin, 'which place men-at-arms are not accustomed to protect, as they hardly expect to find enemies underfoot' (*Vita et Mors Edwardi II*). Hereford's standard-bearer and two other knights were killed, and his son-in-law Roger Clifford severely wounded. Lancaster rushed the ford on horseback, but could not approach the water's edge for dense showers of arrows. Construction of flood defences along the south bank during the 1790s turned up bones and fragments of armour, subsequently lost.

Hereford's death took the fire out of the attackers, who fell back into the town, at first by ones, then by troops. Unable to continue the fight or escape, Lancaster negotiated a truce. While Harcla's men patrolled the northern bank, many rebels slipped away, some posing as beggars in old clothes. Next morning Royalist reinforcements from York helped Harcla across the river, capturing Lancaster and his 95 remaining knights without further loss. Lancaster was jeered through the streets of York, and summarily executed at Pontefract, without parliamentary sanction. Twenty-three other barons and knights were drawn on hurdles and hanged, contemporaries criticizing 'the excessive cruelty of the king and his friends' (*Lanercost*). The savage aftermath of Edward's arm's-length triumph further embittered English politics. Five years later it would be the king's turn to die a death not very different to that of the Earl of Hereford.

Burton-upon-Trent

	Winners	*Losers*
Opponents	Royalist	Rebel
Commanders	Edward II	Thomas, Earl of Lancaster

Boroughbridge

	Winners	*Losers*
Opponents	Royalist	Rebel
Commanders	Andrew Harcla	Thomas, Earl of Lancaster (x) Humphrey, Earl of Hereford (k)
Numbers	4000	*c.*2000

Directions

Boroughbridge is east of the A1, 16 miles (26 km) northwest of York. A modern road bridge occupies the site of the medieval structure at the north end of the main street. Follow a riverside walk along the southern bank to the ford near Milby Lock. A monument to the battle stands on the green in nearby Aldborough.

Byland (Old Byland), *c.* **12 October 1322**

England, North Yorkshire, LR100 SE5182–83

Edward II's last battle shows how far the wheel had turned since his father promenaded through Scotland in 1296. At Byland Scottish mounted infantry operating deep in England stormed a precipitous ridge defended by men-at-arms and archers, plundered the royal baggage train, and 'hadde nigh take the kyng at mete yf he hadde not flowe [fled]' (Ranulf Higden, *Polychronicon*, mid-14th century).

Edward II mounted his last invasion of Scotland in August 1322 with an army from over 30 counties and a ration strength of 14,000 infantry. The Scots refused to fight, withdrawing their cattle and food stocks beyond the Forth. Unable to solve this strategic conundrum, the English retreated, after famine had killed as many of them as dysentery. On 30 September King Robert launched an exceptionally bold and dangerous counter-raid, penetrating as far as Blakehoumor, the old name for the moorland south of the Cleveland Hills.

The Scots had never attacked this inaccessible area before, and were not there by chance. Robert wanted to strike directly at Edward, 'having heard for a certainty from his scouts that the king of England was there' (*Lanercost Chronicle*). The Scots advanced rapidly by secret night marches, 'hoping to capture or at least kill the unwary king' (Thomas Walsingham, *Historia Anglicana*, early 15th century). On 12 October they were at Northallerton, while Edward lay 15 miles (24 km) southeast near Rievaulx Abbey. Most accounts equate references to '*Bella Landa*' with Byland Abbey, 4 miles (6 km) south of Rievaulx. Deeds and tax records, however, identify Blakehoumor with Old Byland, a manor west of Rievaulx. Walsingham leaves no doubt that Edward fled from Rievaulx before the battle, while an archer received pay in March 1323 for 'following the body of the lord king from the conflict had with the Scots at Rievaulx on 14 October'.

The Scots advanced via Thirsk, heading eastwards towards the Hambleton Hills. Accounts of the battle support the commonsense view that the English occupied Sutton Bank, where the road performs two hairpin bends to climb 500 feet (150 m) in half a mile (0.8 km). This is the only line of advance suitable for King Robert's purpose, which above all required speed. Abbot Adam of Melsa wrote of the English on the height of the moor itself, '*super verticem ipsius morae*', attempting to bar the slopes over which the road passed. Barbour places the Scots 'in a plane feld / Fra Biland but a litell space', which fits the re-entrant between Roulston Scar and Whitestone Cliff. Before them, 'A craggy bra ... / And a gret path up for to gang'. The English were already arrayed on the heights, where they displayed their banners, 'and thocht weill to defend the pas'.

Edward had disbanded his invasion army, and had only the retinues of those magnates still with him, besides locally raised forces. King Robert on the other hand had troops from both sides of the Forth, as well as the Western Highlands and Isles. For an operation of such importance, he may have fielded more men than at Bannockburn. Abbot Adam expressly states the English were outnumbered.

Bruce started the battle with a frontal diversionary assault. Moray and the Black Douglas led the pick of the army up the road to draw the enemy fire:

Byland

	Winners	*Losers*
Opponents	Scots	English
Commanders	Robert the Bruce	John of Brittany, Earl of Richmond (p) Aymer de Valence, Earl of Pembroke

> ... arrows fley in gret foysoun [numbers]
> And thai that owe war tumbill down
> Stanys apon thaim fra the hycht.
>
> John Barbour, *The Bruce*

Once Moray had fixed the English, King Robert sent forward his 'Irschery from Argyle', ordering them to leave the path altogether, and climb the crags to gain the heights beyond. It was a 'peralous bargane' even for agile mountain troops. The Earl of Richmond dismounted to lead the defence on foot, but the Highlanders made good their hold on the crest. General English collapse followed, and the earl was captured. English sources confirm that overwhelming numbers of Scots, specifically Highlanders, scaled the steep wooded slopes, scattering their opponents at the first onset. The English were presumably engaged against Moray's forlorn hope, when they were suddenly attacked in flank. Sir Thomas Gray, a contemporary, blamed the defenders' poor morale, 'The Scots were so fierce and their chiefs so daring, and the English so badly cowed, that it was no otherwise between them than as a hare before greyhounds.'

The king took no part in the fighting, 'being ever chicken-hearted and luckless in war' (*Lanercost Chronicle*). More than one source stresses his personal lack of vigilance, '*minus caute*', nearly being captured over lunch in the monastery. He fled '*velociter*', speedily, losing treasury, supplies and silver plate. Total casualties are unknown, but three northern lords lost 42 men-at-arms and hobelars (mounted spearmen) from their retinues, out of a pre-battle strength of 331. A loss rate of 12.6 per cent suggests they had not fled with the alacrity that defeatist chroniclers suggest.

Edward's second narrow escape from capture, this time on his own turf, revealed incompetence well beyond the ordinary, and shook the most loyal subjects. The Archbishop of York permitted religious houses to preserve their property by compounding with the Scots. Andrew Harcla, created Earl of Carlisle for his victory at Boroughbridge, negotiated with Bruce as Robert I of Scotland. Harcla died a traitor's death, but such an initiative showed the war was lost. In March 1323 a 13-year truce was agreed that would outlast the reign.

Directions

Take the A170 east from Thirsk through Sutton-under-Whitestonecliffe, and climb the hairpin bends to the viewpoint at the top of Sutton Bank. Walk the Cleveland Way north and south of the main road, to see the proposed English position and the slopes scaled by the Highlanders. Continue along the A170 to Helmsley, and turn left onto the B1257 to Rievaulx Abbey.

The Gaelic Recovery in Ireland

The Anglo-Norman lordship of Ireland reached its greatest extent in the 1270s, spreading west into Galway and Co. Clare. A century later it had been pushed back southeast of a line from Louth to Limerick, and was increasingly on the defensive. This erosion of English power was not the result of reversals on the battlefield so much as a shift in underlying strategic realities. Gaelic victories illustrate the revival of Gaelic fortunes, but did not cause it.

The population boom that fuelled European expansion in the early Middle Ages levelled off around 1300. Even before the Black Death, English peasants no longer needed to travel to a remote and hazardous frontier to find empty land. In Ireland, Gaelic social patterns reasserted themselves in marginal areas of settlement. The 'degeneration' of established colonists accelerated the process, as they adopted Irish customs, language and haircuts. Royal governments diverted Irish resources to Scotland provoking Edward Bruce's disastrous invasion in 1315.

While English support faltered, the native Irish adapted the invaders' military techniques to local conditions. Irish cavalry still fought overarm with thin 12-foot (3.5-m) lances, but wore round iron helmets, mail coats and throat pieces. Opponents looked so similar that at Dysert O'Dea (1318) Irish reinforcements were mistaken for Normans. Continual warfare fed the market for mercenaries. Bands of *ceithernaigh* or kerns wandered from one employer to another, 'barefooted, bareheaded, and lightly armed', equipped with the traditional Irish darts. Scottish gallowglasses (mercenaries) appeared in the 1250s: 'grim of countenance, tall of stature, big of lime ... chiefly feeding on beefe, porke, and butter'. Equipped with mail shirts or a knee-length leather jack, gallowglasses could fight it out hand-to-hand with long-handled axes, or garrison the castles that Irish lords were beginning to build. Anglo-Irish men-at-arms are said to have fallen behind English developments in protection, but numerous contemporary accounts refer to heavily armed cavalry. Knights worth £20 a year served on barded (armoured) horses, by law. Lesser folk adapted to the fluid conditions of Irish warfare, producing the hobelar or mounted spearman who became a feature of Anglo-Scots warfare.

Aedh O'Connor employed the first gallowglasses, introduced from the Western Isles by his Scottish wife as part of her dowry. Nevertheless, his victory at Athankip (1270) followed a typical Irish running fight, enlivened by treachery. Dysert O'Dea (1318) featured a baited ambush, as well as a stand-up fight. Faughart (1318), the only English victory of Edward II's miserable reign, was won by subterfuge, and the victor, John Bermingham, murdered by settlers at Balibragan (1329).

Athankip, 1270

Ireland, Co. Roscommon, DS33 unlocated

Aedh O'Connor was a lucky survivor of Brian O'Neill's disastrous attack on Downpatrick in 1260 (see Down II above). The conduct of the two battles was as different as their outcome. Aedh fought Athankip on his home ground in Connacht, where the thinly settled countryside favoured the optimum Irish strategy of avoiding action, until fruitless marching had worn out the opposition. As Brian O'Neill had not, Aedh fought only when retreating or pursuing, not closing in hand-to-hand combat until the other side was already beaten. Then he overwhelmed their rearguard in the greatest defeat the English had yet suffered in Ireland.

All the *Gallaibh* (foreigners) of Erin had combined for a full-scale expedition against Connacht, led by Walter de Burgo, Earl of Ulster. The *Annals of Loch Cé* (16th century) set out development of this expedition in detail:

Day 1 The host gathers at Roscommon
Day 2 March to 'Oilfinn', i.e. Elphin
15 miles (24 km)
Day 3 March to 'Port-na-Leice'
9 miles (14.5 km)

The latter 'fort on the hillside' is presumably Lackagh (DS33 M9996), where a rath or ring fort occupies a low hill between the River Shannon and the Jamestown Canal.

Walter de Burgo then went east over the Shannon, crossing at Ath-Caradh-Conaill, an unknown ford near Carrick-on-Shannon. Robert de Ufford remained on the west bank with a small force, to secure the crossing. Aedh awaited the *Gallaibh* at Magh-Nissi

Athankip

	Winners	Losers
Opponents	Irish	Anglo-Irish
Commanders	Aedh O'Connor Turlough O'Brien (k)	Walter de Burgo, Earl of Ulster Robert de Ufford

(pronounced Moynishy), a wooded region thick with lakes and small round hills between Leitrim and Mohill, known as the Woods of Conmaicne (Day 4). Some of Aedh's people opposed the Anglo-Irish advance, and a few foreigners were killed: 'Nevertheless [they] ... desisted not from the expedition until they reached Magh-Nissi, where they rested and encamped the night.'

The Anglo-Irish seem to have developed cold feet, as they sought to make terms, handing over Walter de Burgo's brother William Og in earnest of good faith. Aedh had other intentions. He took William prisoner, and killed two other hostages outright. Learning of this treachery, the Anglo-Irish headed back to the Shannon, making for an unknown crossing called Athankip. The name indicates a ford marked for the benefit of travellers by the stump of a tree. Irish jitter parties delayed the retreat, for the English were two days coming back (Days 5–6) compared with one going out:

> And O'Connor was during these two nights marching round them, as a furious, raging, tearing lion goes about his enemies when killing them, so that he permitted them neither to eat, sleep, nor be at rest.

On the morning of Day 6 the Irish overtook the weary column as it approached Athankip, a few miles south of Carrick-on-Shannon, 'when their rear was dislodged, and their van was routed'. Walter de Burgo escaped after killing Turlough O'Brien, in single combat. Aedh retaliated in kind against William Og. Other Anglo-Irish casualties included nine principal knights slain on the spot, an unknown number of lesser folk, and 100 barded horses captured with their trappings. Aedh followed up by destroying three towns and their castles, including Roscommon: 'Great famine and scarcity in all Erinn *hoc anno*'.

Directions

Athankip lay on the left, i.e. eastern, bank of the Shannon, between the N4 and the river, south of Carrick-on-Shannon. Explore the river bank between Carrick-on-Shannon and Jamestown by minor roads.

Athenry, 10 August 1316

Ireland, Co. Galway, DS 46 unlocated

Dysert O'Dea (Disert Tola), Thursday 10 May 1318

Ireland, Co. Clare, DS 57 R2985

A new style of fighting appeared in Ireland as the Scots Wars of Independence spilled over into Ulster with Edward Bruce's landing at Louth in 1315. Inspired by the Scottish example at Bannockburn, heavily armed Gaelic foot soldiers began to fight it out to the death. Bruce's intervention prompted disturbances in Connacht, culminating in an obscure battle at the gates of Athenry: 'sore fought a long time that no man wist what side the best went'. The *Annals of Loch Cé* filled a page with high-ranking Irish casualties, including the king of Connacht, his standard-bearer and lawgiver, '28 persons entitled to the sovereignty of Ui Maine ... and 100 of his own people along with him'. The victors captured enough armour to pay for new town walls for Athenry, proving the Irish were no longer 'naked men' who fled at the first shock of battle.

More is known of Dysert O'Dea, thanks to the *Triumphs of Turlough*, a contemporary mixture of history, entertainment and panegyric: Froissart with banshees. During the late 13th century the Clare family had established a foothold in the area that shares their name between the Shannon estuary and Galway Bay. In 1318 Richard de Clare interfered in a civil war amongst the O'Briens of Thomond. Murtough O'Brien's men reacted by plundering the outskirts of de Clare's stronghold at Bunratty, provoking retaliation.

Richard slept at Quin Abbey, before crossing the River Fergus, heading for a district known as 'Ruan of the Entrenchments'. At the ford he met a banshee, a manifestation of ancient Irish war goddesses, who fed on men's skulls and foretold the deaths of heroes. The doomed men laughed at the hag's warnings and

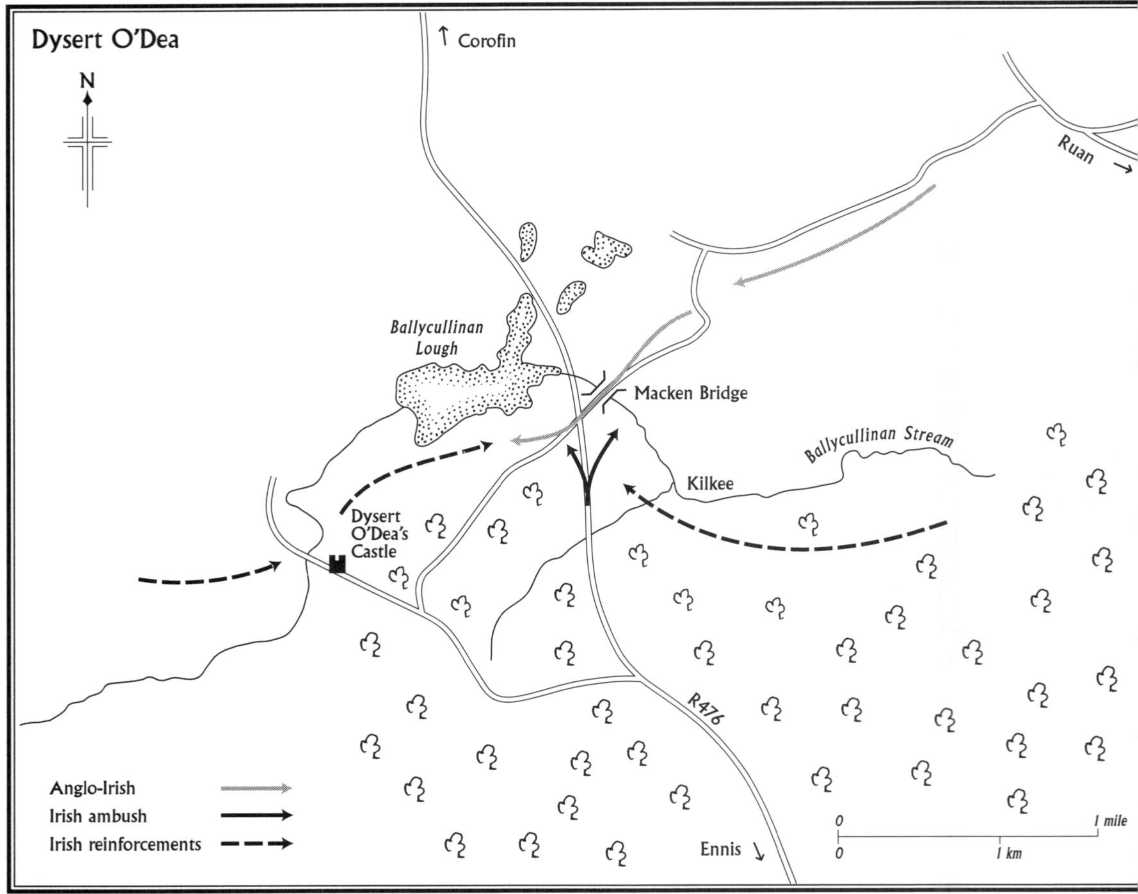

marched on. Meanwhile, a local Irish chieftain, Conor O'Dea, had laid an elaborate ambush in the marshy meadows covering the approaches to Dysert from Ruan, and called on his neighbours for help. Lough Ballicullanin protected Conor's left flank, Ballicullanin stream ran across his front to Kilkee, and hilly ground further south protected his right and rear. The marshes remained a significant obstacle in the 1890s, impassable even after a dry spring.

Richard de Clare advanced into O'Dea's territory, splitting his force into three columns to pillage more thoroughly. Orders of battle are unknown, perhaps a thousand either side: Anglo-Irish men-at-arms and archers against gallowglasses and kerns. In the centre de Clare headed west towards O'Dea's round tower, which stood out over the trees and crags. As the Anglo-Irish approached today's Macken Bridge, they found some kerne driving a herd of cattle, and gave chase. Some they killed, but the survivors crossed Ballicullanin stream, and held the causeway until de

Directions

Dysert O'Dea *Bunratty Castle is 9 miles (19 km) west of Limerick on the N18. Turn right off the N18 along the R462 for Quin, and the R469 to Ennis. Then approach the battlefield from the southeast along the R476. The fighting occurred immediately west of the Macken Bridge, between Lough Ballicullanin and the Dysert road. Scamhal Hill to the west provides an extensive view over the battlefield.*

Athenry

	Winners	Losers
Opponents	Anglo-Irish	Irish
Commanders	William de Burgo, 'Liath' Richard Bermingham	Felim O'Connor (k)

Dysert O'Dea

	Winners	Losers
Opponents	Irish (Thomond)	Anglo-Irish
Commanders	Murtough O'Brien	Richard de Clare (k)

Clare came forward with the pick of his knights to drive them away.

The knights pressed on past Conor's ambush, springing the trap for which the cows had acted as bait. Half the ambushers rushed down to the ford isolating de Clare's 80-strong party beyond the river. The rest took the Anglo-Irish advance guard in flank and wiped them out. When de Clare's main body finally cleared the crossing, Irish reinforcements appeared over Scamhal Hill to the west. Both sides closed ranks and slugged it out. Hemmed in by streams and marshes, neither could retreat. Drawing in their outlying detachments, the Normans strengthened their 'battle-hedge', encircling the Irish forces.

Murtough had heard of de Clare's raid, and was following the trail of burnt houses from the east, through Spancel Hill. The arrival of fresh troops behind the surviving Anglo-Irish was decisive, the *Gallaibh* dying where they stood. Anglo-Irish power in Thomond was destroyed, and never recovered. Richard de Clare's widow, whose eldest son was also killed in the fighting, fled down the Shannon by boat, after setting Bunratty Castle on fire. Murtough had won one of the least-known but greatest Gaelic victories of the day.

Directions

Athenry *12 miles (20 km) east of Galway on the N6 and R348. See the massively forbidding keep built in 1238, and patches of town walls funded from the spoils of battle.*

Faughart (Fochart), 14 October 1318

Ireland, Co. Louth, DS36 J0512

Few medieval battles combine the significance and interest of Faughart. Edward Bruce, 'destroyer of all Erinn in general, both Foreigners and Gaidhel', was slain, ending a three-year nightmare of famine and war. The unlikely instrument of deliverance was a Drogheda butcher 'in a fooles coat', who shook out Bruce's brains 'with a plomd of lead' (*Register of the Mayors of Drogheda*).

Bannockburn (see above) handed the Scots the initiative in their struggle against England. Robert the Bruce may have hoped his brother's invasion of Ireland in May 1315 would create a pan-Celtic empire, divert Anglo-Irish support from the English war effort, or simply remove his brother to a safe distance. Paralysed by faction, lack of money and famine, neither the royal government nor Anglo-Irish magnates could resist Edward's Scottish veterans. In the end it was a scratch force that outfaced the Scots lion.

Edward's fortunes had declined since his proclamation as king of Ireland on May Day 1316, and the heady days when he spread death and destruction as far as Dublin and Limerick. The English had regained control of the sea, cutting Edward off from Scotland. He held out in Ulster until Sir John Bermingham, with the gentry and commons of Counties Louth and Meath, intercepted him near Dundalk, and killed him. The English army was not large: '*exercitu modesto*'. Concrete figures range from 1224 through 1324 to 2000, including 'a great body of bowmen' and 'horsemen clad with iron coats of mail from head to foot'. There were also well-armed townsmen, such as 20 picked men from Drogheda, including John Maupas the butcher. Credible estimates of Bruce's army are 3000 altogether – 2000 Scots plus their Irish allies. Edward also deployed some dissident Anglo-Irish.

The sources name both Dundalk and Faughart, a hill 3 miles (5 km) further north, as the site of the battle, but various indications show the fighting took place nearer the latter. The major Gaelic account, *Cath Fhochairte Brighite* ('Battle of Faughart'), explicitly

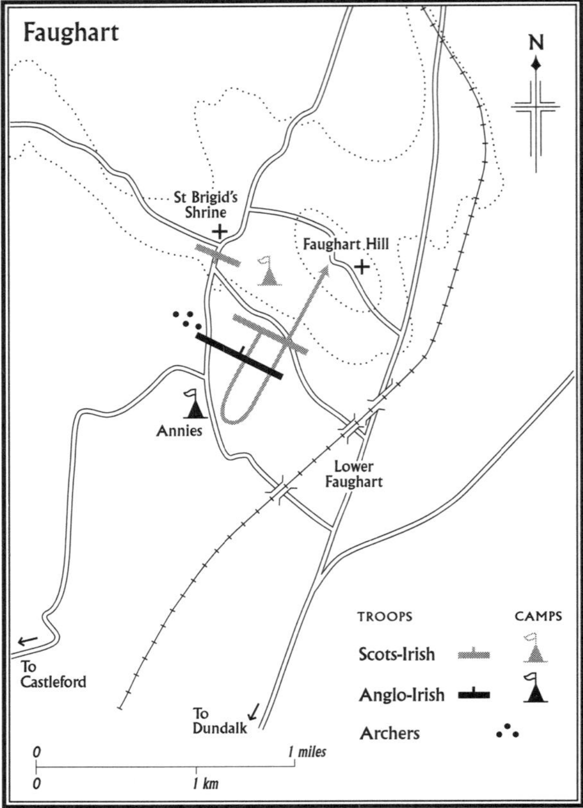

Directions

Follow the N1 north of Dundalk. Take a left fork after Strandfield along a country road to Lower Faughart. Turn left between the houses, across the battlefield. Bear right towards McDermott's Corner, and further right to see Bruce's grave in the churchyard on top of the hill.

declares, 'The Gaels and Scots put themselves in battle array on the brow of the hill.' This suggests the southern slope of Faughart Hill, where a broad shelf affords a sheltered campsite with excellent views southwards. The Anglo-Irish host camped north of Dundalk within half a mile (0.8 km) of the enemy, at a place called 'the Mores', i.e. a marsh. Just below the probable Scots camp is Annies, a place-name adapted from the Gaelic for marsh. Annies neatly covers converging roads from Dundalk and Castletown, by which Bermingham's troops would approach. Conversely, an Anglo-Irish rendezvous at Annies prevented Bruce's further movement south.

Both armies were in position the night before the battle. Edward's formed three divisions echeloned back from left to right, along the southeast–northwest alignment of the slope. The Scots were furthest forward on the left, the dissident *Gallaibh* (i.e. Anglo-Irish) in the centre, while the lightly armed Irish were held back on the right. They had not wanted to fight as Bruce had rejected their advice to await reinforcements, but they agreed to hold their ground. They stood within hailing distance, where the old road runs back over Faughart Hill past St Brigid's Shrine, shown on modern maps as McDermott's Corner.

English sources run different stages of the battle together. They say only that the Anglo-Irish broke through the enemy front line, the Scots fleeing after Edward's death at the hand of John Maupas, whose body was found on top of the king. The *Cath* is more intriguing. The English, as might have been expected, began the action with a shower of arrows, causing heavy losses among the unarmoured Irish on the enemy right. Their heavy cavalry then charged the renegade Anglo-Irish in Bruce's centre, driving them back to the top of the hill. Last of all Bermingham himself attacked Bruce's division. The Anglo-Irish seem to have hoped to push back the Scoto-Irish right, cutting Bruce's line of retreat northwards across Moyry Pass.

The Anglo-Irish were at a disadvantage, attacking uphill against superior numbers. Edward rallied his shaken centre, and led it with his own left wing in a counterattack, driving the enemy back downhill with heavy loss. The Irish abandoned their neutrality to chase off the defenceless archers, who had loosed all

Faughart

	Winners	*Losers*
Opponents	Anglo-Irish	Scoto-Irish
Commanders	John Bermingham	Edward Bruce (k)
Numbers	1200–2000	2000–3000
Losses	50	unknown

their arrows. Some of the Anglo-Irish fled as far as Dundalk, and rich booty was taken, suggesting the Anglo-Irish camp had fallen into enemy hands. Convinced the battle was won, Edward's men sat down to refresh themselves with plundered rations.

During the lull, Edward walked between the armies to view the morning's work. The two forces must have been some distance apart, for when 'a shameless idiot ... enveloped in a bundle of straw ropes' ambled towards Edward and his retinue, the Scots could only surmise he had come from the English position. The counterfeit jester carried an iron ball and chain, with which he professed to do feats of skill excelling all others in Ireland. These included murder: 'finding an opportunity of the king, he gave him a strike of the ball on the head' (*Cath Fhochairte Brighite*), and ran off as fast as he could. Bermingham's forces were ready 'in good order of battle' to exploit their murderous stratagem. They fell upon the leaderless Scots, many destitute of their arms, and drove them up the hill with great slaughter. The lowest English claim of 1500 Scots casualties still seems excessive, for the pursuers soon gave up the chase. John Barbour wrote, 'Thai wencust [vanquished] was sa suddenly, that few intill the place were slayne.' Many could have found refuge with their undefeated Irish allies.

The juggling butcher must have been among the English casualties, for the reward went to his heirs. Bermingham ensured his own payoff by salting Edward Bruce's head and delivering it to Edward II in a wooden pail. The king was 'right blythe' to be thus rid of a 'felon foe', and elevated Bermingham to the earldom of Louth. Bruce's friends recovered his remains after dark and buried them in Faughart churchyard. His legacy was entirely negative. He exposed the impotence of the English crown and undermined the Anglo-Irish magnates, but ruined his natural supporters, the Gaels. The annalist of Loch Cé wrote of his death that, 'no better deed for the men of Erinn was performed since the beginning of the world ... for theft and famine and destruction of men occurred throughout Erinn during his time ... and people used to eat one another without doubt'.

Balibragan (Braganstown), 10 June 1329

Ireland, Co. Louth, DS43 O0394

Athy, 1359

Ireland, Co. Kildare, DS55 unlocated

John Bermingham, victor of Faughart (1318), died at the hands of his own tenants in a disturbance that passed into legend and shocked his contemporaries. The Braganstown Massacre of Whitsunday 1329 was hardly a battle, but it illustrates the violence that disfigured 14th-century Irish society better than the more formal action outside Dundalk.

Edward II had rewarded Bermingham by granting him the earldom of Louth, and the new earl played his part in the treacherous power politics of Edward's later years. He survived Byland (1322) only to fall victim to his inability to deal with fellow Anglo-Irishmen. Bermingham was bred in the wild Leinster marches, where his father was remembered as conqueror of the Irish, '*debellator Hibernicorum*'. He had hunted Irishmen 'as hunter doth the hare', and in 1305 organized the massacre of 32 leading O'Connors during a feast at Carbury Castle. John Bermingham seems to have transferred the uncompromising habits of western Leinster to Louth. He also brought to Louth a private army or 'rout' of Irish kerns, and a taste for Irish culture.

The English settlers of Louth, who resented an outsider's imposition upon them, appreciated neither. They boiled over the Friday before Whitsun. Two of Bermingham's kerne killed Robert Godeknave of Ardee during a quarrel over a limekiln. The townsmen raised hue and cry, killing the culprits. Twenty-two more kerns took sanctuary in the Carmelite chapel, but next morning the townsmen dragged out and killed 19 of them. The survivors escaped by force to Bermingham's house at Balibragan, 5 miles (8 km) northeast of Ardee.

Legal hearings established later that Roger

Gernoun, Robert Godeknave's father-in-law, then conspired to alarm the whole county and raise the posse comitatus, by which all who heard the horns sounding from village to village were obliged to turn out with their legally specified weapons, mostly bows and arrows, and go in pursuit of the criminal. Fifty-eight named accomplices and an unspecified number from Dundalk joined Gernoun overnight by the Braganstown causeway. On Sunday morning they demanded the earl surrender the fugitives, but Bermingham refused, not believing his tenants would attack him in his own manor. His wife and children went out to defuse the situation, escorted by a squire bearing a white wand of peace, but the *posse* assaulted the countess and killed the squire. Bermingham shut the gate, but Gernoun's companions broke in through the haggard, an enclosure for storage of crops, killing the earl (who was still unarmed), 'with 160 and more, with his two brothers and about nine of his name'. The *Book of Howth* claimed 200 soldiers of the Pale were slaughtered, 'a great hindrance to the North of Ireland, for this was the only key and wall thereof'.

The earl was clearly not beloved by his tenants, but the disproportionate slaughter suggests there was more to the business than simple resentment of a change of lordship. Among the casualties were one-eyed Cam O'Kayrwill, supreme exponent of harp and bodhrán, and 20 of his students. The English of Louth meant to wipe out an intrusive pocket of Gaelic culture. The *Book of Howth* recounts a spurious tale of a drunken quarrel over dinner, the cellars treacherously packed with armed men, but its assessment of the massacre's fallout rings true: 'No wonder that Ireland could never be brought to conformity, for God never did permit any to reign that sought earnestly the commodity thereof.' Anglo-Irish feuding after Braganstown halved the colony almost overnight. The colonists could still defeat Irish forces, but the only memorable feature of the Earl of Ormonde's success at Athy (1359) was the theft of English cattle to pay his troops.

Balibragan

	Winners	*Losers*
Opponents	Anglo-Irish	Anglo-Irish
Commanders	Roger Gernoun	John Bermingham, Earl of Louth (k)
Losses	unknown	*c.*200

Athy

	Winners	*Losers*
Opponents	Anglo-Irish	Irish
Commanders	James Butler, Earl of Ormonde	unknown
Losses	*c.*30	unknown

Directions

Balibragan *The Carmelite church in Ardee was in a lane known as Boat Trench. Leaving Ardee by the N52, turn right onto country roads north of the River Dee, and left just before the Drogheda–Dundalk railway. Bermingham's manor house has disappeared, leaving the map squares labelled Braganstown nearly devoid of settlement.*

Athy *Tactical locations unknown.*

PART FOUR

LONGBOW AND BOMBARD

The Later Middle Ages 1332–1497

Any distinctions made between the high Middle Ages (say 1100–1300) and the following two centuries are purely arbitrary. No catastrophic discontinuity like the Norman Conquest separates Edward II's reign from that of later Plantagenets. The knightly class continued to dominate society and its military arrangements, just as castles still dominated the landscape. Contemporaries had no idea that they were living through a transitional period between Ancient and Modern, still less that they were approaching its end. In their own minds they were time's latest handiwork. Significant changes in the organization and conduct of war, however, distinguish the 14th and 15th centuries from earlier medieval periods; changes that made the English, an insular people of no great military reputation, the first soldiers of Europe. Techniques learned fighting the Scots earned undying glory in France, and reappeared on domestic battlefields when defeat overseas and dynastic inadequacy inspired revolution at home.

The strategic pattern of medieval Britain's last two centuries is quite different from that of the previous two. Three-quarters of the battles fought in Britain and Ireland between Dupplin Muir (1332) and Stoke Field (1487) were located in England, compared with less than a third between Northallerton (1138) and Byland (1322). The English turned their energies away from building an insular empire, first into continental adventures, then into fighting one another. Battles trebled in frequency, from one every 17 years to one every 5. Commanders sought prompt decisions on the battlefield, rather than wrecking the English countryside with the protracted devastation they practised elsewhere.

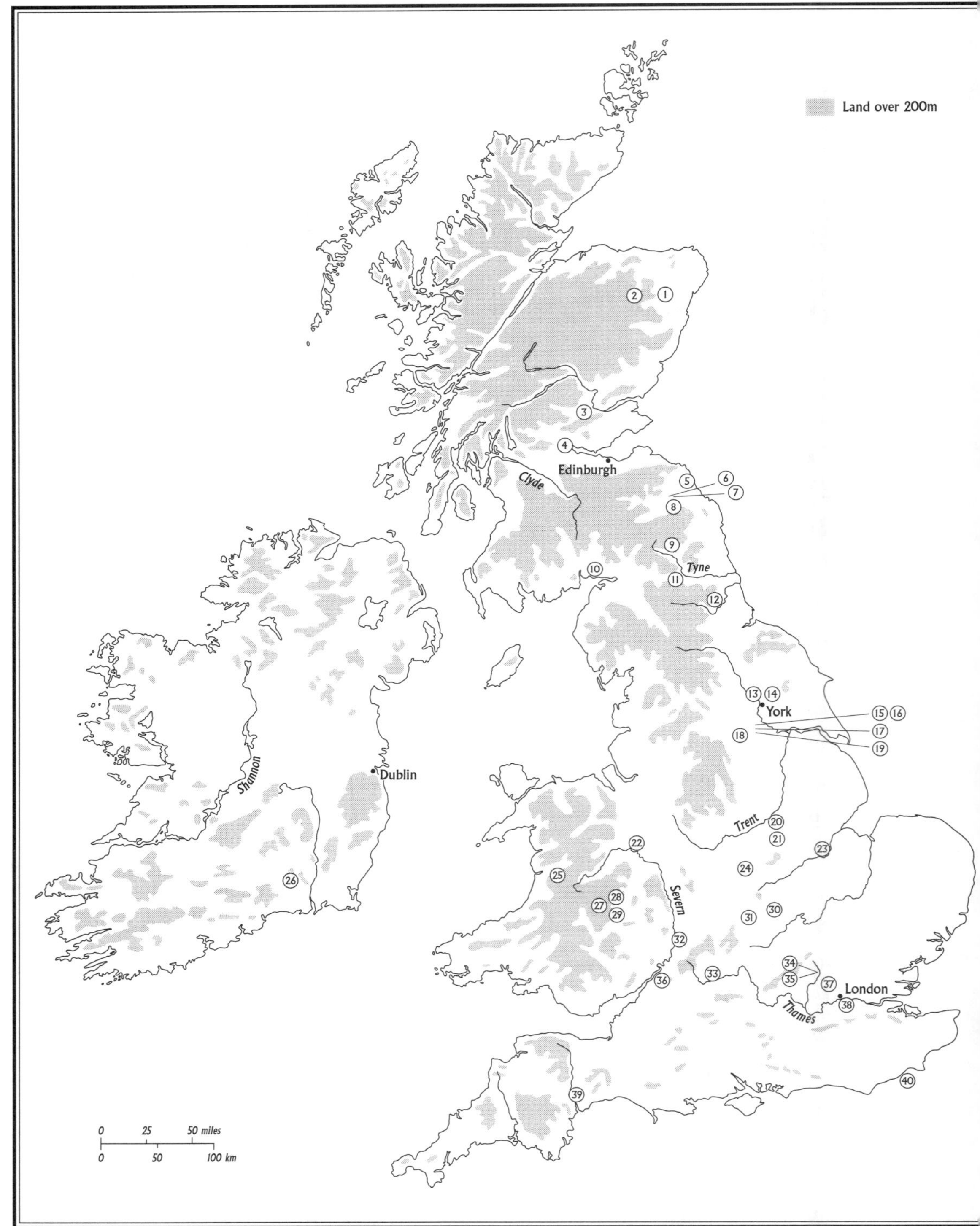

Land over 200m
Edinburgh
Clyde
Tyne
York
Dublin
Shannon
Trent
Severn
London
Thames
1
2
3
4
5
6
7
8
9
10
11
12
13
14
15
16
17
18
19
20
21
22
23
24
25
26
27
28
29
30
31
32
33
34
35
36
37
38
39
40
0 25 50 miles
0 50 100 km

A growing sense of English nationhood failed to enhance political stability. Only one king had been deposed since the Norman Conquest, the notoriously useless Edward II. The 160 years following his murder in 1328 saw one king killed in action (Richard III), and four deposed: Richard II in 1399, Henry VI several times, Edward IV in 1470, and Edward V in 1483. Henry IV and Henry VII had to defend their crown on the battlefields of Shrewsbury (1403) and Stoke Field (1487) respectively. Military success became more significant when resolving dynastic disputes than hereditary right.

The relative quiet amongst England's neighbours reflected her strategic pre-eminence. Bannockburn (1314) ensured Scotland's freedom, but Wales and Ireland remained subordinate or divided. North of the Border Edward III won splendid victories at Dupplin Muir (1332) and Halidon Hill (1333), whose political inconsequence confirmed that a permanent conquest of Scotland was beyond England's reach. English kings never reasserted suzerainty after Otterburn (1388), while the end of the Hundred Years' War in 1457 removed the temptation for French kings to invoke the Auld Alliance. Peace returned to the Tweed after a last English victory at Homildon Hill (1402).

The failure of Owain Glyn Dŵr's prolonged revolt, on the other hand, confirmed the permanence of Edward I's conquest of Wales. Closely bound to England by economic and social ties, Wales was more significant as a dissident recruiting ground than as a battlefield. French troops marched through south Wales in 1405, as Henry Tudor did before Bosworth (1485). The Yorkists raised troops there before Ludford Bridge (1459), and the Lancastrians before Mortimer's Cross (1461). The weakness of Ireland, remote beyond St George's Channel, was not yet an opening for England's enemies. Rulers in London could safely

---

KEY

1 Harlaw 1411
2 Culbean 1335
3 Dupplin Moor 1332
4 Sauchieburn 1488
5 Halidon Hill 1333
6 Homildon Hill 1402
7 Nesbit Muir 1402
8 Hedgeley Moor 1464
9 Otterburn 1388
10 Annan 1332
11 Hexham 1464
12 Neville's Cross 1346
13 Heworth Moor 1453
14 Stamford Bridge 1454
15 Bramham Moor 1408
16 Tadcaster 1487
17 Towton 1461
18 Wakefield 1460
19 Ferrybridge 1461
20 Stoke Field 1487
21 Blore Heath 1459
22 Shrewsbury 1403
23 Lose-Coat Field 1470
24 Bosworth Field 1485
25 Hyddgen 1401
26 Piltown 1462
27 Pilleth 1402
28 Ludford Bridge 1459
29 Mortimer's Cross 1461
30 Northampton 1460
31 Edgcote 1469
32 Tewkesbury 1471
33 Radcot Bridge 1387
34 St Albans I 1455
35 St Albans II 1461
36 Nibley Green 1470
37 Barnet 1471
38 Blackheath 1497
39 Clyst Bridge 1455
40 Winchelsea 1349

ignore its problems. Ireland had avoided conquest, at the price of division between Gaelic and Anglo-Irish, who increasingly retreated within the Pale, their enclave around Dublin. Endemic low-level violence rarely escalated into formal conflict, except when the Wars of the Roses brought Desmonds and Butlers to blows at Piltown (1462). Like Wales, Ireland was significant as a source of instability, providing refuge for Richard, Duke of York in 1459 and Yorkist pretenders in the 1490s.

Other changes accompanied the shift in Britain's strategic centre of gravity. The reign of Edward III coincided with remarkable administrative and tactical developments. Medieval kings had always hired troops to supplement feudal levies serving from tenurial obligation, and attempts to enforce feudal military obligations upon magnates opposed to unpopular foreign wars had contributed to tensions throughout the reigns of Edward I and II. Under Edward III the old feudal approach to raising armies fell entirely out of use. Whole armies received wages from the 1330s, even the Prince of Wales. Rates of pay varied: knights two shillings a day, men-at-arms one shilling, archers threepence, and Welshmen twopence. The king made commercial agreements with his magnates to supply troops. Terms and conditions were set out in documents known as indentures, which made no mention of land or homage. Aristocratic contractors provided infantry as well as cavalry, replacing Edward I's commissioners of array who had scoured localities for whatever ill-armed or incapable recruits they could find. Integration of cavalry and infantry within knightly retinues improved administrative and operational efficiency, as contractors, unlike commissioners, accompanied their men into the field. Contractors could be expected to recruit reliable men among their own tenants, or from the pool of veterans created by successful campaigns overseas.

Financial pressures had begun the shift from quantity to quality before the one 14th-century event most likely to limit military manpower. The Black Death killed 1–2 million people, about a third of the population, during its first outbreak in 1348. After repeated epidemics supplemented by crop failures, the population of England stabilized at half its pre-plague level. Shortage of labour complicated social relations, undermining serfdom and the manorial economy, but had no discernible military impact. The Peasants' Revolt in 1381 passed without significant fighting.

The Wars of the Roses remained a dynastic not a class struggle, despite the Yorkist policy of sparing the commons at the expense of the gentry.

Edward III deployed smaller forces in Scotland than his grandfather, even before the Black Death. In 1334 and 1335 he assembled 4000 and 13,500 men respectively, compared with the 27,000 men at Falkirk (1298). Richard II mobilized similar numbers for his Scottish expedition of 1385: 4590 men-at-arms plus 9144 archers. The civil wars of the next century left little documentary evidence for the numbers engaged. In an emergency the king might call out the shire levies, as Henry IV did for Shrewsbury (1403). However, the breakdown of law and order during Henry VI's reign encouraged men to attach themselves to local grandees, wearing their badges in return for Mafia-style protection. Networks of dependence created by this system of 'livery and maintenance' may have facilitated rapid mobilization of large armies for short, sharp campaigns that left few administrative traces. The Earl of Salisbury, a leading Yorkist in the early battles of the Wars of the Roses, contracted with 40 to 50 retainers, just one of whom could supply 290 armed men, implying a potential force of tens of thousands.

Administrative evidence reveals a much smaller call-up. Indentures show most retainers provided no more than 4 or 5 armed men apiece. The city of Salisbury paid 40 men to assist Edward IV for two months after Towton (1461); York sent just 80 to Bosworth (1485) despite intense local sympathy for Richard III. The Duke of Norfolk, one of the most powerful men in the country, raised 1000 soldiers for the same campaign. Most of them were his tenants, yeomen farmers from East Anglia. Such people were unwilling to travel far from home, reducing the potential for large armies. Norwich mustered 600 men against a French raid in 1457, but sent only 120 to Towton. Military manpower was further limited by reluctance to involve the peasantry, who were prone to settle old scores in the confusion of battle. The Earl of Salisbury offered ransom when captured at Wakefield (1460), 'but the common people of the country who loved him not, took him out of the castle by violence, and smote off his head' (*Davies Chronicle*).

Halidon Hill (1333), 'in which the English archers made great slaughter' (*Melsa Chronicle*), marked the emergence of a new school of tactics that even monastic observers could not miss. They unanimously attributed Edward III's stunning victory, not to the gentility, as social convention demanded, but to the commons:

the 15th-century historian John Capgrave wrote that 'In this batayle wonne the archeres of Ynglond a perpetual laude.' Historians have sought the tactical antecedents of Halidon Hill in previous reigns, but the most likely precursor was the most recent. Exiled Scots lords, who fought alongside Edward III at Halidon, had demolished a vastly superior Scottish army at Dupplin Muir the previous year, with a novel combination of dismounted men-at-arms and archers who enfiladed the enemy masses from the flanks.

Longbows had existed for centuries before they emerged as a battle-winner. The crucial 14th-century innovation was to support very large numbers of archers with men-at-arms, who, contrary to usual practice, dismounted to fight on foot. The Burgundian diplomat Phillippe de Commynes thought archers an essential component of an army, 'though they should be counted in thousands, for in small numbers they are almost useless'. Their exact formation has inspired endless debate. The Canon of Bridlington states that at Halidon the English deployed in three divisions, each flanked by wings, to which the archers were assigned. At Dupplin the central core of men-at-arms occupied '*in longitudine unius stadii*', i.e. just over 200 yards (180 m), a small enough front to be swept by arrows from both flanks. Froissart described the English archers' formation at Crecy as '*en herce*', like a harrow. This may imply triangular wedges of bowmen set forward of the men-at-arms, or may refer to the open grid-like pattern of their ranks and files, meant to give every man a clear field of view. The word may also derive from *hericius*, 'hedgehog', symbolizing prickly invulnerability. Sometimes bows and spears may have mingled individually. Henry VII's herald described the king arraying his people for battle before Stoke Field (1487), 'that is to say, a bow and a bill at his back'. This combination of missile and shock action was the hallmark of the new English tactics, the men-at-arms fighting on foot with the archers until the enemy broke, then recovering their horses to complete the rout. Abroad the system proved so strong that even French knights gave up frontal attacks on well-posted English armies. At home it only failed at Otterburn (1388), when the English insisted on fighting by night.

The proportion of English infantry armed with longbows grew throughout the later Middle Ages, rising from two-thirds to three-quarters, as they supplanted hobelars (mounted spearmen) and Welsh knifemen. Increasing numbers reflected improved social status and equipment. Edwards I's conscripted villeins made way for yeomen of good social standing, with the leisure and diet to support physically demanding archery practice. The Tudor Bishop Hugh Latimer recalled his father teaching him to use the bow, 'not to draw with the arms as other nations do, but with the strength of the body ... for men shall never shoot well unless they are brought up to it'. An Italian visitor in the 1470s thought English bows thicker than elsewhere, requiring arms of iron for their use. Tests on facsimiles of 16th-century bows recovered from the *Mary Rose* suggest a battlefield range of 320 yards (290 m), not dissimilar to modern small arms. Roughly hewn knobbly bows developed a smooth finish indicative of quality and soldierly pride in a weapon's appearance. Archers acquired helmets, brigandines (leather coats covered with mail) and even leg armour. Many rode to battle. Edward III's host of 1335 included similar numbers of men-at-arms (2977), mounted archers (3597) and foot archers (3333). Individual archers loosed ten arrows a minute to create what the St Albans chronicler Thomas Walsingham termed '*imbriferam tempestatem*', the arrow storm. Men used the expression, 'as thick as arrows in an English battle'.

Englishmen who were compelled to fight each other did so on foot, grumbling that where three or four volleys of archery had won battles against mounted knights, battles between infantry armies remained undecided after a hundred. When James, Earl of Douglas, counterattacked an English army at Otterburn, he first gained their flank on horseback before dismounting for the final assault. A fictitious account of Shrewsbury by the Burgundian chronicler Jean de Waurin suggests how one of the new-style battles might have proceeded:

> When they came in sight of each other the archers dismounted uttering a loud and horrible cry, dreadful to hear, and then began to march at a good pace in good order against each other, and the archers to draw so fast and thick that it seemed to the beholders like a thick cloud, for the sun ... lost its brightness so thick were the arrows, and this was helped by the dust which flew about together with the breath of the men who began to get heated, so the air was quite darkened. After the arrows were exhausted they put their hands to swords and axes ...

Full plate armour replaced the compound mail and plate worn at Bannockburn, to improve protection against mail-piercing bodkin-headed arrows. Shields disappeared, freeing both hands for the poleaxes that suited foot fighting better than cut-down lances. These 'ravensbills' were 4 to 6 feet (1.2 to 1.8 m) long, protected by steel strips nailed either side of their wooden shaft, and pointed at each end, with a beak or hammer behind the head. They could break open the strongest armour, or split a helmeted skull to the teeth. Lack of suitable targets for archers may have encouraged a swing back to heavy infantry during the War of Roses. An indenture of 1452 committed a Westmorland squire to follow the Earl of Salisbury with 150 billmen, but only 140 archers. Not everyone had complete protection. Most wounds at Barnet (1471) were to face or lower limbs. John Paston was shot through the right arm below the elbow. Other casualties returned home, according to a contemporary account by Gerhard von Wesel, 'with sorry nags and bandaged faces, some without noses etc. and preferred to stay indoors'.

The most important military innovation of the period was the introduction of firearms. Edward III bought the makings of gunpowder from a Yorkshire apothecary in 1334, but early guns were too unwieldy for field use. A hundred years later, cannon were a regular feature of English battlefields. The Earl of Devon deployed five carts of guns and other ordnance for his private war against the Earl of Wiltshire in the 1450s. Fortified artillery camps appeared at Ludford (1459) and Northampton (1460). Warwick the Kingmaker employed handgunners and cannon at Second St Albans (1461). The latter may have been multi-barrelled *ribaudekins*, 'that would shoot both pellets of lead and arrows of an ell of length with six feathers'. They failed to impress the contemporary author of *Gregory's Chronicle*, for 'in time of need they could shoot not one of these, but the fire turned back upon them'. Nevertheless both sides deployed arquebusiers at Barnet (1471), the Yorkist army including 'a blak and smoky sort of Gunner Flemyngs … to the numbyr of 500' (*Historie of the Arrivall of Edward IV*). Armies with insufficient guns, whether rebels at Lose-Coat Field or Lancastrians at Tewkesbury, could be driven into premature offensives by bombardments to which they had no reply.

Northern Stalemate

The Scots Wars of Independence did not end at Bannockburn. Edward III's reign (1327–77) saw a reprise of earlier campaigns, more dazzling victories, and even the restoration of a Balliol king. Edward III did not feel bound by the shameful Treaty of Northampton/Edinburgh (1328) that recognized Robert the Bruce as king of Scotland. Negotiated during his minority, the agreement reminded Edward of a period of intense personal and national humiliation. King Robert's death in 1329 and the succession of the infant David II ended Scottish strategic dominance, and gave Edward III the chance to pursue unfinished business across the Border.

The Bruce had dispossessed numerous members of the Balliol faction. In 1332 these exiled Scots lords launched a seaborne invasion with covert English support to restore Edward Balliol to his father's throne. Despite victory at Dupplin Muir (1332) 'the Disinherited' could not consolidate Balliol's claim without English help. Extensive campaigns by Edward III and Edward Balliol after their joint victory at Halidon Hill (1333) brought Scotland to the verge of subjection. David II was smuggled away to Château Gaillard in Normandy, while his kingdom descended into civil war. Only an obscure victory at Culblean kept the Bruce cause alive through the winter of 1335.

French support for David II exacerbated the shakiness of Edward III's relations with France, diverting his energies across the English Channel. For the rest of his reign Scotland was a minor theatre in a wider struggle, known today as the Hundred Years' War. The strategic conditions that denied Edward I victory still held good: Scotland's remoteness, lack of an English standing army for garrison duty, and the unwillingness of the English Parliament to fund distant and unprofitable campaigns. Scottish patriots nibbled away at territory ceded by Balliol to his English backers, and in 1346 a recently returned David II felt strong enough to invade England. The Bruce strategic genius was not hereditary, however: David was defeated and captured at Neville's Cross, spending 11 years in captivity. In his absence Robert the Steward, a survivor of Halidon Hill and Neville's Cross, sustained the patriotic cause, succeeding the childless David as Robert II, the first Stewart (later Stuart) king, in 1371.

The death of Edward III in 1377, like that of his grandfather, was Scotland's opportunity. The Scots withheld further instalments of David II's ransom, liquidated English garrisons in Lochmaben and Teviotdale, and faced down a counteroffensive in 1385. Three years later Richard II's political difficulties at home and abroad inspired a final Scottish attempt to force the English to the conference table. For once the Scots won the ensuing battle at Otterburn. No peace treaty ever recognized Scottish independence, but Otterburn established Scotland's strategic equality with England, marking the triumphant conclusion of the Wars of Independence.

Dupplin Muir (Gaskmore Gledesmore), **11 August 1332**

Scotland, Perth and Kinross, LR58 NO0219?

The First Scots War of Independence left antipathies that diplomacy was unlikely to allay. Edward III forbade direct attacks on Scotland from English soil, but did allow disinherited Scots lords to mount an amphibious invasion from the Humber. Edward Balliol, son of King John Balliol, held nominal command, with operational guidance from Henry Beaumont, a veteran of Bannockburn. They landed at Kinghorn in Fife on 6 August, and marched on Dunfermline. Here they learned a Scots army stood ready for battle '*apud Glaskmore*', i.e. on Gask Ridge north of the River Earn, between them and Perth, a crucial objective for Scottish usurpers. The pro-Bruce Scots had divided to cover both shores of the Firth of Forth, giving Balliol the chance of defeating them piecemeal.

When the invaders closed up to Forteviot on the Earn, they found the bridge held against them. Meanwhile the Scots southern army had reached Auchterarder, half a day's march to the west. Caught between converging forces, the Disinherited essayed a bold stroke. Led by a local exile, they crossed the river by night, avoiding the sentries, and climbed the hill to attack the Scots camp. One knight was accidentally drowned, but the rest fell upon the sleeping camp and cut down their foes without mercy, the unfortunate Scots 'flying hither and thither' as they 'ran about naked among the armed men'. Others were burned as the Disinherited fired their lodgings.

The location of the Scots camp is uncertain. Balliol's men initially bivouacked at Millar's Acre, perhaps Milton of Forteviot. Overnight they presumably headed upstream, the most hopeful direction for a ford, perhaps crossing at Dalreoch Bridge. Several nearby locations share the place-name Gask, from Gaelic *gasg*, 'tongue of land'. None is very near the loch and castle that give the battle its modern name. The most significant settlement is Findo Gask, a mile and a half (2.5 km) north of Dalreoch and indubitably on top of the ridge. Well back from the crest, Findo Gask would have been hidden from Scots knights down in the valley, who remained unaware of Balliol's manoeuvre until morning revealed the smoke of burning huts. Another hint is John Capgrave's 'grete bataille in a place thai clepe [call] Gledesmore', perhaps a transliteration of Clathymore, a mile (1.6 km) northeast of Findo Gask.

The Disinherited thought they had disposed of the whole Scots army, until patrols reported otherwise: 'For all the knights and men-at-arms', according to the Canon of Bridlington, 'were guarding the bridge, thinking that the invaders would not know about the ford …'. The appearance of numerous fresh opponents horrified the Disinherited, who momentarily considered flight. The Scots division of their forces implies half their military establishment was present, say 3000 men. Contemporary statistics are consistent with this estimate: Andrew of Wyntoun put the smaller leading echelon of their army at 800; the Canon of Bridlington thought 2000 mounted or armed men fell in action. The Disinherited, on the other hand, had 'litel strengthe unnethe two thowsand', more precisely 500 men-at-arms and 1000 archers. Although outnumbered two-to-one, the invaders had the better force: a balanced combination of shock and missile troops.

Rallied by Balliol, the Disinherited occupied some high ground east of the wrecked Scots camp, '*in sinistra parte*', dominating a steep-sided indentation in the ridge, described as 'an hongen boughte of the more in a streit passage' in the *Brut* (14th century). As the battle developed, this narrow glen would hem the Scots in and stop them using their superior numbers. A mile (1.6 km) east of Findo Gask, the hill rises to 460 feet (140 m), above a re-entrant now covered by Cairnie Wood. Just half a mile (0.8 km)

Dupplin Muir

	Winners	*Losers*
Opponents	Scots (Balliol)	Scots (Bruce)
Commanders	Edward Balliol	Donald, Earl of Mar (k)
Numbers	1500	*c.*3000
Losses	35	*c.*2000

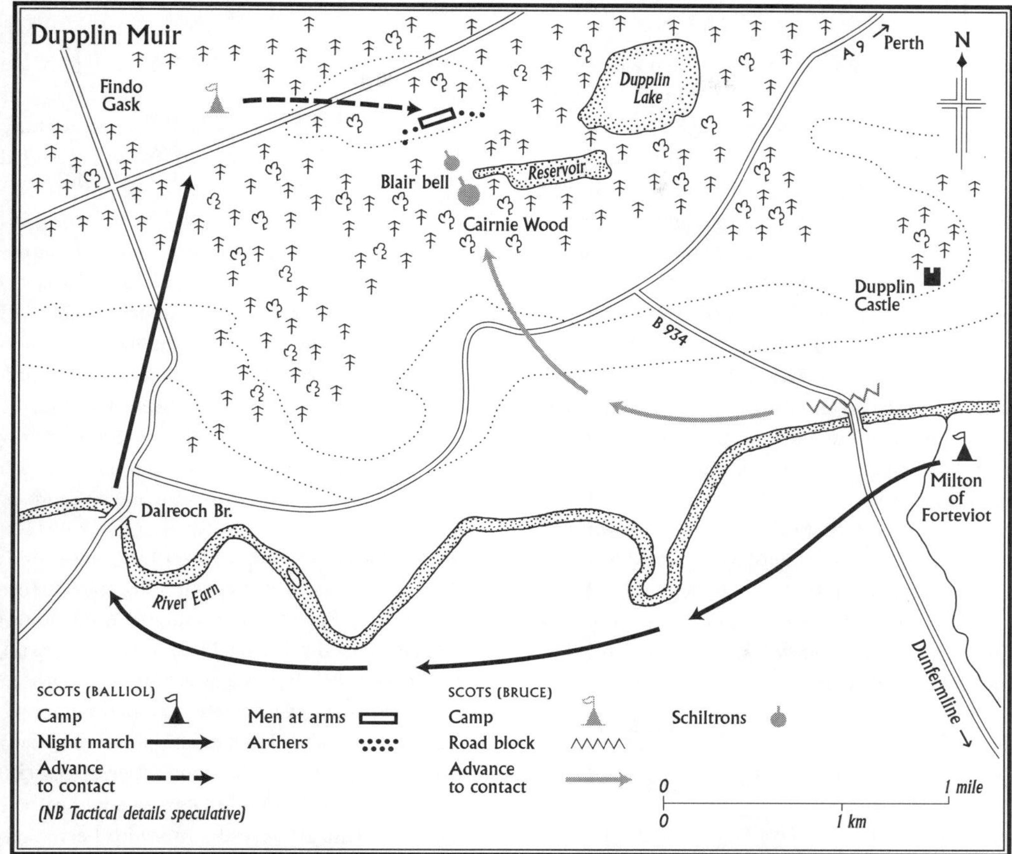

west of Dupplin Loch, and almost directly between Findo Gask and Forteviot Bridge, this is a logical place for the Disinherited to have confronted the Scottish schiltrons.

Resolved to sell their lives dearly, the Disinherited sent away their horses, although 40 German mercenaries remained mounted in the rear. The dismounted troops adopted a novel formation: 'Having so disposed their archers, in order to assail the flanks of the enemy columns, the men-at-arms engaged the main body' (Bridlington). Another contemporary, Robert of Avesbury, provides an unusually precise indication of the frontage occupied: one stadium, i.e. just over 200 yards (180 m). Two ranks deep, each man-at-arms would occupy 30 inches (75 cm), or one pace. The archers may have been more dispersed, presenting no formed body at which the enemy might strike.

As described in the *Lanercost Chronicle*, the Scots attacked in two great masses, supporting Scottish claims that a quarrel among their leaders led to separate, uncoordinated attacks. Nevertheless, they pushed back Balliol's outnumbered men-at-arms, until Ralph, Lord Stafford had them stand side-on to stem the rush with their shoulders. Meanwhile the archers shot the Scots' flanking files to pieces, driving them in upon the centre, to form an inchoate mass: 'jammed together in a small space, one was crushed by another' (Bridlington). The second wave of attackers crashed into the rear of the melee, making matters

Directions

Gask Ridge is 6 miles (10 km) southwest of Perth along the A9(T). Fork right at Crossgates, along the Roman Road to Findo Gask. Just after Dupplin Loch stop on the crest. A track on the left runs down through Cairnie Wood towards the suggested battle area.

worse. More Scots were killed by their friends than by the enemy, as they suffocated in the press, the bodies forming a grisly heap as high as a lance.

The battle was over by the third hour, about quarter past eight at that time of year. When the Scots began to slip away, Beaumont's men-at-arms remounted to ride them down, leaving the archers to run spears through the heap, so that 'not one could be brought out alive'. Three earls were among the countless dead. The English lost two named knights and 33 men-at-arms. The archers got off without a scratch. Medieval chroniclers might be excused for attributing so one-sided a victory to divine intervention: 'Alle men seide it was Goddis hande, and not mannes hande. For the Scots were so many, and English so fewe, that ech of hem bar down othir' (Capgrave). Edward Balliol had effected a political and military revolution. On 24 September he was crowned Edward I of Scotland, for a brief while. Dupplin's tactical legacy lasted longer, providing a model for English armies into Tudor times.

Annan, 17 December 1332

Scotland, Dumfries and Galloway, LR85 unlocated

Annan

	Winners	*Losers*
Opponents	Scots	Scots
Commanders	Sir Archibald Douglas	Edward Balliol

Halidon Hill, 19 July 1333

England, Northumberland, LR75 NT9655–56

Halidon Hill

	Winners	*Losers*
Opponents	English	Scots
Commanders	Edward III	Sir Archibald Douglas (k)
Numbers	*c.*4000	5000–6000
Losses	*c.*12	unknown

Edward III's first victory, at Halidon Hill, was a pivotal moment in English military history. At a stroke he avenged Bannockburn and laid the tactical foundations for immortal successes in France.

Edward Balliol's post-Dupplin rule was short. He went to spend Christmas under truce at Annan, where a treacherous dawn attack overwhelmed his party while asleep. Edward's brother was killed fighting with a staff, while the *soi-disant* king 'brake out through a wall by an Hole in his chambre' and rode off to England without saddle or breeches. To recoup their losses, in March 1333 Balliol's supporters besieged Berwick. Anxious to dispel memories of his father's hapless reign, Edward III joined in.

Berwick was one of two fortified places left to the Scots after King Robert's programme of dismantling castles. North of the Tweed, but close to sources of English manpower, Berwick was especially vulnerable, its narrow landward approach easily held by a besieging force. Archibald Douglas, the new guardian of Scotland, took the fatal decision to relieve Berwick, but moved too slowly. Before Douglas could gather his forces Edward III agreed terms with Berwick's garrison that committed the Scots to fighting their way into Berwick before sunrise on 20 July, or watching it surrender.

Edward III occupied a position the Bruce might have chosen, where one 'mycht dyscumfyte thre' (Andrew of Wyntoun, *Orygynale Cronykil of Scotland*, *c.*1420). Two miles (3 km) northwest of Berwick, Halidon Hill (535 feet/163 m) squarely blocks the path of a relieving army, its front covered by marshes recalled by such place-names as Bogend Farm. River and sea secured Edward's left and right. The situation resembled that before Bannockburn, only in reverse: a superior army with a tradition of victory, but running out of time, had to tackle a defensive position head-on to preserve a symbolic fortress.

No administrative evidence confirms the general view that the Scots outnumbered the English at Halidon Hill. Douglas is said to have summoned 'all the men that worthy war in Scotland' (Wyntoun),

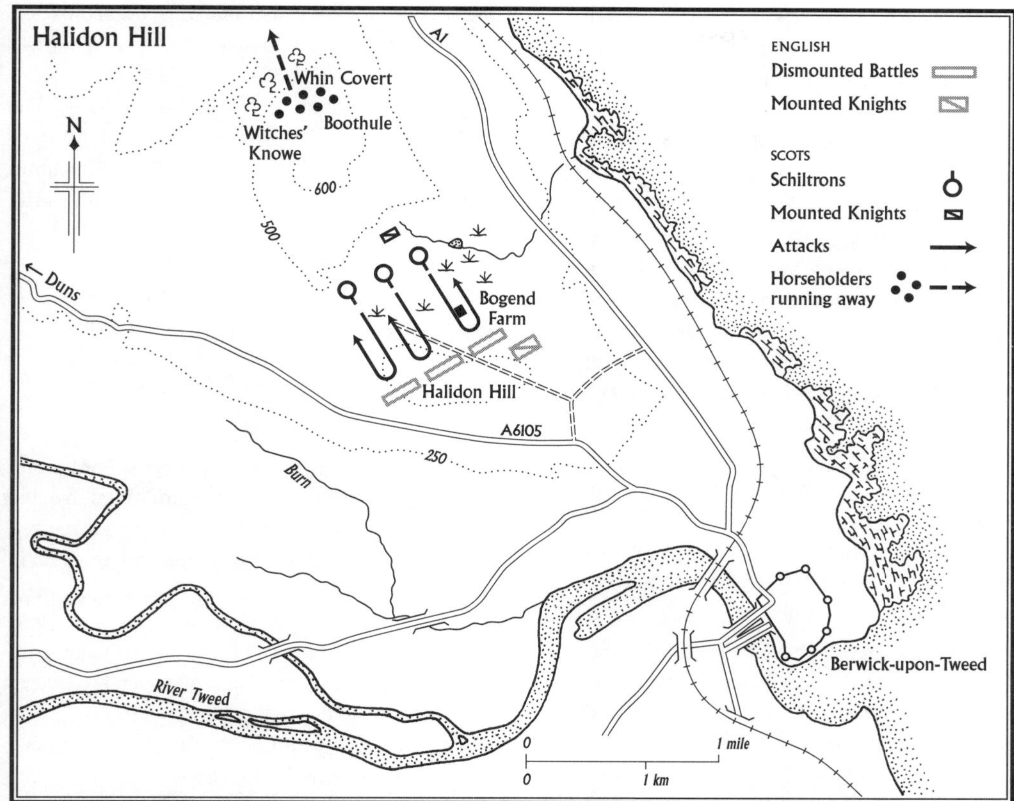

but certainly not 'sexty full thousand'. However, tithes went uncollected for want of labour, suggesting his army exceeded Bruce's at Bannockburn. Edward's forces were probably nearer the 4000 who began the Roxburgh campaign of 1334 than the 13,500 deployed a year later. Pardons issued to criminals who served have inspired claims that the battle was won by murderers, robbers and poachers. However, only two companies of felons (200 men) took the field at Roxburgh, suggesting historians have unfairly blackened the character of Edward's soldiers.

The morning of the battle the Scots army marched from Duns, 13 miles (21 km) west of Berwick, to Witches Knowe (650 feet/198 m), overlooking Halidon Hill from the north. Douglas had to introduce 200 men-at-arms into Berwick under the besiegers' noses, or defeat them in pitched battle under the walls. His plan combined both options. He kept 200 men-at-arms in hand, while the rest dismounted to join the infantry, forming three divisions in line. Horse-holders sheltered in a wood behind the crest, perhaps Whin Covert (NT9557), beyond the spur jutting out from Witches Knowe towards Halidon Hill. Douglas took the left wing, the mounted forlorn hope following on horseback. The three Scottish divisions rolled down the forward slope of Witches Knowe late in the afternoon, at the ninth hour or even later, about vespers.

Directions

From Berwick Castle follow the A6105 towards Duns. Turn right at a signpost to the battlefield, down a farm track through the probable position of the rightmost English division. This must have been on the forward slope, to give the archers a field of fire, not behind the hill where the Ordnance Survey marks the battle site.

Edward III also drew up in three divisions, the English men-at-arms on foot, even the king. Contemporary observers thought this unprecedented, quite contrary to the custom of their fathers who had always fought mounted. Sleeves of archers stood either side of each division: 'had everye Englisshe bataile ij wenges of pris Archiers' (*Brut*). Each individual battle thus resembled the Disinherited order of battle at Dupplin. The two flanking divisions may have been echeloned rearwards in conformity with the rounded slope of the hill, presenting a convex front to the enemy. Five hundred men held the siege lines, while 200 picked knights waited on horseback to intercept any Scots flying column that slipped past.

Few of the Scots can have been adequately protected against the hail of arrows, 'as thyk as motes on the sonnes beme', which struck them as they started up the slope beyond the marsh. Contemporary accounts are laconic:

> At the fulle see [high tide], the Scottes come ageynst Englishe men in thre batailles, all on fote and ungert [i.e. not formed for action] in a place faste beside Berwik that hatte [was called] Boothule [Boothulf] besides Halyngdoun. Englishe men archers beat down the Scottes, and horsemen pursued them for to nycht.
>
> Ranulf Higden, *Polychronicon*

The Canon of Bridlington describes a two-stage attack. First the Scots centre and right attacked the English centre and left respectively: 'But they could not bear the storm of arrows nor the weapons of the knights, and soon they took to flight.' The Melsa chronicler claimed this repulse so depressed the remaining Scots that they fled before making contact. Bridlington, however, describes a second more serious engagement, '*cruenta pugna*', with the English right. This lasted some time, '*maxima parte diei*', claiming the lives of 500 of Scotland's choicest knights, at a place known as Hevyside, perhaps from the boggy going.

Seeing how matters lay, the Scots horse-holders rode off leaving their masters to be slaughtered. As at Dupplin, the victors remounted and pursued their exhausted opponents until nightfall. Douglas and five Scots earls were killed. John of Fordun broke off his catalogue of dead notables in despair. They can never have come to hand strokes. English casualties were one knight, one squire and 7 to 12 infantry. The slaughter left nobody in Scotland capable of raising or commanding an army. Robert the Bruce's kingdom was shattered, and the Disinherited temporarily repossessed.

Culblean, 30 November 1335

Scotland, Aberdeen, LR37 NO4199–4299

Renewed English involvement across the Border after Halidon Hill (see above) further inflamed the civil war between David II's guardians and a revived Balliol faction. The only ray of hope for Scotland in this dark hour was a skirmish in the remote northeast, between two entirely Scottish forces. Sir Andrew Moray, acting for the exiled David II, outmanoeuvred his Balliol counterpart with a professionally executed night march and dawn attack.

Edward Balliol's fortunes reached high watermark in the summer of 1335. While Edward III carved up southern Scotland, Balliol charged David Strathbogie, titular Earl of Atholl, with crushing resistance further north. In the autumn Strathbogie besieged Kildrummy Castle, the last obstacle to Balliol carpetbaggers overrunning the northeast. Kildrummy's chatelaine – Lady Christian de Bruce, sister of the late king and wife of Sir Andrew Moray, David II's new regent – symbolized Scottish resistance.

Moray marched to the rescue with 800 men, 'the floure of that half of the Scotis Se' (Andrew of Wyntoun), i.e. the area north of the Forth/Clyde

Culblean

	Winners	*Losers*
Opponents	Scots (Bruce)	Scots (Balliol)
Commanders	Sir Andrew Moray	David of Strathbogie (k)
Numbers	1100	*c.*3000

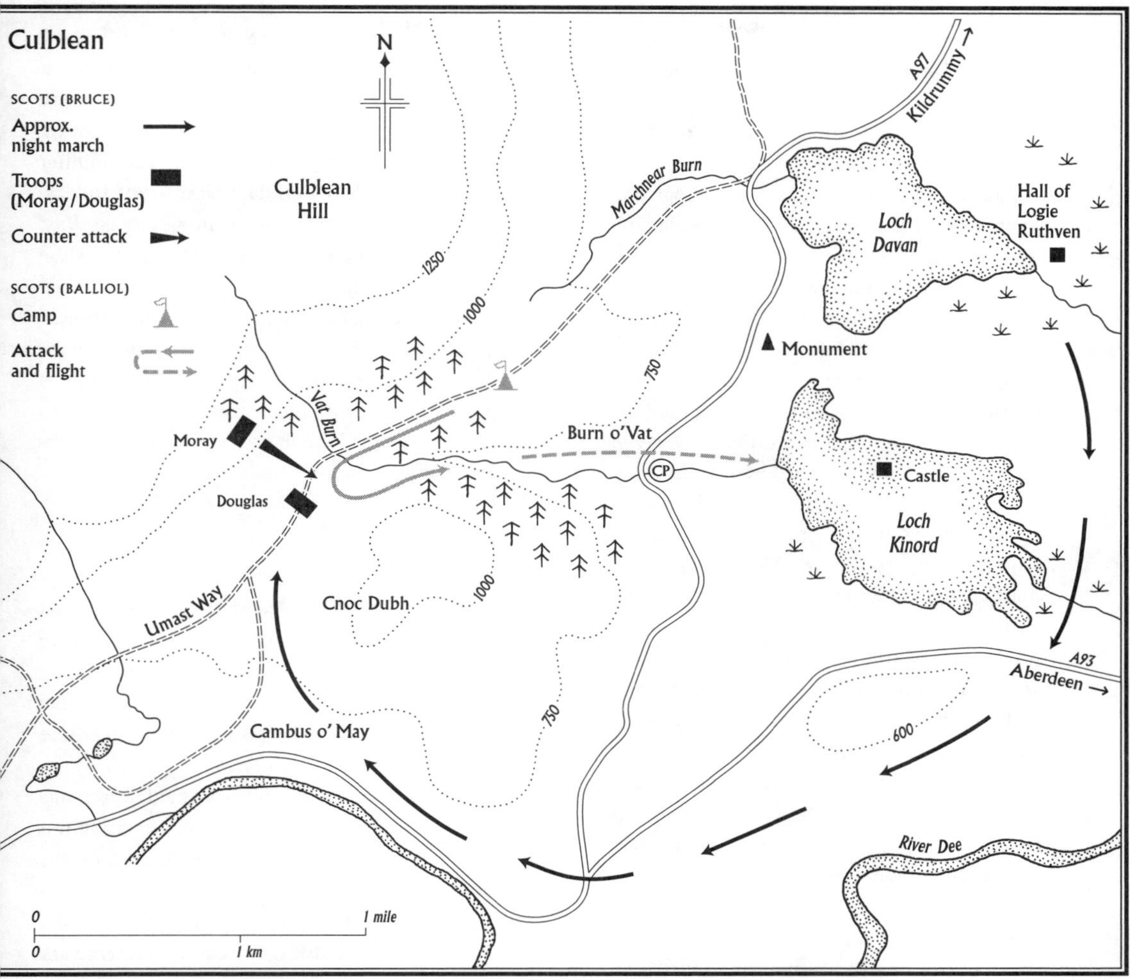

isthmus. By 28 November the patriots were within striking distance of Kildrummy, at the Hall of Logie Rothwayne or Ruthven, a moated homestead east of Loch Davan. Strathbogie abandoned the siege and fell back to the lower slopes of Culblean Hill, 2 miles (3 km) west of Moray's quarters. Here his superior numbers could defy frontal attack, while if Moray moved north across Strathbogie's front, he would expose flank and rear to a counterstroke.

Wyntoun's *Orygynale Cronykil*, the main source for the battle, located Strathbogie's camp near a ford on the higher of two paths through Culblean forest:

Directions

The battlefield is 30 miles (50 km) west of Aberdeen along the A93. Turn right along the B9119 to Burn o'Vat car park. Follow Nature Conservancy trails to Strathbogie's camp to view the alternative battlefields. A monument halfway between Burn o'Vat and Marchnear Burn marks yet another proposed site. To follow Moray's approach as described above, return to the A93, continue west to Cambus o' May, and take forest paths up the hillside. Turn right in map square NO4199, and follow the drove road to Vat Burn 1/2 mile (0.8 km) further on.

the Tothir and Umast (uppermost) Ways. These were probably the modern Deeside road (A93) and the old drove road around Culblean Hill to Tullich. Wyntoun also says Strathbogie lay 'at the est end rycht in the way'. Strathbogie would seem therefore to have occupied the eastern opening of the valley between Culblean and Cnoc Dubh, opposite Logie Ruthven, 'rycht befor thame wear thai lay'. A round hillock at NJ4200 provides observation eastwards, while the Marchnear Burn and the Vat Burn protected Strathbogie's flanks. Moray's situation was uncomfortably reminiscent of that of the Scots before Halidon Hill, facing a hostile force strongly posted on a hill covered by marshy ground. Moray, however, had time and space in which to manoeuvre. On 29 November 300 men from Kildrummy joined him, led by John of the Craig, who knew a way round Strathbogie's position.

Moray's route is a matter of debate. Dr W. Douglas Simpson believed Moray divided his force, marching two columns independently round Loch Davan's northern end to attack Strathbogie on the line of the Marchnear Burn. This view requires wholesale rejection of the main contemporary source, and is militarily implausible. Two separate columns could never have coordinated their movements in the dark to pull off the combined attack described by Wyntoun, and they would still have approached Strathbogie's position head on, rendering the whole risky exercise pointless.

Professor Ranald Nicholson has proposed a more likely route along a continuous line of tracks that run south from Logie Ruthven to the Dee, west along Deeside, then north to pick up Umast Way. Wyntoun expressly says John of the Craig was to lead Moray around the enemy position and into its rear, in his words 'enwerown quhare thare fays lay and behynd'. The decisive confrontation was therefore behind Strathbogie's camp, across the Vat Burn. The Ordnance Survey marked a 'supposed battle' here on the 6-inch map of 1870, but subsequently moved the symbol nearer Marchnear Burn. Douglas Simpson denied that Moray could have travelled so far in the time available, but neglected the customary mobility of Scots armies. Mounted infantry with local guides could easily have marched 7 miles (11 km) in the eight hours between their departure 'sone eftir the mydnycht' and dawn, about 8.40 a.m.

Despite Moray's circuitous approach, Strathbogie's scouts gave the alarm in time for him to about face and occupy the heathery slopes above Vat Burn. Moray had lost strategic surprise, but had another trick to play. While Sir William Douglas of Liddesdale led part of the army north along Umast Way, Moray took the rest uphill to the left, hidden by the oak, birch and juniper that covered the slopes. Seeing the enemy waiting beyond the burn, Douglas halted his detachment. Strathbogie mistook prudence for want of resolution, and charged across the valley. The boulder-strewn slopes threw his ranks into disorder, of which Douglas took immediate advantage. At the same time Moray crashed into Strathbogie's right flank with such force

> That in his cummyng as thai say
> He baire doune buskis [bushes] in his way.
>
> Andrew of Wyntoun, *Orygynale Cronykil*

Strathbogie fought to the last, his back against an oak, but the rank and file scattered. Some hid in the woods; others were driven down the Vat to take refuge in the island castle of Loch Kinnord, where they surrendered next day.

Culblean was not a great decisive battle, but it was a turning point, proving Balliol's cause could not stand on its own feet. Convinced that a cure for the Scottish ulcer lay overseas, Edward III turned his attentions to France. Lacking English support, Edward Balliol's shadow kingdom withered on the vine.

Neville's Cross, 17 October 1346

England, Durham, LR88 NZ2542–2642

Scottish armies were slow to realize how the longbow had tilted the tactical balance further against them. At Neville's Cross the young David II suffered a defeat as catastrophic as Halidon Hill (see above), but to less purpose.

David II returned from exile in France in 1341.

Neville's Cross

	Winners	*Losers*
Opponents	English	Scots
Commanders	Lord Ralph Neville of Raby Lord Henry Percy William de la Zouche, Archbishop of York	David II, King of Scots (p) Robert the Steward
Numbers	*c.*10,000	unknown
Losses	unknown	500–1000

Being, 'stout and right jolly, desirous to see fighting', he responded favourably to French pleas for a diversion, after Edward III thrashed David's French benefactors at Crécy in August 1346. The Scots carried fire and sword down the Roman road through Corbridge to Durham, where they arrived on 16 October. Sir William Douglas counselled against going so far south, but David mocked his advice, claiming there was nobody to oppose them except shepherds and imbecile priests. Scottish military intelligence was at fault, for Edward III had enlisted no troops north of the Trent, leaving a powerful committee of magnates, chaired by the Archbishop of York, to defend the Marches. They 'set their army in order, etc, as was proper' (*Lanercost Chronicle*) at Barnard Castle on 15 October, before moving secretly, '*occulte*' to Bishop's Auckland, 9 miles (14.5 km) south of Durham.

The Prior of Durham wrote to his absent bishop describing how the Scots turned aside from the city, to spend the night at Beaurepaire, now Bear Park, 2 miles (3 km) northwest of Durham. They had no apprehension of attack, and 'made them great mirth' (Andrew of Wyntoun). Next morning Sir William Douglas led 500 men to plunder Kirk Merrington, near Bishop's Auckland, where they unexpectedly heard 'the trampling of horses and the shock of armed men' (*Lanercost Chronicle*). In autumnal mist the raiders had stumbled upon the archbishop's advance guard, who killed half of them and chased the rest back over Sunderland Bridge on the River Wear. Douglas got away with 200 survivors to give the alarm, while the English followed carefully, occupying the hills beyond the Wear.

Contemporary references clearly indicate the general area of the battle. The prior states the Scots prepared to fight in line of battle on the moor 'beside our park'. John of Fordun had them draw out '*super moram de Beaurepair*' and advance to the vicinity of 'Nevillcross' near Durham. This was one of several ancient crosses around the city that by chance shared the name of one of the English leaders. Scots fugitives from the battle could see the banners from 2 miles (3 km) away, placing the struggle on high ground. All this evidence points to the irregular ridge known as Red Hill that falls steeply into Durham on the east and the River Browney on the west. Some 500 yards (460 m) wide, the ridge is best described as *accidenté*, an intricate tangle of slopes likely to disorganize an attacking army.

The chroniclers' generalities could apply to almost anywhere along the ridge, but A.H. Burne argues persuasively for an English start line on the forward slope, 300 yards (275 m) north of the cross, where the A167 Durham bypass crosses the railway. The Scots would have come under archery as they climbed out of the valley east of Arbour House, onto Red Hill. All accounts agree that the ground funnelled the Scots into a defile, presumably between the Browney and the ridge, jamming them together unable to use their weapons: 'a full anoyus plas that nane, but hurt, mycht lyft his hand' (Wyntoun). Their right flank was further impeded by ditches and high wattled fences, 'that brak gretly thaire Aray'.

Both armies drew up on foot in three divisions, although the English may have kept a mounted reserve. Presumably they fought as they did at Halidon Hill, with wings of archers flanking the men-at-arms. Contemporary estimates of immense numbers of Scots are implausible after Scotland's recent calamities, and David may even have been outnumbered. At Hexham he had mustered 2000 men-at-arms and an indeterminate quantity of half-armed camp followers. The most plausible estimate of English numbers was 1200 men-at-arms, 3000 archers and 7000 spearmen and Welsh. The number of bowmen bears comparison with payroll figures from

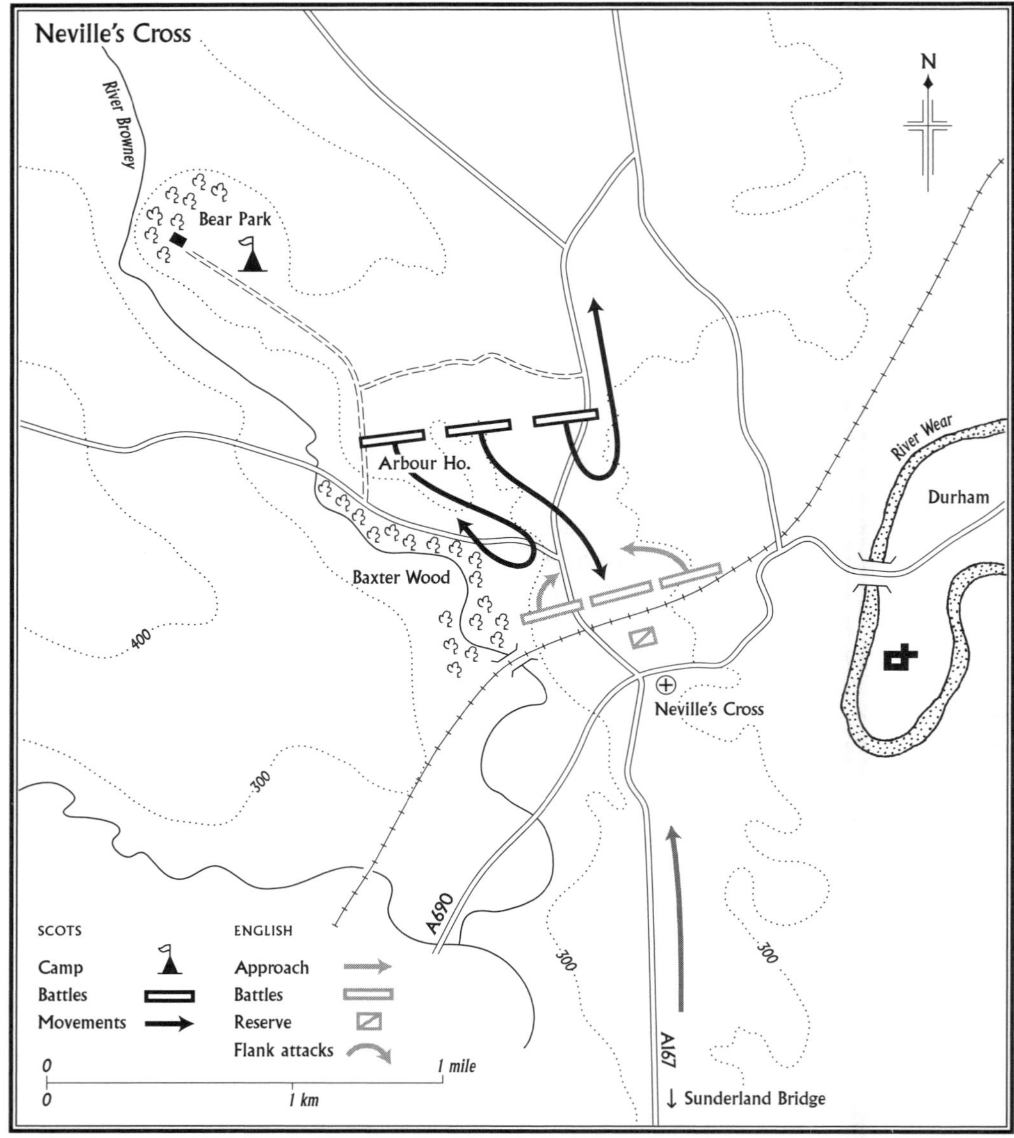

1335, when northern counties fielded 3075 archers. Numerous parish priests turned out, 'swords and arrows under the thigh, bows under the arm ... beating the ears of God and his saints, invoking his mercy and grace' (Henry Knighton of Leicester).

Douglas's round trip to Kirk Merrington and back would have taken mounted troops three hours, bringing the time to 9.30 a.m. The Prior of Durham confirms the two armies stood a moderate distance

Directions

Follow the A690 from the centre of Durham to see the remains of the cross, just before the A167 junction. Turn right along the main road towards a pedestrian footbridge for a view of the built-over battlefield from a position between the lines. Visit Lord Neville of Raby's tomb in Durham Cathedral, and David II's headquarters in the ruins of monastic Bear Park, 1 mile (1.6 km) along footpaths to the northwest.

apart with banners flying, from about the third hour to the ninth. Historians disagree over which side attacked first. Sir Charles Oman saw Neville's Cross as a rare example of an English offensive, their left wing outflanking the disorganized Scots right, swarms of archers crowding them back against the Scots centre, which the English then engaged hand-to-hand. Sir John Graham tried to scatter the English archers with a mounted attack, like Keith's at Bannockburn, but had his horse shot from under him. The Scots left showed little enthusiasm. The Lanercost chronicler joked that Earl Patrick of Dunbar should have been called '*Non Hic*' ('not here'), 'for he stayed all the time afar off like another Peter'. When he and Robert the Steward, a veteran of Halidon, saw the centre and right falter, 'they led off the dance, leaving David to dance as he felt inclined'.

A.H. Burne thought the Scots began the affair, the bend in the Browney crowding their right wing upon the centre, presenting a dense target to English arrows. He produced a contemporary newsletter to show the Scots fought better than the Lanercost chronicler admitted:

> And they charged one another and fought well and long, from the ninth hour until vespers, before the enemy were at last plainly beaten from the field. Twice the archers and common folk on our side fell back, but our men-at-arms fought and held on grimly while the archers and commons reformed.
>
> (Author's translation)

The collapse of the Scots right and the Steward's withdrawal left the Scots centre, led by the king, to be surrounded. Nearly all the nobles and royal household fell around him before David was taken, wounded by an arrow in the face. The prior, an eyewitness, described the dead lying across Beaurepaire moor as far as Fyndoune Hill, their bodies pitifully stripped so that he could tell neither their identity nor number. Scottish chroniclers admitted 500 to 1000 slain, compared with few English. Apart from the butcher's bill the victory was hollow. The Scots were used to doing without a king, and would not submit. David II remained in the Tower until 1356, when he was released for a ten-year truce and the immense ransom of 100,000 marks.

Otterburn (Chevy Chase), 19 August 1388

England, Northumberland, LR80 NY8793

Few battles on English soil have taken such a hold on Anglo-Scots imaginations as Otterburn, fought by moonlight for possession of a lance pennon, and won by a dead man. Ballads written centuries later have concealed Otterburn's wider significance in a welter of poetical carnage, a triumph of obfuscation only rivalled by modern historians, who have devised a range of implausible sites for one of the 14th century's best-known battlefields.

Otterburn was not the isolated product of Border politics. Douglas's army was a national Scottish force, with international objectives. Scottish plans included subversion in Ireland and an invasion of Cumberland, timed to exploit Richard II's humiliation by the Merciless Parliament (see Radcot Bridge below). Otterburn was a deliberate attempt to end the Scots Wars of Independence at a moment of English political weakness. Douglas crossed the Border on 29 June and advanced to Newcastle, where he is supposed to have captured Hotspur's lance pennon. Repulsed at Newcastle, the Scots retreated with their plunder into Redesdale on 18 August. Douglas could have got clean away, but delayed to attack Otterburn Castle, now represented by the Tower Hotel. Hotspur followed next day.

The ensuing battle is variously dated, the most popular variants being the Wednesday–Thursday night before the confusingly assonant feasts of St Oswald or St Oswin, i.e. 5 or 19 August. The latter is more likely. The moon shone as bright as day during the fighting, and full moon was on the 20th. The modern Newcastle–Jedburgh road did not yet exist, so Percy's most likely route would have been the drove road via Belsay and Cambo to Elsdon, then downhill to Otterburn. Clearly his troops were all mounted, as they left Newcastle in the early afternoon and reached the battlefield, 32 miles (51 km) away, before sunset, just after 7.30 p.m.

Two monuments, one of them contemporary,

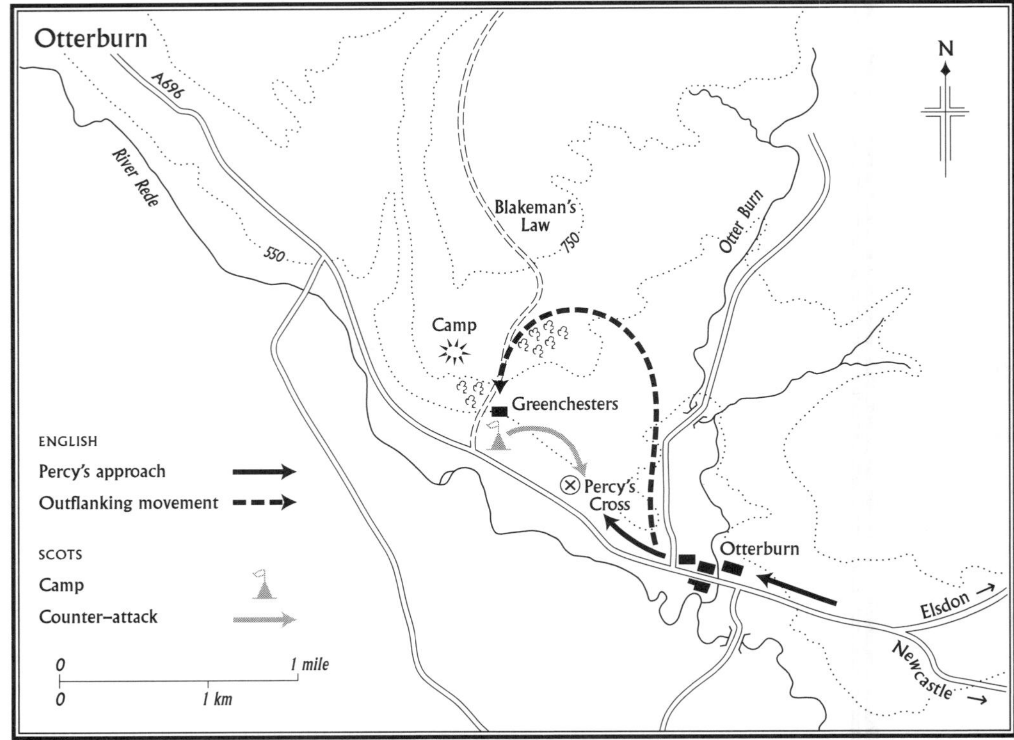

mark the traditional battle site northwest of Otterburn village. This has not prevented historians proposing several other sites, mostly inspired by excessive reliance upon Froissart and an overestimate of the military value of ancient earthworks. A.H. Burne's analysis of the evidence remains pre-eminent. He located the Scots camp in the narrow pass between the swift-flowing River Rede and the slopes of Blakeman's Law (899 feet/274 m), squarely astride their direct road home along the valley, the route now followed by the A696. Douglas would have been aware of the advantages of this position. Froissart, who spoke with survivors, tells us the Scots had examined the ground beforehand and settled what they would do if attacked. Five hundred yards (460 m) in front of the camp, across the only line of approach, is a slight ridge traditionally known as Battle Rigg or Battle Croft. Running gently down to the river, this provided good dry footing on which to fight a battle, and dead ground from which the defending Scots could launch a surprise counterattack.

Directions

Take country roads from Belsay on the A696 to follow Hotspur's approach through Elsdon. Rejoin the A696 east of Otterburn, and continue through the village for 1/2 mile (0.8 km) to the battle site marked on the 1:50,000 Ordnance Survey map. See Percy's Cross on the right. Alternative sites are near Otterburn Mill (NY8892), at the prehistoric settlement (NY8694), or further off at Fawdon and Gallows Hills (NY8993 and NY9392).

A stone obelisk known as the Battle Stone, which stood in the open field 250 yards (230 m) from the roadside, was said to commemorate where Douglas fell. He was of course killed unseen in the dark, but his men held the ground next morning, and could have marked the spot before leaving. If Douglas died in the initial rush, the Battle Stone should represent the position of the English right flank. A more recent monument, the Percy Cross, was constructed beside the road in 1777, from components of the original Battle Stone. This is also on the site of heavy fighting,

Otterburn

	Winners	Losers
Opponents	Scots	English
Commanders	James, Earl of Douglas (k)	Henry Percy, 'Hotspur' (p) Sir Thomas Umfraville Matthew Redeman
Numbers	2400	*c.*3400
Losses	*c.*400	*c.*800

as nearby ploughing has turned up fragments of weapons and horse trappings.

Numbers are speculative. The 10,000 men Andrew of Wyntoun assigned Hotspur would have exceeded Newcastle's entire population. Froissart gave Douglas 300–400 men-at-arms and 2000 mounted infantry; reasonable figures for half the Scottish national army. The English are agreed to have outnumbered the Scots. Wyntoun's ratio of ten-to-seven suggests 3400 English troops, not too many to occupy the 500 yards (460 m) between the Battle Stone and the River Rede. Hotspur did not, however, keep his force together. He detached an unknown number to take the Scots in the rear, '*a tergo*', while he attacked them head on. He may have hoped to throw the Scots into confusion, or he may have intended 'to holde them in that they fled not awaye' (John Hardyng, *fl.* 15th century). Contemporary sources assign command of the outflanking column to several local knights, any of whom might have been expected to know the way.

The English turning movement made a wide sweep as 'they skirted the side of the hill ... hard by' (Froissart), deliberately climbing the slope to approach the Scots camp from the north, perhaps along the track from Greenchesters Farm. They missed Douglas's own outflanking party, which wheeled inside their path, to gain Hotspur's right flank. These mutually oblivious manoeuvres on so narrow a front appear unconvincing, but it was dusk, and the ground less open than today. John of Fordun says Douglas advanced through thickets and thorn brakes. While Percy 'hastened to the fight ... rejoicing at the prospect of their flight', Douglas and his men 'approached the field unseen by the English, with twelve banners [perhaps 1200 men] ... gleaming in the setting sun' (John of Fordun).

Hotspur's men were tired and hungry, having ridden straight into action. John of Malverne criticized Percy for committing his troops to action unformed ('*sine ordinatione*') and in haste. In the gathering darkness the English could make little use of their archers, who in any case were denied a target by Douglas's astute use of terrain. John Swinton, a particularly powerful Scots man-at-arms, broke into the English formation, allowing his comrades 'to penetrate the English line with their spears, so that the English were forced to give ground' (Fordun). Hotspur and his brother were among the prisoners taken in running fights that lasted all night. Douglas never knew of his victory. Distracted from arming himself in the rush to organize the line of battle, he was fatally wounded in face and neck by persons unknown, and found dead in the morning. Hotspur's cut-off party inflicted heavy losses among the Scots rear echelon, chasing some of them as far as the Border, but failed to affect the outcome of the battle. The ballads sang of mutual annihilation:

Of fowre and forty thousand Scottes,
Went but eighteen awaye.

But this is misleading nonsense. The English put their own casualties between 550 and 1000. Even Wyntoun struck a sceptical note:

Sum sayis as thowsands deyd thare
Sum fyftene hundyr; and sum more.

In 1877 the skeletons of 1200 young and middle-aged men were found packed in rows under the 15th-century St Cuthbert's Church at Elsdon. Their presence supports moderate estimates of both numbers and casualties: 1200 dead out of combined strengths of 6000 is one fifth, not an unlikely proportion, two-thirds of them English. Northern England had suffered a devastating blow, redeemed only by the accidental death of Douglas. Despite English threats of a huge Edwardian-style invasion, the war fizzled out in 1389 in a truce that lasted until the death of Richard II. The Scots Wars of Independence were over.

Winchelsea (Espagnols sur Mer), Sunday 29 August 1349

Naval, English Channel, LR189

Sea fighting was a continuous but neglected feature of medieval warfare. The only contemporary to describe Edward III's action off Winchelsea was Froissart, in a passage omitted from early editions of his work. Winchelsea was probably not unique, but it must stand in for other sea fights not graced by the royal presence.

The Spanish kingdom of Castile was western Europe's leading sea power in the 14th century. Enmity between Castilian and Gascon seamen readily spilled over into attacks on the latter's allies. In 1350 a Castilian fleet bearing wool to Flanders enlivened its passage by snapping up English ships. Edward III mobilized shipping and sailors to avenge these outrages, and in August went down to Sussex to dispute the Castilian return passage. Few naval operations were so difficult under medieval conditions as interception of a fleet at sea. Most sea battles occurred in anchorages, like the English victory at Sluys in 1340 over the French. However, Flanders was a common destination for English merchants, and an easy target for Edward's naval intelligence.

Warships of the 14th century were generally merchantmen, taken up from trade. High broad-beamed cogs fitted with castles fore and aft made effective fighting vessels, while a fighting top on the single mast allowed armed men to drop stones into any ship running alongside. No contemporary account of English numbers at Winchelsea survives, beyond the impression that Edward had more ships than the enemy. A Treasury list names 17 vessels prepared for action in May 1350. The largest was the *Thomas*, Edward's flagship, with 100 mariners. Smaller vessels carried 30 to 80 men. Additional fighting men went aboard when ready to sail. An unprecedented following accompanied Edward to Winchelsea: his sons Edward the Black Prince and John of Gaunt, 13 barons and 400 knights. The Spanish had 47 ships, 'packed with warlike men', according to the chronicler Thomas Walsingham (*fl.*1400). Froissart described them as large powerful vessels, much higher than the English ships, their crews well used to sea fighting.

The action was fought a few miles off Winchelsea, in the bay between Dungeness and Hastings, starting about 4 p.m. Froissart did not record the location, but Thomas Walsingham headed his notice '*De Bello apud Wynchelsee*'. A royal pardon for a homicide committed 'before 29 August last', rewarded good service in the late sea battle *juxta Winchelse*. A significant omission from the sources is wind direction, which might have indicated the heading of the opposing fleets. The only clue is that Froissart, a landsman, thought the Spanish ships were going fast enough to have avoided action if they had wished. This implies they had the wind abeam, filling their one square sail to best effect. Lack of a foresail made such ships unhandy, dependent entirely on their rudders for changing course. They may have been unable to get out of Edward's way, when he told his helmsman to steer directly for the leading Spaniard, 'for I want to joust with her'.

The two ships struck with such force that the Castilian's fighting top went overboard, and the *Thomas*'s seams were all sprung. Edward's knights did not tell him the ship was sinking until they had grappled and captured a second Spanish ship. The Black Prince, his ship holed in several places and settling fast, was in similar case, until John of Gaunt's ship took his opponent from the other side. King and prince then abandoned ship, and fought on from their prizes. Despite his preoccupation with the doings of the great, Froissart aptly conveys the flavour

Winchelsea

	Winners	Losers
Opponents	English	Spanish (Castilian)
Commanders	Edward III Edward, the Black Prince	Don Carlos de la Cerda
Numbers	*c.*50 ships	47 ships
Losses	2 ships	14–26 ships

of medieval war at sea. Unconnected skirmishes broke out as ships intermingled, the Spaniards responding to English archery with crossbow bolts and iron bars thrown from fighting tops. Decisive action required grappling with iron hooks and boarding, the winners killing everyone on board. In one conspicuous feat of arms, '*grande appertise d'armes*', a lone boarder immobilized a Spanish ship, cutting her halyards and shrouds with his sword, so that mast and sail fell across the deck, bringing her to a stop.

Edward sounded the ceasefire at sunset, 6.45 p.m., the English fleet making land between Rye and Winchelsea soon after dark. Walsingham thought the battle an atrocious conflict, many dead and wounded on both sides, with so many injuries inflicted that hardly anyone escaped unharmed. The Castilians must have lost several thousand men, thrown over the side of the 14 or 26 prizes they are said to have lost. Froissart says they passed on and escaped, which makes sense if running before the wind. Walsingham, however, says they turned back. In November, the English captain of Calais went to Flanders to negotiate safe passage for Spanish ships still at Sluys, suggesting they had indeed put back, rather than run the gauntlet of Edward's fleet.

Uneasy Lies the Head

The primary function of medieval kings was to provide effective leadership in war. Monarchs unable to fulfil such expectations, such as Henry III or Edward II, suffered accordingly. Richard II, whose words as imagined by Shakespeare head this section, was initially disqualified by age from military leadership, and later by his preference for more cultured activities. He also faced deeper problems. In 1399 these resulted in Richard's deposition and murder by his cousin Henry, Duke of Lancaster, precipitating a decade of conflict.

Richard II succeeded his grandfather Edward III in 1377, inheriting a disastrous legacy. Hostilities with France dragged on, neither side capable of breaking the strategic stalemate. English magnates, denied glory and profit overseas, amused themselves with factional infighting, led by members of Edward III's over-large family. Lesser gentry felt the economic consequences of falling population and rents. They resented paying for unsuccessful campaigns abroad, but criticized diplomatic efforts to stop the fighting. Parliament became a platform for attacks on government extravagance and mismanagement. Richard II was unsuited to the task of resolving his kingdom's malaise. Edward III had involved the magnates in his policies and campaigns, but Richard was an autocrat, his exalted view of royalty confirmed by his boyhood intervention in the Peasants' Revolt. Throughout his reign Richard II showed a taste for arbitrary rule, recruiting companies of Cheshire archers to intimidate judges and parliaments.

Conflict between court and magnates came to a head in 1387, in an obscure campaign ended with minimal bloodshed at Radcot Bridge in Oxfordshire. Richard was not present, but Radcot Bridge was the decisive military event of his reign. The victorious Lords Appellant, so-called after they 'appealed' the king's 'favourites' of treason, used the Merciless Parliament of February 1387 to purge Richard's counsellors. They could not curb his power indefinitely, however. A decade later, Richard killed or exiled all five Appellants. This belated vendetta left the one survivor, Henry Bolingbroke, Duke of Lancaster, with no sure means of securing life and estates short of overthrowing the king, which he did in August 1399.

Henry IV gained the throne without a battle, but spent the rest of his life fighting to keep it. Royal weakness inspired interrelated conflicts in England, Wales and Scotland. Richard II's death invalidated the truce with Scotland, reopening the miserable alternation of English invasion and Scottish counter-raid, two of which came to grief at Nisbet Muir and Homildon Hill (1402). In Wales Richard II's favouritism and the Lancastrian revolution undermined ties of lordship built up since the Edwardian conquest. When Henry failed to deal justly with Owain Glyn Dŵr, a Welsh squire at odds with a royal councillor, he provoked the worst Anglo-Welsh crisis of the later Middle Ages. Royal *chevauchées* through rain-swept mountains were as futile as in Henry II's time, while Glyn Dŵr scored inspirational victories, at Hyddgen (1401) and Pilleth (1402). At the height of the revolt Glyn Dŵr controlled most of North Wales including Edward I's castles at Harlech and Aberystwyth. He styled himself Prince of Wales, held a parliament and opened negotiations with foreign princes.

Welsh rebellion thrived on Henry IV's domestic distractions. In 1405 Glyn Dŵr made a Triple Indenture partitioning England with Henry Percy, Earl of Northumberland, and Edmund Mortimer, Earl of March, who had a better hereditary claim to the throne than Henry IV. The Percys had played a key role in Richard II's deposition, but suffered total defeat at Shrewsbury. Northumberland went on the run in Scotland, Wales and France. He returned to the Borders in 1408, only to be killed at Bramham Moor, ending the threat of serious rebellion. Against all the odds Henry V succeeded his father peacefully, enjoying sufficient domestic security to launch further adventures overseas.

Radcot Bridge, 20 December 1387

England, Oxfordshire, LR163 SU2899

The Radcot Bridge campaign of December 1387 is of remarkable interest for a period often dismissed as devoid of strategy. The victors ensnared the opposition, like beaters driving their prey, and concentrated their forces on the battlefield, an almost impossible feat under medieval conditions, to inflict a decisive defeat on an army led by Richard II's most favoured friend.

Royal government in the 1380s was unpopular and weak, unable to counter criticism of extravagance and incompetence. The Wonderful Parliament of 1386 appointed a 'great and continuall council' to oversee the king, but Richard resented even moderate restraint. In November 1387 five magnates, the Lords Appellant, accused key members of Richard's administration of high treason, the charges to be heard by Parliament the following February.

The only defendant to show fight was Robert de Vere, previously Earl of Oxford, now Marquess of Dublin. De Vere escaped into the Northwest, where he 'assembled great number of men-at-arms and archers, as well from the counties of Lancashire, Cheshire, and Wales, as from several other places' (Act of Attainder). He returned south in December, presumably down Watling Street. Appellant forces at Northampton blocked the direct route to London, so de Vere dodged west, probably along the Fosse Way, reaching Stow-on-the-Wold on the 19th. The Lords Appellant occupied a broad arc of territory behind de Vere, preventing his retreat: '*scilicet Bannebury, Braylles, Chepyngnorton, Campedene, Blokkeleye, et Bourton-sub-Coteswold*' (John of Malverne). De Vere could carry on down the Fosse Way, moving away from Richard in London, or dash through Burford for Radcot Bridge, to put the Thames between himself and his pursuers. The Lords Appellant had clearly

Radcot Bridge

	Winners	*Losers*
Opponents	Lords Appellant	Royalist
Commanders	Thomas, Duke of Gloucester Henry Bolingbroke, Earl of Derby	Robert de Vere, Marquess of Dublin
Numbers	unknown	4000–5000
Losses	none	few

laid a trap, for, when de Vere chose the second option, he found the river held against him.

Tactical details are garbled. The usually reliable St Albans chroniclers went hopelessly astray, placing the battle on the River Windrush, '*iuxta Burford prope Bablakehythe*', an name unknown in that quarter. In some versions de Vere escaped to Rathecotebrigg; others do not mention Radcot at all. Malverne's continuation of Higden's *Polychronicon* also locates the fighting on the Windrush at Witney, which still leaves de Vere the wrong side of the Thames. Other sources leave no doubt the action occurred at Radcot. The Merciless Parliament heard that de Vere rode, 'as far as a place which is called Rottecotebrigge which is near Coteswold'. The *Knighton Chronicle* records that de Vere turned his march '*versus pontem de Radecote*' ('towards the bridge of Radcot'). Circumstantial evidence supports the written sources. Knighton says the bridge was broken in three places: Radcot Bridge has three arches, and needed repairs in 1393. Malverne describes fighting '*in lato campo*', i.e. the wide plain of the Thames not the deep hollow of the Windrush.

Henry of Derby, who anticipated de Vere at Radcot, was also Earl of Leicester, home town of the Knighton chronicler. The latter's account probably came from an eyewitness. Derby placed archers and men-at-arms '*ad caput pontis*' ('at the head of the bridge'), logically at the southern end, and pulled up the roadway so only one horse could cross at a time. To encourage doubters de Vere displayed the royal banner Richard II had entrusted to him, and charged the bridge in person. Finding it effectively blocked, he was first to turn back, shouting 'We are betrayed'. At this unpromising moment fresh Appellant forces appeared behind the Royalists, pinning them against the Thames. The game was up: de Vere threw away his armour, exchanged his warhorse for a swift courser, and disappeared along the riverbank. His second-in-command, Sir Thomas Molyneux, was caught at the water's edge, and knocked on the head. Thoroughly plundered, the rest of the army straggled home in miserable plight.

Accounts of de Vere's flight agree only on his miraculous vanishing act across the Thames, which probably owed more to seasonal mists and darkness than divine intervention. The Royalists might have reached Radcot about midday, assuming a dawn departure at 8 a.m. and an all-mounted force. Evening would have drawn in by the time they had formed up and delivered their unsuccessful assault. De Vere's most hopeful route was downstream, to cross at Bablockhythe, a ferry on the Thames, not the Windrush as the St Alban's chronicler supposed.

The Lords Appellant ruthlessly exploited their advantage, forcing the king to abandon his friends to the Merciless Parliament. Richard reasserted his independence next year, but the Appellants' military achievement was striking: a brilliantly conceived scheme, executed with devastating effect.

Directions

Radcot Bridge is just south of RAF Brize Norton, which sprawls across the direct route from Burford to Faringdon along the B4020 and A4095. Entrenchments on the north bank probably date from the Civil War, not the 14th century. Bablockhythe (SP4304) is 2 miles(3 km) west of Cumnor, outside Oxford on the A420.

Hyddgen (Mynyddhyddgant), *c.* **June 1401**

Wales, Powys, LR135 SN7889

Pilleth (Bryn Glas), **22 June 1402**

Wales, Powys, LR148 SO2567–68

Owain Glyn Dŵr was an unlikely revolutionary. A Denbighshhire landowner, he had served during Richard II's Scottish expedition of 1385. His father-in-law was a judge on King's Bench. Glyn Dŵr revolted after Henry IV denied him justice in a property dispute with Lord Grey of Ruthin, an important Lancastrian supporter.

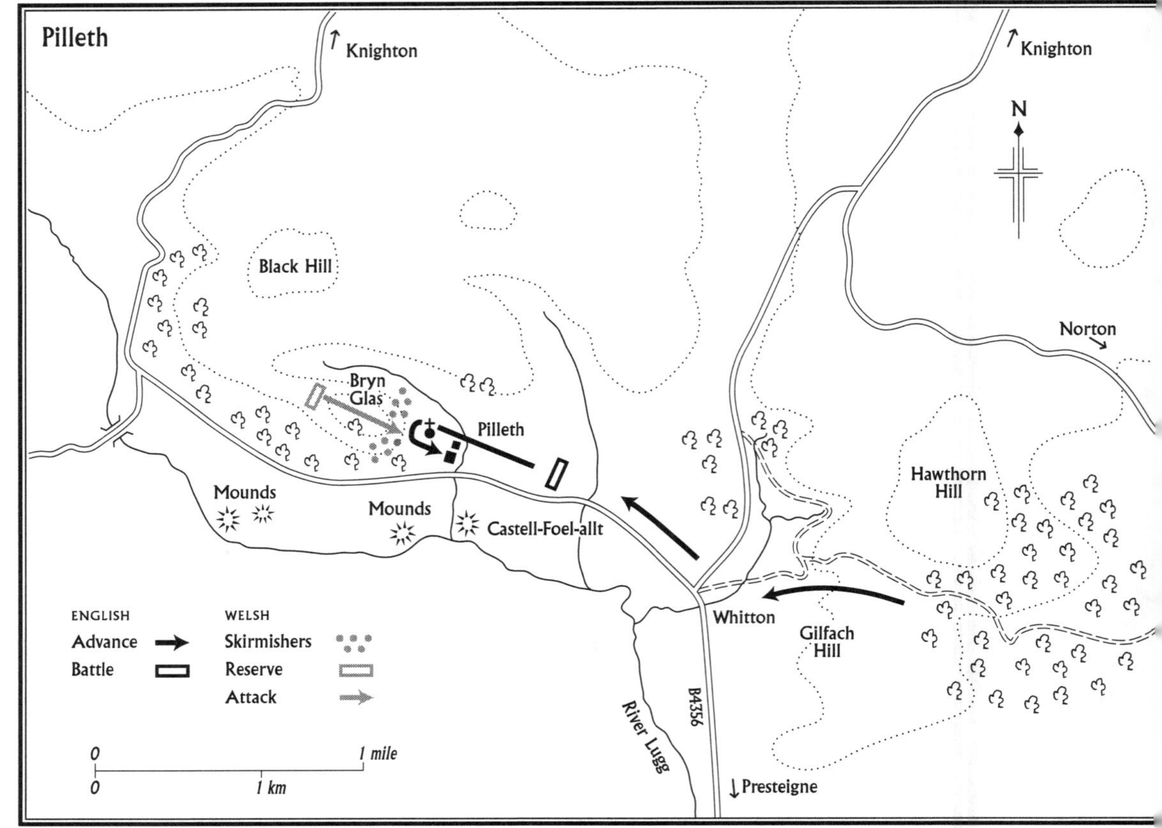

Henry Hotspur, responsible for security operations in North Wales, reported brushes with Glyn Dŵr in June 1401, at Cader Idris and somewhere known as 'M', perhaps Machynlleth. Glyn Dŵr's first victory occurred 6 miles (10 km) further south, in Nant Hyddgen, a remote glen behind Plynlimon. Still inaccessible by road, the area made an ideal guerrilla base, central but secure. Overlooked by Carn Hyddgen (1850 feet/564 m) to the east and Banc Llechwedd-mawr (1781 feet/543 m) to the west, the gently sloping valley is not unsuited to hand-to-hand combat, its bottom covered with grass and short rushes. On the west bank of Afon Hyddgen two white standing stones called Cerrig Cyfamod Owain Glyn Dŵr are said to commemorate where the rebel gathered his men for action, though which way they faced or went subsequently is unknown. The nearest source was the 16th-century bard and herald Gruffyd Hiraethog:

> Owain rose with 120 reckless men and robbers … in warlike fashion to the uplands of Ceridigion [Cardiganshire]; and 1500 men of the lowlands of Ceridigion, and of Rhos and Penfro [Pembroke] assembled there and came to the mountain with the intent to seize Owain. The encounter … was

Directions

Pilleth *Take the B4356 west from Presteigne. Pilleth is on the right, 1 mile(1.6 km) after Whitton. Several tracks lead up the hill past the church. The Ordnance Survey site is at SO2567. Various mounds in the river valley, including the motte and bailey at Castell-foel-allt, are nothing to do with the battle.*

Hyddgen

	Winners	Losers
Opponents	Welsh	English
Commanders	Owain Glyn Dŵr	unknown
Numbers	120	1500
Losses	unknown	200

Pilleth

	Winners	Losers
Opponent	Welsh	English
Commanders	Owain Glyn Dŵr	Sir Edmund Mortimer (p)
Numbers	unknown	1000–2000
Losses	unknown	200–400

at Hyddgant Mountain, and no sooner did the English troops turn their backs, than 200 of them were slain.

A later account says 1500 Flemings of Cardigan 'whom Owain distressed most of all' hemmed him in on all sides, so he could not escape without fighting. As other counterinsurgency forces have found, small bands of desperate men can slip through the tightest net. The 18th-century Anglesey antiquary Thomas Ellis wrote: 'Finding themselves surrounded and hard put to it, they resolved ... to make their way through or perish in the attempt; so falling on furiously with courage whetted by despair they put the enemy ... to confusion.' The enormous disparity between the strengths quoted is consistent with breaking through an overstretched cordon. Glyn Dŵr's 120 could never have fought the whole English force, and are unlikely to have inflicted many casualties, making 200 a literary figure rather than a statistic.

Many joined Glyn Dŵr after Hyddgen: 'the best for love of libertie, the basest for desire of bootie and spoile' (John Hayward, *Life and Reigne of King Henrie IIII*). Glyn Dŵr caught Lord Grey outside Ruthin Castle, and held him for ransom. In summer 1402 he carried the war into the Marches, and 'brent [burnt] a town of the Erle of March ... hight [called] Knighton' (*The Brut*). Welsh sources imply this was part of some larger design, more than just a raiding party:

> Owain arose with a great host from Gwynedd, Powys and the South, and made for Maelienydd [north Radnorshire]; where the knights of Herefordshire gathered against him. The battle between them was fought at Pilleth.
>
> Gruffyd Hiraethog

Pilleth is a settlement in the Lugg valley west of Presteigne, consisting of little more than St Mary's Church and the farm at Pilleth Court. It featured in Domesday Book as Pellelei, from the Welsh Pyllalai.

It is not clear whether Glyn Dŵr wanted a battle, or whether the English took him by surprise. The local marcher lord was Sir Edmund Mortimer, uncle and namesake of the young Earl of March. He was at Ludlow when reports came in of Glyn Dŵr's incendiarism. Contemporary sources say Mortimer sent to his tenants and adherents in Wales for help and 'summoned all the militia of Hereford', but supply no concrete numbers. A thousand or so appears reasonable, mostly English colonists from Ludlow and Wigmore, but also some local Welsh archers. Mortimer could approach the battlefield by three routes: north or south of the Lugg, or further north along the River Teme via Knighton. The first, more direct route would be most likely, picking up troops at Wigmore Castle, continuing through Norton, and across high ground to Whitton, a route still followed by a footpath, avoiding the boggy undrained valley.

The slope above Pilleth rises 'like a great green roof', whence its Welsh name Bryn Glas ('Green Hill'). The name suggests a slope cleared of trees and put to grass. The Ordnance Survey marks the battlefield at the roadside below, between the steep southern hillside of Bryn Glas and the Lugg's swampy banks. However, the closest source to the battle in time and space, a monk at Wigmore, categorically places it 'on the hill of Brynglase'. Other chroniclers say Mortimer 'bravely ascended the hill', although *The Brut* put the action a mile (1.6 km) further 'on the black hyll beside Pynmaren' (SO2469). Archaeological evidence points to the eastern slope of Bryn Glas. Pilleth is a small parish with few burials, but great quantities of bones are said to have been found in the churchyard. Further up the slope above the church four Wellingtonias mark another mass grave found in the 1840s.

Glyn Dŵr seems not to have put all his troops in the shop window, but lured the English on; the contemporary chronicler Thomas Walsingham put it thus: 'Being the stronger forces in the field, they were not afraid of the Welsh, who were in retreat'. Resistance stiffened, perhaps sustained by fresh troops advancing from dead ground, just west of the summit of Bryn Glas: the Elizabethan historian John Hayward wrote of 'a sharp and cruell conflict; not in forme of a loose skirmish, but standing still and maintaining their place'. Mortimer's 'friendly' Welsh turned on their allies: 'As they hastened in their turn to the attack they were betrayed ... unexpectedly defeated by their own archers who turned their own arms against them' (Walsingham). No contemporary description of the English formation survives, but it would make sense for archers to deploy on the men-at-arms' flank, ostensibly to shoot in the assault, but as it turned out to shoot them in the back.

Breathless from the climb and attacked on two sides, the English broke. Welsh sources naturally claim most of them were slain, but English accounts vary: 200, 400, 1100, although this last figure looks impossibly high. Unrecorded Welsh casualties and exhaustion would have limited the victors' appetite for pursuit, allowing the English rank and file to escape. Four named knights were killed, a modest setback compared with actions on the Scottish Border. The Welsh made up for the low body count by obscenely mutilating the corpses. Mortimer was captured and held in Glyn Dŵr's 13-foot (4-m) square stone *cachardy* in Snowdonia. Henry IV refused to ransom him, and he married one of Glyn Dŵr's daughters, dying during the siege of Harlech in 1409.

Battles like Hyddgen and Pilleth were not typical of Glyn Dŵr's guerrilla strategy. He was eventually defeated by poor harvests, rather than on the battlefield. Glyn Dŵr outlived Henry IV, dying in 1415, probably at another daughter's house in the Golden Valley in Herefordshire. His revolt was the last sustained protest against English rule in Wales.

Directions

Hyddgen *Take a tarmac road north from Ponterwyd on the A44, east of Aberystwyth, to the modern Nant-y-moch reservoir. The standing stones that mark Glyn Dŵr's forming-up point are 3 miles (5 km) past the dam by mountain trails, beyond Afon Hengwm. Glyndŵr's Way runs 4 miles (6.5 km) north of the battlefield.*

Nesbit Muir, 22 June 1402

England, Northumberland, LR75 NT9833?

Homildon Hill (Humbleton Hill), 14 September 1402

England, Northumberland, LR75 NT9628–9

One measure adopted to strengthen England's northern frontier during the 14th century was to appoint wardens of the Marches, local magnates responsible for defending the Border. Twice in the summer of 1402 these regional leaders inflicted disaster upon Scots raiders beside the River Till, at Nesbit and Homildon Hill.

The River Till flows north towards the Tweed, forming a strategic corridor between the crossing at Coldstream and the Northumbrian coastal plain. The men of Lothian passed that way in June 1402. Returning 'looslie and licentiouslie, as in a place of great securitie', they were set upon at Nesbit by the head of the Percy family, warden of the East March. The Elizabethan historian John Hayward, quoted above, evoked the ensuing Scots panic: 'Clean destitute both of counsaille and courage, [Sir Patrick Hepburn] ranne up and doune, from one place to another, commaunding many things & presently forbidding them ...'. Hepburn died well enough, 'among the thickest of his enemyes'. English losses were negligible, 'and those of no great service and degree'.

A larger Scots party tried again in September, plundering as far as the Tyne. Medieval estimates of numbers range from 10,000 to twice as many. About

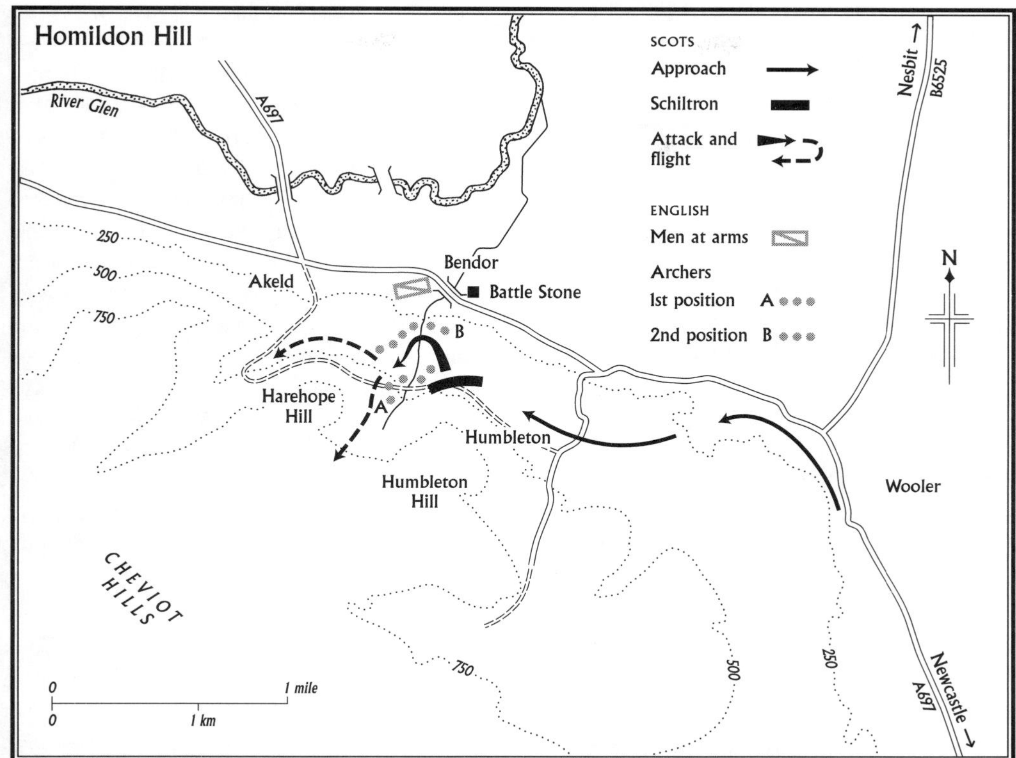

1200 became casualties, making 2500 men a more reasonable figure. They were sufficiently numerous to appear like formal invaders: 'not by soddaine incursions and roades, but with banner displayed, making a brave head, in sett & composed order of battaile'. Returning to the Tweed loaded with plunder, the Scots were once more headed off beside the Till: 'Out of a valley nere to a towne called Hameldown came against them Lord Henrie Peircie, Earle of Northumberland … followed by all the gentry of Northumberland, and about 8000 ordinarie souldiers'. Again the numbers look like an exaggeration, but the English had the better men, 'such as had beene trained & formerlie tried in those frontier warres' (Hayward).

The logical position for Northumberland is across the road before Akeld: left flank on the River Glen, a tributary of the Till; right flank resting on high ground to the south. At this point the Glen approaches the Cheviot Hills, forming a narrow defile some 500 yards (460 m) across. An ancient boulder, the Bendor Stone, marks the spot in Red Rigg field, north of the main road. Douglas needed to fight his way clear, but he chose to defend Humbleton Hill (978 feet/298 m) instead. Humbleton, Homildoun or Halweden Hill is south of the road, terraced in three successive tiers, with a flat top showing traces of prehistoric occupation. A Scottish position part way up the terraced slopes seems more likely than the inaccessible summit, perhaps the footpath that follows the 150 m (492 feet) contour around the northern hillside.

Directions

Homildon Hill *Continue west along the A697 about 2 miles (3 km) to Bendor. Facing south, Homildon Hill is half left, and Harehope Hill half right.*

The contemporary St Albans chronicler Thomas

Nesbit Muir

	Winners	Losers
Opponents	English	Scots
Commanders	Henry Percy, Earl of Northumberland	Sir Patrick Hepburn (k)

Homildon Hill

	Winners	Losers
Opponents	English	Scots
Commanders	Henry Percy, Earl of Northumberland Henry Percy, 'Hotspur'	Archibald, Earl of Douglas (p)
Numbers	unknown	*c.*2500
Losses	none	*c.*1200

Walsingham says the English left the road and climbed a hill facing the Scots, usually taken as Harehope Hill half a mile (0.8 km) west of Humbleton Hill. Their archers then drew up at the foot of the hill, to shoot at the Scots schiltron and provoke it to come down. A re-entrant between the two hills provides a suitable 'dale' from which the English archers could hope to engage a dense target 100–200 yards (90–180 m) above them on the footpath. Had the Scots occupied the summit, they would have been out of range.

Scots archers shot back, but 'endured not long ... being bothe the fewer & the worser bowmen' (Hayward). Lance in hand Douglas led the schiltron down the hill, probably in some disorder. Walsingham's exact word was '*turba*', a rabble. They never made contact: 'The English archers, as the Scottes came towards them, gave ground & drew back, not fearfullie, not disorderly, but with a well measured pace fitting their advantage letting fly in their retreat so thicke as haile among theire enemies' (Hayward). The column melted away before the arrow storm, which 'pierced the armour, perforated the helmets, pitted the swords, split the lances, and pierced all the equipment with ease' (Walsingham). Douglas received five wounds, and was blinded in one eye before he was taken. His ungrateful countrymen nicknamed him the Tyneman or Loser.

The surviving Scots 'committed the safetie of their lives to theire goode footmanshipp' (Hayward), but Percy's archers followed, still shooting. Many surrendered, 'for fear of the death-dealing arrows' (Walsingham). Walsingham attributed victory entirely to the archers, the English men-at-arms remaining idle spectators. Casualties among the rank and file are characteristically obscure, but over 100 knights were slain and 80 captured, along with 500 gentlemen and soldiers. Another 500 were thought drowned in the Tweed. English casualties must have been slight. The true cost of the battle was paid a year later at Shrewsbury. The Percys and Henry IV fell out over the prisoners, who 'raised more malice & mischief in England by being captive, than they possibly could have done if they had fortuned to escape' (Hayward).

Directions

Nesbit Muir *Take the B6525 north from Wooler (which is on the A697, 42 miles/67 km north of Newcastle), and follow a country road on the left.*

Shrewsbury, Sunday 21 July 1403

England, Shropshire, LR126 SJ5117

Henry IV gained but one victory in person: 'the sory bataill of Schrovesbury'. Memorable for the subsequent foundation of Battlefield Church, Shrewsbury was the first pitched battle in which English archers faced each other, and the occasion Henry, Prince of Wales, later Henry V, was 'first fleshed in bloud'.

The Percys played a material role in Henry IV's elevation to the throne, and may have aspired to the crown themselves. Grievances over debts incurred in royal service, and the disposal of prisoners taken at Homildon Hill (1402) left the younger Henry Percy – 'Hotspur' – literally at daggers drawn with the king. In midsummer 1403 he broke out in open revolt. Alternately denouncing Henry IV for the murder of Richard II, and promising to produce the late king in person, Hotspur marched into Cheshire, a focus of pro-Richard feeling: 200 Cheshire knights and squires would die at Shrewsbury. Had Hotspur defeated the king and joined forces with Owain Glyn Dŵr, whose rebellion was at its height, England would have been divided, with incalculable consequences.

Henry IV learned of Hotspur's revolt on 16 July at Burton-on-Trent, and immediately ordered a dozen Midland sheriffs 'to collect knights, esquires, and valets and attend the king as speedily as possible'. Numbers raised are unknown. The Burgundian chronicler Jean de Waurin (d.*c.*1474) opened the bidding at 3000 men-at-arms and 26,000 archers, and went up to 60,000 Lancastrians and 80,000 rebels. The authoritative *Annals of Richard II and Henry IV* says Hotspur deployed 14,000 picked men, but offers no Lancastrian figure. Modern estimates range from Oman's 8000–9000 for both armies together, through A.H. Burne's 12,000 Lancastrians versus 10,000 rebels, up to J.H. Wylie's total of 40,000–50,000. C.R.B. Barrett justifiably objected to the 'impossibility of reconciling the numbers said to have been engaged with the extremely narrow nature of the ground'. It was impossible to get 30,000–40,000 men into 'a six-acre patch, let alone execute either charges or manoeuvres ... in so small an area'. If the armies' frontages were 800–900 yards (730–825 m), they could have numbered between 6000 and 12,000 each, depending on the number of ranks. It is probable the Lancastrians outnumbered the rebels, absorbing a devastating charge and keeping a reserve.

The king moved southwest to Lichfield, blocking the direct route to London down Watling Street, then north to Stafford (28 miles/45 km in three days). Here he must have received intelligence of Hotspur's movements. On 20 July Henry dashed 32 miles (51 km) to Shrewsbury, to find the rebels embattled to assault the town. Henry's forced march turned the tables in Napoleonic fashion: not only did he safeguard the Prince of Wales, who was in Shrewsbury, he also secured the Severn bridge to cut Hotspur off from his Welsh allies. Henry could now destroy the rebels' strategic centre in detail, saving the wings for later. Hotspur's father, the Earl of Northumberland, was still in the north, and Glyn Dŵr was 100 miles (160 km) away in South Wales.

Henry caught up with the rebels next day, 'at Bolefild in the town of Harlescote', now a suburb of Shrewsbury. Hotspur chose as good a position as the locality offered: 'the more advantageous ground, as the King's army ... would have to advance across a broad field thickly sown with pease, which they had further twined and looped together so as to hamper an attacking force' (*Annals*). Three hundred yards (275 m) north of Battlefield Church a gentle ridge forms a slight crest, the one defensible feature in an otherwise flat landscape, and the optimum rebel position. Hotspur's deployment is unspecified, except for archers in front, as were the Earl of Douglas's troop of Scots. Captured at Homildon, they were intent on recovering their freedom through Henry IV's overthrow. The royal army formed two divisions: the left entrusted to the 14-year-old Prince of Wales, the other under the king. The latter was further sub-divided, the Earl of Stafford taking direct command of the front ranks, sometimes described as a vanguard.

Several places are associated with the fighting besides Bull Field: Hayteleyfield, where the church stands; Husseyfield, named after a manor to the west; and King's Croft, where the railway now runs. The heaviest fighting, and therefore casualties, occurred during the rebel attack at the start of the battle. The dead were buried in one large pit, near which the church was built. Victorian excavations north of the chancel are said to have cut through large masses of human bones. Metal-detector surveys along the foot

Shrewsbury

	Winners	*Losers*
Opponents	Lancastrian	Rebel
Commanders	Henry IV	Henry Percy, 'Hotspur' (k)
	Henry, Prince of Wales (w)	Archibald, Earl of Douglas (p)
Numbers	*c.*12,000	*c.*10,000
Losses	4600	5000

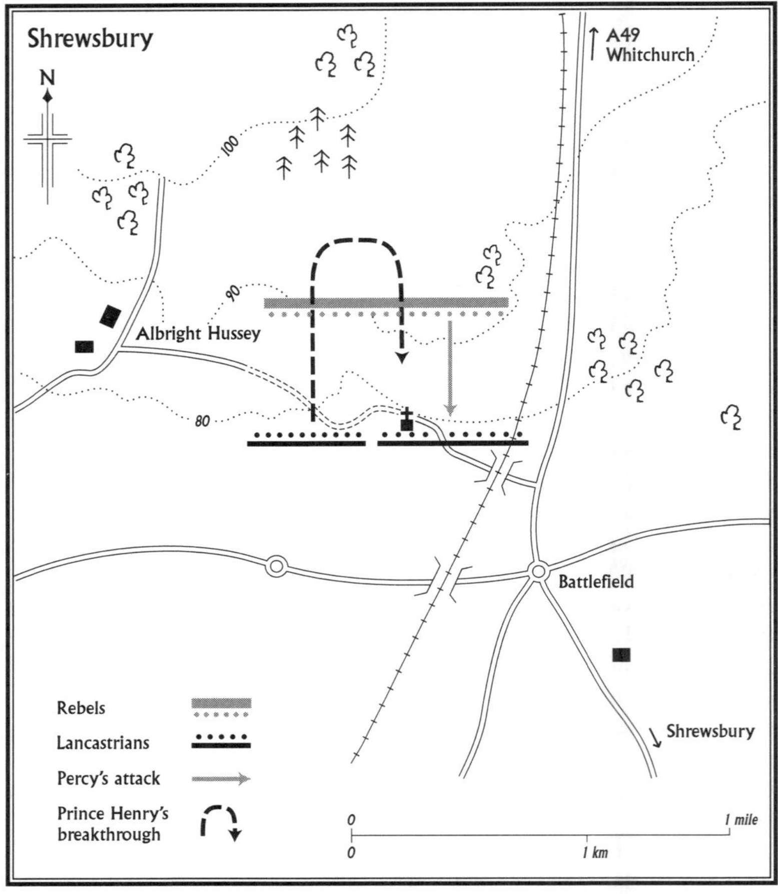

of the hill have confirmed the intensity of the fighting, finding masses of items such as buckles and arrow heads. It would appear likely therefore that the Lancastrian front line ran westwards from the railway, through or just south of the churchyard, conveniently out of arrowshot of the rebels on the forward slope of the hill.

Historians have made much of some mounds and ponds around the church, both ignored by contemporary sources. The ponds are insignificant obstacles, a few inches deep, and invisible in summer. They are best attributed to later excavations, either fishponds or clay pits dug during construction of the vicarage in 1861. Medieval commanders rarely dug in, preferring open battlefields, where masses of men could push each other about unhindered. The only contemporary mention of an obstacle, other than the 'pease', is a tale of a wounded knight murdered under an unlocated hedge. None of these obstacles affected the course of the battle.

Much of the day was spent in diplomacy, until late in the afternoon the king realized Hotspur was prolonging negotiations in hope of reinforcement. No sooner had talks broken down than Hotspur's

Directions

Turn left off the A49 Shrewsbury–Whitchurch road just north of Battlefield roundabout. Go under the railway to Battlefield Church, at the centre of the fighting. The rebel start position is uphill on the right.

Cheshire archers opened the attack, shooting down so many of their opponents that 4000 Lancastrians ran away immediately. The Elizabethan historian John Hayward thought the exchange less one-sided, 'both parties ... shrewdly stricken and galled without any apparent oddes'. The *Annals* confirm 'the destruction dealt by the arrows ... flying like a hailstorm from both sides'. Undaunted by the Lancastrian barrage, Hotspur and Douglas led a personal attack on Henry IV, 'counting him worth 10,000 others'. They overwhelmed the royal vanguard, killing its commander, and broke into the king's main battle. The Earl of Dunbar, a Scot fighting on the other side, pulled the king out of harm's way, as Douglas overthrew the royal standard, killing the bearer and three decoys dressed like the king, 'affirming that he marvailed to see the king soe often to revive' (Hayward).

The rebel concentration against the king may have left fewer men to oppose the Prince of Wales. Despite being 'schot in the heed with an arrowe', he reached the enemy position, 'breaking their line, and overthrowing all opponents. Passing right through he faced about, and thus closed them in between his own division and that of the king' (*Annals*). Modern reconstructions usually interpret this as an outflanking movement, but penetration followed by an attack on the enemy rear was common in Continental battles of the day. It was the natural consequence of a successful attack on a force drawn up in one line like Hotspur's, without reserves.

Meanwhile the king rallied his division, personally killing 30 or 36 of the enemy, and launching a counterattack. The chivalric novelist Jean de Bueil (1406–77) echoed these events, describing a battle at 'Cherausbry', where 'Sir Thomas de Percy' (sic) broke the king's battle. De Bueil said all but 500 of de Percy's men headed off in pursuit, leaving the king with 2000 men still in hand. These he led straight against the thinly attended de Percy, defeated and killed him, winning the battle he had just lost. English accounts confirm that the real Percy's death was decisive: 'Pursuing his enemies too farre, [he] was environed by them and sodeynely slaine by an uncertaine arme' (Hayward).

The combatants fought until they dropped: 'When night came on they did not know which side had won; and they sank down in all directions a chance-medley of weary, wounded, bruised, and bleeding men' (*Annals*). It was clearly very hot. Wounded men, stifling in their armour, sought shade under nearby hedges. Many of the 3000 wounded Lancastrians are said to have died of exhaustion, besides 1600 killed outright. Rebel casualties were similar. Douglas the Tyneman maintained his reputation as a gallant loser. Unhorsed as he fled through Haughmond, 'he brake one of his genitalles', or kneecap in Victorian accounts. Henry IV wept over Hotspur's corpse, but displayed it near Shrewsbury's future Post Office, to convince sceptics of his death.

A dynastic struggle between two usurpers, Shrewsbury settled no great issue of principle. Henry IV's victory did, however, ensure the defeat of all those opposed to the Lancastrian succession, both in Wales and the North of England.

Bramham Moor, Sunday 19 February 1408

England, West Yorkshire, LR105 SE4341

The Earl of Northumberland, head of the Percy family, avoided personal implication in the rebellion that had led to the defeat of his son Harry Hotspur at Shrewsbury. He continued to plot against Henry IV, however, and supported Archbishop Scrope's conspiracy in 1405, fleeing abroad on its failure. He returned in January 1408, to be killed on Bramham Moor.

Northumberland took the ancient invasion route from Scotland, down the Roman Dere Street, now the A68, past Otterburn to Durham, reaching Darlington on 14 February. He exploited 'the common hatred against the king', according to the contemporary chronicler Thomas Walsingham, claiming he had 'come to the succour of the English people, and the relief of evil oppression'. Joined by numerous commoners, Northumberland continued south through Northallerton. At Knaresborough the Sheriff of York, Sir Thomas Rokeby, barred his way across Grimald

Bramham Moor		
	Winners	*Losers*
Opponents	Lancastrian	Rebel
Commanders	Sir Thomas Rokeby	Henry Percy, Earl of Northumberland (k)

Bridge with the knights of the shire ('*cum militibus patriae*'). Unable to cross the River Nidd, the rebels circled eastwards round de la Hay Park, to Wetherby on the River Wharfe.

Next day Northumberland headed east along the Wharfe's northern bank to cross at Tadcaster, 'his crowd following him'. Rokeby chased the rebels through the town, placing outposts so 'they could not escape without a battle'. About 2 p.m. Northumberland 'rode to *Brehamsmore* near *Hesywode* where he chose the place of battle'. Place-names locate the action 2 miles (3 km) south of Bramham village, at Bramham Crossroads, where the Roman road from Castleford forked right for Tadcaster. Hazelwood is still an extensive wood, in the southeast quadrant of the crossroads. The battlefield lies in more open ground to the northeast, between Camp Hill and Spen Farm.

Rokeby accepted Northumberland's challenge without delay, displaying the banner of St George: 'On the other side, the earl unfurled a pennon of his arms, and began a desperate battle in which he preferred to die for his cause than to be captured' (Walsingham). Northumberland was killed and stripped, his head paraded through the capital and displayed on London Bridge. His confederate Sir Thomas Bardolph was taken, but died of wounds. The Abbot of Hayles, 'who had borne arms with the lords', was hanged. Owain Glyn Dŵr's last English allies had gone under, and Henry IV's dynastic position was secure.

Directions

Take the A64 west from Tadcaster towards Leeds. Hazelwood is on the left before the A1(M) interchange. From the junction a minor road leads 1/2 mile (0.8 km) north to the old Roman crossroads, where Spen Common Lane runs east across the battlefield.

Harlaw, 24 July 1411

Scotland, Aberdeenshire, LR38 NJ7524

Few Scottish battles have the fearful reputation of the 'Sair Field o' Harlaw', whether as one of Scotland's bloodiest battles, or as the decisive clash between Gaelic and Anglo-Saxon Scotland. Both claims are exaggerated.

The unlucky capture of James I by English pirates in the early 15th century left the Duke of Albany, James's uncle and regent, free to pursue family interests in the Highlands by the most dubious means. In 1406 Albany misappropriated the inheritance of his ward, heiress to the Earl of Ross, cheating the next heiress in line. She, however, was married to Donald, Lord of the Isles, the one Highland magnate strong enough to resist the Stewarts. Denied legal remedy, Donald resorted to violence. He burnt Inverness, and struck southeast to reclaim the Ross sheriffdoms of Banff, Aberdeen and Kincardine.

The local Stewart magnate was the Earl of Mar. His career nicely illustrates their methods, for he had acquired the earldom by starving his predecessor to death and marrying the widow by force. Mar's response to Donald's approach was equally simple. He sat on the direct route to Aberdeen at Inverurie and summoned the armed strength of Garioch, Angus and Buchan. Both sides fielded large armies by Scottish standards, but that only implies a few thousand each. Ballad references to 'fifty thousand Hielan' men a-marching to Harlaw' are as apocryphal as the 6000 picked men reinforced by 4000 Highlanders claimed by the battle elegy of the MacDonalds. The only administrative evidence is that

Harlaw		
	Winners	*Losers*
Opponents	Lowland	Highland
Commanders	Alexander Stewart, Earl of Mar	Donald, Lord of the Isles
Numbers	unknown	unknown
Losses	600	900

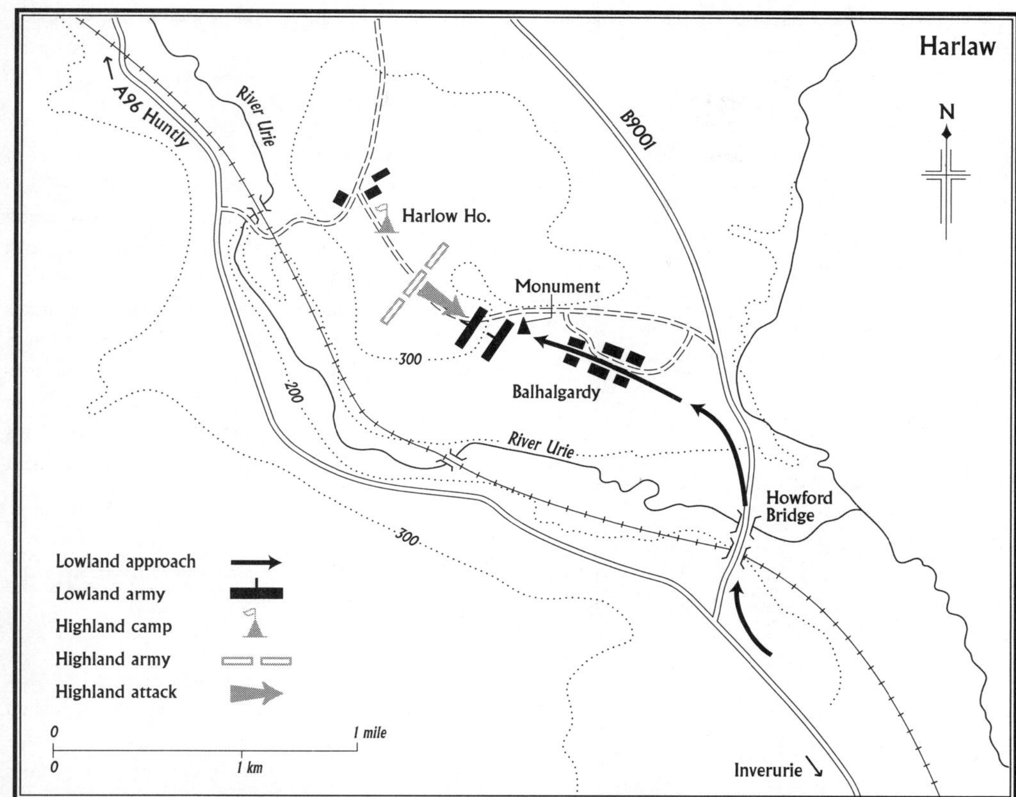

36 citizens of Aberdeen took the field. The appearance of the armies is more certain. The Highlanders, 'comely in form but unsightly in dress' (John of Fordun), wore the plaid and saffron-dyed shirts. In action their leaders sported mail shirts, the rest quilted linen jackets waterproofed with pitch or wax, under deerskin jerkins. Weapons were bow, broadsword and axe. The Lowlanders were more conventional: knights in plate armour, commoners in mail.

The night before the battle, the Gaelic host encamped on the elevated plateau 2 miles (3 km) north of Inverurie in a field known as Pley Fauld. Now covered with barley fields between dry-stone walls, the area was quite open, a bleak and stony heath, with small *farmtouns* at Harlaw and Balhalgardy. The position favoured the Gaels, a long gentle slope to the south to slow an attacker, or to add impetus to a charge. A steeper slope down into the Vale of Urie protected the right flank from an enemy in Inverurie. According to the MacDonald account, the Gaels formed up in three divisions: MacLeans on the right under 'Red Hector of the Battles'; Donald's kinsmen in the centre; Mackintoshes, who had been bribed to fight, on the less honourable left. Mar's formation is less certain. The MacDonald

Directions

Take the B9001 north from Inverurie, and turn left down a minor road signposted to the monument, in the centre of the battlefield. Scattered stones beside a farm track west of Balhalgardy (NJ7523) mark Provost's Cairn, where Robert Davidson, Provost of Aberdeen, was killed. Also see the tombstone of Sir Gilbert de Greenlaw, probably killed at Harlaw, in Kinkell Churchyard south of Inverurie.

elegy suggests three divisions, matching their own deployment. Lowland sources have two, a vanguard leading and a main body in support, led by Mar. A deep formation is reasonable, as the advance from Inverurie would be easier for divisions in column than line abreast.

The Lowlanders crossed Howford bridge at dawn, possibly hoping to catch the Gaels still asleep. In fact, the Highlanders attacked their vanguard near the monument, and pushed it back 'three acres breadth or mair', 60–70 yards (55–65 m) if an acre were a furlong in length. Mar's division came up to stabilize the position, but could do no more. Lowland accounts tell a conventional tale of Highlanders hurling themselves ineffectually on levelled spear points. The elegy claimed the MacLeans entirely routed their opposite numbers, although Red Hector was killed. In the centre the Earl of Mar gave ground, was 'quite defeated', and chased back to Aberdeen. Only the Lowlanders' right flank held out in a cattle fold, presumably at Balhalgardy, emerging at nightfall to plunder the fallen. The monotonous and long drawn out fighting recorded in 'The Battel of Hayrlaw' suggests there was no clear result:

> With doubtsome victory they dealt
> The bludy battel lasted lang.

Medieval commentators agreed each side thought itself beaten, and withdrew. The only known grave is north of the battle site, behind the Highlanders' position. It contained 12 skeletons, scant support for the ballad's gloomy conclusion:

> An sic a weary buryin'
> I'm sure ye never saw
> As wis the Sunday after that
> On the muirs aneath Harlaw.

Harlaw's political results reflected the tactical stalemate. Albany extracted hostages and 'submission' from Donald next year, but the Lord of the Isles kept Ross and his independence.

The Wars of the Roses

The Wars of the Roses between the rival Plantagenet houses of Lancaster and York began with the First Battle of St Albans (1455), and ended 32 years later at Stoke Field (1487). The military history of the struggle is appropriately thorny. Sketchy contemporary accounts are no match for Elizabethan melodrama in forming popular misperceptions of the conflict. Even the period's name is misleading: participants never sported red or white roses to indicate support for the Lancastrian and Yorkist factions. As the name indicates, there was not one war but several, separated by intervals of peace. Modern estimates of active campaigning total at most two years, less than 10 per cent of the whole period.

Yorkist and Tudor propagandists deliberately exaggerated the ferocity and destructiveness of the wars to justify successive usurpations of the crown, first by the Yorkist Edward IV in 1461, then by the Tudor Henry VII in 1485. Shakespeare then transformed the partisan claims of Yorkist Acts of Attainder into accepted fact. Ever since, the overthrow of the Lancastrian Henry VI has been seen as divine retribution for his grandfather's deposition and murder of Richard II in 1399, a national crime only expiated when England's soil had been manured in blood.

The inference is doubly spurious. The Wars of the Roses had no connection with the turbulence of Henry IV's reign; nearly 50 years elapsed between Bramham Moor (1408) and First St Albans (1455). Neither did a generation of English fighting men perish on 15th-century battlefields. The Wars of the Roses were nothing like the Civil Wars of the 1640s, when large national armies contested deeply held causes. Participation and casualties during the Wars of the Roses were limited. 'The Ballad of Bosworth' claimed 'forty thousand and three' turned out for Richard III, but Professor Ross has calculated a more modest 8000–10,000. Chronic overestimates of combat strength destroy the credibility of inflated casualty figures, which numbered hundreds rather than thousands. There is no evidence of labour shortages at harvest, or of noble families dying out more often than usual.

The Wars of the Roses did, however, reflect a deep social and political crisis. Contemporaries complained bitterly of want of good governance. This arose primarily from the character of the king. Henry VI's personality was entirely inappropriate to his station. He failed to control the rivalries of great aristocratic families, or restrain the greed and ambition of favourites, such as the Duke of Somerset. Henry allowed such men to exploit the judicial system for their own benefit, forcing others to take the law into their own hands.

Henry VI fatally neglected the military side of medieval kingship, losing both his father's recent French conquests, and more ancient Plantagenet possessions in Gascony. Present at five battles as a spectator, Henry was captured three times, apparently lacking the initiative to run away. He never developed his own armed following to overawe mighty subjects, but alienated Richard, Duke of York, his most powerful kinsman. In 1453 Henry VI suffered complete mental breakdown, his speechless immobility suggesting catatonic schizophrenia. The king's absence from the centre of power allowed local feuds to spill over into national politics. Magnates active in minor conflicts, like the confrontation at Heworth Moor (1453) or the Fight at Clyst (1455), took the lead in more general hostilities. The Wars of the Roses were not at first a dynastic struggle. Yorkist rebels made fulsome protestations of loyalty to the king, and Richard of York was only driven to attack the king after repeated exclusion from the royal council by Somerset and Henry VI's queen, Margaret of Anjou. Their intrigues denied him the place in government to which his birth entitled him, and even threatened his life.

The Wars of the Roses consisted of three distinct conflicts:

(1) THE YORKIST DRIVE TO POWER (1455–61)
Richard of York acted as Protector during the king's insanity, with some success. He imprisoned Somerset in the Tower of London, but was once more excluded from government on Henry's recovery. Believing his life and property under threat, York took arms against the king's advisers at St Albans in May 1455. The Neville earls of Salisbury and Warwick (father and son) supported him, having their own grievances against Somerset.

Many magnates stayed outside the opening stages of the war. Despite another success at Blore Heath (August 1459), York and his allies underestimated the extent of support for Henry VI, and had to flee the country following the cannonade at Ludford Bridge (October 1459). York's associates returned from Calais next year to defeat the king, or rather the court faction, at Northampton (July 1460). Only now, after five years of bickering, did York advance his own hereditary claim to the throne, which was better than Henry's. The resulting compromise, or Act of Accord, reserved the throne to Henry VI during his life, but made York the heir, disinheriting Henry's son Prince Edward.

Margaret of Anjou made common cause with the heirs of Lancastrians killed at St Albans to assert her son's rights and seek revenge. York and Salisbury again underestimated their opponents. Attempting to disperse Lancastrian forces in the north of England with inadequate numbers, they were defeated and killed at Wakefield (December 1460). Margaret marched on London, beating Warwick at Second St Albans (14 February 1461). Warwick, however, escaped to join his cousin, Edward Earl of March, eldest son of Richard, Duke of York. London refused to admit the Northerners, and as Margaret hesitated, the new Yorkist leaders slipped into the capital, compelling the Lancastrians to withdraw.

March, who inherited his father's claim to the throne, made a striking contrast to Henry VI, possessing all the physical aura of a king. He was also the most successful general of the wars, fighting five battles and losing none. He had already eliminated Lancastrian forces from Wales at Mortimer's Cross (3 February 1461). Two months later he smashed their main army at Towton (29 March 1461), the bloodiest battle of the war. March was crowned Edward IV, and Henry VI imprisoned in the Tower. A flicker of Lancastrian resistance in Ireland was extinguished at Piltown (1462). Warwick's brother Lord Montagu suppressed renewed Lancastrian activity in northern England at Hedgeley Moor and Hexham (April–May 1464), while Margaret of Anjou and the prince took refuge in France. The Lancastrian cause appeared lost.

(2) WARWICK'S COUNTER-REVOLUTION (1469–71)
The alliance between Edward IV and Warwick 'the Kingmaker' soon broke down. The insatiably ambitious earl could not accept the inevitable decline of his influence, as the king grew older and more self-confident. The Kingmaker sought a more amenable puppet in Edward's brother, the false, fleeting and perjured Duke of Clarence, but his machinations produced fruitless battles at Edgcote (1469) and Lose-Coat Field (1470). The conspirators fled to France, where Warwick was improbably reconciled to Margaret of Anjou. He returned to England with French help, forcing Edward to flee in his turn. The short-lived 'Readeption' of Henry VI gave Warwick the ultimate royal dummy, but Edward was back within six months, annihilating Warwick at Barnet (14 April 1471) and wiping out the entire Lancastrian house at Tewkesbury (4 May 1471). Henry VI and Prince Edward were killed, while Margaret of Anjou was captured, ransomed and exiled. The slaughter ensured peace for the remainder of Edward IV's reign.

(3) TUDOR INTERVENTION (1485–7)
Edward IV's premature death in 1483 released explosive tensions within the Yorkist camp. Richard of Gloucester, Edward's surviving brother, seized the throne from his nephew, who should have been Edward V, and ruthlessly eliminated all opposition. Whether Richard was personally responsible for the deaths of the Princes in the Tower will never be known for certain, but his well-attested capacity for drastic action makes him the most likely culprit. The Princes' disappearance split the Yorkist establishment, which failed to support Richard III when he faced the obscure Lancastrian pretender Henry Tudor, Earl of Richmond, at Bosworth (1485). Henry's claim to the throne was tenuous, but he defeated and killed Richard, while most of the royal army looked on. Crowned Henry VII, the new king consolidated his position by marrying Elizabeth, Edward IV's eldest daughter, and ruled with support from both factions. At Stoke Field in 1487 he saw off an even less plausible pretender, whose ludicrous claim to the throne suggests the lack of credible alternatives. Like Edward IV, Henry VII died in his bed, but his heir was of age, and able to look after himself.

Heworth Moor, 24 August 1453

England, York, LR105 SE6256?

The flashpoint of the Wars of the Roses was the struggle between the great northern families of Percy and Neville. Exposed to Scottish attack, their border earldoms of Northumberland and Westmorland, with their shared Yorkshire hinterland, were a breeding ground for soldiers. The opening clashes of the wars occurred here, within a day's march of medieval England's second city.

The Percy earls of Northumberland had been disinherited for rebellion against Henry IV (see above). Henry V rehabilitated them, but they resented the loss of lands forfeited to more orderly neighbours. The Nevilles had expanded by marriage rather than violence, acquiring the heiresses and titles to the earldoms of Salisbury and Warwick. In August 1453 Sir Thomas Neville, Salisbury's third son, married a co-heiress of Lord Cromwell of Tattershall Castle in Lincolnshire, once a Percy possession. This provocation was too much for Lord Egremont, a particularly irascible son of Northumberland. He laid an

Heworth Moor

	Winners	Losers
Opponents	Neville	Percy
Commanders	Sir Thomas Neville Richard Neville, Earl of Salisbury	Thomas Percy, Lord Egremont
Numbers	unknown	*c.*1000

ambush for the bridal party east of York at Heworth Moor, as it rode home to the Neville castle at Sheriff Hutton.

Egremont is said to have raised 5000 men, although subsequent indictments list only 700, mostly Yorkshiremen. Fortunately for the newlyweds, the bridegroom's father came similarly prepared. The two parties met at Huntington, north of York on the road to Sheriff Hutton. Egremont was sufficiently intimidated to let the Nevilles pass, after an exchange of threats and some blows. One of the wounded sued him for 100 marks compensation. The legal records conceal an ugly incident. It was, commented the Neville chronicler, the beginning of all the great sorrows of England (*Annales Rerum Anglicarum* attributed to William Worcester).

Stamford Bridge, 31 October 1454

England, East Yorkshire, LR105 SE7255

The site of Anglo-Saxon England's last victory also saw the Nevilles catch up with Lord Egremont. For more than a year after Heworth Moor, Egremont pursued a reckless career of riot and intimidation. Despairing of royal justice for Heworth, two of Salisbury's sons intercepted Egremont riding west along the Roman road to York, through the Neville manor of Stamford Bridge. Egremont had 200 men from his manor at Pocklington, 7 miles (11 km) to the southeast, but they fled, leaving him in Neville hands. Nearly 100 were killed and many wounded. Condemned to pay impossibly high damages, Egremont remained in Newgate Jail as a debtor

Stamford Bridge

	Winners	Losers
Opponents	Yorkist	Lancastrian
Commanders	John Neville Sir Thomas Neville	Thomas Percy, Lord Egremont (p)
Numbers	unknown	unknown
Losses	unknown	*c.*100

until November 1456, when he bribed a warder to smuggle in arms, released the other prisoners and escaped sword in hand.

St Albans (I), 22 May 1455

England, Hertfordshire, LR166 TL1407

The first full-scale battle of the Wars of the Roses was unique in several ways. At least two eyewitness accounts survive, a rare event in a war when only four out of more than a dozen battles are so described. Unusually, the fighting took place in a built-up area, whose outline still reveals the course of the action.

If Henry VI's insanity was a personal tragedy, his recovery in January 1455 was a national disaster. Within weeks the Duke of Somerset had escaped from the Tower and combined with the Earl of Northumberland to drive York and Salisbury from the king's council. The local feud between Percy and Neville, begun on Heworth Moor, would now be fought out at national level. York and the Nevilles left court without royal permission. Summoned in threatening terms to a Great Council at Leicester, they took up arms and marched on London.

The Yorkist response took Somerset by surprise. Unwilling to fight in the capital, he left for Leicester on 21 May with the king and 11 other peers. Oblivious of its peril, the court proceeded more like a royal progress than an army advancing to contact. Next morning, between Watford and St Albans, the Yorkist lords were reported to have spent the night at Ware, only 14 miles (22 km) north of St Albans. The royal party pressed on, hoping to reach St Albans first and to defuse the crisis by negotiation.

They reached St Albans at 9 a.m., to find Yorkist forces established half a mile (0.8 km) east of the Abbey, in Key and Camp Fields. York had achieved strategic surprise, concentrating superior numbers at the decisive point, before Somerset could mobilize his own forces. York's party included only 3 peers against the king's 12, but contemporary estimates of the armies range from 5000–7000 Yorkists against 2000–3500 Lancastrians. The former are probably exaggerated propaganda figures; the lower Lancastrian numbers come from an eyewitness, Sir William Stoner, the abbey steward. Peers accompanying the king had only their immediate household forces. More had been summoned, but were not due to arrive until the day after the battle.

The Lancastrian position was not a bad one. St Albans stands on the southwest extremity of a ridge, 100 feet (30 m) above the surrounding plain. Formal defences included a ditch, masonry wall and palisades, known collectively as Tonman Ditch. Houses fronting the triangular marketplace north of the abbey provided a second line of defence. Three narrow lines of approach penetrated the defences: Cock Lane (now Hatfield Road), Shropshire or Butts Lane (now Victoria Street), and Sopwell Lane, off Hollywell Street. Wooden barriers or 'bars' blocked Shropshire Lane and Sopwell Lane. The modern London Road did not yet exist.

Henry VI set up his banner 'in Seynt Petrus strete', probably near the Town Hall, 'and commaundeth the warde and barres to be kepte in strong wyse' (Stoner). Several hours elapsed in diplomatic exchanges, 'without ony stroke smeton on eyther partye'. York protested his loyalty, but insisted on surrender of 'hem which hav deserved deth'. Henry refused to hand Somerset over, threatening to 'destrye them ev'y modre sone'. Between 11 and 12 noon, Yorkist patience ran out, and they started to break into the town at three places, presumably the lanes listed above. The king's last order was to give no quarter, which done, 'lord Clyfford kept strongly the barrers that the seyde Duke of York might not in ony wise, with all the power that he hadde, entre ne breke into the town' (Stoner).

St Albans

	Winners	*Losers*
Opponents	Yorkist	Lancastrian
Commanders	Richard, Duke of York	Henry VI (w)
	Richard Neville, Earl of Salisbury	Edmund Beaufort, Duke of Somerset (k)
	Richard Neville, Earl of Warwick	Henry Stafford, Duke of Buckingham
Numbers	c.3000	c.2000
Losses	unknown	60–120

Jammed together on a narrow front, the attackers could not get on, but Warwick infiltrated men through the 'Backsides', that is the gardens between Shropshire and Sopwell Lanes. Yorkist soldiers chopped their way through a house 'betuene the signe of the Keye, and the sygne of the Chekkere in Holwell strete', and appeared in Chequer Street blowing trumpets and crying, 'A Warrewyk, a Warrewyk, a Warrewyk!'. The Paston Letters describe the scene:

> Sir Robert Ocle took 600 men of the Marches [Neville retainers from Westmorland], and took the marketplace ere any man was aware; then the alarum bell was rung, and every man yed to harness [i.e. armed himself], for at that time every man was out of his array, and they joined battle anon ...

Casualties among Henry's entourage confirm the Lancastrians' surprise: four royal bodyguards were shot dead; arrows hit three partially armed magnates in hand or face; another wounded the king in the shoulder. Outflanked, the Lancastrians fell back into the marketplace, fighting around the Clock Tower. Resistance soon crumbled; the Paston correspondent thought 'it was done within half an hour'. The whole action was over by half past two.

Left alone by his attendants' death or flight, Henry VI took cover in a tanner's house, just north of St Peter's Church, on the site now occupied by Hall Place. Somerset defended himself in an inn, until York's men broke down the door. He charged out

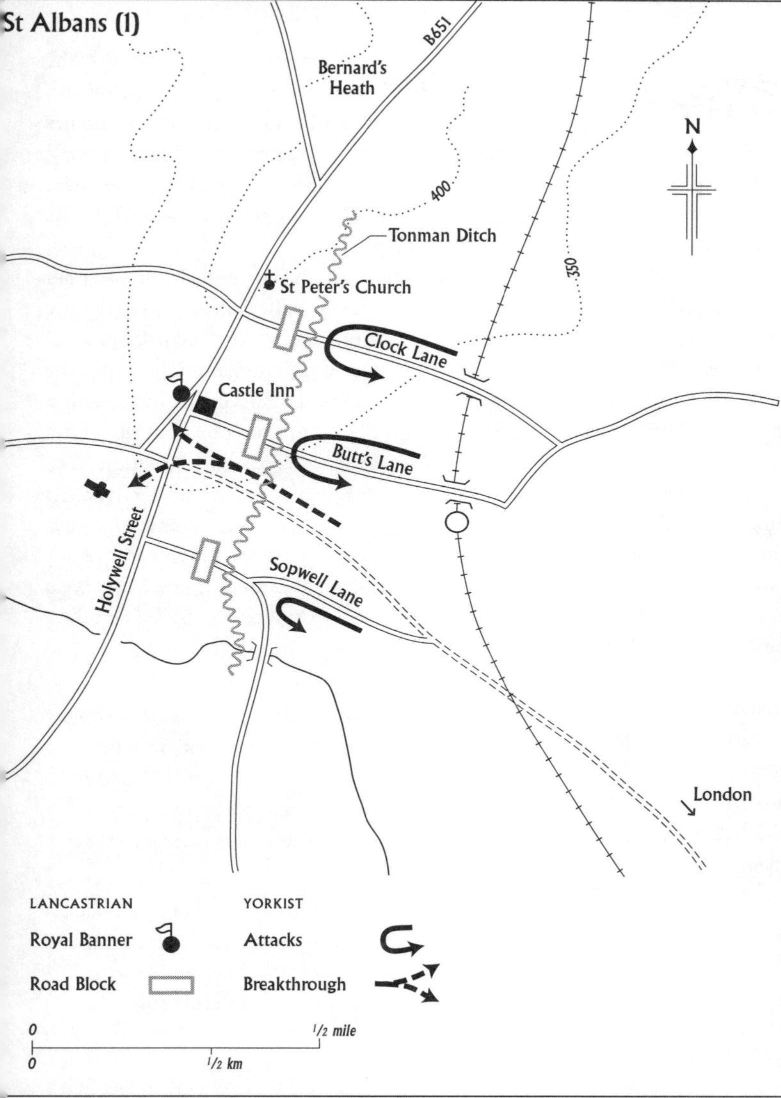

Directions

View the battlefield from the Clock Tower, and see the bell that rang during St Albans' 'mal journey'. Walk to the sites mentioned in the market-place and the abbey. A plaque in memory of Somerset marks the building that has replaced the Castle Inn.

into their midst, killing four before an axe cut him down. A soothsayer had allegedly predicted Somerset's death 'under a castle', and he did indeed die on the steps of The Castle, a pub that once stood on the north corner of Shropshire Lane and Chequer Street. Witnesses put casualties at 48 buried in the abbey, at most no more than six score, compared with the 5000 claimed by the Tudor historian John Stowe. Northumberland and Clifford were among the dead, victims of the Nevilles' private vengeance. Once personal scores had been settled, the Yorkist lords besought the king's grace, led him to safety in the abbey, and proclaimed an immediate ceasefire.

Dismissed as scarcely a battle at all, St Albans had serious consequences. The killing of Lancastrian leaders, essential to prevent their reinstatement in royal favour, ensured lasting bitterness: 'evermore a grouch and wrath had by the heirs of them that were so slain' (*Brut*). For the time being York was first after the king, but his victory would prove hollow.

Clyst Bridge, Monday 15 December 1455

England, Devon, LR192 SX9691

The West of England was as great a source of disorder as the North. Courtenay earls of Devon resented the threat to their hereditary regional predominance posed by newcomers like Sir William Bonville of Shute Barton. Governmental distraction after First St Albans gave Devon his chance to settle private grievances.

Trouble began in October 1455 with the murder of Nicholas Radford, Recorder of the City of Exeter. The earl's sons and a hundred of their tenants plundered Radford's house, tipping his invalid wife out of bed to steal the sheets, and smote him a deadly stroke with a glaive (a long-bladed polearm). A mock jury of Devon's retainers returned a verdict of suicide, crushing Radford's body with rocks to hinder further inquiries.

Devon followed the most notorious private crime of a violent century by besieging his kinsman Sir Philip Courtenay in Powderham Castle, 6 miles (10 km) below Exeter, west of the River Exe. He deployed 1000–1500 men, with 'jakkes and sallettes and harnessed', and on 15 November bombarded the castle for eight hours:

> Great cannon and serpentines were fixed in the earth at different places near the house, and putting into them powder and fire, stones were shot at the mansion of Sir Philip Courtenay, as if they had been in an enemy's country.
>
> Indictment of the Earl of Devon

The assault failed, perhaps because Devon could not concentrate all his forces for siege operations. He had to keep troops in Exeter to cover his rear, as the Mayor and council refused to deny entry to Bonville, daily expected with a relieving force. Devon sentinels guarded the city gates, scrutinizing all-comers like a regular garrison. Bonville's strength is unknown, but he had recruited 600 archers in 1444 to fight the French in Gascony.

Unable to count on the citizens, Devon went out to meet Bonville in the valley of the sluggish little River Clyst, east of Exeter. City records speak of him returning after the fight from 'Clisbrige', the long sandstone bridge at Clyst St Mary. The action probably centred around rough open ground later known as Clyst Heath. Now under Junction 30 of the M5 motorway, this was one of the few flat areas near Exeter, which is otherwise surrounded by hills. When first ploughed during the Napoleonic Wars, the soil yielded masses of human bones, either from 1455 or the Western Rebellion of 1549. The fullest contemporary account comes from Exeter's Mayoral Roll:

> Monday after St Lucie's Day … the said Erle lord of Devon departed out from the City with his people into ye feld by Clist and there bykered and faughte with ye Lord Bonevyle and his people and put them to flight and so returned again that night into the City …

A local Tudor historian wrote of 'a greate feught upon Clyst hethe', where 'was miche hurt donne and many hurted', but undermined his credibility somewhat by claiming 'the occasion thereof was … a dogge'. Casualties were not recorded, but when Devon finally quit Exeter on 21 December he left a number of wounded.

The fight at Clyst blurred local and national divisions. Previously a Court man, Bonville became a supporter of the Duke of York who, as Protector, incarcerated Devon in the Tower of London. The earl adhered to the Lancastrian Court party, which released him without charge after Henry VI resumed power in February 1456. The widening struggle brutally ended the Courtenay–Bonville feud: Bonville was executed at Second St Albans (1461), and Devon's successors at Towton (1461) and Tewkesbury (1471).

Clyst Bridge

	Winners	*Losers*
Opponents	Lancastrian	Yorkist
Commanders	Thomas Courtenay, Earl of Devon	Sir William Bonville
Numbers	c.1000	c.600

Directions

Approach the old bridge at Clyst St Mary through the village from the east. The remnants of the battlefield lie to the west, between the river and motorway. Powderham Castle is open to the public.

Blore Heath, 23 September 1459

England, Staffordshire, LR127 SJ7135

The uneasy truce that followed First St Albans (1455) broke down in the autumn of 1459. Henry VI left London to rally his supporters in the Midlands, where the queen, Margaret of Anjou, recruited many followers in Cheshire, under her son's White Swan livery. Once more excluded from royal councils, the Yorkist lords took up arms as they had in 1455. The first armed clash between the factions was at Blore Heath.

Royal forces in the Midlands separated the Duke of York at Ludlow in the Welsh Marches from the Nevilles in the North, forcing the Earl of Salisbury to follow a circuitous route through Lancashire and Cheshire to join him. Salisbury evaded Lancastrian armies under the queen and Henry VI, but ran into Lord Audley's subsidiary force between Newcastle-under-Lyme and Market Drayton.

More than one source identifies the site: '*Bellum Bloreheth juxta villa Novi Castri sub Lyne*' (John Benet), and 'a grete journaye [fight] at the Blowre Hethe by the Erle of Saulysbury ande the Quenys galentys' (William Gregory). Before the modern fields were enclosed, the area would have been open heath, as its name implies. A monument to Lord Audley stands in a field south of the Newcastle road: 'a square pedestal, seemingly of great age, with a rude stone cross standing upon it, now much battered and injured' (Richard Brooke). First recorded in 1686, the cross is halfway down the forward slope of the Yorkist position, an inconspicuous spot at the culminating point of Audley's attack across the valley.

Two other features identify the site: Hemphill or Wemberton Brook; and the main A53 road, which crosses it 2 miles (3 km) east of Market Drayton. The stream is readily fordable, but flows through a narrow valley between steep slopes. Today the road is straight, bisecting the battlefield, but at the time it bent southwards towards the brook, where it split. One branch went straight on across Hemphill Brook towards Blore village, the other turned back along the north bank, fording the stream near the modern bridge.

A Lancastrian roadblock would probably cross the road at right angles, within longbow range of the stream. Colonel Twemlow's exhaustive study of the battlefield places Audley 300 yards (275 m) south of Hemphill Brook, west of Blore village, along a still extant hedge separating open heath to the north from fields to the south. The Burgundian chronicler Jean de Waurin describes how the Yorkists observed Lancastrian pennons beyond the stream, above '*une grant forest haye* [hedge]'. Twemlow's map depicts a mass of Lancastrian cavalry in the centre, quite close to Blore, screened by archers. They seem more likely to have started the battle on foot, cavalry having no defensive capability, and somewhat further west, although not necessarily across the modern main road as A.H. Burne believed. Five ranks deep, 6000–8000 Lancastrian infantry would occupy nearly three-quarters of a mile (1.2 km), sufficient to block both crossings and dominate the valley between them with archery.

Hemphill Brook, combined with the steep ascent out of the valley on the Drayton side, made a formidable defensive position, especially as Salisbury was outnumbered. A Yorkist source gave him only 3000 men against Audley's 8000 (Benet). The Lancastrian

Blore Heath

	Winners	*Losers*
Opponents	Yorkist	Lancastrian
Commanders	Richard Neville, Earl of Salisbury	James Touchet, Lord Audley (k)
Numbers	5000	6000–8000
Losses	56	2000

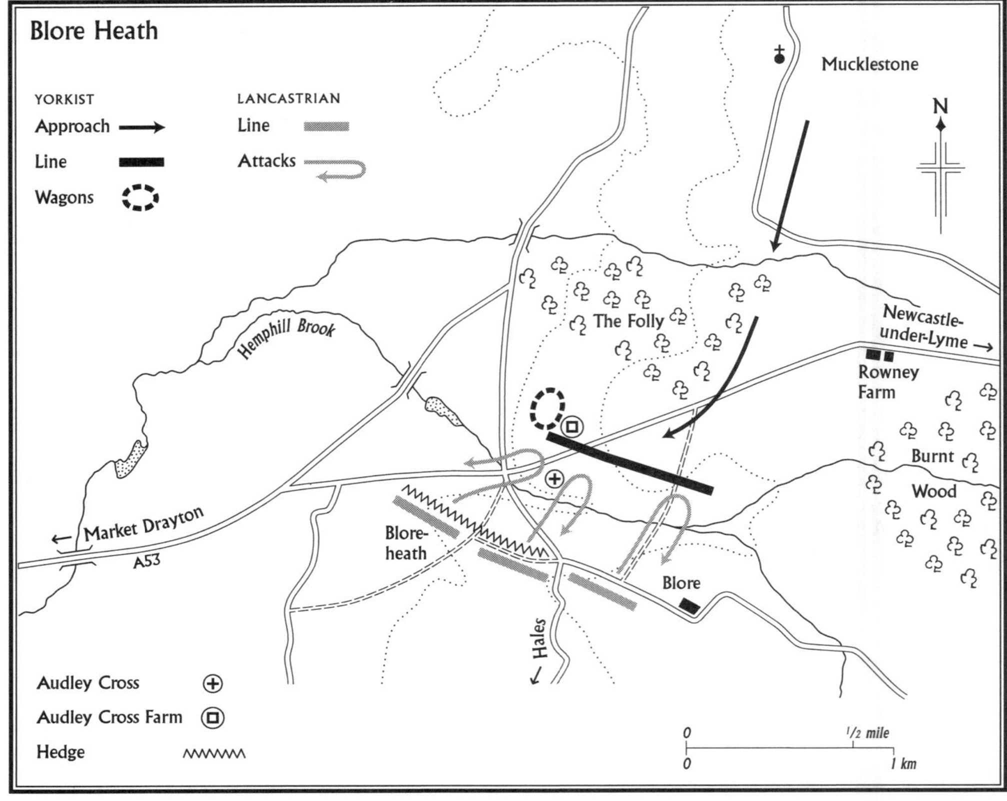

Act of Attainder against Salisbury alleged more: 'a grete multitude to the nombre of VM [5000] persones … arrayed in manere of warre, with their standards displaied'. Only the foreigner de Waurin gives the Yorkists 6000–7000 men. The prudent course for Salisbury was to form up across the old road, out of range of Audley's bowmen. The Yorkist left would rest on the boggy valley bottom; their right was protected by a wagon-laager near Audley Cross Farm on top of the hill. Rounhay Wood behind them, now reduced to The Folly and Burnt Wood, provided a lay-back position, in case of disaster. Neither side seems to have used cannon.

Most accounts of the battle are unnecessarily complicated. Tudor sources say the Lancastrians advanced after the Yorkists staged a false retreat, reoccupying their original line to shoot Audley's men down as they struggled across Hemphill

Directions

Follow the A53 east from Market Drayton towards Newcastle-under-Lyme. Turn right at Hemphill Brook along the front of Audley's initial position towards Blore village. Just after the right fork to Hales, turn left down a sunken footpath, the old main road. Continue across Hemphill Brook to the place of slaughter. Audley Cross is in a private field on the left.

Brook. No contemporary mentions any such manoeuvre. It seems more probable that Audley simply came on when Salisbury admitted his inferiority by stopping.

The Lancastrians certainly attacked, because Audley was killed on the far bank. Beyond that we know very little. De Waurin's narrative is not implausible: a three-stage assault, twice by cavalry, finally by 4000 dismounted troops. Each attack was driven off in detail, the cavalry losing heavily to archery, with many horses killed, before the infantry came to hand-strokes. Such an assault by successive echelons might be the natural consequence of a medieval army's three battles forming column, one behind another, to pass the stream. Audley seems to have died during the second mounted attack. After that the discouraged horsemen took no further part in the action, until 500 of them changed sides and rode down their own infantry to end the battle.

The contemporary London chronicler William Gregory says fighting continued all afternoon, from one until five. The Cheshire gentlemen suffered heavily. A royal pardon recognizing service at Blore Heath recorded 31 killed out of 66 names listed. The Yorkists claimed 2000 Lancastrian dead. According to tradition Hemphill Brook ran red with blood. Less plausible are tales that Margaret of Anjou watched from Mucklestone Church, behind the enemy position, reversing her horse's shoes to cover her escape. Yorkist casualties were possibly buried in a small oblong mound near Audley Cross Farm. Salisbury had cleared the road to Ludlow, but had only dispersed a fraction of the royal forces.

Ludford Bridge, 12 October 1459

England, Shropshire, LR137 SO5173

The Rout of Ludford dramatically illustrates Clausewitz's observation that 'Possible Engagements Are To Be Regarded As Real Ones Because Of Their Consequences'. Insufficiently bloody to attract Shakespeare's attention, the cannonade at Ludford Bridge is undeservedly obscure, for had the action been consummated, the outcome of the Wars of the Roses might have been quite different.

After Blore Heath, the Yorkist lords congregated at Ludlow in the Welsh Marches. No doubt they hoped to approach Henry VI in arms, as they had at St Albans in 1456, to plead their case. The Ludford Bridge campaign, however, exposed the narrowness of their support. When the 6 Yorkist peers neared Worcester in early October, they faced 20 in the royal camp. Worse still, Henry VI had taken the field himself, '*cum Wexillo in facie belli*', flying his banner in warlike style. Nobody wanted to fight the king in person, so the rebels retreated on the Duke of York's castle at Ludlow. A contemporary statement that 40,000 Lancastrians confronted 25,000 Yorkists is wild exaggeration, but the proportion may be right. Salisbury had several thousand survivors from Blore Heath, while Warwick added 500 men from the English garrison at Calais to York's local troops. The Lancastrians may have fielded twice as many.

Undeterred by autumnal rain the royal army followed up through Leominster, then north along the old switchback road through Richard's Castle and Overton to Ludford. Ludlow stands on high ground within a loop in the River Teme. Ludford is across the river to the south, between a steep forested hill on the west and gently sloping meadows to the east. Late on 12 October the Lancastrian host approached the Ludford bridgehead, 'albe the impediment of the ways and straitness, and by let of water, it was nigh even ere ye [Henry VI] might come to take ground convenable for your field' (Act of Attainder, November 1459).

The Yorkists had occupied a strong position: 'fortified their chosen ground, their carts with guns set before their battles, made their eskirmishes, [and] laid their embushments' (Attainder). The exact location of York's battery is uncertain, but the gunners would have enjoyed a good field of fire from the gentle rise south of Ludford House, between the

Ludford Bridge

	Winners	Losers
Opponents	Lancastrian	Yorkist
Commanders	Henry VI	Richard, Duke of York
	Margaret of Anjou	Richard Neville, Earl of Salisbury
		Richard Neville, Earl of Warwick
Numbers	*c.*12,000	6000–7000
Losses	none	none

main road and the river. The London chronicler William Gregory confirms the Yorkists had prepared 'a grete depe dyche and fortifyde it with gonnys, cartys, and stakys'. The Attainder's references to skirmishers and ambushes may be legal flummery, or reflect a more active defence. The Burgundian chronicler de Waurin refers to York 'hoping to find the king's company in disorder, but they did not do so, for the king's people held together'. Unable to catch the Lancastrians off balance before they deployed, the Yorkist contented themselves with firing cannon into the gloom.

Overnight Yorkist morale collapsed, despite their leaders pretending Henry VI had suddenly died, 'to make the people the less dread to take the field'. The cream of York's army was a detachment from the Calais garrison, the nearest equivalent to English regular troops. Their leader Andrew Trollope was Master Porter of Calais, foremost English soldier of the day. Unimpressed by Warwick's charade of masses for the departed king, the professionals withdrew their services. The game was up. During the night the Yorkist leaders 'stole away out of the field under colour they would have refreshed them awhile in the town of Ludlow' (Attainder). With a small following they fled unarmed into Wales, breaking the bridges behind them.

The decision was prudent, but disgraceful. It exposed York's followers to royal vengeance, and left Ludlow to the 'misrule of the king's gallants', who robbed the citizens and raped their women. In November the Parliament of Devils raised the stakes by attainting the rebel lords, stripping them of lands and titles. Margaret of Anjou was triumphant, while the Duke of York's political judgement was compromised. He fled to Dublin, but his eldest son, Edward, Earl of March, accompanied the Nevilles to Calais, forging a partnership with Warwick that would soon recoup Yorkist losses.

Directions

Head south out of Ludlow along the B4361. Turn left 1/4 mile (0.4 km) after Ludford Bridge along a farm track down to the river to the Yorkist position suggested above.

Northampton, 10 July 1460

England, Northamptonshire, LR152 SP7558–7658

The Battle of Northampton marked an intensification of the Wars of the Roses, the last occasion that negotiations preceded the fighting, or Yorkist lords protested personal loyalty to Henry VI. Soon afterwards the Duke of York lodged his own claim to the throne, converting a political struggle into a dynastic one.

The aftermath of the Rout of Ludford (see above) drove the exiled Yorkist leaders to further military action to regain their forfeited lands and titles. Late in June 1460 the earls of March, Salisbury and Warwick landed at Sandwich and bluffed their way into London, where the commons of Kent, Sussex and Surrey joined them in protest at extortionate Lancastrian taxes. Two days later, March and Warwick headed for the Midlands to confront Henry VI before he could assemble his forces. Seven bishops accompanied the rebel army, a curious comment upon ecclesiastical views of Henry VI's piety. Salisbury stayed behind to blockade the Tower of London, too important an arsenal to leave unguarded.

The Lancastrians had dug in south of the River Nene, facing the Yorkist line of approach along Watling Street: 'a strong and mighty field, in the meadows beside the nunnery [i.e. Delapré Abbey], armed and arrayed with guns, having the river at his [the king's] back' (*Davies's English Chronicle*). John of

Northampton

	Winners	*Losers*
Opponents	Yorkist	Lancastrian
Commanders	Edward, Earl of March Richard Neville, Earl of Warwick William Neville, Lord Fauconberg	Humphrey Stafford, Duke of Buckingham (k) Lord John Grey of Ruthin
Numbers	8000–12,000	c.4000
Losses	unknown	300–500

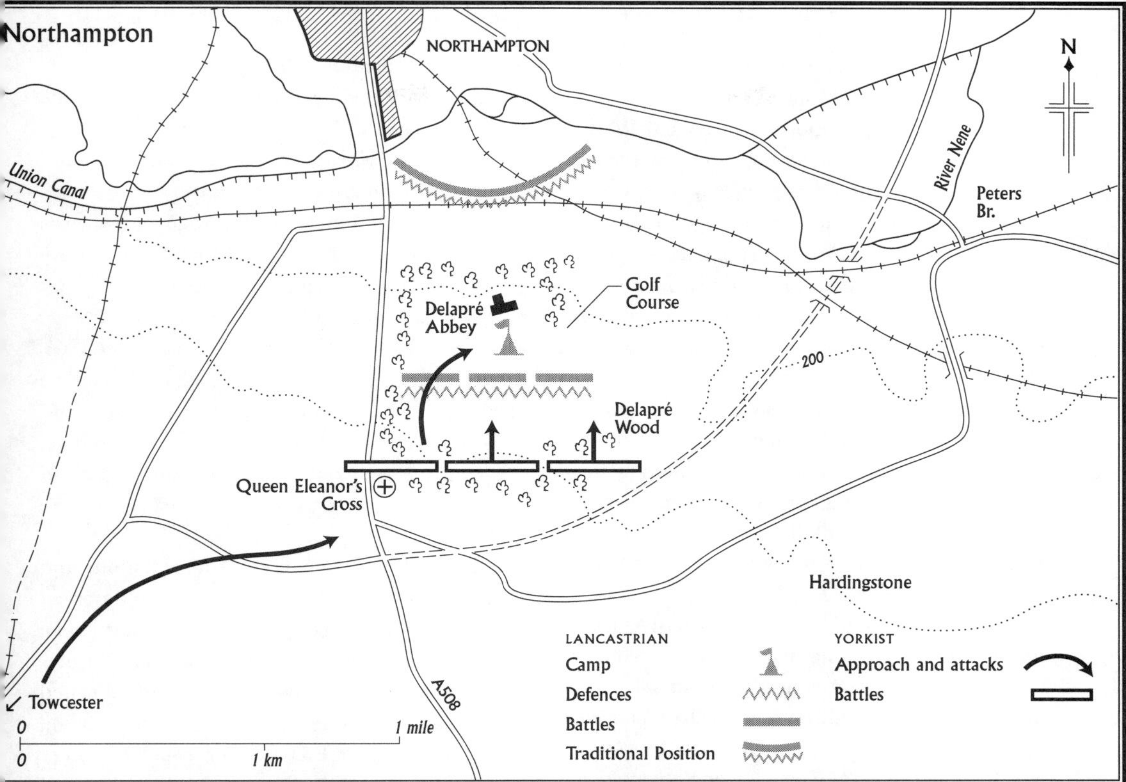

Whethamstede, a contemporary Abbot of St Albans, placed the Lancastrians southeast of Northampton, as did the Tudor historian Sir Edward Hall: 'in the newe fields, betweene Harsyngton [Hardingstone] and Sandifford [Sandford Mill, now St Peter's Bridge] ... with high bankes and deepe trenches'. John Benet also located the king forward of the river, between the village of Hardyngeston and the monastic house called de Pratis (i.e. Delapré). This agrees with the description of the Tudor antiquarian John Leland: 'on the Hille withoute the south Gate, where is a right goodly Crosse, caullid... the Queen's Cross'.

Despite this, traditional reconstructions put the royal camp by the river, with a good field of fire southwards across level tree-fringed meadows, up the gentle rise to the abbey and Queen Eleanor's Cross beyond. Even in the 1850s there were no traces of fieldworks here, and today the area is covered with railways, factories and the Grand Union Canal. Recent interpretations favour the golf course, between the A45 ring road and the abbey. This site is more accessible today, and agrees with the sources.

Directions

Approach Northampton along the A508 from Junction 15 of the M1. See Queen Eleanor's Cross on the right, before the entrance to the abbey grounds, where the fighting probably occurred. The traditional site is between the railway and the Nene, on the right just before crossing the bridge into Northampton.

Numbers are the usual puzzle. Benet claimed 20,000 Lancastrians against 40,000 Yorkists, symbolic values signifying a great many. Other sources give the Yorkists an advantage of two or three to one, including 'an infinite number of commons' (Whethamstede). De Waurin set the Lancastrian van at 1300 or 1400, implying an overall total of 4000. For once the Lancastrians had fewer peers: five against eight or more. They had plenty of firepower, the king's supporters having taken guns from the

Tower of London, as insurance against another surprise like First St Albans.

The Yorkists are thought to have left Watling Street at Towcester, advancing on Northampton from the southwest. Their final approach was along the A508 London Road, turning right before they reached the royal camp to form up in the area of the modern Delapré Wood. Mutual distrust rendered mediation hopeless. The Bishop of Salisbury approached his sovereign under armed escort, 'for suerte of oure persones, for they thet beth aboute the kyng bythe nat oure frendes' (*Davies's Chronicle*). Confident in his fortifications and engines of war, Henry VI's commander-in-chief Buckingham refused to allow Warwick near the king: 'and yef he come he shalle dye'. Warwick was equally obdurate, insisting he would speak with Henry at two in the afternoon, 'or elles dye in the feeld'.

Promptly at 2 p.m. March and Warwick 'let cry through the field that no man should lay hands on the king, ne on the common people, but only on the lords, knights, and squires: then the trumpets blew up, and both hosts countered and fought together half an hour' (*Davies's Chronicle*). The Yorkists fought in the usual three divisions under March, Warwick and their uncle 'little Fauconberg ... a knight of great reverence'. John of Whethamstede described them attacking simultaneously but separately, at different points of the defences. Presumably the Yorkists hoped to overwhelm their overextended opponents with superior numbers. The approach was slippery, obstructed with stakes and small trees cut down as abattis. However, it was treachery not tactics that won the day.

Lord Grey of Ruthin, commanding the Lancastrian van, their rightmost battle, 'brake the feelde and came to the erles party' (*Davies's Chronicle*). The Neville chronicler confirms the king lost the field through Lord Grey's treachery. Whethamstede gave more detail: 'the squadrons coming to the ditch before the rampart and wanting to climb over it, which they could not do quickly because of the height ... Lord Grey met them with his troops and, holding out their right hand, they pulled them ... into the fortified camp'. Grey's motives are obscure, but de Waurin implies premeditation, alleging Warwick had issued orders to spare anyone wearing '*le ravestoc noue*', the Ruthin badge of a black ragged staff.

The betrayal was doubly fatal to the Lancastrians. Grey's defection threw them instantly off balance, and cut them off from the bridge. Many drowned as they fled, the river being unusually full. Royal artillery proved useless, 'for that day was so great rain, that the guns lay in deep water, and so were *queynt* [quenched] and might not be shot' (*Davies's Chronicle*). The Kentishmen killed Buckingham beside the king's tent, along with that bane of the Nevilles, Lord Egremont. As at First St Albans, the Yorkists' sudden irruption overran royal headquarters before it could react. Beyond nobles and gentry, casualties were slight.

Henry VI was once more captured, alone and solitary. The victors treated him with ill-deserved respect, but this time the Duke of York intended more than a reprise of earlier protectorates. Three times he had held and lost power. When York returned from Ireland he asserted a claim to the throne based on his descent from Edward III through Lionel of Clarence, a better hereditary claim than Henry of Lancaster's. The war had entered a new and more dangerous stage.

Wakefield, 30–31 December 1460

England, West Yorkshire, LR110 SE3318–3419

Wakefield was a disaster for the Yorkists, but one that paradoxically ensured their ultimate victory. The Lancastrians took bloody revenge for First St Albans and Northampton, bringing more deadly opponents to the fore.

Richard of York's return from Ireland after Northampton (see above) resembled a king's progress. Parliament would neither deny nor accept his royal pretensions, but compromised, offering York the throne after Henry VI's death. Margaret of Anjou escaped north, and rallied Lancastrian supporters in defence of her son's rights. Henry, Duke of Somerset,

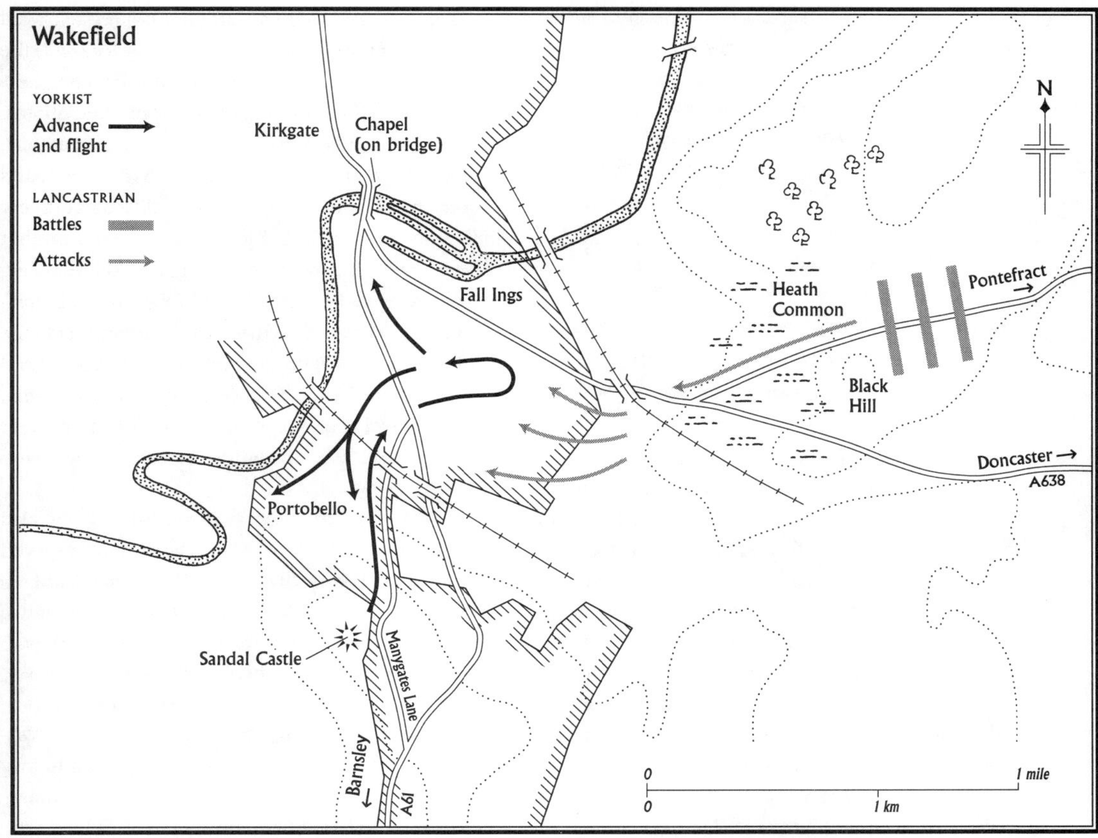

whose father had died at First St Albans, joined the Percys in Yorkshire with forces from southwest England, a double threat the Yorkists could not ignore Somerset set off northwards with the Earl of Salisbury on 9 December 1460. Luckily for the younger generation of Yorkists, the Earl of March went to rally support in the Welsh Marches; Warwick remained in London to guard the king.

York and Salisbury reached Sandal Castle, 2 miles (3 km) south of Wakefield, just before Christmas. Thoroughly slighted during the 1640s, only the massive mound of the keep and the towers' footings reveal Sandal Castle's former strength. The Lancastrians lay at Pontefract, 8 miles (13 km) east, with immensely superior numbers, 15,000–20,000 according to contemporary estimates.

Sandal Castle stands on a slight eminence that slopes gradually north towards Wakefield, beyond the winding River Calder, crossed since the 1350s by a stone bridge. The battle's nearest contemporary location is simply '*apud Wakefelde*', but John Leland, the Tudor antiquary, recorded 'a sore Battel fought in the South Feeldes by this bridge'. Subsequently enclosed and built over, the battlefield was a large open tract of meadowland known as Wakefield Green, between bridge and castle. Richard Brooke,

Directions

See Sandal Castle down a minor road off the A61 at Sandal Magna. Follow the lane north past the Duke of York's monument on the left to rejoin the A61 in the now built-up battle area. Continue north to the 14th-century chapel on Wakefield Bridge, incorrectly said to commemorate the battle.

Wakefield

	Winners	*Losers*
Opponents	Lancastrian	Yorkist
Commanders	Henry Beaufort, Duke of Somerset	Richard, Duke of York (k)
	Henry Percy, Earl of Northumberland	Richard Neville, Earl of Salisbury (k)
	Lord John Clifford	
Numbers	15,000	5000–6000
Losses	unknown	1000–2000

who saw the area before it was built over, placed the fighting half a mile (0.8 km) south of the bridge near the turnpike road, now the A61, extending across the bend in the Calder between Portobello to the west and Fall Ings on the Doncaster Road to the east. Sir Edward Hall, grandson of York's adviser Sir David Hall, placed York's death in 'the plain ground between his castle and the town'. Leland stated that York's son, Edmund, Earl of Rutland, was 'slayne a litle above the Barres beyond the Bridge going up into the Toune'. Despite this weight of opinion, many reconstructions place the battle west of Sandal, remote from either town or bridge.

The Lancastrians' simplest plan was to march directly from Pontefract and approach Wakefield from the east, moving south of the Calder in column of divisions, screened by Black Hill. The *Victoria County History* took this line, disposing the Lancastrians on the common northeast of the castle, 'with their wings skilfully hidden'. Lord Clifford commanded the van, followed by Somerset and Northumberland, all three with scores to settle. Queen Margaret was not present, being in Scotland. The mystery of why the Yorkists rode out against vastly superior numbers in flat open country will never be resolved. Dead men tell no tales, while unsympathetic historians dismiss Wakefield as York's final miscalculation. The puzzle has inspired many ingenious theories, starting with de Waurin's tale of Yorkist renegades masquerading as Neville reinforcements to lure the '*sage et ymaginatif*' Salisbury into the open. The tale must come from Warwick, who was not present, and begs more questions than it resolves.

Other sources present a simpler story. The Lancastrians chose their moment, and took the Yorkists by surprise: 'The Duke of Somerset came as if suddenly upon them' (John Benet); 'When they saw a convenient time ... the last day of December they fell upon the said Duke Richard ...' (*Davies's English Chronicle*). John of Whethamstede, Abbot of St Albans, alleged the Lancastrians broke a truce. Lulled into a false sense of security, the Yorkists were not under arms, but wandered about the country '*pro cumulandis victualibus*'. The Neville chronicle confirms their dispersal in search of food. The duke may have only seen Clifford's vanguard, and gone out to cover his foragers' withdrawal.

Once in the open, the Yorkists were exposed to all three enemy divisions, who deployed successively on Clifford's left: 'Crushing them by the weight of their numbers, they forced many to flee the field' (Whethamstede). The Yorkists would naturally flee west. The greatest slaughter occurred on the banks of the Calder, where workmen found human bones and ironwork while digging the foundations of Portobello House in 1825. Other relics have been found further east, near the Pontefract road. Contemporary estimates of losses among the common soldiery are: 700, about 1000 or 2000, inflated by Tudor historians to 2800.

The Duke of York was slain on the field, or more accurately just west of Manygates Lane, known also as Cock and Bottle Lane. For many years willow trees and a cross in a triangular fenced enclosure marked the spot. Today a 19th-century monument carved with roses and the duke's likeness stands in the grounds of an infants' school. Rutland sought shelter in a poor woman's house in Wakefield near the junction of Kirkgate and Park Street, 'and she for fear shut the door and the erle was killed'. His killer was Clifford, who commanded the Lancastrian van or right wing, conveniently placed to chase fugitives across the bridge. Shakespeare's account of Clifford's brutal dispatch of a 12-year-old boy is sentimental tosh. Rutland was an 18-year-old man-at-arms, and probably gave a good account of himself. Salisbury was captured and held for ransom, but local enemies beheaded him next day at Pontefract.

The triumphant Lancastrians displayed the Yorkist leaders' heads on the Micklegate at York, the duke sporting a paper crown. Lancastrian vindictiveness is unsurprising, but the disaster struck terror into southern England. Observers prophesied greater ruin 'than witnessed for the last thousand years'. However, the Lancastrians now had to deal with a younger and more dangerous generation of Yorkist leaders: the earls of March and Warwick.

Mortimer's Cross, *c.*3 February 1461

England, Herefordshire, LR149 SO4262–63

Military details of Mortimer's Cross are almost entirely lost, except that it began Edward IV's remarkable string of victories. Contemporaries noticed it mainly for the rare meteorological phenomenon known as a parhelion (multiple images of the sun) that accompanied it, additional proof of divine favour for the victors.

Edward, Earl of March was recruiting in the Welsh Marches when his father Richard of York was killed at Wakefield (see above). Edward's response was to exploit his central position between the main Lancastrian army in the North and an ill-found detachment in South Wales to destroy the latter in detail. James Butler, Earl of Wiltshire and Ormond, had joined Jasper Tudor at Pembroke with a mixed bag of Irish, Breton and French mercenaries. Irish troops were notoriously ill armed, while few Breton nobility had plate armour or even gauntlets, essential accessories when fighting with poleaxes. Their leader was of doubtful courage; Wiltshire was the foremost escapologist of the day, fleeing from every battle in which he fought.

Reconstructions of Mortimer's Cross generally follow a single contemporary source, used by the Tudor historian Sir Edward Hall, that says Edward kept Christmas 1460 at Gloucester. From this he is deduced to have dashed northwards to intercept an unexpected Lancastrian advance from Presteigne, engaging superior numbers with his back against the River Lugg. The idea beggars belief. Edward was the most successful commander of the war, and had recently seen the dangers of such a deployment at Northampton (see above). The Yorkists had good intelligence of Jasper's movements, and plenty of time for countermeasures.

Most contemporary sources say Edward heard of his father's death while he was at Shrewsbury, 60 miles (100 km) to the north of Gloucester: 'and from thence went to Wales, where at Candlemas, he had a battle at Mortimer's Cross' (*Brut*). Candlemas was 2 February, a major feast to which events of the 3rd easily became attached. The Neville chronicle describes the action as '*bellum prope Wigmore apud Mortimer Crose*', suggesting Edward approached from Wigmore Castle, 3 miles (5 km) north of Mortimer's Cross. Yorkist forces there would be well placed to block a Lancastrian advance, either across the mountains from the west via Presteigne, or up the Roman road from Hereford, yet another Watling Street.

Yorkist garrisons and freezing weather make the mountain route unlikely. Castles at Builth and Radnor belonged to the earls of Warwick and March, and the road climbs to nearly 1250 feet (380 m) above sea level. The parhelion phenomenon, which is caused by ice crystals in the atmosphere, indicates extreme cold. If Jasper Tudor wished to save his ill-clad troops, he would have followed the route through Brecon and Hay-on-Wye (maximum altitude

Mortimer's Cross

	Winners	*Losers*
Opponents	Yorkist	Lancastrian
Commanders	Edward, Earl of March	Jasper Tudor, Earl of Pembroke James Butler, Earl of Wiltshire Owen Tudor (x)
Numbers	*c.*2000	2000–3000
Losses	unknown	unknown

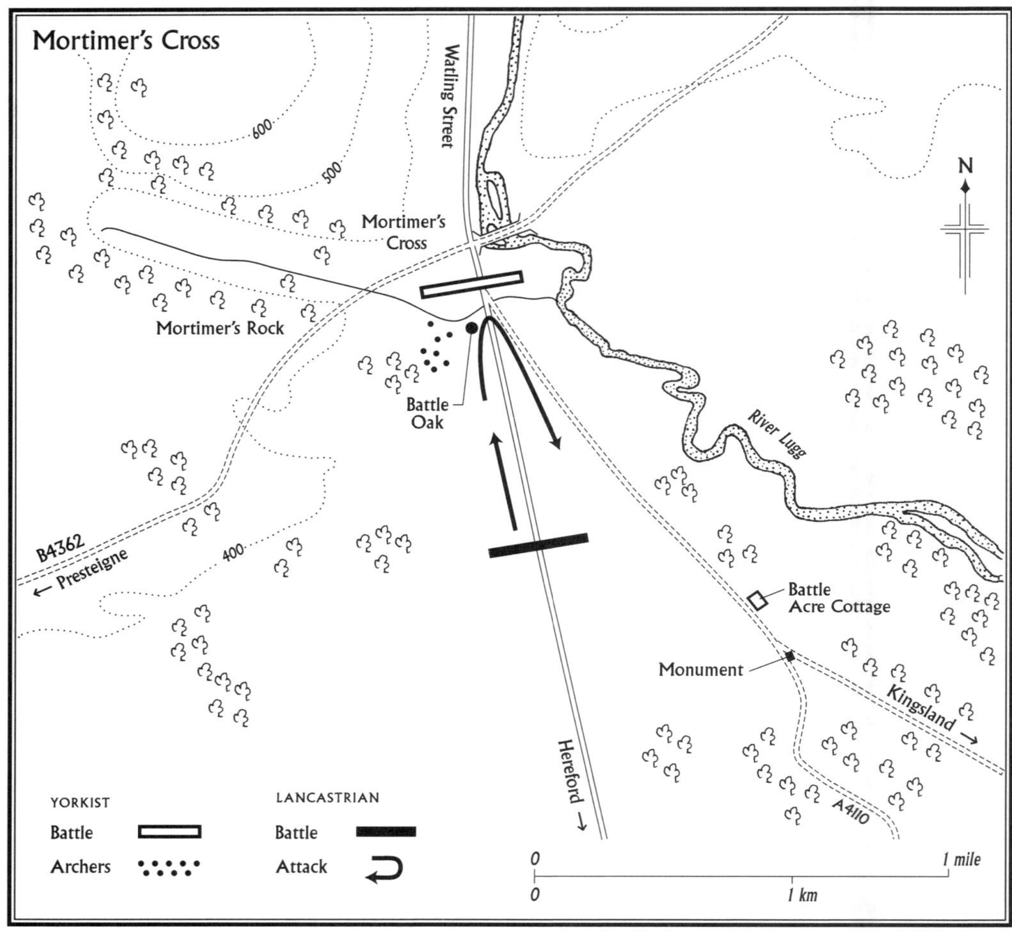

886 feet/270 m). His subsequent approach from the south would have given the opposing troops an optimum view of the sun's unusual behaviour, which they would not have enjoyed had they been facing west.

Mortimer's Cross is ideally suited to meeting an enemy advancing from Brecon. The River Lugg flows north to south, cutting through the limestone hills that define the northern edge of the battle area. Level ground extends southwards, bounded by the river on the east, and more high ground at Mortimer's Rock (456 feet/139 m) on the west. Quite open at the time of the battle, the terrain is now split up by hedged enclosures. An admirable defensive position runs east–west through the junction of Watling Street and the main road, just south of the cross itself. About 500 yards (460 m) across, the site would fit the limited numbers engaged; its flanks rest on natural features preventing anything except a frontal attack, and a stream flows across its front. Nearby place-names are suggestive: the rotten stump of 'Battle Oak' and 'Blue Mantle Cottage', title of a royal herald. Battle

Directions

Take the A44 west from Leominster, turning right at Lowton's Cross onto the A4110. See the 18th-century monument at Kingsland (SO4361). The Yorkist position is south of and parallel to the B4362 to Presteigne.

Acre Cottage further south may recall the Lancastrian bivouac, or their last stand. Victorian ploughmen found ironwork nearby, said to resemble broken swords.

Mortimer's Cross was a small battle. Only three magnates were present. A clue to Yorkist strength is the 2000 marchers they raised for a private campaign in 1456. Jasper may have had more, but not the 8000 attributed to him by the source that gave Edward 51,000. Its result is unsurprising. The Lancastrians were worse equipped, communicated in five different languages, and had just marched 110 miles (176 km) in freezing winter weather. The Yorkists were on home ground, rested and well fed.

The best account of the day viewed the battle as a religious not a military occasion: 'And so by his grace, he had the victory of his enemies, and put the two earls to flight, and slew of the Welshmen to the number of 4,000' (*Davies's English Chronicle*). Tactical details come from an Elizabethan poem:

> The Earl of Ormond ... came in the vanguard
> with his Irishmen
> With darts and skains [daggers] ...
> And as they fall still make their places good.
> That it amazed the Marchers to behold
> Men so ill armed, upon their bows so bold.
>
> Michael Drayton, 'The Miseries of Queen Margaret'

Yorkist archers, echeloned on the hillside, would have shot their ill-protected attackers to pieces, driving them sideways upon their comrades in the centre. Disorder and massacre would commence, as Yorkist men-at-arms wheeled left, pushing survivors of the barrage against the riverbank and into the stream. A *barbute*-style helmet found downstream shows at least one 15th-century soldier got wet.

Quoted casualties of 3000–4000 probably exceed total combatants, although Lancastrian losses may have approached 50 per cent, especially among the mercenaries. Wiltshire got away as usual, but Pembroke's father Owen Tudor was executed at Hereford with eight other Lancastrian captains. Edward had secured his rear with minimal damage to his own forces.

St Albans (II), Shrove Tuesday, 17 February 1461

England, Hertfordshire, LR166 TL1508

Second St Albans revealed a tactical sophistication rarely associated with medieval armies. The Yorkists prepared elaborate defences over a wide frontage, which the Lancastrians turned by a night approach that ended, not with the usual frontal assault, but a series of outflanking movements. Warwick was beaten, but his propaganda cheated Queen Margaret of her victory.

The Lancastrian success at Wakefield (see above) opened the way for them to capture London and rescue Henry VI, a Yorkist prisoner since Northampton (April 1460). The Lancastrian army swept south 'like a whirlwind', down Ermine Street to Royston, 'covering the whole surface of the earth just like so many locusts' (*Croyland Chronicle*). Left to protect London and the king, Warwick was unwilling to move far from his base. He occupied a covering position at St Albans, astride Watling Street. St Albans is west of the direct Lancastrian route along the Great North Road, but Warwick must have had wind of their plans. At Royston Margaret's army swung southwest down the Icknield Way to Dunstable, 12 miles (19 km) northwest of St Albans and also on Watling Street. There the Lancastrians surprised a Yorkist outpost, none of whom escaped to give warning.

Warwick 'took his field beside a little town called Sandridge not far from St Albans, in a place called Nomansland' (*Davies's English Chronicle*). The destruc-

St Albans (II)

	Winners	*Losers*
Opponents	Lancastrian	Yorkist
Commanders	Margaret of Anjou Sir Andrew Trollope (w)	Richard Neville, Earl of Warwick
Numbers	15,000–20,000	25,000
Losses	*c.*1000	*c.*2000

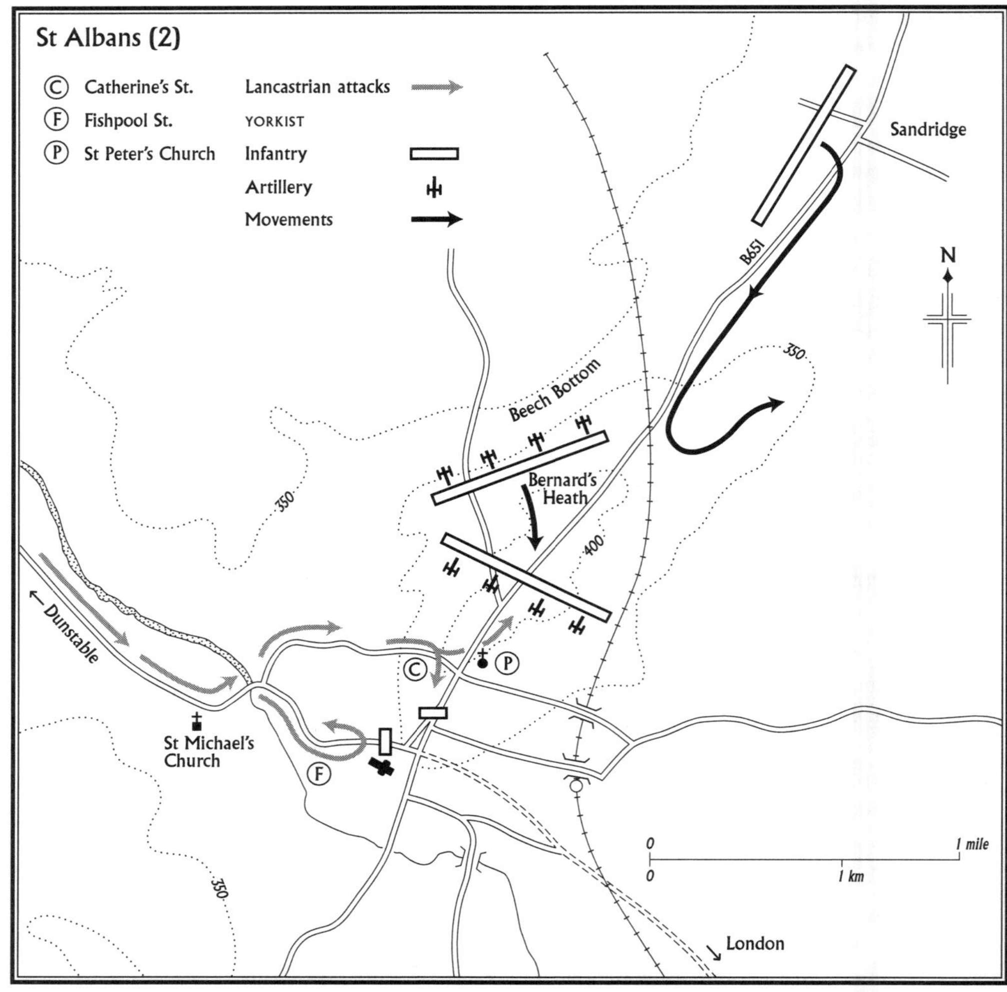

tion of his detachment at Dunstable left Warwick off-balance. Most of his army was spread out along the Sandridge road back to St Albans, 3 miles (5 km) away, making an unusually broad frontage for the time. Warwick strengthened his line with a variety of ordnance, described by William Gregory, who served at St Albans: nets bristling with nails at every other knot; portable shields or pavises; lattice-work fences that unfolded to block gaps in hedges, and numerous caltrops, spiked devices to lame horses. A.H. Burne thought Warwick deployed this impressive armoury along the ancient earthwork that runs

Directions

From the Clock Tower and the site of the Great Cross (demolished 1701), walk west along Fishpool Street to see Watling Street beyond the River Ver. Return along the Lancastrians' second line of advance, past the north end of Branch Road, up Folly Lane and Catherine Street into St Peter's. Turn left up Bowgate to Bernard's Heath. A hundred years ago this was open common, some strips of which remain along the Sandridge road (B651). Beech Bottom crosses Valley Road, downhill on the left.

along Beech Bottom, parallel to the Sandridge road.

The numerical balance between the armies is uncertain. Twelve Lancastrian peers turned out, against nine Yorkists, but the lack of a standard for baronial retinues makes this a poor basis for comparison. The Neville chronicle appears to claim the Lancastrians fielded 80,000 men, unless 'iiii.xx.milia' means four and twenty thousand, comparable with the 25,000 Yorkists given by the Abbot of St Albans. Whatever the totals, Gregory attributed the victory to a few professionals: 'The substance that gate the field were household men and feed men. I ween there were not 5000 men that fought in the Queen's party, for the most part of Northern men fled away.'

Margaret of Anjou drove her army on through the night of 16–17 February. Such operations were unusual, but even in the dark her troops could follow the old Roman road to St Michael's, on the outskirts of town. Strung out in a long thin column, the Lancastrians were slow to make their presence felt. Their initial dawn attack was unsuccessful. Advancing up Fishpool and George Street near Queen Eleanor's Great Cross, they met a handful of Yorkist archers, '*paucos arcitenentes*', who swept the head of the column with arrows.

Beaten back to the eastern outskirts of the town, the Lancastrians tried again further left. Scouts found a way through the fields into Catherine Street, and Lancastrian troops poured into St Peter's Street near the church, where they fought some more Yorkist infantry. After an exchange of casualties the Lancastrians pushed still further left, up Bowgate towards Barnet or Bernard's Heath, where they found more significant opposition. Perhaps 4000–5000 of Warwick's left wing had left their prepared positions along Beech Bottom and formed up across the road to meet the Lancastrian outflanking movement.

The struggle on the heath lasted some time, as the Lancastrians wore the Yorkists down. The abbot attributed this to the Northerners' personal staying power, but it seems more likely they were continually reinforced, while Warwick failed to commit his main body. Abbot John reckoned 20,000 Yorkists never saw action. Gregory blamed the change of plan in the middle of a battle: 'Like unwise men [the Yorkists] brake their array and took another, and ere that they were all sette ... the Queen's party was at hand with them in the town ... and then all thing was to seek and out of order ...' The artillery was particularly inflexible: 'Ere the gunners and borgeners [Burgundian handgunners] could level their guns they were busily fighting and many a gynne [engine] of war was ordained that stood in little avail or nought.' If Warwick tried to commit fresh troops, he was prevented 'by undisposition of the people ... that would not be guided nor governed by their captains' (*Davies's Chronicle*).

Overwhelmed by numbers, Warwick's unsupported left wing eventually broke, scattering among the surrounding thickets. Victorious Lancastrians took horse and rode them down, killing and capturing many. Unwilling to face a night in the open near the buoyant Lancastrians, the remaining Yorkists slipped away in the dark. Low officer casualties show the armies had not been closely engaged. Contemporary totals for both sides include: 1916, 2000, 'well nigh 3000', 3500 and '*quasi iiij milia*'. The higher numbers suggest double counting. Henry VI, who spent the battle under a tree laughing at the discomfiture of his 'allies' was mislaid, and recaptured by his 'friends'. They showed their opinion of royal authority by murdering his escort, two Yorkist knights who had naively accepted their king's guarantee of safety.

London lay open to the victorious Lancastrians. Lurid reports of their misdeeds on the march south, however, persuaded the citizens to deny Margaret entry. She hesitated, falling back to Dunstable, and then York. And that, remarked the Neville chronicler, was the destruction of King Henry and his queen, for had they come to London with their army, they would have had everything at their will.

Ferrybridge, Saturday 28 March 1461

England, West Yorkshire, LR105 SE4824

Towton (Palm Sunday Field), **29 March 1461**

England, North Yorkshire, LR105 SE4737–39

The climactic action of the Wars of the Roses attracts superlatives as dead knights attract crows in a ballad. The biggest, bloodiest, longest, coldest battle of the war, Towton is also among the worst documented. Little certain information exists except for locality, pinpointed by the Act of Attainder passed on the losers: 'a feld between the Townes of Shirbourne in Elmett, and Tadcastre, in the seid shire of York, called Saxtonfeld and Tawtonfeeld'. No eyewitness accounts survive, as if contemporaries were stunned by the horror of the event. Sir Edward Hall's account appeared 80 years later, and enjoys an undeserved influence. Geographically challenged contemporaries ran several distinct fights together: an advanced guard action at Ferrybridge, the Lancastrian withdrawal, and the main encounter at Towton next day.

The English crown hung in the balance in February 1461. Edward, Earl of March, the Yorkist claimant, had destroyed a Lancastrian army at Mortimer's Cross, but the main Lancastrian host had beaten the Earl of Warwick at St Albans and freed Henry VI. Unwilling to storm London, the king and queen retreated to York, allowing March and Warwick to reoccupy the capital 'with a great power of men, but few of name'. Their loss of the king's person forced the Yorkists onto the offensive. Anti-Lancastrian lords agreed to make a king of their own, accepting March as heir to Richard of York, killed at Wakefield (December 1460). Edward was proclaimed king on 4 March, in a secular ceremony. Full coronation was postponed, wrote the papal legate, 'until he has annihilated the other king ... and among other things exacted the vengeance due for the slaughter of his father'. Edward IV had to take the field at once, before support began to waver.

The numbers engaged in the Towton campaign are a vexed question. Edward IV, or someone on his council, had a knack for mobilizing troops. Yorkist sources speak of 'a countless multitude flocking to him', allegedly 200,000 fighting men, '*ducentis milibus hominum bellatorum*'. Such figures, 10 per cent of England's population, are unlikely. Needing over 100 miles (160 km) of road space, they would have starved before they reached Yorkshire. Such estimates do show that contemporaries considered Towton much larger than Second St Albans. If Edward IV deployed twice the contemporary estimates for St Albans, he would have had 50,000 at Towton, an estimate consistent with an alleged payroll figure of 48,640. However, the document has vanished, and may never have existed. Most troops were paid by local authorities, not by the crown.

The Lancastrians are usually said to have outnumbered the Yorkists, with 60,000 men, a figure based on no evidence apart from Warwick's improbable propaganda. Edward IV controlled the richest and most populous parts of the country. The enemy had shot their bolt at St Albans, and could only draw replacements from a restricted area, with limited population. Some historians view even the lowest contemporary estimates of 20,000 a side as too high, approaching the numbers known to have fought at Marston Moor (1644), following a population explosion and a military revolution. The one certainty about the Towton armies is that they were large for their day, and involved half the political establishment: 8 Yorkist peers versus 19 Lancastrian, all intent on ending the chaos of the preceding decade.

Southern chroniclers confused the events of 27–29 March, subsuming two or three days fighting under the name of 'Feurbirga'. The opposed river crossing at Ferrybridge was quite separate from Towton, an essential prelude to the final showdown. The Lancastrians may have hoped to defend the River Aire, but imposed trifling delay on the advancing Yorkists: 'When the forepríckers [scouts] came to Ferrybridge there was a great skirmish ... And thereupon they advanced themselves until they came to Towton ... awaiting the residue of their company' (*Hearne Fragment*). The Burgundian chronicler de Waurin confirms a bitter afternoon's fighting either side of Ferrybridge, costing 3000 casualties altogether. Edward IV reinforced his hard-pressed scouts and forced a passage, described by Warwick's brother George, Archbishop of York: 'Our adversaries had broken the bridge ... and were strongly posted on the other side, so that our men could only cross by a narrow way, which they had made themselves ... But our men forced a way by the sword, and many were slain on both sides.' Warwick got an arrow in the leg. Edward dismounted to lead the attack on foot: '*sic pugnavit rex in pede*', as John Benet put it. Meanwhile Lord Fauconberg turned the Lancastrian line, crossing upstream at Castleford. Some of the defenders were killed as they fled. Clifford was among them, shot in the face and tumbled into a common grave at Dintingdale, almost in sight of the Lancastrian main body.

The Lancastrian host assembled on the low massif that rises above the flat Yorkshire plain south of Tadcaster between the villages of Saxton and Towton. On the south, towards the Yorkists, a gentle upwards slope begins a quarter of a mile (0.4 km) north of Saxton, rising to a narrow plateau that continues north beyond Towton. A mile (1.6 km) from Tadcaster the road descends rapidly to level meadows by the River Cock, marked by the Ordnance Survey as Cock Beck. This Cock Beck is more a large stream than a river: 10 feet (3 m) across, a couple of feet (0.6 m) deep with a firm bottom, its 3-foot (1-m) banks make it a dangerous obstacle. Eastward the massif slopes gently down to level poorly drained ground beyond the modern main road. Westwards the plateau terminates abruptly, plunging down to a narrow belt of meadow beside the Cock. A considerable depression, Towtondale, crosses the plateau from east to west, between the two villages. Westwards the hollow deepens into a re-entrant predictably known as Bloody Meadow. The Lancastrians stood north of Towtondale, their right anchored on bluffs above the re-entrant. As the Yorkists came up they naturally took station facing them along the opposite side of the dip.

Attempts to recreate orders of battle are speculative. Nobody knows into how many battles the armies were divided, or whether they were in line or column. Both sides can be assumed to have put archers in front, but there are no references to cannon. Neither missile weapon could have been much use as it snowed continually, soaking bowstrings and gunpowder, blinding archers and gunners. A Lancastrian ambush party features in most reconstructions, but not in the sources. Its supposed forming-up area in Castle Hill Wood is a death trap: halfway down a steep slope, encircled by Cock Beck on three sides, the only exit through enemy lines.

The only tactical certainty is that while the Lancastrians were concentrated on the field, about a third of the Yorkists had not arrived at dawn of Palm Sunday. Their rearward spent the night south of the Aire, perhaps because its leader Norfolk was sick, perhaps because the rest of the army was still defiling across Ferrybridge. Initially the Lancastrians could have outnumbered the Yorkists three-to-two. Depending how far the armies extended down the eastern slope, they occupied 1000–1300 yards (900–1200 m).

Ferrybridge

	Winners	*Losers*
Opponents	Yorkist	Lancastrian
Commanders	Edward IV	Lord John Clifford (k)
Numbers	unknown	*c.*500

Towton

	Winners	*Losers*
Opponents	Yorkist	Lancastrian
Commanders	Edward IV Richard Neville, Earl of Warwick William Neville, Lord Fauconberg John Mowbray, Duke of Norfolk	Henry Beaufort, Duke of Somerset Henry Percy, Earl of Northumberland (k)
Numbers	*c.*20,000	*c.*20,000
Losses	unknown	unknown

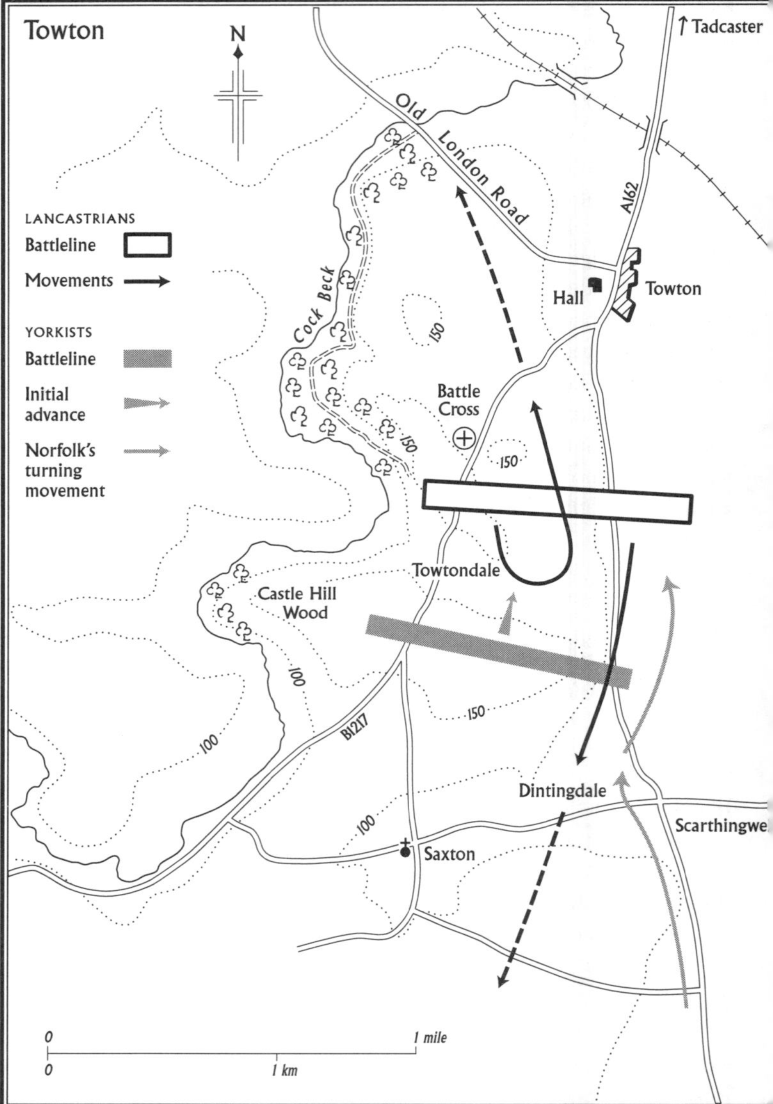

Directions

Towton *The battlefield is west of the A162 Ferrybridge–Tadcaster road. Turn left onto a minor road at Scarthingwell, and bear right through Saxton up to the battlefield. See Lord Dacre's grave in Saxton Churchyard. His cross on the battlefield, beside the B1217, marks the Lancastrian start line. Continue through Towton along Old London Road to Cock Beck.*

Depth would vary with the numbers present, between 9 and 13 ranks respectively for the initial Yorkist and Lancastrian battle lines, allowing one pace per file as at Dupplin Muir (1332).

Everyone agrees Towton was unusually protracted: George Neville's official account described 'a great conflict, which began with the rising of the sun, and lasted until the 10th hour of the night'. Another account seems to describe a night action: 'About four of the clock the two battles joined and fought all night till on the morrow in the afternoon' (*Hearne Fragment*). A better interpretation of 'four of the clock at night' might be 4 a.m. on Palm Sunday, when it was still dark. There is a tendency to exaggerate the battle's duration. One correspondent claimed fighting went on for a day and a half; another that it commenced on Sunday at prime (6 a.m.) and lasted until midday on Tuesday.

It seems likely the battle started at first light with skirmishing between the opposing archers. Hall's old soldier's tale of Yorkist bowmen shooting downwind in a snowstorm to tempt the other side into wasting their arrows presumably derives from this phase. As at Shrewsbury, 'The archers began the battle, but when their arrows were spent the matter was dealt with hand strokes' (Polydore Vergil). The Yorkists had no incentive to force the issue until their rearward arrived. The head of Norfolk's column would come level with Saxton about 9 a.m. if it left Ferrybridge at dawn, requiring another hour or two to move into line. At that point, about 11 a.m., A.H. Burne reckoned the Lancastrians attacked, before they lost their numerical edge. A Yorkist balladeer supports Burne's timing:

> On Palm Sunday, after the noon, they met us in the field;
> Within an hour they were right fain to flee ...

De Waurin, who spoke with Warwick and other veterans, gives the only detailed account of the Lancastrian attack, which may have been on horseback. Edward IV was encouraging his troops when he saw Henry VI's banner advance. He dismounted, and after some final words, placed himself behind his own banner to direct operations. The Lancastrian charge was highly successful, breaking the men-at-arms opposite them and chasing them 11 miles (18 km). The success was incomplete, however: 'They thought ... Northumberland had charged on the other side, unfortunately he had not done so ... ' Edward had time to rally his men, fighting like 'a new Hector, another Achilles'. The sycophancy need not have been undiluted with truth: Edward's skeleton was 6 foot 3½ inches (1.89 m) tall, a fearsome height for the time.

The battle degenerated into a slogging match, 'a very hard fought battle, the result remaining doubtful during the whole of the day' (Richard Beauchamp, Bishop of Salisbury). The decisive moment was Norfolk's arrival 'with a fresh band of good men' (*Hearne Fragment*). By common assumption they turned the Lancastrian left flank, insufficiently protected by boggy ground beyond the main road. The numerically equal Yorkists now pushed the Lancastrians back across the plateau, but 'Ever the northern men they saw or perceived any advantage [they] returned again, and fought with their enemies to the great loss of both parties.'

Disaster came at the northern end of the massif, where the old London Road descends steeply to Cock Beck, entangling the Lancastrian centre and right in a confused heap. As in all medieval battles, slaughter followed the collapse of the fighting line. Many were killed as they stumbled across a stream choked with their fallen friends. The Croyland chronicler wrote of heaps of bodies, a common feature of medieval battles, while 'the blood of the slain, intermingled with the snow ... ran in horrible wise down the furrows and ditches'.

The official death toll was 28,000, bodies covering an area three or four furlongs (600–800 m) across and six miles (10 km) long, further than after Shrewsbury. Sometimes the official figure is inflated to 38,000, nearly twice the fatalities suffered on the British Army's blackest day at the start of the Somme offensive in 1916, a comparison that should inspire scepticism. A more credible estimate is the Neville chronicler's 9000 dead, a figure compatible with Polydore Vergil's total of 20,000 inclusive of prisoners, and John of Whethamstede's '*supra bis x milia*' ('more than twice 10,000'). Vergil's reference to prisoners discredits sensationalist claims that no quarter was given. The latter, relatively non-partisan estimates give the lie to Yorkist exaggerations, reducing the slaughter to a similar level to Marston Moor (1644), denying Towton its claim to have been uniquely bloody.

Whatever the final score, the day was a national disaster, a shocking indictment of Henry VI's misrule. Bodies have turned up all over the battlefield: beside the main road while building the Tadcaster railway; in the cellars of Towton Hall near Richard III's vanished chantry at Chapel Garth; and in All Saints churchyard north and east of Saxton Church. Here the skulls were clearly those of young men, still with perfect teeth. Mass graves were once visible east of the roadside monument. Five Lancastrian peers died in action, and two more were executed soon after. Their cause was smashed. The deposed royals fled to Scotland, while Edward returned to London for his coronation.

Directions

Ferrybridge *From Pontefract follow the A1 across the Aire. See the bridge and river from footpaths along the north bank.*

Piltown (Baile-an-Phoill or the Battle of the Yellow Steed), **August 1462**

Ireland, Co. Kilkenny, DS75 S4321–4621

The Wars of the Roses had few echoes in Ireland. The Lancastrians enjoyed little support among Anglo-Norman settlers, while native Gaels ignored foreign feuds. Henry VI's only Irish supporters were the Butlers, whose titular leader James, Earl of Ormond married the Duke of Somerset's sister. As Earl of Wiltshire he played an inglorious role in several English battles, until his execution after Towton (1461). Wiltshire's brother John Butler of Ormond was attainted, but escaped, arriving in Ireland during the winter of 1461–2, 'with a great number of Saxons' (*Annals of the Four Masters*). His chief supporter in Kilkenny and Tipperary was his cousin Sir Edmund MacRichard Butler. Their quarrel was less with the Yorkists than their Geraldine rivals, in particular Thomas Fitzgerald, 8th Earl of Desmond, who claimed territory the Butlers had long considered theirs.

Fighting broke out early in 1462, the Butlers plundering Westmeath and capturing Waterford. Following Gaelic practice, 'both sides ordained to decide their variances by set battle'. They met in high summer at Piltown in the parish of Fiddown, a mutually convenient spot between Waterford and Carrick-on-Suir, a mile (1.6 km) north of the River Suir. The Butlers owned the nearby manor of Ardclone, while Co. Waterford, across the Suir, was Fitzgerald country. Although the battle was by prior arrangement, the Butlers failed to concentrate: 'Englishmen were accustomed not to give battle on a Monday nor after noone any day, but MacRichard regarded not their superstitious observation, but went on' (*Annals of Ireland*).

Butler strength including Earl John was said to be 5000, bordering on the credible if it includes unarmed men. Similar numbers crossed the Irish Sea before Mortimer's Cross (1461) and Stoke Field (1487). However, the Butlers only drew on two counties within Ireland, and were unlikely to have armed their Gaelic peasantry. MacRichard may only have had the 1000 horsemen 'all wearing helmets' with whom he had ravaged Westmeath. Desmond is said to have raised 20,000 men, a nonsensical figure. By way of comparison, James, 9th Earl of Desmond disposed of 400 horse, eight battles of gallowglasses, one of crossbows and gunners, and 3000 kerns, perhaps 4000 men in all.

The battle seems to have been a running fight. It started west of Piltown near Rogerstown Castle, passed south of the modern water tower and continued along a hollow to the traditional site of a bridge over the River Pill, halfway between village and railway, where the fiercest fighting took place. The Butlers made a stand at the crossing, and had the worst of it. MacRichard was captured, and many of his men drowned. The survivors retreated north-east towards their base in Kilkenny, the battle ending near St Mary's Presbytery.

Eyewitnesses claimed 410 of MacRichard's men were interred, 'besides all that were eaten by doggs and by the fouls of the aire' (*Annals*). Weapons have

Piltown

	Winners	*Losers*
Opponents	Yorkist	Lancastrian
Commanders	Thomas Fitzgerald, Earl of Desmond	Sir Edmund MacRichard Butler (p)
Numbers	unknown	*c.*1000
Losses	unknown	410

been unearthed, but the absence of human remains confirms the implication that the bodies were removed for burial. The battle finished the Butler-Lancastrian revolt. Desmond took Kilkenny and other Butler townships. MacRichard was ransomed for priceless Irish manuscripts, including the Psalter of Cashel, now in the Bodleian Library at Oxford. John of Ormond went abroad, dying in the Holy Land in 1477. The Geraldines would control Ireland until Henry VIII broke their power in 1534.

Directions

Take the N24 northwest from Waterford. Piltown is 1 mile(1.6 km) past Fiddown at the R698 junction. The fighting was south of the main road, between the village and railway. St Mary's Presbytery is on the left approaching from Waterford.

Hedgeley Moor, 25 April 1464

England, Northumberland, LR81 NU0419–20

Hexham, 15 May 1464

England, Northumberland, LR87 NY9662

The Lancastrians held out in the far north for several years after Towton (1461). Northumberland was remote from the Yorkist southeast, defended by mighty castles, and easily succoured from abroad. Not until spring 1464 did the Yorkists extinguish resistance there after battles at Hedgeley Moor and Hexham, whose significance exceeded the numbers engaged.

Edward IV made peace with France in October 1463, cutting off Scottish as well as French support for Henry VI's northern redoubt. Its defenders were driven to make one last effort. The Duke of Somerset, who had come into King Edward's peace, resumed his true colours and tried to interrupt Anglo-Scottish peace talks. Eighty Lancastrian men-at-arms laid an ambush for Montagu, Edward IV's warden of the Marches, as he rode north to escort Scots peace envoys to York. Tipped off, Montagu took another road. Somerset tried again just south of Wooler, where the Devil's Causeway, the Roman road from Hexham to Berwick, crosses Hedgeley Moor. *Gregory's Chronicle* claimed 5000 Lancastrian men-at-arms were present, a gross overestimate.

The battlefield is a level area, between the modern road and disused railway, marshy terrain to the east and rising ground north and west. Absolutely no details of either side's dispositions are recorded, except that Sir Ralph Percy led the Lancastrian charge. He was killed immediately, causing a general *sauve-qui-peut*, as described by Gregory:

> And when that he was dead all the party was discomforted and put to rebuke. And every man avoided and took his way with sorry hearts.

According to local tradition, Sir Ralph's horse was wounded at Percy's Leap, in the centre of the battlefield, its rider fighting his way half a mile (0.8 km) further south before he fell. Percy's Cross marks the spot, a headless stone pillar decorated with the Percy badge of shackle bolts and a crescent. Montagu let the fugitives go. He had more important business on hand.

Once Montagu had safely conveyed the Scots envoys to York, he proceeded to liquidate the survivors of Hedgeley Moor at Hexham. Somerset had regrouped, pushing south into the Tyne valley, near the site of Oswald's victory at Denisesburna (*c*.633). To encourage reluctant Lancastrians, Henry VI was brought down to Bywell Castle. Edward IV prepared a major expedition north with great ordnance, but Montagu struck first: 'the xiiii daye of May, my lorde Mountague toke hys journaye toward Hexham from Newcastelle' (Gregory). Montagu probably rode through Bywell, using the road along the north bank of the Tyne, without encountering opposition. Henry had left the castle perhaps four days before, the Yorkists capturing his sword and byecocket, the deposed monarch's coroneted helmet.

Most descriptions of Hexham follow Sir James Ramsey in placing the battle in meadows known as Hexham Levels, east of Devil's Water and south of Linnel's or Linnold's Bridge. Ramsey himself admitted the area was a death trap, enclosed between a precipitous riverbank and steep wooded heights.

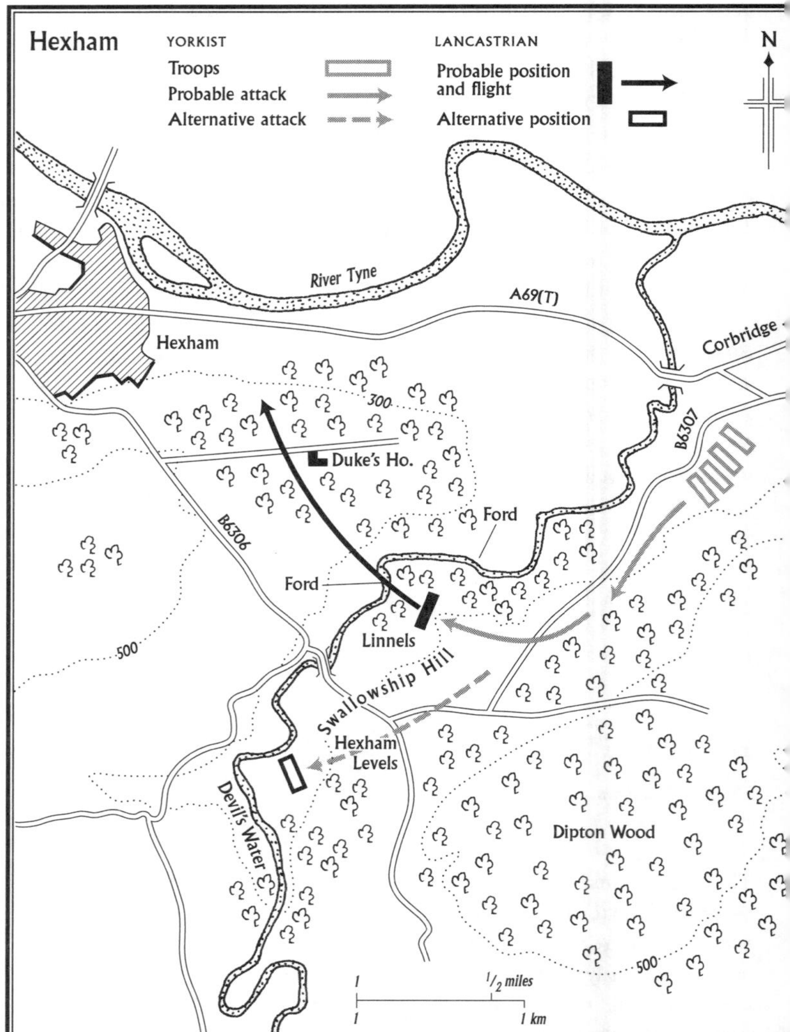

Directions

Hexham *Follow the B6306 southeast from Hexham to Linnel's Bridge, and turn left along the B6307 through Dipton Wood. Swallowship Hill is on the left, between the road and Devil's Water. The Ordnance Survey marks the battle to the right of the B6306 at NY9561.*

Its only tactical advantage was that the troops couldn't run away. Strategically Hexham Levels covers neither Linnel's Bridge nor two fords further downstream. Altogether it seems an odd choice of position for the astute Somerset, victor of Wakefield and Second St Albans.

Contemporary sources do not mention meadows. They specify 'a certain hill one mile from Hexham' (*Neville Chronicle*), while local tradition placed the battle south of Devil's Water. The latter clue suggests a site where the river flows west–east, which it does downstream of Linnel's, a name not associated with the battle until 1778. The best tactical location, which also fits the evidence, is Swallowship Hill (322 feet/ 98 m). This commands the three available river crossings, preventing Montagu cutting Somerset off from his base at Hexham, and providing observation of Yorkist approaches from the north. If it came to a fight, the extent of the position suited the numbers available to defend it, their

Hedgeley Moor

	Winners	*Losers*
Opponents	Yorkist	Lancastrian
Commanders	John Neville, Marquess of Montagu	Henry Beaufort, Duke of Somerset Sir Ralph Percy (k)
Numbers	unknown	500–1500

Hexham

	Winners	*Losers*
Opponents	Yorkist	Lancastrian
Commanders	John Neville, Marquess of Montagu	Henry Beaufort, Duke of Somerset (x)
Numbers	4000	500
Losses	unknown	unknown

flanks protected by slopes down to the stream.

None of the sources give the time or direction of Montagu's attack, which is assumed to have taken the Lancastrians by surprise. The effective pursuit indicates it was early in the day, suggesting the Yorkists had camped nearby. Some accounts give Montagu's men no rest after their 20-mile (32-km) approach, dating the action to the 14th. A local church yearbook, however, fixes the 15th as the day. Other accounts put the battle earlier in the month, or even the previous year, leading some to imagine there were two 15th-century battles near Hexham.

Montagu's capture of Lancastrian leaders south of Hexham suggests he had crossed the Tyne at Corbridge and attacked from the east, chasing fugitives westwards over the ford below Swallowship Hill. The action was more a rout than a battle. As soon as Montagu 'came in sight of the Duke of Somerset's army with 4000 armed men ... the duke with the great part of his army fled, and the whole of his force was broken into pieces' (*Neville Chronicle*). Gregory made more of the affair, claiming Montagu 'took many of the men and slew many one in that journey'.

Somerset was captured running away – '*in chacea*' – and beheaded near Duke's House on the way to Hexham. The other Lancastrian leaders, Lord Roos and Lord Hungerford, were caught '*absconditi*' in nearby woods, and executed later. Not only were their men hopelessly outnumbered, they were unpaid. Henry VI's £2000 war chest had been captured in a coal pit near Newcastle, 'a very wholesome salve' for Montagu's war-weary troopers. Within two months the whole Lancastrian position had collapsed. Henry VI was captured near Clitheroe in Lancashire in July, having taken no part in either battle; the queen had already fled to France. Tales associating her with Queen's Cave on Dipton Burn (NY9061) are romantic inventions. Montagu was rewarded with forfeited Percy lands as a Neville Earl of Northumberland. For the first time since he seized the throne in 1461 Edward IV controlled all England.

Directions

Hedgeley Moor *The battlefield lies across the A697 Morpeth–Wooler road, 1 mile (1.6 km) south of the junction with the B6346 Alnwick–Woolperton road. Percy's Leap is on the right, in a walled enclosure. Half a mile (0.8 km) further on, Percy's Cross is on the left, 500 yards (460 m) from the road.*

Edgcote (Danes Moor), **26 July 1469**

England, Northamptonshire, LR151 SP5145–46

Lose-Coat Field, 12 March 1470

England, Rutland, LR130 SK9711

These Midland battles have more in common than the assonance of their names. They were the first cracks in the York–Neville alliance that had seized the kingdom from the Lancastrians at Towton (1461).

Warwick the Kingmaker resented Edward IV's independence in marital and foreign affairs, and exploited popular discontent to further his own impossible ambitions. Warwick took no personal part in either battle, leaving the fighting to his henchmen.

They were victorious at Edgcote, but Warwick failed to consolidate his gains politically. Lose-Coat Field was a rebel disaster, opening Edward's eyes to the treachery of his closest associates.

Warwick forged an alliance with George, Duke of Clarence, Edward IV's brother, while covertly fomenting rebellion in Yorkshire. Its leader, 'Robin of Redesdale', was probably Sir John Conyers, one of Warwick's northern relatives. While he headed south, Warwick and Clarence issued a manifesto from Calais denouncing seditious persons about the king. On 16 July 1469 they invaded Kent. Surrounded by shadowy threats, Edward IV dithered at Nottingham, while the northern rebels intercepted his reinforcements northeast of Banbury at Edgcote.

The opposing armies were ostensibly equal, though numbers quoted are purely illustrative: 14,000 Welsh spears under Pembroke and 7000 West Country archers under Devon against 20,000 rebels. A better indication of the scale of the affair might be Sir Edward Hall's statement that the rebels' decisive reinforcement was 500 strong, plus 'all the rascal of Northampton and other villages about'. In the king's absence the Yorkist forces had separated. John Warkworth's chronicle, the best English source, says they 'felle into a varyaunce for ther logynge', to which Hall adds a characteristic piece of Tudor gossip, 'for the love of a damosel'. Devon took off, leaving Pembroke outnumbered, with no archers to support his men-at-arms. De Waurin's account was more prosaic. Pembroke and Devon misjudged the proximity of the rebels, and failed to concentrate soon enough.

Warkworth located the fighting 'in a playne byyonde Banbury toune', amplified anonymously as '*ad Hegecote, seu Danysmore, prope Banburiam, dictam Banbery-Felde*'. Hall places the fighting, in 'a fair plain near to a town called Hedgecote, three miles from Banbury, wherein there be three hills, not in equal distance, nor yet in equal quantity, but lying in manner although not fully triangle'. His description fits Danes Moor, which lies south of the River Cherwell in the parish of Edgcote, amid three hills. Now a minor plantation, Danes Moor was a more extensive tract of rough pasture before enclosure. Hall put Pembroke's Welsh and the rebels on the western and southernmost hills respectively, either side of a small stream.

Modern accounts have pressed various hills into service (see map), but the three nearest Danes Moor are at Upper Wardington to the west, Thorpe Mandeville (591 feet/180 m) to the south, and Culworth to the east. If Hall is to be believed, the Yorkists were at Upper Wardington and the rebels at Thorpe Mandeville, having slipped past the king to join their sponsor, Warwick. The medieval road system would have brought them to Northampton, whence Banbury Lane took them southwest across Watling Street at Pattishall to Culworth.

De Waurin, the best contemporary source, says Pembroke rode ahead to secure a river crossing, presumably over the Cherwell at Edgcote, not the later bridge at Trafford Farm. After a skirmish at Edgcote, he then occupied Upper Wardington, renewing the action next morning upon Danes Moor. Pembroke held his ground, despite casualties from archery, which his spearmen could not return. After a pause for lunch, Warwick's advance guard appeared, reportedly 15,000 professional troops from Calais. Their best route from London would have been up Watling Street, picking up Banbury Lane north of Towcester. Thus reinforced the rebels resumed the assault. Devon's archers never showed. Taken in flank,

Edgcote

	Winners	*Losers*
Opponents	Rebel	Yorkist
Commanders	Robin of Redesdale	William Herbert, of Earl of Pembroke (x) Humphrey Stafford, Earl of Devon (x)
Numbers	unknown	unknown
Losses	1500	2000

Lose-Coat Field

	Winners	*Losers*
Opponents	Yorkist	Rebel
Commanders	Edward IV	Sir Robert Welles (x)

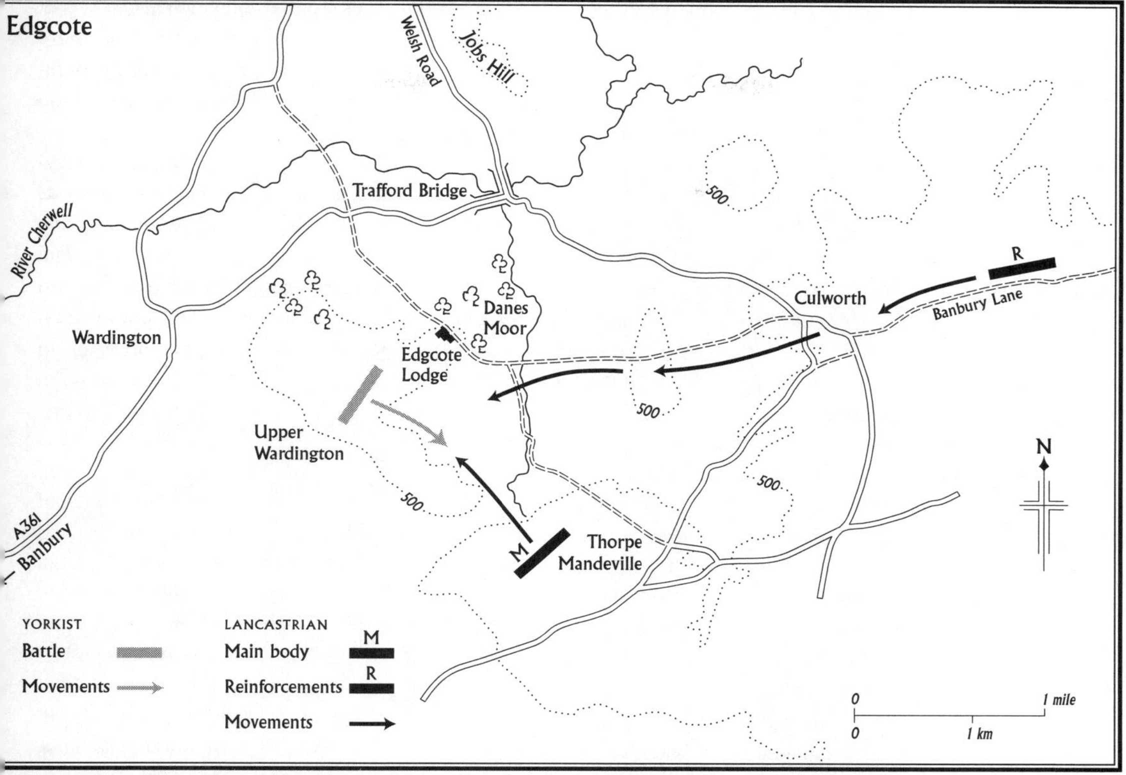

Pembroke's tired and outnumbered spearmen were overwhelmed. Welsh Road beyond the Cherwell is said to commemorate their flight, but the etymology is suspect, such names usually denoting a drove road for Welsh livestock.

Both sides suffered heavy casualties, '*caesi multa milia*'. Welsh bards lamented a national calamity: 168 of their gentry were killed. Warwick executed Pembroke and his brother the next day at Kenilworth out of spite; Devon was killed soon after. For a while the Kingmaker was triumphant, holding Edward IV under house arrest. He had no political platform, however, and could not mobilize troops against a real Lancastrian rebellion in Yorkshire without royal authority. By September the king was free, 'and dyd what hym lykede'. Warwick's attempt to rule through a puppet, as he had in 1455 and 1460, could not succeed against a king who was in full possession of his wits.

Directions

Edgcote *Take the A361 north from Banbury. Turn right onto a minor road at Wardington for Danes Moor and Pembroke's position at Edgcote Lodge, from where footpaths run across the battlefield towards Thorpe Mandeville and Culworth. Banbury Lane exists today as a series of minor roads and footpaths.*

Lose-Coat Field (1470) arose from Warwick's second attempt to find a more manageable king. As in 1469 he exploited a local feud as smokescreen for his ambitions, which were now to install the pliable Clarence in Edward's place. The king was ignorant of Warwick's schemes, but less inclined after Edgcote to let rebellions gather momentum. When Lincolnshire gentlefolk attacked the home of one of Edward's household knights, the king took it personally. The main source for the campaign is a *Chronicle of the Rebellion*, compiled by one of Edward's clerks.

Edward gathered intelligence as he rode north through Huntingdon and Fotheringhay. Sir Robert Welles, 'calling hym self grete capteyn of the commons of Linccolne shire', had summoned troops to his estate at Ranby (6 miles/10 km northeast of Horncastle) in Henry VI's name. He played on popular fears of retribution for the previous year's troubles, alleging 'the king's judges would sit and hang and draw a great number of the commons'. Unfortunately for Welles, his father, Lord Welles and Willoughby, was already in royal custody. Under interrogation he admitted the plot, and wrote to his son advising immediate submission, 'or elles thay for theire seide treasons shulde have dethe'.

The main rebel army marched down Ermine Street as far as Grantham. They 'beganne to chaunge theire way towards Leycestre', presumably via Melton Mowbray, but turned back on receiving Lord Welles's communication. Warwick had promised to meet Welles at Leicester with 20,000 of his own men, but Edward's stratagem divided the rebel forces and wrecked Warwick's plan. Sir Robert Welles had no intention of surrendering, hoping 'to have sett upon the king in Staunford the monday nyght [12–13 March] ... destryt hym and his oost [host], and so rescued his fadre lyf'. Edward, however, was on guard. When he reached Stamford on 11 March he sent his vanguard on towards the rebels, while he 'bayted [fed] himself and his felawship in the toune'. It was the rebels who were unexpectedly brought to action next day as Edward 'incontinent toke the felde, where he undrestoode the saide Sir Robert Welles to be in armes with baniers displaied against hym, disposed to fight'.

The Act of Attainder against the rebels placed the battle 'at Empyngham, in a felde called Hornefelde'. General accounts of the campaign equate this with Empingham village, 5 miles (8 km) west of Stamford towards Leicester. The *Victoria County History* locates the fight in Empingham parish, 3 miles (5 km) northwest of Stamford on a stretch of Ermine Street still known as Horne Lane in 1900. A small wood still known as Bloody Oaks stands nearby, within a mile (1.6 km) of Horn House and Empingham Old Wood. The rebels had presumably regained Ermine Street and formed up across the old road facing south, perhaps on the slight rise (295 feet/90 m) running through Bloody Oaks.

Details of the battle are few. Unwilling to leave traitors in safety while he risked his own neck, Edward began by executing Lord Welles in sight of both armies. Contemporary claims of 30,000 rebels imply they outnumbered royal forces, but they were outclassed. They had few nobles, with their seasoned household troops, and no answer to Edward's artillery:

> The Kynge toke his oste and went towards his enemyes, and losyde his gonnys of his ordynaunce uppone them, and faught with them, and anone the commons flede away.
>
> *Warkworth's Chronicle*

Hall over-eggs the pudding, claiming the action was 'sore fought on both sides', but the contemporary Croyland chronicler says the rebels were beaten at first sight. In their hurry, the fugitives threw off their tell-tale livery, giving the battle its name. Hall's figure of 10,000 killed probably exceeds total combatants, although Warkworth thought 'ther was many manne slayne of Lyncolneschyre'.

Among the dead was a yeoman in Clarence's livery, his helmet containing, 'many mervelous billes, conteining matter of the grete seduccion'. Rebel confessions confirmed suspicions aroused by their battle cry, 'A Clarence! A Warrewike!' On 26 March Edward denounced both as traitors. As their schemes fell apart, the conspirators fled to France. Warwick's second proxy rebellion had collapsed, through the fumbling of his subordinates and Edward's forceful response.

Directions

Lose-Coat Field *Follow the A1 trunk road 4 miles (6 km) north from Stamford. Stop at the Bloody Oaks intersection where a minor road turns left to Empingham. View the battlefield from minor roads alongside the main road. The Ordnance Survey Explorer series marks the battle in the square given above.*

Nibley Green, 20 March 1470

England, Gloucestershire, LR162 ST7295

The Plantagenets were not the only family to fall out over landed property during the 15th century. The row over Thomas Berkeley's inheritance lasted for nearly 200 years after his death in 1417. The struggle was not unrelated to national events. Margaret Talbot, the heir general, had the Duke of Somerset's protection until the duke's death at St Albans (1455). The immunity she enjoyed from legal process enabled her to deprive James Berkeley, the heir male, of his manor at Wotton-under-Edge. She held him hostage in his own castle, while his wife, Isabel, died of neglect in Gloucester jail. Nibley Green (1470), the most violent turn in this savage dispute, coincided with the disorders after Edgcote (1469). Property rights and revenge went together for the Berkeleys, as they did for more prestigious families. Details of the action come from John Smyth's *Lives of the Berkeleys*, compiled in 1618 from family records, and the testimony of villagers, whose grandfathers had sat in trees as children to watch the battle.

Margaret Talbot had left her spoils to the 19-year-old Viscount Lisle, while William Berkeley, son of James and Isabel, headed a new generation on the other side. On 19 March 1470 Lisle sent Berkeley a formal challenge to come forth, 'with all your carts of guns, bows and other ordnance', promising to meet him with 'Englishmen of my own nation and neighbours (not Welshmen as falsely rumoured)'. Berkeley denied the legality of such an appeal to arms, but agreed to fight anyway: 'Fail not tomorrow to be at Nibley Green at eight or nine of the clock … and the truth will be shown by the mercy of God'.

Nibley Green

	Winners	*Losers*
Opponents	Berkeley	Talbot
Commanders	William, Lord Berkeley	Thomas Talbot, Viscount Lisle (k)
Numbers	*c.*1000	*c.*300
Losses	unknown	150

Berkeley did not rely entirely on divine assistance. He summoned his brother from Thornbury, (6 miles/10 km off), who came 'with all the strength that on so short a summons he could make'. Black Will, a character from Victorian romance, brought miners and woodsmen from the Forest of Dean (7 miles/11 km across the Severn), while Berkeley's in-laws travelled up from Bristol (17 miles/27 km). After the battle the city's mayor interrogated 20 persons 'under suspicion … of having sent armed men in manner of war' to Berkeley's assistance. All in all, the Berkeleys outnumbered the Talbots three-to-one.

North Nibley stands below the Cotswold escarpment (*c.*660 feet/200 m) on a rounded foothill falling steeply away to Nibley Green (190 feet/58 m) and the low-lying countryside towards the Severn. Berkeley Castle, where Edward II was murdered, is an hour's march to the northwest. Wotton is closer, in the opposite direction, but the Berkeleys were in position first, 'hidden in the outskirts of Michaelswood Chase'. Michael Wood then grew nearer the Cotswolds, perhaps as close as Bush Street Farm, at the western end of a lane down from Nibley Church. A small stream crosses the lane, running through the meadows between farm and church, a useful obstacle within bowshot of the position.

When Talbot arrived about 10 a.m. Berkeley gave him no chance to form up, breaking cover 'when he first beheld the Lord Lisle with his fellowship descend that hill from Nibley Church'. Lisle was shot before he could adjust his visor: 'the place of meeting was at Fowleshard, whence this Lord William sent upon the Lord Lisle the first shower of his arrows, that one Black Will (so called) shot the Lord Lisle, as his beaver was up'. Half of Lisle's men were cut down as they ran back up the narrow defile. During the 19th century, a mass grave in the churchyard was found to contain 150 skeletons.

The sequel was brutally decisive. Berkeley's men ransacked Wotton Manor, carrying off deeds and other legal documents, besides roof leads and ovens, still to be seen at Berkeley Castle. That night Lisle's widow, 'cast into an abortive travail', miscarried his child. Legal action dragged on until the seventh year of the reign of James I without dislodging the Berkeleys from their repossessed manors: 'Thus did all the sons joyne in revenge of the innocent bloude of that virtuous and princely lady Isobel their mother malitiously spilt at Gloucester seventeen years before.'

Directions

Michael Wood is now a services area on the M5. Approach the battlefield from Berkeley Castle (ST6899) by minor roads through Lower, Middle and Upper Wick to Nibley Green. Go straight up the hill to Nibley Church, or double back right to Bush Street Farm. See the battlefield from viewpoints at Nibley Knoll (ST7495) and Drakestone Point (ST7398).

Barnet, Easter Sunday, 14 April 1471

England, Hertfordshire, LR166 TQ2497

The years 1470–1 saw some of the most dramatic swings of fortune in English history. Kings and nobles experienced exile, power and death in quick succession. Barnet set former comrades in arms against one another, as Warwick the Kingmaker's intrigues split the Yorkist faction. Unequalled sources include the Yorkist *Historie of the Arrivall of Edward IV*, the pro-Lancastrian *Warkworth's Chronicle*, and an impartial newsletter by Gerhard von Wesel, a merchant.

Warwick fled England after Lose-Coat Field (see above), and made an unlikely alliance with his deadliest enemy, Margaret of Anjou. With French support he reran the strategy that nearly paid off in 1469, simulating revolt in northern England, while threatening invasion in the south. Distracted by this two-pronged threat Edward hesitated, lost popular support, and fled abroad. On 3 October 1470 Henry VI was formally restored as king, although real power remained with Warwick. His support for French designs upon Burgundian territory in the Netherlands, however, persuaded Charles the Bold, Duke of Burgundy and Edward IV's brother-in-law, to sponsor a counter-revolution.

Edward landed at Ravenspur on Humberside in March 1471 with 900 English supporters and 300 Flemish handgunners. Meeting a hostile reception in the north, he slipped through Warwick's defensive cordons to London, gathering strength as he went. The Duke of Clarence turned his coat again, bringing Edward's forces up to 7000 men when he entered London on Good Friday 1471. Edward released his wife and a host of Yorkist internal exiles from sanctuary, and put Henry VI back into the Tower.

Warwick moved rapidly south from Coventry towards the capital. He hoped to surprise Edward over the Easter holiday, but Edward IV was not Henry VI. At 4 p.m. on Easter Saturday Edward marched out of London to intercept Warwick. Reconnaissance elements clashed at Hornsey at about 7 p.m., Yorkist scourers chasing Warwick's aforeriders back through Barnet in the dark. Warwick's assortment of Lancastrian die-hards and Neville clients was encamped a mile (1.6 km) north of the village, 'undre an hedge-syde' on Hadley Green, also known as Gladmore Heath. Edward drew up under cover of darkness, 'moche nerer than he had supposed', probably within bowshot, and 'somewhat a-sydes-handed'. Both sides' van or right wing overlapped their opponents' rearward or left, with curious consequences.

Warwick held the crest (430 feet/131 m) of a flat ridge that crosses the main road between Barnet and the point where the road forks to St Albans and Hatfield. Hadley High Stone was erected at the junction in 1740 to commemorate the battle, but the ridge there is too narrow for the forces engaged, and too far from Barnet to agree with the *Arrivall*'s statement that the Yorkists pursued the Lancastrian scouts 'oute of the towne, more some what than a half myle'. Some Victorian accounts thought Warwick lined a roadside hedge facing east, but this is clearly wrong. He would naturally form up at right angles to the road, facing south, rather than present his flank to the enemy. A.H. Burne found the *Arrivall*'s hedge where it should be, running west across Barnet golf course from Old Fold Manor. East of the road Warwick's line passed 150 yards (140 m) north of Hadley Church.

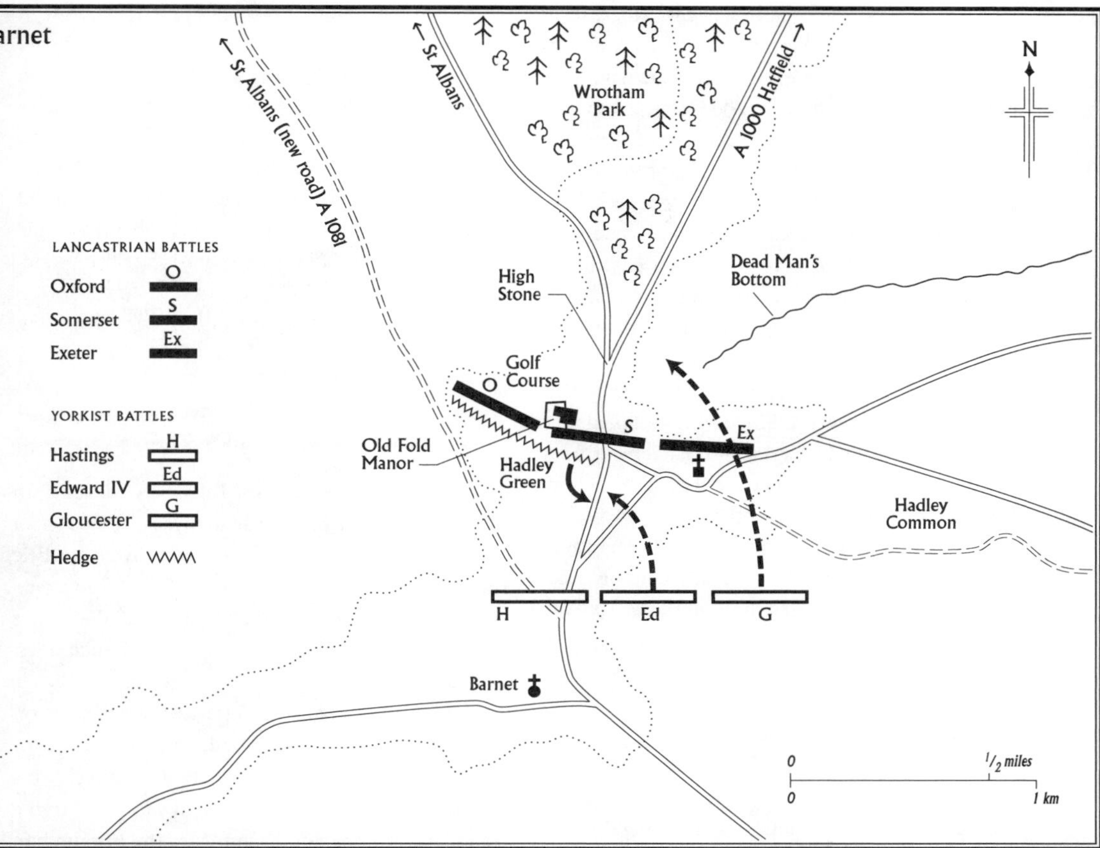

The armies formed up in three divisions in line abreast, with no reserve. Some accounts, misled by Tudor sources, assign the Lancastrian centre to the Duke of Somerset, rather than Warwick's brother Montagu. Contemporary estimates of numbers include:

- 15,000 Yorkists rising to 20,000 (Wesel)
- 20,000 Lancastrians (de Waurin)
- 7000 Yorkists versus 20,000 Lancastrians (Warkworth)
- 9000 Yorkists versus 30,000 Lancastrians (*Arrivall*)

The last figures are Yorkist propaganda, but Warwick had the bigger army, 'a good three or four thousand men more than on king Edward's side'. He also had more guns – arquebuses and 'serpentines' (probably field guns) – which he placed 'immediately opposite the road coming from Barnet' (Wesel). The frontage available across Hadley Green (1200–1500 yards/ 1100–1370 m) would comfortably accommodate 10,000–13,000 men, six or seven ranks deep.

Directions

Follow Barnet High Street (A1000) 1/2 mile (0.8 km) north to Hadley Green, to the golf course and surviving common land on either side of the road. See Hadley High Stone 1/2 mile further on, and Wrotham Wood.

Edward IV may have hoped to offset Warwick's superior numbers by speed and surprise, as Somerset had done at Second St Albans (1461). Edward kept his people still, 'without any mannar langwage or noyse', and made no reply to Warwick's artillery, who 'shotte gunes almost all the nyght'. Not realizing how close the Yorkists lay, the Lancastrian gunners 'overshote the kings hoste, and hurtyd them nothinge' (*Arrivall*). Unusually for the period, Edward attacked before first light, 'betwyxt four of five of the cloke'. Early-morning fog thickened the gloom: 'suche a grete myste, that nether of them might see othere' (Warkworth). The preliminary missile exchange was short but furious. Over 10,000 broken arrows littered the ground, as Edward 'sette upon them, firste with shotte, and then and sone, they joined and came to hand-strokes' (*Arrivall*).

Any advantage the Yorkists gained from their sudden onslaught was nullified by their unbalanced deployment, for 'bothe batteyls was nat directly frount to frount'. The western end of Warwick's line, under the Earl of Oxford, 'ovarrechyd the end of the kings battayle, and so, at that end, they were myche myghtyar than was the kings bataile'. Three thousand of Edward's followers fled through Barnet, pursued by Oxford. The Yorkist right similarly overlapped the Lancastrian left, and pushed them back across Dead Man's Bottom: 'distresyd them theyr gretly, and soo drew nere towards the Kynge, who was abowt the myddest of the battayle' (*Arrivall*). Both armies wheeled counterclockwise, yielding to pressure on their left flanks, until they lined up along the road, the Lancastrians now facing east instead of south. Fighting raged along the new line, 'And dyverse tymes the Erle of Warwyke party had the victory, and supposed that thei hade wonne the felde' (Warkworth):

> There was shotyng of gonnes and arrows plenté
> There was showting and crying that the earth
> did quake
> There was hewing of harnes, peté was to see;
> For fere of that fray many men did shake.
>
> Yorkist ballad

The battle was won by accident, compounded by distrust among Warwick's ill-found host. When 800 of Oxford's men returned from the chase they naturally followed the road, only to encounter the right flank of Montagu's Lancastrian centre where the Yorkist rear had been. Their livery, 'a sterre with stremys', was mistaken for Edward's 'sunne with stremys', and 'the myste was so thycke ... the Erle of Warwikes menne schotte and faughte ayens the Erle of Oxenfordes menne' (Warkworth). Oxford's men fled shouting 'Treasoune!', while one of Warwick's retainers, thinking Montagu meant to change sides, killed him.

Barnet

	Winners	*Losers*
Opponents	Yorkist	Lancastrian
Commanders	Edward IV	Richard Neville, Earl of Warwick (k)
	Richard, Duke of Gloucester	John Neville, Marquess of Montagu (k)
	William, Lord Hastings	John de Vere, Earl of Oxford
		Henry Holland, Duke of Exeter (w)
Numbers	*c.*10,000	*c.*13,000
Losses	1500	2000

The Lancastrians were left leaderless. Exeter, on the left, was down, 'wounded, and left nakede for dede' (Warkworth). Warwick had fled on seeing his brother's disaster in the centre, and was killed trying to escape. Philippe de Commynes, the Burgundian strategic expert, blamed this on Warwick's having fought on foot, contrary to his usual practice. Warkworth thought his horse became entangled in a wood 'where there was no way forthe', perhaps Wrotham Wood beyond the High Stone. One of Edward's men 'came upon hym and kylled him, and despolede hym nakede'. Organized resistance ceased about 8 a.m.

Casualties reflected the evenness of the battle. Wesel thought 1500 fell on both sides. Commynes gave the same figure for the Yorkists, more among the defeated Lancastrians. These neutral estimates fall between John Paston's 1000 'of both parties', and Warkworth's 4000. The decisive casualties were Warwick and Montagu, the Neville faction's political and military leaders. Edward was not yet secure. The same evening Margaret of Anjou, long delayed by contrary winds, landed at Weymouth.

Tewkesbury, Saturday 4 May 1471

England, Gloucestershire, LR150 SO8931

Edward IV's victory at Tewkesbury completed the Yorkist recovery. With customary vigour he denied his Lancastrian opponents time to gather strength, and brought them to battle in circumstances that guaranteed their annihilation.

Undaunted by Warwick's destruction at Barnet (see above), Margaret of Anjou raised an army in the west of England. Edward IV's strategy was to fight as far from London as possible. Within a week of Barnet he marched west up the Thames valley. The Lancastrians refused action at Cirencester on 29 April, resupplied in Bristol, and headed north up the Severn. Margaret hoped to join her allies in Wales and Cheshire, but the bridge at Gloucester was held for Edward IV, forcing her to push on to the tidal ford at Tewkesbury. The march was a feat of endurance: 'xxxvj longe myles, in a fowle contrye, all in lanes and stonny wayes, betwixt woodes, without any good refresshynge' (*Historie of the Arrivall of Edward IV*). Edward followed across the more open Cotswolds. At Cheltenham he heard the exhausted Lancastrians were preparing for battle at Tewkesbury, still east of the Severn. Edward refreshed his troops 'with suche meate and drynke as he had', and drove them on to catch the Lancastrians before a falling tide allowed them to escape.

The armies were smaller than at Barnet, although Edward had summoned replacements, and purveyed 'artilary, and ordinaunce, gonns, and othare, for the filde grete plentye'. He had more guns than his opponents, although they too had acquired guns at Bristol. The Yorkist *Arrivall* gives Edward 'moo then iij milia fotemen', a figure borne out by a payroll for 3436 archers. Total Yorkist strength would depend on the proportion of bills to bows: one-to-two would give the 5000 shown in the table opposite. Although defeated, Margaret is credited with more. Perhaps they were poorer quality, 'as the greater parte of theyr hoste were fotemen'.

The Lancastrians chose a classic English defensive position, in the meadows south of Tewkesbury, 'marvaylous strong grownd … full difficult to be assayled'. A.H. Burne discounted the *Arrivall*'s repeated allusions to its strength as Yorkist propaganda, but Tudor historians who embroidered the original do not contradict it:

> … upon every hand of them, fowle lanes, and depe dikes, and many hedges, with hylls, and valleys, a right evill place to approche …
>
> In the front of theyr field were so evell lanes, and depe dykes, so many hedges, trees, and bushes, that it was right hard to approche them nere, and come to hands.

Two main locations have been canvassed:

(1) A.H. Burne's forward site at Gupshill, between the River Swilgate and Coln Brook, along a lane running west from 'Queen Margaret's Camp'.

(2) Colonel J.D. Blyth's less exposed position on Holm Hill, its flanks resting on the Avon and fishponds south of Gander Lane.

Margaret's Camp is a moated manor that predates the battle. Its name has no bearing on the location of the battle. Nearly contemporary references place the battle in 'the great field which is called Gastons', or, as the Tudor antiquary John Leland put it, '*campum nomine Gastum*'. This was a broad ridge between the above sites, mostly occupied today by a cemetery and housing. Local records suggest that the area was divided into orchards and gardens, with numerous ditches and hedges, supporting the *Arrivall*'s account. The only obstacles at Gupshill are a gentle depression and roadside hedges. The *Arrivall* also places the

Tewkesbury

	Winners	*Losers*
Opponents	Yorkist	Lancastrian
Commanders:	Edward IV Richard, Duke of Gloucester William, Lord Hastings	Margaret of Anjou (p) Prince Edward (k) Henry Beaufort, Duke of Somerset (x)
Numbers	*c.*5000	*c.*6000
Losses	unknown	*c.*2000

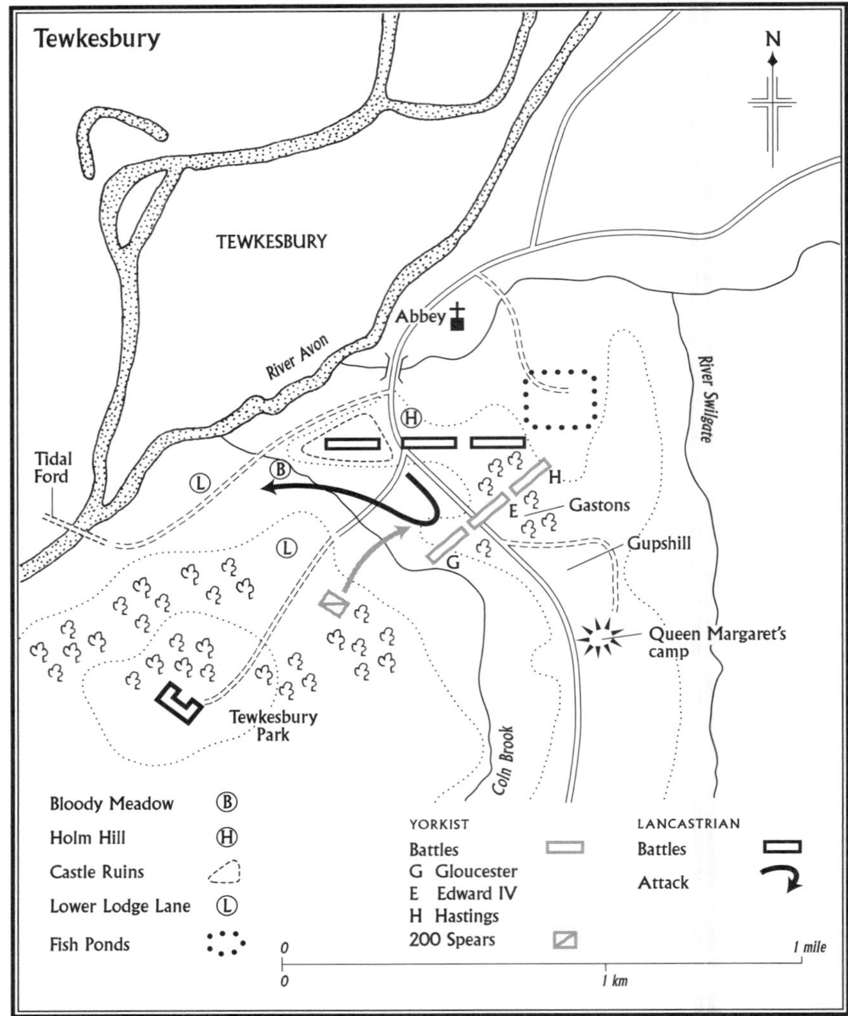

Lancastrians very near Tewkesbury, 'in a close even at the townes end; the towne and the abbey at theyr backs'. Again this supports Holm Hill, which was much the best defensive position available: the frontage was half that at Gupshill; both flanks rested on serious obstacles; and the ruins of Holm Castle provided cover from light artillery. Margaret would have been mad to fight anywhere else.

Next morning, Edward IV attacked with customary alacrity. Fugitives from the battle interrupted the abbey's monks still celebrating Mass, i.e. before 9 a.m. The Yorkists deployed in three divisions, but reversed the usual order: Gloucester's van took the

Directions

See memorials to Prince Edward and the Earl of Devon in Tewkesbury Abbey. Walk south from the abbey across Swilgate, and turn right along a footpath to the Lancastrian position on Gloucester Road. Either turn left along the road towards open ground around Lincoln Green, where the Yorkists advanced, or carry straight on down Lower Lode Lane (the Severn Way) into Bloody Meadow.

left, while Hastings's rearward (defeated at Barnet) took the right. Edward was clearly concerned about his left. He detached 200 mounted spears to occupy a wooded park, 'upon the right hand of theyr field', i.e. the Lancastrian right, 'set ... in a plomp, togethars, nere a qwarter of a myle from the fielde'. Some accounts assume the *Arrivall*'s author did not know his right from his left, helpfully reversing the whole order of battle. The course of the action shows the 200 Yorkist men-at-arms were at Tewkesbury Park, between Edward's army and the Severn.

The Yorkists' best line of attack ran between Coln Brook and Swilgate, wheeling half left through the Gastons. Formed five or six ranks deep they would comfortably fill the 750 yards (685 m) between the two streams. Any further left, and Gloucester's division would have straddled Coln Brook, suffering delay and confusion. Instead, they came into action first, in good order: 'the Kyngs ordinance ... so conveniently layde afore them, and his vaward so sore oppressed them [the Lancastrians], with shott of arrows, that they gave them right-a-sharpe shwre' (*Arrivall*). Edward's centre and right, still obscured among the orchards, held their fire.

The Lancastrian response to Gloucester's bombardment remains unexplained. Tudor historians invented a feigned retreat to lure them forward, but the contemporary *Warkworth's Chronicle* simply says 'Edmunde Duke of Somersett, and Sere Hugh Curteneye, went out of the felde, by the whiche the felde was broken; and the moste part of the peple fledde away from the Prynce'. Field in this context signifies a tactical formation, not an agricultural enclosure. The *Arrivall* offers two explanations: either the Lancastrians were so shaken by Gloucester's bombardment, 'as well with gonnes-shott as with arrows', that they charged out to silence their tormentors, or Somerset was overcome by an excess of chivalry.

The Lancastrian counterattack was premeditated, following 'certayne pathes and wayes ... *afore* purveyed'. This was not the wide-ranging flank attack shown by traditional reconstructions, for its target was not the Yorkist left, but Edward's main battle in the centre. Somerset advanced 'somewhat asyde-hand the Kyngs vawarde', appearing 'even afore the Kynge where he was enbatteled, and from the hill ... set right fiercely upon th'end of the Kyngs battayle' (*Arrivall*). In other words Somerset charged obliquely down the forward slope of Holm Hill, into the left flank of the Yorkist centre.

The move was premature. Edward's troops were not yet engaged. He beat off his attackers with Gloucester's help, and drove them back uphill. Somerset's advance exposed his own flank, not just to Gloucester's division but also to the 200 spears in Tewkesbury Park. 'Seinge no lyklynes of any busshement in the saide wood-corner', they burst out, 'all at ones ... asyde-hand, unadvysed'(*Arrivall*), and routed Somerset's vaward. The Lancastrians fled west into Bloody Meadow, where horse bones and shoes have turned up, suggesting the area deserves its name. Edward left Somerset's men to the cavalry, and stormed the main Lancastrian position: 'such as abode hand-stroks were slayne incontinent', and the rest ran away.

Many drowned 'at a mylene [millpond] in the meadows faste by the towne', presumably in the deep water above Swilgate weir, just behind Holm Hill. No contemporary casualty figures survive, but a third of the defeated army seems not unlikely. Excavations disturbed some of their remains at sewage works in the angle of the Avon and Swilgate. Others fled through the town, or sought sanctuary in the abbey. Many of the latter were dragged out and executed, despite an initial promise of amnesty.

The slaughter has been much exaggerated. Contemporary accounts fail to bear out bloodcurdling tales of Prince Edward's murder by Edward IV's cronies. Warkworth and the *Arrivall* agree he was 'slayne in the fielde', during the rout. Holinshed's sensational account of Somerset braining his fellow Lancastrian Lord Wenlock with an axe, as a traitor, is simply an attempt to find a scapegoat. Edward IV was certainly lucky. Had the Lancastrians managed their counterattack better, or just held their ground, the day might have turned out differently. Instead the extinction of the Beaufort and Lancastrian lines was soon completed by Henry VI's murder. The Yorkists were left undisputed masters of the political as well as the military field.

Bosworth Field (Redemore), Monday 22 August 1485

England, Leicestershire, LR140 SP3899–3998

Bosworth Field is one of the major landmarks in English history, and the last time an English king was killed on the battlefield. A convenient end point for the Middle Ages, Bosworth brought the Tudors to the throne, and is memorable as the only occasion the crown of England was found in a hawthorn tree after a battle. Despite its importance, the battlefield has been misplaced for over 200 years.

The Yorkist hegemony established at Tewkesbury (1471) was wrecked by Edward IV's early death and the ambition of his brother Richard, Duke of Gloucester. Popularly supposed to have murdered his nephews, the Princes in the Tower, Gloucester certainly bastardized his elder brother and massacred his in-laws to secure the throne as Richard III. His ruthlessness split the Yorkist faction, transforming the prospects of the Lancastrian pretender, Henry Tudor. Yorkist refugees joined Henry in exile, while Richard's real and imagined crimes undermined royal credibility at home. After two years of invasion scares, Henry Tudor landed at Milford Haven, Pembrokeshire, on 7 August 1485, with a handful of English émigrés and 3000 French mercenaries.

The invaders marched through Wales to Shrewsbury, gaining few recruits. When Henry reached Stafford on 17 August, he still had insufficient troops to beat the royal army gathering at Nottingham. Most disappointing was the failure of Henry's stepfather, Lord Stanley, to join him. Richard III held Stanley's son, Lord Strange, as hostage, inspiring caution if not loyalty, and had already denounced Lord Stanley's brother Sir William Stanley as a traitor. Aware of Henry's numerical weakness, the king was as anxious to fight as his rival. On 19 August he marched to Leicester, turning west off the Fosse Way to intercept Henry as he moved down Watling Street towards London. Next day Henry reached Merevale Abbey, west of Atherstone, where he spent the night. Discussions with the Stanleys failed to win their open commitment, the brothers retreating towards Richard, to maintain the appearance of loyalty.

Modern accounts of the battle that followed are almost without exception valueless, being inspired by flawed 18th- and 19th-century ideas, derived from wholesale corruption of the sources. The most important of these was a coherent and impartial account by a near contemporary, the Italian humanist Polydore Vergil, based on eyewitness testimony from Bosworth veterans at Henry VII's court. Tudor historians began the process of distorting Vergil's evidence, but the main culprit was the 18th-century amateur William Hutton, who invented most of the elements that make up traditional accounts of Bosworth. In particular Hutton was responsible for placing the action on Ambion Hill (SK3900), about 2 miles (3 km) south of Market Bosworth, and the site of Leicestershire county council's visitor centre. Historians universally followed this fictitious interpretation, until its demolition by the local historian Peter Foss in the 1980s. His key points were:

(1) Local 16th-century sources placed the battle on flat low-lying ground, not on a cramped hilltop. William Burton's *Description of Leicestershire* specifies, 'a large and spacious ground three miles distant from Bosworth'. The Leicestershire-born poet Michael Drayton called it, 'a spacious moore, lying southward from the town'.

(2) The action is first named in the minutes of a York city council meeting on 23 August as 'Redemore apud [at] Leicestre', glossed in the margin as, 'the battayle of Redesmore Heath'. This signifies reed-covered wetland, not a red ploughed field as sometimes said, tallying with Polydore Vergil's reference to a marsh as the key tactical feature. A broad variety of geological and place-name evidence persuaded Foss that Redesmore lay a mile (1.6 km) southwest of Ambion Hill, where several streams cross the partly vanished Roman road to Leicester. Known as Fenn Lane, this leaves Watling Street at Fenny Drayton. This undeveloped area of wasteland and marsh was still known as the Great Moor in the 18th century. Market Bosworth lent the battle its name in the 1530s, as the nearest town. Ambion Hill

first appears as Richard III's campsite somewhat later, before becoming confused with the battlefield itself.

(3) The battlefield was surrounded by high ground, allowing Richard III and the Stanleys to observe the fighting. A Spanish newsletter says the latter were on the left of the royal army, i.e. to the south. If the king occupied Ambion Hill's forward slope, spurs at Dadlington and Stoke Golding provide the obvious place for the Stanleys to await the outcome. The former village's church became a chantry for those killed, their remains often turning up in the churchyard. Stoke Golding lies on Crown Hill, traditional site for the Earl of Richmond's *al fresco* crowning as Henry VII at the end of the day. Lancastrian ballads show the treacherous brothers were in communication throughout the battle, discrediting suggestions that Lord Thomas and Sir William were on opposite sides of the array, the armies arranged in a quadrilateral.

Michael K. Jones has proposed a more radical relocation, 4 miles (6.5 km) further west, in the flat open fields outside Atherstone, on the Warwickshire border. Rejecting Ambion Hill's pretensions, he places the Yorkist camp north of the River Sence at King Dick's Hole, with the Stanleys on Bloody Bank, overlooking Royal Meadow between Atherstone and the River Anker. The main battlefield lay in the angle formed by the Anker and Sence. Henry attacked from the southeast, after circling the town to get the sun at his back, as reported by Polydore Vergil.

Bosworth Field

	Winners	*Losers*
Opponents	Tudor	Yorkist
Commanders	Henry Tudor, Earl of Richmond John de Vere, Earl of Oxford Sir William Stanley (Thomas, Lord Stanley)	Richard III (k) John Howard, Duke of Norfolk (k) Henry Percy, Earl of Northumberland
Numbers	5000–8000	4400–7900
Losses	100	*c.*1000

Support for Jones's view comes from payments Henry VII made to the Abbot of Merevale and the villagers of Mancetter, Witherley, Fenny Drayton and Atterton, as compensation for damage done by Lancastrian forces before and during the battle. Subsequently, the abbot sought the king's favour in a dispute over the lordship of Atherstone. The abbot's suggestion that this would provide a perpetual memorial to Henry's victory is hard to explain if the battle happened elsewhere.

Both revisionist sites are superior to the traditional battlefield at Ambion Hill, which is neither a plain, nor large enough for the forces engaged. On the whole Foss's eastern location at Redemore appears more convincing:

(1) It puts the battle where Burton and Drayton say it happened.

(2) It places the Stanleys on Richard III's left flank as the Spanish newsletter reports. Their position at Atherstone would be on his right.

(3) It places the marsh on Richmond's right flank, as Polydore Vergil says, not his left as Jones's interpretation requires. Either way, the Lancastrian manoeuvre avoids the sun dazzling their archers.

(4) The hills overlooking Redemore are more like the 'mountaines hye' of the ballad tradition, than the gentle slopes around the Sence–Anker confluence. The deeper rivers at Atherstone are a more significant tactical obstacle than the brooks north of Fenn Lane.

(5) The compensation payments could reflect damage done by foraging parties during Richmond's final approach on 21 August. Atterton seems particularly remote from the Atherstone battlefield. Fenny Drayton and Atterton lie directly in Henry's path, however, if he continued eastwards from Atherstone along Fenn Lane, to confront Richard upon Redemore.

The Lancastrians were still very weak. They had only enough men for a vanguard of 4000 under the Earl of Oxford and a 1000-strong bodyguard to ensure Henry's personal safety. In theory Richard outnumbered Henry two-to-one, the contemporary *Great Chronicle of London* breaking his forces down as follows:

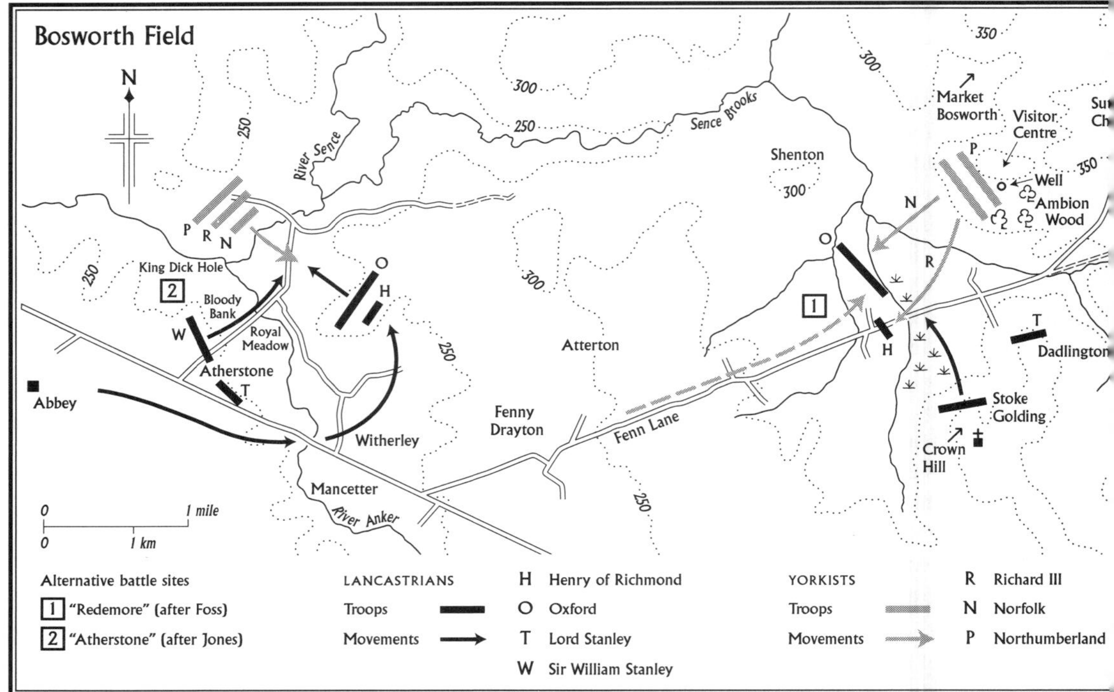

Vaward: Norfolk	1200	bowman flanked by
	200	heavy cavalry
Main: the king	1000	billmen 'empaled' with
	2000	pikes
Rereward:		
Northumberland	2000	with two wings of totalling
	1500	horse
Uncommitted:		
Lord Stanley	2000	'most of them horsemen'
TOTAL	9900	

Only the first two Yorkist echelons saw action. Northumberland and Lord Stanley remained aloof, giving Richard a similar number of effectives to Henry, until Sir William Stanley swung the balance with his independent force of 3000 joining Henry's. Both sides must have had some artillery; a royal army without cannon at this period would be unthinkable. Henry's French mercenaries advised him to attack the Yorkist flank to avoid their fire. Henry himself brought cannon from France, and may have acquired more at Lichfield, where 'gonnes craked' in his honour.

The Yorkists had occupied the place of fight the previous evening. Vergil's informants remembered them on the forward slope, 'so full replenished both with footmen and horsemen that to the beholders afar off it gave a terror ... in the front were placed

Directions

(1) Redemore *from the A5 follow Henry Tudor's approach along Fenn Lane, turning left after 2 miles (3 km) down a minor road along the western edge of the now drained wetland. White Moors picnic site roughly marks Oxford's position. Richard's death probably happened 1/3 mile (0.5 km) further along Fenn Lane from the junction. Continue through Shenton to see the battlefield from Ambion Hill, and visit the Battlefield Centre.*

(2) Atherston *turn off the A5 through Witherley, and bear left beside the River Anker to see Michael K. Jones's alternative site.*

his archers, like a most strong trench and bulwark'. To achieve this effect Richard would have needed to combine his van and main battles, as shown in the map. Drayton described their formation as wedge shaped, following the shape of the hill. Traditional spots associated with the doomed monarch bracket the ridge: Richard's Well at its southwest extremity, Dickon's Nook a tumulus to the east.

The action began 'well early in the morning', taking the Yorkists by surprise: 'at daybreak … when the chaplains on King Richard's side were not ready to celebrate, nor was any breakfast prepared …' (*Crowland History*). The Lancastrian army advanced at 'moderate pace', exploiting Vergil's marsh, 'which Henry of purpose left on the right hand, that it might serve his men instead of a fortress … also he left the sun on his back'. Oxford's northward movement round the marsh brought him in front of Richard's right flank, as one ballad suggests:

> The right hand of them he took
> The sun and wind of them to get.
> 'The Rose of England'

As the Lancastrians cleared the marsh, Richard's van advanced to engage them with archery. Oxford kept well closed up:

> Fearing lest his men … might be environed of the multitude, [he] commanded in every rank that no soldier should go ten feet from the standards; which charge being known, when all men had thronged thick together, and stayed a while from fighting, the enemy were therewith afeared … and forbore the fight a certain space.
> Polydore Vergil

The first stage of the battle thus ended in stalemate. Meanwhile, Richard had observed Henry 'afar off with small force of soldiers'. Rather than reinforce the infantry battle, he resolved on a high-risk mounted attack on his Lancastrian opposite number. Polydore Vergil's words clearly show the eccentric direction of Richard's charge, out of the opposite side, '*ex altero latere*', of the battle line to that just described, i.e. the vanguard bogged down north of Redemore. Richard's southerly movement brought him dangerously close to Sir William Stanley. While Henry defended himself with surprising obstinacy for a novice, Sir William cut in between the king and Northumberland's rereward, which stood three-quarters of a mile (1.2 km) away, neither giving nor receiving blows. Outnumbered three-to-one and taken in the rear, Richard scorned flight and was struck down by a Welsh halberdier.

Several sources place Richard's last stand in a bog. The French chronicler Jean Molinet says the king's horse stumbled in a marsh, from which its rider could not escape. The *Great Chronicle* described Richard's body 'all to besprung with myrr and ffylthe'. A royal circular written immediately after the battle refers to Richard III as 'lately slain at a place called Sandeford within the county of Leicestershire'. This has been identified, on flimsy evidence, with a ford north of Ambion Hill, near the Shenton–Sutton Cheney road. Peter Foss puts Richard's death much further south, where Fenn Lane crosses the Sence brooks. This is more convenient for Richmond's battlefield acclamation on Crown Hill, while the '-ford' ending indicates a causeway such as the Roman road might have followed.

Oxford easily dispersed the leaderless Yorkist vanguard, once the result was no longer in doubt. Prisoners anxious to make their peace with the new regime outnumbered the dead, who may have been as few as 300 altogether. The defeated king, 'despoiled to the skin', was borne off for public display, 'trussed … as a hog or other wild beast'. The *Great Chronicle* thought the God of Battles had spoken: 'had he [Richard III] … suffered the children to have prospered according to his allegiance and fealty, he would have been honourably lauded over all, whereas now his fame is darkened'.

Tadcaster, 10 June 1487

England, North Yorkshire, LR105 unlocated

Stoke Field, Saturday 16 June 1487

England, Nottinghamshire, LR129 SK7448–7548

Blackheath, 17 June 1497

England, London, LR177, unlocated

Henry VII's reign was unlikely to bring instant peace after 30 years of intermittent civil war. He resolved the most dangerous threat to his position at Stoke Field, the last major action of the Wars of the Roses, but revolts persisted, dying away after Blackheath (1497).

One of the few Yorkist claimants to the throne left after Bosworth was Edward, Earl of Warwick, son of Edward IV's brother Clarence. Henry locked him up, but this did not stop malcontents grooming Lambert Simnel, the ten-year-old son of an Oxford joiner, as a counterfeit Warwick. Crowned Edward VI in Dublin, Lambert was a stalking horse for the Earl of Lincoln's own dynastic claims. Funded by Edward IV's sister Margaret, Duchess of Burgundy, Lincoln raised 2000 pike-armed German *Landsknechte*, led by the famous mercenary leader Martin Schwarz, and 'so much Irishmen as would take their part ... for the most part naked' (*Book of Howth*).

The expedition landed at Piel Castle in the Furness peninsula of southern Cumbria on 4 July 1487, and crossed the Pennines into Yorkshire to seek recruits. Denied entry to York, Lincoln bypassed the city, camping on Bramham Moor. Lord Clifford, the Tudor sheriff, entered York the same day with 400 men, and with more courage than sense rode out to intercept the rebels. That night the rebels overran Clifford's camp at Tadcaster, captured his baggage and chased him back to York. However, Lincoln would not fight Tudor reinforcements under the Earl of Northumberland. He continued south, probably following Ryknield Way via Castleford and Rotherham.

Henry VII had occupied a central position in the Midlands. Hearing Lincoln was at Southwell, north of the River Trent near Newark, the king closed with him rapidly, hoping to crush the rebels before they grew too strong. On the eve of battle Henry lay at Radcliffe on Trent, outside Nottingham, 14 miles (22.5 km) from Newark along the Fosse Way. Next morning he heard two Masses, and then advanced along the river's south bank, meeting the enemy at a little village '*quem vocat Stochum*', i.e. East Stoke, 4 miles (6 km) short of Newark. Acts of Attainder confirm the fighting occurred 'at Stoke in the countie of Notyngham'.

Lincoln occupied high ground south of Stoke, where 19th-century rustics pointed out his campsite near a windmill known as the Rampire, or rampart. Lincoln presumably crossed the Trent at Fiskerton, directly between Southwell and East Stoke. His army was in a poor strategic position. One possible line of retreat lay through Newark, a Tudor garrison; a second ran obliquely across his right rear towards the 160-yard (145-m) wide Trent. The ridge did suit Lincoln's tactical purpose, however. It runs east–west across Henry's line of approach, and has extensive views across the low-lying Trent valley. On the west, a cliff falls steeply to Stoke Marsh, a narrow strip of bog beside the Trent, securing the rebel right. The escarpment is now partially wooded, but at the time of the battle the whole area was open and unenclosed. Eastwards the ridge slopes gently down towards Elston. The location is the only suitable defensive position that fits Tudor accounts. Sir Francis Bacon placed Lincoln 'upon the brow or hanging of a hill', while Polydore Vergil says he came down to fight, '*in certamen descendit*'.

The rebel front extended between a half and three-quarters of a mile (0.8–1.2 km), allowing four or five men per yard. The official estimate of their numbers was 'V.M' or 'VIII.M': 'a great multitude of straungers', armed with the statutory 'swerdys, speris, marespikes, bowes, gonnes, harneys, brigandynes, hawberkes, and many other wepyns' (Acts of Attainder). They were fewer than Lincoln had predicted, and Schwarz went into action less in hope of victory than out of loyalty to his Burgundian duchess. No official figure survives for Henry VII's army, but he far outnumbered the opposition. His herald's journal describes Lord Strange's contingent alone as 'a greate hoste, inow to have beten al the kings enemies'. Despite several panics on the march, the core of the army was sound, with veteran leaders: 'I harde of no man of worship that fledde but rascals.'

Older interpretations of Stoke Field reversed the battle lines, with Henry retracing his steps from Newark to attack the rebels from the north. This mistaken view derives from a confused passage in Polydore Vergil, who wrote twenty years after the battle, never visited the site, and does not mention its key feature, the River Trent. The herald, an eye-witness, leaves no doubt that Henry moved directly from Radcliffe to Stoke. Vergil also states that Henry divided his force into the traditional three divisions, '*triplici instructa acie*', but the herald refers only to the Earl of Oxford's 'fowade', and by implication a main body under the king. This two-fold division was Henry's standard practice in all his battles. The royal council of war had established a powerful vanguard before the Stoke Field campaign, with five peers under Oxford's command, and 'many other Gallants of the king's house' as fore-riders, later reinforced by Lord Strange. Henry was a very modern general, organizing victory from behind, leaving operational control to a trusted subordinate.

The herald's journal gives extensive details of Henry's preparations: selection of guides to avoid 'bushements' during the approach from Radcliffe, and disciplinary regulations that filled Loughborough's stocks with 'harlatts and vagabonds'. Unfortunately he says little about the battle:

> And so in good order and array, before 9 of the clok, beside a village called Stook, a large myle out of Newarke, his forwarde recountrede his enemyes and rebells, wher by the helpe of Almighty God, he hadde the victorye.

Other sources say the rebels left the high ground and fought in the 'champion' or plain, presumably opposite the northern end of Lodge Lane. Their élan may suggest they hoped treachery would even the odds, for they 'sped them towards the field with as good courage as they had had twenty thousand men more' (*Great Chronicle of London*). More likely, Lincoln's tactics reflected the rapid advance to contact characteristic of *Landsknechte* and kerne.

The rebel army, with its 'beggarly, naked, and almost unarmed Irishmen', lacking armour and longbows, was ill adapted to English warfare. Undistracted by return fire, Oxford's archers displayed their ancient mastery of the field, despite valiant opposition:

> For these Allmayns [Germans] were very good and apt soldiers, so was their captain Martin Swarthe; his like was not seen in both the armies to all purposes … The Irishmen did as well as any naked men could do.
>
> *Book of Howth*

Tadcaster

	Winners	*Losers*
Opponents	Yorkist	Tudor
Commanders	John de la Pole, Earl of Lincoln	Lord Henry Clifford
Numbers	unknown	400

Stoke Field

	Winners	*Losers*
Opponents	Tudor	Yorkist
Commanders	Henry VII John de Vere, Earl of Oxford	John de la Pole, Earl of Lincoln (k) Martin Schwarz (k) Francis, Viscount Lovell
Numbers	*c.*12,000	5000–8000
Losses	unknown	4000

Blackheath

	Winners	*Losers*
Opponents	Royalist	Rebel
Commanders	Henry VII Lord Daubeney	James Touchet, Lord Audley (x)
Numbers	25,000	15,000

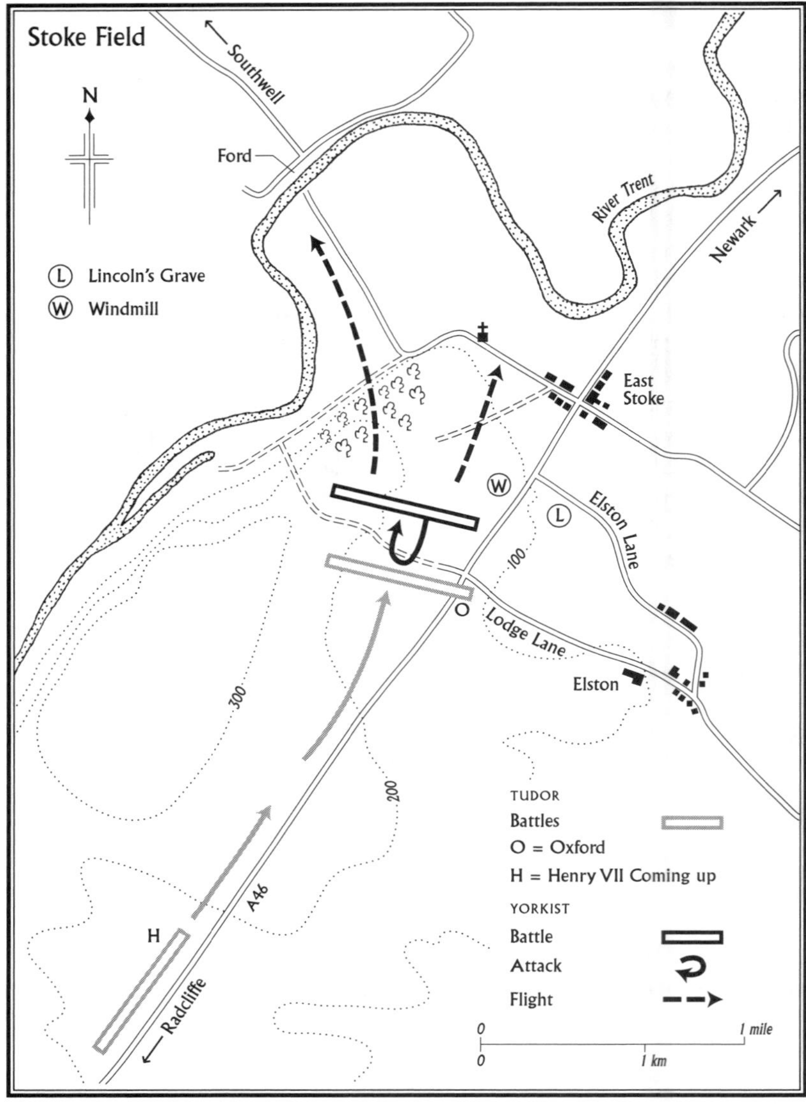

The powerful royal vanguard 'was alone committed to the fray', and won the battle on its own: 'only then when the battle was over … [was it] fully apparent how rash had been the spirit inspiring the enemy soldiers' (Vergil). They fled through the fields south of Stoke, or towards Fiskerton down a ravine since known as Red Gutter for the blood that ran down it. *Indicia* of slaughter have been found in both areas, including rows of bodies in a mass grave in Stoke Hall garden.

Directions

Stoke Field *Follow the A46 south from Newark. Turn right to see Stoke Hall, a monument to the fallen at Stoke Church, and the 'ford' at Fiskerton. A footpath leads south from the village onto the ridge, although there is no public access to Red Gutter. Carry on down the Fosse Way past Elston Lane to the place of slaughter, on the right. According to tradition, Lincoln is buried south of Elston Lane by a spring called Willow Rundle.*

Rebel losses were high and disproportionate. More than one source sets them at 'IIII.M', while Henry VII claimed he won 'without death of any noble or gentleman on our part'. Lincoln and Schwarz died fighting. Lovell was last seen swimming his horse across the Trent. A vault opened at Minster Lovell in 1728 contained a man's seated skeleton, often judged to have been the missing viscount. Lambert Simnel was spared, becoming a royal falconer after a spell as a scullion in the royal kitchens.

The last battle of Henry's reign in 1497 had no dynastic agenda. Cornish taxpayers resented paying for a war against Scotland, and some 15,000 of them marched on the capital to complain. On 16 June they reached 'the Blackheath beside Greenwich', threatening London across the Thames. However, artillery covered the Deptford Creek approach to London Bridge, while Henry diverted Daubeney's Scottish expedition to collect an overwhelming force against the rebels. Many deserted overnight. Perhaps 10,000 faced Daubeney's men-at-arms and archers, when they advanced over Deptford bridge: 'The Cornishmen, being ill-armed and ill-led and without horse or artillery, were with no great difficulty cut in pieces and put to flight' (Sir Francis Bacon). Many died on the field, but only leaders were executed afterwards. Henry's reprisals were financial, giving no excuse for a vendetta.

Directions

Tadcaster *Tactical locations unknown.*
Blackheath *Tactical locations unknown.*

Sauchieburn, 11 June 1488

Scotland, Stirling, LR57 NS8384

The English were not the only British people to depose and kill their kings in the 15th century. The reign of James III of Scotland also ended in violence, ironically near the site of Robert the Bruce's crowning victory at Bannockburn.

James III was that dangerous phenomenon, an unwarlike king who 'desyrit never to heir of weirys [wars] nor the fame thereof, but delytit mair in musik'. He amassed treasure in his 'blak kist [chest]', and pursued détente with England, to his barons' discontent. Seeing treachery on all sides he locked his eldest son, the Duke of Rothesay, in Stirling Castle. In February 1488, Rothesay's jailer handed him over to his father's enemies, an ideal figurehead for rebellion. Royal government collapsed as James III lost ground to a patriotic opposition who denounced 'the perverst counsale of divers persouns', and 'the inbringing of Inglissmen'. Early in June, James III left Edinburgh for the last time, meaning to crush his enemies once and for all. Royal ships patrolled the Firth of Forth, allowing James to avoid the main rebel concentration at Linlithgow. He crossed into Fife, rode up the north shore of the estuary and entered Stirling from the north. His forces chased rebel outposts through the town, but encountered their main army on the River Carron, ready for action.

Sauchieburn

	Winners	*Losers*
Opponents	Rebel	Royalist
Commanders	James, Duke of Rothesay	James III (k)
Numbers	unknown	unknown

The location of 'Sauchieburn' is a case history of how a battlefield can wander. Contemporaries wrote vaguely of 'slauchteris commit and done in the field of Striviline' (Act of Parliament, 1488), or the recovery of Bruce's sword, which James had carried in the battle near Stirling, '*in bello prope Striveling*'. More specific 16th-century accounts locate the fighting, 'at Bannokburne tua myles fra Striuelinge', or in neighbouring Tor Wood. The battle and James's flight could have involved both areas, connected as they are by Scotland's strategic artery, the Roman road from Falkirk through Stirling to Perth. The name 'Sauchie' first appears in the 17th century, when William Drummond of Hawthornden placed James III's army 'the other side of Torwood near a small brook called the Sauchieburn … not far from

… Bannock-burn'. The association with Bruce's victory suggests Drummond meant Sauchinford Burn, which rises near West Plean, between Tor Wood and Bannockburn, right on the line of the road. Subsequent writers have followed Drummond, in order to distinguish the 1488 battle from Stirling Bridge (1297) or Bannockburn (1314).

Unfortunately another stream is also called Sauchie Burn. It rises in the Lennox foothills west of Old Sauchie (NS7688), joining the Bannock Burn above Chartershall Bridge, almost a mile (1.6 km) from the Roman road. The Reverend William Nimmo transferred the battle there in 1777, wrenching it from its strategic context. Sauchieburn was a standard encounter between armies moving in opposite directions along a main road. There are no significant roads at all around Nimmo's site, which is too far west to fit Lindsay of Pitscottie's extensive 16th-century battle narrative. It is hard to imagine what possible purpose could have brought two armies there. Nevertheless, most historians have followed Nimmo, crassly mistranslating '*in bello prope Striveling*' as 'on the field of Sauchie'.

Pitscottie's narrative develops more naturally. James met his enemies south of Stirling, probably along the Roman road. This would be their natural route from Larbert, where a bridge existed by 1651. At the time Tor Wood spread further north, a patchwork of clearings and copses as far as Bannock Burn. James, however, deployed in open fields, therefore south of the wood. He failed to defend any of the obstacles available, such as Tor Burn (NS8385). Perhaps he wanted a decisive result. James took the centre with 'all the burrowis and commons of Scottland', presumably infantry, with Highlanders in the van, their traditional post on the right. Precise numbers and identities of combatants are obscure, except when they were killed, or subsequently arraigned for treason.

Various factors suggest James fought at some disadvantage. One source says he was awaiting northern reinforcements, while the rebel line was well equipped, '*bene instructa*'. No notable fatalities occurred among the rebels, whose leaders had signed a pledge not to harm the king, a step implying confidence rather than moderation. The Duke of Rothesay boldly asserted his right to rule by flying the royal standard, to the probable dismay of the king's army. James was half-hearted in his own cause: 'never hardie nor yeit constant in batell', he was among the first to quit the field.

After fruitless negotiations, the rebels fell upon the royal line with all their strength. James's army retreated into Tor Wood in good order, where they held out until dark. Rothesay then followed up as far as Stirling Bridge, where a Royalist counterattack checked further pursuit. In his flight, James strayed away from the battle's main axis. Heading eastwards for his ships on the Forth, he fell off his horse jumping Bannock Burn. Carried senseless into a nearby watermill, he was 'wnworthelie [sic] slaine', by 'vile and unknown persons'.

Pitscottie blamed a sinister priest, who asked the king whether he might recover, and on receiving a positive reply, 'pullit out ane quhinger [sword] and gif him foure or fyue straikis ewin to the hart'. Sadly Pitscottie had adapted the story from Hector Boece's recently published account of Robert the Bruce's murder of John Comyn in 1306. James III's assassin was more likely a servant of Lord Gray, a rebel diehard, who had the sense to keep quiet afterwards. The first death of a Stewart king at the hands of his own subjects was a shocking affair. It did, however, transfer power from a thoroughly unsatisfactory king to the most successful of late medieval Scottish monarchs. As James IV, Rothesay revived the classic pattern of royal-magnate cooperation, reigning successfully until the disaster at Flodden Field (1513).

Directions

Take the A9 north from Larbert Bridge. Turn left at Glenbervie for Torwood Castle, which is on the line of the Roman Road, in the approximate area of the battlefield.

PART FIVE

HACKBUT AND HALBERD

Renaissance and Reformation 1504–1601

The century that spanned the reigns of Henry VIII and Elizabeth I (1509–1603) marks the strategic transition between medieval and modern Britain. Henry VIII confronted military relationships familiar to Edward III. Before the death of his daughter Elizabeth, these had evolved into a pattern recognizable today. Wales ceased to be a source of military conflict, while Ireland replaced Scotland as England's nearest strategic preoccupation. The loss of Calais, the last remnant of Edward III's conquests, ended 500 years of Continental entanglements. On the battlefield, bows and bills made way for gunpowder weapons. At sea the development of fully rigged ocean-going ships exposed the North Atlantic Archipelago to attack in a way not seen for centuries. For the first time, our knowledge of military events no longer depends on hearsay. Numerous official documents and eyewitness accounts of battles survive, thanks to burgeoning bureaucracy, wider literacy and the printing press.

The Tudor restoration of strong royal government ensured most British warfare during the 16th century occurred outside England. No English monarch was overthrown by a military uprising, despite wide availability of weapons and military training. In contrast to the 15th century, most rebellions collapsed without serious fighting, even when genuine grievances inspired mass protests, such as the Pilgrimage of Grace of 1536. The absence of serious military threats at home allowed Henry VIII to pursue grandiose ambitions abroad. His obsession with re-enacting the Hundred Years' War rekindled hostility along a still smouldering Scottish Border. English Renaissance armies defeated Scots armies as expedi-

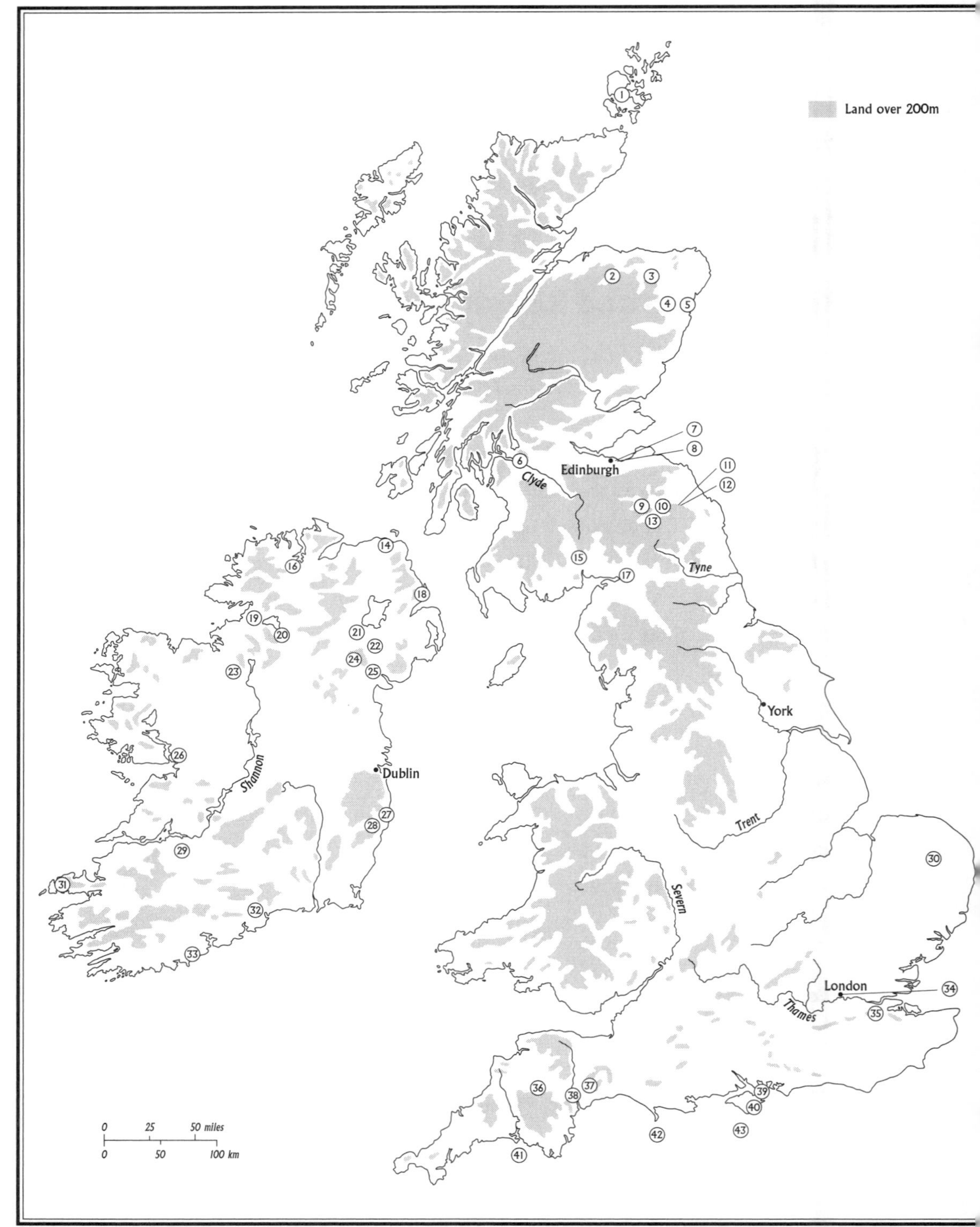

Land over 200m
1
2
3
4
5
7
8
6
Edinburgh
Clyde
11
12
9
10
13
14
16
15
Tyne
17
18
19
20
21
22
24
25
23
York
26
Dublin
Shannon
27
28
Trent
29
30
31
Severn
32
33
London
34
Thames
35
36
38
37
39
40
42
43
41
0
25
50 miles
0
50
100 km

tiously as their medieval predecessors had, but with no more political success: Tudor victories – such as those at Flodden (1513) or Solway Moss (1542) – may have shattered Scottish military self-confidence, but they had the effect of reinforcing the Auld Alliance with France.

The loss of Calais in 1558 ended dreams of Continental conquests, and brought a diplomatic revolution to the Border, as the economical Elizabeth abandoned the testosterone-rich policies of her predecessors. Elizabethan armies visited Scotland by invitation, liquidated pockets of French or Roman Catholic influence, and went quietly home again. The Reformation gave the two British nations a common interest in Protestantism that moderated ancient antagonisms. The unlikely rapprochement between Stewart Scotland and late Tudor England was sustained by the realization that James VI was the most probable successor to his cousin Elizabeth. Armed conflict in late 16th-century Scotland was domestic, inspired by Mary Queen of Scots' marital vagaries, or the cynical power-play of unruly magnates.

The presence of a French garrison at Leith in 1560 reveals how the king of France bestrode Elizabeth's realm. Improvements in ship design and naval administration brought the most serious external threat to Britain and Ireland since the Viking raids. French and Spanish invasion fleets appeared off the southern English coast, the Great Armada (1588) threatening to overturn the entire Elizabethan state. Rumours of amphibious descents upon Ireland in the 1530s became a reality when Catholic troops from Spain and Italy landed at Smerwick (1579–80), provoking a savage response from the English.

As Anglo-Scots hostility approached resolution, Ireland emerged as the major

---

KEY

1 Summerdale 1529
2 Glenlivet 1594
3 Tillyangus 1571
4 Corrichie 1562
5 Craibstane Rout 1571
6 Langside 1568
7 Pinkie 1547
8 Carberry Hill 1567
9 Melrose 1526
10 Hadden Rig 1542
11 Flodden 1513
12 Milfield 1513
13 Ancrum Moor 1545
14 Glentaisie 1656
15 Drumlanrig 1548
16 Farsetmore 1567
17 Solway Moss 1542
18 Carrickfergus 1597
19 Erne Fords 1593
20 Ford of the Biscuits 1594
21 Yellow Ford 1598
22 Mullaghbrack 1595
23 Curlew Mountains 1599
24 Clontibret 1595
25 Moyry Pass 1600
26 Knockdoe 1504
27 Wicklow 1599
28 Glemalur 1580
29 Monasternenagh 1579
30 Dussindale 1549
31 Smerwick 1580
32 Affane c.1565
33 Kinsale 1601
34 Fleet Street 1554
35 Wrotham 1554
36 Stampford Courtenay 1549
37 Fenny Bridges 1549
38 Clyst St Mary 1549
39 Portsmouth 1545
40 Bonchurch 1545
41 Plymouth 1588
42 Portland Bill 1588
43 Isle of Wight 1588

strategic concern for English governments. Irish support for pretenders during the Wars of the Roses had revealed the risks posed by an Ireland largely outside English control. Henry VIII abandoned his predecessors' laissez-faire policy. Medieval English kings had ruled Ireland at arm's-length through Anglo-Norman settlers, leaving the native Gaels largely to themselves. The centralizing Tudor state could not tolerate a self-governing heroic society, hardly changed since the days of Brian Boru. Henry imposed direct rule through an English viceroy (known as the lord deputy), backed by a standing army. Gaelic resistance flared up in a series of rebellions, culminating in Elizabethan England's most serious military challenge, Tyrone's Rebellion, otherwise known as the Nine Years' War.

Hugh O'Neill, Earl of Tyrone, skilfully adapted the latest military techniques to Irish conditions, but developments elsewhere undermined Gaeldom's strategic position. Rising population and higher land prices in mainland Britain encouraged economic migrants from England and Scotland to colonize Ireland's under-utilized countryside. Cultural and religious differences between the settlers and Ireland's existing population precluded assimilation. By the end of the Nine Years' War, the bipolar split between Gael and Anglo-Norman had become a threefold division between Gaelic, Old English and New English. The first two were generally Roman Catholic, for the first time bracketed together as 'Irish'.

The Reformation divided the Gaelic-speaking communities either side of the North Channel, as Protestantism spread into the Western Isles, cutting off the supply of Scots mercenaries or Redshanks to Ireland. The native gallowglasses had their last outing at Kinsale (1601). Adherence to the Counter-Reformation isolated the Irish within a predominantly Protestant archipelago. In future they would seek help from outside powers, concerned more with their own strategic interests than those of their Irish clients.

Population trends confirmed England's emerging hegemony. England's population may have risen by 60 per cent during the 16th century and Scotland's by 13 per cent. Ireland's defied the general trend, and shrank. England had plenty of sturdy beggars to fill the large armies needed for Renaissance warfare. The Duke of Somerset began the campaign that led to Pinkie (1547) with an army of 16,000–19,000 men; English forces in Ireland rose to a similar figure during the

Nine Years' War. Plans to resist the Armada envisaged three armies totalling over 80,000 men.

Henry VII reorganized the county militia to form the basis for Tudor recruitment, as inflation curtailed aristocratic retinues. Even a thinly populated county like Cumberland could raise over 6000 militia during the 1530s. German or Italian mercenaries supplied the deficiency of professional military manpower. The Scots army at Flodden (1513) – some 20,000 men – was the largest ever to cross the Border, though most Scottish mobilizations were less productive. Scotland was poor, and smashing defeats made Scotsmen unwilling to serve, defying fiery crosses and legal bans on such distractions as golf and football. Aristocratic retinues did well at Hadden Rig (1542,) and Ancrum Moor (1545), but became a menace for Mary Queen of Scots.

Irish military manpower was both limited and fragmented. Surveys in the 1520s reckoned 60 to 80 independent Gaelic chiefs controlled 20,000 armed men between them, but individual warbands were small: 200 light horse, rather more kern (lightly armed footsoldiers), and one or two 'battles' of 60–80 gallowglasses: the 'castles of bones' that suited Ireland's fluid warfare better than fixed defences. Social convention limited military service to the aristocracy and their followers. Shane O'Neill in the 1560s was the first chieftain to arm all his subjects, mixing them with 'gunners, galloglass and all other men of war that he conveniently can get'. Hugh O'Neill followed Shane's example, fielding nearly 5000 men at Yellow Ford (1598). Scottish mercenaries remained significant in Irish warfare, despite legislation making their employment a capital offence. When homebred gallowglass proved insufficient to meet demand, they were joined by kilted 'Redshanks' from the Western Isles, transient warriors who campaigned by the season.

In mainland Britain large armies, good communications and advanced urbanization promoted rapid military outcomes. In Ireland limited forces and the absence of towns and roads hampered attempts to seek victory on the battlefield. Guerrilla warfare was normal, bringing hardships upon both sides. Henry Wallop, treasurer of Ireland, wrote of Ormond's march through Munster in December 1579: 'bread but for five days and no drink at all. They passed rivers wading to the stomach seven times a day and then lodged abroad without tent, house or cabin. It is easier to talk at home of Irish wars than to be in them.' Tyrone's Rebellion left Ulster a wasteland, its inhabitants reduced to eating grass and corpses.

Battlefields underwent startling changes during the 16th century, as demi-lances (lightly armoured cavalry) and arquebusiers swept away knights and archers. Gunpowder weapons sparked off a military revolution that substituted mercenary armies for feudal hosts, and low earth-packed bastions for tall stone towers. Armies avoided battle, as they pursued countervalue strategies directed against the enemy's pocket, rather than counterforce strategies aimed at his armies. Geographically remote and culturally detached from the European mainstream, Britain and Ireland, it is said, stood outside these exciting developments.

This simplified view of the 16th-century military scene is open to question. Many aspects of the military revolution continued medieval trends. Paid infantry armies were a longstanding feature of British battlefields, and Robert the Bruce had favoured economic pressure over combat. There is no real evidence that 16th-century England and Scotland were militarily backward where it mattered. James IV imported French veterans before Flodden to teach his men to handle 15-foot (4.5-m) pikes, in the latest 'Almayn [German] manner'. The first Italian-style bastion in Scotland appeared at Eyemouth in 1547, at the same time as the French were building such fortresses along their northern frontier. Henry VIII and his successor Edward VI supplemented local troops with foreign mercenaries, but so did everyone else.

Henry VIII took a keen interest in military technology – the Venetian ambassador thought he had 'enough cannon to conquer hell'. English gun founders were among the best in Europe: they pioneered several technical advances, boring out gun barrels vertically, and standardizing calibres before the French, the recognized experts. The clumsy handguns used at St Albans (1461) had evolved into more sophisticated weapons. Fired from the shoulder, and known as hackbuts or arquebuses, these could pierce the finest plate armour at 100 yards (90 m). In 1547 Henry VIII's probate inventory shows the Tower of London contained 64 bronze cannon, 351 iron guns, 6700 demi-hakes (arquebuses), and 275 'short gonnes for horsemen'.

English infantry had no pressing need to give up the tried combination of bow and bill. Early drill books praised the longbow's 'sharpe and manyefolde hail-shotte'. Gradually, however, the bow fell behind developments in armour and firearms. Thomas Ruthal, Bishop of Durham (d.1523) wrote that the leading Scots ranks at Flodden 'were so surely harnessed with complete harneys Jacks almayn ryvettes splints pavices and other habilments that shote of arrows ... did theim no harme'. Italian arquebusiers outranged rebel archers at Fenny Bridge (1549), and made more noise. Moral commentators blamed the longbow's decay upon a preference for whoring instead of archery practice, but arquebusiers were better paid: 8d. a day, against the archer's 6d.

The English adopted the new weapons gradually, mixing them with the traditional bow and bill. Formations became deeper, with a narrow front to optimize mobility, and a central core of pikes and bills screened and flanked by archers and arquebusiers. Combined-arms formations became typical of infantry throughout the British Isles, predominantly comprising pikes and arquebuses, with some halberds around the colours. Firepower was enhanced by the introduction of the heavier, longer-ranging musket. English armies included powerful cavalry formations. Some carried the lance, as fully armoured *gens d'arme*, or as the cheaper demi-lance, who discarded horse and leg armour in search of greater mobility. Other cavalrymen carried firearms, acting as scouts or as a mobile reserve of firepower. Mounted arquebusiers played an important role at Pinkie (1547), against the flanks of Scots pike squares.

The Scots did their best to keep up. Stewart interest in artillery dated from James II, killed by a burst gun barrel during the siege of Roxburgh (1460). James IV fielded large numbers of home-cast cannon, and his successors imported massive quantities of French firearms in the 1520s and 1540s. Scots pike squares at Flodden imitated the best Continental practice, 4000 men each in a solid mass, 60 men along each side. Superficial likenesses aside, this was a faster, more dangerous formation than the old schiltron, which rarely took the offensive; pike squares, on the other hand, moved rapidly across country. On contact they doubled up their deep open files, rear-rank men filling the gaps between the leaders: 'so hard at their backs, laying their pikes over their foregoers' shoulders; that if they do assail undissevered, no force can well withstand them' (William

Patten, *The expedicion into Scotlande of the most woorthely fortunate prince Edward Duke of Somerset*, 1549). On the defensive, front ranks stooped, bracing pike butts against feet, successive rows of pike points crossed in front of them, 'the whole Ward so thick, that as easily shall a bare finger pierce through the skin of an angry hedgehog, as any encounter the front of their pikes' (Patten). However, the reliance on one weapon type proved disastrous against English combined-arms tactics at Pinkie (1547). In smaller actions the Scots fielded a more balanced weapon mix, their advance guard at Hadden Rig combining 1000 spears, 500 bows and 500 'hagbuttis'.

The most remarkable transfer of 16th-century weapon technology within the British Isles occurred in Ireland. Gaelic armies had not altered much since gallowglass joined the traditional light cavalry and dart-throwing kerne in the 13th century. Now kerns took up the arquebus, often as auxiliaries of the English. Fired from cover, single-shot firearms were ideal for Irish hit-and-run warfare. Hugh O'Neill completed the process, fielding red-coated regiments of well-drilled arquebusiers at Clontibret (1595), many of them deserters from English armies. He acquired arms and powder from Scotland, or seized them guerrilla style from the enemy. Nevertheless, O'Neill gained most of his successes in the traditional way: 'never making good any fight, but bogring [sic] with his shot and flying from bush to bush' (Lord Burgh). Formal operations at Kinsale (1601) confirmed English superiority in the open. Outnumbered two-to-one Lord Mountjoy bottled up nearly 4000 Spanish infantry, the finest in Europe, and broke O'Neill's unshaken pikemen with a cavalry charge, a remarkable vindication of the Tudor art of war.

The Rough Wooing: England in Scotland

The Anglo-Scots Wars of the early 16th century followed the pattern of earlier Scottish wars. Military stalemate proved once more that England could not conquer her northern neighbour, despite battlefield successes surpassing those of Edward I or even Edward III.

Warfare remained an essential means of self-assertion for Renaissance monarchs, as it had been for medieval kings. This had little to do with objective definitions of national interest. James IV's death at Flodden (1513) arose from the desire he shared with Henry VIII to cut a fine figure on the European stage. The Anglo-Scots Treaty of Perpetual Peace (1502), and the marriage of Henry's sister Margaret to James IV, paradoxically heightened tension, as dynastic rivalry sharpened ingrained suspicion. Henry VIII revived defunct claims to the Scottish throne, proclamations of the 1540s referring anachronistically to 'our rebels the Scots'.

James V's accession to the throne after Flodden, aged two, necessarily undermined royal authority in Scotland. For years the young king was held prisoner by his mother's second husband, Archibald Douglas, Earl of Angus. Magnates fought private battles at Melrose (1526) and Summerdale (1529), while cold war prevailed along the Border. Mistrust became so ingrained that in 1541 James V cut a summit meeting at York, for fear of being kidnapped. Henry's response, instructing his lieutenants to 'do to the Scots in spoils, burnings and killings, three hurts to one', was a throwback to Edward I's policies, and just as ineffectual. Neither party could engage the other effectively: the Duke of Norfolk's invasion of October 1542 withdrew 'for skarsitie of vitaylles'; James V's attempted riposte in November ended in humiliation at Solway Moss. His sudden death, attributed to a broken heart, left the week-old Princess Mary as Queen of Scots.

Even Henry VIII baulked at making war on a baby, but his pachydermous attempts to marry her to his son Edward inspired eight years of savage warfare, known as the Rough Wooing. Many Scots enlisted with the enemy as 'assured Scots', giving hostages as security for good behaviour. English state terrorism was counterproductive. The horrors inflicted in pursuit of dynastic unity alienated even Scots who favoured the marriage. Rather than accept the Treaty of Greenwich (1543) and see Mary married to Edward VI, the Scots regency sent her to France, to marry the Dauphin (who was to become Francis II). Only Francis's premature death in 1560 saved England from the nightmare of a French province on her northern Border.

Scotland remained too poor to afford the cavalry and missile troops needed to win at Flodden (1513) or Pinkie (1547), the two great battles that delimit the period. The Scottish rout at Solway Moss (1542) underlined the uselessness of the traditional Scots *levée en masse*, although flying columns did well in smaller actions at Hadden Rig (1542), Ancrum Moor (1545) and Drumlanrig (1548). Distance and poverty remained Scotland's best defence: victorious English armies could not convert military gains into political success before lack of food forced them to withdraw. Destruction of crops in the West Marches hindered even minor operations like Drumlanrig (1548). Attempts to dominate Scotland Roman fashion with chains of forts supplied by sea proved impossibly expensive. The strategy bankrupted the English government, inspired rebellions in Norfolk and western England, and brought the Duke of Somerset, lord protector for the boy-king Edward VI, to the executioner's block. French troops and arms supplies sustained Scots pressure on isolated English garrisons, the last of which were evacuated early in 1550.

Milfield (the Ill Raid), 13 August 1513

England, Northumberland, LR74 NT9334?

Flodden (Branxton Field/Heath), Friday 9 September 1513

England, Northumberland, LR74 NT8937

James IV's death colours all accounts of Flodden. In hindsight the campaign is easily seen as a rash adventure, foredoomed and unpopular. Defeat was harder to accept as the Scots had every advantage of ground, numbers and supply, and should have won. The casualty roll, however, shows that James enjoyed widespread support among his fellow Scots. Facing Henry VIII's mindless belligerence, Scotland had little choice but to stand by France. A limited Border campaign would secure the advantages of the Auld Alliance, with little risk. A document found on the battlefield listed substantial French aid: 25,000 gold crowns, 40 cartloads of gunpowder, hundreds of handguns, thousands of pikes, and French technical experts to explain their use: 'The Scotts lacked no thyng necessary for the warrys but oonly the grace of god' (Thomas Ruthal, Bishop of Durham).

Hostilities began with a raid that went wrong within 4 miles (6 km) of Flodden, near earlier Scottish misadventures at Nesbit Muir and Homildon Hill (1402). Sir William Bulmer circled ahead of the returning Scots, slowed by stolen cattle, and ambushed them near Milfield. Concealed archers shot down 500 raiders from the flank, while Border horsemen 'sette upon and venquysched the chamberlayn of Scotland' (Ruthal), who left his standard and 400–500 prisoners in enemy hands.

The main Scots host crossed the Tweed on 22 August and battered Norham Castle into submission with James IV's new bronze cannon. After that they found an impregnable position 8 miles (13 km) further south at Flodden Edge, and defied the Earl of Surrey, Henry VIII's lieutenant, to turn them out. The Geordie soldier who wrote a *Trewe Encountre or Batayle lately don between Englande ande Scotlande* described James's position 'upon an high hill in the egge [edge] of Cheviotte ... with three great mountaynes, soe that ther was noe passage nor entre unto hym but oon waye, wher was laied marvellous and great ordenance of gonnes'. Surrey described it as 'like a fortress'.

The Scots lampooned the 70-year old Surrey as 'ane cruikit cairll [fellow] liand in ane charieot', but he was too wily to risk a frontal attack against the largest army Scotland ever sent into England. Contemporaries estimated Scottish numbers at 60,000–100,000. Modern scholars suggest 30,000– 40,000 Scots crossed the Border, half deserting before the battle. This left some 20,000 serious fighters, 'every man for the most parte with a kene and a sharp sper of v [five] yards long, and a target afore hym' (*Trewe Encountre*). Some handgunners may also have been present. Exchequer entries for removing captured ordnance from the field of battle included two waggonloads of 'hagbushes and pellets', the 'dyvers small ordenances' to which *Trewe Encountre* refers. Seventeen heavier cannon were dug in upon Flodden Hill, covering the open ground below.

Surrey's army was probably the smaller: *Trewe Encountre* gives a figure of 26,000, while Surrey's accounts show wages for 18,699. He formed them into two divisions, vanward and rearward, recalling Henry VII's tactics. Each division consisted of a centre or 'breste' and two wings, the centres 9000 and 5000 strong respectively, 3000 men to each wing (*Trewe Encountre*). The proportion of archers and men-at-arms are unknown, as are details of Surrey's artillery, although he paid 11 German gunners.

James IV declined Surrey's invitations to come down and fight on the level ground near Milfield, but offered to wait for him until midday on 9 September. Surrey had the unpalatable options of attacking uphill, or disbanding his army, which had run out of beer. He resolved the impasse by marching around the Scots army to place himself across their line of retreat, accepting the risks of fighting with his back to the Tweed. The first part of Surrey's march lay east of the River Till (a tributary of the Tweed), secured from

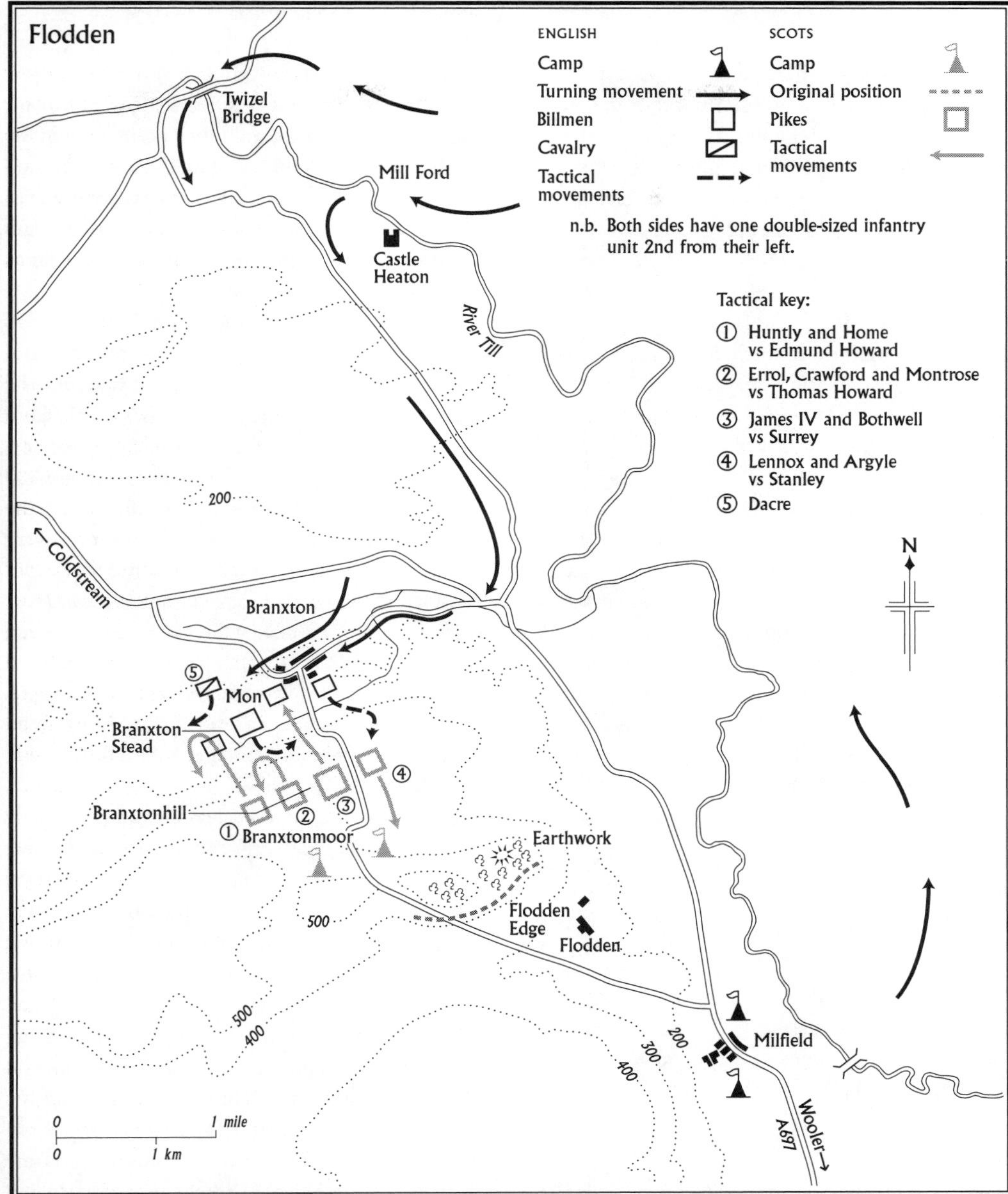

Scots observation by an intervening hill. At 1 a.m. on the 9th he repassed the Till. His son Lord Thomas Howard led the vanward and artillery over Twizel Bridge, a single-arched stone span 5 miles(8 km) north of the battlefield; Surrey and the rearward crossed the ford by Heaton Castle. Surrey has been criticized for dividing his forces, but James IV reacted

Directions

Flodden *Turn left off the A697 Wooler–Coldstream road for Branxton. A granite cross on the left beyond the village is dedicated 'To the Brave of both Nations'. Farm tracks run up to the Scots start line on Branxton Hill. Remains of James's gun positions can be found in the woods on Flodden Hill.*

too slowly to catch him on the move. At the last minute James had to countermarch north across Branxton Moor to deny Surrey the heights behind Flodden Edge. Through rain and smoke from fired bedding straw, the two armies came into sight a mere quarter of a mile (0.4 km) apart.

The Scots array is a matter of debate. The Tudor commentator Sir Edward Hall, who was not present, says they had six divisions. *Trewe Encountre* and Surrey, who were, say four and five respectively: 'each a bowshot distant from the others and all equally distant from the English, in grete plumpes, part of them quadrant, and some pikewise [diamond shaped?]' (Surrey, *Articles of the Bataill*). Each square numbered upwards of 4000 men: 60 files broad and 60 ranks deep, led by the flower of the Scots nobility and the French veterans. Some reconstructions stretch the battle front a mile and a half (2.5 km) eastwards from the Flodden Monument to Pace Hill. The numbers of troops and their deep formation require a much shorter frontage, three-quarters of a mile (1.2 km) across Branxton Hill, 'kepyng the height of the mountain'. According to *Trewe Encountre* Surrey reorganized into four battles, to mark the opposing divisions. Surrey's report simply says Lord Thomas

Milfield

	Winner	*Loser*
Opponents	English	Scots
Commanders	Sir William Bulmer	Alexander, Lord Home
Numbers	700–1000	*c.*3000
Losses	unknown	*c.*1000

Flodden

	Winner	*Loser*
Opponents	English	Scots
Commanders	Thomas Howard, Earl of Surrey Lord Thomas Howard	James IV (k)
Numbers	*c.*20,000	*c.*20,000
Losses	500–1500	10,000–12000

'caused the van to stale [form line of battle] in a little valley, till the rear joined one of the wings of his battle; they both advanced in line against the Scots, who came down the hills and met them'. The 'little valley' suggests the beck flowing east across the English front from Branxton Stead, an unnoticed obstacle that may have thrown the attacking Scots into disorder.

The battle began between 4 and 5 p.m. with an artillery exchange. The English came off best: 'our bullets ... did theme na hurt, but flewe over their heidis' (John Leslie, *Historie of Scotland*). The English guns, however, 'did soe breke and constreyne the Scotisshe great army, that some parte of thaim were enforsed to come down the saide hilles' (*Trewe Encountre*). James IV has been criticized for leaving the high ground, but a brisk attack under cover of pouring rain, which had soaked English bowstrings, would neutralize the deadly longbowmen. James has also been blamed for leading from the front rank of a pike square, but it was his job to set an example. Maximilian the Impecunious, Duke of Burgundy and future Holy Roman Emperor, did the same at Guinegate in 1479.

There were four separate actions, which suggests the *Trewe Encountre's* author was right, or else two pike squares joined up while advancing. From left to right across the Scots front these actions were:

(1) The Earl of Huntly and Lord Home defeated the English right under Lord Thomas Howard's brother Edmund, who was abandoned by his men and beaten to the ground. However, Lord Dacre charged to the rescue with 1500 Borderers who had kept their horses, and stabilized the situation.

(2) The Earls of Errol, Crawford and Montrose attacked Lord Thomas Howard's vanward and were totally defeated: 'soon put to flight and most of them slain' (*Articles*). If Howard had kept most of his 9000 men the result is hardly surprising, as the Scots, a fifth of 20,000, would have been outnumbered two-to-one. Bishop Ruthal saw Howard as the architect of victory, 'the veray ledyr conduytor and setter on with our army'.

(3) James IV, supported by the Earl of Bothwell, attacked Surrey's rearward 'with a great power'. The

two Scottish divisions outnumbered Surrey's 5000 men, and nearly broke through. The king fell within a spear's length of the earl, who was directing operations from his carriage in the English rear, showing how close James came to victory.

(4) The rightmost Scottish division consisted of Highlanders under the Earl of Lennox and the Earl of Argyle. Preparing to 'releiff the said King of Scottes batell', it was attacked and routed by Sir Edward Stanley, 'being at the uttermoste parte of the said rerewarde on th'Est partie' (*Trewe Encountre*). Highlanders wore mail not plate, an easy target for Stanley's bowmen.

Pikes proved less effective at close quarters than the shorter English bills, which 'did beat and hewe thaim downe'. Balladeers in Cheshire sang how, 'we blanked them with bills through all their bright armour', and while an Italian poem recorded 'so many weapons lowered it seemed as if a wood were falling down' ('*La Rotta Scossese*'). Their pikes spent, the Scots fought on silently with their swords: 'so myghtie Large strong and grete men that they wolde not fall whenne iiij or v [four or five] billes strake on oon of theym ... yet they coude not resiste the billes that lighted so thicke and sore upon theym' (Ruthal).

No quarter was given, 'for our folks entending to make all thing sure toke little regarde in taking of prisoners but rid [killed] all that came to hande' (Ruthal). Eyewitnesses estimated Scottish casualties at a frightful 50 per cent, but disagreed over the English losses. Official sources admitted less than 500; *Trewe Encountre* and Bishop Ruthal just over 1000. Hall quoted 1500 from a paybook. James IV headed the Scottish casualty list, followed by an archbishop, at least eight earls and the French ambassador. Some of the French advisers fell in action; others were cut to pieces by aggrieved Scotsmen as the cause of their misfortune. The whole Scots camp fell into enemy hands, with all their guns, immense stores of beef, mutton and cheese, and 4000 feather beds. It was said that not a family in Scotland avoided losing a father, a husband or a son.

Psychological damage outweighed physical losses. Flodden was an undiluted national disaster as Culloden (1746) was not. It ended a golden age of peace and prosperity, and shattered Scottish confidence irretrievably. James IV was the last Scots king to offer battle in England. 'The Flowers of the Forest', a lament (*c.*1750) for Flodden's dead, still haunts Scottish military funerals.

Directions

Milfield *Six miles (10 km) from Wooler along the A697 Coldstream road, before the turning to Flodden Edge. Tactical locations unknown.*

Melrose, 25 July 1526

Scotland, Scottish Borders, LR73 NT5334

Summerdale (Bigswell), 18 May 1529

Scotland, Orkney Islands, LR6 HY3410

James V's minority exposed Scotland to the excesses of aristocratic factionalism, as magnates pursued family interest with little regard for the law or the king's dignity. The skirmish at Melrose was fought for control of James V's person, while Summerdale was a local quarrel over territory.

Archibald Douglas, Earl of Angus, married Queen Margaret, James IV's widow, and ruled in her son's name, holding the prince captive. Young James resented his subjection, and wrote secretly to Sir Walter Scott of Buccleuch, while visiting Jedburgh, requesting help. Sir Walter intercepted the royal party returning to Edinburgh via Melrose, where it slept the night before the fight. The would-be rescuers occupied Skirmis Hill, now the site of the Waverley Castle Hotel, west of Melrose and south of the River Tweed.

Angus left James with his brother, Sir George Douglas, and advanced on foot to meet the challenge. Lord Home and 80 spears vigorously attacked Buccleuch's left flank, driving his outnumbered party

Melrose

	Winner	*Loser*
Opponents	Scots	Scots
Commanders	Archibald Douglas, Earl of Angus	Sir Walter Scott of Buccleuch
Numbers	unknown	600–1000
Losses	100	80

Summerdale

	Winner	*Loser*
Opponents	Orkney	Scots
Commanders	James Sinclair of Brecks	John Sinclair, Earl of Caithness (k) Lord William Sinclair (p)
Numbers	unknown	unknown
Losses	unknown	130

from the field. The defeated party rallied at a steep bank known as Turnagain, one of Buccleuch's followers, Elliot of Stobs, killing the laird of Cessford. This terminated the pursuit, only to begin a major blood feud that ended with Buccleuch's murder in an Edinburgh street fight in 1552. James V remained in Douglas hands until 1528, when he asserted his right to rule. Angus fled to England, next appearing as a renegade fighting for Henry VIII.

The Battle of Summerdale on Mainland, Orkney, was a family quarrel in Scotland's far north. The Orkneys had been pawned to Scotland in 1468, as security for the unpaid dowry of James III's wife Margaret of Denmark, and remained outside effective royal government. They were controlled by local magnates, in particular the Sinclairs, but Lord Henry Sinclair's death at Flodden (1513) split the family. His widow and son, Sir William, became absentee landlords, unable to collect their rents in face of local opposition led by James Sinclair of Brecks, who murdered Sir William's followers and laid the islands waste. Unable to obtain redress in the courts, Sir William and his cousins on the Scottish mainland obtained a royal commission to recover Kirkwall, and punish their enemies.

Sinclair of Brecks was a figure of saga-like proportions: 'kinglike as he war a king in thai parts'. He prepared for trouble in advance: a pardon respiting his adherents for the slaughter of his enemies lists imported Shetlanders as well as Kirkwall men. According to tradition his opponents landed at Waulkmill Bay on the Orphir coast of Mainland southwest of Kirkwall, most readily approached through Hoxa Sound to the south. Scapa Bay is nearer Kirkwall, the only town and the invaders' objective, but a more distant and hence more secure beachhead makes strategic sense. The battle was fought on a line extended northwards from Waulkmill Bay. Caithness may have thought an indirect route through Tuskerbister valley easier going than the moorland that interposed between Orphir and Kirkwall before the modern road was built. Alternatively, Caithness may have been headed off from the direct eastward approach to Kirkwall, and tried to turn Sinclair of Brecks's northern flank through Kirbister. Place-name evidence supports the Ordnance Survey's unnamed site: Summerdale means 'south boundary dale', and lies between Orphir and Stenness parishes.

Details of the fighting are speculative. As the invaders crossed the steep neck in which the Tuskerbister valley ends, they were anticipated by an alert enemy with a shorter distance to travel. Strung out along the line of march, among the hummocks and hollows between Fea farm and the little township of Germiston, they lost 30 men in the first onset, including both leaders, Caithness being killed and Sir William captured. Another hundred were killed fleeing to their boats, including some dragged from sanctuary. Local casualties are unknown, except for one Tuskerbister man, whose mother failed to recognize him in looted finery and cracked his skull with a stone in the toe of a sock. The defeated Sinclairs continued to demand justice, to no purpose. In 1535 James V pardoned the unrepentant rebels.

Directions

Melrose *Waverley Castle Hotel is south of Waverley Road (the B6374), half a mile (0.8 km) from Melrose town centre. West of the hotel the road climbs some rising ground, now built over. This would* *appear the most appropriate location for Scott of Buccleuch's roadblock.*

Summerdale *Two miles (3 km) west of Finstown, turn left off the A965 and continue 2 miles (3 km) along a minor road. The battlefield is 300 yards (275 m) down a footpath on the right just after Nisthouse.*

Hadden Rig (Halydon Rigg), 24 August 1542

Scotland, Scottish Borders, LR74 NT7734?

Solway Moss, 24 November 1542

England, Cumbria, LR85 NY3867

Anglo-Scots border clashes rarely escalated into full-scale battles. Actions at Hadden Rig and Solway Moss were exceptions, although they resembled routs more than formal engagements.

There was no respectable reason for heightened tension in 1542. Henry VIII had sent Sir Robert Bowes to watch the frontier, not to initiate hostilities. Nevertheless he concerted a major foray for the morning of St Bartholomew's Day, involving regular troops from royal garrisons, and Borderers from Tynedale and Redesdale. While Bowes took up a covering position, or 'bushment', on Hadden Rig (541 feet/165 m), he 'shoved forth' two forays to burn villages along the Tweed's southern bank: Maxwell Heugh, Grymesley and Sunlaws. The rendezvous was at Heiton, 5 miles (8 km) southwest of Hadden Rig. The Earl of Angus, currently serving his country's enemies, thought the English were overextended, for 'they had a great ground to ride to return to their main body'.

Meanwhile Sir Walter Lyndsay had crossed the Tweed at Kelso, halfway between the forays and bushment, with a smaller but more concentrated force of Scots. Seeing their 'prickers' or scouts hard after the raiding parties, Bowes rode down to help. Captured livestock was hurried away, the Redesdale men spurring after to secure their plunder, the signal for a general disbandment. According to Angus, the Northumbrian gentlemen 'began to trot, and shortly fell to galloping, and the rest of the host brake rule and fled'. Two gentlemen who 'escaped by speed of horse' confirm that the Redesdale men 'took the gate and fled'. Sir Robert Bowes dismounted with 30 or 40 of his household to stem the rout, but were overrun. Angus watched from the other side of the field, before he 'gat away with great debate of himself', losing 8 out of his immediate retinue of 20, 'but the rest of his following did naught'. John Tempest, who had a company at Wark Castle, lost a similar proportion: but 'fifty came home with great hurts and without weapons or harness'. The English admitted losing 400–500 prisoners. The Scots claimed twice as many, but 'It was not they that won the field, but we that lost it with our misorder' (Angus).

Hadden Rig reinforced Henry VIII's desire to render southern Scotland militarily harmless. The Duke of Norfolk, a veteran of Flodden (when he had been Lord Thomas Howard), overran the Eastern March in October 1542, burning Kelso and destroying incredible quantities of corn. He withdrew after

Hadden Rig

	Winner	*Loser*
Opponents	Scots	English
Commanders	Sir Walter Lyndsay	Sir Robert Bowes (p) Archibald Douglas, Earl of Angus
Numbers	2000	3000
Losses	unknown	400–500

Solway Moss

	Winner	*Loser*
Opponents	English	Scots
Commanders	Sir Thomas Wharton Sir William Musgrave	Robert, Lord Maxwell (p) Oliver Sinclair (p)
Numbers	2000–3000	14,000–18,000
Losses	*c.*10	1200

six days for want of bread and beer, without bringing the Scots to battle. In November a fresh Scots host took advantage of English concentration in the east to threaten Cumberland in the West March. The warden, Sir Thomas Wharton, reported great powers at Langholm and Mortonkirk late on the 23rd. They outnumbered him at least five-to-one, but at Solway Moss Wharton would inflict the most embarrassing defeat ever suffered by a Scots army.

Wharton left Carlisle at daybreak on 24 November, about 4 a.m., with 300 men, picking up more as he went along: 'not one soldier among them, but men of the country' (Wharton). He was on the River Lyne by 6 a.m., watching smoke from burning houses across the Esk and at Oakshaw Hill, the English side of the Border. While mounted skirmishers drew the Scots south towards Arthuret Howes, Wharton occupied Hopesike Hill (69 feet/21 m) with six standards, 1200 men by his reckoning, dismounted ready for action. A committee investigating the battle for the Privy Council in London estimated the 'stale' or line of battle at 1500 men, leaving 500 horsemen, the king's subjects being 'not above 2000'.

The Scots' logical line of advance would be down the modern A7 from Longtown, forming up between St Michael's Church near Howend and the A6071. The Esk lay behind them and to their right, beyond it the tidal marshes of Solway Moss. The Scots army was mainly infantry with artillery, the latter of little use in the mobile combined-arms battle that Wharton meant to fight. The countryside then was less enclosed, allowing his cavalry room for manoeuvre. Wharton ordered them, now rallied on his right, away from the river, to attack the Scots' left flank as they came within range of his archers. However, the cavalry 'thought best to set upon them before the foot battles joined, and so the Grames [Grahams] pursued the horsemen of Scotland, who fled, while Jack Musgrave and 300 gentlemen of the country entered upon the footmen. These seeing them fiercely coming on and the stale following retired and fled towards the water' (Privy Council). The cavalry overtook them at Sandyford, beside Arthuret Mill. The Scots lords dismounted to cover the retreat but were overthrown, the horsemen taking two to five prisoners apiece.

Scots morale had been doubly shaken before they met Wharton's main body. His prickers, hanging upon their flank and cutting up stragglers, 'gatt theym in a shake all the waye' (Wharton), while an astonishing row over who was in command of the Scots host left it leaderless at the critical moment. Both would-be commanders went into the bag, along with 1200 smaller fry. Only 20 Scots died in action, although more must have drowned in the Moss. On their way home survivors were plundered or even killed by their Liddesdale compatriots. The artillery train fell into English hands: 20 carted pieces, six score demi-hakes (arquebuses) and a great number of handguns, besides 30 standards, more than Wharton had brought into the field. He admitted seven dead and one prisoner.

The most fatal casualty of the day was James V. To avoid his father's fate, he watched from a distance, probably from Birrenswark Hill between Lockerbie and Middlebie. Returning to the east coast, James fell ill on 7 December and was dead a week later. Chroniclers attributed the sudden death of a robust 30-year-old to despair over the shattering defeat at Solway Moss. 'What a victory God has sent the King,' wrote the English Privy Council, but the opportunity was lost on Henry VIII.

Directions

Hadden Rig *Take the B6352 southeast from Kelso about 2 miles (3 km), and turn left along the B6396 toward Hadden Rig. Look back from the southwest end of the ridge over the area covered by the forays, and the Scots chase.*

Solway Moss *Take the A7 north from Carlisle. Hopesike Hill is 1½ miles (2.5 km) beyond Westlinton, alongside some woods on the right. Continue through Longtown, across the Esk, to see Solway Moss north of the A6071, where the Ordnance Survey marks the battlefield.*

Ancrum Moor (Lilliard's Edge), **Friday 27 February 1545**

Scotland, Scottish Borders, LR74 NT6127

The Scots rout at Solway Moss (see above) and the death of James V seemed to leave Henry VIII triumphant. The Treaty of Greenwich offered a peaceful outcome to Tudor–Stewart rivalry, with the proposed marriage of Henry's son Edward and the infant Mary Queen of Scots. Bickering over the regency, however, the Scots could neither deliver the wedding nor deter Henry VIII's rhinoceros-like attempts to enforce it. The one bright moment for Scotland during this miserable period came at Ancrum Moor.

The Scots Parliament's refusal to hand over their baby queen to the English brought terrible suffering. Sir Ralph Evers, Henry's warden of the Middle March, kept a 'bloody ledger' of his depredations: 192 villages, towers, barns and churches destroyed; 403 Scots slain and 816 captured; over 22,000 cattle and sheep driven off. The English king granted Sir Ralph whatever land he 'conquered', though by what right is not clear. Much belonged to the Earl of Angus, an erstwhile collaborator, who now promised to inscribe the '*sasine*' or deeds upon Evers's skin, with sharp pen and bloody ink.

Acting upon intelligence that Angus and the Governor or Regent Arran were amassing troops, Evers marched into Scotland on 25 February 1545. He had a powerful force: 1500 English, 3000 foreign mercenaries and 700 assured Scots – 'broken men' or outlaws, who only served out of fear. Arran was heavily outnumbered, having 'under 2000 men' by English estimates, and failed to prevent Evers burning Melrose on the 26th. Evers was less successful the next day. Sir William Petrie reported to the Privy Council from the Border on 5 March: 'his retreat [was] ... so pressed by the Scots that within two miles of Jedburgh [actually five] our men were forced to dismount and fight on foot; in which fight Sir Ralph Evers and Sir Brian Laiton were slain and our men worsted'.

The encounter is generally thought to have occurred near the intersection of Dere Street, the Roman road south of Melrose, and the steep ridge running northeast along Lilliard's Edge to Muirhouse Law (584 feet/178 m). English accounts of the battle refer exclusively to 'Mewrehouse', a moated site north of the battlefield. The Roman causeway was the best route for a column loaded with plunder, the only firm going across Ancrum Moor, where low-lying undulations formed areas of dead ground, places where the Scots could lie in ambush, their flanks covered by marshland. Modern writers do not agree on which direction the English were travelling when they met disaster. They should have been heading southeast towards friendly territory across the River Teviot. In this scenario, the Earl of Angus overtook them and occupied a concealed position across their retreat. This might be just behind Lilliard's Edge, as marked by the Ordnance Survey, or at Penniel Heugh, blocking access to the fords where Dere Street crosses the Teviot.

Most contemporary accounts however favour an alternative reconstruction. The English reached the north bank of the Teviot, but were too hard pressed to cross, as the official account says. They dismounted and defied Angus to attack them. Eventually the Scots broke the stalemate by withdrawing from Penniel Heugh in apparent disorder, tempting the English back along Dere Street. Advancing piecemeal, the invaders ran onto the pikes of a prepositioned ambush, straddling the road. This might

Ancrum Moor

	Winner	*Loser*
Opponents	Scots	English
Commanders	Archibald Douglas, Earl of Angus James Hamilton, Earl of Arran George Gordon, Earl of Huntly	Sir Ralph Evers (k) Sir Brian Laiton (k)
Numbers	2000–2500	5200
Losses	c.200	1300–1400

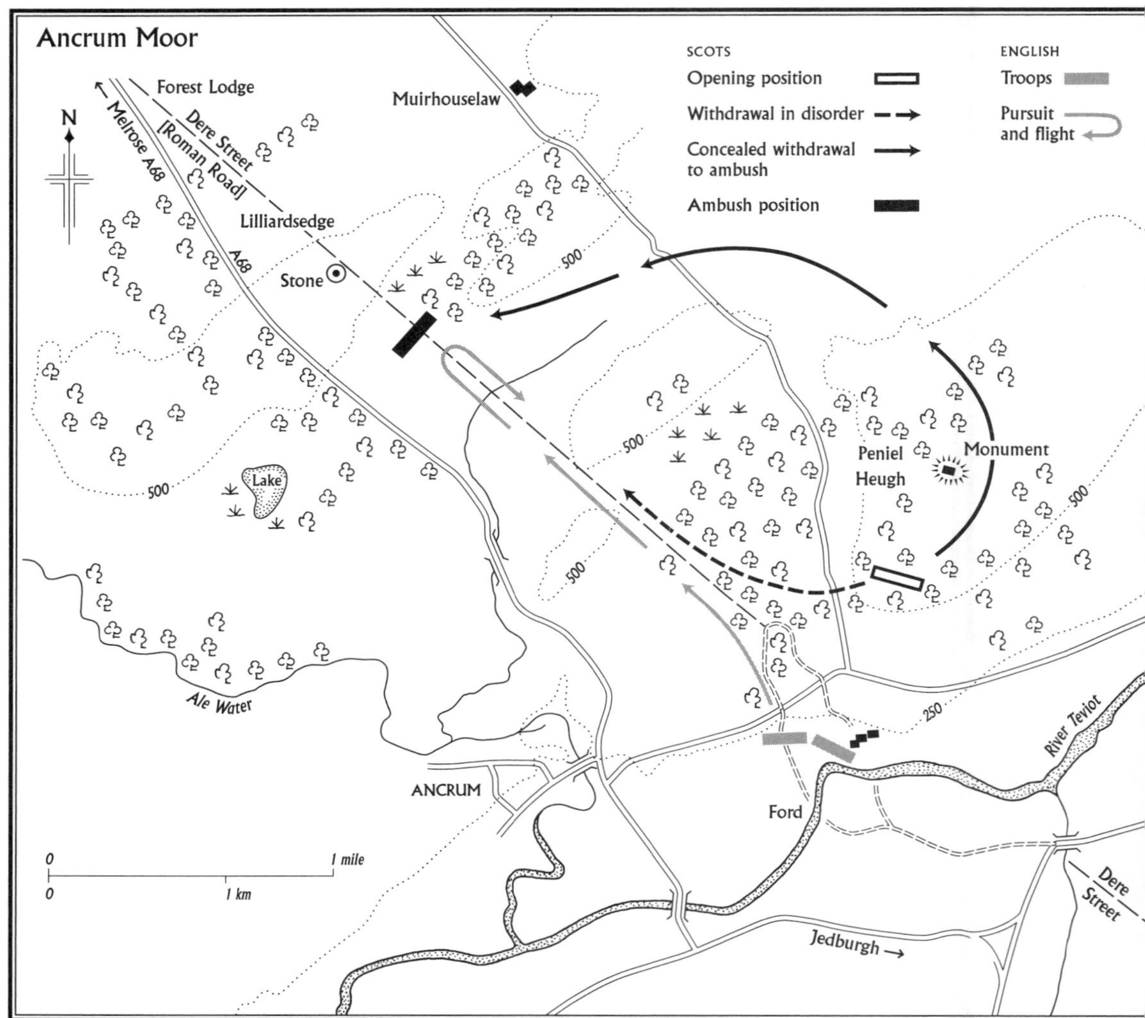

have been at the point shown by the Ordnance Survey, but facing the other way, or further down the slope nearer the burn, out of sight of the approaching English. Proponents of both versions of events refer to the setting sun dazzling the attackers, but this is little help. Sunset in February would have been in the southwest, on the English flank whichever direction they were moving, and therefore not in their eyes.

The overall result was much the same. The leading English troops, stumbling through potholes dug

Directions

Follow the A68 north from Ancrum Bridge across the moor to the ridge, which provides views of the battlefield to the northeast. To reach the Roman road continue along the A68 to Forest Lodge on the right, and turn sharply back along Dere Street to Maid Lilliard's battered sandstone memorial. This bears the date 1544, as the New Year did not then start until 23 March. The more conspicuous monument on Penniel Heugh commemorates the joint Anglo-Scots victory at Waterloo in 1815.

across the road, were thrown back on their supports, breaking their formation and spreading alarm and confusion. Anyone escaping to the flanks stuck fast in the marshes off the causeway. At least one English horseman perished on the wooded slope above Ale Water, where his helmet was found 350 years later. At the psychological moment the assured Scots changed sides, killing or taking more English than their ostensible enemies. English accounts do not blame the defeat entirely on treachery. The Earl of Shrewsbury, in overall command of the Border thought that 'but for the disorder among our men at the joining of the battle, victory might have been ours'. He suspected 'too much adventure or some disorder ... [and] knowing the forwardness of the man [i.e. Evers] had specially warned him to be wary'.

At first the Privy Council believed that up to 1400 English were slain or taken. A week later Shrewsbury reckoned the slaughter 'less than was supposed, for ransomed soldiers come in daily'. Only nine score were still missing 'that should be slain'. As they returned without horse or harness, and their officers remained prisoners, the net effect was similar. The Scots refused to admit any casualties, although numerous countrywomen came enquiring after husbands and sons. The final score, for diplomatic consumption, was 160 English and 200 Scots. Among the latter was the probably apocryphal Maid Lilliard, who had sworn vengeance on the English for killing her lover, as commemorated by a memorial on the moor:

> Upon the English loons,
> She laid monie thumps,
> And when her legs were cuttit off,
> She fought upon her stumps.

Arran wept upon Evers's corpse, 'a cruel man and over-cruel, which many a man and fatherless bairn might rue', then embraced Angus, his old enemy. Their success at Ancrum Moor sent shock waves throughout northern Britain. Many assured Scots resumed their proper loyalties again. Scotland repudiated the Greenwich treaty, regardless of what Henry VIII might do.

Pinkie (Falside/Inveresk/Musselburgh/Pinkiecleugh), **Saturday 10 September 1547**

Scotland, East Lothian, LR66 NT3670-71

The last set-piece battle between an independent England and Scotland occurred 7 miles (11 km) east of Edinburgh, between the River Esk and Falside Hill. Pinkie was the last major British battle before the Civil Wars, almost a century later. A wide range of sources reflect its significance, including eyewitness battle plans and a printed account by William Patten, an English staff officer.

Henry VIII's death in 1547 did not bring peace with Scotland. The Duke of Somerset, regent for the young Edward VI, was just as obsessed with bludgeoning Scotland into union. Disillusioned with the ineffective raiding policy that had resulted in disaster at Ancrum Moor (1545), he planned to install English garrisons around the Lowlands. These would occupy bastioned forts proof against Scottish siege trains, and provide a focus for pro-union Scots. In August 1547 Somerset mustered a major invasion force at Berwick, with 900 carts and 80 ships to carry the necessary tools and stores. He crossed the Border on 4 September, advancing along the coast. The Scots mustered slowly, and too far inland. Their late arrival on the scene of operations forced them to offer battle on Edinburgh's doorstep. Somerset, on the other hand, needed a quick victory to gain a decent harbour, and so ensure communication with the English fleet.

The opposing forces reflected how far the two nations had absorbed the military lessons of the Renaissance. The core of the English army comprised the traditional three infantry divisions, armed with pikes and bills, and flanked by archers: a battle of 4000, supported by a foreward and rereward of 3000 each. A third of the army were cavalry, mixed according to the latest Continental prescription: 4000 men-at-arms and demi-lances in full plate armour, and 2000 light cavalry. Additional fire support came from

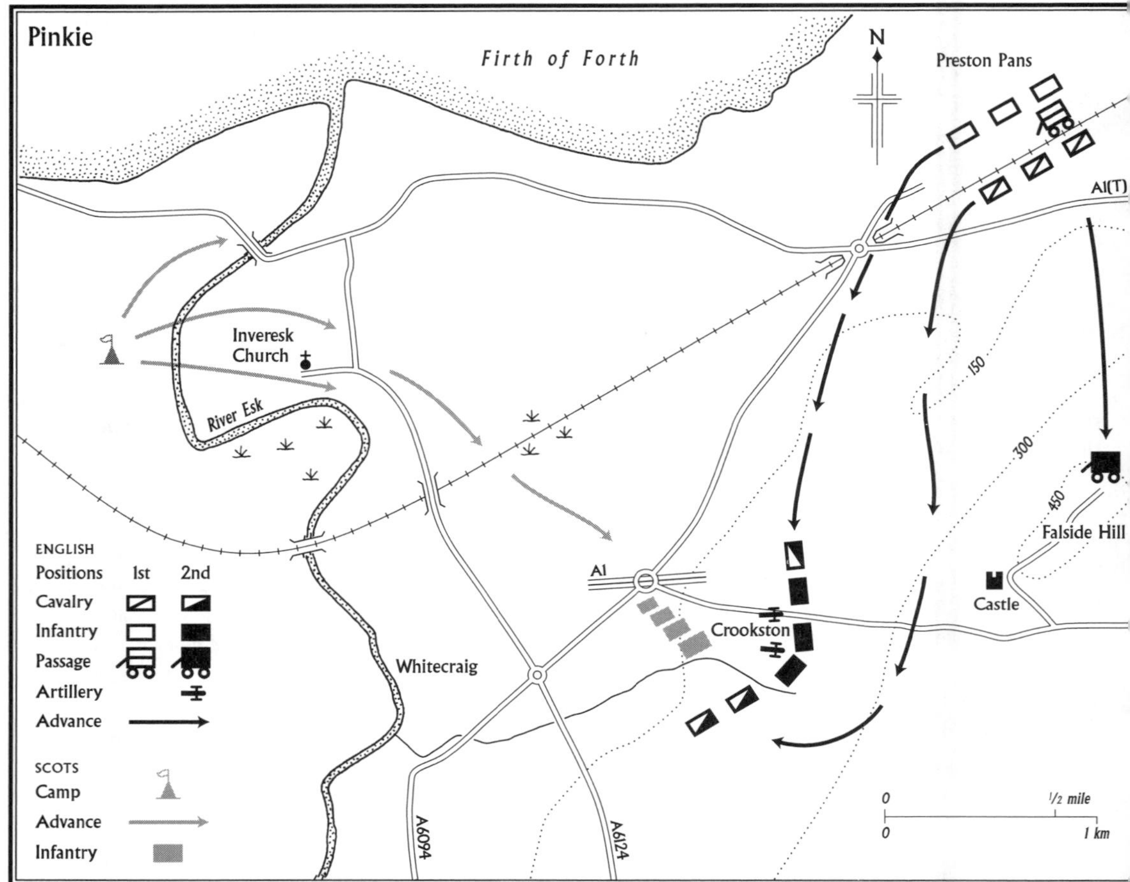

800 foreign arquebusiers (200 of them mounted) and 15 heavy guns drawn by horses.

The Scots host was large, but poorly equipped. They had no hackbutters, and only 4000 Irish or Highland archers. Their 1500 light horse were outnumbered and outclassed. The core of the army was some 20,000 pikemen, formed in three massive squares. Gentlemen not serving with the cavalry left their horses and fought afoot. Patten claimed over 30,000 Scots took part, but Huntly, their rearguard commander, reckoned only 22,000–23,000, a figure supported by Edward VI's *Chronicle*. They also had 25–30 light field guns.

The Scots held a position of great natural strength on the west bank of the River Esk, flanked north and south respectively by the Firth of Forth and a great marsh. The Esk was not particularly deep, but its banks were high and steep, 'as a small sort [company] of resistants might have been able to keep down a great number of comers-up' (Patten). Scots artillery

Directions

Today the A1 trunk road cuts the battlefield in half. Take the A6124 south from Inveresk (Somerset's proposed artillery position), turning left at the A6094 roundabout for Crookston. The crisis of the battle occurred south of the A1/A6094 interchange, not to its north as shown by the Ordnance Survey. Take a minor road through West Mains to Somerset's command post near Falside Castle.

Pinkie		
	Winner	*Loser*
Opponents	English	Scots
Commanders	Edward Seymour, Duke of Somerset	James Hamilton, Earl of Arran
	John Dudley, Lord Lisle	Archibald Douglas, Earl of Angus
	William Grey, Lord de Wilton	George Gordon, Earl of Huntly
Numbers	15,000–19,000	*c.*23,000
Losses	500–600	6000

commanded the bridge between their camp and the Forth, while their horse patrolled Falside Hill, beyond their right.

Somerset reached Prestonpans on 8 September. The constricted ground limited his tactical options to a frontal attack. On Friday 9 September English cavalry cleared the Scots horse away, killing so many that their mounted arm played no part in the fighting next day. Somerset could pushing forward almost as far as Inveresk Church (NT3472). His plan was to place his heavy artillery on the hillock there, and behind the turf wall along the lane running south from Inveresk, now the A6124. Thence he could pound the Scots camp beyond the river, supported by naval gunfire from the Forth.

The English army moved off at 8 a.m. next morning, as it began to rain. They marched in two parallel columns: infantry in column of battles nearest the Forth; cavalry on the open flank, towards the high ground. They were not expecting to fight, so the *gens d'armes* left their horse armour behind. The Scots disappointed the English, for they abandoned their strong place, crossed the river, and moved obliquely across Somerset's front towards Falside. Arran has been much blamed for this decision, but he may have wished to avoid a close-range artillery bombardment, to which his pikemen could make no reply. A position on Falside could take any direct English advance upon Edinburgh in flank, and was out of range of the fleet.

Like the English, the Scots infantry were in column of squares, led front to rear by Angus, Arran and Huntly. Their gunners kept up with them, alternately firing and dragging their guns forward. The Highland archers followed Huntly's rearward, while the remains of Scots cavalry screened the right flank. The speed and direction of the Scots movement placed them across Somerset's line of advance, and threatened to forestall him at Falside. Once there, they could easily turn left into line, and roll up the English battles piecemeal. Somerset pushed his heavy cavalry ahead, to buy time for his infantry to come up, Lord Grey leading a heroic charge against the right flank of Angus's vanward. Cavalry were unlikely to break unshaken infantry, especially attacking across a 'cross ditch or slough', probably the small burn that flows south of Crookston (NT3670), into the Esk near Whitecraig. Angus's men drove Grey's cavalry off, with several high-profile casualties. They reeled back, rallying between the English foreward and battle.

Meanwhile, Somerset's artillery came into action on Falside Hill, enfilading the Scots masses bunched up behind Angus. The English infantry deployed 'sidelong towards the enemy', the foreward well up on the hillside, the battle tailing down to the plain, towards the rereward. Between them, they caught the Scots in a deadly crossfire from hackbutters lining the burn, archers in the main English array, and great ordnance on the hilltop and with the rereward on the other flank.

The Scots vanward turned to face the enemy, but their hastily embodied host lacked the cohesion necessary to manoeuvre under fire. The main battle thought the van's change of front presaged flight, and fled. Arran's political opponents alleged he led the way. Angus retreated upon Huntly's rereward, but in the smoke and rain his men were mistaken for the English. Van and rereward disintegrated, leaving their pikes 'strewed on the ground as rushes in a chamber; impassable they lay so thick, for either horse or man' (Patten). Angus shammed dead until a servant brought his horse, and Huntly defended the Esk bridge until captured. He put Scottish losses at 6000, although Patten claimed 13,000 dead plus prisoners, an unlikely percentage. Most of the Scots casualties fell during the 5-mile (8-km) pursuit, 'in all which space, the dead bodies lay as thick as a man may note cattle grazing in a full replenished pasture' (Patten). Official English accounts admitted only 200 dead, compared with the 500–600 indicated by private letters.

The Scots remembered Pinkie as 'Black Saturday', but the consequences of Somerset's victory did not match its tactical brilliance. The Scots sent Queen Mary away to France, out of England's reach. French troops poured into Scotland to harass Somerset's garrisons. His strategic vision of a Scottish Pale soon proved militarily and financially unsustainable.

Drumlanrig, 23 February 1548

Scotland, Dumfries and Galloway, LR78 NX8599?

This little known action was a running fight more typical of Anglo-Scots warfare than major battles like Pinkie (see above). A severe setback for the victor of Solway Moss, Drumlanrig shook the English hold on southwest Scotland, throwing them onto the defensive.

The English exploited blurred national loyalties to create a protective barrier north of the Border. When Lord Wharton, English warden of the West March, rode out 'to annoy the Douglases' on 20 February 1548, he did so with the support of his Scottish counterpart, John Maxwell. Although Wharton received intelligence of a treacherous plot at Lochmaben on the 21st, he discounted this as an attempt to deter him from his enterprise, believing his force sufficient for the exploit in hand. Wharton, in his report, stated that his main concern was lack of supplies in 'a wasted country, where small relief is to be had'.

Wharton's objective was Drumlanrig Castle, a Douglas stronghold, 15 miles (24 km) north of Dumfries. He left his baggage train at Dumfries, and on 23 February marched up Nithsdale in two echelons. Wharton's son Henry rode ahead with the cavalry to burn Durisdeer, 3 miles (5 km) beyond Drumlanrig on Carron Water. Lord Wharton followed with the infantry. As at Hadden Rig (1542) divided command proved a liability. Angus fell upon the advance guard at Durisdeer (NS8804) with 'a chosen power of men', large numbers of Scots infantry appearing on the surrounding hills. Treachery was confirmed when Maxwell's 400 friendlies displayed a black flag and attacked Wharton's troopers, who, according to Wharton, were 'compelled to the mountains'.

Reports of Henry's death reached Wharton *père* near Drumlanrig, 'but I told the man who brought the news, that if he spoke any more thereof, I would strike his neck asunder'. Grimly he put his men in such order that, 'the enemy coming up ... they dared not fight'. The standoff lasted two hours, during which time Wharton seems to have retreated down the Nith towards Dalswinton. The retreat was not without difficulty. Sir Thomas Holcroft, a visiting official, reported 'some gentlemen of honest houses did not so well that day as they might'. Two hours later, however, Henry Wharton, very much alive, rejoined the main body with most of his party. Turning the tables on the Scots, they drove many of them into the Nith: 'Thus chasing and giving them the overthrow, between Dawswynton and Dusdere, we returned at our order, ease, and will to Dumfries, where we lodged quietly'.

Lord Wharton's report was disingenuous. During his absence the Scots had overrun the baggage guard, who 'if they had done as I commanded, might have kept the town, and annoyed all that were against them'. Protracted hostilities had eroded troop quality: 'Many of them', Wharton complained, 'are most simple creatures, and not like men of war.' Loss of supplies in a devastated countryside was decisive, and Wharton withdrew from Dumfries without further enemy contact.

Drumlanrig

	Winner	*Loser*
Opponents	Scots	English
Commanders	Archibald Douglas, Earl of Angus	Thomas, Lord Wharton
Numbers	unknown	3000
Losses	500	c.400

Wharton minimized his losses, claiming that, 'Of the power appointed with me, and of the horsemen appointed with my son, not one was taken or slain.' He admitted 176 carriage men and 379 horses taken, also mentioning 5 gentlemen prisoners 'taken in a place where they were not commanded to be', and 15 arquebusiers captured at Dumfries. Unusually they had not been released pending ransom: 'but the Scotch men were in great comfort that day'. Holcroft suggests a cover-up: 'Lord Wharton's journey ... did not go so clear with us as reported, for we had 400 taken prisoner and 400 geldings and carriage horses.'

Wharton claimed 500 Scots casualties, 'whereof I have above 200'. These were offset by the defection of many assured Scots, ensuring the expulsion of English garrisons from Dumfries. The demoralized warden was reduced to hanging hostages, as his troops were siphoned off to the more important eastern theatre of war. Hostilities lasted two more years, the English holding out for a general peace settlement not with Scotland, but with France.

Directions

Precise location unknown. Drumlanrig Park is west of the River Nith 1 mile (1.6 km) north of Carronbridge, off the A76 Dumfries–Cumnock road. For Durisdeer continue north, fork right onto the A702 Hamilton road, and right again. Henry Wharton's most convenient route across the hills would lie east of Nithsdale, perhaps the track that climbs Glenaggart, turning south past Bellybought Hill (1453 feet/443 m).

Defence of the Realm

The Spanish Armada of 1588 is one of the most famous episodes in English history, a nation-defining moment stiff with patriotic images. The much larger French invasion fleet of 1545 is less well known, although it lay in the Solent for a week. On both occasions the people of southern England had a grandstand view of the forces prepared for their destruction, a spectacle that they would not enjoy again until the Battle of Britain (1940).

The one constant factor in European politics during the 16th century was competition between the kings of France and the Habsburg rulers of Spain, Austria and the Netherlands. Traditionally England sided with the latter, to maintain trading links with Flanders, particularly the wool trade. A temporary cooling of Anglo-Habsburg relations in 1545 allowed Francis I to concentrate French resources against his cross-Channel neighbour. Possessing bases close to English soil, the French could mobilize an impressive fleet: over 200 vessels, half of them warships. In July this immense force attacked the main English naval base at Portsmouth. The aim was to tie up English naval resources while Francis besieged Boulogne, captured by Henry VIII the previous year. The French forced the outnumbered English fleet onto the defensive, but could not bring it to action among the sandbanks of Spithead. A partial naval engagement on the 19th is remembered mainly for the accidental loss of the *Mary Rose*. After some further skirmishes on the Isle of Wight, notably at Bonchurch, the French withdrew with little to show for their efforts.

The Reformation and the European discovery of America disrupted the traditional pattern of English foreign policy. The Habsburgs' uncompromising defence of the old faith caused inevitable friction with the most significant Protestant power, England. Wholesale slaughter of Dutch Protestants by Spanish troops in the 1560s and 1570s demonstrated the implications of militant Counter-Reformation Catholicism, and threatened England's economic ties with the Low Countries. Religion and economics fuelled the increasingly confident assertion of England's right to share the New World, which Spain sought to monopolize. Drake's freebooting circumnavigation of the world (1577–80) made him a hero amongst his countrymen. In Spanish eyes he was nothing more than a pirate.

The 'Invincible' Armada was the means by which Philip II of Spain hoped to resolve all his foreign-policy problems at once. A fleet from Spain would sweep English ships from the Channel, link up with troops in the Netherlands, and then transport them to Kent. The Spanish Army of Flanders, the best soldiers in Christendom, would cut the English militia to pieces and overthrow the heretical Elizabeth I, who had profited from Drake's piracy and succoured Dutch rebels. The Armada would simultaneously preserve the lifeline to America's silver mines, end the ruinous Dutch Revolt, and prevent further outrages against the Iberian homeland, like that at Cadiz in 1587, when Drake 'singed the king of Spain's beard'.

The often-delayed Armada left Spain on 11 July 1588 (Old Style), and was observed off the Lizard on the 19th. Campaign chronology is confused by Catholic Europe's adoption of the Gregorian calendar in 1582, using dates ten days ahead of the Old Style dates employed in Protestant England. For a week the Armada proceeded eastwards along the south coast of England. It fought three major actions, interrupted by pauses while the English replenished ammunition:

Location	*Day*	*Old Style*	*New Style*
Plymouth	Sunday	21 July	31 July
Portland Bill	Tuesday	23 July	2 August
Isle of Wight	Thursday	25 July	4 August

Neither side had gained any tactical advantage before the Armada anchored off Calais on Saturday 27 July. However, the English did shepherd the Armada past a succession of sheltered anchorages, notably the Solent. The Spanish, on the other hand, failed to bring about the close-quarters boarding action that Medina Sidonia, the Armada's commander, saw was the only way to victory. At Calais the Spanish fleet lay so far to leeward of English landing beaches that it had little realistic chance of beating back against prevailing westerlies, even if the Army of Flanders had been ready to embark. The English victory off Gravelines (Monday 29 July), when fireships broke the Armada's impregnable formation, confirmed Medina Sidonia's strategic failure. Unaware that the enemy were out of ammunition, the Spanish commander took his battered fleet northwards, around Scotland and Ireland. Nearly half the Armada, 63 out of the original 130 ships, failed to return, many being wrecked on the long voyage home.

These unprecedented invasion fleets incorporated revolutionary changes in ship design and armament. Medieval sailing ships had been broad in the beam, powered by a single huge sail, and accustomed to fight at close quarters. During the 16th century warships became specialized naval vessels, increasingly different from merchantmen. Warships became longer and lower, and acquired more masts, improving manoeuvrability and seaworthiness. Gunports cut low down in their sides allowed them to carry more and heavier weapons on gun decks running the length of the ship. Such broadsides outgunned the handful of cannon that galleys could mount in their bows; Spithead was the last major galley action in English waters.

Henceforth ships would fight at a distance by gunfire instead of running alongside an enemy and grappling, as Edward III had done at Winchelsea (1349). In future boarding was relegated to occupation of an enemy ship already pounded into submission. The sporadic artillery exchanges in the Solent in 1545 hinted at this new long-range warfare, although both sides used line-abreast formations inherited from galley warfare. English fighting instructions promulgated in August 1545 laid down a wedge-shaped formation of three ranks of ships in line abreast, the most powerful in front; individual ships half a cable (100 yards/90 m) apart, with two cables (400 yards/360 m) between successive ranks. In 1588 the Spaniards used similar massed formations, either crescent shaped, or in a 'plump' or 'roundel'. The English attacked in more flexible line-astern formations designed to maximize firepower. The Armada battles showed the potential superiority of ships acting as mobile batteries, when Spanish ships packed with infantry could not close with more agile English vessels dependent on gunnery rather than cold steel.

Portsmouth (Spithead), **Sunday 19 July 1545**

Naval, Solent, LR196 SZ6396

Bonchurch, Tuesday 21 July 1545

England, Isle of Wight, LR196 SX5677

The French fleet that appeared in the Solent in July 1545 surpassed any naval force previously seen off British shores. William the Conqueror may have had more ships, but d'Annebault's gun-armed squadrons far outclassed them in fighting power. The French Armada proved a disappointment, however, notable more for its potential than its actual results.

D'Annebault had 150 '*gros vaisseaux ronds*' ('great round ships'), 60 *flouins* or coasters, and 25 galleys from the Mediterranean. Propelled by oars and independent of the wind, the last were ideal for operations in the confined approaches to Portsmouth harbour. French manpower is estimated at 30,000–60,000, including a landing force of 6000 troops. One of their officers, Martin du Bellay, left an eyewitness account of the fighting.

The French appeared on 18 July and fought an indecisive gunnery action with part of the English fleet, 'there beinge never a ship in redynes nore anye suche wynde to serve' (Sir Peter Carew). As evening fell the English withdrew inside the harbour, 'defended by a few forts which stood on the cliff behind them and on the other by hidden shoals and rocks, with only a narrow and oblique entrance for a few ships at a time' (du Bellay). By 'cliff' du Bellay presumably meant the low rocky headland occupied by Southsea Castle. Next morning the Privy Council reported, 'xxij gallees were at anker on this side St Ellen's Point [St Helens Anchorage, the northeast of the Isle of Wight] and better than one hundreth sayle in sight behind them'.

Henry VIII had been at Portsmouth since 15 July, making his headquarters beside Southsea Castle. This was an ideal spot to supervise operations in Spithead, that part of the Solent lying roughly between the Isle of Wight and Portsea Island. As yet, the town of Portsmouth, today's Old Portsmouth, occupied only part of the latter, separated from the castle by Southsea Common. Spithead is deceptively open, affording little real space for fleets to manoeuvre. Its waters are treacherous and shallow, covering a complex drowned river valley, scoured by fierce tides and flanked by extensive sandbanks. A narrow channel winds from St Helens towards the harbour mouth, between Nomansland and Horse Sands. In front of the harbour entrance a triangular sandbank, the Spit Bank, compels deep-draught vessels to run along the beach, under the guns of Henry VIII's castle and older fortifications at the Round and Square Towers.

Lacking local pilots, the French heavy ships dared not enter the harbour approaches, so d'Annebault turned to his shallow-draught galleys. At daybreak on 19 July he sent them in to engage the English with gunfire and draw them out onto the main French battle line of three squadrons of 30–36 ships each. The weather was dead calm, ideal for galleys, five of which got near the harbour. Lying off St Helens in his troopship, du Bellay claimed their fire sank the 91-gun *Mary Rose*, while *Great Harry* 'was so distressed, that if she had not been relieved by the ships … nearest her, she would have undergone the same fate'.

English accounts, and that of the Imperial ambassador, tell a different story. Henry VIII was aboard *Great Harry* dining with his admirals and the ambassador when the French attack was observed. This suggests the galleys spent the morning picking their way through the sandbanks from St Helens, 6 miles to the southeast. The civilians hurried ashore, although the English could not leave harbour at once, for lack of wind. Around midday the usual offshore wind sprung up and the tide changed, allowing the English to get underway. The Cowdray Engraving, a contemporary representation of the action, shows them engaging French galleys in deep water south of Spit Bank, suggesting they used the Swatch Way rather than the main channel past Southsea Castle. The Swatch Way is a shortcut through Spit Bank, on the Gosport side of the spithead, still used by Isle of Wight ferries at high tide.

Benefiting from local knowledge, the English could turn to starboard as soon as they had passed the harbour entrance, pass along the Swatch Way in line astern, and then turn to port, back towards the enemy. The Cowdray Engraving shows *Great Harry* and *Mary Rose* in the lead, except that only the latter's masts are above water. Disaster had struck as *Mary Rose* went about, sinking with almost all hands on the tail of the Spit Bank, in full view of the king and her captain's wife. Not more than 40 men out of 600–700 survived. Among them was a Fleming, who told his fellow countryman, the Imperial ambassador, 'when she heeled over with the wind the water entered by the lowest row of gun ports which had been left open after firing ...' The contemporary historian Sir Edward Hall agreed: 'She was laden with much ordinaunce, and the portes left open, which were very lowe, and the great ordinaunce unbreeched [unsecured], so that when the ship should turne, the water entered, and sodainly she sank.' Modern archaeological investigations have found no shot-holes, indicating accidental loss. Her captain's last words, saying 'he had the sort of knaves whom he could not rule', suggest poor discipline, consonant with failure to fasten the gun ports. Additional troops and light artillery on the upper deck may have further compromised the ship, making her top heavy and bringing the ports dangerously near the water.

The tragedy hardly interrupted the action: 'Notwithstandinge this looste, the service appointed wente forwarde, as soon as wynde and weather woulde serve' (Carew). The galleys, long unhandy vessels, were so close they hardly had time and room to go about when the English ships bore down on them. Du Bellay says they retreated 'to the distance of a cannon-shot ... as most conducive to their main design of drawing the English out of cover'. Sir Peter Carew was less polite: 'The Frenchemen ... licke as a sorte of shepe runnynge into the folde ... shifted awaye, and gate them into theire harborowes, thincking it better to lye theare in a salffe skyne [safe skin].' The English did not, however, approach the French sailing squadrons, contenting themselves with chasing the galleys off with their own oared craft.

Portsmouth

	Winner	*Loser*
Opponents	English	French
Commanders	John Dudley, Lord Lisle	Claude d'Annebault
Numbers	*c.*60 ships, 12,000 men	22–26 galleys
Losses	1 ship, 700 men	none

Bonchurch

	Winner	*Loser*
Opponents	English	French
Commanders	unknown	Le Seigneur de Tais
Numbers	*c.*2500	unknown
Losses	unknown	unknown

D'Annebault now attacked the Isle of Wight, believing this would force Henry VIII to commit his fleet to protect his subjects' property. The Island was less vulnerable than it looks. Sir Edward Bellingham, the English field commander, reported its south coast lacked harbours, while the north was unsuitable for military operations, being 'fowle, full of egerowse, lans, dyks, wods, yll and dale, and in sum places marys [marsh]'. Reinforcements from Hampshire and Wiltshire had brought the local militia up to 5000 men. Too few to defend all possible landing places, they held the high ground, particularly Bembridge and St Boniface Downs, towards the French anchorage.

The French landed at several places over a 10-mile (16-km) front from Seaview to Bonchurch. The presence of the Seigneur de Tais, the overall French military commander, at Bonchurch suggests that was the main landing. Appuldurcombe House, 3 miles (5 km) inland, belonged to Sir Richard Worsley, captain of the Isle of Wight, making it an attractive target. Alternatively, the French may have wanted fresh drinking water, available near Bonchurch. Contemporaries estimated 2000 Frenchmen went ashore altogether; how many at Bonchurch is unknown. The 17th-century antiquarian Sir John Oglander reckoned 'We [the English] had there most of the companies of Hampshire', which mustered later at 2681. Spread between several beachheads, the French must have been locally outnumbered.

The southeast corner of the Isle of Wight rises steeply from the sea to St Boniface Down (771 feet/ 235 m), an average gradient of one in four. C.T. Witherby, a modern local historian, believed the French landed in Horseshoe Bay, then pushed westwards along the modern Newport Road, towards the combe leading to Wroxall. The road runs along a shelf between cliffs that fall away towards Ventnor and the wooded slopes of St Boniface Down. Here the Hampshire militia, 'by hidden ways and screened by the wood had assembled in the most advantageous spot to give us battle. These confident in their position showed a bold front to our men and wounded some of them ... but the rest of our men, marching in array, made them abandon their position and retire precipitately ... where we could only follow them in loose order and in single file' (du Bellay). Witherby located the action near the Hillside Hotel, between Ventnor Junior School and the old railway station. It was a strong position, with impregnable flanks, out of reach of French naval guns. Nevertheless, Oglander admitted the French 'put our men to the rout', dispersing them up narrow paths that still lead to the Down. Captain Fischer, 'a fat gentleman and not being able to make his retreat up the hill ... cried out £100 for a horse, but in that confusion no horse could be had, not for a kingdom'. English casualties may have been heavy: 'not any family of note in the Island but lost a father, brother, or uncle'.

The French failed to press their advantage, perhaps because another landing was in difficulties, at Whitecliff Bay. Here, straggling up Bembridge Down, the French found more militia in ambush behind the crest, and the militiamen – some of them riding cart horses – chased them back to their boats. D'Annebault had to recall the Seigneur de Tais from Bonchurch to restore order. French troops made a fresh attempt to expand the Bonchurch beachhead next morning. The Chevalier d'Aux, a galley captain, led a patrol through White Shute up St Boniface Down, to cover his watering parties. The reorganized defenders ambushed the breathless Frenchmen at the top, shooting the chevalier in the knee with an arrow. His own men deserted him, 'whereupon some country fellow ... clove his head with a brown bill' (Oglander).

D'Annebault's strategic devices had all failed. He re-embarked his troops and withdrew from the Solent, clearing English waters by the 28th. The greatest attempt the French had yet made at sea was a ten-day wonder. An English diplomat in Venice rejoiced 'to see the intollerable crakes [croaks] of Frenchmen reduced to vaine ostentacion'. The more measured judgement of the naval historian Sir Julian Corbett (1854–1922) was that the cannonades in Spithead represented the birth pangs of English naval power. Memories of D'Annebault's repulse would inspire confidence in face of Spanish threats in 1588.

Directions

Portsmouth *View Spithead from Southsea Castle. St Helens is directly south. The wreck of the* Mary Rose *is marked by a buoy, southwest of the nearest of the cylindrical 19th-century sea forts that now defend the anchorage. Walk west along the seafront to the Round Tower overlooking the harbour mouth. Visit Portsmouth dockyard to see the remains of the* Mary Rose *and artefacts from the wreck.*

Bonchurch *From Horseshoe Bay turn left along Newport Road to the area of the initial skirmish, past Leeson Road on the right. Further east along the A3055 retrace the Chevalier d'Aux's steps up a footpath from Upper Bonchurch to the viewpoint at the top of St Boniface Down.*

Plymouth (Eddystone), 21 July 1588

Naval, English Channel, LR201

Portland Bill, 23 July 1588

Naval, English Channel, LR194

Isle of Wight (Dunnose Head), 25 July 1588

Naval, English Channel, LR196

The Armada campaign consisted of several engagements usually lumped together as indistinguishable episodes of one larger battle, whose decisive moment came off Gravelines, out of sight of England. The numbers of ships lost in battle were insignificant compared with the Spanish losses from storm damage, during their return voyage. Nevertheless, the actions off Plymouth, Portland and Dunnose Head were distinct in time and space, tactical steps towards the grand dénouement.

The Armada was the product of Philip II's decision in October 1585 to overthrow Elizabeth I and restore England to the Roman Catholic faith. The overall scheme appeared simple enough: a powerful fleet would sail from Lisbon to Margate, rendezvous with the Spanish Army of Flanders, and convoy it across the English Channel in barges. The plan possessed fatal flaws, however. The Spanish commander, the Duke of Medina Sidonia, had to bring the invasion force's naval and military components together in the presence of a hostile fleet, which he had no way of defeating as long as the more agile English ships kept clear of their less weatherly opponents. Contemporary technology offered no reliable means of two-way communication between a fleet sailing up-Channel before the wind and an army hundreds of miles to leeward in Flanders. Even if Medina Sidonia had coordinated his movements with the Army of Flanders, rebel Dutch flotillas controlled the coastal waterways that the Spanish soldiers had to traverse before linking up with the Armada.

The English did not rely on strategic factors alone for their defence. They assembled a fleet that outclassed the Armada in numbers and fighting power. Official records list 197 ships, 34 of them Her Majesty's ships 'great and small', carrying 15,925 men. The Armada is unlikely to have reached the Channel with more than 125 vessels of all types, carrying not more than 24,000 men. All were sailing ships, apart from four galleasses, a compound type powered by sails and oars, possessing some of the galley's advantages, but more heavily armed and more seaworthy. In all the pioneering naval historian Sir John Knox Laughton (1830–1915) reckoned the Spaniards deployed 62 effective warships, against 49 English.

Elizabethan propaganda has created an enduring but false image of a monstrous force of huge ships miraculously beaten by a puny foe. In fact, the largest ship present was the English *Triumph* (900–1100 tons), nearly twice the size of the captured *San Salvador* (600 tons). Mobility and firepower mattered more than size, however. Spanish ships were leewardly (prone to drifting downwind) and unmanageable, even in a moderate wind. Many of their crews were fair-weather sailors from the Mediterranean, unused to Atlantic weather. English warships carried two sailors to every soldier, a proportion reversed in the Armada, and could outrun their fastest opponents.

Contrary to popular belief Spanish broadsides were not mounted so high that they overshot their low-lying opponents. Neither were short Spanish cannon outranged by long-barrelled English culverins. The effective range of both was less than 200 yards (180 m). The English simply had more heavy guns, firing 16 lb shot or heavier: 251 to 138. Most Spanish guns were light people-killers, firing 4–9 lb shot, making them ineffective against ships. The English had major quality advantages: better-made guns and shot; better-organized gun crews. Spanish shot did not fit poorly cast guns, which burst when fired, while their gun carriages were large and clumsy, preventing reloading inboard. Spanish cannon might fire twice during a day's fighting, while the English kept up a continuous bombardment. Contemporaries thought they sounded more like a fusillade of musketry than great ordnance. During the South Coast battles, however, the English failed to close the range sufficiently to inflict significant damage on their targets. They only did so at Gravelines, with their last barrels of powder.

The action off Plymouth set the pattern for the following week. While the English outmanoeuvred and outshot the Armada, they neither disrupted its formation nor inflicted fatal damage on its components. The Spanish appearance off Land's End on 19 July caught the main English fleet taking on stores at Plymouth, after a failed attempt to destroy the Armada before it left port: 'The southerly wind that brought us back from Spain', wrote Lord Howard of Effingham, the English commander-in-chief, 'brought them out.' The story that Drake refused to interrupt his game of bowls, presumably on Plymouth Hoe, still attracts belief, although it did not appear until 1625.

The Spanish allowed the English to leave harbour overnight, gaining visual contact at 3 p.m. on 20 July between Fowey and Plymouth. Howard sailed boldly across the Armada's front with most of the 54 ships that had left Plymouth so far, turning west to weather the enemy's southern flank. Meanwhile Drake cut in between the enemy and the shore, exploiting local knowledge of the coastal back eddy that runs when the flood tide is at its peak. By dawn 21 July the English had gained the wind, lying west of the enemy, abeam of Eddystone Rock. The appropriately named *Disdain* fired the first shot at 9 a.m.

The Armada formed a great crescent, 2 miles (3 km) from flank to flank, divided into three squadrons: van and rearguard of 20 ships each under Leyva and Recalde respectively trailed to port and starboard, flanking 80 more in the centre under Medina Sidonia. The English ran across the Spanish rear, before the west-northwesterly wind: Howard to engage the Spanish flagship, the other commanders against the Armada's exposed right wing. Spanish sources describe the English as arrayed '*en ala*', in single file, showing they attacked in line astern: 'The fight was so well maintained ... the enemy was constrained to give way and bear up room to the eastward' (Howard). Medina Sidonia admitted that Recalde's flagship withstood the attack alone, two shots striking her foremast, and another cutting her forestay.

Despite heavy gunfire the English would not close. Forty of Howard's ships had still not arrived from Plymouth, besides 'we durst not adventure to put in amongst them their fleet being so strong'. After two hours fighting the English drew off to take stock and conserve ammunition. The Armada carried on eastwards, up the Channel.

The only casualties, both Spanish, were accidental. *Nuestra Senora del Rosario* was involved in a collision, lost her foremast, and became unmanageable, while an explosion in *San Salvador* killed half her crew. Both vessels fell into enemy hands next day, an evil omen that shook Spanish morale. Otherwise the 21st proved English firepower was insufficient to defeat the Armada, while Medina Sidonia confessed he could do no more than keep formation. The English always had the wind, he complained, their ships 'so fast and handy there was nothing which could not be done with them'.

Plymouth

	Winner	*Loser*
Opponents	English	Spanish
Commanders	Charles, Lord Howard of Effingham Sir Francis Drake Sir John Hawkins Sir Martin Frobisher	Duke of Medina Sidonia Don Alonso de Leyva Juan Martinez de Recalde
Numbers	54 ships	*c.*125 ships
Losses	none	2 ships

Portland Bill

	Winner	*Loser*
Opponents	English	Spanish
Numbers	unknown	*c.*123 ships

Isle of Wight

	Winner	*Loser*
Opponents	English	Spanish
Numbers	unknown	*c.*123 ships

The second battle, off Portland Bill, confirmed first impressions. Medina Sidonia had reorganized the Armada: he eliminated the crescent's vulnerable horns, combining the best 43 ships in the van and rear under de Leyva's command. The original centre became the van, under Medina Sidonia. Military police went round the fleet, promising to hang any captains losing station. The two fleets had lost touch after Plymouth, but by the evening of 22 July both were becalmed in Lyme Bay, approaching Portland Bill. A fresh northeasterly breeze next morning gave the Spaniards the weather gauge (i.e. placing them to windward of the English). The English stood in towards land, hoping to regain the wind, but the Armada also tacked, denying the English sea room to manoeuvre. Most of the English cast back to seaward. A dozen galleons attacked them as they came away, 'but all to little purpose, for the enemy, seeing that we endeavoured to come to arm's length, bore away, avoiding our attack, thanks to the lightness of his vessels' (Medina Sidonia).

Six ships, including Sir Martin Frobisher's *Triumph*, were too close to shore to beat off, inviting attack by the galleasses. The fighting straddled an uncomfortable stretch of water, from Chesil Bank in the west, past the rocky headland of Portland (Thomas Hardy's Isle of Slingers), to the Shambles reef in the east. Sometimes the Portland Race, the fiercest tidal rip on the south coast, makes the sea boil here like a cauldron, a major problem for ships dependent on wind and muscle power. In this awkward seaway, the galleasses proved a disappointment, provoking Medina Sidonia to send their admiral 'certain words ... not to his honour'.

Fighting continued for perhaps two hours, when the wind veered southeast then south-southwest, allowing Howard to relieve *Triumph* and her companions. Calling upon neighbouring ships, he 'charged them straitly to follow him, and to set freshly upon the Spaniards, and to go within musket shot of the enemy before they should discharge any one piece of ordnance'. Medina Sidonia met them with 16 ships, 'At which assault after wonderful sharp conflict, the Spaniards were forced to give way, and to flock together like sheep' (Howard). Medina Sidonia, referring to himself in the third person, described the encounter in different terms: 'The enemy's flagship and all the fleet passed him, firing at him ship by ship, while he, on his side, fired his guns very well and quickly, so that half the enemy's fleet did not draw near, but fired at him from a distance.'

It is not surprising that accounts vary. Ships lacked logbooks and chronometers, and fought in ad hoc groups as circumstances required. Orders were transmitted by word of mouth. When the battle died away the Armada shook itself back into formation and carried on towards its rendezvous with the Army of Flanders. Despite fighting all day, and 'the terrible value of great shot' expended, the English had failed to break up the Armada. Short of ammunition, they faced a strategic crisis as the Armada approached the great anchorage between Portsmouth and the Isle of Wight.

Historians disagree whether Medina Sidonia meant to await the Army of Flanders here. The Armada battles all coincide with major harbours, but this probably owed more to English fears than Spanish intentions. Philip II's instructions to make directly for the Margate rendezvous with the Army of Flanders were explicit. Nevertheless the English could not risk Medina Sidonia taking shelter in the Solent, and prepared a concerted effort. Howard organized his fleet into four semi-independent squadrons: Frobisher inshore to port, Hawkins and Howard himself in the centre, Drake to seaward to starboard. As more ships joined they were assigned to a particular squadron. So far Howard's ships had fought as a loose agglomeration; now they had to act together to chivvy the Armada past the Isle of Wight, on towards the Flanders sandbanks.

The Solent's western entrance, past the Needles and the guns of Hurst Castle, was too dangerous for the Armada. If Medina Sidonia meant to enter the Solent, he would do so through the eastern entrance used by the French in 1545. All night on 24–25 July, 300 becalmed ships drifted in brilliant moonlight beneath the Island's southern cliffs. Next morning there was still no wind. Longboats towed Hawkins's squadron into action against one or two Spanish stragglers, coming so close the boats were beaten off by musketry. The attack drew in the galleasses, which needed no wind. Howard claimed to have damaged them so that 'one of them was fain to be carried away on the careen', heeled over to keep shot-holes above water. Another lost her lantern, 'which came swimmingly by', and the third her nose. Nevertheless the galleasses towed the stragglers away, as a 'little gale' sprung up, presumably a southwesterly, allowing the sailing ships to manoeuvre. The main fleets 'began some fight', probably off Dunnose Head, between Ventnor and Shanklin, 'but it continued not long'. Medina Sidonia reported that with growing confidence and calmer weather the English were at last using their heaviest guns at decisive ranges: 'approaching nearer than on the previous day, and firing their lower deck guns'. Damage remained inconsequential: a severed mainstay and some dead soldiers.

Meanwhile Frobisher slipped past the Armada, barring the approach to St Helens, the anchorage northeast of the island. For a while Medina Sidonia entertained hopes of catching *Triumph* becalmed to leeward, but the wind freshened and Frobisher slipped away, leaving his opponents standing, as if at anchor. Seeing he had lost his advantage, and the Isle of Wight lying very near, Medina Sidonia 'fired a gun and proceeded on his course, the rest of the Armada following in very good order, and the enemy remaining far astern'.

As far as commanders-in-chief were concerned, that ended the affair, which had lasted about four hours, 'a very sharp fight for the time' (Howard). Neither mentions Drake's part in the battle, which may have been decisive. While the commanders-in-chief were busy elsewhere, Drake is thought to have worked his squadron to seaward, using the freshening wind to launch a furious attack upon the Armada's right flank, 'in such wise', recalled a Spanish officer, 'that we who were there were cornered, so that, if the Duke [of Medina Sidonia] had not gone about with his flagship ... we should have come out vanquished that day'. Drake's onslaught disrupted Medina Sidonia's dispositions, hurrying him away from the Solent towards Selsey Bill, with no alternative but to make all sail eastwards to avoid the Ower Banks.

The implications of this were not immediately apparent, as ammunition shortages once more reduced the English to shadowing their indestructible enemy. When Medina Sidonia anchored off Calais on 27 July, he seemed to have fulfilled Philip II's orders. However, the battles of 21–25 July had shown the English what they had to do. Before Medina Sidonia could link up with the Army of Flanders, fireships followed by more effective close-range gunnery than ever seen before drove him from his anchorage, sending the Armada off on its fatal voyage homewards around the British Isles.

Directions

View the sea areas fought over as follows:

Plymouth *from Rame Head.*

Portland Bill *from Henry VIII's Castle.*

Isle of Wight *from St Catherine's pre-Reformation lighthouse, the coastal path, and St Boniface Down.*

Rebellion and Disorder

The middle years of Tudor England were an untypical interlude of disorder. Henry VIII's death in 1547 left a country seething with discontent, and a vacuum at the heart of government. The throne was first occupied by the boy-king Edward VI (reigned 1547–53), and then by Mary (1553–8), the first queen regnant since Matilda's inauspicious 'reign' in 1141. Neither was strong enough to deal with the consequences of the turmoil of Henry's reign, which had detached England from the papacy, alienating many without bringing the religious reforms desired by others. England lurched towards Protestantism under Edward, and back to Catholicism under Mary, inspiring three revolts: the Western Rebellion and Kett's

Rebellion of 1549, and Wyatt's Rebellion in 1554. Inflation and changes in land usage added social grievances to religious divisions. Attempts by the Duke of Somerset, lord protector and head of the Council during Edward's early years, to address the country's economic problems further exacerbated the unrest.

The Western Rebellion voiced the religious conservatism of Devon and Cornwall. People there resented replacement of the Latin Mass by an English liturgy, a 'Christmas game', which Cornish speakers claimed not to understand. The rebellion's military leader was Humphrey Arundell, a known troublemaker, but its guiding hand was Robert Walsh, vicar of St Thomas the Apostle, near Exeter. Walsh was subsequently hanged from his own church tower wearing the symbols of his faith: rosary beads, sacring bell and holy-water bucket. East Anglia, by contrast, was a Protestant hotbed. The small farmers and businessmen who followed Robert Kett, an otherwise obscure Norfolk gentleman, had social rather than religious grievances, particularly the enclosure of common land for sheep farming, which had led to the impoverishment of small farmers. The most striking similarity between the revolts of 1549 was the localism that prevented either from advancing on London. Wyatt's Rebellion, centred in Kent, was more dangerous. Sir Thomas Wyatt was a significant local figure, who fused gentry dissatisfaction over Mary's proposed marriage to Philip of Spain with popular hatred of foreigners.

The fact that the revolts of 1549 were simultaneous, and at opposite ends of the country, hampered government efforts to deal with them. The Western Rebellion began at Whitsun as two separate protests, at Bodmin and Sampford Courtenay, inspired by the introduction of the new Book of Common Prayer. By 2 July the rebels had joined up, surrounded Exeter, the provincial capital, and cut the London road at Clyst St Mary. Lord Russell, the government's local commander-in-chief, nervously blockaded the western peninsula with an unreliable handful of militia at Honiton, Devon, while awaiting reinforcements. When the rebels advanced in late July he was compelled to fight and defeat them at Fenny Bridges, showing that rebel numbers and capabilities had been exaggerated. Substantial reinforcements encouraged Russell to advance in his turn, relieving Exeter on the 6th, after two days fighting around Clyst St Mary. Despite heavy casualties, the rebels regrouped at Sampford Courtenay, where Russell finally dispersed them on 18 August.

Kett's Rebellion arose from a brawl at Wymondham, near Norwich, on 7 July 1549, but Robert Kett's unexplained assumption of leadership of the discontents transformed the affair into a national emergency. The seriousness of the revolt forced the Council to commission the Earl of Warwick, the second most powerful magnate in the Council, to suppress the revolt. He reoccupied Norwich on 24 August, provoking two days of confused fighting. The arrival of professional troops released by the relief of Exeter restored the initiative to Warwick, who cut the rebel army to pieces at Dussindale.

Wyatt's Rebellion began as a conspiracy to replace Queen Mary with her Protestant sister Elizabeth, who was to be forcibly married to one of the conspirators, Edward Courtenay, Earl of Devon. The prospective groom, however, betrayed the plot, while the failure of risings in Devon, Leicestershire and Herefordshire isolated Wyatt in Kent. A skirmish at Wrotham further weakened his support, but the defection of 600 troops from London encouraged Wyatt to strike at the capital. Strung out along Fleet Street, the rebel army found the city gates barred, and had to surrender.

Mid-Tudor rebellions had little chance of success. The revolts in the West and Norfolk focused on local grievances, and never spread beyond their immediate geographical setting. Nevertheless, considerable numbers were involved. Modern historians estimate 10,000 rebels were killed or executed. In proportion to Tudor England's small population, the death toll bears comparison with a First World War battle. Wyatt's national agenda made his rebellion more dangerous, but his failure demonstrated the futility of revolt as a vehicle for dissent. In future, gentry would oppose the Crown through Parliament, while Elizabeth's compromise settlement of 1558 assuaged sectarian conflict in England until the Civil Wars of the 1640s. The late Tudor period was as remarkable for its domestic peace as the reign of Henry VIII.

Fenny Bridges, *c*.28 July 1549

England, Devon, LR192 SY1198

The rapid spread of revolt through Devon and Cornwall in June 1549 surprised central government. Not until 10 July did the Duke of Somerset despatch Lord Grey of Wilton to the West Country with professional reinforcements and field artillery. Until they arrived, the regional commander, Lord Russell, had to hold out with local levies. John Hooker, who was besieged in Exeter, wrote, 'Having but a very small guard about him he lived in more fear than feared; for the Rebels daily increased and his company decreased and shrank away, and he not altogether assured of them which remained'. Grey had still not arrived when the rebels advanced up the Roman road from Exeter towards Russell's headquarters at Honiton. About 27 July they approached Fenny Bridges, where the road crosses the River Otter, and drove in Russell's outposts. Next day Russell took the chance to attack them in relatively open countryside.

Russell's army comprised three distinct elements: 650 cavalry from his own retinue, and from the local gentry and their servants; 160 professional Italian arquebusiers; and about 1000 militia infantry. Most of the cavalry would have been demi-lances, 'with a shirt of mail and a sallet [light helmet extending over the neck],' according to the Venetian ambassador, 'and a light long spear, and ... any sort of horse, as they never charge, save in flank'. The militia generally carried bows and bills, like the rebels, with some firearms, although the Venetian ambassador also thought English arquebusiers 'good for little, as only a few of them have had practice south of the Channel'.

Rebel numbers are impossible to gauge. Russell thought he faced 10,000. The Imperial ambassador reported 12,000, 'drawing closer to London'. The Privy Council estimated 'not above vij.m [7000] men tag and rag that should come to fight, and yet some ... they leave behind to keep their houses ... and one thousand of them is in Exeter ... the rebels cannot be thought in the whole against you past iiij.m [4000] and the more part unarmed'. On paper the rebels at Fenny Bridges outnumbered Russell two-to-one, but it is not certain they deployed all their available manpower so far forward. They were a purely infantry force, one-third archers, the rest billmen. Russell's men were better armed, 'with harness and having arquibusses which they have none'.

The Roman road runs southwest from Honiton, beside the Otter as far as Fenny Bridges, where the river turns south under a series of stone bridges. One group of rebels held the far end of these, while the rest formed up in the meadows behind them, presumably in traditional array, bows on the flanks, bills in the centre. Their logical position would be south of the modern railway, between bridge and village. Wooded hills either side of the road forced Russell to attack head-on. Casualties among local gentlemen, shot through arms and legs, suggest dismounted cavalry rushed the bridge, relying on their armour to avoid serious injury, while arquebusiers gave covering fire. The rebel bridge guard fell back on their supports, whereupon the Royalist main body filed across and formed up. When the arquebusiers fired a volley and the cavalry charged, the rebels broke.

Russell's men began pillaging, but the rebels were not yet finished. A Cornish captain, John Smyth of St Germans, brought up 250 men through Fairmile under cover of the hedges, to launch a sudden barrage of arrows, interrupting the looters 'in the middle of their game'. The unexpected counterattack drove Russell's disordered troops back across the stream, but his reserves restored the situation: 'The fight for a time was very sharp and cruel, for the Cornishmen were lusty and fresh and fully bent to fight out the matter' (Russell). Eventually the Cornishmen were beaten off: 'Their Captain whose comb was cut,

Fenny Bridges

	Winner	*Loser*
Opponents	Royalist	Rebel
Commanders	Lord John Russell	Robert Smyth
Numbers	*c*.1800	unknown
Losses	*c*.100	300

showed a clean pair of heels and fled away' (Russell). Legend claims the meadows beside the Otter ran ankle deep in blood.

Russell pushed down the main road to Streteway Hill, but was halted by an incident out of musical comedy. His jester, confused by church bells ringing for evensong, galloped up from Honiton, crying, 'with a foul mouth', that the bells were ringing backwards to raise the country people to attack the royal army from behind. After their previous surprise, tired troops were probably not sorry to return to quarters.

Russell's victory was significant, nevertheless. The rebels had not appeared in overwhelming numbers, and had 'neither weapons, order nor counsel, but being in all things unprovided, were slain like beasts' (Hooker). The longbow's legendary superiority proved illusory, the superior range of the arquebus offsetting the traditional weapon's higher rate of fire. Hungry archers, worn out by marching, failed to draw their bows properly. Royalist archers even had their arrows shot back at them. This was not a problem with firearms: 'The shott of the habirgon pelot [a primitive mortar] is brust [burst], which never returneth.'

Directions

Follow Russell's approach down the A30 from Honiton to the B3177 Alfington turnoff. Go under the railway, and turn right to Fenny Bridges. The Ordnance Survey marks the action north of the A30, although the fighting was presumably to the south, on the older minor road.

Clyst St Mary, Sunday–Monday 4–5 August 1549

England, Devon, LR192 SX9791

The decisive action of the Western Rebellion was fought east of Exeter, on both sides of the River Clyst.

Russell's victory at Fenny Bridges (see above) did not immediately open the road to the besieged city. He was too cautious to penetrate the difficult country west of Honiton without Lord Grey's reinforcements. These arrived shortly after Fenny Bridges, most of them German *Landsknechte*, 'in a great chaff' at missing the battle. The Imperial ambassador reported the English so resented the use of foreign troops against their countrymen 'that they say they won't leave a foreigner alive'. However, reliable infantry were essential for clearing the way to Exeter, a task for which disaffected local militia had neither the training nor inclination.

Russell could advance straight down the Roman road, or take a byway through Ottery St Mary, across Aylesbeare Common, to Clyst St Mary, where the sandstone bridge west of the village provides a direct approach to Exeter. Russell chose this more southerly route. On 3 August he marched from Honiton, camping at Windmill Hill, north of Woodbury Salterton. Rebels came out of Clyst St Mary early next day and attacked his outposts, but found them 'as vigilant as they were forward' (John Hooker), and were driven off.

Russell's force was nearly double that at Fenny Bridges: 950 cavalry, half foreign mercenaries; 200 Italian mounted arquebusiers; 1000 English militia; and 850 *Landsknechte* with pikes and arquebuses. Grey had also brought an unknown quantity of artillery. The army was formed in three battles, perhaps one each for the mounted troops, the English infantry and the German infantry. References to foreward and rearward cavalry, however, suggest the arms were mixed, to provide horsemen on both flanks. The death of the foreward's cavalry commander north of Clyst St Mary would place the van in its traditional place on the right. Rebel numbers are speculative. Edward VI, who had good sources, reckoned about 2000 fought on 4 August. The remainder lay before Exeter or at 'Honiton Bridge', covering the northerly route via Clyst Honiton. Some of these joined in the second day of fighting, west of the river on Clyst Heath. However, Edward VI's estimate of rebel strength on the 5th as 'another two thousand' implies the rebels never converted their general superiority of numbers into superiority on the battlefield.

The rebel position has been pinpointed 500 yards (450 m) east of Tudor Clyst St Mary, along the

Clyst St Mary		
	Winner	*Loser*
Opponents	Royalist	Rebel
Commanders	Lord John Russell William Grey, Lord de Wilton	unknown
Numbers	3000	2000–4000
Losses	unknown	1000–2000

eastern edge of the modern village, squarely blocking the main road. South of the A3052 a deep lane between high banks runs down to Grindle Brook, which secured the rebel right. A surviving hedge east of the lane was probably mirrored by another on the west. The rebels reinforced this formidable obstacle with earth bulwarks, continuing their fieldworks across the main road towards the Clyst Honiton lane, the only other approach to the position. The water-logged banks of the River Clyst protected the rebels' other flank.

Edward VI says Russell attacked three battles up in the front line, covered by small arms fire: 'The rearward of the horsemen ... set upon the one bulwark, the vanguard and battle on the other. Spinola's band [the arquebusiers] kept them occupied at their wall.' English cavalry would naturally dismount to storm redoubts, their armour proof against arrows. Tactically outmatched, the defenders retreated into the village 'to abide the pulse'. As the attackers regrouped, a few stray rebels sounded drum and trumpet from a furze close in the rear, causing a panic-stricken flight back to the Royalist start line 3 miles (5 km) away. Had the rebels possessed even makeshift cavalry to keep the broken Royalists running, they would have won the day. Instead they looted Russell's wagons, while he reformed and tried again.

Russell put in his second attack down the Clyst-Honiton lane, which dips down into the village from the northeast. The rebels dropped stones on the attackers' heads from the high overhanging banks, killing their leader, but the troops gained a foothold on the edge of the village. Firing the thatch, they drove the defenders out of the cottages: 'Some were slain by the sword, some burned in the houses, some shifted for themselves [or] were taken prisoner and many thinking to escape over the water were drowned' (Hooker). A last stand in the middle of the village was overthrown with levelled pikes.

The surviving rebels barricaded Clyst Bridge with tree trunks and cannon. The muddy-bottomed tidal stream is unfordable at that point, but local troopers led the cavalry upstream to Bishop's Clyst mill, where they could cross. Russell offered 400 crowns for volunteers to rush the bridge, but rebel gunners blew the forlorn hope away. Then the cavalry rode up from the flank and cut down the gunners while reloading, so allowing the Royalist infantry to cross. As they climbed the further bank another accident of war, more sinister than the jester's intervention at Fenny Bridges, disrupted the pursuit. Lord Grey thought he saw the gleam of weapons behind the Royalist army, reflecting the sunset. Fearing fresh opponents, Grey ordered his men to kill the day's prisoners, lest they overwhelm their captors.

Overnight (4–5 August) the rebels occupied a new position on Clyst Heath, just west of the Topsham road. Today the area is so cut up by major roads as to be unrecognizable, although place-names like Sandy Pit and Sandy Gate recall the barren heath it was until the 19th century. Here the rebels dug in among the small fields along the roadside, and brought up guns from the siege lines. They opened fire at dawn, provoking an immediate counterattack. While two of Russell's divisions pinned the rebels in front, pioneers gapped the hedges between Clyst Heath and the Topsham road to turn the rebel right, cutting off their retreat: 'Valiantly and stoutly they stood to their tackle, and would not give over as long as life and limb lasted, yet in the end they were all overthrown, and few or none left alive' (Hooker). The hard-bitten Grey, a veteran of Pinkie, admitted 'that he never in all the wars he had been [in] did know the like'. When the area was ploughed during the Napoleonic Wars, it yielded vast numbers of human bones.

Casualty estimates are confused and unreliable. Repeated references to 1000 slain may represent the total for both days, or daily losses. Edward VI's figure of 900 may reflect an official body count. Another 900 prisoners were killed in cold blood, and 600 allegedly fell at Windmill Hill. The protracted slaughter broke the revolt, the rebels abandoning their siege lines overnight. After so many surprises, Russell remained cautious. He refreshed his troops in Topsham, before advancing in battle array to relieve Exeter next day.

Directions

Clyst St Mary is 3 miles (5 km) east of Exeter off the A3052. Continue along the main road to the rebels' first line of defence, or enter the village to see Clyst Bridge and the sunken lane to Clyst Honiton. A footpath north of the public house crosses to the right bank, near the ford used by the cavalry. Clyst Heath is beneath the A379 dual carriageway, west of Junction 30 of the M5.

Sampford Courtenay, Sunday 18 August 1549

England, Devon, LR191 SS6301–6401

Sampford Courtenay		
	Winner	*Loser*
Opponents	Royalist	Rebel
Commanders	Lord John Russell William Grey, Lord de Wilton William Herbert, Earl of Pembroke	Humphrey Arundell
Numbers	8000	2000
Losses	10–12	1200

The Western Rebellion ended where it began. The rebels who survived the Clyst St Mary battles regrouped 30 miles (50 km) to the west at Sampford Courtenay, 'fully bent to maintain their quarrel and abide the battle' (John Hooker). Lord Russell remained in Exeter, restoring order and the food supply. The Privy Council, mindful of Kett's Rebellion in East Anglia, pressed Russell to finish the campaign. On 16 August he advanced on Crediton, the roads 'verie cumbrous', his foreward pushing on next day to North Tawton, 3 miles (5 km) short of their objective.

The Royalist army had undergone major changes at Exeter. The *Landsknechte* withdrew for service in Norfolk, being replaced by 1000 Welsh troops under Sir William Herbert, and as many more from Gloucestershire and Wiltshire. Local recruits, keen to make up for earlier backwardness, brought Russell's numbers to 'above seaven or 8000 persons'. The only mercenaries were Spinola's mounted arquebusiers. The rebels still had 15 or 16 cannon, but were outnumbered four-to-one. To offset lack of numbers, they tried to exploit the enclosed hilly terrain. Half of them fortified a conspicuous vantage point, where they, in Lord John Russell's words, 'lay strongly encamped as well by the seat of the ground as by the entrenching of the same'. The rest waited in concealment for the inevitable Royalist attack to become entangled in the surrounding hedgerows. The most likely campsite is a rise 1 mile (1.6 km) east of Sampford Courtenay (594 feet/181 m), dominating the approach from Exeter and conveniently near a concealed position for the rebel reserve, back towards the village.

Grey's patrols clashed with rebel outposts beside the River Taw early on 18 August. He and Herbert commanded the Royalist advance guard, while Russell brought up the rear. Grey's most direct approach from North Tawton was along a minor road, which at Culm Cross came within gunshot of the rebel camp. Grey and Herbert turned right to attack up the lane that leads northwards from Culm Cross, pioneers covered by artillery fire gapping the hedges. Events suggest Herbert's Welshmen led off on the right, while Spinola's arquebusiers took the left, with Grey's cavalry in support. In the dense patchwork of tiny fields surrounded by high banks and hedges, the Royalists would have been unaware of the trap they were about to spring.

Russell was far behind when Arundell's charge

into Grey's left rear 'wrought such fear in the hearts of our men as we wished our power a great deal more' (Russell). However, the difficult terrain blunted the Cornish onslaught, and Grey's rearmost troops had time to turn and face the new threat. Without surprise, the rebels were 'nothing in order nor in company nor in experience to be compared to the royal forces' (Hooker). The action bogged down into a desultory exchange of fire, while Herbert stormed the rebel camp, supported by fresh troops advancing from North Tawton on his right.

Arundell's party fell back to make their last stand in Sampford Courtenay, where they 'most manfully did abide the fight; and never gave over until that both in the town and in the field they were all for the most part taken or slain'. The village was well prepared for defence with earthworks and a chain blocking the road. A Welsh gentleman was killed 'more boldy than advisedly giving the adventure to enter the rampire at the town's end' (Hooker). Russell's main body came up as the day waxed late, finally ending resistance: 'upon the sight the rebels stomach so fell from them as without any blow they fled' (Russell).

Royalist sources claimed 500–600 rebels killed in the fighting, and 700 in the pursuit to Okehampton, where Russell's cavalry forestalled a final attempt to rally. Russell minimized his own losses: 'many hurt but not passing x or xij slain'. The Western Rebellion was finished. Savage reprisals changed the West for ever. Catholicism was stamped out, while the Cornish language faded away.

Directions

Sampford Courtenay is a picture-postcard village on the A3072, 5 miles(8 km) northeast of Okehampton. Right of the lych gate see Church House, where the first blood of the rebellion was spilled on 10 June. East from the village, fork left to Culm Cross, and left again, up the lane to the rebel camp site.

Dussindale (Ossian's Vale), **27 August 1549**

England, Norfolk, LR134 unlocated

Kett's Rebellion was more serious than its reputation as the most famous sit-down strike in English history suggests. For six weeks up to 20,000 rebels camped at Mousehold Heath on the northeast outskirts of Norwich, terrorizing the 13,000 inhabitants of England's second city and devouring thousands of their class enemy, the sheep. The site of Dussindale, where they were finally dispersed, has been forgotten, but within Norwich many buildings that witnessed the fighting remain.

Mousehold Heath was, according to Edward VI, 'a strong plot of ground upon a hill', proof against cavalry attack. Its occupation placed Norwich, the rebels' main supply centre, between them and any Royalist forces approaching along the ancient route through Cambridge, Newmarket and Thetford. At first this strategic disadvantage proved a tactical asset. Norwich's defences were decayed and extensive, straggling either side of the River Wensum. Its labyrinthine streets soaked up small royal forces, leaving them vulnerable to counterattack from Kett's redoubt on the Heath. The Marquess of Northampton arrived on 31 July with a thousand horse and some arquebusiers, 'who winning the town … kept it one night and the next day … with the loss of 100 men departed out of the town …' (Edward VI). A townsman reported 'all the houses in Holmstreet [modern Bishopgate] afire on both sides', the lead roof of the gatehouse melting in the flames.

Kett's position proved less advantageous against a much larger Royalist army under the Earl of Warwick, who as Lord Lisle had fought at Pinkie (1547). Warwick occupied Norwich on 24 August. For two days fighting flared in the city centre, in Tombland and around St Andrews Hall, as Kett's men cut off stragglers and even carried off ill-guarded artillery pieces. Warwick's militia were poor street fighters, but they held the walls, while Captain 'Poignard' Drury's professional arquebusiers patrolled the streets, dispersing rebel archers with 'a terrible volley of shot (as if it had been a storm of hail)'. On 26 August four ensigns of *Landsknechte* (1040–1100 strong) marched in firing a *feu-de-joie*. Their arrival signalled the end of the revolt. Warwick's cavalry had already cut off rebel food supplies from the countryside, and Kett's men had no hope of regaining control of Norwich now.

Local Tudor historians put Warwick's army at 12,000–14,000 men. The Spanish ambassador preferred 8000–9000, supported by a payroll figure of 9422. Edward VI's estimate of 1500 horse and 6000 infantry would approach the latter, if augmented by local troops and *Landsknechte*. Warwick committed his best troops to the final action, a picked striking force including all the cavalry and the *Landsknechte*, about 4000 in all. The English foot held the town. Rebel numbers are almost certainly exaggerated, the most common estimate of 16,000 including women and non-combatants. The Spanish ambassador reported many deserters, 'and as I hear from some who have been in the field, most of them are now nothing but young serving men and riff-raff'. The remainder were ill-equipped: 'some of them naked and unarmed, some armed with staves, bills and pitchforks'. The accidental capture of Warwick's artillery train was an unlooked for windfall, 'for before they were utterly unprovided of such things'.

The rebels' withdrawal from Mousehold Heath during the night of 26–27 August baffled eyewitnesses. More recently the ensuing battle has been interpreted as a belated rearguard action, or as an attempt to offer battle before hunger depleted rebel numbers. Double-edged prophecies encouraged the rebel rank and file:

The country gruffes Hob, Dick, and Hick
With clubs and clouted shoon,
Shall fill the vale of Dusindale
With slaughtered bodies soon.

The location may have been deliberately forgotten, but must be nearby, 'not past a mile off'. Kett's indictment specifies 'Dussindale in the parishes of Thorpe and Sprowston'. Warwick observed rebel movements from the cathedral tower, and followed them through St Martin's Gate, on the north side of the city, turning east. The site was open and flat, but the rebels 'devised trenches and stakes wherein they and theirs were entrenched, and set up bulwarks of defence before and about, and placed their ordnance all about them'. In front of the position captive gentlemen were chained together as a human shield.

The rebels refused a final offer of pardon with a resolute shout of 'No!', and Kett's master gunner killed Warwick's standard-bearer with a well aimed shot. The *Landsknechte* replied with a devastating volley, and Warwick's cavalry charged the rebels' shattered ranks: 'whereupon instead of abiding the encounter they, like sheep, ran away headlong as quickly as they could'. A few stood fast, but 'such … was the force of the shot and the eagerness of our men to rush upon them … that Kett's army being beaten down and overthrown on every side … was almost with no labour driven from their standing'. Warwick intervened personally to stop the slaughter.

Rebel casualties show this was no mere skirmish. Edward VI put them at 2000, a figure that Holinshed stretched to 3500, perhaps including the Norwich street fighting. Most of the hostages escaped. Kett left early, and was arrested 10 miles (16 km) away near Swannington, by a farmer's wife. After the usual show trial, he was hanged in chains from the walls of Norwich Castle on 7 December. Warwick prevented reprisals like those in Cornwall, asking vengeful gentry, 'Would they be ploughmen themselves and harrow their own land?' The sheep's victory was short-lived, as rising prices revived demand for arable land. The chief beneficiary of Dussindale was Warwick, who replaced Protector Somerset as head of the Council. The rebellions had destroyed Somerset's

Dussindale

	Winner	*Loser*
Opponents	Royalist	Rebel
Commanders	John Dudley, Earl of Warwick	Robert Kett
Numbers	*c.*4000	*c.*12,000
Losses	*c.*250	2000

credibility, and given Warwick and Russell control of the mercenaries. Somerset joined Kett in the Tower, and was himself executed in 1552.

Directions

Mousehold Heath is an open area surrounded by housing (TG2410). In Norwich see St Andrews Hall, and the churches of St Michael (Queen Street) and St Simon and St Jude (Elm Hill), where rebels ambushed Warwick's men. Bishopgate bridge is contemporary.

Wrotham, 28 January 1554

England, Kent, LR188 TQ6059

Fleet Street (Ludgate Hill), Ash Wednesday, 7 February 1554

England, London, LR176 TQ3181–3080

Queen Mary's set intention to marry Philip of Spain excited general fury. Schoolboys pelted Spanish envoys with snowballs, and Her Majesty's guards discharged their arquebuses at them. Popular discontent peaked early in 1554 with an insurrection that threatened the heart of the Tudor regime.

Sir Thomas Wyatt was the type of impoverished firebrand found in every Tudor conspiracy, the unemployed soldier son of the poet and courtier of the same name. Nevertheless, the younger Wyatt claimed to speak 'for the liberty and benefit of the kingdom' when he raised the standard of revolt at Maidstone on 25 January 1554, and occupied Rochester. John Proctor, a Londoner who attended Wyatt's trial, published an account of the rebellion, from the initial skirmish on the slopes of Wrotham Hill to the final rout in London.

Sir Henry Isley set off from Sevenoaks to join Wyatt, but loyal troops had occupied an intermediate position at Malling, well placed to intercept anyone heading for Rochester via the modern road or the Pilgrim's Way. On 28 January Lord Abergavenny advanced through Wrotham Heath to Borough Green. The approaching rebels hoped to reach Rochester without a fight, and 'shrank as secretly as they could by a bye-way', around his right flank. They were spotted climbing Wrotham Hill, 'directly over [against] Yaldham', a mile (1.6 km) northwest of Borough Green. Abergavenny's cavalry pursued at speed, leaving the infantry to follow.

The southern scarp of the Downs runs east–west, just north of Wrotham. It rises 280 feet (85 m) in a third of a mile (0.5 km), steep enough to deter pursuit, but the rebels never made the crest. Abergavenny 'overtook the rebels at a field called Blacksoll Field ... a mile distant from the very top of the hill'. Here the rebels awaited Abergavenny's onslaught, 'thinking to have great advantage by the winning of the hill, [they] displayed their Ensigns bravely: seeming to be in great ruff'. But they were deluded, for the Royalists 'handled them so hot and so fiercely that, after a small shot with long bows by the traitors, and a fierce brag shewed by some of the Horsemen, they took their flight away as fast as they could'. Over 60 were captured in a chase that lasted to nightfall. The leaders hid in Hartley Wood, 4 miles (6 km) to the north, compelled, 'for haste to rip their boots from their legs and run away in the vampage of their hose'.

The same day as Abergavenny's brisk victory, six companies of London 'Whitecoats' went over to Wyatt at Rochester. Their leaders encouraged him to march on the city, where the Venetian ambassador was convinced the people had an understanding with the rebels. Only a personal appeal by the queen at the Guildhall held the citizens in check. When Wyatt appeared in Southwark on 3 February, he found London Bridge drawn up, and armed men on guard. Unable to force London Bridge, Wyatt marched 10 miles (16 km) upstream on 6 February, to cross the Thames at Kingston. Although 30 feet (9 m) of the bridge had been removed, Wyatt got his army and artillery across, and marched back through Knightsbridge, his weary army approaching Hyde Park at 9 a.m. next morning.

London was still very rural. Fields separated Oxford Street and Holborn from the recently paved Strand, which joined two separate centres: the administrative and legislative City of Westminster in the west, the commercial City of London further east, beyond a southward bend in the Thames. The royal palace of Whitehall stood just south of Charing Cross, between the river and St James's Park, which Henry VIII had enclosed for a deer park, stretching north towards Islington and Hampstead. The City of London still had its medieval walls, although its jurisdiction extended westwards to Temple Bar, a gatehouse and prison separating the Strand from the more developed Fleet Street.

The forces inside London consisted of three main elements. Her Majesty was at Whitehall, defended by her guards and loyal gentlemen from the Inns of Court. In the City, the Mayor, aldermen and householders were under arms before dawn, 100 men guarding every gate. The Earl of Pembroke's field army held the high ground north of Charing Cross, facing west, perhaps in front of the village of St Giles (at the east end of what is now Oxford Street, near Foyle's bookshop). They were in formal array with cavalry on either flank – barded horses and demilances on the south; light horsemen to the north: 'The great ordnance being charged to shoot full upon the breast of the rebels coming eastward … the Main Battle of footmen … standing in goodly array … behind the said great ordnance ready to set upon the rebels … coming towards Holborn' (Proctor). John Stow, another contemporary, wrote that Pembroke 'set his troop of horsemen on the hill in the highway … over against St James; his footmen … somewhat lower and nearer Charing Cross, at the lane turning down by the brick wall from Islingtonward, where he had set also certain other horsemen …'. Pembroke's front from Oxford Street towards St Martin's Lane extended just over 1000 yards (900 m), a broad but not impossible frontage.

Wyatt had at most 'fourteen Ensigns in his band and not past four thousand men, although they were accounted of a far greater number'. Proctor reckoned 'most of them naked, void of all policy and skill'. Wyatt had promised to fight pike against pike, but avoided direct confrontation. Instead the rebels fired their artillery at the Royalists, turned half right, and followed the brick wall around St James's Park towards Charing Cross. The queen's main battle stood fast as the rebels crossed their front, perhaps from disloyalty, perhaps as part of a deliberate plan. Once 400 of Wyatt's men had passed, the queen's heavy cavalry came down on their flank, overwhelming the rear of the column: 'The Lord Clinton, observing his time; first with his Demi-lances brake their array, and divided Wyat's Band in two parts. Then came the Light Horsemen, who so hardly pursued the tail of his band, that they slew many, hurt more, and took most of them' (Proctor).

Wyatt continued eastwards along the Strand and Fleet Street, his men in no very good order, crying out, 'The Quene hath pardoned us', a statement at odds with their drawn swords. Heavily armed Londoners watched impassively from either side of the road. At Ludgate, the western entrance to the City of London, Wyatt found the gate shut, and entry denied. For a while he refreshed himself at the Belle Sauvage tavern in Ludgate Hill, until, realizing he had no hope of support within the city, he rode back along Fleet Street. The Londoners who had let him pass, now held Temple Bar against him. Bottled up in Fleet Street, Wyatt was compelled to surrender. Forty of the 300 men still with him were killed. Wyatt himself was executed on 11 April 1555, the people dipping handkerchiefs in his blood.

Wrotham

	Winner	*Loser*
Opponents	Royalist	Rebel
Commanders	Henry Nevill, Lord Abergavenny	Sir Henry Isley
Numbers	600	500
Losses	unknown	60 pw

Fleet Street

	Winner	*Loser*
Opponents	Royalist	Rebel
Commanders	William Herbert, Earl of Pembroke	Sir Thomas Wyatt
Numbers	unknown	*c.*4000
Losses	40	*c.*400

The government had suffered a fright. Wyatt's half-baked plot had failed by the narrowest of margins, London's citizens remaining uncommitted to the last. The failure of the queen's main battle to engage caused panic among the queen's escort, as rebels spilled down Whitehall, loosing arrows through Court Gate, transfixing one unfortunate gentleman through the nose. The miraculous defeat of the rebels confirmed Mary in her obdurate pursuit of the Spanish match and England's restoration to Roman Catholicism. These policies would make her reign the least successful and most reviled in English history.

Directions

Wrotham *The village is 6 miles (10 km) east of Sevenoaks, between the M20 and M26: Blacksoll Field lies west of the village, directly on the Pilgrim's Way.*

Fleet Street *Despite extensive development in central London it is still possible to follow Wyatt's route past St James's Park down the Mall. Bear left at Charing Cross along the Strand and Fleet Street to Ludgate Hill. A garden marks the site of the Belle Sauvage, where the Devil himself was said to have appeared during a performance of Marlowe's* Dr Faustus. *See the plaque in the road outside the Law Courts commemorating Temple Bar.*

Regents and Presbyters

More than ordinary talents were required to rule Scotland in the 16th century. Turmoil under Mary Queen of Scots and her son James VI bespeaks deep-lying social causes rather than personal shortcomings. The Stewarts lacked the economic means to assert themselves. James IV and James V had sold or given away royal lands, while Scotland's weak economy offered few alternative revenues. Royal finances remained medieval: the Exchequer was an occasion, not an institution. Lack of money exposed Scottish rulers to intimidation by powerful magnates, whose main amusement was feuding: 'They bang it out bravely,' wrote James VI, 'he and all his kin against him and all his.' The period produced few battles of consequence, political violence usually taking more limited forms, such as the murder of Cardinal Beaton by Protestant zealots, or the ensuing siege of St Andrews (1546).

Aristocratic excesses that in England were a thing of the past continued in Scotland. Mary's secretary was stabbed to death, and her husband blown up or strangled. She herself was kidnapped and raped by the Earl of Bothwell, forced to abdicate, and driven into exile. James VI enjoyed little more respect. His own treasurer held him captive for a year after the 'Ruthven Raid' of August 1582. Another Bothwell confronted him sword in hand outside the royal privy, while armed men racketed about Holyrood House 'with halbertis ... colveringis [muskets] and pistolles'. Not surprisingly the king resented the magnates' 'feckless arrogant conceit of their greatnesse and power'.

Mary Queen of Scots outfaced the Earl of Huntly at Corrichie (1562), but was herself destroyed by the most cynical filibuster (private military action) of the period. After the shocking murder of her second husband Lord Darnley at Kirk o'Fields in February 1567, Mary confirmed popular suspicions of her involvement in the crime by marrying the probable perpetrator, the Earl of Bothwell. Comprehensively discredited, Mary abdicated after a military standoff at Carberry Hill (1567). She escaped her jailers, only to suffer decisive defeat at Langside (1568). Mary fled to England, never to return.

The men who drove her out ruled in the name of her infant son James VI, whose birth on 19 June 1567 made Mary expendable. The ensuing disturbances are associated with the Scottish Reformation, but religion was not yet a significant source of armed conflict. The Roman Catholic Church in Scotland was not worth fighting for. Crown and nobles had misappropriated its revenues, and the Mass no longer inspired a better-educated laity, drawn to new and exciting Calvinist doctrines of predestination and assurance. Religion signified less than family rivalries. The Gordons who fought Tillyangus and Craibstane (1571) in Queen Mary's name were Catholics, but their main aim was to crush their traditional enemies, the Forbes.

James VI escaped the supervision of his regents in 1582, but had little immediate success in controlling his kingdom. The Catholic-leaning earls of Huntly and Erroll plotted with foreign powers, provoking a rare military expedition by a peaceable and cash-strapped king. James's supporters were beaten at Glenlivet (1594), but the winners would not oppose the king directly, and their leaders fled into exile. The earls' submission in 1597 closed off confessional and familial strands of conflict, as they renounced the old faith and forswore enmity with the Laird of Forbes.

Corrichie, 28 October 1562

Scotland, Aberdeenshire, LR38 NJ6902

Corrichie is a rare example of a Stewart monarch successfully asserting herself against a recalcitrant grandee. It also demonstrated the primacy of family over religion in Scottish politics during the later 16th century. From the start of her personal rule in August 1561 Mary Queen of Scots, herself Roman Catholic, had tolerated the Protestant Kirk, and relied upon her illegitimate half brother Lord James Stewart. In January 1562 she granted him the lapsed earldom of Moray, as a counterweight to Gordon influence in the northeast. At Corrichie the Protestant Moray overthrew Mary's 'natural' Catholic supporters, with the queen's full approval.

The involvement of Huntly's son Sir John Gordon in an Edinburgh street brawl provided an excuse for a royal expedition to Aberdeen in August 1562. Thomas Randolph, the English ambassador, accompanied the queen, and provided full reports. The Gordons inflamed matters by shadowing the royal entourage, and excluding Mary from her own castle at Inverness. Huntly narrowly evaded arrest at Strathbogie, and hid in the wilds of Badenoch, hoping to exhaust Mary's resolve by guerrilla warfare. She was determined, however, to bring the Cock o' the North to utter confusion. On 16 October Huntly was 'put to the horn': anyone at feud with him was at liberty to use whatever force they could against him. Huntly did not await the inevitable betrayal. Encouraged by prophecies that he would lie that night in the Tolbooth of Aberdeen, he marched on the city on 27 October, 'to apprehend the Queen and do with the rest at his will' (Randolph). Huntly miscalculated, for next morning Mary 'sent forth a sufficient number against him', forcing the rebels to retreat from Garlogie, to a commanding position on the Hill of Fare.

Huntly was seriously outnumbered, his force probably less than Randolph's pre-battle estimates of 500, 'friends, tenants, and servants, of whom divers in two nights stole away'. Many of his kin pledged themselves to stay away until the troubles ended. Moray, on the other hand, called up reinforcements from the south: cavalry, pikemen and arquebusiers. Events suggest that, as in the English Western Rebellion, arquebusiers and mounted troops formed an advance guard followed by bodies of traditional infantry. Advancing westwards from Aberdeen to Garlogie, Moray's forces followed Huntly southwest to Corrichie, most readily by the modern B9125, turning the southern flank of Hill of Fare.

Hill of Fare forms a broad horseshoe around the Burn of Corrichie, opening to the southeast. Today the slopes are planted with conifers, but at the time only a few birches or pines fringed open heather moors. The ridge is relatively dry, encircling a peat bog at the source of the burn. The exact location of the fighting is uncertain, despite references to 'Bank-a-fair utherwayis callit Coruchie'.

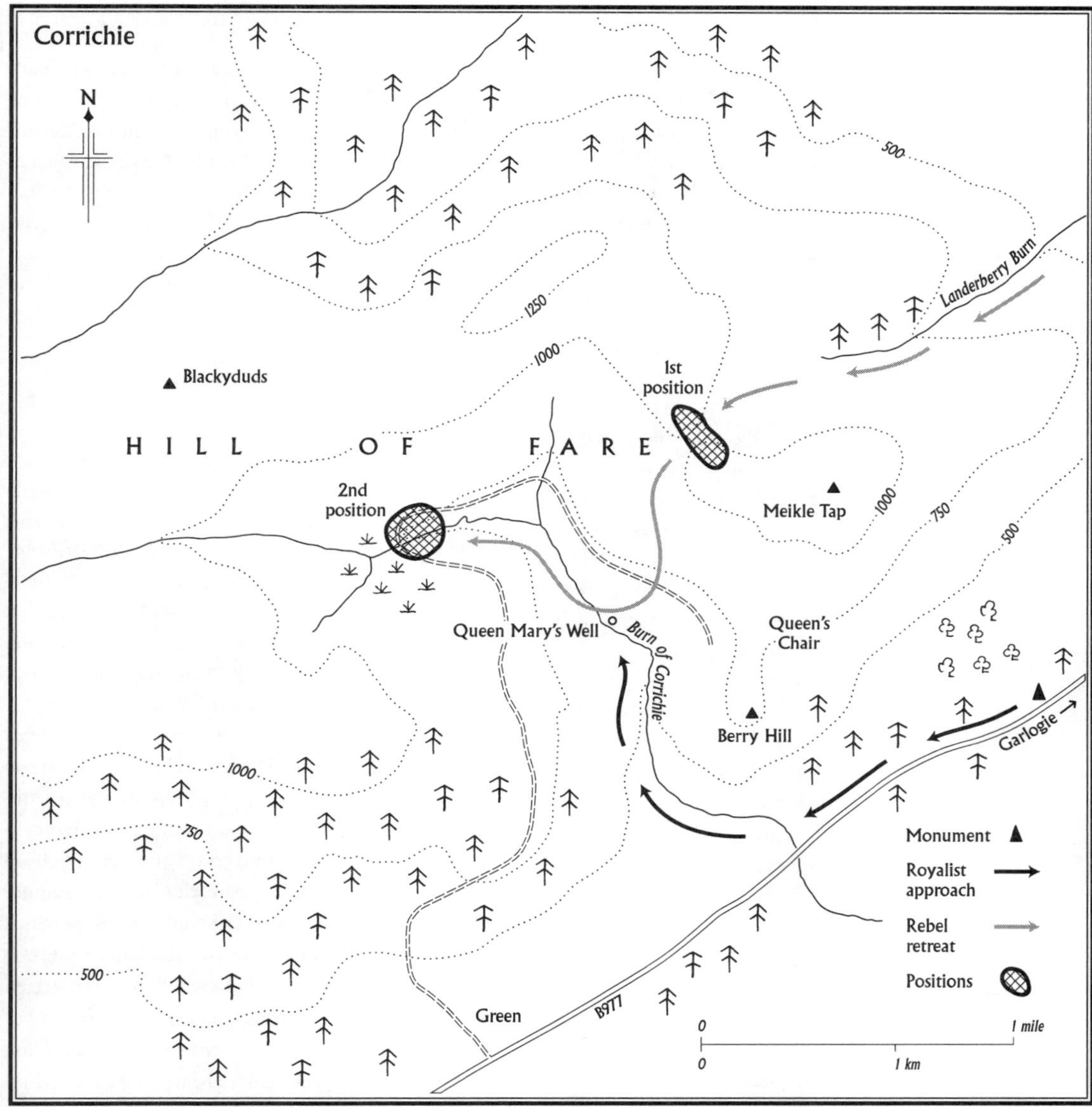

Huntly began the fight on a hilltop, and was finally trapped at the upper end of the burn. He had the choice of several crests. Blackyduds (1421 feet/ 433 m) lies too far west, beyond where Huntly was cornered. In the centre, across the top of Landerberry Burn, a re-entrant between Greymore (1289 feet/ 393 m) and Meikle Tap (1178 feet/359 m) is still known as Gordon's Howe. At the east end of the ridge a more defensible position at Berry Hill (764 feet/ 233 m) looks down steep slopes to Moray's likely

Directions

Huntly's camp was at Gordon's Moss, south of Garlogie bridge, 10 miles (16 km) west of Aberdeen on the B9119. Follow the B9125 and B977 4 miles (6 km) southwest to the 12-foot (3.5-m) granite monument on the right. Berry Hill and Meikle Tap are 1 mile (1.6 km) uphill west and northwest of the monument respectively, obscured by trees. Reach the Gordons' last stand along a forestry track from The Green, 2 miles (3 km) further on the right.

route, 550 feet (170 m) below. Moray's indirect approach outflanked both the latter hilltops, so Huntly must have come down to the burn to meet him, before being driven back up the valley to surrender.

The English ambassador, Thomas Randolph, reported the rebels' defeat thus: 'They had encamped on top of a hill from whence they were driven with shot of harquebus into a low mossy ground where the horsemen dealt with them a good space and at length forced them into a corner.' This was probably north of the burn, at a bend in the forest track below Brown Hill, where the stream crosses the 250 m (820 feet) contour. This is the only substantial bog in the vicinity, and nearby mounds have been identified as mass graves. Huntly hoped Moray's local troops would not fight, but they were given little choice: 'When they came to the shock those of the vanguard gave back, and many cast away their spears ready to run away. The Earl of Moray and his company being behind them, seeing the danger, came so fiercely upon them that he caused the others to turn again, and so stoutly set upon the enemy that incontinently they were taken to the number of six score and about 220 slain' (Randolph). A local source confirms Moray's pikemen 'stuid fermlie still', while the Gordons were 'put upon their bakkis with speiris and thairefter fled'.

The battle was over between 3 and 4 p.m. Moray lost no one killed, 'but divers hurt and many horses slain'. The rebels lost two-thirds of their number, including the obese and apoplectic Huntly. He tried to surrender, 'but ... without blow or stroke ... suddenly fell from his horse stark dead'. Removed in a couple of fish baskets, Huntly was left overnight in the Tolbooth, fulfilling the oracle. Scottish treason trials required a defendant, dead or alive, so his embalmed body was brought before Parliament, and not finally buried until 1565. Mary might have shown more compunction about destroying her greatest Catholic subject, but flagrant treachery had sealed his fate.

Corrichie

	Winner	*Loser*
Opponents	Royalist	Rebel
Commanders	James Stewart, Earl of Moray	George Gordon, Earl of Huntly (k)
Numbers	c.2000	500
Losses	unknown	340

Carberry Hill, 15 June 1567

Scotland, East Lothian, LR66 NT3769

Langside, 13 May 1568

Scotland, Glasgow, LR64 NS5761

The decisive military events of the reign of Mary Queen of Scots were more remarkable for political consequence than casualties. Nobody was killed at Carberry, and not many at Langside. Nevertheless the latter, little more than a tussle in a village street, ended Mary's independent political career.

The dismal tale of Mary's Scottish marriages more than justifies the decision of her English cousin Elizabeth to remain single. Mary married the worthless Lord Darnley in 1564, alienating her other magnates. Darnley was strangled on 10 February 1567 outside the palace of Kirk o'Fields near Edinburgh, just after the building had blown up, crimes for which responsibility has never been established. Mary's authority was doubly shaken when she married Bothwell, the chief suspect. James Douglas, Earl of Morton, who led the Presbyterian Lords of the Congregation into revolt against Mary and Bothwell in June 1567, was thoroughly implicated in Darnley's murder, but won the propaganda war. Mary's popular support fell away, leaving her outnumbered at Carberry Hill. A contemporary engraving shows Mary's army uphill, with four cannon in front of one pike square, menaced by three similar formations flanked by arquebusiers. Bothwell engaged in fruitless parleys, while his army melted away. Mary surrendered to keep the peace, but was brutally humiliated and imprisoned at Loch Leven Castle.

Mary's abdication in favour of James VI, her son

by Darnley, further inflamed aristocratic rivalries. On 2 May 1568 Mary escaped to Hamilton Castle near Glasgow, where she revoked her abdication. Not yet 'myndit to feicht nor hazard battaille', she left Hamilton on 13 May for Dumbarton Castle, to rally support in the northwest. She could have made directly for the north bank of the Clyde via Bothwell Brig. Instead she bore left through Rutherglen, towards Langside, heading for fords downstream from Glasgow, at Govan or Renfrew.

The current regent was Mary's half-brother James Stewart, Earl of Moray. By chance he was at Glasgow when she escaped, between her and Dumbarton. He prepared to fight, gathering artillery from Stirling, and arquebusiers and Royal Archers from Edinburgh. Alerted by a spy, Moray occupied Glasgow Moor, today's Gallowgate, covering Mary's route north of the Clyde, but after some hours learned that she had taken the southern route. He hurried back across the medieval bridge at Bridgend to intercept her, following the old route to Langside via Gorbals Street and Langside Road, interrupted today by the railway. Arquebusiers mounted behind horsemen dashed ahead, followed by the infantry and six guns in carts. Moray forced the opposition to attack him at a disadvantage, or risk a long detour south.

The battlefield forms a triangle: Queen's Park uphill to the north, Clincart Hill to the east, and Langside village to the south. At the time of the battle, the area was unenclosed 'outfield', coarse grass and furze, uncultivated except around Pathhead Farm, since absorbed into the 19th-century park buildings. Langside village ran north–south either side of a narrow street, now Millbrae. At the northern end it bent eastwards towards the western end of Battlefield Road, then known as Langloan. The houses were small and solid with low dry-stone walls.

Moray divided his army in two: the battle uphill on the left in Queen's Park; the vanguard on the right, behind Langside village. Arquebusiers held the houses and gardens, while between the infantry masses Moray placed artillery and light horsemen. Kirkcaldy of Grange, an experienced soldier, was appointed troubleshooter, to deal with emergencies. The Marian army lay 500 yards (460 m) away, just west of Mount Florida railway station, spreading across Prospect Hill into the eastern division of Queen's Park. Two thousand Hamilton retainers formed the vanguard, covered on their right by the cavalry, and supported by seven guns. The Marian main body never came into play, perhaps because Argyle, Mary's lieutenant general, fell sick as the battle started. Mary is said to have watched from Court Knowe near Cathcart Castle, a mile (1.6 km) to the south.

Artillery opened the action, followed by cavalry charges across the hollow now occupied by the Victoria Infirmary. Moray's horsemen were outnumbered and retreated on their gun line, where archers drove back the Marian cavalry in their turn. Meanwhile Mary's vanguard advanced on Langside village along Battlefield Road, 'opposed by two battalions of spearmen, each presenting a dense rampart' (George Buchanan). Jammed into the narrow lane, 'not above Fortie feet broad', both sides strained to push back their opponents. Pikes locked against the opposing front ranks' armour, or became so entangled overhead that stones, daggers and empty pistols hurled at the enemy phalanx lay on the crossed weapons and never reached the ground. Some of Moray's rear ranks ran away, but the deep formation

Carberry Hill

	Winner	*Loser*
Opponents	Confederate	Royalist
Commanders	James Douglas, Earl of Morton	James Hepburn, Earl of Bothwell
Numbers	unknown	1000
Losses	none	none

Langside

	Winner	*Loser*
Opponents	Confederate	Royalist
Commanders	James Stewart, Earl of Moray Sir William Kirkcaldy of Grange	Archibald Campbell, Earl of Argyle
Numbers	4000	5000–6000
Losses	unknown	440

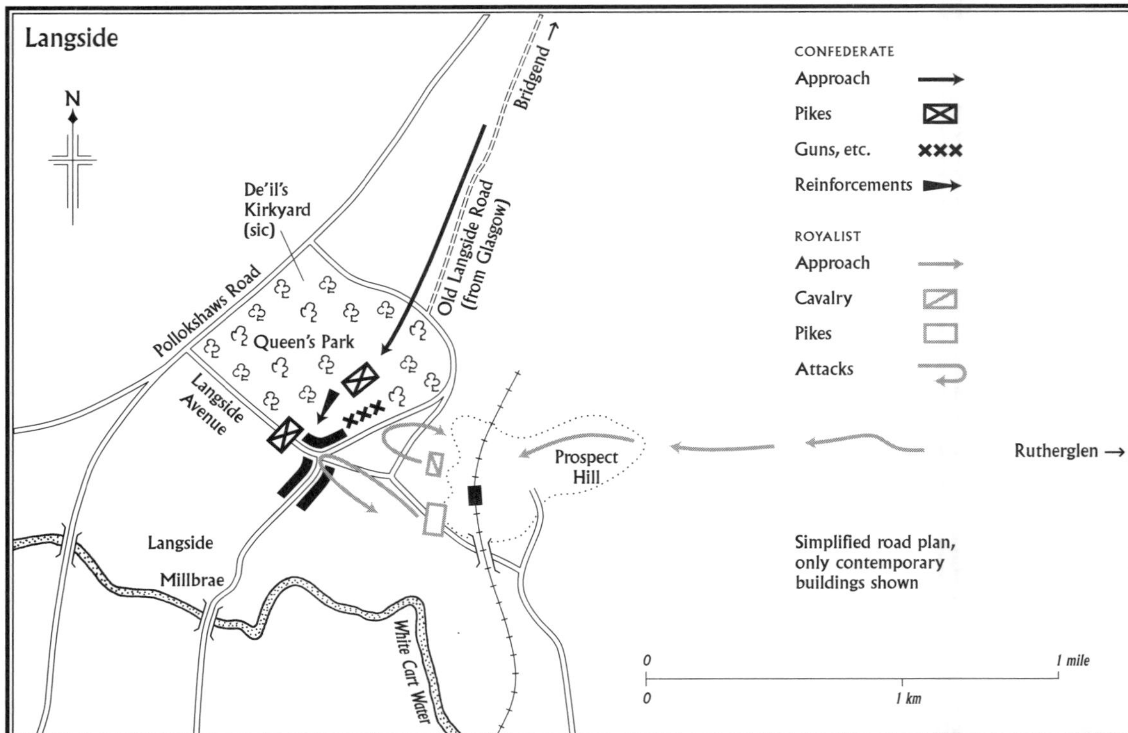

prevented a rout, as those in front could not see behind them.

The Confederate left wing stood fast, watching Mary's rearguard across the valley. Kirkcaldy of Grange, seeing Moray's vanguard in difficulties, rode over to the disengaged battle for reinforcements: 'Quhilk fresche men with ther lowse weapons, straik ther ennemys in ther flankis and faces, quhilk forced them incontinent to geve place and turn bakis' (Sir James Melville). This was enough for the Marian rearguard, who 'fled in lykwyiss'. Some attributed Moray's victory to a charge by 200 MacFarlanes, but others say the Highlanders had ran away, and only returned for the plunder. The whole battle lasted 45 minutes to an hour.

Some reported 'great slaughter, 2000 slain on the queen's side and 1000 on the regent's'. However, Moray had few cavalry, limiting casualties: 'The only slauchter was at the first renconter, be the schot of the soldiours that Grange had planted at the lon [loan, i.e. lane] head behind some dykis' (Melville). A better estimate was six or seven score killed, and 300 prisoners. However, 'divers were taken and not brought in, for there was father against son, and brother against brother'. The dead were allegedly buried in the De'il's Kirkyard, the northern corner of Queen's Park, near Camphill House. During the 1830s, the lodgekeeper's wife reported a procession of spectral warriors, disturbed by recent building work, but

Directions

The medieval bridge across the Clyde no longer exists. Queen's Park lies 1½ miles (2.5 km) south of Victoria Bridge, left of the A77, along Queen's Drive. A lion-topped monument on a traffic island between Langside Avenue and Battlefield Road marks the battle's turning point. Numerous road names commemorate the battle, without locating specific events. An ancient earthwork in Queen's Park played no part in the battle.

drainage operations have uncovered no tangible evidence of casualties. Moray admitted, 'never a man of name slain, but divers sore hurt', although judicial proceedings name at least four killed on his side. The queen's reaction mattered more than the casualties. She fled south, into England, leaving her followers leaderless. Disappointed in hopes for assistance from Elizabeth, Mary began the bleak descent into protective custody and conspiracy that ended with her execution at Fotheringhay Castle on 8 February 1587.

Directions

Carberry Tower is on the left of the A6124, 2½ miles (4km) south of Inveresk. Take the next left (B6414) for Queen Mary's Mount.

Tillyangus, 10 or 17 October 1571

Scotland, Aberdeenshire, LR37 NJ5224

Craibstane Rout, 20 November 1571

Scotland, City of Aberdeen, LR38 NJ9305

Confusion followed the battle of Langside (see above). Mary Queen of Scots fled into England, sowing doubt and indecision among her supporters. Her opponents, the Protestant Lords of the Congregation, fell out among themselves, a sniper assassinating Regent Moray in Linlithgow. In the northeast religion and national politics inflamed local rivalries as the Roman Catholic Gordons, beaten at Corrichie (1562), fell upon their old enemies, the Protestant Forbes.

Sources for these regional conflicts are thin. Even the date of Tillyangus is uncertain. Sir Adam Gordon may have mounted a pre-emptive attack on a Forbes gathering at Druminnor Castle, or the Forbes may have obstructed his passage south from Huntly. Either way the Forbes dug in on the northern slopes of the Correen Hills, overlooking Mains of Tillyangus near a stone circle on White Hill, once known as Gordon's Camp Muir. If the Gordons came from Strathbogie Castle, the Forbes must have faced northeast, towards Clatt; however if the Gordons came eastwards from Rhynie along the 'Mar Road', then the defenders must have faced the other way.

A variety of place-name evidence supports the former view. Forbes survivors fled west, 'evin to the gates of Druminnor', and their dead are supposed to have been buried in Jock's Cairn. 'Black Arthur' was killed as he stopped for a drink, perhaps from the Smallburn. All these locations are west of the White Hill spur, consistent with a Gordon attack from the east, driving the enemy before them. Total forces are given as 1300 to 2000, perhaps divided as shown above. Protestant sources probably exaggerated Gordon numbers, but their capture of an entrenched position on a hill does suggest a significant superiority.

'Black Arthur' divided his men into two companies, taking command of the one nearest the enemy. Sir Adam conformed in a manner reminiscent of Dark Age combats, for example that at Ashdown (871): 'Thus', according to an anonymous contemporary, 'they began a cruell skirmish. The Gordouns, with great courage, did break the Forbesses trenches, and run desperatelie upon the spears of their enemies.' Once the defenders were all engaged, a reserve detachment of Gordons broke in upon them from an unexpected direction, and put them to flight. Protestant sources admit 13 to 17 Forbes killed and 17

Tillyangus

	Winner	*Loser*
Opponents	Gordon	Forbes
Commanders	Sir Adam of Auchindoun	'Black Arthur' of Putachie (k)
Numbers	*c.*1000	*c.*300
Losses	22	30–120

Craibstane Rout

	Winner	*Loser*
Opponents	Gordon	Forbes
Commanders	Sir Adam of Auchindoun	William, Master of Forbes (p)
Numbers	*c.*900	*c.*500
Losses	60	60

captured, against 22 Gordon dead, although higher losses are not impossible.

The Master of Forbes, the laird's eldest son, escaped from Druminnor and acquired a commission as the regency's lieutenant in the north. He mustered 900 men at Brechin – five companies of pikes, 200 arquebusiers and 100 gentlemen horse – and marched north, probably crossing the Dee at Mains of Drum. Here the column divided, the master going on to Aberdeen with part of the force. At the time a single road approached Aberdeen from the southwest. The Hardgate ran through an oat field between Howburn and Denburn, entering the city via a broad street known as The Green, now the eastern end of Union Street. Between the bridges stood a boundary marker: the Crab Stone or Craibstane.

As Forbes neared the Craibstane about 4 p.m. he met a 'gret cumpanie' of Gordons, who had secured the city and impressed some of its inhabitants as reinforcements. The master's troops were hungry and tired from the march, but 'more hastily than wiselie' they resolved to fight:

> Adventuring further in following of the Gordons than their shot of powder would continue, they went so far that, in the end, being out of reach of defence from their company, they were put to fearfull flight by the bowmen of the Gordons …
>
> Raphael Holinshed, *Chronicles of England, Scotlande and Irelande* (1577)

Craibstane was a rare victory for traditional weapons over gunpowder. The Forbes arquebusiers ventured too far from their supporting pikemen and ran out of ammunition, after which the victors 'chacit thame four myullis' (*Diurnal of Remarkable Occurrents*). The Provost of Aberdeen spent £10 Scots burying the dead. The battle confirmed Gordon ascendancy in the northeast. Queen Mary's old opponents would enforce her writ there until the general pacification of February 1573, when they finally admitted defeat.

Directions

Tillyangus *Turn east off the A97 at Rhynie, and follow a minor road to Clatt for 3 miles (5 km), before turning right. Walk up the drove road through Mains of Tillyangus to White Hill. The fighting occurred between the stone circle on the left and Smallburn to the right.*

Craibstane *The whole area is now built over. A brass plate near the junction of Hardgate and Justice Mills Lane commemorates Craibstane and Justice Mills (1644). The massive square stone in the wall beneath may be the original Craibstane.*

Glenlivet (Allt a' Choileachain), **Thursday 3 October 1594**

Scotland, Moray, LR36 NJ2429

Anglo-Spanish hostilities during the 1580s reinvigorated Scottish Catholicism. Conservative magnates, led by the Earl of Huntly, plotted to overthrow king and kirk with foreign support. Even the pacific James VI felt compelled to quench what Robert Bowes, the English ambassador, called 'the fire of Spanish practices'. In September 1594 James launched a two-pronged assault on Huntly and his northeastern associates. James advanced from Stirling, while the Campbells moved in from the west through Blair Atholl and Badenoch.

The court scorned Argyle's Highland army, 'marching without guard of horsemen', and Huntly boasted he would 'rubb his cloake on Argyle's pladd'. Argyle was initially estimated to have 7000–8000 men and boys, including 500 Irish arquebusiers. Bowes's final estimate was 4000 fighting men with 2000 'raskalls and poke bearers', who 'marched at raggle and in plompes without order'. Many were distracted by feuds, or lately revolted from Huntly, with few 'experimented' leaders. Huntly had a smaller, better-equipped force: 800 cavalry, nearly 1200 infantry and six cannon, the first battlefield appearance of artillery so far north.

Huntly's forces gathered at Strathbogie, then marched south to Auchindoun to meet Argyle on the Auchorachan–Achmore road near the head of Glen Rinnes. An eyewitness placed the encounter 'six miles above Auchindoun [presumably country miles], beside the hill Ben Rinnes'. Four miles (6 km) northwards, Ben Rinnes (2756 feet/840 m) is the most prominent feature in a rugged area. The nearest settlement is Glenlivet, 3 miles (5 km) further west. Modern conifers mask the terrain, but pre-afforestation the battlefield was 'an inclined plain … terminating in a flat ridge which descends rapidly to the burn of Altachoylachan, and flanked on the south by a somewhat precipitous shoulder of the contiguous mountain [Carn a' Bhodaich (2149 feet/655 m)]' (*New Statistical Account*). The 'ridge' consists of three flat topped hills, north of the burn: Tom Cullach, Muckle Tomlair and Carn Tighearn (1391 feet/424 m). At the time of the battle, the hilltops were bare, their slopes covered with scrubby pine, birch and juniper. A tangle of ancient drove roads survives as forestry tracks.

The battle consisted of two successive engagements, or 'yokinges', as the opposing forces straggled up the narrow path. The vanguards fought from 11 a.m. until 2 p.m., and the main bodies from 3 p.m. until evening, about 6.30. Argyle was 2 miles (3 km) away at the 'strykinge' of the battle. His arquebusiers and archers had marched ahead, followed more slowly by the pikes and transport. This left Argyle's missile-armed vanguard defenceless against Huntly's cavalry, who drove them back on the main body: 'If it had not beyne neare ther strengthe the horsemen had overthrowne them all.' Argyle complained 'the great part of his army fled from him before they saw any cause of fear … whereupon the enemy was most encouraged to come forward'. Bowes reported 2000 of Argyle's men ran before he could array the spearmen. However, Errol, leading the rebel vanguard, was repulsed, and 'dong backe to the battle'. Huntly renewed the fight with mixed results:

> Errol and Auchindoun with their 100 horsemen charged the shot, killing some of them. The field pieces also playing on them, many fled, [but] many, with the advantage of some bushes near the place of encounter, stood and poured such a volley of bullets and shower of arrows on the horsemen and horses that Auchindoun and other gentlemen of the Gordons with the most part of the horses were slain.
>
> Robert Bowes

Errol was shot through arm and leg, and Sir Patrick Gordon of Auchindoun was dirked and beheaded in the Gaelic manner. The Campbells captured two cavalry standards, though hostile sources claim Argyle hid in a wood while his company fled 'to Stradorone', presumably Strathavon. Most agreed the two parties 'severed of ther owne accordis, without the persuite of any chase'. Argyle was able to bury his dead and remove his wounded on stretchers improvised from 'bowes and pladds'.

Casualty claims vary wildly. The highest estimate of 500 Campbell dead comes from the other side. Bowes reduced this to half a dozen men of credit, with 300–400 'raskalls'. Argyle reported just 50 dead. Huntly admitted one fatality, but Bowes reported 20 rebel gentlemen slain, with 40 or 50 wounded, and 150 horses killed, all in the second phase of fighting. The rebels were in no state to fight again. The chief gentlemen of Huntly's name had suffered heavy losses, while the commons only turned out to prevent the Campbells spoiling the country. Unable to resist the main royal force, Errol and Huntly fled overseas, while James demolished their castles.

Glenlivet

	Winner	*Loser*
Opponents	Rebel	Royalist
Commanders	George Gordon, Earl of Huntly Francis Hay, Earl of Erroll (w)	Archibald Campbell, Earl of Argyle (w)
Numbers	2000	6000
Losses	70	300–400

Directions

Take the B9009 southwest from Dufftown through Glen Rinnes. Turn left before Renaten onto a minor road for Achmore and Auchindoun's cairn beside Allt Cullach at Badeach (NJ2530). Follow the forestry track ¾ mile (1.2 km) up the pass between Tom Cullach and Muckle Tomlair, where the Ordnance Survey marks the battle.

The Tudor Conquest of Ireland

The 16th century saw radical shifts in Anglo-Irish relations, as Tudor efforts to govern Ireland in the same way as Wales or the North of England provoked rebellion rather than stability. Centralization and administrative uniformity clashed with Irish diversity to create the most severe military challenge of Elizabeth's reign.

Late medieval Ireland possessed three distinct cultures. Along the east coast, Old English settlers controlled the Pale, between Dublin and Dundalk. Another anglicized pocket around Galway survived from the 13th-century Anglo-Norman advance into Connacht. Northwest of an irregular line from Limerick to Dundalk, Gaelic chieftains defended the old ways, with outlying redoubts in the Wicklow Mountains and the far southwest. Otherwise Anglo-Norman magnates dominated the south, between Cork and the Pale; notable among them were the Butler earls of Ormond and the Fitzgerald earls of Kildare and Desmond. In the past these gaelicized grandees had done much as they liked, but battles at Knockdoe (1504) and Affane (1565) illustrate Tudor erosion of their autonomy. In 1504 the 'Great Earl' of Kildare could safely assume Henry VII's compliance, but Affane led to judicial proceedings.

Tudor monarchs devolved power in Ireland to a Council at Dublin, headed by governors styled lieutenant, deputy, deputy lieutenant or justiciar. After Henry VIII broke the Fitzgeralds in 1534, the governors were Englishmen, with no sympathy for local conditions. Sir Nicholas Arnold viewed the Irish like 'bears and bandogs, so that he sees them fight earnestly and tug each other well, he cares not who has the worse'. While English aristocrats exchanged local power for influence at court, Irish landowners lost out to government officials on the make. Factional intrigues both sides of St George's Channel prevented policy developments that might have answered London's strategic concerns, while delivering equitable government in Dublin. Administrative reforms that turned Irish chieftains off land they had held for centuries alienated Palesmen and magnates, without reconciling Gaelic peasants to English rule. Religious upheavals made things worse. Old English families adhered to Roman Catholicism, disqualifying themselves from serving a Protestant state. Exclusion from royal favour created common ground between the Gaels and the Old English ruling class. In their stead the Crown depended upon a narrow base of imported administrators, and Protestant New English planters, who colonized Queen's and King's Counties (now Laois and Offaly), Kerry and Limerick.

Elizabeth I faced three major Irish crises, punctuated by battles and usually ended by treachery and famine:

(1) SHANE O'NEILL'S WARS

Shane was Elizabeth's most capable Irish opponent, 'royal heir of Erinn without dispute' (*Annals of Loch Cé*). He was also notorious for drinking bouts, during which he would bury himself underground. Shane remained an Ulster chieftain with local ambitions, defeating MacDonald settlers at Glenshesk (1565), and defeated by the O'Donnells at Farsetmore (1567). He was murdered by his Scots enemies during a final bender.

(2) THE DESMOND REBELLION

The rapacity of court factions during Elizabeth's early reign alienated traditional royal supporters in Ireland, whether Old English or Gaelic. On the religious front, Catholic agitators sought papal support against the abomination of a woman masquerading as Head of the Church. In 1570 Gregory XIII excommunicated Elizabeth, and sponsored armed intervention against the 'she-tyrant'. A minor landing on the Dingle peninsula in September 1579 sparked off revolts in Munster and Wicklow, drawing in the Earl of Desmond. Honours on the battlefield were even: Desmond's sons lost a rare pitched battle at Monasternenagh (October 1579); Feagh MacHugh O'Byrne ambushed the new deputy, Lord Grey, at Glenmalur (August 1580) to deadly effect. A second papal landing was brutally extinguished at Smerwick. Desmond was hunted down and killed by fellow Irishmen in November 1583.

(3) THE NINE YEARS' WAR

English administration was established across Ireland by the 1590s, outside Ulster. Schemes to introduce English governance there threatened local overlords, particularly Hugh O'Neill, Earl of Tyrone, an ambiguous figure, spanning the Anglo-Gaelic cultural divide. Marginalized by English court intrigues, he was drawn into plotting for Irish independence, under Spanish suzerainty. O'Neill cooperated with Sir Henry Bagenal, his brother-in-law, at the Battle of the Erne Fords (1593), but thought his loyalty ill rewarded. He revolted in May 1595, inflicting an unparalleled series of setbacks on English forces, notably at Clontibret (1595) and Yellow Ford (1598). O'Neill raised and paid regular units of horse and arquebusiers. These protected his economic base in Ulster, while his allies overran Connacht and Limerick, driving out the planters. The most spectacular casualty was Elizabeth's favourite, the Earl of Essex, disgraced for making a truce in September 1599, after minor defeats at Wicklow and the Curlew Mountains. Elizabeth's last deputy, Lord Mountjoy, reversed the trend with a bout of trench warfare in the Moyry Pass (1600), while English amphibious forces took Derry in the north, deep in O'Neill's rear. A Spanish landing at Kinsale the following year offered him a last chance of victory, except that Mountjoy had sealed off the beachhead. When O'Neill tried to raise the siege, his army was routed on Christmas Eve 1601. Unable to prevent Mountjoy devastating large areas of Ulster, O'Neill surrendered at Mellifont on 30 March 1603, six days after Elizabeth's death. The war had absorbed over 40,000 men, a fifth of England's military manpower. O'Neill kept his earldom, suggesting he had won, but in 1607 he joined the Flight of the Earls, confirming the defeat of the old Gaelic order.

Knockdoe, 19 August 1504

Ireland, Co. Galway, DS46 M4036

The last great battle over purely Irish issues, uncomplicated by external considerations, Knockdoe falls chronologically within the Tudor period, but owed its context and tactics to an earlier age.

Henry VII governed Ireland through Gerald Fitzmaurice Fitzgerald, 8th Earl of Kildare, the 'Great Earl'. Kildare bridged Ireland's cultural divide, dealing with Gaelic chiefs according to their customs, while retaining English loyalties. Naturally Kildare exploited his unique pre-eminence for personal ends, under the legal veneer of his status as deputy. His expedition into Galway in 1504 can be seen as an official response to O'Brien raids across the Shannon, or a family row with Kildare's son-in-law, Burke of Clanrickard, over custody of the grandchildren.

Pre-battle movements are obscure. The *Annals of Loch Cé* merely refer to the 'overthrow of Cnoc-Tuagh', where, 'Earl Garret, Justiciary of Erinn, mustered the Foreigners and Gaeidhel of the province of Laighen and of Leth-Chuinn [Leinster], and advanced into Clann-Rickard'. The *Book of Howth* provides more detail, with typical bias: Kildare's council of war combines sage deliberation with axe-twirling bravado from the gallowglass captain. The improvident Irish spend the night before battle 'watching, drinking and playing cards, who should have this prisoner and that prisoner'.

Knockdoe is a low round hill (230 feet/70 m), 10 miles (16 km) northeast of Galway City, rising from flat countryside through which winds the River Clare. Kildare presumably approached from the east, and drew up across the hill facing southwest towards Galway, the river on his left. His main body adopted the traditional English array, wings of bowmen

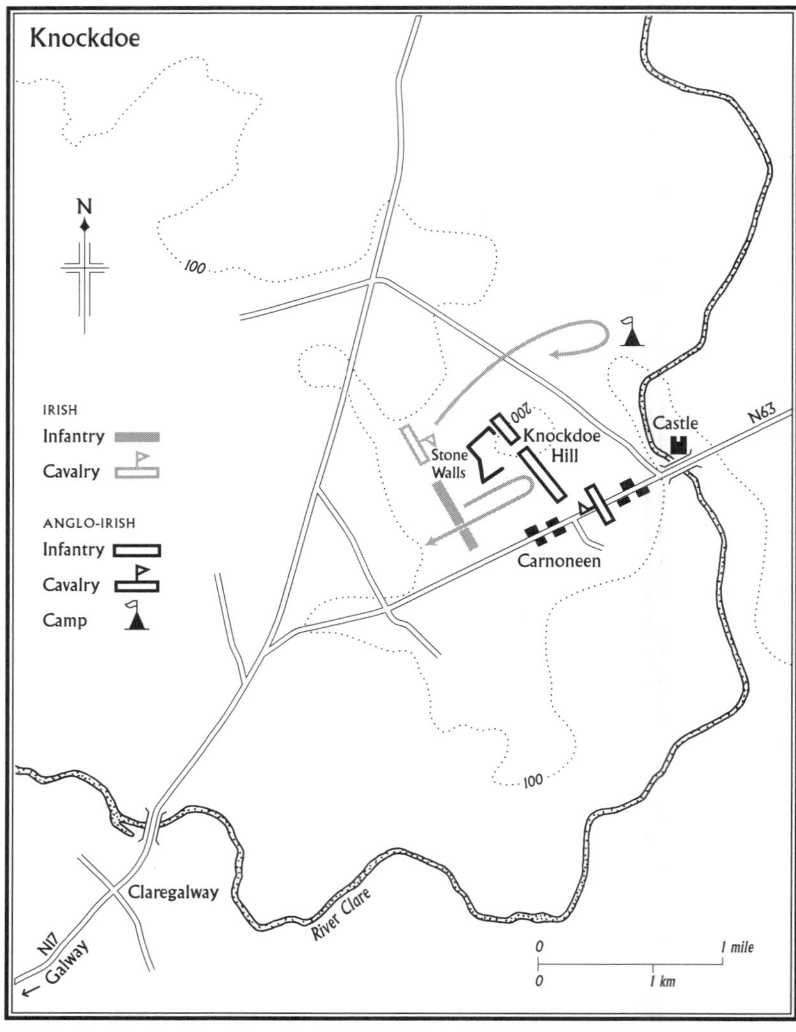

flanking a main battle of billmen, uphill and partly covered by low walls protecting a cornfield. Ordnance Survey maps of the 19th century still showed irregular enclosures on the northwest slope. Kildare's cavalry concentrated on the left, clear of the obstacle, his Irish allies 'in another quarter', presumably the right. No cannon were present, although Kildare had once deployed German handgunners. A Dublin soldier named 'Squyvors' (perhaps Schwarz) brained an Irish cavalryman, using his arquebus as a club. Kildare's son was left out of battle, with 'a chosen company for relief, fearing so great a number of enemies would enclose them about, being far less in number than they' (*Book of Howth*).

No clearer statement survives of numbers. G. A. Hayes-McCoy, the Irish military historian, thought Kildare outnumbered the opposition 6000 to 4000, which is possible given the earl's vice-regal authority. Irish sources mention nine battalions of gallow-

Directions

From Galway take the N17 through Claregalway. Bear right down the N63 through Carnoneen along the southern edge of the battlefield. Just before the main road crosses the River Clare, turn left onto a minor road running behind Kildare's position.

Knockdoe		
	Winner	*Loser*
Opponents	Anglo-Irish	Irish
Commanders	Gerald Fitzgerald, Earl of Kildare	Ulick Burke of Clanrickard Turlough Don O'Brien
Numbers	*c.*6000	*c.*4000
Losses	unknown	*c.*2000

glasses on the other side, 2000 men including auxiliaries, unless they speak poetically, implying large numbers. Burke and O'Brien deployed cavalry and infantry separately, in the traditional Irish manner, 'galoglasse and footmen in one main battle, and all their horsemen on their left side' (*Book of Howth*), away from the river. Kildare dismissed the opposition as a rabble: 'A great number of them hath but one spear and a knife. Without wisdom or good order they march to battle, as drunken as swine to a trough.' This cannot include the gallowglasses, fearsome warriors protected by long, padded surcoats and iron helmets, bristling with darts, two-handed swords and axes. Knockdoe, which signifies 'hill of axes', was their greatest battle.

The battle started with Celtic war whoops that astonished newcomers to the Gaeltacht. Kildare's cavalry commander spurred forward to cast a spear among the enemy, showing the Anglo-Norman's acquired taste for local forms of heroic self-display. Despite disadvantageous numbers and terrain, the Irish gallowglasses attacked. Disregarding 'such a shower of arrows that their weapon and hands were put fast together', they closed with Kildare's battle. MacSweeney, captain of the Irish gallowglasses, beat one opponent to the ground, but received 'such payment that he was satisfied ever after' (*Book of Howth*). Gaelic accounts are unhelpful, concerned less with tactical detail than poetic convention: 'the feats of the champions … the courage and impetuosity of the youths … the prevailing of the nobles over the lowly'.

Most accounts describe a protracted hand-to-hand struggle, although contemporary descriptions of gallowglasses suggest the contrary is more likely: 'powerful swordsmen … by no means inclined to give quarter … should they come to close fighting, they either soon kill or are killed'. Meanwhile 'the field became uneven from those heaps of slaughter, with the multitude of spears and of swords, and of battle-shields, and of corpses cross-thrown'. The *Book of Howth* simply says, 'They fought terrible and bold a while', before the Irish fled. Their only success was in Kildare's rear, where young Fitzgerald prematurely committed his reserve to the dogfight, allowing Irish cavalry to plunder the baggage.

Casualty figures are speculative. The lowest contemporary estimate of 2000 Irish dead is probably too many. The *Book of Howth* claimed 9000, while the *Annals of Loch Cé* thought 'a large number of chiefs of the Foreigners and Gaeidhel were slain; so that no battle equal to it was fought in the late time'. Kildare occupied Galway next day, gaining custody of his grandchildren. Knockdoe was a remarkable demonstration of his power in a remote part of Ireland, but its effects were limited. Against the *Book of Howth*'s claim that the Irish 'durst not fight a battle never after with the English Pale' must be set O'Brien's continued provocations on the Shannon, which he bridged in 1506. Kildare had clipped O'Brien's wings without gaining a decisive victory.

Affane, *c.*8 February 1565

Ireland, Co. Waterford, DS82 X1198–1298

Affane was an extraordinary event, the last private battle fought on British or Irish soil, without pretence of a royal commission on either side. Its judicial consequences illustrate Tudor success in suppressing aristocratic faction fights.

'Black Tom' Butler, 11th Earl of Ormond, preferred the life of a Renaissance nobleman to Anglo-Celtic warlordism. The 14th Earl of Desmond kept the old ways, harassing Ormond's tenants, frustrating his attempts to replace uncertain military exactions with defined rents. Squabbles over land and the wine trade at the port of Youghal exacerbated strategic differences. When Desmond distrained the cattle of Sir Maurice Fitzgerald of Dromana Castle, the latter appealed to Ormond for help. Black Tom gathered his forces at Knocklofty near Clonmel: 100 horsemen, 300 gallowglasses and kerns, plus stragglers 'he knoweth not certeynly the nomber'.

The night before the fight Desmond lay at Lismore, 8 miles (13 km) north and west from Dromana, around the right-angle bend in the Blackwater River at Cappoquin. His own estimate was 56 horsemen, 60 gallowglasses (31 'harnished' in mailshirts), 60 kerns, besides horseboys, a normal travelling retinue. Sir Maurice, a hostile witness, reckoned 60 horsemen and 300–400 foot, 'and of Raskally twise as many'. The participants may have misrepresented their numbers to minimize their offence, but the figures' consistency, in the low hundreds, suggests their accuracy.

Another 60 Geraldine horsemen were due at Lismore, but Desmond left without them, approaching Dromana Castle on the Finisk River, a tributary of the Blackwater, between 8 and 9 a.m. Depositions vary, but essentially Desmond demanded military service of Sir Maurice, rejected arbitration, and continued east along the Finisk valley, camping at Whitechurch. He killed 'thre skore beeffs' for his dinner, but before they could be cooked news came that Ormond had crossed the Knockmealdown Mountains and was advancing rapidly from the north.

The short February day must have been well gone, but Desmond rejected a proposal to await nightfall before attacking the weary Butlers. Instead he rode back across the front of the approaching column, perhaps to regain touch with his reinforcements at Lismore. The enemies collided north of Affane House, near Bogheravaghera crossroads, on Ormond's direct route towards Dromana Castle. Participants told different stories:

(1) Sir Maurice observed Desmond's foot pass the crossroads, stopping when they saw Ormond; Desmond's cavalry, in the rear, left their proper course, 'two or three flight shots on the righte hande', moving 400–600 yards (370–550 m) nearer Ormond's men. Desmond's infantry came up in support, firing their arquebuses when in range.

(2) Desmond alleged Ormond deliberately interposed 'betwene him and his passage to retourne to his owne countrey'. He had followed the infantry to inhibit looters, although a rearguard position was normal for horsemen on a 'prey', to protect the stolen cattle from attack. Desmond claimed Ormond set about his infantry, obliging him to initiate a cavalry encounter.

(3) Ormond affirmed that Desmond 'gave the first chardge', with banners displayed – proving malice aforethought. Had he wished to begin the quarrel, he could have easily disposed of Desmond's unsupported foot, before their horse came up. He fought only in self-defence.

The fighting was soon over: 'Desmond seeing the day lost, gave a violent charge into Ormond's battyle of horse, whereinto being farre entered, and hauing fewe about him, hee was overthrowne from his horse by ... Ormond's brother, who broke his thigh with a shott from his pistol, and was there taken prisoner. His small company were likewise for the most part, cutt in pieces' (*Relation of the Fitzgeralds of Ireland*). The swift conclusion supports the assertion in *The Annals of the Four Masters* (1632–6) that Desmond was 'overpowered by numbers'. One may suspect Desmond's outnumbered horsemen turned tail, leaving their infantry in the lurch.

Casualties went unrecorded, although excavations for a well in 1908 uncovered human remains by the crossroads. Others 'took the water', drowning in the Blackwater. The wounded Desmond was carried off piggy-back, and lodged in Clonmel jail. The queen was furious, summoning both earls to London. Des-

Affane

	Winner	*Loser*
Opponents	Anglo-Irish	Anglo-Irish
Commanders	Thomas Butler, Earl of Ormond	Gerald Fitzgerald, Earl of Desmond (p)
Numbers	400–500	*c.*500
Losses	unknown	unknown

mond was heavily fined, but Ormond remained at court three and a half years, his friendly relations with Elizabeth causing much scandal. The feud with Desmond ended less agreeably, with the latter's rebellion and death in 1583.

Directions

Affane crossroads is 4 miles (6 km) east of Cappoquin on the N72. 1½ miles (2.5 km) north of Affane Cross. On the right of the old road to Clonmel, is 'the Earl's Stone', where Desmond rested pending more serviceable transportation than a man's back.

Glentaisie (Glenshesk), Wednesday 2 May 1565

Ireland, Co. Antrim, DS5 unlocated

Farsetmore (Letterkenny), 8 May 1567

Ireland, Co. Donegal, DS6 C2012

Shane O'Neill of Tyrone was a new type of Gaelic chieftain, one who posed as a defender of Catholicism, dabbled in overseas diplomacy, and armed his tenants. His army's broader social base made Shane the strongest military player in Ireland. Like earlier chiefs, however, he refused to confront English armies. Shane's battles were fought against fellow Gaels.

Ruthless victor in a murderous succession struggle, Shane had two great enemies, apart from the English: the MacDonalds of Antrim in the east, and the O'Donnells of Tyrconnel to the west. Scots from the Western Isles had established a maritime lordship spanning Antrim and Kintyre, with strongholds at Ballycastle and Dunyveg. Signal fires on Tor Head could summon reinforcements across the 15-mile (24-km) wide North Channel in hours. MacDonalds controlled half the coastline between Coleraine and Dublin by the 1560s, and boasted they would soon get the rest. The O'Donnells appeared less threatening. Shane imprisoned his father-in-law Calvagh O'Donnell and cohabited with his own wife's stepmother, his lawful spouse dying of shame. The O'Donnells depended on traditionally limited sources of manpower, but outrage made up for lack of numbers.

Shane attacked the MacDonalds first, egged on by an English government anxious to exclude Scottish influence from Ireland. He struck after Easter 1565, before the Redshanks, a vital component of the MacDonald forcesreturned from winter quarters in Kintyre. Shane advanced rapidly from his stronghold at Edenduffcarrick, now Shane's Castle on Lough Neagh, through Broughshane to Clogh (26–29 April), giving the enemy no time to summon help. On the way he surprised Sorley Boy MacDonald at Knockboy Pass, killing 20 Scots. Shane chased them north-east, down Glenballyemon to Red Bay, where he burnt James MacDonald's castle, a favourite Scots landfall.

Sorley Boy had summoned his brother, who arrived that night (30 April) with part of his force. On Tuesday 1 May the Scots retreated across the hills to Ballycastle, hoping for further reinforcements, perhaps intending to make a stand behind the River Shesk. Shane swung around their flank, marching up Glenaan, and skirting Slieveanorra's northern slopes to gain the Shesk's left bank. The MacDonalds fell back from the now useless Ballycastle position, which Shane occupied unopposed. It was then too late to fight, the two sides camping a mile (1.6 km) apart, in sight of each other.

Shane sent two reports of the battle to the justiciar in Dublin, neither of which specifies its location. Two valleys converge at Ballycastle, and annalists mention both: 'Glenn-sheisg' and 'Gleanntaisi', the Shesk and Tow valleys, east and west of Knocklayd (1686 feet/514 m) respectively. Shane's presence at Ballycastle beforehand suggests the battle was in the latter. Had the Scots not previously withdrawn across the River Tow, Shane could have attacked them on the Tuesday. Glentaisie is the most northerly of the Antrim glens, extending several miles along the western base of Knocklayd, between Ballycastle and Armoy. Perhaps the MacDonalds hoped the rising ground beyond the Tow would offset

Glentaisie

	Winner	Loser
Opponents	Irish	Scoto-Irish
Commanders	Shane O'Neill	James MacDonald of Dunyveg (p) Sorley Boy MacDonald (p)
Numbers	c.2000	c.1000
Losses	60	300–500

Farsetmore

	Winner	Loser
Opponents	Irish	Irish
Commanders	Hugh O'Donnell	Shane O'Neill
Numbers	unknown	unknown
Losses	unknown	613/1300

their relative numerical inferiority.

Shane wrote: 'Early on the next morning [2 May], we advanced upon them in battle array, and the fight was furiously maintained on both sides.' Shane's secretary added: 'He … mett with them about v. of the clock in the morning, to whom he gave the overthrowe, and tooke of their baners and ancients xiii' – enough standards for some 900 gallowglasses. Shane also captured 23 gentlemen, including James MacDonald, 'being veray sore woundid'. The victors claimed 700 dead Scots, although English commentators believed the slaughter exaggerated. Shane had done well to win quickly. That night a third MacDonald brother, Alexander, reached Rathlin Island with 900 men, just too late to even the odds.

Glentaisie crushed the Antrim Scots, reducing Shane's strategic value to the English. After he burnt villages in Co. Louth and attacked Dundalk, they sent a flying column to devastate Co. Tyrone, and restore Calvagh O'Donnell to his lordship. Shane avoided action, but suffered heavy casualties attacking an English fort at Derry. The garrison's subsequent withdrawal after an accidental explosion encouraged Shane to attack Calvagh's successor, Hugh O'Donnell, at dawn on 8 February 1567 at Farsetmore.

The repulse at Derry had cost Shane 'the most of his best footmen, as well galloglass as shot', perhaps 300 out of 5700, and 'many of his Scots for that days work left his service'. He still outnumbered the O'Donnells in May when he crossed Farsead Suilighe, the great ford over the Swilly estuary below Ardingary Hill, between Letterkenny town and golf course. Hugh O'Donnell withdrew into a bog, to await reinforcements, while Shane pitched camp preparatory to laying the area to waste. Irish sources report only 400 O'Donnells, even after Hugh's gallowglasses had turned out, but that is clearly too few to defeat an army of several thousand.

Contemporary accounts of the action are brief and unsatisfactory. An English correspondent wrote simply: 'Sir Hugh O'Donnell with a small band nearly captured Shane O'Neill and slew most of his men.' Modern historians do not even agree whether Hugh took Shane by surprise: Cyril Falls thought the action, 'not so much a battle as a killing'; Hayes-McCoy says O'Neill had warning and came out to fight, the combatants proceeding 'to strike mangle, slaughter, and cut down one another for a long time'. Whether the end was protracted or sudden, O'Neill's men were driven back into the estuary, where the rising tide had covered the sandbanks, which became the graveyard of O'Neill's army. The *Annals of Loch Cé* thought 'it is not possible to reckon or tell all that were lost or drowned there'. Less fastidious annalists claimed 1300 or even 3000 casualties. The English deputy confirmed 'such slaughter of many of his [O'Neill's] best and principall men', reporting 613 bodies found dead.

Shane escaped across a ford 2 miles (3 km) upriver, west of Letterkenny at Scariffhollis, An Scairbh in Irish, meaning the shallows. Unable to collect another army he sought to make a deal with Alexander MacDonald, brokered by the captive Sorley Boy. They met in the MacDonald castle on the shore north of Cushendun in Ballytearim townland (Co. Antrim). Shane was accompanied by just 50 riders. The drinking was going well when words were spoken, the Scots drew their two-handed swords and hacked Shane to pieces. It was, thought Sir Henry Sidney, 'an end hard enough, but not sufficient for his deserts'.

Directions

Glentaisie *The battle site is unknown. See Sorley Boy's tomb at Bonamargy monastery, 1 mile (1.6 km) east of Ballycastle, and Dunluce Castle, his stronghold on the A2 between Portrush and Bushmills Distillery.*

Farsetmore *Take the R245 Rathmelton road out of Letterkenny, and follow the minor road on the right that loops round a bend in the river by the ford.*

Monasternenagh, 3 October 1579

Ireland, Co. Limerick, DS65 R5540

Glenmalur, 25 August 1580

Ireland, Co. Wicklow, DS56 T0793

Smerwick (Dun an Oir/Golden Fort), 7–10 November 1580

Ireland, Co. Kerry, DS70 Q3407

The Desmond Rebellion of 1579–83 initiated a new phase in Anglo-Irish warfare, fuelled by foreign intervention and religious animosity. 'This realm', wrote Sir Peter Carew, killed at Glenmalur, 'was never so dismembered, owing to the quarrel upon religion.' Before the revolt died away, Munster was devastated, and a new standard of atrocity set by the otherwise obscure Massacre of Smerwick.

Sir James Fitzmaurice landed at Smerwick with 60 papal troops in July 1579, and built a small fort. Desmond might have been expected to deal with Fitzmaurice, but the earl's loyalty and mental stability had been doubtful since Affane (1567). While he dithered, his brother, John Fitzgerald of Desmond, dragged him into rebellion by killing royal officials sent to concert action against Fitzmaurice.

Sir Nicholas Malbie, in temporary command in the southwest, was moving north from Kilmallock when a rebel force offered battle at Monasternenagh, near the ancient Cistercian abbey on the River Camoge. Town and abbey lie north and south of the Camoge respectively. The rebels may have hoped to stop Malbie marching on Desmond's stronghold at Askeaton, which the former burnt after the battle. The earl was not present, but added 600 gallowglasses to Sir John's 600, 'gave them his blessing and instructions to fight ... and then departed to Askeaton' (Malbie). The rebels formed up on flat open ground, behind a banner showing Christ's wounds, and 'came on as resolutely minded to fight ... as the best soldiers could' (Sir William Stanley, an English officer). Malbie had 150 cavalry and about 900 infantry, mostly recent recruits. Devonshire ploughboys with modern weapons proved superior to gallowglasses, for 'all their captains were slain saving the two ... who carried away the Pope's standard through the woods and thorns' (Malbie). Irish sources admitted: '[eight] of the noblest of the Clann-Sithigh [Sheehy] were slain and one or two score along with them' (*Annals of Loch Cé*). As usual in Ireland, it was one thing to break up rebel armies, and another to restore peace.

While the Desmonds occupied government forces in the southwest, rebellion spread to Co. Wicklow, where the English suffered a debacle still celebrated by Irish traditional musicians. Even today there is no road out of Glenmalur, the heavily wooded valley of the Avonbeg River, which runs for 4 miles (6 km) along the northeast fringe of Lugnaquilla (3031 feet /924 m), the highest peak in the Wicklow Mountains. The recently arrived deputy, Lord Grey, insisted on pursuing the wily Feagh MacHugh O'Byrne into this ugly corner, despite warnings from old Irish hands, including the commander of the Queen's Kerne.

Sir William Stanley described how his company 'were forced to slide some tymes three or four fedoms [18–24 feet/5.5–7.5 m] or we could staie our feete; it [Glenmalur] was in depth, where we entered, at the least a myle, full of stones, rocks, bogs and woods, in the bottom ... a river full of loose stones, which we were driven to cross diverse tymes'. Halfway up the glen, Stanley's colonel, 'a corpulent man not hable to endure travaile', chose to leave the valley bottom and lead his men up hillsides, 'so steep ... we were forced to use our hands as well to climb as our feet … it was the hottest piece of service for the time that ever I saw'.

Grey's English recruits, conspicuous in new red and blue uniforms, stood about in amazement as they were shot down by an invisible enemy: 'laid all along the wood as we should pass … Yet so long as we kept the bottom we never lost a man, till we were drawn up the hill by our leaders, where … we could have no sight of them [the enemy], but were fain only to beat the places where we saw the smoke of their pieces'. Casualty evacuation was impossible: 'Were a man never so slightly hurt, he was lost, because no man was able to help him up the hill. Some died, being so out of breath'. Sir Peter Carew, suffocating in full armour, 'more fatal than even a red coat', was captured 'and most butcherly slaughtered' (all quotes Stanley).

Irish recruits who had filled up the English ranks refused to fight, taking their weapons over to their countrymen. The recruits wavered; the kerns ran away, and so the gentlemen were lost. The *Annals of Loch Cé* wrote enthusiastically of 'the defeat of Glenn-Malura, in which nine captains were slain and 100 men along with each captain', but folk memories of Saxon gore flowing from Tasagart to Clonmore are exaggerated and geographically inaccurate. Stanley's rearguard lost 8 killed and 10 wounded out of 28 rank and file, a higher proportion than in less exposed units. In total he admitted 6 gentlemen killed and about 30 others. Glenmalur was a bad start for an unpopular deputy, but had little wider significance.

A fresh papal expedition, this time comprising 600 Italian troops, landed at Smerwick on 10 September 1580. Some of the new arrivals joined Desmond in besieging English garrisons. The others refurbished Fitzmaurice's redoubt on the rocky headland of Dun an Oir, west of Smerwick Harbour. Dun an Oir signifies 'Fort of Gold', from the iron pyrites – fool's gold – left by a ship wrecked returning from America. A contemporary illustration shows two fortified positions, linked by a bridge: a redoubt on the jagged promontory shooting out into the bay, and a double bastioned hornwork on the landward side. The former's embrasures could be traced as late as the 1880s, the landward lines still visible under rough pasture.

Local people made much of the fort's strength, but it was too small for the garrison, only 350 by 100 feet (100 by 30 m), and overlooked from every direction. Professionals 'found it a vain toy and of little importance' (Justiciar William Pelham). The Spanish ambassador thought a worse place could not have been found. The nearest fresh water was half a mile (0.8 km) away. Lacking firewood, the garrison burnt their ships. The harbour on the other hand was of strategic importance: 'commodious for the safe keeping of the ships, but also very apte to impedite such foreign aid as might approach to the relief of our western rebels' (Pelham).

The English *Swiftsure* appeared off Smerwick on 17 October, exchanging fire with the fort. Invasion confirmed, Lord Grey left Dublin with 200 cavalry and 600 infantry, but no siege artillery, camping at

Monasternenagh

	Winner	*Loser*
Opponents	English	Irish
Commanders	Sir Nicholas Malbie	John Fitzgerald of Desmond
Numbers	*c.*1000	*c.*2000
Losses	unknown	*c.*50

Glenmalur

	Winner	*Loser*
Opponents	Irish	English
Commanders	Feagh MacHugh O'Byrne	Arthur Grey, Lord de Wilton
Numbers	unknown	unknown
Losses	unknown	*c.*36

Smerwick

	Winner	*Loser*
Opponents	English	Papal
Commanders	Arthur Grey, Lord de Wilton Sir William Winter	Sebastiano di San Guiseppi (p)
Numbers	800	700
Losses	1 killed	*c.*500

Dingle, until Admiral Winter's squadron arrived. Two hundred sailors landed heavy guns over Smerwick beach, and mounted them in 'the marriners trenche', opposite the southern corner of the Italians' hornwork. The English artillery opened fire on 8 November, quickly silencing the two defending guns that faced inland. Warships joined in from seaward.

The papal troops lacked equipment and enthusiasm, using swords as spits and helmets as cooking pots, cursing the pope, 'and as many as sent them' (Earl of Ormond). Numbers are uncertain. *Swiftsure*'s captain estimated 'one thousand poor simple *bisognos* very ragged and a great part of them boys'. They were 'sick and malcontent with the countrye and their evil and hard entertainment'. Prisoners taken before the siege said the garrison numbered 700, but the cold and wet took their toll: 'very many ... do die daily, so that there should not be here of them all left above 500'.

Outgunned and demoralized, the defenders put up a white flag, after Admiral Winter personally directed two shots into a wooden penthouse sheltering the most combative papal arquebusiers. Roman Catholic writers condemn their commander's cowardice and incompetence, but he had little alternative to surrender once his guns were silenced. Desmond had promised to lift the siege with 4000 men, but never appeared. A succession of Spanish and Italian officers discussed terms, hindered by their translator, an Irish priest, who was doomed whatever happened. Official English reports speak of 'simple surrender', with no promise of quarter. Catholic sources say the garrison surrendered on condition of their lives being spared. The confusion was fatal for most of the defenders, and Grey's historical reputation.

A dozen officers emerged from the fort on Friday 11 November, trailing their ensigns in token of surrender. The English secured the defenders' arms and stores, enough to equip 4000 men, set aside 20–30 officers 'to represent in Spain and Italy the poverty and infidelity of their Irish consociates', and killed everyone else, as recorded by an anonymous eyewitness: 'All the Irish men and women were hanged and upwards of 400 Italians, Spaniards, Basques and others put to the sword.' The Spanish ambassador reported 507 soldiers killed, and 17 Irish and English hanged. Among the executioners was Walter Raleigh. Only one English soldier died in action, but raging weather ensured a long sick list.

The massacre was a dark episode in a dark chapter of Irish history, exploited by chauvinists on either side, including Charles Kingsley in his 1855 historical novel *Westward Ho!* The original event drew no protest from the Catholic powers, and bears comparison with equally atrocious Spanish behaviour in the Netherlands. The victims were not prisoners-of-war, but self-confessed filibusters, with no official commission to justify their presence. The queen objected only that Grey had spared the principals, while punishing the accessories. The previous week the Council in Dublin had reported the burning of Rathkeale (Co. Limerick), 'and all the English picked out for slaughter, being the poor families of Harrington's band now with the Deputy [before Smerwick]'. Neither side enjoyed a monopoly in cruelty.

The massacre left the Munster rebels as obdurate as ever. No one could be got to pull down the redundant fort, and the Desmond war dragged on. Not until 1583 would Grey's successor, Ormond, erode his old enemy's support by a classic counter-insurgence mixture of conciliation, night raids and ambushes. Desmond was finally captured and killed in Glenageenty east of Tralee, by a fellow Irishman, exactly three years after the Smerwick Massacre, his severed head sent to England for display on London Bridge.

Directions

Monasternenagh *Follow a minor road east from Croom for 2 miles (3 km). Continue through Monaster and turn right across the Camoge to see the abbey's fragmentary remains. The Ordnance Survey mark the battle at the latter in a loop in the river.*

Glenmalur *Take the R752 from Rathdrum to Ballinclash, and turn right to Drumgoft Bridge. A minor road beyond follows the English line of advance along the Avonbeg.*

Smerwick *Take the R559 north from Dingle, turning right on the west side of Ballyferriter for Dun an Oir and the car park overlooking Smerwick harbour.*

Erne Fords, 10 October 1593

Ireland, Co. Fermanagh, DS17 G9359

Ford of the Biscuits (Drumane Ford), 7 August 1594

Ireland, Co. Fermanagh, DS27 H2336

The opening engagements of the Nine Years' War took place before its leading protagonist, Hugh O'Neill, Earl of Tyrone, had shown his hand. At the Erne Fords he fought alongside the English marshal, Sir Henry Bagenal.

O'Neill's Gaelic sons-in-law were already disaffected: Hugh Roe O'Donnell had recently escaped English detention, while Hugh Maguire resented the English sheriff recently imposed on Fermanagh, and in May 1593 attacked other encroaching officials in Sligo. When Maguire refused O'Neill's mediation and raided into Co. Monaghan, the earl joined Bagenal at Omagh (Co. Tyrone), with 200 horse and 600 foot. O'Neill had organized and trained his private army in the modern fashion, converting gallowglasses into pikemen, and kerns into arquebusiers. The Erne Fords would be their first outing.

The combined force marched west into Fermanagh, camping at Termon M'Grath, where they found the track of the raiding party, on 9 October. The River Termon flows into Lower Lough Erne at Pettigo, showing Bagenal and O'Neill approached the battlefield from the northeast, circling the lough's northern shores. The allies caught up with Maguire next day at 'Athe Coolloyne', the Golune Ford, on the River Erne near Belleek. A contemporary picture map shows the fighting downstream from Belleek Castle, on Bagenal's left. Ballyshannon is away to the right, confirming the allies came from the north. Maguire occupied a fortified bend in the river, presenting three sides to allied fire. Sir Philip Holles, an eyewitness, described Maguire's unusual decision to fight: 'Being earnestly followed [he] forsook the open places ... and fortified himself in a little island within the River Erne, which ... he enstrengthened... to abide all comers.' The Ordnance Survey shows no fords, but there is one suitable bend in the Erne, a quarter of a mile (0.4 km) below Beleek road bridge, where the railway once crossed.

Bagenal trumpeted his victory over Maguire's full strength of 160 horse and 1000 foot, but O'Neill counted only 900 rebels in all: 400–500 arquebusiers, bowmen and gallowglasses held the ford, while Maguire 'staid himself, with the rest of his company about ... a quarter of a mile off'. Bagenal attacked promptly, either to deny Maguire time to further improve his position, or to forestall O'Donnell's arrival with reinforcements from Ballyshannon. Musketeers swept the approaches with fire, while the Anglo-Irish vanguard prepared to enter the ford, leaving the rearguard 'to make a stand'. Bagenal and O'Neill took station with the cavalry on the left, ready to follow the vanguard.

The defenders stood well enough at first, but 'seeing our forces fast upon the river, and the footmen wading through to the arm holes with their shot [arquebusiers] ... without further assault left the hold and hastened towards the woods which were very near, fearing greater danger if they stayed till the

Erne Fords

	Winner	*Loser*
Opponents	Anglo-Irish	Irish
Commanders	Sir Henry Bagenal (w) Hugh O'Neill, Earl of Tyrone (w)	Hugh Maguire
Numbers	1200	900–1160
Losses	*c.*22	*c.*400

Ford of the Biscuits

	Winner	*Loser*
Opponents	Irish	English
Commanders	Hugh Maguire Hugh Roe O'Donnell	Sir Henry Duke Sir Edward Herbert
Numbers	*c.*1000	650
Losses	200	125

horsemen came upon them' (Holles). O'Neill had found the ford broad enough for the cavalry to charge through side by side with the infantry, the two arms arriving together. The combined assault was disastrous for the defenders, who withdrew in good order, but scattered when they saw the cavalry gaining upon them, being chased some 5 miles (8 km). A 17th-century historian attributed the defeat to English fire-power: 'The musketeers in the woods bordering on the river shot down with impunity the Catholics, who stood in the open, while the archers could take no aim at men protected by thick clumps of trees.' The picture map supports this view, showing musketeers on the English right firing at Irish trenches from a wood.

The Irish cavalry did little, although O'Neill took a lance thrust in the thigh. Maguire ran away, 'being on horseback and not near the fight … and never left running till he came to Enniskillen … almost 20 miles from the place of defeat' (Lord Deputy Fitzwilliam). Bagenal's scoutmaster counted 300 Irish dead, excluding three or four score 'drowned and carried away with the stream'. The English admitted one killed, another drowned and 20 hurt. Bagenal was among them, 'bruised by the flat falling of a galloglass axe'.

Maguire escaped with only 60 men, and those without weapons. The following February the English took his castle at Enniskillen in a remarkable amphibious operation, with special landing craft mounting scaling ladders. The new English garrison proved a hostage to fortune, however. O'Donnell invested Enniskillen with 3000 men in June 1594, while Maguire ambushed an English supply column at one of the few clearly identifiable Irish battle sites.

Five miles (8 km) south of Enniskillen the main road crosses the River Arney at Drumane Ford, near its confluence with the Erne, between Upper and Lower Lough Erne. The modern bridge crosses the ford, the road to the north bending right around a hill, which at the time was heavily wooded. English scouts missed Maguire's Redshanks, and the convoy ran straight into them: 'A fierce and vehement conflict and a spirited and hard-contested battle was fought between the two parties, till at length Maguire and his forces routed the others by dint of hard fighting …' (*Annals of the Four Masters*, 1632–6). The English lost 56 killed and 69 wounded, and their commanders were glad to get away. They lost so many rations the name of the ford was changed to Bel-atha-na-in-Briosgadh, 'Mouth of the Ford of the Biscuits'.

Directions

Erne Fords *Follow a minor road out of Beleek, bearing left along the north bank of the Erne.*

Ford of the Biscuits *5 miles (8 km) south of Enniskillen on the A509 Belturbet road.*

Clontibret, Tuesday 27 May 1595

Ireland, Co. Monaghan, DS28 H7629

Mullaghbrack, 5 September 1595

Ireland, Co. Armagh, DS29 unlocated

The Earl of Tyrone wavered for two years before joining the rebellion begun by Hugh Maguire and Hugh Roe O'Donnell. Pressure from both sides forced him to choose between loyalty to an ungrateful Crown and his position as a Gaelic overlord. In February 1595 O'Neill's brother destroyed Blackwater Fort in Co. Armagh. Three months later the earl himself took the field against his old comrades at Clontibret.

The rebels were never strong enough to overthrow the Tudor state, but their defensive aims did not require them to do so. They had only to maintain themselves unbeaten in the field, until the strategic situation altered in their favour. The old queen might die, and the pacific James VI offer terms. Spanish intervention might tip the military balance. O'Neill played for time, avoiding formal battles, but attacking English columns on the march, as they tried to nourish isolated garrisons. When Bagenal marched from Newry to relieve Monaghan Castle on 25 May, he only reached his destination after a ruinous expenditure of irreplaceable gunpowder.

Sir Henry had 19 companies of foot: 14 of veterans

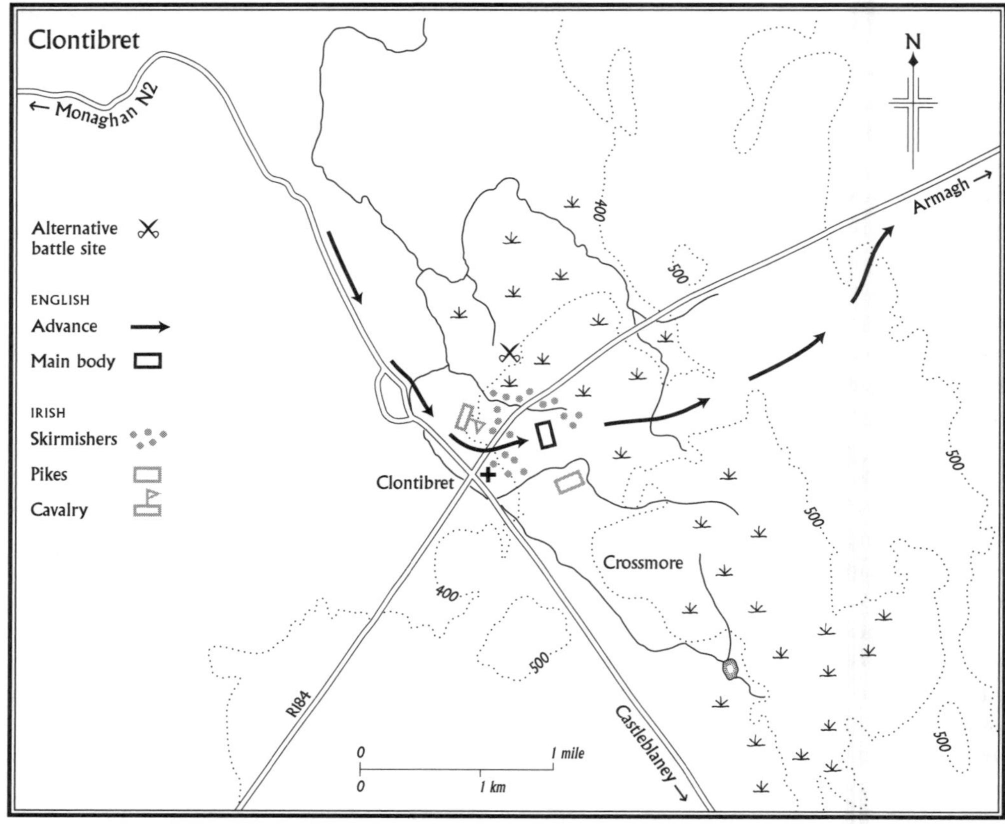

and 5 newly drafted from England. He also had 6 troops of horse. On paper a company numbered 100 (including 6 fictitious 'dead-pays' whose wages went to the captain), but many were understrength. Lieutenant Tutcher Perkins declared Bagenal left Newry with 1500 foot and 250 horse: 80 men per company and 40 horse per troop. Command was weak: companies were unregimented for lack of field officers, and were often commanded by lieutenants. The column was encumbered with 'carriage' – pack horses rather than wheeled vehicles, as the country was rough and lacked roads.

The 'fabulous advertisements' of the defeated English greatly exaggerated O'Neill's numbers. An Irish insider put them at '1800 foot, viz., 1000 shot and the rest pike and others of the bonaghts [mercenaries]'. The rebel leaders together had only 3000

Directions

Follow the N2 6 miles (10 km) southeast from Monaghan; ½ mile (0.8 km) beyond Clontibret turn left onto a minor road around the north side of Crossmore, i.e. Crossaghy Hill. Older Ordnance Survey maps marked the battle site further north, beyond the Clontibret–Keady road.

foot and 800 horse, but O'Donnell, worth a quarter of their strength, was not present at Clontibret. Hugh O'Neill's power lay not in numbers, but in his red-coated arquebusiers, trained in happier days by English captains. Bagenal's cavalry commander affirmed that 'wheresoever he served in all his life he never saw more readier or more perfecter shot'.

Irish firepower had so impressed Bagenal that he took a different route home, southeast towards Castleblaney. O'Neill caught him up near Clontibret church, where the English had to turn east to regain the Newry road around the north side of Crossaghy Hill. Some of O'Neill's men already occupied both sides of the bottleneck, 600–700 pikes uphill to the English right, arquebusiers in the bog to their left. The earl followed with 300 cavalry, more arquebusiers and Scots, ready to assail Bagenal's rear.

Once past the church, the English were attacked on all sides, and brought to a standstill. Sir Francis Stafford, one of several English officers present who left accounts, reported that they were 'charged in the vanguard ... [and] in the rearguard with the Earl and his troops ... their shot and Scots [archers] playing upon our wings, we were fain to abide the whole force the space of three hours and never marched above a quarter of a mile in all that time'. O'Neill skilfully combined infantry and cavalry to prevent the English deploying: 'every troop of shot in the head of a troop of horse, the one never putting forth but seconded by the other, charging our two battles on each flank, holding our horse so short and our shot so close to our pikes ...' (Sir Edward York). After three hours fighting, Bagenal's ammunition was low. O'Neill closed in, 'perceiving our stand of pike, for lack of shot to save them, to grow close together and like to brandle [waver], thinking ... that with the next volley ... that a breech should have been made in both battles to have given an entry to all his horse to their utter overthrow' (Sir Ralph Lane).

Bagenal was saved by a sacrificial charge, in the finest cavalry tradition. A Palesman named Seagrave rode against O'Neill with 40 troopers, the collision knocking both men off their horses. They wrestled on the ground until another Ulsterman cut off Seagrave's arm, while the earl stabbed him under the mail shirt. O'Neill was safe, but the duel paralysed the Irish horse, who stood motionless, while the English army hurried through the strait.

Fighting continued another five hours, as the English pressed on grimly, 'still boggered on by them until nightfall when we encamped in the midst of them' (Perkins). They had only a third of a pound of powder left per piece, but O'Neill's men were no better placed. Next day they allowed the exhausted English to march quietly on to Newry. Bagenal deliberately understated his losses, his muster master later admitting more wounded 'than we have thought fit to be given forth upon the first advertisement'. One company listed as suffering 7 hurt still had 18 men unfit for duty, excluding men killed or previously evacuated. Official figures of 31 killed and 109 wounded should be multiplied at least three times. Reports of 100 Irish killed and thrice that number injured probably require revision the other way.

Irish sources obscured Clontibret's significance, confusing it with a minor action at Mullaghbrack, between Newry and Armagh, near Markethill. Policy makers in Dublin thought Ireland never stood in greater danger. The army was in no state to fight again. Perkins went to Dublin by sea for fresh ammunition, but admitted that 'if they had all the munition in Ireland, they would not have undertaken to come to Dundalk'. Bagenal had escaped disaster by the narrowest of margins, thanks to Seagrave's death-ride. A frustrated O'Neill fined the gentlemen of his guard 40 cows apiece for not following him more closely. Nevertheless he had found the tactical method that would bring him nearer to military victory over the English than any other Irish leader.

Clontibret

	Winner	*Loser*
Opponents	Irish	English
Commanders	Hugh O'Neill, Earl of Tyrone	Sir Henry Bagenal
Numbers	2800	1750
Losses	*c.*130	*c.*420

Mullaghbrack

	Winner	*Loser*
Opponents	Irish	English
Commanders	Hugh O'Neill, Earl of Tyrone	Sir John Norris (w)
Numbers	unknown	unknown
Losses	unknown	unknown

Directions

Mullaghbrack *Tactical location unknown.*

Carrickfergus, 4 November 1597

Ireland, Co. Antrim, DS9/15 J4294–4495

Sir John Chichester's overthrow outside Carrickfergus arose from an entirely unnecessary collision with Antrim Scots. Half the garrison were killed in a mindless quarrel over a few cows.

Carrickfergus, on the northern shore of Belfast Lough, was one of a few English garrisons that still held out in the summer of 1597. Elementary diplomacy would have ensured MacSorley's Antrim Scots remained neutral. His meeting with Chichester on 4 November was at the latter's request, to resolve 'certeine stealthes and other outradges' at issue between MacSorley and officers of the garrison.

The encounter took place 'betwixt Olderfleet and this town', a 9-mile (14.5-km) stretch of hilly country between Carrickfergus and Larne, the site of Olderfleet Castle. Larne Lough flanks the area on the east, and beyond that is the peninsula of Island Magee. The fighting was far enough outside Carrickfergus for Scots cavalry to infiltrate between Chichester and the town. Lieutenant Harte, an officer wounded in the action, placed the initial English position 'About iiij [four] myles from the towne, one myle and a half distant from a hill, whearupon the enimye made their stande'. This suggests either Black Hill (J4294) or Ballagh Hill (J4394), just north of Ballycarry, MacSorley on slightly higher ground beyond Aldfreck (J4495). Harte's distances roughly agree with an estimate by the English commissary James Birt, placing the Scots 'within vi myles of the towne'.

Chichester had five companies of foot and just 40 horse. Harte gives a detailed order of battle, though it totals less than his casualty figures: 'The battle contaynde sixtye pikes or thereabouts ... the forelorne hope contayninge nyne pikes and twelve or fifteen shott ... a whinge of shott to the number of twentye ... two loose winges of shott [20 each], which wear to seconde our horse [40]': 180 in all. Companies were in poor shape after an earlier expedition, 'wherein we had soe tyred our men and wett our powder and munition that ... our shotte wear able to doe no service' (Harte). MacSorley deployed in two echelons, 'which he showede of horse and foote aboute 700 fighting men; yet havinge left aboute two myle behind him in certaine shrubbs an ambushemente of Irish shotte and Scotche bowmen, with sloughes [two-handed swords], swords and pikes, in all 800' (Sir Ralph Lane).

Chichester thought it inexpedient to meddle with the enemy, but changed his mind when Captain Merriman brought up the battle, saying, 'yt was a shame we showld sufer a sort of beggers to brave us in that sort' (Harte). The lieutenant of horse urged the Scots would never stand, 'and if theye weare roundly charged ... they [the English] myghte have a good killinge upon them, or at leaste take a good runne out of them' (Lane).

MacSorley's advanced party refused to cooperate, withdrawing slowly from hill to hill, 'untille they weare drawne to the shrubbie grounde, where the ambushements laid' (Lane). Chichester ordered his horsemen to charge, but only six obeyed, encouraging the enemy to wheel about and disperse the supporting shot. At the same time, MacSorley's 500 arquebusiers opened fire from the shrubs. The English shot had used up their powder, and hid amongst the pikemen, crying out for ammunition, 'which they enimye heeringe, they pursued us soe closely with their horse that they killed our men within two pikes lengthes of our battle, and our horse wowld never geeve them any one chardge, nor all that our commander were able to doe' (Harte).

Already wounded two or three times, Chichester was last seen striking his own men with his sword, before being shot in the head. Charged front and rear, the English battle dissolved and the men cut down, 'some fighting, some running'. A few officers swam

Carrickfergus

	Winner	*Loser*
Opponents	Scoto-Irish	English
Commanders	James MacSorley MacDonald	Sir John Chichester (k)
Numbers	1500	c.350
Losses	unknown	200–300

their horses to Island Magee, suggesting a battlefield near the shallower southern end of Larne Lough. Harte reckoned the English lost eight or nine score killed, and 30 or 40 hurt, 'moste of which recovered'. The muster master general, who had reason to know, thought eight or ten troopers were killed, 'but of the V [five] companies of foote … there were slaine in the feelde 220 footmen or thereabouts, together with 60 Kearne of the contrye'. Fifty or sixty stragglers came in later, 'which hadd coverd themselves dureinge the slaughter, some in the high grass, and some in the ouse [bogholes] up to the shoulders' (Lane). Seventeen officers, sergeants and drummers were listed as killed, over half the establishment.

The disaster had surprisingly little result. MacSorley sent Chichester's head to O'Neill, but treated his prisoners decently. He protested the affair was a ghastly mistake, brought on by Chichester's aggression: 'and as the gentillemen that is heare in hand with us [as prisoners] knoweth, yt behoved the gentillmen that was with me to do for themselves or dye'.

Directions

The exact site is unknown, but a line of hilltops between the two Black Hills, east of the B149 Carrickfergus–Larne road, suits descriptions of the Scots retreat.

Yellow Ford, Monday 14 August 1598

Ireland, Co. Armagh, DS19 H8550

Yellow Ford was the worst disaster an English army ever suffered at the hands of the Irish. Yet it was ill-served by vague chroniclers, and does not appear on modern maps. Almost everything we know about O'Neill's greatest victory comes from postmortem reports by English officers.

The Nine Years' War progressed fitfully between its great crises at Clontibret, Yellow Ford and Kinsale. Ulster's geographical strength balanced English military power. O'Neill's invulnerable economic base allowed him to maintain forces unprecedented in Irish warfare: 1000 cavalry, the same number of pikes, and 4000 arquebusiers, equipped with modern weapons smuggled in from mainland Britain. The struggle was no longer a carefree scramble after defenceless kerns, but a full-scale war against a disciplined and skilful enemy, the largest single drain upon Queen Elizabeth's exchequer.

The English still held Blackwater Fort on the Armagh–Tyrone border, just downstream from the first bend below the modern Blackwatertown bridge. O'Neill moved against this eyesore in the heart of his country in July 1598. Irish troops lay close under the crumbling ramparts, cutting off water and firewood, starving the garrison out. Sir Henry Bagenal advanced to Armagh to relieve the fort, camping east of the River Callan.

Bagenal had concentrated all the English troops available: 3500 infantry in 40 companies, and 300 cavalry. Half the infantry were ill-disciplined recruits, and three-quarters of the rest were Irish, drafted to fill up the ranks. Companies were grouped into regiments of about 600 men, marching in battle order, one behind another at intervals of six or seven score paces:

Vanguard: Colonels Percy and Bagenal
Battle: Colonel Cosbie; Sir Thomas Wingfield
Rear: Colonel Cunie; Captain Billings

Two sleeves or wings of shot preceded the army as a forlorn hope, bodies of cavalry riding between the leading and rearmost pairs of regiments. Bagenal also had four guns, the heaviest a saker, firing a 6lb (2.7 kg) ball. Irish sources put O'Neill's army at 600 horse and 4050 foot.

The ground beyond Armagh is broken up with little round hills, covered in the 1590s with woods and shrubby brushwood, 'plashed' or entangled in the usual defensive fashion. Open areas served as killing grounds for Irish arquebusiers in the neighbouring bogs and woods. The road from Armagh to Dungannon ran, as it still does, west of the Callan before forking northwest for Blackwatertown, straight across three small hills separated by soft ground. The location of Yellow Ford is uncertain, although the

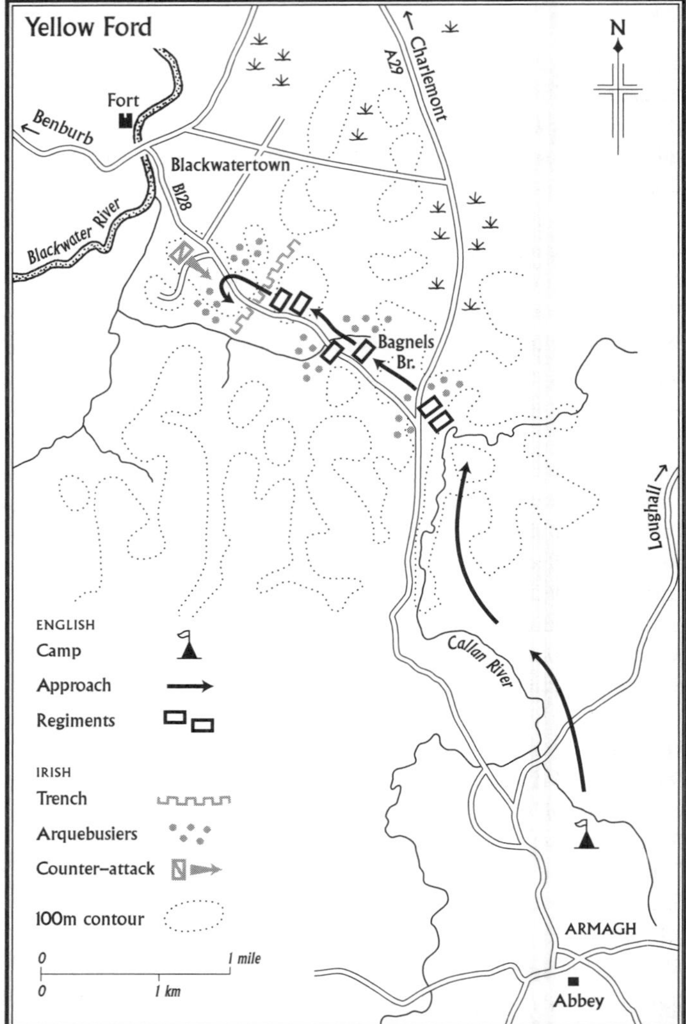

Directions

Take a minor road north from Armagh along the east bank of the Callan, crossing at Allistragh. Cross the A29, and follow the B128 towards Blackwatertown. Yellow Ford was probably at Bagnel's Bridge, and O'Neill's trench beyond the next hill.

colour suggests bog water rather than that of the Callan. Eyewitness accounts suggest it was further on, where the Ordnance Survey marks 'Bagnel's Bridge'.

Bagenal moved off at 8 a.m. At first he advanced east of the Callan, wheeling left across the river to make his final push, 'a mile on the right hand side of the common highway' (Lieutenant William Taafe). The Irish began harassing attacks almost at once, but O'Neill's main position was much further on, too far north to be outflanked. Between the second and third hills, covering the last half mile (0.8 km) of Bagenal's approach to the Blackwater, the Irish had dug a huge ditch, connecting marshy ground either side of the passage, 'a mile long, some five foot deep, and four feet over, with a thorny hedge on the top' (Captain Charles Montague).

Percy's leading regiment stormed the obstacle 'and passed forward to a sconce made upon the top of the hill beyond the same, where they remained a pretty while' (Taafe). Unfortunately for them, the supports were nowhere in sight. Bagenal's regiments had become strung out with the broken terrain and continual harassing fire from either flank. Counter-

Yellow Ford

	Winner	*Loser*
Opponents	Irish	English
Commanders	Hugh O'Neill, Earl of Tyrone Hugh Roe O'Donnell Hugh Maguire	Sir Henry Bagenal (k) Sir Thomas Maria Wingfield
Numbers	4650	3800
Losses	120–300	1200–2000

attacked by Irish horse and foot under O'Neill, and confused by orders to fall back, Percy's regiment 'turned and fell to run, and so were all put to the sword with small resistance' (Montague). When Bagenal reached O'Neill's trench with the cavalry and his own regiment, he was shot in the forehead. The cavalry could not close, 'by reason of a main bog' (Taafe), and the infantry 'advancing themselves in like sort [to Percy's] were all slain' (Montague).

The other regiments had lost touch entirely. Cosbie and Wingfield were stuck between the first and second hills: 'the saker being bogged stayed the battle so long, and the enemies gathered so about them in such multitudes, as that they could not both second the vanguard and save the ordnance' (Captain George Kingsmill). Cosbie led his regiment forward, but they 'fetched off as broken as the rest', after two firkins of gunpowder exploded in their midst.

Out of sight beyond the first hill, Cunie and Billings were fighting a separate battle with O'Donnell and Maguire: 'in an hour and a half they could not march a quarter of a mile forward, by which means they never understood in the rear of the killing of the Marshal [Bagenal], nor of the defeating of the former regiments, until they came up to fetch off the rear of the battle' (Kingsmill). Wingfield's regiment defended the saker until the draught oxen were all killed, when he decided, as senior officer surviving, to withdraw. Leaving the gun irretrievably bogged, the infantry regained Armagh, covered by the horse, who had suffered few casualties.

Half Bagenal's army had been destroyed or routed. An official list shows 855 rank and file killed and 363 hurt, besides 16 named captains killed and 11 colours lost. Between 1800 and 2000 English troops got away, too shattered to do more than fortify themselves in the ruined abbey. Lieutenant Taafe understood enemy losses were 300. The chaunter or precentor of Armagh Cathedral admitted six score while parleying over Bagenal's dead body. O'Neill let the English withdraw, taking the Blackwater garrison with them. He proceeded to turn on Connacht and Limerick, undoing 14 years of English settlement in a few days. Reinforcements from England saved Leinster, but O'Neill was at the height of his power, making his presence felt throughout Ireland.

Wicklow, 29 May 1599

Ireland, Co. Wicklow, DS56 unlocated

Curlew Mountains, 5 August 1599

Ireland, Co. Roscommon, DS33 G7905

Bagenal's defeat at Yellow Ford provoked an unprecedented English response. Elizabeth's forces in Ireland rose to 16,000 foot and 1300 horse, commanded from 15 April 1599 by the first man in the kingdom, Robert Devereux, Earl of Essex, the queen's favourite. Essex dared not confront O'Neill, preferring a futile promenade around the south, symbolized by a skirmish near Ballybrittas (Co. Laois), known as the Pass of Plumes (N5706). Meanwhile, more disasters befell the English, near Wicklow and in the Curlew Mountains.

Sir Henry Harington was posted at Wicklow, one of the most dangerous areas in Ireland, scene of Lord Grey's embarrassment at the hands of Phelim MacFeagh's father at Glenmalur (1581). He had five raw companies: 50 horse and 450 foot in all. Captain Loftus's company was 'all Irish and most of them lately come over from the rebels' (Harington). O'Byrne numbers are not quoted, but their battle consisted of

200 pikes and targeteers with sword and buckler, and many shot.

Harington led a reconnaissance through Rathdrum towards Avonmore on 28 May, 'to learn our men to make cabins and to get fresh flesh' (Captain Linley). He marched 'six miles', presumably double-sized country miles, and camped at 'Bolougbe', perhaps Ballylug, 'a mile or something better from the passage into the Ranelagh, upon which ford the rebels had fortified' (Captain Atherton). Harington reconnoitred the enemy positions, but discovered little in the heavily wooded hills. Overnight Irish harassing parties fired volleys into the camp.

Harington decided to withdraw, hearing 'of all the rebels in those parts gathering ahead of me'. The column formed up next morning, with a vanguard of shot, a main battle of pikes and a rear of shot, screened by loose sleeves of musketeers. The baggage marched between vanguard and battle; cavalry followed behind. Several parleys delayed departure, one initiated by Captain Loftus, enquiring after a deserter, another by the enemy. Captain Linley disliked the delay, thinking it 'a policy of the rebels that they might come near us'.

The English route presumably lay back down the valley connecting Rathdrum and Wicklow. The Irish overtook them after a mile (1.6 km) or so, the English skirmishing successfully for the next two, as they negotiated a 'foul ford', the cavalry charging as the ground afforded opportunity. 'On my faith and credit,' reported Captain Atherton, 'there was not one bullet came near our battle in all this skirmish; but now we were drawing near to another ford and strait.' The distance from Wicklow at this point is uncertain, although reported mileages imply halfway, near Glenealy, where the modern road and stream cross each other several times. A contemporary picture map suggests somewhere nearer town, showing a large building named 'Monisharlee' or 'Monishorle', probably a corruption of Mainister Liath ('grey monastery'), Wicklow's ruined Franciscan friary. Parts of the walls stood in the 1950s, in the presbytery grounds west of the town, left of the Dublin road. The Elizabethan artist drew the ford quite near Monisharlee, but his work is not to scale,

Wicklow

	Winner	*Loser*
Opponents	Irish	English
Commanders	Phelim MacFeagh O'Byrne	Sir Henry Harington
Numbers	unknown	500
Losses	unknown	unknown

Curlew Mountains

	Winner	*Loser*
Opponents	Irish	English
Commanders	Brian Og O'Rourke	Sir Conyers Clifford (k)
Numbers	unknown	1701
Losses	500	449

representing the whole fight, from the initial attack to the final pursuit near Wicklow Castle.

As the English vanguard approached the ford, the Irish main body tried to head them off, crossing upstream to attack the English left: 'the enemies playing very hotly upon us with shot … their battle, marching over the bog, unto a fair green close'. Linley's vanguard won the race, deploying 40–50 musketeers as flank guard behind a ditch bank, 'very convenient for the receiving of their battle', with a clear field of fire across a small plot of ground, presumably the same green close. Atherton sent the cavalry across the ford next, followed by the battle and the loose shot and pike in the rear: 'At which time, in my conscience, there was not one man of ours lost' (Atherton).

The fight was going well for the English, and Atherton was about to attack the enemy battle as it left the bog, when everything fell apart. The musketeers who were told to give covering fire threw down their pieces and fled before the enemy came within range; Atherton's own men refused to charge; Loftus's ensign, one Pierce Walsh, rode away with the company colours. The other musketeers panicked, leaving the pikemen exposed, crowding the narrow strait leading up from the ford: 'At which sight the rebels' battle came very fast up, and charged us in the rear with push of pike, our men coming all of a heap, by reason divers of Captain Loftus his men quit their places ... seeing their colours gone' (Linley). Many of them fell without a fight, their officers imploring them to face about for their own safety, but 'they never offered to turn nor speak, but as men without sense or feeling, ran upon one another's back' (Atherton). A dozen gallant horsemen saved a few colours from the carnage, the remains of the infantry rallying in the abbey.

Total casualties are unknown, but must approach 50 per cent. Linley lost 44 of his company. Everyone blamed Loftus, who would not dismount to rally his men. Disorder had begun in the rear, when his musketeers left their post at the ford and legged it back to Wicklow. Loftus conveniently died of wounds, but all the other officers were cashiered, and Ensign Walsh hanged. The rank and file were sentenced to be decimated, the survivors reduced to pioneers, lowest of the low. The O'Byrnes had shown once more that they were not to be trifled with.

A more serious reverse followed in the Curlew Mountains in the west. The English troops were more numerous and of better quality than at Wicklow, but they were defeated in a set piece attack, not bamboozled in a running fight. Hugh O'Neill's revolt had spread to Connacht, where Hugh O'Donnell besieged O'Connor of Sligo, a notable loyalist, in Collooney Castle. The governor, Sir Conyers Clifford, marched to relieve O'Connor, reaching Boyle late in the afternoon of 5 August. The weather was hot, the troops were tired and hungry, but he pressed on.

The modern highway from Boyle into Co. Sligo loops east, through low ground between the hills and Loch Cé (Lough Key). Clifford's route led directly north, through the Curlew Mountains to Balinafad. The mile-long (1.6-km) defile is only a quarter of a mile (0.4 km) across, the track running between bogs fringed by woods on the right. O'Donnell had detached O'Rourke to dispute the pass, which he did in depth, barricading its southern entrance, where the 180-m (591-foot) contour crosses today's minor road.

Clifford advanced between areas now known as Derrypark and Garrow, on the southern slopes of An Corrshliabh, with 1496 infantry in three regiments, one behind another, as follows:

Vanguard:	186 pike	385 shot	571 total
Battle:	165 pike	256 shot	421 total
Rear:	160 pike	344 shot	504 total

The 205 cavalry stayed behind to escort the baggage through the pass when cleared.

The 400 defenders of the breastworks fired a volley and retired into the defile, followed by the English vanguard. Galled by musketry from both flanks, the advance petered out in a 90-minute fire fight, which ended when the English ran out of powder. Demoralized, the vanguard fell back, carrying away battle and rear. Clifford failed to rally the troops, and received a pike thrust through the body. Only the cavalry prevented a massacre, pushing forward left of the road, '[by] a way that had stones in it six or seven feet broad, lying above ground, and plashes of bogs between them' (Sir John Harington). Despite the unfavourable terrain, they checked the Irish pursuit, allowing the infantry to stream back to Boyle Abbey. Irish sources claimed 100 per cent casualties, but English figures were bad enough: 208 killed and 241 wounded. Clifford's veteran companies were eliminated as offensive units, and Collooney Castle surrendered. The Irish attributed their victory to the Blessed Virgin Mary, the English to sorcery, but the story was similar to Yellow Ford. Irish arquebusiers moving freely through difficult terrain could concentrate fire against individual parts of an English column, with devastating results.

Directions

Wicklow *Follow Harington's path along the R752 from Rathdrum, bearing right through Rathnew along the R750, towards the site of the old abbey.*

Curlew Mountains *See Boyle Abbey's mutilated remains, then follow the Red Earl's Historical Trail 1½ miles (2.5 km) along a minor road off the N61 north of Boyle. The battlefield extends north from a minor crossroads in the mouth of the pass, as marked by the Ordnance Survey.*

Moyry Pass, 20 September–6 October 1600

Ireland, Co. Armagh, DS36 J0613–14

Lord Mountjoy, Elizabeth's most successful Irish governor, succeeded Essex in February 1600. He faced a stalemate that threatened to divide Ireland permanently, between an English-controlled south-east and a Gaelic free state in Ulster and Connacht. To break the deadlock Mountjoy had to re-establish an English presence in Ulster, from which they had been excluded since Yellow Ford (1598). On 20 September 1600 he advanced to Faughart Hill, scene of Edward Bruce's defeat in 1318, with 375 cavalry and 3450 infantry. O'Neill lurked half a mile (0.8 km) further on, in the woods of Moyry.

The Moyry or Moyra Pass, known in Irish as *Bealach an mhaighre*, is a strategic defile, traversed by the old Dundalk–Newry road and the Dublin–Belfast railway. The battlefield remains doubtful territory, the border between Northern Ireland and the Republic running down the road that O'Neill held against Mountjoy. The way through the woods passed between Claret Rock and Slievenabolea (630 feet/192 m), 'two great mountains or rocks with equal ascent, the one of the right hand, the other on the left, their tops being distant more than a musquet shot from one another' (Mountjoy's *Journal of the Campaign in the North*). From them the defenders could observe every English move.

The defile was naturally strong, 'fenced with strong cliffs and thick bushes and trees even to the Three Mile Water', a stream running north of Slievenabolea, under Kilnasaggart Bridge. Further east Feede Mountain inhibited outflanking manoeuvres in that direction. O'Neill had built a series of obstructions across the road: 'three several barracadoes or trenches, a caliver [arquebus] shot distance, flanked from higher ground on the left hand with other works' (*Journal*). Mountjoy's secretary Fynes Moryson described trenches running from bog to bog, 'with huge and high flankers of great stones, mingled with turf and staked on both sides with palisadoes wattled'. Another officer who served at Moyry thought it hard enough 'for swine to pass through, much less men'.

Apart from forcing the pass, Mountjoy had to re-establish English morale. He deliberately hugged O'Neill's works, although it meant fighting for every stick of firewood: 'the better to acquaint our men in lesser factions with the fight of the northern rebel whom they had seldom tasted in later times but to their cost'. Mountjoy hoped to wear O'Neill down, 'to make the war upon him where with greatest difficulty he might sustain it, and where he cannot without great pain draw his men together' (*Journal*). The dogged three-week campaign that followed, in torrential rain, resembles the Somme more than traditional images of Elizabethan warfare.

Fighting became serious on three principal occasions:

(1) THURSDAY 25 SEPTEMBER

An English trench raid on O'Neill's defences, 'to taste them thoroughly'. One hundred volunteers attacked under cover of thick mist, broke into the trenches, and captured the front line. The raiders took the second trench, but lacked means to go further. Finding the surrounding terrain as strong as the fortifications, the attackers withdrew, 'having viewed the trenches and seen how well the Irish could defend them'. The Irish followed up, maintaining a hot fight with detachments posted to cover the retreat.

(2) THURSDAY 2 OCTOBER

'One of the greatest fights that hath been seen in Ireland'. Equinoctial storms delayed operations for a week, until Irish coat-trailing drew out five of Mountjoy's regiments to drive the enemy away from the camp: 'As, however, the enemy did not retreat in the usual way they [the English] were ordered to give home to their trenches and to force them, which accordingly they did and possessed them a good while, maintaining the fight with the rogues in their great strength, almost four hours together'. The attackers entered the pass, but lacked the force to overcome the remaining obstacles, which included O'Neill's cavalry beyond the ford. It was equally

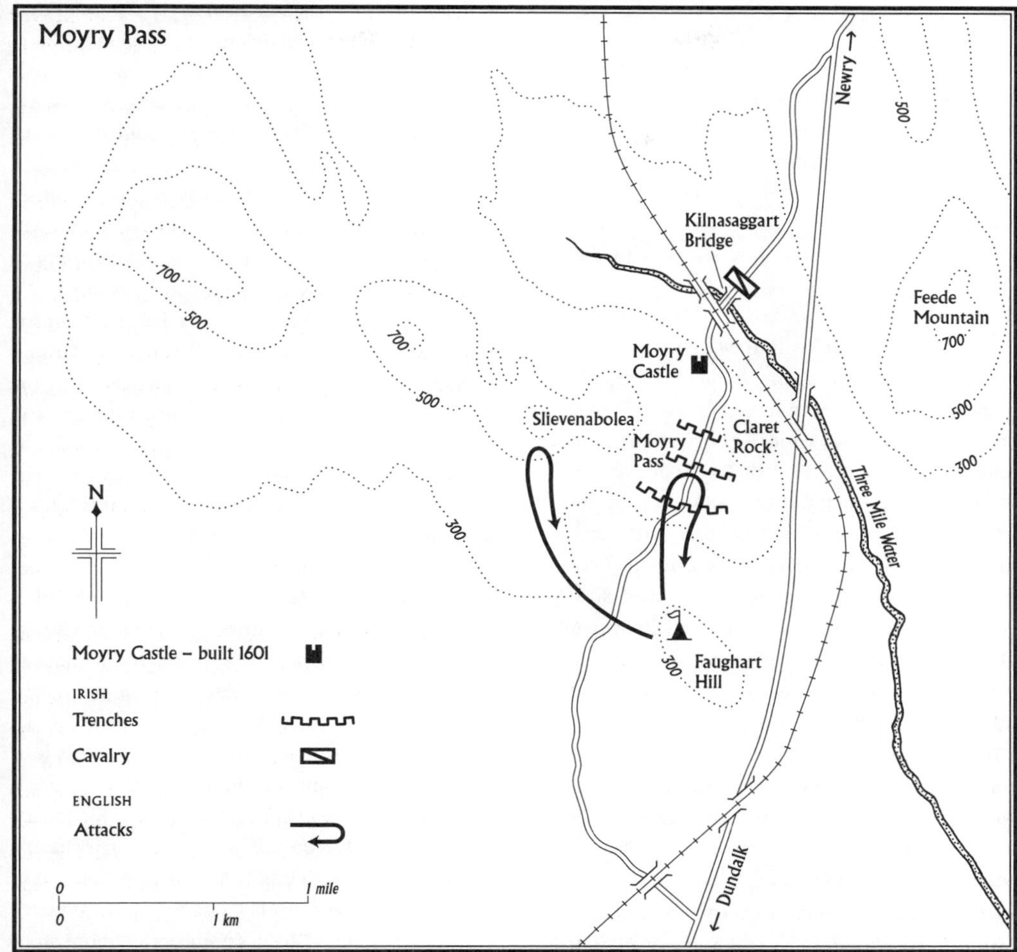

impossible to hold the captured trenches, under fire from both flanks. The English made 'a gallant and orderly retreat', covered by a seasonable cavalry charge across unfavourable ground, 'where never horse served'. Mountjoy reported the Irish 'did call this day's work their great overthrow', believing defeat so near that they sent off their baggage. After an afternoon's fighting at full stretch, however, O'Neill still held his ground.

(3) SUNDAY 5 OCTOBER

'The only fair day we had since we encamped'. Mountjoy sought to seize the western high ground, turning the Irish trenches. He deployed three regiments, echeloned back from left to right. The leading unit, only 230 strong, moved directly against Slievenabolea, with another in support, the third staying in the low ground with some cavalry. Noticing the English spearhead had outpaced its supports, 300 Irish charged them on all sides at once. The English

Directions

From Dundalk follow the N1 north, taking the left fork towards Faughart Hill. Turn left and right along the old Newry road to follow Mountjoy's approach to the pass.

Moyry Pass

	Winner	*Loser*
Opponents	English	Irish
Commanders	Charles Blount, Lord Mountjoy	Hugh O'Neill, Earl of Tyrone
Numbers	3825	3500
Losses	250	500

defended themselves vigorously, killing a dozen of their attackers, before withdrawing unpursued.

Mountjoy's attempt to break the impasse by manoeuvre was no more successful than his previous efforts: 'We are now', wrote Sir Geoffrey Fenton, secretary to the Irish Council, on 9 October, 'but where we were in the beginning.' Next day Mountjoy withdrew his half-drowned dysentery-stricken army to Dundalk. He found it difficult to estimate O'Neill's total losses, claiming between 400 and 800, but admitted 50 of his own men killed and 200 wounded. O'Neill retreated in his own time, perhaps because the English could turn Moyry by the coastal road from Dundalk, around Carlingford Lough. Mountjoy took the undefended pass on 18 October, its strength convincing his officers it 'could not have been won without the great hazard of the whole army'. O'Neill's stand had kept Mountjoy away from the Blackwater, postponing any attack on Co. Tyrone. The deputy gave up his aim of retaking Armagh, and fortified Mountnorris, 8 miles (13 km) north of Newry. He had, however, succeeded in confronting O'Neill on even terms, breaking a cycle of English defeat.

Kinsale, 24 December 1601

Ireland, Co. Cork, DS87 W6151

O'Neill needed foreign help to defeat the English, but he was strategically ill-placed for his allies: the Spanish landing at Kinsale on 22 September 1601 was at the wrong end of Ireland to Ulster. O'Neill had to leave his northern stronghold to cooperate with the invaders, risking an entirely different kind of battle from his usual defensive engagement.

The Spanish expedition (3814 men) was too small for independent field operations. Lord Mountjoy, Queen Elizabeth's deputy, promptly bottled them up in Kinsale and cut them off from seaborne supplies by capturing Rincurren and Castle Park (now Charles's and James's Forts). O'Neill reacted more slowly. He approached Kinsale on 21 December, camping at Coolcarron, 3 miles (5 km) north of Mountjoy's position on Spittle Hill. The war's decisive moment had come. Mountjoy could neither assault Kinsale with O'Neill in his rear, nor maintain the siege for lack of supplies, particularly forage for the cavalry, his key weapon. The Spaniards were trapped, enduring infinite miseries from bombardment and hunger, 'Dogs, cats and garrons [horses] is a feast when they can get it,' commented Sir George Carew, Elizabeth's president of Munster. Far from home, O'Neill forsook his Fabian tactics and gambled on a night attack. Half an hour before dawn on Christmas Eve 1601, English patrols spotted rebel arquebus matches, glowing in the darkness beyond the northwest sector of their siege lines.

Mountjoy was ready for such a move. He had formed eight old companies into a 500 strong *squadron volante* as a mobile covering force under Sir Henry Power. He reinforced this with two more infantry regiments totalling 500, and all the cavalry (300–400). Most of his infantry (*c.*4000) stayed in the trenches to observe Kinsale. O'Neill's numbers are more problematic: 'all the rebels of Ireland ... joined with Spaniards that landed at Castlehaven ... and the greatest part of the Irishry of Munster' (Carew). Hayes-McCoy reckoned they brought 5000 into the field, his detailed figures adding up to 680 cavalry and 5520–5700 infantry, a total of 6380.

The Irish had abandoned their usual dispersed formations: 'Being ... by the Spaniards put in fashion to fight' (Sir Henry Power). The foot came on in three dense masses: the battle under O'Neill, the rear under Captain Richard Tyrrell, and the vanguard last under Hugh Roe O'Donnell. English eyewitnesses estimated O'Neill's battle at 1000–1500 strong, suggesting 3000–4000 Irish pikemen in all, armoured by the

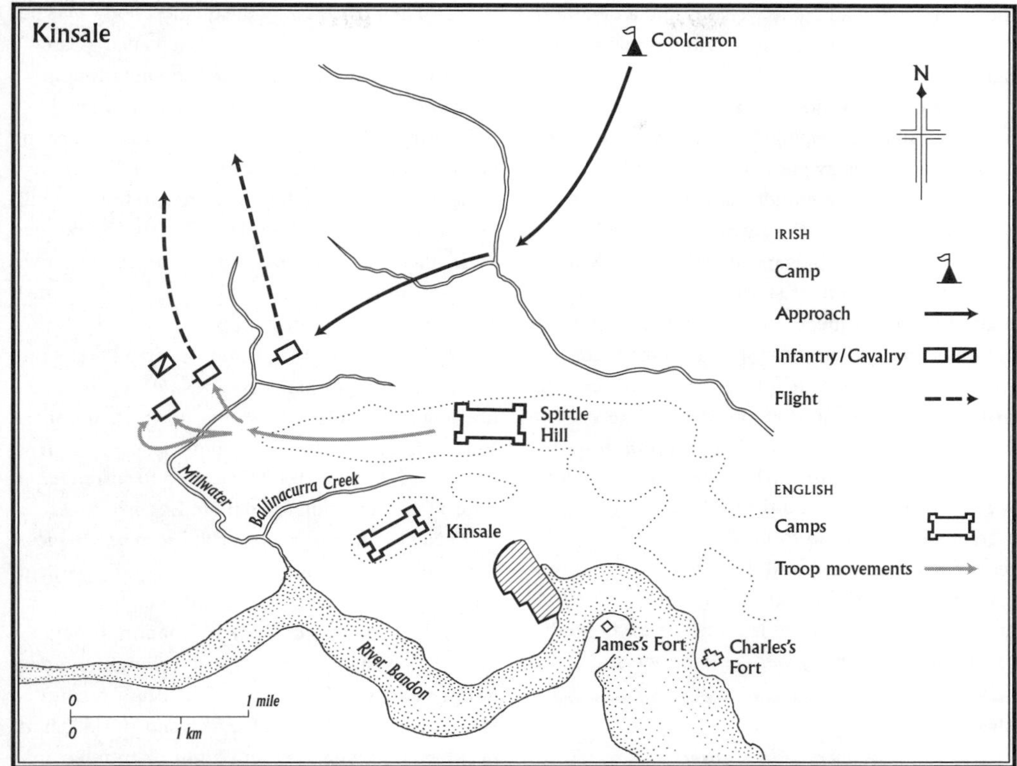

Spaniards with corselets and knee-length tassets. O'Neill's cavalry fought as a single body, but kept in the rear. The unorthodox order of march supports assertions that O'Neill got lost, misled 'by the darkness of the night and ignorance of his guides' (Carew).

Attempts to assign blame for the defeat have obscured Irish intentions. Did Aguila force O'Neill's hand by threatening to surrender if not relieved? Had he promised a simultaneous attack on the English camp, or only agreed to a sortie once O'Neill had committed his forces? Was O'Neill's advance merely a demonstration to cover the introduction of reinforcements into Kinsale? The answers are lost in rumour and recrimination. The alleged betrayal of the plan for a bottle of whiskey is a picturesque but immaterial detail. The result would have been much the same any other night.

Kinsale lies north of the Bandon River, and the English siege lines were protected on the west by Ballinacurra Creek, 'a boggish glynn, and passable with horse only at one ford'. The English were entrenched between creek and town, on higher ground flanked by artillery, 'of great advantage for horse and foot both to be embattled and to fight' (Carew). When O'Neill found the English drawn up ready, he retreated away from Kinsale, across the Millwater. Mountjoy followed, 'But being drawn out some mile further we might perceive the enemy to stand firm upon a ground of very good advantage

Directions

Follow the R605 Kinsale–Inishannon road across Ballinacurra Creek. The Ordnance Survey marks the battle at the R605/R606 junction, but fighting extended further north, over Ballythomas Hill, reached by a right fork beyond Millwater bridge. Also visit Charles's Fort south of Kinsale.

for them, having a bog between us and a deep ford to pass, and in all appearance with an intention to fight' (Carew).

The ground beyond Millwater was an open plain, 'none but a fair champaign'. It offered no scope for O'Neill's customary guerrilla tactics. Mountjoy's advanced-guard commander saw the Irish were disordered after their withdrawal, and as the leading infantry hurried up, 'advanced with some 100 horse ... and gave occasion of skirmish upon the bog side with some 100 arquebusiers. The enemy thereupon put out some of their loose shot from the battle and entertained the fight, their three battalions standing firm on the other side of the bog' (Carew). The English beat the Irish shot back into their battle, pursued by the cavalry, who wheeled to the flank when the pikemen stood firm. The Irish battle gave a great shout, but too soon. Power brought up the rest of his regiment, 'and then the horse and foot together charged through them, [and] brake that gross' (Power). Attacked front and rear, O'Neill's cavalry and main body were overthrown and eliminated: 'Their battle being the greatest body, was put all to the sword, and not above 60 escaped' (Carew).

Kinsale

	Winner	*Loser*
Opponents	English	Allied (Irish and Spanish)
Commanders	Charles Blount, Lord Mountjoy	Hugh O'Neill, Earl of Tyrone Hugh Roe O'Donnell Don Juan del Aguila
Numbers	1300–1400 committed	6380 committed
Losses	10	1500–2000

Tyrrell's division had been observing Mountjoy's rearmost regiment, upon a little hill on the right. Now he sidestepped to cut off the English troops pursuing O'Neill, but the English reserve charged the Irish rear in flank, whereupon they withdrew to the next hill, where they stood a while. Tyrrell's Irish abandoned their allies, who were overrun by the deputy's own troop of horse, and mostly killed. Only 42 Spanish soldiers survived to be captured. O'Donnell's vanguard, safely in the rear, 'ranne away withoute any stroke strickinge'. Back in Kinsale, Aguila knew nothing of what had passed, until the triumphant English fired a *feu-de-joie* and hung out captured Irish flags. On 2 January 1602 he agreed to surrender, in return for evacuation to Spain in English ships.

O'Neill's superior numbers had been beaten piecemeal, allowing Mountjoy to win the only battle of the war that mattered. Sir Edward Wingfield, reporting to the Secretary of State in London, thought it 'a slight skyrmydge for so great a slaughter, and a happy victory unlooked for'. The English counted 800–1200 enemy dead on the field and 700–800 hurt, besides 2000 weapons and eight or nine ensigns captured, 'more than ever they had together before' (Carew). More of the Irish perished on the way home as their own people turned against them. English losses were trifling: one dead and a few wounded, but many horses injured. Power thought 'The adventure was great with so few men ... yet was the best blow given since these wars; and so much the better that the Spaniards were eye-witnesses to it.' O'Neill's military reputation was irretrievably ruined, and with it all hope of Irish victory.

PART SIX

PIKE AND DRUM

The Great Civil War 1639–51

The pre-eminent strategic development in the North Atlantic Archipelago during the early 17th century was its unification under James VI of Scotland and I of England, the homespun Stewarts becoming known more grandly as the House of Stuart. The Union of the Crowns in 1603, combined with the Tudor monopoly of legal violence, bade fair to consolidate the domestic peace typical of late 16th-century Britain. At the same time the Earl of Tyrone's submission at Mellifont (see Part 5 above) re-established peaceful relations within James's Irish kingdom. Within forty years, however, his son Charles I had plunged the three kingdoms into the bloodiest decade of their history. In proportion to population, casualties were comparable with the First World War. Some 34,000 Parliamentarian soldiers and 50,000 English Royalists fell in action. Far more died of disease, including many civilians. Irish casualties are incalculable, perhaps 650,000 out of an estimated population of 1.5 million.

The greatest military upheaval in the modern history of Great Britain and Ireland has no satisfactory name. The expression 'English Civil War' conveys neither the scale of the conflict nor the interconnectedness of events in different parts of the archipelago. Fighting began in Scotland, and spread first to Ireland. The final break between king and Parliament came over control of troops destined for Ulster. The First English Civil War (1642–6) was decided at Marston Moor (1644) by an army that was half Scottish. The central military event of the Second English Civil War of 1648 was a Scots defeat at Preston. Cromwell's elimination of Royalist forces from Ireland and Scotland (1649–50) was an essential

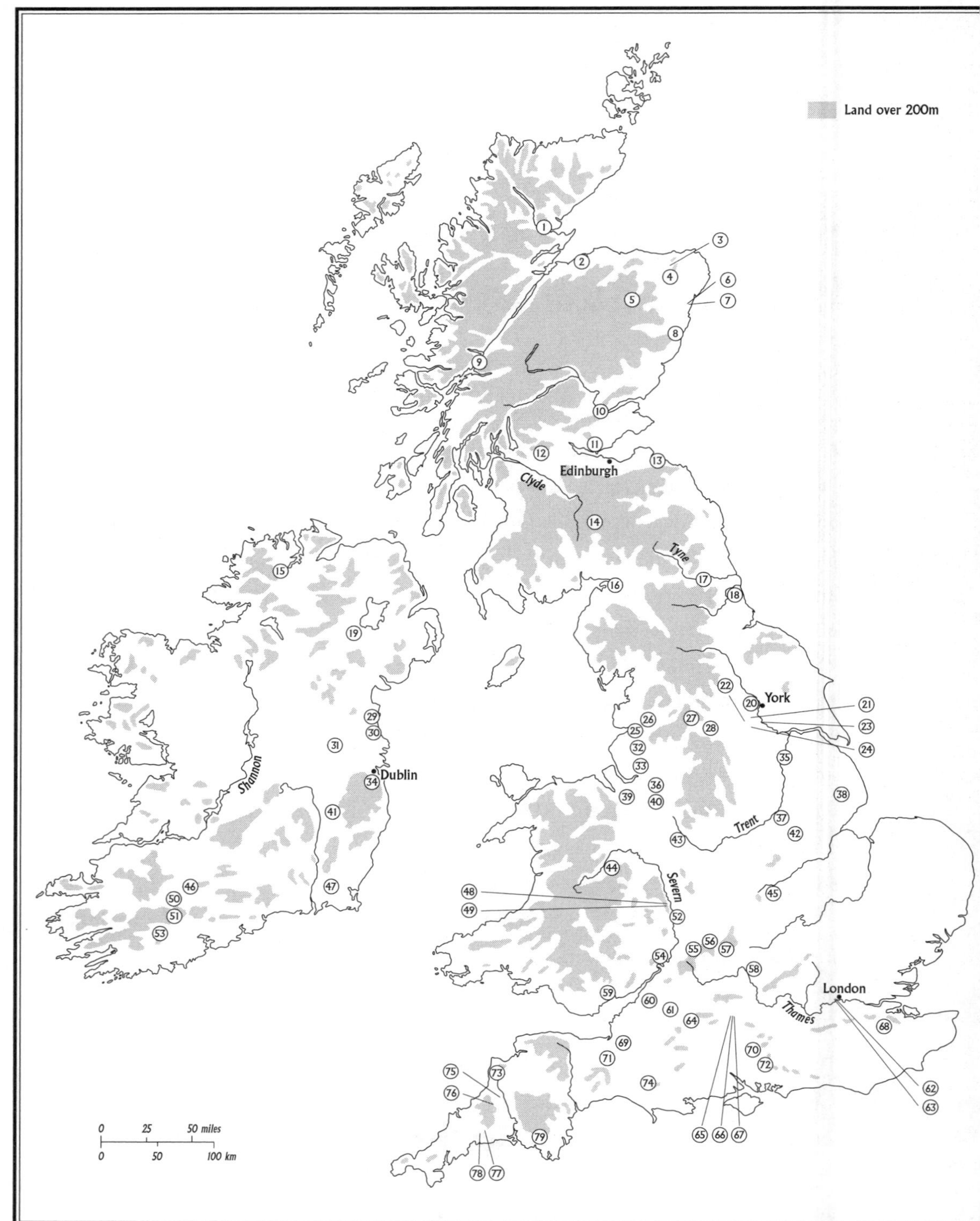

Land over 200m
Edinburgh
Clyde
Tyne
York
Dublin
Shannon
Trent
Severn
London
Thames
0 25 50 miles
0 50 100 km

prerequisite for their final overthrow at Worcester (1651). Contemporaries clearly understood the linkages between geographically separate theatres of war. Charles I regularly tried to use troops from Ireland against his British enemies, and after his military defeat played Scots Covenanters off against English Parliamentarians. 'The Wars of the Three Kingdoms' captures the conflict's multinational character, but lacks popular currency, while only a Royalist like the Earl of Clarendon could write of 'The Great Rebellion'. The 1662 Prayer Book dodged the issue, speaking with Anglican moderation of 'the late unhappy confusions'. At the risk of succumbing to Anglocentrism, the most economical solution may simply be to speak of 'the Civil Wars' in the plural.

Historians still debate the origins of the Civil Wars. Determinists have sought the rolling stone that precipitated the avalanche: 'Ship Money'; the 'Eleven Years' Tyranny' of Charles I's personal rule in the 1630s; the addled Parliaments of James I's reign; even Henry VIII's Dissolution of the Monasteries. Whigs and Marxists traced constitutional or socioeconomic trends, which rarely suit the variety of local circumstance. Some have blamed the rise of the gentry, others their decline; some a revolt of the provinces, others a crisis of central government, unable to resolve the clash of three kingdoms only joined at the head. The Earl of Bedford, one of Charles's privy councillors, complained

---

KEY

1 Carbisdale 1650
2 Auldearn 1645
3 Turriff 1639
4 Fyvie 1644
5 Alford 1645
6 Aberdeen 1644
7 Brig O'Dee 1639
8 Megray Hill 1639
9 Inverlochy 1645
10 Tippermuir 1644
11 Inverkeithing 1651
12 Kilsyth 1645
13 Dunbar 1650
14 Philiphaugh 1645
15 Scarrifhollis 1650
16 Burgh-by-Sands 1645
17 Newburn Ford 1640
18 Boldon Hill 1644
19 Benburb 1646
20 Marston Moor 1644
21 Tadcaster 1642
22 Seacroft Moor 1643
23 Selby 1644
24 Sherburn in Elmet 1645
25 Preston 1648
26 Whalley 1643
27 Adwalton Moor 1643
28 Wakefield 1643
29 Drogheda 1649
30 Julianstown 1641
31 Dungan's Hill 1647
32 Wigan Lane 1651
33 Winwick 1648
34 Rathmines 1649
35 Gainsborough 1643
36 Middlewich 1643
37 Newark 1644
38 Winceby Fight 1643
39 Rowton Heath 1645
40 Nantwich 1644
41 Kilrush 1642
42 Grantham 1643
43 Hopton Heath 1643
44 Montgomery 1644
45 Naseby 1645
46 Liscarroll 1642
47 Old Ross 1643
48 Powick Bridge 1642
49 Worcester 1651
50 Knockanuss 1647
51 Knockbrack 1651
52 Ripple Field 1643
53 Macroom 1650
54 Highnam 1643
55 Stow-on-the-Wold 1646
56 Edgehill 1642
57 Cropredy Bridge 1644
58 Chalgrove Field 1643
59 St Fagans 1648
60 Bristol 1643
61 Lansdown 1643
62 Brentford 1642
63 Turnham Green 1642
64 Roundway Down 1643
65 Newbury I 1643
66 Newbury II 1644 (Oct)
67 Newbury III 1644 (Nov)
68 Maidstone 1648
69 Marshall's Elm 1642
70 Cheriton 1644
71 Langport 1645
72 Alton 1643
73 Stratton 1643
74 Babylon Hill 1642
75 Sourton Down 1643
76 Launceston 1643
77 Braddock Down 1643
78 Lostwithiel 1644
79 Modbury 1643

in 1645 that 'noe body can tell what we have fought about all this whyle'.

Money and religion certainly played a part. There is no doubting the Crown's financial weakness. Elizabeth left enormous debts, while inflation eroded traditional sources of royal revenue. Stuart attempts to expand these, by more or less legal means, infuriated country gentlemen with no sympathy for the problems of central government. Elizabeth's religious settlement of 1559 had never satisfied radical Protestants. Known to their enemies as Puritans, they resented the embargo on further reformation, and opposed attempts by Charles I's bishops to instill uniformity and dignity into church services. The king's marriage to a French Roman Catholic and his taste for ritual inflamed widespread fears of popery in high places. Once hostilities began, religion exerted a powerful negative influence, hindering compromise and justifying atrocities.

More recent historians have viewed the Civil Wars as a bolt from the blue. An old-fashioned clash of personalities offers the most demonstrable explanation of why the wars began when they did. Charles I's chilly ineptitude was an essential factor in the descent of his kingdoms into chaos. Emotionally unfitted for kingship, Charles combined obstinacy with untrustworthiness, and possessed a taste for violence inappropriate in a ruler lacking military resources. His attempts to impose a prayer book and bishops upon the Church of Scotland outraged the Scots, whose Presbyterian religion symbolized their national identity. They raised the largest Scottish army since Pinkie (1547), and defeated a scratch English side at Newburn Ford (1640). Forced to call his first Parliament for 11 years, Charles responded to demands for reform by plotting his critics' violent overthrow. Royalists acquired the nickname Cavaliers, a corruption of *caballeros*, Spanish horsemen notorious from Europe's religious wars. Their opponents became known as Roundheads, after the close-cropped London apprentices who demonstrated noisily in favour of Parliament.

Political paralysis in London offered Catholic Irish landowners a chance to reverse the semi-legal plantation of their land by British settlers, many from Scotland. In October 1641 Ulster burst into revolt, creating panic throughout the three kingdoms and an insoluble crisis. Troops were needed to restore order, but who should control them? The king would not surrender his undoubted right of command. Parliament's more radical leaders, in self-preservation, dared not trust Charles with an army. In January 1642 he proved their point by invading the House of Commons with 400 bravoes, seeking to arrest five prominent opposition leaders, subsequently known as the Five Members.

The military issue split Parliament. Numerous members of both Houses who had criticized Charles remained loyal to the Crown. They resented Puritan attacks on the established church, and could not stomach the Militia Ordinance of March 1642, which gave Parliament authority to raise troops, hitherto a royal prerogative. These moderates formed a Royalist faction strong enough for Charles to make a stand. On 22 August 1642 he raised his standard at Nottingham Castle, formally beginning the English Civil War.

Driven out of London, Charles scoured the provinces for troops to reduce his own capital. He rallied sufficient support to fight a major battle at Edgehill in October, but the bloodless confrontation at Turnham Green revealed the capital's defensive strength. Outnumbered two-to-one Charles withdrew to establish his headquarters at Oxford. Hostilities spread to the regions during 1643, as both sides consolidated their position in the centre. Sir Ralph Hopton made extensive Royalist gains in the southwest, culminating in a major victory at Roundway Down (13 July) and the capture of Bristol, England's second port (26 July). The Earl of Newcastle took Yorkshire for the king after Adwalton Moor (29 June), but his offensive petered out south of the Humber, with some minor actions featuring an obscure Puritan member of Parliament called Oliver Cromwell. In the Thames valley the proximity of the main armies ensured stalemate, despite a potentially decisive confrontation at Newbury (20 September). Some historians perceive in all this a deliberate Royalist pincer movement on London, a strategy unconfirmed by contemporary sources.

English strategists called on the other kingdoms to break the deadlock. Hostilities had dragged on in Ireland, the Dublin government unable to defeat the insurgents without help from mainland Britain. In September 1643 the king sponsored a Cessation of Arms in Ireland, to free regiments sent to suppress the rising. The few troops forthcoming were mostly dispersed by Sir Thomas Fairfax at Nantwich (25 January 1644), while the king's enemies loudly denounced the Royalist use of Catholic troops. Parliament did better with the Scots, who sent 21,000 troops across the Border to help win Marston Moor

(2 July). Events in the south obscured the significance of the allied victory. Sir William Waller defeated Hopton at Cheriton (29 March), but was himself beaten at Cropredy Bridge (29 June). Parliament's commander-in-chief, the Earl of Essex, came to grief at Lostwithiel (31 August), while Charles I beat off superior numbers at Second Newbury (27 October). Summer victories proved winter stories. Invaluable blood, gallantly given, had been poured into a bag full of holes.

Parliament's material superiority was overwhelming by the end of 1644. The Roundheads controlled two-thirds of England, including London and most of the ports. Their forces outnumbered the king's two-to-one, despite startling Royalist successes in Scotland, which paralysed the Covenanter army. Recriminations after Second Newbury convinced Parliament of the need for a 'New Model Army', to replace the miscellany of regional forces that never coalesced long enough to gather the fruits of victory. Oliver Cromwell came into his own as a military organizer, pushing through legislation and lending his own religious fervour to the new formations. For the first time England had an army that believed in what it was fighting for. Cavaliers mocked the 'New Noddle', but it crushed them in months, with smashing victories at Naseby (14 June 1645) and Langport (10 July).

Winning the peace proved harder. Charles I refused all compromise, while the victors fell out. The Scots changed sides, inspiring a coalition of diehard Royalists and Presbyterian Parliamentarians who were unwilling to pay off the soldiers who had won the war. Neither would they grant religious toleration to the independent sects, which flourished among the troops. The Army crushed risings in Kent and Wales, before dealing with the Scots at Preston. Cromwell, and others, now saw Charles as a man of blood, a blasphemer who had challenged the will of God, as expressed at Naseby. The Army purged the House of Commons, going on to try and then execute Charles, not in a corner like a failed medieval king, but openly in Whitehall on 30 January 1649. England became a republic or 'Commonwealth'. Both monarchy and House of Lords were abolished, along with maypoles and mincepies.

Ireland and Scotland, however, recognized Charles II as king, provoking invasions led by Cromwell, who had achieved political and military predominance over the Rump Parliament. Colonel Michael Jones had defeated the main Irish field army at Rathmines (1649), a victory Cromwell consolidated by storming a series of Irish towns, notoriously Drogheda. Recalled to drive Charles II from Scotland, Cromwell won his most impressive victory at Dunbar (1650). Defeated in Scotland, Charles II led a last Scottish army to annihilation at Worcester (1651). The English army was triumphant, but could not devise a durable political settlement. Unable to agree with their employers in Parliament, the Army ruled through Cromwell, as 'Lord Protector'. Like Charles I, Cromwell faced insuperable financial problems, only resolved after his death in 1658, by the restoration of Charles II. A chastened Parliament paid off the troops and admitted it had been wrong all along, passing an 'Act declaring the sole right of the Militia to be in the King'.

The Civil Wars were not long and bloody simply because of the issues at stake. Changes in military technique made armies larger, and battles more frequent. At the height of the First English Civil War (1643–5) up to 150,000 Englishmen were under arms, 10 per cent of the male population. Irish armies totalled between 43,000 and 66,000 men at the end of the decade. Wastage rates were high as men fell sick or deserted, hindering the pursuit of consistent strategies. Infantry-based armies, encumbered with guns and powder wagons, moved slowly, poor roads limiting march rates to 10–13 miles (16–21 km) per day. Nevertheless, significant numbers reached the battlefield. Total combatants often exceeded 10,000, and sometimes approached 30,000. Marston Moor, with 45,000–50,000 combatants, is probably the largest battle on British soil, unless surpassed by Worcester (1651).

Most of these men were raised by compulsion, even in the New Model Army. No county was spared, but Royalist recruits tended to come from Northumberland and Lancashire, Cornwall and Wales. Parliament drew on the populous southeast. London's 400,000 inhabitants included the only significant body of troops in England at the outbreak of war, the London Trained Bands. In the provinces gentlemen and 'Parliamentary Associations' commissioned to raise regiments turned to veterans of Continental wars. Alexander Leslie, Earl of Leven, commander-in-chief of the Scots army at Newburn and Marston Moor, was one such. So were Sir Jacob Astley, Charles I's sergeant-major general, and

Sir Thomas Fairfax, the New Model Army's first commander-in-chief. For the first time inexperienced officers could study printed drill manuals.

The Civil Wars saw a remarkable number of battles, compared with earlier conflicts. Battles had become less decisive, encouraging commanders to fight them. Longer-range weapons kept armies apart, making it easier to break off unfavourable combats. Armies no longer fought in two or three inflexible 'battles', although the terminology survived. They were articulated into more numerous sub-units, regiments, brigades or 'bodies', allowing commanders to probe enemy positions, or cover a withdrawal. Hours of drill gave soldiers a moral cohesion that kept them together in defeat, inhibiting the sudden collapse that decided so many medieval actions.

Larger armies and longer range weapons expanded battlefields. Some battles remained tightly focused on a few acres (Edgehill 1642, Naseby 1645). Others extended over considerable areas (Lostwithiel 1644, Worcester 1651), or involved bold turning movements by several independent columns (Highnam 1643, Second Newbury 1644). Sometimes increased firepower produced a very modern-looking stalemate, victory going to the side that kept its nerve longest (Lansdown 1643). First Newbury (1643) was a sprawling fire fight, decided by the Royalists' ammunition shortage.

Cavalry remained the decisive arm, combining mobility with close-range firepower. Countryside was generally unenclosed, presenting few obstacles to mounted troops. Marston Moor and Naseby, among many other battles, were won by cavalry attacking the enemy infantry's flanks. The favoured proportion between the arms was one horseman to two infantry: the original New Model Army fielded 7600 horse against 14,400 foot. Scots armies rarely reached the tactically desirable ratio. Leven entered England in 1644 with 3000 horse and dragoons against 18,000 foot. Irish armies lacked effective cavalry. Horse breeding had yet to take off in Ireland, and pony-sized garrons made poor chargers.

Two types of horse soldier had become standard since the 1590s, replacing the earlier mixture of fully armoured cuirassiers, unarmoured light lances, and 'shot on horseback', with firearms. Only a few Parliamentarian cavalry turned out in full armour. Otherwise, arquebusiers or horse wore limited defensive equipment: pot helmet, backplate and breastplate over a leather buff coat, sometimes an armoured gauntlet on the left arm. There is no evidence for claims that Royalist horse were more lightly equipped. At Marston Moor they were described as standing 'like an iron wall'. Offensive weapons included carbine or arquebus, several pistols, a sword and sometimes a poleaxe. English cavalry often did without the arquebus, but generally carried them in Scotland and Ireland, where dismounted action was more common. For want of pistols, lancers featured in Scots and Irish armies, for example at Julianstown (1641) and Inverkeithing (1651), as well as at Marston Moor.

The other type of cavalry was dragoons, equipped like infantry musketeers, mounted on cheap nags for mobility. They fought on foot, leaving one man in ten to hold the horses. At Edgehill, Royalist dragoons cleared hedges on the flanks before Rupert's cavalry charged. At Naseby, Colonel John Okey's dragoons enfiladed the Royalist advance from hedges on the flank. Cavalry firearms were better quality than the matchlocks used by the infantry. Pistols and carbines were fired by wheel locks, wound up before action to discharge a stream of sparks into the priming when fired. Dragoons tried to get flintlock muskets, simpler than wheel locks but easier to handle on horseback than matchlocks.

Bills and bows had finally disappeared from English armies, along with halberd and arquebus. Civil War infantrymen, except for a few Scottish Highlanders, consisted of two standard types: pikemen and musketeers, the latter commonly termed 'shot'. The former were usually imprisoned in corselet and headpiece, but the shot went unarmoured. The proportion of pikes to muskets had declined from half to one third, and continued falling throughout the Civil Wars. Until the bayonet made every musketeer his own pikeman, however, pikes remained essential to protect musketeers against cavalry. The 16-foot (5-m) pike was more honourable, but less mobile, and quite useless in sieges or hedgerow fighting. In pitched battles, however, pikes came into their own. Even Prince Rupert's cavalry made no impression on the opposing pikemen at First Newbury.

Musketeers had least prestige, but most future, as firearms became more deadly and easier to use. The musketeer's inconveniences were considerable: the rattling of his wooden cartridges drowned out orders; misfires were as common as one shot in three; lighted matches betrayed night attacks, and caused frequent accidents as soldiers peered into half-empty powder casks, or set themselves on fire.

Nevertheless, the musket's large bullet (12 to the pound/455 g) could smash through armour, and 'spoyle man and horse at six score' paces, although combat ranges were much closer. Deep infantry formations delivered continuous rolling fire by a process known as extraduction or countermarching. The front rank fired and withdrew to the rear to reload, while successive ranks stepped forward to fire in their turn. When every man had fired the first rank were, in theory, ready to fire again. Improvements in drill and weapon design had reduced the number of ranks from ten to the six common in the Civil Wars. Doubling into three ranks allowed aggressive infantry with little ammunition to fire a single devastating volley or 'salvee', followed by an immediate charge.

Civil War field artillery has been unfairly neglected. Its inconspicuous role in well-known encounters such as Marston Moor (1644) and Naseby (1645) has left a misleading impression of tactical irrelevance. Guns were certainly clumsy and immobile. Once in position they moved with difficulty, especially as civilian drivers rarely stood about under fire. Weapons existed in a confusing range of calibres, with exotic and inconsistently applied names: basilisks, culverins, drakes and fawconets. The most common field guns were medium weapons known as minions and sakers. These fired 3 or 6lb (1.4 or 2.75 kg) projectiles respectively, usually solid round shot, perhaps once every four minutes. Ranges were some 360 yards (330 m) at 'point blank' i.e. zero elevation, or 2170 yards (1985 m) 'at utmost random'.

Contemporary generals acquired powerful trains of artillery, despite its technical limitations. The Royalists had 20 guns at Edgehill (1642), from two 24-pounder demi-cannon downwards. The New Model Army under Sir Thomas Fairfax fielded 56 field guns in 1647, besides mortars and siege guns. Fire support was sufficiently important for generals to direct individual guns, as the Earl of Newcastle did at Adwalton Moor (1643). Sir Ralph Hopton attacked at Braddock Down (1643) to forestall the appearance of hostile artillery.

Artillery fulfilled various roles on the battlefield. Lacking range and mobility, lighter pieces were distributed in pairs along the front of the army, for close support. Heavier guns could form a battery and fire overhead, or provide a rallying point for shattered infantry. In sufficient numbers guns might prepare an attack, as the Scottish artillery did at Newburn in 1640. Fairfax prepared the way for a risky cavalry charge at Langport (1645) with a protracted bombardment. Irish armies were particularly skittish under artillery fire. Earl Inchiquin drew the Munster Confederates from an advantageous position at Knocknanuss (1647) by firing guns into their flank.

Overall tactics followed Continental developments, especially those in the Dutch and Swedish armies, where thousands of English and Scots volunteers had served. In principle the infantry formed the centre of the battle line, with cavalry protecting the flanks. Pikemen and musketeers combined for mutual protection against enemy horse, who could pistol unsupported pikemen, or ride down undefended musketeers. Infantry fought six deep in small flexible bodies of about 500, a central stand of pikes flanked by wings of shot. Each file of six occupied a frontage of 3 feet (0.9 m) in 'order', the standard fighting formation. Some writers make this the distance between files, excluding the men. This increases frontages by 50 per cent, but most contemporary authorities support the lesser figure. Individual bodies of foot might therefore occupy 80–100 yards (70–90 m).

These small formations were usually arranged chequerboard fashion in two staggered lines, supporting units covering intervals in the front line. Historians and contemporary drill manuals disagree over the extent of these gaps, which might be very small, as in Robert Streater's contemporary picture map of Naseby. Sometimes more complex brigade formations were used, as deployed by the Royalists at Edgehill. Infantry fighting began with 'forlorn hopes' of musketeers driving in the enemy's skirmishers or *enfants perdus* ('lost children'), while the main bodies advanced more circumspectly. Once within musket shot, these would exchange fire before coming to push of pike, a frightening but not particularly lethal scrum. If neither side broke, both would fall back a few paces, plant their colours in the ground and blaze away until darkness or the cavalry intervened.

Horse were organized in small troops of 40 to 60 men, but usually fought in composite bodies, placed like the infantry in a chequered formation. At the start of the First English Civil War, there were two schools of cavalry tactics. Parliamentarian horse fought six ranks deep, receiving the enemy's charge at a stand in order to blaze away with firearms. Prince Rupert introduced the Swedish practice of charging in three ranks, reserving pistols for the melee. The latter tactic proved more effective, and became general. Cavalry left considerable space between files while manoeuvring, closing up before contact. New Model Army troopers were instructed to charge with knees locked together with those of their neighbours 'as close as they can well endure', troops 100 paces distance behind one another, and 'no man should fire till he came within a horse's length of the enemy'. Mounted troops, therefore, might require 5 feet (1.5 m) per file when drawn up; less during a charge.

Wild images of galloping Cavaliers are misleading. Charges began at an easy trot, building up to 'a round trot and charge'. Prince Rupert swept all before him at Powick Bridge (1642) and Edgehill (1642), but cavalry fights could easily bog down into a confused melee. At Marston Moor (1644) Cromwell's horse stood, as he described it, 'at sword's point a pretty while, hacking one another', before the Royalists broke. At Winceby (1643) Fairfax committed fresh troops to break the deadlock. A broader sample of Civil War battles than Edgehill discredits the myth of the dashing Cavalier unable to rally after a first charge: at Hopton Heath (19 March 1643) and Roundway Down (13 July 1643) Royalist horse charged and rallied repeatedly. On the other hand, Parliamentarian horse pursued their immediate opponents 6 miles (10 km) at Gainsborough (28 July 1643), leaving Cromwell only a few scattered troops to oppose the Royalist reserve. A cynic might attribute the success of Cromwell's cavalry at Marston Moor and Naseby as much to superior numbers as their ability to rally for a second charge.

Cavalry mattered because they were the dominant arm. England's unprecedented conquest of the other two kingdoms depended in the final resort upon its ability to bring superior numbers of good cavalry to the battlefield. Cromwell had more horse than the Scots at Dunbar, despite heavy wastage during the preceding campaign. The English had 1300 cavalry to 500 at Knockbrack (1651), the last battle in Ireland, although they were outnumbered overall. It is entirely appropriate that the best-remembered leaders of the wars should be Rupert and Cromwell.

'Twas Thus that the Wars Began

Charles I's three kingdoms had been a rare example of stability in a Europe torn apart by the Thirty Years' War. This happy state might have continued indefinitely except for royal attempts to enforce ecclesiastical uniformity throughout Britain, a policy that politicized Charles's subjects and revealed his financial weakness.

The Church of England and the Church of Scotland are distinct institutions, reflecting the different paths the Reformation took in those countries. The Scottish Kirk has followed the Presbyterian model of Protestantism, governed by locally elected elders, although James VI had reinstated bishops. Charles I sought to extend episcopal power, even threatening to restore church lands acquired by secular landowners. Introduction of a modified English Prayer Book into Scotland in 1637 was thus a focus for wider grievances. Popular opposition grew from riots in St Giles Cathedral in Edinburgh into the National Covenant of January 1639, a radical manifesto justifying revolt in defence of established law and religion.

Charles I's attempts to crush his opponents in Scotland led to the First and Second Bishops' Wars (1639 and 1640). The first was largely theatre: neither side wanted an old-style Anglo-Scots war. Charles's deliberate advance on the Border failed to impress the politely defiant Scots. English mobilization was a shambles of untrained and unwilling soldiers, with rotten weapons and worse discipline. Alexander Leslie, the Covenanters' commander-in-chief, bluffed the Royalists into believing themselves outnumbered 45,000 to 15,000, and both sides were glad to sign the Treaty of Berwick (18 June) restoring the *status quo ante*. The only fighting was in northeast Scotland, where Covenanters gained control of Aberdeen after skirmishes at Turriff, Megray Hill and Brig o'Dee.

Charles refused to accept the result of the First Bishops' War. He planned a further invasion next year, despite a worsening financial and political situation after he dissolved the Short Parliament in May 1640. The threat persuaded the Scots to launch a preemptive strike, taking the English by surprise. They forced the Tyne at Newburn Ford (28 August), and occupied Newcastle, the source of London's coal. Unable to remove the Scots by military means, Charles had to buy them off, giving him no choice but to call a fresh Parliament. Charles's incompetence in pursuing a war with neither money nor weapons shook his supporters' loyalty, while the continued Scots presence encouraged the disaffected to proceed to extremes.

Parliamentary attacks on royal policies and advisers combined with economic distress to deepen the crisis. Disorder in London made the king strengthen his guards, aggravating distrust of royal intentions. Parliament's impeachment and execution of Thomas Wentworth, Earl of Strafford, for planning to introduce Irish troops into England permanently estranged Charles from the legislature. It also weakened royal government in Ireland, where Strafford's iron rule had alienated all political classes.

Ireland was a British colony, where institutional confiscation of Catholic-owned land by blatant legal chicanery went on in a manner inconceivable in England or Scotland. 'New English' settlers (many of them Scots) ruthlessly exploited 'quirks and quiddities of the law' to prevent the Roman Catholic majority selling or inheriting land. Protestant immigrants benefited from plantation schemes that impoverished Gaelic landowners in Ulster and Connacht. The 'Old English' – descendants of the Anglo-Norman invaders – dabbled in confiscated estates, but rightly feared an alliance between London Puritans, Scots Covenanters and New English against them. During the Bishops' Wars, Charles I plotted with Randal MacDonnell, Earl of Antrim, to use Irish troops against the Campbells of Argyll, leading Covenanters and Antrim's clan rivals. These intrigues destabilized Ulster, where the Scots' assertion of religious independence invited imitation.

Insurrection broke out on 2 October 1641, with attacks across Ulster by dispossessed Gaelic landowners on government forts and British settlers. Some 4000 settlers died, a figure wildly exaggerated by Protestant propagandists to justify disproportionately savage reprisals. The conspirators failed, however, to seize Dublin Castle, allowing the British to pour in reinforcements. By the summer of 1642 the government had some 45,000 regular troops in Ireland, compared to 70,000 rebel militia. However, the outbreak of the English Civil War prevented a speedy conclusion to the struggle, which grew into the Eleven Years' War (also known as the Confederate War), the central event of Irish military history.

After the insurgent success at Julianstown (November 1641) a local populist uprising grew into a regular war. Old English Palesmen joined landless Gaelic gentry and peasants in a Catholic Confederation based at Kilkenny. The Remonstrance of Catholics of Ireland (December 1641) justified their action as self-defence against a Scottish invasion, sword and Bible in hand, directed by the English Parliament. In Ireland there were relatively few formal battles. Government victories at Kilrush and Liscarroll (1642) revealed the insurgents' tactical weakness, presaging their eventual defeat.

Turriff (the Trot of Turriff), **14 May 1639**

Scotland, Aberdeenshire, LR29 NJ7249–50

The opening engagements of the Civil Wars hardly merit the description of 'battle'. The first fatality was one David Prat, shot during an abortive Royalist attempt on Towie Barclay Castle south of Turriff, on 10 May 1639. Four days later his friends tried again at Turriff itself.

A key element in Charles I's strategy against the Covenanters was an amphibious landing in north-east Scotland to support a Royalist uprising by George Gordon, Marquess of Huntly. The naval task force never materialized, and Huntly was arrested, while under safe conduct, and imprisoned at Edinburgh. His followers regrouped at Strathbogie, and decided to beat up their opponents' quarters in the small market town of Turriff. The Covenanters had more men, but the Royalists had 600 proper infantry and two troops of horse, while Colonel Johnstone, a professional, assisted the gentlemen in nominal charge. The Royalists also had four small brass field guns.

Turriff's elevated position gave its defenders good observation over the surrounding countryside, while steep slopes down to the River Deveron and Idoch Water protected the south and west sides of the town, towards Strathbogie. Perhaps for this reason, the Royalists decided on a night approach, some 15 miles (24 km). Their natural route lay along the modern A97 as far as Haddo, then turning east either along the B9024 or following the banks of the Deveron. The latter made for a troublesome march, but led straight on to the objective, preventing the Royalists getting lost.

They arrived at 'peip of day', to the Covenanters' surprise, 'sum war sleeping in their bedis, uther sum drinking and smoaking tabacca' (John Spalding). The Covenanters had no time to assemble their

Turriff

	Winner	*Loser*
Opponents	Royalist	Covenanter
Commanders	Colonel William Johnstone Sir George Ogilvy of Banff	Sir William Hay of Delgaty
Numbers	800	1200
Losses	1 killed	2 killed

superior numbers, although Johnstone took the risky step of marching up the Idoch under the defenders' noses, to gain the east end of the village. This was the best line of attack, 'being open, without any gate or porte, and it capable to receave a number of horse or foote a breaste; beside the feeld harde by the streete levell and usefull for drawing upp a greate number of men for reserve' (James Gordon, Minister of Rothiemay).

Conflicting accounts state the Covenanters either drew up in the open or behind hastily thrown up barricades, the contradiction underlining their confusion. The Royalist artillery fired a couple of rounds and the infantry rushed forward, pulling down the barricades and shooting down the street. The Covenanter infantry refused to stand, despite their leaders' 'faire persusasione and … threttings', and fell back towards the church. A final cannon shot and the appearance of the Royalist horse scattered them at such speed that people subsequently spoke of 'the Trot of Turriff'.

Casualties were few. The Covenanters never stood to fight, and the Royalists let them go, suspecting an ambush. The one Royalist fatality was killed accidentally, 'by the unskillfullnesse of his owne comerades' (Gordon). They insisted on firing a farewell volley over his grave inside the church, nearly shooting the minister, who was hiding in the loft dressed as a woman. Strategic consequences were hardly more significant, although the Gordons briefly occupied Aberdeen. However, lacking external direction they dispersed, and the Covenanters regained control of the city.

Directions

Turriff is on the A947 Aberdeen–Banff road, the town centre northwest of the main road. The battlefield is now built over, but presumably Johnstone crossed the Idoch at Bridgend, and formed up across the Cuminestown road facing left, before advancing down the main street.

Megray Hill (Stonehaven), Saturday 15 June 1639

Scotland, Aberdeenshire, LR45 NO8786–7

Brig o' Dee, Tuesday 18–Wednesday 19 June 1639

Scotland, Aberdeen, LR38 NJ9203

Montrose is one of the great romantic figures of the Civil Wars, responsible for a string of Royalist victories from Tippermuir to Kilsyth (1644–5). He first appeared on a British battlefield on the other side, winning skirmishes for the Covenant at Megray Hill and Brig o' Dee.

After Turriff a Royalist military mission arrived by sea under Huntly's son, Viscount Aboyne, retaking Aberdeen for the king. Less fortunately for the cause, Aboyne brought Colonel Gunn, a veteran of the Thirty Years' War, whose conduct does little for the image of 17th-century military professionalism. On 14 June 1639 Aboyne marched out of Aberdeen to attack a Covenanter garrison at Stonehaven. The enemy commander, hereditary Earl Marischal of Scotland, prepared to dispute Cowie Water, which flows northwest from Stonehaven Bay, along the northern edge of the town. Hill of Megray (400 feet/ 122 m) lies just over a mile (1.6 km) further north, commanding the Muchalls road from Aberdeen. The battlefield makes a triangle, enclosed by Cowie Water on the west, Megray Hill's two round heights to the north, and the coast running northeast from Stonehaven through Cowie.

The Covenanters were at less of a disadvantage than the numbers suggest. Montrose and Keith had 14 guns, two of them 24-pounder demi-cannon, while Aboyne fielded 500 Highlanders, who failed to sustain their military reputation. Keith had ordered his men to leave open the gates of Dunnotar Castle, just south of Stonehaven, to facilitate a speedy retreat, but there was no need. Once the Royalists had occupied Megray Hill soon after dawn on the 15th, they put off further operations while Aboyne and Gunn had breakfast.

Johnstone's frustrated cavalry skirmished with the Covenanter outposts, inexperienced troopers firing at too great distance to do any harm, or falling off horses still unused to the service. Both sides committed their supports, 'such as pleased falling in, and such as wanted courage keeping off'. Whether by accident or design, the Covenanters fell back, drawing the enemy cavalry within range of Stonehaven, where Keith's guns let fly, 'so that now they who but immediately before wer so eager in ther poursuite wer glade to runne of in disorder, not having any enemy to cope withal but canon and muskett shot' (James Gordon, Minister of Rothiemay).

Having repelled the Royalist horse, the Covenanter guns turned on their infantry, drawn out across the brow of Megray Hill, just within range of the two heavy guns: 'some balles went over them ... some fell short and but one lighted amongst them, whereby some were hurt and some slaine, but not many' (Patrick Gordon of Ruthven, *A Short Abridgement of Britane's Distemper*). This was too much for the Highlanders, who retreated over the hill to a bog half a mile (0.8 km) to the rear, presumably the burn that falls into the sea just north of Red Man. The Lowland foot 'beganne now to mutinee against Gunne', who withdrew them onto the reverse slope around Logie Farm (NJ8888), away from Montrose's two cannon. During the afternoon, the Highlanders 'beganne to dropp awaye and marche off in whole companyes'. The Lowlanders followed, leaving only the cavalry to cover the retreat to Aberdeen. The whole affair was 'so ridiculously and grossly managed that in all the warre, nothing can be recounted lycke it' (Gordon).

Megray Hill

	Winner	*Loser*
Opponents	Covenanter	Royalist
Commanders	James Graham, Earl of Montrose	James Gordon, Viscount Aboyne
	William Keith, Earl Marischal	Colonel William Gunn
		Colonel William Johnstone
Numbers	1200	2500
Losses	unknown	unknown

Brig o' Dee

	Winner	*Loser*
Opponents	Covenanter	Royalist
Commanders	James Graham, Earl of Montrose	James Gordon, Viscount Aboyne
	William Keith, Earl Marischal	Colonel William Gunn
		Colonel William Johnstone (w)
Numbers	2300	300–500
Losses	30–40	14–18

Unaware of their victory, the Covenanters did not follow up until the 17th. The disintegration of Aboyne's army left him just 180 Gordon horse and a handful of foot to defend the approach to Aberdeen, across Bridge of Dee. The seven-arched stone bridge, with its turreted gatehouse, was the only practicable crossing, as the river was in spate, blocking fords nearby and upstream at Banchory Devenick. Johnstone had fortified the southern end of the bridge with earthworks, held by a company of Aberdeen militiamen, working in two 50-man shifts. The Royalist horse and remains of the Strathbogie regiment stood by on the Aberdeen side of the river.

Montrose appeared over Kincorth Hill at dawn on 18 June, with some 300 horse, 2000 foot and the guns that did the business at Megray Hill. The demicannon outranged the defenders' muskets and field pieces, but deployed too far back and left of the bridge. Throughout Tuesday their oblique fire was so ineffectual that militiamen's wives served refreshments to the defending troops. Two Covenanter companies from Dundee rushed the bridgehead about noon, but received so hot a welcome they quickly retreated, pursued by whoops of derision from the crowd of spectators. Only one Royalist fatality is recorded on the 18th, and another man 'rakleslie schot in the foot'.

Overnight Montrose moved his artillery east to fire along the bridge, half of whose defenders had gone off to their comrade's funeral. The rest were soon pinned down in their earthwork, as cannonballs flew down the roadway or knocked lumps off the gatehouse. Some Covenanter cavalry drew Gunn's attention in the direction of Banchory, whither he led the Gordon horse, ignoring protests that the ford was impassable. Montrose's artillery redoubled its fire, bringing down a gatehouse turret on top of Johnstone. His men carried him off with a broken leg, leaving the bridge undefended. The Strathbogie men slipped away, allowing a Covenanter storming party across without a fight.

Royalist casualty figures range from 4 to 18 killed, although 48 militia were thrown into the Tolbooth as prisoners of war. The attackers' losses may have been twice as many, the bodies buried in the mosses on the south bank. Colonel Gunn later alleged Montrose and the earl marischal received shots through hat and hair respectively, though his claim to have beaten them off suggests he was romancing. Montrose prevented an immediate sack of the town, which was saved by news of a ceasefire, ending the First Bishops' War.

Directions

Megray Hill *Today the A90 and the Aberdeen–Montrose railway cut through the lower slopes of the hill, where the cavalry skirmished. Follow the B979 north through New Mains of Ury to Forester's Croft where a footpath on the right leads back over the hill through the Royalist position. In Stonehaven a minor road opposite the distillery runs along Cowie Water's right bank, the Covenanter's probable gun line.*

Brig o' Dee *The medieval bridge is still a major river crossing, taken by the A90. View the battlefield from the landscaped riverbanks southwest of the river. Kincorth housing estate now occupies the Covenanter position. A school and roundabout mark the probable location of the Royalist cavalry and supports on the north bank.*

Newburn Ford, 28 August 1640

England, Newcastle-upon-Tyne, LR88 NZ1664–5

The only engagement of the Second Bishops' War took place 5 miles (8 km) west of Newcastle at Newburn Ford on the River Tyne. It was the first major Scots victory over the English since Byland (1322), and did comparable political damage.

Charles's continued quarrel with the Scots over the Prayer Book gave the Covenanters a choice between awaiting invasion or invading first and feeding their troops at English expense. The Covenanter army crossed the Tweed on 20 August 1640, the first Scottish invasion since Flodden (1513), and moved down the old Roman road past Hedgeley Moor (1464). Leslie's ambiguous strategy left the English uncertain as to whether he would strike at Newcastle or Hexham, 20 miles (30 km) further west. In the event he advanced between them, aiming to cross the Tyne at Newburn and approach Newcastle from its unfortified southern side. English forces were few and poor quality: 'cart-horses ... and men that are fit for Bedlam and Bridewell', as the Royalist commander, Viscount Conway, reported. When Leslie appeared at Heddon Law (476 feet/145 m), 3 miles (5 km) northwest of Newburn, on 27 August, he outnumbered the defenders nearly four to one.

Contemporaries put Conway's numbers at 3000–7500; modern historians compromise on 1500 horse and 3000 foot, with 8 field guns. Most of these were at Stella Haugh, a level stretch of ground extending east from Newburn towards a deep bend in the south bank. Within view of the crossing place, they were out of range of artillery north of the river. Some 800 musketeers occupied a couple of sconces or redoubts near the bank, covering the southern exits from two fords: one near the modern bridge, the other further east, in a bend of the river now occupied by a power station. Their exact locations are now uncertain, since the Tyne was straightened during the 19th century. The fords were tidal, too deep to cross at high water.

Leslie's numbers were augmented by a powerful

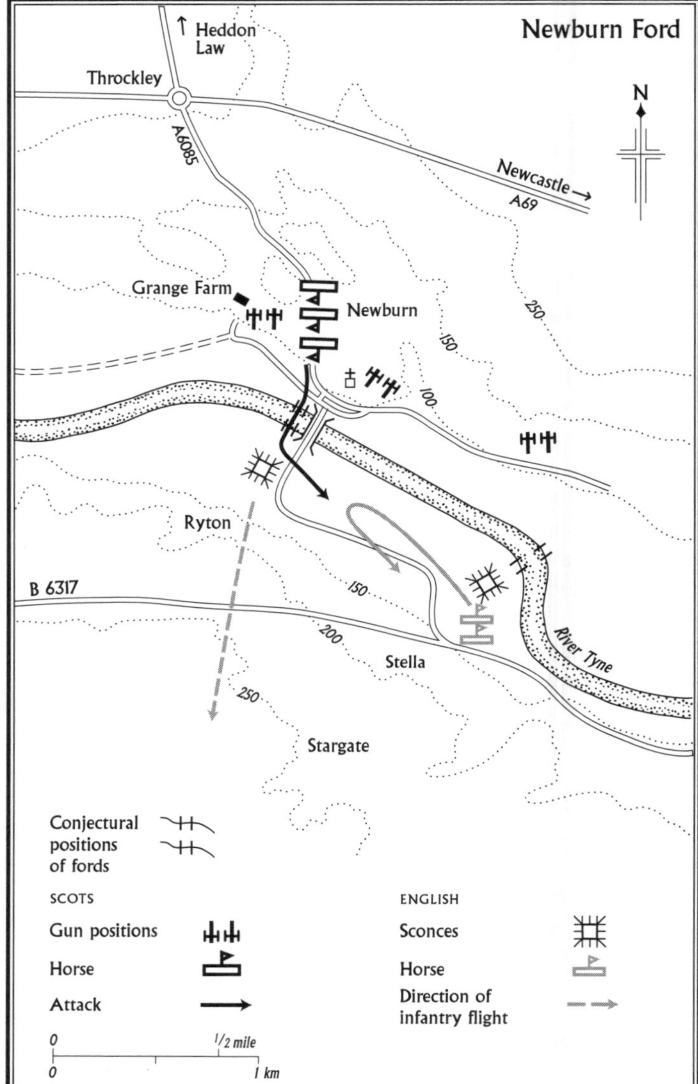

Directions

Turn south off the A69 Newcastle – Hexham road at Throckley to Newburn along the A6085. Head west from the church to the Tyne Riverside Country Park to view the modern bridge and the Scots artillery positions around Grange Farm. An electricity substation covers the site of the cavalry action. Traces of earthworks are said to be visible from footpaths south of Newburn Bridge, where some open ground remains on the round spur above Stella, north of Stargate on the A695.

artillery. He had at least 40 cannon, most of them demi-culverins firing a 9 or 10lb (4 or 4.5 kg) ball, outclassing the 6lb (2.75 kg) shot of Conway's sakers. Leslie concealed his guns on the wooded slopes either side of Newburn, dominating the miserable English breastworks, barely half a yard (0.45 m) high, 'where we lay so exposed to their battery that their great shot was bowled in amongst our men to their great loss and such confusion as made them quit their works' (Captain Thomas Dymoke).

The armies spent the morning of 28 August watering their horses on opposite river banks, until an English musketeer shot a Scottish officer off his horse about 2 p.m. The fusillade became general. About 4 p.m. the Scots mounted two light guns or fframes in Newburn church tower, 'which commaunded our workes and battered them so muche that they that weare in one of them fled and forsooke the work' (Dymoke). Soon after the garrison of the work further downstream decamped, throwing away their

Newburn Ford

	Winner	*Loser*
Opponents	Covenanter	Royalist
Commanders	Sir Alexander Leslie	Edward, Viscount Conway Lord Henry Wilmot (p)
Numbers	17,000	4500
Losses	c.300	c.300

arms and blowing up the ready-use powder store.

Low tide was between two and three, allowing Scots cavalry to pass across, followed by great numbers of infantry. The English horse had been awaiting such a move in the meadow east of the abandoned sconces. They immediately counter-charged, despite raking fire from Scottish guns across the river to their right. Commissary General Wilmot broke in among the Scots horse, killing several with his own hand, and receiving a pistol shot in the face. The Scots staggered, but rallied as the English troopers failed to follow their leaders. Sir Henry Vane, the principal secretary of state with the king, reported to his London counterpart: 'Our horse did not behave well, many ran away and did not second those that were first charged.'

The English foot had retreated up Ryton and Stella Banks, where Sir Jacob Astley rallied them in a wood. As they moved forward to support six troops of horse making a stand on the hillside, more Scots cavalry came up and beat them again: 'The fight was sharp and short, the flight general, and the foot being overrun by the horse in a narrow lane fled for company' (Dymoke). Wilmot was left for dead. The English horse and foot retreated separately, first to Durham and Newcastle respectively, then to York. Only logistical problems halted the Scots at the Tees.

Charles had lost the war in a day. Courtiers could not comprehend what the Earl of Clarendon, in his *History of the Rebellion*, called 'the most shameful and confounding rout that was ever heard of'. Conway more realistically blamed 'the disadvantage of the ground, and the slight fortification, which the shortness of the time would not afford to be better'. Dymoke pointed to the decision to fight 'in a low valley exposed to the enemy's ordnance, which almost encompassed us on the hills'. Casualties were surprisingly few: Secretary Vane thought 100 common soldiers died, against Dymoke's estimate of 300, which might include wounded. Scots losses were similar.

Charles's attempt to make war without parliamentary approval or money had brought tactical and political disaster. He now had to pay the Scots £850 a day living expenses to spare northern England the horror of German-style free quarters made notorious by the Thirty Years' War. On 24 September a Great Council of Peers recommended parliamentary elections as the only way to raise the money, setting the stage for further turmoil.

Julianstown, Monday 29 November 1641

Ireland, Co. Meath, DS43 O1271

The Irish insurrection began as a peasant uprising directed at Protestant settlers. The settlers took refuge in towns such as Drogheda, besieged by 5000–6000 insurgents from 21 November 1641. A relieving column of 50 horse and 600 foot reached Balrothery, 11 miles (18 km) south of Drogheda, on 28 November. Morale was poor. Strafford's Old English companies had been filled up with disaffected Irish or half-trained Anglo-Scots refugees from the North, who had lost their courage along with their goods.

The English commander, Sir Patrick Wemyss, pressed on at first light, through autumnal mist, to Julianstown on the River Nanny. He presumably followed the modern main road, which he described as 'a dirty lane, and a high ditch on every side of us'. Three troopers scouted ahead, but while they ate breakfast in an alehouse, a boy ran away with one of their horses and alerted the enemy. The whole party had just crossed Julianstown bridge when they saw the enemy within musket-shot range, 'advancing towards us in as good order as ever I saw any men'.

Wemyss reported three troops of lancers and two of horse with pistols on the wings, a little in advance of five great bodies of foot in the centre, and two field pieces. He claimed 3000 insurgents, but the commander-in-chief in Dublin, James Butler, Marquess of Ormond, estimated only 1500, 'verie meanly armid with sutch wapines as wold sho them to be a toumoultuarey rable than anything like an armey'. Contemporary depositions confirm Ormond's dim view of rebel equipment, listing clubs and pitchforks alongside firelocks and half-pikes; the English on the other hand 'had as maeny aerms as all the rebells in the kingdoume, and war as well trenid as they'.

Wemyss ordered his officers to deploy in a field beside the road, but a British officer with Sir John Clotworthy's regiment in Ulster wrote that the Irish attack caught the English still in the narrow lane. An English lieutenant 'gave the unseasonable word of counter-march', intending his men to commence firing by rank and filing away to reload, but they misunderstood. Intimidated by the enemy's wild shouting, they fell into disorder and began a general retreat. Wemyss had just sounded the charge when his troopers cried out that 'the foot had left their officers, thrown down their arms, and took themselves to running'. Ormond reported: 'They betook themselves to their heels upon sichtt of the enimey, not onse shouting one shott or streeyking one stroke.' The insurgents were equally confused. Thinking the officer had called out in Irish '*Contuirt bhais!*' ('danger of death'), they fell on sharply and cut the opposition to pieces. Wemyss escaped to Drogheda with about 100 horse, complaining about those who had underestimated the enemy. Drogheda would not be relieved until the following March.

Julianstown

	Winner	*Loser*
Opponents	Irish	English
Commanders	Rory O'Moore	Sir Patrick Wemyss
Numbers	1500	650
Losses	unknown	500

Directions

Follow the N1 from Julianstown towards Drogheda: the battlefield is an unspecified distance north of the river; 1/4 mile (0.4 km) would allow enough road space for the fighting component of Wemyss's force to have got across.

Kilrush (Cnocaterife), 15 April 1642

Ireland, Co. Kildare, DS55 N7601–7802

Ormond's easy victory at Kilrush suggests how readily the English might have suppressed the Irish rebellion without the Civil Wars at home. The lord lieutenant sortied from Dublin on 2 April with 500 horse, 3000 foot and five guns to re-establish communications with his Kilkenny estates. He was at Athy by the 14th, after recapturing various castles without loss, except for detachments left as garrisons. The insurgents took nearly a fortnight to gather sufficient troops at Maganey, 5 miles (8 km) down the River Barrow from Athy, to pursue Ormond: 'being double the number of the Marquis, they thought without difficulty to have cut off his army ... tired and harassed with long marches and want' (Clarendon, *History of the Rebellion*).

The two armies raced for Ballyshannon, where the Athy–Kilcullen road crosses the River Greese, arriving more or less simultaneously. Richard Bellings, secretary to the Catholic Confederation, was its official historian:

> Both armyes marched the next morning in sight one of the other. The English to regain their way, still fell to the right hand and neare the Irish, who moving with the same speed must sooner have come to Kilrush, which was the centre, and crossing them there, the fight was unavoydable.

The collision occurred at Kilrush 7 miles (11 km) northeast of Athy. Numerous place-names, apart from the battle's name, place the action there, for example Battlemount just to the south. The conflict's

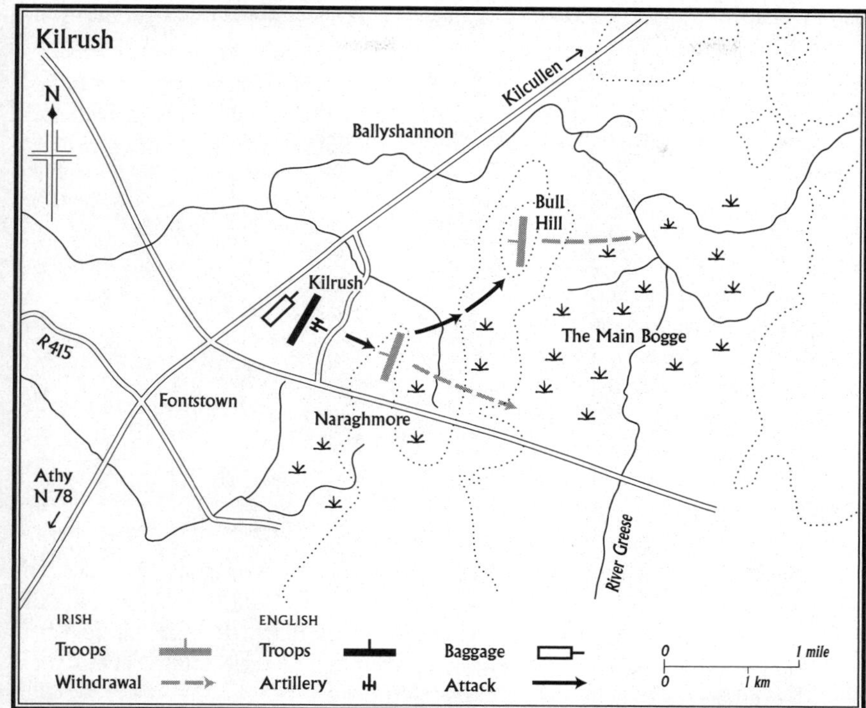

Gaelic name translates as 'Bullhill', a height between Kilrush and Ballyshannon. An Irish gentleman left his sick bed at Mullaghmast, 3 miles (5 km) away, to die in the fighting. After the battle, Ormond slept at Madinestown or Maddenstown a few miles north of Kilrush.

A battle map that accompanied the official English report shows the English with their backs to the Athy road, facing southeast across a deep lane (still extant) towards the main Irish position on a spur of high ground, extending north of Narraghmore. More Confederates occupy a hill on Ormond's left, consistent with the direction of Bullhill, too near Ballyshannon for Ormond to cross the ford without a fight. Innumerable winding streams still drain the 'bogge yet passible' shown on Ormond's right and 'the main bogge they fled unto', beyond Bullhill.

The Confederates outnumbered Ormond two-to-one, but one of their own officers, the anonymous author of *An Aphorismical Discovery of Treasonable Faction*, describes them as 'a rabble of disarmed fresh water souldiers, without armes, ammunition or souldier commanders'. Most were peasants recruited in the last ten days, 'of whom the most parte had never before that time faced an enemy'. Only 100 were cavalry. Munitions consisted of one barrel of powder. Besides these disadvantages, 'being joined but the night before, the command in chiefe was not absolutely established in any one person' (Bellings). MacPhelim O'Byrne was 'of opinion not to give a field at all upon such odds', but Mountgarrett and the commonalty were 'of a contrarie sense' (*Aphorismical Discovery*).

Bellings states the Confederates 'made up three divisions, whereof each was to second the other'. This agrees roughly with the map, which shows two

Directions

Take the N78 northeast from Athy. Turn right just after Fontstown and along a minor road then left into the deep lane along which Ormond formed up. Regain the main road and take the next right to Bullhill.

bodies 'some 3000 in sight' in front of Ormond behind a dry ditch on the hill, a troop of horse on each flank, and 4000 foot in two bodies on Bullhill. The gap in the line may reflect tactical disagreements, one Confederate commander placing himself 'the other side of the enemie ... as not pleased with the managinge of affaires'. Commanded musketeers screened the front, 'without sconce, shelter, or defence ... being not in posture of an armie bodie ...' (*Aphorismical Discovery*). Ormond's army on the other hand consisted of 'disciplined men, disposed into regiments and companies under the command of officers to whose direction they had been used' (Bellings). Their deployment reflected superior tactical ability: eight bodies of 300 foot in two lines of three and four units each, with a reserve; and eight troops of 50 horse, three on the right and five on the left. Second-line units covered the intervals between those in front. The guns stood in front along the lane, half a mile (0.8 km) from the enemy.

Ormond's artillery opened fire and the musketeers advanced, 'by every step gaining ground, advancing to the verie brest of the Irish musketires, seconded by a select and choice troupe of horse'. The Confederate shot promptly 'showed heels', precipitating general panic among their infantry, 'though far from present danger' (*Aphorismical Discovery*). Bellings suggests the Irish stood a little longer: 'The [English] horse that charged the first division in finding some resistance they wheeled about, and coming upon the last division ... that brake and the rest followed'. Sir Charles Coote, 'that inhumaine bloudsucker', charged like a man of 30 rather than 60, 'crying "kill, kill", and with his hand set the example'.

Kilrush

	Winner	*Loser*
Opponents	English	Confederate
Commanders	James Butler, Marquess of Ormond	Colonel Hugh MacPhelim O'Byrne Viscount Mountgarrett
Numbers	2800	6000–7000
Losses	c.100	100–700

Had the bogs not been so near, few Confederates would have escaped. Bellings thought 'scarce 100 men killed and noe prisoners taken', although Protestant sources claimed 700 dead. The makeshift Irish army disintegrated, everyone to their own home. Dublin officials reported a great victory, but dared not stir out of town without a troop of horse. They wrote plaintively of finishing the war quickly, 'if our troops were come that are designed'. Kilrush remained a portent of what might have been.

Liscarroll, Saturday 3 September 1642

Ireland, Co. Cork, DS73 R4411–4511

The pattern of the Eleven Years' War was fixed early in Munster. Baron Inchiquin's tactical success at Liscarroll saved Cork for the English, but logistical weakness prevented him regaining rebel-held areas further west.

Limerick fell to the Confederates on 24 July 1642. Spoils included a 32-pounder demi-cannon and two lighter guns. These were used to reduce English strongholds in west Munster, 25 yoke of oxen dragging the 3-ton demi-cannon across near-impassable bogs in a hollowed tree trunk. In August General Barry moved to eliminate the Protestants' last redoubt in Co. Cork, appearing before Liscarroll, the northern entry to the Blackwater valley on Tuesday the 30th. Helpless before the Confederate battery piece, the 30-man garrison of Liscarroll Castle surrendered on Friday. Barry's next objective was Doneraile, 9 miles (14.5 km) further east, but Inchiquin forestalled him. The Munster Protestants, for whom 'English' was a political rather than ethnic label, preferred fighting two-to-one odds to leaving their fortresses to be picked off piecemeal. They concentrated their garrisons at Mallow, and appeared before the startled Confederates early on Saturday 3 September.

Barry had gathered a large army, 500 horse and 6000 foot, ill furnished with arms and undisciplined. Inchiquin's initial strength was 400 horse, 250 pikes and 1600 shot, reinforced overnight by 500 unspecified infantry, perhaps pikemen left behind during the forced march. He did not advance directly from Mallow, preferring the Limerick road through Buttevant, where cavalry had been stationed to observe Confederate operations. Next morning Inchiquin marched east, presumably along the modern R255 to Liscarroll. The infantry followed 2 miles (3 km) behind the cavalry, who beat in the enemy scouts, and advanced to the top of an unidentified hill near Liscarroll to view the Confederate camp.

South and west of Liscarroll the country was suitable for military operations, although according to the anonymous eyewitness author of *A Discourse of the Battell at Liscarroll*, 'in the North and East it abounds with woods boggs waters furzes not usefull for the service of Horse'. Barry had a choice of positions: open ground clear of the castle and village to the west, or the ridge south of Liscarroll, which runs obliquely across the direct road from Mallow and that via Buttevant. Contemporary accounts fit either location: 'The ground between them was a valley, which neither ... could pass without great disorder' (Richard Bellings); the terrain was also described as 'a plaine flat valley ... about twenty score [a quarter mile (0.4 km)] in breadth'. All agree Barry was advantageously posted, left flank resting on the castle, his guns 'upon a little round hill neere the Castle where they were first planted and verie well fortified' (*Discourse*). Inchiquin's corresponding locations would either be on the ridge, uncomfortably close to the enemy-held castle, or further southeast, on the high ground towards Gurteenroe, where the road from Buttevant would have brought him. In the latter scenario, whose grid references appear above, Barry's infantry would comfortably fit the mile-long (1.6-km) ridge, in three large bodies of 2000 each. His cavalry were 'all in one intire body' on the right.

Fighting began with a nearly harmless artillery duel, except for five Confederate infantry killed in file by a single shot. Musketeers and commanded horse bickered over a ditch 100 yards (90 m) in front of the Confederate position, perhaps the stream flowing northeast below the Liscarroll and Gurteenroe ridges. The Irish having the worst of it, a few English horse crossed the ditch. The whole Confederate cavalry advanced, incidentally presenting their flank to the body of English horse. Inchiquin naturally charged the open flank, 'being resolved to putt the whole stake upon the game' (*Discourse*). Despite their disadvantage, the Irish horse countercharged with equal determination, denying the better-equipped English time to fire their pistols. Charging pell-mell, the Irish caught the English in mid-caracole, the latters' front ranks wheeling to the rear to reload. The English rear ranks mistook the manoeuvre for a retreat, and, 'unable to resist the enemy's shocke and the violence of the impression they [the Irish] made, turned and ran away' (Bellings). Wounded and alone, Inchiquin was nearly captured by the opposing cavalry commander, 'hooded downe with his helmet', until Inchiquin's foster brother 'layed his pistol unawares on the gentleman's eyepiece and shott him through his head' (*Aphorismical Discovery*).

Meanwhile the English foot repelled an advance by 'the whole bodie of the Rebell Army', buying Inchiquin time to rally his cavalry and counterattack the Confederate horse, 'At this time ... scattered all over the field in pursuit of the English soe as hardly could twenty of them be seen in a body' (*Discourse*). Deprived of their own leader, the Irish horse fell back and broke. Few were killed before Inchiquin saw formed troops still on the Confederate position, and turned back to relieve his infantry: 'but when they came there they found it a grosse mistake and that it was their owne foote'(*Discourse*). Forsaken by their cavalry, the Confederate infantry had taken to their heels, abandoning their cannon and leaving the castle doors wide open. Inchiquin resumed his pursuit too

Liscarroll

	Winner	*Loser*
Opponents	English	Confederate
Commanders	Murrough O'Brien, Lord Inchiquin (w)	General Garrett Barry
Numbers	2750	6500
Losses	32	600–700

late. Most of the enemy had escaped northwards into the bogs around Kilbolane (R4221).

Richard Bellings thought 'the losse of men very inconsiderable on the one side or the other'. Modern historians accept Dublin's official report of 600–700 dead. The most serious Confederate loss was 50 officers captured and hanged next morning. The two-hour fight was a great success for Inchiquin, who frustrated Confederate plans at a critical point of the war, at the cost of 12 dead and about 20 wounded. He lacked means to exploit the victory, being unable to pay or feed his troops, who plundered the Protestant refugees they were meant to defend. The victors marched back to Mallow, 'taking care for the bringing away thither of the great (captive) peece of Ordnannce with the other two as the chiefe Trophies of this victorie' (*Discourse*), and dispersed into winter quarters.

Directions

From Mallow take the N20 north to Buttevant. Turn left along the R522 to Liscarroll, where the battlefield is on the ridge left of the road into the village. See the castle's restored 13th-century curtain wall.

Victory Deferred: 1642

The Civil Wars spread to England after the king quit London in January 1642. Local enthusiasts bickered over county armouries, while ordinary people kept out of the way. Parliament drew on London's military and financial resources to raise a field army of 20 regiments of foot and numerous independent troops of horse, commanded by the Earl of Essex, a veteran of the Dutch service. The king created an army almost from nothing, with the help of the landed aristocracy and gentry. Nevertheless, when Charles raised his standard at Nottingham, his safety could not be guaranteed in face of Essex's superior forces. The Royalists withdrew to Shrewsbury to recruit, drawing Essex unwillingly westwards.

The first clash between the opposing cavalry came further down the Severn valley, at Powick Bridge outside Worcester (9 September). The Royalists withdrew after their brisk little victory, which allowed Essex to occupy the city, exposing his communications with London. The main Royalist army marched southeast from Shrewsbury, cutting Essex off from the capital. Essex caught up with the king at Edgehill (23 October), where the Parliamentarian commander fought the first of several battles he would fight with the enemy between him and home. Edgehill was a tactical draw, but a moral victory for Charles I, as Essex abandoned the field, losing seven guns.

The Royalists' sluggish exploitation of the battle gave Essex time to slip around them. On 8 November he regained the capital, whose citizens were phlegmatically raising fresh troops to replace those lost at Edgehill. When Prince Rupert chased in Parliamentarian outposts at Brentford (12 November), the immediate shock of Edgehill had faded. Next day, overwhelming numbers of Londoners poured out of the city to Turnham Green, to face down the Royalist army. Charles I had won the first major battle of the First English Civil War, but Essex had won the campaign.

Powick Bridge, 23 September 1642

England, Worcestershire, LR150 SO8352

The starting point for many accounts of the First English Civil War is the cavalry skirmish at Powick Bridge, south of Worcester. Numerically unimportant, the action demonstrated the Royalist cavalry's quality, setting the tone for much that followed.

While the king gathered troops at Shrewsbury, Sir John Byron with a few Royalist horse brought away Oxford University's silver plate, for conversion into cash. His convoy had reached Worcester by 20 September, pursued by Parliamentarian cavalry from Alcester, followed by Essex's main army. Byron had no chance of holding Worcester, its ancient walls 'open enough to have been entered in many places', its rotten gates without lock or bolt. All day on the 23rd the Parliamentarian cavalry under Colonel John Brown waited in the meadows south of the River Teme at Powick Hams, expecting Byron's withdrawal westwards before Essex. The flood plain either side of the Teme is level and probably higher now than in 1642, but the banks are steep, the bridge the only way across.

Brown's failure to push scouts forward or post a lookout in Powick church tower left him ignorant of Prince Rupert's arrival from Bridgwater to cover Byron's escape. The Royalists deployed in a fold in the ground just north of Powick Bridge at Wick Field. Their dragoons occupied hedges either side of the lane up from the Teme, while weary Cavaliers took off their armour and rested in a field on the right of the road. Rupert had about 1000 men, half of them dragoons, against a similar number of Parliamentarians: ten troops of horse, and five companies of dragoons.

About 4 p.m. Brown heard that Byron was pulling out and sent Colonel Edwin Sandys forward across the narrow bridge. He advanced rapidly, no doubt hoping to traverse the defile, only wide enough for four riders at a time, as quickly as possible. The enemy remained out of sight, behind a gently rising shoulder of high ground at Manor Farm. Their dismounted dragoons gave notice of Sandys's approach, however, firing into his column at point-blank range.

The two sides were within musket shot before the Royalist horse realized they were under attack: 'scarce time to get upon their horses and none to consult what was to be done' (Clarendon, *History of the Rebellion*). Rupert declared 'that he would charge', and led a forlorn hope of senior Royalist officers forward, without armour or pistols, before half the Parliamentarians had deployed. Nathaniel Fiennes's troop shattered their attackers with close-range carbine fire, but those on either flank melted away as Rupert's seconds came up, leaving Fiennes to cut his way back to the bridge. It was a victory of offensive spirit over superior armament. The Parliamentarians were 'completely armed both for offence and defence ... yet in a short time, many of their best men being killed and Colonel Sandys ... the whole body was routed, fled, and was pursued by the conquerors for one mile' (Clarendon).

Brown's dragoons held the bridge and checked the Royalist pursuit, falling back unmolested to Upton-upon-Severn. The Parliamentarian horse had still not rallied at Pershore, 15 miles (24 km) away, where they carried away some of Essex's Lifeguards in their flight. Clarendon reckoned the slain as 'not many ... not above 40 or 50'. Nathaniel Wharton, who entered Worcester with Essex's army, counted 28 dead on both sides, after he had inspected the graves and checked the parish registers. Prisoners, drownings and desertions may have brought Brown's losses to 150; 'of the king's party none of name was lost', although Lord Wilmot suffered his second wound in the king's service. A less fortunate outcome to Rupert's headlong dash might have decapitated the Royalist horse before the war had started.

Powick Bridge

	Winner	*Loser*
Opponents	Royalist	Parliamentarian
Commanders	Prince Rupert	Colonel John Brown
Numbers	1000	800–1000
Losses	unknown	100–150

Powick Bridge had little strategic significance. Rupert retreated to Tenbury, allowing Parliamentarian hacks to claim a propaganda victory. From a moral point of view, the action proved 'of unspeakable advantage and benefit to the king' (Clarendon), establishing the superiority of his cavalry and rendering Prince Rupert's name terrible to his enemies. It would take more than parliamentary votes to end the business now.

Directions

Powick Bridge is 1½ miles (2.4 km) southwest of Worcester. Turn right onto a minor road opposite Manor Farm, to cross the old bridge, repaired after the Battle of Worcester (1651), just west of the modern A449 crossing. Much of the battlefield is now built over.

Edgehill, Sunday 23 October 1642

England, Warwickshire, LR151 SP3548–3649

The first major action of the English Civil Wars was the largest fought on British soil since Pinkie in 1547. Like many battles between raw armies, it was notable for wild swings of fortune, 'some of both sides did extreamly well, and others did as ill, and deserve to be hanged' (Official Parliamentary Account). Edgehill could have ended the war at a stroke, but the scale of the opposing forces and the significance of the issues at stake made outright victory in a single encounter unlikely. Tactically indecisive, Edgehill marked a political turning point, as Kipling's 'first dry rattle of new drawn steel' changed the world for ever.

The Earl of Essex had occupied Worcester after Powick Bridge, pushing outposts up the Severn valley to Kidderminster. The Royalists still held Shrewsbury, with cavalry at Bridgnorth. From Worcester Essex prevented the Royalists recruiting in South Wales, and covered Bristol, England's second city and a major seaport. He did not, however, cover his communications with London, his own base and the king's objective. On 12 October Charles I marched southeast from Shrewsbury, screened by Rupert's cavalry. The Royalists had chosen not to fight Essex in the heavily enclosed Worcestershire countryside, making instead for more open cavalry country in the Midlands. On 19 October they were at Kenilworth, with a clear road to London.

Essex groped after them. Newly raised cavalry make poor scouts, while mounted units represented only a fifth of Essex's strength, some of them demoralized after Powick Bridge. The two armies re-established contact late on Saturday 22 October, as their quartermasters clashed at Wormleighton in Warwickshire. Prince Rupert's patrols soon located Essex's main body in the little market town of Kineton, and the king issued midnight orders to concentrate the Royalist army on Edgehill, squarely across Essex's route to London. The Parliamentarian leaders had meant to spend the Sabbath resting, while the artillery and its escort came up. They were outside Kineton church, about 8 or 9 a.m., when news arrived of the enemy's presence 2 miles (3 km) away.

Essex was temperamentally unwilling to fight; he expected reinforcements, and the Royalist forming-up area on Edgehill was unassailable. The 3-mile (5-km) long scarp rises 330 feet (100 m) from the plain, reaching a gradient of 1 in 4. Now covered in trees, in 1642 the ridge was open. It remains the dominant feature of the battlefield, the battle lines conforming to its alignment northeast to southwest. Essex took up a defensive position, occupying 'a great broad Field under that Hill, called the *Vale of the Red Horse* ... some half a Mile from the Foot of the Hill, and there drew into Battalia' (Official Parliamentary Account). The Royalists forced the issue by coming down from the hill about 2 p.m. Unlike Essex, they had no reinforcements on hand. Hostile country people had denied them food and hidden stocks of horseshoes. Many companies 'had scarce eaten bread in eight and forty hours ... The only way to cure this was a victory'. At 3 p.m. the king gave the word to attack. The weather was 'as fair a day as that season could yield, the sun clear, no wind or cloud appearing' (Clarendon, *History of the Rebellion*).

Clarendon, an eyewitness, approved Essex's choice of ground, 'between the hill and town a fair champaign [plain], save that near the town it was narrower and on the right hand [of Essex's army] some hedges and inclosures so that he placed musketeers, and not above two regiments of horse, where the ground was narrowest, but on his left wing he placed a body of a thousand horse. The reserve of horse was a good one.' Red Horse Field was an unenclosed expanse of ridge and furrow, offering no obstacle to troop movements. From the foot of the hill at Radway village the ground falls away gently for 2 miles (3 km) towards Kineton and the River Dene, whose tributary streams cut up the battlefield. Two roughly parallel roads between Edgehill and Kineton mark the axes of advance of the Royalist cavalry.

Rupert's Walloon engineer, Sir Bernard de Gomme, sketched the Royalist deployment. He showed two equal cavalry wings, flanking five tertias or brigades of infantry, cruciform arrangements of pikes in the centre, musketeers on each flank or tucked behind the central pike blocks. Three tertias were in front, the intervals between them covered by the two in support. This complicated-looking formation divided the Royalist high command: Lord Lindsey, the lord general and a veteran of the Dutch service, wanted a plainer order of battle, but was overruled by more recent graduates of Continental warfare, Prince Rupert and Patrick Ruthven (later Lord Forth), who appealed to Swedish practice. Historians usually side with Lindsey, but the Swedish brigade may have suited an army short of firearms intent on shock action. Some 400 of Charles's infantry were only armed with cudgels until they could pick up weapons from the fallen.

Edgehill

	Winner	*Loser*
Opponents	Royalist	Parliamentarian
Commanders	Charles I Robert Bertie, Earl Lindsey (k) Prince Rupert	Robert Devereux, Earl of Essex Sir James Ramsey Sir William Balfour
Numbers	14,300	14,650–14,900
Losses	1500	1500

De Gomme put Royalist numbers at 2500 cavalry and 10,000 infantry, forgetting two brigades of 500 dragoons, deployed on either flank. Brigadier Peter Young, who revitalized Civil War studies in the 1960s, has expanded these figures to 10,500 foot and 2800 horse (excluding dragoons) to reach the total shown below: 27 troops concentrated on the right under Rupert (1695); 14–15 troops under Lord Henry Wilmot on the left (1055). Stuart Reid's more recent analysis stays with de Gomme, putting the infantry brigades at 1800–1900 each and dividing the cavalry equally, except for the 300-strong King's Lifeguard. Piqued by remarks that they were 'The Troop of Shew', the Lifeguard had joined Rupert, leaving Charles with no uncommitted cavalry except his personal escort of 50 gentlemen pensioners. A third of each cavalry wing were in support, but they were too near the front line, and their officers too inexperienced, to act as an independent reserve. Contemporaries support the view that the cavalry were distributed heavily in favour of Rupert, who faced the majority of the Parliamentarian horse. The authors of the Official Parliamentary Account were shocked to learn afterwards that the king had indeed raised 14,000 men. The Royalist artillery train provided two light guns for each tertia, plus a heavier six-gun battery held back on the slopes of Edgehill to fire overhead. Their most likely position is in Grange Park behind Radway, reached by a track down from the vicinity of the obelisk at the top of the hill.

Essex's army was incomplete. Two of his best infantry regiments and one of horse missed the battle, the latter including Oliver Cromwell. The Official Parliamentary Account put their forces at: '11 Regiments of Foot, 42 Troops of Horse, and about 700 Dragoons, in all about 10,000 Men'. Sir James Ramsey, a Scottish mercenary, had 24 troops (1200 men) on the left, 'in posture Defensive and Offensive, interlining the squadrons with a convenient number of Musketeers'. Another 300 *enfants perdus* lined a hedge on the outer flank to enfilade attackers. Ramsey's troops were probably in pairs, deployed in two lines. The infantry consisted of three brigades of four regiments each, despite the Official Account:

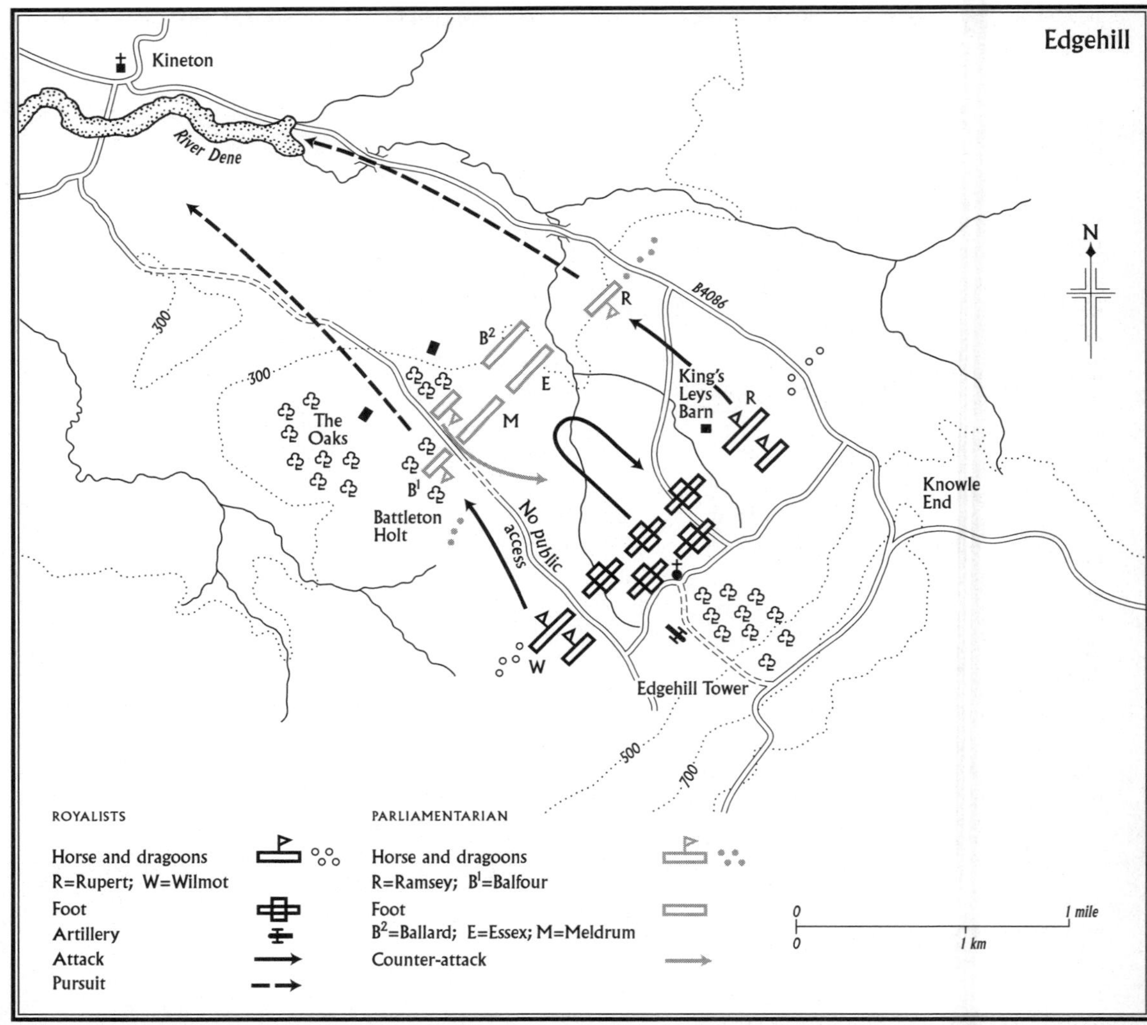

12,000 foot if nearly up to strength. The Official Account quaintly termed these van, battle and rear, under Sir John Meldrum, Sir Charles Essex (no relation) and Colonel Thomas Ballard respectively. The first two were in front, all four regiments up in line, with Ballard's brigade behind the battle in support. Parliamentarian regiments used the simpler Dutch formation, wings of shot flanking a central stand of pikes. Eight ranks deep, they would occupy less space than the enemy foot in six ranks, which might explain the gaps Royalist commentators

Directions

Take the B4100 (ex-A41) north from Banbury, turning left at Warmington along the B4086 for Kineton. Turn left along the top of Edgehill to view the battlefield to the northwest from the Castle Inn's garden. Returning to the B4086, go down the hill and turn left through Radway, behind the Royalist start line. Most of the battlefield – including much of the minor Radway–Kineton road – belongs to the Ministry of Defence, and is usually inaccessible. The modern copses do not reflect 1640s land usage.

observed in the opposing Parliamentarian line.

The deployment of Essex's right wing is less clear. Balfour should have had the remaining 18 troops (900 men). Some of them, however, began the battle behind Meldrum's van, in lieu of the missing infantry regiments. Peter Young thought two complete regiments were in reserve, leaving only six troops of Lord Fielding's regiment to continue the line. Stuart Reid places all three regiments on the flank, leaving only three large troops of cuirassiers to support Meldrum. Opinions vary as to the artillery available to Essex, from the 7 guns known to have been captured, up to the 30–37 pieces Peter Young thought present.

None of the contemporary sources mention specific landmarks to anchor Essex's start line, or define the frontages occupied. Peter Young, following his old associate A.H. Burne, located the Parliamentarians a mile (1.6 km) from the Royalists, on a line from The Oaks through Battle and Thistle Farms to the cylindrical monument on the south verge of the B4086 Kineton road. This line conforms with the Ordnance Survey symbol (SP3549), local place-names and traditional grave sites between Graveyard Coppice and Battleton Holt. It is tactically convenient, on top of a small rise, clear of a brook between Battleton Holt and Radway. It does not agree with the Parliamentarian estimate of the distance from Edgehill, half a mile (0.8 km), and is out of artillery range of the Royalists. Most authorities place them nearer the foot of Edgehill, just northwest of Radway, Essex's presence inhibiting any further advance. Stuart Reid places Essex further forward, between Battleton Holt and the junction of the B4086 with the side road to Radway past King's Ley Barn, near point 106. This position is the right distance from the bottom of Edgehill, and puts Ramsey's cavalry at a high point on the main road, as described by the Official Parliamentary Account, and by the commander of the King's Lifeguard, who charged uphill to get at them.

Opinions also differ over the extent of ground occupied. The horse at the northern end of the opposing lines is sometimes shown beyond and sometimes athwart the B4086. This displaces the opposing foot more or less southwest, lying entirely between the two roads, or extending across the minor road by Battleton Holt. The horse on the southern flank is consequently deployed across the minor road, or beyond it, with dragoons further southwest. Colonel Rogers extended the front still further, to the Stratford road from Sun Rising Hill, by putting the whole Parliamentarian army in the shop window. This seems unlikely. Numerous contemporary sources place Ballard's brigade and some of the horse back in support.

The general course of events at Edgehill is straightforward, despite 'many notable accidents, which if they had been pursued by either side would have produced other effects' (Clarendon). Fighting began with an artillery exchange, initiated by Essex, who directed several shots at the king's retinue. This caused few casualties, but persuaded His Majesty to retire to Bullet Hill, a spur at the northern end of Edgehill, below Knowle End. The Royalist dragoons then advanced to clear the flanks preparatory to a charge, 'which they very well performed; whereupon our army advanced in very good Order, the Ordnance of both sides playing very fast' (Official Royalist Account).

Just before the horse moved off, Rupert reminded them 'to march as close as was possible, keeping their Ranks with Sword in Hand, to receive the Enemy's Shot without firing either Carbin or Pistol, till we broke in amongst the Enemy, and then to make use of our Fire-Arms as need should require' (Sir Richard Bulstrode, Prince of Wales' Regiment of Horse). These orders were carried out with startling success. Ramsey's wing awaited the charge at a stand, relying on their carbines and supporting musketeers, but they either fired too soon or into the air, and promptly fled, shamefully abandoning their musketeers. Royalists unkindly suggested they didn't stop until they reached St Albans. Many saved their lives by shouting 'For God and King Charles' as they ran. A complete troop, raised by Sir Faithfull Fortescue for service in Ireland and shanghaied into Essex's army, changed sides. Unfortunately for Charles I, the Royalist second line thought 'nothing more to be done, but to pursue those that fled' (Clarendon). The whole mass of cavalry, except three troops rallied by Rupert, chased after Ramsey's fugitives towards Kineton, 3 miles (5 km) away. Much the same happened on the other flank. Lord Henry Wilmot swept over ditches and hedges lined with shot to smash the opposing cavalry and Meldrum's rightmost infantry regiment. Again the commander of the supports 'gave more Testimony of his Courage than of Conduct' and joined the pursuit, leaving the Royalist infantry 'naked' in the centre.

The Royalist foot had advanced in conformity with the horse, only more slowly, both sides' musketeers opening fire as they came into range. The two supporting tertias filled the intervals in the front line, but not all of them came to push of pike. Sir Charles Essex's whole brigade disbanded at the first volley, following Ramsey's cavalry to the rear. Remarkably, Ballard was 'not dismaied', and marched up the hill to replace Essex's battle. The commander-in-chief joined them pike in hand. Only 6000 or so Parliamentarian infantry were left facing 10,000 Royalists. Nevertheless they stopped them, perhaps with superior firepower, having a higher proportion of muskets, or by sheer bloody-mindedness, as James II (then the young Duke of York) thought: 'it were reasonable to imagine that one side should run and be disorder'd, but it happened otherwise, for each as if by mutuall consent retired some few paces, and they stuck down their coulours, continuing to fire at one another even till night'.

While the infantry slugged it out, the Parliamentarian cavalry reserve launched a counterattack against the unsupported Royalist foot. One body of horse was repulsed. Edmund Ludlow of Essex's Lifeguard recalled 'some loss from their pike though very little from their shot'. Another party under Balfour drove a regiment with green colours as far as the Royalist battery, where they broke. By a narrow margin the Parliamentarians failed to capture the Prince of Wales and Duke of York, who had been sent to the rear for safety. Unable to spike the guns for want of nails, Balfour returned to put in a joint attack with two of Meldrum's regiments, 'who did it so home thrice together, that they forced all the Musqueteers, of two of their left Regiments, to run in and shrowd themselves within their Pikes, not daring to shoot a shot' (Ludlow). Two more regiments joined in from Ballard's brigade, to break Charles's Lifeguard and the Lord General's Regiment in the Royalist centre. The royal standard was captured, and Earl Lindsey mortally wounded.

Three out of five tertias never broke, but 'retired orderly and at last made a stand; and having the Assistance of Cannon and a Ditch ... held us in play very handsomely' (Official Parliamentary Account). The Royalist cavalry straggled back to stabilize the situation as dusk fell. Their dragoons fired a few volleys, but it was growing so dark the officers 'durst not Charge for fear of mistaking Friends for Foes' (Official Royalist Account). Regiments had disintegrated, 'where many soldiers of one troop or regiment were rallied ... the officers were wanting; and where the officers were ready ... the soldiers were not together; and neither desired to move without those who properly belonged to them' (Clarendon). About 6 p.m., an hour after sunset, the two sides separated, the Parliamentarians holding the disputed ground, the Royalists withdrawing up the hill.

Neither side had rallied after a night in the open, 'starving with cold': 'the field was covered with the dead, yet nobody could tell to what party they belonged ... the enemy's [Parliamentarian] troops appeared as thin or broken, and as dispirited as they [the Royalists] could wish, so that they who could longest endure ... were likely to remain masters of the field' (Clarendon). Essex's nerve broke first. Later on Monday the 24th he retreated to Warwick, abandoning 7 guns and 30 wagons, conceding a moral victory to the king. Essex lost 70 colours and cornets, against only 16 Royalist ensigns, the royal standard being recovered by heroism or trickery, depending on one's point of view.

Human losses are less certain. The author of the Official Royalist Account later estimated 1000 dead for both sides, after investigating the graves. This compares with James II's figure of 'not above fifteen hundred bodys of both partys remaining on the field of battell'. The common ratio of two wounded per fatal casualty brings losses to 10 per cent, a reasonable proportion in a battle with no sustained pursuit. Claims that the Royalists killed five to one, or that 300 Parliamentarians were lost for 3000 Royalists are propaganda. Ludlow, who helped break the Royalist centre, observed, 'the greatest slaughter on our side was of such as ran away, and on the enemy's side of those that stood firm'.

Charles I's faulty dispositions, without a dedicated reserve, had cost him outright victory, while the Parliamentarian success in the centre was frustrated by darkness and the return of the Royalist horse. After Edgehill the king had the chance of a strategic victory, if he could reach London before Essex. Instead he 'trifled away his Time in taking Banbury and Broughton House ... Places of little Consideration' (Bulstrode). More significant was the king's occupation of Oxford on 29 October, but, 'While he refresht his men, Essex stole by other roads as many of his army to London, as he could' (Sir Philip Warwick, King's Lifeguard). When Charles approached the capital in November, he would find that he had missed his chance.

Brentford

	Winner	Loser
Opponents	Royalist	Parliamentarian
Commanders	Patrick Ruthven, Lord Forth Prince Rupert	Robert Devereux, Earl of Essex
Numbers	c.3400	c.2500
Losses	unknown	500

Turnham Green

	Winner	Loser
Opponents	Parliamentarian	Royalist
Commanders	Robert Devereux, Earl of Essex	Charles I Prince Rupert
Numbers	c.12,000	24,000
Losses	none	none

Brentford, 12 November 1642

England, London, LR176 TQ1776–7

Turnham Green, 13 November 1642

England, London, LR176 TQ2077–8

The closest Charles I came to re-entering London as a free agent was at Brentford and Turnham Green, three weeks after Edgehill, at the culminating point of the first Royalist offensive of the war. The king's arrival at Colnbrook, on the western edge of what is now Heathrow Airport, moved Parliament to propose terms on 11 November. Charles was more interested in submission than negotiation, and ordered Rupert to drive in the Parliamentarian outpost at Brentford, covering London's western approaches, 8 miles (13 km) from the Houses of Parliament at Westminster.

Brentford lies north of the Thames, east of the River Brent. The garrison consisted of a few horse and two regiments of foot (Lord Brooke's and Denzil Holles's) from Ballard's brigade. Both had suffered severely at Edgehill, and probably numbered only 1000 men between them. Late in the day two more regiments (Hampden's and Lord Robartes's) covered their survivors' withdrawal. The defenders appear to have awaited the enemy in front of Brentford, west of the river, near Sir Richard Wynn's house in Syon Park, 'having barricaded the narrow passes to the town, and cast up some little breastworks at the most convenient places' (Clarendon, *History of the Rebellion*). Rupert approached from Hounslow Heath to the west. He had four regiments of horse, 1300 strong at Edgehill, supported by Wentworth's brigade of foot, under Forth's overall command.

Rupert's cavalry tried to bounce the defenders under cover of early morning fog, but met considerable opposition. The Prince of Wales's Regiment discovered hostile cannon in a hedge behind which they had formed up, and withdrew after losing several casualties. The Royalist infantry renewed the attack. The Parliamentarians disputed the passage 'with unspeakable courage', according to Edmund Ludlow of Essex's Lifeguard, but the Royalist foot 'beat them from one Brainford to the other, and from thence to the open field, with a resolute and expeditious fighting, that after once firing suddenly to advance up to push of pikes and the butt end of muskets' (John Gwynne, Sir Thomas Salusbury's [sic] Regiment of Foot).

Fighting continued until the afternoon, when the Parliamentarians were surrounded by horse and foot, and driven into the river, possibly down Dock Road or Ferry Lane, site of the ancient ford, later covered by Brentford Dock. Meanwhile Rupert detached troops to Syon House, where they sank 'two great Barks in the River of Thames, with many Soldiers' (Sir Richard Bulstrode, Prince of Wales' Regiment of Horse). Other Parliamentarian losses included 500 prisoners, 11 colours and 15 guns. An unknown number were killed or drowned, Brooke's and Holles's regiments disappearing from the Parliamentarian order of battle.

The victory 'proved not at all fortunate to His Majesty' (Clarendon). The 'massacre' of Holles's Londoners, allegedly in breach of a ceasefire, rallied support for Parliament. Next morning an unprecedented number of regular and part-time soldiers gathered under Essex's command at Turnham Green, 2 miles (3 km) east of Brentford along the Chiswick High Road. To rub in their superiority over the king's handful of weather-beaten and half-starved troops, the London Trained Bands wore their best uniforms, while their wives brought them dinner in the field. It would have been madness for Charles to fight both his chief enemies, Parliament and the City, at once. He stood in line of battle to receive their attack, but Essex only bombarded the Royalist position, killing four or five horses. The doubtful offensive value of the troops excuses his failure to take more decisive action. That night the Royalists withdrew through Hounslow and Reading to Oxford, where they went into winter quarters. Turnham Green was the Valmy of the English Civil War, the decisive cannonade that preserved a revolutionary government, and ensured a long war.

Directions

Brentford *From Brentford Central railway station turn left down Boston Manor Road, and right along Brentford High Street (A315), the axis of the battle. Cross the bridge to Syon Park south of the main road, the Ordnance Survey battle site. See the 1909 monument in the High Street opposite Dock Road, also commemorating battles supposedly fought by Julius Caesar (54 BC) and Edmund Ironside (1016).*

Turnham Green *The Parliamentarian position was on Chiswick Common and Acton Green Common, two remnants of the 17th-century heath. Essex's huge army could have occupied several miles, stretching south across the A4 as far as Chiswick House.*

Hopton's Campaign in the West: 1642–3

Fighting broke out in western England before Charles I raised his standard at Nottingham. Englishmen fired their first shots at other Englishmen at Marshall's Elm in Somerset, Parliament securing the county before Edgehill. Remote from the clash of great armies, the West had a disproportionate significance, as small Royalist forces might capture a major port, such as Plymouth or Exeter, allowing them to challenge Parliament's maritime supremacy. Western Royalists failed to shake Parliament's grip on the coastal towns, but proved invincible in the countryside. The campaign consisted of three phases:

(1) SPORADIC FIGHTING IN SOMERSET (JULY–SEPTEMBER 1642)

Both sides despatched grandees to overcome local neutralism: the Earl of Bedford for Parliament; the Marquess of Hertford for the king. The Royalists enjoyed minor tactical successes at Marshall's Elm and Babylon Hill, but faced overwhelming Parliamentarian numbers. Hertford evacuated his infantry and guns by sea, leaving Sir Ralph Hopton to slip through North Devon to Cornwall with a few cavalry. Bedford withdrew to fight at Edgehill creating a temporary lull in the west.

(2) INDECISIVE FORAYS BACK AND FORTH ACROSS THE RIVER TAMAR (DECEMBER 1642–FEBRUARY 1643)
Hopton rallied the Cornish Trained Bands to the king, but they would not cross the Tamar which formed the border with Parliamentarian Devon. A Royalist attempt to raise the Devon posse comitatus at Modbury collapsed on 6 December, 'the Gentlemen of the Country being so transported with the jollity of the thing, that noe man was capable of the labour and care of discipline' (Hopton, *Bellum Civile*). Meanwhile, Hopton raised five regular regiments of foot, who defeated a Parliamentarian counter-invasion of Cornwall at Braddock Down (19 January 1643). He invaded Devon again, blockading Plymouth until the Parliamentarians broke through the siege lines at Modbury (21 February). Hostilities were then suspended by a local truce.

(3) REASSERTION OF ROYAL CONTROL THROUGHOUT THE WEST (APRIL–MAY 1643)
Hopton beat off a renewed Parliamentarian invasion at Launceston (23 April), and after an unlucky panic on Sourton Down (25 April) smashed the Parliamentarians' western army at Stratton (16 May). This remarkable victory confirmed Hopton's military reputation, confined Parliamentarian influence in the West to a few towns, and opened the way for the western Royalists to join the potentially decisive struggle for the strategic corridor between London, Oxford and Bristol.

Marshall's Elm, 4 August 1642

England, Somerset, LR182 ST4834

Royalist efforts to maintain King Charles's cause in Somerset during the summer of 1642 were brief and unsuccessful. Their propagandists made the most of the skirmish at Marshall's Elm.

The campaign began with rival groups of gentry competing for the support of the local militia. Several hundred horse joined the Marquess of Hertford at Wells, but many more foot turned out for the Parliamentarians. Justifiably nervous, Hertford sent out a patrol, which reached the southern escarpment of the Polden Hills (203 feet/62 m) at Marshall's Elm early in the evening. From here they spotted an enemy column 2 miles (3 km) off in a corn field, marching from Taunton to join other Parliamentarian forces threatening Wells. The Parliamentarians had presumably followed the A378 around the Somerset Levels, turning north at Somerton, to cross the Poldens at Marshall's Elm, where the road climbs a cutting in the eastern slope of a re-entrant between Ivy Thorn Hill and Collard Hill.

The main sources for the skirmish are Sir Ralph Hopton's *Bellum Civile* and a pamphlet published soon afterwards (Thomason Tract E112.33). They quote comparable numbers: three or four score mounted Royalists, against 500–600 foot. Stowell's horse drew up in single rank along the brow of the hill, 'so that their thinnes might not be perceived', their three weak troops, 'so advantageouslie placed by meanes of the uneavennes of the ground that the enemy discovered no part of them but their heads and some of their swords'. Fourteen dragoons hid in 'two quarry-pitts, which the deep hollow way divided 150 paces before the horse in the declining of the hill' (*Bellum Civile*).

Sir John Stowell asked the Parliamentarian leaders not to precipitate hostilities by continuing their march, but the parley proved abortive. Meanwhile Colonel Lunsford had taken post in one of the pits, ordering none of the Royalists to stir 'till they saw him with his company come forth … shouting and discharging their Carbines, which being done they should all doe the like' (T.T. E112.33). The enemy now advanced within musket shot and opened fire 'verie thicke'. Lunsford let them come within 120 paces before returning fire, killing the leader of the Parliamentarian van, 'a violent Grandjury man', with a shot in the head. This made their whole body stagger: 'who being hurt by they knew not whom, nor hardly from whence, and the Cavaliers with the same expedition comming in their faces, were so

Marshall's Elm

	Winner	*Loser*
Opponents	Royalist	Parliamentarian
Commanders	Sir John Stowell	John Pyne
Numbers	60–80	500–600
Losses	unknown	*c.*70

distracted that they knew not which way to flie, some throwing down their arms and running into Corners, others fled, some ran into the Corne to hide' (T.T. E112.33).

Some Royalists followed the chase 3 miles (5 km), although they claimed to have killed no one as they fled, and left their prisoners at Somerton. Casualty figures bear this out. Those 'kill'd upon the place' numbered only single figures, although deaths from wounds brought Parliamentarian fatalities to 19 or 25. Despite their victory, the Royalists were unable to maintain themselves at Wells as thousands of country people gathered on the hills outside: 'some bringing Pitchforks, Dungpecks, and suchlike weapons, not knowing (poor soules) whom to fight against, but afraid ... of the papists' (T.T. E.112.33). On 6 August Hertford retreated 20 miles (32 km) south to Sherborne, where he prepared the castle to withstand a siege.

Directions

Marshall's Elm is 3 miles (5 km) south of Glastonbury on the B3151. A track runs along the crest of the hill either side of the main road.

Babylon Hill, 7 September 1642

England, Somerset, LR183 ST5815–16

This reconnaissance in force was not the first skirmish of the Civil Wars, although it should have been, Babylon being at once a Puritan image for Charles I's despotism, and Babel a symbol of his kingdom's descent into confusion.

The Marquess of Hertford's handful of Royalists remained undisturbed at Sherborne for nearly a month after they abandoned Wells. Fearing their designs upon Wiltshire, Parliament detached the Earl of Bedford from the Earl of Essex's army to deal with them. On 2 September Bedford appeared with 7000 men outside Sherborne, which they besieged half-heartedly until the 6th, when they retreated to Yeovil. Next day about 2 p.m., Hertford sent Hopton after them, 'to give him an account of their mocions'.

Hopton later recalled (in his *Bellum Civile*) taking 'all the horse and dragoones and sevenscore muskettiers', but a contemporary letter from the governor of Sherborne Castle puts the Royalist force at 150 horse and 200 foot. Parliamentarian numbers are not stated, but a report to the king gave them 'a like number'. Hopton recorded that he marched to Raborn Hill, 'which look'd downe upon Yeovill-Bridge, which hee found possest of the Enemy with a guard of foote and cannon'. Yeovil lies west of the River Yeo. To the east, dominating the bridge, was Babylon Hill (358 feet/109 m), whose steepness has encouraged development of alternative routes down to the Yeo, either side of the main road. These hedged hollow ways proved tactically significant, allowing Parliamentarian troops to approach the top of the hill undetected. Today a footpath still runs across the golf course towards Tilly's Hill, south of the main road; early Ordnance Survey maps showed another lane to the north, a more direct approach than that via Over Compton.

Hopton secured the approaches to his position with musketeers and dragoons. Drawing up the horse upon the hill, 'with the rest of the muskettiers he played from the side of the Hill on the guard which was upon the bridge'. About 6 p.m., 'within halfe an houre of sun sette', the Royalists decided to withdraw, but the foot were not yet clear of the hill, when the enemy appeared, 'marching out of Yeovell by a secret way that they had made over the fields, and some of their horse were neere gotten up to the topp of the Hill upon the left hand [i.e. Tilly's Hill]'. Hopton recalled the infantry and drew up his four troops of horse. The result was more muddle than battle.

Captain Edward Stowell charged the enemy on

the left, 'but withal (his troope consisting of new horse, and the Enemy being more in number) was rowted himselfe; and Captain Moreton, being a little too neere him was likewise broaken with the same shocke, and the trueth is in verie short tyme, all the horse on both sides weer in a confusion'. Another Parliamentarian troop charged unopposed up the hollow way on Hopton's right, where the musketeers had been withdrawn. Gaining the hilltop somewhere near point 99 on the Landranger map, they were halted by a fluke: 'James Colborne with a fowling gunne shott at the Captain in the head of the troope, and at the same instant Mr John Stowell charg'd him singly ... the Captain was slayne, and the troope (being rawe fellows) immedyatly rowted'. In this moment of 'extreame confusion' Sir Ralph sent off his foot, covered by a few gentlemen, escaping to Sherborne under cover of darkness.

A local Parliamentarian correspondent saw the two-pronged assault on the hill from a different perspective, although he failed to distinguish right and left. Captain Askew's troop charged through the Royalist horse, discharging carbines and pistols, killing 8. Captain Thomson, on the other flank, routed his opponents, before falling on the enemy foot, killing 30 or 40. The casualties are exaggerated, Royalist sources admitting only 15 killed and 1 officer prisoner. The Parliamentarians acknowledged 3 dead, a long way from the 100–140 of Royalist claims, including 9 officers buried next day in church.

Babylon Hill was pretty much a draw: 'This ruffe medley gave apprehension to both parts ... but the Enemy liked their bargaine so ill that they marched cleere away from Yeovill that night or the next morning very early' (*Bellum Civile*). The Royalists were equally cast down by news of the surrender of Portsmouth to Parliamentarian forces. Against Hopton's advice, Hertford withdrew on 22 September to Minehead, where he evacuated his guns and infantry in Welsh coal barges. There was no shipping for the 160 mounted troops. Hopton led them south into Cornwall, to become the nucleus of a new Royalist army.

Babylon Hill

	Winner	*Loser*
Opponents	Parliamentarian	Royalist
Commanders	Francis Russell, Earl of Bedford	Sir Ralph Hopton
Numbers	*c.*350	350
Losses	unknown	16

Directions

From the A30 roundabout by Yeovil Bridge, follow the right hand Parliamentarian column across the golf course towards Tilly's Hill, where several minor roads lead around the hilltop.

Braddock Down, 19 January 1643

England, Cornwall, LR201 SX1561/SX1763

New Year 1643 found the Cornish Royalists under pressure from superior Parliamentarian forces in Devon, under the Scots mercenary Colonel William Ruthven. On 13 January Ruthven crossed the Tamar at Newbridge and Saltash, his troops converging on Liskeard. Sir Ralph Hopton's outnumbered regular troops withdrew to Bodmin, 'where the storm being foreseene, orders were sent some dayes before for conventing of the Posse' (Hopton, *Bellum Civile*). The Trained Bands turned out in strength, equipped with arms taken from Parliamentarian ships recently driven into Falmouth by storms. With this accession of strength Hopton countermarched, lodging overnight on 17–18 January in Boconnoc Park between Lostwithiel and Liskeard. Both sides were anxious, for different reasons, to fight before the Earl of Stamford, Parliament's newly appointed lord general in the West, arrived with reinforcements, to supersede Ruthven.

No authoritative figures exist for the numbers engaged at Braddock Down. Hopton led 2900 regular troops out of Cornwall in May, and it seems reasonable that volunteers and militia should double his numbers on home ground. The numbers quoted for

Ruthven's army are also reasonable: enough to force Hopton's regular army to withdraw; too few to overcome the county's concentrated resources. Parliamentarian cavalry outnumbered the Royalist horse two-to-one, but difficult terrain made infantry the decisive arm. The only guns present were two small 'minion drakes', 3-pounders brought up from Lord Mohun's house at Boconnoc and placed 'upon a little Borough [i.e. a tumulus] within randome-shott of the Enymies bodyes'. These had a point-blank range of some 300 yards (275 m), the distance in this case being rather more. So far the Cornish army had been led by committee, useful for mobilizing support, but inconvenient in battle. Sensibly they resigned operational command to Hopton.

The area of Braddock Down appears on modern maps as Broadoak Common. The battlefield has altered substantially since 1643, following the emparkment of the Boconnoc estate in the 18th century. Before then the open heathland was a wasteland of low scrub, pitted with ancient earthworks and crossed by hedged lanes. Today its southern parts are thickly wooded, although tracks still run uphill from Boconnoc northeastward past Broadoak Church towards Middle Taphouse on the main Liskeard road. Reconstructions of the battle locate it either at Middle Taphouse, or on the spur running southwest of Broadoak Church. Hopton says only that the enemy were 'already drawen up upon the east side of Bradock Downe at the end of the Lane coming out from Lyskeard', while he deployed on the west. Sir Bevil Grenville, one of Hopton's colonels, wrote that the enemy 'were possessed of a pretty rising ground which was in the way to Liskerd [sic], and we planted ourselves upon such another against them within musket shot'. Parliamentarian sources assert the Royalists emerged from 'a thick wood of a park of My Lord Mohun's joining to the way', suggesting they had not long left their bivouac.

Braddock Down

	Winner	*Loser*
Opponents	Royalist	Parliamentarian
Commanders	Sir Ralph Hopton	Colonel William Ruthven (Ruthin)
Numbers	*c.*5000	3000–4000
Losses	none	1250 prisoners

These imprecise indications might support either site. Both have tumuli for Hopton's artillery. Both have opposing areas of high ground separated by valleys several hundred yards across, at 'randomeshott'. The traditional site places Ruthven on the slope forward of Broadoak Church, which none of the sources mention, facing southwest across the Royalist approach from Boconnoc. The Middle Taphouse site is more consistent with Hopton's description, lying more obviously east–west, at the far side of the common, the opposing hillsides being rather more clearly defined.

Hopton formed up conventionally, his infantry in the centre: 'having placed a forlorne of muskettiers in little inclosures that lay before him, and winged all with the few horse and dragoones hee had' (*Bellum Civile*). Both sides kept their advantageous positions and limited themselves to an exchange of musketry. After a couple of hours Hopton realized Ruthven's artillery was missing, formed his infantry in two waves, and attacked. Grenville's regiment was in front: 'I ledd my part away, who followed me with so good courage, bothe downe the hill and up the other, it strooke a terror into them, while the second came up gallantly after me, and the winges of horse charged both sides, but their courage so faild them, as they stood not our first charge, but fled in great disorder'. Defending musketeers lined hedges behind to cover the retreat, to no purpose: 'The Cornish so briskly bestirred themselves and pressed them so hard on every side, being indeed excellent at hedge work and that kind of fight that they quickly won that ground too' (Clarendon, *History of the Rebellion*). A Parliamentarian letter writer confirms the rout: 'Both our horse and foot were suddenly routed and every man divided and dispersed, ran and rode as fast as fear could carry them towards Saltash'.

The Parliamentarians broke too quickly to suffer many casualties, while the Cornish refused to kill men without weapons in their hands. They took plenty of prisoners, most of the enemy's colours and

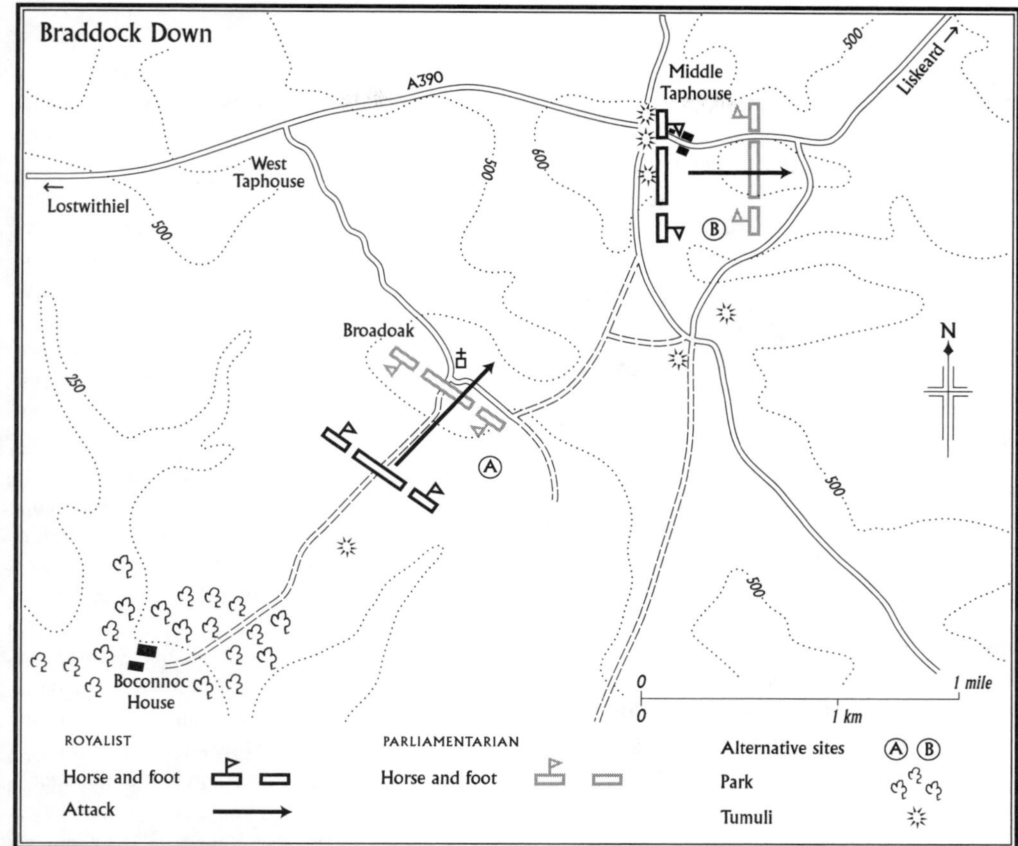

Directions

Take the A390 west from Liskeard, and turn left at the crossroads in Middle Taphouse, following the Royalist start line for the northern location of the battle. Ruthven would have been 1/4 mile (0.4 km) back to the east. Half a mile (0.8 km) further on, fork right along a track past Penventon to Broadoak, for the traditional southern site. This may also be reached by turning down a minor road further along the A390, at West Taphouse.

arms, and their artillery train, stuck in the narrow dirty lanes. Grenville boasted, 'but for their horses speed had all been in our hands ... we lost not a man'. Hopton's first proper battle, with thousands of combatants, had proved him more than just a partisan leader. It had also secured Cornwall, a Royalist redoubt that held out to the end.

Modbury, Tuesday 21 February 1643

England, Devon, LR202 SX6651

Hopton followed up his success at Braddock Down (see above) by investing Plymouth. The Cornish Trained Bands would not serve beyond their own county, so the Royalist siege lines were overstretched. An improbable number of Devonshire Clubmen, the local defence force, gathered at Kingsbridge, to relieve Plymouth, possibly led by the dynamic James Chudleigh (see Launceston, etc., below). Some time between noon and 3 p.m. on 21 February they fell upon the Royalist quarters at Modbury, covering the eastern approaches to Plymouth, 'and stormed it with very great fury all that afternoone and the most part of the night, with musket and cannon shot' (Hopton, *Bellum Civile*). The Royalists held out until their

Modbury

	Winner	Loser
Opponents	Parliamentarian	Royalist
Commanders	James Chudleigh?	Sir Nicholas Slanning
Numbers	9000?	*c.*1500–1600
Losses	unknown	250

powder ran short, when they were beaten back from the hedges into the blazing town. Forced to retreat on Plympton, they left 100 dead, 150 prisoners, 1100 muskets and five guns. The same day, the Earl of Stamford attacked Hopton's batteries, forcing the Royalists to withdraw to Tavistock, and breaking the siege. Hopton's second invasion of Devon had failed. Both sides needed to reorganize, and concluded a truce on 28 February.

Directions

Follow the A379 west from Kingsbridge. Turn right at Harraton, and fork left to Ayleston Cross, where the left-hand road leads over a hill east of Modbury, marked by the Ordnance Survey as the battle site.

Launceston, Sunday 23 April 1643

England, Cornwall, LR201 SX3384

The final phase of Hopton's campaign in the West began with a demonstration of the defensive/offensive capability of Cornish troops at Launceston, a day-long holding action ended by a counterattack at dusk.

The opposing factions in Devon and Cornwall spun out the truce agreed after Modbury until midnight on 22–23 April. During this period the Royalists quartered their forces at a distance from the county border, to spread the burden of their subsistence. On expiry of the truce, the Parliamentarians exploited this dispersal by attacking a single Royalist regiment posted at Launceston, before it could be reinforced. Hopton had ordered his own army to rendezvous there during forenoon of the 23rd, but the Parliamentarian leader, James Chudleigh, had already concentrated at Lifton, 3 miles (5 km) to the east. He beat off some Royalist dragoons guarding Polson Bridge, and advanced on Launceston while Hopton's men were in church.

The most detailed Parliamentarian source gives Chudleigh 1500 shot, 200 pike and 5 troops of horse. He also had two or three brass guns, and was subsequently reinforced later by 100 horse and Lord Stamford's grey-coated regiment of 700 foot from Plymouth. Hopton began the day with Sir Bevil Grenville's foot and some dragoons. Two more regiments and the cavalry came in just after fighting began at 10 a.m., the other two regular regiments appearing later, about the same time as the enemy reinforcements. This gave Hopton a sufficient numerical superiority to encircle the enemy. Assuming limited casualties, Royalist numbers at Launceston were probably similar to those at Sourton Down two days later: 3000 foot and 600 mounted troops.

The fighting at Launceston centred around the eastern slopes of 'the Beacon Hill over the Towne' (Hopton, *Bellum Civile*). Now known as Windmill Hill, the 492-feet (150-m) hill south of Launceston's centre dominates the road from Polson Bridge, along the south bank of the River Kensey. In 1643 Launceston was smaller, clustered around church and castle, leaving Windmill Hill a distinct feature separate from the town. While Parliamentarian pioneers gapped hedgerows for their infantry to advance across the fields towards Launceston, Hopton led out Grenville's regiment to receive them. The main body held the hilltop, which was prepared for defence. Municipal accounts record payments for 'carrying away wall by the door in the back lane'. Royalist musketeers lined hedges at the foot of the hill, 'half a mile off the Towne' (Thomason Tract E100.20), resting

Launceston

	Winner	Loser
Opponents	Royalist	Parliamentarian
Commanders	Sir Ralph Hopton	James Chudleigh
Numbers	1200–3600	1950–2750
Losses	unknown	*c.*50

their left flank on the stream west of Kensey Vean.

Most of the day, Hopton could only keep the ground he had. Parliamentarian sources speak of beating Royalist musketeers from their hedges 'like sheepe', but it was mid-afternoon 'til they were come neere home to the towne'. The Cornish, 'gathered into a body', suffered much from the Parliamentarian guns, which 'beate them home unto the walls'. Cornwall's high sheriff was killed , 'shot in two by our brasse peeces, blessed be God for this mercie' (T.T. E100.20). Towards evening both sides received reinforcements, at 7 p.m. according to Hopton, rather earlier according to the enemy. The Royalists divided their foot, 'and three severall wayes charg'd upon the Enemies body, which with the losses they had before received, and the opportunytie they had of the night approaching for them to escape away quickly disordered them ...' (*Bellum Civile*). Hopton's converging attack 'plaid upon them on every side whereat our men [the Parliamentarians] began to be dismayed and about 400 shrank away'. Polson Bridge would have been lost, but for the appearance of Lord Stamford's greycoats 'in the very nick' to secure the Parliamentarian retreat (T.T. E100.6).

Darkness and narrow lanes covered Chudleigh's escape, assisted by the accidental explosion of some gunpowder left in a barn. The day's casualties support the impression of an evenly balanced exchange. The Royalists admitted 'noe great losse of their part', despite Parliamentarian claims to have killed 'above twenty for one', while losing only 7 dead and 40 wounded themselves. Certainly there was no rout. That night Chudleigh retreated to Lifton, and then Okehampton, undisturbed by the Royalists, whose rank and file celebrated, 'according to their usual custome after a fight' (*Bellum Civile*), with a mutiny.

Directions

Follow the A388 west towards Launceston, from the old Polson Bridge north of the A30 trunk road. The slopes of Windmill Hill are ahead and to the left, just after the left turn to Higher Bamham. The A388 Tavistock road runs below Hopton's position on the brow of the hill, now thoroughly built over.

Sourton Down, 25 April 1643

England, Devon, LR191 SX5491

The sequel to Chudleigh's setback at Launceston was a Royalist rout on Sourton Down, one of the funnier episodes of the English Civil War, which lost nothing in the hands of the rival propagandists:

> Do you not know, not a fortnight ago,
> How they bragged of a Western Wonder?
> When a hundred ten slew five thousand men,
> With the help of Lightning and Thunder.

Two days after Launceston, the Cornish army advanced to Bridestowe, along the old Okehampton road through the Lew valley, on the northern fringe of Dartmoor. Encouraged by reports of 'great disquyett and feare' among the enemy at Okehampton, Hopton resolved to surprise them, after a night approach across Sourton Down. By chance, a Parliamentarian quartermaster spotted the Royalists, just 'two miles' (clearly old miles) from Okehampton. Sourton Down is at least 3 miles (5 km) from the town, a defile half a mile (0.8 km) wide between South Down (1227 feet/374 m) and Bowerland (820 feet/250m). Hopton's advance confronted Chudleigh with a dilemma, 'to loose the Ordnance and all that we had here ... or to hazard a desperate charge' (Thomason Tract E100.17).

Chudleigh's army had dwindled since Launceston, leaving him three or four troops of horse and not above 600 foot. After blaming 'the intollerable neglect of our lying deputy Scout Master', Chudleigh left his infantry at the end of town, and deployed the cavalry, consisting of 108 troopers, across the east end of Sourton Down, 'close as an Ambuscade under the side of a hill, by many small divisions, with great space between; wee spreading more ground than the enemies whole body'. Another account places them at 'the brow of a hill where the enemie was to passe'. The logical position is northeast of the watershed of the Rivers Lew and Okement, an ancient crossroads marked by a cross and earthworks, and now the A30(T)/A386 interchange. Below the crest, Chudleigh's men would be out of sight, able to see

Sourton Down

	Winner	*Loser*
Opponents	Parliamentarian	Royalist
Commanders	James Chudleigh	Sir Ralph Hopton
Numbers	700	3600
Losses	12	60 (k)

approaching Royalists skylined as they reached the crest. No man was to show himself, 'upon paine of death … till the enemy should march full upon them' (T.T. E100.20 & 17).

Hopton had 3000 foot, 300 horse and 300 dragoons, the latter 'new leavyed'. When they drew out on the western slopes of Sourton Down, he thought them 'the handsoms't body of men that had bene gotten together in those parts all that warr'. The Royalists advanced tactically, preceded by scouts, 'halfe of their dragoones, halfe of their horse, and halfe of their foote in the van, their ordnance in the middle, and th'other halfe of the foote after the ordenance, the left whing of the horse in the next place, and the left whing of the dragoones in the rear of all' (Hopton, *Bellum Civile*).

Hopton and other officers were 'carelessly enterteyning themselves in the head of the dragoones' about 11 p.m., when they rode smack into one of Chudleigh's ambush parties. The Parliamentarian commander 'put spurs to horse, and charged the enemies Horse and Dragoones, giving the shout "Fall on, fall on!", pistolled the first man he met; knockt out the brains of the next with his poll axe, and so made through for the rest of his squadron' (T.T. E100.20). Hopton's raw dragoons panicked and fell back onto the horse, 'and so the Enemy riding mixt with them rowted halfe of the army up to the cannon' (*Bellum Civile*). Parliamentarian accounts make much of how they rode through and through the enemy column; the hostile multitudes defending themselves with musket butt and sword, or firing upon one another in the darkness, finally sticking close to their artillery, 'which made them more confidence [sic] than Sir Ralph Hopton's soldiership …' (T.T. E100.17).

Taking advantage of an old earthwork the Royalists made a stand around the guns, planting iron-shod stakes, known as Swedish feathers across their front, while Hopton brought up fresh troops from the rear. Chudleigh found himself deserted 'by the more ignoble part of our troops'. His own foot had little taste for night fighting, 'hearing onely of two shot of the enemies Ordnance without any more hurt, all forsooke us and ran away'. He was left with his officers, 'and about a Dozen Souldiers, which I was forced to perswade back with a battoone'. Setting burning matches in gorse bushes, to simulate a line of musketeers, Chudleigh imposed upon the enemy until dawn, when they withdrew to Bridestowe.

Royalist discomfiture was completed by a storm which broke just as the action commenced, 'extream weather, lightning and thunder and much Raine, which beate into the Enemies face having neither Hedge nor Ditch'. One propagandist alleged the lightning fired the gunpowder in Royalist bandoleers, scorching their bodies, and providing an excuse for much implausible moralizing (T.T. E100.16 & E102.9).

Hopton admitted 60 Royalists killed. Chudleigh claimed 20 dead, the same number captured, 'and not a man of ours lost'. Another Parliamentarian source admitted 12 wounded, 'not above two that are dangerous'. The victors picked up hundreds of muskets and broke a multitude of pikes, not worth removing. Several senior Royalists had narrow escapes: Hopton lost his helmet, 'and was almost chokt therby'; Lord Mohun was 'taken and stript and not being known let goe'; the high sheriff of Devonshire had his horse shot under him, 'and thence recovered his owne house in South Hams in a womans apparrell' (T.T. E100.16 & 17; *Bellum Civile*). Hopton's captured cloak bag was 'worth a million', containing Royalist subscription lists and orders from Charles I for Hopton to rejoin his old commander-in-chief Hertford in Somerset. Within weeks, this intelligence would bring about the denouement of the western campaign, at Stratton.

Directions

Much of the battlefield is under the A30(T)/A386 interchange west of Okehampton. Follow the B3260 from

Okehampton, and fork right onto a minor road after Highslade farm, along the north side of the A30(T), possibly through Chudleigh's ambush position. Hopton's earthwork may have been near the motel at the top of the pass. He approached along the less traumatized road from Bridestowe, southwest of the junction.

Stratton (Stamford Hill), **16 May 1643**

England, Cornwall, LR190 SS2206–7

The Royalist position in the West remained precarious until May 1643. Hopton's remarkable victory at Stratton saved a reputation shaken by Sourton Down, and transformed the wider strategic situation.

Parliament knew of Royalist intentions to unite Hopton's Cornish army with a detachment from their main Oxford army under the Marquess of Hertford and Prince Maurice, Rupert's younger brother. To prevent this, the Devonshire Parliamentarians once more invaded Cornwall, 'the king's small forces being not half the number and unsupplied with every useful thing' (Clarendon, *History of the Rebellion*). The Earl of Stamford, the Parliamentarian commander, split his forces, sending 1000 cavalry to disperse the posse comitatus at Bodmin, while his infantry occupied a naturally strong position between Bude and Stratton, in northern Cornwall. Resolved to hazard battle while Stamford's cavalry were absent, the Cornish Royalists marched north from Launceston, through North Petherwick and Week St Mary, cutting between the Parliamentarian forces. By sunset of 15 May, 'they were advanced as far as Efford House being within the parish of Stratton' (Hopton, *Bellum Civile*).

The Parliamentarian army lay within a southward loop in the River Neet or Strat, 'strongly encamped and barracadoed upon the flat top of a very high hill that had very steepe ascents to them every way' (*Bellum Civile*). Stamford Hill, renamed after the defeated commander, is a lozenge-shaped plateau, separated by a sharp dip from the last southern spur of a ridge running north–south, parallel with the coast, a mile (1.6 km) to the west. It is notoriously impregnable upon the east, falling steeply to the Neet, but Hopton attacked from the other side. He advanced well to the west of Stamford Hill, passing the river lower down, at Efford Mill. House and mill are gone, but Ordnance Survey maps still show Efford Beacon, near Bude on the coast. Hopton drove Stamford's musketeers away from the crossing, securing a bridgehead beyond the golf course, somewhere near Burn.

Stamford had 5400 infantry, about half of them Trained Band militiamen, the rest volunteers and the Greycoat regiment that had covered Chudleigh's retreat from Launceston in April. Descriptions of the fighting suggest he formed two echelons, the militia in support. The Parliamentarians also had 200 horse, who achieved little, 13 brass pieces and a mortar. These are often said to have been in the oval earthwork atop Stamford Hill, but the structure is ancient and unsuitable as a battery. Contemporary sources ignore it.

Hopton had 500 cavalry, 2400 infantry and 8 field pieces. He divided infantry and guns into four equal storming parties, the rightmost opposite the south side of Stamford's camp, facing northeast. Many reconstructions of Stratton follow Clarendon's interpretation of Hopton's fourfold deployment as an attack from all four points of the compass. This is a military nonsense that ignores the problems of coordinating such a dispersed advance, without being defeated in detail, let alone getting up the sheer eastern slope, where the woods still defy developers. The Royalists were aware of the ground, as Sir Bevil Grenville, one of Hopton's colonels, lived nearby, and had clearly

Stratton

	Winner	*Loser*
Opponents	Royalist	Parliamentarian
Commanders	Sir Ralph Hopton	Henry Grey, Earl of Stamford James Chudleigh (p)
Numbers	2900	5600
Losses	*c.*90	2000

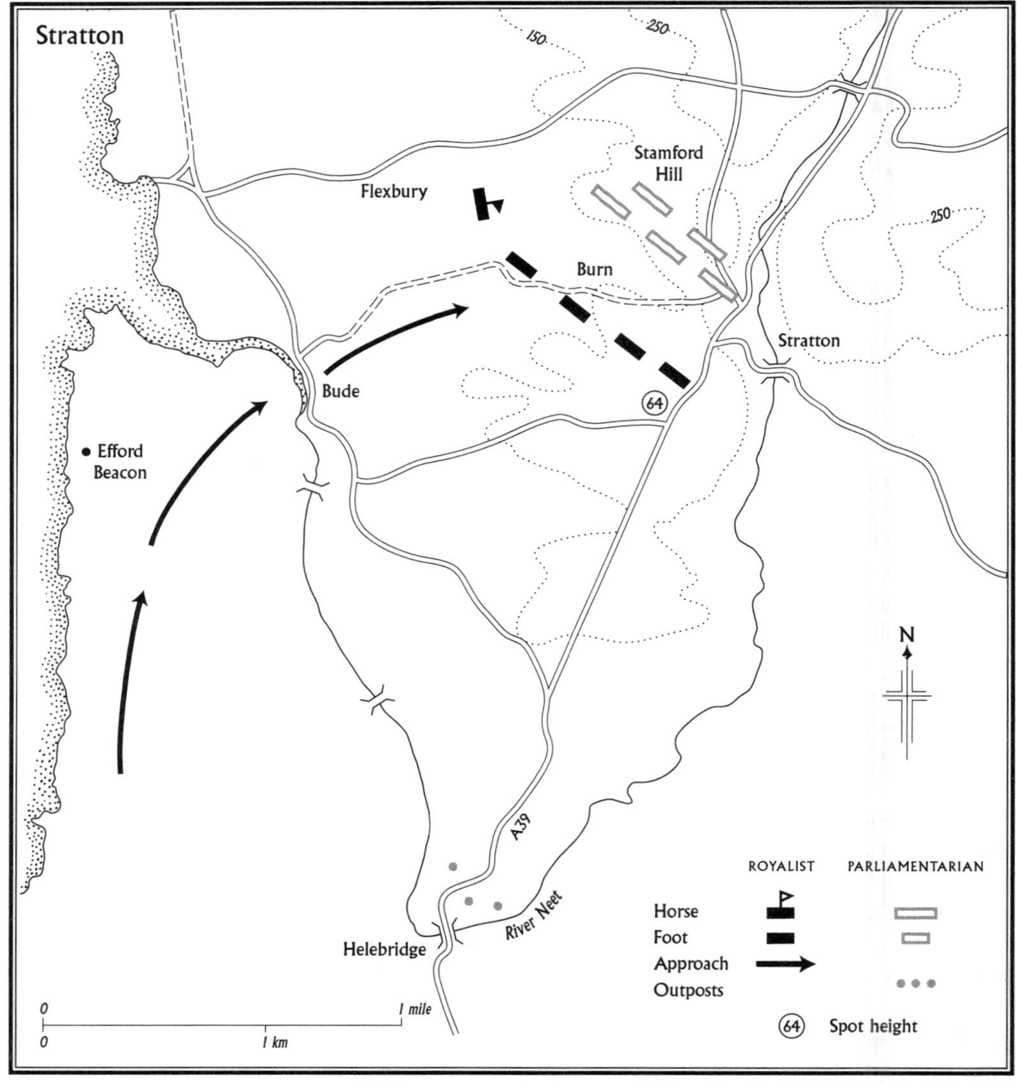

manoeuvred to gain the gentler slopes to seaward. Hopton's start line probably ran northwest from point 64 around the foot of the hill, half a musket shot from the enemy musketeers lining the hedges up to Broomhill House. He held his mounted troops back 'upon a Sandy-Common, where there was a way leading up to the Enemye Campe ... to charge anything that should come downe that way'. This was probably near Flexbury, covering the lane towards

Directions

Various lanes and footpaths cross the battlefield, now surrounded by suburban villas. Follow the footpath across Bude golf course to Hopton's start line near Burn. Alternatively, take the A39(T) into Stratton, fork left opposite the hospital, and climb up to the battle site as marked by the Ordnance Survey. See the monument on the hill, and a wall plaque outside the Tree Inn in Stratton.

Stamford Hill, via Broomhill. The cavalry's orders and location are consistent with their securing Hopton's left flank. Stamford could anchor his left on the steep slope down to the Neet, but his right was more open. A Parliamentarian officer describes relieving the outpost line, 'South West of Warmington's House downe towards the sea sandes' (Captain Robert Bennett). 'Warmington's House' was either Broomhill Manor or Hill House, on the northwest shoulder of Stamford Hill.

Hedge fighting began at first light, and 'continued doubtfull with many countenances of various events till about three of the clock in the afternoone' (*Bellum Civile*). When it ended, the Royalists had run out of ammunition, without shifting the enemy. Hopton's commanders agreed 'by messengers to one another … to advance their full main bodies [i.e. the pikes], without making any more shot, till they reached the top of the hill, and so might be on even ground with the enemy' (Clarendon). The Royalist ability to coordinate such an assault supports the more compact deployment described above.

The defenders may have been demoralized by the silent Royalist advance, or just worn out by ten hours of skirmishing. The burden of the fire fight seems to have fallen upon Stamford's first line, 'in all which time our poore Gray-coats and Voluntiers did their parts very manfully; but our base cow-hearted trained Souldiers, as soone as they came to doe service ran all away' (Thomason Tract E103.12). James Chudleigh led a Parliamentarian counterattack on Grenville's party, the second from the right. Grenville was knocked over, but Royalist musketeers on the flanks restored the situation, capturing Chudleigh, 'and the Van of a brave Army killed, taken, and routed with him [sic]' (T.T. E67.27). Captain Bennett confirms the rot set in on that side, maintaining his own position 'till the enemy came in upon our Reare by reason that the left winge fayled'.

Stamford still had 3000 men, 'but no intreaty could perswade above thirty of them to stay'. The earl's enemies claimed that he had fled already, but a Parliamentarian colonel avers he stayed to the last, firing the guns before he withdrew. Royalist columns converged on the hilltop between 3 and 4 p.m., turning the enemy's own guns upon them to complete their rout. Pinned against the sheer drop to the east, 1700 Parliamentarians were captured, beside 300 previously killed. Clarendon supplies Hopton's estimate of 'not above four score' Royalists killed, with many more wounded, ten of whom died. Two thousand arms were taken, all the Parliamentarian guns, 70 barrels of gunpowder and a great quantity of biscuit, 'a verie seasonable blessing to the Cornish Army that had suffered very great want of foode for 3 or 4 dayes before, and had not fower barrels of powder left in the world' (*Bellum Civile*). Hopton's astonishing victory over superior numbers, materiel and position ended the Civil Wars' opening period in Cornwall. It freed him to lead his Cornish army onto a wider stage.

Deadlock in the Centre: 1643

The Edgehill campaign left a strategic impasse in the Thames valley. The main Parliamentarian army under Essex commanded London's western approaches, but lacked the numbers and resolve to evict the king from his headquarters at Oxford, behind its outer ring of fortified towns: Reading, Abingdon and Banbury. This central theatre of the war saw no great strategic movements in early 1643. Skirmishes at Hopton Heath (19 March) and Chalgrove Field (18 June) involved Royalist detachments striking out from Oxford's defences. Essex limited himself to the siege of Reading, captured on 27 April.

More significant were the activities of Sir William Waller, who had secured the south coast for Parliament, including the great naval base at Portsmouth, the previous year. Early in 1643 he 'made a cavalcade or two into the west … not only beat up some loose quarters, but had surprised a fixed and fortified quarter, made by the Lord Harbert of Ragland, near Glocester [sic]' (Clarendon, *History of the Rebellion*). Waller's Highnam victory (24 March) won him a great reputation and the nickname 'William the Conqueror'. His appearance in the Severn valley, where Parliament already held Bristol and Gloucester, threatened Oxford's communications with the Welsh Marches. Prince Maurice was detached from the main Royalist army to secure these, defeating Waller at Ripple Field (13 April). Maurice's subsequent junction with Sir Ralph Hopton's Cornish army intensified the struggle for western England, provoking the fiercest actions of the war so far, at Lansdown (5 July) and Roundway Down (13 July).

A fortnight after the destruction of Waller's army at Roundway Down, troops from Oxford joined the Royalist western army to storm Bristol (26 July). The subsequent siege of Gloucester in August stirred even the comatose Essex to action. Reinforcing his army with London Trained Bands, he marched around Oxford's northern outposts to relieve Gloucester (5 September). On his return, the Royalists intercepted him at Newbury, one of the war's greatest missed opportunities. The armies fought themselves to a standstill (20 September), but the Royalists ran short of ammunition and allowed Parliament's main army to escape. The Royalists recapture of Reading on 3 October showed how little the situation on the central front had changed since spring. Neither side was strong enough to win the war without outside help.

Hopton Heath, Sunday 19 March 1643

England, Staffordshire, LR127 SJ9526

Fighting flared across the Midlands as rival gentry struggled for control of their localities. The little-known encounter at Hopton Heath was one outcome of these internecine struggles.

Parliamentarian forces took Lichfield on 6 March 1643. The Earl of Northampton, commander of the Oxford Cavaliers' northernmost outpost at Banbury, went to support Staffordshire's Royalists, and recover the cathedral city. Meanwhile, Parliamentarian columns from Derbyshire and Cheshire were converging on Stafford under Sir John Gell and Sir William Brereton respectively. Their plan was to rendezvous at Hopton Heath, 3 miles (5 km) northeast of Stafford, at 2 p.m. on 19 March. Gell crossed the Trent at Weston. Brereton approached from the north through Sandon, perhaps along Salt Heath Lane. His late arrival allowed the Royalists to attack Gell, before Brereton's infantry came up.

Hopton Heath was a rare encounter between mounted troops and an all-arms force. Peter Young has calculated Northampton had 25 troops of horse (800 strong), 300 dragoons and perhaps 100 Banbury foot. His artillery consisted of one 29-pounder called 'Roaring Meg'. The Parliamentarians had more men of lesser quality: six troops (400), five companies of dragoons (300), 500 shot and perhaps 250 pikes: 'the most licentious, ungovernable wretches that belong to Parliament' (Lucy Hutchinson). Gell also had some 'Moorlanders', 'a great rubble [sic] of all sorts … neither disciplined nor armed; some with birding guns, others with only clubs, others with pieces of scythes, very few with muskets'. He had a powerful artillery for so small a force: eight 3-pounder drakes and three heavier pieces.

The Weston and Sandon roads run 2000 yards (1830 m) apart across an east–west ridge between Stafford and the Trent. Salt Heath and Hopton Heath lie between these roads, physically continuous, but separated by Brick-kiln Lane. They made a good defensive position, enclosures on either flank for dismounted dragoons, and rising ground behind for the guns. In the centre an unknown Royalist recalled a rabbit warren, 'full of coney holes where horse could not charge without great danger and hazard', which protected Gell's ill-trained foot against Northampton's horse.

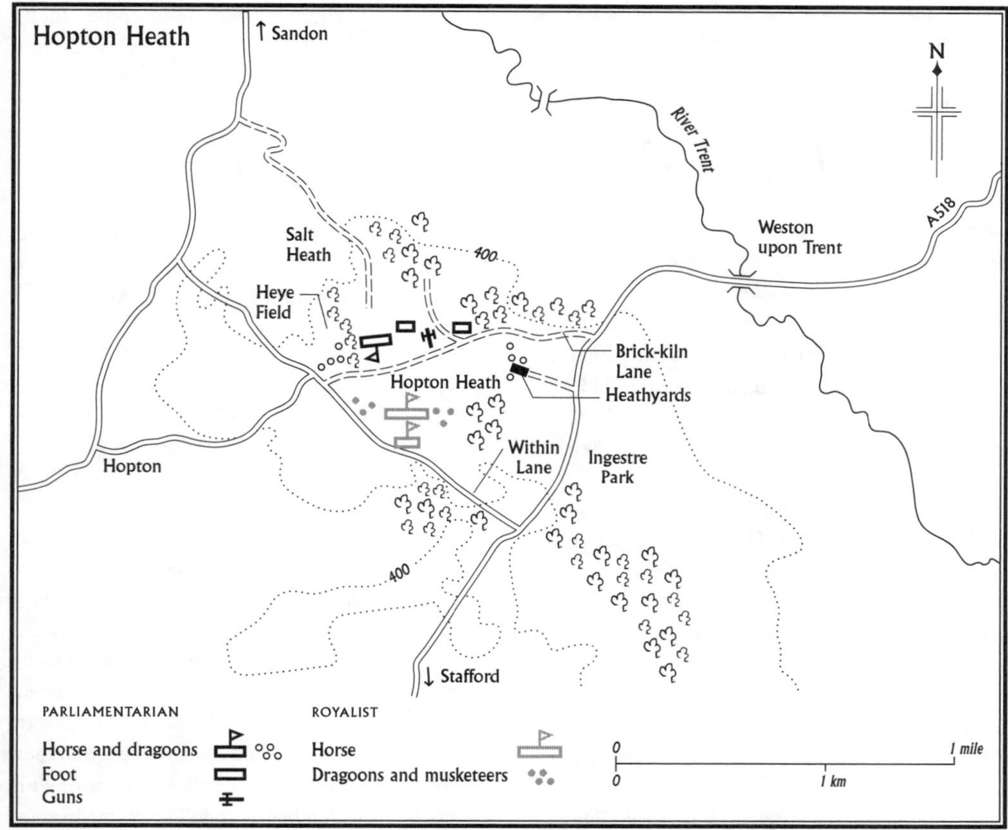

A.H. Burne located the Parliamentarian left by the stone wall of Ingestre Park, on the Stafford–Weston road, their front running northwest through Heathyards Farm, and across the heath. Even he thought the 1500-yard (1370-m) frontage excessive for the numbers available. A more recent reconstruction, based on a sketch drawn for a 16th-century lawsuit, pulls the left in towards the Parliamentarian centre, reducing the front to half a mile (0.8 km) between the stone wall around Heathyards and the hedges of Heye Field, down a gentle slope to the west. Parliamentarian dragoons occupied both enclosures, infantry and guns on the sandy hillocks across Brick-kiln Lane, now wooded, cavalry in five or six ranks filling in between the guns and Heye Field.

Northampton arrived about 3 p.m., and drew up within half cannon shot, perhaps 400 yards (370 m) to the south, where the Ordnance Survey marks the battle site. He would have formed up in three ranks, his four Oxford regiments in front, supported by four Staffordshire troops, perhaps 600 and 200 in each echelon. Royalist dragoons started the battle by clearing the enclosures to right and left, while

Directions

Take the A518 northeast from Stafford, continuing uphill past the Agricultural Show Ground to Heathyards' entrance on the left. The northern end of Brick-kiln Lane, leading back to the Parliamentarian position on the heath, is next left, by the disused quarry. The Royalist forming-up area beyond Within Lane is now obscured by RAF Stafford. Battlefield Ridge and Cromwell Close in Hopton village are spurious, but see a plaque in Willmorehill Lane.

Hopton Heath		
	Winner	*Loser*
Opponents	Royalist	Parliamentarian
Commanders	Spencer Compton, Earl of Northampton (k)	Sir John Gell Sir William Brereton
Numbers	1200	*c.*1450
Losses	50	300

'Roaring Meg' softened up the Parliamentarian centre. Her first shot killed six and wounded four, the second 'making such a lane through them,' according to an anonymous Royalist, 'that they had little mind to close again'.

Northampton's first cavalry charge saw off most of the Parliamentarian horse. He then launched a more desperate attempt against the remaining enemy cavalry, who had taken shelter amongst their infantry. The Roundheads' first volley 'did perform mighty great execution', but the Royalists rode over much of their foot, and 'almost routed the Parliament party' (Sir William Brereton). The victorious horse took eight guns, but fell back, pelted with musketry, allowing the enemy to repossess their battery. In the melee, Northampton was separated from his men, unhorsed and his helmet knocked off with a musket butt. Scorning to take quarter 'from such base rogues as you are', he was killed with a halberd blow to the back of the head.

The Cavaliers came on again, retaking the guns and clearing the last Parliamentarian horse from the field. However, the Roundhead foot stood fast. Over half the Royalist troop commanders were down, night was falling, and 'the field which they thought so fair, was found full of coalpits and holes dangerous for horse' (Clarendon, *History of the Rebellion*). Perforce the exhausted Royalists held off until next morning. By then the enemy had slipped away, leaving behind their baggage and ammunition.

The refusal of Gell's foot to run away and, in the chilling expression of the day, suffer execution at the hands of the victorious Royalist cavalry, kept down the casualties. The Royalist tabloid, *Mercurius Aulicus*, claimed 100 Parliamentarian dead and as many prisoners, perhaps 300 including wounded. Clarendon put Royalist losses at 25 dead and the same hurt. The *Victoria County History* perversely presents the result as a Royalist defeat. While Lichfield remained in Parliamentarian hands for the moment, Northampton had forestalled Gell's and Brereton's designs on Stafford. Their divergent withdrawal, to Uttoxeter and Stone, left nobody to prevent Prince Rupert retaking Lichfield a month later on 21 April.

Highnam, 24 March 1643

England, Gloucestershire, LR162 SO7919

One of the most decisive engagements of the early Civil War was Sir William Waller's capture of an entire Royalist army at Highnam, yet most accounts of the conflict barely mention it.

Charles I depended heavily on magnates raising troops for his army. One of the greatest moneyed men in the kingdom was the Marquess of Worcester, whose estates were in the southern Welsh Marches. His son Lord Herbert spent £60,000 recruiting his tenants to clear Pembroke and Gloucestershire for the king. In mid-February they advanced on Gloucester, through the Forest of Dean, perhaps as part of a wider plan calling for Prince Maurice to attack the city from the east. Otherwise it is hard to explain what the Welsh hoped to achieve by entrenching the old bishop's palace at Highnam Court, a mile (1.6 km) west of the long bridge leading to Gloucester on the opposite bank of the Severn. John Corbet, chaplain to Edward Massey, Gloucester's Parliamentarian governor, derided their inactivity: 'five weeks in a stinking nest, they were basely baffled, never attempted our outguard, never undertook the least party that issued forth'.

The unfortunate Welsh faced two of Parliament's most effective commanders. Massey's sorties 'never failed to beat the enemys into their works, kill and take prisoners ... so that the name of our blew [-coated] regiment became a terror to those miserable Welshmen' (Corbet). Waller had recently taken command of the Parliamentarian Western Association, formed from Somerset, Gloucestershire, Worcestershire, Wiltshire, Shropshire and Bristol. On 21 March he stormed Malmesbury, and 'making a face at Cirencester … by a sudden night march posted to the River Severn six miles west of Gloucester' (Clarendon, *History of the Rebellion*). By prior arrangement, Massey had sent flat boats down to Framilode, allowing Waller to slip across the river to Huntley, between the Welsh and home, 'the guard of the river being either treacherously or sottishly neglected' (Clarendon). Meanwhile Waller had ordered Massey 'to draw forth both horse and shot before Highnam, and to keepe them in continuall action, that they might not understand his approach' (Corbet).

Parliamentarian numbers are uncertain. Massey drew 500 men from his garrison, of whom 300 might have been horse. Waller had 'a light party of horse and dragoons, near 2000' (Clarendon), but not all of them saw action at Highnam. Royalist prisoners after the battle equalled or outnumbered Waller's whole force, suggesting the total shown below. Herbert had raised 'a body of above 1500 foot and near 500 horse, very well and sufficiently armed' (Clarendon). Nearly as numerous as Hopton's Cornish army, the Welsh Royalists lacked effective leaders. Lord John Somerset in command of the horse, was 'a maiden soldier', while the infantry commander, 'a bold and sprightly officer', had been killed during the approach march. Herbert was absent on political business at Oxford.

Massey performed his diversion with distinction, 'brought up the ordnance neere the house and kept them in the heat of play till the evening' (Corbet). At dusk on the 23rd he flung a picket line around the enemy to prevent their escape, although they were dug in with artillery, and outnumbered him three-to-one. Next morning some Welsh horse tried to break out, driving Massey's cavalry back on their infantry supports, who nearly lost their cannon in the melee. Corbet continues:

> In this point of the action Sir William Waller came up and shot his warning piece on the other side, which dasht the enemy, and so revived our men that they ran up with fury, [and] stormed a redoubt.

Waller had only 150 foot soldiers, but sufficient colours for two infantry regiments, which he placed 'in the best advantage for show', while directing his artillery against the house. His sudden appearance in their rear so shook the inexperienced Royalists that 'after his approach not a man of the enemy was slaine or hurt, yet the common souldiers would do anything but fight' (Corbet). To Clarendon's disgust, 'without giving or receiving blow they … kindly delivered up themselves and their arms upon the single grant of quarter'.

Corbet counted nearly 1500 prisoners lodged in St Mary de Lode and Trinity churches in Westgate Street, where they lived on turnip tops and cabbage leaves. Waller claimed 1400 'common prisoners well armed'; 'commanders and gentlemen about 150' (Thomason Tract E97.1). Clarendon recorded nearly 1300 foot and three troops of horse taken. Lord John Somerset had remained at a safe distance with three or four troops more. Some of them came unstuck 2 miles (3 km) northwest of Highnam, where, in 1868, 86 skeletons were found at Barber's Bridge on a tributary of the River Leadon. More appeared during road widening in the 1970s. Waller admitted two casualties.

Highnam was a major Royalist disaster whose consequences have escaped notice. Clarendon wrote of a 'mushrump army, which grew up and perished so soon that the loss of it was scarce apprehended at Oxford'. Had the Herberts' money been better spent, 'the war might have been ended the next summer'.

Highnam

	Winner	*Loser*
Opponents	Parliamentarian	Royalist
Commanders	Sir William Waller Colonel Edward Massey	Sir Jerome Brett (p)
Numbers	*c.*1500	2000
Losses	unknown	1550 (p)

Directions

Highnam Court was damaged in the battle, and rebuilt during the 1650s. Its landscaped Victorian gardens are open to the public. Follow the A40 Ross-on-Wye road west from Gloucester, and take the right hand exit off the A48 roundabout. Remains of Welsh trenches 3–6-feet (1–2-m) high survive near Highnam Church. A large monument marks the mass grave near Barber's Bridge, right of the B4215 heading to Newent.

Ripple Field, Thursday 13 April 1643

England, Worcestershire, LR150 SO8737–8

The Royalist defeat at Highnam provoked a response similar to that which followed the loss of Lichfield. A local setback attracted reinforcements from the king's main army. Prince Maurice's Oxford Cavaliers provided stiffer opposition at Ripple Field than Herbert's Welshmen had at Highnam.

Maurice pursued Waller into the Forest of Dean, crossing the Severn at Tewkesbury by a pontoon bridge. Waller doubled back to Gloucester, 'by bypathes and unsuspected waies', according to the Royalist newspaper *Mercurius Aulicus* and sent Massey to break Maurice's bridge. The prince's approach on the evening of 12 April drew Waller to Tewkesbury, but his horses were too worn out to go further. Pushing north next morning to block the permanent bridge at Upton-on-Severn, Waller found Maurice had already regained the Severn's eastern bank.

Waller left Tewkesbury by the King John Bridge across the River Avon, climbing The Mythe or Royal Hill, before turning along the old Worcester road, left of the modern A38. He met Maurice beyond Ripple village, 'his army drawn up and divided into three bodies, besides the hedges lined with musketeers' (John Corbet). The ground slopes upwards from Ripple for 400 yards (370 m) to the crest of Old Nan's Hill, perhaps a corruption of Ordnance Hill, a reminder of where Waller deployed his artillery. The ridge runs east–west from Ripple School towards Uckinghall village. Northwards it falls away steeply to Ripple Field, a flat area intersected with hedges, the first two enclosures known significantly as Deadland Furlong and Scarlett Close.

Maurice lay within cannon shot, perhaps at the crossroads half a mile (0.8 km) north of Old Nan's Hill. He had at least two regiments of horse, one of dragoons and one of foot. Waller had some 1300 mounted troops and one company of Massey's blue-coated foot, enough to dispute a bridge, but insufficient to fight an all-arms force in the open. Sun and wind were against the Parliamentarians, whose retreat lay down a narrow tree-lined lane, some 2 miles (3 km) long.

Ripple Field was not one of Waller's better days. He revealed his numerical weakness by occupying the forward slope, instead of lining the crest, 'to deceive the enemy with the semblance of a greater power behind'. His cannon proved ineffective, 'having neither shot prepared nor cannoneers that understood their business'. A half-hearted cavalry reconnaissance, 'discovered their [i.e. Maurice's] ambuscades within the hedges', and Waller decided to withdraw, 'commanding a party of dragoons to face the prince's army, and the musketeers to stand at the corners of the lane within the hedges to make good their retreat' (Corbet).

Maurice thought Waller meant to draw him into an ambush, 'knowing whom he was to deal with, having repulsed the horse sent out to brave him pursued no further than the Countrie was free and open, and then commanded some of his choicest foote to scoure the hedges' (*Mercurius Aulicus*). Having

Ripple Field

	Winner	*Loser*
Opponents	Royalist	Parliamentarian
Commanders	Prince Maurice	Sir William Waller Colonel Edward Massey
Numbers	*c.*2000	*c.*1400
Losses	2 killed	*c.*200

cleared up the situation, the Royalists suddenly attacked with devastating effect: 'not a man of those dragoons would stand ... but hurried away, broke over the hedge, fell among and disordered our owne musketeers, the enemy clapt in among them, cut downe four or five of the foot, and took as many prisoners' (Corbet).

Sir Arthur Hesilrige, a leading rebel and one of the Five Members (see introduction to Part 6), countercharged with his own troop of arquebusiers, 'put the enemy to a stand, and in part took off the foulnesse of the retreat through that strait passage'. A foot soldier shut a farm gate in the Royalists' faces by an old barn just north of Ripple, gaining time for the horse to show front; 'for a while they stood in a maze, but on a suddaine faced about, ran flock meale, the enemy upon their backs'. Luckily for Waller's cavalry, some infantry from Tewkesbury eventually formed a rearguard 'at the entrance of a strait passage neare the Mythe Hill' (Corbet), where they stopped the chase.

Mercurius Aulicus admitted two Royalist fatalities, while claiming 80 Parliamentarians killed, 'beside as many more ... who flying from the sword, fell into the river, and were there drowned'. Prince Maurice is usually eclipsed by his elder brother Rupert, but he was the first Royalist commander to check William Waller. He failed to retake Tewkesbury, however, being recalled to Oxford to help relieve Reading. Paradoxically Ripple Field left 'William the Conqueror' master of the Severn valley.

Directions

Follow the A38 north from Tewkesbury, up the Mythe. Turn left after 2 miles (3 km) along Bow Lane, a minor road through Puckrup to Ripple. Pass over the M50, which runs less than 1 mile (1.6 km) south of Ripple across the scene of the later cavalry action. Turn right and left through narrow winding village streets between half-timbered houses to Waller's position at the south end of Ripple Field.

Chalgrove Field, Sunday 18 June 1643

England, Oxfordshire, LR165 SU6497–6598

The rearguard skirmish at Chalgrove Field had little military significance. Its celebrity arises from the consequent death of John Hampden, MP, an inveterate opponent of Charles I.

The Earl of Essex moved a little nearer Oxford after taking Reading (27 April 1643), spreading his forces to cover the Home Counties. This dispersal invited Royalist cavalry raids. At 5 p.m. on 17 June Prince Rupert left Oxford by Magdalen Bridge, in response to intelligence of a Parliamentarian pay convoy bound for Essex's headquarters at Thame. Bypassing an enemy outpost at Tetsworth, Rupert fell upon Postcombe and Chinnor at 2 a.m. next day. The Royalist assaults were well executed, but noisy. The pay convoy hid in the Chiltern foothills, and several troops of Parliamentarian horse turned out to give chase. Rupert retired on Chiselhampton, where Royalist infantry secured his route home across the River Thame. He approached the narrow lane leading to the bridge at about 8 a.m. on a hot sunny morning. Hard-pressed by Essex's cavalry, the prince resolved to turn and fight rather than risk being caught strung out along the defile.

The road Rupert used is now the B480. It once ran east–west along the top of a gently sloping plateau, a quarter of a mile (0.4 km) north of Chalgrove. It has since been rerouted downhill, nearer the village, to make way for an airfield. English Heritage places the action either side of a 'Great Hedge' east of the airfield buildings. Halfway between Chalgrove and Warpsgrove House, this obstacle marked the northern edge of the unenclosed arable land of Chalgrove Field. At the time of the battle it probably continued in a northwesterly direction towards Chalgrove Common, where Haseley Brook deterred cavalry movements around the hedge's northern extremity.

The site is over 3 miles (5 km) from Chiselhampton Bridge, and at first appears too far east. The official Royalist account, reproduced in the English

Heritage Battlefield Report, put Rupert 1½ miles (2.4 km) from the bridge when the Parliamentarians were seen approaching over Golder Hill to the east. Clarendon, at Royalist headquarters in Oxford, believed the bridge was 'yet two miles [3 km] from them'. These estimates would put the Royalists at the other end of the airfield, near Rofford Hall.

This westerly location does not, however, match the official Royalist account of how the enemy 'drew down to the bottom of a great Close or Pasture'. This is later identified with a tree-lined enclosure around Warpsgrove House, where the Parliamentarians placed their reserve, a position too far back to support troops engaged beyond the airfield. In addition there is no suitable 'bottom' near Rofford Hall, although a convenient stream between Warpsgrove and Golder Manor might be the feature in question. It must be assumed, therefore, that the contemporary accounts gave distances in 'great' miles, placing Rupert significantly nearer the northern boundary of Chalgrove Field.

Rupert had left Oxford with three regiments of horse (1000–1200 men), supported by 'a great body of dragoons' (350) and 500 foot. Only the horse saw action at Chalgrove, the rest lining the hedges through Stadhampton down to Chiselhampton Bridge. The official Royalist account claims the Parliamentarians had eight troops in front, three in support at Warpsgrove, and two more 'higher up the hill'. Depending on one's assumptions about troop strengths, this would make 650–910 Parliamentarians. Essex reported that three troops responded to the first alarm, reinforced by another troop and 50 commanded horse, besides a troop of dragoons (Thomason Tract E55.19). Altogether this made 'not above 300 horse', probably an underestimate.

Chalgrove Field

	Winner	*Loser*
Opponents	Royalist	Parliamentarian
Commanders	Prince Rupert	Sir Philip Stapleton John Hampden (k)
Numbers	1000–1200	350–900
Losses	45 (k)	10–12 (k)

The outnumbered Parliamentarians approached in some disorder, 'in the pursuit as they thought, of a flying enemy' (Clarendon, *History of the Rebellion*). The Royalists were debating whether to draw the enemy further into their ambush when enemy dragoons shot at Rupert from the hedge in front: 'Yea (saith he) their insolency is not to be endured.' Setting spurs to horse he leapt the hedge 'in the very face of the dragooners', while 'the rest of his troop of Lifeguards (every man as he could) jumbled over after him' (Official Account).

Parliamentarian cavalry had not yet abandoned their disastrous preference for firepower over shock action. They slowed down while the prince formed line, and blazed away as the Royalists came on, 'yea, they had time for their second pistols, ere ours could charge them'. Nevertheless, 'they stood our first charge of pistols and swords, better than the rebels have ever yet done since their first beating at Worcester [Powick Bridge, 1642]' (Official Account). Superior tactics and numbers soon told: 'The Enemy being so very strong, kept a body of Horse for his reserve and with that Body, wheeled about and charged our men in the Reare, so that being encompassed and overborne with multitude, they broke and fled' (T.T. E55.19).

According to the Royalist account, the decisive move was a right flanking attack by Rupert's Lifeguard, which broke the Parliamentarian left. The Parliamentarian reserve near Warpsgrove House were carried away in the rout, the pursuit continuing 'a full mile and a quarter ... from the place of the first encounter'. Essex claimed that Sir Philip Stapleton rallied the fugitives, and showed front for about an hour, but if he did it was beyond the hill, out of sight of the enemy.

Rupert withdrew unmolested, regaining Oxford at noon, with nearly 200 prisoners from Chinnor, seven cornets and four ensigns. Essex reported 45 dead altogether, mostly Royalists. The latter reversed the proportion. The most serious casualty on either side was Hampden, hit in the shoulder during the first charge. A Parliamentarian pamphleteer thought this 'more likely to be a badge of honour than any danger', but Hampden died on 24 June, 'to as great consternation of all that party as if their whole army had been defeated and cut off' (Clarendon). Hampden's death ensured his fame among Parliamentarian sympathizers, making Chalgrove Field part of Civil War mythology. Clarendon, by contrast, thought Parliament's loss 'a great deliverance to the nation', which would have recompensed a considerable defeat.

Directions

Chalgrove is 8 miles (13 km) southeast of Oxford. Follow the B480 to Chiselhampton, across the Thame and towards Chalgrove airfield. Skirting its southern edge, turn left along a minor road to Hampden's memorial, confusingly erected behind the Royalist start line. Continue northeast 1/3 mile (500 m) to Rupert's Hedge, on the left opposite the depot shown on the Landranger map. Warpsgrove House is no longer standing, having burned down since the battle.

Lansdown, 5 July 1643

England, Somerset, LR172 ST7269–71

The English Civil War's first summer saw regional and national struggles coalesce, producing larger, more desperate battles. Lansdown gained the Cornish infantry immortal glory, but at a shocking price.

Sir Ralph Hopton's victory at Stratton (see above) cleared the way for a rendezvous with a force of Oxford Royalists at Chard, on 4 June. The Marquess of Hertford held nominal command, but Hopton and Prince Maurice made the tactical decisions. They soon encountered Sir William Waller's Western Association army, plentifully supplied from Bristol, while the Royalists found the country 'so disaffected that only force could bring in any supply' (Clarendon, *History of the Rebellion*). Waller occupied Bath, a naturally strong place surrounded by steep hills, covering his own base, and threatening Royalist communications with Oxford. Historians disagree on which of the three cities – Bath, Bristol or Gloucester – constituted the Royalist objective. Clarendon suggests they simply wanted to fight Waller before he got any stronger. After several days failing to contrive an engagement on even terms southeast of Bath, the Royalists' progressive turning movements brought them to Tog Hill, on the Bristol–Oxford road north of Bath. Operating on internal lines, Waller was already deployed a mile (1.6 km) away on Lansdown Hill, a long flat-topped hill running northwest from Bath, ending in an abrupt 150–200-foot (45–60-m) drop. His position appeared so strong that after some hours skirmishing the Royalists withdrew towards Marshfield, as if heading for Oxford, 'presuming that by this means they should draw the enemy from the place of advantage, their chief business [i.e. Waller's] being to hinder them from joining with the king' (Clarendon).

Waller had better cavalry, but fewer infantry. Exact Parliamentarian numbers are unknown, but included most of Stamford's 1200 Devonshire horse (see Stratton above). More horse had come from London, as a counterweight to Maurice, including a regiment of cuirassiers, or 'Lobsters', raised by Sir Arthur Hesilrige since Ripple Field, and perhaps 500 dragoons. A week later Waller had about 2000 foot at Roundway Down, and it is hard to see how he could have held his own at Lansdown with less. Combined Royalist strength was: Hopton with 500 horse, 300 dragoons, 3000 incomparable Cornish infantry and 4 or 5 guns; Maurice with 1600–1700 horse, 1000 newly raised foot and 7 or 8 guns.

Waller's position on Lansdown Hill justified his reputation as 'the best shifter and chooser of ground when he was not Master of the field' (Sir Walter Slingsby). Clarendon described it as 'a place almost inaccessible', the brow of the hill strengthened with earthworks and cannon: 'On either flank grew a pretty thick wood towards the declining of the hill, in which strong parties of musketeers were placed; at the rear [beyond the crest] was a very fair plain where the reserves of horse and foot stood ranged.' A Royalist cavalry officer described Tog Hill and Freezing Hill where he stood to the north as a wedge-shaped eminence, 'like a straight horn about six score yards over at the end towards Marshfield, and twenty score over at the end towards their army; on both sides enclosed with a hedge and woods without that' (Captain Richard Atkyns). The road from 'Friznoll' dips steeply into the valley, before winding up the Lansdown escarpment. A stone wall provides some cover along the road, as may the dead ground in front of Waller's breastworks. The woods to either flank still exist, somewhat closer than in 1643, those to the east shown on OS maps as 'Battlefields'.

The Battle of Lansdown consists of two separate actions. The first began about 3 p.m., when Waller sent parties of horse and dragoons to attack the Royalist flank and rear, as they retreated across Tog Hill. Atkyns thought this 'the boldest thing I ever saw the enemy do; for a party of less than 1000 to charge an army of 6000 horse foot and cannon, in their own ground, at least a mile and a half from their body'. Nevertheless, they threw the whole Royalist army into disorder. Dragoons advanced unseen through the hedgerows, and shot up the Royalist cavalry, crowding them back onto their own foot. Hesilrige's cuirassiers routed two bodies of horse, 'and gave so great a terror to the king's horse, who had never before turned from an enemy that no example of their officers ... could make them charge' (Clarendon)'. Only the Cornish musketeers supporting the cavalry held their ground, until successive countercharges drove the Parliamentarians back into the valley between Freezing Hill and Lansdown. After two hours fighting they recovered their original position, with 'all the symptoms of a flying army; as of blowing up of powder, horse and foot running distractedly upon the edge of the hill, for we could see no further' (Atkyns).

Thus encouraged the Cornish foot insisted that Hopton, 'lett us fetch those cannon', precipitating a second quite unnecessary battle. The lie of the land, open in the centre, woods on the flanks, inspired Hopton to reverse the usual tactical sequence. Pikes and cavalry advanced up 'that broad way that leads to Lansdowne ... sending out as they wente strong parties of muskettiers on eache hand ... to endeavour under the couvert of the inclosed groundes to gaine the flanck of the Enimy on the topp of the Hill' (Hopton, *Bellum Civile*).

The initial attack was repulsed by Waller's horse,

Lansdown		
	Winner	*Loser*
Opponents	Royalist	Parliamentarian
Commanders	Prince Maurice	Sir William Waller
	Sir Ralph Hopton (w)	Sir Arthur Hesilrige (w)
Numbers	6400–6500	*c.*4500
Losses	*c.*200	*c.*20 (k)

and rallied by Sir Bevil Grenville, who stormed the works despite a hail of fire and repeated cavalry charges. Grenville fell to a blow on the head from a poleaxe, but his Cornish pikemen stood fast on a ledge just below the crest, 'as upon the eaves of a house for steepness, but as unmovable as a rock'. Atkyns had followed Grenville up the hill, but could not find his own regiment, 'for the air was so darkened by the smoke of the powder, that for a quarter of an hour together ... there was no light seen, but what the fire of the volleys of shot gave'. Waller claimed the like had never been seen in England, 'the famous fights in France were but a play in comparison of this. Not a regiment of ours but charged their Horse and Foot 4 or 5 times'. *Parliamentary Scout* reported the Hoptonians fought as if the survivors were to be made barons: 'all those that had a mind to fight had enough of it before the action ceased' (Thomason Tracts E60.12, E60.8).

As Hopton's outflanking movements took effect, the Parliamentarians withdrew to a stone wall further south, within demi-culverin shot. They held this till nightfall, the battered armies still pelting one another with round shot. About midnight the Parliamentarians fired a last volley and stole away, leaving a line of burning matches on their wall to discourage the curious. Next morning the Royalists possessed the field and other ensigns of victory, but had insufficient cavalry or ammunition to fight another action. Two-thirds of their horse had fled to Oxford, spreading the customary reports that all was lost. Just 18 barrels of powder remained, compared with 80 used the previous day.

No proper casualty figures exist, beyond the

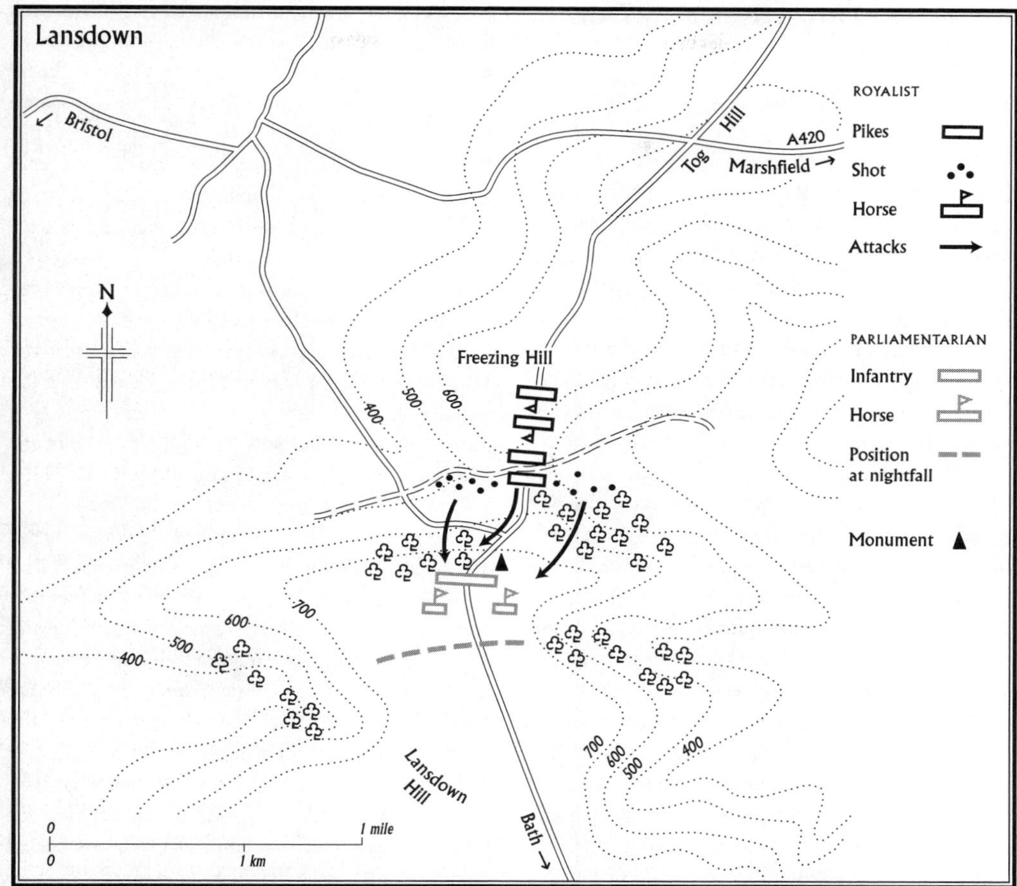

Parliamentary Scout's claim that 1500 Royalists had died, against 20 Parliamentarians: 'but its more probable that there were more ran away by far than was slaine'. Clarendon thought the dead more evenly distributed, 'on the king's part ... more officers and gentlemen of quality were slain than common men, and more hurt than slain'. Waller's army was 'rather surprised and discomforted with the incredible boldness of the Cornish foot, than much weakened by the numbers slain'.

The narrow Royalist victory turned into disaster about 8 a.m. Some prisoners blew themselves up while smoking on the powder cart, along with half the remaining ammunition and Sir Ralph Hopton. Burnt and blinded, he was looked upon as dead for many days. Cast down by this final blow, the Royalists resumed their march on Oxford, pursued by a reinvigorated Waller, his losses more than replaced from Bristol's reserves.

Directions

One mile (1.6 km) west of the A46/A420 junction near Cold Ashton, turn left down a minor road for Tog and Freezing Hills, where the initial cavalry action was fought. View Waller's position before crossing the woody vale that separated the armies to follow Grenville's route up Lansdown Hill. His monument is just below the crest on the left. Waller's layback position is probably the stone wall 400 yards further on, left of the Bath road.

Roundway Down (Runaway Down), 13 July 1643

England, Wiltshire, LR173 SU0264

If Lansdown's ear-splitting conclusion demonstrated the role of chance in war, Roundway Down saw another violent swing of the pendulum, Wilmot pulling off one of the most total victories of the English Civil War.

The western Royalists withdrew from Lansdown, having lost all their ammunition and the badly singed Sir Ralph Hopton, 'whom the people took to be the soul of that army' (Clarendon, *History of the Rebellion*). Waller hustled them eastwards along the old Chippenham road, reaching Devizes on 9 July. The Royalist infantry could not risk further retreat over the open downland between Devizes and Oxford before Waller's superior cavalry. Overnight (10–11 July) Maurice broke out with the Royalist horse, riding 45 miles (72 km) to the king's headquarters for assistance. Within 24 hours Lord Wilmot marched for Marlborough, whence the relief force took the old Bath road for Devizes on the morning of 13 July. Waller had notice of Wilmot's approach at 2 p.m., and prepared to meet him 'on an open plain piece of ground upon the top of a steep hill from the town, and about a mile's distance from thence called Roundway Hill, where the enemy was to pass' (Clarendon).

Location and deployment of the opposing armies remain controversial. Every account differs from the last. A.H. Burne had no doubt the battle was fought on top of Roundway Down (not Hill), a natural arena formed by four hills, 'like the four corners of a dye, in such a champaign as 40,000 men might fight in' (Captain Richard Atkyns). These features are generally agreed to be: King's Play Hill, Morgan's Hill, Roughridge Hill and Roundway Hill. The latter is sometimes known as Bagnall or Bagdon Hill, which 19th-century historians sometimes confused with Beacon Hill, a mile and a half (2.5 km) away. The 1500 yards (1370 m) distance between King's Play Hill and Roundway Hill provides easily enough space for Waller's force, and lies firmly across the old road. This turned left for Devizes further west than the modern A361, nearer point 184 than point 169. Burne located Waller 300 yards (275 m) east of the Ordnance Survey's battle site, directly blocking Wilmot's advance down the old road.

More recent reconstructions place Waller nearer the A361, at Roundway Hill's eastern end. The position does not block the old road to Devizes directly, but it can be seen from Devizes, as several contemporaries report. Sir John Byron reported that the Royalists fired signal guns 'from an high hill that overlooks the town', while Hopton states that the relieving force 'appeared miles off upon the hills'. The only suitable high ground is Roughridge Hill. Wilmot's force, being entirely mounted, was not confined to the road, and could easily have wheeled south across the open downland, crossing Wansdyke at Shepherd's Shore. Roughridge Hill has line of sight into Devizes, and lies across Waller's flank, as located by Burne, explaining the piecemeal destruction of Waller's cavalry, right wing first.

Estimates of Waller's numbers come from exclusively Royalist sources: 2000–2500 horse, 1800–2500 foot, 500 dragoons, who did not feature in the battle, and 7 or 8 brass guns. Reinforcements had flocked to Waller after Lansdown, so he should have had more infantry than at Lansdown: 'well armed and well bodied, [but] very vulgarly spirited and officered' (Clarendon). Waller deployed conventionally: two great bodies of foot in the centre, guns in front and wings of horse. However, his cavalry were over-extended and masked their guns, an eyewitness 'observing that Waller had placed all his horse in

Roundway Down

	Winner	*Loser*
Opponents	Royalist	Parliamentarian
Commanders	Lord Henry Wilmot	Sir William Waller
	Prince Maurice	Sir Arthur Hesilrige (w)
	Sir Ralph Hopton	
Numbers	1700–1900	3800–5000
Losses	few	1400–1800

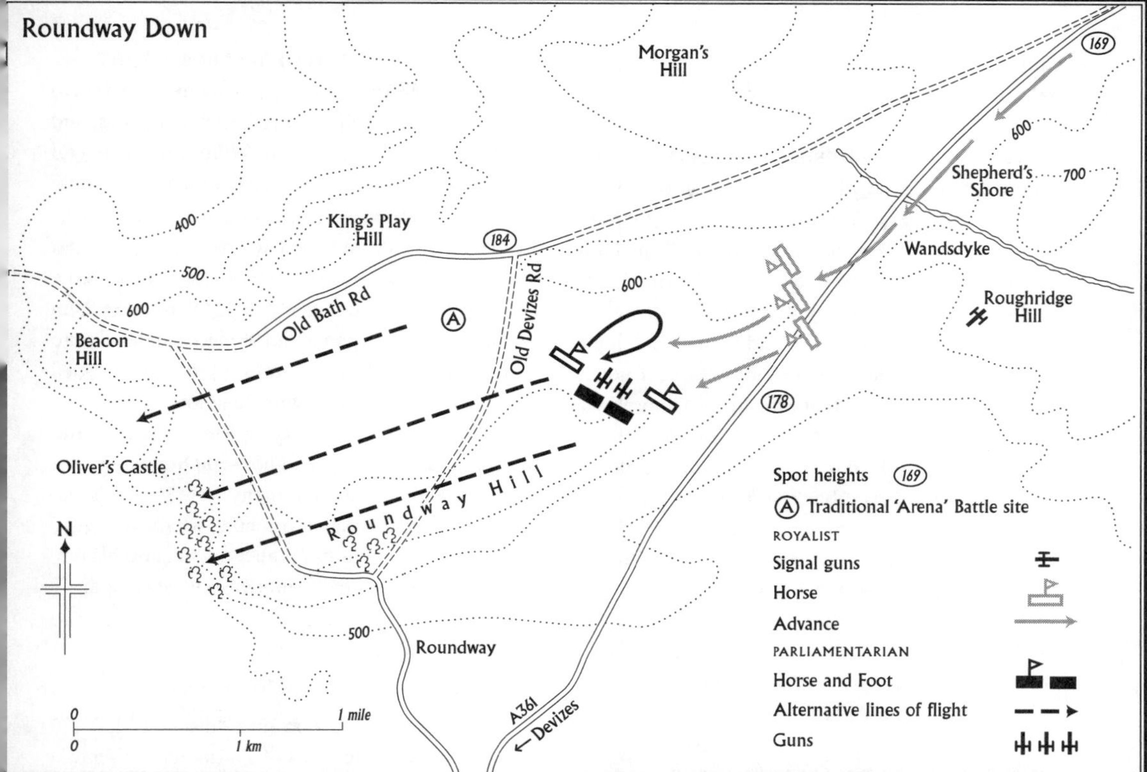

several small bodies at some distance, each from other, and all between them [the Royalists], and his foot and cannon' (Clarendon).

Wilmot was outnumbered by the Parliamentarian cavalry, even after combining his two brigades (1200 men) with the Earl of Crawford's brigade (500–700), sent to reinforce Maurice on news of Lansdown. Incompatible reports have inspired contradictory accounts of Wilmot's formation. Captain Atkyns is generally supposed to have fought with Wilmot's brigade. He positively identifies Waller's right wing as cuirassiers, stating that his regiment charged 'the uttermost man of their right wing', leaving Royalist troops further left unopposed. This would put Wilmot on the Royalist left. Sir John Byron's account, however, appears to place his brigade on the Royalist left, instead of Wilmot, reversing the most common scheme. Historians do agree that a forlorn hope of 300 screened the Royalist main body, and Wilmot led the charge, seconded by Byron.

Directions

From Devizes either (a) turn off the A361 for Roundway village, and walk up the track onto Roundway Hill, or (b) continue 2 miles (3 km) to point 178 where a minor road runs northwards, between Roundway and Roughridge Hills. St James's Church in Devizes still shows signs of Waller's bombardment from a battery on the hill east of Devizes, just above the town's name on the Landranger map (SU0161). View the 'steep place' from the Rowde–Roundway road.

Crawford was in reserve, the three brigades in echelon or a reverse arrowhead, depending on whether Wilmot is supposed to have been on the left or in the centre. Hopton's infantry played no active part in the fighting.

The Devizes Royalists ignored Wilmot's signals, suspecting a ruse. Wilmot had no time to wait, as Waller advanced at once, 'with his whole body of horse ... appointing Sir Arthur Hesilrige with his cuirassiers to make the first impression'. The action falls into three stages:

(1) THE DEFEAT OF HESILRIGE'S CUIRASSIERS

About 3 p.m. the Royalist forlorn hope drove in their opposite numbers, drawing the Lobsters forward. Wilmot charged so suddenly Atkyns hardly had time to put on his helmet: 'We advanced a full trot 3 deep, and kept in order [not knee to knee]; the enemy kept their station [i.e. stood still], and their right wing of horse being cuirassiers, were I'm sure five if not six deep, in so close order, that Punchinello himself had he been there, could not have gotten in to them.' Overlapped on the flanks, and standing still, the Lobsters were driven back and finally broken by Byron's brigade coming up in support of Wilmot. Atkyns nearly captured Hesilrige, by killing his horse, the rider's armour being proof against firearms discharged when touching. His Majesty joked on hearing the tale that 'had he been victualled as well as fortified, he might have endured a siege of seven years', a rare example of Stuart humour.

(2) THE DEFEAT OF WALLER'S HORSE

While Wilmot's brigade rallied, Byron dealt with the Parliamentarian left, despite close-range cannon fire which killed two of his men. Tactics were those used at Edgehill, 'First they gave us a volley of their carbines, then of their pistols, and then we fell in with them, and gave them ours in their teeth, yet they would not quit their ground but stood pushing it for a pretty space' (Byron). Then the Parliamentarian horse fled westwards over the downs, watched by Walter Slingsby from Devizes, 'our Horse in close body firing in their rear, till they had chased them down the hill in a steep place, where never horse went down nor up before'. Byron claimed 'many of them brake both their own and their horse's necks', although a survivor admitted only 50 killed. Traditional historians locate this disaster between Beacon Hill and Oliver's Castle, where 'Bloody Ditch' skirts the foot of the slope. The vicinity of Roundway Wood would be more convenient for observers in Devizes.

(3) THE DESTRUCTION OF WALLER'S FOOT

Meanwhile the Parliamentarian infantry prepared to receive cavalry, 'their muskets lined with pikes, and fronting every way' (Atkyns). Wilmot made several ineffective charges over the next hour and a half, until the appearance of Royalist foot persuaded the Parliamentarians to withdraw. They made for the nearest enclosures, 'but drawing over the downes seeing severall bodies of our horse pressing hard upon them on all sides, they began to fall in pieces and melt into … disorder' (Sir Walter Slingsby): 600 were killed and 800–1200 captured, with 36 colours.

Wilmot's victory was complete. A month later Waller could still only field 500–600 horse. Royalist fatalities were few, though many were hurt. Clarendon remembered 'a day of triumph', which 'redeemed the king's whole affairs'. Waller's army and his reputation as 'William the Conqueror' were ruined:

> Great William the Con
> So fast he did run
> That he left half his name behind him

This dismal defeat, soon after Adwalton Moor (30 June), contained the seeds of Parliament's eventual victory. On 19 July Parliamentarian envoys were despatched to Edinburgh, to invite Scottish assistance in a war that Parliament despaired of winning.

Bristol, Wednesday 26 July 1643

England, Bristol, LR172 ST5772, ST5872–3, ST5972

The proper outcome of a major victory in the field during the 17th century was the capture of some important town. Excepting London, nowhere in England was more significant than Bristol, the Royalists' strategic reward for Roundway Down.

Powerful Royalist forces promptly converged on Bristol. Maurice's western army invested the city's southern side towards Somerset; Rupert covered the northern Gloucestershire side with a contingent of Oxford Cavaliers. Sir William Waller had wisely slipped away to Evesham with '15 pittyful weake Troopes', the survivors of Roundway Down. In the absence of a relieving army, the Royalists could choose their tactics. The northern defences were weak, the ground hard and rocky, favouring an immediate assault over sapping and mining. The defences were stronger on the south, the ground easily dug, favouring regular siege operations. After two days wearing down the defenders with a round-the-clock bombardment (24–25 July), the Royalists decided to storm the whole line next morning just before daybreak. Once the infantry had penetrated the defences, they were to pull down the breastworks and fill in the ditch, to let in the horse.

Medieval Bristol lay 4 miles (6 km) from the Severn, between the Wiltshire Avon and the River Frome. Today the Floating Harbour follows the Avon's old course, before construction of the New Cut, while the Frome has vanished underneath Nelson Street and Broad Weir. Bristol Castle, between Peter Street and Castle Green, barred the neck of the peninsula created by the rivers. By the 1640s, however, Bristol had expanded south across the Avon into a bend in the river, and northwards beyond the Frome. Bernard de Gomme, the Royalist military engineer, reported: 'The Citye of Bristoll stands in a hole, & upon the Northside towards Durdham Downe, be 3 eminenter knolls or rocky hills, now crowned with so many forts'. A line of palisaded forts joined by a low wall and ditch dominated the high ground beyond the northern suburbs, from Brandon Hill in the west, through the modern university, curving round to the Gloucester road, 'in the bottome of the hill in the medow calld Stokes Croft' (Sir Bernard de Gomme, *Journal of the Siege of Bristol*). Defences continued south across Old Market Street, reaching the Avon opposite Temple Meads Station. Beyond the Avon the curtain ran through Temple and Redcliffe gates, at the southern ends of those streets. Portwall Lane still reflects the line of the fortifications. De Gomme considered the curtain wall 'of meane strength & not comparable to those of Oxford', being 4 1/2–6-feet (1.4–1.8-m) high and 3- feet (1-m) thick at the top. The ditch or 'graff' was commonly 6-feet (1.8-m) wide and 5-feet (1.5-m) deep, but less in rocky areas. South of the Avon the ditch was deeper and the wall 'better flankered'. Additional works included a spur outside Stoke Croft Gate, and redoubts on St Michael's Hill (at the Tyndall Road junction) and Park Street ('Essex Work').

The 5-mile (8-km) perimeter was excessive for the number of defenders. Waller had drawn heavily on the Bristol garrison, leaving Colonel Nathaniel Fiennes, the Parliamentary commander, just 300 regular horse and 1500 foot, reinforced by pro-Parliament townsmen. They had 99 real guns, '& diverse small iron hammerd peeces', made up by a country blacksmith. The Royalists had overwhelming numbers. Rupert had 3 tertias of 14 regiments of foot 'all very weake', 2 brigades of horse, and 9 companies of dragoons. Maurice presumably had Hopton's 3000 Cornish infantry, plus his own cavalry from Lansdown.

The Cornish jumped the gun, attacking at 3 a.m., before Rupert's signal. Three storming parties of a few hundred men each formed up outside what is now Temple Meads Station to assault the southern curtain, west of the Temple Circus Gyratory System. Wagons full of faggots were driven into the ditch to help the troops across, but the graff was deep and full of water, leaving Maurice's men 'with no provision for such work but the courage of the assailants' (Clarendon, *History of the Rebellion*). After half an hour the Cornish retreated, minus a third of their number, 'the common soldiers, after their chief officers were killed or desperately wounded, finding it a bootless attempt' (Clarendon).

Two of Rupert's tertias did no better between St Michael's Hill and Stoke Croft. A petard failed to blow the gate, faggots and scaling ladders were left behind in the rush, and the attackers fell back under a hail of bullets and stones, their dead filling the

Bristol

	Winner	*Loser*
Opponents	Royalist	Parliamentarian
Commanders	Prince Rupert (w) Prince Maurice	Colonel Nathaniel Fiennes
Numbers	unknown	1800–2500
Losses	*c.*500	unknown

ditches. Prince Rupert, himself injured in the fighting, called off the attack after an hour and a half.

Meanwhile, Rupert's third tertia under Colonel Henry Wentworth had found a way through the enemy lines. His officers had decided against attacking Brandon and Windmill Hill forts, preferring to try the dead ground between them, which, 'in respect of the forts, was a hollow bottome at the foot of both the hills' (de Gomme). The forts saluted them with 'iron shot, prick-shot, & what they pleased from theyr Canon', but once up to the curtain, at the junction of Park Street and Park Row, the assault troops were out of sight. Hand grenades drove off the defending infantry, and the Royalists were over, tearing down the breastworks with halberds and bare hands. First across were some dragoons, who named the spot Washington's Breach, after their colonel.

Fiennes had troops of horse ready to counterattack, but the first got 'a round Salvoe' from 50 musketeers in a hedge, and refused. The second were beaten off by officers running upon them with fire pikes, which 'neyther men nor horses were able to endure' (de Gomme). Some of the Royalists, unformed from crossing the curtain, ran away down Park Street towards Essex Work. Mistaking haste for determination, the Parliamentarian defenders fled, opening the way into the suburbs. Rupert poured troops through the breach, some pushing on past College Green and the cathedral towards the quayside, the opposing musketeers 'skolding at one another, out of windows'. Others bore half left towards Frome Gate, now at the junction of Rupert Street and Broad Street. Desperate fighting continued outside for two hours, while women and children barricaded the gate with woolsacks filled with earth. Numbers told, and the exhausted Royalists beat the defenders back inside the gate, after heavy casualties on Christmas Steps.

Shut up inside the medieval fortifications, the Parliamentarian soldiers dropped away from their colours. Out of 12 or 14 companies Fiennes could not rally a hundred men, 'and yet the enemy drew down thick upon the back, and it began to be low water in the key, so that they might wade over at their pleasure' (Thomason Tract E70.1). Many of Fiennes's men had already paddled across to surrender. Rupert was bringing up Cornish regiments and preparing petards, 'when to the exceeding comfort of generals and soldiers, the city beat a parley' (Clarendon). Generous terms were agreed, preserving lives and property, and allowing the defenders to march away next morning. Ships in the harbour fired 60 guns in celebration.

The reduction of Bristol was 'a full tide of prosperity to the king' (Clarendon), purchased at heavy cost: 'as gallant men as ever drew sword ... lay upon the ground like rotten sheep' (Captain Richard Atkyns). Its fall gave the Royalists a major port, ships and arms, making Charles I 'master of all the tract between Shrewsbury and the Lizard Point' (T.T. E70.1). Fiennes was court-martialled, and narrowly escaped death. By year end the only Parliamentarian garrisons left in Devon were Plymouth and Lyme.

Directions

The battlefield is spread out over Bristol; see text for specific locations. The partial outline of a bastion can be seen on Brandon Hill, which is less built over than some areas (ST579729).

Newbury (I), Wednesday 20 September 1643

England, Berkshire, LR174 SU4564–6

The tide of Royalist success faltered in the autumn of 1643. The Earl of Essex won First Newbury by default when the Royalists ran out of gunpowder after a prolonged artillery duel, making it one of the few battles of the English Civil War decided by that arm.

The last Parliamentarian stronghold in the Severn valley after the loss of Bristol (see above) was Gloucester. Unwilling to risk another bloody storm, the Royalists invested Gloucester on 10 August, giving Parliament time to gather a relief force. Essex reinforced his army to 15,000 men with London Trained Bands regiments, previously uncommitted to field operations. He left Colnbrook on 26 August,

Newbury		
	Winner	*Loser*
Opponents	Parliamentarian	Royalist
Commanders	Robert Devereux, Earl of Essex Major General Philip Skippon	Charles I Prince Rupert
Numbers	12,000–14,000	12,000–14,000
Losses	*c.*500	*c.*500

sidestepping Royalist outposts north of Oxford and penetrating Rupert's cavalry screen to lift the siege on 5 September. Essex now had to retrace his steps in the face of a concentrated Royalist army intent on his destruction. He feinted north towards Tewkesbury on 10 September, then countermarched for Cirencester and Swindon, 'through that deep and enclosed country of North Wiltshire' (Clarendon, *History of the Rebellion*), passing the semi-mythical Mons Badonicus (*c.*495) as he went. By the 18th Essex was at Hungerford, 9 miles (14.5 km) from the communications hub of Newbury. The king lay further off, at Wantage, but Essex was too slow. Approaching Newbury late on 19 September, he found the Royalists barring the road to London. The Parliamentarians spent the night in the fields, in pouring rain, with no food and little sleep.

First Newbury is one of the most confusing battles of the whole conflict. S.R. Gardiner, the pioneering historian of the Civil Wars, thought it presented difficulties 'incapable of a positive solution'. Graphic but disconnected accounts omit the specific times and locations necessary for a coherent narrative. Hedges and lanes that determined the course of the action were already gone by the 19th century. Newbury's southward development has further obscured the terrain. Fortunately, the recent bypass follows the disused railway, clear of the main areas of conflict.

The battlefield's essential feature is the 400-foot (120-m) contour that delineates a long flat-topped ridge running east–west from Greenham across the Newbury–Andover road. Its northern slope runs gently down to the River Kennet. Two spurs at the plateau's northwest corner saw the fiercest infantry fighting. The Ordnance Survey designates the eastern one as the battle site; the other is generally recognized as 'the little enclosed hill commanding the town of Newbury and the plaine, where His Majesty in person was drawn up' (*Mercurius Aulicus*). Contemporaries knew it as 'the Hill of Greatest Concernment'; modern historians as the 'Round Hill'. At the time of the battle, this area was thickly enclosed, the boundary hedge of Newbury parish forming a particularly impenetrable barrier. The cavalry clashed further south, on the 'open campania' of Wash Common and Enborne Heath. A.H. Burne lamented the heathland's destruction in 1950, but Wash Common Farm survives at the western end of the ridge. Nearby tumuli are nothing to do with the battle.

Numbers were roughly equal, but the Royalists had more cavalry both absolutely and proportionally. They deployed four rather worn brigades of foot west of the Andover road, between the river and high ground, supported by part of Sir John Byron's cavalry brigade. The remaining four and a half brigades of horse extended the line onto the plateau, beyond the Falkland Monument. In darkness and rain they failed to occupy Round Hill, with serious consequences next day. Otherwise, they had all the advantages of the defensive – choice of ground and shelter for the troops. A Royalist inventory lists 20 guns, from demi-cannon downwards.

Essex encamped between Skinner's Green and the Kennet, his headquarters in Enborne, and impedimenta back in Hamstead Park. Some accounts suggest Essex slept at Biggs Cottage, over a mile (1.6 km) south of the Parliamentarian line of march. This is unlikely, despite alleged apparitions of the lord general's ghost still fretting over his dispositions. The mislocation may derive from Clarendon, who probably confused 'Biggs Hill' with the 'big hill' at Enborne, a much better site for a command post. Essex had some 3500 horse, four brigades of regular foot, originally 5000 strong, as many in the five Trained Bands regiments, and 15–20 guns.

The Parliamentarians had no choice but to attack, a difficult business against an enemy with superior cavalry and guns on the ground. Round Hill out-

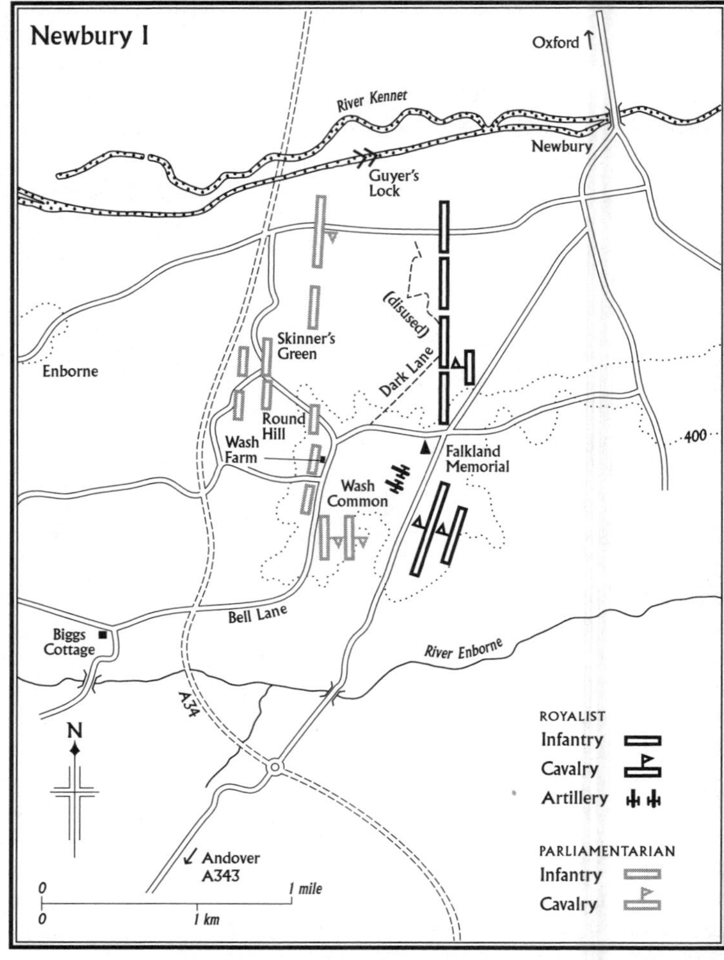

flanked any direct advance on Newbury, while a detour south of Enborne River would take the Roundheads further from home. Their best option was a limited right flanking movement to secure the high ground around Wash Common. Overnight Essex occupied the undefended western end of the ridge: two regular brigades along the hedgerows of Bell Lane, which continues Biggs Hill Lane onto the common, another under Skippon on Round Hill, and the fourth towards the Kennet. The Trained Band regiments were in reserve around Skinners Green. His cavalry was divided between the flanks, the left wing on the Newbury–Enborne road with some commanded shot

Directions

Follow the A343 Andover road southwest from Newbury and turn right into Essex Street by the Gun Inn. See Falkland's monument across the road near Rupert's artillery position. Turn left down Charles Street and across the recreation ground to Wash Common Farm. Head right to Round Hill, then back towards Essex Street, where Dark Lane is now a footpath running part way down the hill, opposite Battle Street. Alternatively turn left along Enborne Street to where Stapleton's cavalry stood.

and four 3-pounder drakes, the right on the open heath.

Against all probability Essex had regained the initiative, forcing the Royalists to attack him in order to regain Round Hill: 'not suspected nor observed by us the night before, from whence a battery would command all the plain before Newbury ... unless we possessed ourselves of that hill, there was no holding of that plain' (Lord George Digby). The battle was unusually disjointed: 'a kind of a hedge fight, for neither army was drawn out into the field; and if it had it would never have held from six in the morning till ten at night. But they fought for advantage; sometimes one side had the better, sometimes the other ...' (*Memoir of a Cavalier*). There were three unrelated struggles:

(1) THE NORTH

The Parliamentarian left 'could not be engaged but in small parties by reason of the hedges' (*True Relation of the Late Expedition ... with the Fight at Newbury*). Fighting degenerated into a static fire fight that continued all day, except for a late flare-up near Guyer's Lock, where the Kennet seems to have been fordable. The most noteworthy event was the arrest of a witch, 'taken as she was standing on a small planck board and sailing it over the river' (Thomason Tract E69.2).

(2) THE SOUTH

Once his two rightmost brigades had secured the ground south of Wash Common Farm, Essex passed through his right wing of horse: four regiments and three commanded troops under Sir Philip Stapleton. No sooner had they deployed beyond the lane's end onto the plateau than several great bodies of enemy horse charged them. Stapleton repulsed two Royalist charges, before being surrounded and attacked, 'front and flank, his whole regiment having spent both their pistols ... and our men at last were forced towards the lane's end where they first came in' (*True Relation*). Here the Parliamentarian infantry stopped the pursuit, killing any Royalist cavalry who entered the lane. Fighting continued until after dark. Rupert's horse dominated the open ground, but his foot, 'having found a hillock in the heath which sheltered them from the enemies cannon could not be drawn a foot thence' (Digby).

(3) THE CENTRE

Unexpectedly finding the enemy on Round Hill, the Royalists advanced parties of commanded shot to drive them off. Heavy fire pinned them down along Dark Lane, an embanked track that ran obliquely from the eastern spur, just west of modern housing along the Andover road, towards Enborne House on the Kintsbury road. The musketeers called for cavalry, and Sir John Byron came up to reconnoitre, finding the ground 'enclosed with a high quick hedge and no passage into it, but by a narrow gap through which but one horse at a time could go'. While Byron was having the gap widened, Lord Falkland, the king's secretary of state and long sick of the war, rode his horse through the opening and was instantly killed. Byron launched three regimental charges, driving the Parliamentarians out of the close, and 'had not left a man of them unkilled but that the hedge were so high the horse could not pursue' (Sir John Byron). Tradition claims Skinner's Green Lane was so choked with dead it had to be cleared before Parliamentarian supports could move up.

Byron cleared Round Hill, but the Royalist infantry once more 'played the poltroons', allowing Skippon to reoccupy the position. The battle now developed into an artillery exchange, the Red and Blue Auxiliary regiments covering deployment of 9-pounder demi-culverins 'at the end of the lane at the top of the hill' (*True Relation*). Rupert had planted his own battery half a mile (0.8 km) to the east: 'They did some execution among us at the first and were somewhat dreadfull when men's bowels and brains flew in our faces; but we kept our ground and after a while feared them not; our ordnance did very great execution upon them; for we stood at so near a distance upon a plain field, that we could not lightly miss one another' (Sergeant Henry Foster, Red Regiment, London Trained Bands). Foster's own colonel was killed laying a gun. Royalist cavalry and infantry attacked the Londoners' right flank 'so that we were glad to retreat a little way into the field until we had rallied our men'. The Royalists do not seem to have pushed the Londoners off the ridge, where 'they stood like so many stakes against the shot of the cannon' (Foster). Clarendon admitted the Trained

Bands 'behaved themselves to a wonder, and were the preservation of that army that day; for they stood as a bulwark and rampire to defend the rest'.

Nightfall found both armies roughly on their start lines. Essex had failed to break through, but the Royalists could no longer dispute his passage, 'not having Powder enough left for half suche another day' (Digby). When the Parliamentarians stood to at dawn, the enemy were gone. Losses were 'not so great as in a hot day might have been looked for, yet very many officers and gentlemen were hurt' (Clarendon). A Parliamentarian letter writer denied wilder casualty claims: 'I viewed the field, and cannot guess above 500'. Townspeople alleged the Royalists removed 50–60 wagonloads of dead and wounded, 'such crying there was for surgeons, as never was the like heard' (T.T. E69.2). Sergeant Foster's hard-pressed regiment lost 60–70 dead, plus wounded.

The Parliamentarians buried the dead and marched for Aldermaston and Reading, which they reached on 22 September. Public thanksgiving was held for 'the great victory', which even Clarendon reckoned 'amongst the most soldierly actions of this unhappy war'. Essex had brought off a remarkable strategic success, leaving the Royalists bitterly divided over their failure to destroy his army and end the war. Falkland's death was a political disaster, as the strategic scatterbrain Digby took his place. The second failure within a year to achieve a military decision encouraged both sides to seek help outside England.

Royalist Gains in the North: 1643

Royalist strategy during 1643 resembles a concentric advance on London from north and west, while the king's army at Oxford pinned Parliamentarian forces in the centre. The northern pincer was commanded by William Cavendish, Earl of Newcastle, who raised an army in the northeast, equipped with foreign arms imported through Newcastle. Opposition to the Earl was divided between Yorkshire and the Eastern Association, separated by the no-man's-land of Lincolnshire, which hampered Parliamentarian efforts to halt Newcastle's advance.

Newcastle first brought his army south to help the Yorkshire Royalists, who had been weakened by the departure of local Cavaliers to fight at Edgehill. He crossed the Tees on 1 December 1642 with 2000 horse and 4000 foot, disarmed the North Riding and occupied York. At Tadcaster (6 December) he drove a wedge between the West Riding woollen towns and the Parliamentarian stronghold at Hull, leaving him 'absolute master of the field' in Yorkshire. He even seized the key river crossing at Newark on the River Trent, reaching out to the Oxford army and threatening Parliamentarian counties in the Midlands. Short of ammunition, Newcastle went into winter quarters, awaiting the arrival of Queen Henrietta Maria from the Continent with fresh supplies.

Newcastle's chief opponents were Ferdinando, Lord Fairfax, and his son, Sir Thomas Fairfax or Black Tom, the most inspired Parliamentarian commander of the war. His energy was out of all proportion to his forces, initially 21 companies of foot, 7 troops of horse and 1 of dragoons, just 1500 men. Trailing his coat on Seacroft Moor, Sir Thomas was overwhelmed by Newcastle's more numerous cavalry (30 March), but he levelled the score raiding Wakefield (21 May). Meanwhile, the Lancashire Parliamentarians had secured the West Riding's rear by defeating the Earl of Derby in the small but decisive skirmish at Whalley (20 April). Newcastle was handicapped for a time by his responsibility for the safety of the queen, who landed at Bridlington on 22 February 1643. Her departure for Oxford on 4 June freed him to deal with the Fairfaxes. He crushed their army at Adwalton Moor (30 June), and captured Bradford and Leeds, eliminating Parliament's position in the West Riding. Father and son took refuge in Hull, the only remaining Parliamentarian foothold in Yorkshire.

Essex, Suffolk, Norfolk, Cambridgeshire and Hertfordshire formed the Eastern Association on 20 December 1642. Oliver Cromwell was just one of its leaders, chiefly notable for his eccentric policy of recruiting religious soldiers. The Association benefited from the resistance put up by the Fairfaxes. Not until April 1643 could Newcastle spare a brigade of horse, under his cousin Charles Cavendish, to support the Lincolnshire Royalists. Cromwell wrote a glowing report of the ensuing skirmish at Grantham (13 May), but Cavendish re-occupied the village ten days later.

Newcastle pushed his forces south after Adwalton Moor, taking Gainsborough on 31 July, despite Charles Cavendish's death in action south of the town on the 28th. The Royalists captured Lincoln, but that was the culminating point of Newcastle's advance. He fell back to besiege Hull (2 September), where Lord Fairfax had raised a new army. Newcastle, however, failed to invest the south bank of the Humber. Sir Thomas Fairfax ferried his cavalry across the estuary to join Eastern Association forces in southern Lincolnshire. Together Fairfax and Cromwell's cavalry equalled the Newark Royalists, whom they beat at Winceby (11 October), securing Lincolnshire for Parliament, and forging a war-winning partnership.

Tadcaster, Tuesday 6 December 1642

England, North Yorkshire, LR105 SE4843–4943

The Fairfaxes were lucky to survive their first encounter with Newcastle. They had cleared Bradford and Leeds of Royalists during November 1642, and advanced to Tadcaster on the River Wharfe, 'that we might have more room, & be less burthensome to our friends' (Sir Thomas Fairfax, *A Short Memorial*). Their position was dangerously exposed after Newcastle's arrival at York. The Parliamentarians were about to retire, when Newcastle appeared east of the town at dawn, after a night approach march.

Most of Tadcaster lay beyond the Wharfe, a broad river, 'not fordable in any place thereabout'. The only passage from York was across a stone bridge, partly broken down. The Duchess of Newcastle claimed the enemy had strengthened the bridgehead with guns and a fort, 'on top of a hill, leading eastward from that bridge', perhaps Gallows Hill, half a mile (0.8 km) northeast of what is now Commercial Street. The defenders only mention 'some breastworks for our musketeers', and 'a slight work above the bridge'. Some Parliamentarian foot remained there to cover the retreat, and more were brought over in response to enemy pressure.

Newcastle had no intention of attacking the bridge head-on, and sent his cavalry off to the right, to cross the river 6 miles (10 km) upstream at Wetherby. If they arrived in time, he might bag the whole Parliamentarian army. Meanwhile, 4000 Royalist infantry formed up in brigades and stormed the works. The defenders opened fire at close range, 'to so good purpose as forced them to retreat & shelter themselves behind the ridges that were hard by' (Fairfax). Fighting went on all day. At one point the Royalists took a house by the bridge, cutting off Parliamentarian troops to the east from their supports in the town, but were ejected with heavy losses. An attack at another unspecified location was also driven off.

Tadcaster

	Winner	*Loser*
Opponents	Royalist	Parliamentarian
Commanders	William Cavendish, Earl of Newcastle	Ferdinando, Lord Fairfax Sir Thomas Fairfax
Numbers	4000	900
Losses	200	*c.*100

As Newcastle's cavalry failed to appear by nightfall, his infantry pulled back, intending to try again next day. Fairfax claimed they left 200 dead and wounded. His own troops, being under cover, probably suffered less. The Parliamentarians had used up all their ammunition, however. They withdrew to Selby, away from their friends in the West Riding, but avoiding destruction.

Directions

Tadcaster is 9 miles (14.5 km) southwest of York along the A64. Turn off the bypass north of Tadcaster onto the A659, to approach the bridge along the course of the old Roman road that Newcastle would have used.

Seacroft Moor, 30 March 1643

England, West Yorkshire, LR104 SE3637?

Not all Civil War battles were formal set piece affairs: Tadcaster (see above) was an assault on an entrenched bridgehead; Seacroft Moor was a running fight, spread along 8 or 9 miles (13 or 14.5 km) of road.

The queen's arrival in February 1643 split Yorkshire Parliamentarians. Sir Hugh Cholmley, governor of Scarborough, changed sides, while Sir John Hotham at Hull refused Lord Fairfax any further help. The latter abandoned Selby, retreating to his original base in the West Riding, covered by a show of force against Tadcaster led by Sir Thomas. This threw Newcastle's preparations to intercept Lord Fairfax's march into confusion. He pulled back his main army, estimated at 10,000 men, and sent his cavalry commander, the dynamic if dissolute Lord George Goring, to clear up the situation. Outnumbered in horse, Sir Thomas broke down Tadcaster bridge and retreated across Bramham Moor.

Goring had 500 horse in 20 understrength troops. Fairfax had three troops (perhaps 150 horse), plus an unspecified number of regular infantry, all musketeers, and rustic levies. The foot numbered at least a thousand if Goring's casualty claims were true.

The Tadcaster–Leeds road ran between enclosed fields and woods, alternating with open expanses of common pasture: Bramham Moor, Thorner Moor and Whin Moor. Seacroft Moor does not appear on Ordnance Survey maps. The village of that name is now a suburb of Leeds, the built-up area extending up the moorland's western edge to Whin Moor. The action's final stages probably unfolded there, rather than on the steep slopes down to the village.

Fairfax sent his foot on ahead, while the horse disputed the narrow lanes leading onto Bramham Moor: 'Here was much firing one at another, but in regard of their [the Royalists'] great number, as they advanced we were forced to give way' (Sir Thomas Fairfax, *A Short Memorial*). Thinking the infantry out of danger, Fairfax regained the moor, only to find the infantry stood about waiting for him, 'which troubled me much, the enemy being close upon us, & a great plain to go over'. He did his best, sending the infantry on in two divisions, the cavalry in the rear. The enemy followed within musket shot, 'in 3 Good bodies'.

Bramham Moor passed without incident: 'But having again gotten to some little enclosure, beyond which was another moor, called Sea Croft Moor (much less than the first), here our men, thinking themselves more secure, were more careless in keeping order' (Fairfax). Desperate for a drink on a hot day, the soldiers dispersed among some houses, located by the *Victoria County History* at Potterton, a lost village 4 miles (6 km) short of Seacroft (SE4038). Whilst Fairfax's officers rounded up their stragglers, Goring pushed on by another way, reaching the open ground beyond as soon as the Parliamentarians.

Fairfax nearly got away with it: 'But when we had

Seacroft Moor

	Winner	*Loser*
Opponents	Royalist	Parliamentarian
Commanders	Lord George Goring	Sir Thomas Fairfax
Numbers	500	unknown
Losses	unknown	1000

almost passed this plain also, they seeing us in some disorder charged us both in flank & rear. The countrymen presently cast down their arms & fled; & the Foot soon after, which for want of pikes were not able for to stand their horse.' The obvious location for the disaster would be where Grimes Dyke crosses the road just a mile (1.6 km) from Seacroft, a tangle of drains and streams sufficient to disorder veterans. Few of the Parliamentarian horse stood the charge, leaving their infantry to be killed or captured. Fairfax escaped with difficulty, his own cornet being taken. Goring reckoned he killed 200 and took 800, 'one of the greatest losses we ever received' (Fairfax). Nevertheless, Lord Fairfax had reached Leeds safely. Sir Thomas could reflect that he had distracted Newcastle from falling upon his father's column with his whole army.

Directions

Take the A64 west across the moors from Tadcaster towards Leeds. The fatal stretch of road begins at Saw Wood, after the turning for Barwick-in-Elmet.

Whalley (Sabden Brook), **Thursday 20 April 1643**

England, Lancashire, LR103 SD7535

Before the Industrial Revolution, Lancashire was poor and isolated. Its usual strategic role was to provide a corridor for Scottish armies heading for the Cheshire Gap. Most Lancastrian battles were fought against the Scots, with the major exception of Whalley, the decisive action of the Civil War in Lancashire.

Royalist prospects in Lancashire looked good at the start of the First Civil War. The chief men generally supported the king, backed by a largely Roman Catholic population. They held the strong places of the county, and secured most of its arms and ammunition. The departure of many Royalists to fight at Edgehill, however, exposed Lancashire to the 'restless spirit of the seditious party'. The Earl of Derby, the leading magnate, was loyal but ineffectual: 'insensibly [he] found Lancashire to be almost possessed against him; the rebels every day gaining and fortifying all the strong towns, and surprising his troops without any considerable encounter' (Clarendon, *History of the Rebellion*). At the start of 1643, the Royalists held Wigan, Warrington and Liverpool; Parliament had Manchester, Lancaster, Preston, Blackburn and Bolton, known from its Presbyterian leanings as the Geneva of the North.

In March, Derby sacked Lancaster and retook Preston, a town of crucial importance as the lowest crossing place over the Ribble. A Parliamentarian reverse at Warrington (5 April) encouraged Derby to continue his offensive with an attack on the disorganized survivors in Blackburn Hundred. On the 19 April he advanced from Preston, crossing the Ribble at Salesbury by ferry, and quartered in Whalley Abbey. Colonel Richard Shuttleworth, the local Parliamentarian commander, was east of Padiham at Gawthorpe Hall. He had three troops of horse and some 500 foot, mostly musketeers if Adwalton Moor (see below) is any guide. Derby outnumbered them, with 11 troops of horse and 700 regular foot, besides numerous ill armed and ill trained Clubmen from the Fylde.

Whalley and Padiham are 4 miles (6 km) apart, on the north bank of the River Calder, which flows east–west into the Ribble. Sabden Brook, which joins the Calder roughly halfway between the towns, forms a steep-sided valley flanked by spurs running down from Pendle Hill to the northeast. The main road follows the Calder's northern bank, but Shuttleworth took higher ground north of the main road, and east of Sabden Brook near Read Hall, a mile and

Whalley

	Winner	*Loser*
Opponents	Parliamentarian	Royalist
Commanders	Colonel Richard Shuttleworth	James Stanley, Earl of Derby
Numbers	*c.*750	*c.*4000
Losses	unknown	unknown

a half (2.5 km) from Whalley. From there an old Roman road, now a secluded lane, runs steeply down to Sabden Brook, continuing over the hill (404 feet/123 m) past the golf course to rejoin the main road near Whalley.

The Parliamentarian commanders were alarmed by Derby's overwhelming numbers and prepared to withdraw, but the soldiers insisted on a fight, 'bidding them [their leaders] take what course they pleased for their safety, yet they would adventure themselves, see the enemy and have one bout with them, if God will'. Accordingly, they lined the stone walls either side of the lane with musketeers, and lay in wait for the enemy.

Derby was slow to advance, and did so without the precautions the broken country demanded. As the Royalists rode up the lane towards High House, 'mounting out of a Hollow dingle between Ashterley and Reed-head' (*Minute Narrative*), they were surprised by a sudden volley. 'Ashterley' equates with Easterley Farm just west of Sabden Brook, and the 'hollow dingle' the depression through which the stream flows. The Royalists fled in panic, carrying away the troops still at Whalley. Ignoring Derby's attempts to rally them the whole lot ran through Langho, strewing the country with discarded weapons, and waded the Ribble, which luckily for them was only neck deep. The river prevented further pursuit, but the rout continued to Preston.

Parliament's supremacy in Lancashire was never in doubt after Whalley. Derby left the county seeking reinforcements, which never came, while the rebels mopped up. By June they held the whole county except for Lathom Hall and Greenhalgh Castle. Soon Parliamentarian troops from Lancashire would appear in Yorkshire and Cheshire, to assist their neighbours at Adwalton Moor (1643) and Nantwich (1644).

Directions

Whalley is 6 miles (10 km) west of Burnley along the A671. Turn right at Read along the byroad used by Shuttleworth, bearing left past High House and down the hill through the ambush site. See Whalley Abbey and the bluebell woods.

Grantham, 13 May 1643

England, Lincolnshire, LR130 SK9238

Cromwell's presence has exaggerated the significance of this minor skirmish. S.R. Gardiner claimed it held the whole fortune of the Civil War, but the records are thin, and its results of no obvious importance. At most Grantham represents a stage in Cromwell's military education.

In early 1643 the country between the Royalist garrison at Newark on the Trent and the Eastern Association's northern border along the Ouse was disputed territory. When Parliamentarian cavalry advanced to Grantham on 11 May to threaten Newark, they attracted a prompt response. Their intended victims secretly concentrated north of Grantham during the night of 12–13 May, and surprised three of Willoughby's troops of horse in their quarters at Belton, killing 70 and capturing 45. The Royalist success paralysed the other Parliamentarians, who sat quietly in Grantham until late on the 13th.

No local traditions survive to locate the fighting. One clue is from Cromwell: 'They came and faced us within two miles of the town.' Gardiner and others place the action northwest of Grantham, on the Great North Road to Newark. A more likely place is on the left bank of the River Witham between Grantham and the Royalists' last reported position at Belton, just 2 miles (3 km) north. West of the Witham (157 feet/48 m) the ground slopes up towards Great Gonerby (328 feet/100 m), a slight incline compared with the escarpment beyond, which Cromwell might well have mentioned, had he ridden over it. The two sides stood a little above musket shot apart, perhaps either side of the re-entrant traversed by the side road from Mansthorpe Mill to Gonerby.

Cromwell reports the enemy had 21 colours of horse, and three or four of dragoons: 1250 men at 50 per troop. Gardiner accepted Cromwell's estimate that the Parliamentarians were outnumbered two-to-one, with only 12 troops, 'whereof some of them so poor and broken, that you shall seldom see worse ...'. As usual Cromwell understated his strength. Another report gives him 2000 men, excluding Willoughby and Hotham. Their discipline was proverbial: 'No man swears but he pays his 12 pence; if he be drunk he is set in the stocks … if one calls the other "Roundhead" he is cashiered.' Parliamentarian units were more likely to be up to strength than Royalists, probably making 12 troops equivalent to 21.

The unwillingness of either side to press matters also suggests that they were evenly matched. The opposing bodies stood 'for the space of half an hour or more, they not advancing towards us' (Cromwell), while the dragoons potted away. Eventually the Parliamentarian leaders agreed to charge, 'came on with our troops at a pretty round trot, they standing firm to receive us; and our men charging fiercely upon them, by God's providence, they were immediately routed and ran all away …'.

Cromwell claimed 45 prisoners and 'very little less than 100 slain'. Captured troopers could be counted, but the body count is implausibly high, given the Royalists' abrupt departure. The Parliamentarians lost 'but two men at the most'. Cromwell's biographers make much of the demonstration that Roundhead cavalry could defeat Cavaliers. Professional cavalry officers, like Goring or Balfour, would not have needed to be taught that cavalry standing to receive a charge were already beaten. The winners gained little by their victory, giving up their designs on Newark and withdrawing to Lincoln.

Directions

Take the A607 north from Grantham to Belton. The suggested battlefield is just beyond the built-up area, in the low-lying ground by the river.

Grantham

	Winner	*Loser*
Opponents	Parliamentarian	Royalist
Commanders	Francis, Lord Willoughby of Parham Sir John Hotham Oliver Cromwell	General Charles Cavendish Sir John Henderson
Numbers	*c.*1000	1250
Losses	unknown	45

Wakefield, Whit Sunday 21 May 1643

England, West Yorkshire, LR110 SE3320

The Parliamentarian storming of Wakefield shows the tit-for-tat nature of the Civil Wars, and the half-baked planning behind many of its operations. Fairfax's aim was to capture prisoners for exchange against his own men taken at Seacroft Moor (30 March 1643). Far from surprising Wakefield's Royalist garrison, he found them waiting for him, in unexpected numbers.

Wakefield occupied a hilltop half a mile (0.8 km) north of the River Calder, built around All Saints Church and the Market Place. Four main streets converged either side of the centre: Northgate and Westgate on the west; Warrengate and Kirkgate on the east. Goring had barricaded the exits, holding reserves of horse and foot in the centre. The official Parliamentarian order of battle was 1000 foot, eight or nine troops of horse, and three companies of dragoons, some 1500 men altogether. Fairfax put his forces at 1100, a mixture of regular and irregular troops. He believed 'the enemy had not above 8 or 900 men in the Town'. After clearing the place, he found they had numbered 3000, drawn from three cavalry and six infantry regiments.

Fairfax approached indirectly from Leeds, through Stanley on the A642 to the northeast, coming before the town 'early in the morning'. Dawn would be 4.15 a.m., 'but they had notice of our coming, & had manned all their Works, & set about 500 musketeers to line the hedges about the town' (Sir Thomas Fairfax, *A Short Memorial*). Notwithstanding, the Parliamentarians stormed the town at three points, forcing the Warrengate barricade after two hours dispute. Fairfax immediately led three troops of horse up Warrengate, as tanks might spearhead an advance today, ploughing through the infantry who filled the street, leaving them to be mopped up by his own foot, who followed close behind.

Goring was sick in bed, but jumped on a horse in his nightshirt to lead a counterattack; 'after a hot encounter', his men were slain, and he himself taken prisoner. Fairfax had pushed ahead on his own, with

Wakefield

	Winner	*Loser*
Opponents	Parliamentarian	Royalist
Commanders	Sir Thomas Fairfax	Lord George Goring (p)
Numbers	1100–1500	3000
Losses	unknown	1500 (p)

two captured officers, when he was trapped in a side street between a regiment of Royalist foot in the market and a 'Corps du guard of the enemy', who asked his prisoners for orders. These did nothing to break their parole, but Fairfax thought it better to put his horse to a nearby barricade and leave them to it.

Meanwhile, Fairfax's infantry had planted a captured gun in the churchyard, to prepare another charge against Royalist troops in the Market Place. Most of the Royalist horse fled down Westgate, but 1400 infantry and 80 officers surrendered, with 28 colours 'and great store of Ammunition, which we much wanted'. Other casualties are obscure. The victors admitted seven dead and many gunshot wounds. Abashed by the quantity of prisoners, Fairfax attributed his success to the Almighty, 'seeing this was more a miracle than a victory'. It did little to reduce Newcastle's overall preponderance, as Fairfax promptly withdrew to Leeds.

Directions

All Saints Church is now Wakefield Cathedral, with the Market Place to the north, and a pedestrian precinct south and west. Street names given are still extant.

Adwalton Moor (Adderton/ Atherton Moor)**, 30 June 1643**

England, West Yorkshire, LR104 SE2228

Adwalton Moor is a largely forgotten battle. Opposing accounts do not even agree on its name. Yet it was a major action involving nearly 14,000 combatants, Yorkshire's second most significant Civil War engagement, exceeded only by Marston Moor.

The Earl of Newcastle could not march south while Lord Fairfax remained active in the West Riding. During the last week of June 1643, Newcastle advanced to eliminate Fairfax's headquarters at Bradford. The town was quite indefensible, commanded all round by hills within half a musket shot. The Parliamentarian commanders arranged a spoiling attack on Newcastle's quarters for dawn 30 June, but set off too late. Marching down the Bradford–Wakefield road (now the B6135), some time after 8 a.m., they encountered Newcastle's advanced guard at Weskitt (now Westgate) Hill, where musket balls still turned up in the 1800s.

Newcastle's army was strung out along the line of march, unable to exploit their superior numbers. The Royalist forlorn hope withdrew, gaining time for their main body to deploy, some distance in the rear. Fighting ranged along an undulating ridge, about a quarter of a mile (0.4 km) wide, running southeast from Westgate Hill, roughly parallel to the B6135, to Hungar Hill (also known as Penfield), a triangular feature south of Adwalton village. It was most intense around the enclosures north and west of Hungar Hill, across Adwalton Moor. David Johnson's painstaking study of the battle shows that these lay either sides of the A58 Whitehall Road, between the B6135 Bradford Road and Hodgson Lane, the battlefield's southern edge. Masses of bullets, bridle bits and horseshoes of unusual pattern have turned up around the northern end of Warrens Lane, at the east end of Hodgson Lane, and finds of military debris continue across the moor's western edge. Drighlington did not then occupy its current position on the Bradford Road, lying 500 yards (450 m) further north. The battle consequently took its name from Adwalton instead, the nearest settlement.

Orders of battle are problematical. The most detailed Parliamentarian source gives them less than 4000 armed men, made up as follows: 13 half-strength troops of horse (500), infantry formations from Leeds and Halifax (1700), 12 full-strength companies from Lancashire (1500), 7 companies from Bradford (300 by subtraction), and 4 brass guns. An unknown number of Clubmen of limited fighting value followed the army, so-called because they represented local defence associations, not because they carried sticks.

Royalist sources are vague about their own numbers. Sir Thomas Fairfax thought Newcastle's whole army of 10,000–12,000 men was present, roughly consistent with the evidence of Thomas Stockdale, a Parliamentarian eyewitness. He observed 80 Royalist cornets (i.e. troops), which at 50 men each agrees with his overall estimate of 4000. The Duchess of Newcastle slightly overstated the Parliamentarian foot at 5000, believing the Royalist shot (musketeers) were only half as numerous. Assuming the same number of pikes, this would make 5000 Royalist infantry, with almost as many cavalry. Such a high percentage of horse was common in Royalist armies, for example at Naseby.

Having pushed back the Royalist advance guard, the Parliamentarians drew up west of the enclosures, on the forward slope north of the A58/A650 intersection. Fairfax recalled forming two wings, each of 1000 foot and five troops of Yorkshire horse. He commanded the Parliamentarian right. Stockdale describes a threefold deployment, 'the van coming up fell upon the enemies at the left hand, and the main battle upon those on the right hand ... the rear fell on in the middle'. Presumably the remaining 1500 regular foot formed Lord Fairfax's reserve in the centre, with the three troops of Lancashire horse. No gun positions are noted.

Stockdale places Newcastle's army very specifically: 'Upon Atherton Moor they planted their ordnance and ordered their battalia, but they manned divers houses standing in the enclosed grounds betwixt Bradford and Atherton Moor with musketeers.' In other words the main body drew up parallel with Moorside Road, southwest of Adwalton, while the shot disputed the hedges. Drake Lane may commemorate Royalist guns, tactically sited on Hungar Hill to fire overhead. Royalist complaints that old coal pits hampered their cavalry are confirmed by 19th-century Ordnance Survey maps, which show such workings right in the middle of the moor. The tussocks of coarse grass that still grow on parts of the moor would have concealed such obstacles, making them doubly awkward. Presumably Newcastle placed most of his cavalry either side of the infantry, possibly with a mounted reserve to the rear.

Newcastle's outnumbered musketeers were soon driven from the enclosures. *Mercurius Aulicus* described the Parliamentarian attack as, 'so strong and violent that His Majesty's forces were fain to give ground until they came within reach of their own cannon'. Sir Thomas Fairfax then lined the hedges west of the moor with musketeers, holding his cavalry in support. Ten or 12 Royalist troops countercharged a gap in the obstacle, but 'after some Dispute, those that entered the pass found sharp entertainment, and those that were not yet entered, as hot welcome from the Musketeers that flanked them in the hedges' (Fairfax). The Royalist colonel was killed, and his men withdrew.

Both Lord Fairfax's wings 'gained ground', presumably leaving the shelter of the hedges for the open moor. Another 13 or 14 troops attacked Sir Thomas, who beat them off with difficulty, 'many having gotten in among us'. At the height of their advance, the Parliamentarians nearly reached the Royalist gun line. A.H. Burne and Peter Young believed Fairfax advanced down Hodgson Lane, halting at Warren Lane, or a little further if the name of Drake Lane signifies anything. Recent demolition of a property in Moorside Road revealed musket balls and metal buttons, which may derive from this stage of the battle.

Newcastle was considering withdrawal when one of his officers, 'a wild and desperate man', requested permission to make one last charge: 'At last the pikes

Adwalton Moor

	Winner	*Loser*
Opponents	Royalist	Parliamentarian
Commanders	William Cavendish, Earl of Newcastle	Ferdinando, Lord Fairfax Sir Thomas Fairfax
Numbers	9000	4500
Losses	*c.*60	*c.*400/1900

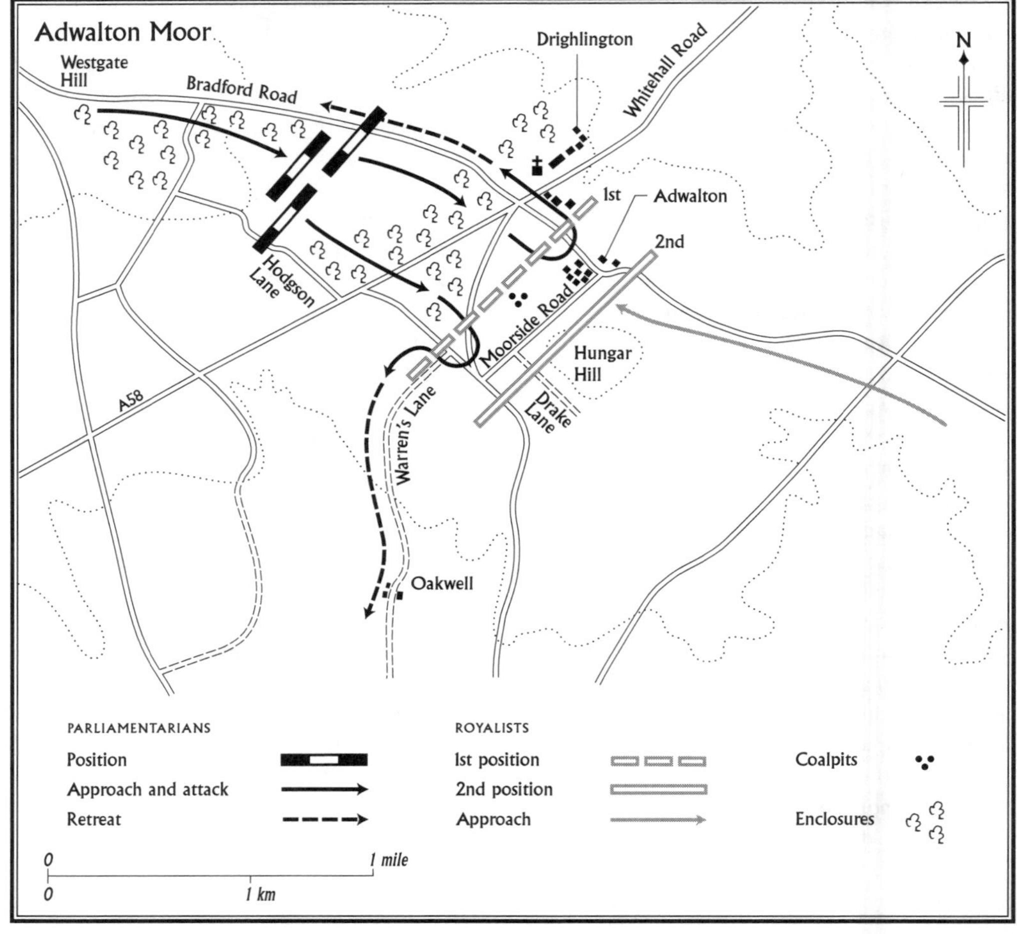

of my lord's army, having had no employment all the day, were drawn against the enemy left wing, and particularly those of my lord's own regiment ... who fell so furiously upon the enemy that they forsook their hedges, and fell to their heels'. At the same instant, a couple of lucky cannon shots disordered the Parliamentarian horse. As Lord Fairfax's reserve wavered, Royalist cavalry broke through the hedges, 'dispersedly two on abreast; and as soon as some considerable number was gotten over, and drawn up, they charged the enemy and routed them' (Duchess of Newcastle).

Stockdale confirms that 'the success of our men at the first drew them unawares to engage themselves

Directions

Follow the A650 east from Bradford over Westgate Hill, continuing along the B6135 to Drighlington and Adwalton. Turn right at the former into Whitehall Road, bearing left along Station Road, approximately following the Parliamentarian front line after they took the enclosures. Newcastle's original position was towards Moorside Road on the remaining fragment of moorland. The high ground where he withdrew is now largely built over. Cromwell Court (off Hodgson Lane) is an affront to all Yorkshiremen and admirers of Sir Thomas Fairfax, who goes uncommemorated. Beyond the A650 the country is undeveloped, with footpaths to Oakwell Hall, which witnessed Black Tom's retreat.

too far upon the enemies, who having the advantage of ground, and infinitely exceeded us in numbers' (sic). Once clear of the hedges, the Parliamentarian left wing was vulnerable to a flank attack, the Royalists sending horse and foot 'to encompass our army and fall on their rear, which forced us to retreat and our men, being unacquainted with field service, would not be drawn off in any order, but instead of marching fell into running'.

By the time Sir Thomas received orders to retreat, the enemy had cut him off from Bradford, compelling him to take the long way home through Halifax. Newcastle chased the rest of Lord Fairfax's army 2 miles (3 km) down the Bradford Road, killing 500 and taking 1400 prisoners. Sir Thomas admitted only 60 killed and 300 taken 'of those that fled', while a dozen more were lost cutting their way out to Halifax. The Royalists admitted many hurt, but 'not above twenty common soldiers slain', besides the two cavalry colonels.

Bradford was less tenable than before. Newcastle brought up 'Gog' and 'Magog', his two cannon, to batter the town, forcing Sir Thomas to follow his father, who had fled Bradford the evening of the battle. After a desperate 60-mile (100-km) ride, they reached Hull with a few horse. Their army was destroyed, Sir Thomas wounded and his wife and daughter prisoners, until the courteous Newcastle handed them back. Adwalton Moor appeared to guarantee Royalist hegemony in the North. In the longer term, it inspired Parliament's determination to seek Scottish help. The following year this would decisively shift the strategic balance against the king.

Gainsborough, Friday 28 July 1643

England, Lincolnshire, LR112 SK8287–8

Gainsborough was a complex action that ended in a Parliamentarian setback. Fresh Royalist forces negated Meldrum's initial success, forcing him to conduct a fighting withdrawal on spent horses. It owes its celebrity to Cromwell's presence.

The Newark Royalists kept up the pressure on the Eastern Association after Grantham, taking Stamford and threatening Cambridgeshire. On 20 July Lord Willoughby responded by raiding Royalist quarters at Gainsborough, 'to suppress and stop the violence of the enimy in this country of Lincolnshir'. He took 400 prisoners, but was himself surprised and trapped there. A Parliamentarian relief force under Sir John Meldrum gathered at North Scarle, off the Newark–Gainsborough road to the south.

Meldrum moved off at 2 a.m. on the 28th, giving his numbers as 'seaveenteene hundred troopers, dragooners and commaunded musketeers, without ordinance or foote'. He had 19–20 troops of horse and 3–4 companies of dragoons, comprising: 5 Midland troops and a dragoon company of his own; 6 or 7 Eastern Association troops and 2 dragoon companies under Cromwell; plus Willoughby's Lincolnshire horse. The closely fought battle that ensued suggests equal numbers. Cavendish had 30 troops of horse and dragoons, at most 1500 men.

Contact was made east of the Trent, a mile or two (1.5–2.5 km) south of 'the town's end', between Gainsborough and Lea. Fighting spread up onto the long ridge that runs parallel with the river, 'The enemy being upon the top of a very steep hill over our heads'. The ridge is of no great height (110 feet/ 33 m), except by comparison with the surrounding lowlands, but it was steep, sandy and full of rabbit holes. Cromwell refers several times to the difficulties of deploying in a 'coney warren'. It is tempting to locate the confrontation with Cavendish's main body at Warren Wood, just east of the railway, at the southern end of a track running along the ridge from Gainsborough. Planted on the site of Warren House, the modern wood is the logical place for a blockading force to await a relieving column from the south.

The Parliamentarian dragoons enjoyed little success against the Royalist forlorn hope: 'not alighting from their horses, the enemy charged them, and beat some 4 or 5 of them off their horses' (Cromwell). The Parliamentarian horse pushed the Royalists back in their turn, pressing up the side of the ridge. The Lincolns went first, followed by Meldrum's 300 Nottingham and Leicestershire troopers. Cromwell was in the rear. The enemy waited within musket shot, 'well set in two bodies, the foremost a large fair body, the other [Cavendish's own regiment] a reserve of 6 or 7 troops'. The Royalists attacked before the Parliamentarians were ready, forcing them to countercharge. Cromwell continues his account thus:

> But with those troops we could get up, came up to the sword's point, and disputed it so a little with them, that all our men pressing heavily upon them, they could not bear it, but all their body ran away, some on the one side of their reserve ... others on the other.

Most of the Parliamentarians chased the fugitives, as the Royalist horse had done at Edgehill. Cavendish's regiment stood fast, alternately facing some Lincolnshire troops, 'much scattered', and three troops of Cromwell's, which he endeavoured 'with much ado, to get into a body'. At last, Cavendish charged the Lincolns, only to be taken in the rear by Cromwell, broken and driven down into a quagmire at the bottom of the hill:

> One of Colonel Cromwell's men cut him [Cavendish] on the head, by reason whereof he fell off his horse; and his Captain Lieutenant thrust him into the side, whereof within two hours he died.
>
> Lincolnshire Committee

In the 1840s Thomas Carlyle recorded a meadow known as Cavendish's Bog, west of the ridge, between road and river, just inside the Gainsborough parish boundary. Redcoats Field lay on the ridge, and Graves Field nearer the town. The victorious Parliamentarians entered Gainsborough, 'believing our work was all at an end' (Lincolnshire Committee).

Meldrum pressed on through the town after some enemy horse who had escaped 'towards a bridge where their ordinaunce were, and where my Lord of Newcastle his secourse did pass' (Meldrum). Neither Meldrum not Cromwell explicitly say where this was, but the ensuing encounter was on the right bank, north of Gainsborough, 'a little on the *other* side of the town, about a mile off us' (Cromwell; author's italics). The Trent has no permanent bridge between Gainsborough and Scunthorpe, but Lucy Hutchinson, wife of Nottingham's Parliamentarian governor, explains how the trick was done: 'My Lord of Newcastle ... by a bridge of boats, passed all his army over and came near Gainsborough, just in a season to behold the rout of all his men.'

Gainsborough

	Winner	*Loser*
Opponents	Parliamentarian	Royalist
Commanders	Sir John Meldrum Oliver Cromwell Francis, Lord Willoughby of Parham	General Charles Cavendish (k) William Cavendish, Earl of Newcastle
Numbers	1700	*c.*1500
Losses	unknown	unknown

Meldrum and Cromwell borrowed some musketeers from Willoughby, and went to deal with the Royalist 'stragglers'. They beat them over a rise and into a village, presumably Morton, which lies barely a mile (1.6 km) north of Gainsborough, concealed beyond the broadening slopes of Castle Hill. It still possesses a windmill as mentioned by Cromwell. From the high ground, Meldrum and Cromwell saw a succession of infantry regiments in the low ground beyond: 50 colours, Newcastle's whole army coming to besiege Gainsborough. Willoughby's musketeers ran back into town, 'not much a quarter of a mile from them', while the horse, 'wearied and unexpectedly pressed by this new force so great, gave off, not being able to brave the charge'(Cromwell).

Eight troops covered the retreat, though 'exceedingly tired', after their early start, marching 15 miles (24 km), and charging twice. Nevertheless, Cromwell describes a classic rearguard action, withdrawing by alternate squadrons, the enemy snapping at their heels within carbine range. Meldrum thought it 'an honorable retreat made with as much saftie as could have been expected on such an occasion', and praised Cromwell's 'discreet and valiant' carriage.

Parliamentarians claimed 'a notable victory' (Cromwell), with 'none of note lost on our side' (Meldrum). Lucy Hutchinson believed the Royalists lost 'many more commanders [besides Cavendish] and some hundreds of soldiers'. The rebels could not stem Newcastle's advance, however. Willoughby surrendered Gainsborough after a short bombardment, and evacuated Lincoln, the hearts of his men 'so deaded that we have lost most of them by running away'. Cromwell withdrew into Cambridgeshire, while the Lincolnshire Roundheads were bottled up behind the Fens at Boston.

Directions

Gainsborough lies at the A631/A156 junction, 14 miles(22.5 km) northwest of Lincoln. Turn right off the A156 3/4 mile (1.2 km) north of Lea, along a track (possibly one of Cromwell's 'tracts') over the railway cutting to Warren Wood. Lea Marsh, where Cavendish met his end, lies between the village and the river.

Winceby Fight (Horncastle Fight), **Wednesday 11 October 1643**

England, Lincolnshire, LR122 TF3168

The 1643 campaigning season ended with a Parliamentarian rally in eastern England. Newcastle abandoned the siege of Hull, and Parliamentarian cavalry won a brilliant action at Winceby.

Military operations in Lincolnshire languished during August–September 1643, as Newcastle's army besieged Hull, while the Eastern Association's new commander-in-chief, the Earl of Manchester, suppressed a Royalist outbreak at King's Lynn. The latter's surrender on 15 September freed Manchester's subordinate Cromwell to extricate Sir Thomas Fairfax from Hull, where his cavalry horses were perishing of thirst. Newcastle's horse shadowed the united Parliamentarians south, towards their rendezvous with Manchester's 6000 infantry at East Kirkby on 10 October. The Parliamentarians then invested Old Bolingbroke Castle, 'which did enslave all those parts', drawing Sir William Widdrington down to relieve its Royalist garrison. Manchester ignored Cromwell's plea that his horses were too tired to fight, and insisted on confronting the approaching Royalists.

Next morning Manchester occupied Bolingbroke Hill, 'where he would expect the enemy, being the only convenient ground to fight with him' (John Vicars, *God's Arke O'ertopping the World's Waves*). The road east of Horncastle would naturally bring the Royalists along a ridge of dry ground through Winceby, Snipe Dale's marshes inhibiting manoeuvre to the north. About noon Manchester heard the Royalists were coming, and advanced a mile (1.6 km) up the road towards the little hamlet of Winceby, 'and met them midway upon a plain field' (Vicars). The Parliamentarian horse deployed on a slight crest near the north end of Hameringham Lane, where the Ordnance Survey marks the battlefield. The enemy were 600 yards (550 m) away on the next ridge, beyond a gentle dip. Except for a parish boundary hedge a few hundred yards from the Parliamentarian left, the open ground presents no obstacle to cavalry.

Five Parliamentarian troops pushed down the forward slope, supported by Manchester's and Cromwell's regiments, Fairfax in reserve. Their foot had fallen behind, so Manchester went back for them, leaving Cromwell in charge of the leading bodies of horse. The Royalists had 74 colours of horse and 21 of dragoons, 1500 and 700 men respectively. Many of the latter were musketeers mounted on nags, of little value in a melee. The Parliamentarians had half as many standards, but their troops were 'fuller'. Widdrington grumbled the enemy were 'very good and extraordinarily armed ... 50 or 60 troops, being very

Winceby Fight

	Winner	*Loser*
Opponents	Parliamentarian	Royalist
Commanders	Edward Montagu, Earl of Manchester Sir Thomas Fairfax Oliver Cromwell	Sir William Widdrington Sir John Henderson
Numbers	1500	2200
Losses	*c.*60	1200

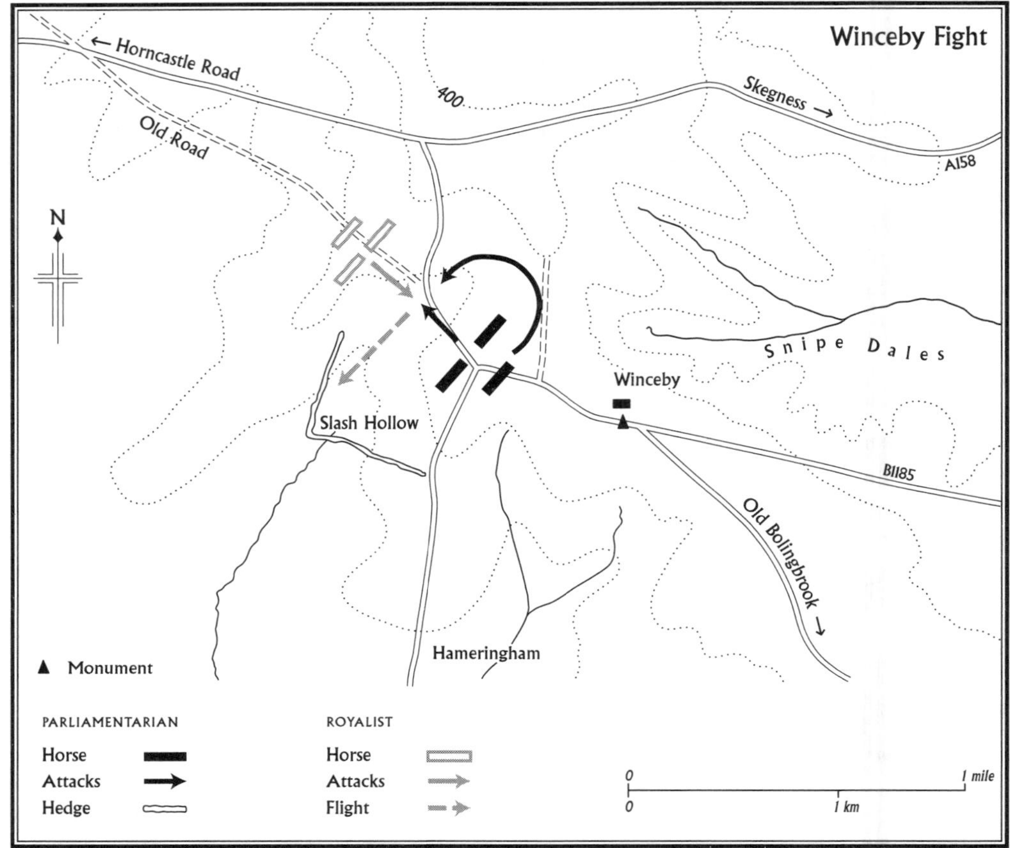

strong'. The Royalists conformed roughly to the Parliamentarian deployment: dismounted dragoons, supported by three divisions of horse, with a reserve.

The parties faced one another for an hour, before Royalist dragoons advanced down their side of the dip, seconded by their horse. Cromwell's men countercharged, singing psalms. Their field word or rallying cry, shouted in the melee to distinguish friends from foe, was 'Religion'. They must have moved quite slowly, allowing the enemy to fire at them twice:

> Colonel Cromwell fell with brave Resolution upon the Enemy, immediately after the Dragooners had given him the first volley, yet they were so nimble as that within half pistol shot they gave him another. His horse was killed under him at the first charge and fell upon him; and as he rose up, he was knocked down again …
>
> John Vicars, *God's Arke O'ertopping the World's Waves*

Directions

Follow the A158 east from Horncastle, turning right along the B1195. At the time the Horncastle–Spilsby road ran along a modern footpath, rejoining Slash Lane west of Winceby, where the B1195 bears left across the Roundhead start line. A footpath north of the B1195 follows the line of Fairfax's turning movement. See the roadside monument at Winceby Farm, and the ruins of Old Bolingbroke Castle 3 miles (5 km) further on. Horncastle Church has a monument to Sir Ingram Hopton, killed fighting Cromwell.

Vicars claimed that this first charge was 'so home given … that the enemy stood not another', but he exaggerates. Shot off his horse and beaten to the ground, Cromwell was in no state to carry the action through to a successful outcome.

It was Fairfax's uncommitted reserve that won

the day. His modest account simply says, 'The Bodies met in the Plain where the Fight was hot for half an hour, but then we forced them to a rout.' Another narrative reveals his contribution in more detail:

> Sir Thomas Fairfax, being in the rear of Col. Cromwell's regiment with his first body, fell in towards the flank of the enemy's body; which they perceiving the enemy's body broke, and so Sir Thomas had the chase and execution of them a great way.
>
> *An Exact Relation of the Victory, etc.*

Historians interpret this as meaning that the boundary hedge prevented Fairfax intervening on the Parliamentarian left, so he led his regiment around the Parliamentarian right, screened by dead ground beyond the crest northeast of the melee, and suddenly appeared on the Royalist left flank. The latter panicked at once, fleeing south into Slash Hollow. Manchester's report confirms the decisive effect of Fairfax's attack, 'after the second charge our men had little else to do but pursue a flying enemy'. Fairfax claimed 200 enemy killed and 2000 prisoners. *An Exact Relation* put total Royalist casualties at 1200, admitting 'very many of our [i.e. Parliamentarian] men are wounded, but we do not hear of above twenty killed'. Country people reported several hundred Royalists drowned in the River Bain at Horncastle.

The consequences of Winceby were enhanced by events further north; during the battle the combatants had heard 'great shooting of Ordnance toward Hull', as a dramatic Parliamentarian sortie broke the Earl of Newcastle's siege. Newcastle's march on London, if it ever was a realistic prospect, had ground to a halt.

The Turning Point: 1644

The campaigns of 1643 disappointed both king and Parliament. Neither was strong enough to impose terms upon the other, and both turned to outside forces to gain the upper hand: the Royalists to Ireland, the Parliamentarians to Scotland. Their points of entry, at Chester and Berwick, made northern England the decisive theatre of the First English Civil War.

Scotland had been at peace since the Second Bishop's War of 1640. Ireland, on the other hand, had been continuously at war since the Ulster rebellion in 1641 (see Kilrush, 1642, above, and Old Ross, 1643, below). Charles I was anxious to restore peace in Ireland, in order to release British troops sent to deal with the rising. On 15 September 1643, Charles's lord lieutenant, the Marquess of Ormond, concluded a 12-month 'Cessation of Arms' with the Irish Confederates. The king's enemies in England and Scotland knew of these manoeuvres. Defeats at Adwalton Moor (29 June 1643) and Roundway Down (13 July 1643) encouraged Parliament to approach the Scots Covenanters for assistance. Ten days after the Cessation of Arms, members of Parliament accepted the Solemn League and Covenant, imposing Presbyterian forms of worship upon England in return for Scottish military intervention in the English Civil War. Parliament had the better deal. Charles's reinforcements from Ireland were limited to 1 regiment of horse and 12 of foot shipped over piecemeal to Bristol and Chester, dodging Parliament's naval blockade. The Scots, on the other hand, contracted to provide 2000 horse, 1000 dragoons and 18,000 foot. Actual numbers were less, but they arrived together as a functioning army, crossing the Border on 19 January 1644. Parliamentarian propagandists made much of the king's deployment of Irish papists, though there was not an Irishman among them.

Royalist forces in the northeast were already on the defensive after Winceby Fight (see above). The Scottish threat drew most of them north, reducing pressure on Yorkshire's Parliamentarians. This allowed Sir Thomas Fairfax to relieve his beleaguered allies in Cheshire. His victory at Nantwich (25 January 1644) disrupted Royalist plans to form a second northern army around Irish regiments based in Chester. The disaster drew Prince Rupert to Chester to restore the situation. He began in fine style with the relief of Newark (21 March), hard-pressed since the departure of Newcastle (now a marquess) to fight the Scots.

Newcastle was no match for a larger Scots army led by a pupil of Gustavus Adolphus. Alexander Leslie, the Scottish commander-in-chief, had been ennobled after Newburn (1640) as Earl of Leven. Despite atrocious weather, he drove Newcastle back 70 miles (110 km) from Tyneside to York in a campaign of movement worthy of the Swedish king. The most serious clash was at Boldon or Down Hill outside Sunderland (24 March). Manoeuvred out of Durham, Newcastle was at Barnard Castle when he received news of a disaster in his rear, at Selby (11 April). The Fairfaxes had reunited to destroy the forces Newcastle had left to secure Yorkshire.

The marquess had no choice but to retreat on York, to protect the natural capital of northern England. Leven left an unreduced Royalist garrison at Newcastle, across his communications, and boldly pressed on south to rendezvous with the Fairfaxes. On 23 April their combined forces invested York, where the Eastern Association army joined them in June. Prince Rupert marched to relieve York, which he did without a battle on 1 July. The next day his close pursuit of the retreating Allies precipitated the decisive battle of the war, at Marston Moor (2 July). Newcastle's army was destroyed, leaving Rupert to withdraw across the Pennines, and then to Bristol. Sir John, now Lord, Byron was left at Chester to hold the northwest, with predictable results. In September 1644 local forces destroyed the last remnants of his Irish army at Montgomery.

Middlewich, 13 March 1643

England, Cheshire, LR118 SJ7066

Nantwich, 25 January 1644

England, Cheshire, LR118 SJ6353

The first break in the stalemate between king and Parliament came in the northwest, a strategic backwater since Charles I passed through on the way to Edgehill (1642). However, the arrival of Irish regiments at Chester in November 1643 attracted outside forces seeking to expedite or prevent their onward march to Oxford. In the event they got no further than Nantwich.

Outside Royalist Chester, Nantwich was the only town in Cheshire large enough to act as Parliament's county headquarters. Local Parliamentarians occupied Nantwich early in 1643, fortifying it with earth walls and sconces at the street ends. In March they frustrated a Royalist attempt to disrupt their activities, capturing most of the Wirral Trained Bands at Middlewich. Threatened by Sir William Brereton's horse west of the River Wheelock, and Parliamentarian foot from Nantwich to the south, Sir Thomas Aston's inexperienced Royalist army fell apart. His own regiment of horse retired eastwards down Kinderton Road, while most of the infantry hid in St Michael's Church, 'wedged up like billets in a wood-pile'. The Parliamentarians blew in the door, bagging 600 soldiers and most of their officers. Aston returned to regimental duties at Oxford, while Brereton went on to fight at Hopton Heath (see above).

The Royalist debacle at Middlewich allowed Brereton to invade North Wales and besiege Chester. The threat to Royalist communications with Ireland became intolerable after the Cessation of Arms. 'The Bloody Bragadochio Byron' was sent from Oxford to secure the disembarkation of the troops expected from Ireland, and to clear up the situation in Cheshire. Byron defeated Brereton on Boxing Day 1643, with heavy loss (200 killed, 300 prisoners), 'in a broad lane between Middlewich and Northwich'. Cheshire's Parliamentarians fled to Manchester, or took refuge in Nantwich, where Byron boxed them in.

Parliament directed Sir Thomas Fairfax, in winter quarters after Winceby Fight (see above), to relieve his northwestern comrades. Marching in the coldest season of the year, he rallied local forces at Manchester, before heading south, through Delamere Forest. He made visual contact with the enemy at Hurlestone, 2 miles (3 km) northwest of Nantwich, at about 2p.m. on the 25 January. Fairfax had 4 cavalry regiments, and 5 of infantry: 1800 horse, 500 dragoons, and 2500–3000 Cheshire or Lancashire foot. He estimated the enemy as 1800 horse and above 3000 foot. Modern historians give Byron 1000 horse and up to 4000 foot, including nearly 3000 from Ireland. However, he had lost 300 dead in a failed assault on 18 January, besides wagonloads of wounded carted off to Chester.

Only half Byron's army was present when Fairfax came in sight. The Royalists were in difficulty, threatened by an equal relieving force, divided by the 20-foot (6-m) wide River Weaver, which flows north–south past the western side of Nantwich. Most of the Royalist infantry were around Acton church to the west, and most of the cavalry with some foot at Beam Heath on the northeast. Communications were assured by a ferry at Beambridge. Unluckily for Byron, a thaw set in. Melting snow overflowed the Weaver's banks, washing away the improvised crossing. When Fairfax appeared, Byron faced a lengthy circuit to regain touch with his infantry. A.H. Burne believed the Royalists went north, crossing at Minshull. Local historians prefer the claim of Shrewbridge, south of Nantwich. The latter seems quicker and more prudent, as it would bring the cavalry up on the left flank of their friends at Acton, rather than behind enemy lines.

The battlefield's location is uncertain, beyond Fairfax's reference to Acton church. Most historians follow A.H. Burne's initial Royalist deployment across the Chester–Nantwich road, where it climbs the northern edge of a low plateau that extends 400 yards (370 m) north from Acton. The rise is the obvious place to await the Parliamentarian approach, and is visible from Hurlestone across the valley, as Fairfax reports. Sufficient Royalist infantry were available to occupy the front, allowing for a detachment left, under Sir Fulke Hunck, to cover the Welsh Row exit from Nantwich.

While Fairfax and his officers debated whether to attack the divided Royalists in their works, the rest of Byron's men came up. The Parliamentarians consequently decided to cut across the fields, and join the Nantwich garrison before offering battle. This entailed a tedious flank march, through gaps cut in the hedgerows by pioneers. Fairfax's route is unknown, but logically lies east of the Shropshire Union Canal (built later), across the modern ring road, towards Nantwich. The Royalists presumably wheeled right, to intercept Fairfax between Henhullbridge and Welshman's Green, attacking the Parliamentarian column in flank. Byron's left, those cavalry who had passed the river, went for Fairfax's rear. The Royalist right, 'those that were drawn up under their works', then attacked Fairfax's vanguard.

Byron had the better of it at first, but Fairfax's cavalry recovered the situation, 'beating the enemy's Horse out of the lanes that flanked the Foot'. Thus encouraged, the Parliamentarian infantry 'made them retire from hedge to hedge, till at length they were forced to flee to their works' (Fairfax, *A Short Memorial*). Clarendon, no eyewitness, thought that 'the body of the horse ... were placed too far from the foot, and

Middlewich

	Winner	*Loser*
Opponents	Parliamentarian	Royalist
Commanders	Sir William Brereton	Sir Thomas Aston
Numbers	unknown	*c.*1300
Losses	unknown	700 (p)

Nantwich

	Winner	*Loser*
Opponents	Parliamentarian	Royalist
Commanders	Sir Thomas Fairfax	John, Lord Byron
Numbers	4800–5300	4800
Losses	unknown	*c.*2000

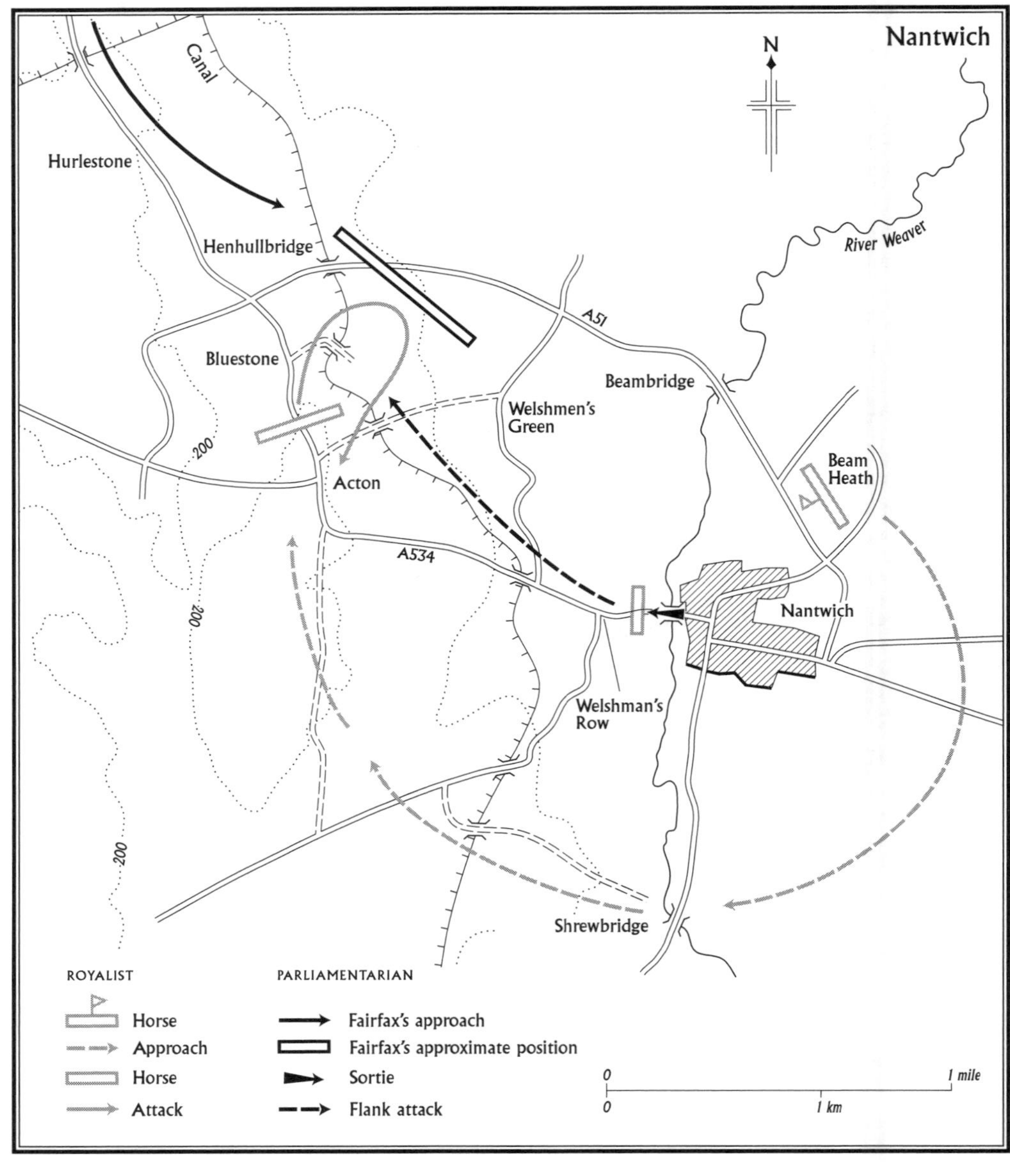

made no stand, but was presently routed' (*History of the Rebellion*). After a good start, Byron's right was attacked in the rear by 700–800 musketeers from Welsh Row, despite the party detailed to prevent this. The encircled Royalists retreated into the church, 'where they were caught, as in a Trap'. Byron's horse withdrew, unable to save their infantry, 'by reason of

Directions

Nantwich *From Welsh Row, take the A534 Wrexham road to Acton. The church is left of the junction with Monks Lane. Carry straight on towards Bluestone, the Royalist forming up area. Footpaths down to the canal towpath from Bluestone and Acton provide access to the likely site of the fighting.*

the deep ways with the sudden thaw, and narrow lanes, and great hedges'. Why these hindered the Royalists more than the enemy is not clear, except that the Parliamentarians turned up together. Byron's cavalry had a 4-mile (6-km) march to join their infantry, and may simply have arrived too late.

Fighting lasted about two hours, although the troops in the church held out until morning. Prisoners included 150 officers and 1500 rank and file. Six hundred of the latter promptly changed sides. Fatal casualties are estimated at 300, mostly Royalists. Some 1200 fugitives rejoined Byron at Chester, but his army had been smashed. Fairfax had won Parliament's most clear-cut victory to date, establishing his reputation as Parliament's most effective field commander. Clarendon lamented 'the most sensible blow to the king, he had yet sustained', which, 'almost nipped all hopes of getting an army into the field'. Outside Chester and Lathom Hall, all Cheshire and Lancashire fell into Parliamentarian hands.

Directions
Middlewich *See text.*

Newark, Thursday 21 March 1644

England, Nottinghamshire, LR121 SK8154

Prince Rupert's relief of Newark deserves to be better known. Short on casualties, it was long on strategic significance.

Newark lies at the junction of the Fosse Way and the Great North Road, where the latter crosses the River Trent. It was a vital link between Charles I's capital at Oxford and the Marquess of Newcastle's headquarters at York. Early in March 1644 Sir John Meldrum invested Newark, and Rupert received positive orders to go to its relief on the 12th. The prince was reorganizing Chester's defences after Nantwich, and had few troops in hand. He had to gather an army as he went, marching through Lichfield to reach Bingham, east of rebel-held Nottingham, on the 20th.

Meldrum had some 2000 horse and 5000 foot, mainly from the Eastern Association, reinforced from neighbouring counties. Their officers drove Meldrum to distraction, 'so piquing in all punctilios of superiority,' wrote Lucy Hutchinson, wife of the Parliamentarian governor of Nottingham, 'that it galled the poor old gentleman to the heart'. The Royalist garrison had some 300 horse and 1200 foot. Brigadier Peter Young calculated Rupert's force at 3430–3530 horse and 3120 foot, all musketeers.

Newark is on the right bank of the Trent, which divides a mile and a half (2.5 km) west of the town to form the 'Island', a low-lying area 2 miles (3 km) long from north to south. The Great North Road runs across this, passing the main branch of the Trent at Muskham Bridge. The area's dominating feature is Beacon Hill (131 feet/40 m), a mile (1.6 km) east of Newark, across the Coddington Road. Meldrum was dug in around the Spittal, a burnt-out house northeast of Newark, between Northgate and the river, beyond the railway. Some of his cavalry deployed on Beacon Hill, withdrawing towards the Spittal on Rupert's approach. The rest were in the Island, covering infantry sent to fortify Muskham Bridge. A pontoon bridge near the modern weir assured their communications with Spittal.

Rupert feared Meldrum might withdraw, and had marched from Bingham at 2 a.m., presumably up the Fosse Way. Swinging right through Balderton, he appeared on Beacon Hill between 9 and 10 a.m., with just 800 cavalry. The Parliamentarian horse were on the northwest slopes of Beacon Hill, deployed in four large bodies, two up and two back. Rupert also formed two lines of two regiments each, with a troop in reserve. Numbers were roughly equal, due to Meldrum's detachment in the Island. To keep them there, Rupert slipped an enigmatic message into Newark,

Newark

	Winner	*Loser*
Opponents	Royalist	Parliamentarian
Commanders	Prince Rupert	Sir John Meldrum
Numbers	8100	7000
Losses	c.100	200

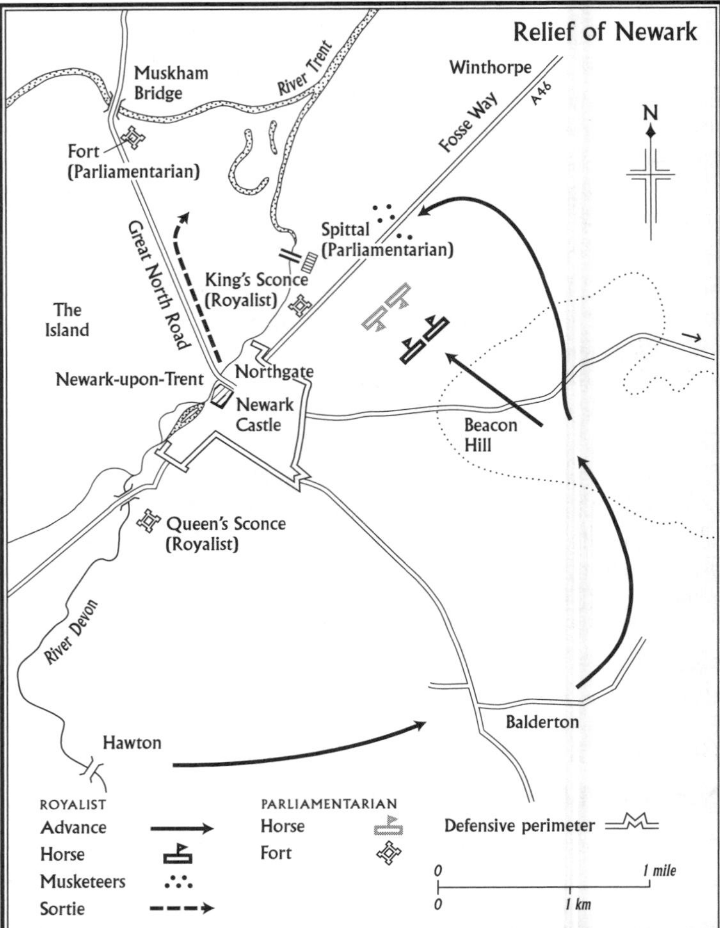

Directions

Industrial works and housing along Beacon Hill Road now obscure the cavalry battlefield marked by the Ordnance Survey. Most of the town's Civil War defences have gone, including the Spittal. Queen's Sconce survives in Devon Park (SK7953), south of the town centre. Also see the castle, Royalist head-quarters during several sieges.

inviting the defenders to create a diversion beyond the Trent: 'Let the old drum on the north side be beaten early in the morning.'

Still concerned Meldrum might escape, Rupert launched a holding attack, with the few cavalry he had. The Parliamentarian left did well enough. Charging six ranks deep, they stood several counter-attacks before they were beaten off. On their right the supports ran away, allowing Rupert to demolish the leading wave of Nottingham horse:

> Colonel Thornhagh [right] and Major Rossiter [left] gave them [the Royalists] a very brave charge, routed those they first encountered, and took prisoners ... and had they been seconded by the rest of the horse, had utterly defeated the prince's army; but the Lincolnshire troops fled away before ever they charged, and left Colonel Thornhagh engaged with only his own horse, with the prince's whole body.
>
> Lucy Hutchinson

Thornhagh escaped with two wounds. One unfortunate Parliamentarian laid his hand on Rupert's collar, and had his arm hacked off for his impertinence.

Both sides withdrew, Rupert to await reinforcements, Meldrum to contemplate withdrawal across the pontoon bridge. He was interrupted by Rupert's infantry, who fetched a detour around Beacon Hill to attack down the Fosse Way. Finding Meldrum too strong, they sat down across his line of retreat to Lincoln. Meanwhile, Newark's defenders had sortied across the town bridge to cut Meldrum off from Muskham Bridge, his alternative escape route. The Parliamentarian cavalry fled, and the commander of their supporting infantry disappeared, telling his men he was going to buy bread. Without orders or food, 'nor bullet more than their muskets were loaded withal' (Lucy Hutchinson), the foot slipped away after dark, leaving lighted matches and squibs to deceive the enemy.

Meldrum was already negotiating terms. Next morning he marched out with his remaining troops, handing over 3000–4000 muskets, two mortars and 11 brass guns, including a 32-pounder cannon known variously as 'Basiliske of Hull' or less puritanically as 'Sweet Lips'. Rupert's rapid advance and bold front had won a complete victory. Newark would remain in Royalist hands until the end of the war, only surrendering on the king's direct order.

Boldon Hill (Down Hill/Hilton), **Sunday 24 March 1644**

England, South Tyneside, LR 88 NZ3560

The second Scottish invasion of the 1640s pitted the professional Leven against the wealthy amateur Newcastle. Leven pursued a canny strategy, outmanoeuvring his enemies rather than fighting pitched battles. Newcastle sought action at Boldon, but failed to impose his preferred combat strategy upon Leven.

Newcastle amused the Scots on the Tyne until late February 1644. Then Leven masked Royalist positions around Newcastle upon Tyne and crossed the river higher up. Abandoning his communications, he marched south to Parliamentarian Sunderland, on the River Wear. Here he could supply his own army by sea, while blocking Newcastle's communications southwards. The Royalist field army withdrew to Durham. Most of March passed in countermarching through blizzards. On the 20th the Scots stormed a Royalist fort at South Shields, tightening the screw on Newcastle town. The marquess responded by crossing the Wear at Chester-le-Street and occupying high ground west of Sunderland on 23 March. Next day a Scottish newsletter reported that he 'marched towards our Quarters intending to have set upon us in Sermon time, and being a foggie day to have surprised us'.

The site of the ensuing confrontation has become unnecessarily confused. The newsletter clearly describes Newcastle's musketeers advancing from 'Bouden Hill', i.e. Boldon Hill, the western continuation of Down Hill. Its estimate of Royalist losses came from the 'Constable of Bouden'. Many accounts misname the battle 'Hilton', following another newsletter that claims Newcastle 'drew up on the north side of Ware, at a place called Hilton, two and a half miles [4 km] from Sunderland'. Hylton Castle (sic) is between Down Hill and the Wear, and saw no fighting. Newcastle's report is less help than it might be, only saying 'he got the Scots out to West Bedwick near Hilton Castle ... where they sat fast upon Bedwick Hill'. The last named is presumably near Biddick Hall (NZ3563), north of Down Hill, although the campaign's chief historian locates Leven at 'Saddick Hill', marked on antique maps near Sunderland.

The most satisfactory interpretation is that Newcastle occupied Down Hill, facing northeast across a low flat moor, the River Don between him and the enemy. Numerous enclosures cut up the moor, not just around the villages of East and West Boldon. After the battle a Scots participant described how the Royalists remained 'inaccessible by us without great disadvantages in regard of the many hedges and ditches betwixt us'. Another source describes musketeers of both sides lining the hedgerows, 'for the Armies could not joyn, the Field between us being so full of hedges and ditches'.

The Solemn League and Covenant had committed the Scots to fielding over 20,000 men, but Leven had considerably fewer at Boldon. He had crossed the Border with 52 troops of horse and 198 colours (i.e. companies) of foot, which at 50 men each gives him 2600 cavalry and 9900 infantry. This agrees roughly with Newcastle's estimate of 14,000 Scots. However, Leven had detached 3000 foot to invest Tyneside, and had sustained further losses from bad weather. The indecisive nature of Boldon suggests the sides were roughly even, 5000–6000 infantry each and a few thousand cavalry, of limited use in the awkward terrain. Newcastle still thought he was outnumbered, assuring Rupert that 'the Scots are as big again in foot as I am, and their horse, I doubt, much better'.

The battle started slowly. The Scots version is that 'After the Armies had faced each other most part of that day, toward five aclock the Cannon began to play ... though to little purpose, and withall the commanded Foot fell to it to drive one another from their hedges, and continued shooting till eleven at night'. Newcastle thought the action began two hours earlier. Failing to draw the enemy out, 'with overtures of many advantageous opportunities ... four regiments of his Excellency's foot fell to work with six regiments of the rebels'. The Scots claimed to have gained ground, inspiring suggestions that they took East Boldon about midnight. Newcastle reported fighting until daybreak, 'the rebels all this time being upon their own *Mickle Midding* [great dungheap], and there they lay all night'.

The standoff resumed next day, when the Scots withdrew into Sunderland. Newcastle retreated to Durham, after another freezing night in the open. The Scots claimed a 'laudable victory', but the Royalists did not feel beaten, 'for as yet they [the Scots] never looked the Marquis in the face'. The Royalists claimed a four-to-one advantage in casualties, while 'Their foot ran twice, and could not stand longer than their officers forced them on with the sword'. The Scots believed the losses favoured them, 'as we understood by the dead bodies we found next day upon their ground, beside the seven Waggons draught of dead and hurt men not able to walk'. Total losses might be three or four times more than the numbers of killed, given above. Whatever the truth, Newcastle had not inflicted sufficient damage to prevent Leven resuming his advance in April, when the weather improved.

Boldon Hill

	Winner	*Loser*
Opponents	Scots	Royalist
Commanders	Alexander Leslie, Earl of Leven	William Cavendish, Marquess of Newcastle
Numbers	c.7500	5000–6000
Losses	1000?	240

Directions

The northeast slope of Down Hill is now a golf course surrounded by housing. Two roads cross Newcastle's position: Downhill Lane from the A19(T)/A1290 interchange to the A184 through West Boldon, and Hylton Lane back south from St Nicholas's Church. See Hylton Castle's 15th-century gatehouse down Washington Road to the left.

Selby, Thursday 11 April 1644

England, North Yorkshire, LR105 SE6132

The departure of the Marquess of Newcastle's army to confront the Scots encouraged a Parliamentarian revival in Yorkshire. At Selby the Fairfaxes united their forces to eliminate the troops Newcastle had left to protect his rear, opening the Earl of Leven's road southwards.

Sir Thomas Fairfax spent the months after Nantwich (see above) consolidating Parliament's position in Cheshire and Lancashire. He crossed the Pennines in April 1644 to join his father in an attack upon the Royalist quarter at Selby, 12 miles (19 km) south of York. The city's governor, Sir John Bellasis (also spelled Belasyse or Bellasses), occupied Selby to prevent the junction, securing his own communications with York by a pontoon bridge. Sir Thomas and his father made their rendezvous upstream, at Ferrybridge, advancing on Selby on 10 April. They drove in Bellasis's outposts, and bivouacked a mile (1.6 km) outside the town.

Selby

	Winner	*Loser*
Opponents	Parliamentarian	Royalist
Commanders	Ferdinando, Lord Fairfax Sir Thomas Fairfax Sir John Meldrum	Sir John Bellasis (p)
Numbers	4000	3300
Losses	unknown	2100 (p)

Selby is a market town on the right bank of the Ouse, at the elbow of a sharp westward bend in the river, open to attack on all sides except the northeast. The Parliamentarian foot attacked from the south in three columns: along the river bank (right), where Victorian maps still showed considerable open space between Ousegate and the River Ouse; by Brayton Lane/Bawtry Road (centre); and by Doncaster Road/Brook Street to Gowthorpe (left). Sir Thomas stood by with the horse to support whoever might prove successful. His father reported the attackers numbered 2000 mounted troops and 2000 infantry, against 1500 Royalist horse and 1800 foot, about three-quarters of York's garrison.

The Royalists defended their barricades for two hours or thereabouts. Even when they fell back, the Parliamentarian foot could get no further because of the enemy horse within. Eventually Sir Thomas broke down a barricade on the right, 'which let us in between the Houses and the river', and rushed in. He charged one body of Royalist horse, who fled across the bridge of boats, and was unhorsed in a second encounter, 'being single, a little before my men, who presently relieved me, and forced the enemy back, who retreated also to York' (Fairfax, *A Short Memorial*). Sir John Bellasis was captured in this charge. Meanwhile, Parliamentarian foot entered the town, taking numerous prisoners, although most of the enemy horse got away northwards and even southwest, to Cawood and Pontefract.

Casualty reports were vague: Lord Fairfax admitted losing 'divers gallant Commanders and Souldiers, and very many sore wounded', while Royalist dead were 'strewed in the way to York for four miles [6 km] together'. Prisoners included 72 named officers, 1600 common soldiers and above 500 cavalry. The disaster 'put them into great Distractions and fears at York', and caused Newcastle's immediate withdrawal from County Durham. Disregarding his lines of communication, Leven followed, meeting the Fairfaxes at Wetherby on 18 April. Together they besieged Newcastle in York, creating the strategic conditions for the war's decisive encounter at Marston Moor.

Directions

Selby is at the junction of the A19 and A63. Southward development, particularly the railway, has obscured the Parliamentarian lines of attack.

Marston Moor, Tuesday 2 July 1644

England, North Yorkshire, LR105 SE4752–4951

The decisive battle of the English Civil War was Marston Moor, the largest ever fought on British soil, except perhaps for Worcester (1651). The only successful example of Anglo-Scottish cooperation on a Civil War battlefield, Marston Moor marked the rise of Oliver Cromwell and the eclipse of Prince Rupert.

During March 1644 the Marquess of Newcastle failed to check either Leven's invading Scots or the renascent Yorkshire Parliamentarians under Fairfax. They besieged Newcastle in York, the Earl of Manchester's Eastern Association forces joining them on 3 June. York's only hope of relief lay in Prince Rupert, posted to Shrewsbury to repair the effects of the Royalist defeat at Nantwich (see above). As a first step Rupert invaded Lancashire, storming Bolton and Liverpool. Within two months Rupert had created a new army, and with this he crossed the Pennines, following the Roman road from Preston through Clitheroe to Skipton. On 30 July he reached Knaresborough, 17 miles (27 km) west of York.

Spread out around the besieged city, and divided by the River Ouse, the Allies feared to meet Rupert's attack in their siege lines. They broke up the siege and prepared to defend the direct route from Knaresborough to York, on Marston Moor. Rupert sidestepped their blocking position, swinging north behind a cavalry screen. He crossed the River Ure at Boroughbridge and pushed down the east bank of the Ouse to York, his advanced guard entering the city without a fight during the evening of 1 July.

Leven was unwilling to engage the combined forces of Rupert and Newcastle. Early on 2 July he withdrew towards Tadcaster, intending to cross the River Wharfe. Behind the river line the allied Army of Both Kingdoms could avoid action, preserve its communications with Hull, and bar a further Royalist advance into Lincolnshire. The leading Scottish infantry were a mile (1.6 km) from Tadcaster when their rearguard on Marston Hill reported Royalist horse advancing across the moor. Believing Rupert meant to attack him strung out in column of march, Leven countermarched his army, a difficult and time-consuming process.

The Allies were saved by dissension among the Royalist high command. Rupert believed he had unequivocal instructions to relieve York and defeat the Scots. A modern staff officer might be hard pressed to interpret the king's impenetrable sub-clauses as a direct order to fight, but contemporary professionals accepted Charles's aggressive intentions: 'he [Rupert] haiffing ane order which was intercepted from the King, that nothing but Impossibilities should stay him from beating the Scots' (Major General Sir James Lumsden). 'Before God,' exclaimed Lord Culpepper, when he learned of the despatch at Royalist headquarters, 'you are undone, for upon this peremptory order he will fight, whatever comes on't.'

Anxious to defeat the enemy while they were still rattled, Prince Rupert had pressed on after them without ensuring the effective cooperation of York's much-tried garrison. Newcastle agreed, unwillingly, to fight, but failed to inspire any haste in James King, Lord Eythin, his military amanuensis. Rupert and Newcastle met on Marston Moor at 10 a.m., still hoping for a glorious day, but Eythin did not appear until 4 p.m. His infantry arrived later still, 'and those all drunk'. By then the Allies had been in position for hours, singing psalms and cannonading the Royalist lines below.

Marston Moor

	Winner	*Loser*
Opponents	Parliamentarian	Royalist
Commanders	Alexander Leslie, Earl of Leven Edward Montagu, Earl of Manchester Ferdinando, Lord Fairfax	Prince Rupert William Cavendish, Marquess of Newcastle Lord George Goring
Numbers	21,500–28,500	17,500–23,000
Losses	*c.*1000	10,650

The battlefield lies within a triangle formed by Wilstrop Wood to the north and the villages of Tockwith on the west and Long Marston on the southeast. Between the settlements ran Marston or Tockwith Road, separating the two armies. North of the road the Royalists occupied 'ane plain field 3 myles in length and in breidth, the fairest ground for such use that I have seen in England' (Lumsden). The Allies stood to the south on the forward slope of Marston Hill, which at the time was covered with standing corn. The ridge falls sharply from Cromwell Plump (125 feet/38 m), which provides commanding views as far as York Minster, levelling out towards the 75 foot/23 m contour line where the Allies deployed. On the west, Marston Hill slopes down through Bilton Bream towards Sike Beck, the western edge of the battlefield.

Two rough tracks fringed with bushes and scrubby trees ran northeast from Marston Road: Atterwith Lane and Moor Lane, christened Bloody Lane by Victorian antiquaries. Three-quarters of a mile (1.2 km) north of the main road, Moor Lane met the now demolished pack road from York at Four Lanes Meet. Newcastle probably took this route from Micklegate through Hessay village, to approach the battlefield obliquely from the flank. Contemporary accounts speak of 'Hessammoore' rather than Marston Moor.

Three hundred yards (275 m) north of Marston Road the lighter cultivable soil changes to heavy

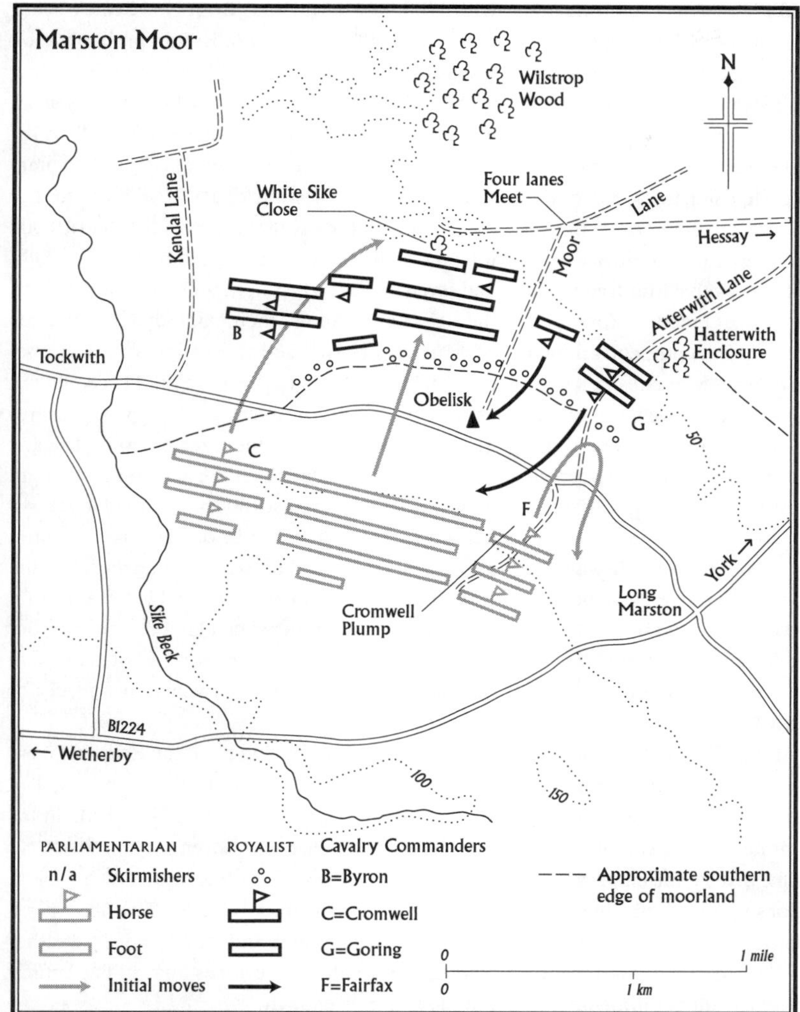

moorland clay. The moor is now enclosed, but in 1644 it was dead flat open ground, with scrubby grass, thorn and gorse. The plan drawn by Rupert's chief of staff, Bernard de Gomme, shows a curved line across the Royalist front, labelled 'These hedges was Lined with musquetiers.' Other sources suggest a less continuous boundary of banks, hedges and ditches between the cornfields and the moor. Several witnesses thought this would deter an attack by either side, as it would 'disturb their order, and the other would be ready in good ground and order, to charge

Directions

Take the B1224 Wetherby road from York, turning right in Long Marston for Tockwith. View the battlefield from the monument at the end of Moor Lane, or from Cromwell Plump, accessible by a footpath across Marston Road. Walk up Atterwith and Moor Lanes to the alternative sites of the white-coats' last stand, in the Atterwith enclosures or White Sike Close, right and left of the tracks respectively. Kendal Lane, on the right near Tockwith, postdates the battle, but shadows the outer flank of Cromwell's first charge.

them before they could recover it' (Scoutmaster General Lionel Watson). In practice, the 'ditch' had little effect except between Atterwith Lane and Moor Lane. Today it is only visible where the boundary crossed the two lanes.

Contemporaries saw both armies as exceptionally large, more than 20,000 each, rising to 27,000 for the Allies, a remarkable figure for the period. Leven enjoyed considerable numerical superiority over Rupert, 'having in the front twelve hundred more than hee', according to a Mr Ogden, a Yorkshire Royalist. The Allies drew up in depth, constrained by the villages on either flank. Manchester's lieutenant general of horse, Oliver Cromwell, was on the left with 3000–4000 Eastern Association horse and dragoons, in two lines. A third line of 1000 Scottish light horse was held in reserve. Sir Thomas Fairfax took the right with 2000 Northern Association horse, supported by another 1000 Scots. Each wave of cavalry was subdivided into four, five or six bodies, interlarded with musketeers, making 600 commanded shot on each wing. The Allied infantry was unusually intermingled, after their hasty return to the battlefield: 4000 Eastern Association, 2500–3000 Northern Association and 8000–13,500 Scots. Sir James Turner, a Scots observer with service in Germany and Ireland, described the latter as 'lustie, well clothed and well moneyd, bot raw, untrained and undisciplined'. Like the cavalry, the infantry were in three lines: ten battalions in front, with eight each in the second and third lines, and two more in reserve. Allied forces totalled 7000–8000 mounted troops and 14,500–20,500 infantry, depending on the source. Artillery strength is unknown, but numerous 6-pounder balls have been found on the field, and one culverin shot behind the Royalist centre.

Rupert's order of battle is less certain, as de Gomme's map may represent planned rather than actual dispositions, particularly in the case of Newcastle's belated infantry. De Gomme shows that besides the usual cavalry wings, Rupert withheld a considerable mounted reserve. Lord Byron commanded the right flank towards Tockwith, with 2500 of Rupert's own horse in two lines, interlarded with 500 shot. Lord George Goring led the other flank with 2100 Northern Horse from Newcastle's army, and 500 more *enfants perdus*. Eythin probably took responsibility for the centre, Newcastle's foot filling up behind Rupert's infantry, who 'had in many small bodies bespread themselves' to secure the Royalist start line (*A Continuation of True Intelligence*, Thomason Tract E2.1). Allowing for 1000 commanded shot detached with the cavalry, the Royalists had 10,000 infantry in the centre, deployed in two lines of eight and seven bodies respectively, with four more behind the right flank. Across their front 'divers regiments of Musketters so lined the hedge and ditch betwixt themselves and us that our Souldiers could not assault them, without very great apparent prejudice'(*True Intelligence*). One three-battalion brigade was pushed forward to cover the junction of the right wing and centre. At least 1300 horse stood in reserve behind the infantry, while de Gomme counted another 500 unlocated horse. Including the latter, the Royalists had 6500 cavalry and 11,000 infantry. Cromwell's scoutmaster general put them somewhat higher: 'some fourteen thousand Foot, and nine thousand Horse, and some twenty-five peeces of Ordnance'.

The armies stood so long that the Royalists postponed further operations until the following day. Rupert called for provisions, and Newcastle lit his pipe. Their relaxation was Leven's signal to attack: 'Our Army in its severall parts moving down the Hill ... like unto so many thicke clouds' (*True Intelligence*). The time was between 5 and 7 p.m., cloudy weather inspiring unusually imprecise estimates. The battle's outline is simple enough:

(1) THE ALLIES' INITIAL ONSET

The Allies' sudden advance gave defending musketeers no time to develop their fire, while the ditch proved a disappointment, particularly on the Royalist right. Byron has attracted general condemnation for the rapid collapse of his wing. Critics allege he threw away the advantages of his position by countercharging over the ditch, masking the fire of his infantry. Rupert's diary notes 'how by ye improper charge of ye Ld Byron much harm was done'. Another contemporary observed that Byron 'did not attend till the foe forced their way unto him, but gave his men the trouble to pass over the ditch; the occasion of much disorder'. The enemy observed nothing of all this, apparently crossing the obstacle before contact, 'In a moment we were passed the ditch into the Moore, upon equall grounds with the enemy, our men going in a running march' (Watson). Surprised and outnumbered by Cromwell's Ironsides, Parliament's best cavalry, Byron's first line was broken beyond recovery.

Carried forward by the success of the cavalry on their left, Leven's infantry soon beat the Royalist musketeers from their hedges. They crossed the ditch, which in front of Manchester's brigade on the left flank of the main battle was no obstacle at all, and pushed back the Royalist front line, taking their guns.

Leven's only check came on his right, where Sir Thomas Fairfax's horse 'answered not our expectatioun, nor his worth' (Lumsden). The Northern Association cavalry were fewer and less solid than the Ironsides, and faced more serious opposition. A steep bank between Atterwith and Moor Lanes prevented them advancing: 'above 3 or 4 in front, upon the one side of the Lane was a Ditch, and on the other an Hedge, both whereof were lined with Musketiers' (*A Full Relation*, T.T. E54.19). When the bank was levelled in the 1960s hundreds of musket balls were uncovered, justifying Fairfax's claim that 'in this charge as many were hurt and killed as in the whole [Allied] Army besides'. Unable to deploy, and countercharged by Goring's hard-bitten Northern Horse, Fairfax's men were driven back on their infantry, 'broke them wholly, and trod the most part of them under foot' (*Full Relation*). Some fled as far as Hull and Lincoln, while others plundered their own baggage train. Only Sir Thomas and a few men broke through the Royalist lines, despite the obstacles and enemy fire. His Scottish supports disputed the junction of Marston Lane and Atterwith Lane for a while, but they too were overwhelmed.

(2) ROYALIST REACTION

Royalist commanders reacted quickly to Leven's offensive. Rupert set off for his right flank with 700 reserve horse, rallying his own regiment on the way: 'Swounds,' said he, 'do you run, follow me.' Reinforcing Byron's second line, he brought the enemy horse to a stand: '*Cromwels* own division had a hard pull of it: for they were charged by *Ruperts* bravest men, both in Front and Flank: they stood at the swords point a little while, hacking one another: but at last ... he [Cromwell] brake through them, scattering them before him like a little dust' (Watson). Other sources show the decisive blow was struck by David Leslie's Scottish horse, coming in on the Royalist flank, text-book cavalry tactics. Cromwell's political opponents exploited this circumstance – and his temporary absence seeking treatment for a neck wound – to attribute the success to others. However, Sir James Lumsden, a Presbyterian Scot and not Cromwell's natural ally, credited him and Leslie equally, 'under God'.

Newcastle tried and failed to rally Byron's fugitives, the terrified troopers killing their own officers and running over a girl who opened the gate for them northeast of Wilstrop Wood, perhaps at Hunters Great Gate (SE489541). Newcastle's white-coated infantry did better, furiously assaulting the Allied centre and driving them back in disorder. Another reserve brigade of Royalist horse charged through the Parliamentarian foot to the top of Marston Hill. Newcastle joined in, killing three of the enemy with his page's half-leaden sword, not bad for a dilettante. Prodigious numbers of Scottish infantry ran away, 'But one Regiment of the Earle of Manchesters Foote seeing the Enemy, both Horse and Foot, pursuing an advantage, did wheele on the right hand, upon their Flanck, and gave them so hot a charge, that they were forced to flie back disbanded into the Moore' (*True Intelligence*).

Meanwhile, Goring's cavalry on the Royalist left had swept the opposing cavalry from the field, his supports wheeling into the exposed flank of the Allied infantry, 'so that they had the Foot upon their front and the whole Cavalry of the enemies left wing to fight with'. For almost an hour a few devoted Scots regiments, musketeers interlined with pikemen, held out against repeated attacks.

An hour into the battle, victory was wide open:

'The truth is wee had the victory but knew it not' (Ogden). Both sides had triumphed on the left. The Royalist centre was holding the Allied attack, except where Manchester's infantry had wheeled into the flank of Newcastle's counterattack. The opposing battle lines had consequently slewed around like a vast rugby scrum, forming a new front between White Sike Close and the obelisk at the southern end of Moor Lane. Arthur Trevor, a Royalist dispatch rider, reported 'horrible distraction' as far away as Skipton Castle, 'here meeting with a shoal of Scots crying out *Weys us, weys us we are all undone* ... and anon ... a ragged troop reduced to four and a Cornet; by and by with a little foot officer without hat, band, sword or indeed anything but feet and so much tongue as would serve to enquire the way to the next garrison'.

(3) ALLIED COUNTERSTROKES LEADING TO THEIR VICTORY

Both commanders-in-chief were out of action. Leven's staff had hurried him away to Leeds, while Rupert was hiding in a bean patch. Old Lord Fairfax went home to Cawood Castle and put himself to bed. Manchester was commanding an infantry battalion in the middle of the fight. Only Cromwell and David Leslie retained control over their troops, or any coherent view of the battle. While the former kept his regiments in hand to charge fresh enemy units, the latter 'with his little light Scotch nags' fell upon broken regiments, 'doing execution upon them, and keeping them from rallying again' (Lord Saye). Several troops of horse had escaped the debacle on the Allied right, including their leader, who removed the white Royalist field sign from his hat, and rode across the enemy rear to join Cromwell and Leslie.

Together the Allies' junior commanders initiated the decisive manoeuvre of the battle, wheeling around the Royalist right rear to deal with the disordered but victorious remnants of Goring's Northern Horse: 'And here came the business of the day (nay almost of the Kingdome) to be disputed upon this second charge' (Watson). The Allied turning movement brought Cromwell to where Goring had started the battle, while the Royalist horse now stood on the disadvantageous ground originally occupied by Sir Thomas Fairfax. Numbers, terrain and disorder all told against the Northern Horse, who broke and fled: 'After which we set upon the reare of their Foot, and with the assistance of our main battell, which all this time stood firm, we put them wholly to the rout' (*True Intelligence*).

The only opposition came from Newcastle's white-coats who 'got into a small parcel of ground ditched in, and not easy of access of horse' (Captain Camby). They held out for an hour at push of pike, until Scots dragoons shot holes in their ranks, allowing the Roundhead horse to break in, Camby among them, every Royalist falling 'in the same order and rank where he had fought' (James Somerville). Only 30 Royalists are said to have survived. Details of this celebrated stand are obscure, the number of victims varying from the whole brigade of 4000 white-coats to a single regiment. Its traditional location was White Sike Close, west of Four Lanes Meet, although this has been challenged. Dr Peter Newman placed the action in the Atterwith enclosures, which, unlike White Sike Close, did exist at the time. Newman argued the white-coats had been cut off from their allotted place behind the right centre by the Allied attack, and fouled the outer flank of Cromwell's turning movement. However, several accounts specifically mention Newcastle's foot in the centre, so the case appears unproven.

Allied accounts claim the battlefield was cleared by 9 p.m., although bodies of broken Royalist horse hung about until midnight, awaiting orders that never came. Newcastle was among the last to leave. Leven had won a staggering victory in his absence. Country people reported burying 4150 bodies in mass graves traditionally located at Four Lanes Meet, White Sike Close and near Wilstrop Wood. Drainage operations in 1859 are said to have found hundreds of skeletons 4 feet (1.2 m) below the moor. Another 5000 Royalist wounded were reported at York, and at least 1500 were captured. Casualties fell disproportionately upon Rupert's old soldiers and gentry, the recent conscripts running away. Among the dead was Prince Rupert's poodle, alleged to have been his familiar spirit. The

Allies admitted only a few hundred dead, although Lord Fairfax's army lost over 1000 wounded. The Eastern Association and Scots armies were virtually intact, once their runaways had returned.

Newcastle's army was destroyed, along with Royalist influence in the northeast. Unwilling to endure the laughter at court, the marquess led his officers into exile. The remnants of the Northern Horse followed Rupert south, leaving York to surrender on 16 July. Only the separation of the Allied armies to pursue individual strategic concerns limited the immediate consequences of the battle, preventing a speedy end to the war. Nevertheless, Marston Moor left the king outnumbered, and on the strategic defensive.

Montgomery, 18 September 1644

Wales, Powys, LR137 SO2298

One of the least-known battles of the Civil Wars, Montgomery was of major strategic significance, cutting off the king's armies from their recruiting grounds, and debilitating Royalist garrisons at Chester and Shrewsbury.

Sir Thomas Myddleton's capture of Oswestry on 22 June 1644 cleared the way for a Parliamentarian invasion of Wales. On 4 September Myddleton took Montgomery and its castle, 'one of the goodliest and strongest places I ever looked upon' (Sir John Meldrum, Thomason Tract E10.4). Local Royalists descended on the town in force, shutting up Myddleton's infantry in the castle, while he rode northwards for help.

The Parliamentarian commanders Sir John Meldrum and Sir William Brereton were blockading Liverpool and Chester respectively, and promptly mobilized a relief force with contingents from Yorkshire, Lancashire and Cheshire. On the evening of 17 September the Parliamentarians approached Salt Bridge, where the Welshpool road crosses the River Camlad 2 miles (3 km) north of Montgomery. They spent the night in the Royalist quarters, probably in the meadows just south of the Camlad, which the enemy 'diserted at our coming thither, placing themselves upon the mountain above the castle, a place of great advantage for them' (Brereton, T.T. E10.4). At first sight this appears to mean the Iron Age fort at Ffridd Faldwyn northwest of Montgomery, an implausibly steep campsite for an army. The Royalist commander Lord Byron seems more likely to have withdrawn south of Montgomery to Town Hill, or westwards past Hen Dolmen, where the valley provides water and a less vertiginous resting place.

Montgomery Castle lies on a steep spur north of the town, commanding the plain north and east. The only practicable approach is from the south, but the Royalists had no siege guns. Their problem was to maintain the blockade while fending off the relieving force, one of the most dangerous of strategic operations. Parliamentarian accounts put the Royalists at 4000–5000 men: 500 horse and 2500 foot from Shrewsbury and other local garrisons, reinforced just before the Parliamentarians arrived by Lord Byron, with 1000 horse and 500 foot. Meldrum had 3000 men, half horse and half foot, with another 500 Parliamentarian foot in the castle. Byron's numerical superiority may have been more apparent than real. He had no more cavalry than the enemy, and had to leave part of his force to watch the castle. Royalist morale must have been brittle after defeats at Nantwich and Marston Moor.

The battlefield consists of a slightly rolling plain 2 by $1^{1}/_{2}$ miles (3 by 2.5 km), northeast of Montgomery. Clockwise from the north it is bounded by the Camlad, Offa's Dyke, the town and the hills to the west. The steeply banked Welshpool road crosses it from north to south. The hedged fields east of the road are large enough for formed bodies of troops,

Montgomery

	Winner	*Loser*
Opponents	Parliamentarian	Royalist
Commanders	Sir John Meldrum Sir William Brereton Sir Thomas Myddleton	John, Lord Byron
Numbers	3500	4500
Losses	100	1600–2000

Directions

Montgomery is 8 miles (13 km) south of Welshpool on the B4388, which crosses the battlefield south of Salt Bridge. A footpath runs southeast from point 93 towards Offa's Dyke. See the remains of the castle, where ditch restoration uncovered Civil War bullets and broken armour. A cavalry helmet with the owner's skull inside was found in Lymore Park, southeast of the town, during the 19th century.

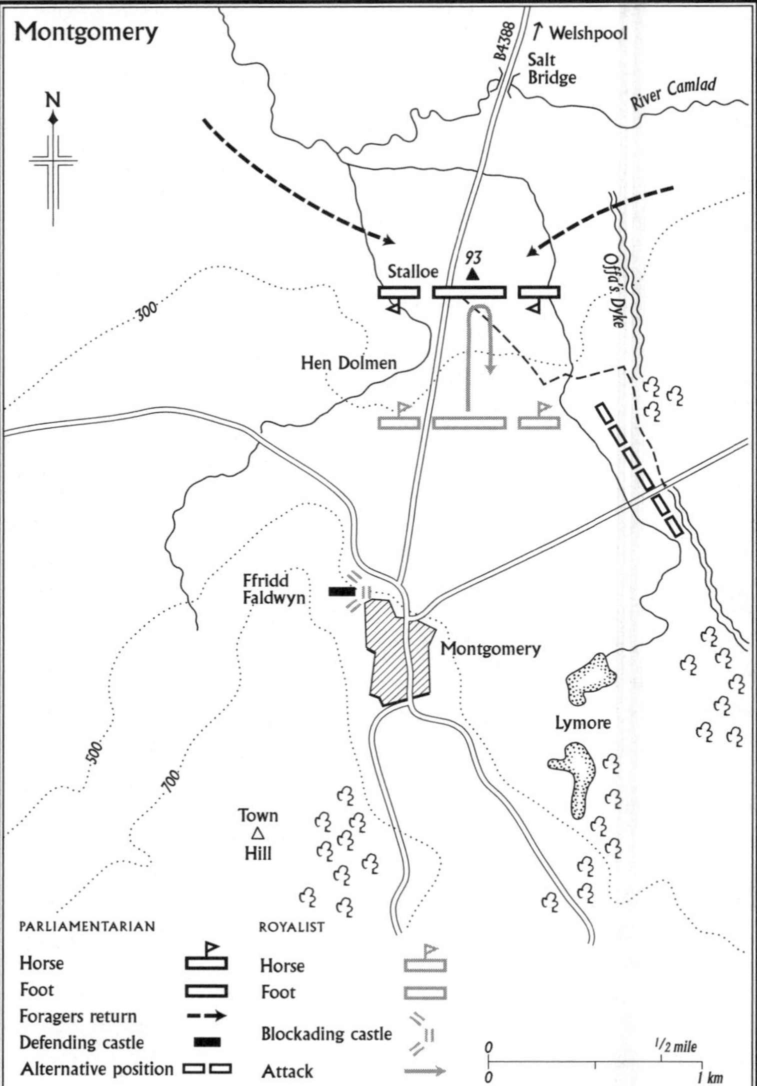

and present relatively firm going. To the west the ground is more broken, with ditches and hillocks. Modern descriptions of the dispositions are largely conjectural. One interpretation of events has Meldrum facing west at SO2398, his back against Offa's Dyke, the stream that marks the Shropshire county boundary across his front. A more credible reconstruction places the Parliamentarians on a small hill (305 feet/93 m) at Stalloe, a mile (1.6 km) north of Montgomery on the Welshpool road, directly covering their line of retreat across Salt Bridge. Streams either side of the road protect the flanks, but if the day went badly wrong the whole army could end up in the Camlad.

Meldrum's primary objective was to resupply the castle. Early on 18 September a third of his cavalry went out foraging, 'which the enemy perceiving, they marched down a body both Horse and Foot ... and came up to our ground and gave us battle' (Myddleton, T.T. E10.4). The axis of Byron's advance would depend on which side of Montgomery he had bivouacked. In the Stalloe position Meldrum could meet a Royalist attack from either south or west, wheeling to cover the bridge, while retaining the hill: 'they came on, with great courage, resolving to break through our forces, and to make themselves masters of a Bridge we had gained the night before; which would have cut off the passage of our retreat' (Meldrum).

At first the Royalists drove all before them: 'it came to push of Pike wherein they were much too hard for us having many more Pikes. Our Horse also at the beginning ... were wasted and retreated'. Sir William Fairfax, leading the Yorkshire horse, was badly wounded, captured and then rescued. Somehow the battered Parliamentarians rallied, resolving to fight it out to the last man: 'Indeed there could be no other hope or expectation of safety or escape ... all passages being entirely in the enemies power' (Brereton). Meldrum gave the credit to Brereton's Cheshire foot, who 'carried themselves more like Lyons than men'. Perhaps the mounted foraging party returned to even the odds. As the Royalists lost their original impetus they simply collapsed: 'We were found too light (of foot at least) for, in plain English, our men ran shamefully when they had no cause of so great fear, so that we were ordained to be the mocking stock of the war' (Arthur Trevor).

The battle was over in an hour. Myddleton thought it 'as great a victory as hath been gained in any part of the kingdom' (*Calendar of State Papers*). As usual the defeated infantry provided most of the casualties, 400–500 dead and 1200–1500 prisoners, 'and some few Horse, the rest all fleeing away' (Myddleton). Local Royalist garrisons were denuded of ammunition and defenders: 'by the blow here given the best of their Foot are taken away' (Meldrum). On the other side, 'we lost not 40 men slaine, and I doe believe, there was not 60 wounded' (Brereton). Byron had trifled away the last of the king's Irish reinforcements, and it was now impossible to replace them: 'North Wales (which formerly hath been the nurseries of the King's armies) in all likelihood will strike off that yoke of servitude ... and will be reduced to the obedience of King and Parliament [sic]' (Meldrum). Montgomery was a fitting conclusion to the work begun at Marston Moor.

Hard Knocks in the South: 1644

In hindsight 1644 was a year of relentless Parliamentarian progress. The strategic shift was clearest in northern England, where Marston Moor permanently extinguished Royalist influence. It was less obvious in the south, where dissension among Parliament's senior commanders presented the king with unlooked for victories.

The year began badly for the Royalists, whose Oxford army was played out after First Newbury (see above). The recently ennobled Lord Hopton was commissioned to advance on London through the southern counties (Hampshire, Sussex and Kent) with an improvised army. Hopton took Arundel, but was too weak to do more, before entering winter quarters. His old opponent, Sir William Waller, took advantage of Royalist dispersal to destroy a detachment at Alton (13 December 1643) and recapture Arundel, finally defeating Hopton in person at Cheriton (29 March).

The destruction of Hopton's army, and Prince Rupert's absence rescuing beleaguered garrisons in the North and Midlands (see above), left Charles I outnumbered by the combined forces of Waller and the Earl of Essex, still lurking in the Thames valley.

Between them they chased him out of Oxford, as far as Bewdley (Worcestershire), before mutual jealousy persuaded them to part company at Chipping Norton (6 June). This was a major blunder, exposing Parliament's two southern armies to defeat in detail. Charles doubled back to Oxford to pick up his guns and pikemen, before defeating Waller at Cropredy Bridge (29 July). He then pursued Essex into the West Country, forcing the latter's infantry to surrender at Lostwithiel, the most striking Royalist success of the war.

These defeats reopened the prospect of a Royalist advance on London, which Parliament only prevented by bringing the Earl of Manchester's Eastern Association forces south. The season ended with a second battle at Newbury (27 October), where Charles was encircled by an unhappy amalgam of survivors from Waller's and Essex's armies, and Manchester's veterans of Marston Moor. After a tense couple of hours, the king slipped away under cover of darkness, apparently none the worse for his second year's campaigning. The bitter disagreements that followed Newbury among the Parliamentarians, however, paved the way for their final victory.

Alton, Wednesday 13 December 1643

England, Hampshire, LR186 SU7139

Autumn 1643 saw a resumption of the duel between Sir William Waller and Sir Ralph Hopton, recently ennobled as Lord Hopton. Parliament's western setbacks (see Roundway Down above) brought operations eastwards into Hampshire and West Sussex, where local Royalists seized Winchester and Arundel. Hopton had too few men to consolidate his success, spreading his troops in a thin screen from Arundel to Alton. The latter made a tempting target for one of Waller's characteristic night operations.

Waller had rebuilt his army with London regiments, and held Farnham, 10 miles (16 km) northeast of Alton. Alton's defenders were heavily outnumbered, consisting of Lord Crawford's regiment of 300 horse and a scratch unit of foot under Colonel Sir Richard Bolle, also spelled Boles, Bolles or Bowles. Drawn from Royalist garrisons in the Thames valley, Bolle's men may have numbered as few as 500, double that if Parliamentarian claims for the numbers of prisoners taken are true.

Hopton warned Crawford to be on his guard: 'But Sir William Waller had verie politiquely, and souldier-like taken advantage of the woodines of that Country, and drawen his men, and his light leather-gunnes into the woods, and with pioneers, made his way through them, without coming into any of the highways' (Hopton, *Bellum Civile*). Waller marched in great secrecy at 7 p.m. on 12 December. He feinted towards the Royalist stronghold at Basing House, before turning south about 1 a.m. towards Alton, 'passing exactly between the hills,' according to a soldier of the Westminster Regiment, 'till they obtained within half a mile of the said Town, altogether undiscovered by the Enemy'. Another Parliamentarian wrote, 'about 9 a clock … came upon the *West* side of the Towne, where we had both the winde and hill to friende'. The hill is presumably the wooded triangle of high ground (571–650 feet/174–198 m) between the A339 and B3349 Basingstoke and Odiham roads, 1 km or half an old mile west of Alton.

Crawford's horse fled south, leaving the infantry to it. Elements of three Parliamentarian regiments attacked north and northwest of the town, 'linying of hedges and the like', but made little impression on buildings and barricades, 'especially one great

Alton

	Winner	*Loser*
Opponents	Parliamentarian	Royalist
Commanders	Sir William Waller	Colonel Richard Bolle (k)
Numbers	5000	1300
Losses	17	915

brick house neere the Church … out of which windows they fired very fast' (Captain Elias Archer, Yellow Auxiliary Regiment). Waller deployed artillery at the foot of the hill, to clear the brick house, while the London regiments 'came downe the hill', to attack a half moon and breastwork on the west side. On the extreme right, the Green Auxiliaries advanced south of 'a little river', the head waters of the Wey, presumably along Lenten Street. Firing a thatched cottage, they blinded the half moon's defenders with smoke, and broke into the High Street with colours flying.

Hemmed in north and south, the Royalists retreated into the churchyard and another earthwork north of the church, 'all which they kept nere upon two houres very stoutly and (having made scaffolds in the Church to fire out of the windows) fired very thick from every place' (Archer). The attackers' concentric fire eventually drove the Royalists from the southeast churchyard, where they left muskets sticking up over the wall, 'as if some of the men had still lyn there in Ambush'. A bold sergeant looked inside, found the enemy still firing from the south and west sides, and waved his comrades forward, to drive them into the church.

The Royalist defenders of the earthwork north of the churchyard counterattacked, but the leading ranks were driven back on their own pikemen, suffering heavy casualties and breaking the pikes: 'By this time the Church-yard was full of our men, laying about them stoutly with their Halberts, Swords, and Musquet-stocks, while some threw hand-granadoes in the Church windows, others attempting to enter the Church' (Archer). The first man in was shot through the thigh, 'whereof he is very ill', but his comrades stormed in, overpowering the defenders. Refusing offers of quarter, Colonel Bolle was brained by a musketeer, reputedly in the pulpit, then in the centre of the church.

The victors buried about 40 Royalists north of the church, perhaps in their own trenches, and captured 875. Half changed sides, and the rest were marched off to Farnham, tied together with slow match. Parliamentarian losses were under twenty, including 'six scorched with powder, by reason of their owne negligence' (Westminster Soldier). Hopton pulled his troops back, isolating Arundel, which Waller retook on 6 January 1644.

Directions

Alton has grown since Clarendon described it as 'a great village', obscuring Waller's lines of attack, except as indicated above. See the church in the town centre, its internal walls retaining bullet holes with lead inside them. The main door, removed from its contemporary position at the west end, is loop-holed and scarred by pike thrusts.

Cheriton (Alresford), **Friday 29 March 1644**

England, Hampshire, LR185 SU5929

The Royalist defeat at Cheriton was an unimpressive battle from a command perspective. One Parliamentarian remarked, 'it was indeed a victory, but the worst possible I ever saw'. Nevertheless, it eliminated the lower jaw of Charles I's pincer movement on London, a southern equivalent of Marston Moor.

Waller resumed operations in Hampshire after the cold weather of early 1644. On 26 March he lay between Warnford and West Meon; Hopton 10 miles (16 km) further west at Winchester. When the Royalists advanced to Warnford on the 27th, Waller occupied a typically inaccessible position on Westbury Hill, before trying to turn Hopton's left flank. Both armies raced for Alresford, the Parliamentarians via Bramdean, the Royalists on a parallel road to the south, through Hinton Ampner. Hopton arrived first, threatening Waller's direct communications with London. Next day the two sides bickered over the downs between Alresford and Hinton Ampner, where Waller had encamped. By evening the Royalists had gained the ridge north of Hinton Ampner, looking into the Parliamentarian quarters. These lay in Lamborough Field, sometimes known as Little London, perhaps recalling Waller's Trained Bands infantrymen. Faced with abject retreat or fighting at a

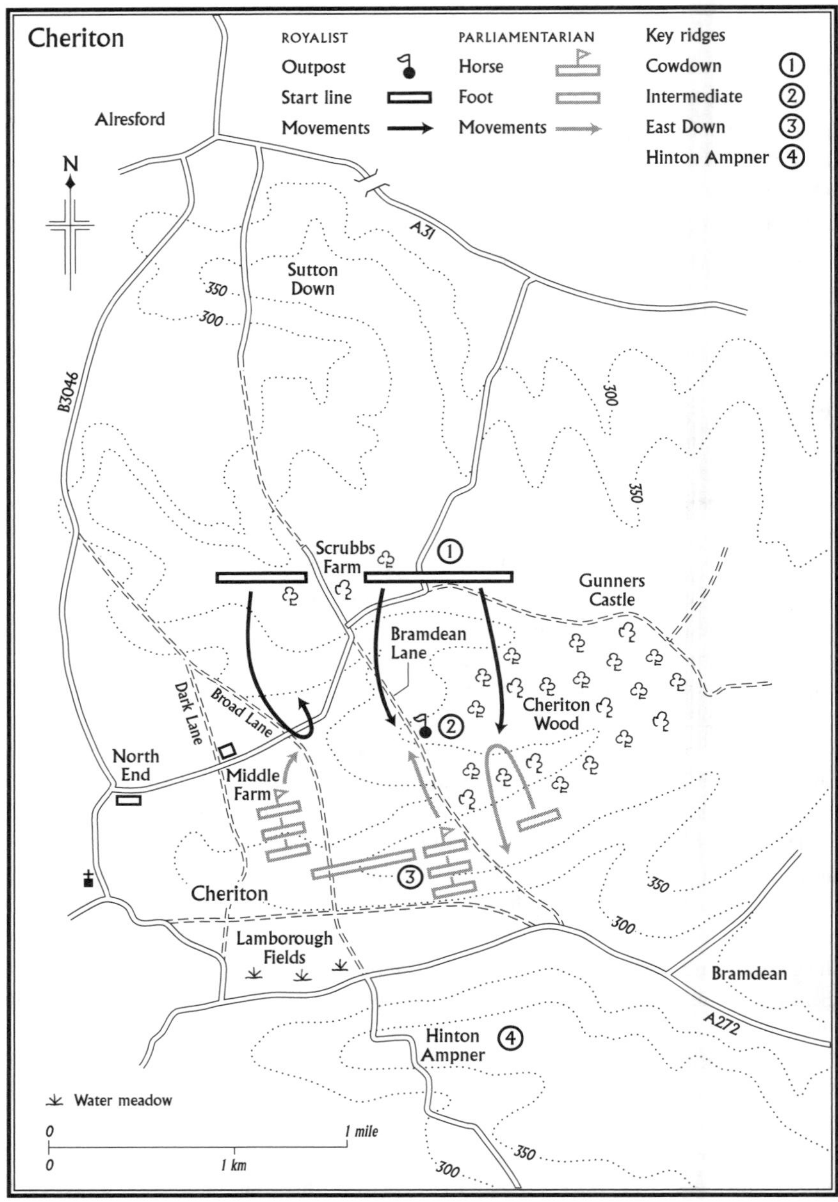

Directions

Eight miles (13 km) west of Winchester along the A272 Petersfield road. Stop opposite Hinton House at the southern end of Broad Lane to see Waller's camping ground on the left. Continue 1000 yards (900 m) to where Bramdean Lane joins the main road, just short of the village. Both lanes lead up East Down to the compromise battlefield. John Adair's site is in the valley either side of the A272. Alternatively, head north along the B3046 through Cheriton, turning right at North End to see the traditional Royalist position, and the roadside monument by the Bishop's Sutton junction in SU5930.

disadvantage, Waller laid on one of his celebrated night operations.

A.H. Burne claimed the battle's location was indisputable, but his optimism was misplaced. His grave pits are prehistoric, the contemporary records are ambiguous, and the ground confusing. Cheriton Wood anchors the eastern flank of the fighting, but is now larger and thicker than it was. Four ridges run east–west across the battlefield, providing a variety of possible start lines:

(1) Cowdown, north of Cheriton wood, between Gunner's Castle and Scrubb's Copse, extending west towards Tichbourne;
(2) A smaller nameless ridge marked by the Ordnance Survey's crossed swords;
(3) East Down, north of the Itchen and Lamborough Field;
(4) Hinton Ampner, south of the River Itchen.

A fifth ridge at Sutton Down, near Alresford railway station, served as a Royalist layback after the battle. Several lanes connect the ridges: Bramdean Lane to the east besides Cheriton Wood, Broad Lane in the centre, and Dark Lane through Middle Farm further west. The battlefield enjoys three possible locations:

(1) The traditional site described by S.R. Gardiner in the 1890s, and generally accepted until the 1970s: the Royalists stood on Cowdown, and the Parliamentarians on East Down. Most of the fighting occurred between these in the shallow 'vale' or 'arena', which broadens out from the wood into a wide, deep valley. The bottom was open common, the slopes covered with enclosed fields. As at First Newbury, these were more densely hedged than now.
(2) A radically different location proposed by John Adair in 1973: he placed the Royalists on East Down, and the Parliamentarians on the Hinton Ampner ridge and the slopes between Bramdean village and Cheriton Wood. The fighting took place across the Itchen valley, and up the southern slopes of East Down.
(3) William Seymour's compromise site: the Royalists held the intermediate ridge, facing Waller on East Down. Unlike the previous scenarios, these positions are within artillery range of each other, as stated by contemporaries. As with the traditional location, much of the fighting would be in the 'arena'.

The Adair interpretation has influenced many battlefield guides, but some combination of the traditional and compromise views seems more likely. Captain John Jones of a London regiment provides the most precise contemporary identification, 'the Enemy lay in Sutton Down, we lay in Lumborne field, we fought in East Down between Cheriton and Alesford [sic]'. Many contemporaries refer to heath or common land, which tradition and tithe maps place only to the north of East Down. Adair's battlefield lies in a quite different landscape – the Itchen's lush water meadows, which still flood in springtime, although nobody mentions fighting in a lake. Waller's right certainly hinged upon Cheriton Wood. So accomplished a tactician seems unlikely to have drawn his other flank back to Hinton Ampner, presenting an oblique front to the enemy's line of advance, awkwardly spanning two ridges rather than lining the crest of one. Hopton's outposts did occupy East Down overnight, but most accounts agree they had withdrawn before fighting began on the 29th, allowing the Parliamentarians to gain the high ground, commanding the Royalist position.

Both armies had received reinforcements. Hopton had been joined by Charles I's chief military adviser Lord Forth, with much 'straining of courtesies' before that gouty veteran would agree to share command. Forth brought 800 horse and 1200 foot from Oxford. Hopton already had some 2000 cavalry and 2400 infantry, and 12 cannon. The Earl of Essex responded to Forth's detachment by sending Sir William Balfour to join Waller, with several thousand extra cavalry and dragoons. Altogether the Parliamentarians probably fielded 5000 horse, 500–800 dragoons and 5000 foot. John Adair gives them 3000 horse and 5000 foot, which seems too few cavalry. Their ordnance included a demi-culverin named 'Kill Cow', five drakes of different calibres, and 60 rounds per gun.

The Battle of Cheriton falls into several well-known episodes: the Parliamentarian capture of the wood, and their ejection; an unintended and disastrous forward movement on the Royalist right; piecemeal destruction of the Royalist horse in an extended and perhaps unpremeditated cavalry battle; the Royalist withdrawal through Alresford after dusk. The exact relationships between these events are less easy to unravel.

Waller's overnight advance into the wood with 300 horse and 1000 shot threatened Hopton's outpost line. This may have stayed on East Down all night. Alternatively it may have fallen back to the intermediate ridge, to enjoy a better view of enemy movement on the skyline above, as contemporary tactical manuals advise. Several sources confirm that the outposts were commanded 'by another hill very well set with hedges and trees (such as Waller loves)' (*Mercurius Aulicus*). At dawn Hopton was unable to see the enemy for mist. He brought up the rest of the army, probably to the intermediate ridge. Forth's men took the right, and Hopton's the left, the latter out of sight in a hollow within musket shot of Cheriton Wood. Modern accounts assume Hopton's cavalry were in the centre, probably on Bramdean Lane, an unusual deployment reflecting the unfavourable ground further left. Waller's order of battle was also unusual, cavalry massed forward on the left, in front of the infantry, who extended along East Down from the wood. Balfour's cavalry is usually shown on the Parliamentarian right, ready to confront Royalists advancing down Bramdean Lane, although exactly how they debouched from a position so encumbered with hedges and friendly troops is unclear.

Cheriton

	Winner	*Loser*
Opponents	Parliamentarian	Royalist
Commanders	Sir William Waller Sir William Balfour	Patrick Ruthven, Lord Forth Lord Hopton (formerly Sir Ralph)
Numbers	10,500–10,800	6400
Losses	*c.*400	*c.*400

When the mist lifted, Hopton sent 1000 musketeers to clear the wood, whose defenders fled shamefully: 'Noe sooner they did see that the bullets would come otherwise than they would have them but they made a foule retreate – I am confident I smelt them' (Captain Robert Harley, Waller's Regiment of Horse). Cheriton Wood gave the Royalists a perfect covered approach to roll up Waller's line from right to left. Hopton was all for pressing on, but Forth preferred to wait while the discouraged enemy melted away.

The sight of enemy soldiers running away by 30s and 40s was too much for some junior Royalist commanders. As Hopton rode over to consult with Forth, 'being neere the midd-way upon the brow of the hill he saw troopes of the right wing too farr advanced, and hotly engaged with the Enemy in the foote of the hill' (Hopton, *Bellum Civile*). Many accounts describe the errant Royalists as cavalrymen of Sir Henry Bard's regiment, cut off by Sir Arthur Hesilrige's Lobsters. However, Bard was commanding an infantry brigade at Cheriton, which Hesilrige's account confirms: 'Sir Arthur seeing they sent their foote from their horse sente out of every of our troope 10 to beat against their foote before their horse could rescue them we kilde many and took their Coll. Sir H Beard.' Losing an arm at Cheriton, Bard would survive Naseby, only to asphyxiate during an Arabian sandstorm in 1660.

Hesilrige's success inspired Balfour, on the Parliamentarian right, to attack Hopton's foot. Sir Walter Slingsby's tertia of foot repelled three separate Parliamentarian charges, 'not firing till within two pikes length, and then three rankes att a time, after turning up the butt end of theire muskets, charging theire pikes, and standing close' (Slingsby). As fighting flared across the whole front, Forth asked Hopton to clear Hesilrige's Lobsters from the heath below the hill. Clarendon claimed 'the king's horse never behaved themselves so ill as they did that day' (*History of the Rebellion*), but everything was against them. The enemy lay in wait, 'rang'd in nine faire bodies', while the Royalists, 'having one laines end only to passe into it [the plain], they came upon great disadvantages, for by that time one body was in the ground and drawne up (before another could second it), it was over charged with number' (Slingsby). Each brigade was defeated in turn, their best officers killed or captured. The fatal defile is usually identified with Bramdean Lane, the precise spot depending on where one imagines it crossed the Royalist frontline: at Scrubbs Copse, the intermediate ridge, or even East Down. It might equally well be Broad or Dark Lane, the latter traditionally running with blood.

After three or four hours 'the whole horse were in disorder, and the Lo: Hopton had much adoe to gett to the number of 300 horse to stand with him at the entrance into the Common' (*Bellum Civile*). Meanwhile, Parliamentarian infantry had been gaining ground, 'about 5 we beate them out of the hill clered the wood on our right hande and the Kentishmen beate them out of the field' (Hesilrige).

Forth and Hopton cut their losses, 'and making our reare as good as we could with some of the best of our horse and dragoons, we recovered our first ground upon the ridge of the hill by Alsforde-towne', probably Sutton Down. Here they waited an hour, before firing the town and retreating north to Basing House, without further loss. Forth and his page were last to leave. Waller followed 'soberly', unwilling to hazard a close pursuit. The Parliamentarian soldier Edmund Ludlow complained that Parliament 'got little more than the field and the reputation of victory'. Harley thought casualties were light, 'considering howe long wee did fight': no more than 60 Parliamentarians and 300 enemy. *Mercurius Aulicus* mocked exaggerated casualty claims, although the *Parliamentary Scout*'s 400 a side agrees with Charles I's estimate, 'the Rebels loss being certainly more'.

Cheriton's strategic results were more substantial. Hopton's survivors joined the Oxford army, freeing Waller to cooperate with Essex against the Royalist capital. The defeat 'altered the whole scheme of the king's counsels: for whereas before he hoped to enter the field early, and to have acted an offensive part, he now discovered he was wholly to be upon the defensive part; and that was likely to be a very hard part too' (Clarendon).

Cropredy Bridge, Saturday 29 June 1644

England, Oxfordshire, LR151 SP4745–4847

Few Civil War battles entirely fit the formal stereotype of two armies neatly drawn up in conventional array. Cropredy departs from the pattern more than most: it was an unintended collision, in which one commander seized a fleeting opportunity to attack the other on the line of march.

Charles I left Oxford in June 1644 to escape the combined attentions of Waller and the Earl of Essex, retreating with a lightly armed column into Worcestershire. The Parliamentarian commanders failed to bring him to battle, and against all reason divided their forces. Essex marched into the West, leaving Waller to pursue the king back into the Home Counties. By 26 June Charles was at Buckingham, after a rendezvous at Witney with the infantry he had left to hold Oxford. Waller lay at Hanwell, near Banbury. As before Edgehill (1642), Charles was nearer the capital than his Parliamentarian opponents. Hoping to defeat Waller while Essex was absent, the Royalists marched on Banbury on 28 June.

That night the armies faced one another across the River Cherwell, south of Banbury. Waller was on Crouch Hill, Charles I in the bottom at Grimsbury. Early next day, realizing Waller would not 'quitt his strength', the Royalists marched north along the Daventry road, 'to observe Waller's motion, & to expect a fitter opportunity & place to give him Battell'. Waller coasted after them, west of the Cherwell. About 10 a.m. the armies were a couple of miles (3 km) apart, in full view across the valley: the Royalists between Williamscot and Wardington, Waller on Bourton Hill above Cropredy: 'at such a distance that Wee did not at all believe they would have attempted Vs' (Sir Edward Walker, Charles I's secretary).

The river was not a major obstacle, 'the water being low by the long dry and hot weather' (Clarendon, *History of the Rebellion*). At the time, before

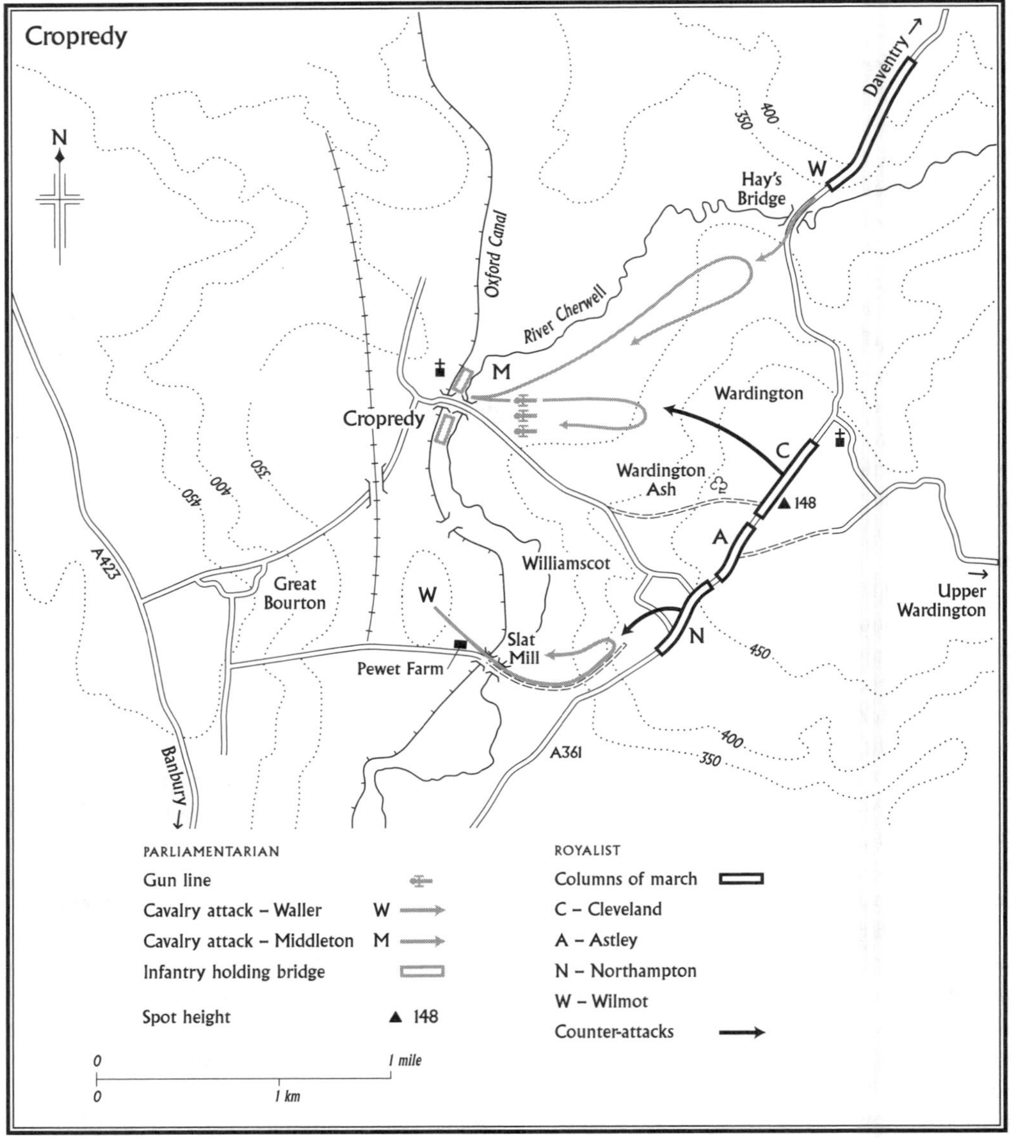

construction of the Oxford Canal, the Cherwell would have been wider, and hence shallower, than today. There were two crossing places:

(1) *Cropredy Bridge*: a narrow pack-horse bridge with no parapet, dating from the 14th century, probably supplemented by a ford. Piles found during reconstruction suggest the original was downstream from today's bridge. A minor road climbs from Cropredy to

Directions

Four miles (6 km) north of Banbury by the A423(T) through Little Bourton to Cropredy, or the A361 to Williamscot and Wardington. An inscription on Cropredy Bridge commemorates the battle. Cleveland began his second charge from a great ash tree, whose successor stands on the northern edge of a track west of the A361 between Williamscot and Wardington opposite point 148. See also Edgcote (1469) above.

Cropredy Bridge

	Winner	*Loser*
Opponents	Royalist	Parliamentarian
Commanders	Charles I	Sir William Waller
	Thomas Wentworth, Earl Cleveland	Lieutenant General John Middleton
	James Compton, Earl of Northampton	
Number	9000–10,000	*c.*6800
Losses	*c.*100	700

Williamscot, connecting the lines of march.

(2) *Slat Mill*: a rather poor ford, a mile (1.6 km) south of Cropredy and 70 yards (65 m) from the mill, now crossed by a footbridge, and still used by the bridleway from Pewet Farm to Williamscot.

North of Cropredy, the Cherwell winds eastwards to Edgcote, intersecting the Daventry road at Hay's Bridge. Charles had mustered 4000–5000 horse in four brigades, some 5000 foot and 12 guns. Cleveland's and Northampton's brigades of horse formed the rearguard with Sir Jacob Astley's tertia of foot, sometimes described as 1000 commanded men. Astley supported both cavalry formations in the battle, so probably marched between them. Waller's strength is uncertain, beyond the number of regiments: seven of horse, one of dragoons and eight of foot. A reasonable estimate, at 50 men per troop or company, comes to 2500 horse, 300 dragoons and 4000 foot. The cavalry figure agrees with Waller's battle report. He also had 11 conventional guns and two multi-barrelled battery guns – 'Blinders' or 'Barricadoes of wood drawen with wheeles in each 7 small brasse and leather Gunns charged with case shott'.

The Royalist tabloid *Mercurius Aulicus* mocked Waller's position on Bourton Hill: 'You know his condition of old, hils, boggs, hedges, ditches, these you must grant him, hee'll not fight else.' Sir William had also appreciated his position's offensive potential, 'which brought me full in upon the flank of the enemy and gave me a very great advantage'. Late in the morning, a gap appeared in the enemy column, providing the cautious Waller with the opportunity to attack. The Royalist van and battle had hastened their march, hoping to cut off 300 Parliamentarian horse reported beyond Hay's Bridge. Nobody told the rear, who trailed behind, sweating up the hill past Williamscot.

Waller launched a two-pronged attack. His lieutenant general, John Middleton, led 1500 horse and 1000 foot across Cropredy Bridge into the gap; the commander-in-chief took another 1000 horse across Slat Mill ford, 'to bite the heele according to his custom' (*Mercurius Aulicus*). The Parliamentarian field word was 'Victory without Quarter', revealing dangerous optimism. Middleton easily chased off the Royalist dragoons left to secure the bridge. Most of his cavalry pursued them northwards along the river bank to Hay's Bridge: 'being enformed that their whole bodie was marched away, when as a third part of them were left behinde unknowne to us' (Thomas Ellis, Heselrige's Horse).

The Parliamentarians had miscalculated. Royalist musketeers barricaded the northern bridge against them, while Cleveland and the rearguard's leading cavalry brigade reacted with such vigour 'that their horse [Middleton's], though twice as many and backed with foot and cannon, thought the devil had come upon them in a cloud of dust, fled back over the pass, routed their own foot, and left us masters of nine or ten colours and eleven pieces of cannon' (Lord George Digby).

As Middleton's horse withdrew, they found their supporting infantry already beaten, Royalist horse and foot blocking their own escape across Cropredy Bridge. Subsequent events are understandably confused. The king, on high ground north of the Cherwell, could see Middleton's horse menacing Cleveland's flank, 'as he was following the execution', and commanded his Lifeguard to recross Hay's Bridge to prevent them. The Lifeguard's intervention gained Cleveland time to reform, on the hill between Wardington and Williamscot. Charging again, Cleveland routed Middleton's horse, driving them back through their gun line by Cropredy Bridge. Ellis does not mention the Lifeguard's diversion, but admits being 'necessitated to retreat very disorderly, having put their body of horse into a combustion'. Lord Wilmot's brigade of horse (from the Royalist main body north of Hay's Bridge) joined in, its commander suffering his third wound in the king's service.

Meanwhile, Northampton had faced about to deal with Waller's Slat Mill detachment, 'and forced the Rebells to a speedy flight over the passe but with little losse they being not willing to abide a Second charge' (Walker). Waller himself had already turned back 'for reinforcements', before his leading unit gained the hilltop, inspiring *Mercurius Aulicus* to remark, 'the Knight was very carefull of his health'.

The cavalry action was over by 3 p.m., leaving enough daylight for the Royalist infantry to assault the river line. They got across at Slat Mill, but failed at Cropredy after some 'hot service', in which the Tower Hamlets regiment were credited with saving the whole Parliamentarian army. As evening fell, the action dwindled into an artillery exchange. Several roundshot were directed at 'the King's Sacred Body', giving the lie to Parliamentarian claims that they only fought to rescue him from 'Evil Counsellors', who were all in Oxford. Charles in turn sent Waller a message of grace and pardon, but the Parliamentarians refused to treat. The standoff continued until the evening of the following day, when the hungry Royalists marched away to Evesham, out of Waller's reach.

The Royalists admitted 3 officers and 14 other ranks killed, but a Parliamentarian witness, Richard Coe, saw 'many dead corps lying naked and unburied, 40 graves in the highway, and many stately horses'. Waller claimed 60 prisoners. Estimates of Parliamentarian losses vary from 100 or six score to 200 dead and 200 prisoners, but hundreds more deserted. The allied victory at Marston Moor meant little in the southern counties. The London regiments resumed 'their old song of home, home', and on 6 July assaulted their own major general. The relatively minor defeat at Cropredy, after months of weary marching, had broken the heart of Waller's army. It never fought again.

Lostwithiel (Castle Dore), **31 August 1644**

England, Cornwall, LR200 SX1054

The most striking Royalist success of the Civil Wars was among the least typical actions of the age. Operations around Lostwithiel lasted more than three weeks, extending over 20–30 square miles (50–80 square km). The only battle was a running fight, concluded near Castle Dore on 31 August.

The disintegration of Sir William Waller's army after Cropredy freed Charles I to pursue Essex into the West. The latter had relieved several Parliamentarian garrisons, notably Plymouth, but failed to defeat Prince Maurice's local Royalist army. Parliamentarian activists urged 'Old Robin', to continue westwards. On 26 July he invaded Cornwall, apparently unaware of Charles's army behind him at Exeter. A week later Charles was at Launceston, and Essex at Bodmin, complaining that the country was rising unanimously against him. Essex withdrew south to Lostwithiel, hoping to gain contact with the fleet and resupply his army through the little fishing port of Fowey.

Prevailing westerly winds brought pouring rain, and ensured the fleet never arrived. Essex was bottled up in the valley of the River Fowey, between its lowest crossing at Lostwithiel and the estuary 6 miles (10 km) south. On 11 August the Cornish Royalists linked up with Charles I's army at Respryn Bridge, 3 miles (5 km) north of Lostwithiel. The king completed Essex's isolation by establishing a line of posts east of the River Fowey: at Cliff, Penpoll Creek, Hall Farm above Bodinnick (Clarendon's Hall View) and Polruan Castle, where Royalist heavy guns commanded the haven. The Parliamentarians lacked either the inclination or the ability to interfere.

Essex made the best of a bad job. A close defence would deny his cavalry forage, so he occupied a wide front: from Restormel Castle (SX1061) a mile (1.6 km) north of Lostwithiel on the west bank of the Fowey, across the river to Druid's Hill (SX1261), then south along a 330-foot (100-m) ridge to Beacon Hill

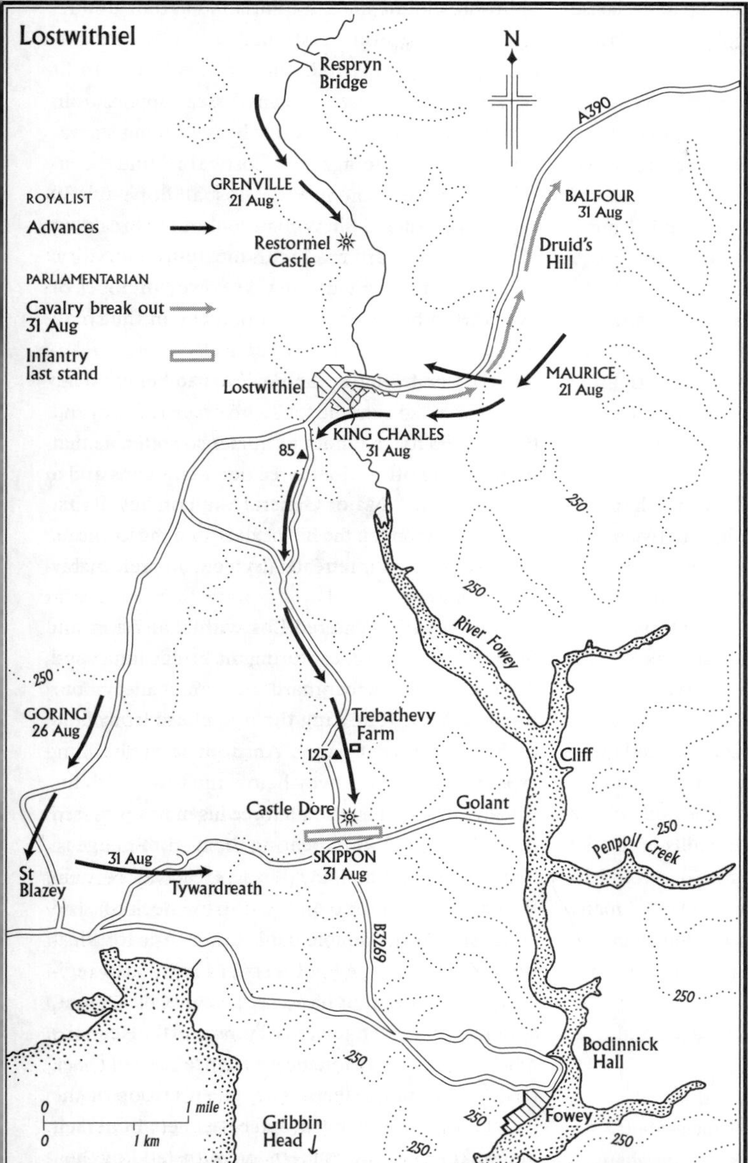

Directions

Lostwithiel is on the A390 between Liskeard and St Austell. See the old bridge north of the railway station, Restormel Castle's circular shell keep, built within the 12th-century motte and bailey, and Lanhydrock House. St Nectan's Chapel is marked on Explorer maps, down a track south of the A390 in the middle of a field. Follow the fighting of 31 August along a minor road south from Lostwithiel through Castle, turning left for Fowey down the B3269. Castle Dore is on the left, just before a side road to Golant, running behind Skippon's right flank, to the Fowey and Penpoll Creek.

(SX1259). A thousand infantry held the port of Fowey against a *coup de main*, the rest of the army holding the front line. Communications ran back along a narrow spine of high ground (413 feet/126 m) between Tywardreath and Golant, where the Parliamentarians would make their last stand. The Fowey's flooded river valley protected the road on the east, although its west side looks less secure. The whole country was very close, with steep hills and hedges, 'which are all cannon proofe and have no avenues wider than one or in some places 2 horse can approach at a time' (Richard Symonds, King's

Lifeguard). High ground extends right up to the coast, to Gribbin Head (243 feet/74 m), between Fowey and St Austell Bay.

The Parliamentarian army included seven regiments of horse (2785 strong excluding officers) and ten of foot (5291), plus 1300 volunteers from Plymouth and the West. Charles had five brigades of horse (3600), three tertias of foot (4700) and 28 guns; Maurice about 1800 horse and 2500 foot, besides 600 horse and 1800 foot from Cornwall.

The Lostwithiel campaign was a blockade, the Royalists hoping hunger would force Essex to surrender or attack at hopeless odds. Serious fighting occurred twice. On 21 August the Royalists launched a very modern synchronized advance on a 4-mile (6-km) front against Essex's perimeter, described by Richard Symonds. On the west 700 Cornish troops 'pelted the rogues from their hedges between the Lord Robarte's house [Lanhydrock] and Listithiel'. Restormel Castle was taken, together with 'divers barrels of beefe', outflanking Parliamentarian positions east of the River Fowey. Maurice took Beacon Hill at 7 a.m., looking down into Lostwithiel: 'The small cottages which were on this hill next the towne were all this forenoone a burning. Our foot and theirs pelting one at another all day: small harme done to ours.' Maurice continued at dusk: 'The body of the king's foot gott into the closes on the hills of the left and right side of the playne that goes down to Listithiel [i.e. Bridgend], and in the night planted many pieces of cannon.' Royalist musketeers dug in around St Nectan's Chapel, on Beacon Hill, its steeple providing an aiming mark for Parliamentarian gunfire.

Lostwithiel

	Winner	*Loser*
Opponents	Royalist	Parliamentarian
Commanders	Charles I Prince Maurice Lord George Goring	Robert Devereux, Earl of Essex Major General Philip Skippon Sir William Balfour
Numbers	15,000	10,000
Losses	unknown	unknown

Sporadic fighting continued, as the screw tightened. Goring took half the Royalist horse to St Blazey, west of Fowey, to deny Essex supplies from that quarter. With his cavalry horses facing starvation for want of forage, and Lostwithiel under continuous bombardment, Essex lost all hope. On 30 August he ordered Sir William Balfour to break out along the Liskeard road with most of the cavalry, while the infantry withdrew to Fowey in hopes of evacuation by sea. Balfour got away in the small hours, the Royalist cavalry being elsewhere. Meanwhile Essex fell back, the Fowey road being, in his own words, 'so extreme foul with excessive rain, and the harness for the draught horses so rotten as that in marching off we lost three demi-culverins and a brass piece ...'. Major General Skippon held a first layback position 'on the hill next beyond the towne ... to make good their retreate' (Symonds), presumably near point 85.

The Royalists entered Lostwithiel at 7 a.m. on Saturday 31 August, capturing the bridge intact and driving Skippon's rearguard off with artillery: 'our forlorne hope following them in chase from field to field in a great pace'. An hour later the king crossed the River Fowey below the town with his Lifeguard: 'With this small force his majesty chased them 2 myles [3 km], beating them from hedge to hedge.' About 11 a.m. the pursuers reached the main Parliamentarian line on the narrow neck of land either side of the double-banked Iron Age fortification of Castle Dore (374 feet/114 m). Three regiments held the right hand sector towards Golant, another two the left towards Tywardreath. Here 'the rebels made a more forcible resistance', driving back the Cornish musketeers. The queen's troop of the Lifeguard countercharged 'and beate them from their hedge, killing many of them, notwithstanding their musquets made abundance of shott' (Symonds). Shot through the left arm, their captain was going for first aid when the king knighted him on horseback with his own sword, a unique honour, unlikely to be repeated.

Fighting swayed across the gentle slopes from Trebathevy Farm (410 feet/125 m) down to Castle

Dore, as Royalist reinforcements came up: 'Shooting continued much on both sides, more on theirs, wee still gaining ground.' About 4 p.m. the few remaining Parliamentarian horse made a charge, retreating when the Lifeguard stood firm: 'Now was our foot in great bodies gott upon the high hill just in the narrowest passage of land between Trewardreth parish church and the passage over the river ... Just ay [sic] 6 of the clock the enemy made a very bold charge both of cannon, muskets, and horse, to gaine this hill [point 125], as likewise the passe by St Veepe, but were valiantly beaten off.' Once more the Lifeguard drew out, 'but the room was too little for horse and our troopers to charge'(Symonds). As darkness fell the Parliamentarians crumbled away. Their Western recruits, who had abandoned Restormel without orders, went first, leaving a great gap near Golant.

While His Majesty slept among his troops in pouring rain, Essex escaped in a fishing boat, 'it being a greater terror to me to be a slave to their contempts than a thousand Deaths ...'. The Royalist newspaper *Mercurius Aulicus* wondered 'why the rebels voted to live and die with the Earl of Essex since the Earl of Essex hath decided that he will not live and die with them'. Skippon was left to get the best terms he could. These were lenient, as the Royalists could not feed themselves, let alone prisoners of war. Six thousand Parliamentarian infantry were disarmed and paroled as far as Portsmouth, marching away 'all of a heape like sheep, though not so innocent'. Plundered by country people eager to take revenge on their tormentors, 3000–4000 reached friendly territory at Southampton. A London newspaper thought that 'by that miscarriage we are brought a whole summer's travel back', but Charles had won a purely defensive victory. He had preserved his base in Cornwall and inflicted a heavy blow on Old Robin's army, but no startling capitulations followed, as they had after Roundway Down (1643). Lostwithiel was the high point of the king's personal command and the end of the Lord General's military career.

Newbury (II), Sunday 27 October 1644

England, Berkshire, LR174 SU4568–4768

Newbury (III), 9–10 November 1644

England, Berkshire, LR174 SU4668

The 1644 campaign ended with a second indecisive battle at Newbury. With a little more luck Sir William Waller might have ended the war in an afternoon, through Charles's I's capture or death in action. The bloodless standoff at Third Newbury a fortnight later confirmed that Parliament's military system could not achieve the victory its material superiority warranted.

Parliamentarian defeats at Cropredy and Lostwithiel (see above) once more exposed London to Royalist attack. Charles I's main concern, however, was to relieve beleaguered garrisons at Banbury Castle, Donnington Castle and Basing House. His leisurely return from the West gave Parliament time to concentrate its scattered forces, including the Earl of Manchester's Eastern Association army, largely unemployed since Marston Moor. Charles reached Newbury on 23 October, resupplied Donnington Castle and detached 800 horse to succour Banbury. Hoping to do the same for Basing House, he delayed withdrawal to Oxford until the appearance of superior Parliamentarian forces at Clay Hill on 26 October forced him to offer battle northeast of Newbury, between the rivers Kennet and Lambourn.

The Earl of Essex, Parliament's overall commander-in-chief, was sick. Command devolved upon a committee headed by Waller and Manchester, and including Oliver Cromwell and Essex's subordinates, Major General Philip Skippon and Sir William Balfour. Finding Charles's position too strong to attack frontally, they decided to march most of the army around the Royalists and attack from the west. Manchester remained at Clay Hill to hold the enemy's attention. Like all double envelopments, the plan was

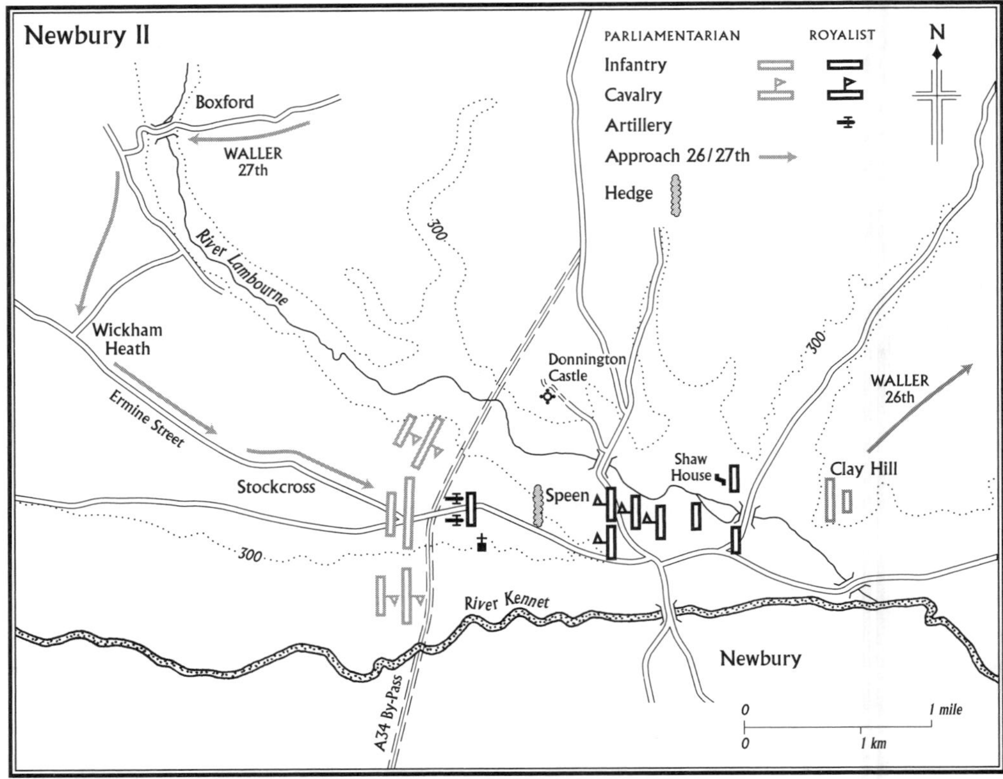

risky, even with superior numbers, but potentially decisive. Waller seems to have commanded the outflanking force, and probably devised the plan. Skippon, Balfour and Cromwell led its infantry and the right and left cavalry wings respectively. Stuart Reid calculates Parliamentarian strength as 6500–7000 horse and 9000 foot, of whom Manchester retained 1500 and 3300 respectively.

Waller marched overnight to Hermitage (SU5073), and west through Chieveley to North Heath (SU4574), where he encamped. Next morning he continued southwest through Boxford and Wickham Heath, to Stockcross on the high ground behind the Royalist army (SU4368). The distance is about 13 miles (21 km), a long day's march for the period. Waller failed to achieve strategic surprise as the Royalists had already deployed Prince Maurice's troops at Speen, to cover their rear.

The Banbury detachment had reduced the Royalists to 4500 cavalry and 5000 infantry: four brigades of Oxford horse, three of foot, and Maurice's combined-arms force. They held a strong position, prepared for all-round defence. The town and the River Kennet secured their right flank and rear, while

Directions

Shaw House is part of Trinity School, and can be seen from the gate in Church Road, off Shaw Hill (B4009). Speen is 1 mile (1.6 km) west of central Newbury along the Old Bath Road from Oxford Street, a little to the south of the A4. Skippon attacked down Ermin Street (B4000), across the A34 Newbury bypass. Speen and Newbury Fields are largely built over, although several street names recall Royalist officers: Cleveland Grove, Lisle Close and Bennett Close. Take the B4494 Oxford Road across Lockett's Bridge, turning left along Castle Lane to view the battlefield from the ruins of Donnington Castle, on the right after the car park.

Newbury (II)

	Winner	Loser
Opponents	Royalist	Parliamentarian
Commanders	Charles I	Sir William Waller
	Prince Maurice	Edward Montagu, Earl of Manchester
Numbers	9500	15,500–16,000
Losses	*c.*500	*c.*500

Newbury (III)

	Winner	Loser
Opponents	Royalist	Parliamentarian
Commanders	Charles I	Sir William Waller
	Prince Rupert	Edward Montagu, Earl of Manchester
Numbers	15,000	15,000–15,500

Shaw House, a Jacobean mansion surrounded by earth ramparts, provided a bastion in the centre. Donnington Castle commanded the Lambourn's north bank, its guns covering Prince Maurice's northern flank. Four more guns were dug in to sweep the open heath west of Speen, hedges obstructing the lower ground on either flank. The king occupied a central position with most of the cavalry and a reserve infantry brigade in two large open fields north of Newbury known as Speen and Newbury Fields, near the A4/B4494 roundabout. The other two Oxford brigades held the eastern side of the position.

Encirclement battles easily go wrong. Second Newbury broke down into three separate actions: a show of strength by Manchester at dawn; Waller's attack on Speen at 2 or 3 p.m.; and Manchester's attack on Shaw House after nightfall (about 4.30 p.m.). Heavy fighting lasted about three hours, continuing an hour by moonlight.

A thousand of Manchester's foot crossed the Lambourn at Shaw, driving the pickets back on the main guard. These counterattacked, 'and not only routed them, but compelled them to rout two other bodies ... coming to second them' (*History of the Rebellion*). Clarendon claimed very many slain or drowned, and 200 arms captured, which Richard Symonds of the King's Lifeguard reduced to 'some' and 100: 'then they lay quiet till 3 afternoone, onely our cannon and theirs played'.

Waller did achieve tactical surprise, Royalist scouts having deserted their posts along the Lambourn: 'having thus got the river they marched in good order with great bodies of foot winged with horse towards the heath'. Maurice's cavalry showed little fight, 'by reason the major part of them, upon confidence of the security of the pass, were gone to provide forage for their horses' (Clarendon). Waller naturally stressed the attackers' difficulties: 'Upon our approach their cannon played hard upon us. The place being a narrow heath gave not leave to bring up our body. The hedges hindered our horse very much. Their cannon made our ground very hot. There was no way left but to fall on with horse and foot, and that without delay, we put into execution.' With an hour's daylight left, Skippon's foot stormed the battery and village, recovering nine guns surrendered at Lostwithiel. They then stopped, as Maurice's infantry doggedly fell back, 'to the hedge next the large field between Speen and Newbury, which they made good' (Clarendon). Old Ordnance Survey maps show this a quarter of a mile (0.4 km) east of Speen, crossing the modern Bath Road opposite Battle Close.

Balfour's cavalry pushed down the north bank of the Kennet, past Speen church and into the open field beyond Speen Lane, throwing the Royalist cavalry into disorder. His Majesty was rescued by the Queen's Regiment and the Lifeguard, who drove the Parliamentarians off with heavy losses, 'besides musqueteers that had lined the hedges and playd upon us in the chase till wee cutt their throats' (Richard Symonds). Cromwell's apparent inactivity north of Speen has puzzled historians. Clarendon records a successful charge by Lord George Goring with the Earl of Cleveland's brigade of horse, driving 'Old Ironsides' back across two hedges, despite the fire of three supporting bodies of foot. The Committee of Both Kingdoms, on the other hand, heard that their horse had gallantly endured Royalist artillery fire, 'and by charging the enemy put them to a retreat taking the Earl of Cleveland'. Symonds bears this out. Most of Cleveland's officers became casualties, 'his men beaten, being overpowered with horse and foot'. The latter outcome is not surprising. Cromwell had a numerical superiority of two- or three-to-one, but night fell before he could exploit it.

Manchester did not resume operations until half an hour after sunset, 'about which time we on the other side (having gained most of the hedges towards Newberry Field) did cease and draw our men together to avoid confusion in the dark' (Cromwell). Manchester's delay has attracted much criticism, not only from his political enemies. Manchester had a clear view from Clay Hill of enemy troops retreating around Speen. His own officers begged him to attack. When he finally did so at 5 p.m. 'his men presently fell foul one upon another' in the darkness and attacked Shaw House where it was most strongly defended. They advanced across Shaw Field in two columns, singing psalms. One party was charged by horse, enfiladed from Shaw House garden, and set upon with musket butts, 'till they had not only beaten them from the hedges, but quite out of the field, leaving two drakes, some colours, and many dead bodies behind them' (Clarendon). The other received similar entertainment at the house itself.

Events elsewhere had shaken the king's confidence. As night fell, he rode away to Bath with the Lifeguard, leaving Maurice to extricate the army across Lockett's Bridge under cover of darkness. In the absence of any effective pursuit, casualties were probably even. Skippon estimated 200–300 a side, while Clarendon claimed 1000 all told, mostly Parliamentarians. The king's flight allowed the latter to claim victory, but their mutual recriminations tell another story.

The king's army was in better shape than he had thought. While the enemy were still arguing, Charles returned in strength to recover guns and wounded left in Donnington Castle. Once more the Royalists drew up in the fields between Speen and Newbury, but the Parliamentarians refused to fight. Next day Charles withdrew, honour regained, 'having passed his army over the river in the face of theirs, and offered them battle, which they durst not accept' (Clarendon). On 23 November he went into winter quarters, after a flying column had resupplied Basing House. In the short term Charles came out well from the confrontations at Newbury. Their long-term political and military repercussions, however, would make them his last victories.

Scottish Diversion

The Marquess of Montrose's year of victories beginning in September 1644 was the most consequential result of Charles I's attempts to mobilize the periphery of the three kingdoms against the centre. With a handful of Irish infantry and fluctuating Scottish support, Montrose shook the Covenanter regime to its core.

Following the Cessation of Arms of September 1643 Charles I commissioned the Earl of Antrim to raise 2000 Irish troops for service in Scotland, where a Royalist rising was planned for 1 April. It was to be led by Montrose, now a marquess, as Charles's lieutenant general. Montrose had fought for the Covenant at Megray Hill and Brig o'Dee (1639), but alienated by the Covenanter leadership, had changed sides.

Neither Montrose nor the Irish arrived in time. Marston Moor destroyed the former's chances of help from northern English Royalists, so he slipped into Scotland with just two companions to raise his native Northeast. Scottish Royalists had already risen in April without success, and refused to cooperate. Montrose's luck changed after a chance rendezvous with the delayed Irish Brigade at Blair Atholl on 29 August. The Ulster freebooter Alasdair MacColla MacDonnell had landed in Ardnamurchan in July with three regiments of 1600 experienced infantry. MacColla's military muscle and Montrose's commission generated enough support for a guerrilla campaign.

Montrose remained very weak. Despite victories

at Tippermuir and Aberdeen (September 1644), he lacked the cavalry to venture far from the mountains, and constantly risked surprises like that at Fyvie (October 1644). The Royalists survived by rapid marches of 20–25 miles (32–40 km) per day, leading their better-equipped enemies round in circles. This raiding phase of the Scottish Civil War lasted until Inverlochy (February 1645), when MacDonalds from both sides of the North Channel demolished a Campbell host. After Inverlochy the previously pro-Covenant Lord Gordon changed sides. His regular cavalry and infantry allowed Montrose to win battles in lowland terrain, at Auldearn (May 1645) and Alford (July 1645). At Kilsyth (August 1645) a combination of Gordon horse, Irish foot and Highlanders destroyed the last Covenanter army left on Scottish soil.

Montrose now occupied Glasgow, Scotland's second city, and summoned a Parliament. Covenanting leaders fled abroad, but Montrose failed to hold his fragile coalition together. MacColla and the clansmen withdrew to the Highlands. Lord Gordon had been killed at Alford, and his brother, Viscount Aboyne, quarrelled with Montrose about promotion. Montrose was reduced to a few Irish and the promises of faithless Border lords. Less than a month after Kilsyth he suffered a fatal defeat at Philiphaugh at the hands of first-line Scottish troops returning from England. Nevertheless, he continued the guerrilla struggle until the captive Charles I ordered him to suspend operations in June 1646.

Montrose's success depended on superior tactics. He was a poor strategist, prone to reckless gambles and inadequate reconnaissance. At least three of his battles, possibly five, began with the Royalists being surprised. Montrose's victories are sometimes attributed to MacColla's introduction of the so-called Highland charge from Ireland, in which Gaelic troops equipped with musket, targe (round shield) and broadsword swept all before them under cover of the smoke from a single volley. MacColla played a crucial if sometimes neglected role in Montrose's victories, but evidence for the Highland charge is elusive. Often it derives from 18th-century accounts of Jacobite hosts, applied retrospectively to earlier 'Celtic' armies. Witnesses of the Civil Wars rarely notice the specific combination of musket, sword and targe, excluding pikes. The Irish Confederate author of *An Aphorismical Discovery of Treasonable Faction* described MacColla's war band in 1642 as 'well appointed with muskets, swords, pickes, bowes and arrowes', but no targes. During the First Bishop's War, Highland equipment varied: 'left to their owne election of their weapons; some carry onely a sword and targe, others musquetts, and the greater part bow and arrows, with a quiver to hold about 6 shafts' (John Aston, *Journal*). Weapon inventories show only a quarter of clansmen possessed the 'true' Highlander's weapons.

References to swordsmen usually apply to officers and gentlemen, which is not surprising. Swords are an aristocratic speciality, requiring financial outlay and leisure to practise. Gaelic accounts naturally focus on heroic leaders like MacColla or Raghnall MacCeanain of Mull, shot through the cheeks with an arrow at Auldearn while holding off five pikemen with targe and pistol. A British officer of Clotworthy's regiment describes MacColla charging at Knocknanuss (1647) with 'a select band of targeteers and Broad Swords ... being seconded by his own men', as if some Redshanks attacked sword in hand, the rest following with other weapons. Only a proportion of MacColla's veterans were Highlanders. Many were Irish Palesmen, with no tradition of sword fighting, organized like other Catholic Confederation regiments, except that 'All to a few were musketyers.' Montrose's Irish won their early fights at Tippermuir and Aberdeen after prolonged fire fights, not by a single throwaway volley. At Inverlochy they shook their opponents with a close-range volley, the Swedish *salvee*, and came immediately to push of pike. Royalist victories at Auldearn, Alford and Kilsyth were won by cavalry charges and hard fighting.

Montrose's intervention came too late to prevent the main Scots army winning the war for Parliament at Marston Moor. When he took Glasgow, the king was already on the run after Naseby (June 1645). Before MacColla and Aboyne defected, Montrose had barely 3600 men, compared with the New Model Army's 22,000. Once sufficient regular Scots troops could be spared from England, Montrose's enterprise was doomed.

Tippermuir (Tibbermore), Sunday 1 September 1644

Scotland, Perth and Kinross, LR 52 NO0623

Tippermuir was the first of Montrose's six classic victories. It defined an image of outnumbered Royalists inflicting enormous losses on masses of hapless Covenanters. The image is more picturesque than accurate and derives from uncritical acceptance of largely Royalist narrative sources.

Montrose quickly took the initiative, after meeting Alasdair MacColla at Blair Atholl. Three Covenanter armies were chasing them already. Montrose struck at the nearest, under Lord Elcho, at Perth. Capture of this strategic gateway to the Highlands would augment Royalist prestige, ease supply and encourage recruits. Montrose marched south from Atholl, through Aberfeldy into Glen Almond, probably along the route of the A826 and A822. On 31 August the Royalists bivouacked on Tippermuir, a broad expanse of moorland around Tibbermore village. Gask Ridge, site of the Battle of Dupplin Muir (1332), rises to the south, while Methven (1306) is 3 miles (5 km) northwest.

Contemporary accounts leave doubt whether the battle occurred east or west of Tibbermore. Parish records show no service for the day of the battle, which may mean the mainly Catholic Royalists were in possession. All sources agree, however, that Elcho marched 3 miles (5 km) out of Perth. This would place the Covenanters athwart a small burn, between Tibbermore and Glendevon Farm, just beyond the A9 west of Perth.

Most reconstructions accept generous Royalist estimates of Covenanter numbers: 700–1000 cavalry and 6000 foot. However, Stuart Reid's recent analysis suggests these figures should be halved. None of the Covenanter troops came from first-line formations, and Elcho had no great character as a soldier. He adopted a conventional formation: three bodies of foot, flanked by wings of cavalry; dragoons and musketeers in front. Montrose also deployed in three bodies:

Right: 500 Atholl Highlanders under himself.
Centre: 1500 Irish and 500 Badenoch Highlanders under MacColla.
Left: 500 Lowlanders under Kilpont.

Some accounts put all the Highlanders on the right. Most claim the left wing were archers, but they probably carried pike and musket. The Atholls were less well armed: a Bishops' War survey shows most had swords or dirks, but only 100 possessed muskets, and 124 targes. Montrose had no cavalry. To avoid being outflanked he extended his line by doubling into three ranks. Most accounts apply this to the whole army, but Gordon of Ruthven explicitly states only the wings were so formed. The Royalist front would then match the Covenanters', about 600 yards (550 m), easily fitting between the stream and Lamberkine ridge (361 feet/110 m) to the south. Montrose was at less of a disadvantage than is usually claimed, especially given the quality of his Irish infantry.

Montrose offered Elcho's men a chance to submit, but Elcho detained the envoy and issued the field-word 'Jesus and no quarter'. The Covenanters moved first, sending in their forlorn hope, which the Irish repulsed with a heavy fire before launching their own attack. Details of what happened next are usually lost in gory evocations of the Highland charge. Ruthven describes how the Covenanter infantry in the centre were 'played upon with hotte alarums and continuall fyre', suggesting a prolonged fire fight by extraduction (a drill involving continuous rolling fire), rather than a single volley. Being 'ontryed men and

Tippermuir

	Winner	*Loser*
Opponents	Royalist	Covenanter
Commanders	James Graham, Marquess of Montrose Alasdair MacColla MacDonnell John Graham, Lord Kilpont	David Wemyss, Lord Elcho
Numbers	3000	*c.*3500
Losses	unknown	1300

freshwater shouldiers', the Covenanters lacked the veterans' coolness under fire: 'ther first and second ranks ... fallin to the ground erre the third ranke resolved what to doe'. Encouraged by this wavering, MacColla's men 'pressed so hard on their retreat that at last they broke and fled' (Rev. George Wishart, Montrose's chaplain and biographer).

The flanks also failed to conform to the stereotypical image of 'a yell and a rush from behind the smoke, and headlong panic' (S.R.Gardiner). The Atholls fired a *salvee* and threw stones at the cavalry opposite them, which checked the Covenanters' advance sufficiently for the Highlanders to drive them off sword in hand. Kilpont's men had recently changed sides and showed no enthusiasm for fighting their old comrades. Elcho's right wing cavalry stood about, until their centre broke when they were caught up in the general rout.

Royalist sources claim 1300 to 2000 Covenanters perished, mostly from Fife, although only 400 Fife militia were present. Montrose claimed 'men might have walked upon dead corps to the town', but the Perth burgh guard tried to mount watch after the battle as usual, implying most of them survived unscathed. Nine or ten townsmen are known to have died from exhaustion, being 'so forefainted and bursted with running'. Wishart says more Covenanters were captured than killed. Estimates of 800–1000 prisoners suggest that total casualties did not exceed the lower figure for deaths.

Otherwise the Battle of Tippermuir had limited results. Montrose occupied Perth, replenishing arms and ammunition, and clothing his Irish troops in requisitioned stuff. However, few recruits came forward, while the Highlanders deserted with their plunder, leaving Montrose unable to maintain his exposed position.

Directions

Heading west from Perth along the A85, fork left at Huntingtower along a minor road to Tibbermore. A track on the left just short of the village zigzags across the Royalist rear. Alternatively turn north off the A9 down a farm track from Lamberkine ridge (361 feet/ 110 m) to the site marked by the Ordnance Survey.

Aberdeen (Justice Mills), **Friday 13 September 1644**

Scotland, Aberdeen, LR 38 NJ9305

Montrose was too weak to hold Perth against a fresh Covenanter army approaching from the west under the Marquess of Argyle. The Royalists withdrew northeast, into Montrose's home country, threatening Aberdeen, where he won his second victory against the odds.

Montrose crossed the Dee at Banchory on 11 September, and marched down the north bank. The old Dee road or Hardgate approached Aberdeen across two streams: Howburn, now piped under Willowbank Road, and Denburn, which ran down the valley now occupied by the railway. Since levelled and built over, the contours of the battlefield are masked by 19th-century urban development.

Montrose marched up Hardgate, through Two Mile Cross, now the suburb of Garthdee, and wheeled north to face the enemy beyond Howburn. The Covenanters were deployed on the forward slope, their forlorn hope occupying houses and gardens abutting the lane up to their position. The Covenanters had six bodies of foot: three trained regiments and three weaker units of Aberdeenshire levies, totalling 2000–2400 men. The horse were perhaps only 300 strong, although most accounts accept the 500 given by George Wishart. Covenanter numbers were sufficient to occupy the half mile (0.8 km) from Denburn, by the railway station, to the millponds beyond Justice Mills Lane. Leadership and morale were doubtful. Lord Balfour, president of the Northern Committee of Estates, left his subordinates without orders, and many of them did nothing. The Aberdeen troops were unenthusiastic, 'no Covenanteris but harlitt [hauled] out sore against their willis to fight against the kingis livetenant [sic]' (John Spalding of Aberdeen).

For once Montrose was as outnumbered as his eulogists suggest: only a few irregular horse under Nathaniel Gordon augmenting MacColla's 1500 Irish. The Royalists deployed along Willowbank, extending further east of Hardgate than S.R. Gardiner's *History of the Great Civil War* suggests. Detachments of musketeers supported the thirty or so horse on either flank. The day was damp and overcast, the wind behind the Royalists, blowing their smoke into the Covenanters' faces. As at Tippermuir, Montrose summoned the enemy to surrender, but some trooper marred the city council's polite refusal by shooting the drummer entrusted with the mission. Modern accounts describe the victim as a boy, but Civil War drummers were grown men, selected for their diplomatic skills.

The Irish started by clearing the enemy's forlorn hope from the houses around Justice Mills. Balfour responded by infiltrating an infantry regiment around Montrose's left, covered by two troops of horse. Moving along a sunken path behind the crest, probably Justice Mills Lane, they gained Montrose's left rear, but unaccountably failed to roll up the Royalist line. While the detached Irish shot held them off from the buildings, Montrose brought another 100 musketeers across from the right, to eliminate the intruders.

The Covenanter horse on the other flank now attacked MacColla's exposed right. Two troops prepared the attack with their pistols, but the second line hung back, 'not for want of good will to feght, but for want of experience, not knowing that it was there time to charge' (Gordon of Ruthven, *A Short Abridgement of Britane's Distemper*). Covenanter failures on the flanks encouraged Montrose to order a general advance. Some accounts describe this as a wild charge, although the only troops available were MacColla's disciplined Irish troops, Gardiner admitted who 'could be counted on to fight in a very different manner from the wielders of the Highland broadsword'.

This became apparent as two troops of Covenanter horse charged O'Cahan's regiment on the left. The Irish, 'being so well trained men as the world could afford no other', formed company-sized clumps, let the cavalry into the gaps, and shot them to pieces. Meanwhile the remaining infantry engaged in a prolonged fire fight. Ruthven specifically says 'it was disputed hard for a long time'. John Spalding, a survivor of the battle, thought the fighting lasted two hours suggesting there was no sudden breakthrough there. The Aberdeenshire levies defending Hardgate seem to have broken first, escaping northwards to Old Aberdeen. O'Cahan's regiment then rolled the Covenanters up from right to left. The Aberdeen and Fife regiments seem to have held out until ordered to retire: 'there wes littell slauchter in the fight, bot horribill wes the slauchter ... fleeing bak to the toune' (Spalding).

Local sources place Covenanter losses at 520, plus 118 Aberdonians named by Spalding, besides 'sum' country people and soldiers from Fife. Ruthven and MacColla admitted seven and four dead respectively, obvious understatements. Civilian casualties may have been considerable, as the Royalists sacked Aberdeen in retaliation for their drummer's murder. Witnesses recalled seeing 20–30 corpses in the streets, and few recruits joined Montrose. As Argyle's army drew near, the Royalists once more retreated: MacColla took two of his regiments off to their western bridgehead to recruit; Montrose withdrew up Strathdon into Speyside, where Argyle hesitated to follow.

Aberdeen

	Winner	*Loser*
Opponents	Royalist	Covenanter
Commanders	James Graham, Marquess of Montrose Alasdair MacColla MacDonnell	Robert, Lord Balfour of Burleigh
Numbers	*c.*1600	2300–2700
Losses	unknown	638

Directions

The battlefield overlaps with Craibstane Rout (1571). Turn right off Holburn Street (A9013) into Hardgate to follow O'Cahan's line of attack. The boulder set in the wall near the junction of Hardgate and Justice Mills Lane marks the Covenanter position, which can be viewed from public open ground below Bon Accord Crescent.

Fyvie, 28 October 1644

Scotland, Aberdeenshire, LR 29 NJ7639–7739

Fyvie

	Winner	*Loser*
Opponents	Royalist	Covenanter
Commanders	James Graham, Marquess of Montrose	Archibald Campbell, Marquess of Argyle
Numbers	1100–1500	2400–2700
Losses	unknown	unknown

The autumn of 1644 found Montrose in the classic guerrilla situation of being able to embarrass the government, but unable to hold territory or attract significant popular support. He spent six weeks after Aberdeen (see above) circling northeast Scotland in search of recruits, but could not take Inverness or overcome the hostility of local people, who resented Royalist plundering. In an unfriendly country with few cavalry, Montrose was at constant danger of an unexpected encounter. Early on 28 October the Marquess of Argyle caught up with him at Fyvie on the River Ythan.

Montrose was surprised and outnumbered. He had O'Cahan's Irish regiment, originally 400 strong, plus 500 locally recruited infantry, 200 Atholl Highlanders and 50 cavalry. This totals 1150, less than the Rev. George Wishart's estimate of 1500. Argyle had 2000 foot, half of them Highlanders, and 14 troops of horse, some 400–700 cavalry. Montrose chose a good defensive position above Parkburn Glen, on the brae or 'craggy hill' east of Fyvie Castle. The castle itself was indefensible, but its pewter pots made bullets for Montrose's musketeers. The Royalist right was protected by steep slopes down to the Ythan, and their left by Parkburn. Today the latter collects in a small loch, but at that time it flowed into the river across Montrose's front. An oblong rise between castle and hill, known as Broom Hill, further complicates the approach to Montrose's position, the western slopes of which were rough and uneven, cut up with agricultural dykes and ditches, an area known as Montrose's Camp.

Argyle approached from the southwest, crossing the Ythan by the wooden bridge between Fordoun Burn and Mill of Pettie. He wheeled left through the village of Fyvie, and then half right to attack northeast, across Parkburn towards Broom Hill. Hampered by the terrain, Argyle restricted himself to probing attacks on a narrow front. Montrose's Lowland infantry promptly deserted, possibly allowing Covenanter infantry into the enclosures on Broom Hill. Royalist sources speak of fierce fighting, but only admit 15 or 16 dead. Montrose counterattacked and drove the Covenanters out again. Argyle pushed five troops of horse over Parkburn, the Royalists once more abandoning the enclosures. Montrose may have hoped to ambush the cavalry in dead ground beyond Broom Hill, but the Atholl men fired too soon and gave the game away. Four troops of Covenanters immediately turned tail, covered by a sacrificial charge by the fifth. Another infantry assault was 'bravely encountered' by Royalist musketeers behind their fences, after which Argyle gave up. The ground was unsuitable for cavalry, and his infantry had made no impression on the Royalist position. Argyle's objective was to contain Montrose and prevent him recruiting, both of which he could do without risking an all-out assault.

The two sides hung about for two days, blaming each other for the stalemate. Eventually lack of forage forced the Covenanters to withdraw. Ruthven thought 'Fyvie deserved not the name of a battell', and it has never ranked with Montrose's six victories. It is remembered in a folk song, the 'Bonnie Lass o' Fyvie', commemorating a doomed, and probably imaginary, captain of Irish dragoons who fell for the chambermaid of Fyvie-o. Montrose slipped away to Strathbogie, and then to his mountain stronghold at Blair Atholl.

Directions

Fyvie is halfway between Aberdeen and Banff on the A947. See Fyvie Castle, which belongs to the National Trust for Scotland. The fighting was just to the east, probably between Old Home Farm and Parkburn.

Inverlochy, Sunday 2 February 1645

Scotland, Highland, LR 41 NN1275

The unlikely Royalist victory at Inverlochy assured Montrose's place in Scotland's national mythology. His winter approach march through the mountains and heroic victory over two-to-one odds made an epic tale that transcends the struggle of king and Covenant. It has lost nothing in the retelling, whether by historians or the Bard of Keppoch, Ian Lom, who guided Montrose through the glens, and watched the fight from the brae above Inverlochy Castle. The facts have never recovered.

Despite Tippermuir and Aberdeen, the Covenanters had contained Montrose's rebellion by November 1644. Montrose and his men faced starvation in Atholl until MacColla's return with 1000 western Highlanders. Hatred of the Campbells and lack of food inspired a strategic shift westwards. In December 1644 MacColla's men devastated the Campbell heartland, sacking Inverary on Loch Fyne, the regional capital of the Marquess of Argyle, 'MacCailein Mor', the head chief of Clan Campbell. At the end of January 1645 Montrose was at Kilcumin, now Fort Augustus on Loch Ness, between the Covenanter garrison of Inverness and Argyle's pursuing army at Inverlochy, on Loch Linnhe. The Royalist leaders resolved on a bold stroke against Argyle, persecutor of Catholics and MacDonalds either side of the Irish Sea.

The Royalists took an indirect route, to avoid being trapped in the Great Glen. They marched up Glen Tarff and into Glen Roy, either over the Corrieyairack Pass, or else 'the nearest way', as MacColla reported, via the Calder Burn gorge and Spey headwaters. From Keppoch in Glen Spean they headed west, through Leanachan Forest, perhaps along the route of General Wade's military road. Tom na Brataich, 'banner knoll', may recall where Montrose's regiments planted their colours (NN1879). On the night of 1–2 February Montrose's men camped below the northwest shoulder of Ben Nevis, after having marched 30 miles (48 km) in 36 hours by snow-blocked paths known only to poets and cowherds.

Reconstructions of Inverlochy often show Montrose attacking from east to west, directly off the mountain slopes. Low ground to the northeast, now a golf course, provides an approach better suited to the limitations of early modern armies and the Royalist line of march. The subsequent slaughter of Covenanter fugitives at the River Nevis and below Cow Hill at Fort William confirms the southwards thrust of Montrose's attack. Argyle's army met it with their left flank on Inverlochy Castle beside the River Lochy, south of Victoria Bridge, their line extending 500–600 yards (450–550 m) southeast across the railway towards the aluminium works.

Desertion had reduced the Royalists to a core of Irish regulars and a few Highlanders. MacColla took the right with 400 Irish; Montrose the centre with 500 Highlanders, supported by 300 Irish and a few cavalry; the remaining 300 Irish formed the left. The larger Covenanter force mirrored Montrose's formation. Sixteen companies from different regiments from the Earl of Leven's army in England formed the wings, 550 each. Five hundred Highlanders with guns, bows and axes stood in front of the Covenanter centre, possibly Argyle's own regiment recalled from Ireland. Their colonel, Campbell of Auchinbreck, took overall command, as MacCailein Mor had retired to his galley following a riding accident. Behind the regulars stood a mass of Campbell clansmen: 'lest if they were allowed to charge, they might disorder the ranks of their unwarlike and untrained comrades' (S.R. Gardiner), an odd way to describe the veterans

Inverlochy

	Winner	*Loser*
Opponents	Royalist	Covenanter
Commanders	James Graham, Marquess of Montrose Alasdair MacColla MacDonnell	Sir Duncan Campbell of Auchinbreck (k)
Numbers	1500	*c.*3000
Losses	*c.*200	1500

of Marston Moor and three years service in Ulster.

Montrose wrote that the armies met 'a little after the sun was up ... the prime of the Campbells giving the first onset, as men that deserved to fight in a better cause. Our men having a nobler cause came immediately to push of pike and dint of sword, after this first firing'. Montrose's victory is commonly ascribed to the Highland charge, but such explanations beg the question how a few hungry and exhausted MacDonalds could so defeat three or four times their number of well-fed and rested Campbells, drawn from a similar military and geographical background.

Montrose held his clansmen back, leading on the flanks with the Irish. Unlike previous battles, they held fire to the last moment, firing a *salvee* in the Lowlanders' beards. Gordon of Ruthven wrote that the Irish then dropped their firelocks, and fell on with broadsword and targe, but Montrose's eyewitness description was more conventional. Either way, the Lowlanders broke and fled. Montrose now led the MacDonalds forward against the Campbell centre. Taken in either flank by Irish troops wheeling inwards, Argyle's regiment fired one volley and fled, carrying away the clansmen. The collapse is not particularly surprising. Heroic societies, like that of the Highlands, are adapted for rapine, not organized warfare. Only the gentlemen who fought in the front rank with sword and targe had any military value. Little reliance could be placed upon their ill-armed retainers in the rear ranks.

Royalist estimates of 1500–2000 Covenanter dead are as implausible as the claims of prolonged pursuit after a 30-mile approach march on empty stomachs. Everyone agrees that the Lowlanders received quarter, so the unamended figures would imply a Campbell loss rate rising above 100 per cent – obvious nonsense. Most of the Campbell clansmen must have escaped, being fresh, while their leaders were cut down. Even Alasdair MacColla gave up the chase after 7 miles (11 km), at Lundavra in the mountains between Loch Linnhe and Loch Leven, where he built a cairn. Every passing Campbell sympathizer is said to remove the top stone, and every MacDonald puts one back. Few Royalist losses were admitted: three, four or seven dead, and 200 wounded.

Inverlochy was a clan battle, with international consequences, forcing the Scots army in England to detach troops for home defence, and limit its operations. Overestimating Highland enthusiasm, Montrose wrote to Charles I offering to make 'rebels in England, as well as in Scotland, feel the just rewards of Rebellion'. MacCailein Mor's prestige had suffered a deadly blow, while his enemies were correspondingly elevated.

Directions

The battlefield is 1 mile (1.6 km) northeast of Fort William, running across the A82 from the castle ruins on the left. Modern Inverlochy Castle, 1 mile (1.6 km) further on, is a hotel.

Auldearn, 9 May 1645

Scotland, Highland, LR 27 NH9155

Auldearn was Montrose's first conventional victory, with a balanced force of horse and foot. Lord Gordon had changed sides, bringing over his regular regiments of horse and foot. These enabled Montrose to march into the Lowlands, but his Highlanders deserted with their plunder, forcing the weakened Royalists to retreat into the hills before General Baillie. Hoping to draw Montrose out, Baillie sent Sir John Urry or Hurry to threaten Gordon territory in the northeast. Urry was a serial turncoat who would die a Royalist after Carbisdale (1650), but he was a competent professional. He led Montrose through Elgin and Forres towards Nairn, a pro-Covenanter area where the Royalists would receive little warning of hostile movements. While Montrose made camp at Auldearn on the evening of 8 May, Urry picked up reinforcements from Inverness, and doubled back. Wet weather favoured his plan to surprise Montrose's men in their billets, until his musketeers gave the alarm by clearing their damp muskets.

Montrose admitted having 250 horse and 1400

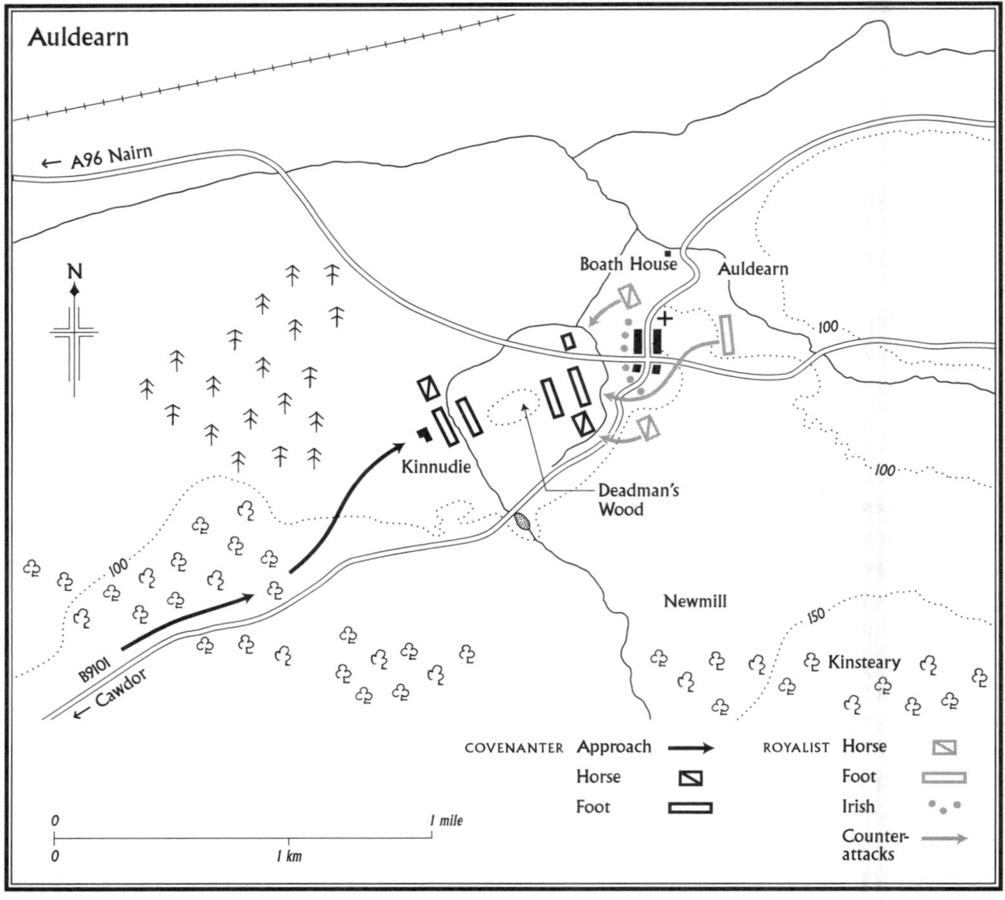

foot: 700–800 Irish (including some Highlanders) and 600–800 Gordons of the Strathbogie regiment. Sometimes described as Gaelic, the force was conventionally equipped, except for the officers' broadswords. For the first time Montrose had enough cavalry to play an independent battlefield role. Royalist sources put the Covenanters at 4000–5000, but modern calculations give 1600–2000 regular foot, 1000–1600 Seaforth and Sutherland militia, and 300–400 horse. Montrose claimed Urry had four of the best-trained regiments in the three kingdoms, but two were unblooded and another only formed in March 1645.

At the time of the battle, Auldearn village ran north–south from St Colm's church along Boath Road, rather than east–west as it does today. The settlement lay on a western slope, stone-walled enclosures running down to a marshy bottom created by Auldearn burn. Another burn encircles a small oval hill to the west, once covered with undergrowth:

Directions

Take the A96 from Nairn to Auldearn, leaving the main road just before the village, passing Deadman's wood on the right after crossing the burn. View the battlefield from Boath Dovecot (National Trust for Scotland), and see memorials to two of Montrose's officers in the churchyard. The Ordnance Survey marks the battle further south, where Gardiner believed Montrose's counterattack began.

Deadman's Wood or Garlic Hill, site of a mass grave traditionally dating from the battle.

There are three versions of events:

(1) The standard interpretation developed by S.R. Gardiner, who visited the site in the 1880s and viewed Auldearn as an elaborate ambush. MacColla provided the bait with 500 infantry spread out from Castle Hill, west of the church, in a dogleg through the village. Montrose waited under cover at Newmill, southeast of the B9101, ready to attack Urry's right flank, once he was preoccupied with MacColla in the village. All the cavalry were on this flank, the only area clear of bogs and fences. Urry approached from Nairn from the northwest, along the modern main road, although this was not built until the 19th century.

(2) David Stevenson's revisionist account, in which MacColla launched a spoiling attack to buy Montrose time to form up east of Auldearn. The Royalists then counterattacked through the village, disregarding the difficulties of inserting fresh troops into an existing fire fight over ground cluttered with buildings. Cavalry operated both sides of the village. In this version Urry approached from the southwest, along the 17th-century road from Cawdor (now the B9101), through the site of Gardiner's putative ambush.

(3) Stuart Reid's variant of the above. MacColla did not await Urry's cross-country approach through Kinnudie, but advanced, 'towards a marishe and som bushes … strong ground and fencible against horsemen' (*Chronicles of the Frasers*), presumably Deadman's Wood. Urry formed up in several echelons, two regular regiments in both the first two, cavalry on the flanks, northern militia in the rear. MacColla was pushed back behind Auldearn's natural defences at pike point, losing four standard-bearers and breaking his sword. Royalist cavalry attacks on either flank shook the Covenanters, who regrouped on the hill. Their right-wing horse mistakenly wheeled left rather than right, exposing their backs to their attackers, who drove them into Lawes's Foot, one of their own infantry regiments, capturing several colours. On the other flank Lord Gordon launched the first Scottish example of a Swedish-style cavalry charge, without preliminary pistol fire. The Gordon troopers trampled along the battle line, regrouping south of the fighting around Kinsteary (NH9254) where numerous casualties were found later.

Montrose's report to the king seems to describe this late stage of the battle, neglecting MacColla's holding action:

> They [the Covenanters] being confident both of their men and their number fell hotly on, but being set backe, seimed to coole of their fury … which perceiving, I divided myself into two wings (which was all the ground would suffer) and marched upon them most unexpectedly, and after some hot salvyes of musket and a litell dealing with sword and pike, they took the chase.

Urry's reserves were still too far off to intervene when Montrose led the Strathbogie regiment round the south end of Auldearn, against the disordered Covenanters on the hill. Ill-prepared to resist an attack by fresh troops, they were 'for the most part cut af, fighting to the death most valiauntlie' (John Spalding). The northern militia left them to it, and fled.

Montrose shamelessly overstated Covenanter losses at 3000 dead, but reality was bad enough. Lawes's regiment buried 11 officers and 200 men, half their strength. Extrapolated to other regiments, the figure supports Covenanter estimates that Urry lost 1000–1200 infantry. On the Royalist side Gordon of Ruthven admitted 'twenty-four gentlemen hurt … and sum few Irishes killit'; 200 might be more accurate. A second Covenanter army had been eliminated, leaving only William Baillie in the field.

Auldearn

	Winner	*Loser*
Opponents	Royalist	Covenanter
Commanders	James Graham, Marquess of Montrose George, Lord Gordon Alasdair MacColla MacDonnell	Sir John Urry
Numbers	1650–1850	3000–4000
Losses	222	1200

Alford, 2 July 1645

Scotland, Aberdeenshire, LR 37 NJ5616–5716

A period of manoeuvring followed Auldearn. Montrose's new opponent William Baillie avoided battle, except on unacceptable terms. After a standoff at Keith on 24 June, the Royalists marched south. Baillie followed, catching up with Montrose on the northern skirts of the Correen Hills, near the site of the Battle of Tillyangus (1571). Montrose withdrew along the Suie Road, crossed the Don at Boat of Forbes, now Bridge of Alford, and occupied Gallowhill (623 feet/ 190 m), a mile (1.6 km) to the south. Baillie sidestepped east before he followed, spending the night at Leslie. The diversion is significant in view of the disputed location of the subsequent battle.

Most modern accounts assume that Baillie, a notably cautious commander, followed Montrose across the ford at Boat of Forbes and formed up under the noses of the Royalists, in a swamp, with his back to the river. Modern Alford is said to date from the coming of the railway (since dismantled), contemporary references to the place being supposed to mean Muir of Alford, 2 miles (3 km) further west. There are good reasons, however, for locating the crossing downstream at Montgarrie, as S.R. Gardiner did. It is further from Gallowhill, to some extent turning the Royalist position. Montrose was near Boat of Forbes on the morning of 2 July when he heard Baillie was a mile distant, and hurriedly returned to Gallowhill 'to order his battle'. This would have been unnecessary if the Covenanters were approaching directly from the north, as the Royalists were already facing that way. Ballad references to Mill Hill, just north of Montgarrie, confirm that Baillie crossed the hills further east, between Knock Saul (1352 feet/412 m) and Satter Hill (1181 feet/360 m). As for the railway, Gardiner went over the battlefield in the 1880s, and heard nothing of Alford's recent appearance.

Montrose had at least equal numbers, as well as better ground. Royalist forces totalled 200–250 horse and 2000 foot: 1000 Scots in the centre, supported by two wings, each of 300 Irish and 100 cavalry. Assuming Baillie followed Gardiner's route, Montrose stood on the northern slope of Gallowhill facing northeast, his line extending along the 490-foot (150-m) contour. Baillie put the Covenanters 'betwixt twelve and thirteen hundred foot and about 260 horsemen', estimating Montrose 'a little above our strength in horsemen and twyse als [sic] strong in foot'. Gardiner dismissed this as the exaggeration of a beaten man, but it is credible, the Covenanters doubling ranks to match Montrose's frontage six in file. Modern accounts decry the Covenanter infantry, but they were veterans of Boldon Hill and Marston Moor. An extra troop of Aberdeen horse brought Baillie up to 300 cavalry, which Wishart doubles unnecessarily. Baillie's force would fit comfortably between Alford and the river, aligned on the main A944 road, facing Gallowhill, east of the A980 junction where the Ordnance Survey marks the battle. Today the ground is cut up by roads and hedges, but at the time of the battle the hill was probably unenclosed common land, its gentle slopes providing an unobstructed run downhill for the Royalist cavalry.

Lord Gordon started the ball, leading his horse down the hill against Baillie's left wing. Allegedly he was provoked by the sight of stolen Gordon cattle in enemy lines, although how he recognized them a mile off is not explained. More likely he just responded to Balcarres probing the Royalist right, as Wishart says. The action was, 'courageously foughten on both sides for a long tyme' (Gordon of Ruthven). Gordon drove Balcarres's first troop back onto

Alford

	Winner	Loser
Opponents	Royalist	Covenanter
Commanders	James Graham, Marquess of Montrose George, Lord Gordon (k)	General William Baillie Alexander Lindsay, Earl Balcarres
Numbers	2200–2250	1500–1600
Losses	unknown	700–1600

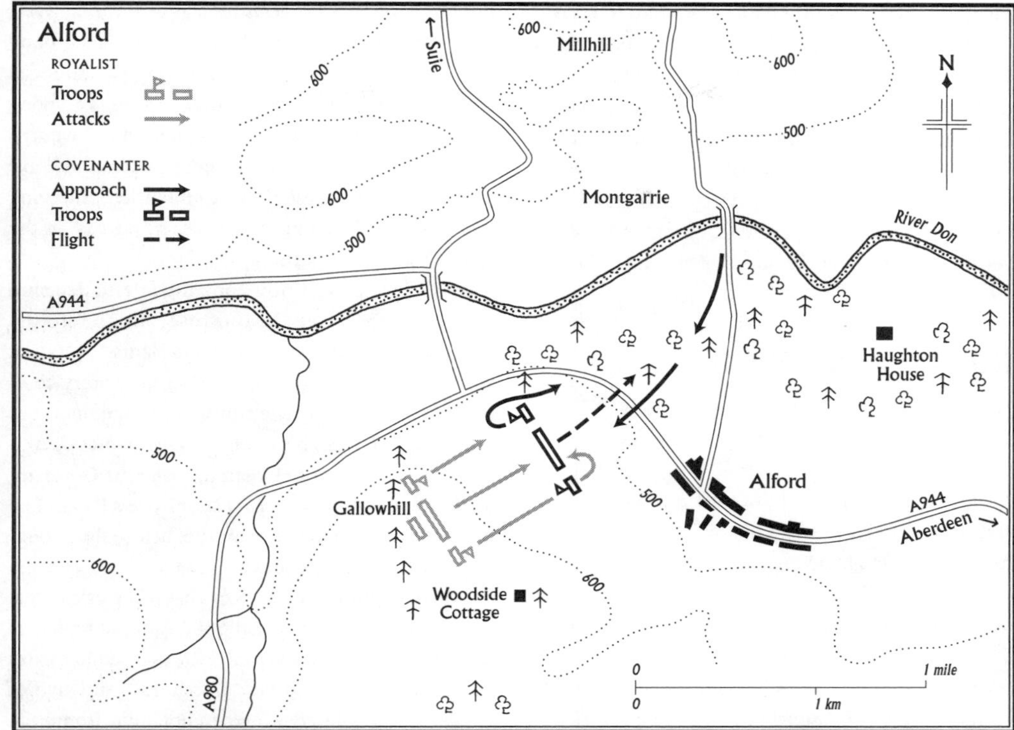

the second, which checked the Royalist advance. The third troop was directed against Gordon's flank, a winning move, but they 'went straight up in their comrades reare, and there stood until they were all broken' (Baillie). With Balcarres's horsemen committed, the Irish musketeers on Montrose's right ran in among them with their dirks, hamstringing the horses and creating instant panic. When Balcarres gave way, so did the troopers on Baillie's other flank; they were survivors of Auldearn, and readily intimidated.

His flanks secure, Montrose repeated the tactics of Aberdeen and Inverlochy, sending in his main body to destroy the enemy infantry. Some narratives feature the attack as a Highland charge, but half Montrose's centre consisted of the Strathbogie regiment, conventional pike and shot. What did for Baillie's veterans was a combined-arms attack: 'Our foot stood with myself and behaved themselves as became them, until the enemie's horse charged in our rear, and in front we were overcharged with their foot …' (Baillie). The general got away, but the troops were cut to pieces in Feight Faulds, just north of Alford. Two of the regiments could only field 100 men each at Kilsyth in August. Ruthven claimed 1600 dead, although they were too scattered to be counted. Modern historians suggest 700–1000. At least one trooper was mired in the bogs along the riverside, his body found by a peat cutter in the 18th century.

Wishart claimed the Royalists lost no rank and

Directions

Alford is 22 miles(35 km) northwest of Aberdeen on the A944. View the battlefield(s) from Montrose's vantage point on the minor road south of Bridge of Alford, and visit Haughton House Country Park where Baillie's infantry made their last stand. The Ordnance Survey showed Gardiner's site until 1974, when they relocated the crossed swords to the 'corrected' location near Ardgathen crossroads.

file at all, although other sources admit 'a considerable losse upon Montrose his side also'. Lord Gordon's troop lost 20 out of 80, including their commander shot in the back during a last charge midway between Gallowhill and Alford. A rough boulder marked the spot, until it disappeared under the village rubbish dump. News of Naseby coincided with Gordon's funeral, tempering Covenanter despair at yet another defeat at the hands of the ungodly.

Kilsyth, 15 August 1645

Scotland, North Lanarkshire, LR 64 NS7478–9

Montrose's last victory bore little resemblance to a conventional 17th-century battle. Kilsyth was a confused melee, fought before either side was ready, with units thrown piecemeal into the fighting. Historians of Kilsyth have further obscured the picture, ignoring the best source, Baillie's explanation of his defeat, in favour of highly coloured Royalist accounts, celebrating patrons and kinsmen.

Montrose was slow to exploit Alford. He plundered the Mearns and menaced Perth, then moved southwest towards Glasgow. Baillie retained executive command of the last Covenanter army, subject to acrimonious direction from a Scottish parliamentary committee. The Covenanters shadowed Montrose through Stirling and Denny Bridge, into the extended strath below the Kilsyth Hills. The Royalists camped east of Kilsyth, in a large meadow now under Townhead Reservoir, otherwise known as Banton Loch. Surrounded by hills, Montrose's position would be indefensible today, but the rough slopes made an insuperable obstacle for a contemporary army, with short-ranged weapons unable to reach his position. Montrose's deployment is obscure, but presumably he faced southeast, along the now submerged burn, watching the likely Covenanter approach along the main A803 road.

Baillie had camped 2 miles (3 km) off at Banknock. Next day he moved cross-country 'through the corns and over the braes, until the unpassible ground did hold us up'. This suggests he was at Banton, overlooking Montrose's left flank. The intervening ground was extremely rough, broken by large hummocks and falling away more steeply into the now flooded meadow. Historians disagree whether the Covenanter army was in view of the enemy, but Baillie says he rode over the crest after he embattled, implying the troops deployed on the reverse slope, east of the Kelvinhead–Banton road.

The Covenanters now took the fateful decision to move right, around Montrose's flank into the glen running southwest from High Banton. Modern accounts are scathing about the parliamentary committee overruling Baillie's military judgement, but the difficult terrain between the two armies diminished the risks of a flank march, as did the Covenanters' oblique position across Montrose's flank. The Royalists had to change front too, before they could react to Baillie's manoeuvre.

Most accounts accept Royalist force estimates: 800 Covenanter horse and 6000 foot, against 300 Royalist horse and 4,400 foot. However, Baillie states he had only two regiments of horse, and five of regular infantry, besides three militia units from Fife: 300 horse and 3000–3500 foot altogether. Three regular units formed the front line with a combined battalion of musketeers. Two more regular units flanked the militia in support. Balcarres's cavalry concentrated on the right flank. Modern accounts insist Baillie wanted to wait for reinforcements, but

Kilsyth

	Winner	*Loser*
Opponents	Royalist	Covenanter
Commanders	James Graham, Marquess of Montrose Alasdair MacColla MacDonnell James Gordon, Viscount Aboyne	General William Baillie Alexander Lindsay, Earl Balcarres
Numbers	3560	3300–3800
Losses	unknown	unknown

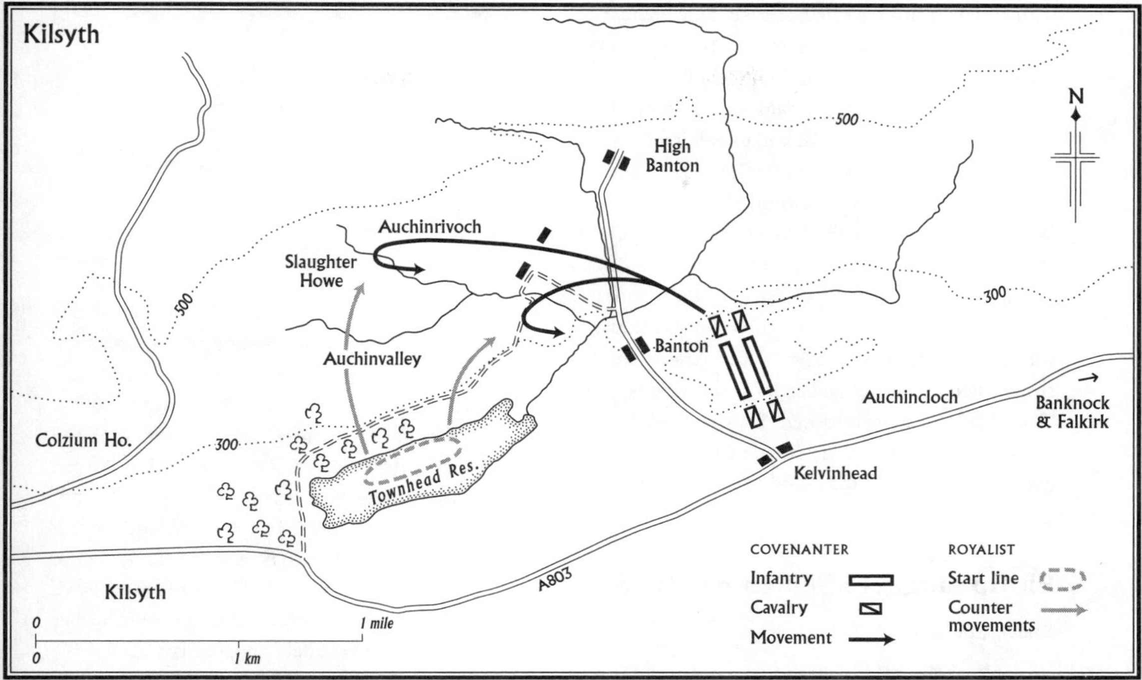

his apologia never mentions them. Montrose had about 600 Irish infantry, 800 Gordons and some 1600 Highlanders. His superiority in mounted troops, three units 360, 120 and 80 strong, proved decisive in the mobile battle that the Covenanters had chosen to fight.

Baillie preserved his order of battle during the flank march by advancing in two parallel columns, on a six-man frontage. Each file had only to face left to present a continuous front to the enemy, regiments maintaining their original position in the line. Cavalry and musketeers led the way. Modern accounts, starting with Gardiner, describe the consequences as the classic result of a flank march in face of the enemy: Highlanders smashing through the centre of the thin Covenanter line, while Gordon horse wrecked the column's head.

The battle's duration and the culminating point of Balcarres's advance at Slaughter Howe, well beyond Auchinrivoch and behind Royalist lines, suggest something more complex. Contrary to orders, Baillie's leading musketeers became entangled with some of Montrose's Highlanders moving up the glen. This may have happened between Banton and the initial Royalist position in the reservoir, or more likely in Auchinvalley. Baillie further lost his grip as his strongest regiment, recently recalled from Ireland and having no time for Gaels, advanced directly west among the Auchinvalley enclosures. The Covenanters were attacking the Highlanders, not vice versa, pinning them down behind the stone walls with a hail of musketry. Meanwhile Balcarres's horse, after some initial success, had succumbed to a series of Royalist cavalry charges. Thus encouraged, the Highlanders pressed home their attack on Baillie's front line, 'In the end the rebels leapt over the dyke, and

Directions

Turn left off the A803 east of Kilsyth town to explore several minor roads crossing the battlefield. The decisive action probably took place at Auchinvalley, north of the reservoir. Visit Colzium House Estate to see the memorial, and view the battlefield from the grounds.

with downe heads fell on and broke these regiments'. Baillie rode back for the reserve, 'bot before we could come at them, they were in flight' (Baillie).

Once broken, the Covenanters would not rally. The cavalry fled 11 miles (18 km) to Falkirk. Gardiner claimed scarcely 100 out of 6000 Covenanter infantry escaped, but numerous dismounted officers reappear later, as do several of the broken regiments. Gardiner's figure is no more credible than claims that small bones found on Auchincloch Farm in 1829 belonged to dead drummer boys rather than sheep. Montrose was finally master of Scotland, and Argyle and his cronies fled abroad. Royalist partisans were ecstatic: 'The Golden Age is returned, his Majesty's Crown re-established, the many headed monster nearly quelled' (William Drummond of Hawthornden).

Philiphaugh, 13 September 1645

Scotland, Borders, LR 73 NT4528

Philiphaugh		
	Winner	*Loser*
Opponents	Covenanter	Royalist
Commanders	David Leslie	James Graham, Marquess of Montrose
Numbers	3400 commited	1700
Losses	*c.*100	200–350

Montrose's defeat at Philiphaugh exposed the narrow basis of his support. Two hours fighting destroyed Montrose's military credibility, ending Charles I's hopes of Scottish intervention in his favour.

The Royalist coalition that won Kilsyth soon disintegrated. MacColla and Aboyne withdrew to pursue personal interests in the Highlands. Montrose was left with 500 Irish infantry, and dubious promises from shifty Lowland magnates. A recruiting drive on the Borders produced only 1200 horsemen, a rabble of gentlemen's younger sons, for 'not a man of the middle classes would serve under him'.

The Scots army in England was already moving to crush the Royalist threat in their rear. David Leslie, a leading figure at Marston Moor, was pursuing Charles I northwards after Naseby. Hearing of Kilsyth he resolved to return home, crossing the Border at Berwick on 6 September. Montrose was unwilling to advance into England with Leslie's veterans on his flank. He withdrew through Jedburgh to Selkirk on Ettrick Water, camping on the haugh, flat ground on the riverbank opposite the town. Acting on intelligence, Leslie followed Montrose down Gala Water into the Tweed valley at Sunderland, a tiny settlement 2 miles (3 km) north of the unsuspecting Royalists.

Some accounts, not unreasonably, place the battle at Philiphaugh itself, near the confluence of the Yarrow and Ettrick. A wood that the Irish occupied is often identified with nearby Harehead Wood, which was not yet planted. The Royalist battle line, if not their camp site, needs to be nearer Selkirk Bridge. Montrose was in town when the Covenanters attacked, and would have been cut off if his troops were further south. There are two suitable positions:

(1) Linglie Burn 3/4 of a mile (1.2 km) north of Selkirk on the A707 (NT4629); and more likely:

(2) Long Philip Burn nearer the bridge, where a prominent re-entrant and the enclosures of Philiphaugh Farm would cover the Royalist left flank.

Leslie's approach is equally debatable. Covenanter accounts give no place-names. Gordon of Ruthven just says he was 'invironed with woodes in a deep valley'. The Philiphaugh ballad can be understood to say Leslie split his forces, sending half through the trackless mosses between Peat Law (1398 feet/426 m) and Linglie Hill (1122 feet/342 m) to take Montrose in the rear: 'Let ae half keep the waterside, / The rest gae round the hill.' Leslie's report says nothing of all this. Any cut-off party was more likely detached nearer the objective, perhaps at Linglie Burn to secure Selkirk, while Leslie moved directly along the left bank.

Leslie's numbers are known, because his troops received a bounty. He had five experienced cavalry regiments from England (2000 men) and a new Scots

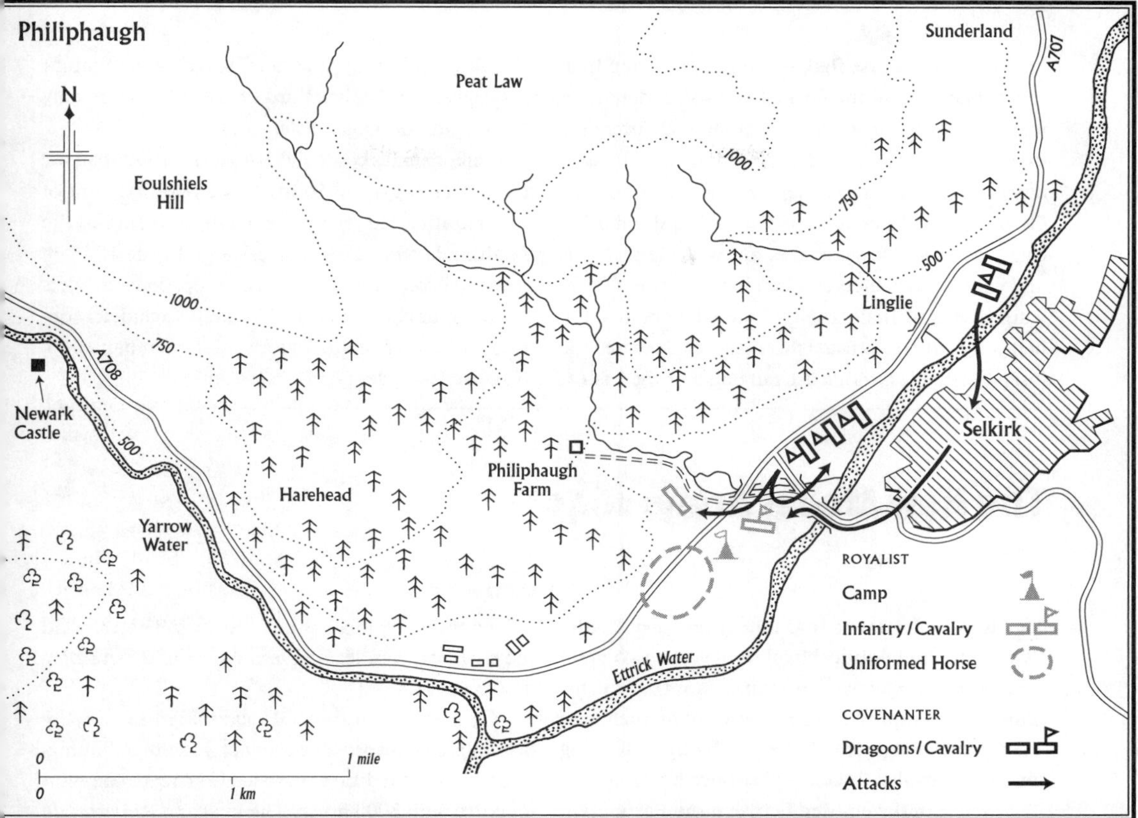

regiment, making 3000 horse, besides 400 dragoons and 700 foot. The latter do not appear in the fighting, and may have been left behind. Montrose's notional strength has no significance. Leslie's appearance at 10 a.m. threw the Royalist camp into uproar, the Irish hastily sending away their baggage, the newly raised horse milling about the haugh in small bodies which never fired a shot. Perhaps 200 Irish formed up on the Royalist left, and 100–200 cavalry in the open ground by the river. As usual the Irish made the best of their position, casting up ditches and lining the hedges with musketeers.

The main Covenanter column drove in Montrose's forlorn hope, and charged the burn in waves. The narrow valley would make it difficult to deploy more than one regiment at a time. Two attacks were driven off, allowing some of Montrose's horse to break out northwards. This left Montrose with 40–50 cavalry in the gap between his infantry and the river. The third attack was decisive. Leslie ignored the enemy cavalry, and wheeled into the Irish right flank, 'charging very desperately upon the head of his own regiment, [he] broke the body of the enemy's Foot, after which they all went in confusion and disorder' (Leslie). Meanwhile, the outflanking column appeared in the Royalist rear, after clearing Selkirk, another point in favour of a battle site near the bridge, as there are no suitable crossing places further upstream.

Directions

Cross the A708 opposite Selkirk into the minor road leading to Philiphaugh Farm to see the Royalist position behind Philiphope Burn. Modern housing obscures Leslie's approach down the A707, but the decisive area south of the burn and marked by the Ordnance Survey is relatively undeveloped. Head west along the A708 to Newark Castle, in private hands, on the left beyond the Yarrow.

The Border horse fled, while 100 surviving Irish regrouped around the farm. They surrendered, on terms as they thought, but were all shot. Quarter only extended to the officers, two of whom were hanged anyway. More Irish prisoners were killed at Newark Castle, in 'the dowie dens of Yarrow', and some 300 camp followers: 'boyes, cookes, and a rabble of rascals and women with their children in their arms' (Ruthven). Myths of Irish cruelty, fostered by both sides, had come home. As usual the victors exaggerated the losers' casualties, Montrose rallying half the Irish at Peebles. Including prisoners, Royalist combatant losses were probably a third of the 1000 claimed by Covenanter propagandists.

Philiphaugh's consequences were greater than the casualties suggest. Montrose had lost his aura of invincibility. He resumed guerrilla warfare in the Highlands, with little success. On 2 June 1646 he received orders from the king, now a prisoner in Scots hands, to disband. A general amnesty excluded Montrose, who escaped in a Norwegian merchant ship, disguised as a clergyman's servant.

The New Model Army: 1645

The Royalist defeats of 1645 cruelly revealed Charles I's strategic and political bankruptcy. His two main armies were destroyed within a month, and his schemes to employ foreign Catholic mercenaries against his own people betrayed. By the following spring no Royalist force could survive in the field.

Seven months elapsed between the Parliamentarian attempt to encircle the king at Second Newbury (see above), and the next major encounter. Despite general war-weariness, the opposing leaderships were more entrenched than ever. Parliament's proposed Treaty of Uxbridge effectively demanded abdication. Charles spun out negotiations to keep his less enthusiastic supporters onside, and gain time for foreign intervention.

Meanwhile Parliament addressed the command problems revealed at Second Newbury. On 19 December the Commons passed a Self-Denying Ordinance excluding politicians from military leadership, the first step towards forming a national New Model Army to replace the regional forces that had failed to get the better of the king. Sir Thomas Fairfax, a non-political soldier, took command of an amalgam of Parliament's three southern armies, with a paper establishment of 22,000 men: 11 regiments of 600 horse, 1 of dragoons (1000) and 12 of foot (1200 each). Besides the New Model Army, Parliament disposed of four more regional or allied armies. The king had no such reserves, leaving him vulnerable to a single knockout blow.

Charles began the 1645 campaign in May by assembling a respectable army of 11,600, but immediately detached Lord George Goring to the west country with 3000 horse. The king and Rupert rode north to join Montrose, who had just won the battle of Auldearn (see above). Fears for his ill-supplied headquarters at Oxford, however, drew Charles back to the Midlands.

Parliamentarian strategy was no better. The Committee of Both Kingdoms fragmented its unitary army, and tied up Fairfax in front of Oxford's defences. Fairfax's chaplain, Joshua Sprigge, grumbled that the campaign had been 'blasted in the bud'. Rupert's brutal sack of Leicester (30 May) changed the Committee's priorities, freeing Fairfax to make the enemy army his main objective. A fortnight later he overtook Charles at Naseby (14 June), and won the war in under two hours. Naseby was a truly decisive battle. It destroyed the last Royalist army capable of operations on more than a regional scale, and sounded the death knell of absolute government in Britain.

The only substantial Royalist force left was Goring's western army. Fairfax immediately moved to crush it at Langport (10 July), while the king diverted himself amid the splendours of Raglan Castle. The king's position continued to deteriorate, as Rupert surrendered Bristol on 10 September. Charles failed to raise a fresh army in South Wales, leaving him dependent on far-fetched schemes for Scots, Irish, French, even Papal intervention. Trapped between the neutralist Welsh 'Peaceable Army' and Parliamentarian flying columns, Charles once more headed for Scotland. His second attempt to join Montrose ended in disaster at Rowton Heath (24 September), a fortnight after the latter's defeat at Philiphaugh (see above). A flying column detached to revive the Royalist cause in Yorkshire came to grief at Sherburn in Elmet three weeks later.

Charles I wandered the Midlands, plundering his subjects to subsist, while the New Model Army mopped up Royalist garrisons. Still hoping for foreign help, the king wintered in Oxford, resolved to continue the struggle next spring, 'though without any fixed design' (Clarendon, *History of the Rebellion*). His last hopes were dashed at Stow-on-the-Wold (21 March 1646), when a scratch force making for a rendezvous near Oxford was compelled to surrender. Charles left Oxford for the last time on 27 April, his hair and beard cut short like a serving-man's. On 5 May he surrendered to the Scots at the Saracen's Head inn in Southwell (Nottinghamshire). Outside a few remote castles the First Civil War was over.

Naseby, Saturday 14 June 1645

England, Northamptonshire, LR141 SP6880

The climactic battle of the First English Civil War was fought in the very centre of the kingdom, on the watershed of the rivers Welland and Avon, which respectively flow east into the Wash and west into the Bristol Channel. Within a couple of hours, a shorter time than earlier, less decisive battles, the New Model Army eliminated Charles I's veteran infantry, destroying any chance of the Royalists winning the war.

The attrition of 1644 had seriously weakened both sides. Cheriton, Marston Moor and Montgomery destroyed Royalist armies in the south, north and northwest. Cropredy, Lostwithiel and Second Newbury were equally destructive of the reputations of Parliamentarian commanders, persuading Parliament to concentrate their surviving southern armies under Sir Thomas Fairfax, an inspired and apolitical battlefield leader. The Self-Denying Ordinance excluded members of both Houses of Parliament from command, most notably Essex, Waller and Manchester. A few exceptions were allowed, including Cromwell and Brereton, whose tactical and organizational abilities made them indispensable.

Fairfax was at Blandford on 8 May 1645, with orders to relieve Taunton. Cromwell had just finished a sweep around Oxford, frightening the Royalist high command out of their wits. Charles was considering his options at Stow-on-the-Wold. Unwilling to be trapped in Oxford, he was unable to reconcile competing advice, either to fight Fairfax in the west, before the New Model Army settled down, or to head north via Chester to defeat Leven's depleted Scots army, and join Montrose. Incredibly the king split his forces, sending Lord George Goring with 3000 horse to Somerset. Charles then rode north, inspiring panic among the Parliamentarians besieging Chester, until Fairfax's investment of Oxford on 19 May drew the king back.

The Royalists sought to defend Oxford indirectly, by picking off Parliamentarian garrisons in the Midlands, such as that at Leicester. This proved too effective. Fairfax was ordered to break up his blockade of Oxford and march after the king, who was awaiting reinforcements near Daventry on Borough Hill. On 12 June Fairfax's advanced troops appeared without warning at Kislingbury, just 7 miles (11 km) away towards Northampton. Overnight the outnumbered Royalists retreated northeast to Market Harborough. Fairfax knew from captured letters that Goring was elsewhere, and on the 13th followed the king to Guilsborough, 10 miles (16 km) south of Market Harborough. That evening Parliamentarian troopers surprised a Royalist outpost at dinner in Naseby. Fairfax was now too close for the Royalists to escape without a fight. Early next morning Rupert deployed the king's army in a strong defensive position 2 miles (3 km) south of Market Harborough, on a long irregular ridge between East Farndon and Oxenden (SP7184–7285). The narrow front suited a weaker defending force, and flanked both the roads along which Fairfax might advance.

The Royalists' strategic situation required that they postpone a decision. They had failed to concentrate their available forces, and should have remained on the defensive pending reinforcement. However, the Royalists despised the tradesmen and religious cranks who made up the 'New Noddle Army'. Rupert committed them to an unnecessary offensive, apparently believing the enemy meant to avoid action: 'supposing by their Motion, or being flatered into an Opinion they were upon a Retreate' (Sir Edward Walker, Charles I's secretary). Rupert had scouted towards Naseby, along the Clipston road, and seen Parliamentarian cavalry 'marching up that side of the hill to that place where after they imbattl'd [deployed] their whole army' (Colonel Sir Henry Slingsby, Northern Horse). The ground in front was poor going, 'by reason the place between us & them was full of burts and water'. Rupert wheeled right, probably at the crossroads south of Clipston, to find better cavalry country a mile (1.6 km) west at Dust Hill: 'a fair piece of ground partly corn and partly heath, under Nasby, about Half a mile distant from the place' (Slingsby).

The Parliamentarians closed up around Naseby before dawn. They were unsure of the enemy's location or intentions, but enjoyed a good view of Rupert's approach from the high ground north of the village. The Royalists on the other hand had a limited appreciation of the forces opposite them, 'as they lay without our sight, having the Hill to cover them' (Slingsby). Fairfax conformed to Rupert's westward movement, occupying 'a large fallow field on the Northwest side of Naseby, flanked on the left hand with a hedge … possessing the ledge of a Hill running from East to West' (Joshua Sprigge, *Anglia Rediviva*). The Parliamentarian front extended a mile (1.6 km) from the Sulby Hedges, north of Red Hill Farm, to Naseby Covert, beyond the Naseby– Sibbertoft road. The baggage train lay behind their left flank, between Fenny Hill and Naseby. As the Parliamentarians deployed, Rupert ordered up the Royalist main body, still between East Farndon and Oxenden, to occupy the ridge from Dust Hill to Long Hold Spinney, facing the enemy across Broad Moor valley, where the Ordnance Survey marks the battlefield. If the Royalists had to fight, this was as good a place as any, the gentle unenclosed slopes offering no obstacle to disrupt their charge. Fairfax encouraged them to come on, withdrawing behind the crest to conceal any confusion in his partly trained ranks consequent upon forming up.

Most Royalist sources understate their own numbers, at some 7500 men. The detailed order of battle given by Richard Symonds, of the King's Lifeguard, lists 5300 foot at Stow and 5520 horse before Leicester. Garrison troops picked up en route probably exceeded any losses suffered to date, leaving the Royalists with well over 10,000 men. Had Goring been present, the king's army might have equalled their opponents. As it was, Sprigge claimed there was 'not 500 odds' in it. The Royalist deployment is clear in outline, though historians distribute the numbers differently. Rupert commanded the right wing with 1500–2000 horse and 200 commanded shot. Sir Marmaduke Langdale took the left with 1700 cavalry, survivors of the Northern Horse defeated at Marston Moor, and 200 more shot. The centre is less clear. Lord Astley's foot are put at 3500–5000, supported by 880 horse. However, Charles's Lifeguard of foot and Rupert's own regiment were held in reserve, under the king's personal control. These numbered 1200 according to Symonds, which leaves Astley 3700 foot after deducting the *enfants perdus* with the cavalry. The reserve also included the king's mounted Lifeguard, 500 strong, and by some accounts 800 garrison horse from Newark. The Lifeguard was hardly an elite formation, its ranks swollen by 'a rabble of gentility', who never drilled and only turned out in a crisis. Other regiments were under strength,

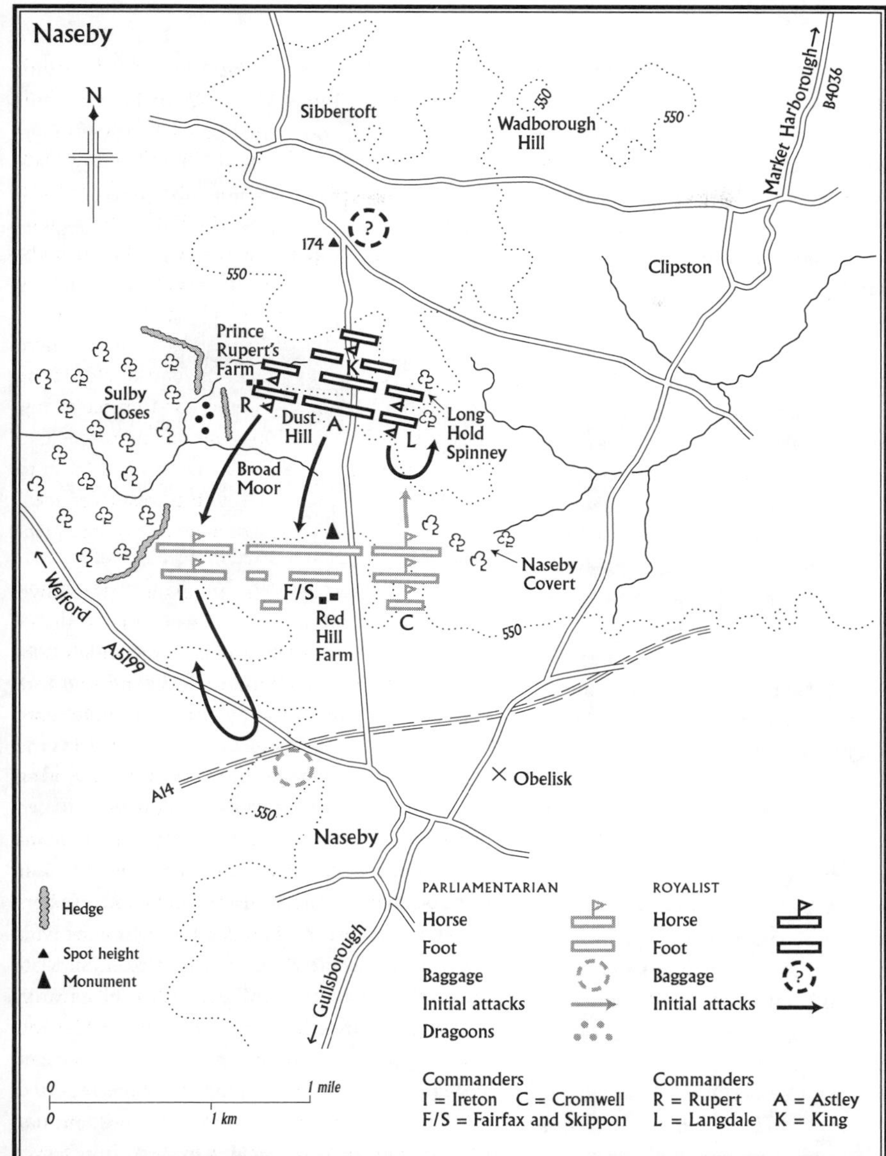

Directions

Naseby is 14 miles (22.5 km) north of Northampton turning right off the A5199 (ex-A50) along the old B4036. Striking northwest from the village turn right off the Welford road, for Sibbertoft. See the monument on the left: intended to commemorate Cromwell's start line, it marks Skippon's front line. The Royalist position is 1/2 mile (0.8 km) further north across the valley. An obelisk by the Clipston road is well clear of the fighting, unlike the A14 link road, which separates Naseby village from the battlefield. From Market Harborough follow Rupert's approach along the B4036, turning right south of Clipston, and left at point 174 to Dust Hill, just past Prince Rupert's Farm.

so they were reorganized into bodies of a more convenient size, formed in several lines. The engraving that accompanies Sprigge's account exaggerates Royalist strength, showing them spread out to match their opponents. However, the general arrangement is plausible: each cavalry wing in two lines, four bodies up, and three in support, covering the intervals in front; Astley's infantry in two lines, four bodies up and three back, with two more bodies in reserve behind them.

Fairfax adopted a similar layout to the Royalists, without a reserve. Cromwell commanded the right wing, opposite Langdale, with six and a half regiments, 3000–4000 horse depending on one's assumptions about their completeness. Cromwell's son-in-law Ireton was commissary general, commanding the left opposite Rupert, with five and a half regiments or 2500–3300 horse. Skippon's eight foot regiments in the centre were under strength, numbering only 7031 a week before the battle. Like the Royalists, they drew up Swedish fashion, supporting units covering the intervals in the front line. Skippon had five regiments up, with three in support, his front screened by 300 musketeers, 'down the steep of the hill towards the enemy, somewhere more than Carbine shot from the Main battail, who were ordered to retreat to the battail, whensoever they should be hard pressed' (Sprigge). The cavalry fought in half-regimental squadrons, ostensibly 300 men each. Ireton deployed six up and five back. Cromwell had more men than were convenient, his front constricted by gorse and a rabbit warren on the right, since absorbed in Naseby Covert. He formed three waves of six, four and three squadrons respectively. Colonel Okey's 1000 dragoons lurked beyond the Sulby Hedges to secure Ireton's left flank and sweep his front with musketry. Traditionally Okey is shown just forward of the Parliamentarian line. Metal-detector surveys have found impressive concentrations of musket balls much closer to the Royalist forming-up area.

The Royalists attacked between 10 and 11 a.m. Sources close to the king complained that 'the Heat of Prince Rupert, and his Opinion they durst not stand him, engaged us before we had either turned our Canon or chosen fit Ground to fight on' (Walker). The prince, however, may have hoped to catch the less experienced opposition off balance. Joshua Sprigge describes how 'the Enemy came on a main in passing good order, while our Army was yet in disorder, or the order of it but an Embrio'. Colonel Okey confirms 'they were ready to advance upon us, before wee were drawn up into a Battalia for to incounter with them'. The battle narrative falls into three main stages:

(1) Opening clashes between the opposing wings and centre of each army.

(2) Charles I's failed attempt to commit his reserve.

(3) Destruction of the Royalist foot, and the flight of their horse.

None of these episodes lasted more than half an hour.

Prince Rupert led the Royalist right against Ireton's horse, timing his onset to coincide with that of Astley's foot on his left. The Parliamentarian horse did not collapse as they had at Edgehill. Some of them stood and fired their pistols; others countercharged to break right through their opponents before Rupert's second line came on 'and routed us clear beyond our carriages'. The Royalists fell to plundering the Parliamentarian wagons, 'but a great many of our horse went clear to *Northampton* and could never be stopt' (Captain Edward Wogan, Okey's Dragoons). Rupert is blamed for losing control, but he needed his whole wing to defeat Ireton's superior numbers, leaving no formed reserve on which to rally the scattered Royalist troopers.

Astley's veteran foot simultaneously charged home upon Skippon's infantry in the centre. These had come forward to the brow of the hill, but had time for only one volley, which missed: 'ours falling in with Sword and butt end of the Musquet did notable Execution; so much as I saw their Colours fall, and their Foot in great Disorder' (Walker). Most of Skippon's front line gave ground, reforming behind the supports or running clean away, depending who you believe. Skippon was desperately wounded in the belly, his officers joining the reserves with their colours, 'choosing rather there to fight and die, then to quit the ground they stood on' (Sprigge). Ireton's rightmost squadron, avoiding the general wreck of his wing, wheeled into the melee, gaining time for the Parliamentarian foot to regroup. Ireton's horse was shot from under him, while he was run through the thigh with a pike, wounded in the face with a halberd, and captured. As Astley's advance ran out of steam, the infantry action bogged down in a fire fight, as attested by the scatter of musket balls recently discovered by metal detectors.

The king's right and centre had nearly won a glorious victory, in just half an hour. The Northern Horse on his left were less fortunate, having to deal with twice their own number of Parliamentarian cavalry, led by the inimitable Cromwell, 'who beside the Advantage of Number had that of the Ground, ours marching up the Hill to encounter them' (Walker). Unlike Rupert and Ireton who led from in front, Cromwell stayed with his second wave, feeding reserves into the fighting as required. Quite properly, he refused to await Langdale's charge, advancing down the slope just east of the Sibbertoft road. His left-hand squadrons made contact first, 'firing at a very close charge', before coming to the sword, to drive their opponents back on Prince Rupert's Foot, in the Royalist third line. Meanwhile, Cromwell's rightmost squadrons struggled through furze bushes and rabbit holes to outflank the rest of the Northern Horse, 'whom they routed and put into great confusion, not one body of the enemies horse which they charged, but they routed, and forced to flie beyond all their Foot, except some that were sheltered by the Brigade of Foot [Rupert's] before mentioned' (Sprigge).

Naseby

	Winners	*Losers*
Opponents	Parliamentarian	Royalist
Commanders	Sir Thomas Fairfax	Charles I
	Oliver Cromwell	Prince Rupert
	Major General Philip Skippon (w)	Jacob, Lord Astley
	Henry Ireton (w)	Sir Marmaduke Langdale
Numbers	13,500–15,300	10,800
Losses	200	*c.*5000

Unlike Rupert, Cromwell had sufficient reserves of men and character to prevent a general chase. Only 4 of his 13 squadrons pursued Langdale's broken horsemen, leaving the rest to charge the Royalist foot in flank.

At this crisis, the king sought to commit his reserve. Rupert's Foot and some of the Newark Horse had been absorbed in the dogfight, but Charles still had his Lifeguards of horse and foot, and 400 Newarkers. They were 'even ready to charge the enemy horse who followed those of the left wing, when, on a sudden, such a panic fear seized upon them that they all ran near a quarter of a mile without'. The Earl of Carnwath had seized the king's bridle with a mouthful of Scotch oaths, saying, 'Will you go upon your death in an instant?', and turned his horse's head away from the enemy: 'Upon this they all turned their horses and rode upon the spur, as if they were every man for himself' (Clarendon, *History of the Rebellion*). This extraordinary and fatal incident cost Charles the war. Before the Royalist reserve could rally, Parliamentarian horse, foot and dragoons combined to destroy the Royalist infantry.

Astley's advance had not engaged Fairfax's own regiment of foot on the extreme right of the Parliamentarian centre. The disintegration of the Northern Horse freed them to cooperate with Cromwell's reserve squadrons against the left flank of Astley's infantry, still fighting Skippon's second line. About the same time, Prince Rupert's wing rejoined the king, 'but they having done their part, and not being in Order, could never be brought to charge again' (Walker). The Royalist foot were left to fight it out unassisted, until they were forced to surrender. Even Okey's dragoons mounted up and charged into the melee, taking 500 prisoners. Traditional accounts of the battle assume the king's foot were overwhelmed near the original Parliamentarian frontline on Red Hill. Recent archaeological investigations suggest they fought their way 2 miles (3 km) back past Moot Hill (617 feet/188 m) to Wadborough Hill (SK6982), where they surrendered upon being offered quarter.

If this is the case, then the Royalist horse must have fallen back without even trying to save their foot.

Sir John Belasyse's secretary commented, 'The horse knew well how to save themselves, tho' not their honours, by hasty and shameful flight to Leicester.' The king and Prince Rupert stayed to the end, labouring to make their remaining horsemen stand. They only withdrew when Fairfax drew up his own cavalry in two wings, 'within Carbine shot of the enemy, leaving a wide space for the battail of foot to fall in, whereby there was framed, as it were in a trice, a second good Batalia at the latter end of the day' (Sprigge). Unwilling to face a second charge, the shattered Royalists fled as soon as Okey's indefatigable dragoons opened fire.

Most of the Royalist horse got away, but their old infantry was annihilated, 4508 rank and file falling into enemy hands; 'but two Footmen went into Leicester' (Okey). Cromwell claimed about 5000 Royalists killed or taken. Parliament's resident Commissioners with the Army reported, 'nigh 4000 prisoners; some 600 slayne ... of ours not above 200'. All the Royalist guns and the baggage train in Chapel Close (SK6881–2) fell into Parliamentarian hands, including King Charles's secret correspondence. Published as *The King's Cabinet Opened*, this provided devastating evidence of royal duplicity, revealing how the head of the Anglican Church had sought to employ Catholic Irish and French mercenaries against his Protestant subjects.

The king made his way west from Leicester, in the futile hope of raising a new army in South Wales, an area already 'vexed and worn out with the oppressions of his own troops' (Clarendon). The best Royalist army was gone beyond hope of replacement, making Naseby the last great battle of the First Civil War.

Langport (Lamport), **10 July 1645**

England, Somerset, LR193 ST4327–4427

The sequel to the Royalist defeat at Naseby followed swiftly. The New Model Army's persistence and tactical skill contrast sharply with the fumbling exploitation of earlier Parliamentarian victories. At Langport, Goring's ill-disciplined troops were no match for their enemy's artillery and enthusiasm.

Fairfax moved quickly to eliminate Goring's western army, the king's last remaining field force. By 5 July Fairfax had advanced to Crewkerne, driving Goring behind the Rivers Yeo and Parret. Royalist headquarters was at Long Sutton, east of Langport, blocking the direct approach from Crewkerne across Load Bridge. Fairfax feinted at Goring's centre, then broke the river line at Yeovil, the Royalists retreating west into Langport. On 9 July Fairfax closed up to Long Sutton, 'farre from our own Garrisons, without much Ammunition, in a place extreamly wanting in provisions' (Cromwell, Thomason Tract E100.20). Next morning, about 7 a.m., a Parliamentarian council was discussing withdrawal, 'but it pleased God to end the business by an Alarm ... that the Enemy had possessed the Passe in Pissbury Bottom' (T.T. E292.28).

Goring had occupied a strong rearguard position, a mile (1.6 km) in advance of Langport, to cover the withdrawal of his guns and 'other lumber', to Bridgwater. Royalist musketeers held the west bank of the Wagg Rhyne, a marshy stream flowing southwards through Huish Episcopi before joining the Yeo, half a mile (0.8 km) below the latter's junction with the Parrett at Langport. Goring's horse occupied the hill behind, with two small guns covering the lane leading up from the Rhyne. The Parliamentarians drew up opposite, 'in a Campania [plain] within a mile of Langport upon one hill they [the Royalists] being on another, ... betwixt us a small valley, and only a roadway to passe through, the sides of the valley being enclosed grounds by hedges and a small brook running in the bottom' (Captain Blackwell, T.T. E293.8).

Parliamentarian reports stress the difficulties of the approach, 'being so streight that four horse could hardly pass abrest and that up to the belly in water' (Fairfax, T.T. E261.4). The ford was 'deepe and dirty and very narrow', covered by fire from the hedges on both sides, 'making the passage for our Horse mortall to every man' (T.T. E293.3 and E 292.30). Outflanking manoeuvres were impractical: the Yeo on Fairfax's left was uncrossable, while a right flanking movement

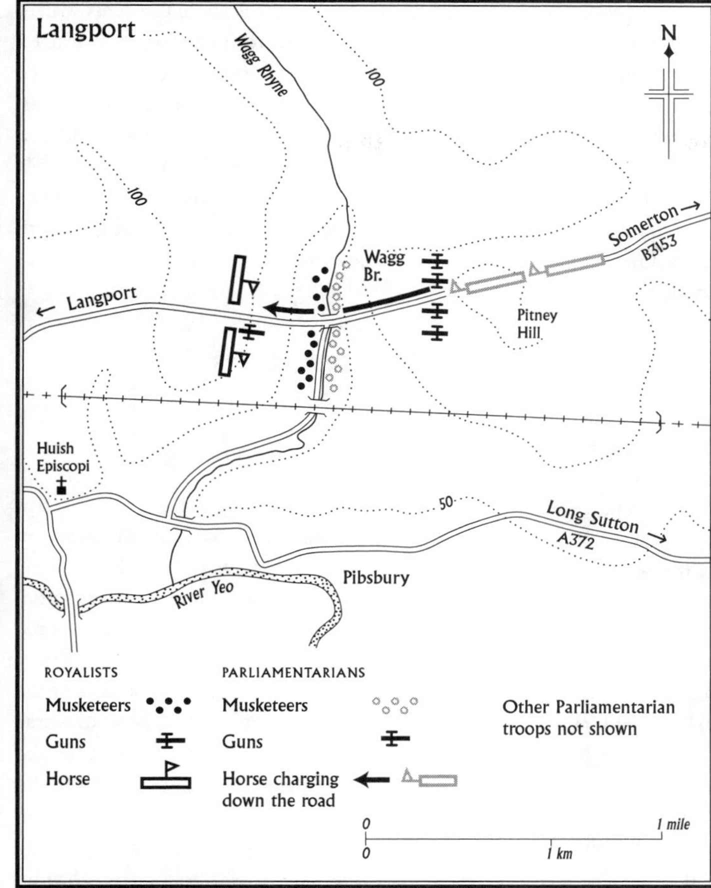

Directions

View the battlefield from Huish Episcopi church tower. Follow the cycle route north of the A372 up the Wagg Rhyne valley under the railway to Wagg Bridge. Banks and hedges line the B3153, either side of the Rhyne, although the boggy stream bottom is now drained. Tengore Lane behind Fairfax's left flank provides a safer viewpoint than the main road.

would have allowed Goring time to escape. Fairfax had two possible crossing places. Huish Episcopi is unlikely. It already had a bridge, not a ford, and the slopes there are too slight to be convincing. Wagg Bridge on the Somerton road seems more probable. The crossing there was still a ford, and it fits Fairfax's initial location, 'by the windmills between Lamport and Somerton'.

Opposing numbers usually appear as given over the page, more than actually feature in contemporary accounts of the fighting. Fairfax reported he had seven cavalry regiments, 'not in all 2000 horse; of foot we had all but the musketeers of three regiments'. Nine foot regiments at their Naseby establishment should have numbered just over 8000, of whom only a forlorn hope of 1000–1500 musketeers saw action. Goring's Royalist critics claimed he had 'at least' 2000 musketeers, and two bodies of 1000 horse.

Langport was an unusually effective example of infantry–artillery cooperation for the period. Between 10 and 11 o'clock Fairfax deployed his artillery train on Pitney Hill (148 feet/45 m), the ridge east of Wagg Bridge, 'which did us good service and made the other side of the Hill so hot, that they could not come down to relieve their men; presently the forlorn hope were ordered down to clear the hedges' (T.T. E292.28). Goring's adjutant general claimed his raw musketeers fired on each other in panic. Captain Blackwell describes stiffer resistance, 'but having drawn up our great Guns, and given them fifty or sixty great shot, their horse began to retreat, and their foot could not abide so much heat as they found in our musquettiers … whereupon our horse began to advance up the way'.

At 1 p.m. two Parliamentarian squadrons of three troops each charged successively up the lane in column of fours, dashed across the ford and gained the ridge. Each troop that came up gained a little more space for its successor to deploy and provide a refuge where its predecessor could rally, before continuing the attack. Finally, all six troops charged together, 'and having disputed it soundly with their swords, the foot marching up furiously … God took away the enemies courage and away they run' (T.T. E293.3). As few as 400 troopers had charged into the middle of a hostile army, and utterly routed it. Fairfax justifiably described the episode as, 'the most excellent piece of service that ever was in England'.

Once the passage was secure, Cromwell consolidated the victory. Goring fired twenty houses either side of Bow Street to cover his escape, but Parliamentarian cavalry charged through the flames to chase fugitives as far as Bridgwater, 'a good store of them … forced into the Ditches'. Royalist infantry threw their weapons into the adjoining river, hid in cornfields and surrendered in droves: 'the whole Foot of the enemy were dispersed, killed and taken, but few killed thanks to hedges and heels' (T.T. E292.28). Infuriated Royalists slew 'some of their own … who would not march with them' (Blackwell). Three hundred were found 'dead on the place', and 2000 captured, with 40 colours and six colonels, some of them 'notorious Incendiaries'. The winners thought it 'a very cheap victory', admitting only 20–30 common soldiers killed, although the leading troop in the charge lost 14 or 16 wounded.

Langport

	Winners	*Losers*
Opponents	Parliamentarian	Royalist
Commanders	Sir Thomas Fairfax	Lord George Goring
Numbers	10,000	7000
Losses	*c.*50	2300

Langport destroyed the western Cavaliers' will to resist. Goring retreated to Barnstaple, 'so great a terror and distraction amongst his men … they could not be brought to fight against half their number' (Clarendon). On 21 July Bridgwater surrendered under threat of bombardment. Cromwell predictably saw the face of God in all this, but others at Fairfax's HQ were equally exalted: 'Our Word was God with us, and he made it good.'

Rowton Heath (Chester), **Wednesday 24 September 1645**

England, Cheshire, LR117 SJ4562 and SJ4464

Charles I had lost almost all freedom of manoeuvre by the summer of 1645. He would not make peace, and could hardly make war. A final strategic initiative foundered at Rowton Heath, his last personal appearance on the battlefield.

Naseby and Langport had left the king without a balanced field army. A dwindling band of horse assured his personal security, but without foot he could no longer conduct effective operations. Charles spent August 1645 wandering between the Welsh Marches and Yorkshire. By mid-September he lay at Hereford, 'in great perplexity and irresolution' (Clarendon, *History of the Rebellion*). Ill-founded confidence in Montrose, who had recently taken Glasgow, inspired a desperate resolve to ride to Scotland, through Lancashire. Charles reached Chirk on 22 September, to learn that his garrison in Chester was about to fall. To the Royalists 'the unexpected coming of his majesty looked like a design of Providence, for the preservation of so important a place' (Clarendon). Next day they rode to the rescue, the king entering the city by the Dee bridge with Lord Gerard. Langdale crossed the river upstream at Holt, and bivouacked on Milners Heath, also called Millers or Milne Heath, 4 miles (6 km) southeast of Chester. The plan was to encircle the besiegers, trapping them in the suburbs they had just stormed, outside Eastgate.

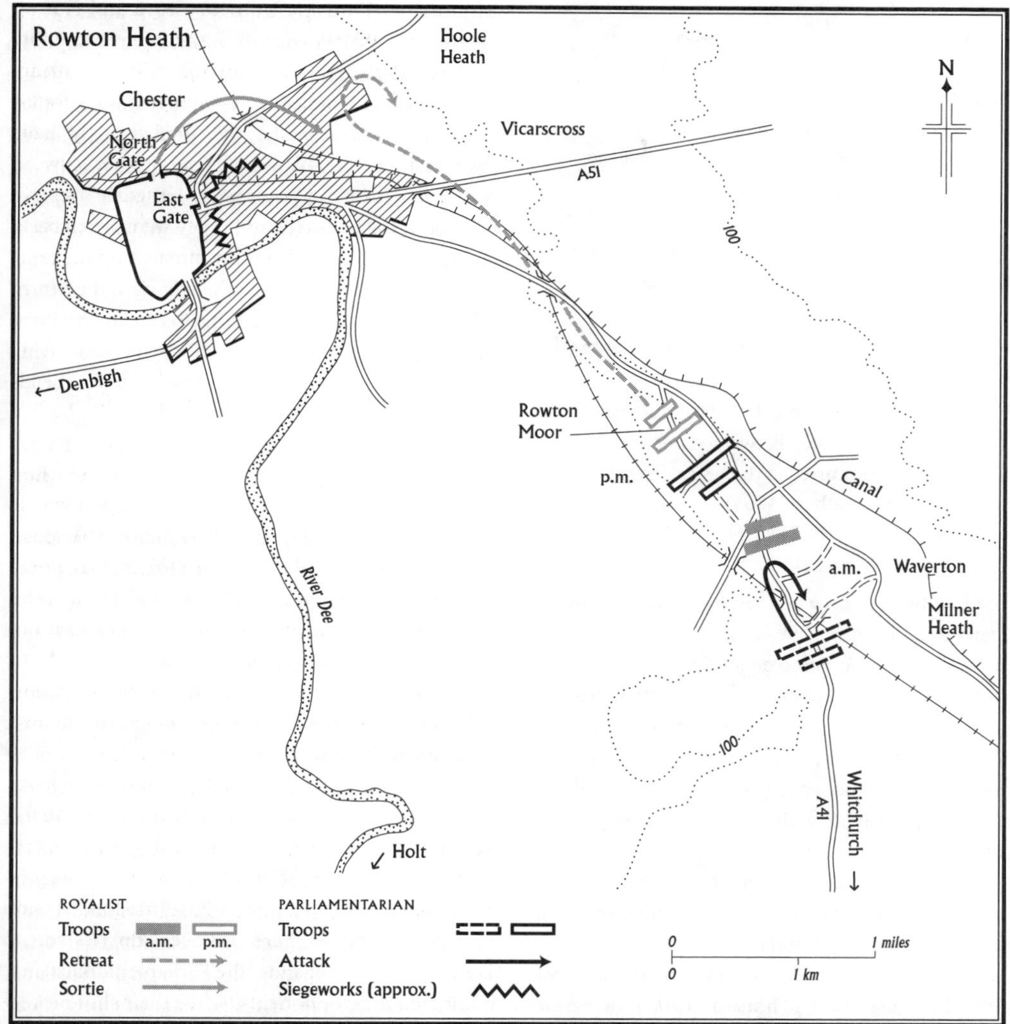

Colonel Sydenham Poyntz was a professional soldier, who had replaced Lord Fairfax in command of Northern Association troops when the Self-Denying Ordinance took effect. He had shadowed the king from Hereford, reaching Whitchurch, 18 miles (29 km) south of Chester, on the evening of 23 September. Receiving a plea for help from Colonel Jones, commanding the besiegers, Poyntz pressed on, reaching Hatton Heath, a mile (1.6 km) south of Langdale's quarters, at dawn on the 24th.

The battle area extends along a low ridge (108–121

Directions

The first two actions are 3 and 4 miles (5 and 6 km) from the centre of Chester respectively, heading south-east along the A41(T). Fork right for Rowton Moor, now a mixture of suburbs and green fields. Regain the A41(T), and cross the railway to view the area of the initial encounter from a footpath either side of the main road. The final clash spread north from Vicars Cross on the A51(T) across Hoole Heath, much of which is built up. See Phoenix Tower at the northeast corner of the city walls, where Charles watched the disaster.

Rowton Heath

	Winners	*Losers*
Opponents	Parliamentarian	Royalist
Commanders	Colonel Sydenham Poyntz Colonel Michael Jones	Charles I Sir Marmaduke Langdale (w) Charles, Lord Gerard of Brandon (w)
Numbers	4000–5000	3000–4000
Losses	unknown	1500

feet/33–37 m) running northwest to southeast, a mile (1.6 km) east of Chester, between the Rivers Dee and Gowy. Fighting occurred in three successive locations:

(1) Milners Heath (SJ4563)

(2) Rowton Moor (SJ4464)

(3) Hoole Heath (SJ4367)

The first two are now crossed by the railway line to Crewe and the Shropshire Union Canal, which some cartographers have mistaken for the River Dee. Open heathland was broken by 'narrow, dirty lanes' and hedged enclosures, providing cover for musketeers. Nearer Chester, the besiegers were dug in southeast of the city, with 'mud walls', while the defenders had blocked up Eastgate with dung, leaving only Northgate available for a sortie.

Parliamentarian accounts claim the Royalists fielded 5000–6000 men, 'having drained their garrisons'. Richard Symonds of the King's Lifeguard listed rather less. Langdale had 1900 horse, while Gerard commanded 640 horse and 200 foot, besides Chester's unquantified garrison. Colonel Parsons, Poyntz's quartermaster general, claimed the Parliamentarians had 'not above 2500 horse', although Clarendon gives them 3000 horse and dragoons. The besiegers sent out two parties during the battle, 800 and 400 men respectively, leaving enough in the trenches to repel a sortie.

Fighting began with a violent encounter between Poyntz and Langdale's cavalry, 'in a narrow passe on top of the heath' (Poyntz). The Royalists had intercepted Jones's messenger returning, and were drawn up ready to fight 'in the midst of a Lane betwixt two Moores': presumably Milners Heath and Hatton Heath, south of Waverton. Langdale presumably held the slight rise north of the railway cutting. Poyntz attacked immediately, without waiting for his main body to come up. His men fired pistols at 'halfe Pikes distance', and drove the enemy back at sword point, only to be overpowered by Langdale's reserve waiting 'at the Lanes mouth'. They were driven back, losing 20 dead. The Cavaliers pursued up the lane, where Poyntz's reserve beat them back in their turn: 'after this the Generall perceiving the enemy lay upon his advantage, only skirmished him with some flying parties, while he held correspondency with his friends in Chester suburbs' (Parsons).

Hearing that Poyntz kept his ground, the Parliamentarians outside Chester agreed to reinforce him with 500 Horse and 300 musketeers, 'upon whose appearing the enemy quitted their station' (Parsons). Langdale retreated about a mile (1.6 km), to where the Ordnance Survey marks the battlefield. The modern road bypasses Rowton, but in 1645 it ran directly through the village. Poyntz drew up 'into many small divisions and reserves, being much outnumbered', placing his few musketeers 'in the two outmost intervals of horse' (Parsons).

Fighting began afresh at 4 or 5 p.m. Langdale advanced his whole body, receiving a volley from the Parliamentarian shot, upon which Poyntz counterattacked with his front line: 'charging the enemy in Front and Flank ... being continually seconded with reserves as often as there was occasion' (Parsons). Despite their propaganda, the Parliamentarians outnumbered their opponents, while their shot picked off the Cavaliers from the hedgerows: 'our Musketeers so galled their horse, that their Rear fled, perceiving their losse by them, upon whom they made no Execution. Their van perceiving that, faced about, and fled also' (*A True Relation*, T.T. E303.18).

Langdale had sent for help, the messenger crossing the Dee in an old tub used for collecting pigs' blood, but the Eastgate was still blocked up. Gerard did not sortie from Northgate until 3 p.m., with 640 horse and 200 foot. Fighting recommenced on Hoole Heath, where the Royalists rallied 'in a great more [moor] wide of Chester in two vast bodies'. Another Parliamentarian reported, 'After we thought the work was ended, the enemy made head againe ... for they were desperate seeing they had lost the day' (*True Relation*). However Gerard's troops became entangled with Langdale's fleeing troopers in the narrow lanes, 'which were so unfit for horse to fight upon' (Clarendon). Taken in flank by 200 Parliamentarian horse from the suburbs and as many foot, the Royalists ran in every direction: west to Holt, north to Trafford Bridge. One formation carried away a hostile regiment in its flight, driving it against the outworks of the suburbs, where the guards fired impartially on friend and foe alike: 'mud walls, fields and the roads were filled with the bodies' (*Parliament's Post*, T.T. E303.24).

The hapless king watched the denouement from the city walls, a stray shot killing the man next to him. The battle was a crushing defeat that ended any hope of combining with Montrose, and dispersed the horse that had attended Charles since Naseby. Poyntz's final score was at least 300 Royalist dead, plus 124 officers and 1200 soldiers captured. The winners gave no account of their own losses, 'but that it is very small'. Charles left Chester next morning with just 500 horse, crossing the Dee bridge behind screens raised against Parliamentarian snipers. That evening, at Denbigh, he learned of Montrose's defeat at Philiphaugh.

Sherburn in Elmet, Wednesday 15 October 1645

England, North Yorkshire, LR105 SE4932–4

Burgh by Sands (Carlisle Sands), 24 October 1645

England, Cumbria, LR 85 NY3060?

As the Royalist war effort foundered, a few of the Marquess of Newcastle's Northern Horse who had survived Marston Moor, Naseby and Rowton Heath tried to return home. For them the First Civil War ended at Sherburn in Elmet and Burgh by Sands, battlefields overshadowed by earlier, more consequential engagements, at Towton and Solway Moss (1461, 1542).

A summer of disasters failed to dampen the enthusiasm of the king's featherbrained secretary of state, Lord George Digby. Hoping to revive Royalist fortunes in Yorkshire and hold out a hand to Montrose's phantom army, Digby parted company from Charles at Welbeck Abbey in Nottinghamshire on 14 October. Taking Langdale's 600–700 Northern Horse and up to 1000 other Cavaliers, he surprised some Parliamentarian quarters at Cusworth in Doncaster's western outskirts, and next morning crossed the River Aire at Ferrybridge. At Sherburn he ran into some Parliamentarian infantry, whose cavalry was still south of the Aire under Colonel Copley. Sherburn in Elmet therefore saw two separate actions. In the first the Royalists captured the unsupported infantry, whose cavalry then came up and defeated them before they could get away.

Copley's report simply says the Royalists 'beat Colonel Wrins regiment at the north side of Sherburne', presumably on Sherburn Common (SE4934). A local sympathizer adds: 'our men were preparing for their coming, by being drawne up into the field about 800 foot beside Horse, but the Enemy soon routed the Horse (being but a handful to them) and tooke all the Foot prisoners, [and] laid all their Armes in a great heap in Sherburn street, till they could get carriages to send them away' (Thomason Tract E305.14).

Copley gave the Royalists no time to carry off their spoil. He had followed Digby across Ferrybridge soon after first light, and spotted the Royalists on Sherburn Common from Betteras Hill, near point 37 on the A162 a mile (1.6 km) before South Milford. Copley prepared for action, forming 'Bodies for Charges and Reserves as before I had given orders to the Officers'. He had two regiments: the Lord General's on the right, probably the best cavalry in Britain, and his own on the left, some 1250 altogether.

Although the encounter with Wrin's infantry took place north of Sherburn, Copley's report shows the decisive cavalry action was to the south, probably on

Sherburn in Elmet

	Winners	*Losers*
Opponents	Parliamentarian	Royalist
Commanders	Colonel Lionel Copley	George, Lord Digby (w) Sir Marmaduke Langdale
Numbers	*c.*2050	1200–1600
Losses	unknown	440

Burgh by Sands

	Winners	*Losers*
Opponents	Parliamentarian	Royalist
Commanders	Sir John Brown (w)	George, Lord Digby Sir Marmaduke Langdale
Numbers	300	950
Losses	80	unknown

the gentle slopes around point 24, north of the railway station (SE4932). Fearing an ambush by Royalist dragoons, Copley had bypassed South Milford. He manoeuvred along the higher ground to his left, passing 'above the Towne, through the Hedges which was some inconvenience'. Approaching Sherburn the Parliamentarians encountered 'an impassable Brooke we knew not of, having much adoe to bring our Bodies again into Order'. The most likely obstacle is Mill Dyke, which lay across Copley's line of advance as he edged around South Milford. This momentary confusion, 'might have occasioned the loss of the day, had not the Enemy been too late in drawing out of the town'. The countryman quoted above describes a race to deploy, 'both sides striving who should be soonest in Battalia'.

Sherburn was less extensive than today. Langdale probably formed up inside the modern built-up area, at an angle to the main road, facing Copley on the rise just east of Mill Dyke. The two sides seem to have charged simultaneously, routing each other's left wing. Copley pleaded in extenuation that his regiment faced 'the only Gallant men [they had], the Reformadoes', that is a troop formed entirely from officers of disbanded regiments. The Lord General's regiment saved the day, while Langdale's supports failed to second his initial success. Less than half the Royalists escaped to Skipton Castle. A 3-mile (5-km) chase yielded 300–400 prisoners, 'whereof many are escaped by negligence of the Soldiers who regarded the Spoyle more than the Glory' (Copley). Parliamentarian accounts claim 40 Royalist dead against 10 of their own, with many wounded on both sides.

Digby's tattered remnant slipped into Westmorland, apparently making for Dumfries. Sir John Brown intercepted them at Burgh Marsh, on the tidal fringes of the Solway estuary. He reckoned he faced 600 survivors of Sherburn, 150 garrison troopers from Skipton and 200 local recruits, his own regiment of local horse 'not being above 300 strong' (T.T. E308.7). Royalist morale must have been pretty ragged, by this time. Brown drew up in two echelons, a forlorn hope and a reserve, sent away his colours for safety, and, according to his own account, 'betwixt hope and despair did charge them. They not knowing which way to goe did stand to it very well, for it was full sea [high tide] soe that they could not goe back to England.' After a bitter skirmish Brown's reserve broke the Royalist main body, whose reserves ran away. Parliamentarian losses of 30 killed and 50 wounded indicate the severity of the fighting. Digby lost 100 dead, with many wounded prisoners, and several drowned. Digby and Langdale got away on a ship to the Isle of Man, but the Northern Horse were no more.

Directions

Sherburn in Elmet *Leave the A1 1 mile (1.6 km) north of Ferrybridge, and take the A162 Tadcaster road. Turn off at the South Milford roundabout, along the old road through the village that Copley avoided. The cavalry battle was on the left between South Milford station and Sherburn. A footpath runs between Mill Lane (off South Milford High Street) and Highfield Gardens in Sherburn.*

Burgh by Sands *The village is on Hadrian's Wall, 5 miles (8 km) northwest of Carlisle along a minor road off the B5307. Several footpaths north of the village lead into Burgh Marsh. See also Edward I's monument nearby.*

Stow-on-the-Wold, Saturday 21 March 1646

England, Gloucestershire, LR163 SP1728/SP1827

The last pitched battle of the First Civil War took place near Stow-on-the-Wold, a postscript to the previous campaigning season. Contemporary pamphlets were imprinted '1645', as the New Year began on 25 March, leading unwary moderns to misdate the action before Naseby.

The king's supporters were reduced by 1646 to a few garrisons. Charles awaited events at Oxford with 1500 horse, while Lord Astley collected infantry in the Welsh Marches for a new field army. Colonel Thomas Morgan, Parliamentarian governor of Gloucester and a veteran of the Thirty Years' War, was instructed to intercept Astley's recruits. Morgan 'rendezvoused seasonably betwixt Evesham and Warwick', and patrolled the River Avon, which Astley had to pass. Realizing Astley would not risk an opposed crossing, Morgan fell back on 19 March to Chipping Campden, 'the most convenient place wheresoever he made his passage' (Thomason Tract E329.7). Astley chose Bidford, on the Avon 7 miles (11 km) east of Evesham.

Morgan was not Astley's only problem. Sir William Brereton was behind him with 1000 horse, manoeuvring between Stratford-upon-Avon and Birmingham to prevent the Royalists turning back. On the 20th Brereton learned Astley was across the Avon, but that Morgan would contest Campden Hills while awaiting reinforcements. Brereton immediately countermarched to Stratford, his troopers filing singly across the war-damaged bridge.

Morgan kept Astley in play, 'skirmishing with him by parties, and keeping my Body drawn up in a most advantageous place for pursuit in case he should passe by me ... which about nine o'clock that night he did'. Brereton caught Morgan up between 1 and 2 a.m. on the 21st, after a 30-mile (50-km) approach march. The combined Parliamentarians were a mile (1.6 km) behind the enemy, somewhere near Longborough, on the road from Chipping Campden to Stow-on-the Wold. Armies had regularly visited Stow during the Civil Wars, His Majesty staying at the King's Arms before Naseby. The little market town was a significant communications centre, where the Fosse Way crosses the Cotswold Ridgeway and the Droitwich saltway to Burford, where Morgan suspected Charles was awaiting Astley.

Morgan reckoned his total numbers equalled Astley's, which he estimated at 3000, although Clarendon's *History of the Rebellion* allowed Astley only 2000 horse and foot, which may include as few as 100 cavalry. Names of captured officers show that elements of four cavalry and two infantry regiments were present. Brereton's hard marching had reduced him to 800 horse, suggesting Morgan originally fielded 2200. They formed up in three bodies: Brereton on the right with his own horse; the Gloucestershire horse on the left; Morgan in the centre with the foot.

Astley's dispositions are unknown, except that 'he made choice of his ground and had the wind with him'. Modern authors agree he fought on the Donnington side of Stow. Morgan was determined to prevent Astley joining the king, sending 400 horse and 200 firelocks ahead to 'charge home his Rearguard to put them to a stand before he should passe through Stow-upon-the-Wold'. The Royalists' best chance was to hold the narrow boot-shaped spur of high ground (656 feet/200 m) south of Horsington Plantation, where the ground falls away steeply either side of the main road, a mile (1.6 km) west of Donnington. Another possible reconstruction places Astley nearer Stow, on the next rise, east of the main road, at SP1827. In either case, the Parliamentarian

Stow-on-the-Wold

	Winners	*Losers*
Opponents	Parliamentarian	Royalist
Commanders	Colonel Thomas Morgan Sir William Brereton	Jacob, Lord Astley (p)
Numbers	3000	2000–3000
Losses	unknown	1900

left had to climb a steep slope to reach the enemy, 100 feet (30 m) above them, while the right enjoyed an easier approach. The woodland east of the main road did not then exist.

Clarendon describes a surprise attack, falling upon Astley's weary troops just as they thought they had evaded hostile attentions. A Parliamentarian eyewitness suggests more deliberation: 'after we discovered them standing in Batalia we faced them an houre before we fought, both sides waiting for day light' (*A True and Fuller Relation*). Morgan attacked half an hour before dawn. Both right wings did well, the Cavaliers possibly helped by the steep hillside to their front. The eyewitness continued: 'Upon the first Charge the Enemy forced the left Wing to a disorderly Retreat by overpowering of them; so that it seemed something doubtfull, But Sir Will: Brereton with our Right Wing of Horse charged their left both of Horse and Foot, and totally Routed them, pursuing them into Stow; killing and wounding many in the town: and the meanwhile our Left rallied.' Local tradition alleges Digbeth Street ran with blood. Astley's position may have been intrinsically strong, but the wide open slopes between it and Stow provided neither shelter not rallying point in case of defeat.

Astley's whole army fell into Morgan's hands: 100 killed, Lord Astley with 70 officers and 1730 common soldiers taken prisoner, 'whereof many being wounded I gave them liberty to go to their own homes'. Two thousand arms were captured: 'the few who escaped were so scattered and dispersed that they never came together again' (Clarendon). The winners glossed over their own casualties as usual, admitting only two officers killed and one wounded. Parliamentarian commentators justifiably rejoiced over 'so great and seasonable a victory ... by which means the last visible field force of the enemy hath been so wholly broken, that all possibility is taken from him of appearing with an army in the field' (*Calendar of State Papers*). Lord Astley's often quoted words to his captors would, with hindsight, assume the status of inspired prophecy: 'You have done your work, boys, and may go play, unless you will fall out among yourselves.'

Directions

See Stow Market Square where Lord Astley sat on a drum to tease his captors, and St Edward's Church, once crammed with 1500 prisoners. Also see the half-length figure of Captain Hastings Keyt, who was buried in the chancel. Follow the A424 northwest to the battle sites. One is along the southern edge of the modern woods south of Longborough; the alternative is 500 yards(450 m) sooner, off the A424 on the right, beside the Donnington road.

Renewed Hostilities: The Second Civil War

Parliament's attempts to convert military victory into lasting peace failed miserably. Hardly two years after Lord Astley's surrender at Stow-on-the-Wold, disagreements among the winners of the First English Civil War precipitated fresh hostilities, culminating in revolution.

General attachment to monarchical government strengthened the hand of a powerless, and hence popular, king. Nevertheless Parliament would not moderate the demands of the Newcastle Propositions (July 1646) that Charles abandon episcopacy and the Prayer Book. The lifetime exclusion of Royalist combatants from public office that was enshrined in the Propositions justified Charles I's refusal to abandon his friends, and rendered desperate those Royalists who had paid heavy fines to avoid prosecution for their 'malignancy'. The constitutional impasse remained unresolved in January 1647 when the Scots army handed Charles over to Parliament and returned home.

A self-inflicted financial crisis accompanied political failure. The House of Lords had blocked the taxes that paid the New Model Army, creating an unmanageable military debt. Infantry pay was 18 weeks in arrears, the cavalry's 43. A shabby attempt by the Commons' Presbyterian majority to disband troops with only 6 weeks' money in March 1647 provoked outrage. The Army seized the king (4 June) and issued its own constitutional programme, the Heads of the Proposals. Charles would no more accept these than Parliament's Newcastle Propositions. His escape to the Isle of Wight in November abruptly terminated the Army's attempts at negotiation.

In less straitened confinement at Carisbrooke Castle, Charles negotiated an 'Engagement' with the Scots, agreeing to impose Presbyterianism throughout Britain in return for military assistance. The Engagers resented the New Model Army's anti-Presbyterian stance, and demanded Parliament suppress 'that army of sectaries'. They formed an unlikely coalition with unreconciled Royalists and disaffected Parliamentarians. Sick of high taxes, free quarter and socio-religious change masquerading as reform, most people longed for 'an old King and a new parliament', but were unwilling to risk their necks to get them. Lacking unity of command or common political objectives, the English rebels were too hasty, and the Scots invaders too slow. Northern Royalists seized Berwick and Carlisle in April 1648, before the Scots began to mobilize. Presbyterian MPs who denounced soldiers' just pay demands as sedition failed to condemn Scottish outrages in Cumbria. The New Model Army thrashed them all.

To speak of a specifically 'English' Second Civil War is misleading. The flashpoint was in Pembroke, where Welsh Royalists wearing the slogan 'We long to see our King' in their hats joined Parliamentarian officers anxious to avoid investigation of their financial irregularities. Despite odds of three-to-one in their favour, they were crushed near Cardiff at St Fagans (8 May). Popular reaction against the Puritan ban on Christmas exploded into a general uprising at Rochester on 22 May, dangerously near the capital. The Lord General Fairfax dispersed the rebels at Maidstone (1 June), but enough escaped to Essex to tie down half the New Model Army besieging Colchester until the crisis was over. It fell to Cromwell to eliminate the main threat in his first major campaign as overall commander. At Preston he annihilated the invading Scots on 17 August, ending the military emergency.

The war inspired savage exasperation amongst the soldiers, making them impatient of Parliament's futile attempts to continue negotiations with the king. Even before fighting broke out, an officers' prayer meeting at Windsor had agreed 'to call Charles Stuart, that man of blood, to an account for that blood he had shed, and the mischief he had done …'. The king's defeated lieutenants at Colchester had already suffered judicial reprisals. If they were guilty, so was he. In November 1648 the Remonstrance of the Army proposed that the king be put on trial, and that the monarchy be abolished. Pride's Purge on 6 December reduced the Commons to 154 MPs, ready to do the Army's business. Ignoring Charles's denial of their jurisdiction, the Rump Parliament sentenced him to death 'as a tyrant, traitor, and murderer'. On 30 January 1649 he was beheaded in Whitehall. England became a Republic.

St Fagans, Monday 8 May 1648

Wales, Cardiff, LR171 ST1077

Wales's largest battle was appropriately fought on the western outskirts of its capital, Cardiff. St Fagans is remembered as a sideshow, but it merited a public day of thanksgiving in London and rallied Parliamentarian support at a critical moment.

The immediate spark of the Second Civil War was the refusal of Colonel John Poyer, an erstwhile Parliamentarian, to surrender Pembroke Castle to a new governor in March 1647. His stand drew in other discontented Parliamentarians such as Rowland Laugharne, and attracted a mass following. Some were old soldiers, 'disbanded men from England', but most were simple countrymen, 'by reason of the malignity of the Gentry, who lead the common sort of people every way they please' (Colonel Thomas Horton, Thomason Tract E442.8). Horton was sent to deal with Poyer, but force of numbers drove him back to Brecon. In early May he got wind of a Royalist advance into Glamorgan, 'having a Design upon Cardiff'.

Horton marched south across the mountains to occupy St Fagans, which covers the bridges leading to Cardiff, 'whither the enemy intended to advance the same night'. Laugharne halted 2 miles (3 km) away at St Nicholas, beyond the River Ely, 'a place much to their advantage, where we could make no use of our horse'. The Royalists withdrew westwards on Friday 5 May, advancing again on Sunday to Peterston-super-Ely. Cromwell was bringing reinforcements, and the Royalists needed a decision before he arrived: 'about seven in the morning our scouts discovered their body about a mile and a half from our quarters, upon which we drew out, and took the best ground we could' (Horton).

Parliamentarian dispositions are unclear, beyond Colonel John Okey's reference to 'our present station, which was at St Fagans'. Local tradition puts Horton's horse lines behind the modern village, on the slopes of Pentrebane ridge (253 feet/77 m). The high ground runs northwest from the rain-swollen Ely, obliquely to the Royalist approach. Horton seems to have defended the ridge's lower slopes, around the crossroads on St Bride's Road north of St Fagans, protecting his quarters: 'wee, being loth to retreat upon a little hill near St Fagans made good our ground' (Okey).

Horton had nine troops of New Model Army horse, Okey's six companies of dragoons and eight companies of Overton's Foot. Another 160–200 firelocks, i.e. musketeers with flintlocks, are also mentioned. Local Parliamentarians provided four more troops of horse, a dragoon company and two infantry companies. At full strength this would give Horton about 3000 men, but allowances must be made for losses from 'unseasonable weather, and rugged ways, want of necessaries, and other inconveniences' (Okey). Royalist prisoners told Horton they had 8000 horse and foot, 'about 2500 musketeers by their own confession, besides bills, pikes, and clubs'. Two-thirds of the infantry were hastily embodied Clubmen, kept in line by the 500 cavalry: 'employed at the rear to keep up their foot, and we never saw … above sixty horse in a body all the fight' (Horton). Neither side had any artillery. Horton drew up conventionally: horse and dragoons on the flanks, infantry in the centre, probably with a reserve of horse. The Royalists brought successive bodies of troops into action as the fight progressed, implying they had either deployed in depth, or been attacked in column of march.

Horton's forlorn hope began by dislodging their opposite numbers, 500 foot with a few horse, from their hedges. They drove them back about a mile (1.6 km), across the low flat ground where the Ordnance Survey marks the battlefield, between the Ely and higher ground to the north. The terrain is greatly

St Fagans

	Winner	*Loser*
Opponents	Parliamentarian	Royalist
Commanders	Colonel Thomas Horton	Rowland Laugharne Colonel John Poyer (x)
Numbers	2500–3000	8000
Losses	unknown	3200

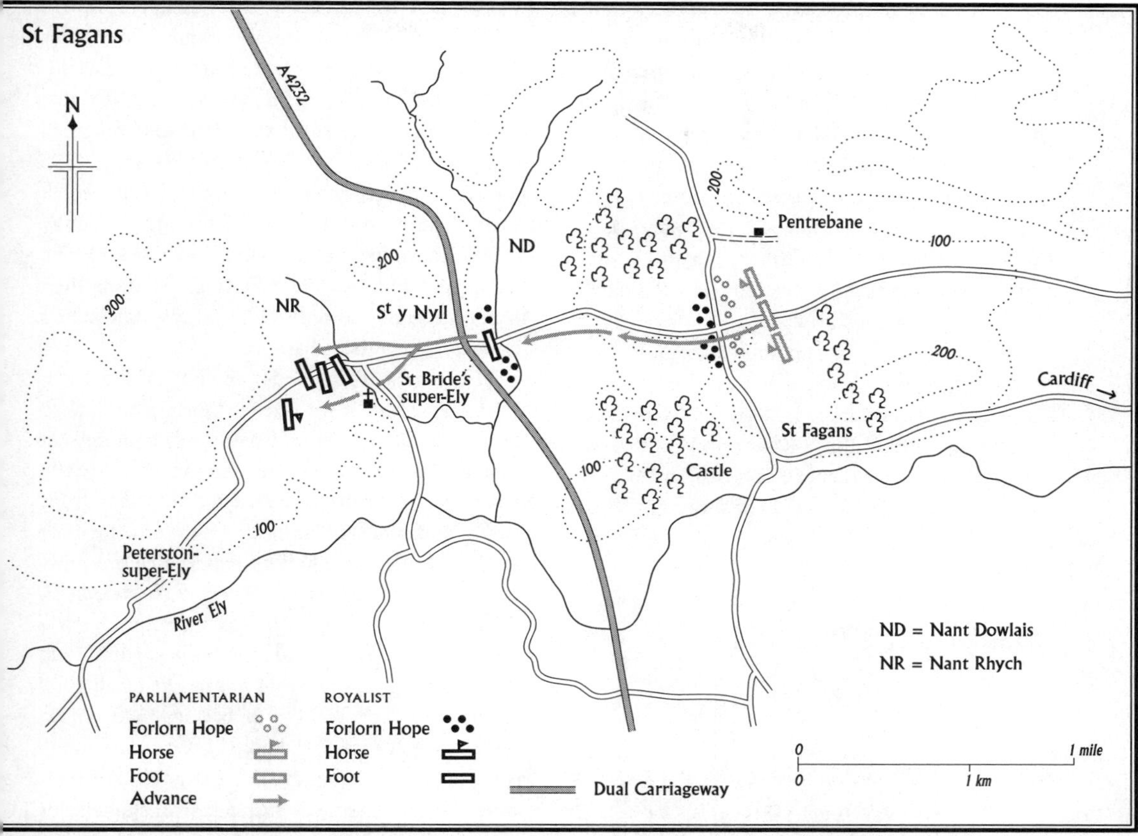

altered. Two streams, Nant Dowlais and Nant Rhych, still flow into the Ely across Horton's line of advance, but a dual carriageway now separates the streams, slicing through the hill at Sant y Nyll. The Royalists, 'having so many reserves of foote behind every hedge … made a stand with a new party … But at the end hee was beat … to a water [Nant Dowlais], and from thence over a river [Nant Rhych], where again he made good his stand' (Okey). Horton confirms capture of the first 'little brook', and a more protracted defence of a bridge, 'where the enemy's greatest body were placed'.

Horton's leading cavalry stopped between Nant Rhych and the dual carriageway, until the infantry caught up. The first division of foot 'fell close to the enemy's front', presumably a frontal holding attack on the bridge, while the second 'got over the little brook on the left flank of the enemy', somewhere near St Bride's Church. The cavalry on Horton's left followed, in time to drive off the only Royalist cavalry charge of the day. Meanwhile the right hand pincer crossed upstream: 'the enemy's foot standing very stoutly to it, until our horse began to surround them, and then they presently all ran, and we cleared the field, pursueing them for eight or ten miles' (Horton).

Directions

Follow St Bride's Road west from Llandaff through Pentrebane, turning left along Crofft-y-Genau Road to see St Fagans Castle, an Elizabethan house of limited tactical value, and the Welsh Folk Museum's collection of contemporary buildings. Go back, and continue west under the A4232 dual carriageway to St Bride's, the Royalists' final stand.

With no cavalry to cover the rout, the Royalist army was annihilated. Horton claimed over 200 killed, 400 officers and gentlemen captured, along with 2600 common soldiers, and '4000 Clubmen dispersed to their severall habitations'. He characterized his own casualties as 'not many', admitting, 'a great loss in horses, our Horse being forced to stand the Enemy's shot, to second our foot'. Okey was shot through the hat, without further injury. Eighteenth-century fantasies that the River Ely flowed red below Nant Dowlais are just that.

Horton's victory had an immediate and salutary effect, swinging waverers behind the Army: the Parliamentarian Edmund Ludlow thought it 'a great discouragement to the contrary party'. Poyer and Laugharne were sentenced to death for their part, drawing lots for which of them should die. Poyer lost.

Maidstone, 1 June 1648

England, Kent, LR188 TQ7655

Events at Maidstone on the evening of 1 June 1648 were less a battle than a street fight, the New Model Army proving that rebels who would not face them in the open stood no more chance behind barricades.

Royalist leaders in the southeast meant to await Scottish intervention before taking up arms. Government action against Christmas rioters, however, provoked an explosion of anti-Parliamentarian feeling in Kent, just when the Royalist defeat at St Fagans should have inspired caution. Insurgents advanced on London, placing guns on the high road at Deptford, echoing the confrontation at Blackheath in 1497. The risings were more a protest movement than a rebellion. Unwilling to fight the Army, the insurgents promptly abandoned Deptford when Fairfax occupied Blackheath on 30 May. Next day Fairfax advanced on the focal point of the rising, at Rochester, where he found the drawbridge pulled up against him.

Unable to force the Medway, Fairfax edged southwest, around the bend in the river, through Meopham to East Malling. Meanwhile thousands of protesters gathered on Penenden Heath northwest of Maidstone, a traditional Kentish rallying point. Royalist detachments at Aylesford and Maidstone prepared to dispute the crossings there (cf. Aegelesthrep *c.*455). Fairfax continued south over Barming Heath, which extended further east than today, crossing the Medway at Farleigh Bridge, 2 miles (3 km) west of Maidstone and lightly guarded. The Parliamentarians then turned left along Lower Road, towards Maidstone's unprotected southern flank.

The Royalist commander, the Earl of Norwich, was the father of Lord George Goring, but lacked his son's military abilities. He was only appointed at noon on 1 June, and has received mixed notices: 'a man fitter to have drawn such a body together by his frolick and pleasant humour ... than to form or conduct them ... He had no experience or knowledge of war' (Clarendon, *History of the Rebellion*). Norwich was uncertain of his own numbers, 'a matter of 7000 as they did say', besides 1000–1500 at Aylesford. Prisoners told Fairfax he faced 8000 Royalists on Penenden Heath, besides 3000 in both Maidstone and Aylesford, 'those of Aylesford coming as a fresh supply to relieve those engaged at Maidstone'. Fairfax disposed of four or five regiments of horse, and three of foot. At full strength he could have had 3000 cavalry and as many infantry, but several sources specify 4000 altogether, which is likely, allowing for detachments and wastage.

The battlefield is now thoroughly built over, the main action taking place along Stone Street, between Maidstone Grammar School and the town centre. Fairfax's line of approach ran south of the Medway

Maidstone

	Winner	*Loser*
Opponents	Parliamentarian	Royalist
Commanders	Sir Thomas Fairfax	George Goring, Earl of Norwich
Numbers	4000	6000
Losses	unknown	1600

across Tovil Brook, then up Old Tovil Road. Casualties from a clash at East Farleigh were traditionally buried here, left of Lower Road. More burials took place in Postley Field, now a commercial centre, where Fairfax's men broke into Upper Stone Street. The main road runs down a long hill into Maidstone before crossing the River Len, which flows through Mote Park on the right, under the Ring Road, and into the Medway. The Parliamentarian advance then carried them up Gabriel's Hill into the High Street, where entrenched cannon commanded all four ways into the town.

The Parliamentarians reached the outskirts of Maidstone at 7 p.m. Fairfax meant to attack next day, but the leading dragoons engaged the enemy too closely, 'which necessitated the drawing down of the greatest part of the foot with some horse'. Despite darkness and their ignorance of the town, the soldiers stormed ahead through abattis and breastworks. The insurgents withdrew from house to house, shooting from the windows and defending their barricades until driven back at push of pike. John Rushworth, Fairfax's secretary, wrote: 'The like service, though I have been a member of this army ever since the first going out and have seen desperate service in several stormings, I have not seen before; for every street was got by inches'. The fight ended about midnight as the Parliamentarians stormed the battery at the top of Gabriel's Hill.

Fairfax reckoned he killed 300 and took 1300, 'in the woods, hop yards, and fields, whither they fled', besides 3000 arms, 9 foot colours and 8 guns. The Penenden Heath mob took no part in the fighting, and dispersed peacefully. Norwich drew off some 3000 men, some of whom crossed the Thames to join Royalist insurgents in Essex. Trapped in Colchester they endured a horrific siege, which tied down the main army of both sides for the duration of the war.

Directions

Follow Fairfax's approach along the B2010 Lower Road through Tovil, and turn left along Stone Street (A229) into Maidstone. Casualties killed inside the town were buried in St Faith's Church.

Preston, 17 August 1648

England, Lancashire, LR102 SD5530–5631

Winwick (Red Bank), 19 August 1648

England, Lancashire, LR109 SJ5993–4

The so-called Battle of Preston was a sprawling three-day affair, extending nearly 30 miles (50 km) from the Ribble to the Mersey. More by luck than judgement Cromwell fell upon the flank of a straggling Scots army, and tumbled it piecemeal to its ruin.

Scottish intervention was the cornerstone of Royalist strategy, but the Kirk opposed the new war, and recruiting was slow. Hamilton did not cross the Border until 8 July 1648, bringing 10,500 men, only a third of the agreed number, to join Langdale's Northern Royalists. Further progress was delayed by the wettest summer in living memory, wrangling among the senior officers and lack of transport. Starving Scots ran off sheep and cattle, requisitioned cart horses and abducted children for ransom. Hamilton greatly outnumbered Lambert's Parliamentarian forces in Yorkshire, but made no attempt to defeat them before Cromwell arrived from South Wales, where he had been besieging Pembroke Castle until 11 July.

Hamilton decided to advance through Lancashire rather than confront Lambert in Yorkshire, heading directly for Preston, west of the Forest of Bowland. Langdale swung east through Settle to cover the left flank, or, as Clarendon suspected, to bear the first brunt, weakening the Episcopalian interest. Cromwell had already joined Lambert at Knaresborough. By the 15th he was across the Pennines at Gisburn, close behind Langdale.

Ignorant of Cromwell's presence, the Royalist column stretched 50 miles (80 km) from Warrington to Kirkby Lonsdale, Sir James Turner, a senior Scots officer, commenting, 'left hand not aware of what the right was doing'. Callander was in front with the horse, Hamilton at Preston with the newly raised Scots foot, Langdale's English away to his left. Major General George Monro's Ulster veterans trailed behind. On 16 August Cromwell's Council of War took the crucial decision to move along the northern bank of the Ribble, threatening to cut Hamilton off if he continued southwards. That night Cromwell slept at Stonyhurst Hall between Clitheroe and Longridge, nearer Preston than either of Hamilton's Scottish subordinates.

Cromwell reported that he had 2500 horse and dragoons of 'your old army' and 4000 similar foot, besides 500 Lancashire horse and 1500 Lancashire foot, 'in all about 8600'. This tallies with Captain Hodgson's account, 'betwixt Eight or Nine Thousand: a fine smart Army and fit for Action'. Some sources give more, suggesting Parliamentarian reinforcements arrived during the battle. Scots numbers are commonly overstated. Monro and most of the 4000 Scots cavalry missed the decisive clash at Preston, the horse only fighting during the subsequent retreat. None of the infantry regiments mustered even half strength when they surrendered at Warrington. Had 50 men accompanied each of the 150 colours captured, Hamilton would have fielded 7500 foot. Langdale claimed 600 horse and 3000 foot, a total of 11,100 Royalists out of a potential 16,700. Neither side had artillery.

Preston

	Winner	*Loser*
Opponents	Parliamentarian	Royalist
Commanders	Oliver Cromwell Major General John Lambert	James Hamilton, Duke of Hamilton James Livingstone, Earl of Callander General William Baillie Sir Marmaduke Langdale
Numbers	8600	16,700 (11,000 engaged)
Losses	unknown	5000

Winwick

	Winner	*Loser*
Opponents	Parliamentarian	Royalist
Commanders	Oliver Cromwell Major General John Lambert	James Hamilton, Duke of Hamilton (x) Lieutenant General John Middleton General William Baillie
Numbers	5500	7000
Losses	unknown	3000

On 17 August Baillie's infantry were set to continue south across Ribble Bridge, covered by Langdale to the northeast. It was late afternoon before Cromwell's forlorn hope (200 horse and 400 foot) closed with the enemy, 'in the enclosed grounds by Preston, on that side next us'. S.R. Gardiner identified the battlefield with Ribble Moor, where Ribbleton Lane, now the B6243 Longridge road, crosses Eaves Brook. The area is now largely built over, although a few open spaces around Ribbleton cemetery and the stream suggest the ground's original appearance. The Ordnance Survey marks another site, near Fulwood Barracks (SD5532), but this is well clear of Cromwell's generally accepted line of advance, taking him north of Preston, rather than south to Ribble Bridge, where he ended up.

The position was, according to Cromwell, 'totally inconvenient for our horse, being all enclosures and miry ground ... There being a lane, very deep and ill.' Elsewhere Cromwell called it 'as dirty a place as ever I saw horse stand in'. Langdale put his shot into the enclosures behind Eaves Brook, blocking the lane with 'a stand of pikes and a great body of colours' (Hodgson). Langdale told Clarendon he had requested the Scots to occupy a lane 'that would flank his men on the retreat', but this was not done. Unfortunately for the Royalists, the narrow five-arched Ribble Bridge lay on the Parliamentarian side of Preston, not beyond it. It proved impossible to defend, when exposed by Langdale's retreat, high ground at Frenchwood overlooking the open 'champaign' on the southern bank. Less than half a mile (0.8 km) beyond Ribble Bridge the road south crosses a second bridge over the River Darwen, past the village of Walton-le-Dale.

Cromwell's leading cavalry drove in the enemy

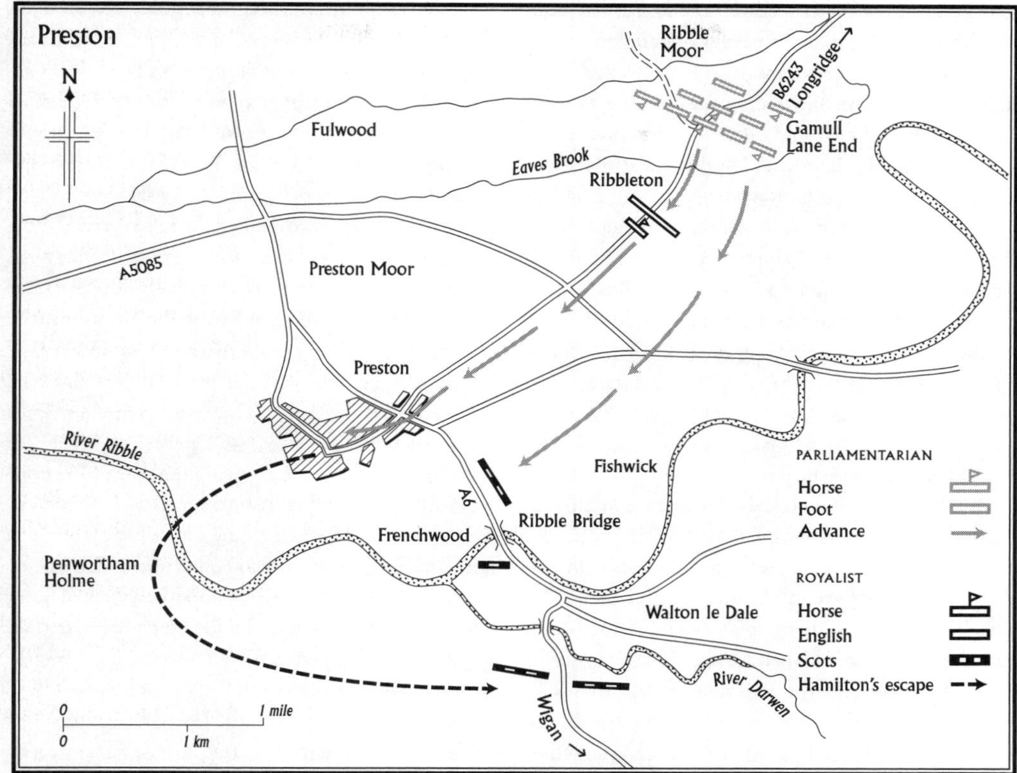

outposts, 'holding this dispute with them until our forlorn of foot came up for their justification, and by those we had opportunity to bring up our whole army'. The New Model Army had considerable expertise in hedge fighting, while Langdale's newly raised men 'shot at the skies, which did so encourage our men, that they were willing to venture upon any attempt ... we came up to the hedge end, and the enemy, many of them threw down their arms, and ran to their party, where was their stand of pikes' (Hodgson).

Meanwhile Cromwell drew up 'into as good a posture as the ground would bear', probably along Gamull Lane, 500 yards (450 m) east of Eaves Brook. He followed the example of Langport (1645), placing two regiments of horse in the centre to charge down the lane, with infantry to clear the enclosures either side, three regiments right and two left. More cavalry covered the outer flanks, the Lancashire troops in

Directions

Preston *Take the B6243 from the centre of town past the Blackpool Road (A5085) in Ribbleton, passing Cromwell Road on the left, to Brookfield where Eaves Brook crosses the main road, just short of the M6 motorway. Also see the monument on the modern A6 Ribble Bridge, built upstream from the old crossing. Darwen Bridge was replaced in its original location.*

reserve with another regiment of horse. The assault went in about four: 'At last we came to a hedge dispute, the greatest impression of the enemy being on our left wing, and upon the battle on both sides the lane, and upon our horse in the lane' (Cromwell). Hodgson's regiment was heavily engaged on the left, experiencing 'nothing but fire and smoke'. Lambert sent him to bring up the Lancashire foot, 'as good fighters and as great plunderers as ever went to a field'. If we believe Hodgson, their intervention south of Ribbleton Lane was decisive, 'and losing that wing the whole [Royalist] army gave way and fled'.

Cromwell describes a more general advance either side of the lane, 'in all which places the enemy were forced from their ground, after four hours dispute, until we came to the town'. Despite the disparity in numbers, success was hard won, 'the enemy shogging [moving intermittently] down towards the Bridge, and keeping almost all in reserve, that so he might bring fresh hands often to fight'. Langdale claimed to have defended the pass for six hours, until 'most of the Scots were drawn over the bridge, the Parliament forces pressed upon me in van and flanks, and so drove me into the town'. Later he told Clarendon 'that if one thousand foot had been sent to him he should have gained the day'.

Langdale's prolonged resistance gave Hamilton plenty of time to change the course of the battle. He failed to do so, allegedly saying, 'Let them alone – the English dogs are but killing one another.' The duke did try to draw up his infantry on Preston Moor, now Moor Park, but Callander had ridden back from Warrington without any troops, and argued Cromwell's horse would easily break Baillie's naked foot on the open ground. Langdale was left to his fate, while Baillie crossed the bridge, leaving two brigades on the north bank.

Cromwell's advance drove a wedge between the English and Scots Royalists. Four troops of Parliamentarian horse charged into Preston and cleared Church Street, while the leftmost foot broke through to the bridge along Fishwick Lane, destroying the two Scots brigades left there. Langdale's surviving infantry surrendered, while his cavalry fled towards Lancaster. Hamilton was trapped north of the river. He made a gallant stand with his mounted escort in Church Street, before swimming the Ribble at Penwortham Holme to rejoin his army at Walton Hall beyond the Darwen, 'where Lieutenant General Baillie had advantageously lodged the foot, on top of a hill, among very fencible enclosures'. Callander interfered again, sending 600 shot to contest Ribble Bridge, which the enemy commanded from the northern bank: 'So that our musketeers, having no shelter were forced to receive all the musket shot of Cromwell's infantry, which was secure within thick hedges; and after the loss of many men, were forced to run back to our foot' (Turner). As night fell, Parliamentarian foot stormed both bridges at push of pike, occupying the houses at Walton Green. Only darkness prevented further Royalist losses, so far amounting to 1000 dead and 4000 prisoners.

Against Baillie's advice, Hamilton accepted Callander's proposal to withdraw under cover of darkness, leaving the reserve ammunition behind. Morning found the Scots at Wigan Moor, 'half our number less than we were – most of the faint and weary having lagged behind' (Turner). The cavalry had rejoined, so Hamilton still outnumbered Cromwell, following with 2500 horse and 3000 foot. The other Parliamentarians were covering the rear at Preston, with orders to kill the prisoners if Monro appeared. The Scots considered fighting on Wigan Moor, but according to Turner it was 'environed with enclosures which commanded it', and many lacked powder or arms. They pressed on for Warrington, hoping to put the Mersey between themselves and the enemy.

Cromwell caught up with the Scots next day. Three miles (5 km) north of Warrington the A49 crosses Newton Brook at Red Bank, a prominent bluff between Newton-le-Willows and Winwick: 'a strait passage in that lane that they made very strong and forcible'. The Scots made a stand with pikes and lined the hedges with shot, 'who so roundly entertained the pursuing Enemy, that they were compelled to stop until the coming up of Colonel Pride's regiment'. Cromwell reported a resolute defence for many hours, 'coming to push of pike and very close charges'. Eventually country people showed the Parliamentarian soldiers a way round, 'so that they drove them up to that little green place of ground short of Winwick church, and there made a great slaughter of them'. Many ran into the church, 2000 Scots being taken prisoner, besides 1000 killed.

The Scots cavalry rode off at Warrington 'to preserve themselves for a better time', leaving Baillie's infantry to make the best terms they could. Cromwell granted quarter for life and civil usage, his horses being too exhausted to move beyond a walk. Hamilton surrendered at Uttoxeter on the 25th, after high words with Callander, 'each blaming the other for the misfortune and miscarriage of our affairs' (Turner). Callander escaped, but Hamilton was executed in March 1649. The final bill was 2000 dead and 8000–9000 prisoners, 'besides what are lurking in hedges and private places, whom the country people daily bring in or destroy'. The victors lost under 100 killed, 'yet many wounded ... our horse so exceedingly battered as I never saw in all my life' (Cromwell).

Preston crushed Royalist hopes, and deflated Presbyterian intrigues in London. Monro withdrew to Scotland, where the Kirk soon regained control after the Whiggamore Raid – the first historical use of 'Whig', a term of political abuse that lasted into the 19th century. Colchester surrendered on 27 August, its garrison reduced to eating rotten dog meat. Cromwell's despatch from Warrington urged speedy destruction of those who 'will not leave troubling the land'. Intended to rescue the king, Hamilton's expedition had sealed his fate.

Directions

Winwick *Fork left at the A49 roundabout north of junction 9 of the M62, passing church and green on the right. Red Bank is 1 mile (1.6 km) further, in Hermitage Green Lane.*

The Eleven Years' War

The Ulster rising of 1641 developed into an Eleven Years' War against English rule throughout Ireland. In June 1642 Irish Catholics of English and Gaelic origin formed the Confederation of Kilkenny to defend property and liberty against Protestant depredations. Early battles of the war are described above, under the heading, ''Twas Thus that the Wars Began'. The complexity of subsequent events defies ready summarization. Factional feuding prolonged hostilities, ensuring the insurgents achieved none of their aims. The Cromwellian settlement of the 1650s was disastrous for Irish Catholics, who saw their clergy exiled, their land confiscated and many transported to Connacht or the West Indies.

More than one observer blamed the Confederates for wasting the chance that the Civil Wars offered of reversing English colonization and establishing religious freedom for the Irish majority: 'It was not lack of manpower, provisions, equipment or enemy strength which took Ireland from them, but they themselves lost it for each other.' The Confederation held two-thirds of Ireland, including the wealthy southeast, but never eliminated English bridgeheads around Dublin and Cork. Personal jealousies hampered cooperation between provincial commanders: Thomas Preston in Leinster, Theobald Taafe in Munster, and Owen Roe O'Neill in Ulster. The Protestant Roger Boyle, Lord Broghill, thought them 'a people strangely given to destruction'.

The consequences of Confederate disunion were not immediately apparent. Their opponents were equally divided: English enclaves in Dublin under the Anglo-Irish Earl of Ormond (Marquess from October 1642) and in Cork under Lord Inchiquin; Presbyterian Scots in Ulster. The Covenanters had sent troops to protect Scottish planters when the 1641 rebellion started, the Scots remaining a power in northern Ireland until their defeat at Benburb (1646). Inchiquin, born Catholic but a political Protestant, changed sides twice. Nicknamed 'Murrough of the Burnings', his home-grown atrocities surpassed Cromwell's. As long as civil war continued at home, British forces could not crush the insurgents, who maintained a guerrilla war of attrition.

Despite Ormond's victory at Old Ross, Confederate troops overran all Ireland during 1643, except the coastal strip northeast of Dublin, and the Cork pocket. The Ormond ceasefire in September prevented the Confederates pinching out the last English footholds, and may have cost them the war. O'Neill destroyed the Scots army at Benburb too late to affect events in Britain, where the Royalists had just lost Naseby. Ultimately Ormond preferred English rebels to Irish. In July 1647 he surrendered Dublin to the Parliamentarian Colonel Jones, who promptly destroyed the Confederate army of Leinster at Dungan's Hill. The erstwhile Royalist Inchiquin joined the winners, and defeated the Munster Confederates at Knocknanuss (November 1647). Renewed civil war at home postponed English victory, however, until Jones had defeated an Ormondist–Confederate coalition at Rathmines (August 1649). After Charles I's execution, the Irish opponents of the Commonwealth fought for Charles's son, although personnel were mostly Catholic Irishmen, pursuing Confederate war aims. When Cromwell landed at Dublin on 15 August 1649, he proceeded to exploit Jones's destruction of the enemy's field armies by eliminating their fortresses, starting with Drogheda. Nothing has left such a stain upon Cromwell's reputation, but most Irish battles of the period ended with a massacre, including the Confederates' only major victory at Benburb. Later actions, such as Macroom (1650) and Knockbrack (1651), were incidental to sieges. The exception was Scarrifhollis (July 1650), where British settlers destroyed the army of Ulster, leaderless since O'Neill's death in November 1649.

Confederate and Royalist–Confederate armies were notably unsuccessful on the battlefield. Their defeats are sometimes attributed to the supposedly primitive nature of Celtic warfare. However, the Confederate armies used orthodox Continental tactics, picked up from veterans of the Spanish Army of Flanders who returned to Ireland during 1642. Garrett Barry, defeated at Liscarroll (1642), had published a manual recommending the Swedish formations O'Neill used at Benburb. Pikes and muskets replaced the improvised weapons of the original insurgents. The Supreme Council of the Confederation insisted companies muster 100 strong, 'two parts armed with muskets well fixed and a third part with serviceable pikes … upon pain of the captains' loss of their companies' (*Calendar of State Papers*).

Similarities between the hit-and-run tactics of the insurgents in 1641 and those of earlier Gaels arise from the circumstances of the insurgents rather than an atavistic fixation with obsolete tactics. Lacking the weapons and training to confront regular English troops, the insurgents launched opportunistic attacks on marching columns, hoping speed would neutralize enemy firepower. Zulu and Sudanese spearmen adopted similar tactics in the 19th century. The only troops who may have fought in some peculiarly Gaelic manner were Scottish Redshanks, from the Western Isles. Alasdair MacColla MacDonnell allegedly used the Highland charge against British planters in Ulster, before taking it to Scotland for Montrose's campaign (see above).

Weak discipline and deficient cavalry are better explanations for the poor performance of Irish armies. The rank and file often demanded action, against their commander's better judgement, only to break at the first shock at Kilrush and Rathmines. It took a great leader to hold them steady under artillery fire, as O'Neill did at Benburb. Irish armies rarely fielded more than 10 per cent horse, a third the favoured proportion. Most lacked armour, and some carried lances, suggesting a scarcity of pistols. At Liscarroll the Munster horse charged sword in hand, in order to close as rapidly as possible, giving the English no time to fire their carbines and pistols. Irish commanders often wasted their cavalry. At Scarrifhollis 'all the Irish horse, as well for want of grounde as for being devoide of management, was all the while idle spectators of this bloudie cathostrophe' (*An Aphorismical Discovery of Treasonable Faction*). Perhaps veterans of the enclosed countryside of Flanders misunderstood cavalry. Thomas Preston twice sent his down a narrow lane in column of threes, at Old Ross and Dungan's Hill. Often Irish cavalry rode off the battlefield, leaving their infantry to be cut to pieces. Such behaviour helps explain the allegations of treachery frequently levelled at Confederate commanders. Even in battle they could not escape the factionalism that blighted their cause.

Old Ross (Ballinvegga), **Saturday 18 March 1643**

Ireland, Co. Wexford, DS76 S7832–7931

Ormond began the 1643 campaigning season with an attempt to take the bridge over the River Barrow at New Ross, hoping to isolate Kilkenny from Confederate ports at Wexford and Waterford. A surprise attack narrowly failed, and Ormond became trapped between a reinforced garrison and Preston's Leinster army, 'not as before naked, now well armed and having a wise, warrlicke warrior their commander' (*An Aphorismical Discovery of Treasonable Faction*). Ormond was lucky to extricate himself after a narrow victory at Ballinvegga.

The Royalists abandoned the siege of New Ross on 17 March, and withdrew eastwards to Old Ross, 'intendinge ... to marche towards the mountains, the next way to Dublin, though sure to lose their ordinance by the bargane'. Preston only needed to hang on the Royalist flank and catch them strung out in some defile. Instead, 'he must compelle them to a stand ... and consequently to a battle' (*Aphorismical Discovery*). The armies met at 10 a.m. next morning, 3 miles (5 km) north of Old Ross, in the sparsely inhabited townland of Ballinvegga or Ballinafeeg. Ormond was heading north for the Templeludigan Gap between the Barrow and the Blackstairs Mountains, possibly at the suggestion of a Confederate double agent.

Preston lay on the right flank of Ormond's line of march, occupying 'a badd peece of roughe, marishe and boggish waie', separated from the enemy by 'a little foorde, where three horse at the most might come in brest deepe'. Contemporary Irish commentators criticized Preston's choice of position, 'setting it thicker with men than bore proportion with the place', and for its lack of offensive potential, 'a foolish posture of fight, rather of slaughter, if ever you intended to advance'. Ormond wheeled half right from the line of march, placing his cannon 'upon a hillocke in a goodly plaine, at the mouth of a narrow lane, *ex diametro* oppositt unto the said foorde, soe that none could pass ... without eminent danger of fallinge under the fumie reache of that murtheringe troncke [gun barrel]' (*Aphorismical Discovery*). English accounts distinguish between Ormond's initial hillside position west of Ballinvegga, and an advanced location on a small round hill nearer the River Aughennacrew, the stream separating the two armies. While the Royalists moved up, the Irish also pushed forward, crossing the stream to bring the opposing armies within musket shot.

Old Ross

	Winner	*Loser*
Opponents	Royalist	Confederate
Commanders	James Butler, Marquess of Ormond	Thomas Preston
Numbers	2700–3000	5650
Losses	20	200

Ormond had left Dublin with 800 horse, 2500 foot, two culverins and four field guns. Clarendon, in his *History of the Rebellion*, reduced these to 500 horse and 2200 foot at Ballinvegga; parliamentary reports specified 3000. The crews of two English ships sunk during the siege of New Ross manned Ormond's guns, a small but useful reinforcement. Old Ross was one Civil War battle where artillery mattered. Contemporary English sources claimed 6000–7000 Irish, but historians prefer the figure given by Richard Bellings, the Confederation's secretary, of 650 horse and 5000 infantry. The weather was in Ormond's favour, a strong southwesterly blowing rain and snow into the enemy's faces.

Between 2 and 3 p.m. Preston launched a cavalry attack down the covered *borreen* or lane between the opposing armies, in the teeth of the English guns, as described by Bellings:

> Immediately the ordinance played from the eminence where they were planted upon the first squadron of horse ... with such successe, as they were forced to break their rankes, and having noe roome in the ground whereas they were engaged, whither to retire or rally, and being placed in the head of the foote, they forced their way back, and disordered the army.

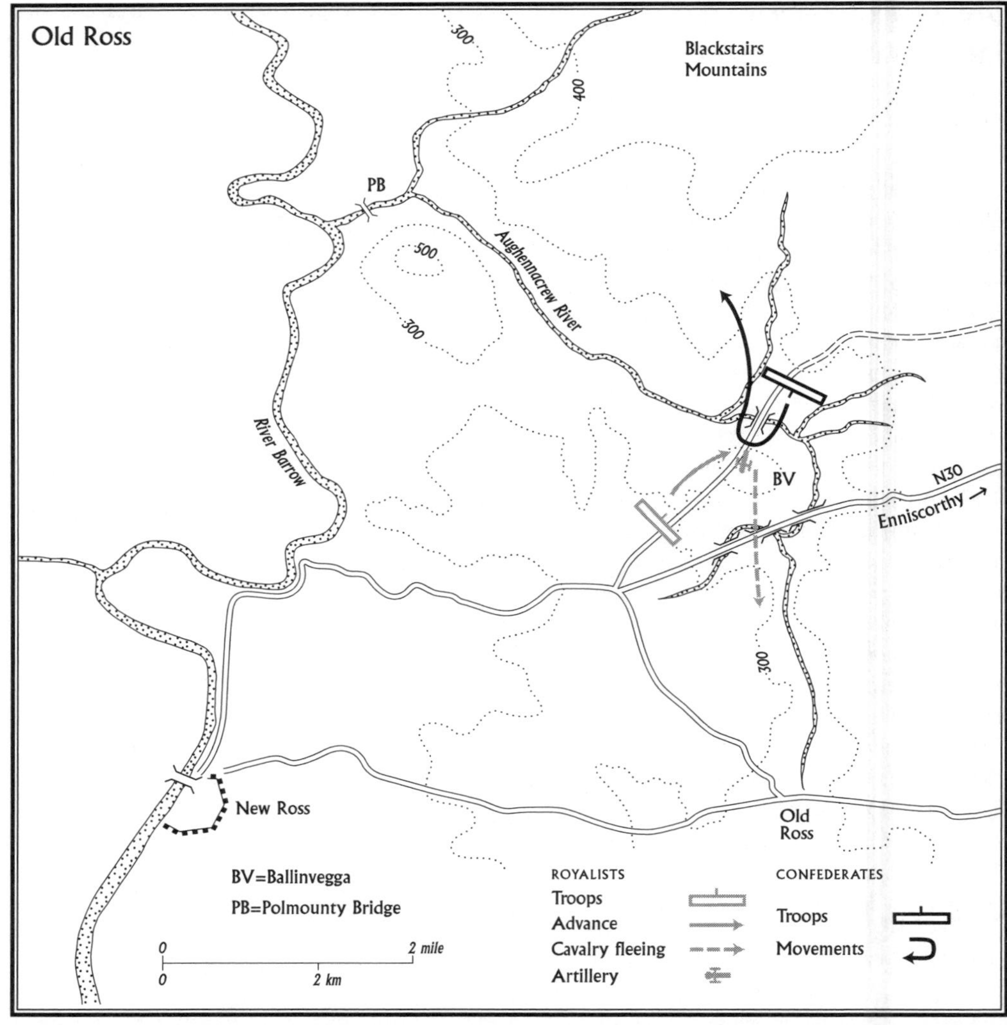

Another body of Confederate horse did better, driving back the Royalist right wing cavalry. One of the latter wrote: 'Suddenly they [the mingled cavalry] went all away slashing each other, leaving both armies of foot standing in the fields' (Sir Francis Willoughby). Hostile witnesses testified to hearing the Royalist cavalry commander call out, desperate to reach the nearest seaport, 'Ten pounds for a guide to Duncannon! Twenty pounds for a guide to Duncannon!' Irish horse penetrated the Royalist gun line, but were either killed or captured. Still discomposed and under artillery fire, the Irish foot never stirred to second their cavalry, 'wherein' thought the *Aphorismical Discovery*, 'the generall proved either drunk, a foole, or a traytor'.

Ormond refused to quit his infantry at this critical

Directions

The battlefield is just north of the N30 New Ross–Enniscorthy road. Fork left at Corcoran's Cross Roads, 3½ miles (5.5 km) east of New Ross, along a minor road. Ballinvegga is 1½ (2.5 km) miles further moment, quelling panic, while the tactical experts debated what to do. Finally the Royalist infantry officers decided to launch an immediate assault, supported by the still intact cavalry from their left wing. Preston's infantry crumbled and 'brake all into pieces' as more English horse returned to the field, Ormond's chaplain George Creichton describing the fugitives twinkling through the powder smoke 'like motes in the sun'.

The victory was marred by the escape of the Irish infantry over the Barrow at Graiguenamanagh; Ormond's ragged troopers were too busy stripping the dead to pursue the living. In any case the English were unwilling to push beyond the obstacles that disrupted Preston's attacks. Bellings claimed the loss was 'very inconsiderable ... for soe greate a victory, there being scarce 100 men slaine upon the place'. An Englishman who 'viewed the field from one end to another' reckoned double that. The Royalists admitted 20 dead, with no figure for wounded.

Old Ross had no immediate consequence. Ormond's tactical success concealed his strategic failure, while Preston's survival robbed his defeat of meaning. The battle underlined the stalemate between government and insurgents, possibly contributing to the ceasefire later that year.

Benburb, Friday 5 June 1646

Ireland, Co. Tyrone, DS19 H7952–8052

Benburb

	Winner	*Loser*
Opponents	Confederate	Scots
Commanders	Owen Roe O'Neill	General Robert Monro
Numbers	5500	5600–5800
Losses	100–270	*c.*2500

The Scots army in Ulster was remote from Dublin and Kilkenny, on the fringes of the Eleven Years' War. It was left largely undisturbed until in 1646 its commander-in-chief, General Monro, attempted something more ambitious than the usual cattle raid, precipitating the one Protestant disaster of the war, at Benburb.

The Scots left their quarters in Co. Down and Co. Antrim on 2 June, intending to rendezvous with British forces from Derry and Coleraine. Documents found on the battlefield suggest Monro's ultimate objective was the Confederation's headquarters at Kilkenny. The recent arrival in Ireland of a papal nuncio, Cardinal Rinuccini, with money and arms, gave Owen Roe O'Neill, the Confederation's commander in Ulster, the means to frustrate Monro's grand concept. O'Neill occupied Benburb, a central position between Monro's scattered forces. The Scots advanced from Armagh to eliminate the threat to their allies, but found O'Neill secure behind the River Blackwater, not far from the place of his uncle's victory at Yellow Ford (1598). Monro committed his weary army to a circuitous outflanking manoeuvre through Caledon, 'to cross the water there and so to draw the enemy from his advantage'. He finally came up with O'Neill a mile (1.6 km) west of Benburb, late on 5 June.

Monro reported his numbers as 3400 foot, 11 troops of horse (perhaps 550), and 6 field guns. Independent sources suggest he had more: 6 Scots infantry regiments and 4 British at 500 apiece, and 600–800 cavalry. O'Neill had used Rinuccini's cash to create the best Confederate army of the war, 5000 thoroughly trained infantry in 7 regiments with 500 cavalry in 9 troops, but no guns. Only half the foot had muskets, but an anonymous British Officer of Sir John Clotworthy's regiment thought the pikes 'longer by a foot or two than the Scottish pikes, and farr better to pierce, being four square and small'.

O'Neill held a strong position at Drumflugh, a hill overgrown with scrub, his front covered by 'scrogs and bushes' and a stream flowing across his front into the Blackwater on his left. He put four regiments in front, three more in support covering the intervals. O'Neill was not ready to fight, having detached most of his horse to Dungannon to eliminate a smaller British column approaching his rear from Coleraine. He sent the remaining troop and

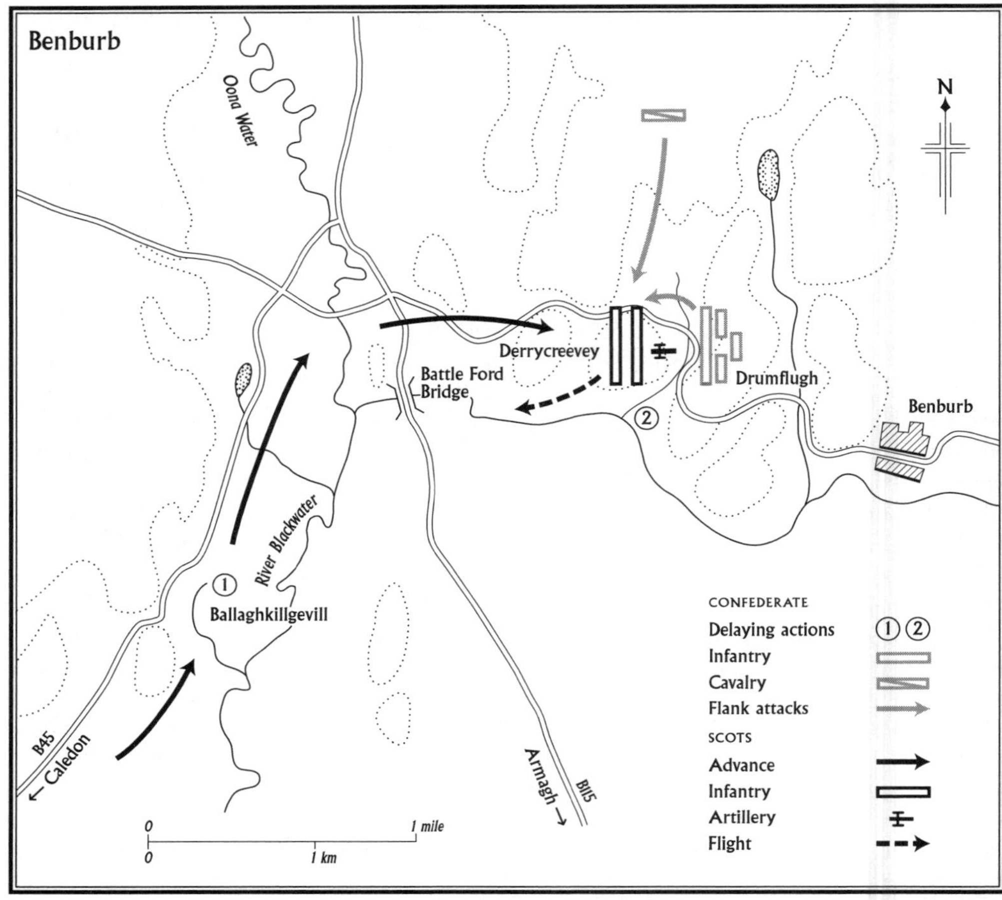

1000 musketeers down the left bank of the Blackwater to delay Monro's approach. The Confederate forlorn hope met the Scots cavalry at Ballaghkillgevill (H7751), 'where they saluted one another very roughly ... and then retired through places as secure from Horse as they could, giving Fire in the Rear' (British Officer). The area was presumably more wooded than today.

By six in the evening Monro had beaten in O'Neill's commanded men, and occupied Derrycreevey hill, 'having the Blackwater on the right hand and a marsh bog on the left wing ... being drawn up in the plaine ... our peeces before us and our horsemen behind [as] our reserve ... it being impossible for the enemy to charge us but in our van'. Monro also enjoyed the weather gauge, 'wind and sun shining and blowing in his back and in the verie face of the Irish' (*An Aphorismical Discovery of Treasonable Faction*).

Scots cavalry and musketeers tried several times to force the Irish left, 'down next the river in scroggie woods ... often put to the worse and beaten back' (British Officer). Artillery fire overshot the target, landing awkwardly above them on the hillside. O'Neill's infantry clamoured to advance, but he held

Directions

Follow Monro's route west from Armagh along the A28 to Caledon, and north along the B45. Turn right at the bend in the Blackwater along the B128, passing north of Derrycreevey and across Drumflugh.

them back. An hour before sunset the Confederate cavalry reappeared, sweaty but victorious, and both sides prepared for closer action.

O'Neill finally sent his men forward after sunset: 'In the name of the Father, Son, and Holy Ghost advance, and give not Fire till you are within Pike-Length.' Monro sent cavalry to disrupt the attack, but the troopers were Irish and refused to charge: the Confederates overran Monro's gun line 'and broke upon the enemie to their very battalion' (*Aphorismical Discovery*). According to Monro, 'our foot stood to it, and received the enemies battalions body to body with push of pike', but the Scots were exhausted after hours marching and standing about under fire. 'Faint and heartless', they failed to back their officers as they should have done. O'Neill's own regiment, on the right of his line, wheeled into the melee's outer flank, slewing the Scots around, with the setting sun in their eyes and the river at their backs. A final Scots cavalry charge broke, and 'fell pell-mell among our foot', leaving their shattered infantry 'no way of retreat but to wade the Blackwater where it was scarcely fordable' (Monro).

Most of Monro's foot perished between Derrycreevey and today's Battlefield Bridge. Casualty figures vary from Monro's 500–600 to the tabloid headline 'bloody fight at Blackwater in Ireland, where almost 5000 Protestants were put to the sword'. The actual toll probably lay between the anonymous British Officer's 1800–1900 plus 150 officer prisoners, and the official Irish bodycount of 3000. Spoils included Monro's wig and 30 colours, beside flags cut up for hatbands and 'such like foperies'. Camp followers searched for loved ones among the dead:

> The tail behinde made known the English race,
> The blewe chapt yarde [bonnet] bewrayed the
> Scottish face.
>
> Contemporary ballad

Much to everyone's surprise this overwhelming success failed to secure Ulster for the Confederates. Instead O'Neill turned his army against members of the Confederation wanting to treat with Ormond. The only Irish victory of the war was thrown away as the Confederates squabbled among themselves.

Dungan's Hill, Sunday 8 August 1647

Ireland, Co. Meath, DS49 N8546

The annihilation of a Confederate army at Dungan's Hill is largely forgotten, its grim reality offering little scope for nationalist myth-making. Nevertheless, it helped split the Confederation, paving the way for Cromwell's reconquest of Ireland.

Confederate divisions prevented them occupying Dublin after Benburb. Cardinal Rinuccini vetoed renewal of the Ormond ceasefire, but countermanded a promising advance on Dublin by the Leinster army, whose leaders he distrusted. Preston loitered near Dublin after Ormond's surrender to Parliament, ignoring intelligence regarding the aggressive intentions of the new Parliamentarian commander, Colonel Michael Jones. Preston took Naas and Maynooth in July 1647, and besieged Trim, Jones's last significant outpost inland.

Jones reacted promptly. On 1 August he joined forces with British garrisons at Drogheda and Dundalk, compelling Preston to withdraw to Portlester on the Stonyford River, an old refuge of O'Neill's. When Jones invested Tremblestown Castle, northwest of Trim, Preston slipped south, hoping to surprise Dublin's skeleton garrison. He spent the night of 7–8 August at Agher, but got away too slowly next morning. Preston had hardly gone 2 miles (3 km) when Jones overtook him about 10 o'clock, near Drumlargan on the Trim–Maynooth road: 'the very untowardest place that nature cold devise'.

Two miles (3 km) south of Cnoc an Linsigh or Lynch's Hill, near Summerhill, the highway crosses a ridge at right angles, passing between a ruinous church and a copse known as Cruachan or Crookahane. Preston's infantry formed up on the forward slope, facing north, 'in a brave field of wheate, not yet reepe, the rigges soe toughe and highe and the corne so extraordinarie high growen, that neither horse nor foote could doe much service there' (*An Aphorismical Discovery of Treasonable Faction*). The outline of a large square field delineated by a thick

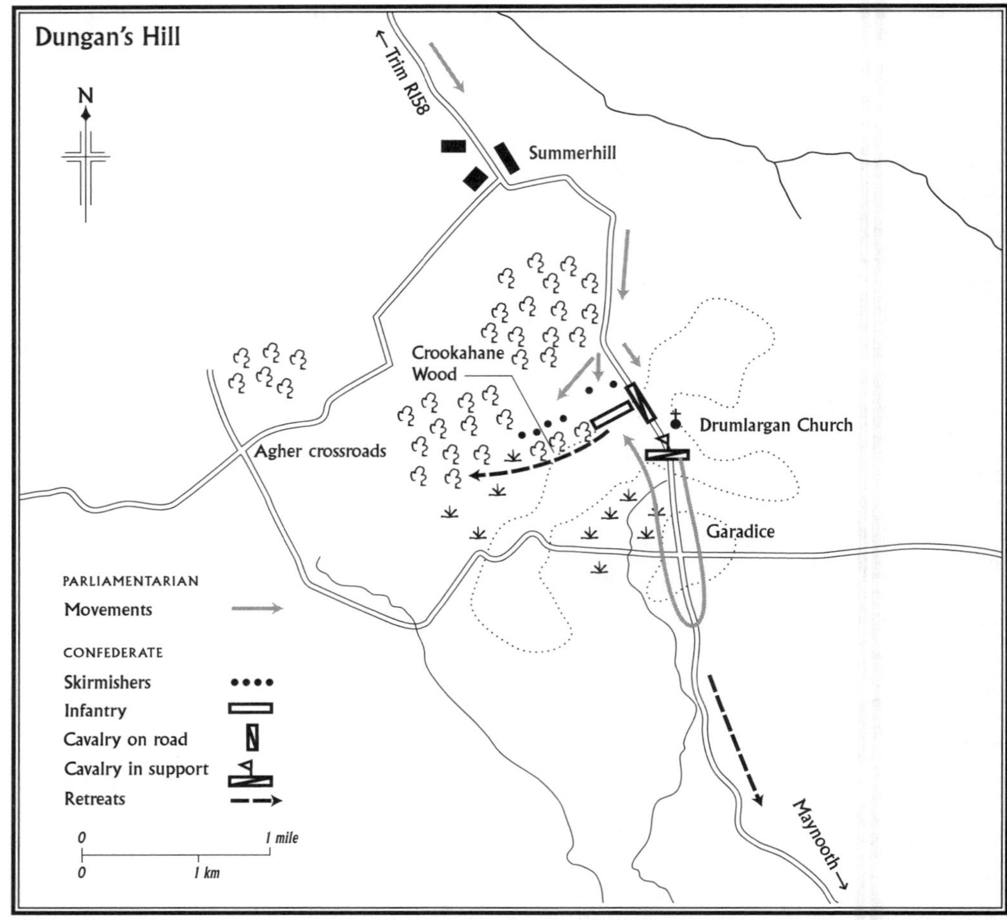

embankment can still be distinguished amidst the later patchwork of smaller enclosures.

Pay records show Preston had nine regiments numbering 5498 foot, of whom the muster master reckoned 4000 fought at Dungan's Hill. Regular cavalry numbered 596 in 15 troops, reinforced by a similar number of temporary troopers. He divided these into three bodies:

> (1) four troops (200) on the right of the foot, 'unto a narrow lane that three onely horse might goe in breste on either side with high strong ditches with twenty years growth of quick sett [hazel hedge]';
> (2) 650 men in support, probably in right rear of the corn field, the only good going;
> (3) seven troops (350) quarter of a mile (0.4 km) further back, 'in a vallie and upon a straight, who could neither see nor come to any of the said parties' (*Aphorismical Discovery*).

Right of the road was 'a goodly plaine made fallow and already harrowed'. Further left, 800 Red-

Directions

Follow the R158 northwest from Maynooth. The battlefield is 1 mile (1.6 km) past Garadice, just north of the crossroads by Drumlargan church. Dungan's Hill is distinct from Dangan's Castle north of Summerhill, which played no part in the battle.

shanks occupied a bog, whose location has caused much difficulty. G. A. Hayes-McCoy, placed them right of the road, but contemporary maps show another bog 'southe and by west of the said fallowe', where swampy ground went undrained until 1812. The Redshanks were veterans of Montrose's campaign, Scots Highlanders under Irish command. Descriptions of the battle emphasize their ferocity, but lack of pikes made them vulnerable to cavalry, explaining their occupation of the bog. Preston's well equipped artillery train included four demi-culverins, heavy 9-pounder field guns.

Jones brought 1500 horse and 5000 foot to the field, with nine guns. They went straight into action from the line of march, meeting the enemy too suddenly for elaborate manoeuvres: 'The enemie arriving in their full marche, never offering to plant theire field peeces, or other warrlicke posture, but as they were advanced towards the horse in the said lane, pell mell ran towards them, as deepe as they pleased'. Five hundred Parliamentarian horse attacked Preston's cavalry, who were trapped in a defile, 'not able to stir forward, backwards, or on either side, for want of ground' (*Aphorismical Discovery*). Some escaped through gaps opened in the hedges by friendly infantry. Thirty were killed. The Parliamentarians pressed on, overrunning Preston's guns and driving the remaining cavalry before them in a 2-mile (3-km) flight.

Meanwhile Jones's infantry advanced upon the main Confederate position. They also tangled with the Redshanks, 'whoe bravelie opposed, causing the bould enemie to stagger, [and] three several times broke upon them'(*Aphorismical Discovery*). The Parliamentarians made little impression upon the Confederate regular infantry inside their ditches. They soon realized these prevented anyone helping the Redshanks, and concentrated against the latter, who 'broke through those that charged them, with some loss, and escaped through a moss where no horse could follow' (British Officer).

The return of Jones's horse sealed the fate of Preston's foot. Attacked front and rear, the Leinster infantry 'for a long time resisted and often beat off the horse [but] were at length forced to retire to a bog near adjoining' (Richard Bellings). This was presumably the ground beyond Preston's initial position, originally occupied by the Redshanks. His infantry were therefore retreating forwards, into a pocket surrounded by the enemy. Perhaps a thousand escaped the trap, leaving the rest to seek quarter. Between 1500 and 3000 were massacred, before or after surrender; English and Irish sources disagree which. Their graves were unknown until the 1980s, when bones were ploughed up near Drumlargan church. Some 500 prisoners were taken, and 'convoyed unto Dublin in a most miserable condition'.

Parliament's immediate attempts to exploit Jones's victory stalled, but Dungan's Hill combined with Knocknanuss in November to tear the Confederation apart. Military defeat weakened the conciliatory Old English, shifting the balance of power in favour of diehard fanatics, dependent upon Cardinal Rinuccini and O'Neill's Catholic army of Ulster.

Dungan's Hill

	Winner	*Loser*
Opponents	Parliamentarian	Confederate
Commanders	Colonel Michael Jones	Thomas Preston
Numbers	6500	6000
Losses	60	2000–3000

Knocknanuss (Knocknegoall), **Saturday 13 November 1647**

Ireland, Co. Cork, DS73 R4304

The largest battle ever fought in Munster would be entirely forgotten except for the death of Montrose's lieutenant, Alasdair MacColla MacDonnell. And yet Knocknanuss was no provincial foray, but a decisive downturn in Confederate fortunes.

Murrough O'Brien, Earl Inchiquin, was the hard-boiled victor of Liscarroll (1642). His latest exploit was to sack Cashel, his troops piling turfs of peat against the Rock to incinerate its defenders. Taafe

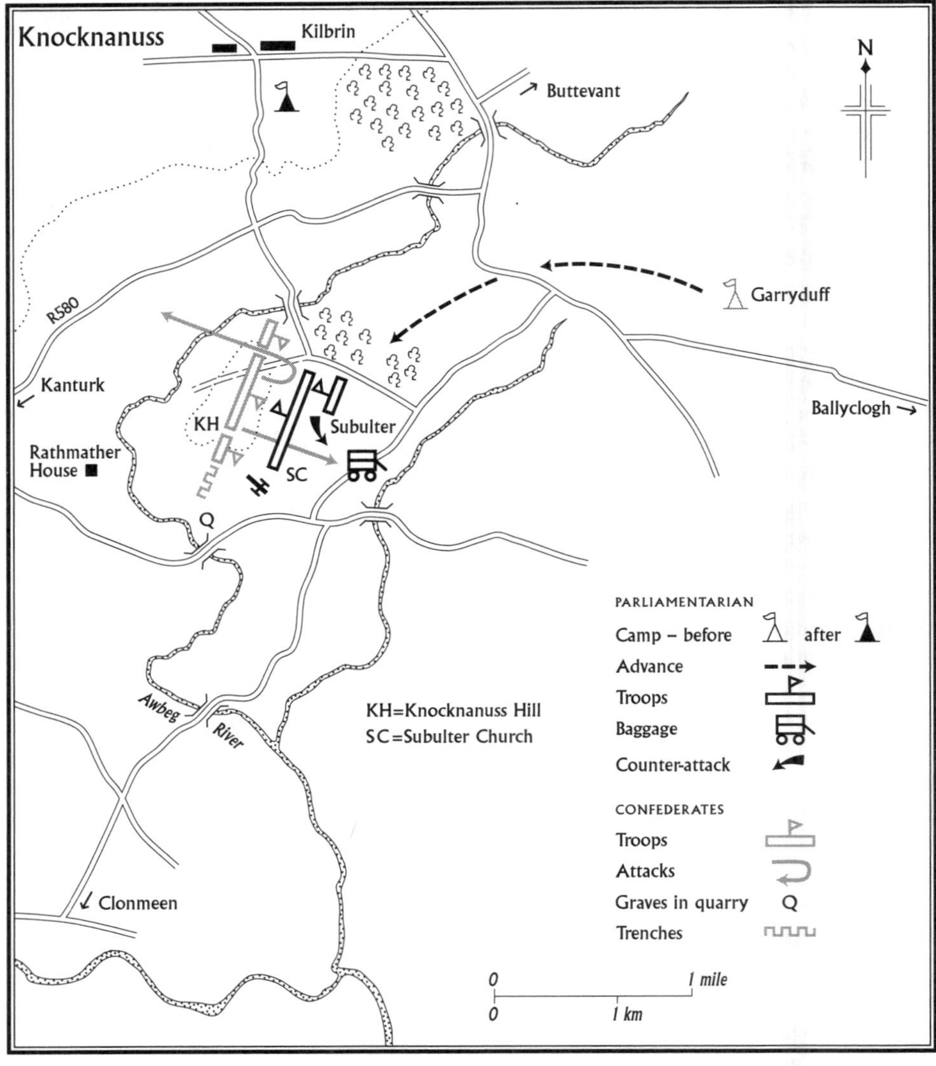

was a simple Cavalier, 'a fencer, a runner of a tilte, a brave generous gamester, and an exceedingly good potator in any liquor you please' (*An Aphorismical Discovery of Treasonable Faction*). He kept clear of the dread 'Murrough of the Burnings' until reinforced by three Connacht regiments and MacColla's 1500 Redshanks for a descent upon Inchiquin's winter quarters: 'a season as unapt for action to the naked English, as opportune for the Irish better inured and accommodated to the hardships of that Country'

Directions

From Kanturk follow the R580 Buttevant road 4 miles (6 km) eastwards. Turn right onto a minor road across the Awbeg, to a T-junction where a farm track on the right leads over Knocknanuss. MacColla was reputedly buried in Clonmeen churchyard, 1 mile (1.6 km) east of Banteer. Other combatants' bones were removed to the crypt of St Mary's Abbey, south of Buttevant on the N20.

Knocknanuss		
	Winner	*Loser*
Opponents	Parliamentarian	Confederate
Commanders	Murrough O'Brien, Earl Inchiquin	Taafe, Lord Theobald Alasdair MacColla MacDonnell (k)
Numbers	c.5200	c.8540
Losses	c.1000	c.3000

(*A Perfect Narrative of the Battell of Knocknones*).

Inchiquin mustered at Mallow on 12 November, and headed northwest through Ballyclogh to meet Taafe at Knocknanuss, a wedge-shaped hill 3 miles (5 km) west of Kanturk. Knocknanuss – from the Irish *Cnoc na nos*, 'Hill of the Fawns' – is also known as Shrubhill or Englishman's Hill, hence the battle's alternative name, Knocknegoall (Irish *gall*, 'foreigner'). It rises steeply to its highest point at the southwest corner, and gradually declines eastwards to level fields, divided by hedges and ditches. The short November day being spent, Inchiquin halted 2 miles (3 km) short of the enemy, at Garryduff.

Some reconstructions of the battle place Taafe's army across the northern tip of Knocknanuss, looking north, presenting its right flank to Inchiquin. This is inherently unlikely. Taafe would naturally occupy the length of the hill, facing the enemy, the River Awbeg securing his flanks and rear:

(1) Armies usually form up across their line of approach, which in Taafe's case was from Kanturk, directly west of Knocknanuss. Inchiquin reports that the enemy occupied the hill immediately the two sides established visual contact, when he was still at Garryduff. Therefore Taafe faced east.

(2) The *Perfect Narrative* describes 'the enemie ranging their battell in a plaine front all along the hill', not across one end of it.

(3) The Awbeg loops northwards around Knocknanuss, impeding offensive movements. Accounts of the battle provide no evidence of such an obstruction.

(4) Inchiquin deliberately took ground to his left at the start of the battle, to neutralize sun and wind. The time was early afternoon, when the sun would be southwest, the prevailing wind direction. Had Inchiquin's troops initially faced south rather than west, advancing their left would have brought sun and wind more directly into their faces.

(5) Field names and relics associate fighting with the southerly end of the ridge. Entrenchments in 'the hollow glen of battle' south-southwest of Knocknanuss, have yielded skulls, spurs and musket balls. The dead were deposited still further south, in a quarry towards the river.

(6) The Irish fled through Kanturk, Newmarket and Liscarroll. The latter is north of Knocknanuss, an unlikely direction to retreat if Inchiquin attacked from that quarter.

It seems more probable that Inchiquin continued his approach from the east, wheeling through Ballyrusheen, the Awbeg on his right, and on his left a smaller stream flowing towards Bannagh Bridge. He then swung down into the fields around Subulter church, bringing sun and wind onto his left, threatening Taafe's open southern flank.

A paper recovered from MacColla's body showed the Confederates mustered 1076 horse and 7464 foot, compared with 1200 and 4000 Parliamentarians respectively. However, most of Taafe's infantry had pikes, while two-thirds of Inchiquin's were musketeers. Taafe's Munster army took the left, MacColla's reinforcements the right, nine divisions of foot in all, winged by three bodies of horse on each flank. Inchiquin marshalled his foot in three divisions of two regiments each, seven troops of horse on the right and six on the left. The Confederate deployment had the serious flaw that the hill stopped the two halves of their army seeing each other, exacerbating their usual lack of cohesion.

Inchiquin had no intention of tackling Taafe directly, preferring to draw him down by fire and movement: 'We drew to the right hand of them and found a piece of ground, within a convenient distance to play with ordnance upon their right wing [i.e. within half a mile], where I caused two pieces to play … that I might discompose the form they were in …'At the same time, Inchiquin pushed infantry forward to a ditch at the foot of the hill, 'that they might be ready to fall on'. The Munster Confederates took two rounds from the artillery before they charged down the hill, cavalry first. Inchiquin's right-hand musketeers 'poured such showers of hail upon them (that it proved a funeral peall to many) the rest retired foul and routed their own foot' (*Perfect Narrative*). Taafe's main body of foot and left wing of horse ran clean away, ignoring all his efforts to stop them.

The Irish did better on the other flank. Their horse broke one of Inchiquin's squadrons, the rest of whom were too busy to notice MacColla's Redshanks charging through the powder smoke, 'thundering down without the least sense of danger ... rouling downe like a torrent'. They overran the forlorn hope and their outnumbered supports, captured two guns, turning one of them upon its owners, 'and so tearing down all before them got to our wagons and there fell a plundering' (*Perfect Narrative*). MacColla's last hurrah is ironically the best-documented example of a Highland charge during the Civil Wars. Cardinal Rinuccini, from Confederation headquarters in Kilkenny, described how, 'after firing one or two vollies', the Redshanks 'threw away the musket, and seizing the sword rushed upon the enemy with such fury that they pursued for three miles'. Opinions on the charge's effect vary. Rinuccini claimed the Redshanks killed 2000 Parliamentarians, more than their opponent's total number. Inchiquin and the *Perfect Narrative* admitted only 40 or 50 common soldiers slain, besides 'divers of our galantest commanders', who stood and fought to the death.

Taafe's flight left MacColla isolated, allowing Inchiquin's cavalry reserves from the right wing to deal with the Redshanks. *Aphorismical Discovery* suggests this was the only serious fighting, as they 'gave a wheel and came in rear of the redshanks ... then began the mortalitie on either side, the event doubtful'. The heroic Scots 'never yieldinge, but rather gaining grounde, were all for the most part slaughtered'. MacColla may have got quarter, but not for long. The most likely story is that a local gentleman, 'coming to him with a naked sword, did thrust him through contrarie to all lawes of both armes and nations'. MacColla had never treated his own enemies any better. The battle started just before 2 p.m., by Inchiquin's watch, 'and lasted not above half a quarter of an hour'.

Inchiquin reckoned 3000 Irish died, nearly half Taafe's infantry, 'though we were killing till night as fast as we could'. Apart from MacColla's three regiments, 'the rest made the best use they could of their heels'. The victors recovered 38 colours and nearly 6000 arms, 'so much the more considerable a loss, because scarcity of arms amongst them is very great' (Inchiquin). The victors overran the surrounding country, 'notwithstanding the violence of the weather', the soldiers crying out 'Home! Home! it being a deepe snow, and his men almost naked' (*Perfect Narrative*). The Supreme Council of the Confederation despaired at the twin disasters of Dungan's Hill and Knocknanuss, by which 'our two most flourishing armies [were] defeated and brought to nought'.

Rathmines (Baggot Rath), **2 August 1649**

Ireland, Co. Dublin, DS50 O1631–2

The last battle in Dublin before the Easter Rising of 1916 was appropriately decisive. Rathmines opened the way for overwhelming English forces to enter Ireland, ending any residual hope of a political settlement to the Eleven Years' War.

Charles I's execution and the destruction of two out of three Confederate armies at Dungan's Hill and Knocknanuss inspired an unstable coalition of Royalists, moderate Confederates and Parliamentarian turncoats, under Ormond's overall leadership. Inchiquin switched sides again, leaving O'Neill the only Irish leader outside this last-ditch alliance against English Puritanism. Michael Jones could not withstand their combined efforts. By July 1649 only Dublin remained in Parliamentarian hands.

Ormond approached the city on 24 July with the largest Irish army of the Civil Wars, 'no less than seven thousand foot and about four thousand horse' (Clarendon, *History of the Rebellion*). Not trusting his mutually hostile and often defeated soldiers to storm the city, he left 2500 men to blockade the north side, taking the rest across the River Liffey to invest the south. He camped near Rathmines at Palmerston Park, a quarter of a mile (0.4 km) west of Milltown Bridge. Before the area was built over, Rathmines commanded a fine prospect of Dublin's defences, from the Coombe past the top of Grafton Street to Trinity College.

Ormond may have only had 7000–8000 men under command, after Inchiquin withdrew to oppose a possible English landing in Munster. The battlefield was unusually wide, extending across open fields between St Stephen's Green and the River Dodder, taking in the modern suburbs of Ranelagh, Ballsbridge and Donnybrook. The investing detachments were not mutually supporting and neglected to build sconces and forts, leaving them 'exposed to the blunt of all hazard' (*An Aphorismical Discovery of Treasonable Faction*). The Royalists also failed to mount cannon at Ringside on the southern shore of Dublin Bay, permitting powerful English reinforcements to arrive by sea on 25 July. The new arrivals gave Jones as many troops as Ormond, 1900 horse and 6000 foot, but of superior quality.

Rather than withdraw, Ormond's junior ranks insisted on pressing the siege more closely. They argued the occupation of Baggotrath Castle would deny the enemy access to grazing between Dublin and the Dodder, and force them to surrender. Baggotrath Castle was less than a mile (1.6 km) outside Dublin's defences, near Macartney Bridge, where Baggot Street crosses the Grand Canal (O1632). On the night of 1–2 August, Ormond sent a strong party to repossess the castle, 1500 foot with pioneers and materials for repairs. He himself stood by all night with the rest of the army. Next morning Ormond found the work incomplete, the officer responsible claiming he had got lost in the dark. There was no sign of a hostile response, so Ormond appointed another officer to complete the task, and about 9 o'clock went to lie down in his tent. Other Royalist officers followed his example, and left their posts.

Rathmines

	Winner	*Loser*
Opponents	Parliamentarian	Royalist
Commanders	Colonel Michael Jones	James Butler, Marquess of Ormond
Numbers	7900	7000–8000
Losses	46 dead	3117

The Parliamentarian commanders, however, had 'taken the occasion by the foretopp'. At dawn they were ready, under cover of burnt-out houses at Lazar's or Lowsey Hill near Pearse Station, and in a hollow between the Liffey and Baggotrath. At 10 o'clock they advanced briskly on Baggotrath, across the meadows between the future Merrion Square and Grand Canal. With 1200 horse and 4000 foot, Jones soon overran the unsupported 1500 Royalist foot around the castle, 'who finding their horse not so ready to assist them as they expected, quitted the place with all imaginable confusion' (Clarendon). Cavalry intended to support the working parties failed to do so, '2000 horse lyinge in the same field, never offered to relieve those until they were broken' (*Aphorismical Discovery*). Ormond's commissary general of horse charged with what troopers he could collect, but was killed, his men fleeing across the Dodder. Ormond led two more regiments forward, but they too were scattered with the loss of their colonels: 'After which there was no more fighting worthy relating, but all took the Run' (British Officer).

Encouraged by the Royalists' disorder, Jones carried on, wheeling to his right through Ranelagh, 'across a large ploughed field looking towards the castle'. Meanwhile the cavalry took a broader arc along the left bank of the Dodder, through Donnybrook and Clonskeagh. This brought them behind Ormond's centre, composed of Inchiquin's erstwhile Parliamentarian regiments, who made little difficulty about surrendering at Rathgar Wood.

There is no record of where Ormond's left flank went, but presumably they escaped in good time, as did their comrades north of the Liffey: 'in lesse than two howers, never a man of Ormond's partie was founde neere Dublin, other than such as weer killed, taken prisoner, or became of the enemie partie' (*Aphorismical Discovery*). The Royalists were surprised, and beaten in detail: 'most of them never thought that fighting would come to their turn, and so were gaping on till they were Routed without fighting' (British Officer). In Ormond's defence, Clarendon found 'nothing strange that so well governed and disciplined soldiers [the Parliamentarians] should overcome a less number of raw, new levied, and unpractised men under inexperienced officers'.

The Royalists' speedy collapse limited the butcher's bill to 600 (though Jones claimed 4000 killed), but they lost 2517 prisoners, many of whom took service with the enemy. The moral effect of Rathmines was immense, turning the tide of the war. Ormond admitted 'the dejection it brings on the best inclined'. A fortnight later Cromwell landed at Dublin, his task greatly simplified.

Directions

Follow Baggot Street southeast from St Stephen's Green across the Grand Canal, where the battle swung west across the main N11 and R117 roads. Suburban development obscures the lie of the land, although Ormond Road commemorates the Royalist stand opposite Rathmines College, the site of Rathmines Castle, off Palmerston Road. Visit Rathfarnham Castle, taken by the Royalists before the battle.

Drogheda (Tredagh), Tuesday 11 September 1649

Ireland, Co. Louth, DS43 O0975

The fall of Drogheda and its attendant massacre have assumed mythical significance as one of the horror stories of Irish history. No other event has so damaged Cromwell's reputation, though other defeats had as dire consequences for Irish freedom, and cost more lives.

Cromwell gave the Royalists no time to rebuild their field army after Rathmines. Just a week after his own troops had landed, he left Dublin for Drogheda, with a picked force: six horse regiments and eight foot, some 4000 and 8000 men respectively. The siege train, the best yet seen in Ireland, went by sea.

Drogheda

	Winner	*Loser*
Opponents	Parliamentarian	Royalist
Commanders	Oliver Cromwell	Sir George Aston (k)
Numbers	10,000–12,000	3100
Losses	150	3500 [sic]

Drogheda is the River Boyne's lowest crossing place, linking Ormond's forces in Leinster with the anti-Parliamentarian Ulster Scots. Ormond held it with eight troops of horse and four foot regiments, 319 and 2221 men, 'almost all their prime soldiers'. However, they lacked guns and ammunition for a successful defence.

The Boyne divides Drogheda into two distinct sectors, each on a steep slope down to the river, joined by a drawbridge on the site of the modern bridge. The town's medieval walls stood 20 feet (6 m) high and 6 feet (1.8 m) thick, tapering to 4 feet (1.2 m) at the top, hopelessly tall and thin in face of Cromwell's heavy guns. Despite eight years of civil war, nobody had bothered piling earth against the ancient curtain to keep out cannonballs, or to make a firing platform. Nevertheless, Aston was confident 'he who could take Drogheda could take hell'.

Even a large force could not invest both sides of the town. Cromwell concentrated against the south, a triangular salient, protected on the north by the Boyne and on the southeast by a ravine. An outwork or *tenaille* between Duleek Gate and the corner tower flanked the southern wall, behind which stood St Mary's Church and the prehistoric Mill Mount, 'a place very strong and of difficult access, being exceedingly high, having a good graft, and strongly palisadoed' (Cromwell).

Cromwell appeared before Drogheda on 2 September. The defenders' lack of artillery allowed him to entrench within musket shot, dispensing with the tedious preliminaries of sapping forward. Cromwell had learned in England not to waste time in slow approaches, but to plant powerful siege batteries and batter places into submission. At Drogheda he had 11 heavy guns, including four cannon of 8- or 7-inch calibre, firing 48 and 42lb shot (22 and 19 kg) . These were ready by 9 September, one battery east of the ravine on Cromwell's Mount, and another to the south, between the Duleek and Dublin roads. Next day Cromwell formally summoned Aston to surrender, 'to the end effusion of blood may be prevented … If this be refused you will have no cause to blame me.'

Receiving no satisfactory reply, the besiegers hoisted the red flag, to indicate no quarter, and opened fire. By nightfall on 10 September the batteries had breached the wall near St Mary's Church, and beat down the steeple. The cannonade continued next day, opening a long level breach in the south wall and bringing down the southeast corner tower. To contain hostile troops penetrating the battered defences, the Royalists prepared three lines of retrenchments between the Duleek Gate and the eastern wall, left and right of the church.

Seven or eight hundred Parliamentarian infantry stormed the breaches in the southern wall at 5 p.m., but were driven out with loss. They took the *tenaille*, but corpses blocked the sally port through the wall. Cromwell personally led on fresh troops, cannon sweeping the breaches before them with grapeshot: 'Whereupon the enemy's foot being abandoned by their horse, whom our shot had forced to retire, began to break and shift for themselves' (Edmund Ludlow, Parliamentarian officer).

Some of the defenders rallied round Aston on Mill Mount. A few had already surrendered when Cromwell came up, 'being in the heat of the action', and ordered that no one taken in arms be spared. One account has Aston's brains beaten out with his own wooden leg, which the soldiers believed was made of gold. Other Royalists fled for the bridge, followed so closely they were overtaken and prevented from drawing it up. The Royalists ran up Ship Street from the river, and along St Peter's Street, taking refuge in St Peter's Church and St Sunday's steeple at the end of Magdalen Street. When they refused to surrender, church furniture was piled against St Peter's wooden steeple and set alight, burning the defenders alive. Those holding out in other towers were starved out. One in ten were shot, and the survivors shipped to the West Indies.

It was considered entirely proper to refuse quarter to a garrison that rejected a formal summons, in order to discourage futile resistance in future; what Cromwell called 'the satisfactory grounds to such actions, which otherwise cannot but work remorse and regret'. However, even Cromwell's apologists feel he went too far at Drogheda. Casualties exceeded the total garrison, and official bulletins admitted the deaths of many inhabitants. Captured officers were killed in cold blood several days later, one of them in Cromwell's presence. Cromwell's defence of the slaughter as 'a righteous judgment of God upon these barbarous wretches, who have imbrued their hands in so much innocent blood' betrays an indefensible confusion between those responsible for the Ulster atrocities of 1641 and the Irish population in general.

Controversy continues over the scale of the massacre. Ormond wrote of the unimaginable terror that Cromwell's success inspired, so stupefying the Irish they could do nothing for their own preservation. However, both sides exaggerated the salutary effects of Drogheda's drastic treatment. Southern Irish towns learned how to withstand the New Model Army, ensuring more bloodshed before the struggle ended.

Directions

See Millmount Museum off Barrack Street, and remains of the walls near St Mary's Church. Follow the fleeing Royalists north across the bridge, up Ship Street (now Shop Street) to St Peter's Church off William Street. Turn right along St Laurence's Street to see an extant gatehouse with drum towers and curtain wall.

Macroom, 10 April 1650

Ireland, Co. Cork, DS79 W3372–73

Cromwell's conquest of Ireland was not unopposed, despite Drogheda. Parliamentarian forces suffered defeat at Waterford and heavy losses at Clonmel. Before the latter surrendered on terms, the Munster Protestant leader Lord Broghill had to disperse a Royalist relief force at Macroom.

Inchiquin's troops had mostly joined the Cromwellians, leaving the Old Irish Catholics to continue the war alone. Early in 1650, 300 Kerry horse and 4000 foot advanced on Macroom, occupying Carrigadrohid Castle on the River Lee as an advanced post to the east. Cromwell detached Broghill to disperse them, with a column reported variously as six troops (perhaps 400 horse) and 800 foot, or 1500 of each. Leaving his infantry to watch Carrigadrohid Castle, Broghill pressed on with the cavalry to Macroom. The fighting appears to have taken place in the town itself, where the castellated gate of the ruined castle stands in the main street.

The Royalists mistakenly thought Broghill had artillery, so they fired the castle and formed up in the park, 'a place the worst for horse I ever saw, and where 100 musketeers might have kept off all the horse of Ireland' (Broghill). Nevertheless, he fell on without preparation or delay, and routed the half-trained Kerrymen in no time. Eight colours and 1000 arms were taken, suggesting few of the Royalists were properly equipped. Bishop MacEgan, one of the Royalist commanders, was among the prisoners. Broghill summoned the garrison of Carrigadrohid Castle to surrender, threatening to hang their erstwhile commander: 'The former not being done, the latter was …' (Broghill).

Direction

Macroom is on the N22 between Cork and Killarney, the castle park now open to the public. The ruins of Carrigadrohid Castle are 4 miles (6 km) east along the R618, north of the flooded Lee valley, near the power station.

Macroom

	Winner	*Loser*
Opponents	Parliamentarian	Royalist
Commanders	Roger Boyle, Lord Broghill	David Roche, Viscount Fermoy Boetius MacEgan, Bishop of Ross (x)
Numbers	1200–3000	4300
Losses	unknown	400–500

Scarrifhollis (Letterkenny), **Friday 21 June 1650**

Ireland, Co. Donegal, DS6 C1410

Ormond's only effective force by 1650 was the undefeated Army of the North, deprived of its leader by O'Neill's death on 6 November 1649. In his place, the northern Catholics chose Heber MacMahon, a good bishop but a poor general. His opponents were the 'Laggan Army', not formal Parliamentarians but British regiments who had been fighting Irish 'rebels' since 1641. Their commander, Sir Charles Coote, was son of the 'inhumaine bloudsucker' of Kilrush (1642).

In June 1650 MacMahon raided into northern Ireland, reaching Antrim before he retreated westwards across the River Foyle near Lifford. Coote bickered with his rearguard, then fell back to Protestant Londonderry to pick up reinforcements. Short of provisions, MacMahon continued into Donegal, crossing the River Swilly on 21 June, 1 or 2 miles (1.5–3 km) upstream from Letterkenny. Coote now marched up south of the river, to find the enemy 'encamped on this side of a mountain, inaccessible to either horse or foot', presumably Glendoon Hill outside Letterkenny.

The unnamed battlefield is usually equated with the Scarrifhollis where Shane O'Neill crossed the Swilly after Farsetmore (1567), 'being a Forde where an old Castle is on the River' (British Officer). The first modern crossing upstream of Letterkenny is at Newmills, 3 miles (5 km) further west. The narrow steep-sided valley there leaves little room for manoeuvre, however. A mile (1.6 km) nearer Letterkenny, a re-entrant at Ballymoe better fits the British Officer's description of MacMahon's encampment as 'a plane Field amongst the Rocks on the North side of that River close to it'. The place-name hints at a crossing, meaning 'mouth of the ford of Mó'.

Official British numbers were 600 horse and 1800 foot, but it is unclear whether this includes Coote's 1000 reinforcements or 'the Gentlemen of the Country on Horseback' who had all turned out for a day's sport. MacMahon's Latin biographer gave him 3 *legiones* and 500 *equites*, which the enemy translated as 4000 foot and 600 horse. The bishop may have had that many at Lifford, but 1300–1400 men had gone 'to bring in Beeves [cattle] from the Country', reducing him to the 3000 infantry mentioned by the British Officer. Nevertheless, Coote is unlikely to have enjoyed the two- or three-to-one superiority that Royalist sources allege.

Coote's arrival took the Royalists by surprise, '*ex improviso*', but they had no need to fight, as MacMahon's council of war told him. They were '*in loco satis munito*', a well-protected position, on a mountain behind a river. Inappropriately for a man of the cloth, the bishop rejected the professional's advice, '*concilio bello refragante*', and accused O'Neill's veterans of cowardice. His corrosive language 'did soe distemper the warlike deportment of those heroes ... that oblivious of all military advantage ... [they put] themselves in a distracted posture of battle' (*An Aphorismical Discovery of Treasonable Faction*). The British, knowing nothing of the enemy's personal differences, congratulated themselves on having skilfully provoked the enemy into fighting at a disadvantage.

Coote simply records that 'they drew forth to a part of ground which though extreme bad ... we presently engaged them ... and after an hour's hot dispute with great resolution on both sides, we wholly routed them'. The British Officer, who on this occasion fought for the Royalists, provides more detail. The bishop passed his infantry over the river to occupy a bog, presumably meadows south of the Swilly, 'where no Horse could fight'. Coote counterattacked with a brigade of foot. The forlorn hopes exchanged fire, and then the main bodies, dropping the leading British colonel. A second British brigade coming up, and the Royalists fell back across a ditch just behind them, hoping to hold out there until their own supports appeared. However, the British followed so closely the Irish had no time to about face again. Thrown into confusion, they fell foul of another brigade of their own, disordering them also. Another of Coote's brigades now charged the whole lot in flank, driving them back to the ford, 'thinking to maintain the same. But instead of that they all run from it.'

The *Aphorismical Discovery* was predictably kinder to the Irish, claiming the enemy fell down dead 'as thicke as haile in whole regiments'. Coote's horse physically stopped their own foot retreating, and then charged the heroic Irish infantry, cutting them down where they stood, while the Irish horse did nothing. However, Coote's total losses were under 100, while the British Officer categorically states it was an infantry battle: 'none of the Cavalry fought, there being no ground for it'.

The day ended with the usual massacre, Coote imitating his appalling father's sanguinary behaviour at Kilrush (1642). The anonymous British Officer reckoned 1500 Irish died fighting, while those that got quarter and were brought before Coote 'were shott or hacked down by his Orders: for his Officers and private Soldiers ... had more Mercy than he had'. Coote reckoned 2000–3000 were killed, 'the country people as well as the soldiers eagerly pursuing and killing them for two days after'. His humbug rivalled Cromwell's: 'It is God's doing, and it is marvellous in our sight ... To his name be the whole glory ascribed.' The British Officer thought it a day 'where neither conduct or noble acts appeared'.

The dead included most of O'Neill's officers, without whom the army could never be rebuilt. Without a field army, the last Royalist garrisons were doomed. MacMahon was captured two days afterwards, his horses foundered from flight, his leg broken in an ambush. Kept prisoner 'till his Thigh bone was knit and sound again', the bishop was hanged and quartered, his head set on the gate of Londonderry. Ormond was finally discredited, leaving Ireland for the last time on 6 December.

Scarrifhollis

	Winner	*Loser*
Opponents	Parliamentarian	Royalist
Commanders	Sir Charles Coote	Heber MacMahon, Bishop of Clogher (x)
Numbers	2400–3400	3500
Losses	*c.*100	2000–3000

Directions

Take a minor road southwest from Letterkenny, through Old Town, along the south bank of the Swilly. The suggested battlefield lies on the right, between the river and road.

Knockbrack (Knocknaclashy/ Dromagh), **Friday 25 July 1651**

Ireland, Co. Cork, DS79 W3796

The last significant action of the Eleven Years' War occurred not far from earlier encounters at Liscarroll and Knocknanuss. Broghill's victory at Knockbrack disrupted Royalist plans to relieve their stronghold of Limerick, besieged by Henry Ireton since 6 June, ensuring its fall and a final end of hostilities.

Broghill was detached to prevent Muskerry's army from Co. Kerry joining other Royalists at Galbally, 20 miles (30 km) southeast of Limerick. For nearly a week Broghill and Muskerry chased each other around the Blackwater valley in appalling weather. Broghill beat up Muskerry's outposts at Castle Lishen near Milford (Co. Cork) on 22 July, 'in a horrid storm of rain and wind', the Irish retreating into wild country, 'that the very Teigues [Irish] themselves could hardly march in', probably the Mullaghareirk Mountains. Driven off the direct line to Limerick, Muskerry did not give up. On the 24th he crossed the Blackwater to harbour in Drishane woods, near Millstreet. Broghill followed next morning, but running out of bread he prepared to withdraw along the south bank to resupply. His drummers were beating for a march when the rearguard reported four bodies of horse following them.

Broghill immediately drew up 'on a fair moor over which I had just passed'. State papers refer only to 'a repulse … near Dromagh', a castle 2 or 3 miles (3 or 5 km) further west. Fortunately the Parliamentarian army diary specifically locates the battlefield at 'Knockbrackt': 'a plaine three or four miles over without bogge or wood', usually identified with the relatively level area between Mount Hillary and the Blackwater, southwest of Banteer railway station.

The army diarist gave Broghill's numbers at 700 horse, 300 dragoons and 1500 foot. Other estimates range from 1000 to 3100. After a week countermarching in the rain, Broghill's men were desperate for action: 'I never saw men more ready to fight'. Parliamentarian sources reckoned Muskerry's force at 350 horse and 5500 foot. Irish estimates are more modest: 500 cavalry and 3000 foot, mostly pikes. Broghill deployed in three divisions: cavalry wings and infantry centre. Each consisted of five bodies, three-up and two-back. An 11th squadron remained in reserve. The Royalist formation is nowhere specified, but Broghill's account suggests Muskerry also had cavalry on the flanks, his foot in large masses in the centre: a leftmost battalion of 1000 musketeers, supported by 1200 pikemen without wings of shot.

Broghill led his right wing through the enemy's fire: 'They marched to the charge … we fired in each other's faces and mingled.' He killed the officer leading the division opposite him, and 'after a sound dispute' routed Muskerry's whole left wing: 'though we were so very much outnumbered and winged that they charged us in flank and rear' (Broghill). After most of Muskerry's left had fled, his pikemen charged home against the Parliamentarian horse, a rare event. They might have saved the day, had Parliamentarian cavalry not broken in at the corners of the battalion. Broghill was himself wounded by a pike, the Irish crying, 'Kill the fellow with the gold laced coat!'

The Royalists did better on the other flank, where the Parliamentarian left had moved off more slowly. Broghill was rallying some horse to assist when he was charged in the rear, perhaps by Irish horse returning from pillaging the baggage: 'We were necessi-

Knockbrack

	Winner	*Loser*
Opponents	Parliamentarian	Royalist
Commanders	Roger Boyle, Lord Broghill (w)	Donough MacCarthy, Viscount Muskerry
Numbers	2500	3500–5850
Losses	56–200	293

tated to mind ourselves, and by that time we had beaten these importunate fellows, God was pleased to give Major Wallis' wing the like success to what he had given mine.'

Broghill confessed that 'there was never known better knocking in Ireland'. The whole front rank of his own troop, 33 men, were either killed or wounded. He admitted 'our army is much shattered', but only conceded 26 dead and 30 wounded against 500 dead Irish. High-value prisoners were taken, 'All their foot field officers charged on foot with pikes in their hands, so that few of them got off ... being too far from any bogs or woods.' Muskerry's casualty figures are more credible: 200 English against 104 Irish dead, 108 wounded, and 9 prisoners.

Henry Ireton, besieging Limerick, recognized the victory with 'a night of triumph by volleys of shott, sounding of drums and trumpets'. With no prospect of relief, Limerick's defenders surrendered on 27 October, the rank and file taking service in Catholic Spain. Although the last capitulation was at Cloughoughter (Co. Cavan) on 27 April 1653, the Eleven Years' War had ended.

Directions

Take the N72 west from Mallow, turning left onto the R579 across the Blackwater to Banteer. In the village turn right along a minor road to Rathcool, following the railway. Fighting took place between Knockaun, 'the little hill', from where Broghill observed the enemy advance, and Knockbrack, a larger wooded hill (787 feet/240 m) to the southwest.

Cromwell and the Scots

The Wars of the Three Kingdoms ended, as they began, with an international conflict, the last between independent English and Scottish states.

Support for Charles I's execution was thin in England. In Scotland it provoked counter-revolution. The Kirkmen, who had regained control after the Engagers' defeat at Preston (1648), proclaimed the exiled Charles II king on 5 February 1649, a first step towards what Cromwell called 'a Covenant made with death and hell'. The Presbyterians imposed intolerable conditions on their impoverished monarch, who had no intention of observing any of them once he was strong enough to break his word. While entertaining the Kirk's negotiators, Charles sponsored a last filibuster by the Marquess of Montrose, abruptly terminated at Carbisdale (27 April 1650). The king took the Covenant, while the Scots raised a new army of 5440 horse and 13,400 foot.

The rapprochement between Charles II and the Kirkmen sowed mistrust between English Republicans and their erstwhile Scottish allies. In June the Council of State resolved to forestall a Scottish invasion, concentrating 16,000 troops at Newcastle under Cromwell. He entered Scotland on 22 July, beseeching the Covenanters in the bowels of Christ to think it possible they might be mistaken.

Ancient strategic realities reasserted themselves. The old Earl of Leven, with David Leslie in operational command, adopted a traditional scorched-earth policy, leaving nothing to eat in the Lowlands. Scotland's summer killed more English soldiers than the Scottish army, which sat tight behind impregnable trenches covering Leith and Edinburgh. Baulked in his repeated attempts to turn Leslie's line, Cromwell retreated to Dunbar, to resupply and evacuate his sick by sea. The pursuing Scots grew overconfident. They came down from the Lammermuir Hills at Dunbar, not 2 miles (3 km) from the scene of their defeat in 1296, and were cut to pieces. Cromwell took Edinburgh, but sufficient Scots survived the 'Race of Dunbar' to contest the Forth/Clyde isthmus. Cromwell refused to risk a frontal attack on Stirling, and military stalemate set in. Mosstroopers harassed English communications, and

Cromwell fell sick. Charles II's coronation at Scone, near Perth, on 1 January 1651 symbolized the recovery in Royalist fortunes.

Both sides were reinforced over the winter, the Scots re-enlisting thousands of Royalists purged before Dunbar. Nevertheless, Cromwell outnumbered Leslie, with 21,000 men against 15,000–16,000. The margin was sufficient for Cromwell to divide his forces. On 17 July English troops landed from flat boats at North Queensferry, threatening the Scottish economic base in northeastern Scotland. A Scots attempt to liquidate the bridgehead came to grief at Inverkeithing (20 July), allowing Cromwell to ship more forces across the Forth, and invest Perth.

Cromwell's advance left open the way to England, perhaps deliberately. Facing logistical disaster, the Royalists marched south before Perth fell on 2 August, hoping to exploit English disillusionment with the Republic. It was a profound miscalculation. Few joined them, even in Roman Catholic Lancashire, where a Royalist recruiting party was eliminated in the Battle of Wigan Lane (25 August). Republican contingency plans were well laid. Regular forces shadowed the dwindling Scots army south, while thousands of militia turned out to surround the foreign invaders. At Worcester (3 September) the Royalists suffered a disaster comparable with Preston.

Worcester was the last throw of the opponents of the Republic. The king was left a discredited fugitive, escaping to France on 13 October. General Monck had already bagged most of the Scottish 'Committee of Estates' at Alyth on 27 September, leaving the country without a government. During the winter of 1651–2 Monck rounded up the last mosstroopers, imposing a peace of exhaustion upon a shattered Scotland. The resulting union lasted until the Restoration, after Cromwell's death in 1658 – on the anniversary of both Dunbar and Worcester – had removed the only figure able to resolve the Commonwealth's internal contradictions.

Carbisdale, Saturday 27 April 1650

Scotland, Highland, LR21 NH5694

It is difficult not to see Montrose's last campaign as a hare-brained adventure, its sudden extinction at Carbisdale the inevitable result of habitually betting against the odds.

Charles II was in penurious exile in the Netherlands after his father's death. Negotiating with the Kirk from a position of desperate weakness, he tried to improve his hand by raising the spectre of a Highland revolt, led by the charismatic Montrose. In March 1650 the marquess arrived at Kirkwall in Orkney with a few Danish mercenaries and the usual handful of desperate Cavaliers. In the absence of a Covenanter navy, he landed at John o' Groats on 12 April, heading down the east coast of Caithness to Dunrobin Castle. Finding this held against him, Montrose turned inland along Strath Fleet to Lairg, then south to the Kyle of Sutherland. Few would rally to the royal standard while the king was treating with those whom Montrose was inviting them to attack. Montrose was forced back towards the coast, onto more open terrain exposed to the Covenanters' superior cavalry.

The Scottish Army gave Montrose no time to gather support. On 27 April Colonel Strachan was at Tain, south of the Dornoch Firth, where he heard Montrose was within reach. Strachan had three troops of 230 horse, 36 regular musketeers and 400 Highlanders, 'upon whom no dependence could be placed' (S.R. Gardiner). Montrose had just 40 mounted men (would-be officers rather than horse), 450 Danish regular infantry and 750 Orkney recruits.

Carbisdale Castle is a 20th-century structure north of the modern hamlet of Culrain. Tradition and the Ordnance Survey place the battle southwest of both, at the foot of the glen where Culrain Burn leaves the hills. The battlefield was an open, rugged piece of ground, sloping down to the stream, flanked by a bog. Behind it rose the spurs of Creag a' Choineachan, the Mossy Hill, thinly covered as late as the

Carbisdale

	Winner	Loser
Opponents	Covenanter	Royalist
Commanders	Colonel Archibald Strachan	James Graham, Marquess of Montrose
Numbers	660	1240
Losses	unknown	all

1890s with birch, poor shelter against cavalry attack.

Montrose's position provided limited visibility south, but he failed to post scouts on Invercharron Hill to watch the old ford between Soyal and Dounie. Irregular hillsides covered with dense broom thickets concealed Strachan's advance south of the Kyle of Sutherland, probably as far as Balinoe, just short of where Culrain Burn falls into the loch. The Covenanters had foreseen that Montrose would retreat into the hills if threatened by cavalry. When they finally encountered the Royalist horse, they agreed 'to send out one troop only, that the enemy might perceive them, and to let the rest of the troops be still in the broom, that the enemy might think they were no more' (Gordon of Sallagh). Strachan's remaining horsemen presumably hid in the gullies that intersect the northeast slopes of Invercharron Hill. Montrose's patrol obligingly rode back to report just a small body of Covenanter horse. Some reconstructions of the battle place Strachan's ambuscade at Wester Fearns, 8 miles (13 km) riding from Montrose, instead of the mile and a half (2.5 km) given by Gordon of Sallagh, the greater distance hardly squaring with Strachan's subsequent surprise attack.

While Montrose was busy drawing up his 'van' and 'body' in the open strath above Culrain, the Covenanters burst out upon them. Too late the marquess ordered his troops back into the wood. Despite the 'ill-riding ground', Strachan's troopers broke the Royalist horse and Orkney men on their first charge, and pursued the more practised Danes into the 'scroggie' (scrubby) birch wood. This was insufficient to stop the cavalry, and resistance collapsed after a harmless volley. Most of Strachan's Highlanders sat out the battle, but 80 joined in the pursuit. Scarce 100 Royalists are said to have escaped.

Montrose escaped over the mountains to the west, hoping for a fishing boat back to Kirkwall. But Highland loyalties had shifted since 1645. Montrose was captured by Neil Macleod, sheriff depute of Assynt, and handed over to those whose armies he had boasted of slaughtering at Tippermuir (1644) and Auldearn (1645). Charles II did nothing to save his most loyal servant, who was hanged in Edinburgh on 21 May, a copy of Wishart's *Memoirs of James Marquis of Montrose* around his neck.

Directions

Leave the A836 at Ardgay, carrying straight on along a minor road through Cornhill towards Culrain. Strachan's ambush was probably south of the railway bridge at Balinoe (NH5793). Continue to Culrain station and turn left for the battlefield, on the right between two arms of the burn.

Dunbar, Tuesday 3 September 1650

Scotland, East Lothian, LR67 NT6976–7076

The Race or Drove of Dunbar was Cromwell's most dramatic victory. Pinned against an inhospitable coast he turned his strategically beaten army against a stronger enemy, and overthrew them by simple tactical genius.

The Scots' response to Cromwell's invasion in July 1650 was a masterly defensive, showing the hand of the old Earl of Leven. Entrenched from Leith to Edinburgh Castle, the numerically superior Scots countered all attempts to turn them out. The English offensive reached its culminating point south of Gogar, just south of Edinburgh Airport, on 27 August, just short of cutting Edinburgh off from the rest of Scotland. Unwilling to fight through a tangle of bogs and stone walls, Cromwell retreated down the coast to Dunbar, where his 'poor, shattered, hungry, discouraged army' (Captain John Hodgson) arrived on Sunday 1 September.

The Scots cut across the arc of the jagged shoreline to block Cromwell's road to Berwick, seizing the Cockburnspath defile, 'where ten men to hinder are better than forty to make way' (Cromwell). The Scots' main army occupied Doun Hill (581 feet/177 m), south of Dunbar, 'having got us into a pound as they reckoned' (Hodgson). Here they flanked Cromwell's line of retreat, perhaps hoping to lure him into a disastrous break out, like that at Lostwithiel (1644). Cromwell wrote of being offered 'a golden bridge', an ancient strategic concept, misconstrued by 19th-century historians as a pecuniary rather than a military inducement.

The English were not drawn, 'standing in battalia in the town fields between the Scotch Army and the town, ready to engage' (Hodgson), their left flank covered by Broxburn House, a large house in a walled park, also known as Broxmouth. About 4 p.m. on Monday 2 September the Scots left the hills, transferring two-thirds of their left wing of horse to the right, 'shogging also their foot and train much to the right, causing their right wing of horse to edge down towards the sea' (Cromwell). This brought them onto the gentler northern slopes of the Lammermuir Hills, exposed to Cromwell's cavalry. Historians disagree over responsibility for the move. Some blame tactically illiterate presbyters, others the Scots council of war, led by David Leslie, a less cautious strategist than Leven. An official inquiry after the battle cleared Leslie, blaming 'the Committee's order, contrarie to his mind, to stop the enemies retreat, and for that end to storm Broxburn House as soon as possible'. The Scottish army must have been pleased to avoid a second night on the rainswept hilltops, but both Cromwell and Lambert realized the tactical opportunity presented by the Scots redeployment.

Dunbar lies on a peninsula between Belhaven Bay and Brock Burn (now Spott Burn) to the east. Richard Cadwell, the bearer of Cromwell's dispatch, described 'a great dyke about 40 or 50 feet wide, and as deep as broad, with a little rundle of water running in the middle of it ... so that either army's marching over first was a great disadvantage to them'. Upstream the ravine was nearer 100 feet (30 m) deep, its sides so straight that it resembled a ditch. Impassable after days of rain, it was an unsatisfactory start line if Leslie meant to attack Broxburn House. There were three possible crossings:

(1) At 'the pass upon the roadway between Dunbar and Berwick', now the A1087, and a minor road past the cement works.
(2) The 'low and shelving banks' at Brants Mill (now vanished), between the A1087 and the railway.
(3) Downstream of Broxmouth, across the golf course.

Cromwell would use all of these.

Traditional interpretations of Dunbar, starting with Thomas Carlyle and still followed by many, align the forces parallel to Brock Burn, the Scots facing northwest or even west, their cavalry north of the Berwick road. Sir Charles Firth, in his detailed analysis of the battle, placed them south of the main road, however, facing the sea. Followed by S.R. Gardiner, this view agrees with older sources, in particular Fitzpayne Fisher's picture plan, engraved for Cromwell, with input from veterans of the battle. Fisher clearly shows the English attacking uphill, across not along the main road, a direction supported by Hodgson's assertion that the Scots 'had a great mountain behind them'. This could not be true of a line across the main road, which runs almost level to East Barns. More than one eyewitness refers to the Scots' elevated location. During the battle General Monck charged pike in hand, 'up the hills that are above the town from the seaside'. Afterwards many Scots were captured as they 'ran away over the sands to Belhaven', an unlikely direction if they started the battle facing west.

The main Scots position, therefore, probably lay as Firth proposed, around Oxwell Mains, in front of Little and Meikle Pinkerton. How far their line extended east towards Dry Burn depends on one's assumptions about Scots numbers and formation density. One Englishman observed 'intervals in their bodies upon the brink of the hill that our horse might march a troop at once, and so the foot'. Leslie's left was crowded between Doun Hill and Brock Burn, so that, 'if we beat their right wing we hazarded their

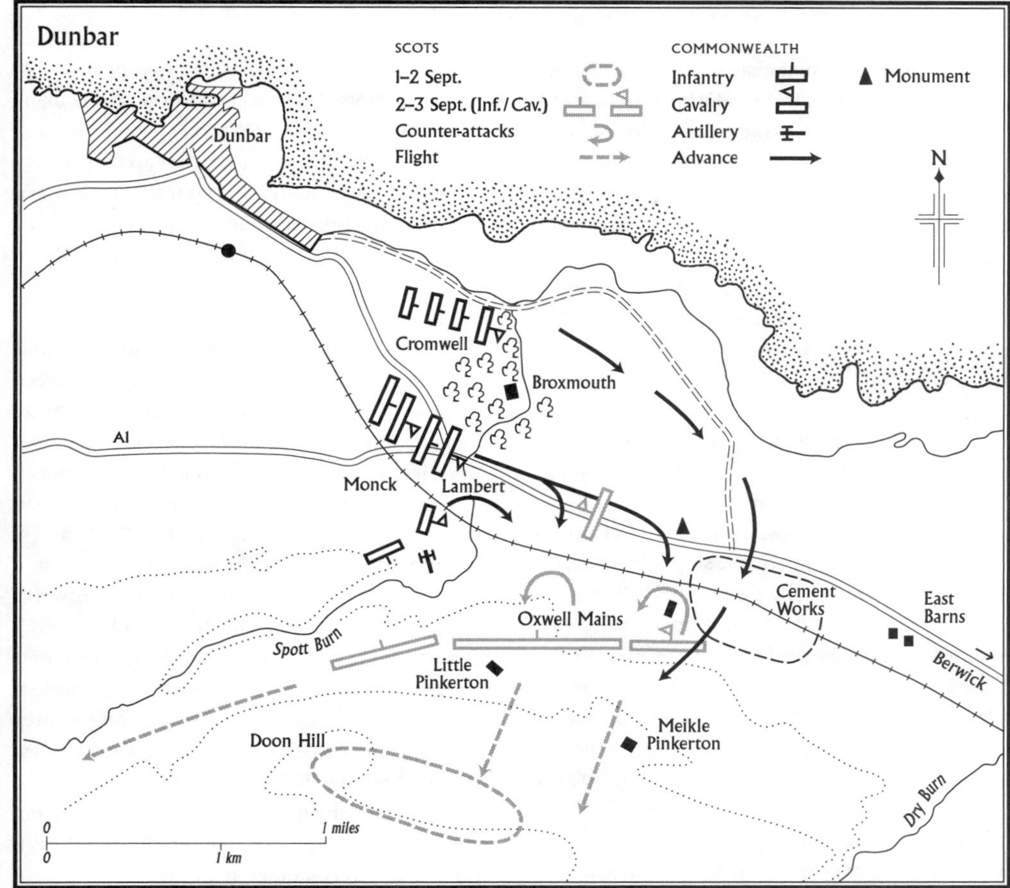

whole army … in regard they had not great ground to traverse their regiments between the mountain and the clough [ravine]' (Hodgson). In front of the main position, Scots cavalry occupied an isolated farmhouse 200–300 yards (180–275 m) on the Berwick side of Brock Burn, near the southern lodge of Broxburn House.

Leslie probably had fewer men than is usually thought. Cromwell's figure of 6000 horse and 16,000 foot tallies with the 19 cavalry and 18 infantry regiments the Scots had, but at full strength. Muster rolls suggest the Scots were below establishment, perhaps 3000 horse and 8000–9000 foot, with 32 guns, including leather fframes. Leslie would have had more men if the Kirk had not purged 4000 Royalist and Engager 'malignants', regardless of military efficiency. Captain Cold and Captain Hunger had reduced the English,

Directions

Take the A1087 from Dunbar across Broxburn, where a path runs down to the sea along the burn. The main road has been rerouted south of the old Berwick road, the A1087 joining the A1(T) in the middle of the battlefield. Either go straight over and up a minor road to Little Pinkerton, behind Leslie's centre, or turn left along the A1(T) and left again past the cement works to see the monument by the old Berwick road marking Carlyle's 'brunt or essential agony of the battle of Dunbar'.

'as to sound men, to about 7500 foot and 3500 horse' (Cromwell), eight regiments of each. His artillery strength is unknown, but each infantry regiment had two light pieces, while the heavier guns formed a battery at the salient in Brock Burn just south of the railway, where they 'might have fair play at their left wing while we were fighting their right' (Hodgson).

Cromwell's response to the Scots closing up to Brock Burn was to sidle to the left, massing his whole army under cover of darkness opposite the crossings either side of Broxburn House. The main concentration was on the Berwick road: six regiments of horse under Lambert, three and a half of foot under Monck. Cromwell's own horse and Pride's three foot regiments were nearer the sea, the remaining regiment and a half escorting the artillery. The eighth cavalry regiment was also in reserve; Fisher shows it near Brants Mill. The move took all night, Cromwell riding about on a little Scotch nag, biting his lip till the blood ran down his chin.

The battle falls into two phases: the fight at the pass, and the main action on the slopes of Pinkerton Hill. Lambert's leading three regiments 'fell upon the horse guards and made them retire' (Sir Edward Walker, formerly Charles I's secretary), killing some of the Scots troopers in their tents. Meanwhile two infantry regiments made good the ford for the second wave of cavalry: 'Firing very hard upon one another, the dispute lasted an hour, and was very hot, the great guns playing on both sides very hot on each other's main body; it being moonlight ...' (Cadwell). Before the Scots could take up their stations, the English were across the burn and deployed along the road with the sea at their backs, Brock Burn on their right.

The Scots responded slowly. It was 'a drakie nycht full of wind and weit'; 'Our Scottis army were cairless and secure, expecting no assault'. About 2 a.m. Major General Holborne had the musketeers put out their matches, except the file leaders, who could hardly keep theirs alight for the rain. The infantry 'made themselves shelter of the corn new reapt and went to sleep. The horse likewise went to forage, and many unsaddled their horses' (Walker). Their eventual response was fierce: 'The enemy horse charged very resolutely, all their frontiers [front rank] being armed with lances: our brigade of horse [Lambert] gave way a little, being charged by the enemy coming down the hill upon them' (Cadwell). Monck's foot were similarly 'overpowered with the enemy'.

Cromwell still had reserves in hand, the four regiments splashing across the Brock Burn between the house and sea. Leslie's remaining troops were jammed in the ravine on his left. While Pride's two leading infantry regiments supported Lambert directly, Cromwell himself directed the third to incline to the left, clear of the fighting line. The English now outnumbered Leslie's right wing three-to-two, a decisive edge when combined with Cromwell's turning movement, and the New Model Army's superior fighting value: 'I never beheld a more terrible charge of foot than was given by our army, our foot alone making the Scots foot give ground for three quarters of a mile together' (John Rushworth). A few regiments armed with flintlocks stood fast, until the cavalry charged them in flank. Leslie's left wing ran away without a fight, the English chasing them 8 miles (13 km) to Haddington.

Cromwell claimed 3000 enemy dead and 10,000 prisoners, more than the total number of Scots combatants. Five thousand were marched south into captivity, tallying with Walker's estimate of 6000 prisoners, of whom 1000 wounded were released next day. That number of wounded implies 300–500 dead, an estimate validated by observers at Worcester, next year, who believed the 2000 Royalist fatalities there exceeded the Scottish death toll at Dunbar.

English acclamation of 'this great and wonderful and signal victorie' was proportional to their strategic plight beforehand. Gardiner ranked Dunbar with Naseby, though it failed to end the war. Leslie rallied 4000–5000 men at Stirling, deterring an assault two weeks later. Dunbar's political consequences were more significant, undermining the Kirk's arrogant pretensions and its ambitions to impose Presbyterianism beyond the Border.

Dunbar

	Winner	*Loser*
Opponents	Commonwealth	Scots
Commanders	Oliver Cromwell Major General John Lambert	David Leslie
Numbers	11,000	12,000
Losses	20 (k)	*c.*6000

Inverkeithing, Sunday 20 July 1651

Scotland, Fife, LR65 NT1182–1282

The decisive action of the last Anglo-Scots war is almost unknown, although thousands of motorists and railway passengers pass over the battlefield every day while crossing the Forth Bridges.

After Dunbar the English were held up in front of Stirling, unwilling to tackle obstacles that had thwarted Edwardian armies at Stirling Bridge (1297) and Bannockburn (1314). Cromwell's build-up to over 20,000 men in early 1651 allowed him to mount an amphibious turning movement across the Firth of Forth, using landing craft purpose built over the winter. On Thursday 17 July, 1600 English troops landed by surprise on the neck of the North Queensferry isthmus and entrenched Ferry Hills (239 feet/ 73 m) to consolidate the bridgehead. David Leslie, the Scots commander at Dunbar, detached Major General Holborne with a small force to counter the threat, leaving the main Scots army still strong enough to prevent Cromwell breaking through at Torwood, south of Stirling, the next day. Concerned for his landing party's safety, Cromwell sent Major General Lambert to reinforce them with two more regiments apiece of horse and foot. On Saturday night Holborne encamped at Dunfermline, while the English laboured to ship their horse across the Forth, 'and before the last came to shore on the Lord's Day, the enemy was advanced very near us' (Lambert).

It is impossible now to visualize the scene as it was, thanks to naval scrap yards, railway viaducts, quarries and the approaches to the Forth Road Bridge. At first Lambert stood on the defensive, placing his foot 'obscure on the side of the hill' (Scoutmaster George Downing). Holborne probably drew up on gently sloping ground north of the isthmus, a mixture of cornland and rocky patches. The arrival of a second English cavalry regiment encouraged Lambert to advance, especially as the enemy 'began to wheel, as if he meant either to march away, or to take the advantage of a steep mountain'. Lambert was presumably referring to the double eminence of Castlandhill (279 feet/85 m) between Inverkeithing and Rosyth, hardly a mountain by Scottish standards.

Having failed to persuade the enemy to attack Ferry Hills Lambert sent forward some horse to fix the enemy rear, causing Holborne to draw up 'in battalia'. The English were 'more in number in my judgement by at least 500 or 600, but on the other side the enemy had the advantage of the ground, our left wing of horse being on a very ill ground, where there was a pass lined by the enemy's musketeers' (Lambert). This was presumably the neck between Castlandhill's two summits, since deepened for the A90 dual carriageway.

Lambert reckoned Holborne had 4000 men at Dunfermline, 'a recruit of 500 [joining] the next day'. Cromwell reported four or five Scots regiments of horse and five of foot, which squares with the 40–50 colours lost at Inverkeithing. Stuart Reid identifies six cavalry and four infantry regiments that fought there, with another three foot regiments possible. At 150 troopers or 500 foot soldiers apiece, typical regimental strengths at Dunbar, this would make nearly 4500 Scots, as Lambert estimated. Cromwell put Lambert's force at 'two regiments of horse and about 400 of horse and dragoons more, and three regiments of foot'. Lambert names three cavalry and four infantry units. He clearly planned to lead with his right, where he placed his own regiment of horse, and four more troops, leaving only six for the left wing. In the centre the infantry formed the 'battle', two regiments up and two in support.

Neither side wanted to start, Lambert recalling:

Inverkeithing

	Winner	*Loser*
Opponents	Commonwealth	Scots
Commanders	Major General John Lambert	Major General James Holborne Major General John Browne of Fordell (d)
Numbers	5000	4500
Losses	80?	2200

'We continued facing one another about an hour and a half, supposing they would come to us, having come so far to seek us; but finding they delayed ... it was resolved we should climb the hill to them.' Lambert relates only that 'through the lord's strength by a very short dispute, [we] put them to an absolute rout'. The hottest service was on his left, a newspaper reporting: 'the Scots with their lances and stoutness of their men gave our horse such charges as did disorder them and charged quite through the first body; to which our gallant Major-General Lambert, coming up with a reserve, in one quarter of an hour put them to the rout which were of the left wing' (*Mercurius Politicus*). One imagines the English foot stormed the eastern hilltop, turning left down the relatively easy descent to the pass, to roll up the Scots position.

Scottish sources accused Holborne of fleeing at the first shot: 'Hellish Holborne came not up, which if he had the Scotch had carried it' (*Fraser Chronicle*). Locals asserted he had conferred with Lambert through a speaking trumpet, from East Ness, although a court martial cleared him of all wrongdoing. His colleague Major General Browne was less fortunate, dying of wounds in the enemy camp, as did five Scottish regimental commanders.

One-sided Commonwealth casualty claims excite disbelief. Lambert reported 2000 'killed upon the place (as most judge)', and 1400 prisoners, three-quarters of the Scots army. Most hard hit were two Highland regiments, said to have been cut down at 'The Hedges of Death' near Pitreavie, beside the A90/A823 interchange: 'divers of them were Highlanders and had very ill quarter ... few of them escaped without a knock' (Lambert). A succession of loyal clansmen are said to have thrown themselves in front of Colonel Hector Maclean of Duart, crying, 'Another for Hector!' St Margaret's Stone ran red with gore.

Such tales deserve no more credence than Holborne's treachery. Duart's regiment in fact lost 140 men out of 800, about a sixth. Applied across the Scots force, this proportion gives 750 casualties, nearly Robert Balfour's contemporary estimate of 800. Lambert's admission of only eight Commonwealth dead suggests government spin doctors removed a zero, although his wife admitted many wounded, 'most of which was in my husband's ridgment of horse'. Lambert's horse was also hurt, 'and a brace of bullets found betwixt his cot and armes'.

Cromwell described Inverkeithing as an 'unspeakable mercy', admitting he had stalled at Torwood: 'We were gone as far as we could ... and we did say to one another, "we knew not what to do".' Lambert had unlocked the strategic impasse, 'for the loss of Inverkeithing had so quared [queered or spoilt] the minds of many ... that his majesty could hardly any more make a defensive war' (Duke of Hamilton). Charles II had two options: attack Cromwell in Fife, or invade England with a foreign army, an infallible recipe for disaster.

Directions

From Inverkeithing station go south along the B981, turning right uphill past the museum, where the town now extends over Castlandhill's more easterly summit. Cross the A90 cutting to the western half of the ridge, the only undeveloped part of the battlefield.

Wigan Lane, Monday 25 August 1651

England, Lancashire, LR108 SD5806

The only Royalist rising to accompany Charles II's advance into England was in Lancashire. It was crushed with contemptuous ease just north of Wigan.

The Earl of Derby landed from his stronghold in the Isle of Man at Preesall Sands in the Wyre estuary on 15 August, too late to join Charles's army as it passed through Lancashire. Derby equally failed to reconcile his old Presbyterian enemies to the royal cause, 'nor did any considerable number come unto him, and those that did were the trash of the county' (*Calendar of State Papers*). He went to raise recruits at Preston, shadowed by Colonel Lilburne's regiment of horse. Early on the 25th Lilburne received intelli-

Wigan Lane

	Winner	*Loser*
Opponents	Commonwealth	Royalist
Commanders	Colonel Robert Lilburne	James Stanley, Earl of Derby (w) Sir Thomas Tyldesley (k)
Numbers	800	1300–1600
Losses	10 (k)	400–500

gence the Royalists had left, 'which I thought was a running away from us, being they began at eleven in the night'. When he caught them up near Wigan, Lilburne found his mistake: 'When we appeared here, (thinking we had been, as it were, pursuing a flying enemy,) they shewed a great deal of courage by a mighty shout they gave beyond the town in sight of us, in the way towards Manchester ... [which] put us upon new thoughts.' This sounds unlikely, but Lilburne is clear, 'they were at one end of the town and we were at the other'.

Lilburne did not want a fight, 'they exceeding us much in foot, and we having no grounds to fight our horse upon'. He preferred to sidle leftwards around the Royalists, to join another Commonwealth regiment at Manchester, 'but they seeing it, presently drew through the town to fall upon us: which we observing and being so neare to them, resolved to trust God with the issue'. Eyewitnesses give Derby 500–600 horse and 800–1000 foot. The former included many gentlemen, veterans of Edgehill and Marston Moor, for whom Wigan Lane was a last heroic death ride. Lilburne fielded 'three companies of foot [*c.*300], about fifty or sixty dragoons, and about thirty horse from Liverpool, with my own wearied and somewhat shattered regiment [*c.*450]'.

Wigan had suffered much during the Civil Wars, being 'a great and poor town and very malignant'. Scots fugitives from Preston had plundered it 'to the skin' in 1648, while Cromwell had beaten their rearguard in the same lane where Lilburne now fought Derby. S.R. Gardiner located the 1651 action south of Wigan, but from Chorley Lilburne would necessarily approach from the north, along Wigan Lane. This was then a broad sandy lane passing between the hedged enclosures around the town, falling steeply away to the River Douglas on the east. Altogether it was most unsuitable ground for cavalry.

Lilburne wrote two reports. Neither gives much detail, except that the dispute lasted an hour, starting about 3 p.m. The outcome was initially doubtful: 'Our horse not being able to do any service, but in lanes, and they overpowering us so much in foot.' Royalist officer casualties suggest they charged with suicidal gallantry, before being driven back down Standishgate into the Market Place, in what Lilburne described as 'a total rout of our enemies'. Derby was sore hurt, his beaver hat captured with 13 sword cuts upon it. Tyldesley, the Royalist major general, was unhorsed and shot, at the place his post-Restoration monument now stands.

Other Royalist casualties in this 'comfortable success' included 'very considerable persons of great quality' and about 60 soldiers killed and 300–400 prisoners. Lilburne lost no officers, 'nor above ten soldiers that I can hear of, but many horses killed and spoiled with their pikes'. In September the Council of State reminded local militia commissioners that 'divers soldiers of Colonel Lilburne's regiment and others in that service against the Earl of Derby and his party were wounded and remain in your county unable to go up to the army'. Derby escaped after dark, joining the king at Worcester two days before the battle. Taken after that debacle, he was executed in Bolton on 15 October in a clear example of victor's justice.

Directions

Modern Wigan spreads north over the battlefield, Wigan Lane being the A49 to Standish. Tyldesley's memorial is on the right 1 mile (1.6 km) north of Wigan town centre, just before Monument Road, set back from the A49 inside a low fence. Some surviving woodland backs onto Widdrington Road (off Monument Road), which commemorates Lord Widdrington, another senior Royalist fatality.

Worcester, Wednesday 3 September 1651

England, Worcestershire, LR150 SO8452–8654

The Civil Wars ended by curious coincidence, 'at Worcester where England's sorrows began'. After all the slaughter, Commonwealth observers remembered those slain at Powick Bridge near Worcester in 1642, 'whose blood cried and had audience in heaven this day'. The Battle of Worcester was also the last confrontation of regular armies on English soil.

Cromwell's advance on Perth after Inverkeithing made it logistically impossible for Charles II to remain in Scotland. On 5 August he crossed the Border, following the western route through Lancashire. Cromwell was already back in Leith, while his subordinates carried out prearranged moves to counter the invasion. Enormous concentrations of militia at Daventry, St Albans and Barnet blocked the way to London, while Lambert's cavalry dogged the Royalists southwards. Shepherded away from London, Charles II headed for his father's recruiting grounds in the Welsh Marches. On 22 August he entered Worcester, the last city to surrender to Parliament in 1646. Worn out by incessant marches in an unfriendly country, the Scots infantry insisted on a rest. Two days later Cromwell's infantry joined Lambert at Warwick, advancing to Evesham, 14 miles (22.5 km) east of Worcester on the 27th.

Royalist strategy was now to hold Worcester as a defensive bridgehead on the east bank of the Severn, while supporters flocked in. Meanwhile the city's fortifications would deter the usually cautious Cromwell from a potentially bloody showdown. Royalist engineers strengthened the medieval defences with earth banks, built new ones to the southeast at Fort Royal, and broke down bridges at Upton and Bewdley to hinder turning movements. Worcester was not Edinburgh or Stirling, however. Cromwell was in the heart of his own country, with overwhelming odds in his favour, and with every reason to seek a decision, regardless of loss. On 28 August he occupied Red Hill, less than a mile (1.6 km) from Fort Royal, while Lambert seized the incompletely demolished bridge at Upton to gain a foothold west of the Severn. Once sufficient bridging material had been prepared to ensure a coordinated attack, Cromwell could close in along both banks of the river: 'The enemy is in Worcester,' he reported, 'and within a few days will have to fight or fly.'

Worcester

	Winner	*Loser*
Opponents	Commonwealth	Royalist
Commanders	Oliver Cromwell Lieutenant General Charles Fleetwood Major General John Lambert	Charles II David Leslie (p) William, Duke of Hamilton (d)
Numbers	28,000–32,000	16,000
Losses	400	12,000

Worcester is at least the second largest battle on English soil, a unique encounter between a Scottish national army with English auxiliaries and an English national army supported by militia. If lower estimates for the earlier battle are correct, Worcester even exceeds Marston Moor. Some Scots troops had stayed behind, reducing Charles's army to 10,000–12,000 at the Border. However, the Council of State thought 'many persons withdrew from their houses', suggesting English Royalists made up his numbers to the 16,000 Cromwell reported. From the fragmentary evidence, Malcolm Atkin has identified some 24 Royalist regiments of horse and 37 foot, all very weak, roughly distributed around the city as follows:

West – in the angle formed by the Rivers Severn and Teme:	4 horse, 9 foot
North – at Pitchcroft, now the Race Course, under Leslie:	4 horse
Inside or just outside to the east:	4 horse, 4 foot
Uncertain – infantry mostly inside, cavalry at Pitchcroft:	12 horse, 24 foot

Artillery was scarce, only 16 leather guns according to one Royalist.

Cromwell outnumbered the Royalists two-to-one, allowing him to fight both sides of the Severn. He

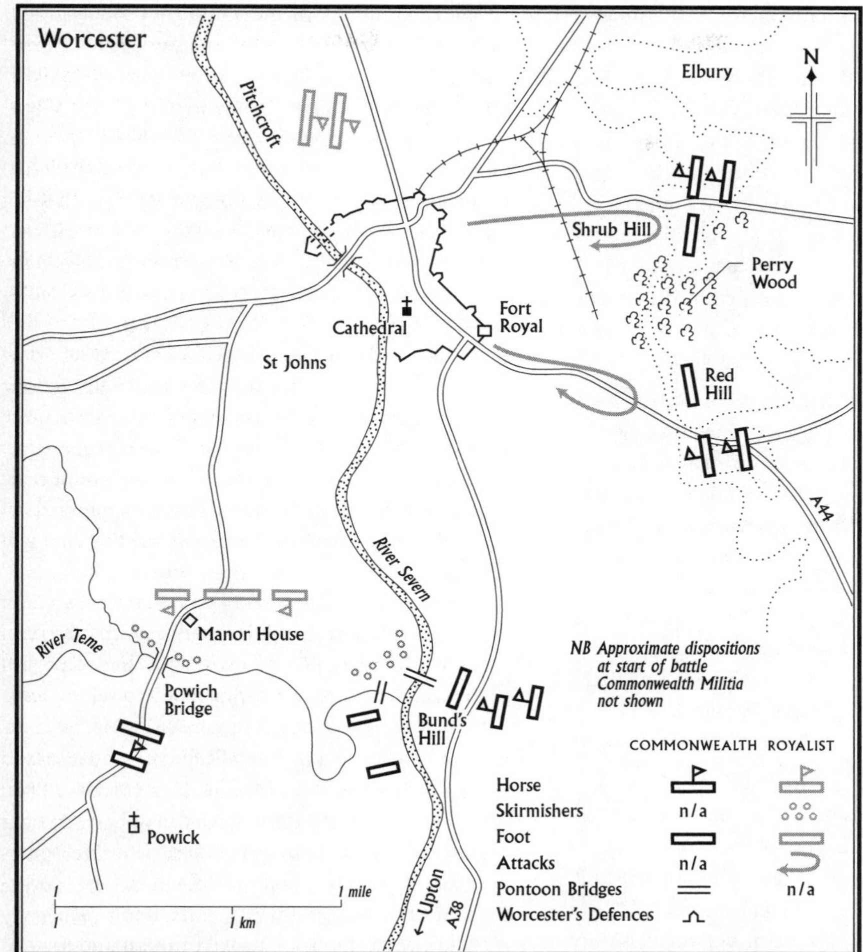

Directions

Much of the battlefield is built over:

City centre *See the cathedral where the Duke of Hamilton is buried, King Charles's House in New Street, and the remains of St Martin's Gate in City Walls Road. The original Severn drawbridge was between today's road and railway bridges.*

East of Worcester *Leave by Sidbury Street, crossing the canal where East Gate stood. See the Commandery Museum, where Hamilton died of his wounds on 8 September, and Fort Royal Park nearby. Continue up London Road (A44) to Red Hill, now the A422 Alcester roundabout.*

Perry Wood *See 'Cromwell's Trenches' north of the wood, in an open area off Humber Road that is little altered.*

South of Worcester *Footpaths in the Teme meadows and east of the Severn follow the river bank around the bridgehead. Alternatively see Cromwell's crossing place from the viewpoint near the A38 Malvern roundabout.*

Powick *See evidence of Civil War damage to the church tower and bridge, whose northern two spans have been repaired.*

himself took command on the east, blocking any movement towards London, on an arc from Elbury Hill in the north, through Perry Wood and Red Hill, to Bund's Hill in the south. West of the Severn and south of the Teme, Lieutenant General Fleetwood covered Bristol and threatened Royalist communications with Wales. His role in the battle was to bring up boats and planks to throw pontoon bridges across both rivers at their confluence half a mile (0.8 km) downsteam from Worcester, permitting Cromwell to switch troops from one sector to another as required. Regiments were distributed as follows:

East bank – assault force (Cromwell):
3 horse, 4 foot

East bank – Red Hill (Lambert & Harrison):
7 horse, 4 foot + militia

West bank – bridging force (Fleetwood):
0 horse, 4 foot

West bank – Powick assault force:
1 horse, 3 foot

West bank – to Bransford Bridge:
3 horse/dragoons

North – cut-off party at Bewdley:
3 horse/dragoons

Lambert's militia included six regiments from Cheshire and Essex, and an unknown number of locals, supported by the artillery train.

Cromwell's preparations were complete by 2 September. According to *A True and Faithfull Narrative of Oliver Cromwell's Compact with the Devil*, these included bargaining with Satan in a cottage at Perry Wood for victory and another seven years' prosperity. Next morning Fleetwood's columns moved off at 5 or 6 a.m., tracking 20 great boats upstream to the junction of the two rivers. Arriving between 2 and 3 p.m., they threw across two bridges in 30 minutes, within pistol shot of one another. Cannon balls found near Manor Farm suggest artillery fire cleared the far bank while civilian boatmen patched the bridges together for the assault troops to scramble across: 'The dispute was from hedge to hedge and very hot; sometimes more with foot than with horse and foot. The lifeguard made a gallant charge, and so did my lord general's regiment of horse ... The dispute continued to the evening, all along with great heat; and about sunset, we had beaten them into Worcester, and our men possessed of St John's at the bridge end' (Scoutmaster George Downing). The greatest stress was about Powick Bridge, where the Scots lined the hedges with musketeers, and defended a house. Driven from these vantage points the Scots skirmishers fell back on their main body, 'that stood in Wick Field; where the first blood was shed in that cause by the late king' (Thomas Scot and Richard Salway, Commonwealth councillors of state).

Charles II had a good view of the fighting from the cathedral tower, and launched his counterstroke on the eastern bank while Cromwell's best troops were committed on the west: '[the enemy] drew out his main body at the same instant, in the heat of that engagement, and marched up to what remained of ours this side, where was not above the third part of our [regular] forces, and many foot of yours new' (Scot and Salway). An anonymous Royalist says the plan was 'to divide the army into two parties; the one to goe upon the one side of Perry Wood, and the other on the other reserving a body to fall on and assist where need should require'. His Majesty led out the right wing through Sidbury or East Gate, along the A44 to Red Hill. The Duke of Hamilton advanced on his left from St Martin's Gate, passing south of Shrub Hill railway station. They had some success: 'Duke Hamilton was shot in the first charge which he performed with great honour at Perry Wood; where the King broke through and forced back their horse to their body of foot'. Superior numbers soon told, however: 'upon the enemy's second firing, they [the Royalists] were so dispersed that they rallied no more, but gave back violently, and forced the king to make into the town' (anonymous Royalist). Clarendon confirms the Royalists 'beat the body that charged them back, but they were quickly overpowered ... such a general consternation possessed the whole army, that the rest of the horse fled and all the foot threw down their arms before they were charged' (*History of the Rebellion*). Leslie conspicuously failed to commit the Royalist reserve at Pitchcroft, but 'rode up and down as one amazed or seeking to fly' (anonymous Royalist).

Cromwell had returned to the east bank, and quickly exploited the Royalist retreat. Fort Royal was summoned to surrender, 'which they denying and shooting at the messenger, our foot most resolutely ran into and possessed it, and despatched the enemy there' (Scot and Salway). The Essex militia, who only the day before had fallen flat on their faces when shot at, planted their colours on the ramparts and turned the fort's guns on Royalists crowding back through Sidbury Gate, 'much readier to cut each other's throats than to defend [themselves] against the enemy' (anonymous Royalist). The king rallied a few men for a counterattack, only to find himself alone, except for his servants. He ordered the gates closed, 'but all was confusion; there were few to command, and none to obey' (Clarendon). Charles retreated to his quarters at King Charles's House in Cornmarket, escaping through the back door as Commonwealth dragoons came in the front. Covered by diversionary charges down High Street and Sidbury Street, he got away through St Martin's Gate, hidden in the press of fugitives.

Cromwell was unusually ecstatic, writing of 'a very glorious mercy', and 'an absolute victory … a total defeat and ruin of the enemy's army'. Nobody could estimate the casualties, 'but they are very many; and must needs be so, because the dispute was long and very near at hand, and often at push of pike, and from one defence to another'. Royalist losses were above 2000 slain, 640 officer prisoners (plus 9 chaplains), a staggering 10,000 other ranks taken, with 158 colours, the king's coach and horses, and the Mayor of Worcester. Commonwealth losses were posted as 100 dead and 300 wounded, with two officers in each category.

Worcester wrecked the Royalist cause for a decade, and legitimized the Commonwealth. The militia's massive presence and impressive battlefield performance showed that, whatever Englishmen thought about the Republic, they liked foreigners even less. The shocking scale of the victory prevented further military challenges to Republican rule. England had proved strong enough to frustrate Scottish and Irish attempts to decide how the Three Kingdoms should be governed, a result that would endure until the 20th century.

PART SEVEN

FLINTLOCK AND BAYONET

The Age of Enlightenment 1652–1798

The century and a half that followed the Battle of Worcester (1651) saw the end of conventional warfare in the North Atlantic Archipelago. In future there might be riots, aerial bombardments or terrorist outrages, but the area's last formal battles were fought in Ireland in 1798, half a century after the 1745 Jacobite Rising had seen the English and Scottish equivalents. This long internal peace, hardly interrupted by the serio-comic French landing at Fishguard in 1793, contrasts sharply with the turmoil that preceded it. The Civil Wars had seen battles in the very heart of England. After 1660 such events were confined to more remote areas. Maritime struggles against the Dutch foreshadowed a new phase, in which an effectively united Great Britain and Ireland would make its military history overseas. Political developments moderated violence within these islands, while military and economic changes made internal strife unprofitable and (outside Ireland) unthinkable.

Charles II's Restoration in 1660 re-established constitutional legality after the military dictatorship of the 1650s. When Cromwell died in 1658, on the anniversary of Dunbar and Worcester, his generals fell out, opening the way for George Monck to engineer a compromise settlement. The king returned with reduced prerogatives, as did the bishops, though most of the Long Parliament's early reforms survived. The New Model Army was paid off, and a few particularly notorious rebels executed. The indispensable Monck became Duke of Albemarle, lord general and master general of the ordnance. The Protector's unions with Ireland and Scotland were dissolved, although England's central role in the Restoration left no doubt where the Three Kingdoms' political centre of gravity lay, a strategic reality underlined by demography. Figures remain uncertain before the 1801 census, but England and Wales probably represented two-thirds of the population of Restoration Britain and Ireland, 5.5 million out of 7 or 8 million. The most astonishing population change of the period was Ireland's recovery from the losses of the Civil Wars. It passed 2 million in the 1680s to reach 5.2 million by 1801 (out of 15.9 million for the British Isles as a whole), figures justifying English fears and Irish hopes.

Any serious contender for power had to control London, the most populous city in Europe. When the Protestant Duke of Monmouth, one of Charles II's bastards, tried to overthrow his Catholic uncle James II in 1685 he got no nearer than Bath, before he was defeated at Sedgemoor. The last successful invasion of England came three years later, when James's son-in-law William of Orange, Stadtholder of the United Provinces, landed at Torbay. Ostensibly coming to preserve English liberties, his personal objective was to secure England's resources for his projected war with France. James panicked and fled. William III and Mary II (James's Protestant daughter) ascended the throne jointly, consummating a bloodless and therefore 'Glorious Revolution'.

Resistance was confined to the fringes. Highland clans rose in support of the deposed king, earning the label Jacobite (from *Jacobus*, the Latin for James). They decimated a Williamite column at Killiecrankie (1689), but failed to exploit their victory. Ireland's Roman Catholic majority made a determined bid for independence, before suffering disaster at the Boyne (1690) and Aughrim (1691). The dependence of James's heirs upon Highland loyalists limited their chances. The Jacobite armies of 1715 and 1745 came no nearer London than Preston and Derby respectively. The little-known adventure of 1719 ended well north of the Border, at Glenshiel.

The most serious military threat to English territory during this period arose from the three Dutch Wars fought against the Protestant United Provinces between 1652 and 1674. Their recurrence under Commonwealth and king illustrates how economic rather than religious or constitutional issues now shaped

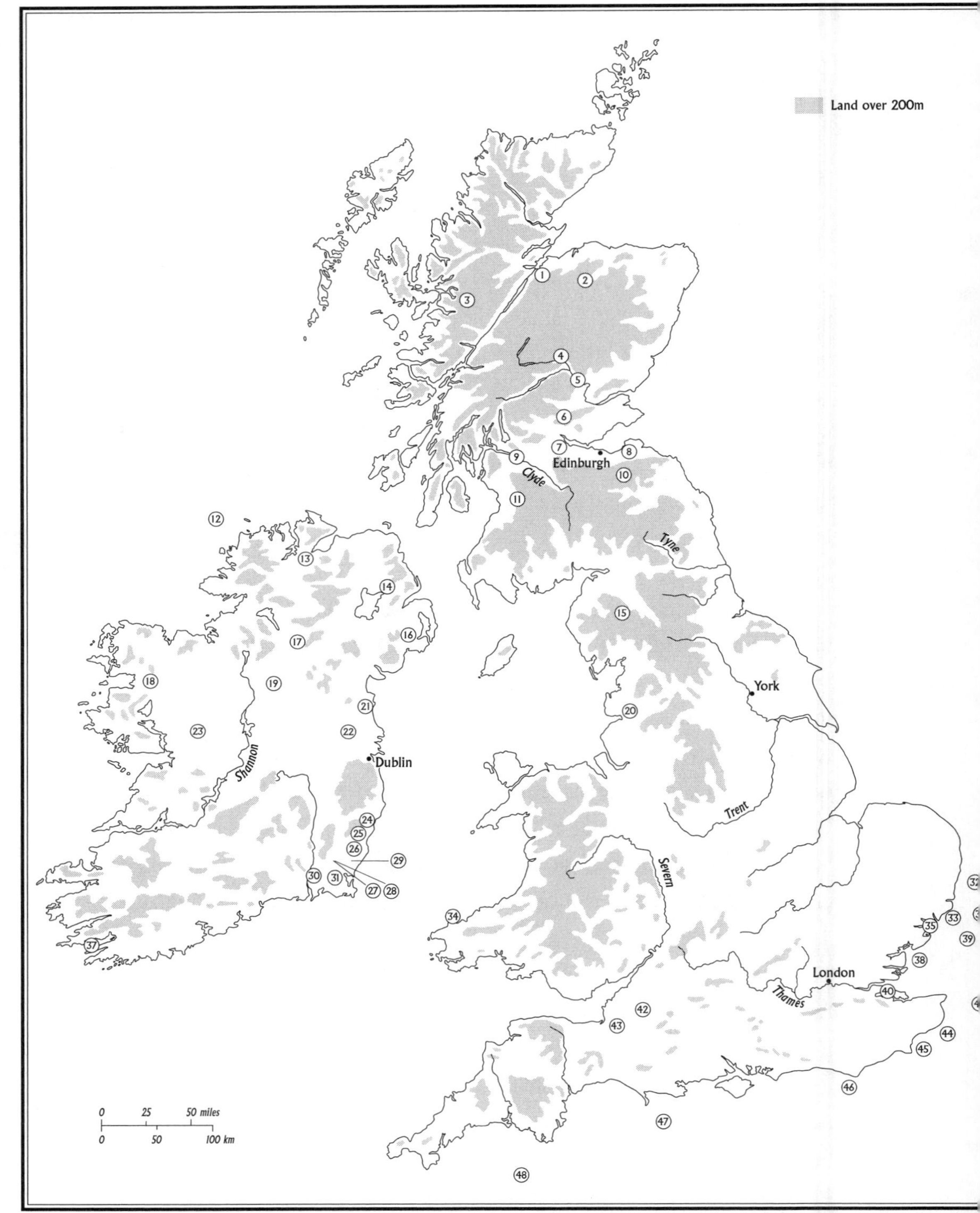
Land over 200m
Edinburgh
Clyde
Tyne
York
Dublin
Shannon
Trent
Severn
London
Thames
0 25 50 miles
0 50 100 km
1
2
3
4
5
6
7
8
9
10
11
12
13
14
15
16
17
18
19
20
21
22
23
24
25
26
27
28
29
30
31
33
34
35
37
38
39
40
42
43
44
45
46
47
48

foreign policy. Anglo-Dutch commercial rivalry inspired a new style of naval warfare, in which huge fleets mounting thousands of cannon fought for national economic objectives. Survivors of Sole Bay (1672) 'believed there never were so many guns fired in one day before'. Naval broadsides comparable in numbers of guns to First World War bombardments shook houses and ships up to 40 miles (64 km) away, and were audible in London. Listeners ashore took heart from reductions in volume, which implied a Dutch retreat. Many battles occurred within sight of land, 'the whole country ... in smoke and stench of the powder, they fighting so near the shore'. A land-based observer of Sole Bay was so near he saw 'almost every broadside, and was in hearing and whistling of the shot' (*Calendar of State Papers*). Inshore naval battles, however, reflected obsolescent strategic conditions. In future the Royal Navy would limit intrusions into British territorial waters. The last fleet action on the English coast was fought off Beachy Head in 1690, although French forays into Irish waters persisted until the 1790s.

Dissolution of the Protector's union left Restoration Scotland with insufficient troops to maintain order, and no money to pay them. The Kirk had lost its ambition to export Presbyterianism, but still resisted the imposition of bishops. Its more extreme followers roamed Scotland's southern hills in armed bands, an intolerable threat to any government. Open warfare broke out twice: in 1666 at Rullion Green, and in 1679 at Drumclog and Bothwell Bridge. More persistent difficulties arose in the Highlands, which assumed a brief and disproportionate importance in British history. Highland society remained largely feudal.

KEY

1 Culloden 1746
2 Haughs of Cromdale 1690
3 Glenshiel 1719
4 Killiecrankie 1689
5 Dunkeld 1689
6 Sheriffmuir 1715
7 Falkirk II 1746
8 Prestonpans 1745
9 Bothwell Bridge 1679
10 Rullion Green 1666
11 Drumclog 1679
12 Lough Swilly 1798
13 Londonderry, Relief of 1689
14 Antrim 1798
15 Clifton Moor 1745
16 Ballynahinch 1798
17 Newton Butler 1689
18 Castlebar Races 1798
19 Ballinamuck 1798
20 Preston 1715
21 Boyne, The 1690
22 Tara 1798
23 Aughrim 1691
24 Arklow 1798
25 Tubberneering 1798
26 Kilthomas 1798
27 Enniscorthy 1798
28 Vinegar Hill 1798
29 Oulart Hill 1798
30 New Ross 1798
31 Goff's Bridge 1798
32 Lowestoft 1665
33 Sole Bay 1672
34 Fishguard 1797
35 Landguard Fort 1667
36 Gabbard Bank 1653
37 Bantry Bay 1689
38 St James's Day Fight 1666
39 Kentish Knock 1652
40 Dutch in the Medway 1667
41 Four Days' Fight 1666
42 Norton St Philip 1685
43 Sedgemoor 1685
44 Dover 1652
45 Dungeness 1652
46 Beachy Head 1690
47 Portland 1653
48 Plymouth 1652

Land was held in exchange for military service, and weapons were part of everyday male attire. Lack of gainful employment other than cattle rustling created a readily mobilized pool of manpower inured to arms. The Stuart dynasty had little sympathy for the Highlands, but cynically exploited the loyalty of some clans in its attempts to regain the throne. Jacobite risings in 1689, 1715, 1719 and 1745 finally provoked the British government to take drastic measures to disarm the clans after Culloden, ending their ancient way of life.

The Glorious Revolution fatally undermined Scottish independence. Drawn willy-nilly into William III's Nine Years' War with France (1689–97), while excluded from England's colonial trade, Scotland became poorer, unable even to mint its own coins. Mary II died childless in 1694, and her sister Anne, who succeeded William in 1702, appeared likely to do the same. Lacking a Protestant Stuart heir to the throne, England's Parliament unilaterally settled the succession on the queen's second cousin George, Elector of Hanover. A Jacobite restoration in Scotland would have entailed inevitable conflict with its more powerful southern neighbour, as James II's heirs always regarded themselves as kings of Great Britain as a whole. The 1707 Act of Union was a marriage of least inconvenience; the lesser of two evils. The Scots surrendered their separate Parliament in exchange for access to English markets, accepting the Hanoverian Succession to avert civil war. The Union inspired little enthusiasm. Its opponents adopted a passive Jacobitism, encouraging ill-fated rebellions that foundered for lack of active support. The Jacobite defeat at Culloden finally exorcized the ghosts of 1688, confirming Scotland's place within Hanoverian Britain.

William III's victory at Aughrim in 1691 crushed Irish Catholics for a generation. Throughout the 18th century Ireland was governed at arm's length by a lord lieutenant appointed in London, and by a gerrymandered Parliament run in the interests of the Anglican minority, known as the Protestant Ascendancy. Presbyterians and Roman Catholics were second- and third-class citizens respectively. Penal laws denied papists the right to vote, bear arms or inherit land. Nevertheless, a degree of prosperity and 10,000 regular troops kept the peace until the 1790s, when war with Revolutionary France and growing population pressure undermined the Ascendancy. In 1798 the Dublin government's brutal policies provoked revolutionary outbreaks throughout Ireland's eastern counties, the richest part of the island. The Ninety-Eight revived old traditions of armed resistance and foreign intervention, inspiring a new ideal of an independent republic that challenged the traditional relationship with the English throne. The Irish Act of Union of 1801 reaffirmed England's political primacy in the British Isles for the time being, although the unwilling presence of a large Irish population within the Union threatened its long-term survival.

The Civil Wars left central government with fewer prerogatives, but with more practical power. Charles II could not raise taxes without Parliament, but he did have a standing army and a sound naval administration. The Commonwealth's army stood down in 1660, but Charles II retained enough old soldiers, both Royalist and Parliamentarian, to create a permanent standing army of 8865 guards and garrisons. Senior regiments of the British Army still trace descent from units of Charles II's army. The Scottish standing army remained separate, consisting in 1679 of 'two regiments of foot, each 1000 men, four troops of horse, and three companies of dragoons' (*Calendar of State Papers*).

In many respects the Restoration army followed Civil War practice. Colonels still owned their regiments, which consisted of a varying number of companies or troops, depending on financial constraints as much as operational requirements. At full establishment a foot regiment had 12 companies of roughly 100 men each; regiments of horse were smaller, typically 6 troops of 50 rank and file each. Artillery had no permanent organization until the Royal Regiment of Artillery was established in 1716.

Small by European standards, the late Stuart army secured the king's person and deterred plotters. Just 2850 royal troops saw off 3000–4000 rebels at Sedgemoor (1685). The total effective strength of the army rose throughout the late 17th century, following a general European trend. During the Nine Years' War the English establishment passed 90,000, mostly posted overseas. Nearer home only Boyne and Aughrim approached Continental battles in size. With 60,000 combatants the former is the largest battle ever fought anywhere in Britain or Ireland. The relatively small numbers of British troops deployed at Culloden reflect limited opposition, rather than military unpreparedness. In 1762, towards the end of the Seven Years' War, the British army numbered 111,583, with 24,000 more in Ireland. Even reduced peacetime strengths represented forces far in excess of those available to governments before the Civil Wars. At the same time, the restructuring of Highland society after Culloden (1746) confirmed the Crown's monopoly of lethal force. Targes found new employment as lids for barrels of buttermilk.

Cromwell's other legacy was the navy: not just the 229 ships on the books in 1660, but its administrative infrastructure: the Navy Board, the Commissioners of Victualling, and the Sick and Hurt Board. Renamed the Royal Navy by Charles II, the fleet's main purpose was home defence. Despite high-profile failures such as the Dutch raid on the Medway in 1667 or William of Orange's descent on Torbay in 1688, it had pushed Britain's frontiers back to the Continental coast by the late 1690s. If an invasion force slipped through, the navy could still cut off its supplies. Admiral Herbert failed to prevent the French landing stores at Bantry Bay in 1689, but HMS *Lyon* did intercept the *Elisabeth* in 1745, en route to Scotland with arms for the Young Pretender. The weather remained these islands' most sure defence. Storms dispersed a Jacobite squadron in 1719, and frustrated General Hoche's Bantry Bay expedition in 1796. Insularity was a positive advantage in emergencies, troops redeploying swiftly by sea from Flanders in 1745, and from England to Ireland in 1798. The Jacobites controlled most of Ireland in 1690, but without a fleet could not prevent William III disembarking an army at Carrickfergus.

While the standing army and navy reduced the frequency of battles by deterring military adventurers, political stability provided more mundane disincentives. Parliamentary government under a constitutionally limited monarchy made it possible to change administrations without the use of force. However violent by modern standards, opposition now represented competition for office, rather than subversion. Established to finance William III's campaigns in the 1690s, the national debt and the Bank of England stabilized the regime by giving government stockholders a pecuniary interest in its survival. Modest economic progress from the 1730s demonstrated the benefits of the Hanoverian Settlement, as Union with England offered Scotsmen an escape from the 'Cow and Kale Yard'. Internal migration permitted all four nations to share England's commercial prosperity as Britain approached industrial takeoff. In 1776, a Scot living in London named Adam Smith published *The Wealth of Nations*, the starting point for modern economics, and a more appropriate symbol of Britain's future than romantic images of dispossessed Highlanders.

On the battlefield technical developments favoured the professional over the amateur, making rebellion less attractive. Battle lines thinned out to develop maximum firepower, making drill essential to prevent disorder on the move and panic under fire. The first official English drill manual appeared in 1678. Untrained troops of any nationality were at a hopeless disadvantage. Irish Jacobites never learned to fight in the open, preferring to defend rivers and bogs at the Boyne and Aughrim. Sir John Cope's raw recruits ran away at Prestonpans (1745). Prince Charles Edward's Highlanders did their best to imitate a regular army, fighting Culloden on level ground rather than withdrawing into the mountains to wage a guerrilla war.

The most prominent tactical development of the late 17th century was enhanced infantry firepower. The proportion of pikes fell to a fifth of infantry numbers, compared with a third during the Civil Wars. By the 1790s the once 'puissant pike' had become a joke weapon wielded by Irish peasants. Its demise, however, left infantry vulnerable to cavalry, until the adoption of the bayonet. From the 1670s English musketeers used plug bayonets, whose handle fitted inside the muzzle of the infantryman's firearm. This stopped him firing just before physical contact with the enemy, an interruption that contributed to the Williamite debacle at Killiecrankie. The socket bayonet, which fitted under rather than inside the muzzle, solved the roblem, becoming standard in the English service, though not the Irish, before the Boyne.

The second element in the period's dominant weapon system was the flintlock musket, introduced gradually between the Restoration and the Glorious Revolution. Like the earlier matchlock, flintlocks were smooth-bore muzzle-loading weapons with a maximum range of some 200 yards (180 m). However, they replaced the matchlock's constantly burning slow match with a shower of sparks; generated when the user pulled the trigger, and directed into the priming pan. Flintlocks were more reliable, reducing misfires to one-third instead of half. They were lighter and took fewer movements to reload, doubling rates of fire to two rounds a minute, with no loss of accuracy. Overall their users enjoyed a three-to-one edge over matchlocks. Flintlocks were also safer. Eliminating the slow match allowed infantry to stand closer together without blowing themselves up, so producing more firepower along a given frontage. Paper cartridges in a waterproof cartouche box replaced the wooden powder bottles carried by Civil War musketeers, further improving safety and reliability. It was firearms that decided battles now, not cold steel.

The separate blocks of pike and shot of the Civil Wars made way for shallower continuous lines of musketeers, in three ranks instead of six. In large battles, such as Culloden, this provided a surplus of men for a second line 300 paces behind the firing line, insurance against tactical emergencies. The sudden outcome of smaller actions such as Killiecrankie or Prestonpans can be attributed to lack of sufficient troops to form a support line. Armies evolved complex procedures to direct musketry to best effect. During the Nine Years' War English infantry adopted the Dutch method of firing by platoons (18 of them per regiment) to deliver a continual rolling fire. This ensured a proportion of men were always ready to fire, while generating more noise and casualties than the French system of firing by ranks.

The British Army retained platoon firing as the basis of its infantry tactics throughout the 18th century. Its main competitor was the attack *à prest*, in which troops closed with the enemy as quickly as possible to avoid their fire, discharged a single volley, dropped their muskets and set to with their swords. The main users of this tactic in Britain were Highlanders, who carried all before them at Prestonpans and Killiecrankie, enjoyed mixed success at Sheriffmuir and Falkirk, and suffered total disaster at Culloden. Their successes, like those of Alasdair MacColla MacDonnell during the Civil Wars (see Part 6), are usually attributed to their speed and heavy armament of musket, pistol, broadsword, targe and dirk. Sceptics might point to extraneous factors: the defenders' plug bayonets at

Killiecrankie; poor training at Prestonpans; bad weather at Falkirk; the opposition's lack of artillery at all those battles. General Mackay noted after Killiecrankie that Highlanders never fought without a mountain at their backs, to which they fled if their opponents stood firm. More commonly infantry sought to shake the enemy by fire, leaving cavalry to deliver the *coup de grâce*, as they did at Sedgemoor and Aughrim.

Cavalry became the main offensive arm, using superior mobility and relative ease of deployment to attack the flanks of the opposing infantry's overextended lines. Horse and dragoons merged into a general-purpose mounted arm, the former giving up their armour, the latter learning to charge sword in hand. English dragoons still carried muskets and bayonets, fighting on foot at Preston (1715) and Clifton (1745). Cavalry combined missile and close-quarter weapons, giving them a choice of tactics: a rapid loose-order charge to avoid enemy fire, or a slower advance in close order, firing pistols and carbines. As bayonets made every musketeer his own pikeman, mounted troops lost their advantage, performing poorly against musket-armed Highlanders during the Forty-Five.

Artillery remained an auxiliary arm at the start of the period, although the decapitation of the French commander at Aughrim by a cannon ball might be seen as a decisive intervention. Cannon changed little in appearance thereafter, undergoing an imperceptible process of technical improvement throughout the 18th century. Lack of trained personnel neutralized the Hanoverian artillery during the Forty-Five, until the Duke of Cumberland's reforms before Culloden. Lighter carriages, improved elevation gear and increased lethality derived from closer tolerances between gun-bore and projectile gave cannon a decisive role in Ireland's last battles in the 1790s.

Naval warfare showed a similar trend towards formal linear tactics based on firepower, as seamen recognized the tactical logic of placing guns along their ships' broadsides. Fleets began to form close line of battle, instead of clustering around a flagship before charging through the enemy in line abreast. The new tactic prevented the enemy concentrating fire on single ships, or attacking the ends of vessels unable to fire ahead or astern. It also prevented overlapping ships firing into their comrades, as the Dutch did at Kentish Knock (1652). Because ships moved at right angles to their line of fire, fleets could not advance directly upon the enemy while firing. They formed parallel lines a few hundred yards apart, and exchanged broadsides until one side broke, or darkness intervened. Admirals learned to trade off the offensive advantages of holding the weather gauge, i.e. remaining to windward of the enemy, against lying to leeward in order to escape downwind when hard pressed.

The *Fighting Instructions* used at Gabbard Bank (1653) prescribed tactics that remained largely unchanged until Nelson's time. Warships evolved into specialized ships of the line, strong enough to withstand the prolonged close-range battering by heavy guns typical of naval actions. Usually ships engaged at musket range, in theory one-tenth that of their main armament. Land soldiers went to sea to sweep the enemy decks with small-arms fire and grenades. The Dutch Admiral de With complained how much better the English managed both great guns and small shot. The only other type of warship was the fireship, stuffed with explosives and floated down wind to disorganize the enemy line or finish off individual cripples.

The large homogeneous fleets and armies of the late 17th century created strategic stalemate, particularly at sea. Fleets could not easily bring an enemy of comparable mobility to action against their will. When they did, poor quality guns and ammunition prevented rapid destruction of hostile fleets, even when heavily outnumbered, as the Duke of Albemarle was during the Four Days' Fight of 1666. Naval battles declined in frequency generally, as well as in home waters. Ashore only the Irish campaigns of the 1690s approached the Continental scale of operations, requiring several years to reach a decision. Hostilities within the British Isles usually ended more quickly, the superior numbers, training and equipment of government forces proving decisive. The Fifteen and the Forty-Five were over in months; other risings in weeks. A heavily armed and centralized state, with a broad base of popular consent, left little room for armed expressions of discontent.

Trade Wars

Anglo-Dutch friction during the mid-17th century provoked a series of desperate sea battles fought out within hearing, and often sight, of southeastern England. The United Provinces obdurately refused to allow anyone else – including England, their erstwhile ally against Spain – a share in Europe's seaborne trade. Dutch warships harassed English fishermen, and their Danish allies closed the Sound, denying England access to Baltic naval stores. In 1623 Dutch officials had massacred English traders at Amboyna in the East Indies. The Civil Wars delayed a settling of accounts until Parliament's final victory. Within a month of Worcester the Navigation Act of 9 October 1651 had prohibited imports in foreign, i.e. Dutch, ships. As George Monck, who fought in the First and Second Dutch Wars, put it, 'The Dutch have too much trade and the English are resolved to take it from them.'

England was well placed to attack Dutch commerce. The south coast flanks the direct route for Dutch vessels plying to or from the Mediterranean and Far East. Concentrated in home waters, rather than dispersed around the world's trade routes, English seamen and ships could force Dutch merchantmen to run the gauntlet up Channel, or sail north around Scotland. Half the battles of the First Dutch War were convoy actions. Prevailing westerly winds hindered Dutch counterattacks on English harbours, although they carried more than one shattered fleet home to the Netherlands and Zealand. Administrative centralization favoured the English, with just one Admiralty Board controlling their war effort. The so-called United Provinces had five.

The First Dutch War (1652–5) began without formal declaration, as an English attempt to make a Dutch flagship strike its flag in salute escalated into a fleet action off Dover (19 May 1652). After four more battles with varying results, the English gained control of the Channel in a three-day fight between Portland and Cap Gris Nez (18–20 February 1653), crippling Dutch commerce. With grass sprouting in Amsterdam's streets, the Dutch made a final sortie, only to be defeated at Gabbard Bank (2 June 1653) by new line-ahead tactics. In April 1654 the Treaty of Westminster acknowledged the rights of the English flag to appropriate courtesies, and submitted outstanding grievances to arbitration.

A Second Dutch War (1665–7) arose from continued disagreements over the Navigation Acts, which were extended under Charles II to include exports, and from the continued Dutch refusal to open the East Indies to English trade. Reprisals against Dutch shipping escalated into a blockade of the Dutch coast and a limited English victory at Lowestoft (3 June 1665). France now allied itself with the United Provinces, dividing the English fleet, which engaged twice its own number of Dutch ships in the epic Four Days' Fight (1–4 June 1666). Heroic efforts by dockyards and seamen refitted shattered English warships within weeks, and the Royal Navy regained control of the North Sea in the St James's Day Fight (25 July 1666). As peace talks dragged on, an impoverished Charles II demobilized the fleet, opening the way for one of the most embarrassing incidents in English history, the Dutch descent on the Medway (10–14 June 1667). Landguard Fort, near Harwich, saw off another landing on 2 July, but the Dutch hovered offshore until the Treaty of Breda was signed on the 21st. Confirming the honour of the seas to England, this modified the Navigation Acts in favour of the Dutch, and confirmed English possession of New York, previously New Amsterdam.

The Third Dutch War (1672–4) followed the secret Treaty of Dover (1 June 1670), when Charles II joined Louis XIV to eliminate the United Provinces. There was just one battle on the English coast, at Sole Bay (28 May 1672), which frustrated an Anglo-French descent on the Netherlands. After further unsatisfactory actions off the Dutch coast, England concluded the second Treaty of Westminster (9 February 1674), restoring the *status quo ante* between the Protestant commercial powers.

Naval tactics before the First Dutch War revolved around attempts to charge through the enemy line piecemeal, hoping to overwhelm one or two enemy ships in the confusion. The results were correspondingly limited. After Portland, the leading English Admiral Robert Blake issued new *Fighting Instructions* on 29 March 1653. In their next battle at Gabbard Bank, English ships kept to windward, 'in file at half cannon shot, from whence they battered the Hollanders furiously all the day ...' (Letter from the Hague, 10 June 1653). Twenty Dutch ships were lost and no English. Linear tactics made best use of the English navy's heavier broadsides and superior discipline. Dutch admirals complained that the lightest English frigates outgunned the heaviest Dutch ships, while Dutch captains regularly overlapped and fired into their friends, fell foul of them, or just ran away. The English had already adopted their classic gunnery techniques of firing more rapidly than the opposition, and targeting enemy hulls to maximize casualties, rather than shooting at masts and rigging, as the Dutch did. The Dutch were already sure after Kentish Knock (28 September 1652) that the English 'fired smarter and quicker than did many of ours'. Warships grew rapidly in size and power. Blake's flagship at Dover had half the guns carried by the Duke of York's at Sole Bay. Before Lowestoft, the English discussed concentrating their biggest warships, to achieve decisive superiority at one point of their line, although the Dutch attacked before the scheme could be implemented. A new era of rational naval tactics had arrived, based on calculated cooperation rather than individual heroism.

NB: Dates given below are Julian Old Style, as used in England, ten days behind the Gregorian New Style used in Dutch reports. Numbers and losses for naval battles usually show warships, fireships and armed merchantmen, excluding small craft and non-combatant merchantmen.

Dover, Wednesday 19 May 1652

Naval, English Channel, LR179

The first action of the Dutch Wars happened by chance. Both sides accused the other of firing first, but open conflict was the probable result of confrontational policies pursued by both governments. The seizure of French goods from neutral Dutch ships by English privateers threatened the Hollanders' carrying trade, the basis of their prosperity. While the action off Dover began with Blake's attempt to force Tromp to strike his flag, the latter's main concern was to protect Dutch merchant shipping.

On 18 May, Blake lay in Rye Bay, 30 miles (48 km) west of Dover, with 12 ships, his flag in the 48-gun *James*. Bourne, with 9 ships, was at the Downs, the roadstead off the east Kent coast between Deal and the Goodwin Sands. Wind was from the northeast, the weather hazy. At 10 a.m. Bourne observed 'a great fleet on the back of the Goodwin Sand'; the fleet sent in two ships to explain that rough weather had driven Tromp's fleet off the French coast. Tromp was 'not willing to breed any difference about his flag', so stayed outside the Downs. While Bourne prepared to defend the anchorage, the Dutch continued down Channel past South Sand Head, into Dover Road, 'off the South Foreland in the fair way', where they spent the afternoon practising small shot.

Next day the wind was easterly, the weather fair. Blake beat up Channel towards Bourne, who left the Downs at noon to join him. As Bourne cleared the South Foreland he saw the Dutch in the middle of the Channel, 'plying to windward towards Calais'. Almost immediately Tromp reversed course onto the starboard tack, i.e. with the wind coming from his right, and bore down on Blake, who prepared for action 'judging they had a resolution to engage'. Blake brought his ships onto the same tack, in line

Dover

	Winner	Loser
Opponents	Commonwealth	Dutch
Commanders	Robert Blake	Marten Harpertszoon
	Nehemiah Bourne	Tromp
Numbers	21–23	40–42
Losses	0 ships;	2 ships;
	men unknown	men unknown

ahead of the *James*, and ran out his lower tier of guns.

Tromp had not meant to precipitate an international incident. Approaching Calais, he learned of seven valuable Dutch merchantmen menaced by English cruisers off Fairlight, east of Hastings. He could see Blake and other ships near the Varne, a sandbank 10 miles (16 km) south-southeast of Folkestone, sometimes called the Ripraps. Unable to distinguish friend from foe at that distance, Tromp hurried back to rescue the merchantmen. The reversal of both fleets inadvertently brought the English and Dutch flagships together, at the rear and head of their lines respectively, the Dutch to windward.

Accounts differ as to what happened next. Blake and other English witnesses say Blake fired three guns: two 'thwart Tromp's forefoot', and a third through his sails. Tromp then ran alongside Blake to starboard, and opened fire, delivering 12 broadsides to the *James*'s 2. The Dutch admiral only reported firing once, well clear of the *James*: 'At once he [Blake] gives me a broadside, being within musket shot, and shot all his broadside through our ship and sails. Some of our men were wounded, some with the loss of their arms, some otherwise; whereupon we presently gave him our broadside.' Tromp hung out the red flag, the signal for action, and firing became general.

While Blake and Tromp ran downwind firing on both sides, Bourne got the wind, and at 4.30 p.m. brought his division astern of the Dutch, who 'did their utmost to decline us and avoid our coming near'. Most of the enemy ships 'shot themselves to leeward of us', while Bourne tried to cut off the rearmost, 'wherein they shuffled themselves into clusters, but by reason many of our ships and frigates sailed very heavy, by reason they are foul, we could not fully attain our desire upon them'. Only two prizes were taken, before darkness ended the action.

Blake spent the night refitting 3 or 4 leagues (about 9–12 miles, or 15–20 km) off Dungeness, and next day the Dutch could be seen from the masthead, making for Dieppe. One of the prizes had been left in a sinking condition, the captain of the other crying out against Tromp and the others, 'for their cowardly carriage in leaving them to our mercy' (Bourne). Blake lost no ships, although his 12 fought Tromp's 40 for two hours before Bourne joined in. The *James* took 70 great shot in her hull and rigging, losing 6 men dead, 9 or 10 desperately wounded and 'twenty-five more not without danger'. Other ships suffered proportionately less.

Blake accused the Dutch of 'being first in the breach, and seeking an occasion to quarrel', but a collision was the likely consequence of brinkmanship and inadequate signalling techniques. Tromp's alleged aggression justified further attacks on Dutch shipping, forcing the latter to adopt convoys, setting the stage for larger, more considered actions.

Directions

The fighting occurred 5 or 6 miles (8–10 km) offshore, in East Wear Bay between the Varne Light and South Foreland, athwart the Dover–Calais ferry lanes.

Plymouth, 16 August 1652

Naval, English Channel, LR201

The first deliberate battle of the First Dutch War was a convoy action off Plymouth. Tromp fell under a cloud after Dover (see above), and de Ruyter replaced him as Dutch commander-in-chief. The latter left Calais Roads on 11 August 1652 with 50–60 outward bound merchantmen, and met Sir George Ayscue in mid-Channel off Plymouth between 1 and 2 p.m. on the 19th.

The English had cleared Plymouth the day before.

They were 7 leagues out (about 20 miles or 32 km) on the morning of the 16th heading towards the French coast, before a northeasterly wind. De Ruyter was due south of Dodman's Point in Cornwall and just 10 leagues (30 miles or 50 km) from the Ile de Batz when he sighted Ayscue, and beat up northwards to meet him. As the Channel is over 100 miles (160 km) wide at this point, the encounter was nearer the French than the English coast.

Ayscue put his own fleet at 38 warships, 4 fireships and 4 small craft known as galliots, not far off de Ruyter's estimate of 40 warships and 5 fireships. The English observed 90 Dutch vessels, including 30 merchantmen, 'who left their fleet upon the first engagement, and kept their course to the southward'. De Ruyter listed in his own fleet 30 warships, the largest 2 mounting 40 guns apiece, the rest 24–30. He also had 6 fireships, 3 galliots and about 20 merchantmen who stayed to fight, figures consistent with English estimates of 55 Dutchmen.

The action began between 4 and 5 p.m., Ayscue charging through the enemy line with 7 ships. They received numerous hits, including sundry great shot through the admiral's cabin, 'but more in their masts, sails and rigging, the enemy's main design being to spoil them, in hope thereby to make the better use of their fireships …' (Ayscue). However, the Dutch leeward position rendered these ineffective; otherwise, de Ruyter thought, 'we should soon have made an end of them'. Avoiding the fireships, Ayscue tacked, weathered the enemy line and charged again, 'and so continued still engaged in the body of their fleet, till it was dark night' (Ayscue). Despite the closeness of the action, neither side succeeded in boarding the enemy.

De Ruyter confirms the English account, 'we having twice fought our way through their fleet; but if we had been able to get the wind of them … as they did of ours, we should, with God's help, have utterly routed the foremost of them; for I with six or seven of our ships was in the middle of their fleet'. Fighting stopped between 7 and 8 p.m., when de Ruyter claimed the English took flight to the north, or as they described it, put back to Plymouth to refit.

Ayscue suffered one total loss, a fireship set ablaze to prevent her capture. *George* and *Bonaventure* were unofficially reported 'much shattered and ready to sink'. Ayscue admitted 'divers slain and many wounded, for the enemy charged us one after another in order'. A letter from Plymouth says 15 were killed and about 60 wounded, mostly from the fireship, which blew up unexpectedly. Several correspondents suggest the admiral was ill-supported: 'Some captains … were cowards, and did not their parts.' The English claimed 2 Dutch ships sunk. De Ruyter reported losing 50–60 killed and 40–50 wounded, although 'our ships and men were in a bad condition before the action, and are consequently now in a worse one …'. Plymouth was a strategic success for de Ruyter, who achieved his aim of taking his convoy safely down the Channel.

Plymouth

	Winner	*Loser*
Opponents	Dutch	Commonwealth
Commanders	Michiel Adrienszoon de Ruyter	Sir George Ayscue
Numbers	36	42
Losses	0 ships; *c.*100 men	1 ship; 75 men

Directions

West of the Plymouth–Roscoff ferry route, nearer the French coast.

Kentish Knock, Tuesday 28 September 1652

Naval, North Sea

Kentish Knock was the first of many inconclusive Anglo-Dutch encounters. The Dutch hoped to regain control of the sea, appointing de With, known as 'the Bellicose', to clear their coasts of English cruisers.

De Ruyter prowled off the Lizard for a month after his success at Plymouth, joining de With off

Calais on 22 September. The combined fleets appeared off the Goodwins on the 25th, but a southwesterly gale prevented them attacking Blake in the Downs. The wind moderating two days later, Blake left the anchorage early on 28 September, heading up-Channel. Wind direction is recorded variously as southwesterly, west-southwesterly, westerly, and even 'a fresh gale at west by north'.

The leading English ships saw the Dutch at noon, hove-to in the lee of Kentish Knock, a sandbank 18 miles (29 km) north-northeast of North Foreland, and 27 miles (43 km) east of Foulness Point. This was a strong position, the sands inhibiting English attempts to weather the Dutch line. Vice Admiral Penn reported 59 enemy sail, supporting de With's statement that he had collected all but 5 of his 64 ships since the storm. The English outnumbered the Dutch, who put them at 'two or three and seventy sail'. De With's ships were in a compact body, standing close by the wind on the port tack in four divisions. Blake's were heading north in three divisions, in rough line ahead, the wind on their port quarter, sandbanks on the port bow, the enemy lying north-northwest on the starboard bow.

Most of Blake's fleet lay 6 miles (10 km) astern, 'by reason of their late weighing in the Downs ... occasioned by the late storm', so he waited until they came up. Sufficient ships had gathered by 4 or 5 p.m. for Blake to bear downwind against the head of the Dutch column. More or less simultaneously, de With turned south, running alongside Blake's leading division to starboard, 'so that there passed many broadsides between us and them ...' (Blake).

During the delay, Penn had pulled ahead of Blake, to port, bringing him amidst the shoals. Turning to follow Blake's attack he ran aground in 3 fathoms (5.5 m), and had to tack clear of the sands. This brought him back across de With's path: 'for as the Dutch fleet cleared themselves of our General [i.e. Blake], he standing to the northward and they to the southward, we fell pat to receive them, and so stayed by them till the night caused our separation' (Penn). Bourne, in the rear, similarly fell across de With's bows, the battle degenerating into a confused melee. Captain Badily was so closely beset on either side 'that one might have flung biscuits out of his frigate into the Dutch ships' (*Letter from the Downs*).

De With complained bitterly of superior English firepower, and his own crews' poor morale. Tromp's old flagship had refused to have de With onboard, forcing him to fly his flag from the worst sailer in the fleet. Nevertheless, he found himself foremost in the action, 'by reason of the holding off and standing away of the others, who could have kept the wind much better than we'. To add injury to insult, de With's laggardly captains shot through him from behind as he lay crippled by English fire, 'damaged and unmanageable, not able to put about on either bow'.

Firing ceased about 7 p.m., the two sides drifting overnight. Penn reported the Dutch 'did flag very much in the latter part of it', and thought they could not have held out another hour. The *Letter from the Downs* contrasted their behaviour with that of the English seamen and soldiers, 'who plied their work ... though some of the men were up to the middle in water in some of the ships'. Next day the English chased the Dutch north, expending much powder and shot to no purpose. That night the English kept their lights burning, 'but the Hollanders showed none, but most poorly and sneakingly stole away' (Captain John Mildmay). With only 49 sail still under command, de With took refuge in the Schelde estuary at Goree.

Dutch losses were at least one sunk and one taken. The *Letter from the Downs* reported two sunk and two captured, 'neither of which did much oppose us after

Kentish Knock

	Winner	*Loser*
Opponents	Commonwealth	Dutch
Commanders	Robert Blake Sir William Penn Nehemiah Bourne	Witte Corneliszoon de With Michiel Adrienszoon de Ruyter Jan Evertsen Gideon de Wildt
Numbers	*c.*70	59
Losses	0 ships; men unknown	2–6 ships; *c.*2000 men

we attempted to board them. By which we perceived that their hearts are much broken.' Another source claimed three of each. An observer at the Hague reported 2000 wounded brought ashore; the dead were unknown: 'they can be no small number considering the torn condition of their fleet'. The English fleet was also 'much rent and torn'. The English newspaper *Mercurius Politicus* reported 'about forty slain ... and not many wounded', but Badily's ship alone lost 20 or 60 killed, and with 100 hull shots had to put into Yarmouth to avoid sinking. The Dutch fleet would not sortie again, until Tromp's return to command in November.

Directions

Kentish Knock is in the middle of the Thames estuary, east of a line from North Foreland to Orfordness.

Dungeness, 30 November 1652

Naval, English Channel, LR189

The last Anglo-Dutch battle of 1652 was a successful Dutch convoy action. Unable to leave port after their defeat at Kentish Knock, they were equally unwilling to make peace. Restored to command on 21 November, Tromp prepared to escort the Bordeaux wine fleet south to collect the new vintage. On the 24th he was seen from Margate steeple with 200 sail. Driven back to Ostend by a southwesterly gale, Tromp reappeared 'on the back of Goodwin Sands' on 29 November, having left his merchant ships on the Flemish shore. Blake left the Downs to meet him, but a northwesterly gale prevented the fleets coming into action. Overnight Blake took shelter below the cliffs in Dover Roads, Tromp lying 2 leagues (6 miles or 10 km) off, in the lee of South Foreland.

Next morning the wind moderated, blowing north-northwest. Both fleets made sail at 11 a.m. and followed the English coast west. Blake kept the weather gauge, Tromp 'taking all pains to get at them'. The English fleet had been reduced by detachments, leaving Blake with perhaps 37 fighting ships and a few tenders. Some of Tromp's fleet had parted company in the storm, probably leaving him the 60 warships and 12 fireships reported in the eyewitness account *News from the Fleet*. Historians have puzzled over Blake's accepting battle at such heavy odds. L. Carr Laughton thought Blake underestimated Tromp's numbers in the poor visibility. S.R. Gardiner considered Blake always meant to fight once he had cleared the Ripraps (south-southeast of Folkestone), trusting in his fleet's superior gunnery.

Whatever Blake intended, the southward trend of the coast beyond Folkestone gave him little chance of avoiding action, as the Dutch could sail directly across the bay to intercept him off Dungeness. Tromp's best sailers opened fire between noon and 1 p.m., the main action beginning at 3, 'about the pitch of the Ness' (Blake). *A Letter from the Fleet* placed the battle 'near the same place where our first engagement was', i.e. within sight of Dover, whose inhabitants came down to the shore to watch, confident of English victory. The town's governor followed the fleets in a boat, 'almost as far as Folkestone ... near unto which place the fight began' (*News from the Fleet*).

The action was the usual shapeless melee, for while the Dutch had formed three squadrons, 'ours continued in one entire body' (*A Perfect Account, etc.*, another contemporary report). Blake's numerical inferiority was rendered catastrophic by the defection of half his fleet: 'not twenty came to the engagement, the rest pretending want of men ... among them that did engage, not above eight stood to it to any purpose' (*Letter from the Fleet*). Blake thought this was down to 'baseness of spirit, not among the

Dungeness

	Winner	*Loser*
Opponents	Dutch	Commonwealth
Commanders	Marten Harpertszoon Tromp Jan Evertsen	Robert Blake
Numbers	72	37
Losses	1 ship; men unknown	5 ships; men unknown

merchantmen only, but many of the State's ships'.

Fighting odds of three- or four-to-one, English losses were heavy. *Vanguard* and *Victory* were 'desperately engaged with twenty of the Dutch ... at last they got off well, though much battered ...'. Towards evening Tromp and Evertsen attacked the *Garland*, Tromp breaking his bowsprit on her lee quarter: 'and for want of men [she] was taken after the blowing up of all her decks'. *Bonaventure* came to *Garland*'s aid, the four ships laying on board one another, side by side, for about an hour. *Bonaventure* too was taken, and her captain killed, 'fighting as a private man' (*Letter from the Fleet*). Blake could not help, the fore topmast of his ship, the *Triumph*, being shot away, 'so that we could not work our ship to go to their relief ... night coming on we were saved ourselves, who were then left almost alone'.

Blake got back into the Downs, while Tromp lay off Dungeness for several days refitting. Total English losses were three sunk and two captured. The Dutch lost one ship accidentally blown up. The battered English ignored the Dutch bravado, Tromp continuing down Channel after stealing 200 cattle from Romney Marsh. A more serious loss was the *Hercules*, captured on her way from Portsmouth to reinforce Blake. Tromp left his merchantmen at Ile de Rhé off La Rochelle, where he awaited their return. The nursery story of the broom attached to Tromp's masthead, in token of his sweeping the English from the sea, presumably relates to this period. If the legend has any truth at all, the broom would have been hoisted over his prizes, the traditional sign that they were for sale.

Blake offered to resign, but the Commonwealth preferred to reinforce his disciplinary powers, appointing generals-at-sea to assist him. Canterbury Cathedral was put up for sale, and army regiments disbanded to fund ships and seamen's pay. Tromp would find his return less easy.

Directions

See the battle area from the coastal road between Dymchurch and Dungeness, 3 or 4 miles (5 or 6 km) offshore between the Varne Light, south of the Ripraps, and Dungeness.

Portland (the Three Days' Battle), **Friday–Sunday 18–20 February 1653**

Naval, English Channel, LR194

Dutch shipping ran the English Channel at its peril, the escorts of outward-bound convoys having to fight their way back with damaged ships and depleted ammunition. While Tromp wintered at Ile St Martin after Dungeness (see above), the English prepared a hot reception against his return. The resulting battle ran nearly the length of the Channel, from Portland Bill to Cap Gris Nez, between Calais and Boulogne.

The English fleet concentrated at Dover on 12 February, then zigzagged down Channel, past Seine Head, Beachy Head and the Isle of Wight to Alderney. Late on the 17th they heard Tromp was 20 leagues (some 60 miles or 100 km) westwards, and stood across to England to meet him. Next morning the wind was in the northwest, the weather cold and dirty. Five leagues (about 15 miles or 24 km) off Portland, close-hauled on the starboard tack, the English spotted the Dutch fleet to windward, between them and the coast. Tromp might have run for it. Instead he put his convoy to windward and attacked Blake's division, being furthest upwind, hoping to inflict enough damage to deter further pursuit.

C.T. Atkinson, co-editor of the Navy Records Society volumes on the war, reckoned the Dutch had 75 ships of the line, a fireship and 5 auxiliaries, besides 150 merchantmen. Blake's numbers are more problematical, as vessels dropped in and out during the action. Tromp estimated 69 to 70 enemy ships, 'the majority of them being large vessels'. For the first time the English were formed into squadrons, in very rough line abreast, Blake and Deane right (Red), Penn centre (Blue), and Monck on the far left (White). They were heading west, well spread out, 'Sir William Penn and his division being a little way ahead of the two Generals [Blake and Deane] ... Sir John Lawson [Vice Admiral of the Red] was about a mile on the Generals' quarter, and General Monck and many leewardly ships of other divisions a league or more on the larboard [port] quarter, right to leeward of the Generals when the fight began' (Captain Richard Gibson).

Blake had to withstand Tromp's opening attack with just 20 ships, but the new squadron organization ensured that he was not left unsupported for long. As the Dutch bore down on Blake in a body, 'Sir William Penn tacked, and his division, with their larboard tacks ... stood through the Dutch fleet one way, as Sir John Lawson did the other'. Gibson's ship the *Assurance* lost 17 dead and 72 wounded, following Penn. Casualties might have been higher except the Dutch shot into the English rigging, while an anonymous Dutch captain complained the English 'aimed always at our round timbers [hulls], and never shot in a hurry'. Tromp commented: 'Divers of our captains are not as staunch as they ought to be; they did not second myself ... as the English did, for I observed in attacking Blake that before I could get at him, I had such a welcome from three of four of his ships that everything on board was on fire, and Blake was still unhurt.'

The Dutch took no English ships, despite repeated attempts to board, and only crippled one, whose surviving crew were rescued before she was left to sink. The English on the other hand destroyed seven or eight ships, the Dutch admitting four sunk, two burnt and two captured. Among them was *Ostrich*, her people too drunk to take a tow. Monck's leeward division made itself felt about 4 p.m., forcing Tromp to break off the action as the better-sailing English ships, close-hauled on the starboard tack, weathered the western end of the Dutch line, threatening the convoy. Blake's squadron drew off to refit, Monck continuing in action till nightfall.

Portland

	Winner	*Loser*
Opponents	Commonwealth	Dutch
Commanders	Robert Blake (w) Richard Deane Sir William Penn George Monck	Admiral Marten Harpertszoon Tromp Jan Evertsen Michiel Adrienszoon de Ruyter
Numbers	60–80	76
Losses	1 warship; *c.*1000 men	11–12 warships; *c.*3000 men

Overnight Tromp steered directly up Channel on a slight westerly. Dawn on Saturday found the fleets 3 or 4 leagues (around 9–12 miles, or 15–20 km) south of the Isle of Wight. Firing was heard in Portsmouth from 9 a.m., as English frigates pushed on to cut off stragglers. Their main body did not come up until early afternoon, claiming five more Dutch warships before darkness. Tromp admitted two, and 'a few small merchant vessels'. Fighting was intermittent but heavy, the English still firing into the 'round timbers'. *Advice* ran into Portsmouth, 'much hurt after an engagement with five Dutch men of war', of whom she sank two, with all but seven of their crew: 'They [*Advice's* crew] have flung thirty dead men overboard, and have forty wounded'.

Fighting recommenced off Beachy Head on Sunday morning, when the generals 'fell close with them with some five great ships and all the frigates of strength' (*Official Despatch*). The wind continued northwesterly, 'dirty weather with more cold'. Having expended their ammunition, the Dutch scattered: 'divers of their ships, both men of war and merchantmen, began to fly from their body towards the coast of France' (*News from the Fleet*). Tromp rallied 25–30 ships that still had some powder and shot, forming a great arc to cover the rear. Smaller English craft worked to leeward, gleaning merchantmen that had ignored Tromp's previous urgings to make more sail, and now ran afoul of one another in their panic.

Two hours before sunset, 3½ leagues (some 10 miles or 16 km) west of Cap Gris Nez, Blake massed his ships to cut off the Dutch escape northwards, but, 'to our great good fortune, the English ships veered off, for if we had fought half an hour longer, we should have exhausted all the ammunition we had left, and must inevitably have fallen into the enemy's hands' (Tromp). Blake's pilots never imagined Tromp could weather the headland, but against all the odds of wind, tide and battle damage, he led his remaining ships to safety, rallying 76 vessels off Calais. Fearing to stay on a lee shore with their battered ships, the English put back to St Helens anchorage off the Isle of Wight, on the 22nd.

The English estimated total Dutch losses as 17–18 warships and 50–60 merchantmen. The Dutch admitted 11–12 and 30 respectively. Human casualties are uncertain. Officials in Portsmouth reported that 'our loss is great ... but that of the Dutch is treble'. A local correspondent claimed 2000 wounded prisoners had come ashore, against 300 English dead and 300 hurt. The latter figure appears too low. Portsmouth and Gosport were full of wounded, 'the few surgeons found have their hands full ... there are more prisoners than there is room for' (*Calendar of State Papers*). Tromp's own ship had 30 killed and 56 wounded, 'some of whom die every day'.

Portland was a great English victory, proving the vulnerability of convoys, even when escorted by the foremost admiral of the day.

Directions

View the sea areas fought over as follows:
Day 1 *from Henry VIII's Castle on Portland;*
Day 2 *from the Isle of Wight as for the Armada: Tromp's merchant ships lay east of Dunnose Head;*
Day 3 *eastwards from Beachy Head.*

Gabbard Bank (First North Foreland), Thursday 2 June 1653

Naval, North Sea

Unlike previous Anglo-Dutch encounters, Gabbard Bank was a deliberate trial of strength between full-strength fleets, unencumbered by non-combatant merchantmen.

Peace negotiations stalled, as the United Provinces refused extreme English demands that threatened their national independence. Commerce languished while both sides pursued military victory. When the blockading English withdrew from the Texel to resupply, Tromp tried to surprise them off the

Gabbard Bank

	Winner	*Loser*
Opponents	Commonwealth	Dutch
Commanders	George Monck Richard Deane (k) John Lawson Sir William Penn	Marten Harpertszoon Tromp Michiel Adrienszoon de Ruyter Pieter Floriszoon Witte Corneliszoon de With
Numbers	123 ships; 16,269 men	104 ships
Losses	0 ships; 362 men	19 ships; *c.*2200 men

Thames estuary. On 1 June 1653 Monck and Deane lay 2 miles (3 km) 'within the south head of the Gaber', a sand bank also known as the Gable or Gabbard Shoal, about 40 miles (60 km) east of Harwich. Tromp anchored 4 leagues (about 12 miles or 20 km) northeast of the North Foreland, hence the battle's alternative title. Other names, such as Lowestoft, Dunkirk or Nieuwpoort, are incorrect. The fleets hove into sight next morning, the English 'right in the wind which was N. by E.' (Tromp). Other accounts make the wind north-northwest or north, suggesting it veered during the night and morning.

The English listed 105 ships of the line, carrying 3840 guns, an enormous proportion of guns to crew. They also deployed 5 fireships, and another 13 ships joined next day under Blake. The Dutch had 98 ships of the line and 6 fireships. Both fleets are usually shown heading east on the port tack, in parallel lines, the English 'separated into three squadrons, a battle and two wings, sailing free at a good distance apart, as it seemed to enclose us in a half-moon' (Tromp). Lawson led, followed by Monck and Deane both in the *Resolution*, with Penn in the rear. The Dutch were initially 2 leagues (about 6 miles or 10 km) to windward, de Ruyter and Floriszoon leading, followed by Tromp, and then de With.

The English approached the Dutch line slowly, at an acute angle, not coming into range until 11 a.m.

One of the first shots killed Deane, leaving Monck in sole command. Accounts of Dutch movements vary. Tromp reported doing his best 'to beat up towards them', but Monck's chaplain describes them 'lashing away', that is lasking or dropping downwind. C.T. Atkinson interpreted this as drifting before the light wind, while hove-to to keep formation. The wind shifted eastwards during the cannonade, allowing the Dutch to exploit the gap between Lawson and the main body. Bringing his division onto the starboard tack, Tromp advanced through the English line, concentrating de Ruyter's and his own fire against Lawson: 'and for three hours the dispute was very sharp on both sides, which continued from three until six in the evening' (Monck).

Contemporary ordnance lacked the power to make Tromp's manoeuvre as decisive as it might have been under Nelson. The Dutch failed to sink a single English ship, losing one of their own instead. At dusk 'the enemy [i.e. Tromp] bore right away before the wind and little more was done' (Monck). De Ruyter reported driving the enemy in flight, but Tromp wrote of them tacking north, while the Dutch lay to the south to refit. Soon after dark a second Dutch ship blew up by accident, with most of her crew.

The decisive factor in the day's outcome was Blake's new tactical system, laid down after Portland. For the first time the English fleet made no attempt to break into the enemy line, preferring to pound the lightly built Dutch ships from a distance: 'It was [for the most part] with the ordnance, the ships of either side coming seldom within musket shot ... for the English having the wind and more and greater guns made use of these advantages.' The Dutch vainly sought to close, 'but the English by the favour of the wind, still prevented them, so as they could do little hurt to the rebels [the English republicans], who kept them still at a great distance, which was so great a terror to most of the State's fleet, as few of their ships durst bear up to abide them'. Twenty Dutch ships stole away after dark, 'pretending that they were parted by storms' (Letter from the Hague, 9 June).

Overnight the fleets drifted south, towards Flanders. Tromp sought to renew the action next morning, but lost the wind at a critical moment. The English resumed long-range battering, 'refusing to board them [the Dutch] upon equal terms ... until they found some of them disordered and foul one against another, whom they presently boarded with their frigates' (Letter from the Hague, 10 June). An English spy at Nieuwpoort observed half the Dutch fleet still in action on Friday, local fishermen reporting them 'in a lamentable, tottered and distracted condition'. Tromp's account degenerates into a litany of collisions, parted tows, shot-away rudders, accidental fires and abject surrenders. Next day he made for the banks of the Wielings, between Ostend and the Schelde, 'and as the water is so showle [shoal], we durst not adventure after them' (Blake and Monck).

Dutch losses included 6 ships sunk, 2 blown up and 11 captured. Dead and prisoners numbered 800 and 1300–1400 respectively. English losses were 126 killed and 236 wounded: 'The ships were but lightly damaged, some masts, sails and bowsprits torn, but no ships lost' (*Triumph*'s lieutenant). The result was a clear-cut English victory, allowing them to blockade the Dutch coast and stifle their trade. When Tromp attempted to leave the Maas in August to join de With at the Texel, he was intercepted off Scheveningen, and killed in the ensuing battle. Both sides were now prepared to compromise. England gained her commercial objectives; the Dutch preserved their independence.

Directions

Fighting extended over an immense area, mostly out of sight of land.

Lowestoft, Saturday 3 June 1665

Naval, North Sea, LR134–152

The first battle of the Second Dutch War was fought within hearing though not sight of Lowestoft. The earlier Anglo-Dutch war had left the differences of the two sides unresolved. Dutch obstruction of English trade in the Far East provoked reprisals closer to home. Formal hostilities followed an English attack

Lowestoft		
	Winner	*Loser*
Opponents	English	Dutch
Commanders	James, Duke of York Prince Rupert Edward Montagu, Earl of Sandwich (w)	Jacob van Wassenaer, Lord Opdam (k) Jan Evertsen Cornelis Martenszoon Tromp
Numbers	130 ships; 22,000 men	114 ships; 21,000 men
Losses	1–2 ships; 623 men	20 ships; 6000 men

on the Smyrna convey off Lisbon, on 19 December 1664.

The English fleet was ready first, blockading the Texel until supply difficulties forced the Duke of York, Charles II's brother and lord high admiral, back into Harwich at the end of May 1665. Learning that the Dutch were at sea, he concentrated the fleet in Sole Bay, a less confined anchorage 5 miles (8 km) offshore. On 1 June the Dutch were discovered at midday 6 leagues (about 18 miles or 29 km) to windward, bearing east-southeast. They kept their distance, James following them northwards that day and the next. About 8 p.m. on the 2nd he was 8 leagues (some 24 miles or 38 km) southeast of Lowestoft, the Dutch 3 leagues (9 miles or 15 km) away, heading out to sea on the starboard tack. Between 2 and 3 a.m. on the 3rd the wind veered, giving the English the weather gauge, 'being as we suppose about fourteen leagues from Lestoffe [sic] south-east southerly' (*Narrative of the Signal Victory*). Sandwich put the fleets 10 or 11 leagues (30–33 miles or 48–53 km) from Southwold, east-by-south or east-southeast, 'wind at south-south-west, then south-west-by-south, a fine chasing gale'. With daylight the Dutch tacked towards the English, the battle starting by 4 a.m.

The English had 109 ships of the line, 21 fireships and 7 ketches, against 103 ships of the line, 11 fireships, and 7 'avisos' or dispatch boats. Opdam's ships were outclassed as well as outnumbered, but he had categorical orders to fight. The English were sailing southeast in three squadrons in line ahead, Rupert (White) leading, James (Red) centre, Sandwich (Blue) in the rear. Opdam had five divisions, 'stemming westward'. The fleets were therefore converging on opposite tacks, port to port, 'and so both fleets passed their broadsides as they crossed by one the other, we to windward of the enemy' (Sandwich). The range was too great to do much damage. Many English ships failed to keep station, 'but luffed up to windward, [so] that we were in ranks 3, 4 or 5 broad ... divers out of reach of the enemy fired over us, and several into us and did us hurt' (Sandwich).

Rupert tacked northwards after this first pass, following the enemy. Opdam also reversed course, possibly trying to gain the wind. The English were now heading west-northwest, the Dutch south-southeast. A second exchange of fire on opposite courses began about 9 a.m., close enough for Sandwich to be wounded by a musket shot. As the lines cleared, the English tacked again, this time by squadrons together rather than in succession, reversing their sailing order. This should have brought Sandwich's Blue squadron into the lead, but the Duke of York made sail to run ahead of him. Rupert followed in the rear. The Dutch kept a parallel course, 'heads to the south-eastwards, and knocked it out with us for several hours, sometimes at great distance and sometimes fair by' (Sandwich). Sir Thomas Allin, a professional naval officer, complained the battle was fought 'very far off, that few shot reached, and those laid at random'. Various English ships suffered damage attempting to close, 'but it was observed, that as we bore in upon them, they altered their course, so that whereas they might have layn South South East, they bore off to the East South East' (*Signal Victory*). The English kept the wind throughout, frustrating the Dutch fireships.

The decisive moment came between 3 and 4 p.m. when James's and Opdam's flagships exchanged broadsides, 'at so near a distance, that the enemy began to shrink apace, though not absolutely to run' (*Signal Victory*). A chain-shot cut down three of the duke's staff at his side, spraying his coat with their blood. Then Opdam's ship blew up, killing all but five of her crew, and demoralizing the Dutch fleet. Sandwich now fell among the enemy, some of whom gave way, while others ran foul of one another, providing targets for English fireships. At the same time Rupert's squadron 'made them downright bear up before the wind and run with studding sails, cutting off their boats and using all advantages of flight' (Sandwich). By 6 p.m. the Dutch were in general retreat towards the Maas and Texel.

The Dutch lost 13 named prizes, and at least 6 ships burnt, besides Opdam's flagship. Laird Clowes, the naval historian, reckoned 32 were taken or destroyed all told. English accounts admit 1 ship captured; the Dutch claim 2. Sandwich recorded 283 dead and 340 wounded, against 4000 Dutch dead and 2000 prisoners. Losses might have been heavier if the English had possessed more fireships, or pressed the pursuit into shoal water. The action's strategic consequences were inconsequential. The Dutch avoided further action, while Tromp rebuilt the fleet and de Ruyter ran convoys under the noses of the blockading English.

Directions

The battle was out of sight from the coast, 30–60 miles (50–100 km) east of Southwold, on the Suffolk coast below Lowestoft. Broadsides were audible in Deal 80 miles(130 km) away.

The Four Days' Fight, Friday–Monday 1–4 July 1666

Naval, North Sea

The Four Days' Fight remains one of the longest and hardest fought fleet actions of all time, 'the sharpest conflict ever known on the ocean' (*Calendar of State Papers*). The English divided their fleet, giving the Dutch temporary superiority, despite which they failed to achieve a decisive success.

France declared war against England on 16 January 1666, in alliance with the United Provinces. When the English navy mobilized at the Downs on 29 May, Prince Rupert took 20 ships of the line and 4 fireships down to the Isle of Wight, to observe the French, while Albemarle remained at the Downs with 56 ships of the line and 4 fireships. They might still cooperate against de Ruyter, as a fair wind for the Dutch admiral would carry Albemarle down to Rupert's squadron. On 31 May, however, Albemarle sailed north towards the Gunfleet, a deep channel protected by the shoals off Clacton, to join ships preparing for sea in the Thames and Medway. He anchored 5 leagues (some 15 miles or 24 km) offshore, the North Foreland bearing northwest by west.

Next morning Albemarle continued north, his scouts reporting enemy ships to the east at 6 a.m, the North Foreland then bearing southwest by south. A council of war decided 'to bear with them', and the main Dutch fleet came in sight to leeward at 10 a.m., variously described as 'off Dunkirk towards the mid-seas', 'seven leagues off Ostend' and 'riding at anchor in a long line, on the coast of Flanders'. Albemarle decided to attack, despite being outnumbered, as he thought, by 75 ships to 60. In reality de Ruyter had 85 ships of the line and 9 fireships.

The action began between noon and 2 p.m., as the Dutch cut their cables and made sail. Modern maps show three squadrons lying north–south or west–east, in the order: Evertsen, de Ruyter, Tromp. Albemarle passed the first two at long range, to concentrate on Tromp: 'we standing towards the south-eastward, a fresh gale ... at the southwest so that we could not carry out our lower tier [of guns], and for fear of the sands where we found but 15 fathom we bore up and came to the other tack' (*A True Narrative of the Engagement between His Majesty's Fleet and that of Holland, etc.*). Returning westward through the whole Dutch fleet, the English suffered heavy damage. The sails of Albemarle's flagship were shot to pieces, forcing her 'in the sight of the enemy to chop to an anchor till she had brought new sails to the yards' (*True Narrative*). Fighting continued so long as there was light, Albemarle anchoring to refit a league and a half (about 4 miles or 6 km) west of de Ruyter.

Fighting recommenced on the Saturday between 7 and 8 a.m. The wind was now from the east, Albe-

The Four Days' Fight

	Winner	*Loser*
Opponents	Dutch	English
Commanders	Michiel Adrienszoon de Ruyter Cornelis Evertsen 'the Old' (k) Cornelis Martenszoon Tromp	George Monck, Duke of Albemarle Prince Rupert
Numbers	94; 22,000 men	60 + 24; 21,000 men
Losses	6–7 ships; 2000 dead	10–22 ships; 5000–7000 men

marle beating to windward to engage. The fleets passed on opposite tacks, 'the headmost ships of our fleet engaging first the headmost of theirs: so passing on by their fleet in a line, firing all the way, and as soon as the rear of one fleet was clear from the rear of the other, then each fleet tacked in the van [i.e. in succession], standing almost stem for stem with one another to engage again: by which means there was at least an hour's respite between every encounter' (*An Account of the Battle between the English and Dutch Fleets, etc.*).

After three passes, backwards and forwards, Albemarle was down to 34 ships in fighting order, mostly through desertion. An official report considered some of the English captains deserved hanging. Of the 34 survivors, many were 'quite disabled for the present, and all extremely shattered, especially in their sails and rigging' (*Account*). When Albemarle came onto the westward tack about 3 p.m. he kept on towards Harwich, gaining at least a league (about 3 miles or 5 km) before the Dutch had finished turning in succession.

On Whitsunday the small northeasterly breeze died away, the fleets continuing slowly west. Albemarle formed a rearguard from his least damaged ships, 'placing his weak and disabled ships before in a line and sixteen of his greatest and best in a rank in the rear as a bulwark for them'. The fastest sailing Dutch ships came on piecemeal, 'but finding it too hot service ... stayed for the rest of their fleet' (*True Narrative*). At 3 p.m. Prince Rupert's squadron appeared, outside the sands of Kentish Knock. Edging south to meet him, Albemarle's squadron took ground on the northern tail of the Galloper, a sandbank northeast of Kentish Knock, and 30 miles (50 km) east of Harwich. Most of them got off again, but *Royal Prince* stuck fast. Surrounded by shallow-draft Dutch warships, while the tide carried her friends to leeward, her crew surrendered, 'without firing ten guns in defence'. Seeing the English squadrons united, and failing to decoy Rupert onto the sands, the Dutch burnt *Royal Prince*, after evacuating her crew, and about 9 p.m. retreated towards their own coasts.

The English admirals followed, Rupert's fresh ships leading. At dawn on the 4th the wind was fresh, from the southwest. The Dutch were discovered at 8 a.m., 'and they having the weather gage put themselves in a line a little to windward of us' (*True Narrative*). Total numbers were now 58–60 English against 78 Dutch. Modern maps show both fleets heading west, sailing on the same tack, a tactic not employed until the St James's Day Fight. Major English sources all describe the fleets passing on opposite tacks, as they had earlier in the battle. Rupert and Sir Thomas Allin both state they lay on the starboard tack, supporting Albemarle's report that he initially stood eastward, with the enemy on the weather bow. Looking at the battle area as a clock face, the key bearings at the start of the fourth day appear, therefore, to have been as follows:

- the wind blowing from seven o'clock
- the English fleet at nine o'clock, heading east
- the Dutch fleet lying between four and five o'clock, heading west.

Fighting continued with a series of passes, the first too far apart to warrant firing. Rupert then closed the range, leading the whole fleet through the Dutch centre, who 'raked him fore and aft, plyed him on both sides (upon the starboard and larboard bows and quarters) ... clapping two fireships upon him' (*True Narrative*). As soon as the prince weathered the end of the Dutch line, he and Albermarle tacked back together, 'and so we stood along, the enemies' fleet being some to leeward and some to windward of us both, backward and forward, which course was four times repeated' (Rupert).

Generally the Dutch lay to windward, 'at so much distance as to be able to reach our sails and rigging with their shot, and to keep themselves out of the reach of our guns' (*True Narrative*). On the fourth pass they kept so far away that Allin's ships scorned to fire back. A report from Albermarle's flagship estimated that only 30 or 40 of de Ruyter's original 90 ships were still in action. Between 7 and 8 p.m. Rupert's ship was dismasted beginning her fifth pass, the Dutch massing against the crippled flagship. Albemarle made to support his colleague on the port tack, 'but they [the Dutch] having made that counterfeit, their Admiral on a sudden fired a gun to call in the straggling remains of his tattered fleet ... and bore away towards Flushing' (*True Narrative*). Lack of ammunition, exhaustion and heavy casualties prevented any pursuit.

English sources admit 9 or 10 ships lost, with 1800 killed, 1500 wounded and 1500–1800 taken prisoner. The naval historian Laird Clowes reckoned as many as 19–22 ships burnt, sunk or taken, with 5000 dead or wounded and 2000 prisoners. Such immense losses, a third of the English complement, are hard to reconcile with the Dutch tendency to aim high. The Dutch admitted 6–7 ships lost, which agrees with Albemarle's report, although a renegade Dutch captain, hoping to please, listed 15 vessels burnt or sunk. An English spy reported '50 sail, towed 3 or 4 together, all lamentably shattered', but undermined his credibility by claiming de Ruyter was killed and Tromp's right leg shot off. British government spokesmen presented the result as a draw, but *An Account of the Battle* confessed the Dutch 'had all the marks of victory on their side ... all that can be said to make it seem a drawn battle, is, that the two fleets parted in the Channel half seas over, both sides sufficiently shattered, and almost beaten to pieces'.

Directions

East of the Thames estuary, between the Ramsgate–Ostend and Felixstowe–Zeebrugge ferry lanes.

St James's Day Fight (Second North Foreland), Wednesday 25 July 1666

Naval, North Sea

The decisive battle of the Second Anglo-Dutch War was fought on St James's Day off the broad Thames estuary, between Orfordness and North Foreland, from which it sometimes takes its name. The hagiological title distinguishes the action from Gabbard Bank, which shares the same topographical label.

English losses in the Four Days' Fight inspired feverish preparations to put a fresh fleet to sea, before Franco-Dutch invasion plans could mature. On 22 July Albemarle and Prince Rupert led a 10-mile (16-km) column of ships out through the Thames Narrows into King's Channel, to anchor south of Harwich in the Gunfleet, driving de Ruyter from his blockading station beyond Long Sand to the east. Contrary winds prevented the English leaving the sands until the 24th, when they anchored 11 leagues (around 33 miles or 53 km) east of Orfordness, the Dutch bearing southeast-by-south. The English weighed anchor next day at 2 a.m., sailing east in a fine north-northeasterly gale to sight the enemy, 4 leagues (some 12 miles or 19 km) to leeward, and 'bore lasking upon them to engage van to van which by 10 we effected' (Sir Thomas Clifford, volunteer).

There is no agreement over numbers. Several contemporaries made the fleets equal, at 90 men-of-war and 17 fireships each. Laird Clowes reckoned the English had 81 and 18 respectively, mounting 4460 guns, against 88 and 20 Dutch of each type, mounting 4704 guns. Twenty-three English ships were new against only eight of the Dutch: 'never was a braver fleet seen at sea'. The English sailed in three squadrons on the port tack: the van under Sir Thomas Allin (White), the centre under the generals in *Royal Charles* (Red), and the rear under Sir Jeremy Smyth (Blue). Station keeping was poor. Despite regulations threatening death to captains firing over their friends, 'our people were very slow to get into a lyne, and some never did, but shot thorow severall of our ships' (Allin).

The Dutch were in three squadrons heading east, loosely formed in a half moon, with the wind, which had veered northwest, on their port quarter: Jan Evertsen was in the van, de Ruyter centre, and Tromp rear. The slight wind and the Dutch crescent formation brought the English squadrons into action successively, between 10 a.m. and noon, lying on the same tack as the enemy. New fighting instructions specified 'standing all along the same tacks aboard as the enemy', keeping them under continuous fire. This proved more effective than the spasmodic exchanges of fire on opposite tacks practised during the Four Days' Fight, and became standard.

The St James's Day Fight consisted of two distinct actions: one between the opposing vans and centres; another between the rear squadrons. The new tactics produced a more straightforward battle. Allin simply records, 'We fell in close and in 4 hours time put them to beare from us.' Evertsen, brother of the Cornelis Evertsen lost in the Four Days' Fight, was killed early on. At 10.30 a.m. an English fireship was expended ineffectually. Several of Allin's ships fell out of line to refit, but at 1 p.m. 'their whole van gave way and bore up before the wind', peeling off southeastwards. Meanwhile the centres fought a desperate battle. Following their new instructions, the English 'plied them so close they could not tack upon us' (*Victory over the Fleet of the States General, etc.*). *Royal Charles* engaged de Ruyter's flagship 'hand to hand much within musket shot' (*London Gazette*), until compelled to fall out to repair masts and sails. After a further hour and a half's mutual destruction, de Ruyter gave way at 3 p.m., his topmast over the side. *Royal Charles* was so shattered that boats towed her out of the line: 'Now at 4 of the clock de Ruyter began to make all sail he could and run, but with great gallantry would make several tacks to fetch off his maimed ships' (Clifford).

St James's Day Fight

	Winner	Loser
Opponents	English	Dutch
Commanders	George Monck, Duke of Albemarle	Michiel Adrienszoon de Ruyter
	Prince Rupert	Jan Evertsen (k)
	Sir Thomas Allin	Marten Harpertszoon Tromp
	Sir Jeremy Smyth	
Numbers	*c.*107	*c.*107
Losses	1 ship; men unknown	2 ships; *c.*1000 men

While the main fleets continued generally southeastwards, Tromp had tacked northwest through the English line, cutting off Smyth's Blue squadron in the rear. Tromp outnumbered Smyth, and was better concentrated than the English, 'because being heavy sailers, some of them were long before they could fall into line, so that the headmost had very hot service' (Silas Taylor, Harwich dockyard official). Tromp's fireship burnt *Resolution*, her crew escaping in boats. Smyth could not make the enemy bear up, and the two rear squadrons disappeared northwards in disorder, firing until nightfall.

Overnight the battered fleets drifted down to the Dutch coast, the English taking and burning two Dutch warships. Next day the wind dropped so even the lightest frigates could not overtake de Ruyter, who 'spoomed away' to hide among the Schelde's sand banks. Mistaken orders allowed Tromp to slip past the generals early on the 27th, making for Schouwen Island in the Oosterschelde. Dutch losses were far fewer than the 26 ships burnt and sunk that the English claimed, or even the 'nine blown up and many more sunk' reported by a spy who 'got by stealth into the Maes'. Modern historians accept the two destroyed in the chase, discounting numerous eyewitness reports of exploding ships. Human casualties must have been high, though fewer than Laird Clowes's estimate of 4000 dead and 3000 wounded. One of the captured ships had lost 50 of each before she surrendered.

English casualties varied wildly. *Elizabeth* put into Aldeburgh unscathed, her captain in silk morning coat and powdered hair. On the other hand *Victory* was said to have lost 80 men, *Vanguard* 60. At least 300 wounded came ashore at Ipswich. Bonfires, guns and bells were rung to celebrate the victory, but it failed to end the war, or even keep the Dutch in harbour. De Ruyter was at sea a month later, offering battle off the North Foreland.

Directions

Between Orford and Walcheren, across the ferry lanes from Harwich to Hamburg and Hook of Holland.

Dutch in the Medway, Monday–Friday 10–14 June 1667

England, Kent, LR178 TQ7869 and TQ7570

The Dutch raid on the Medway remains one of the most notorious failures in British defence policy. Charles II attempted to fight the Dutch on the cheap, and laid up his battle fleet, hoping that attacks on Dutch trade would compel them to make peace. His underestimate of enemy enterprise and capability invited a devastating surprise attack.

De Ruyter's fleet appeared off North Foreland on 7 June, and an inshore squadron penetrated the Thames estuary as far as Hope Reach. Finding wind and tide against them, the Dutch switched their attack to Sheerness on the Isle of Sheppey, where the Medway joins the Thames, 10 miles (16 km) northeast of Chatham. Both Sheerness and Chatham were royal dockyards, packed with naval stores, the winding channel between them sheltering numerous warships in varying states of unpreparedness.

Landward defences were little better. The fort at Sheerness was unfinished, its gun platforms unable to support the recoil of the sixteen 18-pounder guns mounted there. The garrison was insufficient and poorly motivated. The main obstacle to riverine attack was a 350-yard (320-m) iron chain between Gillingham and Hoo Ness. Like the similar chain at Portsmouth, this usually lay on the bottom, being raised to block the channel when necessary. Small batteries covered either end of the chain, reinforced by three warships. Blockships sunk below the chain were badly placed, and failed to close the channel. Two miles (3 km) upstream, round the bend in the river formed by St Mary's Island, Upnor Castle lay on the left bank, i.e. the Dutch right. Built in the 1560s, Upnor Castle's single bastion and keep mounted eight guns, covering the final approach to Chatham Reach, and the Royal Navy's premier dockyard on the right bank.

De Ruyter's heavy ships remained in the Thames to secure the retreat of the Medway assault force, which comprised 27 warships, 15 fireships and 20 smaller craft, commanded by van Ghent, a Dutch marine officer. He entered the Medway at noon on 10 June, engaging Sheerness Fort at 5 p.m., capturing it two hours later. Masses of naval stores fell into Dutch hands or were burnt, the smoke visible in Rochester. The invaders spent next day reconnoitring the intricate channel through the estuary, while Albemarle arrived at Chatham to coordinate defensive measures. Only 3 out of 1100 dockyard workers would assist the duke. He requested their pay be stopped – to little purpose, as government wages were months in arrears already. English voices called out from Dutch ships, 'We did heretofore fight for tickets; now we fight for dollars.'

The Dutch advanced at dawn on Wednesday the 12th, taking advantage of a northeasterly breeze and a spring tide. Their fireships negotiated the badly placed blockships, and at noon attacked the chain, which broke under the weight of ships pressing against it on a floodtide. A contemporary suggests it was only fastened with cable yarn. Outside the chain's Gillingham end, *Unity* (44 guns) was abandoned by her pressed crew of Thames watermen. Inside the obstacle, *Matthias* caught fire and blew up, while *Carolus Quintus* was taken, the Dutch using her guns to silence the shore batteries. Despite Albemarle's orders, *Royal Charles*, veteran of the St James's Day Fight, still lay in Short Reach above Gillingham. She opened fire with the 30 guns she had mounted, until

Dutch in the Medway

	Winner	*Loser*
Opponents	Dutch	English
Commanders	Michiel Adrienszoon de Ruyter Willem van Ghent	George Monck, Duke of Albemarle Sir Edward Spragge
Numbers	42	19
Losses	13 fireships; 150 men	9 ships; 500 men

her scratch crew ran short of ammunition and fled, allowing the Dutch commander to conduct operations from an English flagship. That night van Ghent anchored in Gillingham Reach.

Albemarle left the fighting around the chain to Sir Edward Spragge, while he 'put things in the best posture he could' at the dockyard. Heavy guns brought overland from the Tower of London were mounted in the New Dockyard. Smaller vessels were towed as far upstream as possible, larger ones scuttled to prevent their removal or burning. On the 13th the Dutch waited for the tide before advancing, a northeasterly wind still in their favour. Their men-of-war attacked Upnor Castle at 2 p.m., 'where they were as warmly handled ... as could be desired, but yet they lay battering till their fireships came up, two of which attempted to fire the *Royal Oak*; but missing their design, and a third arriving, they fired the *Royal James* and *Loyal London*, and then retired' (John Conny, an eyewitness). Another witness saw 'all three flaming', but the Dutch had finally shot their bolt. They withdrew the following afternoon, taking *Unity* and *Royal Charles*, whose stern carvings now decorate the Rijks Museum in Amsterdam.

The English lost another seven ships burnt or sunk, although there were hopes of recovering the latter. The Dutch expended all but two of their fireships. De Ruyter's exploit deeply shocked English opinion, with treachery suspected in the highest places. Unruly persons cut down the trees around Clarendon House, home of the lord chancellor, and smashed his windows. Some said things were better ordered in Cromwell's time, 'for then the seamen had their pay, were not allowed to swear, but were clapped in the bilboes [leg irons]'. In London the disaster was considered worse than the Great Fire, 'the nation having lost its honour at sea for ever' (*Calendar of State Papers*).

Directions

See Gillingham Reach from the Saxon Shore Way, or from the pier opposite Hoo Ness, off Pier Road (A289). Visit Upnor Castle off the A228 northeast of Rochester to see the culminating point of the Dutch offensive. Also visit Chatham Historic Dockyard.

Landguard Fort, Tuesday 2 July 1667

England, Suffolk, LR169 TM2831 and TM3134

The Dutch assault on Landguard Fort, near Harwich, was the largest overseas incursion upon English soil since Bonchurch (1544). Its successful defence was a modest restorative for English morale after the Dutch intrusion into the Medway.

De Ruyter still cruised off southeast England, threatening outrages from Harwich to Portsmouth. On 30 June, 70 Dutch ships appeared in the Sledway, the deep-water channel off Felixstowe, before describing a large northward circle past Aldeburgh. They returned on 2 July, before a light northeasterly, perfect for landing operations. At 11 a.m. it fell flat calm and very hot, de Ruyter hoisted a red flag, and Dutch landing barges rowed ashore, commanded by Colonel Thomas Dolman, an English renegade.

The beachhead (TM3134) was 'at the bottom of Filstow Cliff in a plaine', half way along the 5-mile (8-km) shoreline between the River Deben to the north and Landguard Fort (TM2831) to the south. A break in the cliffs just south of Cobbolds Point led via Foxgrove and Maybush Lanes to Walton and Old Felixstowe, then small villages three-quarters of a mile (1.2 km) inland. The Dutch objective was the fort, built in the 1620s to defend the sand spit across the harbour from Harwich, 'a point of land, shooting out from the mainland about a mile; the main sea not being above 20 or 30 yards from the foot of the fort at low water, and not above 12 yards at high water' (Surveyor General's Report, 1645). A contemporary illustration shows a standard fortification of the period, four earth bastions mounting cannon at the corners, drawbridge and gateway in the north curtain wall, a guardhouse and ranges of buildings against east and south curtains. A participant in the Dutch attack remarked its good ditch and counterscarp, filled with well disciplined and alert soldiers.

The garrison consisted of two companies of the Lord Admiral's Regiment, the Stuart predecessor of

Landguard Fort

	Winner	Loser
Opponents	English	Dutch
Commanders	James Howard, Earl of Suffolk	Michiel Adrienszoon de Ruyter
	Captain Nathaniel Darell (w)	Colonel Thomas Dolman
Numbers	*c.*2000	1650
Losses	unknown	*c.*150

the Royal Marines, a couple of hundred strong, commanded by Nathaniel Darell, the senior captain. A number of sailors were also present, presumably to man the 59 guns, mostly culverins and demi-culverins. Outside the fort, the Suffolk militia eventually brought 1500 foot and three troops of horse into action. Across the harbour entrance seven colliers were moored as blockships, 'all with jack, ensign and pendant as though they were men of war, and with holes cut ready to be sunk in case of any attempt of the enemy' (*Calendar of State Papers*). Small vessels inside the harbour provided additional fire support.

The Dutch landing force consisted of 842 land soldiers with pikes and matchlock muskets, 408 marines with flintlocks, 400 sailors and some light field guns. De Ruyter had planned a naval bombardment on three sides of the fort, but the shallows kept his ships outside effective range. The blockships were another worry, 'not knowing whether they were men-of-war or fireships, but wondering more to see them sink' (Silas Taylor, Harwich dockyard official). About 4 p.m. the landing party were told to press on across Landguard Common without naval support: '300 or 400, covered by the smoke from the ships, made up to Landguard Fort, with scaling ladders of 20 feet, hand granadoes, drawn cutlasses, and muskets, and came up close to the fort; their reception was brisk when discovered, and they were repulsed after half an hour's assault' (Taylor). The Dutch had followed the sea wall, and were unwilling to leave its shelter, especially when English warships fired on them from the harbour: 'An hour after they tried again, but ran away, leaving some of their ladders and arms' (Taylor).

Meanwhile, the Dutch boat guards were under pressure. The Suffolk militia had followed de Ruyter's manoeuvre north of the River Deben on 1 July, and could not easily return, as Dutch gunboats interrupted the Felixstowe–Bawdsey ferry. As the tide fell, however, the Dutch inshore squadron withdrew, allowing the militia to return across the estuary, threatening the beachhead's northern flank: 'At 4 or 5 o'clock, the Suffolk forces came to them in inclosures; 400 or 500 were detached from the Dutch main body to meet them, with a strong body of pikes and two or three drakes, with which they maintained the lanes and hedges; so that the horse being excluded from service, the Earl of Suffolk got his ground but by inches' (Taylor). Firing continued until 9 p.m., when a rising tide floated off the Dutch boats, and their forces safely re-embarked, taking their artillery with them.

De Ruyter admitted 7 killed and 35 wounded, compared with English claims of 'about the *fforte* [sic] 8 dead', or 150 all told. Anxious to please, a deserter alleged that 60–80 Dutch had been slain in the battle. Reports came in daily of gruesome discoveries washed ashore, or uncovered on the beach. Half a dozen 'dead carcasses of the enemy' were found in a broom field, 'where our foot engaged them'. The *London Gazette* admitted 'only 3 or 4 men [dead], and as many hurt', including Darell, wounded in the shoulder. Pepys thought little of the victory, and historians have followed his lead. De Ruyter achieved little more in the remaining month of hostilities, despite sowing terror as far west as Milford Haven. 'By God,' swore Admiral Sir William Batten, 'I think the Devil shits Dutchmen.'

Directions

Approaching from Ipswich along the A14, turn right after Port of Felixstowe along Carr Road (A154) for Landguard Fort. Extensively rebuilt in the 18th century, this is now a listed monument. A plaque commemorates Darell 's part in the action. The beachhead is in Undercliff Road East, down High Street East and Brook Lane from Felixstowe railway station.

Sole Bay (Southwold Bay), **Tuesday 28 May 1672**

Naval, North Sea, LR156

Sole Bay was the only battle of the Third Dutch War with an English name, reflecting the changed strategic balance between Britain and the United Provinces. The former could now participate as much or as little in Continental wars as she wished, while the Dutch confronted a deadly threat from Louis XIV's France.

Inefficient Dutch mobilization prevented de Ruyter attacking the English fleet before the Comte d'Estrées joined it off Portsmouth with a French squadron on 7 May 1672. The joint fleet then beat up the Channel to support French land operations in Flanders. They made and lost contact with the Dutch near the Gunfleet on 19 May, anchoring in Sole Bay to replenish water and victuals. Learning of their exposed position on 27 May, de Ruyter was encouraged by the easterly wind to launch a spoiling attack at dawn on the 28th.

Sole Bay was then a significant indentation in the Suffolk coast, of which erosion has left little trace. The Allies lay between Aldeburgh and Southwold, less than 2 miles (3 km) offshore, roughly parallel to the coast, in three squadrons lying north to south: Blue under Sandwich; Red under the Duke of York; White (French) under d'Estrées. R.C. Anderson's Navy Records Society volume lists 82 Allied warships, including 8 of less than 40 guns; Laird Clowes counted 98 warships and 30 fireships, carrying 6018 guns and 34,496 men.

De Ruyter had 75 line-of-battle ships and 36 fireships, carrying over 4000 guns and 20,738 men. He attacked from east-northeast a little before 3 a.m., in two grand divisions: an advanced echelon of 18 warships, 6 from each squadron, and many fireships, with the main body behind in line abreast: Van Ghent right; de Ruyter centre; Banckert left. The Dutch had the weather gauge, the wind variously described as east-northeast, east-by-south or east-southeast. Sir Charles Lyttelton of the Lord Admiral's Regiment complained there was so little wind 'our ships could not work, which was the reason our fleet fought very scattering'. In other ways the light wind favoured the Allies. It prevented the Dutch running fireships among the unformed Anglo-French fleet, and allowed the heavier English ships to run out their lower deck guns. Sandwich fired the opening shots between 6.30 and 7 a.m., the whole fleets engaging an hour later.

The battle's key tactical feature is the still unexplained division of the Allied fleet. Ordered to keep close to the wind, d'Estrées sailed south, away from the other two squadrons. English historians have accused him of treacherously following secret instructions to avoid combat, but the White squadron was nominally the van, and James never communicated his intention of reversing the sailing order, giving Sandwich's rear squadron the lead. The split may have been entirely accidental, as the flood tide put the heads of the English ships to the north, making it easier for them to continue on the starboard tack, forgetting in the emergency to tell their allies.

D'Estrées ran south exchanging fire with Banckert, who turned into line on the port tack to follow him. The Dutch failed to close, which they might have done, as the coast prevented the French bearing away before the wind. Heavy French casualties, 67 in the flagship alone, give the lie to subsequent English accusations of French cowardice. D'Estrées's contemporaries wrote warmly of their allies' gallantry.

Sandwich and the Duke of York ran north, heavily engaged by van Ghent and de Ruyter. The

Sole Bay

	Winner	*Loser*
Opponents	Dutch	Allied
Commanders	Michiel Adrienszoon de Ruyter Adriaen Banckert Willem van Ghent (k)	James, Duke of York Edward Montagu, Earl of Sandwich (k) Jean, Comte d'Estrées
Numbers	111	128
Losses	2–3 ships; *c.*2000 men	1 ship; *c.*2000 men

Dutch fell 'ungenerously' upon Sandwich's flagship the *Royal James* (100 guns), 'who being the windermost ship and a good sailer, got so deep into their fleet that she never had less than three or four of their stoutest ships on her, which yet she continued to keep off, having sunk two fireships that were laying her aboard' (Joseph Williamson, head of British intelligence). An observer near Southwold described Sandwich 'all in fire and smoke, that nothing but his flag was seen from seven till about one'. Sandwich's supporting divisions could provide little support. Sir Joseph Jordan had tacked through the Dutch line on Sandwich's orders, to attack de Ruyter from the windward, 'and in this smoke and hurry we could not well discern what was done to leeward'. Sir John Kempthorne was entangled all day with de Ruyter.

Groot Hollandia (60 guns) got across the *Royal James*'s bow, 'raked them through and through, and dismounted twelve of their guns on the lower and middle decks, they not being able to stand by one gun to return on them' (Robert Edmunds, survivor). Attacked by van Ghent on the starboard side, *Royal James* suffered heavily before cutting herself free, only to succumb to another fireship, which ran in covered by the smoke of the broadsides. Sandwich was drowned escaping in a boat. His scorched body washed up 40 miles away (64 km), identifiable only by the rings in his pockets.

Approaching the shoals off Lowestoft about 11 a.m., the Duke of York went about and ran south on the port tack, followed by de Ruyter. Both fleets were in disorder. Van Ghent had been killed fighting *Royal James*, and the duke forced to shift his flag from *Prince* (100 guns) into *St Michael* (90). On the whole the Dutch kept the weather gauge, and the two sides continued battering one another without intermission. About 5 p.m. they were back off their starting place, the northeasterly wind and ebb tide carrying them towards Aldeburgh, smoke driving in upon the coast. Soon after the duke shifted into *London* (96) and d'Estrées came back into sight on the opposite tack. Firing continued, shaking windows at Landguard Fort, until 8 p.m., when de Ruyter bore away southwards, joined by Banckert.

Next day saw the usual chase across the North Sea, dense fog denying the Allies a second chance, just as the duke hung out the 'Blody Flagg'. Both sides claimed victory. The Dutch had the best of it strategically, delaying projected attacks on their coastline. English veterans admitted 'never was so sharp a bout'. The Dutch lost one ship sunk by gunfire, one captured, and another blown up accidentally on the 29th. Besides *Royal James* burnt to the water line, English dockyard officials reported seven maimed, including a forerunner of Nelson's *Victory*, 'so paid away with shot in our hull that we had near seven feet of water in the hold'. *Henry* put into Aldeburgh, 'not an officer left on board alive, and half their men killed' (Lyttelton). *Katherine* was in Dutch hands for three hours until her people, shut in the hold, shouted, 'The ship sinks!', and overpowered the prize crew when they let them up on deck. Incomplete lists show 535 Dutch dead and 952 wounded, against 737 Allied dead and as many wounded, besides unknown losses in *Royal James*. Four out of twelve captains in the Lord Admiral's Regiment were killed, the corps earning its first official praise as 'Marines'.

Defeats ashore now diverted Dutch resources from the naval war, where bad weather and de Ruyter's strategy frustrated the Allies' amphibious plans. Popular dissatisfaction with the French alliance forced Charles II to make peace, ending a unique period of tactical innovation and closely fought battles.

Directions

Sole Bay is northeast of Southwold, off the A12 between Woodbridge and Lowestoft, down the A1095. The battle travelled northwards, Royal James blowing up off Kessingland, where the Suffolk Coastal and Heath Path approaches the shore to cross Hundred River.

King and Covenant

The Restoration in Scotland was followed by an ugly cycle of protest and repression. A government intent on imposing royal supremacy and bishops upon the Kirk confronted ministers and congregations equally intent on preserving its Presbyterian character, as laid down in the Solemn League and Covenant of 1639. The resulting disturbances hardly deserve the name of battles, surviving more as legends than military events.

Charles II's experiences before Dunbar (1650) had convinced him Presbyterianism was no religion for a gentleman. Like his father, he saw bishops as a way of managing the Kirk's political pretensions, but unlike him had no wish to subvert its Calvinist doctrine. Unhappily the clerical purge that accompanied the religious settlement of 1661 created an irreconcilable clique of dispossessed ministers bitterly opposed to Charles's Episcopalian Kirk. Disgruntled congregations followed their ministers, who held open-air conventicles. Government attempts to suppress these gatherings by force still divide historians, some viewing their members as dangerous fanatics, some as martyrs.

Restoration Covenanters never represented a majority of contemporary Scottish opinion, but they have won the propaganda battle since. Lending their nickname of 'Whig', to the main beneficiaries of the Glorious Revolution in 1688, they have acquired an entirely bogus image as defenders of religious freedom, a concept alien to the 17th century. Covenanters sought an intolerant theocracy, ruled, 'not after a carnal manner by the plurality of votes ... but according to the word of God'. Self-confessed terrorists, they considered assaults on Episcopalian ministers as 'so many acceptable services to God', quoting Psalm 149's revolutionary verses in their justification:

> Let the high praises of God be in their mouth,
> And a two-edged sword in their hand;
> To execute vengeance upon the heathen,
> And punishments upon the people;
> To bind their kings with chains,
> And their nobles with fetters of iron ...

Their embittered obstinacy combined with the government's brutality to produce one of the most miserable periods in Scottish history.

The worst excesses occurred in southwestern Scotland, in Ayrshire, Lanarkshire and Dumfries and Galloway, an isolated and economically depressed area. There were two major crises. The Pentland Hills Rising of 1666 began in Ayrshire, and escalated into an armed protest march on Edinburgh to seek redress of grievances. Finding the citizens in arms against them, the 'rude and undigested rabble' set off home, to be intercepted at Rullion Green by the Scottish standing army.

The Western Rebellion of 1679 drew in more support, but never represented the same threat. Alternate conciliation and repression had culminated in the brutal murder of James Sharp, Archbishop of St Andrews, on Magus Moor in Fife on 3 May. The assassins fled into the southwest, where Covenanters continued to gather in spectacular numbers. Three of the murderers joined a conventicle led by one Robert Hamilton, inspiring him to stage an armed demonstration against the royal supremacy at Rutherglen, south of Glasgow. An attempt to extinguish the incipient rebellion failed disastrously at Drumclog on 1 June, and the Duke of Monmouth, Charles II's illegitimate son, was rushed north to crush the politically divided and militarily incompetent rebels at Bothwell Bridge three weeks later.

Trouble dragged on through the 1680s. Then the Episcopalians handed the game to the Presbyterians. Refusing to endorse William III's accession in 1688, the bishops compelled the new regime to abolish episcopacy in Scotland, and with it the contentious royal supremacy in ecclesiastical affairs north of the Border.

Rullion Green (Pentland Hills), 23 November 1666

Scotland, Midlothian, LR66 NT2262–3

The Covenanters' most serious challenge to the Scottish government was the Pentland Rising of 1666, when they came within sight of Edinburgh before turning back to meet disaster at Rullion Green.

The rising began on 13 November 1666 when three soldiers threatened to grill a Dalry farmer on his own gridiron for not paying fines for non-attendance at church. The scuffle soon escalated into a minor revolt. Several hundred armed men carried off Sir James Turner, Royalist commander at Dumfries and a veteran of Preston (1648), in his nightshirt, along with the profits of his exactions. Like 16th-century English rebels (see Part 5), participants protested their loyalty to the king, and apparently they expected little resistance: 'They were not to fight, but God would arise and scatter their enemies before them. Never were such deluded creatures' (*Calendar of State Papers*). Some claimed a general rising against bishops was planned in all three kingdoms. Others blamed the oppressions of Sir James Turner and the influence of deposed ministers. Subsequently denounced as 'the first stirrer up of the rebellion', Colonel James Wallace, a veteran of Kilsyth (1645) and Dunbar (1650), only joined the rising after its original leader had disappeared, taking Turner's money with him.

When the rebels approached Colinton, south of Edinburgh, on 27 November, Charles II was of course elsewhere, while the Scottish Privy Council were 'no ways satisfied' with insurgent attempts at negotiation. At best the rebels might petition for mercy, if they laid down their arms immediately. Wallace sought safer quarters in the Pentland Hills, withdrawing east past Dreghorn Castle, before turning homewards along the A702 West Linton road: 'Some four or five miles from Edenburgh, at a place called Gallows Hill, (ane ominous name), they made ane halt ... waiting for their reare, for many had stayd behind looking for their breakfasts' (Turner).

'Tam' Dalyell, the Royalist commander-in-chief, was an old Cavalier, his waist-length beard said to have been untrimmed in mourning for Charles I's death since 1649. Country folk alleged he was bullet proof, and that he boiled water in his boots. The rebels had led him a sad march through seasonably boisterous weather, destroying bridges and ferries behind them. Dalyell heard of Wallace's change of direction at Currie, 11 miles (18 km) northwest of Rullion Green, and turned east across the Pentland Hills to cut off their retreat. The track he followed still runs up by Kenleith Burn, between Harbour Hill and Bell's Hill (1332 feet/406 m), past St Catherine's Chapel, now under Glencorse Reservoir, and into the steep-sided glen northwest of the rebel leaguer.

Wallace saw the Royalists coming about noon, and led his troops in a clockwise circle through dead ground behind Marchwell or Lawhead Hill (Turner's Gallows Hill). He reappeared on the eastern slope of Turnhouse Hill: 'the westmost, greatest and highest off pentlandhill, and the tope of it doeth just resemble the tope [of] Arthur's seat [in Edinburgh]' (Maitland of Hatton). Here Wallace drew up along the 300-m (984-foot) contour, either side of the point shown by modern Ordnance Survey maps, facing northeast across a re-entrant running up from the glen. Several small woods now mark the rebel position, the southernmost concealing the 18th-century Martyrs' Tomb. Accessible only after a stiff ascent, the position was so steep that when Royalist dragoons rode up two men per horse, the hindmost fell off.

Wallace's cavalry covered the rebel flanks, 'the poor unarmed foot men' taking the centre. Most

Rullion Green

	Winner	*Loser*
Opponents	Royalist	Covenanter
Commanders	Sir Thomas Dalyell Lieutenant General William Drummond	Colonel James Wallace
Numbers	2600	1100–1500
Losses	few	130

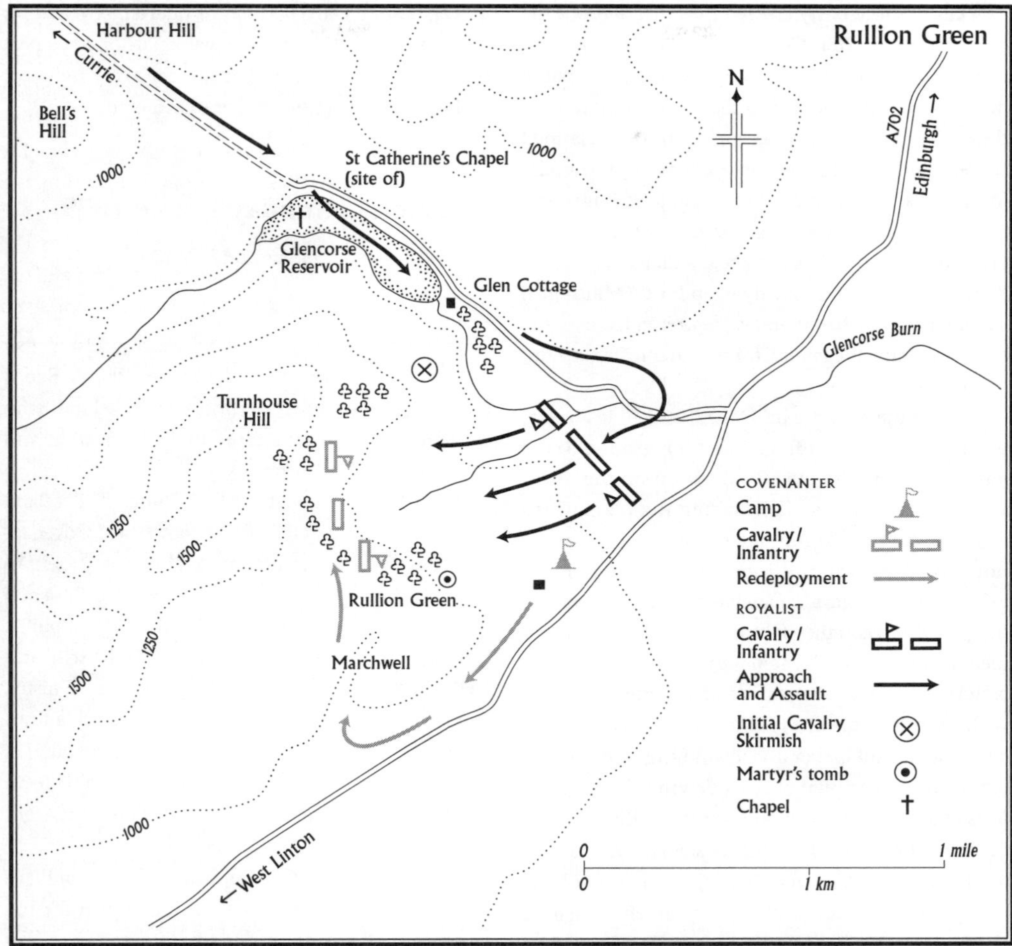

accounts exaggerate rebel numbers. Turner reckoned they never had more than 1100 under arms, mustering 440 horse and over 500 foot at Lesmahagow in Lanarkshire. The former were well enough armed with swords and pistols, the latter with muskets, agricultural implements or 'staves great and long'. Rebel numbers had since been diminished by terrible night marches, during which they tied themselves together to keep in touch. An observer at Newbridge thought them 'rather like dyeing men than souldiers going to conquer'. Dalyell's troops appeared piecemeal opposite the rebel left: a fore-party of 80–100 mounted men; the main body of 500 horse, 8 troops in all; finally 2 regiments of foot, 2000 strong, the men falling down for want of food after marching 24 miles (38 km) a day on rebel leftovers.

Directions

Rullion Green is in Pentland Hills Regional Park. Head south along the A702, and turn right at the visitor centre along a minor road to Glencorse Reservoir for the early locations of the battle. Return to the main road and continue south just under 1 mile (1.6 km) to reach the rebel position by a track on the right, near the radio mast on Lawhead Hill. Martyrs' Tomb, erected in 1788, claims to mark the Covenanter graves.

Dalyell's fore-party crossed the burn to probe the rebel left near Glen Cottage. Wallace detached a similar force, meeting the Royalists on a rare patch of level ground lower down the slope, perhaps near the eastern end of the reservoir. Both sides claimed success, but Dalyell's men broke contact to await reinforcements, who arrived after a couple of hours. Initially the Royalist horse joined their fore-party west of Glencorse Burn, behind 'a great sidlens or presipes … wher horse could hardly keep foot' (Maitland). Threatened by rebel infantry, they retreated over the burn, watching the enemy from a safer distance until the infantry came up.

Some time after 3 p.m. Dalyell had all his troops to hand. As daylight failed, he took ground to the left, recrossing the burn to draw up on the lower slopes of Turnhouse Hill, facing the plantations around Martyrs' Tomb. He placed four troops of horse on the right and four on the left, with the infantry in the centre, somewhat behind the mounted troops: 'Nor could they fyr unless they had killed our men out of the horse' (Maitland). Dalyell led off with attacks on the rebel left, the cavalry fighting at length with swords, 'until they mixed like chess-men in a bag' (Lieutenant General William Drummond). The rebels held their own at first, driving the Royalist horse back onto their own infantry in disorder. At the third attempt the Royalists pushed the rebels back up the hill. The Covenanters' right wing quit their own position to help, 'and so gave our left wing their slack'. Dalyell's left wing now led off, followed by the infantry, drums beating and colours flying: 'by the tyme we had received ther fyre, thos off ther left wing that were reilling thrust amongst ther oun foot [and] disordered them. And tho pressing to assist, ther right wing of hors yet helped to put them in confusion. And soe all off them rune for it through the hills' (Drummond).

The rebels were decisively beaten: 'The army say they never saw men fight more gallantly … nor endure more; the general was forced to use stratagem to defeat them. Now not one dares call himself a Whig' (*Calendar of State Papers*). Royalist losses were trivial. Wallace put his own casualties at 50 killed and 80 prisoners. About 30 were executed by the civil power, despite Dalyell's offer of quarter. A year after Rullion Green the survivors were pardoned as part of a conciliatory policy that saw the army reduced, and its more rapacious officers cashiered.

Drumclog, Sunday 1 June 1679

Scotland, South Lanarkshire, LR71 NS6239

'The Rencounter at Drumclog' was more skirmish than battle. It owes its fame to Sir Walter Scott, and the presence of Claverhouse and Cleland, who achieved posthumous fame at Killiecrankie and Dunkeld (1689) respectively.

Opposition to the established Church of Scotland persisted throughout the 1670s, with armed Covenanters attacking, and sometimes killing, troops sent to disperse them. Tension deepened with Archbishop Sharp's murder in May 1679. On the 29th, a public holiday commemorating Charles II's birth and Restoration, Robert Hamilton, an itinerant minister, supported by 60–80 armed horsemen, fixed 'a testimony against the iniquity of the times' to the market cross at Rutherglen, declaring the kingdom of Jesus Christ and styling the king a usurper. This overt act of rebellion could not go unpunished.

John Graham of Claverhouse had yet to achieve his now legendary status as an uncompromising champion of Stuart despotism. Created Viscount Dundee in 1688, he is known as 'Bluidy Clavers' or 'Bonnie Dundee' depending on one's politics. In 1679 he was sheriff depute of Dumfries and a plain captain of horse, leading his own troop and a company of dragoons in pursuit of the Rutherglen demonstrators. Eating breakfast in Strathaven at 6 a.m. on 1 June, Claverhouse learnt of a conventicle 7 miles (11 km) to the southwest, at Glaisterlaw or Hairlaw. This is now Harelea Hill (NS6038), near Robert Bruce's Loudoun Hill encounter with Aymer de Valence in 1307.

Claverhouse's probable line of advance ran north of the A71, through Letham and Crewburn to High Drumclog, where he found the enemy 'drawn up in battle upon a most advantageous ground, to which there was no coming but through mosses and lakes'. His final approach was probably through Coldwakning (sic), the direction of his subsequent retreat, rather than along the main road through Drumclog. The Covenanters scorned the shelter of numerous impenetrable mosses and advanced to confront Claverhouse across the re-entrant between High Drumclog and Stobieside House. The slopes either side were arable, separated at the bottom by a piece of marsh or 'misk ground' a few yards wide, in some places too soft to support horses. Sir Walter Scott's *Old Mortality* misrepresents the terrain, exaggerating its steepness and the extent of the bog. William Aiton, who knew the area, and whose great-grandfather fought there, reckoned the slope up to the Covenanter position was a gentle one in twenty.

Claverhouse had about 70 horse and three score dragoons. Covenanter numbers go up to 8000–9000, including numerous non-combatants. Official accounts gave them 1400–1500 men, 'well armed and in good order'. Aiton reckoned 'about 50 horsemen, ill provided with arms, 50 footmen with muskets, and about 150 more with halberds and forks'. Claverhouse reported 'four battalions of foot, and all well armed with fusils and pitchforks, and three squadrons of horse'.

The numerical disparity discouraged the Royalists from making a direct attack, both sides' skirmishers exchanging fire across the bog. Traditional secondary accounts say the Covenanters fell flat to escape the bullets, except one obstinate predestinarian, who stood up to be shot. Claverhouse then charged the Covenanters, who counterattacked his disordered troopers as they floundered in the bog.

Drumclog

	Winner	*Loser*
Opponents	Covenanter	Royalist
Commanders	Robert Hamilton William Cleland	John Graham of Claverhouse
Numbers	250	c.130
Losses	unknown	36–42

Claverhouse's report tells another story. It says the Royalist skirmishers, including all 60 dragoons, twice made their counterparts run away, 'But in the end (they perceiving that we had the better of them in skirmish) they resolved a general engagement, and immediately advanced with their foot, the horse following.' A Whig participant, James Russell, one of Sharp's murderers, confirms this: 'The honest party [sic] having but few guns, was not able to stand, and being very confused at coming off, one of the last party cried out for the Lord's sake go on; and immediately they ran violently forward, and Claverhouse was tooming [pouring] the shot all the time on them.' Both eyewitness sources agree the rebel infantry charged across the marsh, 'louping ower', receiving a volley at ten paces before coming to close quarters. A pitchfork man disembowelled Claverhouse's horse, which dashed off with its guts hanging out, 'which so discouraged our men that they sustained not the shock, but fell into disorder'.

The Covenanter cavalry gave the Royalists no chance to recover, pursuing them to Calder Water, nearly 3 miles (5 km) away. Claverhouse escaped by mounting the horse of his trumpeter, who was killed near Coldwakning in his place. Two dragoons were refused quarter near Hillhead, their graves visible between that farm and Hookhead until the 1750s. In Strathaven the inhabitants attacked the fugitives in a lane called Hole-closs, 'but we took courage and fell to them, made them run, leaving a dozen on the place' (Claverhouse).

Total Royalist losses depend on which side provided the unlucky 'dozen'. Claverhouse admitted 3 officers and 8 or 10 men killed, besides an unspecified number wounded. The dragoons lost perhaps twice as many, presumably because they were on foot. Whig sources confirm 30 to 36 Royalists died. Half a dozen were captured, one of whom Hamilton killed in cold blood, with appropriate scriptural justification. The others were allowed to escape. Whig losses are uncertain. Claverhouse 'saw several of them fall before we came to the shock', so Russell's 3 killed and as many wounded is probably an underestimate. One of Archbishop Sharp's killers was among the dead.

The action justified government fears, Claverhouse counting it 'the beginning of the rebellion'. The rebels occupied Glasgow, but failed to agree their aims or formulate a defensive strategy. Drumclog remained the only Covenanter victory.

Directions

Turn right at Roundhill, 4 miles (6 km) southwest of Strathaven along the A71, taking a minor road through Coldwakning. The Ordnance Survey marks the battlefield and monument 1 mile (1.6 km) further on the right, just past High Drumclog. The marsh has been drained, and is no longer visible.

Bothwell Bridge, 22 June 1679

Scotland, South Lanarkshire, LR64 NS7157

Bothwell Bridge was the most significant confrontation during the struggle against the Covenanters, and the only real battle of that conflict. A simple enough river crossing in face of a disorganized rabble, its military detail is obscured by the falsehoods spun around it.

The victors of Drumclog hung together, if only to avoid hanging individually. They took Scotland's second city, Glasgow, after Royalist forces withdrew to cover Edinburgh and Stirling, but never agreed any political aims, not even who should preach, nor about what. While they debated church–state relations the government mobilized the Scottish militia and dispatched the Duke of Monmouth to take command. He joined the Royalist army at Blackburn in West Lothian on 19 June, advancing on Glasgow next day, down the M8 corridor.

Meanwhile the Covenanters had retreated across the Clyde, camping south of Bothwell Bridge on Hamilton Moor. As Monmouth closed in, the rebel leadership continued arguing, as if there was no opposition within a thousand miles. Few of their men had ammunition to shoot twice: 'I was not halfe an hour there until I feared the Lord was not with them, seeing no Authoritie in discipline ... [and] perceaving much devision among those that should have guided the rest' (James Nimmo).

Royalist forces consisted of the Scottish standing army, some 2500 regulars, plus as many militia. Monmouth approached from the north, down the spur of high ground then occupied by Bothwell Muir, cutting off the rebels from Glasgow but committing him to an opposed river crossing. Rivers make poor tactical obstacles, however. The Covenanters were less safe behind the Clyde in face of a regular army with artillery than critics suggest. By 7 a.m. on 22 June the Royalist advanced guard of one troop of horse and five of dragoons, with 300 commanded foot, were within pistol shot of the barricaded bridge, where they dug in to cover deployment of cannon on the slope behind them. The Covenanters tried to parley, but Monmouth refused, giving them an hour to lay down their weapons – 'and hang next,' commented Hamilton.

Rebel strength had dwindled, leaving 6000–7000 'drawn up in two Lines, or Bodies rather, half a Mile one from the other; one near the Bridge, which was the weakest in number; the other near their Camp as high as the Little Park' (*London Gazette*). The latter does not appear as such on modern maps, but may be the public park across Bothwell Road from Hamilton Park Race Course, on the brow of the hill, the appropriate distance from the bridge. The latter was very different to the modern structure, being long and narrow with four arches. Not more than 12 feet (3.5 m) wide, it rose 20 feet (6 m) in the middle, with a fortified gateway nearer the rebel end. The banks of the Clyde were fringed with hazel and alder thickets, giving way to the plain open field where the main body of insurgents drew up. Their advanced

Bothwell Bridge

	Winner	*Loser*
Opponents	Royalist	Covenanter
Commanders	James Scott, Duke of Monmouth	Robert Hamilton
Numbers	5000	6000–7000
Losses	*c.*10	*c.*2000

party at the bridge originally included three troops of horse, two companies of foot and their only cannon. When the burning matches of Monmouth's advanced guard appeared in the pre-dawn darkness, extra infantry were drawn down 'hard upon the water-side against the west end of the bridge' (James Ure of Shargarton). Two hundred of the defenders had no arms except pikes and halberds.

When the Covenanters' artillery opened fire, Monmouth's gunners briefly took cover, but soon rallied to silence their solitary opponent. When rebel ammunition ran out, Royalist dragoons stormed the bridge, pressing on uphill towards the Covenanters' main body, who chased them back down the slope. Royalist reinforcements consolidated the bridgehead, occupying the houses that contemporary illustrations show around the southern end of the bridge. Today they presumably lie under the A725, which crosses the Covenanters' advanced positions.

Monmouth then passed his main body over, forming line across Back Muir Plantation, the armies 'but two carabine's shot asunder', perhaps 200 yards (180 m). The Royalists would fit neatly between Park Burn on their right and the southwards bend of the Clyde on their left. Before Monmouth finished deploying, the rebels attacked his right flank under cover of some hollow ground, presumably the gully formed by Park Burn. They disordered some Highlanders in front, pushing them back onto their supporting dragoons.

A few rounds from Monmouth's guns settled the affair, the rebel foot unable to cope with cavalry and artillery together: 'The right hand stood a little, but not so long as to put on a pair of gloves' (Ure of Shargarton). The official account suggests the Covenanter cavalry broke first, 'Their horse began to run and scatter upon all corners, leaving their flying foot to the mercy of our army ...' It was, the Privy Council assured His Majesty, 'a total rout and discomfiture of these insolent rebels'.

Robert Hamilton was among the first to fly. Some 700–800 of his followers were killed in the pursuit, and 1100–1500 captured, depending on who you believe. The Royalists are supposed to have lost no more than two or three common soldiers. Much has been made of Claverhouse's sinister role at Bothwell Bridge, and his massacre of fleeing Covenanters in defiance of orders. Claverhouse was still a simple captain, promoted colonel by Sir Walter Scott in *Old Mortality* for dramatic effect. His troop was one of

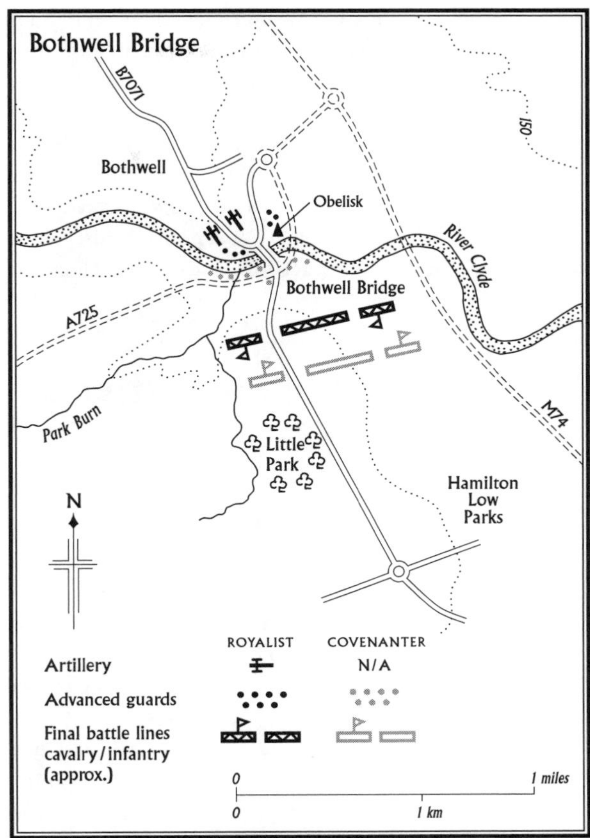

Directions

Follow the B7071 Old Bothwell Road southeast across the modern bridge. An obelisk on the left near Bellshill Road commemorates the Covenanters' supposed defence of civil and religious liberty. Like the Ordnance Survey battle symbol, the monument is the wrong side of the river, as most of the fighting occurred south of the bridge. Outlying areas at Back Muir Plantation and Hamilton Low Parks have escaped development, but factories and motorways occupy the centre of the battlefield.

eight committed to the pursuit. Otherwise, it is not even certain where Claverhouse was stationed, only that he had no part in the broader conduct of the battle.

Monmouth's personal sympathy with Protestant dissenters moderated subsequent retribution. Most of the prisoners were released on giving sureties for good behaviour, though Whig propagandists make much of the accidental drowning of several hundred irreconcilables, shipwrecked in the Orkneys on their way into self-imposed exile. Fines for non-attendance at church were remitted, and private conventicles permitted indoors. Hamilton's imbecile leadership at Bothwell discredited the extreme Covenanters. A few diehards maintained the struggle into the so-called 'Killing Times' of the 1680s. As in more recent people's wars, military victory proved easier to achieve than peace.

The Wars of the British Succession

The death of Charles II in February 1685 began a struggle for the crowns of England, Scotland and Ireland that lasted into the 1690s. Monmouth's Rebellion (1685), the Glorious Revolution (1688–9), and the Irish War of the Two Kings (1689–91) all formed parts of this dynastic crisis. Potential claimants to the throne included:

(1) Charles's illegitimate son, James Scott, Duke of Monmouth and Buccleuch. He was handsome, popular and Protestant, the victor of Bothwell Bridge (1679), but a worthless featherweight, in exile since 1683.

(2) Charles's brother, James, who had recently returned from exile. He was elderly, legitimate and seemingly competent, but a Roman Catholic.

(3) Mary and Anne, James's daughters by his first wife. They were both legitimate and staunchly Protestant.

The morbid English fear of popery is now hard to understand. It derived from folk memories of Guy Fawkes and the largely imaginary Irish atrocities of the 1640s, given new life by genuine fears of Louis XIV's Catholic absolutism. Only the prospective succession of Mary, safely married to the Protestant Prince of Orange, made James II's accession tolerable as a short-term necessity.

Charles II's attachment to dynastic legitimacy ensured his brother's accession, despite James's religion. Monmouth's Rebellion, which soon followed, strengthened James's position, encouraging Parliament to vote him taxes for life, and justifying the standing army that crushed the rebels at Sedgemoor (6 July 1685). Within three years, however, James had shattered the Restoration settlement. He undermined the Church of England by suspending the Test Acts, driving doggedly non-resistant bishops into opposition. He threatened civil liberties by packing town corporations – key bodies in elections – with government nominees, and by massing troops on Hounslow Heath. Most seriously he governed through new men, army officers and Catholic converts, alienating the country's natural rulers.

The unexpected pregnancy of James's second wife in 1688 was the last straw. It created a community of interest between anti-popish elements in England and William of Orange, Stadtholder of the United Provinces and leader of the grand alliance forming against France, known as the League of Augsburg. William had two concerns: to secure English financial and naval help against Louis XIV, and to safeguard his wife's inheritance from the potential consequences of the queen's 'pretended bigness': a male Catholic heir to the English throne. England's demilitarized aristocracy could not challenge James's regular army, so they called secretly for William's assistance. The Protestant wind that carried the Dutch invasion force down the Channel trapped the English fleet south of Harwich in the Gunfleet, unable to contest William's passage. On 5 November, already an auspicious date for Protestants, William of Orange landed at Torbay with 4000 horse and 11,000 foot, the largest disciplined army ever to invade England. James II's army outnumbered them, but key defections broke his nerve. Rather than brazen it out, James fled the country, a dereliction of duty gratefully interpreted as abdication. On 23 February 1689 William and Mary took the vacant throne as co-rulers, ensuring English participation in the forthcoming Nine Years' War against France. At home, the Declaration of Rights outlawed James's absolutist policies, and became the basis of England's unwritten constitution. Annual Mutiny Acts brought the Army under parliamentary control.

In Scotland James's flight dramatically reversed the status quo. Presbyterian fanatics from the south-west, survivors of the 'Killing Times' (see above) dominated the hastily assembled Convention of Scottish Estates in Edinburgh, ensuring William secured Scotland. Jacobitism was confined north of the Tay, where John Graham of Claverhouse, now Viscount Dundee, mobilized the more raffish Highland clans on James's behalf. Dundee's death at Killiecrankie (27 July 1689) exposed the slender basis of his rebellion. Highlanders could neither take towns nor operate in open country. A handful of proper infantry beat them off from Dunkeld (21 August 1689), while mounted troops broke up a last foray at Cromdale (1 May 1690). Dundee's counter-revolution was more the old regime's dying spasm than the birth of a major opposition movement. Only the London government's neglect of Scottish affairs in favour of foreign wars permitted the Jacobite recovery that would lead to Sheriffmuir (1715) and Culloden (1746).

In Ireland the Glorious Revolution precipitated a major crisis, whose reverberations continue to this day. The War of the Two Kings, *Cogadh an Dá Rí*, formed part of a wider European struggle. Louis XIV used Ireland to divert Allied resources from the decisive theatre of war in Flanders. For the price of a few thousand broken muskets and more misery for the Irish, the French spun out hostilities for nearly three years. The conflict was also the climax of the 100-year-old struggle between Anglo-Scots Protestant settlers and Ireland's established inhabitants, both Gaelic and Old English. James's lord lieutenant, Richard Talbot, Earl of Tyrconnell, had been the only Royalist officer to survive the storming of Drogheda (1649). Now he mobilized Ireland's Catholic inhabitants to reverse the Cromwellian land settlement that had survived the Restoration.

James II landed at Kinsale on 12 March 1689 without interference from the Royal Navy, which also failed to stop French troops landing at Bantry Bay (1 May 1689). Jacobite forces overran all Ireland except Protestant enclaves at Londonderry and Enniskillen, relieved on the 28 and 31 July respectively after the celebrated breaking of the boom across the River Foyle, and a ferocious action at Newton Butler. Geographically remote, James's setbacks in Ireland coincide neatly in time with Killiecrankie.

Continued Jacobite resistance demanded William III's personal intervention in Ireland, despite the risks of his leaving England for a remote dependency. William's victory at the Boyne (1 July 1690) remains Ireland's largest and most famous battle, an event comparable in European significance to the relief of Vienna from its Turkish besiegers in 1683. The Williamite success was incomplete, however. The Jacobite army escaped to Limerick, fighting on into the following year without James II, who had incontinently taken ship for France, leaving the Irish as disgusted with *Seamus an Chaca*, 'James the Shite', as he was with them.

William's failure to include the Irish leaders in peace terms offered after the Boyne prolonged the war into 1691. He returned home, as did the French contingent, while a reduced Allied army eliminated Irish resistance beyond the Shannon at Aughrim (12 July). The bloodiest battle in Irish history, Aughrim broke the Jacobite army, the survivors fleeing abroad to win undying glory as the Wild Geese. It would be over a century before Irishmen renewed the struggle for freedom, as Jacobins rather than Jacobites.

Norton St Philip, 27 June 1685

England, Somerset, LR172 ST7756

Sedgemoor, 6 July 1685

England, Somerset, LR182 ST3535

When thy star is in trine,
Between darkness and shine,
Duke Monmouth, Duke Monmouth,
Beware of the Rhine!
Soothsayer (*c.*1672)

Monmouth's Rebellion was the last popular uprising in England, and culminated in the last pitched battle on English soil. Sedgemoor was a stark warning that home-grown armies with pitchforks stood no chance against professional regular soldiers.

Monmouth landed at Lyme Regis on 11 June with 150 adventurers, and denounced James II as a usurper. Marching through Taunton and Bridgwater, he raised an army of 5000 unemployed lead miners and woollen workers, but few gentry. He failed to take Bristol, capturing the bridge over the Avon at Keynsham on 25 June, the day after the Royalist commander, the Earl of Feversham, secured England's second city. The rebels retreated through Bath, fighting a successful rearguard action at Norton St Philip. The battered Royalists withdrew to Bradford on Avon, 'having stood two houres a fair mark, shooting at hedges ... in desperate rainy weather' (Edward Dummer, Royalist artilleryman). Monmouth continued to Frome, but fearing to expose his ill-trained followers to royal cavalry on Salisbury Plain, he retreated to Bridgwater.

While Monmouth dithered, Feversham closed up through Somerton, camping 3 miles (5 km) south-east of Bridgwater around Westonzoyland. It was a strong position, 'bequirt [surrounded] with a dry (but in some places mirey) ditch ... fronting the moor; a place copious and commodious for fighting' (Dummer). Learning Feversham had not dug in, and that the Royalist troops were sampling the local cider, Monmouth gambled on a night attack. Between 9 and 10 p.m. on 5 July the rebels left Bridgwater by the old Bristol Road, known then as Long Causey, and now as the A39. While the transport trundled northwards, as if making for Bristol, the fighting troops turned right along Marsh Lane to Bradney, hoping to take the Royalists by surprise.

Contrary to Monmouth's expectations, Feversham had made elaborate security arrangements. Dragoons secured Burrow Bridge across the River Parrett behind his left, and infantry occupied a sheep-fold near Penzoy Farm to his left front, covering the A372 Bridgwater–Westonzoyland road. Horse and dragoons at Chedzoy watched the moor directly in front, while more cavalry patrolled to the right, towards Bradney and the Bridgwater–Bristol road. Feversham himself remained on the moor 'till neare one after midnight', when he handed over to his second-in-command, John Churchill, later Duke of Marlborough, probably the safest pair of hands in military history.

The moors and levels between Bridgwater and Westonzoyland are more enclosed now than in 1685, and the drainage quite altered. King's Sedgemoor Drain has absorbed Black Ditch whose western bank Monmouth followed, while new watercourses have replaced the Langmoor Rhine and Bussex Rhine which crossed his line of march, fulfilling the soothsayer's prophecy. Both Rhines have been filled in, leaving their sites conjectural. Bussex Rhine's value as a physical obstacle is debatable. The season was dry, and Royalist infantry crossed it during the battle. Cavalry may have found it more difficult, only crossing the Upper and Lower Plungeons, flanking the Royalist line.

The Royal army had encamped tactically: infantry before Westonzoyland, leaving a clear forming-up space between their tents and the Bussex Rhine, which ran across their front; cavalry and artillerymen quartered in the village behind them; the militia 2 miles (3 km) further off at Middlezoy. The 1900 regular foot formed six small battalions, two from 1st Foot Guards, supported by 750 horse and dragoons. The 200 ordnance personnel parked their 26 guns where the Bridgwater road crossed the Bussex Rhine. Feversham's infantry had flintlocks, except

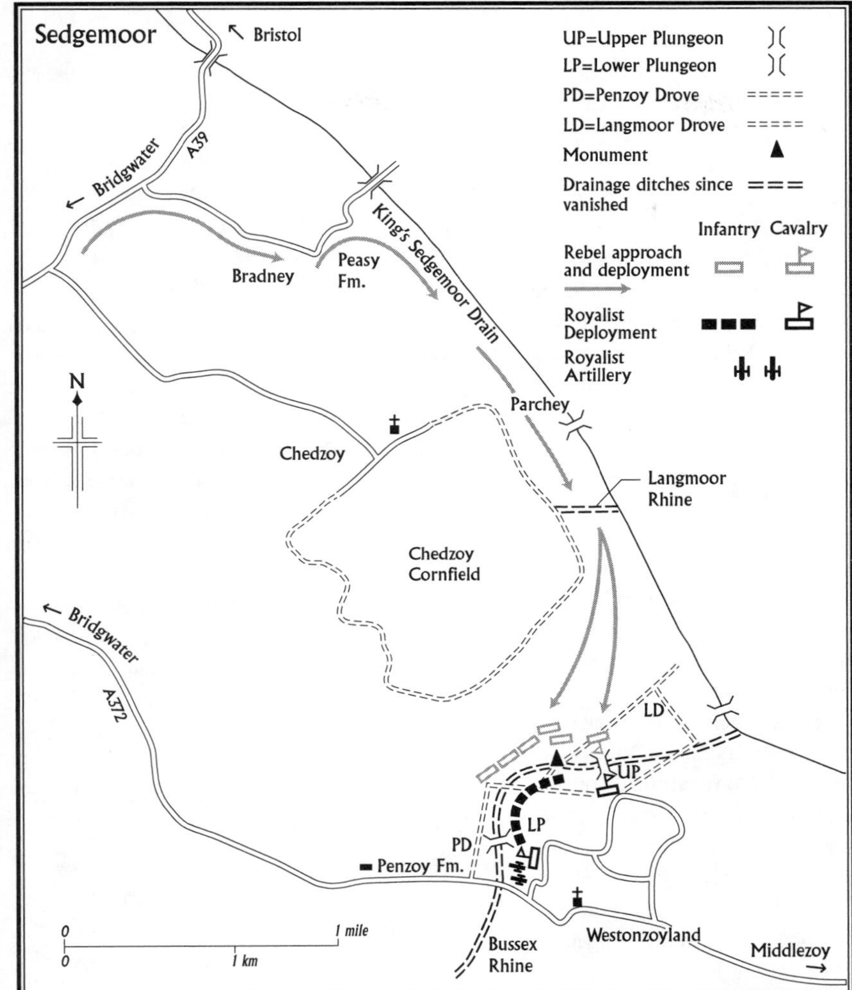

for Dumbarton's Regiment on the Royalist right. The 3000 militia took no direct part in the fighting.

One of their number reckoned the rebels 'were never four thousand when they fought'. The campaign's historian David Chandler puts them at 600 cavalry and 2980 infantry in five colour-coded regiments, plus four guns, one of which broke down en route. Firearms were scarce, many infantry carrying pitchforks or scythes mounted on poles. The cavalry took the lead at Peasy Farm, narrowly avoiding Feversham's patrols. Monmouth's luck ran out four hedgerows south of Parchey Bridge, where the column missed the Langmoor Rhine crossing and attracted

Directions

Sedgemoor *Follow the A372 south from Bridgwater past the Royalist-held sheepfold near Penzoy Farm. Turn left just short of Westonzoyland along Penzoy Drove, leaving the vanished Bussex Rhine and Feversham's front line on the right. Fork left into Langmoor Drove to see the monument (erected 1927) before Kirke's Lambs' second position. Northwest lies the Gravefield where the Red and Yellow Regiments fought, and many of their dead were buried. In the village see St Mary's Church where 500 prisoners were held. Follow Monmouth's march from Peasy Farm along King's Sedgemoor Drain, turning right into Langmoor Drove.*

the attention of an unknown trooper of the Blues. Discharging his piece, he rode back to alarm the camp at about 1.30 a.m. The battle unfolded in three stages:

(1) REBEL CAVALRY ACTION.
Monmouth's horsemen dashed on ahead, hoping to cross the Upper Plungeon before the unformed Royalists were ready for action. Instead they ran into the Chedzoy vedette, which reached the Plungeon first and held it against them. While 200 rebel horse disputed the crossing, the rest rode right along the Royalist front, until dispersed by a volley from the Foot Guards. Fleeing riders disordered the leading rebel foot and carried away the ammunition detail at Peasy Farm.

(2) FIREFIGHT ACROSS THE BUSSEX RHINE.
The Red Regiment deployed 40 or perhaps 80 paces from the ditch opposite the Royalist centre, meaning to charge when ready. The Yellow Regiment on their left opened fire prematurely, however, 'After wch. they could never make their men advance one foot, but stood firing as they were' (James II). Rebel musketeers shot high, but Dumbarton's Regiment suffered heavily from Monmouth's artillery, 116 paces from the ditch, the gunners aiming at their lighted matches. Only four of Dumbarton's officers escaped unhurt. Realizing the rebels overlapped the Royalist right, Churchill moved the two leftmost regiments, Kirke's and Trelawney's, behind the Foot Guards, onto Dumbarton's right. The Ordnance Board's civilian drivers having fled with their teams, the Bishop of Winchester, Feversham's guest for dinner, harnessed his coach horses to six of the guns uselessly parked on the far left. Deployed between the Royalist battalions, they silenced the opposing artillery, their shot carving lanes through the deep rebel formations.

(3) ROYALIST COUNTERATTACK.
Feversham was awake by 3 a.m. He approved the various countermoves, but prohibited any forward movement until daylight. By then rebel powder had failed and Monmouth had left the field, before his last regiment even reached the battlefield. About 4 a.m. Feversham pushed cavalry across the Upper and Lower Plungeons, against the rebel flanks. When the rebel pikes began to open out, a sure sign of distress, Royalist foot swarmed over the Rhine with a great shout, 'wch. the Reb. seeing, ran before they came to bandy blows' (James II).

Monmouth's losses are uncertain, perhaps 400 killed in the battle and 1000 in the pursuit. Country people buried 1384, 'Beside many more they did believe lay dead unfound in the corn' (Adam Wheeler, militia drummer). The greatest slaughter was at the ditch forming Chedzoy Cornfield's southwestern edge. Numbers of prisoners vary between 500 and 1500. The Royalists lost about 80 dead and 200 wounded, a not insignificant percentage, which may explain the notorious severity of the mopping-up operations, which gained 'Kirke's Lambs' an abiding nickname.

Civil reprisals were worse, becoming notorious as the Bloody Assizes. Judge Jeffries, a peculiarly savage law officer even by late Stuart standards, sentenced 333 alleged rebels to death, and 814 to transportation. Monmouth was captured in a ditch, near Blandford Forum, and executed on 15 July.

Norton St Philip

	Winner	*Loser*
Opponents	Rebel	Royalist
Commanders	James Scott, Duke of Monmouth	Louis Duras, Earl of Feversham
Numbers	*c.*2000	2500
Losses	30–50	30–80

Sedgemoor

	Winner	*Loser*
Opponents	Royalist	Rebel
Commanders	Louis Duras, Earl of Feversham John Churchill	James Scott, Duke of Monmouth (x) Forde Grey, Lord of Wark
Numbers	2850	3580
Losses	280	2900

Directions

Norton St Philip *Situated 4 miles (6 km) south of Bath at the B3110/A366 junction.*

Bantry Bay, Wednesday 1 May 1689

Ireland, Co. Cork, DS85/88

The first military action to arise from the Williamite coup of 1688 was at sea. Both sides in the War of the Two Kings depended on external arms supplies and expeditionary forces. Control of the waters between Britain and France remained in dispute until the Allied victory at Barfleur/La Hougue, eight months after hostilities had ended in Ireland. Bantry Bay was the only fleet action caused by French and English attempts to ship troops into Ireland. It was the largest naval battle fought in Irish waters, and began over 100 years of Anglo-French naval conflict.

The French fleet was ready sooner than a Royal Navy still shaken by revolution. Châteaurenault left Brest on 26 April 1689 to convoy French military advisers and 3000 British Jacobites to Ireland. He reached the Irish coast before Herbert, who was fog bound at Milford Haven. The fleets made contact off Kinsale on the 29th, Châteaurenault continuing west round Cape Clear to enter Bantry Bay next morning. He anchored south of the entrance, close inshore under Sheep's Head, while smaller French ships landed troops and supplies 12 miles (19 km) further up at Bantry Creek. Herbert anchored overnight in line of battle 4 miles (6 km) off Mizen Head, the next promontory south of Bantry Bay. At 5 a.m. next morning he sailed northwards, sighting the enemy as he rounded Sheep's Head.

Herbert reported the French as 'a very orderly line, composed of twenty-eight men of war and four fireships'. Châteaurenault admitted only 24 ships of the line, suggesting that Herbert's estimate includes the four French frigates. Twenty-two named English ships suffered damage in the battle: 18 of the line, the 5th-rate *Dartmouth* and 3 fireships, broadly agreeing with Châteaurenault's figures. The crucial odds were 24 French ships of the line (1264 guns), against 19 English (1056 guns). The French formed 3 squadrons of 8 ships each, the flagship in the centre. Herbert seems not to have organized separate squadrons, fighting instead in one continuous line.

The French slipped their cables and tacked northeast against a fine fresh east-northeasterly gale, blowing directly out of the bay. Châteaurenault wanted to gain time for the landing operations, but about 11 a.m. the tide turned and the English van overtook the French fleet, pressing them to fight. Châteaurenault turned onto the starboard tack, across the bay, forcing Herbert to conform. How far Châteaurenault had travelled up the bay's rocky southeastern shore from his overnight anchorage is uncertain, but the encounter cannot have begun far south of Bantry. The bay at this point is at best 5 miles (8 km) across, a restricted area for 50 warships.

As the fleets came within pistol shot, the leading French ships opened fire with musketry, forcing the English to close their gun ports. Firing spread down the lines from front to rear. As the opposite shore approached, Herbert changed tack, running southeast before the wind on the port tack, the fleets still fighting ship to ship. Herbert described what happened next:

> I stretcht off to sea, as well to gett owr ships into line as by that way to have got the wind of them but found them soe cautious in bearing doune that wee never could gett an opportunity to do it, so continued battering upon a stretch till about five a clock in the afternoone …

Throughout the afternoon the French kept their distance, concentrating fire on the English masts and rigging. By late afternoon the fleets were nearly back

Bantry Bay

	Winner	*Loser*
Opponents	French	English
Commanders	Louis François de Rousselet, Comte de Châteaurenault	Arthur Herbert, Earl of Torrington
Numbers	28 ships; 6880 men	22 ships; 5850 men
Losses	0 ships; 133 men	0 ships; 365 men

at sea, Dursey Island to starboard and Mizen Head to port. Rather than risk Herbert gaining the weather gauge in open water, Châteaurenault hauled down his bloody flag, the signal for closer action, and tacked back inside Bantry Bay. The English were in no state to pursue.

Both sides claimed victory, although Herbert admitted the French had gained their point, completing their landing operations unhindered. Châteaurenault blamed his subordinates for not supporting him during the run south. They blamed him for disrupting his own battle line by taking the lead. English casualties considerably exceeded the French: 96 killed and 269 wounded against 40 and 93 respectively.

Jacobite Dublin greeted the victory with fireworks and calls for amphibious operations against the British mainland, but Châteaurenault had already sailed home, his strategic task achieved. Herbert left George Rooke to patrol the Irish Sea with light forces, and put back to Portsmouth to refit. There were no further naval encounters that year.

Directions

View Bantry Bay's deep, turbulent waters from the northern coast of Sheep's Head peninsula, as the country people did in 1689, lifting their hands in prayer for a French victory. The French Armada Exhibition at Bantry House is devoted to Wolfe Tone's attempt to land in 1796, which was less successful than Châteaurenault's effort.

Killiecrankie, 27 July 1689

Scotland, Perth and Kinross, LR43 NN9063

James II was even less popular in Scotland than in England. His only supporters were a few professional swordsmen, whose leader was killed in their first major action.

Viscount Dundee had played a leading role in the persecution of Covenanters under Charles II (see above). When his enemies gained power after the Glorious Revolution, Dundee fled Edinburgh on 18 March 1689 and launched a half-baked rebellion without arms, money or even a commission from his deposed king. Dundee spent May 'skipping from one hill to another like wildfire' before withdrawing into the Jacobite fastness of Lochaber to await help from Ireland. This eventually amounted to just 300 naked, undisciplined recruits, discrediting Dundee's promises of foreign aid. In late July he left his Highland refuge to disrupt the half-hearted attempts of Blair Castle's owners to eject a Jacobite garrison. Blair Castle was the seat of the Marquess of Atholl, a sensitive strategic spot, controlling north–south communications through the Grampian Mountains.

General Mackay, William III's commander-in-chief in Scotland, marched up through Pitlochry to assist the besiegers. At noon on 27 July he entered the Pass of Killiecrankie, a steep defile whose tree-clad slopes fall sheer to the River Garry's rocky bed. The road in 1689 was more rugged and nearer river level than today, comprising a narrow path where three men might walk abreast only with difficulty. Nevertheless, Mackay safely reached Aldgirnaig or Killiecrankie, where the defile opens out. Here he halted 'upon a field of corn along the side of the river', for the baggage to catch up (Mackay, *Memoirs of the War in Scotland*).

Observing small parties of enemy a short mile further up the pass at the foot of the mountain towards Blair, Mackay advanced to face them, occupying a crest 'steep and difficult of ascent, full of trees and shrubs', within carbine shot of the road. Modern reconstructions vary wildly, either depicting the Williamites facing north towards Creag Eallaich, the River Garry behind them, or west across Allt Chluain burn. Mackay describes each battalion making a right wheel, a *quart de conversion* or quarter wheel of 90 degrees, which would strictly have brought them round to face Creag Eallaich. However, Dundee's biographer, C.S. Terry, suggests that the turn was not completed, leaving the Williamites facing north-west towards the Jacobite approach from Blair Castle. In this case, Mackay's line ran along the false crest from Lettoch down to the woods and marshy grounds skirting the highway on their left. It was 'a ground fair enough to receive the enemy, but not to

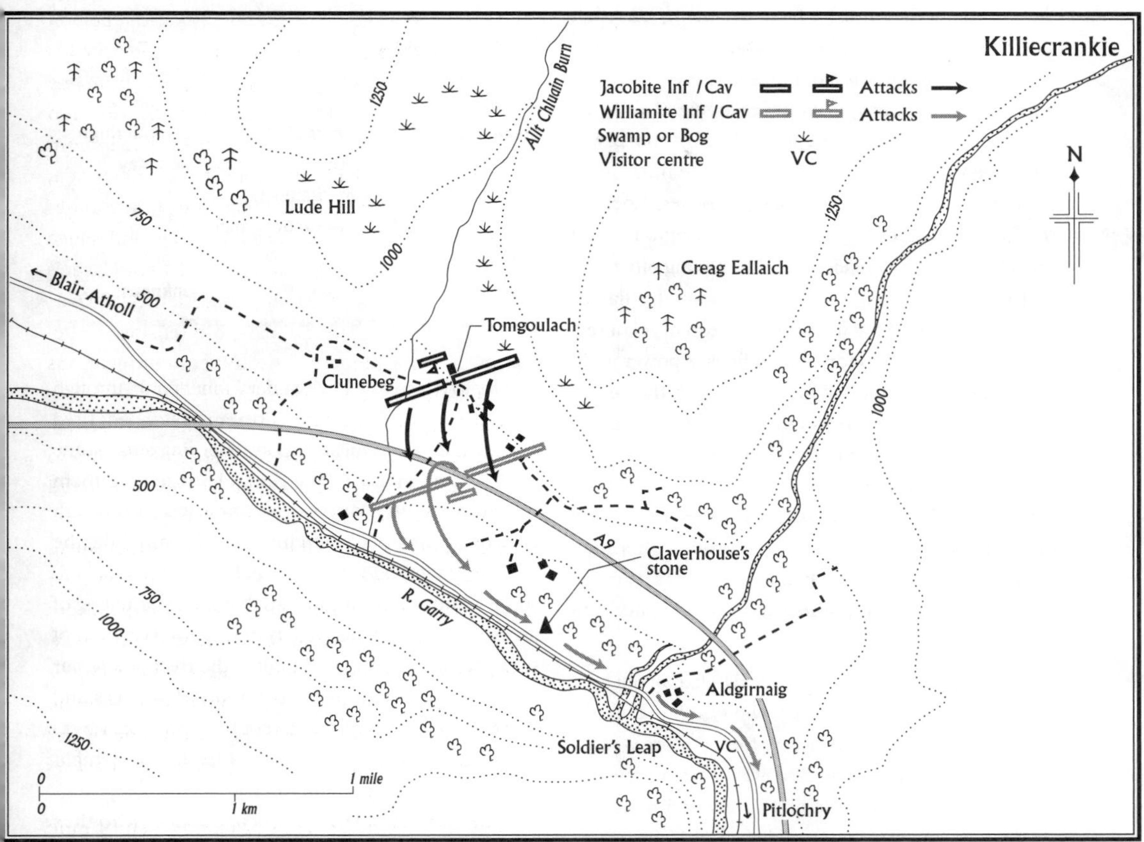

attack them, there being, within a short musket shot to it, another eminence before our front … whereof Dundee had already got possession …' (Mackay).

The Jacobite position was 150 feet (45 m) higher up, roughly along the Tomgoulach–Clunebeg footpath, out of sight from the road. Lude Hill's eastern slope was behind them, consistent with 'the ordinary maxim of Highlanders, who never fight against regular forces upon any thing of equal terms, without a sure retreat at their back' (Mackay). Old Ordnance Survey maps marked the battlefield further down the pass, between Urrard House and the river. This seems unlikely, as Mackay's survivors retreated past the house after the battle.

Mackay had six infantry regiments, two troops of horse and three small guns adapted for transport on pack horses. Three infantry units were the old Scots regiments of the Dutch army. The rest, including the cavalry, were newly raised. All were strangers to Highland warfare. The position was too extensive for Mackay's numbers, so he put all his infantry in front, three ranks deep for extra frontage. He left a gap in the centre for the cavalry to charge through when the

Directions

Follow the B8079 (the old A9) north from Pitlochry through the Pass of Killiecrankie, visiting Soldier's Leap and the National Trust for Scotland visitor centre at Killiecrankie. The battlefield is further north on private land, either side of the dual carriageway of the present A9, beside tracks running uphill from Ardclune to Lettoch. Like other battle stones, Claverhouse's Stone is actually prehistoric. A memorial tablet marks where Dundee was buried in the old kirk at Blair.

line had spent their fire, 'to flank the enemy on either side, as occasion should offer'.

Dundee's army was a dubious mixture of outlaws and malcontents, few of whom recognized any government. MacDonald of Keppoch, 'Coll of the Cows', had recently attacked Inverness, while pursuing a personal vendetta with the Mackintoshes. Lochiel, the Cameron chief, a gentleman 'of upright life and proven honour', was celebrated for having bitten out an English officer's throat. Worried about his flanks, Dundee increased the intervals between his clan regiments, leaving their individual offensive power undiminished. Like Mackay he left a gap in the centre covered by his single troop of horse, mostly gentlemen or deserters from his old regiment.

Several hours delay ensued, enlivened by Mackay's cannon, until their improvised carriages broke. Half an hour before sunset Dundee ordered his men forward. Donald Macbean, a Highlander serving in the Williamite army, published a dramatic account of the charge:

> The sun going down caused the Highlandmen to advance on us like madmen, without shoe or stocking, covering themselves from our fire with their targes; at last they cast away their musquets, drew their broadswords, and advanced furiously upon us, and were in the middle of us before we could fire three shots apiece, broke us and obliged us to retreat.

Mackay's right wing came under attack first, either because the lines were closer together there or because Dundee's other flank stood fast when his left advanced. The three rightmost Williamite regiments opened a brisk platoon fire at 100 paces. They killed numerous MacDonalds, but failed to stop the attackers, who came to close quarters before the soldiers could fix their plug bayonets into the muzzles of their muskets. Only Hastings's Regiment on the extreme right was unshaken, as the slope diverted the Highlanders downhill and away from them, supporting Terry's view that the charge ran obliquely across the contour lines from the northwest, not straight down from the foot of Creag Eallaich.

As his infantry gave way Mackay ordered the

Killiecrankie

	Winner	*Loser*
Opponents	Jacobite	Williamite
Commanders	John Graham of Claverhouse, Viscount Dundee (k) Colonel Alexander Cannon	General Hugh MacKay
Numbers	2500	4000
Losses	800	unknown

cavalry to charge the Highlanders' inner flank, through the central gap. The untried horsemen stopped, fired their carbines and turned about, carrying away some of their own infantry. The general himself led them on, but was left alone riding unmolested through crowds of disordered Highlanders. Meanwhile, the Williamite left had run away before it was attacked, some without firing a shot, 'so that in the twinkling of an eye ... our men, as well as the enemy, were out of sight, being got doun pall mall to the river where our baggage was stood' (Mackay). Only Hastings's and some of Leven's Regiment kept their ground. It was with these remnants that Mackay left the field, night concealing their small numbers.

One of the last volleys killed Dundee, who thus passed instantly from history to immortality with untarnished laurels. Other casualties are less certain. Mackay reckoned the enemy lost six-to-one on the field, 'the fire to our right having been continued and brisk'. Jacobite sources admitted losing a third of their number. Mackay probably lost half his strength killed, taken or deserted, the temptations of the baggage train buying time for many runaways to escape. Donald Macbean claimed to have jumped 18 feet (5.5 m) across the Garry at the Soldier's Leap, below Aldgirnaig, losing one of his shoes but saving his life. Mackay's Regiment, second from the right and hardest hit, lost its lieutenant colonel, 2 captains and 5 subalterns killed, with 3 more captains wounded, from an establishment of 39 commissioned officers.

Killiecrankie's significance has been played up to offset subsequent Jacobite defeats. However, Dundee's ragbag of marginal clans lacked the military muscle to effect a counter-revolution. His death pricked the strategic bubble that his overblown claims of Franco-Irish support had created. Sated with plunder and bereft of their romantic leader, the victors of Killiecrankie went home as soon as they ran into serious opposition three weeks later at Dunkeld.

Relief of Londonderry, Sunday 28 July 1689

Ireland, Co. Londonderry, DS7 C4317–4722

The Siege of Londonderry is one of the most celebrated episodes in Irish history, part of an international Protestant iconography that included the equally heroic defences of Leiden (1573–4) and La Rochelle (1627–8). It gave Northern Ireland's Protestant community its watchword of 'No Surrender', and encouraged an abiding distrust of a British government that seemed unduly slow to rescue its beleaguered partisans. Compared with their 105-day ordeal, the relief of 28 July was a pushover. There is some confusion over the latter date. Macaulay, arch-proponent of Whig Protestant historiography, gives 30 July (Old Style), despite the *London Gazette*, an error compounded by the Apprentice Boys of Derry, who incorrectly adjusted the date of their annual commemoration to 12 August (New Style).

Londonderry had been a Protestant rallying point since the original Nine Years' War in the 1590s (see Part 5). It was a natural focus for resistance to the Catholic counter-revolution that followed William III's coup d'état. It closed its gates against the Earl of Antrim's Redshanks in December 1688, while 20,000–30,000 refugees flooded in, fearing a general massacre of Protestants. The common view of the siege as part of a universal Protestant confrontation with Roman Catholicism is of course nonsense: the Pope backed William of Orange, and James II only wanted Ulster as a stepping stone back to Britain. The numerous protections James issued to his erstwhile Protestant subjects undermined Jacobite efforts to take the city. Nevertheless, when James appeared before Londonderry on 17 April 1689, thinking it would infallibly surrender, the inhabitants shot at him.

The siege quickly developed into a blockade. The ill-equipped besiegers, many armed with nothing more deadly than pointed sticks, were too few for an assault, and lacked the skills for a formal siege. Some 20,000 Jacobite troops served before Londonderry, less than half at any one time. They were outnumbered and outgunned by the 7361 defenders. Londonderry was well adapted to defence, occupying an oval hill surrounded on three sides by the River Foyle. Its mile-long (1.6-km) circuit of stone walls was backed with earth to make it artillery proof, and reinforced by eight small bastions, mounting 20 elderly cannon. A more recent earthwork covered Bishop's Gate to the west.

The Jacobites camped along Creggan Heights northwest of the city, their sod huts extending north through Brooke Park to Magee Campus. They had a mortar platform on the high ground above Eastway, and a battery opposite Butcher's Gate, in the orchard now occupied by William Street and Great James Street. Their siege train was totally inadequate: one 24-pounder, one 18-pounder and two mortars, one of which cracked. On 5–6 May the Jacobites captured and then lost the outwork at Windmill Hill, 500 yards (450 m) southwest of Bishop's Gate, where St Columb's College now stands. An attempt to blow up Gunner's Bastion at Butcher's Gate ended with the deaths of the miners. By mid-July the frustrated besiegers were considering withdrawal.

Relief of Londonderry

	Winner	*Loser*
Opponents	Williamite	Jacobite
Commanders	Major General Percy Kirke Captain John Leake	Conrad, Count de Rosen Lieutenant General Richard Hamilton
Numbers	unknown	unknown
Losses	unknown	unknown

Poor intelligence and contrary winds delayed Williamite relief efforts. Major General Kirke did not reach Lough Foyle until 13 June, shortly after Jacobite shore batteries had nearly sunk the 16-gun *Greyhound* during its attempt to reach the city. A conference of senior officers decided existing information about conditions inside Londonderry did not justify hazarding another ship, with the risk of adding her guns to the enemy siege train. Instead, the squadron sailed round to Inch Island in Lough Swilly, to secure a bridgehead and cut off the besiegers' supplies. Kirke has been execrated for this decision, usually attributed to residual loyalty to his previous employer, James II, but he reacted promptly enough to definite intelligence of the city's plight on 20 July. About 4300 of the garrison remained alive, living on salt hides, tallow pancakes and dogs fattened on corpses, the survivors 'so weak that they can scarce creep to the walls, where many of them dye every night at their post ... God knows what will become of us' (George Walker).

Londonderry lies about 5 miles (8 km) from the mouth of the Foyle, in the teeth of the prevailing southwesterly winds. The river is a quarter of a mile (0.4 km) across, exposing ships in midstream to close-range artillery fire from both banks. Culmore Fort at the mouth (C4722) was a single triangular bastion, well placed to command the channel. Halfway between Culmore and the city, at the bend below the modern Foyle Bridge (C4519), were three more batteries: Charles and New Fort on the left bank, Grange Fort on the right. Between them floated a boom 200 yards (180 m) long and 5 to 6 feet (1.5–1.8 m) thick, constructed from fir beams held together with cables and iron spikes. The boom lay obliquely across the river, its west end fixed to a huge rock in the grounds of Boom Hall, still visible in the 1890s.

The relieving squadron consisted of Captain Leake's 36-gun *Dartmouth* and three victuallers, two of which ran the blockade: the *Mountjoy* of Derry, and *Phoenix* of Coleraine. Kirke remained offshore in *Swallow*, whose longboat accompanied the leading victualler, 'well baricado'd and armed with seamen to cut the Boume'. Being sailing ships they had to await a favourable wind and tide. At 6 p.m. on Sunday 28 July a moderate gale sprung up, from the north-northwest, just before slack water off Culmore, giving the ships a flooding tide to carry them up to the city. Leake had agreed with the victuallers' captains that he would engage Culmore while they ran past under full sail to break the boom. He held fire until he had rounded Culmore Point, anchoring within musket shot of the fort. There *Dartmouth* remained until 8 a.m. next day, 'the Castle still saluting her and she returning 5 or 6 for one' (Kirke).

No sooner had the leading ships passed Culmore than the wind dropped, becalming the third victualler. *Mountjoy* lost way, rebounded off the boom, and ran sternmost onto the left bank. The Jacobites swarmed around, 'firing their great and small shot, and preparing their boats to board her; which however was not to be done so easily as they imagined' (*Life of Sir John Leake*). The recoil of *Mountjoy*'s stern chase guns combined with the rising tide to float her off, with the loss of Micaiah Browning, her captain. Meantime *Swallow*'s longboat, 'a boat with a house on it' said the Irish, pulled up to the boom; the boatswain's mate in command cut the cables, 'so that the weight of the ship [*Mountjoy*] broke it and the shipps went up but so little wind that the longboat towed her all the way ...' (Kirke). Harried all the way by Jacobite small arms and field guns dragged along the bank, the ships reached Derry Quay (C4317) about 10 p.m., to unload their cargo of meal, dried peas, salt beef and biscuit.

The Jacobites blamed their defeat upon treachery, claiming the English had got the king's gunners drunk. A better explanation was lack of cannon and trained artillerymen: only 5 out of 36 French gunners present were fit for duty. Their ambassador blamed poor construction of the boom, which wind and tide had broken several times before. Casualties among the relieving force were few: five or six soldiers in the victuallers, presumably returning fire over the bulwarks; *Swallow*'s boatswain's mate wounded in the thigh with a splinter; one soldier killed and one wounded in *Dartmouth*. Losses during the siege were much worse. A Treasury paper of 1702 reckoned 12,000 perished by sword and famine. *A Jacobite*

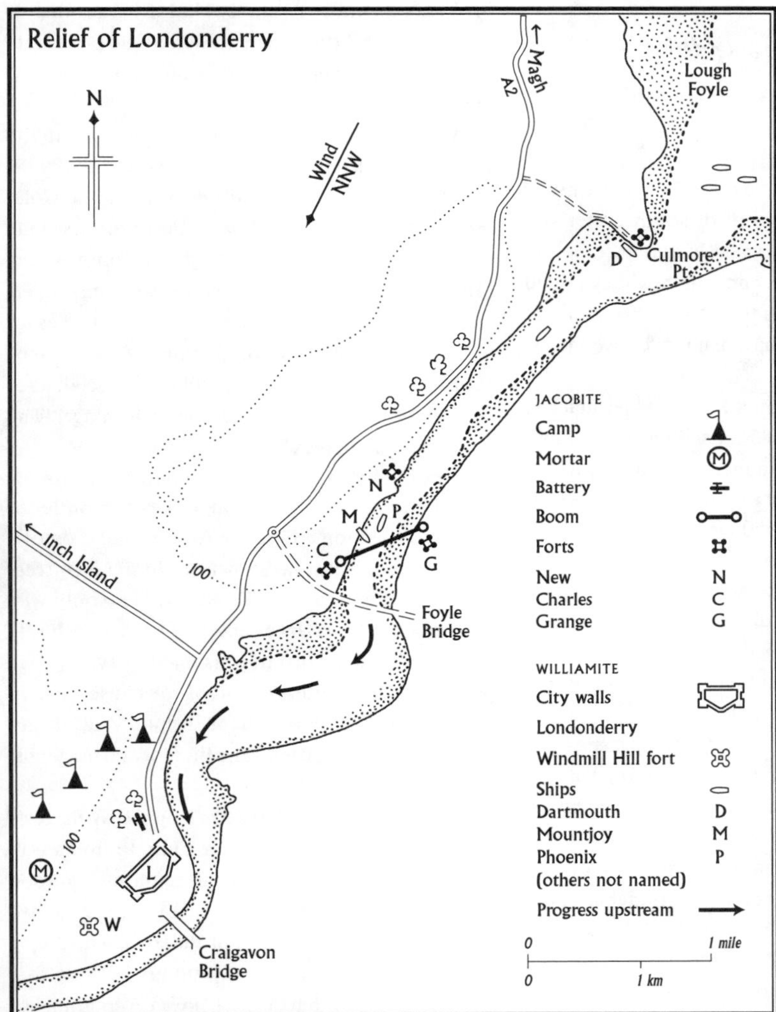

Narrative of the War in Ireland put their losses 'first and last' at 2000.

Breaking the boom was a decisive action. The Jacobites broke camp during the night of 31 July–1 August and retreated south, clearing the way for massive Williamite reinforcements to land at Carrickfergus. Londonderry's defence and last-minute relief were a turning point in the local struggle between William III and James II, and in the wider Continental war against James's French sponsor, Louis XIV.

Directions

Londonderry's walls provide a continuous walkway around the ancient part of the city, connecting the bastions, which are now gardens. See 'Roaring Meg', one of the guns used during the siege, at Royal Bastion. A statue of George Walker, the leader of the defenders, stood here until the IRA blew it up in 1973, making this the longest continuously contested piece of ground in the United Kingdom. Boom Hall is off the Culmore Road roundabout at the west end of Foyle Bridge. Culmore Fort is on the right off the A2, before Magh.

Newton Butler, Wednesday 31 July 1689

Ireland, Co. Fermanagh, DS27 H4224–5

Spared the attentions of the main Jacobite army at Londonderry, the Protestants of south Ulster and north Connacht maintained a lively resistance. Secure amidst Fermanagh's lakes and marshes, they raided Jacobite communications from their stronghold at Enniskillen, finally defeating a major offensive against them at Newton Butler.

Late in July 1689 Viscount Mountcashel attacked Crom Castle, southeast of Enniskillen on the shore of Lough Erne (H3524), 'to make the way more easy for the expugnation of the said Enniskillen' (*Jacobite Narrative of the War in Ireland*). Crom Castle occupied a promontory nearly surrounded by water, an earthwork covering the landward approach. The Jacobites took the outwork on 30 July, but lacked artillery to breach the stone walls beyond. Next day the approach of a relieving force under Colonel William Berry forced them to abandon the siege.

Major General Kirke had no troops to spare from operations around Londonderry (see above), but sent two officers by ship to assist Enniskillen's defenders, who communicated with the sea by Ballyshannon. The senior adviser, Colonel William Wolseley, put total Protestant numbers at Newton Butler as 2200; another source gives 800 horse and 1200 foot, with no artillery. Mountcashel's 'small flying camp' was 4000 strong: three infantry regiments and 16 troops of horse or dragoons, reinforced by a further 13 troops of dragoons under Anthony Hamilton, brother of the besieger of Londonderry. Their 8 field pieces presumably resembled the leather-bound tin gun that burst at Crom Castle.

Newton Butler

	Winner	*Loser*
Opponents	Williamite	Jacobite
Commanders	Colonel William Wolseley	Justin MacCarthy, Viscount Mountcashel (p)
	Colonel William Berry	Brigadier Anthony Hamilton (w)
Numbers	2200	*c.*4800
Losses	70	2500

Mountcashel sent Hamilton's dragoons up the B514 Enniskillen road, meeting Berry north of Newton Butler, on a narrow causeway along the Colebrooke River's marshy left bank. Berry surprised the dismounted dragoons, wounding their commanding officer, whose orders to left wheel were misunderstood, leading to general panic. Hamilton fled as far as Navan (Co. Meath) over 50 miles (80 km) away. Wolseley now joined Berry, and they agreed, after consulting the troops, to press their advantage: 'The word was "no popery".'

Finding his advanced guard had fled, Mountcashel withdrew south through Newton Butler to occupy a position where the Cavan road crosses a stream flowing east–west, before climbing 100 feet (30 m) to the hamlet of Kilgarrett. The only way through in 1689 was by a causeway flanked by boggy pools and quagmires, impassable to cavalry: 'He planted at the [southern] end of the causeway two or three small pieces of cannon, behind which he set a troop of horse, on each hand his foot and dragoons' (*Jacobite Narrative*).

Mountcashel's artillery fire stopped Wolseley's advance down the road, forcing him to find a way round: 'They drew back and passed through a wood that was at one end of the said morass, and marched unperceived against the rear of the Irish, who seeing the foe coming surprisingly upon them in that posture, took their retreat ...' (*Jacobite Narrative*). For what it is worth, a small wood survives on Mountcashel's right front, down the slope near the A34/B143 junction. The Enniskillen foot and dragoons dispatched the Jacobite gunners, allowing their horse to rush the causeway. In an echo of Irish battles of the 1640s, the Jacobite cavalry abandoned their infantry and fled without a blow: 'Though the foot fought with great obstinacy, and the general did all that could be expected ... yet the king's horse giving way the rest were totally routed' (James II).

The ensuing slaughter also recalled the Eleven Years' War. The Enniskilleners pushed on, and took

Wattle Bridge across the River Erne, cutting off Mountcashel's retreat. Ignorant of the terrain, his Munstermen were hunted down, or blundered into the area's numerous lakes and marshes. Wolseley claimed 1500 killed in the pursuit, 500 drowned and only 500 prisoners. Mountcashel was among the latter, wounded in several places, one potentially fatal bullet intercepted by his watch. Protestant losses were 20 killed and 50 wounded. The third Jacobite setback in four days, Newton Butler was a striking victory that enhanced the Enniskilleners' reputation, while further depressing the Jacobites' already low morale.

Directions

Kilgarrett is ½ mile (0.8 km) south of Newton Butler on the B road which, south of the border, becomes the N54 to Butler's Bridge. Hamilton was presumably ambushed near Ballindarragh Bridge, where the B514 follows the north bank of Colebrooke. See Crom Castle's ruins on a finely wooded promontory overlooking Lough Erne, 3 miles (5 km) southwest of Newton Butler. Also, in Enniskillen, visit the regimental museum of the Royal Inniskilling Fusiliers, formed from troops who fought at Newton Butler.

Dunkeld, 21 August 1689

Scotland, Perth and Kinross, LR 53 NO0242

The defence of Dunkeld revealed the alteration in Scottish politics made by the Glorious Revolution. The garrison were ex-Covenanters, now fighting for the Government, and their commanding officer a veteran of Drumclog (1679).

The Highland Jacobites dared not leave the mountains, despite their victory at Killiecrankie (see above). Colonel Cannon, who replaced Viscount Dundee, marched north through Braemar into Strathbogie, threatening Aberdeen. General Mackay followed with a mounted column, but was left behind when Cannon doubled back southwards into the hills. Meanwhile the Council in Edinburgh, 'without consideration of the insufficiencie of the place for defence, ordered the Earl of Angus's Regiment to Dunkeld, 10 miles (16 km) above Perth, separate from all speedy succour, and exposed to be carried by insult …' (Mackay).

The regiment had been formed on 16 April from followers of Richard Cameron, a diehard Covenanter killed in 1680. Mackay thought William Cleland, their commander, 'a sensible resolute man, though not much of a soldier'. Their enemies called them the Cameronian Regiment, 'whose oppression against all such as were not of their own sentiment made them generally hated and feared in the northern countries'. The Atholl men had declared for King James after Killiecrankie, and informed Cannon of the chance to catch their arch-opponents at Dunkeld, 'an open useless place, ill provided of all things, and in the midst of the Enemies' (*Exact Narrative of the Conflict at Dunkeld … Collected from Several Officers of that Regiment*).

Modern Dunkeld is directly north of the 19th-century Telford bridge over the River Tay. Before the battle the settlement was further west, around the cathedral, near the original crossing place from Inver. On a 7th-century monastic site, the medieval cathedral's mainly roofless ruins lie amidst idyllic lawns and trees. In 1689 they were surrounded by 'stone yard dykes' – low garden walls – in most places not 4 feet (1.2 m) high. West of Stanley Hill, an artificially enhanced eminence 100–200 yards (90–180 m) north of the cathedral, lay the Marquess of Atholl's more substantial dwelling, not to be confused with today's Dunkeld House, a mile (1.6 km) further west.

Most accounts assign the Cameronians their full establishment of 1200, i.e. 20 companies of 60 men. By their own account (*Exact Narrative*) only 700–800

Dunkeld

	Winner	*Loser*
Opponents	Williamite	Jacobite
Commanders	William Cleland (k)	Colonel Alexander Cannon
Numbers	700–800	c.5000
Losses	50	c.300

men entered Dunkeld on the evening of 17–18 August. They placed musketeers in the square cathedral tower, entrenched the marquess's yard dykes, 'the old breaches whereof they made up with loose stones', and scaffolded the dykes to make firing platforms. Beyond the buildings they placed outposts (18–24 men apiece) below the surrounding hills, and barricaded the Mercat (Market) Cross to the east. The Cameronians put the enemy at 5000 men with 1000 pack horses, a figure supported by Mackay's estimate of 4000. This included three troops of horse, with back, breast and headpiece. Luckily for Dunkeld's defenders the Jacobite artillery lacked ammunition.

The Highlanders appeared at daylight on 21 August, 'standing in order, covering all the hills about'. About 7 a.m. they advanced cannon, 'down to the face of a little hill, close upon the Town', covered by cavalry either side. One troop went southwest 'betwixt the Foord of the River and the Church'; two more northeast of the town near the Mercat Cross, 'who in the time of conflict shewed much eagerness to encourage and push on the Foot' (*Exact Narrative*). The northern Cameronian outpost was driven back, 'firing from one little dyke to another', and withdrew into the Marquess of Atholl's house. The Cameronians to the west 'fired sharply upon the Enemies Horse, until great numbers of Foot attacked their Dyke, and forced them to the Church', where the Mercat Cross detachment joined them:

> All the outposts being forced, the Rebels advanced most boldly upon the yard dykes all around, even upon those parts which stood within less than forty paces from the River; where they crowded in multitudes, without regard to the Shot liberally poured in their Faces; and struck with their Swords at the Souldiers upon the Dyk, who with their Pikes and Halberts returnd their Blows with Interest ...

Others fired into the yard dykes from the houses, shooting Cleland through head and liver, and mortally wounding his second-in-command. Their replacement sent out fire parties, 'with burning Faggots upon the points of their Pikes, who fired the Houses; and where they found the keys in the Doors, lock't them and burnt all within ...'. All the houses, except three the Cameronians still held, were destroyed, the surviving inhabitants sheltering in the cathedral.

Fighting continued until 11 a.m. when the Highlanders, 'wearied with so many fruitless and expensive assaults', withdrew to the hills. The Cameronians beat their drums, flourished their colours, 'and hallowed after them with all Expressions of Contempt and Provocations to return', but the Highlanders refused to charge again, saying, 'they could fight against Men, but it was not fit to fight any more against devils' (*Exact Narrative*). Mackay thought it a providential victory, one that destroyed Cannon's credit among his flighty allies, and proved their inability to overrun the simplest obstacles defended by fire. He reckoned the Jacobites only lost 20 men, although the victors claimed over 300 slain. Including officers the Cameronians lost 17 dead and 33 wounded. Within a month the Atholl men, the main cause of Mackay's troubles, had made peace, while autumnal rain halted operations for the rest of the year.

Directions

Dunkeld is 10 miles (16 km) north of Perth, just off the A9 to Pitlochry. The fighting was mostly around the cathedral, west of the modern town. See Cleland's tombstone in the nave. Other casualties were buried outside the south wall. A fountain has replaced the Mercat Cross in the town centre. The Cameronians, later the 26th Foot and 1st Scottish Rifles, were disbanded in 1968. Their regimental museum is at Hamilton, near the site of Bothwell Bridge (see above).

Haughs of Cromdale, 1 May 1690

Scotland, Highland, LR36 NJ0628–0727

After the high drama of Killiecrankie and Dunkeld, Jacobite insurgency in the Highlands ended with a whimper at the Haughs of Cromdale. King James's new commander in Scotland, General Buchan, found little support among western clans harassed by the Williamite navy. On 20 April 1690 he left Lochaber

Haughs of Cromdale

	Winner	*Loser*
Opponents	Williamite	Jacobite
Commanders	Sir Thomas Livingstone	Major General Thomas Buchan Colonel Alexander Cannon
Numbers	1200	1200
Losses	0	400

for Strathspey, with 800 of the worst clansmen, joined en route by 400 from Badenoch.

Fearing Buchan's column would gather strength if not speedily opposed, Sir Thomas Livingstone, the Williamite commander in Inverness, concentrated his own forces between Nairn and Strathspey: two troops of horse and 300 dragoons (making 400 cavalry in all), 700 conventional infantry and '100 brisk Highlanders of Lord Rae's men, which the General had taken into the service a twelvemonth before' (General Hugh Mackay, *Memoirs of the War in Scotland*). During the afternoon of 30 April, Livingstone received news of Buchan's whereabouts. Not realizing how close the Jacobites were, he marched for Grantown-on-Spey, reaching the hilltop of Derraid above Castle Grant (NJ0430) by 2 a.m. on May Day.

The Williamite officer commanding Castle Grant pointed out the enemy camp fires across the valley at Lethandry, a village between the Spey and the Haughs of Cromdale, low ground in the bend of the river, rising south-astwards to the hills beyond. Mackay thought this a double providence. Had Livingstone known the enemy were so near, he would never have ventured into the pass at night, 'not being very confident of the people of that country'. Had Buchan suspected Livingstone's approach, he would never have left the hills 'to camp upon a plain ground a great mile and a half from any strong ground, just as if they had been led thither by the hand, as an ox to the slaughter'.

Livingstone gave his weary men 30 minutes rest, then pressed on under Tomvaich Wood, down a covered way to the river. The first ford, perhaps by Mains of Cromdale, was held by 100 Highlanders. Leaving a detachment to amuse them, Livingstone 'marched his gross to another foord below that a quarter of a mile', perhaps Boat of Cromdale (NJ0628–29). Lord Rae's Highland company led the way, followed by three troops of dragoons and one of horse, the rudely awakened enemy 'moving confusedly as irresolute men'. Sending back orders for his main body to follow, Livingstone attacked with what he had, 'pushing betwixt the Highlanders and the hills'.

Livingstone's own Highlanders outran his galloping horse, and cut off the Jacobites from the hills, 'who seeing him so weak, resolved to stand; but upon the sight of the rest of his party, which was following with all the speed they could make, they began to run for it ...'. Livingstone's mounted troops mixed with the fugitives, killing or taking 400 of them for the loss of 7 or 8 horses. Few Jacobites would have escaped except for a sudden fog. The Ordnance Survey marks the battle east of Lethandry in Claggersnich Wood (NJ0927), but the direction of the attack would have carried the action more southwards, up the Spey valley. A Jacobite party was intercepted next day at Aviemore, 16 miles (25 km) upstream. They suffered another 100 killed, the survivors sheltering amongst the rocks of Craigellachie (NH8811–12).

Buchan was not quite finished, raiding into Aberdeen with 600 Braemar Highlanders, but his sponsors had had enough. Their chiefs offered no resistance when Mackay appeared in Lochaber with 3000 men to fortify Inverlochy, renamed Fort William. The first Jacobite rising was over.

Directions

Grantown-on-Spey is 20 miles (32 km) south of Nairn along the A939. See Castle Grant on the left, 1 mile (1.6 km) north of the town. Turn left along the B9102 towards a standing stone (NJ0529), where forestry tracks (perhaps the 'covered way') head down to Mains of Cromdale. Cross the modern bridge and continue past Cromdale village to Lethandry. Alternatively, drive through Grantown to Speybridge, turning left along the A95, and right at the Lethandry junction.

Beachy Head (Beveziers), **Monday 30 June 1690**

Naval, English Channel, LR199

The most dangerous moment for the Williamites in the War of the Two Kings occurred not in Scotland or Ireland, but off Beachy Head. The strategic balance in the English Channel had altered in France's favour since the 1670s (see above). England faced a real danger of invasion in the early 1690s, for which, unlike Charles II's Dutch opponents, the French had both the means and motive. The appearance of Gardes Françaises at Whitehall would have guaranteed a counter-revolution, knocking England out of the Nine Years' War.

The combined Dutch and English fleets should have outnumbered the French, but the Admiralty had yielded to commercial pressure, dispersing its ships to protect trade. Meanwhile the French concentrated their Mediterranean and Atlantic squadrons at Brest, the largest fleet France had ever sent to sea. When Tourville approached the Isle of Wight on 25 June 1690, he outnumbered Torrington by 68 ships of the line (4122 guns) to 56 (3696 guns). Torrington's critics argue he could have fought and won, as Nelson did at Trafalgar against similar odds. The conditions were quite different, however. The Royal Navy had yet to establish its tradition of victory, and it was the weaker Anglo-Dutch fleet that suffered from divided command.

The Allies withdrew eastwards, up Channel, generally in sight of the enemy, although light winds prevented either fleet closing. On 29 June Torrington received categorical orders to fight from Queen Mary, head of government during William's absence in Ireland. A fresh northeasterly gale next morning gave the Allies the weather gauge, and no excuse for further evasion. Torrington formed his fleet in three squadrons and bore down on the enemy in line abreast: van upon van, centre upon centre, rear upon rear. The French awaited them on the starboard tack, head sails aback, heading north-northwest. Beachy Head lay 10 or 12 miles (16–19 km) northward, crowds of country people lining the top of the chalk cliffs to watch.

The Dutch took the Allied van, led by Evertsen, a veteran of Sole Bay (1672), whose father had died in the Four Days' Fight (1666). Turning closer to the wind, they came together onto the starboard tack, parallel with the enemy van, opening fire at 9 a.m. Torrington's centre squadron opened fire an hour later. The French maintained correct distance between ships throughout their fleet, their three divisions keeping well together. The centre sagged to leeward, however, creating a bend in the middle of their line away from the enemy. Individual Allied ships kept station well enough, but gaps opened up between the three divisions of Torrington's squadron, and between him and the Allied van and rear. Perhaps for this reason, he remained at long gunshot from the enemy centre, which outnumbered him 25 ships (1518 guns) to 21 (1410 guns).

Conspiracy theorists claim Torrington deliberately left the Dutch to bear the brunt of the fighting. That was certainly the effect of his reticence. About 1 p.m. the disengaged ships heading the French van doubled back to put Evertsen between two fires, while Tourville's leading ships, from the insufficiently engaged centre, pulled ahead to put further pressure on the Allied van. Only a sudden calm at 3 p.m. saved Evertsen from annihilation. While the French lower-

Beachy Head

	Winner	*Loser*
Opponents	French	Allied
Commanders	Anne Hilarion de Cotentin, Comte de Tourville Louis François de Rousselet, Comte de Châteaurenault Victor Marie, Comte d'Estrées	Arthur Herbert, Earl of Torrington Cornelis Evertsen 'the Youngest' Vice Admiral Sir Ralph Delaval
Numbers	68	56
Losses	0 ships; men unknown	9–10 ships; men unknown

ed boats to tow their ships nearer the enemy, the Allies dropped anchor, and at 5 p.m. the ebb tide carried the French out of range to the southwest, ending the action. When the tide reversed direction that evening, the Allies sailed eastwards up Channel, towing their most damaged ships with them.

Tourville pursued deliberately, keeping formation rather than ordering general chase, which might have taken numerous prizes. He gave up off Dover, the Allies anchoring off the Nore. They had lost 8–9 ships of the line, all but one destroyed in the pursuit to prevent their capture. The French claimed to have captured 1 and destroyed 14, which presumably includes expended fireships. Human casualties were heavy, but unknown.

Panic reigned in London, where a French descent was imminently expected, though they had prepared neither troops nor transports. Torrington survived the ensuing court martial, but was never employed again. In his defence he argued the French dared not invade as long as the Allies avoided a decision, preserving their fleet as a deterrent against invasion, the first formulation of the 'fleet in being' concept of naval strategy. The threat of invasion was lifted next year, when the Allies smashed Tourville's Brest squadron off Cape Barfleur (19 May 1692), and burnt the surviving vessels in La Hougue Bay, where low spring tides exposed their ribs until the 19th century.

Directions

Turn off the A259 Eastbourne–Seaford road at East Dean, and follow the South Downs Way around Beachy Head, looking southward to where the Newhaven–Dieppe ferries used to pass through the battle area.

The Boyne (Drogheda), **Tuesday 1 July 1690**

Ireland, Co. Meath, DS43 O0474–5

The largest and most famous Irish battle occurred 3 miles (5 km) upstream from Drogheda, the scene of the island's most notorious atrocity (see Part 6). Still celebrated by Ulster Protestants as the origin of their freedom, religion and laws, the Boyne saw two kings, neither of whom cared a jot for Ireland, supported by international armies, fighting beside an Irish river for the throne of England and the liberties of Europe.

Continued Jacobite resistance after the Relief of Londonderry (see above) persuaded William III to take personal command in Ireland. He landed at Carrickfergus (Co. Antrim) in June 1690, and marched south to bring James II to battle. The latter failed to hold Moyry Pass, scene of Tyrone's struggle with Mountjoy in 1600 (see Part 5), and withdrew across the River Boyne, the only practical line of defence in front of Dublin, 'the old Rubicon of the Pale, and the frontier of the corn country' (*A Jacobite Narrative of the War in Ireland*). William caught up with him at noon on Monday 30 June.

James's supporters sought to minimize the Boyne: 'but a skirmish … for the defending and gaining a few passes upon a shallow river; and after the passes gained there happened a running fight' (*Jacobite Narrative*). Rivers certainly make poor defensive lines. Armies either disperse to cover all the crossings, and get beaten in detail, or concentrate at the obvious places, and get surrounded. Williamite scouts, however, assessed the position as 'not only difficult but almost impracticable', a more respectable reason for not attacking immediately than William III's often quoted dislike of Mondays.

The Boyne's two lowest bridges were 8 miles (13 km) apart, at Drogheda and Slane. Jacobite forces had occupied the former, and partly demolished the latter. In between, the river forms two large bends, southwards from Slane around Rosnaree and New Grange, then northwards to Tullyallen and Oldbridge, whence it flows east through Drogheda to the sea. Northwards, Hill of Slane and high ground at Tullyallen provided good observation of Jacobite movements; to the south Roughgrange dominates the whole valley, while Donore Hill closes the Oldbridge loop.

The Boyne was tidal, limiting crossings below Oldbridge to specific times and places:

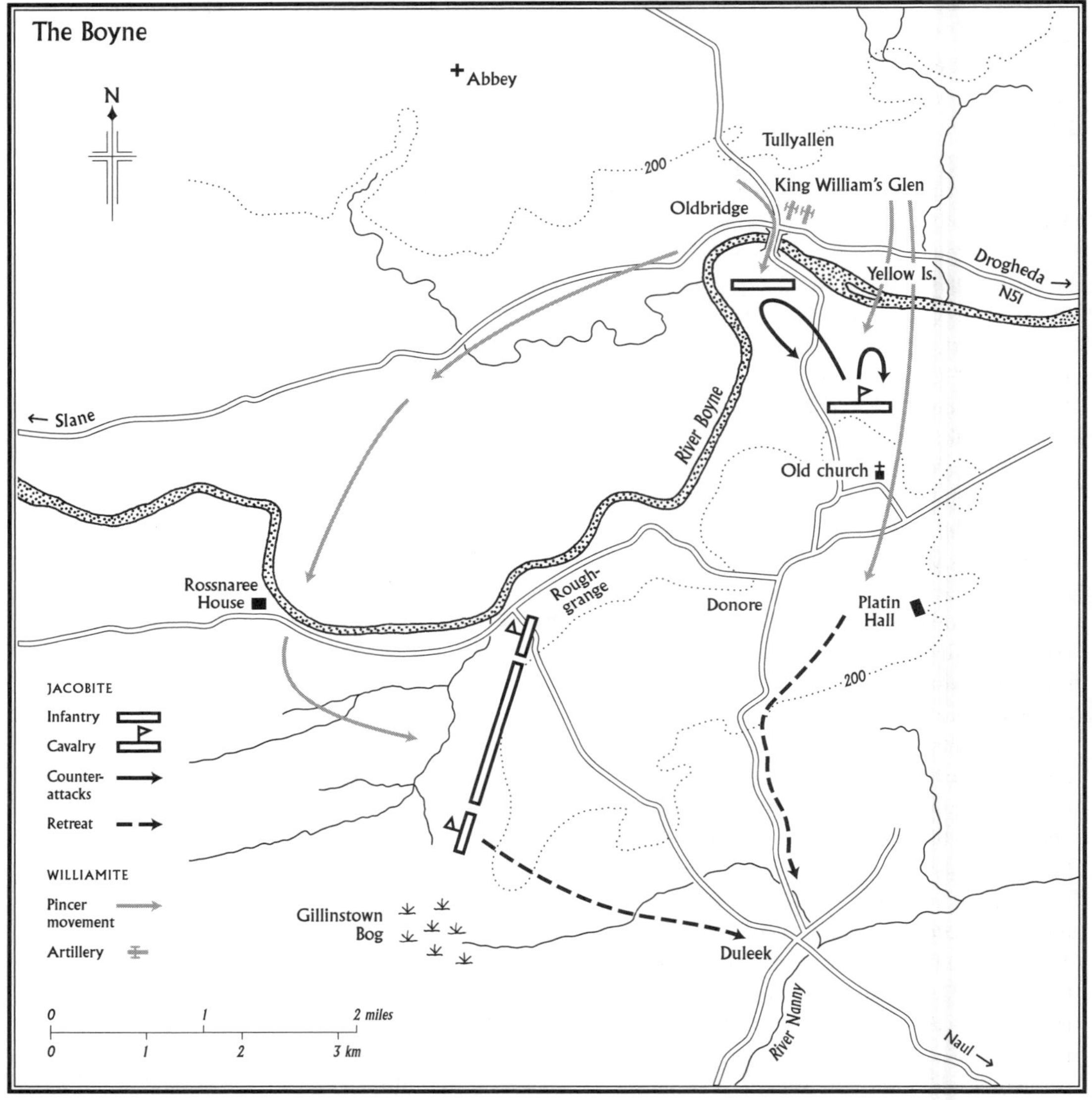

(1) *The old ford*: 200–300 yards (180–270 m) from King William's Glen, knee deep at low water;
(2) *Grove Island and Yellow Island*: half a mile (0.8 km) downstream;
(3) *Mill Ford*: also named Drybridge from a nearby crossing over the stream that joins the Boyne just east of the motorway.

Directions

Take the N51 west from Drogheda, past Drybridge and Yellow Island, to the 19th-century bridge at the foot of King William's Glen. See the plinth of the obelisk built in the 18th century, and blown up by the IRA in 1923. Turn left across the bridge to see the area fought over. Continue through Donore to reach James II's position, near the information centre.

The Boyne

	Winner	*Loser*
Opponents	Williamite	Jacobite
Commanders	William III	James II
	Friedrich Herman, Count Schomberg (k)	Antonin de Caumont, Comte de Lauzun
Numbers	37,000	25,000
Losses	1000	*c*.4000

The next ford upriver from Oldbridge was at Rosnaree. The Ordnance Survey locates this east of Rosnaree House; Colonel O'Carroll puts it to the west. The battlefield has altered greatly: a bridge has replaced Oldbridge ford, where the hamlet has vanished; a canal follows the river's south bank; and the islands are overgrown. Modern Donore lies a mile (1.6 km) southwest of the ruined church marking the old settlement.

Contemporary military doctrine cautioned against fighting at worse odds than three-to-four, so James should have avoided action. Williamite muster rolls compiled after the battle show 7772 mounted troops and 22,528 infantry. Allowing a fifth more for officers and NCOs, plus the casualties, this approaches the tabulated figure. James II put his own army at 5000 horse and 20,000 foot. His French advisers suggested burning Dublin and retreating behind the Shannon, but the king found the Boyne an indifferent good post, 'and indeed the country afforded no better'. James resolved 'not to be walked out of Ireland without having at least one blow for it'. His army was the largest ever raised in Ireland, but ill armed and of uneven quality. A quarter of the infantry had pikes, compared with a seventh or none at all in Allied units, who carried bayonets, swine feathers and spiky *chevaux-de-frise* (both types of spikes for deterring cavalry) instead. Allied flintlocks outclassed Jacobite matchlocks in a fire fight. On the other hand, James's 7000 French infantry were excellent, while his Old English cavalry, heirs to the high-quality Leinster horse of the Eleven Years' War, were fighting for their land and survival as a class.

The Jacobites deployed in two lines: infantry forward in Oldbridge's gardens, cavalry uphill in support, the French on the left. One regiment of dragoons watched the Rosnaree ford. James was apparently unaware of the Drybridge crossing. William originally deployed directly opposite, downstream from King William's Glen, as shown by the map in the Reverend George Story's semi-official account, *An Impartial History of the Affairs of Ireland*. At dusk, however, he took ground westwards, his headquarters at Mellifont Abbey, his right wing menacing Rosnaree.

William III's plan is much debated. Pádraig Lenihan characterizes it as a three-pronged pincer movement: a right flanking move via Rosnaree, combined with simultaneous attacks between Oldbridge and Drybridge. Unwilling to risk such a combination in darkness, William started the right flanking column at first light, 5 or 6 a.m. Williamite accounts allocate 10,000–19,000 men to this manoeuvre, a quarter to half the whole army. It seems that the smaller force that initially crossed at Rosnaree attracted a disproportionate Jacobite response. Alarmed at the potential annihilation of his outflanking detachment, William sent reinforcements, leaving just half his army for the frontal attack.

Two factors saved the Williamite battle plan: firstly James II overreacted, moving two-thirds of his army to meet the turning movement; secondly the bogs, ditches and ravines between Rosnaree and Roughgrange prevented the two sides coming together on the western flank of the battlefield. The 8000 Jacobites left at Oldbridge faced twice their number of Williamites, while the best portion of their army did nothing. The day was hot and bright, 'as if the sun itself had a mind to see what would happen' (Story).

Unaware of the impasse on his right, William began the main attack. English artillery softened up the defenders around Oldbridge, and at 10 a.m. the Dutch Guards stormed the ford, clearing the immediate bank and taking the village. Irish infantry counterattacked from dead ground south of the village, but were beaten back by crushing platoon volleys. Armed with pikes and matchlocks, they were a Civil War army facing 18th-century opposition.

Meanwhile Huguenot regiments, Protestant refugees from Louis XIV's France, crossed downstream, 100 yards (90 m) to the left of the Dutch Guards. As the Jacobite infantry withdrew, their cavalry emerged from hollows southeast of Oldbridge, apparently rising from the ground. The Dutch met them with bayonets and swine feathers, backed by rolling volleys. The Irish charged 'like madmen', with 'unspeakable bravery', their enemies claiming they were all drunk. They broke through the Huguenots, who lacked bayonets, killing old Marshal Schomberg in the melee, but the Dutch held firm: 'Nothing was to be seen but smoke and dust nor anything to be heard but one continued fire for nigh on half an hour' (Story). One 300-strong Jacobite unit had just 30 men left after three or four charges. It was a cavalry fight without equal in Ireland's history.

Once the Jacobite cavalry were committed, more Williamites pushed across the Boyne. Danish infantry waded over from Yellow Island, water up to their chests, holding their cartridges and their commanding officer over their heads. They dispersed a hostile dragoon regiment, then stuck fast behind their *chevaux-de-frise*. Further downstream, William led 2000 Dutch, Danish and Enniskillen cavalry over Mill Ford at 11 a.m., the asthmatic king struggling through mud left by the receding tide. For more than half a mile (0.8 km) downstream from Oldbridge, foliage stuck in Williamite hats as a field sign made the river a thicket of green boughs.

William's crossing was the moment when 'the one hope of Mother Ireland died', yet the Allied cavalry charge up Donore Hill was disappointing. William failed to coordinate different national contingents, who collided in the smoke and dust and suffered heavy losses in confused fighting around the hilltop. Not until 2 p.m. did the last Jacobite cavalry give way near Platin House, east of Donore.

All this time, most of the Jacobites were quietly observing William III's right-hand pincer, north of Gillinstown Bog. Learning of events further east, James proposed an immediate attack, only to find the ditches to his front were impassable. Behind him, his lines of retreat converged on Duleek, where the Dublin road crosses the River Nanny. Fearing encirclement, James's co-commander the Comte de Lauzun hastily marched off by the left, harassed by Allied dragoons. As they approached the Duleek bottleneck, the Jacobite columns became entangled. Panic-stricken cavalry trampled their own infantry, causing more damage than the enemy. Williamite disorganization, however, prevented an effective pursuit in face of steady French rearguards. The last shots were fired about 10 p.m., at Naul on the Delvin River.

Williamite sources claim 1000 Jacobite dead, which implies 2000 wounded, and 1000 deserters. They admit 500 dead on their own side, and the same number wounded. Jacobite sources reverse the proportion, but were in no position to know. James II abandoned his troops and fled to Dublin, his leaderless army falling apart. Next morning he denounced its performance in terms even Williamites thought unfair, before continuing south in a state of nervous collapse. Early on the 23rd, James took ship for France at Duncannon, in Waterford Harbour. The contrast with William III, who suffered several near misses during the battle and led the pursuit to Neal, could not have been more stark: 'Change but kings with us,' said the Jacobite general Patrick Sarsfield, 'and we will fight you over again.' In the following century Orangemen would eat sheep's trotters in memory of James's hasty departure.

The Boyne was a signal success for William III, greeted with rejoicing by Louis XIV's enemies in Catholic Austria and Spain. Sadly, however, there is no truth in the story that the pope celebrated this famous Protestant victory with a Te Deum. The Battle of the Boyne more than offset the Allied setback at Beachy Head (see above). On 6 July William III entered Dublin, the political and strategic key to Ireland. The escape of three-quarters of the Jacobite army, however, ensured another battle would be needed. This took place at Aughrim, on 12 July 1691 Old Style. Not until the 1790s, after the calendar adjustment of 1752, did the Boyne become a key date in the Orangeman's marching calendar, 12 July New Style.

Aughrim, Sunday 12 July 1691

Ireland, Co. Galway, D47 M7827

The 'Break of Aughrim' was the greatest defeat in Irish military history, though less famous abroad than the Boyne. Aughrim was a local disaster, ending a war that its French and Jacobite sponsors had given up as lost, and finishing off the Old English gentry as a factor in Irish politics.

James II's flight after the Boyne and the withdrawal of French troops left the Irish Jacobites alone, except for a handful of French officers. Excluded from William III's uncompromising Finglas Declaration of 7 July 1690, their leaders prepared to fight to the end behind the Shannon. William ordered the Dutch general Baron de Ginkel to eliminate this final pocket of resistance and take Galway and Limerick, the last Jacobite ports. On 30 June 1691 Ginkel breached the Shannon at Athlone, after a ten-day siege. The new Jacobite commander, the French Marquis de St Ruth, rallied his troops on the River Suck, 12 miles (19 km) to the west. Ginkel followed on 11 July, camping at Ballinasloe. Reconnoitring through Garbally, he found the Jacobites 3 miles (5 km) further on at Aughrim.

St Ruth had chosen an excellent defensive position astride the road through Loughrea to Galway, the Aughrim–Kilcommadan ridge rising like a breastwork above the waterlogged countryside. Extending a mile and a half (2.5 km) from Aughrim Castle along the Melehan River, which flows south then east into the Suck, the high ground stretches as far as the modern Tristaun bridge on the Aughrim–Laurencetown road. Surrounded by swamps, it was approached by two narrow 'passes', one on either flank:

> On their [Jacobite] left ran a small Brook, having steep Hills, and little Boggs on each side, next to which was a large Red Bogg, almost a Mile over … passable to Horse nowhere but just at the Castle, by reason of a small River [the Melehan], which running through moist Ground made the whole a Morass of Bogg … all along to the Enemies Right, where was another Pass called Urachree, having a rising Ground on each side of it.
>
> George Story, *A Continuation of the Impartial History of the Wars of Ireland* (1691)

The Jacobite camp ran along the ridge, the intervening space down to the bog divided into numerous small enclosures by quickset hedges, banks and ditches which still impede the battlefield visitor.

The whole Jacobite field army was present: 14,000 foot in 37 regiments, 2500 horse and 3500 dragoons, formed in two lines – infantry in the centre, cavalry on the wings, opposite the passes. Some dragoons loitered east of Tristaun brook, towards Urraghry village. St Ruth's front line ran through the enclosures, 'for he knew that the Irish naturally loved a Breastwork between them and Bullets'. The second was in more open ground along the road. Two or three regiments supported by three guns held the castle: 'an old ruinous Building, with some Walls and Ditches about it, and never … a place of any strength'. Aughrim was just a hamlet, 'half a score little cabins … with the Ruins of a little Church and a Priory …' (Story).

Ginkel also deployed in two lines with cavalry wings, occupying the high ground between Melehan Bridge and the Urraghry Pass. Story reckoned he 'could not make up 17,000 Horse and Foot', though modern estimates are higher: 47–49 squadrons at 100 each, and 28 infantry regiments at 450 rank and file. Twelve guns supported Ginkel's right, and 18 the left. The published order of battle was modified before fighting commenced, several squadrons moving from right to left, the infantry closing up into a single line.

Aughrim

	Winner	*Loser*
Opponents	Williamite	Jacobite
Commanders	Godard van Reede, Baron de Ginkel General Hugh MacKay	Charles Chalmont, Marquis de St Ruth (k) Jean-Baptiste de Frouly, Comte de Tesse (w)
Numbers	17,400	20,000
Losses	1744	7950

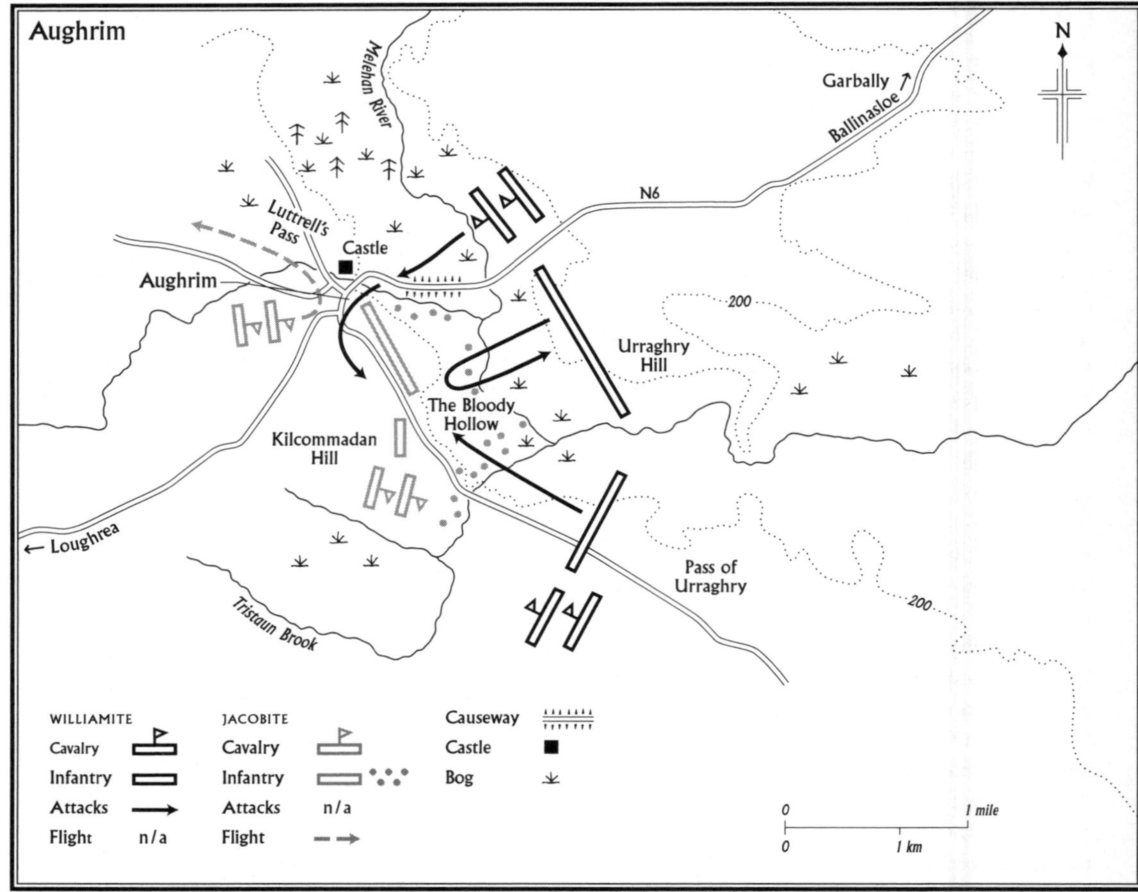

Fighting began about 2 p.m., on the Williamite left, where the ford offered better prospects than the 60-foot (18-m) long causeway past the castle. After an hour's skirmishing, Ginkel's dragoons secured the east bank of Tristaun brook. He considered suspending operations until next day, 'but then perceiving the Enemy to be in some Disorder by what had already happened, they concluded not to delay their Attack, lest the Enemy should March off in the Night'. Ginkel resumed the offensive at 4.30 p.m., hoping to draw Jacobite reserves south and give General Mackay's right wing an easier passage at the castle: 'by five the Battel began afresh' (Story).

The Irish infantry stoutly defended their ditches, 'like men of another nation', said Story unkindly, 'for they would maintain one side until our men put their Pieces over at the other; and then having lines of communication from one Ditch to another, they would presently post themselves again and flank us'. Ginkel's attack across the Tristaun brook stopped just west of the Melehan, his Huguenot infantry

Directions

Follow the N6 southwest from Ballinasloe, past Ginkel's artillery position on Uraghry Hill (M8127), over the causeway. Pass the castle on the right, into Aughrim village. See the Aughrim Experience, and a plaque commemorating St Ruth's death. His grave is unknown.

pinned down in 'Bloody Hollow' (M7926), behind their 'turnpikes' or *chevaux-de-frise*.

Sufficient Jacobite troops were drawn off by 6 p.m. to trigger the attack's second stage. Mackay's cavalry refused to tackle the broken-down causeway, only wide enough for two riders abreast, but the infantry waded chest deep into the Melehan: 'at the narrowest place where the Hedges on the Enemies side ran furthest into the Bogg'. They beat the Irish front line back upon the main battle, but the defenders had cleared lanes through the enclosures, 'by which means they poured great numbers both of Horse and Foot upon us … being both flanked and fronted, as also exposed to all the Enemies shot from the adjoining Ditches; our Men were forced to quit their Ground, and betake themselves to the Bogg again' (Story). Ten battalions were pushed back over the stream, losing two colonels killed. Clubbing their muskets, the Irish foot stormed the far bank, momentarily silencing the guns on Urraghry Hill. Back on Kilcommadan ridge, St Ruth cried out, '*Le jour est à nous, mes enfants*' – 'The day is ours.'

In these desperate circumstances, the Williamites launched a combined-arms attack next to the castle. Two battalions gained a lodgement in the ditch, close under the castle walls, while cavalry scrambled over the causeway under a shower of bullets. The Jacobites had eight mounted regiments covering the pass, but they never moved. As St Ruth rode down the forward slope to lead them on, a single great shot from Urraghry Hill struck off his head, traditionally 1000 yards (900 m) south of Aughrim rectory. His lifeguard went about, followed by the other Irish horse, who abandoned their foot as their grandfathers had at Liscarroll (1642): 'And so', said the infantryman responsible for *A Jacobite Narrative of the War in Ireland*, 'let them keep their priding cavalry to stop bottles with.' The cavalry commander lived to collect a pension from William III, a rare justification for the usual allegations of treachery. His name is commemorated by Luttrell's Pass, just north of Aughrim village.

Williamite cavalry poured across the causeway, rolling up the Irish infantry from left to right, 'surprised at their hard fate while they were mowing the field of honour' (*Jacobite Narrative*). Ginkel's infantry renewed their attacks along the line, 'till being beat from Ditch to Ditch, they [the Jacobites] were driven up to the Top of the Hill of Kilcommadan, where their camp was laid, which being levelled and they exposed to our Shot more openly, they began now to run … the Foot towards a great Bogg behind them on their left, and the Horse on the highway towards Loughrea' (Story). It was all over by 9 p.m.

Aughrim was a shattering blow for the Jacobites, 'the last effort *pro aris et focis* [for altar and hearth], in which the gasping honour of all the Catholic nobility and gentry of the kingdom struggled to do its utmost' (*Exact Journal of the Victorious Progress of Their Majesties' Forces*). The flower of the Jacobite army perished: 500 officers and 7000 common soldiers miserably slaughtered before misty rain stopped the pursuit, 'lying most of them by the Ditches where they were shot, and the rest … like a great flock of sheep scattered up and down the country for almost four miles round' (Story). Another 450 were captured, along with all 9 guns. Williamite casualties were 673 killed and 1071 wounded.

Galway capitulated on 26 July. Limerick held out until October, Ginkel granting generous terms in order to release Allied forces tied up in Ireland. Unfortunately the Treaty of Limerick did not prevent the penal laws of Queen Anne's reign storing up trouble for future generations. Meanwhile, William III had secured Ireland, finally consolidating his grip on the three kingdoms.

The White Cockade, 1715–46

The final outcome of the Glorious Revolution of 1689 remained in doubt throughout the first half of the 18th century, as James II's heirs sought to reclaim their lost kingdoms.

The failure of William and Mary, and their successor Queen Anne, to produce an heir persuaded Protestant Englishmen to confer the throne upon the Stuarts' Hanoverian cousins instead of James II's Roman Catholic descendants. The 1701 Act of Settlement excluded the latter from the English succession, and strengthened the political case for Union with Scotland, lest the Scots offer the crown to the son of James II, Prince James Edward, known as the Old Pretender.

The Act of Union in 1707 outraged many Scots, who used Jacobitism as a way of expressing their dissatisfaction with the Union and the consequent accession of George I in 1714. During the sporadic civil wars that followed, the sides were distinguished by the colour of the cockades worn in their hats; white for the Jacobites, black for the Hanoverians. The dynastic label 'Hanoverian' used for the incumbent regime is unsatisfactory, as it was the British Army that confronted Jacobite rebels, not the forces of Hanover. 'British' won't do, however, as the Stuarts also saw themselves as British, the rulers of Great Britain and Ireland, not just Scotland. They cared little for Scotland – except as a stepping stone towards the greater prize of England – and even less for the Scottish Highlands. When the Young Pretender – Charles Edward Stuart, also known as Bonnie Prince Charlie – first tried Highland dress, he joked that he only needed 'the Itch' to be taken for the real thing. For their part, many Scots defended the Hanoverian settlement. Three of Cumberland's 15 infantry regiments at Culloden were Lowland Scots fighting against 'a merciless despotick Tyranny' fostered, as they saw it, by papists. Only 4000 out of 32,000 Highlanders of military age fought for the Pretender at Culloden, less than the number mobilized against him.

There were three major Jacobite risings against the Hanoverians, known from the year they broke out:

(1) The Fifteen (September 1715–February 1716), the most dangerous of the three risings, and the only occasion English Jacobites came out in significant numbers. The Fifteen had three strategic elements: the Old Pretender was to land in southwest England with French support; the Earl of Mar, spurned by the new regime, would whip up Scots' resentment of George I, the 'wee bit German lairdie'; while English Jacobites raised the North of England. The Pretender's secretary of state, however, shared a mistress with a pro-Hanoverian member of the French government, who forewarned George I's ministers. The Royal Navy interdicted arms shipments meant for the West Country, and Hanoverian regiments from Ireland reached the strategic bottleneck at Stirling in time to prevent Mar's Highlanders joining the Northumberland rebels. When overoptimistic estimates of Lancashire's Jacobite potential tempted the latter south, Hanoverian dragoons surrounded them at Preston and forced them to surrender. Meanwhile a drawn battle at Sheriffmuir broke the back of the rebellion. Prince James Edward briefly held court at Perth, until Argyll's army advanced on the city in January 1716, when the Pretender took ship for France, his clansmen dispersing into the snow-covered mountains.

(2) The Nineteen (April–June 1719), an obscure fiasco confined to the Western Highlands. It ended at Glenshiel, a day's march from the rebels' original landfall.

(3) The Forty-Five (July 1745–April 1746), the last chance of Stuart restoration, after 56 years and two generations in exile. The Fifteen and Nineteen had left Highland society unaltered, Jacobitism

feeding upon clan loyalties founded on 'Notions of Vice and Virtue ... very different from the more civilized part of mankind' (General Wade). Worsening Anglo-French relations during the 1740s and the emergence of a new leader untainted by failure inspired fresh hope amongst irreconcilable Jacobites. Highland chiefs cautioned the Young Pretender against rash adventures, but he ignored them. When he landed in Arisaig on 25 July 1745, they felt honour bound to support him.

The British Army had few effective units in Scotland, its garrisons more caretakers than rapid reaction force. Sir John Cope, Hanoverian commander-in-chief in Scotland, was beaten at Prestonpans (21 September), handing Scotland to the Jacobites. On 31 October 1745, 5500 rebels crossed the English border and marched down the west coast, reaching Derby on 4 December. Prince Charles Edward was only six days' hard marching from London, whose defenders outnumbered the Highland army only by a slender margin. The Pretender would have pressed on, but Lord George Murray and the Lowland officers complained of inadequate English support, and the absence of a French invasion. They insisted on turning back on 6 December, 'Black Friday', as George II prepared to fight for his crown at Finchley, and the Bank of England paid its creditors in sixpences to stem the run on its reserves.

The invaders got clean away, except for a brisk rearguard at Clifton (18 December). Their retreat returned the initiative to the Hanoverians, who reoccupied Edinburgh. A last Jacobite victory at Falkirk (17 January 1746) failed to arrest the decline in the prince's fortunes, and Lord George Murray led a further withdrawal into the Highlands. William, Duke of Cumberland, George II's unprepossessing but militarily expert son, followed remorselessly, beating the prince at Culloden, the last battle on Scottish soil.

The three rebellions displayed common features. Jacobite leaders repeatedly drew their followers into hopeless undertakings, leaving them to shift for themselves in the face of government reprisals. Foreign governments happily played the Jacobite card, but rarely delivered the assistance they promised. The weather did not help. Prevailing westerly winds frustrated more than one seaborne intervention. Arms shipments that escaped shipwreck faced interception by an increasingly powerful Royal Navy.

Battles ashore were short and sharp, with the exception of the street fighting at Preston. Falkirk was over in 10 minutes, Culloden in 25. Despite government setbacks, the period showed the superiority of the three-deep line of infantry armed with musket and bayonet over other weapon systems. A Highland charge, led by a front rank of broadsword-wielding gentlemen, worked best against impressionable recruits over dry, flat ground, as at Prestonpans. Ravines and bogs broke the impetus of charges at Falkirk and Culloden, while imperfectly disciplined Highlanders had no answer to government mortars at Glenshiel, or the dragoons who surrounded them at Preston.

Pacification followed social change rather than military action, however. Highland chiefs lost their powers of 'pit and gallows' in 1747. No longer able to compel tenants to fight by burning down their cottages, they started to turn them off their land. Long before the 19th-century Clearances, thousands of Scots emigrated voluntarily, removing the demographic basis for militant Jacobitism and Highland insurgency.

Preston, 12–14 November 1715

England, Lancashire, LR102 SD5429

The Jacobite capitulation at Preston supports Karl Marx's remark that history repeats itself, first as tragedy, secondly as farce. The 1715 fighting was as decisive as Cromwell's victory of 1648, although it lacked the high drama and moral tone of the earlier battle.

Thomas Forster, a dissident member of Parliament, raised the Jacobite gentry of Northumberland at Hexham on 6 October 1715. He failed to take Newcastle from the local Whigs, achieving little even when the Earl of Mar detached 1500 Scots to support the English rising, under Brigadier William Mackintosh of Borlum. Mutually antipathetic, the two parties could never agree to anything tending to their advantage. They drifted southwest along the Border, before turning south into Roman Catholic Lancashire, which might be expected to support the Jacobite cause. Increasingly demoralized, the rebels pushed on through pouring rain to Preston. Believing there was no opposition within 40 miles (60 km), Forster retired happily to bed, having 'received some little damage in the course of a convivial entertainment'.

Government forces were also converging on the 'metropolis of the North'. General Wills and General Carpenter had 2200 and 2500 men respectively, some of them veterans of Marlborough's campaigns. In the open their mounted troops would be more than a match for Old Borlum's recruits, armed with rusty swords, old muskets, fowling pieces and even pitchforks. Preston was a small market town, 'a short mile' north of the River Ribble, at the junction of roads from Lancaster, Clitheroe, Wigan and Liverpool. The Hanoverians approached along the south bank of the Ribble, Wills from Wigan, Carpenter from Clitheroe. Borlum refused to dispute the bridge Cromwell had forced in 1648, where an outflanking movement across nearby fords would trap the defenders. He preferred to hold the built-up area, which suited the individual fighting skills of his remaining Highlanders, considering that 'The body of the Town was the security of the Army'. The Jacobites barricaded the four roads that converged on the marketplace in Fishergate, mounting two small guns on each, and occupying St John's parish church as an observation post. They also held Houghton House, a mansion at the east end of the town, dominating the road up from Ribble Bridge.

Wills arrived at 1 p.m. on 12 November and ordered his regular infantry to clear the Wigan road barricades beyond the bridge, while cavalry surrounded the town and militia secured the river line. The main attack soon followed, described by an English Jacobite called Peter Clarke: 'Abt 2 a clock … 200 of General Wills men entered the Churchgate street, and the Highlanders firing out of the cellrs and windows, in 10 minuits time kiled 120 of them'. Jacobite artillery fire brought down a chimney pot, whether from 'too little judgement or too much Ale' is not clear. Hanoverian casualties were probably nearer 50, enough to stop the frontal attack. The brigadier in command, 'finding that the taking of the Barricade would cost him a great number of men, thought it properer to take possession of two great Houses within fifty yards of it [including Houghton House] by which he secured his Men from the Fire of the Rebels … and annoyed them very much from the Windows' (*London Gazette*).

Dismounted dragoons attacking from the north down the Lancaster road, made less progress, despite firing the houses up to the Friargate barricade. Forster ordered a sortie, but Borlum refused to cooperate,

Preston

	Winner	*Loser*
Opponents	Hanoverian	Jacobite
Commanders	Lieutenant General George Carpenter Major General Sir Charles Wills	'General' Thomas Forster, MP (p) Brigadier William Mackintosh of Borlum (p) James Radcliffe, Earl of Derwentwater (x)
Numbers	4700	3000
Losses	276	1527 (1485 p)

suspecting the English cavalry would leave his Scots infantry in the lurch. Stalemate set in as darkness fell. The Hanoverian dragoons stood at their horses' heads all night, but left the Liverpool road unguarded, allowing many Jacobites to slip away across Penwortham Ford.

General Carpenter's arrival next day with 750 dragoons and 1750 militia trapped the Jacobites. The Highlanders would have charged out to die, 'like Men of Honour, with their swords in their Hands', but their leaders were already seeking terms. Early on 14 November the Jacobites surrendered, to be treated as the victor chose, after Wills threatened to storm the town and massacre its defenders. The Jacobite leaders were escorted to London for trial, some receiving death sentences; common rebels were dealt with locally. Wills was promoted within the week. Carpenter blamed him for 'losing so many men to no purpose, except to serve his ambition', but the victory was salutary, dissuading future English Jacobites from 'venturing their Carcasses any further than the tavern' (Rev. Robert Patten).

Directions

Preston's development has left little evidence of the battlefield. See St John's parish church south of Churchgate, where Jacobite prisoners were confined, and displays in the Harris Museum, near Forster's headquarters in the Mitre Inn.

Sheriffmuir, 13 November 1715

Scotland, Stirling, LR57 NN8101–8202

There's some say that we wan, and some say that
they wan,
And some say that nane wan at a', man;
But ae thing I am sure, that at Sheriffmuir
A battle there was, that I saw, man;
And we ran and they ran, and they ran and we ran,
But Florence [the Earl of Huntly's horse] ran
fastest of all, man!

Traditional song, ascribed to the contemporary poet Murdoch McLennan

Sheriffmuir was one of those tactically unsatisfactory battles with disproportionately significant consequences. Half of each army ran away, leaving the remaining combatants on the enemy position, facing their own start line.

The Earl of Mar had raised the Stuart standard at Braemar on 6 September 1715, and by October had 12,000 Jacobites under arms. Fortunately for the House of Hanover, Bobbing John, as Mar was nicknamed, made a better raiser of armies than battlefield commander. Borlum's detachment to help the English Jacobites (see above) was a brilliant stroke, but it failed to distract the Duke of Argyll's Hanoverian army from defending the Forth/Clyde isthmus. On 10 November Mar led the main Jacobite army south from Perth to confront Argyll directly.

Warned by spies, Argyll forestalled them north of Stirling in Strathallan, on 12 November. He chose to fight in front of the river line, for 'the Grounds near Dumblain were much more advantagious for his Horse ... and besides this by Frost then beginning, the Forth might become more passable'. Despite severe cold, the armies slept on their arms: Argyll's on the high ground east of Dunblane, near Dykedale Farm, Mar's to the north at Kinbuck.

Recent muster strengths were as given below, though numbers appear to have been reduced in the field. The Jacobites formed up near Whitestone about 6 a.m. on the 13th, in two roughly equal lines of nine clan regiments, each 200–700 strong, a total of 3335 infantry in front, 2920 in support. The Jacobite horse, 'never so constant in anything as being disorderlie' (John, Master of Sinclair), were divided unequally: 657 on the right, 260 on the left. Outnumbered nearly three-to-one, Argyll put more in the shop window: six battalions in front (1440), with two regiments of dragoons on each flank (720 altogether); just two battalions in support (570), with a single dragoon regiment and some gentlemen volunteers in the second line (240 altogether). All the Hanoverian regiments were very weak.

Mar was uncertain of Argyll's whereabouts, and did nothing until 11 a.m., when he ordered his army to form two columns and advance towards the high ground. Mar led the right column, formed from the

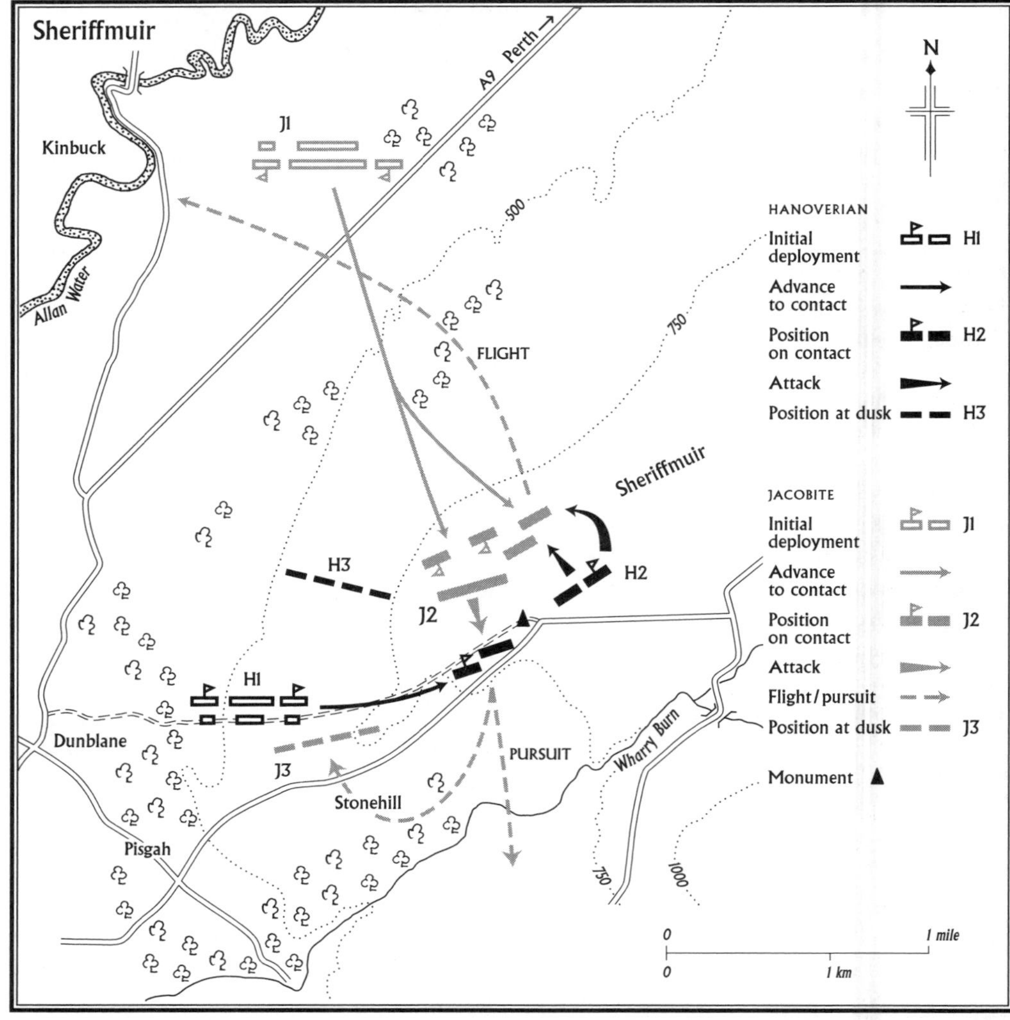

original front line. Hamilton took the second line, now the left. Most battlefield guides show the armies lined up formally at right angles to Wharry Burn, the Jacobites facing west, their backs to the high ground. John Baynes's detailed study of the action places its axis north–south, the Jacobites climbing the northern slope of Sheriffmuir from their bivouac near Kinburn. This more dynamic reconstruction explains how the Jacobite cavalry lost touch with its infantry during the advance, falling behind the army and denuding its left flank of mounted troops.

Watching Jacobite movements, Argyll thought they meant to turn his own right flank, where boggy moorland had frozen solid overnight. To counter the threat, he ordered his army to 'stretch out to the Right', to occupy the Sheriffmuir ridge before the enemy. This worked very well against Hamilton's understrength left wing, straggling back down the hill:

Directions

Dunblane is 5 miles (8 km) north of Stirling off the A9. on the B8033. Turn east for Sheriffmuir along the minor road to Blackford through Pisgah. A monument to the Macraes stands where the armies probably collided, beside the footpath from Dykedale on the left.

Sheriffmuir

	Winner	*Loser*
Opponents	Hanoverian	Jacobite
Commanders	John Campbell, Duke of Argyll	John Erskine, Earl of Mar General George Hamilton
Numbers	3210	8797
Losses	663	232

> As the Right of our Army came over against the Left of the Rebels, which they had put to a Morass, his Grace finding they were not quite formed, gave Orders immediately to fall on, and charged both their Horse and Foot. They received us very briskly, but after some Resistance they were broke through, and were pursued above 2 miles …
>
> *London Gazette*

While Argyll's foot held the Highlanders in play with musketry, his cavalry repeatedly attacked the Jacobites' open flank. A Whig pamphleteer, posing as a survivor of Mar's army, described the dragoons 'trampling down our men like Mice … and hewing them down like Cabbage stalks'. In fact it took all afternoon to drive the Jacobites back across the Allan Water.

On the western flank fortunes were reversed. Argyll's left had fallen behind during its flank march. Still unformed, it sustained a classic Highland charge, 2000 clansmen running forward to draw the Hanoverian fire:

> No sooner that begun, the Highlandmen threw themselves flat on their bellies; and when it slackned, they started to their feet. Most threw away their suzies [plaids?], and drawing their swords, pierced them [the Hanoverians] everie where with ane incredible vigour and rapidity, in four minutes time from receaving the order to attack.
>
> John, Master of Sinclair

At least three, perhaps five, of Argyll's battalions fled before the charge with their supporting cavalry, the Highlanders mercilessly cutting down the fugitives by Wharry Burn, and cruelly mutilating the wounded.

The duke was near Allan Water, when he discovered the disaster to his left flank at 3 p.m. He called off the pursuit, and turned to face the Earl of Mar, who had rallied 2000–4000 of his men on the spur between Stone Hill and Argyll's original position at Dykedale. Argyll had perhaps a thousand men, three or five battalions sheltering behind some mud walls, and the remains of his right wing cavalry. As darkness fell, the Jacobites edged forwards, but Mar failed to press his advantage: 'The Highlandmen were so fatigued they had lost spirits, and would not attack, and … he could not find it in his heart to risque the gentlemen [i.e. the cavalry]' (Sinclair). Faced with another freezing night in the open both sides withdrew.

Argyll returned next day to retrieve his wounded and weapons dropped by charging Highlanders. He put a brave face on his narrow escape, claiming: 'The Courage of British Troops was never keener than on this Occasion.' Privately he admitted that 'some of our troops behaved as ill as ever any did', while the enemy were 'ten times more formidable than our friends in England ever believed'. Nevertheless, Mar's failure to annihilate Argyll's remnant at the end of the day was a strategic defeat for the Jacobites, underlined by Prince James Edward's belated arrival, without French support.

Glenshiel, 10 June 1719

Scotland, Highland, LR33 NG9913

The outcome of the Fifteen irritated rather than depressed Scots Jacobites. Government reprisals were half-hearted, the 1716 Disarming Act merely encouraging Highlanders to hand in broken muskets at exorbitant prices. A brief Anglo-Spanish war in 1719 gave the Jacobites a brief opportunity to repeat the Fifteen's strategy of foreign intervention in western England combined with diversionary landings in Scotland. Gales scattered the main expedition, making the diversion the central attraction.

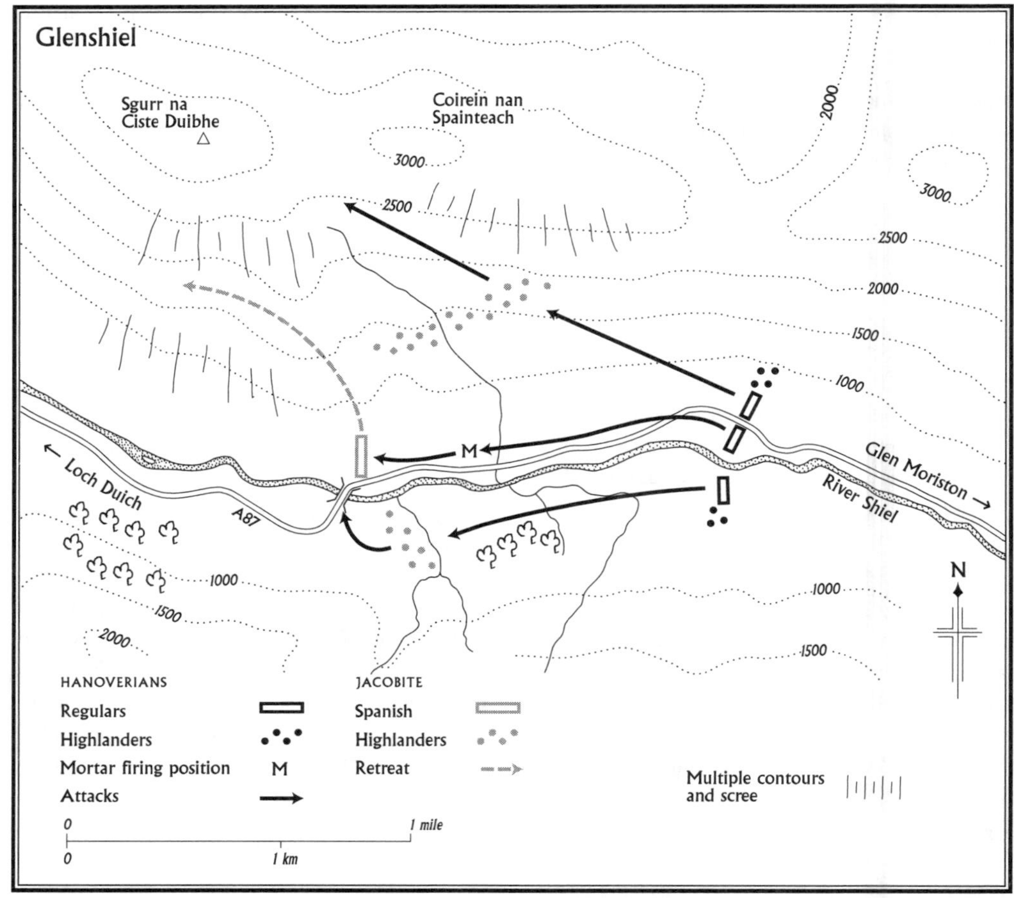

Two Spanish frigates landed the hereditary earl marischal of Scotland with 307 Spanish infantry at Loch Alsh on 16 April 1719, where Tullibardine joined them with another group of émigrés. The factions disputed command and disagreed about their response to the main expedition's non-arrival. Relationships became so tense that Tullibardine and the Spaniards moved camp 3 miles (5 km) away from the others. On 10 May the Royal Navy destroyed the main Jacobite magazine in Eilean Donan Castle, at the mouth of Loch Duich, striking great terror among the other rebels. The captain of HMS *Assurance* affirmed 'they would surrender upon the first summons from a body of regular Troops'.

Government reaction to the landing was prompt and determined. General Wightman, a veteran of Sheriffmuir, concentrated two British infantry regiments at Inverness, reinforced by dragoons and Scottish irregulars, plus a battalion and a half of Dutch infantry. On 5 June he marched via Loch Ness and Glen Moriston into the Western Highlands.

Directions

The battlefield is 5 miles (8 km) above Invershiel, along the A87 from Loch Duich, 1/2 mile (0.8 km) above the new bridge. See a monument to one of Wightman's officers. Also see Eilean Donan Castle, restored in the 1920s. Coirein nan Spainteach, the peak whose name commemorates the Spanish presence, lies 1 mile (1.6 km) north of the fighting, behind Hanoverian lines.

Glenshiel		
	Winner	*Loser*
Opponents	Hanoverian	Jacobite
Commanders	Major General Joseph Wightman	William Murray, Marquess of Tullibardine George Keith, Earl Marischal
Numbers	*c.*1286	*c.*1000
Losses	142	*c.*10

Tullibardine had advanced 'to view the narrow passes in the little Glen, hoping to maintain the Rough Ground till People that were expected should come up', but Wightman's rapid advance anticipated the reinforcements. He drove in the Jacobite outposts and met their main body about 4 p.m. on 10 June, just above the present stone bridge below Sgurr na Ciste Duibhe (3369 feet/1027 m), one of the Five Sisters of Kintail. The site enjoys several names: the Pass of Strachell in Wightman's despatch, Glenshielbeg according to Tullibardine, and Lub-innis-na-seangan in the local Gaelic tradition, meaning 'the bend of the river at the island of ants'.

Beyond the bridge the road skirts the north side of the river, entering the pass on a narrow shelf below steep slopes covered with heather, bracken and scattered birch trees, running steeply down to the roaring torrent. A shoulder of the mountain juts into the glen on its northern side, restricting the valley to a narrow gorge. 'Their Dispositions for Defence', wrote Wightman, 'were extraordinary, with the Advantage of Rocks, Mountains, and Intrenchments.' The Jacobites deployed both sides of the river. The Spanish regulars were in the centre holding some breastworks on the hillside and a barricade across the road. Highlanders extended up the precipitous slopes either side of the glen. Most were north of the river, leaving only 150 with Tullibardine's brother Lord George Murray on the south bank.

Tullibardine had left 'no means untried to get people together so as to keep life in the affair', but could only find takers for a fifth of the 2000 stand of arms shipped from Spain. Wightman put the Jacobites at '1640 Highlanders, besides 300 Spaniards, and a Corps apart of 500 Highlanders ... posted on a hill to make themselves masters of our Baggage ... always one of their chief Aims'. Tullibardine's not unbiased account put his strength nearer a thousand, principally 150 Camerons and 500 Mackenzies from Seaforth, 'who it was thought would heartily defend their own country'. Rob Roy sent 80 MacGregors, who sat out the battle, as they did at Sheriffmuir.

Wightman deployed on both banks. He gives various numbers for his own strength, excluding the Dutch, who may have numbered an extra 600. Figures usually give the Hanoverians 850 regular infantry, 120 dragoons and 136 loyal Highlanders. Detailed analysis gives them: 56 friendlies and 150 grenadiers on the right, next to 490 British infantry (Montagu's and Harrison's regiments); an unspecified number of Dutch and 120 dragoons in the centre in the glen; 390 British regulars south of the river, with four score (i.e. 80) Highlanders on their outer flank.

The general took post in the centre, 'where everyone had free access to him for orders'. Four light coehorn mortars shelled the Jacobite trenches, wounding several of the leaders, while infantry turned the flanks, first on the left beyond the river, then on the right. The rugged and steep ground that made it impossible to come at them also prevented the Highlanders mounting a charge: 'always as they had fired their Muskets skipping off, and never venturing to come to a Close Engagement ... driven from Rock to Rock, our Men chacing them before them for above Three Hours, till we gained the Top of the Hill, where they were immediately dispersed' (Wightman). Meanwhile, dismounted dragoons stormed the breastworks commanding the pass, the Spanish infantry withdrawing up the mountainside.

Losses during the uphill assault were heavy: 21 dead and 121 wounded. The Jacobites' prompt retreat saved them casualties, but next morning they had hardly anyone still together. The earl marischal 'went off without any more adoe or so much as taking leave' (Tullibardine). The king's troops lay on their arms all night to bring off the wounded, incidentally taking 274 Spanish prisoners, who had refused to fight on without being fed.

Wightman spent the rest of June 'taking a Tour thro' all the difficult Parts of the Seaforth country, to terrify the Rebels, by burning the Houses of the Guilty, and preserving those of the Honest' (*London Gazette*). Tullibardine confessed 'the whole episode verged on the farcical'. This self-inflicted Jacobite defeat 'bid fair to ruin the king's Interest ... seeing we came with hardly anything that was really necessary for such an undertaking'. The cause was crippled for a quarter of a century.

Prestonpans (Gladsmuir), 21 September 1745

Scotland, East Lothian, LR66 NT4074

The first action of the Forty-Five was a bolt from the blue after the mediocre showing of Highland armies at Sheriffmuir and Glenshiel (above). Prince Charles Edward's routing of Sir John Cope's army at Prestonpans was a stunning propaganda victory that has come to be regarded as the archetypal Hanoverian–Jacobite encounter.

Sir John Cope, commander-in-chief Scotland, had only two and a half mobile battalions and a couple of newly raised dragoon regiments with which to confront the Young Pretender. Ordered north into the Highlands to nip the rebellion in the bud, Cope left the Stirling gap unguarded, allowing the Jacobites to capture Edinburgh. Shipping his troops back south from Inverness, Cope met the prince's army near Musselburgh on 20 September, in an area already notable for its battlefields – Pinkie (1547) and Dunbar (1296, 1650). While the Jacobites swung inland over Falside Hill, Sir John occupied a strong position on flat ground just south of Prestonpans: 'on his right two enclosures surrounded by stone walls from six to seven feet high [Preston and Bankton parks] ... Before him was another enclosure, surrounded by a deep ditch filled with water and from ten to twelve feet broad ... On his left was a marsh [Tranent Meadows] which terminated in a deep pond [Seton Millpond], and behind him was the sea' (Chevalier James Johnstone). None of Cope's regiments were satisfactory, their ranks recently filled up with Scots ploughboys.

Cope made optimum use of his shaky army. All the infantry (1440 rank and file) were in the front line, maximizing their firepower. A regiment of dragoons on each flank were deployed in two rather than the usual three ranks, to make the most of them (650 all told). Ten small guns were massed on the flank to allow the few gunners available to work them, while 180 'friendly' Highlanders were left out of battle at Cockenzie.

Initially Cope faced west, turning south, west and south again in response to Jacobite movements around Tranent. As night fell he posted extra pickets and lit fires along his front. He was right to be nervous, for Lord George Murray had evolved a plan that neutralized Cope's topographical advantages. At 4 a.m. on the 21st the Highland army stole down through Riggonhead Farm, around the eastern end of the morass, where the only obstacle was a 4-foot (1.2-m) ditch crossed by a plank bridge. Once over the Jacobites formed up in three divisions facing west, about 1000 yards (900 m) from Cope's left flank: the Duke of Perth on the right with some 850 men, and Murray on the left with 900. Perth went too far north before facing left, leaving the prince's 600-strong reserve to cover the gap. The Jacobites had no artillery, and only 50 light horse.

Contrary to legend Cope was not asleep when a cavalry patrol gave the alarm. The Hanoverians wheeled left by platoons, and marched north, facing east to meet the Jacobite attack. The rebels charged across ideal terrain, described by a loyalist volunteer, John Home, as: 'an extensive cornfield, plain and

Prestonpans

	Winner	*Loser*
Opponents	Jacobite	Hanoverian
Commanders	Prince Charles Edward Lord George Murray	Lieutenant General Sir John Cope
Numbers	2400	2500
Losses	c.100	c.1600

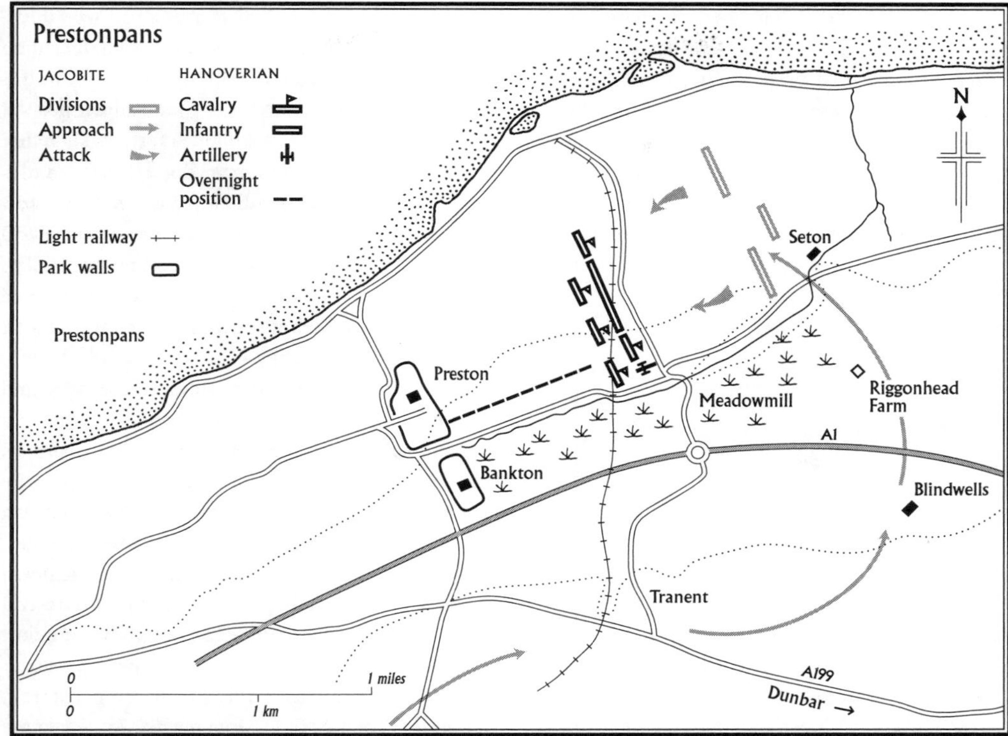

level, without a tree'. Nevertheless the Highlanders lost formation, clustering in dense masses, 20 files across and 30 ranks deep. As they came out of the mist, Cope's scratch gun crews of invalids and tipsy sailors bolted, leaving two officers to fire the pre-loaded guns. The Jacobite line gave 'a great Shake', then cheered and advanced 'with a swiftness not to be conceived', firing as they came.

Ordered to countercharge, the raw Hanoverian dragoons refused to follow their officers, 'immediately the Rear Rank began to run away, and the Rest followed in Tens and Twelves'. Deserted by their supporting arms, the infantry gave a straggling fire, as successive waves of swordsmen broke through them from right and left, where Perth overlapped the northern Hanoverian flank. Cope rode through the wreckage calling out, 'For Shame, Gentlemen, behave like Britons', but the soldiers ignored him, and fled as best they could in boots, gaiters and cross-belts. Many were killed against the walls of Preston Park,

Directions

Much of the area has been restored after opencast coal mining, so may bear scant resemblance to the original battlefield. Follow the B6414 from the Jacobite starting position near Tranent, over the A1 and the railway to the Meadowmill roundabout, to see the battlefield from a viewpoint between the opposing lines.

which the day before had secured their right flank. Others got away down 'Johnny Cope's road', past Bankton House. A captured Hanoverian reckoned the whole army was broken within four and a half minutes from the first shots being fired.

Staff officers collected 450 dragoons at pistol point, but could not get them to charge. Riding away to Berwick, they met the veteran Lord Mark Kerr, who swore that in all his battles he had never known general officers bring the first news of their defeat – a gibe Jacobite songwriters applied to Cope himself. All but 170 of the Hanoverian infantry were killed or captured, the battlefield 'a spectacle of horror, being covered with heads, legs, and arms, and mutilated bodies'. Jacobite propagandists exaggerated the fatalities, which were 200–300 rather than 500, but at least 1300 redcoats were taken. Two-thirds were unwounded, reflecting the lack of serious resistance, and the Jacobite officers' efforts to restrain their men. All Scotland, except a few fortresses, fell into the Pretender's hands, encouraging waverers and a lukewarm French government. The Highland charge appeared for the moment to be invincible.

Clifton (Clifton Moor), **18 December 1745**

England, Cumbria, LR90 NY5325–6

The only significant fighting in England during the Forty-Five was the rearguard action at Clifton, a clash whose interest as the last battle on English soil exceeds both its numerical or strategic importance.

The Duke of Cumberland followed the retreating Jacobites north from Derby with dragoons and infantry mounted on country horses. Despite French invasion scares and roads slippery with ice, he caught up with their rearguard during the afternoon of 18 December.

Lord George Murray held Clifton with the Glengarry Highlanders, John Roy Stuart's Edinburgh regiment and a few light horse. They ambushed the road at Town End Farm Cottage, 300 yards (275 m) south of Clifton, but the farm's Quaker owners warned Cumberland's troopers as they rode down Brackenber Hill. The Hanoverians withdrew after an indecisive skirmish, the Jacobites crowding back through the narrow village street. Some of Murray's cavalry galloped back to the prince's headquarters at Penrith, reporting 'that if those of the escort ... were not immediately supported they would be infallibly cut to pieces'. Fearing his rearguard would be overwhelmed, the prince sent back two more clan regiments, Cluny Macpherson's and the Stewarts of Appin.

Clifton village consisted of 'one street with poor houses and enclosures all made about with dry stone walls and thick hedges' (Colonel John O'Sullivan). Cumberland thought it 'one of the strongest posts I ever saw'. The enclosures extended further down the western side of the road from Kendal than on the eastern side, forming a salient from which enfilading fire could be brought across the front of the main position. The Glengarries occupied the salient, the other two clan regiments lying beyond the road on Scalebarrs Hill, facing south, their front protected by hedges and boggy ground. The Edinburgh regiment, held in reserve, busied itself looting the village.

Cumberland had only 1000 dragoons at the front, who formed up on foot, from right to left: Bland's 3rd, Cobham's 10th, and Kerr's 11th. Two regiments of horse remained in support, while another 1000 mounted infantry saw no action. After marching ten hours through exceedingly bad country with intelligence 'not certainly to be relied on', they were not ready to attack Clifton until it was dark, perhaps 5 p.m.

There was much confusion in the gathering darkness. When Lord George pushed his left wing forward to find a better hedge, they unexpectedly ran into Bland's Dragoons, who opened fire at 150 paces, long range in poor light. Nevertheless, an anonymous correspondent of the *Gentleman's Magazine* saw some scores of rebels fall before a second volley at 50 yards (45 m), 'and I am sure they never rose again while I kept my station'. While the Hanoverians were reloading, Cluny's men, on the Jacobite left, rushed their position, which lay along the bottom ditch, between moor and enclosures. Bullets flew thick and hot about Murray's head, as

Clifton

	Winner	*Loser*
Opponents	Jacobite	Hanoverian
Commanders	Lord George Murray	William Duke of Cumberland
Numbers	1000	1000
Losses	*c.*40	*c.*60

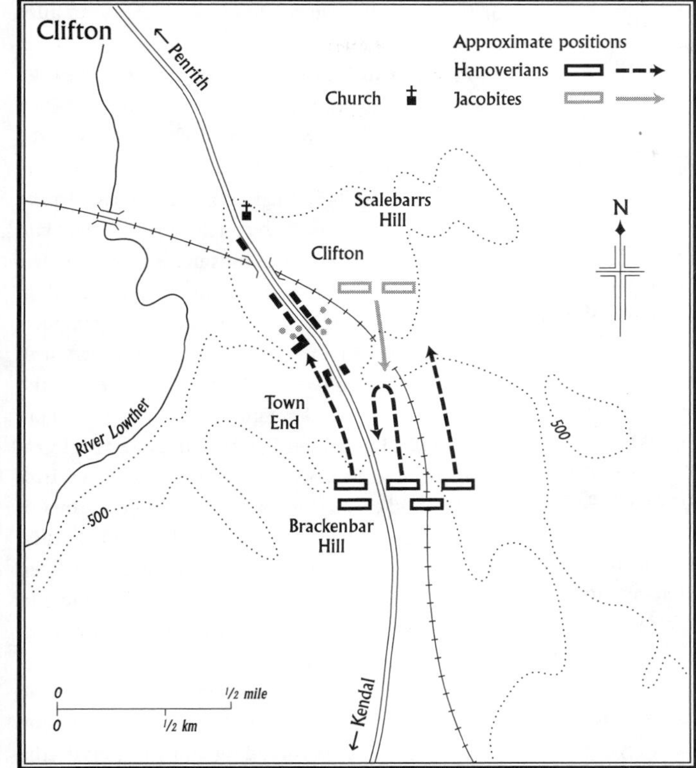

Directions

Clifton is 6 miles (10 km) south of Penrith on the A6. See a modern headstone in the churchyard, left of the main road, erected in memory of Bland's dragoons. The battlefield is 1 mile (1.6 km) further on, now crossed by the railway and M6 motorway. See the 'Battle Oak' and small monument opposite Town End Farm, where the Jacobite dead were buried.

the rebels 'received a full fire from the king's men within a few yards'.

Murray claimed 'a good many of the enemy' were killed fighting hand to hand, though only ten were buried in St Cuthbert's churchyard next day. Many were saved by the steel skullcaps they wore under their hats. Cumberland alleged the Macphersons cried, 'No Quarter – Murder them', as they mutilated the wounded. Bland's Dragoons fell back, some being killed as they pulled off their boots to run quicker. Murray stopped at the ditch for fear of friendly fire from his right, where Cobham's and Kerr's maintained a fire fight with the Appin men and Glengarries until they too were driven off at sword point.

Lord George fell back after half an hour's fighting, his men retrieving their discarded muskets and regimental colours as they went. Cluny noted the loss of a sergeant and 12 men killed, implying about 40 Jacobite casualties altogether, including wounded. The other Highland regiments were protected by their hedges and dark clothes. Advancing in the open, the dragoons' yellow cross belts had made them an easy mark. Cumberland reported 40 rank and file killed and wounded, besides 4 officers hurt. His ADC thought 20–30 were killed, consistent with Jacobite intelligence reports of 40 Hanoverian wounded.

The Hanoverians occupied Clifton about 6 p.m., darkness and difficult country preventing any immediate pursuit. The next day Cumberland pressed on to Penrith, but the Jacobites had gone. On 20 December they waded the River Esk to regain Scottish soil, dancing themselves dry to the sound of the bagpipes. Cumberland took credit for having 'shewed the Nation that they are far from being such terrible people … [and] that other troops can march as well as they'. Otherwise Clifton was the inconsequential sequel to an almost bloodless campaign of manoeuvre.

Falkirk (II), 17 January 1746

Scotland, Falkirk, LR65 NS8679–8778

The largest engagement of the Forty-Five took place in a howling storm, in pitch darkness, and large numbers of both sides ran away. It is unsurprising that the location and course of the Second Battle of Falkirk should be the subject of some dispute.

Hanoverian forces reoccupied Edinburgh during the Highland army's march to Derby, General Hawley taking command in January 1746. Meanwhile Prince Charles Edward, having returned from England, laid siege to Stirling Castle. Hawley marched from Edinburgh on 13 January to relieve the besieged fortress, reaching Falkirk three days later. The Jacobite army drew up 6 miles (10 km) away on Plean Muir to cover their siege works. They had to fight or withdraw, as they lacked tents, and dared not disperse to seek shelter so close to the enemy. Just after noon on 17 January the Jacobites advanced on to Falkirk Muir, crossing the River Carron at Dunipace Steps.

Most accounts of Falkirk pretend the Jacobites took Hawley unawares, the general hurrying back from a luncheon party at Callendar House. In reality the Jacobite approach was noticed as early as 11 a.m. Nothing was done about it, however, until Hawley ordered a left flank march across the Jacobite line of advance at 2 p.m., moving past Bantaskin House towards the unreconnoitred high ground that rises steeply southeast of the town. Falkirk Muir (407 feet/124 m) runs roughly northwest–southeast, between Glen Burn to the south and the Union Canal to the north. It was covered with heather and low bushes, its patches of rough grazing broken by dry stone walls. A steep-sided ravine, a postglacial coastal chine, ran northwards from the summit down to the low ground where the canal was subsequently built.

Hawley's army was the strongest yet to confront the prince, with 12 infantry battalions and 3 dragoon regiments. Two of the latter were survivors of Prestonpans, and as useless as ever. The artillery remained a makeshift collection of small pieces operated by sailors and conscripted yokels. Most of the guns stuck in the mud, to be captured after the battle.

Recent studies of the battle disagree over the numbers engaged. Stuart Reid gives Hawley 4100 infantry and 770 cavalry, with 1500 Scots loyalists. Christopher Duffy allows 5850 and 800 regulars respectively, and 1450 friendlies. Everyone agrees the dragoons led the way, followed by the infantry in two parallel columns, six battalions in the front line, five in the second, and one in reserve (or just straggling) on the extreme right. Militia and friendly Highlanders were kept out of harm's way on the flanks. The Jacobites also formed two lines with a reserve, though calculations of their strength vary. Duffy gives them some 3000 Highlanders in front, supported by 1500–2500, mostly Lowlanders, with 600–700 Franco-Irish regulars and cavalry in reserve. The Prince's chief of staff, Colonel O'Sullivan, found the latter 'not fit to be set in line of battle … [being] not well mounted enough to resist the enemy's choc [shock]'. Reid puts more Jacobites in the shop window, with correspondingly fewer in support.

Historians also disagree over which way the two armies were facing. Most accounts follow contemporary plans showing the dragoons lined up north–south to form an angle with their infantry, who inclined back to the northeast. The space between the lines widens towards the Hanoverian right, which stands behind the ravine. The prince's front line conformed, facing slightly south of east. Different factions within this tradition put the lines of battle near the modern hospital, or further west near the monument, adjusting the ravine accordingly. Christo-

Falkirk (II)

	Winner	*Loser*
Opponents	Jacobite	Hanoverian
Commanders	Prince Charles Edward	Lieutenant General Henry Hawley
	Lord George Murray	Major General John Huske
Numbers	5100–6200	6370–8100
Losses	110–130	350–400

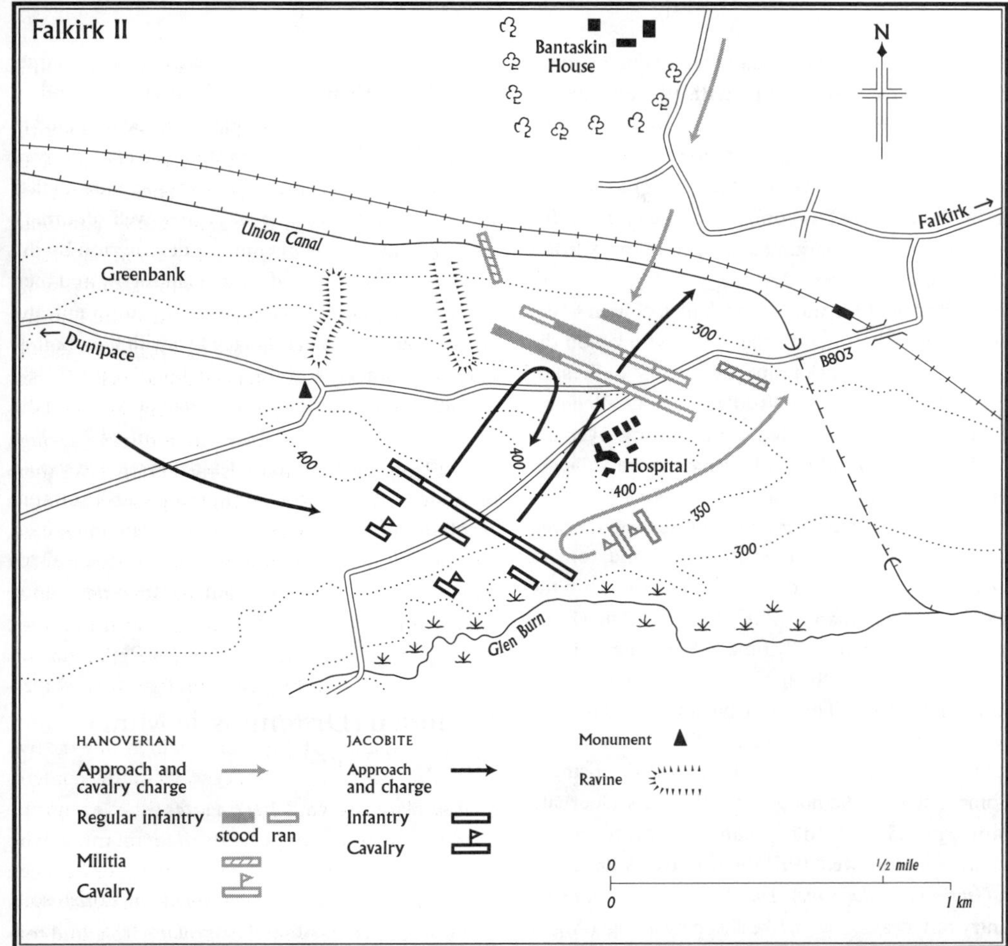

pher Duffy makes a strong case for the Hanoverians facing south, not west. The Jacobites had stretched out their right flank to Glen Burn, wheeling half left to get the freshening southwesterly wind behind them. In this scenario, the ravine ran clear of Hawley's right flank, not between the opposing lines, acting as a prop rather than a direct defence.

The weather had deteriorated by 3.30 p.m., 'blowing Strong in the faces of the Dragoons as they ascended the Hill, it was with much difficulty the Standards were kept upright' (Anonymous *Journal of the King's Army*). Approaching the summit the horsemen converged with the leading Highlanders, until boggy ground prevented further movement across the moorland plateau. Both sides wheeled to face the enemy, but wet ground stopped the Hanoverian left reaching so far as the Jacobite right.

The Hanoverian cavalry began the action about

Directions

Some of the battlefield is built over, obscuring Hawley's approach. Head west from Falkirk along the B803, bearing right at the hospital along a minor road towards Bantaskin Park and the ravine, on the right. See the 1927 monument at the fork near Greenbank Farm. Alternatively, continue along the B803 past the hospital towards the Jacobite right flank near Seafield. Different vintages of Ordnance Survey map place the battle at various points between Bantaskin House and the hospital.

4 p.m. Perhaps Hawley imagined the enemy more afraid of horse than foot; perhaps 'the Speedy approach of the Rebels oblidg'd the Dragoons to attack, which on the left, they did with Resolution, but the Briskness of the Enemy, the Raynyness of the night in the Face of the Dragoons ... caused a fatal disorder' (Journal). Charging unshaken infantry frontally, the cavalry received a volley at 10 yards (9 m), which sent the 13th and 14th reeling. Cobham's 10th closed with Clanranald's regiment, who lay on the ground to thrust dirks into the horses' bellies, or dragged riders from the saddle to be pistolled and stabbed. The cavalry fled, some riding over the loyalist Glasgow militia, who gave them a volley in return. Others broke to the right.

Unable to reload their empty muskets in the wet, the Jacobite centre charged sword in hand, 'one of the boldest and finest actions, that any troops in the world cou'd be capable of' (O'Sullivan). The Hanoverian infantry had hardly time to form, their left traditionally reaching the top of the hill, the right still down in the valley. They were breathless and blinded by the rain, which had soaked their ammunition. A quarter of the muskets missed fire. Not surprisingly, 'Some foot Reg[ts] did not perform Wonders' (Journal). Panic spread, and, 'like a catching infection, the whole front followed' (Private of Barrell's Regiment in *Gentleman's Magazine*). Two-thirds of Hawley's infantry ran away, 'driven, like sheep by a dog' (Argyll militiaman). Only the rightmost battalions of the second line held out, either sheltered by the ravine, or escaping the first onset because Hawley's right overlapped the Jacobite left. Either way, Barrell's 4th and Ligonier's 59th Foot fired into the Jacobite flank, putting their front line to a stand:

> One party of them came running upon us, and fired, but at too great a distance ... they threw away their guns, being their usual way of fighting, and advanced sword in hand; we gave them a volley of shot, and kept a reserve [of loaded muskets], which caused them to halt and shake their swords at us; we gave them three huzza's and another volley, which caused them to run ...
>
> Private of Barrell's Regiment

Cobham's Dragoons threatened a fresh charge, but fell back before Prince Charles's handful of Franco-Irish infantry. Both sides were too shattered to make a fresh effort. The Hanoverians retired, covered by Barrell's Grenadiers, who 'always kept up regular ranks of three deep and Behav'd very well' (Journal). Rather than expose his men to destruction by the elements, Hawley withdrew to Linlithgow and then Edinburgh, abandoning tents and equipment, the civilian transport drivers having fled with their horses.

The winners admitted 50 killed and 60–80 wounded, claiming 800 Hanoverian dead left on the field and 300 prisoners. Hawley admitted 27 killed and 280 missing, to which at least 50 wounded should be added. Possession of the field substantiated Jacobite claims of victory, but they were in no condition to follow up, and returned to their siege. Falkirk was an embarrassing but temporary setback for Hanoverian arms.

Culloden (Drummossie Muir), **16 April 1746**

Scotland, Highland, LR27 NH7345–7444

Culloden was the last pitched battle on British soil, and one of the most controversial. Seldom has a battle inspired so many differing maps. The historical disagreements mirror the Jacobite dissensions that contributed to the Young Pretender's defeat.

When a reinforced Hanoverian army, under the Duke of Cumberland, renewed its advance after Falkirk, Prince Charles's officers would not risk another battle. While the Jacobites retreated into the Highlands, Cumberland followed cautiously to Aberdeen, going into winter quarters in February 1746. He recommenced operations on 8 April, advancing rapidly through Inverurie and Banff to Fochabers in Speyside. His speed surprised the Jacobites, who had dispersed to ease their subsistence. The prince now had no choice but to fight for Inverness, his great magazine of oatmeal and ammunition. Colonel O'Sullivan, his adjutant general or chief of staff, had

Culloden

	Winner	Loser
Opponents	Hanoverian	Jacobite
Commanders	William, Duke of Cumberland	Prince Charles Edward
	Lieutenant General Henry Hawley	Lord George Murray
		Colonel John O'Sullivan
Numbers	8151	6754
Losses	320	*c.*2000

previously reconnoitred a position at Culloden on Drummossie Muir, a stretch of gently undulating moor and rough pasture between the Nairn valley to the south and the Moray Firth.

Lord George Murray, the Jacobite executive commander, objected to 'so plain a field'. Finding the prince set against retreat, he suggested a night attack on the Hanoverian camp at Nairn, hoping to catch them 'as drunk as beggars' on Cumberland's birthday. The night march, in single file through trackless quagmires, was a shambles. Murray called it off unilaterally, within sight of the enemy campfires, depriving the prince of his last thin chance of victory. The Jacobite army was left hopelessly off balance, its soldiers befuddled with hunger and fatigue, 2000 of them straggling about in search of food and shelter. Its leaders were no longer on speaking terms. Lord George spoke grimly of 'putting an end to a bad business'.

Cumberland's main concern was to bring his army onto the field in good order, with morale intact and weapons serviceable. Kerr's 11th Dragoons and Kingston's 10th Horse had replaced the Prestonpans runaways, and his infantry were eager to retrieve the disgrace of Falkirk. For the first time the Hanoverians possessed effective artillery manned by trained gunners of the Royal Artillery: twelve 3-pounder guns and six light mortars. Cumberland had allowed a rest day before seeking battle, ordering extra cheese and brandy for the troops. Reveille sounded at 4 a.m.: 'a very cold rainy Morning, and nothing to buy to comfort us; but we had the Ammunition loaf, thank God' (Alexander Taylor, Royal Scots). The weather was at the army's back, unlike at Falkirk, helping the soldiers preserve their muskets from the rain: 'Scarce one in a regiment missed firing, for we kept them dry with our coatlaps' (Edward Linn).

Cumberland's infantry marched in three columns, each of five battalions, cavalry on the left, Highland auxiliaries probing ahead. Twice the army halted to form line of battle, the second and fourth battalions of each column occupying the intervals between the units in front, to make two lines of six battalions, the last three battalions remaining in third line as reserve: 'On our approach near the enemy, the army was formed in an instant' (*Gentleman's Magazine*). Pairs of guns stood between the frontline battalions, mortar batteries either side of the supports. A morass secured the Hanoverian right, so Cumberland's two dragoon regiments concentrated on the left under General Hawley, 'to endeavour to fall upon the Right flank of the Rebels' (Cumberland). Kingston's Horse joined the reserve. The duke spoke to every battalion, 'yea, almost to every platoon' (*Gentleman's Magazine*). His message was simple and confident: 'Depend, my lads, on your bayonets; let them mingle with you; let them know the men they have to deal with.'

This steady and resolute approach contrasted with the disorder of previous encounters, and with the wretched state of the opposition. A French observer feared the day was already lost. The Jacobite line faced northeast, between the stone walls of Culloden Park on the left and the Culwhiniac enclosures, running down to the River Nairn, on their right. Except for this dead ground, the battlefield was flat, if boggy. Murray condemned O'Sullivan's choice as 'an open muir … not proper for Highlanders', claiming it favoured Cumberland's superior cavalry and artillery. Supporting arms had achieved little in previous battles, however, and the Highlanders' sudden charge needed flat open ground. Lord George also demurred at taking the right flank for a second day, but as O'Sullivan pointed out, 'It is no time to change the order of battle in the enemy's presence.'

Murray's men initially stood against the western corner of the Culwhiniac enclosures, moving forward to clear some now vanished turf walls. This extended the Jacobite line, as the MacDonalds on the left

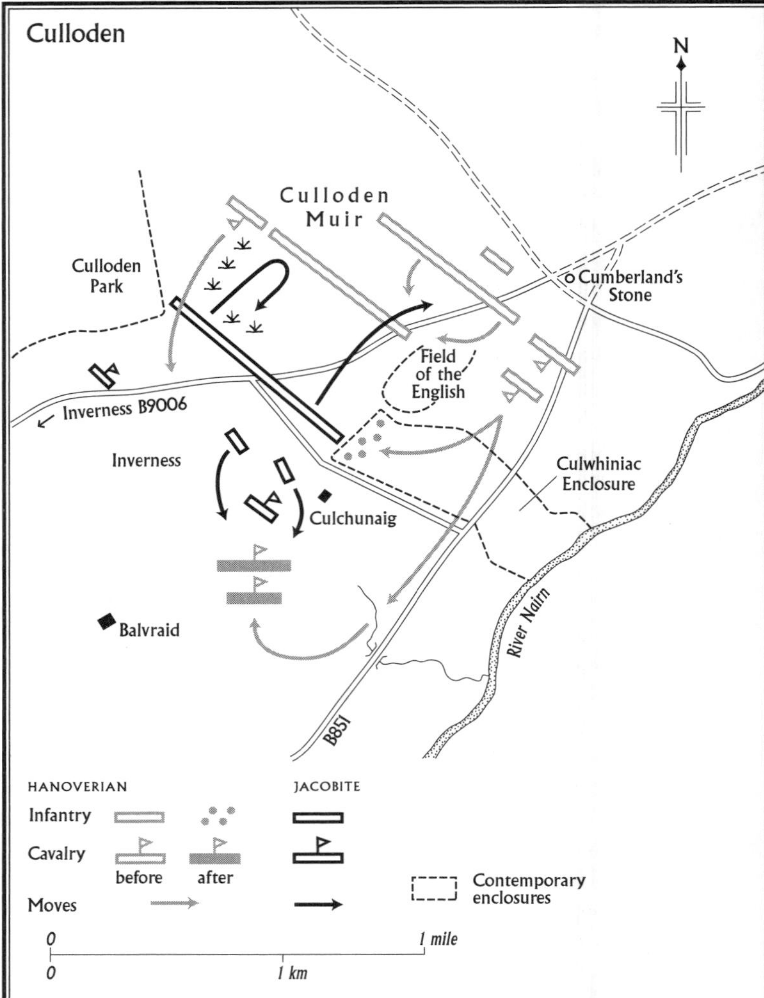

Directions
Culloden battlefield is owned by the National Trust for Scotland, who have cleared the trees that once infested the battlefield. Turn off the A9 5 miles (8 km) southeast of Inverness, along the B9006. The visitor centre is on the right, just after the Graves of the Clans.

refused to advance beyond the wall of Culloden Park. Often attributed to pique at losing their customary place on the right, MacDonald reluctance had some justification. Cumberland had strengthened the flank opposite them with two reserve battalions and Kingston's Horse, making his final line-up: seven battalions in front (3804), seven in support (3005), one more in reserve (356). Most of the cavalry were on the left (486) with 200 red-coated Highlanders. The remaining 300 mounted troops were on the right.

In theory the Jacobites also formed two lines: 3832 Highlanders in front, with 2020 more Scots in support and 652 Franco-Irish regular infantry and perhaps 250 cavalry in reserve. In practice, a third of the army were missing after the night march fiasco, and O'Sullivan had to weaken the thin second line to plug the gaps that appeared when Murray doubled the depth of frontline units to improve their offensive power.

More Jacobites moved right to watch the Culwhiniac enclosures, an obvious covered approach for Hawley's dragoons. The antipathy between Murray and O'Sullivan ensured the Jacobites occupied neither front nor rear walls of the enclosures, allowing loyalist Campbell Highlanders to break through them, followed by Hawley's dragoons. Rather than lining the walls, a tactical nonsense for cavalry, the latter passed through the enclosures to threaten the enemy rear. Redeployment of scarce Jacobite reserves delayed Hawley a while, the re-entrant between Balvraid and Culchunaig forming an obstacle that 'neither side could pass safely in the presence of the other' (Major James Maxwell, Elcho's Lifeguards). The dragoons' restraint, unlike the ill-considered charges that began Prestonpans and Falkirk, was not the least factor behind Culloden's different outcome.

Fighting began about 1 p.m. with a ripple of fire from the Jacobite artillery, 'which was extremely ill-served and ill-pointed' (Cumberland): they had 11 captured 3-pounders, but few trained gunners. When the Royal Artillery opened fire, most of the Jacobite gun detachments ran. The duration and effect of the Hanoverian gunfire have been wildly exaggerated. Firing ball for at most 15 minutes, at the guns' maximum range of 500–700 yards (450–650 m), over ground too soft for ricochet fire, a dozen 3-pounders are unlikely to have caused more than 150 casualties. This is hardly the massacre some writers describe. The psychological effect of the bombardment, upon partially disciplined troops unaccustomed to standing under fire, was more significant: 'our Gunners galling their lines, they betook them to their small Arms, Sword and Pistol, and came running upon our Front Line like Troops of Hungry Wolves' (Taylor).

Disregarding the prince's orders not to throw away their muskets, the Jacobite right and centre streamed forward in two great clusters against the Hanoverians' apparently open left flank. At 300 yards (275 m) the defending guns began firing case-shot against the dense masses of charging Highlanders with devastating effect, 'the men dropping down by wholesale'. Unable to sustain the brisk small-arms fire opened upon them at 50 yards (45 m), or confused by the smoke blowing through their ranks, the Jacobite centre swerved right, becoming entangled with Murray's column. Together they crashed into Barrell's and Monro's 4th and 37th regiments, on the extreme left of the Hanoverian front line, killing the supporting gunners and carrying the infantry back past the Well of the Dead. In contrast to Falkirk, the supports stood firm, and shot down any Highlander who penetrated the front line. The novel combination of fire action by the rear ranks, covered by the bayonets of the front, 'staggered the enemy', who confessed later 'they never seed the English fight in such a Manner, for they thought we were all Mad Men that fought so' (Linn).

Prevented from retreating by the battalions behind them, the Hanoverian front line 'fairly beat them with their bayonets. There was scarce a Soldier or Officer of Barrell's and of that part of Monro's which engaged, who did not kill at least one or two men each with their Bayonets and Spontoons' (Cumberland). Numerous injuries to the left side of Barrell's wounded suggest the obstinacy of their resistance: 'After the battle there was not a bayonet in this regiment that was not either bloody or bent' (*Gentleman's Magazine*).

Meanwhile Wolfe's 8th Regiment, leftmost in the second line, swung forward onto the Highlanders' right flank, and 'wheeled in upon them; the whole then gave them 5 or 6 fires with vast execution' (Captain Lieutenant Thomas Ashe Lee, Wolfe's Regiment). Monro's fired nine rounds per man, emptying their pouches. Twenty to thirty ranks deep, the Highlanders could make no reply, beyond throwing stones and dirks. They suffered enormous casualties in the cross fire, one company losing 30 men out of 33. So desperate was the fighting 'that the soldiers' bayonets were stain'd and clotted with the blood of the rebels up to the muzzles of their muskets' (*Gentleman's Magazine*).

The Jacobite left never made contact. Nervous of Kingston's Horse to their flank, and ill-supported by swordless regiments from the second line, the MacDonalds failed to press their charge through knee-deep water: 'They came down three several times within a Hundred yards of our Men, firing their Pistols, and brandishing their Swords; but the Royals and Pulteney's [1st and 13th] hardly took their Firelocks from their Shoulders' (Cumberland). As the MacDonalds faltered, Cumberland threw in the cavalry from his right flank, 'upon which, rather like Devils than Men they broke through the Enemy's Flank, and a Total Rout followed' (*Newcastle Journal*). The Jacobite collapse on the other flank was equally sudden, their right and centre giving way 'in the greatest hurry and confusion imaginable; and scarce was their flight begun before they were out of our sight' (*Gentleman's Magazine*). As firing in the centre died away, Hawley put his dragoons at the Balvraid stream, the two wings of cavalry meeting in the centre of the enemy position.

Only a few Jacobite units held together. The well-drilled Forfar men marched off in square. The French regulars withdrew in good order until, convinced all was lost, the survivors surrendered. The prince was on his second horse of the day, collecting runaways, when O'Sullivan persuaded him to save himself, as 'all is going to pot'. Jacobite losses were estimated as a thousand on the field, and 'as many by the Campbells and dragoons in their flight'. If 'Cut hard, pay 'em home' seems a cruel policy, the function of cavalry in pursuit was to place a defeated army beyond all possibility of further use, preventing further bloodshed.

Less defensible was the deliberate killing of Jacobite wounded, but, as Cumberland's contemporary biographer Andrew Henderson wrote, 'The Troops were enraged at their Hardships and Fatigues during a Winter campaign; the habit of the enemy was strange, their language was still stranger, and their mode of fighting unusual; the Fields of Preston and Falkirk were still fresh in their Memories.' Jacobite propagandists had gleefully exaggerated the slaughter of redcoats after previous battles. At Culloden the boot was on the other foot. Only 154 Scots prisoners were taken compared with 222 Franco-Irish, and over 1500 Jacobites were killed. Cumberland probably understated his own losses at 50 dead and 270 wounded, 126 of whom came from Barrell's regiment alone.

Culloden was a decisive Hanoverian success, depriving the Jacobites of the northeastern lowlands, without whose resources resistance could not continue. Two days later the remains of the Highland army gathered at Ruthven Barracks in Strathspey, without the prince, who had no interest in leading a last-ditch guerrilla struggle. He sent a message inviting his supporters to save themselves, before taking to the heather himself. Unfortunately for everyone, the Jacobite chiefs did not disperse their people at once. Some were still under arms in August, to some extent justifying the reprisals that Cumberland was not unwilling to begin.

There was no repetition of the leniency that followed the Fifteen and Nineteen. Cumberland was set on destroying the socio-economic conditions that made the Highlands a nursery of rebellion. Hanoverian reprisals (120 judicial executions and 1000 transportations) were comparable with those that the Young Pretender's grandfather had found appropriate after Sedgemoor (1688). The Forty-Five's repercussions appear more shocking because they so closely preceded social and economic changes that have made such medieval severity as anachronistic as the romanticized adventurism that provoked it.

The Year Ninety-Eight

The Irish rebellion of 1798 produced the last conventional land campaign fought in the North Atlantic Archipelago. It followed the usual pattern of popular uprisings: initial rebel successes over scattered government detachments were stemmed piecemeal by makeshift columns, finally allowing the massed forces of repression to crush the insurgents with overwhelming firepower.

The political issues defy such straightforward categorization. Survivors played down their involvement, obscuring the rebellion's revolutionary antecedents, while the viceregal government in Dublin exaggerated rebel outrages, trading on Protestant folk memories of 1641 and 1689 to give the impression of another popish plot. This was the reverse of the truth. Atrocities by the government's paramilitary forces were routine and deliberate. They pre-dated the rising, and always exceeded those perpetrated by the insurgents. More recent accounts are still clouded by partisan rhetoric, however. The Roman Catholic hierarchy in the 19th century was nervous of secret societies such as the United Irishmen, and presented the rising as the spontaneous reaction of frightened peasants to loyalist terrorism. Thomas Pakenham's popular modern account perpetuates traditional views of the United Irishmen as an aimless and bloodthirsty rabble. Some Irish historians have floated the understandable but unlikely suggestion that the imperial government in London, under William Pitt the Younger, deliberately fomented rebellion to justify Union with Great Britain. Only recently has the Ninety-Eight been set alongside other 18th-century revolutions as a coherent movement with a rational political aim: establishment of an independent secular Irish republic, like those in France and the United States.

The 1790s saw a general crisis in Anglo-Irish relations. Population growth in Ireland sharpened land hunger and religious divisions. The American and French Revolutions of 1776 and 1789 provided new political models, more attractive to Irishmen than the Glorious Revolution of 1689, which had reduced Presbyterians and Catholics to second- or third-class citizens. In 1791 the non-sectarian Society of United Irishmen was formed in Belfast and Dublin to pursue constitutional reform and Catholic emancipation. Relaxation of the penal laws, however, inflamed Protestant sectarianism, symbolized by the foundation of the Orange Order in 1795. War with Revolutionary France from 1793 exacerbated economic distress, while increasing Ireland's strategic importance to the imperial government in London. Proscribed on the outbreak of war, the United Irishmen formed an underground army. They sought French help, inspiring abortive invasions at Bantry Bay (Christmas 1796) and Fishguard (February 1797), French military planners seemingly unaware of the distinction between Ireland and Wales.

The beleaguered Protestant Ascendancy, beneficiary of the penal laws and the land confiscations of the 17th century, launched an officially condoned campaign of torture and intimidation. Loyalist paramilitaries flogged suspected revolutionaries, or 'pitch-capped' them – gluing gunpowder to their scalps with tar, and setting fire to it. The onslaught threw the United Irishmen into disarray, but encouraged survivors to strike while they could. They failed to take the capital, however, while outbreaks throughout the Midland counties of Dublin, Meath and Kildare (23–27 May 1798) were suppressed with heavy casualties.

Only in County Wexford did the insurgents achieve any success, winning battles at Oulart Hill (27 May), Enniscorthy (28 May) and Tubberneering (4 June). Government troops abandoned Wexford, where the insurgents declared a short-lived republic. A belated rising in Ulster was swiftly suppressed at Antrim (7 June) and Ballynahinch (12–13 June), while the Wexford rebels suffered heavy defeats at New Ross (5 June) and Arklow (9 June), attempting to break out into the Midlands. Government forces then mounted a concentric advance against the survivors. One column had a stiff fight at Goff's Bridge (20 June), but others surrounded half the insurgent army on Vinegar Hill, breaking the back of the rebellion on 21 June.

The expected French invasion arrived at Killala Bay in Connacht on 22 August, two months too late. Despite a runaway victory at Castlebar (27 August), the French failed to join rebels in Westmeath and Longford, and were forced to surrender at Ballinamuck (8 September). The Royal Navy intercepted another expedition near Lough Swilly (12 October), capturing half its ships and Wolfe Tone, the United Irishmen's charismatic leader-in-exile.

The United Irishmen were not an inchoate rabble. Their cellular organization, typical of later revolutionary movements, exploited local loyalties to create cohesive tactical units. Townlands supplied platoons of 12 under a sergeant, parishes companies of 120 under a captain, and baronies regiments of 1200 under a colonel. However, training was sketchy and arms inadequate: 'scythes, hay knives, scrapers, currying knives, and old rusty bayonets fixed on poles'. Except for fowling pieces, firearms were taken from the enemy. Ammunition was scarce and marksmanship poor. The United Irishmen had no answer to the light field pieces that accompanied every government force, capable of firing three rounds of case shot a minute up to 300 yards (275 m), or two round shot to 800 yards (730 m). Nevertheless, the terrain of County Wexford – a dense *bocage* of small, irregularly shaped fields, hedges and copses – posed a severe challenge for government forces, every hill and ditch forming a rebel strongpoint. The offensive tactics of the rebels usually consisted of bold rushes by dense masses of pikemen. At New Ross Colonel Robert Craufurd reported the rebels, 'made as severe an attack as is possible for any troops with such arms'. Strategic leadership was poor. The Wexford insurgents gave the British commanders time to occupy New Ross and Arklow in force, and failed to concentrate at Vinegar Hill. They made no use of night attacks or the guerrilla tactics that might have neutralized superior British firepower.

The Irish government had no regular infantry battalions at the start of the rising, although several poor-quality dragoon regiments were available, demoralized by easy living. One regiment was disbanded after the rebellion, and the rest shipped out to relearn their business. The government depended on second-line paramilitaries of different types, formidable to everyone but the enemy: (1) Irish militia battalions, with Protestant officers and Catholic soldiers, conscripted by ballot to serve only within Ireland; (2) Irish Yeomanry, both infantry and cavalry, usually described as Protestant fanatics; they were volunteers serving within their own county; (3) British Fencibles, who were Scots, English or Welsh volunteers, enlisted for service within Great Britain and Ireland. The last were more reliable in action, but no better at civil–military relations. All three randomly murdered and tortured innocent country people, outraging humane officers such as Lord Cornwallis, appointed lord lieutenant on 22 June, or Major General (later Sir) John Moore. The Irish militia fought surprisingly well, but were otherwise ungovernable. Unfairly blamed for the humiliation of the 'Castlebar Races', they became a recruiting vehicle for the regular army. The Ninety-Eight also discredited the semi-independent government in Dublin. The Act of Union swept it away on 1 January 1801, without delivering the Catholic emancipation that might have reconciled the mass of the population to the new constitution. Rather than transcending Ireland's sectarian divisions, as the United Irishmen hoped, the Ninety-Eight ensured their perpetuation.

Fishguard, Friday 24 February 1797

Wales, Pembrokeshire, LR157 SM9437

This final invasion of British soil was a futile attempt to divert attention from French designs against Ireland. Two months after storms scattered the main effort at Bantry Bay, Tate's expeditionary force capitulated on Goodwick Sands, near the small port of Fishguard.

General Tate and Commodore Castagnier left Brest with four ships on 16 February 1797. Prevented from entering the Bristol Channel by an easterly wind, they continued west around St David's Head, dropping anchor off Carregwastad Point at 2 p.m. on the 22nd. One ship rounded Pen Anglas and entered Fishguard Harbour, putting back when saluted with blanks by the battery of 9-pounders at Old Fort. As evening fell, Tate's troops rowed ashore in ships' boats and scaled the cliffs west of Carregwastad.

The invasion force consisted of the Légion Noire, so-called from their dark brown jackets. They were mostly convicts, described by their own leaders as, '*gens perdus, de bandits, et des massacreurs*'. Tate was an Irish-American renegade, court-martialled in the USA for keeping false muster rolls. His orders were to raise insurrection around Bristol or Chester, interrupt commerce and generally spread terror and confusion. No regular troops were available to oppose him. Fishguard's immediate defence depended on two companies of Fencibles and three Royal Artillery invalids at Old Fort, less than 150 men altogether.

Fishguard

	Winner	*Loser*
Opponents	British	French
Commanders	John Campbell, Lord Cawdor	General de Brigade William Tate (p) Commodore Jean Castagnier
Numbers	650–750	1400
Losses	none	1400 (mostly prisoners)

The Cardigan militia and more Fencibles were stationed at Pembroke and Newport. Including the Castlemartin Yeomanry and armed bluejackets, the British eventually concentrated 40–50 cavalry, 600–700 infantry and two naval guns on carts.

Tate camped around the solid two-storey farmhouse at Trehowel (SM9139), with an outpost looking towards Fishguard at Garnwnda (SM9339). His men seemed 'more bent on cooking than conquering', washing down half-fried goose with wine and brandy that the inhabitants had salved from a recent shipwreck. The French made no effort to extend their bridgehead, beyond stealing the communion plate from Llanwnda church and shooting an eight-day clock at Brestgarn Farm. They had thoroughly misjudged the local mood. Thousands turned out with pikes and scythes to attack marauders and defend their property.

The initial military response was to abandon Fishguard, but it was reoccupied when reinforcements arrived with Lord Cawdor, who made his headquarters at a house in Fishguard Square, now the Royal Oak public house. The troops remained outside town, lining the turnpike from Haverfordwest (now the A40). Several hundred Welsh women in scarlet 'whittles' or cloaks gave the impression of more soldiers on Manorowen Hill and Bigney Hill, contributing to French demoralization. Many French soldiers were, by now, 'in a very displeasing state of body and mind in consequence of rash indulgence in port wine and poultry boiled in butter' (Rev. Daniel Rowlands). Morale was not enhanced by the departure of Castagnier's ships. At 9 p.m. on the 23rd Tate proposed a ceasefire, but Cawdor insisted on unconditional surrender, subject only to 'that consideration it is ever the wish of British troops to show an enemy whose number's are inferior …'.

At 2 p.m. next day, the Légion Noire marched down the steep road from Llanwnda to surrender on Goodwick Sands, hemmed in between the sea and the marsh inland of the bay. A contemporary painting shows the Yeomanry drawn up in line across one end of the beach, the sea on their left, the Légion Noire facing them in three lines. Red- and blue-coated infantry mass behind them, on the high ground east of the bay towards Fishguard, giving the French no opportunity to change their minds. Cawdor's main problem was to protect his prisoners from the population, kept back by Yeomanry with drawn swords. Tate and his officers were disarmed separately at Trehowel, to preserve them from their own soldiers.

Fatal casualties hardly reached double figures, including 8 men drowned on landing. Nearly 1400 prisoners were marched off to Haverfordwest for internment: 700 in St Mary's Church, 500 in the town hall, the rest in warehouses. Most were repatriated, spoiling a 'fine stroke of political economy', by which the French government had packed them off to be killed or imprisoned at the enemy's expense. The affair was a welcome boost for British morale. It demonstrated the effectiveness of their counter-invasion preparations, and provoked an outburst of Anglo-Welsh patriotism that reverberated into the 19th century, Queen Victoria awarding the Castlemartin Yeomanry the unique battle honour 'Fishguard' in 1853.

Directions

Goodwick Sands, where a plaque commemorates the surrender, are 1 mile (1.6 km) west of Fishguard along the A40(T). Follow a steep minor road from the bay to Llanwnda and Trehowel, whence footpaths converge on the cliff-top monument commemorating the landing (SM9240). Alternatively take the Pembroke Coast Path from Goodwick to Carregwastad. See a table at the Royal Oak on which the capitulation was signed, and the remains of Old Fort at Castle Point (SM9637), 1 mile (1.6 km) northeast of Fishguard off the A487 Newport road.

Tara, Sunday 27 May 1798

Ireland, Co. Meath, DS43 N9259

Kilthomas, Sunday 27 May 1798

Ireland, Co. Wexford, DS69 T0153

Oulart Hill, Sunday 27 May 1798

Ireland, Co. Wexford, DS69 T0840

The outbreak of the Irish rebellion in May 1798 was almost uniformly disastrous for the insurgents. Only at Oulart Hill did the United Irishmen achieve sufficient success to sustain their cause for more than a few days.

The plan was for metropolitan United Irishmen to capture Dublin in a *coup de main*, while risings in the surrounding counties pinned down government troops. When the scheme was betrayed and its leading players arrested, the diversionary attacks went ahead anyway. Most were put down with ease. Three companies of Scottish Fencibles from Dunshaughlin with their battalion gun sufficed to disperse the United Irishmen army of Meath, encamped south of Navan in a strong position at Tara Hill, the ancient seat of the high kings of Ireland.

News of the Midland risings reached Wexford during Saturday 26 May, encouraging the local United Irishmen to mobilize. The first fatalities happened during Saturday evening. An illegal 'peat-cutting' party under their parish priest, Father John Murphy, confronted 20 Yeomanry on the road from Harrow to Tinnacross, just south of Bookey's stream (T0546), killing a lieutenant of that name and a trooper.

Insurgent arms raids and Yeomanry house burnings continued all night. As part of the government's policy of breaking up potentially subversive gatherings, 100 cavalry and 200 infantry attacked a confused multitude of both sexes and all ages on the hill north of Kilthomas crossroads at ten o'clock next morning. While the infantry advanced across the fields to the south firing volleys, the cavalry climbed a narrow lane a quarter of a mile (0.4 km) to the west, turning the supposed insurgents' right flank. When the latter panicked, they were ridden down. How far the victims were rebels, or refugees from the Yeomanry's indiscriminate attacks, is debatable.

Meanwhile, Father John Murphy, who seems to have missed his true vocation, had gathered 400–600 men, and conducted a circular arms sweep south and east of Oulart. They returned to Oulart Hill in the early afternoon of 27 May, about 1000 strong, to join a similar number of unarmed refugees. During the morning a small government column, 110 North Cork militia and 19 Shelmalier Cavalry, had left Wexford,to deal with Father Murphy's growing band. They passed through Ballinamonabeg, and about 3 p.m. appeared on Bolabee or Bolaboy Ridge, just over a mile (1.6 km) south of the insurgent position.

Oulart was a market village straggling along the old Dublin coach road from Gorey to Wexford.

Tara

	Winner	*Loser*
Opponents	British	United Irishmen
Commanders	Captain Blanche	unknown
Numbers	300	unknown
Losses	41	350

Kilthomas

	Winner	*Loser*
Opponents	British	United Irishmen
Commanders	Captain Wainwright	Father Michael Murphy
Numbers	300	unknown
Losses	1 wounded	100–150

Oulart Hill

	Winner	*Loser*
Opponents	United Irishmen	British
Commanders	Father John Murphy Edward Roche	Colonel Foote
Numbers	1000	129
Losses	6 dead	105

Known in Gaelic as An Screig, 'stony ground', Oulart Hill (568 feet/173 m) is a mile-long whale-shaped ridge running northwest of the village. Its summit provides a 360-degree view of the surrounding countryside, making it a good defensive position for infantry beset by mounted troops. Steep on the north and west, it sloped gradually towards the approaching militia on the other sides. Streams flowing away from the hill tended to channel advancing troops towards Father Murphy's position, and small patches of woodland covered the rebels' rear.

Small fields pressing up to the top on all sides provided cover for the defenders, who prepared an L-shaped ambush on the southeast slope just below the crest. The shorter leg ran some 200 yards (180 m) northeast along the summit ditch from Father Murphy's monument, turning through 90 degrees to head southeast towards the village. The 40–50 insurgents with firearms were hidden on the right, their rear protected by a hedge and ditch, probably constructed in advance. The mass of pikemen were on the other flank, in plain view of Colonel Foote's men across the valley, drawing them on. Behind them were the unarmed people.

Most narratives repeat Foote's subsequent assertion that he never meant to attack so strong a position, but that his subordinates (all safely dead) had pressed on regardless. Tactical movements on the ground suggest a deliberate pincer movement, like that at Kilthomas, under less favourable circumstances. The attackers paused to burn some cabins in the village, then the cavalry branched off along the old Enniscorthy road on the left, turning up a *borreen* or sunken lane west of the hill, behind the insurgent right. The militia appear to have advanced directly on the United Irishmen, menacing their open left flank. To rattle the defenders, as recommended by tactical manuals of the day, they opened fire at 30 perches, literally 165 yards (151 m), rather long range. Some of the rebels slipped away, halving the number of armed men on the position. The gunmen, however, resolved 'to stand together and not to fire until our enemy would be quite close to us and then to fire and rush in amongst them' (Peter Foley).

As the North Cork militia approached the insurgent position, most of the defending pikemen withdrew into the next field behind them, confirming the attackers' impression that they were driving the enemy before them onto the waiting cavalry. As the militia fired a last volley and dashed forward, the ambushers opened a deadly fire into their left flank

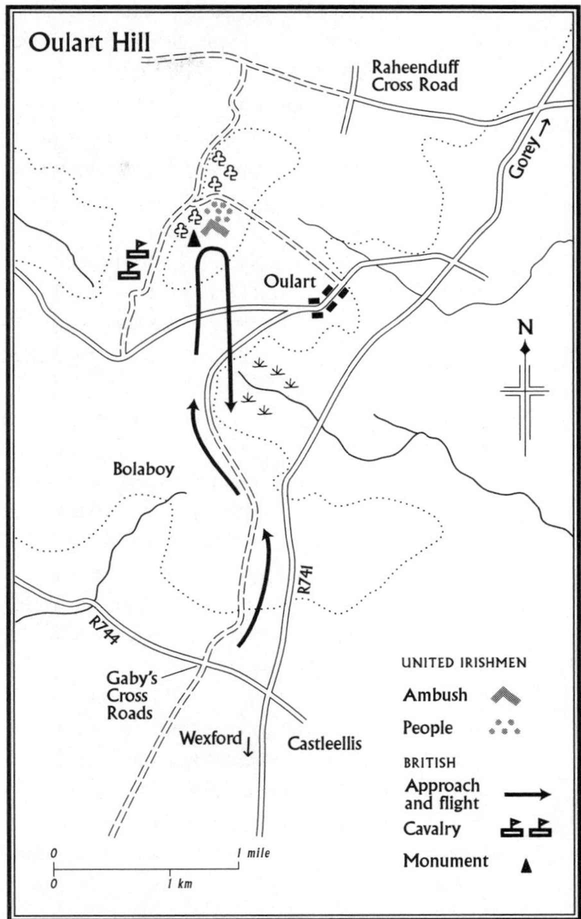

Directions

Oulart Hill *From Wexford follow the R741 north to the R744 junction at Castleellis. Turn left and right onto the old road across Bolaboy Ridge into Oulart, from where a minor road runs up the hill, across the rear of the insurgent position, and into the* borreen. *See Father Murphy's monument in the fields atop the hill.*

at not more than 15 yards (14 m), while the pikemen worked round both flanks in the shelter of the parallel earthen banks or hedges: 'At this opportune moment they leapt over and bore down all opposition' (Foley).

The surviving soldiers fled downhill, 'the insurgents in amongst them knocking them down with their various weapons, numbers of them with stones of which the hill offered a plentiful supply' (Foley). Most were killed in the boggy valley bottom, perhaps in North Cork Lane by the Ferns road, or making for Bolaboy Ridge. The last couple fell 2 miles (3 km) away at Gaby's Cross (T0837). Foote and four other ranks escaped on horseback. The Shelmaliers, unable to see what was happening beyond the crest, only left the *borreen* to withdraw. The insurgents captured over 100 firelocks, with 60 rounds apiece, trebling their firepower.

Oulart Hill was a catalytic victory. It sowed panic among local loyalists, hundreds of whom fled their homes. Thousands of recruits rallied to the insurgent camp on Carrigroe Hill, north of Oulart, providing sufficient momentum to sustain the cause for weeks.

Directions

Tara *Hill of Tara is down a minor road 1 mile (1.6 km) west of the N3 Dunshaughlin–Navan road. The most desperate resistance was round the churchyard gate, the Fencibles advancing from the south.*

Kilthomas *Half a mile (0.8 km) north of Ferns turn left off the N11 Gorey road for Kilthomas crossroads. The battle (or massacre) was on the hill beyond.*

Enniscorthy, Monday 28 May 1798

Ireland, Co. Wexford, DS69 S9739

Enniscorthy

	Winner	*Loser*
Opponents	United Irishmen	British
Commanders	Father John Murphy Edward Roche	Captain William Snowe
Numbers	5000–8000	331
Losses	200–500	*c.*100

Enniscorthy, the site of the United Irishmen's only offensive victory, sits astride the shallow tidal estuary of the River Slaney, at the strategic centre of Co. Wexford. Its possession allowed the rebels to strike west towards New Ross, or south against Wexford. Enniscorthy itself is tactically indefensible, its streets sprawling either side of the river, which was easily fordable after weeks of dry weather. It lacked perimeter walls, although the castle and Market House made useful redoubts inside the town. Cabins along the approach roads obstructed the defenders' fields of fire, and sheltered a population sympathetic to the insurgents. Troops holding the bridge below the castle could not see the western and northern approaches to the town, hidden by the rim of the slope up from the riverbank.

The victors of Oulart Hill left Carrigroe Hill during the morning of 28 May. They marched southwest through Ferns and Scarawalsh Bridge, where the N11 now crosses the Slaney, joining the survivors of Kilthomas at Ballyorrill Hill, north of Enniscorthy (see map for Vinegar Hill, page 620). Estimates of their combined strength come from pro-British sources, and are probably exaggerations. Enniscorthy's defenders officially totalled 13 officers and 318 other ranks: 70 were North Cork militia, the rest local Yeomanry, including 50 cavalry. Captain Snowe left the east bank undefended, holding the bridge with the militia, his best troops. A hundred Enniscorthy infantry covered Duffry Gate at the west end of town, with cavalry and more infantry in support on Castle Hill and in the streets along the western river bank. Neither side had any artillery.

The rebels converged on Duffry Gate about 1 p.m., advancing down the Ballyorril road or through Milehouse, their column a mile (1.6 km) in length, and 'so thick as to fill up the road'. As they approached, they threw out flanking columns right and left, turning Duffry Gate. Accounts of the initial encounters are confused, some ascribing a futile cavalry charge to this part of the battle. The first definite move was a determined assault on Duffry Gate, rebel pikemen closely following 30–40 cows stampeded through the defenders, driving them back into Market Square. More insurgents fought their way into Irish Street, on the north side of town. With few firearms, they suffered heavily from sharpshooters in place behind barricades and in upper windows, whose muzzle flashes set light to the thatched roofs. Smoke filled the streets, concealing the charging pikemen until they were on top of the Yeomanry, while the overarching flames scorched the soldiers' hair and bearskin caps.

Meanwhile the insurgents' left pincer had gained an island north of the bridge. The North Cork recklessly exposed themselves above the parapet to drive them off with musketry, but were themselves distracted from reinforcing the hard-pressed defenders of Market Square. Eventually the rebels crossed the Slaney further north at Blackstoops, advancing down its left bank to threaten the eastern end of the bridge: 'A small number of them only had firearms, but the pikemen, wonderfully tall, stout, able fellows fought with their pikes in the most furious and desperate manner.'

After three hours fighting Snowe evacuated the town, covered by the smoke, retiring down the road to St Johns, west of the river. As they went, demoralized Yeomanry shot at every countryman they passed, the officers tearing off their epaulettes to pass for soldiers. Back in the blazing town, exasperated rebels piked loyalists, leaving their bodies in the street for the pigs to eat. Scenes of panic gripped Wexford, while thousands of insurgent recruits, voluntary and otherwise, gathered east of Enniscorthy on Vinegar Hill. Next day the rebels advanced on Forth Mountain west of Wexford, whose garrison slipped away to Duncannon on the 30th. The insurgents gained control of the whole county, except a few peripheral towns: New Ross, Bunclody and Gorey.

Directions

Enniscorthy is halfway between New Ross and Gorey along the N30 and N11. The main insurgent attack was eastwards down the R702 through Duffry Gate. See the National 1798 Visitor Centre, and the County Museum in the castle. The old bridge held by the North Cork militia stands between modern road and railway bridges.

Tubberneering (the Gorey Races), **Monday 4 June 1798**

Ireland, Co. Wexford, DS69 T1254–55

For a few days in early June the United Irishmen were triumphant throughout Co. Wexford. The pinnacle of their military success was the encounter battle at Tubberneering (or Toberanierin), 'which the soldiers called Gorey Races, because each strove to outrun his fellows' (Sergeant Archibald M'laren, Dumbarton Fencibles).

After capturing Wexford the United Irishmen divided their forces, now 15,000 strong. Some went west to Carrickbyrne Hill to threaten New Ross; the rest to Carrigroe Hill to protect the northern part of the county. Meanwhile, the commander-in-chief in Ireland, Lieutenant General Gerard Lake, prepared a three-pronged counteroffensive against the Wexford rebels. While General Johnson occupied New Ross (see below), General Loftus was to march south from Gorey, driving the rebels back against a force advancing from Bunclody to Ferns. Loftus and his unruly subordinate Colonel Walpole left Gorey at 9 a.m. on 4 June with 5 guns and the best part of 1500 men. They divided forces a few hundred yards west of the town: Walpole carried on down the main road towards Clogh, while Loftus forked left to Ballycanew. They quickly lost contact in the enclosed countryside, despite Loftus detaching 150 Antrim militia at Ballyminaun Hill (T1455) to maintain touch. He had 'no intelligence to be depended on respecting the actual situation and force of the enemy', but Walpole was confident he had a force 'equal to anything they could do'. Loftus claimed afterwards the rebels had fielded 15,000 men. Half that is probably too many.

The insurgents were aware of Loftus's plans, and left Carrigroe Hill early on the 4th. They marched north through Ballyoughter to meet Walpole, who left the main road at Clogh. South of that place the road became deep, narrow and intricate, flanked by clay banks with wide ditches at the base and rows of close bushes on top. Fields were small and difficult, covered with standing corn, potatoes and uncut grass.

Tubberneering

	Winner	Loser
Opponents	United Irishmen	British
Commanders	Edward Roche Father Philip Roche	Major General William Loftus Colonel Lambert Theodore Walpole (k)
Numbers	c.7500	1200
Losses	unknown	54

Walpole was a Dublin Castle 'dangler', a courtier not a fighting soldier. He advanced in column of march without flanking parties or scouts, only a few dragoons in front of the infantry, and four guns in the centre. Half a mile (0.8 km) south of Clogh he blundered into an ambush in the townland of Tubberneering, where the road bends east and south skirting a large rocky outcrop 100 yards (90 m) west of the road.

Rebels on the crag watched Walpole's troops pass down the road towards the main insurgent force, somewhere south of the modern railway bridge. More rebels lined the hedges either side of the road, and shot down the gun teams. The redcoats could neither fight nor retreat, the rebel pikes reaching across the narrow road. Those who escaped the opening volley were transfixed from behind, by invisible opponents. Walpole, a conspicuous target on a grey horse, was hit immediately. His men returned fire as best they could, while insurgents infiltrated round their flanks covered by hedges and crops. A nearly anonymous survivor, 'W.G.H.', wrote: 'In a little time their [i.e. the rebels'] line broke, which we took to be an omen of their defeat; but this only to deceive us for their two wings set up the *war-hoop* and made for Gorey to cut off our retreat …' Abandoning three guns and their wounded, the soldiers fell back past Tubberneen Rock, firing and loading as they ran, dodging the fire of their own guns, which were now turned against them. Enough of them kept together to prevent a massacre. A black bandsman of the Armagh militia, who swapped his drumsticks for a musket, boasted afterwards, 'Sare, de army ran away – de Armagh retreat.' Standing briefly at Clogh, the shattered column continued its retreat through Gorey to Arklow.

The fighting was over in 10–20 minutes. Loftus heard the firing from Ballycanew, but had no time to react. The Antrims at Ballyminaun reached Clogh too late, and were themselves cut to pieces. Meanwhile Loftus assumed Walpole had dispersed the opposition. He pushed on through Ballymore below Carrigroe Hill, and turned north up the Ballyoughter road, previously traversed by the insurgents. Presumably a trail of bodies disillusioned him before he caught up with the enemy on Gorey Hill (T1459), 'in such force and so advantageously posted that it would have been madness to have attacked them' (Loftus). Guided by local Yeomanry, Loftus withdrew westwards, over the hills to Carnew and Tullow.

Tubberneering was a remarkable victory, against a strong force well equipped with guns. It disrupted Lake's counteroffensive, restoring the initiative to the Wexford insurgents, who could now attempt to break out into adjacent counties.

Directions

Clogh is 3 miles (5 km) south of Gorey along the N11. Turn left into the minor road to Ballyoughter, past Tubberneen Rock on the right, to the ambush area.

New Ross, Tuesday 5 June 1798

Ireland, Co. Wexford, DS76 S7127–7227

New Ross is the lowest road crossing on the River Barrow, and the obvious route for the United Irishmen to carry the Wexford rebellion westwards. However, their national plan had assigned the county a defensive role, as a bridgehead for the projected French invasion. By the time the leaders at Carrickbyrne Hill adopted a more aggressive strategy, it was too late. Their attempt to break into Co. Waterford ended in shattering defeat.

The United Irishmen's Carrickbyrne division occupied Corbet Hill, a mile (1.6 km) southeast of

New Ross, on 4 June. Loyalist estimates probably double insurgent numbers, already reduced by numerous defections. Perhaps a quarter had firearms, with poor quality powder and no cartridges. Johnson had entered New Ross the same day, with detachments from the Clare, Donegal and Dublin militia, 5th and 9th Dragoons, mounted Yeomanry, and at least six guns.

New Ross lay east of the River Barrow, a significant obstacle, navigable as far as the town by 400-ton vessels. Three narrow thoroughfares ran parallel to the river: Custom and Block House Quays, South Street and Neville or Nevin Street. Across these ran Market Street, Mary Street, Michael Street and Cross Lane, sloping steeply down to the river. The medieval town walls with nine flanking towers, somewhat slighted in the 1650s, formed the basis of the defence. Labourers hastily entrenched Market or Bishop's Gate and Three Bullet Gate, at the northeast and southeast corners respectively. The latter work was sited at an angle to sweep both the Wexford road past Corbet Hill, and the road south of Priory Gate, beside the river. The Clare militia held Market Gate, and the Dublins Three Bullet Gate, with interior strong points at St Mary's Churchyard, the barracks in Michael Street and the Main Guard at the junction of Mary and South Street. Cavalry occupied the quayside, ready to counterattack.

The rebel leader Bagenal Harvey tried to summon Johnson to surrender early on 5 June, but militia sentries shot the insurgent envoy under his white flag. At 5.30 a.m. the enraged rebels surged forward in three columns against the Market, Three Bullet and Priory Gates. The rightmost column never made contact, leaving the field without a shot fired. In the centre the main attack stalled in face of the Dublins' musketry and the fire of two field guns. A disastrous sortie by 5th Dragoons revived the assault, the United Irishmen pursuing the broken cavalry back through Three Bullet Gate, down Neville Street into Church Lane and Mary Street. Here they were stopped by a field gun in a dominating position in the churchyard, and another in Chapel Lane firing into Mary Street.

More insurgents turned left down Michael Street to join the Priory Gate column on the quayside, persuading half Johnson's men to retreat over the bridge: 'Between six and seven o'clock it was supposed there were three thousand rebels in the town, the upper part of which was set on fire by them' (Jordan Roche, surgeon). However, Market Gate and the Main Guard posts held firm, the Donegal militia at the latter inflicting heavy casualties with their swivel guns. While thirsty rebels dispersed in search of food and drink, or blundered about in the smoke, Johnson rallied his men west of the river beyond Rosbercon. Harvey had plenty of reserves, but made no effort to relieve his exhausted firing line, or isolate the town by pulling up the drawbridge.

The Dublins counterattacked over the bridge at about 9 a.m., taking the disorganized rebels by surprise. Short of ammunition and lacking decisive leadership, the United Irishmen were cleared from the streets by 1 p.m., retreating to Corbet Hill in good order. So fierce was the fighting that some of the militia fired 120 rounds per man, twice the contents of their pouches, while Mary Street was swept by 23 successive discharges of grapeshot. One rebel leader was said to have stuffed his wig into a gun muzzle, his last words, 'Come on boys, her mouths stopt.'

Rebel and civilian casualties were incalculable and indistinguishable. James Alexander, a British medical officer, reckoned the United Irishmen lost 2806 killed: 'Next to Main Street, the greatest slaughter was round the Town Walls where the battle raged. Next the Chapel Lane twas horrible; next Brogue Makers Lane, Michael's Street and the Cross Lane.' In Chapel Lane bodies lay three deep. Ancient residents interviewed in the 19th century agreed as many were shot afterwards or suffocated in the blazing

New Ross

	Winner	*Loser*
Opponents	British	United Irishmen
Commanders	Major General Henry Johnson	Bagenal Harvey
Numbers	2678	8000
Losses	230	2806

houses as were killed outright. Johnson reported 172 soldiers killed or missing, and 58 wounded.

Indiscriminate reprisals continued for days, despite Johnson's efforts to restore discipline. Meanwhile, retreating United Irishmen massacred over 100 loyalist hostages at Scullabogue, the worst rebel atrocity of the Ninety-Eight. New Ross ended all insurgent hopes of cooperation with neighbouring counties to the west, a strategic setback confirmed at Arklow four days later.

Directions

New Ross is 12 miles (19 km) northeast of Waterford along the N25. From the bridge climb the steep back alleys to the top of the town, to see the ruins of St Mary's.

Antrim, Thursday 7 June 1798

Ireland, Co. Antrim, DS14 J1486–1586

The north of Ireland saw separate risings in Co. Antrim and Co. Down, dealt with respectively at Antrim and Ballynahinch.

The northern leaders of the United Irishmen meant to await French intervention, but their more militant supporters overrode them. On 7 June Henry Joy McCracken, a Presbyterian cotton manufacturer, raised the flag of revolt at Craigarogan Fort southeast of Templepatrick, on the old straight road to Glengormley. The plan was to capture the town of Antrim, strategically placed on the main Belfast–Derry road, along with the local magistrates, who were due to assemble there that day. Meanwhile rebel forces across the county were to persuade local militia detachments to change sides. However, Major General George Nugent, in command at Belfast, was tipped off in time to warn the magistrates and despatch reinforcements. The militiamen remained loyal.

McCracken approached Antrim through Templepatrick and Dunadry, meeting several thousand more supporters from Donegore Hill (896 feet/273 m) just east of the town. His numbers are probably exaggerated, as many United Irishmen failed to turn out. Their only artillery was a brass 6-pounder mounted on old carriage wheels, and fired with a pot of burning turf for want of slow match. Meanwhile another group of insurgents from Randalstown were expected to converge on Antrim from the northwest.

Antrim's garrison consisted of 70 Light Dragoons, 50 Yeomanry infantry, and 30–40 armed civilians. They occupied the Market House and Castle Gardens at the head of Main Street, looking east towards the church. Six Mile Water protected their right flank, though Castle Street on their left (then Bow Lane) was wide open to the Randalstown rebels. McCracken's left and rear were equally exposed to government reinforcements: Colonel Clavering approaching Massereene Bridge from the south, with 150 troopers of 22nd Light Dragoons, 2 battalions (not engaged) and 4 guns; Colonel Durham approaching from the east through Templepatrick, with 250 militia, an unspecified number of mounted troops, and 2 6-pounder guns. Some 500 troops definitely participated in the action, plus Durham's cavalry, making about 700 altogether.

McCracken's force entered Antrim about 2 p.m. in two columns. One went along the continuation of Main Street known as Church Street (formerly Scotch Quarter), the other circling north by Railway Street (formerly Patie Lane). Heavy fire swept Main Street, preventing the latter re-emerging opposite the churchyard. The main body was held up by the sudden appearance of Clavering's mounted advance guard across Massereene Bridge, who wheeled two guns out of the lane below the church to open fire on the insurgents, but were soon driven off. Casualty claims

Antrim

	Winner	*Loser*
Opponents	British	United Irishmen
Commanders	Colonel Clavering Colonel James Durham	Henry Joy McCracken (x)
Numbers	c.700	6000–8000
Losses	60	300

vary from 'some men killed and a few horse' (Colonel Durham), to 5 officers and 47 men. Unable to shake the enemy pikemen, the remaining dragoons withdrew. Some went back across Six Mile Water, others into Bow Lane.

The insurgents occupied the churchyard, but continual musketry from Castle Gardens held up further progress. McCracken led a party behind the houses north of Main Street to turn the defenders' left flank, dislodging the dragoons in Bow Lane instead, just as the Randalstown column came in sight. Mistaking the fleeing dragoons for a cavalry attack, the Randalstown men fled, their panic spreading to McCracken's own followers. Simultaneously Colonel Durham's 6-pounders opened fire from Sentry Hill, just south of the A6/B95 junction, where the railway cutting now runs.

The United Irishmen cleared out before Durham was ready to advance. A few rallied at Donegore Hill, but the rest dispersed in every direction. As usual the senior British officers had difficulty preventing their troops mistreating innocent inhabitants, many of whom were killed. Overall casualties were low compared with further south, however. Next day Nugent published a general amnesty, encouraging insurgent rank and file to abandon the struggle. McCracken remained at large for a month, until he was caught making for Carrickfergus harbour. He was hanged in Belfast on 17 July.

Directions

Antrim is 15 miles (24 km) northwest of Belfast. Follow McCracken's approach march (and Durham's) along the A6 from Templepatrick (M22 junction 5) through Muckamore. See the churchyard and Castle Gardens.

Arklow, Saturday 9 June 1798

Ireland, Co. Wicklow, DS62 T2373–2473

Arklow

	Winner	*Loser*
Opponents	British	United Irishmen
Commanders	Major General Francis Needham	Anthony Perry Father Michael Murphy
Numbers	1824	*c.*5000
Losses	46	500

The decisive engagement of the Wexford insurgency, and hence of the Ninety-Eight, was at Arklow, a river crossing on the road to Dublin. The victors of Oulart Hill and Tubberneering (see above) had failed to take Arklow when they had the chance, General Needham reoccupying the place on 6 June. If the Wexford rebels could still push north into Wicklow, they might mobilize fresh support, and once more threaten the capital. At 10 a.m. on 9 June, after much wrangling, their northern army left Gorey for Arklow. The direct road was not yet built so they marched westwards through Coolgreany.

Arklow was a small town at the mouth of the River Avoca, its single main street running parallel with the river's southern bank. At the western end, beyond the present Parade, was the barracks, now demolished. The bridge is still in use at the eastern end, from where the town's poorer quarter, the Fisheries, extended south towards the sand dunes fringing the golf links. A stream, now culverted under the Gorey road pavement, flowed into a ravine under the barrack wall. Not much of an obstacle in itself, its open, gently sloping banks provided a natural killing ground that the insurgents had to cross to reach the town. In general the ground sloped northeast towards the estuary, intersected with hedges and banks, as it still was before recent building activity between the Gorey road and the N11 bypass further west.

Needham's position resembled a Wellington boot – its heel at the barracks; the toe pointing south down the railway; the shin curving east towards the Fisheries at the top. He placed some militia in the barracks, and three of his five guns behind a barricade across the Coolgreany road, outside today's Bank of Ireland. The Durham Fencibles, who bore the brunt of the fighting, occupied the boot's toe, facing west

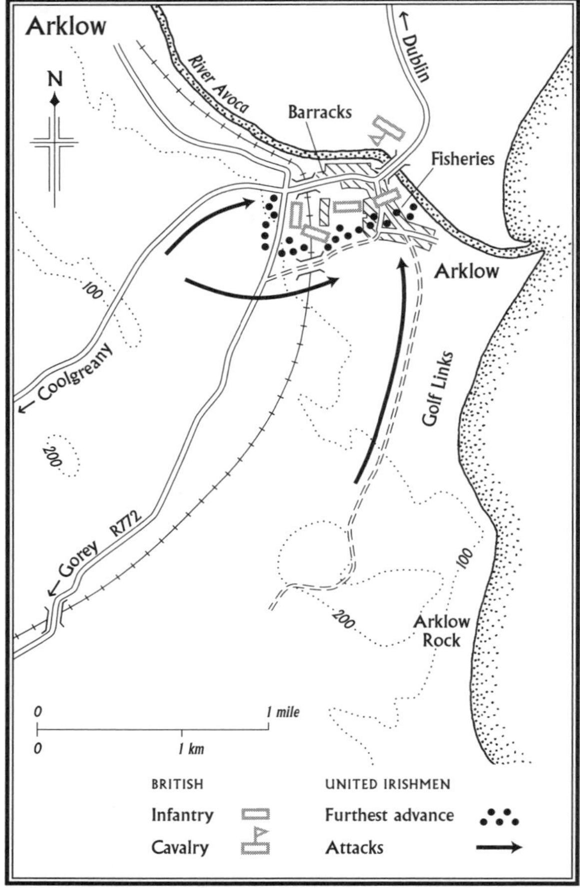

Directions

The appearance of the battlefield is greatly altered by modern building, particularly along the R772 Gorey road. A footpath follows the insurgents' eastern line of advance across the golf links.

along a gentle rise between the Gorey road and railway, commanding the stream. The Cavan militia continued the line eastwards, along the backs of the houses, as far as the old Fisheries road, which they barricaded south of the bridge, with two more guns. The Dumbarton Fencibles occupied some ditches flanking the rebel line of advance from Coolgreany, a quarter of a mile (0.4 km) in front of the main position. Needham's cavalry were held back north of the river. Maxwell's *History of the Irish Rebellion* tabulates the defenders as follows:

Fencibles	479
Cavan militia	362
Regular and yeomanry cavalry	414
Dismounted yeomanry	77
Survivors from Tubberneering	492
Total	1824

The United Irishmen cannot be enumerated with such precision. Hayes-McCoy, the battle's most thorough historian, reckoned there were 5000 armed rebels, less than most estimates, perhaps two-fifths with firearms. They had several field guns, and captured militiamen to work them. One was on high ground 1000 yards (900 m) south of the barracks, another beside the Coolgreany road 600 yards (550 m) west of the barracks – a more effective range for 6-pounder round shot.

The insurgents appeared about 4 p.m. Most of them advanced from Coolgreany, others through the sand hills by the shore, using a no longer extant road across the golf links from Arklow Rock. Needham reported two immense columns, his entire front crowded by a rabble armed with pikes and firearms, bearing down on him without any regular order. The Coolgreany column drove in the Dumbarton skirmishers easily enough, but was halted by the fire of three field guns at the future roundabout, where the Gorey road joins the old roads from Coolgreany and Woodenbridge. Unable to progress that way, successive masses of United Irishmen spread out south of the junction, along the line of the modern road, to exchange fire with the Durham Fencibles beyond the stream. Groups of pikemen broke cover in repeated attempts to reach the enemy, but there is no evidence they ever made contact.

The United Irishmen did better at the Fisheries. Their pikemen saw off several cavalry charges, and got in amongst the blazing cabins. Every attempt to break into the town, however, was met by crushing fire from the barricade and old churchyard, grapeshot tumbling the insurgents down in twenties. The Cavan militia's brass 6-pounder became so hot that after the battle it was condemned as unserviceable. The attackers' impressed artillerymen fired deliberately wide, until United Irishmen took over as gun layers. They hit a limber, a gun carriage and a pub beyond the barracks, before one gun was silenced by return fire, and the other ran out of ammunition.

The crisis came at 8 p.m., as ammunition on both sides ran low. Father Michael Murphy, last seen at Kilthomas (see above), led a final charge up the Coolgreany road, falling within 50 yards (45 m) of the barricade. Allegedly he had claimed to be able to pluck musket balls from the air, but had not vouched for 6-pounder grapeshot. The leaderless pikemen fell back followed by the musketeers, their powder spent. All round the field the attackers 'drew off with a sulky reluctance'. Needham's cavalry recrossed the bridge to cut off stragglers among the sand dunes, but ventured no further in the darkness.

While Needham's men stood to, expecting fresh attacks, the insurgents marched sullenly back to Gorey. The highest figures for British losses are 18 dead and 28 wounded. Estimates for rebel losses range from 200–300 up to 1000, the truth probably lying in between. Most of these would be dead, as no wounded prisoners were taken. Arklow's strategic consequences were considerable. As at New Ross (see above), the United Irishmen had again failed to capture a defended town. They were thrown back on the defensive, with no realistic hope of conventional military victory.

Ballynahinch, Tuesday–Wednesday 12–13 June 1798

Ireland, Co. Down, DS20 J3651–3752

The second rising in the north of Ireland was defeated at Ballynahinch, nearly a week after the first was crushed at Antrim (see above).

At first the Co. Down insurgents encamped at Creevy Rocks near Saintfield, shifting south to Ballynahinch on 12 June. Their main camp was on Ednavady Hill, south of Ballynahinch River in Lord Moira's demesne at Montalto Park. Ballynahinch lay beyond the bridge, between the river and a wedge of hilly ground to the north that ends in a mass of small round hills outside the town. An advanced detachment occupied Windmill Hill, half a mile (0.8 km) northeast of Ballynahinch, covering the old Saintfield and Downpatrick roads. Traces of earthworks were still visible in the 1950s.

The insurgents were the usual motley crowd of men, women and children, in their Sunday best. Numbers are difficult to gauge, owing to numerous defections before and during the battle. General Nugent reckoned there were 5000 rebels on the evening of the 12th, 'many pressed and almost entirely unarmed', and did not suppose there were so many in the morning. Few local inhabitants would hazard their lives for the cause, preferring to hide in the mountains to the south. Most of the United Irishmen had pikes, though some only carried swords 'of the least efficient kind', or even pitchforks. Only the higher class had guns. Visiting the camp, James Thomson observed seven or eight very small cannon mounted on carts, which 'were not calculated to produce much effect'.

General Nugent at Belfast had to strike a balance between denuding the city of troops, and leaving the insurgency to spread in the countryside unchecked. By 12 June he felt able to launch an offensive against the Saintfield rebels in conjunction with a Colonel Stewart from Downpatrick. Finding Saintfield deserted, Nugent pressed on to await Stewart at Bell's Bridge, just short of Windmill Hill. Thomson estimated total British numbers at 2000–3000, the lower figure being more likely. Nugent mentions the following, without further enumeration:

> *From Belfast*: Fife Fencibles, Monaghan militia (incomplete), 22nd Light Dragoons (60 men), six 6-pounders, and two howitzers.
> *From Downpatrick*: Argyle and York Fencibles (100 of the latter), some dragoons, three companies of Yeomanry infantry, and one gun.

Initially the Monaghans drew up in line fronting Windmill Hill, the Fifes massed behind their right to

Ballynahinch

	Winner	Loser
Opponents	British	United Irishmen
Commanders	Major General George Nugent	Henry Monro (x)
Numbers	2000	c.5000
Losses	unknown	500

counter hosts of pikemen who appeared in that quarter, threatening Nugent's flank. Stewart's arrival on the British left restored the situation, however. The Argyles drove the United Irishmen off Windmill Hill, the rebels fleeing back through the town. Nugent moved his guns up to Windmill Hill, cannonading Ballynahinch and Montalto Park until night fell at about 9 p.m. He then occupied the battered town with infantry and guns, leaving the cavalry back at Windmill Hill. Large numbers of United Irishmen took the opportunity to disappear into the darkness, despite loyalist detachments placed on the Hillsborough and Downpatrick roads to prevent their escape.

Fighting resumed at first light, about 3 a.m. Successive bodies of pikemen charged up Bridge Street 'like bloodhounds', taking several guns and driving the Monaghans back into the houses, 'where they kept up a kind of broken fire' (anonymous insurgent). Further pikemen turned right after crossing the bridge, and fought their way past the parish church, rejoining the main body in Market Square. Despite heavy losses crossing the open space, they drove Nugent's troops back up Windmill Street. The United Irishmen had shot their bolt by 7 a.m., however, their numbers diminished by desertion, and their ammunition running low.

The decisive move came south of the river. Colonel Stewart had taken the Argyles, three companies of dismounted Yeomanry and two guns across Mill Bridge (J3751) to the vicinity of Magheradroll Old Church, whence his guns enfiladed Montalto Park from the east. Advancing within 200 yards (180 m) of the enemy's main body, he withstood 'three different attempts with their musquetry, supported by a very great number of Pikemen, to dislodge him' (Nugent). Having inflicted heavy casualties with grapeshot, Stewart overran the rebel camp, guns and baggage, while Nugent's shaken troops reoccupied the town. Monro, a descendant of the Scottish general defeated at Benburb (1646), was among the last to leave the field. Two days later he was captured at Clontymagullion, 2 miles (3 km) west of Ballynahinch, and hanged outside his own draper's shop in Lisburn.

Total insurgent losses, including reprisals, are unknowable. Nugent claimed 300 killed in the battle and 200 in the pursuit, admitting only 6 of his own men killed and 15 wounded, besides a few Yeomanry. Half the town was destroyed in the fighting, which in 1800 remained a heap of ruins. The losers were so disheartened they surrendered two days after the battle, on promise of pardon. Organized resistance in the north was at an end.

Directions

Ballynahinch is 15 miles (24 km) south of Belfast, halfway between Dromore and Downpatrick on the B2. Approaching from the former, Montalto Park is on the right, just before the bridge. Continue up Bridge Street, bearing right along the B7 for Windmill Hill and Bell's Bridge.

Goff's Bridge (Foulkes Mill), **Wednesday 20 June 1798**

Ireland, Co. Wexford, DS69 S8618

Vinegar Hill, Thursday 21 June 1798

Ireland, Co. Wexford, DS69 S9839

Reinforcements from mainland Britain allowed General Lake to revive the concentric advance against the Wexford rebels that had been disrupted at Tubberneering (see above). This time, after their defeats at New Ross and Arklow, he would encircle the demoralized United Irishmen in central Wexford, and destroy them at Vinegar Hill.

Lake's forces advanced in a wide arc from Arklow, through Carnew and Bunclody, to New Ross. The insurgents' northern army withdrew to the United Irishmen's main camp at Vinegar Hill, outside Enniscorthy, but the southern army failed to join them before the decisive battle. Edward Roche was in Wexford, trying to stop the massacre of loyalist prisoners. His clerical namesake had marched west through Taghmon to intercept Lake's southernmost pincer, under General Moore.

Moore and Father Roche met at Goff's Bridge, on a tributary of the River Corock, near Foulkesmill. Moore repulsed the leading insurgents with riflemen and artillery on the high ground at Stoneenrath crossroads, driving them back across the bridge in confusion. More United Irishmen crossed further upstream, probably at Cullenstown, driving in the British left through the woods around Raheenduff House. Moore rallied his retreating troops: '[I] took off my hat, put my horse into a trot, gave a huzza, and got them to make a push. The tide immediately turned and we drove the rebels before us and killed a great many.' The encounter prevented Moore reaching Vinegar Hill, but left his opponents unable to dispute his subsequent advance on Wexford. Meanwhile other British columns were converging on Enniscorthy: Lake from Carnew and Bunclody was 2 miles (3 km) northeast at Solsborough; Johnson from New Ross was to the west, approaching through Clonroche; and Needham from Arklow was at Oulart, 7 miles (11 km) to the east.

Overnight Needham was ordered to circle southeast of Vinegar Hill, to block the insurgents' retreat, while Lake attacked them frontally. Lake advanced down the Enniscorthy road at 3 a.m., his forces fanning out where a byroad makes directly for Vinegar Hill: the right carried on towards Enniscorthy to enfilade the rebels' forward line of defence; the centre took the byroad; the left marched cross-country towards Clonhasten crossroads. Changes in the road system obscure Lake's dispositions, which probably extended along the modern Oulart–Enniscorthy road, within easy artillery range of the rebel position.

Vinegar Hill lies on the eastern outskirts of Enniscorthy, south of the Oulart road. It looks defensible enough from the west, but 'from the east all appearance of elevation disappears, and the whole hill lies vulnerable from that side' (Charles Dickson, *The Wexford Rising in 1798, etc.*). The United Irishmen had done nothing to improve its defences, apart from hanging their green flag and tree of liberty from the ruinous windmill near the summit:

> … the vast hedges and ditches which surround it on three sides and which should have been levelled to the ground for at least a cannon shot, or half a mile … were all left untouched. The English forces [sic] availing themselves of these defences advanced from field to field, bringing with them their cannon, which they placed … under cover of the hedges and fences, whilst our men were exposed to a terrible fire … without being able to drive them back from their strongholds in these fields.
>
> Miles Byrne (émigré soldier of fortune)

Reports of 30,000 insurgents double their likely numbers. Deducting a few thousand combatants in

Goff's Bridge

	Winner	*Loser*
Opponents	British	United Irishmen
Commanders	Major General [Sir] John Moore	Father Philip Roche
Numbers	*c.*1300	5000–6000
Losses	55	200–300

Vinegar Hill

	Winner	*Loser*
Opponents	British	United Irishmen
Commanders	Lieutenant General Gerard Lake Major General Henry Johnson Major General Francis Needham	Anthony Perry Edward Roche
Numbers	10,000	*c.*15,000
Losses	95	unknown

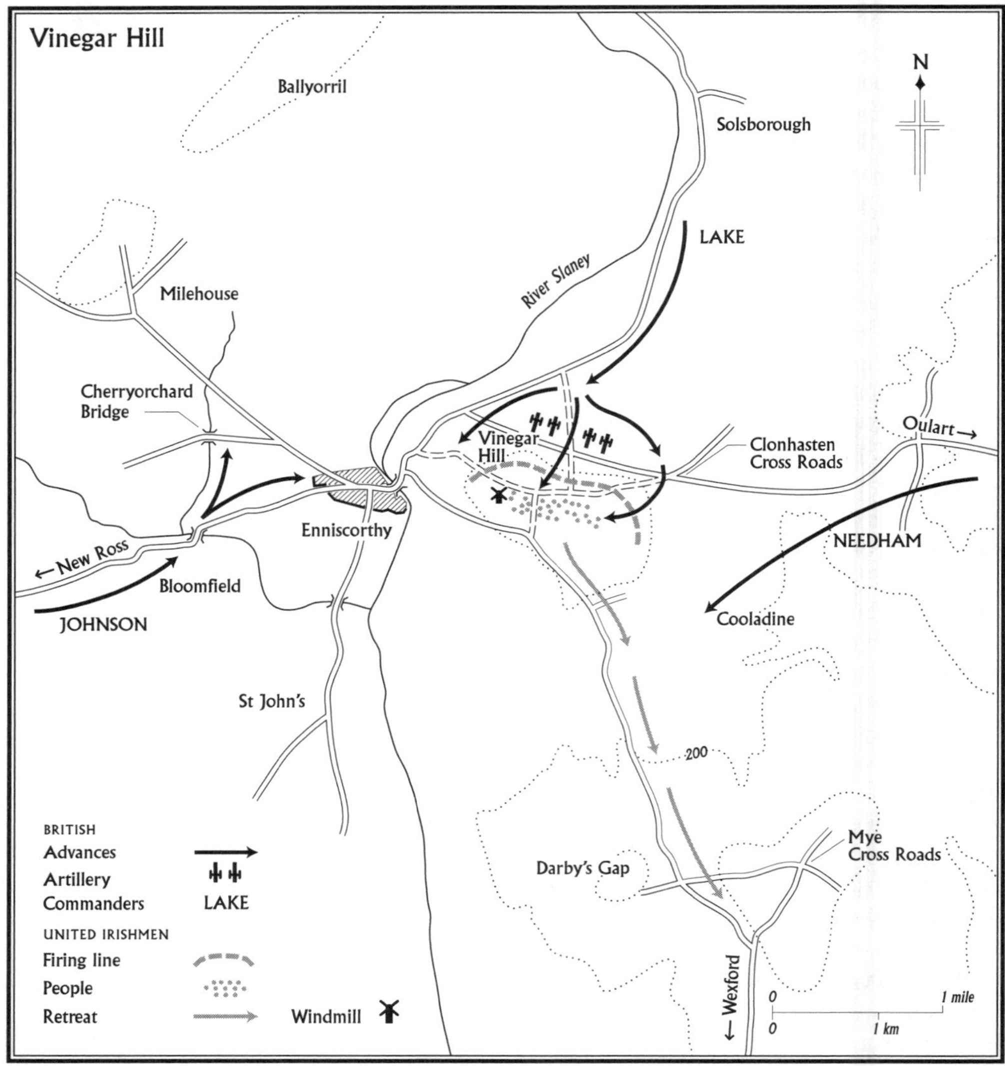

Enniscorthy, 10,000 pikemen would fit comfortably between Vinegar Hill's two high points, musket men lining a ditch at the foot of the hill, whence they kept up a very smart fire. Half a dozen cannon were available 'to vomit forth the thunder of rebellion', but their rhetorical effect exceeded their physical value. Oddly, no account refers to fighting along the high-banked lane across the hilltop, just north of the summit, an obvious last line of defence.

The 12 British guns north of Vinegar Hill opened fire at 4 a.m., causing heavy casualties among the crowds on the open summit. A large body of insurgents forced their way down the east end of the hill, 'but the Light Brigade under Colonel Campbell who

Directions

Vinegar Hill *See the National 1798 Visitor Centre in Enniscorthy, before crossing the bridge to pass south of Vinegar Hill, turning left and left again to see the windmill and view the battlefield from the car park at the top. Also see a monument to Father Clinch between Darby's Gap and Mye's Cross, where he fell.*

occupied that post saluted them with a shower of hail stones something harder than dried peas, drove them back and pursued them up the hill' (Sergeant Archibald M'laren, Dumbarton Fencibles). West of Enniscorthy, General Johnson captured Bloomfield and Cherryorchard Bridge by 7 a.m., and then cleared the town, 'pikemen disputing the streets, and their musketry firing on the advancing troops from the windows' (Maxwell, *History of the Irish Rebellion*). There was still no sign of Roche's southern insurgent army.

Crammed together on Vinegar Hill, the United Irishmen presented an ever denser target to the guns below. About 9 a.m. they withdrew down the old Wexford road through Darby Gap, covered by a rearguard action led by Father Thomas Clinch, galloping up and down upon a white horse. Watching from the top of a ditch Sergeant M'laren described 'a general foot race ... among the Croppies' as British infantry stormed the hill, 'every man firing as he thought proper, and so eager ... to get at the enemy that the swiftest man was the foremost regardless of any order'.

Needham's brigade, which included the Dumbartons, had reached the eastern foot of Vinegar Hill, probably near Cooladine, but from exhaustion or confused orders it failed to intercept the fleeing rebels. Army wits spoke of 'Needham's Gap' and 'General Needless'. British cavalry on the other hand are said to have cut down 500 stragglers, strewing the road south with bodies for two and a half miles (4 km). Lake's biographer understated insurgent losses at 300, the general himself reporting, 'the numbers killed yesterday were very great indeed'. He admitted losing 95 officers and men, against Maxwell's figure of 20 British dead, 68 wounded and 6 missing. An early battlefield visitor found numerous burial pits, 'actually elastic as we stood upon them'.

Moore reached Wexford late on the 21st, averting a general massacre of loyalists. Many United Irishmen just went home. Others fled to the north and east, pursued by flying columns through Wicklow into Kildare, and beyond. Their last formed body was scattered on 14 July at Ballyboghil, near today's Dublin airport.

Directions

Goff's Bridge *Turn left off the R736 7 miles (11 km) southwest of New Ross along a minor road for Foulkesmill. The battlefield is around the crossroads 1 mile (1.6 km) past Foulkesmill.*

Castlebar Races, Monday 27 August 1798

Ireland, Co. Mayo, DS31 M1492

The only French troops to land in Ireland in any numbers during the Ninety-Eight were the 50 officers and 1000 men of General Humbert's expedition, which descended on Killala Bay in the remote northwest of Connacht, on 22 August. The nickname of their first action suggests what the French might have achieved had they intervened sooner, or in greater strength.

Humbert's orders were to await reinforcements, but he also needed to expand his beachhead. On 25 August he occupied Ballina, 7 miles (11 km) from Killala, continuing southwards on the 26th. There were two routes from Ballina to Castlebar, Co. Mayo's chief town. British troops blocked the mail coach road east of Lough Conn through Foxford, so Humbert took a mountain track to the west, through Crossmolina and Lahardaun to the variously spelt Barnageeha Pass, 7 miles (11 km) north of Castlebar. Lashed by rain, his troops left one of their two light guns on the mountainside, but at 8 a.m. next morning they reached Slievenagark, a ridge north of

Castlebar Races

	Winner	*Loser*
Opponents	Franco-Irish	British
Commanders	General Joseph Amable Humbert	Lieutenant General Gerard Lake General Francis Hutchinson
Numbers	1540	1700
Losses	unknown	366

Directions

Castlebar is 10 miles (17 km) east of Westport on the N5. Take the R310 Lough Conn road north from the town centre, and fork left almost immediately to the British position on Sion Hill. Mount Humbert is 1200 yards (1100 m) further north up the Barnageeha road. A granite obelisk along a minor road past the golf course commemorates the cavalry killed at French Hill (M1785).

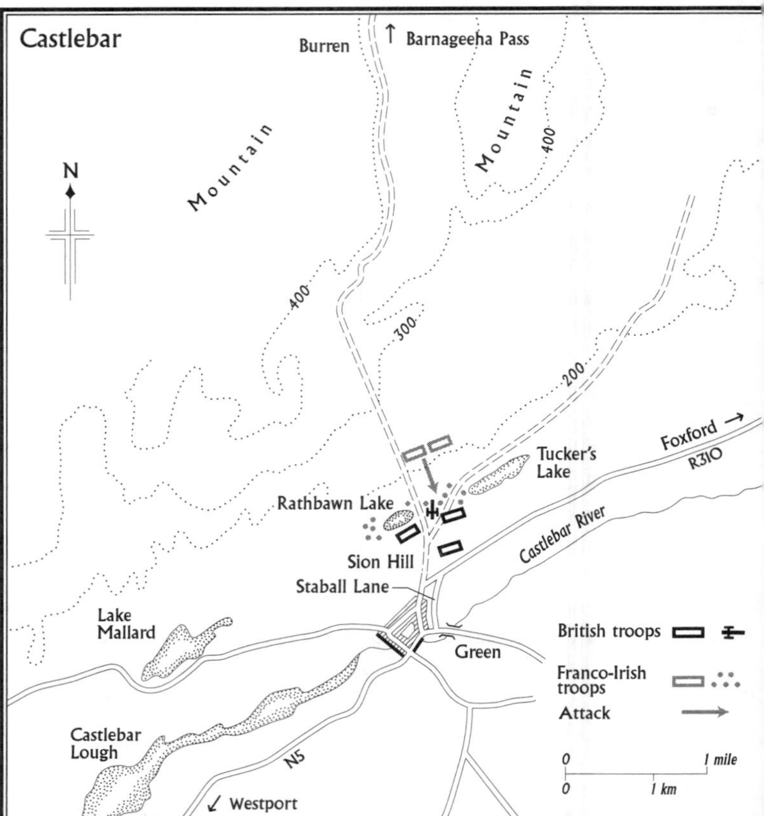

Castlebar, known ever since as Mount Humbert.

Much has been made of Humbert's unexpected line of advance, but there is no evidence that this affected the battle's outcome. A loyalist farmer from the Burren had warned the British of the enemy approach, giving them ample time to occupy a position General Hutchinson had previously marked out at Sion Hill, on Castlebar's northern outskirts. General Lake had recently taken overall command, but left Hutchinson's dispositions unaltered.

The British extended across the Barnageeha road about a mile (1.6 km) from the town centre, between Tucker's Lake and Rathbawn Lake. The line ran east–west along a range of rocky heights, commanding the rising ground where Humbert stood, compelling him to advance 800–1200 yards (730–1100 m) under artillery fire. The ground between the armies has changed little: a rolling plain intersected by rough pathways, stone walls and hedges, with tracts of bogland, furze, and bracken.

Estimates of British numbers vary wildly. Humbert claimed he beat 6400; Hutchinson reported only 1700, which Sir Henry McAnally, historian of the Irish militia, broke down into 500 cavalry, 1100 infantry and a few gunners. They were drawn up as two close-order lines, 'in the true Dundas style': Longford and Kilkenny militia in front with detachments of the regular 6th Foot and the Prince of Wales's Fencibles on their right; and Fraser Highland Fencibles and Galway Yeomanry in support. Detachments of regular and paramilitary cavalry stood behind the front line. Three guns were right of the road, and two on the left. Humbert had 800 French infantry, 700 Irish auxiliaries, a light gun and 40 light cavalry.

Initially Humbert attacked down the road in close order, a massed column of Irish volunteers in the centre, flanked by parties of French grenadiers. The latter took cover from the British artillery, but the Irish pressed on bravely, until at 100 yards (90 m) the defending gunners blew great lanes through their ranks with case-shot, 'balls and bullets fell everywhere like hail whereupon the survivors of the desperate fire broke and dispersed' (Captain Jobit, French grenadier officer). A second attack shielded by cattle also failed when the terrified beasts stampeded back through the Franco-Irish ranks.

Humbert now changed his approach and advanced in open order, 'deploying rapidly from his centre with open files, until he formed line, mostly in rank entire, nearly parallel with the royal [i.e. British] position' (Maxwell, *History of the Irish Rebellion*). Against this attenuated target, the defenders' fire had little effect. Conflicting accounts obscure exactly what happened next. Shaken by the steady advance of the French, the defending militia may have opened fire too soon, panicked and fled pell-mell through Castlebar, leaving their gunners to be cut down. Alternatively, French skirmishers infiltrated across the British front through broken ground, turned their left and shot up the Kilkennys and Longfords from beyond Lake Rathbawn, precipitating their collapse. Other accounts say the British cavalry broke first, trampling their infantry as they galloped down Staball Lane, across the bridge into Castlebar's main street, and south across the Green: 'Like a dam bursting its banks,' wrote a resident, 'a mixture of soldiers of all kinds rushed in at every avenue.' Some Frasers and Longfords made a stand in the Market Square and at the bridge, until dislodged by Humbert's few cavalry. The French were too tired for a protracted pursuit, but some British cavalrymen did not stop before Tuam, 30 miles (48 km) away.

The French wildly exaggerated English casualties. Most historians prefer English estimates of 53 killed, 34 wounded and 279 missing. Many of the latter changed sides, literally turning their coats inside out. Humbert's own losses were unsustainably high: 40 Frenchmen killed and 80 wounded, or 186 all told, depending on one's source. This included a few hussars killed at French Hill, 3 miles (5 km) southeast of Castlebar. Nobody bothered to record losses among the Irish insurgents.

Castlebar remains one of the most ignominious defeats in British military history, although a contemporary comparison with Saratoga was exaggerated. Humbert was a long way from France, unable to profit from risings in Westmeath and Longford before they were crushed. Soon he would be enmeshed in a web of hostile forces, vastly superior in quantity if not quality.

Ballinamuck, Saturday 8 September 1798

Ireland, Co. Longford, DS34 N1891–1990

The otherwise obscure village of Ballinamuck witnessed the last land battle of the Ninety-Eight, to date the last conventional action on Irish soil, or anywhere else in the North Atlantic Archipelago. Today a statue of a wounded pikeman recalls the rebellion's heroic tradition, while a garden of remembrance expresses modern hopes for peace.

Humbert's victory at Castlebar (see above) did not provoke the expected rebellion across Connacht. To keep the initiative he marched northeast into Sligo, turning southwards towards insurgencies reported in Westmeath and Longford. Humbert crossed the Shannon at Ballintra on 7 September, British cavalry hustling him eastwards through Fenagh. At 6 that evening Humbert's weary troops stopped at Cloone, an astonishing halfway between Killala Bay and Dublin.

The British had massed overwhelming numbers against their nimble opponent. Lake was close behind with 14,000 men; Lord Cornwallis, recently appointed viceroy, was on Humbert's right at Carrick-on-Shannon with another 15,000. Late on the 7th Cornwallis marched to interpose between Humbert and the still smouldering revolt in the Midlands, ordering Lake to hang upon the enemy rear. Humbert had come 105 miles (168 km) in four days, and his exhausted troops did not leave Cloone until 5 a.m. on the 8th. They took the mountain road past Keeldra Lough, dumping artillery ammunition as they went, to reach Ballinamuck between 8 and 9 a.m. The rearguard was about a mile (1.6 km) behind, at Kiltycrevagh, when Lake's leading troops overtook them.

Humbert had about 850 French and 1500 Irish, some in French uniforms, others in corduroy knee breeches and frieze tailcoats with brass buttons. Two guns remained of those taken at Castlebar, the others having been jettisoned to hasten the march. Cornwallis had 5000 men at Ballinalee (St Johnstown) 6 miles (10 km) ahead of Humbert, while Lake had nearly as many behind him, though only the cavalry and two battalions saw action.

Three major features cross the battlefield, running down from northeast to southwest, at right angles to the road through Ballinamuck. Fighting occurred around each in turn:

(1) Kiltycrevagh ridge to the north (N1892), where the Cloone road passes between two loughs, before running steeply down the hill towards Ballinamuck. A local farmer reckoned in the 1930s that Humbert should have fought there, flanked by the lakes.

(2) A stream between Kiltycrevagh and the village, running through a solid-looking morass, in which French grenadiers sank waist deep.

(3) An area of high ground to the southeast, Shanmullagh Hill (N1991), from which projects a round spur east of the village, sometimes called Humbert's Hill.

The commander of Lake's advanced guard was Robert Craufurd, 'Black Bob' of Peninsular War fame. He gave Humbert no time to organize his defence. Riding boldly up to the 200-strong French rearguard 'on the height of the road' at Kiltycrevagh, Craufurd begged its commander 'not to sacrifice the heroes of Castlebar'. According to British accounts the French surrendered at once. French accounts describe a brief exchange of fire, after commander and men had been separated on the pretext of discussing terms. Either way the rearguard promptly went into the bag.

Captain Jobit's French grenadier company was further down the road, near the future site of the chapel. They faced down some cavalry and tried to turn the British flank, only to stick fast in the bog. Regaining the road, Jobit found the valley filling up with British troops, and was also forced to surrender. His men 'fought like lions', but, as he later said, 'what could these 400 Frenchmen do against the 28,000 troops that surrounded them? [sic]'.

Humbert deployed his remaining 400 French and half the Irish behind Ballinamuck, on Shanmullagh Hill. After Jobit's surrender, 'General' Blake withdrew down the road with the remaining Irish and two cannon towards Gaig Cross, a mile (1.6 km) southeast of the village. Repulsed in a frontal attack, Lake passed troops around to his left. Unobserved below the swell of Shanmullagh Hill, the cavalry suddenly burst out of the fold in the ground, at which point the French as suddenly 'threw up their arms with caps on them, yielding themselves prisoners'. Posing to the last, Humbert was taken sword in hand.

Humbert's Irish, for whom surrender was not an option, withdrew into the boggy ground behind the hill, presumably where the Irish Ordnance Survey marks the battle (N1990). Charged in front by British dragoons, and under fire from both flanks, they stood it for half an hour and then ran. Blake led his pikemen across to assist, too late to avert disaster. Gunner Magee, lately of the Longford militia, exchanged fire with British artillery by the chapel, reportedly exploding a limber and mowing down a column advancing in fours. Running out of conventional shot, he fired off a load of broken iron pots from nearby cottages, then stood by his gun until overrun.

At midday some 500 insurgents lay dead on the

Ballinamuck

	Winner	*Loser*
Opponents	British	Franco-Irish
Commanders	Lieutenant General Gerard Lake	General Joseph Amable Humbert (p)
	Lieutenant Colonel Robert Craufurd	George Blake (x)
Numbers	*c.*5000	2350
Losses	*c.*100	*c.*1450

field, an indefinite number cut down as they fled. A loyalist commented, 'Tis incredible the number of them, exclusive of the French, lay on the field ... we had a most glorious day.' Over 100 insurgents were captured, many to be hanged later, including Blake and Gunner Magee. James O'Neill, whose great-uncle fought in the battle, had never heard of any French casualties, though the British captured 96 officers and 748 men. Lake's report minimized the fighting's duration and severity – half an hour, 3 killed and 16 wounded or missing. Tradition inflated British losses to about 100.

Humbert and his men travelled back to Dublin by canal for repatriation, assuring their captors of their shared contempt for their ragamuffin allies. Only a handful of United Irishmen remained under arms at Killala, to be liquidated in the usual depressing fashion on 23 September.

Directions

Ballinamuck is 10 miles (16 km) north of Longford, left of the R198, which runs through the eastern fringes of the battlefield. The old police barracks contains a Battlefield Centre, and signs identify key sites round the village.

Lough Swilly (Warren's Action), **12 October 1798**

Naval, North Atlantic, DS2

Admiral Warren's capture of the *Hoche* off Tory Island ended all prospects of further French intervention in the Ninety-Eight. Commodore Bompart reached the place with which the battle is commonly identified only when his flagship was towed into Lough Swilly as a British prize.

Bompart left Brest on the evening of 16 September, eight days after General Humbert's capitulation at Ballinamuck (see above). His squadron carried 2800 troops, masses of warlike stores, and Wolfe Tone, the United Irishmen's exiled leader. British cruisers dogged his movements until Warren caught him up at daybreak on 11 October, five or six leagues (some 15–18 miles, or 24–29 km) west of Tory Island, on Ireland's extreme northwestern coast. The opposing squadrons comprised:

BRITISH
SHIPS OF THE LINE *Canada* (74 guns), *Foudroyant* (80), *Robust* (74)
FRIGATES *Amelia* (44), *Anson* (44), *Ethalion* (38), *Magnanime* (44), *Melampus* (36)

FRENCH
(* denotes captured):
SHIPS OF THE LINE *Hoche* (74)*
FRIGATES (40-GUN) *Immortalité**, *Loire**, *Romaine*
FRIGATES (36-GUN) *Bellone**, *Coquille**, *Embuscade**, *Résolue**, *Sémillante*
SCHOONER *Biche*

Warren chased Bompart eastwards, and at nightfall the French were 10–12 miles (16–19 km) ahead of HMS *Canada*. After dark the wind blew hard from the north-northwest, the weather very bad and boisterous, 'with a hollow sea'. *Hoche* lost her main topmast, bringing down the fore and mizzen topgallant masts, and shredding her mainsail. Soon afterwards *Résolue* sprang a leak. Unwilling to fight in this crippled state, Bompart turned and ran southwest, back past the British, hoping to land his troops anywhere that might offer. *Résolue*'s captain was ordered to create a diversion by running ashore and burning blue lights, but failed to do so. Overnight the wind dropped, carrying Bompart less far to leeward than he expected. At daybreak on the 12th (5.30 a.m.) he found British warships close on every side, except to windward, closing every avenue of escape.

Contemporary naval historians disagreed on the course of the action. Rear Admiral Charles Ekins's *Naval Battles of Great Britain* (1828) followed a sketch drawn many years later by *Robust*'s captain to put the French and some of the British ships on the port tack at first light, heading east. Captain William James's *Naval History of Great Britain* (1837) relied on contemporary logbooks, which put both squadrons on the starboard tack, heading west. This agrees with Warren's dispatch and a midshipman's journal from HMS *Foudroyant* published in the 1920s. The weight

Lough Swilly

	Winner	*Loser*
Opponents	British	French
Commanders	Rear Admiral Sir John Borlase Warren	Commodore Jean Baptiste Bompart (p)
Numbers	8 ships	10 ships
Losses	0 ships; 88 men	7 ships; 462 men

of evidence, therefore, supports the view that both squadrons were on the starboard tack. Bearings given for the start of the action are also contradictory:

> From HMS *Canada* to the Rosses: five leagues south-southwest, putting her uncomfortably near dry land, if not ashore on Tory Island.
>
> From HMS *Foudroyant* to the Aran Islands: six leagues south-by-east, locating her safely out in the Atlantic.

The latter appears more likely as the Rosses are obscured from the direction given from HMS *Canada* by Bloody Foreland, a feature named for the colour of its vegetation rather than nearby events.

Following James, it would appear *Robust* and *Magnanime* were directly astern of the French before a variable to light northwesterly wind. *Canada* was on the enemy's lee bow, and *Foudroyant* on their lee beam, cutting them off from the coast. The other British frigates lay between *Robust* and *Foudroyant*, except *Anson*, which was out of sight to the south, having rolled out her main topmast the previous evening. About 7 a.m. Bompart formed the eight French ships still in company into a straggling line ahead: *Sémillante*, *Romaine*, *Bellone*, *Immortalité*, *Loire*, *Hoche*, *Coquille* and *Embuscade*. Warren then ordered his ships to close, *Robust* leading, 'the rest of the ships to form in succession in rear of the van'. *Robust* exchanged shots with the sternmost French frigates, then bore down to engage *Hoche*'s leeward side at 8.50. *Magnanime* followed, ranging to leeward of *Robust*'s disengaged port side, before turning into the wind to gain a raking position across the French flagship's bow. The three Frenchmen immediately ahead of *Hoche* bore out of line to rake *Magnanime* during this manoeuvre, but soon desisted, making sail to the southwest, away from the action.

Effectively abandoned, *Hoche* surrendered at 10.50 after a heroic resistance – her masts tottering, 25 guns dismounted, 5 (1.5 m) of water in the hold, and 270 of her 1237 crew dead or wounded. *Embuscade* struck her colours soon afterwards, most of the British ships pursuing, while *Robust* and *Magnanime* stood by their prizes. Two more French ships had struck their colours by nightfall, and another three were captured on the way home.

British casualties were 13 killed and 75 wounded, reflecting their material superiority. Their ships crowded with troops, the French suffered disproportionately. *Hoche* nearly sank before reaching harbour, but was later renamed, serving the Royal Navy as HMS *Donegal*. Wolfe Tone was captured and condemned to death for treason, but cut his throat first, dying on 19 November. With this gruesome sequel, Warren's action not only frustrated the last French invasion of British or Irish territory, but brought the United Irishmen movement to its tragic end.

Directions

Tory Island is notoriously inaccessible, but may be reached by ferry from Bunbeag and Magheroarty in the summer. The battle occurred west of the island.

PART EIGHT

RIFLE AND RADAR

Britain's Last Battles? 1916 – 40

The 120 years following the Act of Union form a unique period in the history of Britain and Ireland. For the only time in its history, the North Atlantic Archipelago was a single political entity: the United Kingdom of Great Britain and Ireland. This unprecedented unity coincided with an almost total absence of conventional military conflict from British or Irish soil. Frequency of battles fell from roughly one every five years, as experienced since Julius Caesar's invasion in 55 BC, to less than one a century.

Battles did not die out in the wider world, where British forces saw more than their share of fighting. The Royal Navy, however, ensured the security of the home base, its maritime supremacy unchallenged for nearly a century after Trafalgar (1805). European competitors were distracted by the aftermath of the Napoleonic Wars: internal dissension in France and Spain, wars of national unification in Germany and Italy. At home, the pre-revolutionary tensions of the 1840s were contained by Methodism, professional civilian policing and gradual reform. Even Ireland, the least happy part of the United Kingdom, preferred the constitutional resistance of Daniel O'Connell's 'Monster Meetings' in the 1830s, which ended with three cheers for Queen Victoria, to the disastrous bloodshed of 1798. The Battle of Widow MacCormack's Cabbage Patch (1848) and the fiasco of the 1867 Fenian Rising discredited the men of violence for another generation. From the 1880s, the Westminster government held out the promise of Home Rule and moved towards a resolution of the land question by helping Irish tenant farmers to buy out their landlords.

Two factors threatened this benign strategic environment in the early 20th century.

New naval powers, Germany in particular, threatened the United Kingdom's strategic isolation. In Ireland, Westminster proved unable to satisfy the national majority's wish for limited self-government from Dublin, in the face of entrenched opposition from Ulster's Protestants, a local majority in the six counties that now form Northern Ireland. Both sides raised and equipped private armies, 100,000 Ulster Volunteers against 180,000 Irish Volunteers. Only the patriotic fervour that accompanied the outbreak of the First World War in August 1914 averted civil war.

A century of peace had seen more dramatic changes in Britain and Ireland than the preceding millennium. As the United Kingdom became the world's first industrial superpower, its population trebled from 15.5 million in 1801 to 47.4 million in 1911. Only Ireland held out against the trend, as mass emigration followed the Famine (1845–9). The Irish population fell from a peak of nearly 7 million to 4.4 million on the eve of the First World War. Industrial development and urbanization transformed the British landscape, though Ireland was emptier than in the 1790s. The immediate effect of this upon battlefield history to the east of St George's Channel was to encourage antiquarian interest in sites threatened by urban sprawl. West of the Irish Sea, a less developed countryside would provide refuge for IRA flying columns.

The Industrial Revolution transformed the military art. Steam power freed navies from dependence on the wind, and armies from the limitations of their soldiers' legs. Ranges and rates of fire increased by a factor of five. Rifled small arms and field artillery reached out to about 1000 and 6000 yards (900 and 5400 m) respectively, firing up to ten rounds a minute. Together they swept horsed cavalry off battlefields that the mounted arm had dominated since Hastings (1066). Armour reappeared after two centuries of absence, to protect soldiers from the hail of steel. Armoured lorries roamed Dublin's streets months before the British Army's first official use of tanks on the Somme, in September 1916.

Armies had still not absorbed the military consequences of the first Industrial Revolution when a second technological revolution began, with aircraft and electronic communications. No military aircraft circled Dublin at Easter 1916, but both sides used wireless: the government to summon reinforcements, the rebels to broadcast propaganda. The new technologies would be fundamental to Britain's defence in the 1940s.

Mainland Britain escaped invasion and civil war throughout the 20th century, despite two world wars. Ireland was less fortunate. The First World War encouraged a handful of activists to seek their long-deferred freedom through violence, while British attention was focused elsewhere. The Irish Volunteers had split in August 1914: 170,000 National Volunteers followed the constitutional nationalists in supporting the British war effort, while the remaining 10,000, heavily penetrated by the secret Irish Republican Brotherhood, prepared for insurrection.

The Easter Rising of 1916 was the only land engagement of any size fought in Britain and Ireland in the 20th century. By standards of the time it was insignificant, coinciding very briefly with the Battle of Verdun, which had just entered its third month. British reprisals united a previously sceptical Catholic population in support of the surviving revolutionary nationalists, who pursued their objectives under the Sinn Féin label, literally 'Ourselves Alone'.

The Anglo-Irish War (September 1919–July 1921) was fought entirely by unconventional means: hunger strikes, murder and ambush – the modern equivalent of Gaelic tactics at Clais an Chro (1169) and Athankip (1270). It was ended by the Anglo-Irish Treaty of December 1921, which dissolved the Act of Union, separating Britain from Ireland, and the Protestant Unionists of Northern Ireland from the Irish Free State, later known as Eire or the Irish Republic. The Civil War between the Free State and dissident anti-Treaty republicans (28 June 1922–24 May 1923) was no more productive of old-fashioned battlefields than the Anglo-Irish War.

The formation of the Royal Air Force on 1 April 1918 reflected the air arm's vital role in the First World War. Aviation developments over the next twenty years shifted responsibility for Britain's frontline defence from the Royal Navy to the RAF. A year into the Second World War RAF Fighter Command proved emphatically that the bomber need not always get through. Appropriately named the Battle of Britain, the conflict's duration and geographical spread so far eclipsed earlier scuffles as to stretch the concept of 'battle' beyond all meaning. The Battle of Britain did not win the Second World War, but it did spare the country from becoming the scene of more localized fighting.

Dublin (the Easter Rising), **Monday–Saturday 24–29 April 1916**

Ireland, Dublin, DS50 O1534

Few events have come to possess the significance for Anglo-Irish relations as the Dublin Easter Rising of 1916, although this was less than obvious at the time. Far from being a national uprising, the rebellion was the action of a narrow clique, whose martyrdom lent inadvertent legitimacy to their cause.

When the First World War broke out, John Redmond's Irish Nationalist Party appeared finally to have secured a measure of self-government with the Home Rule Act of 18 September 1914, although its operation was suspended for the duration of hostilities. A few revolutionary nationalists of the Irish Revolutionary Brotherhood (IRB) were mindful, however, that England's danger was Ireland's opportunity. They resolved to overthrow British rule by force, using those Irish Volunteers who had rejected Redmond's call to support the imperial war effort. Their plans were concealed from most of the Volunteers, including Eoin MacNeill, the commander-in-chief.

Germany agreed to assist a rising at Easter 1916, but on Good Friday the Royal Navy intercepted the promised shipment of 20,000 rifles off Co. Kerry in Tralee Bay. The same day the IRB's international fixer, Sir Roger Casement, was arrested nearby at Banna Strand, landing from a German U-boat. This double blow entirely disrupted the insurgents' plans. Brought into the picture at the last minute, MacNeill insisted on cancelling Easter Sunday's manoeuvres, which had been intended as the springboard for a general rising. Patrick Pearse, MacNeill's director of organization, issued secret orders for a more limited rising on Monday, confined almost exclusively to the capital. A leading figure in the IRB, Pearse was obsessed with poetic notions of a 'blood sacrifice' to revive the cause of Irish freedom, which the Home Rulers had sold out.

Despite its presentation as a 'Poet's Insurrection', the Easter Rising was well executed, within the limitations of the numbers available to the insurgents. Fighting in built-up areas favours a weaker force on the defensive. Cities provide cover and concealment for defending troops, while channelling the attacker along well-defined routes, easily blocked by barricades and overlooked from bullet-proof buildings. The dense terrain provides numerous alternative positions, easily reached by pre-arranged escape routes, cut through intervening buildings. If driven from one position, the defenders can fight on from another.

Central Dublin is cut in half by the River Liffey, and protected north and south by the Royal and Grand Canals. All three are significant obstacles, only crossable at their bridges. The rebels occupied strong mutually supporting positions either side of the Liffey, surrounding the centre of government at Dublin Castle, which they cut off from numerous barracks around the capital, and the railway stations through which British reinforcements would come. The Volunteers had no heavy weapons, only rifles and pistols. No written details of their plans survive, one survivor stating they were no more than 'the surprise seizure of previously selected buildings, fortifying them as best we could, and holding them as long as possible' (Commandant W.J. Brennan Whitmore).

About 1000 insurgents turned out on Easter Monday, including 220 militant trade unionists of James Connolly's Irish Citizen Army. Another 800 joined later in the week. They were distributed as follows, the Volunteers organized as four notional battalions:

NORTH OF THE LIFFEY

1st Battalion: 150 at the Four Courts and Mendicity Institute, King and Church Streets

HQ: 210 in the GPO at the corner of Henry Street and Sackville (now O'Connell) Street

SOUTH OF THE LIFFEY

2nd Battalion: 150 at Jacobs' Biscuit Factory, Kevin and Camden Streets

3rd Battalion: 130 at Boland's Bakery, covering Mount Bridge over the Grand Canal

4th Battalion: 150 at the South Dublin Union Workhouse in James's Street

Citizen Army: 180 around St Stephen's Green and City Hall

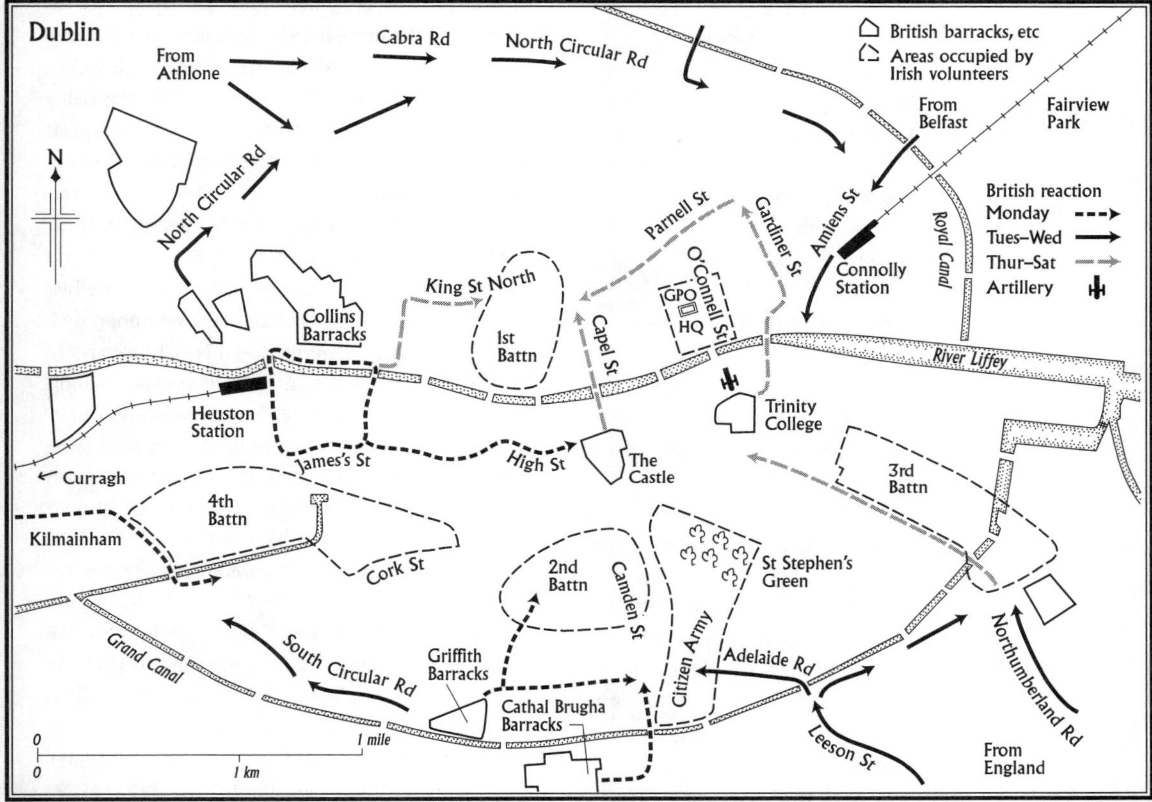

Another 50 Volunteers attacked Dublin Castle. The chief deficiency in their dispositions was their failure to hold Trinity College, overlooking the GPO from beyond the river. Its occupation by the British would allow their artillery to fire directly at rebel headquarters. None of the insurgent positions fell to direct assault, being either set alight by shell fire, or surrendered on the commanders' orders.

The British outnumbered the insurgents from the start, and rapidly assembled forces to crush the rising. The Dublin garrison comprised 2400 fighting troops, of whom 400 were immediately available, under arms. Most were on leave for the bank holiday, including their commander Major General C.B. Friend. Communications were faster than in earlier Irish rebellions, the British calling up reinforcements by telephone, and via the naval transmitter at Kingstown (now Dún Laoghaire). They arrived as follows:

Monday: Curragh Mobile Column	1600
Tuesday: Detachments from other Irish garrisons	2600
Wednesday: 178th Brigade (4 battalions) from England	4000
Thursday: 176th Brigade (4 battalions) fromEngland	400

Directions

Key locations given in text. See bullet marks left outside the restored GPO in O'Connell Street. In 1916 Collins Barracks in Benburb Street was the Royal Barracks, housing the 10th Royal Dublin Fusiliers. Built in 1701, it is now an annexe of the National Museum. Fourteen of the executed leaders are buried north of the barracks, in Arbour Hill Cemetery.

Dublin		
	Winners	*Losers*
Opponents	British	Irish Volunteers
Commanders	Lieutenant General Sir John Maxwell Brigadier General W.H.M. Lowe	Patrick Pearse (x) James Connolly (x)
Numbers	*c.*14,600	*c.*1800
Losses	532	196

The infantry were initially from Irish regiments. English reinforcements came from 59th (North Midland) Division, a Territorial Force unit still under training. Many accounts speak of 'heavy artillery', but the only guns deployed were four 18-pounder quick-firers from the Curragh, a naval 1-pounder on a lorry, and two 12-pounder guns mounted on the Admiralty's armed steam yacht *Helga*, in the Liffey. The British Army's massive expansion since 1914 had diluted the quality of the troops, who came from depots and second-line units. The Volunteers were better shots, fighting on home ground, advantages reflected in the casualty figures.

The first shots were fired at noon, when Irish Citizen Army men killed a policeman at Upper Castle Yard Gate and captured the guardroom. Half an hour later the Irish tricolour was hoisted outside the GPO, and Pearse proclaimed the Republic, in the name of God and the dead generations from whom Ireland received her old tradition of nationhood. Just after 1 p.m. some Lancers rode down Sackville Street, probably by accident, and were dispersed by rifle fire. Insurgents at the Four Courts and the South Dublin Union prevented some British troops from reaching the Castle, but others got through. Yet more began to throw a cordon around rebel positions.

The process of isolation continued next day as more reinforcements arrived, and Brigadier General Lowe from the Curragh took command. By Tuesday afternoon the British had divided the insurgents with a line of posts from Kingsbridge (now Heuston) Station along Victoria Quay and Thomas Street to Trinity College, where they deployed two 18-pounders. Two more field guns destroyed barricades on the Cabra and North Circular Roads, while troops from Belfast pushed in Volunteer outposts from Ballybough and Fairview, establishing the cordon at Amiens Street (now Connolly) Station, northeast of the insurgent enclave.

Wednesday saw the week's heaviest fighting, as 178th Brigade disembarked at Kingstown and advanced towards Dublin in two columns. Its two westerly battalions reached Kilmainham unopposed. The other two, advancing down Northumberland Road with no tactical security, ran into the Boland's Bakery rebels, at the Haddington Road junction. Seventeen riflemen held the British up for hours, inflicting 234 casualties, before they were driven off with grenades and a light naval 'pompom' gun on a truck.

The British tightened the cordon around the insurgent headquarters at the GPO during Thursday and Friday. Generally they avoided frontal attacks on other insurgent positions, concentrating their fire on the rebel leadership. The Trinity College 18-pounders pounded Sackville Street from Butt Bridge and the junction of D'Ollier and College Streets. By Friday evening the target area was well ablaze, the sky over the city centre a mass of flames. Pearse evacuated the GPO at 8.40 p.m. on Friday, moving to temporary headquarters at the Moore Street end of Henry Place. He surrendered next day at 3.45 p.m., much to the surprise of the other insurgents, many of whom had hardly been engaged. Total casualties were approximately:

	Killed	*Wounded*
Troops and police	132	400
Insurgents	76	120
Civilians	300	2000

The salutary effect of General Lowe's prompt suppression of the rising was entirely thrown away by General Maxwell's execution of 15 rebel leaders over the next few weeks. The deaths ended with Connolly on 12 May, shot in a chair because his wounded foot prevented him standing. The Dublin population had regarded the rebels as 'f***ing slackers', and greeted the troops with tea and biscuits. However, British reprisals, followed by the internment of suspected nationalists and anxieties about conscription, turned public opinion in favour of the insurgents. Sinn Féin eliminated Redmond's constitutional Nationalist Party in the 'khaki election' of November 1918, and the refusal by Sinn Féin MPs to sit in the Westminster Parliament set in train the events that would lead to the Anglo-Irish War, and eventual independence.

Battle of Britain, 10 July–31 October 1940

The air battles over southeast England in the summer of 1940 appear to have little in common with other conflicts described in this book, yet the Battle of Britain recalled earlier struggles in many ways. Like medieval knights, a handful of airmen depended on untold numbers of unknown helpers. German pilots pursued a chivalric ideal of personal combat, which no more precluded them burning the houses of the common people over their heads than it had restricted knightly incendiarism. With his usual historical awareness, the British prime minister, Winston Churchill, compared the Battle of Britain with the Armada, which it closely resembles in geographical spread and potential consequence.

The nightmare of an unstoppable bomber offensive had been a major contributory factor to British paralysis in the face of German aggression during the 1930s. By June 1940 German forces had reached the Channel, within sight of England's southern coast. Goering, head of the German air force or Luftwaffe, issued orders for air operations against Britain to start on 30 June, anticipating Hitler's approval of Operation Sealion, the German invasion plan, on 16 July.

The failure of either nightmare or invasion to become reality is attributable to a revolution in air-defence technology during the 1930s. Fast single-engined eight-gunned monoplane fighter aircraft were developed, capable of shooting down any bomber they met, unless prevented by another fighter. RAF Fighter Command deployed two types of fighter in 1940. The Supermarine Spitfire remains indelibly fixed in the public mind as the icon of victory, with its classic lines and speed in excess of 350 mph (560 kph) at 18,000 feet (6000 m). The Hawker Hurricane was slower but more numerous and durable, though it burned easily. At the height of the battle Air Vice Marshal Park recognized the complementary virtues of the two types by scrambling pairs of Hurricane and Spitfire squadrons to tackle German bombers and their fighter escort respectively. The RAF also deployed the Boulton Paul Defiant, a two-seater fighter mounting four machine guns in a rotating turret. It proved a death trap, and was speedily withdrawn from daylight action.

Less exciting than the fighters was the control system that brought them into contact with intruding enemy aircraft in sufficient time and strength to prevent the latter completing their mission. The front end of the system consisted of a chain of coastal radar stations from the Firth of Forth to Land's End, with a west-facing outpost in Pembrokeshire. Inland it was supplemented by the Observer Corps' visual reporting. In July 1940 there were 21 'Chain Home' stations with fixed masts providing long-range detection, supplemented by 30 'Chain Home Low' stations with rotating aerials for tracking ships and low-flying aircraft. Reports of approaching threats were passed through Air Chief Marshal Dowding's headquarters at Bentley Priory in Stanmore, on the edge of London, to the operations rooms of Fighter Command's subordinate groups. These in turn controlled sector stations, each responsible for two to four fighter squadrons at an individual airfield. To gain maximum time to react, the radars were placed on the coast, as far forward as possible, while sector stations generally lay inland. Luftwaffe intelligence never understood the structure or significance of this organization. Although the Germans had radar, the Luftwaffe had never applied it to controlling aerial warfare, or considered how such control should be exercised. Dowding's system was one of the first examples of modern cybernetic warfare, and remains the basis of modern air-defence systems.

The German arrival on the Channel coast probably surprised them as much as everyone else. They were not ready to invade the United Kingdom, and supplemented Sealion with peace feelers, which the British definitively rejected on 22 July. Goering's air offensive was part of the build-up to Sealion. If it succeeded, it might avoid the necessity for a risky Channel crossing in the face of an undefeated Royal Navy. For the first time in history an attempt was to be made to force an enemy to surrender by air power alone.

The conflict's duration is moot. Churchill had first spoken of the forthcoming Battle of Britain on 18 June. Most historians start with the first dogfight involving over 100 aircraft on 10 July. HMSO's account arbitrarily assigned 8 August and 31 October as the start and end dates, though Hitler had indefinitely postponed Sealion on 17 September, and the last significant daylight raid was at Southampton on 5 October. Key dates within the period were *Adlertag*, or Eagle Day, on 13 August, the start of the Luftwaffe's direct attack on Fighter Command, and 15 September, still commemorated as Battle of Britain Day.

The aircraft used in the Battle of Britain moved roughly 100 times faster than leg infantry. The battlefield was correspondingly larger, taking in the whole of southern England, extending on occasion to Portland or Newcastle-upon-Tyne, and the French and Dutch coasts. The brunt of the battle fell upon Park's 11 Group in the southeast, the only area within range of the Luftwaffe's fighter bases in Normandy and the Pas-de-Calais. Park's headquarters, from where he controlled the day-to-day tactical battle, was at Uxbridge in Middlesex, 60 feet (18 m) underground. Geography and the short operating radius of the Luftwaffe's fighters limited 10 and 12 Group in the southwest and Midlands respectively to a supporting role. Further north 13 Group came under attack only once.

Numbers are difficult to assess, and vary over the course of the battle: aircraft and squadrons moved between groups; not all aircraft or pilots were available for operations; and combat damage and the flow of replacements affected daily battle strengths in a manner unknown in earlier, shorter battles. Fighter Command deployed 548 Hurricanes and Spitfires on 1 July 1940, of which 11 Group had 310 in 25 squadrons. By 1 September Park had 259 fighters in 21 squadrons, out of Fighter Command's total of 558. The other key index was the number of operational single-engined fighter pilots, 1200 and 1422 at those dates respectively (Richard Overy, *The Battle*). Britain did not stand entirely alone, and many pilots came from the Commonwealth or countries overrun by Germany. Total Fighter Command air crew engaged throughout the whole battle was 2917. They were the crucial individuals in the immediate battle for air superiority, but Bomber and Coastal Command aircrew ran similar or greater risks attacking German air bases and invasion ports. Total RAF strength in the United Kingdom in October 1940 was 437,473 (Stephen Bungay, *Most Dangerous Enemy*). Most of them had been involved in the Battle of Britain, one way or another.

The Luftwaffe did not possess the superiority of numbers or equipment usually attributed to it. Designed for army cooperation, it was unsuited to the task of bringing Britain to its knees independently. It was operating from improvised airfields in recently occupied France, and had no idea of the opposition it faced. Numbers of aircraft were insufficient. Churchill's famous reference to 'the Few' on 20 August was concerned more with the disproportionate debt of gratitude owed by the many than with the material balance of the opposing forces, though inevitably it has been applied to the latter. The decisive type in a battle for air superiority was the single-engined fighter. Only 702 out of the 2355 Luftwaffe aircraft operational on 10 August, just before *Adlertag*, fell into this category (Hough and Richards: *The Battle of Britain*). The Germans' 998 medium bombers were too slow and poorly armed to face high-performance fighters without escort. The single-engined Ju 87 Stuka dive bombers were a death trap in contested air space, and had to be preserved for ground support during Sealion. The twin-engined Me 110 was ineffective in its assigned role as a long-range fighter escort, requiring protection itself.

The Germans' main asset was their pool of high-

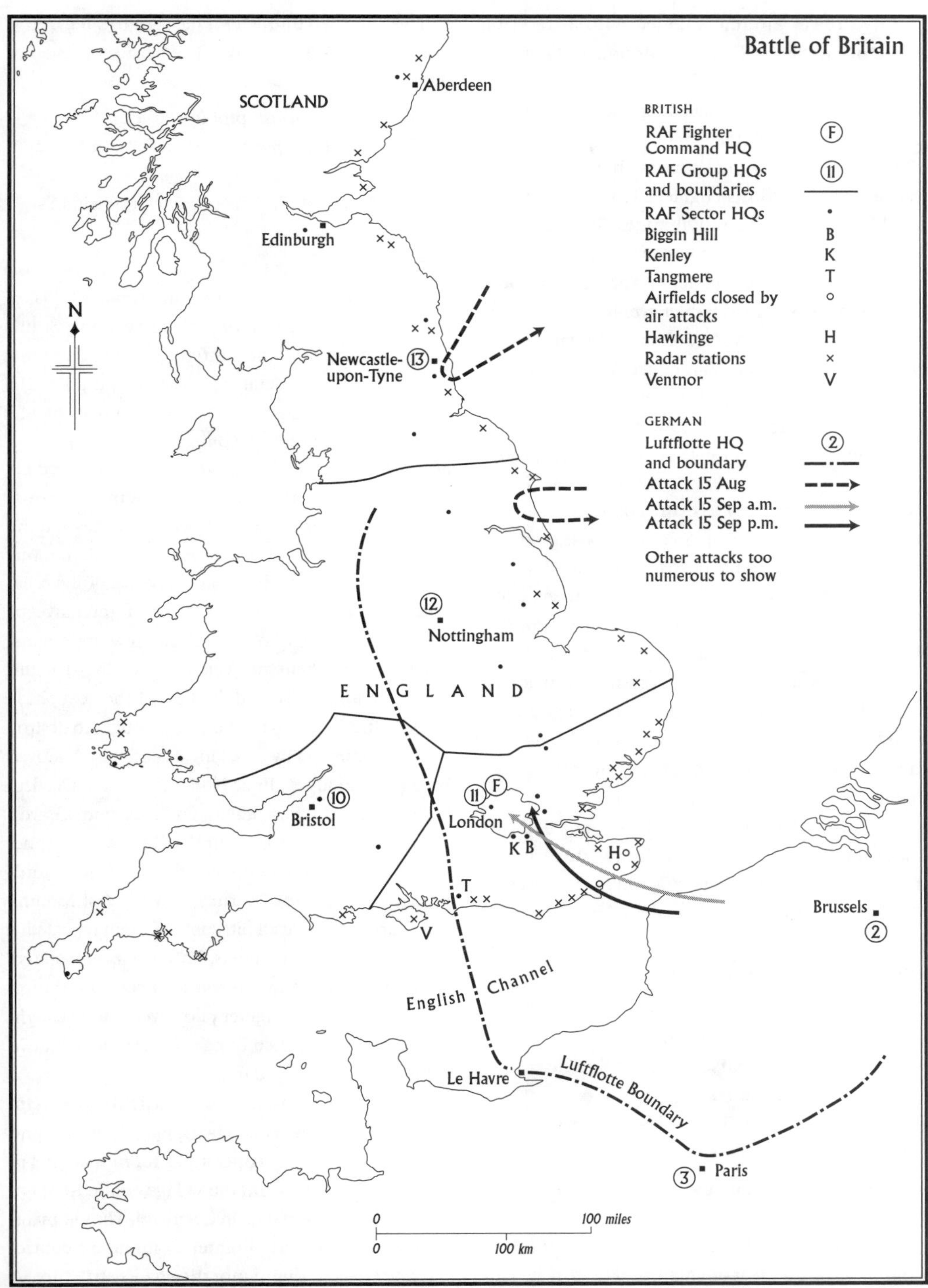

Battle of Britain
BRITISH
RAF Fighter Command HQ
RAF Group HQs and boundaries
RAF Sector HQs
Biggin Hill B
Kenley K
Tangmere T
Airfields closed by air attacks
Hawkinge H
Radar stations
Ventnor V
GERMAN
Luftflotte HQ and boundary
Attack 15 Aug
Attack 15 Sep a.m.
Attack 15 Sep p.m.
Other attacks too numerous to show
SCOTLAND
Aberdeen
Edinburgh
Newcastle-upon-Tyne
Nottingham
ENGLAND
Bristol
London
English Channel
Le Havre
Luftflotte Boundary
Brussels
Paris
0 100 miles
0 100 km

quality prewar aircrew, imbued with a tradition of victory in Spain, Poland and France. Their key weapon system, the Me 109 single-engined fighter, was very good indeed. It had a top speed of 334 mph (534 kph) at 19,000 feet (5800 m), and was more effective in dogfights at altitudes above 20,000 feet than either of the British fighters. However, German bombers operated at lower altitudes, forcing the Me 109s to fly at heights that better suited the opposition, where both the Hurricane and Spitfire could out turn them. German fighter armament was more powerful than the RAF's .303-inch Brownings, the Me 109 mounting two 20-mm cannon firing explosive shells, plus two machine guns.

Superior German tactics were a more serious advantage. RAF squadrons operated in tight groups of three aircraft flying in an inverted 'V' or 'vic', a suicidal formation that German pilots dubbed *Idiotenreihe*. The Luftwaffe flew in *Schwärme*, loose groups of four formed of two pairs or *Rotte*, a system the RAF adopted later as the 'finger-four' arrangement, a formation that is still in general use. Air battles inverted the usual military calculation that 'The more you use, the less you lose.' Large formations provided a target-rich environment for smaller, more agile units, who could spend less time avoiding collisions with their neighbours, and more time shooting at the enemy.

Unlike the RAF, which kept fighters and bombers under separate commands, the Luftwaffe deployed mixed formations known as *Luftflotte*, whose commanders reported directly to Hitler's deputy, the First World War ace, Herman Goering. Three *Luftflotte* took part in the Battle of Britain:

Luftflotte 2	Feldmarschall Albert Kesselring HQ at Brussels
Luftflotte 3	Feldmarschall Hugo Sperrle HQ at Paris
Luftflotte 5	Generaloberst Hans Stumpf HQ at Oslo

The last participated in just one disastrous raid, on 15 August.

Luftwaffe strategy was to draw RAF Fighter Command into a great dogfight, and destroy it. This aim was pursued throughout the summer, regardless of the immediate objective. The battle consisted of three phases:

(1) *10 July–7 August*: probing attacks.
(2) *8 August–6 September*: battle for command of the air.
(3) *7 September–31 October*: attack on Britain's economy.

The first phase brought German attacks on British convoys through the Channel, and smaller raids on Bristol, Portsmouth, Norwich, Liverpool, South Wales and the Midlands, often by night. The Luftwaffe suffered considerable losses to no purpose: 216 aircraft by 11 August, against British losses of 115 fighters and 64 bombers (Bungay). The RAF tested its untried control systems while Park conserved his forces, committing individual squadrons against much larger German formations. This has fed the myth of the Few, but was probably less dangerous than it looked, given air warfare's reversal of the usual rules of economy of force. German fighter sweeps unaccompanied by bombers found few opponents, as Park denied them the decisive action they sought.

Bad weather obscured the start of the next phase of the battle, in which the Luftwaffe sought to destroy Fighter Command by attacking its airfields. Andover, Biggin Hill, Bradwell, Brize Norton, Croydon, Debden, Detling, Driffield, Eastchurch, Ford, Gosport, Gravesend, Hawkinge, Hornchurch, Kenley, Lympne, Manston, Middle Wallop, North Weald, Rochford, Sealand, Tangmere, Thorney Island, West Malling and Warmwell were all hit, some of them repeatedly. Airfields are difficult targets, however. Bomb craters are easily filled, and alternative accommodation readily improvised. Fighter pilots were rarely caught on the ground. Stephen Bungay reckons less than 20 fighters were destroyed that way.

Only three exposed coastal airfields were temporarily shut down, at Hawkinge, Lympne and Manston. Biggin Hill's operations room was hit, but continued working from the village, while Kenley's moved into a sausage shop in Caterham. The Germans' total failure to disrupt Fighter Command's control system reflected their ignorance of its structure. A third of the raids hit Training or Bomber Command airfields of limited relevance to the battle in progress. This intelligence failure also accounts for the German failure to target radar stations, with the significant exception of Ventnor, temporarily blinded in mid-August.

RAF losses were not small: 410 fighters were destroyed between 6 August and 2 September. The 31st was Fighter Command's worst day ever for casualties in the air. Strain on pilots and ground crew was intense. The Luftwaffe suffered also, losing nearly 900 aircraft, 443 of them fighters (Overy). Sickness rates soared among German pilots exhausted by cross-Channel operations. Nevertheless, their exaggerated claims suggested half the RAF's fighter force had been destroyed by the end of August, leaving Dowding just 100 operational fighters. Fighter Command actually started September with 701 serviceable aircraft, and over 200 in store (Overy). A bigger problem for Dowding was the attrition of trained pilots, which forced him to concentrate the survivors in 11 Group's frontline squadrons. Category 'C' squadrons in 12 and 13 Groups might have only 6 experienced pilots out of an establishment of 20. Even so the RAF ended August with more operational fighter pilots than in July, and nearly twice as many as the Luftwaffe: 1422 to 735.

Once more cloud marked the beginning of a new phase in the battle. The enforced lull helped convince Goering that Fighter Command was beaten, and that it was time to attack the British economy directly. There is no real evidence for the claim that Hitler's decision to bomb London in retaliation for British raids on Berlin saved Fighter Command from imminent defeat. The Berlin attacks were at best an excuse for the next stage in an agreed programme, while the figures quoted above show clearly that, so far from running down, Fighter Command was in a better state by September than the Luftwaffe.

The period 7–15 September certainly proved decisive, but not in the way Goering expected. In nine days the Luftwaffe lost nearly 300 aircraft, a third of them fighters. Worse still they met ferocious resistance from an enemy their leaders had told them was finished. Named 'Loge', after the ancient German fire god, the mass attack of 7 September on the Isle of Dogs surprised RAF controllers at first. Their scrappy interceptions were insufficient to stop the Germans, who ploughed through by weight of numbers: 348 bombers covered by 617 Me 109 and Me 110 fighters. They left the Docklands blazing, over 1000 aircraft mixing it in a huge dogfight over the Isle of Sheppey as they came away. More bombers returned after dark to stoke the flames.

Cloudy weather limited further attacks until 15 September, when Kesselring's Luftflotte 2 launched the Luftwaffe's last great effort. Nearly 500 bombers and 120 Me 110s were available, more than could be used, and over 500 Me 109s. Dowding had 630 fighters with frontline squadrons, half of them in 11 Group. Kesselring launched two attacks. The morning raid was the smaller: 25 bombers, 21 fighter-bombers and 150 fighters. Intended to draw Fighter Command's teeth, it crossed the coast between Dover and Folkestone, flying over Ashford, Maidstone and Lewisham, to arrive over London about noon. The RAF scrambled 254 Hurricanes and Spitfires, peeling away the German escorts over Kent, and setting about the bombers as they completed bombing runs over Clapham Junction and Battersea Power Station. One Dornier, abandoned by its crew, jettisoned its bombs over Buckingham Palace, before crashing in the forecourt of Victoria Station. A disappointing six bombers succumbed to the 100 or so fighters that swarmed around them, though claims were much higher.

Battle of Britain

	Winners	*Losers*
Opponents	British	German
Commanders	Air Chief Marshal, Sir Hugh Dowding	Reichsmarschall Herman Goering
	Air Vice Marshal Keith Park	Feldmarschall Albert Kesselring
		Feldmarschall Hugo Sperrle
Numbers	see text	
Losses	1547 aircraft; 1494 airmen	1887 aircraft; 2698 airmen

The afternoon raid was the larger: 114 bombers, 20 fighter-bombers and 340 fighters. It crossed the English coast further west, at Dungeness, flying north towards Maidstone in three great columns. Interceptions began over Romney Marsh and continued across Kent. Confident that Kesselring had nothing left, Park committed every squadron, and summoned help from 12 Group. Churchill was present in Park's operations room, the first time the head of His Majesty's Government had followed a battle on British soil so closely since William III led the charge at the Boyne, 250 years before.

Aircraft filled the sky between Gravesend and London's eastern outskirts, stripping away the German fighter escorts. When the bombers reached their targets in Docklands they found them covered in cloud and turned away, dropping their bombs over Bexley, Dartford, Crayford, West Ham and Bromley-by-Bow. Another 21 bombers were shot down. Total German aircraft losses for the whole day were 56, against 28 British. Twenty more German bombers were badly hit, bringing their effective losses to an unsustainable one in three. The day of these attacks – 15 September – had been the date chosen for Operation Sealion, but the invasion never came. Another big raid was beaten off with heavy losses on 18 September, after which the bombers came by night, though fighter-bombers conducted offensive sweeps through October and early November.

The Luftwaffe had been outgeneralled and outfought, victory apparently snatched away at the last moment by means beyond its comprehension. Its precious prewar cadres suffered irreplaceable losses, the survivors demoralized by the disparity between their own experience and their leaders' overconfident assertions. Accounts of total losses vary, and it is impossible to count all those injured while engaged in supporting roles. The scoreboard reflects Stephen Bungay's recent figures. His totals are higher than most, including 524 aircraft from Coastal and Bomber Command. A total of 544 Fighter Command pilots are thought to have died, and the full human cost to all RAF commands now exceeds the 1494 listed on the roll of honour in the Battle of Britain chapel in Westminster Abbey.

Fighter Command had won a partial victory. The air-defence battle continued through the winter, until Hitler's invasion of Russia in June 1941 changed the whole character of the war. Nevertheless, the Battle of Britain can be seen as the decisive battle of the Second World War, the first check inflicted on those attempting to change the world order by force since Japan invaded Manchuria in 1931. British morale was consolidated and national purpose reaffirmed, ending any possibility of a negotiated peace with the Third Reich.

Directions

No one site can provide a representative overview of an event the size of the Battle of Britain, except perhaps for Park's operations room at RAF Uxbridge, open by prior arrangement with the curator. Also see the Battle of Britain Hall at the RAF Museum in Hendon, with a reproduction of Dowding's control room at Bentley Priory and period aircraft. His statue stands outside St Clement Dane's Church in the Strand. The Imperial War Museum has more contemporary aircraft at Duxford, a 12 Group station in Cambridgeshire. Other airfields with displays open to the public are at Tangmere, near Chichester, and Hawkinge, Kent.

Glossary

Arquebus. Light musket.

Barony. Irish unit of local government, between parish and county.

Burghal Hidage. West Saxon list of garrisons.

Caliver. Light musket (16th–17th centuries).

Chevauchée (French 'ride'). Mounted expedition or raid.

Colours. Company of foot or troop of horse possessing their own colours.

Commanded horse/shot. Selected men detached to act at a distance from their unit.

Cornet. Cavalry standard.

Corslet. Body armour.

Demi-lance. Lightly armoured Tudor cavalry soldier.

Dragoon. Cavalry soldier armed and trained to fight on foot.

Enfants perdus (French 'lost children'). Advanced party of skirmishers (17th century).

Extraduction. Drill intended to deliver a continuous rolling fire (17th century).

Fframe. Light Scottish field gun (17th century).

Foreward. Right or leading wing of a Tudor army, i.e. the van.

Forlorn hope. Advanced party of skirmishers (17th century).

Fusil. Flintlock musket.

Hide. Old English land measure between 60 and 120 acres (25–50 ha).

Hornwork. Trapezoid fortification, often with projections of 'horns' at the broad end towards the enemy.

Horse. Cavalry of the mid-17th century.

IRA. Irish Republican Army.

IRB. Irish Republican Brotherhood.

Jack. Light padded armour (15th–16th century).

Kern. Lightly armed Irish foot soldier(s) (13th–16th centuries).

League. Archaic unit of distance, usually 3 miles (5 km).

Mark. Medieval unit of exchange worth 13/4d or 67 decimal pence.

Oppidum. Fortified Celtic stronghold.

Pilum. Heavy Roman throwing spear.

Rearward or **Rereward.** Left wing or rear of a medieval army.

Reformadoes. Officers of disbanded regiments formed into ad hoc units.

Refused (of a position, commonly on a flank) Deliberately held back from the enemy.

Slight. To damage a fortification rendering it indefensible.

Swine feathers. Iron-tipped stakes stuck in the ground against cavalry; also known as Swedish feathers.

Targe. Target or round shield.

Tassets. Armour for the upper leg (16th–17th centuries).

Teigues. Catholic Irish.

Trained Band. Militia regiment, usually from London (17th century).

Vanward. Right or leading wing of a medieval army.

Weather gauge. Position to windward (in relation to enemy fleet).

Further Reading

Battles only exist as events because people have written about them in the past. Readers wishing to explore the subject further should consult the secondary accounts listed below, whose footnotes and bibliographies will point them towards the original source material. Some modern accounts, such as Brigadier Peter Young's Civil War monographs, reproduce relevant sources in full. Victorian scholars edited and published numerous primary sources, forming the basis of modern English historiography, most notably in the Rolls Series of medieval chronicles. Many official documents appear in the Calendars of State Papers for Domestic or Foreign Affairs, with separate series for Ireland and Scotland. Unfortunately these Victorian compilations are rarely found outside university libraries, making them nearly as inaccessible as the original documents.

Readily available primary sources include:

– *English Historical Documents*, published by Oxford University Press since the 1950s in eight large volumes.

– New dual language editions from the same publisher, for example: *Bede's Ecclesiastical History* (ed. B. Colgrave and R.A.B. Mynors) and *Gesta Stephani* (ed. K.R. Potter and R.H.C. Davis).

– Older dual language editions of classical authors from Loeb.

– English translations published as Penguin Classics, for example: Caesar's *Conquest of Gaul*, Tacitus' *Agricola*, Bede's *Ecclesiastical History*, Gerald of Wales's *Journey through Wales*.

– Numerous volumes published by the Navy Records Society dealing with naval history.

An invaluable source for students of the Civil Wars are the Thomason Tracts, pamphlets and newsletters collected by a contemporary bookseller of that name. These are now held in the British Library, where they are available as photocopies and also on microfiche. Relevant reference numbers appear throughout Part 6.

Secondary works on battlefield history continue to appear in large numbers, some too recently to feature below. Articles in learned journals are often particularly useful. Photocopies of these may be obtained from the British Lending Library at minimal cost, through the public library system.

Books are identified by author, title and publication date; entries for articles also specify the name of the publishing journal, volume and page numbers, abbreviations as below:

AA	*Archaeologia Aeliana*
(ed.)	editor
HER	*English Historical Review*
IS	*Irish Sword*
Jnl	Journal
JSAHR	*Journal of the Society for Army Historical Research*
n.d.	no date
NRS	Navy Records Society
NS	New Series
SHR	*Scottish Historical Review*
Soc.	Society
Trans.	Transactions
TRHS	*Transactions of the Royal Historical Society*
WHR	*Welsh History Review*

General

Bartlett, T. and Jeffery, T., *A Military History of Ireland* (1996)

Burne, A.H., *The Battlefields of England* (1950)

Burne, A.H., *More Battlefields of England* (1952)

Hayes-McCoy, G.A., *Irish Battles: A Military History of Ireland* (1989)

Hayes-McCoy, G.A. (ed.), *The Irish at War* (1964)

Laird Clowes, W., *The Royal Navy: A History from the Earliest Times to 1900* (7 vols) (1903)

MacDougall, N., *Scotland and War AD 79–1918* (1991)

Marren, P., *Grampian Battlefields: The Historic Battles of North East Scotland* (1990)

Rayner, M., *English Battlefields* (2004)

Rodger, N.A.M., *The Safeguard of the Sea: A Naval History of Britain* 1 *660–1649* (1997)

1 Sword and Javelin

Frere, S., *Britannia: A History of Roman Britain* (1978)

Hanson, W.S., *Agricola and the Conquest of the North* (1987)

Thornhill, P., *A Lower Thames Ford and the Campaigns of 54 BC and AD 43* (1976) – *Archaeologia Cantiarum* XCII pp.119–128

Webster, G., *The Roman Invasion of Britain* (1993)

Webster, G., *Boudicca: The British Revolt Against Rome AD 60* (1999)

Webster, G., *Rome Against Caratacus: The Roman Campaigns in Britain AD 48–58* (1993)

2 Shieldwall

Alcock, L., *Arthur's Britain, History and Archaeology AD 367–634* (1971)

Bassett, S., *The Origins of the English Kingdoms* (1989)

Campbell, A., *The Battle of Brunanburh* (1938)

Collingwood, W.G., *The Battle of Stainmoor in Legend and History* (1901) – *Trans. of the Cumberland and Westmorland Antiquarian and Archaeological Soc.* NS II pp.231–41

Cooper, J., *The Battle of Maldon: Fiction or Fact* (1993)

Duncan, A.A.M., *The Battle of Carham* (1976) – *SHR* 55 pp.1–28

Dymond, C.W., *Identification of the Site of "Buttingdene", etc* (1921) – *Montgomeryshire Collections* 31 pp.336–46

Hart, C.R., *The Danelaw* (1992)

Hooper, N., *Anglo-Saxon Warfare on the Eve of the Conquest: A Brief Survey* (1979) – *Anglo-Norman Studies I* pp.84–94

Kirby, D.P., *The Earliest English Kings* (1991)

Magoun, F.P., *King Alfred's Naval and Beach Battle with the Danes in 896* (1942) – *Modern Language Review* XXXVII pp.409–14

Meehan, B., *The siege of Durham, the battle of Carham and the cession of Lothian* (1976) – *SHR* IV pp.1–19

Myres, J.N.L., *The English Settlements* (1986)

Peddie, J., *Alfred: Warrior King* (1999)

Rawlence, E.A., *On the Site of the Battle of Ethandune* (1921) – *Antiquaries Jnl* I pp.105–17

Revill, S., *King Edwin and the Battle of Heathfield* (1975) – *Trans. Thoroton Soc.* LXXIX 40–9

Ryan, Rev J., *The Battle of Clontarf* (1938) – *Jnl of the Royal Soc of Antiquaries of Ireland* LXVIII pp.1–41

Scragg, D.G. (ed.), *The Battle of Maldon* (1991)

Smyth, A.P., *Scandinavian York and Dublin* (1987)

Strickland, M., *Anglo-Norman Warfare* (1992)

Swanton, M. (ed.), *The Anglo-Saxon Chronicles* (2000)

Thorpe, L., *The Bayeux Tapestry and the Norman Invasion* (1973)

Wainwright, F.T., *Nechtanesmere* (1948) – *Antiquity* 22 pp.82–97

Walker, J.W., *The Battle of the Winwaed AD 655* (1944) – *Yorkshire Archaeological Jnl* 36 pp.394–408

3 Knight and Castle

Barrow, G.W.S., *Robert Bruce* (1988)

Bartlett, R., *England Under the Norman and Angevin Kings* (2000)

Beeler, J., *Warfare in England 1066–1189* (1966)

Cannon, H.L., *The Battle of Sandwich and Eustace the Monk* (1912) – *EHR* XXVII pp.649–670

Carpenter, D.A., *The Battles of Lewes and Evesham 1264–5* (1987)

Cathcart King, D.J., *Henry II and the Fight at Coleshill* (1964–5) – *WHR* 2 pp.367–73

Edwards, J.G., *Henry II and the Fight at Coleshill: Some Further Reflections* (1966–7) – *WHR* 3 pp.251–63

Edwards, J.G., *The Site of the Battle of 'Meis Medoc'* (1931) – *EHR* XLVI pp.262–5

Hill, R., *The Battle of Stockbridge 1141* (1989) – in C. Harper Bill, *Studies in Medieval History Presented to R Allen Brown* pp.173–8

Laborderie, O. de, Maddicott, J.R., Carpenter, D.A., *The Last Hours of Simon de Montfort* (2000) – *EHR* CXV pp.378–412

Lloyd, J.E., *A History of Wales from the Earliest Times to the Edwardian Conquest* (1939)

Lydon, J.F., *The Braganstown Massacre, 1329* (1977) – *Louth Archaeological Jnl* XIX pp.5–16

Mac Carthaigh, P., *Ireland versus England: The First Battle – Clais an Chro* (1972) – *Old Kilkenny Review* 24 pp.37–41

MacIomhair, Rev D., *The Battle of Fochart (Co Louth)* 1318 (1968) – *IS* VIII (32) pp.193–209

Mackay-Mackenzie, W., *The Battle of Bannockburn* (1913)

Meldrum, E., *Bruce's Buchan Campaign* (1966) – *Deeside Field* pp.20–6

Morris, J.E., *The Welsh Wars of Edward I* (1901)

Myres, J.N.L., *The Campaign of Radcot Bridge in December 1387* (1927) – *EHR* XLII pp.20–33

Norgate, K., *The Minority of Henry III* (1912)

Oman, Sir C., *The History of the Art of War in the Middle Ages* (2 vols) (1924)

Prestwich, M., *Armies and Warfare in the Middle Ages: The English Experience* (1996)

Smith, L.B., *The Death of Llywelyn ap Gruffydd: The Narratives Reconsidered* (1982–3) – *WHR* 14 pp.200–14

Verbruggen, J.F., *The Art of Warfare in Western Europe During the Middle Ages* (2002)

Walker, R.F., *The Hagnaby Chronicle and the Battle of Maes Moydog* (1976–7) – *WHR* 8 pp.125–30

4 Longbow and Bombard

Ashdown, C.H., *Battles and Battlefields of St Albans* (n.d.)

Blow, J., *Nibley Green 1469: The Last Private Battle fought in England* (1952) – *History Today* 2 pp.598–610

Blyth, J.D., *The Battle of Tewkesbury* (1961) – *Trans. Bristol and Gloucestershire Archaeological Soc.* LXX pp.99–120

Brooke, R., *Visits to Fields of Battle in England of the 15th Century* (1857)

Butler, G., *The Battle of Piltown (Co Kilkenny)* (1964) – *IS* VI (24) pp.197–212

Charlesworth, D., *The Battle of Hexham 1464* (1952) – *AA* 30 pp.57–68

Dockray, K., *Three Chronicles of the Reign of Edward IV* (1988)

Foss, P.J., *The Field of Redemore: The Battle of Bosworth 1485* (1990)

Gillingham, J., *The Wars of the Roses* (1981)

Goodman, A., *The Wars of the Roses Military Activity and English Society 1452–97* (1990)

Goodman, A. and Tuck A. (eds.), *War and Border Societies in the Middle Ages* (1992)

Hodges, G., *Ludford Bridge and Mortimer's Cross* (1989)

Hodges, G., *Owain Gly Dwr and the War of Independence in the Welsh Borders* (1995)

Jack, R.I., *A Quincentenary: The Battle of Northampton July 10th 1460* (1960) – *Northamptonshire Past and Present* III pp.21–5

Jones, M.K., *Bosworth 1485: Psychology of a Battle* (2003)

Lander, J.R., *The Wars of the Roses* (1990)

Markham, Sir C.R., *The Battle of Towton* (1889) – *Yorkshire Archaeological Jnl* 10 pp.1–34

Markham, Sir C.R., *The Battle of Wakefield* (1886) – *Yorkshire Archaeological Jnl* 9 pp.105–23

Nicholson, R., *Scotland: The Later Middle Ages* (1974)

Nicholson, R., *Edward III and the Scots* (1965)

Radford, Mrs G.H., *The Fight at Clyst in 1455* (1912) – *Trans Devonshire Assoc* XLIV pp.252–65

Twemlow, F.R., *The Battle of Blore Heath 1459* (1995)

White, R., *The Battle of Neville's Cross, Fought 17 Oct 1346* (1857) – *AA* NS I pp.271–303

Wylie, J.H., *The Battle of Shrewsbury (quincentenary)* (1903) – *Trans. of the Shropshire Archaeological and Natural History Soc.* Series 3 III pp.139–49

5 Hackbut and Halberd

Butler, G., *The Battle of Affane (Co Waterford)* (1967) – *IS* VIII (30) pp.33–47

Clouston, J.S., *The Battle of Summersdale* (1909) – *Old Lore Miscellany* II p.2

Corbett, J., *Drake and the Tudor Navy* (1899)

Cornwall, J., *Revolt of the Peasantry 1549* (1977)

Falls, C., *Elizabeth's Irish Wars* (1950)

Fissel, M.C., *English Warfare 1511–1642* (2001)

Hill, G., *Shane O'Neill's Expedition against the Antrim Scots 1565* (1861) – *Ulster Jnl of Archaeology* pp.122–41

Land, S.K., *Kett's Rebellion: The Norfolk Rising of 1549* (1977)

Longmate, N., *Defending the Island: From Caesar to the Armada* (1989)

Martin, C.J.M., *Ancrum Moor: A Day of Reckoning* (1965) – *The Scots Magazine* 83 pp.146–52

Martin, C. and Parker, G., *The Spanish Armada* (1988)

Mooney, C., *The Battle near Wicklow in 1599 – An Identification* (1955) – *IS* II (7) pp.231–3

Patten, W., *The Expedition into Scotland in 1547* – in A.F. Pollard, *Tudor Tracts* (1903)

Petrie, Sir C., *The Hispano-Papal Landing at Smerwick* (1969) – *IS* IX (35) pp.82–94

Phillips, G., *The Anglo-Scots Wars 1513–50* (1999)

Pinkerton, W., *The "Overthrow" of Sir John Chichester at Carrickfergus in 1597* (1857)

Proctor, J., *The History of Wyatt's Rebellion, etc.* – in Prof. Arber, *An English Garland* (1880)

Rose-Troup, F., *The Western Rebellion of 1549* (1913)

Scott, A.M., *The Battle of Langside 1568* (1885)

Witherby, C.T., *The Battle of Bonchurch* (1962)

6 Pike and Drum

Abbott, W.C. (ed.), *The Writings and Speeches of Oliver Cromwell* (1939)

Abram, A., *Montgomery, 1644* (1993)

Adair, J., *Cheriton 1644* (1973)

Atkin, M., *Cromwell's Crowning Mercy: The Battle of Worcester 1651* (1998)

Broxap, E., *The Great Civil War in Lancashire 1642–51* (1910)

Coate, M., *Cornwall in the Great Civil War and Interregnum 1642–60* (1933)

Dore, R.N., *The Civil Wars in Cheshire* (1966)

Fairfax, Sir T., *Short Memorial of the Northern Actions in which ... engaged 1642–4* (1926) – *JSAHR* V pp.119–25 and 160–74

Firth, Sir C.H., *Cromwell's Army* (1967)

Firth, Sir C.H., *De Gomme's 'Bristol taken by Prince Rupert...'* (1925) – *JSAHR* IV pp.180–203

Firth, Sir C.H., *Dunbar* (1900) – *TRHS* XIV pp.19–52

Fissel, M., *The Bishop's Wars: Charles I's Campaigns against Scotland 1638–40* (1994)

Foard, G., *Naseby: The Decisive Campaign* (1995)

Gardiner, S.R., *History of the Great Civil War 1642–49* (1894)

Gardiner, S.R., *History of the Commonwealth and Protectorate* (1903)

Gardiner, S.R., *The Last Campaign of Montrose* (1894) – *Edinburgh Review* CLXXIX pp.140–8

Gentles, I., *The New Model Army in England, Scotland and Ireland 1645–53* (1992)

Grainger, J., *Cromwell Against the Scots* (1997)

Hogan, E. (ed), *History of the Warr of Ireland 1641–1653 by a British Officer...* (1873)

Holmes, R., *Preston 1648* (*British Battlefields Series*) (1985)

Hyde, Earl of Clarendon, E., *History of the Rebellion and Civil Wars in England* (ed.W.D. Macray) (1969)

Johnson, D., *Adwalton Moor 1643: The Battle That Changed A War* (2003)

Kenyon, J., and Ohlmeyer, J., *The Civil Wars: A Military History of England, Scotland, and Ireland 1638–1660* (1998)

Lenihan, P., *Confederate Catholics at War 1641–49* (2001)

Lenihan, P., *The Leinster Army and the Battle of Dungan's Hill, 1647* (1991) – *IS* XVIII (71) pp.139–53

Miller, A.C., *The Battle of Ross: A Controversial Military Event (March 1643)* (1971) – *IS* X (39) pp.141–58

Newman, Dr P., *The Battle of Marston Moor 1644* (1981)

O'Brien, B., *Munster at War* (1971)

Peachey, S. (ed.), *Richard Symonds: The Complete Military Diary* (1989)

Reid, S., *All the King's Armies: A Military History of the English Civil War* (1998)

Reid, S., *The Campaigns of Montrose ... the Civil War in Scotland 1639–1646* (1990)

Rogers, H.C.B., *Battles and Generals of the Civil Wars 1642–1651* (1968)

Stevenson, Prof. D., *Highland Warrior: Alasdair MacColla and the Civil Wars* (1994)

Terry, C.S., *The Life and Campaigns of Alexander Leslie, First Earl of Leven* (1899)

Toynbee, M., and Young, P., *Cropredy Bridge 1644* (1970)

Wicks, A., *Bellum Civile: Sir Ralph Hopton's Memoirs ... 1642–1644* (1988)

Woolrych, A., *Battles of the English Civil War* (1991)

Young, P., *Edgehill 1642* (1967)

Young, P., *Marston Moor 1644* (1970)

Young, P., *Naseby 1645* (1985)

Young, P., *The Battle of Hopton Heath 19 March 1643* (1955) – *JSAHR* XXXIII pp.35–9

Young, P., and Holmes, R., *The English Civil War: A Military History of the Three Civil Wars* (2000)

Young, P., and Tucker, N. (eds.), *Military Memoirs – The Civil War* (1967)

7 Flintlock and Bayonet

Aiton, W., *The Rencounter at Drumclog and Battle at Bothwell Bridge etc.* (1821)

Anderson, R.C. (ed.), *Journals and Narratives of the Third Dutch War* (1946) – *NRS*

Baynes, J., *The Jacobite Rising of 1715* (1970)

Chandler, D.G., *Sedgemoor 1685: An Account and An Anthology* (1985)

Dickson, C., *Revolt in the North: Antrim and Down in 1798* (1960)

Dickson, C., *The Wexford Rising in 1798: Its causes and its course* (1997)

Duffy, C., *The '45* (2003)

Gardiner, S.R., and Atkinson, C.T. (eds.), *Letters and Papers Relating to the First Dutch War 1652–1654* (1899) – *NRS*

Hayes, R.D., *The Battle of Castlebar 1798* (1957) – *IS* III (11) pp.107–14

Hayes, R.D., *The Last Invasion of Ireland* (1937)

Hayes-McCoy, G.A., *The Topography of a Battlefield: Arklow 1798* (1949) – *IS* I (1) pp.50–6

Keogh, D., Furlong, N. (eds.), *The Mighty Wave: The 1798 Rebellion in Wexford* (1996)

Le Fevre, P., *The Battle of Bantry Bay, 1 May 1689* (1990) – *IS* XVIII (70) pp.1–16

Lenihan, P., *1690 Battle of the Boyne* (2003)

Lenman, B., *The Jacobite Risings in Britain 1689–1746* (1984)

Longmate, N., *Island Fortress: The Defence of Great Britain 1603–1945* (1991)

Mackay, Major General H., *Memoirs of the War in Scotland 1689–1691* (1833)

Martin-Leake, S., *The Life of Sir John Leake, etc* (ed. Geoffrey Callendar) (1920) – *NRS*

O'Carroll, D., *An Indifferent Good Post: The Battlefield of the Boyne* (1990) – *IS* XVIII (70) pp.49–56

Pakenham, T., *The Year of Liberty: The Great Irish Rebellion of 1798* (1998)

Powell, J.R., and Timmings, E.K. (eds.), *The Rupert and Monck Letter Book* (1969) – *NRS*

Powley, E.B., *The Naval Side of King William's War* (1972)

Reid, S., *1745: A Military History of the Last Jacobite Rising* (2001)

Simms, J.G., *Eyewitnesses of the Boyne* (1963) – *IS* VI (22) pp.16–27

Simms, J.G., *Jacobite Ireland 1689–91* (1969)

Simms, J.G., *The Siege of Derry* (1964) – *IS* VI (25) pp.221–33

Tedder, A.W., *The Navy of the Restoration* (1970)

Terry, C.S., *John Graham of Claverhouse, Viscount Dundee, 1648–1689* (1905)

Terry, C.S., *The Pentland Rising and Rullion Green* (1905)

8 Rifle and Radar

Bungay, S., *Most Dangerous Enemy: A History of the Battle of Britain* (2000)

Hally, Col P.J., *The Easter 1916 Rising in Dublin – The Military Aspects (1)* (1966) – *IS* VII (29) pp.311–26

Hally, Col P.J., *The Easter 1916 Rising in Dublin – The Military Aspects (2)* (1967) – *IS* VIII (30) pp.48–57

Overy, R., *The Battle* (2001)

Terraine, J., *The Right of the Line: The RAF in the European War 1939–1945* (1985)

The Battlefields Trust is a charity dedicated to the preservation and interpretation of battlefield sites; aims which deserve every support. It organizes walks and conferences, and publishes a quarterly journal. For details contact:

Michael Rayner

Meadow Cottage, 33 High Green, Brooke, Norwich NR15 1HR

Email: BattlefieldTrust@aol.com

Chronological List of Battles

55BC	26 August	Dover (Porta Dubris)
54BC	8 July	Bigbury Camp
54BC	21 July	Cassivellaunus' Fight
43		Medway
51		Caradoc's Last Stand (Cefn Carnedd)
60		Boudicca's Revolt (Mancetter/Paulerspury)
60		Menai Straits
83		Mons Graupius
c. 429		Alleluia Victory
c. 455		Aegelesthrep (Aylesford)
c. 456		Crecganford (Crayford)
*c.*465		Wippedsfleot (Ebbsfleet)
*c.*491		Anderitum (Pevensey)
*c.*495		Mons Badonicus (Mount Badon)
*c.*501		Portesmutha (Portchester Castle)
*c.*508		Natanleag (Cerdicesleag)
*c.*519		Cerdicesford (Charford)
552		Searoburg (Old Sarum)
556		Beranburh (Barbury Castle)
568		Wibbandun (Wibba's Mount)
571		Biedcanford (Bedford)
*c.*573		Arfderydd (Arthuret)
577		Dyrham (Deorham)
*c.*580		Caer Greu
584		Fethanleag (Stoke Lyne)
*c.*590		Lindisfarne (Metcaud)

592		Wodnesbeorh (Woden's Barrow)
597		Circinn (Howe of the Mearns)
*c.*598		Catraeth (Catterick)
603		Degsastan (Dawston Rigg)
*c.*616		Chester (Caer Legionis)
*c.*617		Idle River
628		Cirencester
*c.*632	12 October	Haethfelth (Hatfield Chase)
*c.*633		Denisesburna (Hefenfelth)
637		Mag Rath (Moira)
639		Calathros (Dun Nosebridge)
641	5 August	Maserfelth (Maes Cogwy)
642		Strathcarron
652		Bradford-on-Avon
*c.*654	15 November	Winwaed (Winwidfeld)
658		Peonnum (Penselwood)
*c.*678		Trent
685	20 May	Nechtanesmere (Dunnichen Moss)
718		Kells
722		Allen
779		Bensington (Benson)
796		Don's Mouth
798	2 April	Whalley
825		Ellendun
825		Gafolford (Galford)
836		Carhampton
837		Portland
837		Southampton
838		Hengestesdune (Hingston Down)
843		Carhampton
848		Parret River
850		Aclea (Oak Glade/Oak Leigh)
850		Sandwich
850		Wicganbeorg (Wigborough)
853		Thanet
c. 860		Winchester
867	21 March	York
870	31 December	Englefield
871	4 January	Reading
871	8 January	Ashdown

871	22 January	Basing
871	March	Meretun (Merantune)
871	May	Wilton
877		Strangford Lough
878		Cynwit (Cannington/Countisbury)
878	May	Ethandun (Edington)
884		Rochester
893		Benfleet
893		Buttington
893		Farnham
896		Sea Battle
903	8 December	Holme, The
910	6 August	Tettenhall (Wednesfield)
914		Corbridge
918		Corbridge
918		Tempsford
919	15 September	Dublin
926	5 January	Anagassan
937		Brunanburh (Bruneswald/Wendune)
948		Castleford
954		Stainmoor (Stainmore)
980		Tara
988		Watchet
991	11 August	Maldon
*c.*995		Skidamyre (Skithmore)
999		Glen Mama
1001		Aethelingadene (Atheling's Valley)
1001		Pinhoe
1004		Thetford
1005		Monzievaird
c. 1005		Mortlach
c. 1006		Burgus
1006		Kennet
1010	5 May	Ringmere (Rymer)
1014	23 April	Clontarf
1016		Penselwood
1016	June	Sherston
1016	July	Brentford
1016	18 October	Assandune (Ashdon/Ashingdon)
1018	September	Carham
1022		Abergwyli

1039		Durham (Siege)
1039		Rhyd-y-Groes
1040	14 August	Torfnes (Burghead/Torness)
1054	27 July	Dunsinane Hill (Seven Sleepers, Day of)
1055	24 October	Hereford
1057	15 August	Lumphanan
1066	20 September	Fulford (Gate Fulford)
1066	25 September	Stamford Bridge
1066	14 October	Hastings (Senlac)
1093	13 November	Alnwick I
1098	July	Priestholm (Anglesey Sound)
1116		Aberystwyth
1136		Maes Gwenllian
1136	October	Crug Mawr (Cardigan/Crugmore)
1138	10 June	Clitheroe
1138	22 August	Northallerton (The Standard)
1141	2 February	Lincoln
1141	1 August –14 September	Winchester
1141	14 September	Stockbridge
1143	1 July	Wilton
1157		Coleshill (Coed Eulo)
1169		Clais an Chro (Clashacrow/Dinin River)
1171	16 May	Dublin
1171	1 September	Dublin (Castle Knock)
1173	17 October	Fornham
1174	13 July	Alnwick II
1177	February	Down I (Downpatrick)
1217	20 May	Lincoln
1217	24 August	Sandwich
1257	2 June	Cymerau (Coed Llathen)
1260	14 May	Down II (Drumderg)
1263	2 October	Largs
1264	14 May	Lewes
1265	2 August	Kenilworth
1265	4 August	Evesham
1270		Athankip
1282	11 December	Irfon Bridge (Orewin Bridge)
1295	5 March	Maes Moydog (Maes Madog/Meismedoc)
1296	27 April	Dunbar
1297	11 September	Stirling Bridge (Cambuskenneth)
1298	22 July	Falkirk (I)

1306	19 June	Methven
1306	11 August	Dail Righ (Dalrigh)
c. 1307	10 May	Loudoun Hill
c. 1307	12 June	Glen Trool
c. 1307	25 December	Slioch
c. 1308	23 May	Barra (Inverurie/Meldrum)
c. 1309	15 August	Pass of Brander (Ben Cruachan)
1314	23–24 June	Bannockburn
1316	10 August	Athenry
1318	10 May	Dysart O'Dea (Disert Tola)
1318	14 October	Faughart (Fochart)
c. 1319	20 September	Myton-on-Swale (Chapter of Myton)
1322	10 March	Burton-upon-Trent
1322	16 March	Boroughbridge
c. 1322	12 October	Byland (Old Byland)
1329	10 June	Balibragan (Braganstown)
1332	11 August	Dupplin Muir (Gaskmore/Gledesmore)
1332	17 December	Annan
1333	19 July	Halidon Hill
1335	30 November	Culblean
1346	17 October	Neville's Cross
1349	29 August	Winchelsea (Espagnols sur Mer)
1359		Athy
1387	20 December	Radcot Bridge
1388	19 August	Otterburn (Chevy Chase)
c. 1401	June	Hyddgen (Mynyddhyddgant)
1402	22 June	Nesbit Muir
1402	22 June	Pilleth (Bryn Glas)
1402	14 September	Homildon Hill (Humbleton Hill)
1403	21 July	Shrewsbury
1408	19 February	Bramham Moor
1411	24 July	Harlaw
1453	24 August	Heworth Moor
1454	31 October	Stamford Bridge
1455	22 May	St Albans I
1455	15 December	Clyst Bridge
1459	23 September	Blore Heath
1459	12 October	Ludford Bridge
1460	10 July	Northampton
1460	30 December	Wakefield
c. 1461	3 February	Mortimer's Cross
1461	17 February	St Albans II

1461	28 March	Ferrybridge
1461	29 March	Towton (Palm Sunday Field)
c. 1462	August	Piltown (Baile-an-Phoill)
1464	25 April	Hedgeley Moor
1464	15 May	Hexham
1469	26 July	Edgcote (Danes Moor)
1470	12 March	Lose-Coat Field
1470	20 March	Nibley Green
1471	14 April	Barnet
1471	4 May	Tewkesbury
1485	22 August	Bosworth Field (Redemore)
1487	10 June	Tadcaster
1487	16 June	Stoke Field
1488	11 June	Sauchieburn
1497	17 June	Blackheath
1504	19 August	Knockdoe
1513	13 August	Milfield (Ill Raid)
1513	9 September	Flodden (Branxton Field/Heath)
1526	25 July	Melrose
1529	18 May	Summerdale (Bigswell)
1542	24 August	Hadden Rig (Halydon Rigg)
1542	24 November	Solway Moss
1545	27 February	Ancrum Moor (Lilliard's Edge)
1545	19 July	Portsmouth (Spithead)
1545	21 July	Bonchurch
1547	10 September	Pinkie (Pinkiecleugh/Falside/Inveresk/Musselburgh)
1548	23 February	Drumlanrig
c. 1549	28 July	Fenny Bridges
1549	4–5 August	Clyst St Mary
1549	18 August	Sampford Courtenay
1549	27 August	Dussindale (Ossian's Vale)
1554	28 January	Wrotham
1554	7 February	Fleet Street (Ludgate Hill)
1562	28 October	Corrichie
c. 1565	8 February	Affane
1565	2 May	Glentaisie (Glenshesk)
1567	8 May	Farsetmore (Letterkenny)
1567	15 June	Carberry Hill
1568	13 May	Langside
1571	10 October	Tillyangus
1571	20 November	Craibstane Rout
1579	3 October	Monasternenagh

1580	25 August	Glenmalur
1580	10 November	Smerwick (Dun an Oir/Golden Fort)
1588	21 July	Plymouth (Eddystone)
1588	23 July	Portland Bill
1588	25 July	Isle of Wight (Dunnose Head)
1593	10 October	Erne Fords
1594	7 August	Ford of the Biscuits (Drumane Ford)
1594	3 October	Glenlivet (Allt a'Choileachain)
1595	27 May	Clontibret
1595	5 September	Mullaghbrack
1597	4 November	Carrickfergus
1598	14 August	Yellow Ford
1599	29 May	Wicklow
1599	5 August	Curlew Mountains
1600	20 September – 6 October	Moyry Pass
1601	24 December	Kinsale
1639	14 May	Turriff (Trot of Turriff)
1639	15 June	Megray Hill (Stonehaven)
1639	19 June	Brig o'Dee
1640	28 August	Newburn Ford
1641	29 November	Julianstown
1642	15 April	Kilrush (Cnocaterife)
1642	4 August	Marshall's Elm
1642	3 September	Liscarroll
1642	7 September	Babylon Hill
1642	23 September	Powick Bridge
1642	23 October	Edgehill
1642	12 November	Brentford
1642	13 November	Turnham Green
1642	6 December	Tadcaster
1643	19 January	Braddock Down
1643	21 February	Modbury
1643	13 March	Middlewich
1643	18 March	Old Ross (Ballinvegga)
1643	19 March	Hopton Heath
1643	24 March	Highnam
1643	30 March	Seacroft Moor
1643	13 April	Ripple Field
1643	20 April	Whalley (Sabden Bridge)
1643	23 April	Launceston
1643	25 April	Sourton Down

1643	13 May	Grantham
1643	16 May	Stratton (Stamford Hill)
1643	21 May	Wakefield
1643	18 June	Chalgrove Field
1643	30 June	Adwalton Moor (Adderton/Atherton Moor)
1643	5 July	Lansdown
1643	13 July	Roundway Down (Runaway Down)
1643	26 July	Bristol
1643	28 July	Gainsborough
1643	20 September	Newbury (I)
1643	11 October	Winceby Fight (Horncastle Fight)
1643	13 December	Alton
1644	25 January	Nantwich
1644	21 March	Newark
1644	24 March	Boldon Hill (Down Hill/Hilton)
1644	29 March	Cheriton (Alresford)
1644	11 April	Selby
1644	29 June	Cropredy Bridge
1644	2 July	Marston Moor
1644	31 August	Lostwithiel (Castle Dore)
1644	1 September	Tippermuir (Tibbermore)
1644	13 September	Aberdeen (Justice Mills)
1644	18 September	Montgomery
1644	27 October	Newbury (II)
1644	28 October	Fyvie
1644	9 November	Newbury (III)
1645	2 February	Inverlochy
1645	9 May	Auldearn
1645	14 June	Naseby
1645	2 July	Alford
1645	10 July	Langport (Lamport)
1645	15 August	Kilsyth
1645	13 September	Philiphaugh
1645	24 September	Rowton Heath (Chester)
1645	15 October	Sherburn in Elmet
1645	24 October	Burgh-by-Sands (Carlisle Sands)
1646	21 March	Stow-on-the-Wold
1646	5 June	Benburb
1647	8 August	Dungan's Hill
1647	13 November	Knocknanuss (Knocknegoall)
1648	8 May	St Fagan's
1648	1 June	Maidstone
1648	17 August	Preston

1648	19 August	Winwick (Red Bank)
1649	2 August	Rathmines (Baggot Rath)
1649	11 September	Drogheda (Tredagh)
1650	10 April	Macroom
1650	27 April	Carbisdale
1650	21 June	Scarrifhollis (Letterkenny)
1650	3 September	Dunbar
1651	20 July	Inverkeithing
1651	25 July	Knockbrack (Knocknaclashy/Dromagh)
1651	25 August	Wigan Lane
1651	3 September	Worcester
1652	19 May	Dover
1652	16 August	Plymouth
1652	28 September	Kentish Knock
1652	30 November	Dungeness
1653	18–20 February	Portland (Three Days Battle)
1653	2 June	Gabbard Bank (North Foreland, First)
1665	3 June	Lowestoft
1666	1–4 July	The Four Days' Fight
1666	25 July	St James's Day Fight North Foreland, Second
1666	28 November	Rullion Green (Pentland Hills)
1667	10–14 June	Dutch in the Medway
1667	2 July	Landguard Fort
1672	28 May	Sole Bay (Southwold Bay)
1679	1 June	Drumclog
1679	22 June	Bothwell Bridge
1685	27 June	Norton St Philip
1685	6 July	Sedgemoor
1689	1 May	Bantry Bay
1689	27 July	Killiecrankie
1689	28 July	Londonderry, Relief of
1689	31 July	Newton Butler
1689	21 August	Dunkeld
1690	1 May	Haughs of Cromdale
1690	30 June	Beachy Head (Beveziers)
1690	1 July	Boyne, The (Drogheda)
1691	12 July	Aughrim
1715	12–14 November	Preston
1715	13 November	Sheriffmuir
1719	10 June	Glenshiel
1745	21 September	Prestonpans (Gladsmuir)
1745	18 December	Clifton (Clifton Moor)

1746	17 January	Falkirk (II)
1746	16 April	Culloden (Drummossie Muir)
1797	24 February	Fishguard
1798	27 May	Kilthomas
1798	27 May	Oulart Hill
1798	27 May	Tara
1798	28 May	Enniscorthy
1798	4 June	Tubberneering (Gorey Races)
1798	5 June	New Ross
1798	7 June	Antrim
1798	9 June	Arklow
1798	12 June	Ballynahinch
1798	20 June	Goff's Bridge (Foulkes's Mill)
1798	21 June	Vinegar Hill
1798	27 August	Castlebar Races
1798	8 September	Ballinamuck
1798	12 October	Lough Swilly (Warren's Action)
1916	24–29 April	Dublin (Easter Rising)
1940	10 July –31 October	Battle of Britain

List of Battles

by County/Unitary Authority

England	
Battle of Britain	1940
Bedfordshire	
Biedcanford (Bedford)	571
Tempsford	918
Berkshire	
Ashdown	871
Englefield	870
Kennet	1006
Newbury (I)	1643
Newbury (II)	1644
Newbury (III)	1644
Reading	871
Bristol	
Bristol	1643
Cambridgeshire	
Holme, The	903
Cheshire	
Chester (Caer Legionis)	*c.* 616
Rowton Heath (Chester)	1645
Middlewich	1643
Nantwich	1644
Cornwall	
Braddock Down	1643
Hengestesdune (Hingston Down)	838
Launceston	1643
Lostwithiel (Castle Dore)	1644
Stratton (Stamford Hill)	1643
Cumbria	
Arfderydd (Arthuret)	*c.* 573
Burgh-by-Sands (Carlisle Sands)	1645
Burgus	*c.* 1006
Clifton (Clifton Moor)	1745
Solway Moss	1542
Devon	
Clyst Bridge	1455
Cynwit (Cannington/Countisbury)	878
Fenny Bridges	1549
Gafolford (Galford)	825
Modbury	1643
Pinhoe	1001
Sampford Courtenay	1549
Sourton Down	1643
Clyst St Mary	1549
Doncaster	
Idle River	*c.* 617
Dorset	
Portland	837
Parret River	848
Durham	
Durham (Siege)	1039
Neville's Cross	1346
Stainmoor (Stainmore)	954

Essex

Assandune (Ashdon/Ashingdon)	1016
Benfleet	893
Maldon	991

Gloucestershire

Cirencester	628
Dyrham (Deorham)	577
Highnam	1643
Nibley Green	1470
Stow-on-the-Wold	1646
Tewkesbury	1471

Hampshire

Alton	1643
Basing	871
Cerdicesford (Charford)	*c.* 519
Cheriton (Alresford)	1644
Natanleag (Cerdicesleag)	*c.* 508
Portesmutha (Portchester Castle)	*c.* 501
Southampton	837
Stockbridge	1141
Winchester	*c.* 860
Winchester	1141

Herefordshire

Hereford	1055
Mortimer's Cross	1461

Hertfordshire

Barnet	1471
St Albans I	1455
St Albans II	1461

Isle of Wight

Bonchurch	1545

Kent

Aclea (Oak Glade/Oak Leigh)	850
Aegelesthrep (Aylesford)	*c.* 455
Bigbury Camp	54 BC
Cassivellaunus Fight	54 BC
Crecganford (Crayford)	*c.* 456
Dover (Porta Dubris)	55 BC
Maidstone	1648
Medway	43
Dutch in the Medway	1667
Rochester	884
Thanet	853
Wippedsfleot (Ebbsfleet)	*c.* 465
Wrotham	1554

Lancashire

Clitheroe	1138
Preston	1648
Preston	1715
Whalley	798
Whalley (Sabden Bridge)	1643
Wigan Lane	1651
Winwick (Red Bank)	1648

Leicestershire

Bosworth Field (Redemore)	1485

Lincolnshire

Gainsborough	1643
Grantham	1643
Lincoln	1141
Lincoln	1217
Winceby Fight (Horncastle Fight)	1643

London

Blackheath	1497
Brentford	1016
Brentford	1642
Turnham Green	642
Fleet Street (Ludgate Hill)	1554

Newcastle-upon-Tyne

Newburn Ford	1640

Norfolk

Dussindale (Ossian's Vale)	1549
Ringmere (Rymer)	1010
Thetford	1004

Northamptonshire

Edgcote (Danes Moor)	1469
Naseby	1645
Northampton	1460

Northumberland

Alnwick I	1093
Alnwick II	1174

Carham	1018
Corbridge	914
Corbridge	918
Flodden (Branxton Field/Heath)	1513
Halidon Hill	1333
Hedgeley Moor	1464
Denisesburna (Hefenfelth)	*c.* 633
Hexham	1464
Homildon Hill (Humbleton Hill)	1402
Lindisfarne (Metcaud)	*c.* 590
Milfield (Ill Raid)	1513
Nesbit Muir	1402
Otterburn (Chevy Chase)	1388

Nottinghamshire

Haethfelth (Hatfield Chase)	632
Newark	1644
Stoke Field	1487

Oxfordshire

Bensington (Benson)	779
Chalgrove Field	1643
Cropredy Bridge	1644
Fethanleag (Stoke Lyne)	584
Radcot Bridge	1387

Rutland

Lose-Coat Field	1470

Shropshire

Ludford Bridge	1459
Maserfelth (Maes Cogwy)	641
Shrewsbury	1403

Somerset

Babylon Hill	1642
Carhampton	836
Carhampton	843
Cynwit (Cannington/Countisbury)	878
Langport (Lamport)	1645
Lansdown	1643
Marshall's Elm	1642
Norton St Philip	1685
Parret River	848
Peonnum (Penselwood)	658
Penselwood	1016
Sedgemoor	1685
Watchet	988
Wicganbeorg (Wigborough)	850

South Tyne

Boldon Hill (Down Hill/Hilton)	1644
Don's Mouth	796

Staffordshire

Blore Heath	1459
Burton-upon-Trent	1322
Hopton Heath	1643
Tettenhall (Wednesfield)	910

Suffolk

Fornham	1173
Landguard Fort	1667

Surrey

Farnham	893
Wibbandun (Wibba's Mount)	568

Sussex, East

Anderitum (Pevensey)	*c.* 491
Hastings (Senlac)	1066
Lewes	1264

Sussex, West

Aethelingadene (Atheling's Valley)	1001

Warwickshire

Edgehill	1642
Kenilworth	1265

Wiltshire

Beranburh (Barbury Castle)	556
Bradford-on-Avon	652
Ellendun	825
Ethandun (Edington)	878
Meretun (Merantune)	871
Mons Badonicus (Mount Badon)	*c.* 495
Searoburg (Old Sarum)	552
Roundway Down (Runaway Down)	1643
Sherston	1016
Wilton	871
Wilton	1143
Wodnesbeorh (Woden's Barrow)	592

Worcestershire

Evesham	1265
Powick Bridge	1642
Ripple Field	1643
Worcester	1651

York

Fulford (Gate Fulford)	1066
Heworth Moor	1453
York	867

Yorkshire, East

Stamford Bridge	1066
Stamford Bridge	1454

Yorkshire, North

Boroughbridge	1322
Byland (Old Byland)	1322
Catraeth (Catterick)	*c.* 598
Marston Moor	1644
Myton-on-Swale (Chapter of Myton)	1319
Northallerton (Standard, The)	1138
Selby	1644
Sherburn in Elmet	1645
Tadcaster	1487
Tadcaster	1642
Towton (Palm Sunday Field)	1461

Yorkshire, West

Adwalton Moor (Adderton/Atherton Moor)	1643
Bramham Moor	1408
Castleford	948
Ferrybridge	1461
Seacroft Moor	1643
Wakefield	1460
Wakefield	1643
Winwaed (Winwidfeld)	654

IRELAND

Co. Antrim

Antrim	1798
Carrickfergus	1597
Glentaisie (Glenshesk)	1565

Co. Armagh

Moyry Pass	1600
Mullaghbrack	1595
Yellow Ford	1598

Co. Clare

Dysart O'Dea (Disert Tola)	1318

Co. Cork

Bantry Bay	1689
Kinsale	1601
Knockbrack (Knocknaclashy/Dromagh)	1651
Knocknanuss (Knocknegoall)	1647
Liscarroll	1642
Macroom	1650

Co. Donegal

Farsetmore (Letterkenny)	1567
Scarrifhollis (Letterkenny)	1650

Co. Down

Ballynahinch	1798
Down I (Downpatrick)	1177
Down II (Drumderg)	1260
Mag Rath (Moira)	637
Strangford Lough	877

Co. Dublin

Clontarf	1014
Dublin	919
Dublin	1171
Dublin (Castle Knock)	1171
Dublin (Easter Rising)	1916
Glen Mama	999
Rathmines (Baggot Rath)	1649

Co. Fermanagh

Ford of the Biscuits (Drumane Ford)	1594
Erne Fords	1593
Newton Butler	1689

Co. Galway

Athenry	1316
Aughrim	1691
Knockdoe	1504

Co. Kerry

Smerwick (Dun an Oir/ Golden Fort)	1580

Co. Kildare

Allen	722
Athy	1359
Kilrush (Cnocaterife)	1642

Co. Kilkenny

Clais an Chro (Clashacrow/ Dinin River)	1169
Piltown (Baile-an-Phoill)	1462

Co. Leitrim

Athankip	1270

Co. Limerick

Monasternenagh	1579

Co. Londonderry

Londonderry, Relief of	1689

Co. Longford

Ballinamuck	1798

Co. Louth

Anagassan	926
Balibragan (Braganstown)	1329
Drogheda (Tredagh)	1649
Faughart (Fochart)	1318

Co. Mayo

Castlebar Races	1798

Co. Meath

Boyne, The (Drogheda)	1690
Dungan's Hill	1647
Julianstown	1641
Kells	718
Tara	980
Tara	1798

Co. Monaghan

Clontibret	1595

Co. Roscommon

Curlew Mountains	1599

Co. Tyrone

Benburb	1646

Co. Waterford

Affane	1565

Co. Wexford

Enniscorthy	1798
Goff's Bridge (Foulkes's Mill)	1798
Kilthomas	1798
New Ross	1798
Oulart Hill	1798
Old Ross (Ballinvegga)	1643
Tubberneering (Gorey Races)	1798
Vinegar Hill	1798

Co. Wicklow

Arklow	1798
Glenmalur	1580
Wicklow	1599

NAVAL

English Channel

Beachy Head (Beveziers)	1690
Dover	1652
Dungeness	1652
Plymouth (Eddystone)	1588
Plymouth	1652
Portland Bill	1588
Portland (Three Days Battle)	1653
Sandwich	850
Sandwich	1217
Isle of Wight (Dunnose Head)	1588
Winchelsea (Espagnols sur Mer)	1349

North Atlantic

Lough Swilly (Warren's Action)	1798

North Sea

The Four Days' Fight	1666
Gabbard Bank (North Foreland, First)	1653
Kentish Knock	1652
Lowestoft	1665

St James's Day Fight (North Foreland, Second) 1666
Sole Bay (Southwold Bay) 1672

Solent
Portsmouth (Spithead) 1545
Sea Battle 896

SCOTLAND

Aberdeen
Aberdeen (Justice Mills) 1644
Brig o'Dee 1639
Craibstane Rout 1571

Aberdeenshire
Alford 1645
Barra (Inverurie/Meldrum) 1308
Circinn (Howe of the Mearns) 597
Corrichie 1562
Culblean 1335
Fyvie 1644
Harlaw 1411
Lumphanan 1057
Megray Hill (Stonehaven) 1639
Mons Graupius 83
Slioch 1307
Tillyangus 1571
Turriff (Trot of Turriff) 1639

Angus
Nechtanesmere (Dunnichen Moss) 685

Argyll & Bute
Pass of Brander (Ben Cruachan) 1309
Calathros (Dun Nosebridge) 639

Ayrshire, East
Loudoun Hill 1307

Ayrshire, North
Largs 1263

Dumfries & Galloway
Annan 1332
Drumlanrig 1548
Glen Trool 1307

Falkirk
Falkirk (I) 1298
Falkirk (II) 1746
Strathcarron 642

Fife
Inverkeithing 1651

Glasgow
Langside 1568

Highland
Auldearn 1645
Carbisdale 1650
Haughs of Cromdale 1690
Culloden (Drummossie Muir) 1746
Glenshiel 1719
Inverlochy 1645
Skidamyre (Skithmore) *c.* 995

Lanarkshire, North
Kilsyth 1645

Lanarkshire, South
Bothwell Bridge 1679
Drumclog 1679

Lothian, East
Carberry Hill 1567
Dunbar 1296
Dunbar 1650
Pinkie (Falside/Inveresk/Musselburgh) 1547
Prestonpans (Gladsmuir) 1745

Midlothian
Rullion Green (Pentland Hills) 1666

Moray
Glenlivet (Allt a'Choileachain) 1594
Mortlach *c.* 1005
Torfnes (Burghead/Torness) 1040

Orkney Islands
Summerdale (Bigswell) 1529

Perth & Kinross
Dunkeld 1689

Dunsinane Hill (Seven Sleepers, Day of)	1054
Dupplin Muir (Gaskmore/ Gledesmore)	1332
Killiecrankie	1689
Methven	1306
Monzievaird	1005
Tippermuir (Tibbermore)	1644

Scottish Borders

Ancrum Moor (Lilliard's Edge)	1545
Degsastan (Dawston Rigg)	603
Hadden Rig (Halydon Rigg)	1542
Melrose	1526
Philiphaugh	1645

Stirling

Bannockburn	1314
Dail Righ (Dalrigh)	1306
Sauchieburn	1488
Sheriffmuir	1715
Stirling Bridge (Cambuskenneth)	1297

WALES

Anglesey

Menai Straits	60
Priestholm (Anglesey Sound)	1098

Cardiff

St Fagan's	1648

Carmarthenshire

Abergwyli	1022
Cymerau (Coed Llathen)	1257
Maes Gwenllian	1136

Ceredigion

Aberystwyth	1116
Crug Mawr (Cardigan/Crugmore)	1136

Flintshire

Coleshill (Coed Eulo)	1157

Pembrokeshire

Fishguard	1797

Powys

Buttington	893
Caradoc's Last Stand (Cefn Carnedd)	51
Hyddgen (Mynyddhyddgant)	1401
Maes Moydog (Maes Madog/ Meismedoc)	1295
Montgomery	1644
Irfon Bridge (Orewin Bridge)	1282
Pilleth (Bryn Glas)	1402
Rhyd-y-Groes	1039

UNLOCATED

Alleluia Victory	*c.* 429
Boudicca's Revolt (Mancetter/Paulerspury)	60
Brunanburh (Bruneswald/Wendune)	937
Caer Greu	*c.* 580
Trent	*c.* 678

Index of Battles

This index gives the page reference for the main battle entry only.

General Index

This index is arranged alphabetically in word-by-word order. Place-names followed by a date indicate a battle. Where a heading/subheading has a number of page references, those in **bold** indicate the most significant. Page references for national armies are only shown where the armies fought in a country other than their own. Alternative battle names are cross referred to the index entry for the main battle name. This index includes entries for all military commanders mentioned in the book. It should be noted that these entries commence with references to mentions in general text followed by subentries giving, in bold, the page references for the battles in which they fought as commanders.